(Continued on back endsheets)

British Short-Fiction Writers, 1915–1945

British Short-Fiction Writers, 1915–1945

Edited by
John H. Rogers
Vincennes University

A Bruccoli Clark Layman Book
Gale Research Inc.
Detroit, Washington, D.C., London

The paper used in this publication meets the minimum requirements
of American National Standard for Information Sciences–Permanence
Paper for Printed Library Materials, ANSI Z39.48-1984. ∞ ™

Library of Congress Catalog Card Number 96-075180

ISBN 0-8103-9357-3

10 9 8 7 6 5 4 3 2 1

Contents

Plan of the Series

. . . Almost the most prodigious asset of a country, and perhaps its most precious possession, is its native literary product – when that product is fine and noble and enduring.

Mark Twain*

The advisory board, the editors, and the publisher of the *Dictionary of Literary Biography* are joined in endorsing Mark Twain's declaration. The literature of a nation provides an inexhaustible resource of permanent worth. We intend to make literature and its creators better understood and more accessible to students and the reading public, while satisfying the standards of teachers and scholars.

To meet these requirements, *literary biography* has been construed in terms of the author's achievement. The most important thing about a writer is his writing. Accordingly, the entries in *DLB* are career biographies, tracing the development of the author's canon and the evolution of his reputation.

The purpose of *DLB* is not only to provide reliable information in a convenient format but also to place the figures in the larger perspective of literary history and to offer appraisals of their accomplishments by qualified scholars.

The publication plan for *DLB* resulted from two years of preparation. The project was proposed to Bruccoli Clark by Frederick C. Ruffner, president of the Gale Research Company, in November 1975. After specimen entries were prepared and typeset, an advisory board was formed to refine the entry format and develop the series rationale. In meetings held during 1976, the publisher, series editors, and advisory board approved the scheme for a comprehensive biographical dictionary of persons who contributed to North American literature. Editorial work on the first volume began in January 1977, and it was published in 1978. In order to make *DLB* more than a reference tool and to compile volumes that individually have claim to status as literary history, it was decided to organize volumes by topic, period, or genre. Each of these free-standing volumes provides a biographical-bibliographical guide and overview for a particular area of literature. We are convinced that this organization – as opposed to a single alphabet method – constitutes a valuable innovation in the presentation of reference material. The volume plan necessarily requires many decisions for the placement and treatment of authors who might properly be included in two or three volumes. In some instances a major figure will be included in separate volumes, but with different entries emphasizing the aspect of his career appropriate to each volume. Ernest Hemingway, for example, is represented in *American Writers in Paris, 1920–1939* by an entry focusing on his expatriate apprenticeship; he is also in *American Novelists, 1910–1945* with an entry surveying his entire career. Each volume includes a cumulative index of the subject authors and articles. Comprehensive indexes to the entire series are planned.

With volume ten in 1982 it was decided to enlarge the scope of *DLB*. By the end of 1986 twenty-one volumes treating British literature had been published, and volumes for Commonwealth and Modern European literature were in progress. The series has been further augmented by the *DLB Yearbooks* (since 1981) which update published entries and add new entries to keep the *DLB* current with contemporary activity. There have also been *DLB Documentary Series* volumes which provide biographical and critical source materials for figures whose work is judged to have particular interest for students. One of these companion volumes is entirely devoted to Tennessee Williams.

We define literature as the *intellectual commerce of a nation:* not merely as belles lettres but as that ample and complex process by which ideas are generated, shaped, and transmitted. *DLB* entries are not limited to "creative writers" but extend to other figures who in their time and in their way influenced the mind of a people. Thus the series encompasses historians, journalists, publishers, and screenwriters. By this means readers of *DLB* may be aided to perceive literature not as cult scripture in the keeping of intellectual high priests but firmly positioned at the center of a nation's life.

*From an unpublished section of Mark Twain's autobiography, copyright by the Mark Twain Company

DLB includes the major writers appropriate to each volume and those standing in the ranks immediately behind them. Scholarly and critical counsel has been sought in deciding which minor figures to include and how full their entries should be. Wherever possible, useful references are made to figures who do not warrant separate entries.

Each *DLB* volume has a volume editor responsible for planning the volume, selecting the figures for inclusion, and assigning the entries. Volume editors are also responsible for preparing, where appropriate, appendices surveying the major periodicals and literary and intellectual movements for their volumes, as well as lists of further readings. Work on the series as a whole is coordinated at the Bruccoli Clark Layman editorial center in Columbia, South Carolina, where the editorial staff is responsible for accuracy of the published volumes.

One feature that distinguishes *DLB* is the illustration policy – its concern with the iconography of literature. Just as an author is influenced by his surroundings, so is the reader's understanding of the author enhanced by a knowledge of his environment. Therefore *DLB* volumes include not only drawings, paintings, and photographs of authors, often depicting them at various stages in their careers, but also illustrations of their families and places where they lived. Title pages are regularly reproduced in facsimile along with dust jackets for modern authors. The dust jackets are a special feature of *DLB* because they often document better than anything else the way in which an author's work was perceived in its own time. Specimens of the writers' manuscripts are included when feasible.

Samuel Johnson rightly decreed that "The chief glory of every people arises from its authors." The purpose of the *Dictionary of Literary Biography* is to compile literary history in the surest way available to us – by accurate and comprehensive treatment of the lives and work of those who contributed to it.

The *DLB* Advisory Board

Introduction

The history of the short story can be seen as either extensive or very brief, depending on how the term is defined. Some form of the short narrative can be traced back to antiquity, but the short story as we now think of it is a recent literary form, one that had its origins in the mid-nineteenth century and in England reached its maturity in the twentieth. The modern British short story grew particularly slowly, following by nearly fifty years the origins of the form in the United States, France, and Russia.

The short story found an early and congenial home in America. Nathaniel Hawthorne in his moral fables and Edgar Allan Poe in both his fiction and his critical writings helped to define the nature of the modern short story and to make of it a respectable literary form. Following Hawthorne and Poe, such writers as Bret Harte and Sarah Orne Jewett showed the use and value of regional settings, while Ambrose Bierce and Stephen Crane added greater psychological depth and a more natural style. O. Henry, overly dependent on the trick ending as most of his work is, nonetheless encouraged the growth and development of the short story through the enormous popularity of his work.

In France Gustave Flaubert influenced other writers by his "desire to give verse-rhythms to prose, yet to leave it prose and very much prose, and to write about ordinary life as histories and epics, yet without falsifying the subject," ideas that led to a greater detachment and objectivity and to an emphasis on form and style. Flaubert's disciple Guy de Maupassant popularized a more naturalistic approach and what many readers considered sordid subject matter. De Maupassant's stories of French lower-class life – stories such as "Boule de Suif," "The Tellier House," and "The Story of a Farm Girl" – provided early instances of an earthy realism and had a direct and immediate impact on other short-story writers. The most important influence on the modern British short story, however, came from Russia – from Nikolay Gogol, Count Leo Tolstoy, the Ivan Turgenev of *Sportsman's Sketches,* and especially from the stories of Anton Chekhov, without whom the modern British story would surely have developed in a very different way.

Although Chekhov modestly remarked of his innovations that "Maupassant in France, and I in Russia began writing very short stories. There's your new movement in literature," his stories were something new. Most other short-story writers of the time, including de Maupassant, relied on unusual settings and characters, strong and often contrived plot, and direct personal narration for their effects. Chekhov, who believed that "First of all . . . we must get rid of lies. . . . [Y]ou cannot practice deception in art," wrote of the ordinary, externally undramatic lives of the Russian peasants, civil servants, teachers, and scientists whom he knew intimately. He wrote of all aspects of their lives with scrupulous detachment, believing that "a writer must be as objective as a chemist, he must lay aside his personal subjective standpoint and must understand that muck-heaps play a very respectable part in the landscape, and that the inherent bad passions are as inherent as the good ones."

Chekhov's restrained treatment of all aspects of the life around him, including the emotional muck-heaps and the great varieties of human passion, was undergirded with sympathy and frequent humor and presented in a style at once thoroughly natural and highly poetic. W. Somerset Maugham, who in his own work was a follower of de Maupassant, provided a perceptive response to Chekhov's stories when he wrote in *A Writer's Notebook* that "with Chekhov you do not seem to be reading stories at all. There is no obvious cleverness in them, and you might think that anyone could write them, but for the fact that nobody does. The author has had an emotion, and he is able so to put it into words, that you receive it in your turn. You become his collaborator. Yet if you try to tell one of his stories there is nothing to tell." The importance of Chekhov cannot be overestimated. His style and approach set the standard for many of the more-innovative British short-story writers during the first half of the twentieth century.

Given the interest in and development of the short story in the United States, France, and Russia, it is curious that the new form came so late to England. It is of course impossible to explain fully why any literary form flourishes or fails to flourish at a particular time and place, but several features of nineteenth-century English life may have retarded the development of the British short story.

William Dean Howells suggested that the form was more congenial to American than to English readers because America had a hastier and more impatient culture than that of England. Howells' generalization is not completely convincing, but it is true that in literary terms English fiction writers and readers were accustomed to the dominance of the Victorian novel. The form and structure of these usually three-volume novels – with their leisurely pace, expansive language, large cast of characters, and reliance on a strong, direct narrative voice – is at the furthest remove from the Chekhovian story, as is much of their subject matter.

The Victorian novelists also tended, with certain notable exceptions, to concentrate on the lives of characters in society and not only to write about but to accept the strict and severe social hierarchy of the time. Virginia Woolf commented in her essay "The Leaning Tower" that to nineteenth-century writers life must have seemed a landscape cut into separate fields, each inhabited by a different group of people, with each group having "its own traditions; its own manners; its own speech; its own dress; its own occupation" and that the typical writer of the time avoided making attempts to change these conditions because he "accepted them so completely that he became unconscious of them." Though overstated, Woolf's comment sums up the opinion that many of the modern writers held of their predecessors and indicates some of the things that their own works were reacting against.

In addition to a class structure that had limited the range of acceptable material for short fiction, the morality of many nineteenth-century readers further limited its scope. A reading public that had been prepared to ban and burn such longer fiction as Thomas Hardy's *Tess of the D'Urbervilles* (1891) and *Jude the Obscure* (1895) was hardly ready for the strong fare that D. H. Lawrence and James Joyce were soon to serve them. And even had there been a more receptive audience, there was still no satisfactory market for the short story.

This market began to be supplied by the appearance of such British magazines as *The Yellow Book,* and after 1850 American, French, and Russian influences slowly penetrated English writing and led to the beginning of the British short story. Robert Louis Stevenson's tale about François Villon, "A Lodging for the Night," often considered the first British short story, was published in *Temple Bar* in October 1877. Stevenson's talent for romantic adventure was best suited to the novel, but such atmospheric tales as "Thrawn Janet," "Markheim," and "The Beach at Falesa" gave impetus to the new

form, and Stevenson's tales were soon followed by the great flood of short-story writing that occurred during the 1890s.

In his introduction to *The Country of the Blind* H. G. Wells recalled this era as "a good and stimulating period for the short story writer," because "people talked about them tremendously, compared them, and ranked them. That was the thing that mattered." It is now difficult to comprehend precisely what Wells was referring to. Many short stories were certainly written and published in England during the 1890s, but most were written by authors such as Joseph Conrad, Henry James, John Galsworthy, and Wells himself – writers who had trained as novelists and who tended to see and write the short story more as an abbreviated novel than as a distinct literary form. Many of their plots were anecdotal, and their stories continued to rely heavily on the personal narrator. The great exception was Rudyard Kipling, who was devoted to the short-story form and who was easily its most popular exponent. What later writers saw as Kipling's excessive bellicosity of subject and style, however, kept them from responding to the quality of his writing, and for most British writers between the world wars Kipling was an influence to be avoided.

Whatever other writers may have thought of Kipling, to readers he was by far the most popular short-story writer of his time. A similarly ambivalent position in the twentieth-century British short story is held by Maugham, who continued to champion an older kind of fiction both during and after the world wars. Maugham is an important figure in any consideration of the British short story not so much because of his fiction but because he best represents the continuing power and popularity of the strongly plotted, clearly narrated tale, a type that became so characteristic of the British short story that James Thurber could easily parody it in "The Man Who Was Wetly." Maugham wrote of his own kind of fiction that "one thing you will notice about it is that you can tell it over the dinner table or in a ship's smoking-room and it will hold the attention of the listener."

Maugham's stories do hold the attention of the listener, but often only on a first reading, for his stories are filled with clichés, retain the old narrative tradition of telling rather than showing, and, as befits a successful playwright, frequently depend upon coincidence and melodrama. As T. O. Beachcroft wrote of one of Maugham's stories, "One almost wants to clap at the end." Despite these weaknesses, however, Maugham's stories were enormously popular, and the great prestige that readers accorded him made Maugham an imposing figure in its history, a formidable spokesman for the idea of the short story as professional entertainment.

Although he was an important figure in the British short story, however, Maugham was, much as Kipling had been, not an especially influential one — for compared to the work of his contemporaries, Maugham's stories must have seemed rather old-fashioned even when they first appeared. The new century brought forth a new social climate and with it a new generation of writers with new ideas and new ways of expressing them. World War I brought an abrupt and brutal end to the stable social world described by Virginia Woolf, and the war led to the general feeling of disillusionment and lost idealism expressed in Wilfred Owen's poetry and Robert Graves's *Goodbye To All That* (1929). Somewhat paradoxically, the disillusionment born by the war was followed by a social revolution that fostered a new sense of freedom from the old conventions and the old hierarchies of class and gender. It thus provided the necessary climate for innovation.

Such innovation was seen in all the arts, and activity in other arts influenced the course of the short story. The post-impressionism exhibits arranged by Roger Fry at the Grafton Galleries in 1910 and 1912 championed a new artistic vision. The mutually useful relationship between the short story and the new medium of motion pictures was noticed by both A. E. Coppard and by Elizabeth Bowen, the latter of whom acutely pointed out that "neither is sponsored by a tradition; both are, accordingly, free; both, still, are self-conscious, show a self-imposed discipline and regard for form; both have, to work on, immense matter — the disoriented romanticism of the age." Many writers of the time also expressed their belief that the short story was more closely related to the drama and, especially, to the lyric poem than to the novel.

In addition to these changes, around the turn of the century Constance Garnett's translations of Russian writers had begun to appear and to exert an enormous influence on the development of the British short story. Moreover, new magazines such as the *Savoy,* T. S. Eliot's *Criterion,* J. C. Squire's *London Mercury,* and John Middleton Murry's *Adelphi* provided an outlet for writers and readers interested in short stories rather than serialized novels. E. J. O'Brien's annual publication of *The Best Short Stories of the Year* in both Britain and America provided more recognition than the form had previously received. Such changes in the social and artistic environs made the 1920s and 1930s an exceptionally fertile period for British literature, and young short-story writers were quick to take advantage of it.

Two other seminal influences on the British short story first appeared just before the outbreak of World War I, with the publication in 1914 of D. H. Lawrence's *The Prussian Officer* and James Joyce's *Dubliners.* Although for many readers today Lawrence's most powerful work is to be found in his novels, these early stories offered readers a new and distinctive voice and were in some ways more satisfactory than his novels, because they were more controlled than some of those later works. From the beginning Lawrence's fiction reflected the intense power of a dominant personality and developed many of the themes that were to occupy him for the rest of his career. The stories in *The Prussian Officer* concern the nature of the physical world, the split between the north and south of England, and the mysterious relations between the sexes and the generations. They express a withering contempt for the upper classes and a belief that it was essential to infuse this rapidly decaying class with the greater sexual and moral vitality of the working classes.

These ideas and Lawrence's presentation of them opened up vast new possibilities for the short story. Perhaps Lawrence's greatest early contribution to the short story, though, was simply that his early stories were firmly based on his personal knowledge of the lives of ordinary men and women in the Nottinghamshire and Derbyshire coal fields. Lawrence thus helped open the British short story to new scenes and subjects. He taught other writers to write of the life around them, and he helped to prepare a fictional climate amenable to Rhys Davies's stories of life in the Welsh mines, Malachi Whitaker's grim tales of Yorkshire, L. A. G. Strong's stories of the Irish fishing coasts, H. H. Manhood's depictions of English country life, James Hanley's of Liverpool, and Leslie Halward's of working-class Birmingham. Lawrence helped to change the course of the British short story by using the regional to stand for the universal.

Another writer who used the life around him to embody universal themes, though in a thoroughly different way, was James Joyce. As if to prove Carlos Fuentes's remark that every time the literary language of English gets lazy, some Irishman comes along to give it a kick in the arse, Joyce's *Dubliners* appeared in 1914 and performed this function admirably. *Dubliners* does owe something to George Moore's stories in *The Untilled Field* (1903), but Joyce, perhaps showing some anxiety about acknowledging influence, later described Moore's tales as "damned stupid!" The fifteen stories in Joyce's book, however, as L. A. G. Strong rightly remarked, "Pricked the fabric of the contemporary short story.... For all their quietness, their drab tones, they are as violently original as anything written in this century."

In one sense the originality of *Dubliners* consists in the absolute realism of its treatment of the often drab, solitary lives of the Dublin citizens who are its subjects. Joyce wrote that he had written *Dubliners* "for the most part in a style of scrupulous meanness," because "he is a very bold man who dares to alter in the presentment, still more to deform whatever he has seen and heard." Joyce certainly did not deform the reality of life in Dublin, but he did transform it by replacing the anecdotal basis of earlier stories with "slices of life." Joyce also employed a more subtle form of symbolism than any earlier short-story writer had mastered, so that these stories of depressing and unfulfilled lives are charged with a deep significance, a significance conveyed entirely through implication rather than direct statement. The stories are, moreover, written in a language that frequently approaches the poetic, a language that, in Frank O'Connor's happy phrase, uses words "not to describe an experience, but so far as possible to duplicate it." In *Dubliners* Joyce achieved the goal famously stated by E. M. Forster in *Howard's End* – to "only connect . . . the poetry and the prose." Joyce's successful blending of prosaic subject matter and poetic prose, his ability to use language and symbol to transform the ordinary into the extraordinary, made him the most influential writer between the wars.

Joyce's poetic language and to some extent his subject matter also characterize the work of two otherwise very different writers whose best stories appeared at the beginning of the 1920s, Katherine Mansfield and A. E. Coppard. Mansfield's earliest volume of short stories, *In a German Pension,* had been published in 1911, but she later dismissed these mostly satiric sketches of German characters as youthful and unsuccessful experiments. Her volume *Bliss,* published in 1920 and signaling the first successful appearance in English of the Chekhovian approach, became the first and most immediately influential example of the modern British story. Like Chekhov's stories, Mansfield's offered little in the way of narrative, and in them what was omitted was as important as what was described – techniques that invited the same criticism often addressed to Chekhov: that the stories "aren't about anything."

They are, of course, about the inner lives of the characters, lives heightened by Mansfield's re-markable creation of mood and an almost palpable atmosphere, presented with what T. O. Beachcroft called Mansfield's "Traherne-like quality of perception." She took a small fragment of life and, as Scott James remarked in *Fifty Years of English Literature,* "observed it minutely, described it simply and objectively, and at the end the point had been made without apparent effort, leaving the reader thrilled, disturbed or emotionally enlightened." Like Chekhov and Joyce, Mansfield wrote of the extraordinary nature of ordinary lives and the significance of the commonplace. She also introduced a fresh perspective into the British short story, because in her stories women and their lives were seen and described from a woman's point of view. Both something of Mansfield's sensibility and of her ability to see the poetry of daily life were shared by her contemporaries Virginia Woolf and Elizabeth Bowen, who added, respectively, a more intensely personal vision and a more worldly, ironic one.

Another writer who attempted to suffuse the ordinary with poetry, though again in a rather different way, was A. E. Coppard, something of a transitional figure linking the generation of Thomas Hardy with that of Mansfield. His first story collection, *Adam and Eve and Pinch Me,* appeared in 1921 when Coppard was more than forty years old. Like Katherine Mansfield, Coppard was completely devoted to the short-story form, which he described in his autobiography, *It's Me, O Lord!,* as "a work of literary perfection, supreme though small, a phoenix, a paragon."

Coppard wrote two kinds of stories – those concerned with the magical and the fantastic (stories often weakened by the stylistic influence of Henry James), and the better and more-influential tales that exalted simplicity and an earthy realism, tales that inspired many other writers, notably H. E. Bates, to set their stories in the English countryside. Coppard sometimes relied too heavily on Hardy-esque coincidence – he mentioned Hardy's *Life's Little Ironies* (1894) as a major influence – and occasionally fell into a Victorian lavishness of style, but in his best stories Coppard gave new life to a distinctive English tradition, one at least as old as Daniel Defoe: he wrote about ordinary things in a direct, matter-of-fact style. Coppard, who always insisted that his works were tales, not stories, and that the short story was an oral rather than a written art, largely depended on the anecdote and on a direct description of setting and character. Because he was thus not an innovator in the sense that Lawrence, Joyce, and Mansfield were, Coppard may not be a "modern" writer in the usual sense, but his tales of the English countryside and provincial town, presented with a kind of folk poetry, preserved and renewed an old English literary tradition and made him a highly respected figure during the period between the world wars.

With the work of Joyce, Lawrence, and Mansfield the short story in England reached heights that remain unsurpassed, but such innovative writers constitute only one strand in the rich fabric of the British short story written between the wars. The great diversity of subjects, styles, and techniques used by a variety of writers was one of the principal strengths of the short story during this period. For the first time many writers found the short story a congenial form, and new writers both in England and in other English-speaking countries appeared almost yearly.

In England older writers such as Maugham and Kipling remained extremely popular and influential, and these did some of their best work during this period. Two other writers from an earlier generation ridiculed the aristocratic classes through their continued use of the traditional comedy of manners – Saki (H. H. Munro), with a mordant and malicious wit, and P. G. Wodehouse, in the spirit of pure farce. The strongly individual, at times eccentric, work of such unclassifiable writers as Walter de la Mare, T. F. Powys, J. D. Beresford, and Coppard added their unique visions to the short story written between the wars, a genre that at this time came to attract many writers now little known. While these secondary figures are now almost completely forgotten and are not included in this volume, they deserve at least brief mention in any consideration of the history of the short story between the wars.

Stacy Aumonier's stories, frequently amounting to no more than slick vehicles for slick magazines, were widely popular during the 1920s and are completely of their period. Occasionally, however, in such stories as "Them Others" – about the mother of a soldier who, following her son's return home, finds an unexpected fellow feeling for her former German neighbors, the Stellings – or "The Great Unimpressionable," about Ned Picklekin, who endures the most harrowing wartime experiences by thinking of his home and his dog – only to break down when he returns home to find that his dog has died – Aumonier achieves some real emotion, but even his best stories are flawed by a false simplicity and by his failure to provide incidents capable of containing the strong emotions he wishes to convey.

Constance Holme, better known for her novels, continued the regional tradition in her somewhat old-fashioned stories of English country life, as did Malachi Whitaker in her short stories set in Yorkshire. Leslie Halward, like Lawrence and Coppard a product of the English working class, had been a toolmaker and plasterer before he decided to learn to write short stories by reading Chekhov. Halward achieved considerable success at the end of the 1930s and seemed to promise a new proletarian voice in the short story. In such character sketches as "Arch Anderson" and "Belcher's Hod," sketches that applied naturalism to working-class life, Halward sometimes achieves Chekhov's bare simplicity of style but misses completely the poetry and emotion of his Russian mentor. After his brief success Halward published no more fiction for the last thirty-five years of his life. These writers, along with Nora Hoult, T. O. Beachcroft, L. A. G. Strong, and H. H. Manhood, perhaps added nothing really new to the short story, but their work in the genre continued to attest to its growing prominence and vitality.

The British short story was further vitalized and enhanced by writers beyond the shores of England. The strongest and best-known influences came, as has so often been the case, from Ireland. While both the Irish and English short story between the wars formed part of a new international literature, Irish writers and their work were products of a different background and different social forces. The three most important Irish short-story writers of this period – Liam O'Flaherty, Seán O'Faoláin, and Frank O'Connor – were influenced not so much by World War I as by the Irish Revolution, a conflict that was fruitful, according to Anglo-Irish writer Elizabeth Bowen, because the "long hopeless romantic quarrel has bred literature."

During the 1920s Liam O'Flaherty began writing stories in the de Maupassant manner, but when told by Edward Garnett that he should return to Ireland and "write a story about a cow," O'Flaherty did so. The best of his short stories are stark, instinctive tales about animals and the Irish peasantry, who are seen in much the same way – as usually helpless victims of an impersonal and unforgiving natural world. The events of his stories are presented completely factually, with no comment or interpretation – so much so that O'Flaherty has sometimes been falsely considered a "primitive" writer. No such charge could be leveled at his two contemporaries, Seán O'Faoláin and Frank O'Connor.

Although the later work of these two writers changed considerably in both form and content, the early stories of both O'Faoláin and O'Connor grew from their youthful experiences as members of the Irish Republican Army during "The Troubles" of the 1920s. O'Faoláin's early stories tend to be concerned with solitary and disillusioned young men and women whose idealism is rapidly fading, and they are often written in a lush, romantic style that O'Faoláin later repudiated. These stories of romantic disillusion at times reflect about Ireland a pessimism worthy of Joyce himself, as in the clear echoes of Joyce's "The Dead" that appear in the conclusion of O'Faoláin's "A Broken World": "under that white shroud covering the whole of Ireland, life was lying broken and hardly breathing."

Frank O'Connor was neither so romantic nor so disillusioned as O'Faoláin. Although "Guests of the Nation," his most famous story, is a classic portrayal not only of the particular conflict between England and Ireland but also the broader, deeper, and more-universal tensions between individual feeling and nationalist responsibility, most of O'Connor's stories are concerned with the daily lives of the men and women of Cork, and they take as their subjects the lives of the individual characters interacting within this community. The stories are not so atmospheric as O'Flaherty's or O'Faoláin's and are narrated in a more direct and personal style. O'Connor felt that such stylists as Mansfield and Joyce "had so fashioned the short story that it no longer rang with the tone of a man's voice speaking," and he tried to instill a personal voice into his own work. Although O'Flaherty, O'Faoláin, and O'Connor are often grouped together as the "post-Joyce" generation of Irish writers, a cursory glance at their work will show that each added a new and distinctive voice to the modern British short story.

Though they have never been so familiar or influential as the Irish, writers from other areas of the British Commonwealth and the former empire also added new voices to the British short story between the wars. The harsh, brutal stories of the peasants of West Wales in Carodoc Evans's *My People* (1915), narrated in a difficult, compressed style designed, according to Gwyn Jones, to "lay bare the mental processes of the spiritual troglodytes who inhabit the stories and give them a savor all their own," so dominated the Welsh short story during the first half of the twentieth century that those works sometimes seem to have a certain sameness of style and content. Rhys Davies's stories of life in the Welsh coal-mining communities, however, present a somewhat different experience of Welsh life, as does the work of Alun Lewis, a poet whose few short stories suggest that he might

have become a major British short-story writer had he not been killed during World War II.

Like the Anglo-Irish and the Anglo-Welsh, English writers born in South Africa — the "stranded gentry," as William Plomer termed them — introduced new subject matter and new, multiple perspectives into the British short story. The South African story reached its most impressive heights following World War II, but Pauline Smith's stories of Boer farmers in *The Little Karoo* (1925) and Plomer's early stories that, according to Laurens van der Post, displayed "the first imagination to allow the black man to enter it in his own right," set the pattern for many later South African writers.

Such a proliferation of new voices, together with the new experiences that had followed World War I, led many to assume confidently that the years after World War II would be as fruitful a period for the short story as the years following the earlier war had been. H. E. Bates felt that the period after World War II, with "its inevitable aftermath of still more distrustful dislocation," would find the short story "the essential medium for whatever it has to say," because "if no other good comes out of wars, stories will." In a May 1945 article in *Britain To-Day* Elizabeth Bowen offered a similar view that "wartime London, blitzed, cosmopolitan, electric with anticipation now teems, I feel, with untold but tellable stories, glitters with scenes that cry aloud for the pen." Such predictions were reasonable but proved to be incorrect. The best stories to emerge from World War II were in fact by these two established writers — Bowen's stories of wartime London collected in *Ivy Gripped The Steps* (1946) and Bates's anonymously published stories of military service that were collected in *Stories of Flying Officer X* (1952).

The writers who emerged after World War II had little to say about it, and they found a declining market. The few magazines that had provided a new avenue for the short story rapidly disappeared after the war, and writers grew interested in other forms. By this time the possibilities that the Chekhov type of story afforded, the most important stimulant to the development of short fiction between the wars, had been largely exhausted, and nothing arose afterward to take its place. The short story lost much of the excitement that had characterized it during this period, when almost every year saw the emergence of new writers, new subjects, and new styles. New writers continued to appear after World War II, of course, but it seems fair to say that none of them has proven as influential with other writers or as popular with readers as the major figures of the 1920s and 1930s had been with their contemporaries. The short but extremely fertile period between the two world wars remains the high point of the British short story.

– *John H. Rogers*

Acknowledgments

This book was produced by Bruccoli Clark Layman, Inc. Karen L. Rood is senior editor for the *Dictionary of Literary Biography* series. Denis Thomas was the in-house editor.

Production coordinator is James W. Hipp. Photography editors are Julie E. Frick and Margaret Meriwether. Photographic copy work was performed by Joseph M. Bruccoli. Layout and graphics supervisor is Emily Ruth Sharpe. Copyediting supervisor is Laurel M. Gladden. Typesetting supervisor is Kathleen M. Flanagan. Systems manager is George F. Dodge. Laura Pleicones and L. Kay Webster are editorial associates. The production staff includes Phyllis A. Avant, Ann M. Cheschi, Melody W. Clegg, Patricia Coate, Joyce Fowler, Stephanie C. Hatchell, Kathy Lawler Merlette, Jeff Miller, Pamela D. Norton, Delores Plastow, William L. Thomas Jr., and Allison Trussell.

Walter W. Ross and Steven Gross did library research. They were assisted by the following librarians at the Thomas Cooper Library of the University of South Carolina: Linda Holderfield and the interlibrary-loan staff; reference-department head Virginia Weathers; reference librarians Marilee Birchfield, Stefanie Buck, Stefanie DuBose, Rebecca Feind, Karen Joseph, Donna Lehman, Charlene Loope, Anthony McKissick, Jean Rhyne, Kwamine Simpson, and Virginia Weathers; circulation-department head Caroline Taylor; and acquisitions-searching supervisor David Haggard.

British Short-Fiction Writers, 1915–1945

Dictionary of Literary Biography

Michael Arlen
(16 November 1895 – 23 June 1956)

Jan Peter F. van Rosevelt
University of South Carolina

See also the Arlen entries in *DLB 36: British Novelists, 1890–1929: Modernists* and *DLB 77: British Mystery Writers, 1920–1939.*

BOOKS: *The London Venture* (London: Heinemann, 1920; New York: Doran, 1920);

The Romantic Lady (London: Collins, 1921; New York: Dodd, Mead, 1921);

"Piracy" (London: Collins, 1922; New York: Doran, 1923);

These Charming People (London: Collins, 1923; New York: Doran, 1924);

The Green Hat (London: Collins, 1924; New York: Doran, 1924);

May Fair (London: Collins, 1925; New York: Doran, 1925);

The Acting Version of the Green Hat (New York: Doran, 1925);

Young Men in Love (London: Hutchinson, 1927; New York: Doran, 1927);

The Zoo: A Comedy in Three Acts, by Arlen and Winchell Smith (New York & London: French, 1927);

Lily Christine (Garden City, N.Y.: Doubleday, Doran, 1928; London: Hutchinson, 1929);

Babes in the Wood (London: Hutchinson, 1929; Garden City, N.Y.: Doubleday, Doran, 1929);

Men Dislike Women (London: Heinemann, 1931; Garden City, N.Y.: Doubleday, Doran, 1931);

A Young Man Comes to London (London: Keliher, 1931);

Man's Mortality (London: Heinemann, 1933; Garden City, N.Y.: Doubleday, Doran, 1933);

The Short Stories (London: Collins, 1933);

Michael Arlen

Good Losers, by Arlen and Walter Hackett (London: French, 1934);

Hell! Said the Duchess (London: Heinemann, 1934; Garden City, N.Y.: Doubleday, Doran, 1934);

The Crooked Coronet (London & Toronto: Heinemann, 1937; Garden City, N.Y.: Doubleday, Doran, 1937);

3

The Flying Dutchman (London & Toronto: Heinemann, 1939; Garden City, N.Y.: Doubleday, Doran, 1939).

PLAY PRODUCTIONS: *Dear Father,* London, New Scala Theatre, 30 November 1924; revised as *These Charming People,* New York, Gaiety Theater, 6 October 1925;

The Green Hat, London, Adelphi Theatre, 2 September 1925; New York, Broadhurst Theater, 15 September 1925;

Why She Was Late For Dinner, London, Everyman Theatre, 27 November 1926;

The Zoo, by Arlen and Winchell Smith, London, King's Theatre, 23 May 1927;

Good Losers, by Arlen and Walter Hackett, London, Whitehall Theatre, 16 February 1931.

MOTION PICTURE: *The Heavenly Body,* screenplay by Arlen and Walter Reisch, M-G-M, 1944.

SELECTED PERIODICAL PUBLICATIONS – UNCOLLECTED: "The Fall of Lady Toni," *English Review,* 30 (April 1920): 336–347;

"The Ci-Divant," *Dial,* 69 (August 1920): 125–131;

"Tea at the Ritz," *Smart Set,* 66 (December 1921): 127–128;

"Lark Among Crows," *Everybody's Magazine,* 50 (January 1924): 175–179;

"Dancer of Paris," *Everybody's Magazine,* 50 (February 1924): 177–179;

"Punctilious Parbold," *Everybody's Magazine,* 50 (March 1924): 25–30;

"The Sheik of Alabam," *Everybody's Magazine,* 50 (April 1924): 41–48;

"One Gold Coin," *Bookman,* 60 (January 1925): 556–564; 60 (February 1925): 699–709;

"The Legend of Isolda," *Redbook,* 44 (March 1925): 38–41, 107–110;

"The Knife Thrower," *Redbook,* 45 (July 1925): 46–49, 135–140;

"Portrait of a Lady with Grey Eyes on Fifth Avenue," *Liberty,* 2 (16 January 1926): 7–8;

"Portrait of a Girl on Hollywood Boulevard," *Liberty,* 2 (20 February 1926): 22–24;

"Why Men Join Clubs," *Redbook,* 47 (August 1926): 68–71, 146;

"Eyes of the Blind," *Redbook,* 47 (September 1926): 54–57, 106;

"Love in Eternity," *Redbook,* 50 (January 1928): 39–41, 130–135;

"The Great Emerald Mystery," *Redbook,* 50 (February 1928): 49–51, 90–94;

"First Love," *Liberty,* 6 (20 April 1929): 13–22;

"O Chivalry!" *Liberty,* 6 (20 July 1929): 13–22;

"An Affair of the Heart," *Cosmopolitan,* 86 (October 1929): 76–79, 117–125;

"The Good Friend," *Strand,* 94 (March 1938): 495–504;

"Knight of Glamour," *Strand,* 95 (May 1938): 13–21;

"Even a Worm Can Earn," *Strand,* 95 (July 1938): 236–245;

"Midnight Adventure," *Strand,* 96 (November 1938): 14–23;

"The Red Cavalier," *Strand,* 96 (January 1939): 258–266;

"Poor Little Rich Boy," *Strand,* 96 (March 1939): 496–505;

"You Only Live Once," *Strand,* 96 (April 1939): 604–613;

"Storm on the Blue Train," *Strand,* 97 (October 1939): 562–572;

"Gay Falcon," *Strand,* 98 (January 1940): 218–230;

"Twilight of a Smile," *Strand,* 111 (April 1946): 83–88.

Michael Arlen is remembered primarily as a novelist, the author of the extraordinarily successful novel *The Green Hat* (1924); however, he wrote many short stories in the 1920s and 1930s — more than forty between 1920 and 1925. His style was distinctive: by 1924 critic David Martin could declare that the term *Arlenesque* was a part of the literary vocabulary.

Arlen was born Dikran Kouyoumdjian on 16 November 1895, in Rostock, Bulgaria, the youngest son of Sarkis Kouyoumdjian. The family had left Armenia, and Turkish repression there, three years before. In 1901 they immigrated to England, where Kouyoumdjian attended Malvern College, then briefly studied medicine at the University of Edinburgh in 1913 before dropping out and going to London. He was on the fringes of the literary-artistic set and was meeting people like D. H. Lawrence, George Moore, and Katherine Mansfield. He became an editor and writer for the Anglo-Armenian magazine *Ararat* and a contributor to A. R. Orage's leftist journal of opinion, *The New Age.* The later *New Age* pieces became his first book, *The London Venture* (1920). When his publisher, William Heinemann, advised Kouyoumdjian to use a more commercial pen name, he became "Michael Arlen," adopting the name legally when he took British citizenship in 1922. Although framed as a novel, *The London Venture* is actually a pastiche of literary essays, semi-autobiographical sketches, and stories told by Shelmerdene, a sorrowful beauty who was to reappear often in Arlen's fiction. Taking Lawrence's advice to give up realism, Arlen developed an almost hallucinatory, playfully ornate style. Alec Waugh remarks that Arlen, using this style, "did not tell a story so much as embroider one."

The Romantic Lady (1921) was Arlen's first collection of stories. Arlen often used Joseph Conrad's technique of indirect narration, with the story framed as an oral performance and the narrative persona acting as listener. In "Fay Richmond" this device is again used. Howard Wentworth, dying of influenza, tells the narrator of his unhappy, long-ago love affair with Fay Richmond. As the narrator leaves Wentworth's deathbed, a nurse – calling him "Mr. Arlen" – tells him of the sad case of another patient, a beautiful young woman who has just died – obviously Fay Richmond. The narrator reflects that "it was like the end of a tale by a sentimentalist, for he had compromised with the angels and brought together in the end . . . the bodies of a man and a woman who had loved so unhappily and so incompletely." Nearly all of Arlen's fiction shares this semi-ironic, strong narrative presence and self-reflective awareness of the "literariness" of the story, and this awareness caused Elizabeth A. Drew to call Arlen's writing "cynically sentimental."

The novella that concludes the volume, "The Romance of Iris Poole," begins with a reflection on the "trained artificiality of the craft of tale-telling," alluding to Henry James's notion of "the figure in the carpet." James did influence Arlen's treatment of human relationships. Brothers Roger and Antony Poole are lifelong rivals for Iris, whom Roger, the successful brother, has wed. After Antony convinces Roger to make fraudulent investments, Roger becomes criminally liable, and, with the law closing in, he denounces Antony and shoots himself. Harry Keyishian argues that the real interest of the story lies not in the melodramatic plot of brotherly treachery but in its Jamesian exploration of how Iris comes to know her husband: "her heart had opened to him, not artificially before his weakness of health, but from a more profound realisation of the man himself."

These Charming People was published by Collins in June 1923; Arlen's American publisher, George H. Doran, recalled that when the American edition appeared a year later it sold one hundred thousand copies, "almost a record for a book of short stories." Arlen also made a large sale to *Everybody's Magazine*, one of the most popular American periodicals, which published several of his stories, beginning with "The Broken Nose." This was an early version of "The Man with the Broken Nose," which had first appeared in *The Strand* and which Arlen revised for publication in *These Charming People*. Arlen frequently revised stories extensively after their initial publication: "The Broken Nose" differs from "The Man with the Broken Nose" in having 293 words cut from the opening and having many changes throughout, but it is arguably the same story. Sometimes Arlen's revisions clearly result in a new story, as with "Tea at the Ritz," which became "The Luck of Captain Fortune" after Arlen rewrote it. But nearly all the collected stories differ in some degree from the periodical versions. Another story published by *Everybody's Magazine* in February 1924, "Dancer of Paris," was never collected, but became the basis for a motion picture by First National in 1926.

Of the fifteen stories included in *These Charming People,* three of them – "The Man with the Broken Nose," "Salute the Cavalier!" and "The Cavalier of the Streets" – feature Michael Wagstaffe as the Cavalier, a likable scoundrel resembling E. W. Hornung's gentleman burglar, Raffles. In the first story George Tarlyon and Ralph Wyndham Trevor encounter the Cavalier, who calls himself an Armenian. They believe him, because "no one would say he was an Armenian when he wasn't" and are hoodwinked into aiding him. Thinking themselves to be rescuing a young girl from a rapacious Turk, they are in fact robbing a respectable English gentleman of his coin collection. Enjoying his own "oriental" background, Arlen mocks the conventions of orientalism in popular literature. He adapted other conventions of the adventure story in *The Strand,* where the first two of these stories appeared originally: the hero acts outside the law, yet operates within his own code of conduct and sense of justice.

The piece that opens *These Charming People,* "Introducing a Lady of No Importance and a Gentleman of Even Less," retells an episode from *The London Venture,* a tale of love gone wrong told by Shelmerdene, one of Arlen's positive female characters – sexually adventurous, yet adhering to her personal code. In "When the Nightingale Sang in Berkeley Square" and "The Hunter After Wild Beasts," married couples deceive each other or fail to communicate their needs. In "Major Cypress Goes off the Deep End" Hugo Cypress woos and weds Miss Shirley St. George, sister of George Tarlyon. The unidentified narrator, whose source of information is "my cousin John Fitzroy Pullman," warns the reader at the start that "[t]his story has no point. No story that has anything to do with Hugo

Cypress could have a point, for Hugo is an utterly pointless man."

Arlen was to write many "my cousin Pullman" stories – in some of which Pullman is a main character, in others merely the unnamed narrator's informant. All of these stories are light, comic entertainments like those of P. G. Wodehouse, mostly tales of impoverished upper-class twits wooing and wedding. "Consuelo Brown" concerns a seemingly innocent young girl of eighteen, but the narrator learns that she has already betrayed a man and driven his brother to suicide. If Shelmerdene represents one type of Arlen heroine, the sexually experienced but sensitive woman, Consuelo Brown represents another type identified by Keyishian as "the voracious, depraved woman who has the power to fascinate but lacks kindness and restraint." "The Ancient Sin" is a story of patricide and the supernatural. "The Smell in the Library," a sequel to the "The Romance of Iris Poole," has a remorseful Antony dropping dead from terror because he thinks he smells the smoke of Roger's suicide gun, but George Tarlyon and Ralph Wyndham Trevor discover that Roger's mute Creole wife, whom he abused, has created the smoke. Arlen concludes the volume as he opened it, with a tale of the human heart in "The Real Reason Shelmerdene Was Late For Dinner." This story originated in a play, "The Ci-Divant," published in *The Dial* in 1920, and in 1926 Arlen again transformed the story into a successful London stage play, *Why She Was Late For Dinner.*

Arlen attained his greatest fame in 1924. Doran had published the American edition of *These Charming People* early in the year, but real success came with the novel *The Green Hat.* It sold more than two hundred thousand copies within a few years, and its dramatic and motion picture adaptations made Arlen rich. With its sexually "progressive" heroine, Iris March, and sophisticated melodrama, it captured the spirit of the postwar generation.

May Fair (1925), his third collection of short stories, did not sell as well as *The Green Hat* or *These Charming People,* although it returned to characters and themes of the latter. In 1926 "The Ace of Cads" became a motion picture starring Adolph Menjou as Beau Maturin, another of Arlen's honorable rogues. In "A Romance in Old Brandy" and "The Three-Cornered Moon" Arlen returns to his theme of domestic quarreling and reconciliation, a theme sardonically treated in "The Revolting Doom of a Gentleman Who Would Not Dance with His Wife."

Other stories in the collection are varied in subject and tone. "Where the Pigeons Go to Die" has an ironic twist worthy of the short stories of O. Henry; "The Battle of Berkeley Square" recalls the works of American humorist Thorne Smith, as George Tarlyon finds himself sharing all the physical sensations – including childbirth – that his sister experiences. "The Prince of the Jews" is a "rattling" adventure clearly patterned after the Bulldog Drummond stories of "Sapper" (H. C. McNeile), as George Tarlyon and Fasset-Smith hunt for arch-criminal Julian Raphael in a story marred by what Dorothy Goldman calls a "dreadfully sentimental" conclusion, in which Fasset-Smith and Raphael are reconciled in the afterlife. Arlen's most frequently anthologized work is "The Gentleman From America," a macabre story that depends on a surprise ending for impact. Two Englishmen challenge an American to stay in a haunted house and impersonate a ghost. Years later they reencounter the American and find him driven mad by the experience.

In "To Lamoir," "Farewell These Charming People," and "The Ghoul of Golders Green" Arlen turns to the supernatural. "To Lamoir" echoes Rudyard Kipling's "The Brushwood Boy" with its imaginary playmate who becomes real. "Farewell, These Charming People" features a tale of a diabolic visitation to a dinner party – a tale subsequently revealed as a hoax. "The Ghoul of Golders Green" begins well, as Ralph Wyndham Trevor and Beau Maturin witness supernatural occurrences in the heart of London; then, as Keyishian observes, Arlen "throws it away with a silly twist of plot" – the occult events are abruptly revealed as the work of a low-budget motion picture company. Arlen called O. Henry "the master technician of the short story" and made the ending with a surprising twist a staple of his own short fiction, but it was not always effective.

Arlen's success faltered, as a sort of backlash at his popularity began. The eagerly anticipated novel *Young Men in Love* (1927), his first after *The Green Hat,* met ambivalent reviews and disappointing sales. Sober in tone and more realistic in style, it differed from Arlen's earlier work, and Arlen's career suffered. F. Scott Fitzgerald, in a letter of 1 May 1930, remarked to editor Maxwell Perkins that Michael Arlen had, like other writers, fallen "through the eternal trapdoor of trying [to] cheat the public, no matter what their public is, with substitutes." Arlen's health also suffered. Convalescing from tuberculosis in November 1927, Arlen met D. H. Lawrence in Florence, Italy, and in a letter dated 18 November 1927 to Richard Aldington,

Lawrence described Arlen as having about him "something sort of outcast, [like a] dog that people throw stones at by instinct, and who doesn't feel all pious and Jesusy on the strength of it . . . but wants to bite 'em – which is good." In revising *Lady Chatterley's Lover* (1928) for the third time, Lawrence depicted Arlen as Michaelis, the Irish playwright despised as an alien in spite of his success.

Arlen married the Greek Countess Atalanta Mercati 1 May 1928 in Cannes, where they lived with their son, Michael John, born in 1930, and daughter, Venetia, born in 1933, until World War II. Arlen's writing pace slowed, but he continued to command top dollar. For serialization rights to *Lily Christine* (1928) Arlen received $50,000 from *Cosmopolitan* – about double the usual rate of that magazine – and advances totaling $35,000 for British and American book sales.

Arlen's next collection of stories was *Babes in the Wood* (1929); subtitled "A Relaxation For Those Who Are Always Travelling But Never Reaching A Destination," it had mediocre sales. The first story, "Confessions of A Naturalized Englishman," is about the experiences of a first-person narrator (an alienated young Armenian writer) and his relationship with Priscilla, who resembles Nancy Cunard, the model for the character of Iris March in *The Green Hat*. Although serious at times, the overall tone of the story is gently ironic and self-mocking, as when the narrator remarks that his ties were "the jolly, flashy-coloured ties which foreigners naturally prefer." "Portrait of a Gentleman" is a gentle Jamesian story of an elderly bachelor who falls in love with a much younger widow and proposes marriage; she refuses, knowing him to be too much of a bachelor ever to be happy as a husband, but honoring him for persisting in proposing after he, too, has come to that realization. "Nettles in Arcady" repeats this theme with the sexual roles reversed, while "A Girl With A Future" is a cheerful parody of romance. In contrast, "The 'Lost Generation' " is a disturbing work with a protagonist named Hemingway, "one of those men whom you don't associate with romance, and even less with sentimentality." He prevents a romance between his former lover and a younger man, ostensibly to save the young man from corruption, but he realizes that he is self-deluded. After the protagonist nearly strangles her, they make love. Arlen may have intended to evoke recognition of Ernest Hemingway, whom he knew personally, in this uncharacteristic story.

Arlen's novel *Men Dislike Women* (1931) had only moderate success. A 1931 short story, "Trans-

atlantic," appearing in *Liberty* is worth noting as another departure from Arlen's norm; its depiction of an alcoholic woman's doomed romance with a wealthy socialite is somewhat sentimentalized, but it has a stark and poignant atmosphere lacking Arlen's usual playfulness. *The Short Stories* (1933), which included this story and reprinted selections from earlier collections, was poorly received in England and was not published in the United States.

Arlen attempted new things in his next novels. *Man's Mortality* (1933) was a critically well-received work of speculative fiction. The following year in *Hell! Said the Duchess* (1934) Arlen elaborated on a story, "O Chivalry," that had appeared in *Liberty* in 1931. In this novel Colonel Tarrant spins a tale of an artist so obsessed with the idea of painting absolute evil that he has a practitioner of black magic, Aleister Fox (an allusion to Aleister Crowley), conjure up an evil spirit in the form of a beautiful woman. The novel handles the supernatural fairly deftly, but the trick ending is anticlimactic, and Arlen's attempt to expand the tale into political and moral allegory is muddled. The reviewer for the 5 July 1934 *Times Literary Supplement* called Arlen "floundering beyond his depth," striving too hard to be taken seriously.

If Arlen's popularity had abated somewhat with the lackluster reception of his later novels, his earnings still put him in the top ranks of magazine writers. P. G. Wodehouse, for example, whom Richard Usborne terms "one of the golden boys of the magazines," was paid by *The Strand* about £525 per story in the 1930s, but its editor, Reginald Pound, reports that Michael Arlen commanded £900 per story "no matter how short . . . [and] whether or not they were published."

The Crooked Coronet (1937), Arlen's last collection of short stories, included pieces that had originally appeared in *The Strand*. The titles of all the stories except the title story itself are prefixed "The Legend of . . . ," and the stories are mostly "entertainments." The title story features the reappearance of Michael Wagstaffe, the Cavalier of the Streets, who attempts to blackmail Lady Quorn out of her adulterous ways but ends up being seduced by her. In "The Legend of the Golden Ass" a young newspaperman and Daisy Appledooley, an American heiress, arrange a marriage of convenience. He gains leisure and money to write a novel; she gains respite from fortune hunters. The two do not end in love, as the reader expects, but rather in divorce; the overall effect is as though American short-story writer Ring Lardner had rewritten Henry James's novel *The Portrait of a Lady*. The motion picture ad-

"*I* am afraid, Lady Quorn," he said, " that it is no good
appealing to the better instincts of a blackmailer."

*Illustration by Arthur Wragg for "The Crooked Coronet" (*The
Strand, *November 1934)*

aptation, *The Golden Arrow* (1936), featured actress Bette Davis.

"The Legend of the Bearded Golfer" echoes works of Saki (H. H. Munro). In this story a man on a train tells a transfixed young lady that he has committed the perfect murder — but the appearance of a white cat proves otherwise. Three of the pieces in *The Crooked Coronet* — "The Legend of the Storm over Piccadilly," "The Legend of the Phantom of Pimlico," and "The Legend of the Policeman in Pince-Nez" — are attributed to "my cousin John Fitzroy Pullman." The first two are lighthearted Wodehousean romps, but the last is more macabre, as Ralph Wyndham Trevor and Beau Rockneil are inveigled into assisting a mysterious Doctor Ulzer overcome a "gangster" disguised as a New York publisher. A genial self-parody of Arlen's earlier stories, the story suddenly darkens into a gruesome murder with an ending that, while jarring, again seems forced in its surprise or twist.

In "The Legend of the Black Archangel" Arlen is clearly trying to expand his scope, and the results,

as Keyishian observes, are "unfortunate." Set in Africa, the story features an African-American who, learning that blacks have special muscles that enable them to fly, becomes determined to use a flying army to free Africa from white colonialism. He befriends a white alcoholic who, by betraying him, forces him to realize that "the highest of the blacks is worthy of friendship only with the lowest of the whites." Occasionally in Arlen's writing such ideas and language appear that are now offensive. Arlen is usually being ironic, however, and, judged in his historical context, he was not racist. Other stories are more successful, if predictable: "The Legend of the Old School Tie," another of Arlen's stories about marital estrangement, is cast as a duologue; "The Legend of the Agreeable Widower" (originally "Fool Proof") is a competent detective story; and "The Legend of the Gorilla of Mayfair" recounts the meeting between "my cousin Pullman" and the Cavalier of the Streets.

Arlen's final novel, *The Flying Dutchman* (1939), was another serious work that sold poorly. Returning to England before the war began, he became a London magazine columnist for *The Tatler* and continued to publish short stories in *The Strand*. Being entertainments like the slighter pieces in *The Crooked Coronet,* these stories were never collected and are not among Arlen's best. Arlen's last major success was with the story "Gay Falcon," which was first published in *The Strand* in 1940 and which inspired a series of "B" motion pictures produced by R-K-O. Gay Stanhope Falcon, the title character, is a tougher version of the Michael Wagstaffe figure, the Cavalier of the Streets.

Arlen was appointed public relations officer for the West Midlands Region Civil Defence in late November 1940 and weathered the blitz in Coventry. In January 1941, however, a parliamentary question arose about a "Bulgarian" serving in a position with security implications. Bitterly hurt, Arlen resigned and rejoined his family, whom he had earlier sent to safety in North America.

He spent the next years contracted to M-G-M in Hollywood, where he wrote *The Heavenly Body* (1944) with Walter Reisch. In 1946 Arlen settled in New York City and spent the next decade in retirement. On 23 June 1956 he died of lung cancer.

Arlen's writing is witty and romantic, characterized by a lush, idiosyncratic prose style that readers identified as "oriental" or exotic and that critic Gorham B. Munson disparaged as an "opium dream style." He created a world of well-bred but destitute cavaliers and world-weary courtesans in his stories, characters whose appeal to his contemporary readers was largely because of the distinctively sardonic persona of the narrator. He is customarily dismissed by critics as a one-novel writer, and his works are now neglected. *The Green Hat* undeniably did mark the high point of his career, for in it Arlen somehow touched the pulse of the age. Never a favorite of the critics, his fall from popularity in the 1930s and after has been largely because of the same reaction that saw F. Scott Fitzgerald's reputation eclipsed – he was too closely identified with a time that had come to be seen as frivolous and inconsequential. Novelist Rebecca West has caustically remarked of Arlen's writing that it was "a mixture of the genuine article and advertising copy." In his short stories "the genuine article" predominates.

Biography:
Michael John Arlen, *Exiles* (New York: Farrar, Straus, 1970).

Reference:
Harry Keyishian, *Michael Arlen* (Boston: Twayne, 1975).

H. E. Bates
(16 May 1905 – 31 January 1974)

J. P. Lovering
Canisius College

BOOKS: *The Two Sisters* (London: Cape, 1926; New York: Viking, 1926);

The Seekers (London: J. & E. Bumpus, 1926);

The Last Bread: A Play in One Act (London: Labour Publishing, 1926);

The Spring Song and *In View of the Fact That* (London: E. Archer, 1927);

Day's End and Other Stories (London: Cape, 1928; New York: Viking, 1928);

Catherine Foster (London: Cape, 1929; New York: Viking, 1929);

Seven Tales and Alexander (London: Scholastic Press, 1929; New York: Viking, 1930);

The Hessian Prisoner (London: William Jackson Books, 1930);

The Tree (London: E. Lahr, 1930);

Charlotte's Row (London: Cape, 1931; New York: Cape & Smith, 1931);

Mrs. Esmond's Life (London: Privately printed, 1931);

A Threshing Day (London: W. & G. Foyle, 1931);

The Black Boxer (London: Pharos Editions, 1932; New York: Ballon, 1932);

Sally Go Round the Moon (London: White Owl Press, 1932);

A German Idyll (Waltham Saint Lawrence, Berkshire: Golden Cockerel Press, 1932);

The Fallow Land (London: Cape, 1932);

The Story Without an End and *The Country Doctor* (London: White Owl Press, 1932);

The House with the Apricot and Two Other Tales (London: Golden Cockerel Press, 1933);

The Woman Who Had Imagination and Other Stories (London & Toronto: Cape, 1934; New York: Macmillan, 1934);

Thirty Tales (London: Cape, 1934);

Flowers and Faces (London: Golden Cockerel Press, 1935);

The Poacher (London: Cape, 1935; New York: Macmillan, 1935);

The Duet (London: Grayson & Grayson, 1935);

Cut and Come Again: 14 Stories (London: Cape, 1935);

Lilly Library, Indiana University

Through the Woods: The English Woodland, April to April (London: Gollancz, 1936; New York: Macmillan, 1936);

A House of Women (London: Cape, 1936; New York: Holt, 1936);

Down the River (London: Gollancz, 1937; New York: Holt, 1937);

Something Short and Sweet (London: Cape, 1937);

Spella Ho (London: Cape, 1938; Boston: Little, Brown, 1938);

The Flying Goat (London: Cape, 1939);

My Uncle Silas (London: Cape, 1939);

Country Tales: Collected Short Stories (London: Cape, 1940);

The Seasons and the Gardener (Cambridge: Cambridge University Press, 1940);

The Beauty of the Dead and Other Stories (London: Cape, 1940);

The Modern Short Story: A Critical Survey (London: T. Nelson, 1941; New York: T. Nelson, 1941);

In the Heart of the Country (London: Country Life, 1942);

The Greatest People in the World and Other Stories (London: Cape, 1942); republished as *There's Something in the Air* (New York: Knopf, 1943);

The Bride Comes to Evensford (London: Cape, 1943);

How Sleep the Brave and Other Stories (London: Cape, 1943);

Country Life (London & Harmondsworth: Penguin, 1943);

O More Than Happy Countryman (London: Country Life, 1943);

Fair Stood the Wind for France (London: M. Joseph, 1944; Boston: Little, Brown, 1944);

Something in the Air (London: Cape, 1944) — comprises *The Greatest People in the World and Other Stories* and *How Sleep the Brave and Other Stories*; republished as *The Stories of Flying Officer X* (London: Cape, 1952);

There's Freedom in the Air: The Official Story of the Allied Air Forces from the Occupied Countries (London: H.M.S.O., 1944);

The Day of Glory: A Play in Three Acts (London: M. Joseph, 1945);

The Cruise of the Breadwinner (London: M. Joseph, 1946; Boston: Little, Brown, 1947);

The Tinkers of Elstow (London: Bemrose & Sons, 1946);

The Purple Plain (London: M. Joseph, 1947; Boston: Little, Brown, 1947);

Otters and Men (London: National Society for the Abolition of Cruel Sports, 1947);

Thirty-One Selected Tales (London: Cape, 1947);

The Jacaranda Tree (London: M. Joseph, 1949; Boston: Little, Brown, 1949);

The Bride Comes to Evensford and Other Tales (London: Cape, 1949);

The Country Heart (London: M. Joseph, 1949), revised and amended edition of *O More Than Happy Countryman* and *In the Heart of the Country*;

Dear Life (Boston: Little, Brown, 1949; London: M. Joseph, 1949);

Edward Garnett: A Memoir (London: Parrish, 1950);

The Scarlet Sword (London: M. Joseph, 1950; Boston: Little, Brown, 1951);

Colonel Julian and Other Stories (London: M. Joseph, 1951; Boston: Little, Brown, 1952);

Selected Short Stories of H. E. Bates (London: Pocket Books, 1951);

Twenty Tales (London: Cape, 1951);

The Country of White Clover (London: M. Joseph, 1952);

The Face of England (London: Batsford, 1952);

Love for Lydia (London: M. Joseph, 1952; Boston: Little, Brown, 1953);

The Nature of Love: Three Short Novels (London: M. Joseph, 1953; Boston: Little, Brown, 1954);

The Feast of July (London: M. Joseph, 1954; Boston: Little, Brown, 1954);

The Daffodil Sky (London: M. Joseph, 1955; Boston: Little, Brown, 1956);

The Sleepless Moon (London: M. Joseph, 1956; Boston: Little, Brown, 1957);

Death of a Huntsman: Four Short Novels (London: M. Joseph, 1957); republished as *Summer in Salandar* (Boston: Little, Brown, 1957);

Sugar for the Horse (London: M. Joseph, 1957);

Selected Stories (Harmondsworth: Penguin, 1957);

The Darling Buds of May (London: M. Joseph, 1958; Boston: Little, Brown, 1958);

A Breath of French Air (London: M. Joseph, 1959; Boston: Little, Brown, 1959);

The Watercress Girl and Other Stories (London: M. Joseph, 1959; Boston: Little, Brown, 1960);

An Aspidistra in Babylon: Four Novellas (London: M. Joseph, 1960); republished as *The Grapes of Paradise: Four Short Novels* (Boston: Little, Brown, 1960);

When the Green Woods Laugh (London: M. Joseph, 1960); republished as *Hark, Hark, the Lark!* (Boston: Little, Brown, 1961);

Now Sleeps the Crimson Petal and Other Short Stories (London: M. Joseph, 1961); republished as *The Enchantress and Other Stories* (Boston: Little, Brown, 1961);

The Day of the Tortoise (London: M. Joseph, 1961);

The Golden Oriole: Five Novellas (London: M. Joseph, 1962; Boston: Little, Brown, 1962);

A Crown of Wild Myrtle (London: M. Joseph, 1962; New York: Farrar, Straus, 1963);

Achilles the Donkey (London: Dobson, 1962; New York: Watts, 1963);

Seven by Five: Stories, 1926–1961 (London: M. Joseph, 1963); republished as *The Best of H. E. Bates* (Boston: Little, Brown, 1963);

Achilles and Diana (London: Dobson, 1963; New York: Watts, 1964);

Oh! To Be In England (London: M. Joseph, 1963; New York: Farrar, Straus, 1964);

The Fabulous Mrs. V (London: M. Joseph, 1964);

A Moment in Time (London: M. Joseph, 1964; New York: Farrar, Straus, 1964);

Achilles and the Twins (London: Dobson, 1964; New York: Watts, 1965);

The Wedding Party (London: M. Joseph, 1965);

The Distant Horns of Summer (London: M. Joseph, 1967);

The Four Beauties: Four Novellas (London: M. Joseph, 1968);

The White Admiral (London: Dobson, 1968);

The Wild Cherry Tree (London: M. Joseph, 1968);

The Vanished World: An Autobiography (London: M. Joseph, 1969; Columbia: University of Missouri Press, 1969);

A Little of What You Fancy (London: M. Joseph, 1970);

The Triple Echo (London: M. Joseph, 1970);

The Blossoming World: An Autobiography (London: M. Joseph, 1971; Columbia: University of Missouri Press, 1971);

A Love of Flowers (London: M. Joseph, 1971);

The Song of the Wren (London: M. Joseph, 1972);

The World in Ripeness (London: M. Joseph, 1972; Columbia: University of Missouri Press, 1972);

A Fountain of Flowers (London: M. Joseph, 1974);

The Good Corn and Other Stories, edited by Geoffrey Halson (London: Longman, 1975);

H. E. Bates: Stories, edited by Alan Cattell (London: Harrap, 1975);

The Poison Ladies and Other Stories, edited by Mike Poulton and John L. Foster (Exeter: A. Wheaton, 1976);

The Yellow Meads of Asphodel (London: M. Joseph, 1976).

OTHER: W. H. Hudson, *Green Mansions,* introduction by Bates (London: Collins, 1957), pp. 11–16.

SELECTED PERIODICAL PUBLICATIONS –
UNCOLLECTED: "Stephen Crane: A Neglected Genius," *Bookman,* 81 (October 1931): 10–11;

"Why I Live in the Country," *Countryman,* 12 (January 1936): 494–499;

"The Novelist's Ear," *Fortnightly,* 145 (March 1936): 277–282.

The term *Midlands* is not very descriptive when applied to those counties in central England whose towns and cities in the nineteenth and twentieth centuries were outgrowths of the Industrial Revolution. Yet this same territory also makes up some of the most scenic beauty in the country. The Midlands is the area in which the Middle English dialect developed and hence, also, our modern English. Rushden in Northamptonshire is in the heart of the Midlands, and Herbert Bates was born there on 16 May 1905.

He became, before his death on 31 January 1974, one of the more notable of English short-fiction writers in an age when this form of literature flourished, and the quality of the short fiction he produced during forty-four years of writing was sustained. Bates is also well known for his large output of novels, and he successfully wrote descriptive nature books about his native land. But there is reason to believe that he loved the short narrative best of all. He returned to it constantly during his long writing career, and he found novel writing to be a helpful way of insuring a steady income that would permit him to continue composing his shorter stories. Especially in his later years marketing conditions surely favored the sale of novels rather than books of short stories.

An appreciation of Bates's development as a writer is illuminated by some knowledge of his educational background. His attendance at local schools culminated in an opportunity to attend the grammar school at Kettering tuition-free. As a teenager he showed an ardent interest in football and in painting, but he failed to gain a scholarship for the public school at Wellingborough. Another kind of education was provided by his paternal grandfather, George William Lucas, who devoted himself to introducing the young boy to Midland landscapes and flowers. When the boy finished at Kettering School, his father, Albert, counseled him not to attempt university training – it being unwarranted in the light of the family's means and prospects. In 1922 Herbert therefore accepted a job as apprentice reporter on the *Northampton Chronicle,* but this job was short-lived, as Bates found the editor a troublesome person to work for. He turned to other employment in his hometown, which was mainly a shoemaking town: for two years he worked as a bookkeeper in a warehouse that supplied raw materials to shoe factories. With some encouragement from friends, the seventeen-year-old Bates continued to read and to write poetry, short stories, and a novel – this last of which, *The Two Sisters,* he worked on for about eight years until it was published by Jonathan Cape in 1926. Bates's inability to attend Cambridge University was, as his career unfolded, a crucial one, for most well-known writers of English literature typically have taken some formal university education. And in the lives of the few who did not, it is interesting to question how this affected their overall development.

Occasionally Bates's work is downgraded for its failure to carry a theme or to resolve a problem satisfactorily, with the implication that the author is not as much at home with handling ideas as are many other illustrious fiction writers. Bates (unlike D. H. Lawrence) did not have such a wide-ranging coterie of followers. To his good fortune, however, Bates was "discovered" by the well-known critic Edward Garnett, who was instrumental in getting *The Two Sisters* published, and this friendly relationship lasted until the death of Garnett in 1937, when Garnett's son David then became Bates's supporter. Novelist Graham Greene was also at least partly responsible for helping Bates get a post as a writer with the Royal Air Force during World War II, a development that led to Bates's stories finally gaining a much larger audience. And he was able to hold this larger audience until the end of his life, especially with his successful short novel series on Pop Larkin and his family.

But certainly the cocktail-party pursuit was not what Bates sought. A family man of lower-class origins who loved to write and keep his close ties with the surrounding beauties of nature, Bates loved the ordinary folk. Another benefit of such a simple lifestyle was that he learned how to deal directly with his publishers. Publishers have not been known to be particularly generous in profit sharing, but Bates, although he never attained a large fortune through his writing, did manage successfully his own business affairs.

Bates married Marjorie Helen Cox on 18 July 1931 in the Methodist church in Rushden, where he maintained that he had been a victim of excessively long sermons and Sunday school sessions all his early life. "Madge," whom he had long known, proved to be a happy choice, as she supported Bates in their long struggle to make a living and to build a career in the early years of their lifelong marriage. The Bateses had four children in their first nine years: two daughters, Ann Catharine and Judith, and then two sons, Richard Lucas and Jonathan.

Shortly before the two were married, however, they had decided to leave Rushden and to relocate in the village of Little Chart in Kent, near the town of Ashford. There they worked to restore an old stone building called the Granary and continued to live for the rest of their lives. They traveled frequently to Europe and elsewhere when Bates's income as a writer eventually permitted it. The happiness of the family may be compared with that of Bates's comical portrayal of his fictional Larkin family, which has been adapted and presented in a television series. Author Herbert Bates's family life

H. E. Bates at the Granary, his house in rural Kent, circa 1932 (courtesy of Stanley Bates)

and values may have resembled those of his fictional creation Pop Larkin in several ways: in the love of family, the spirit of fun and innocence, the disdain toward government forces that intrude upon their lives, and a spirit of entrepreneuring or "larking."

Bates's first collection of short stories was *Day's End and Other Stories* (1928), twenty-five works written largely when the author was in his late teens and early twenties while he was trying to publish *The Two Sisters*. The stories reveal a writer who is always clear about what he has to say and who can deftly and unobtrusively incorporate natural description into the plot, the character's actions, and the theme of the story. The settings are generally the rural England of Northamptonshire and the small village that Bates knew so well. The main characters are young or old, male or female, but are generally selected from the less fortunate people of the Midlands. Most of the stories are written with third-person narration and are approximately ten pages long, with the exception of the title story "Day's End," which is about three times longer than the rest. It might be labeled a novella, but it does not demonstrate the artistry of the novella, a genre in which Bates became very proficient as his career unfolded.

Reading Bates's fiction with success and pleasure requires some realization that he was, from the start, departing from the prevailing mode of such English short-fiction writers of the 1890s and early 1900s as Robert Louis Stevenson and Rudyard Kipling. They were more formal in diction and given to close plotting of narratives that were more heavily thematic. In the late 1920s and in the 1930s Bates became aware of the revolution in narrative style engendered mainly by Hemingway — a newly impressionistic and oblique manner. In his *The Modern Short Story* (1941) Bates discusses some of the major influences on the narrative style of the English short story: non-British writers such as Ivan Turgenev, Anton Chekhov, and Guy de Maupassant — and still later Hemingway, Sherwood Anderson, and other Americans. James Joyce and George Moore, among Ireland's fine short-fiction artists, and Katherine Mansfield and A. E. Coppard among the British, were all inclined to follow the new narrative obliqueness in storytelling.

In the opening title story of *Day's End* the main character, seventy-year-old Israel Rentshaw, is living with his daughter Henrietta, who is in her late thirties. They have received an eviction notice because their rented farm is directly in the way of a proposed highway. The old farmer is in failing health and will not pay close attention to the foreclosure notices in spite of his daughter's gentle reminders. A real tension mounts steadily and is conveyed primarily through the consciousness of Israel. Bates crafts extemely well Israel's hallucinations, his sinking spirits, and the familiar objects that he encounters in his daily rounds. These objects slowly become elusive for him. On his deathbed these objects, like the fir tree he had promised to cut down at Henrietta's request, haunt his dying reflections:

> His body felt light and frail, like a shell. Yet he longed for the tree to fall, cease its agony and cover him.
> And suddenly in the branches of the tree a lovely commotion began, as of gladness and relief, all the leaves seemed to shake with laughter, and the tree did fall.
> And in that moment his beard gave a sleepy droop, his hands fell away from his chest, and he paused to draw a long breath in which, too, was relief, thankfulness and an end.

In this story Bates is not laboring one of his central concerns or themes — the transition in rural Britain from an agricultural economy to one of shoe manufacture. But his story brings home the plight of the small English town.

"Blossoms," the last story of this first collection, similarly demonstrates an ironic and futile human relationship between mother and son. Frances, a widow, loves to ride her young son to school on a bicycle, applying the brakes halfway down the hill and coasting to their destination. Bates describes the ride: "Through the streets they glided serenely, . . . Francie with her simple, moon-like face looking neither to right nor left, the boy resting stupidly one frightened cheek on the back of her tender body." It is spring, and the mother pauses to gaze at the "soft, reddish dust" under the trees. She carefully explains nature's process to the boy, who seems only confused by her words. Francie speaks openly to the boy of her desire that he might become perhaps a great opera singer one day. (She herself had climaxed her own musical career by being part of a large chorale in London.) But her daily explanations are always forgotten by the boy as soon as they are uttered.

In his second collection, *Seven Tales and Alexander* (1929), Bates continued to work with characters of the rustic Midlands. Dennis Vannatta comments on the general tone of the new volume: "Certainly the world of *Seven Tales and Alexander* is far removed from the harsh realities of life in the crises years of the late 1920s in England." "Alexander" is the best of the eight stories in this volume.

Alexander is an eleven- or twelve-year-old boy who takes a day's journey with his uncle to visit a wealthy old widow who owns some large fruit orchards. The story is loosely structured in four parts, in order to bring out the sensitive young boy's first experience of love during a chance encounter with a young girl his own age. When his Uncle Bishop stops for a brief visit at a friend's house, Alexander accidentally meets a girl in the orchard. She is friendly but not aggressively so, and she tries to engage the boy in some innocent play. But he is carried away by a vision of love that controls his demeanor for the rest of his day and evening. The situation recalls the love experience of James Joyce's unnamed narrator in "Araby," as the imaginations of both boys are wholly consumed by their experiences. The story continues in its episodic structure as the uncle drives on to the goal of the day's ride. But Alexander's soul remains riveted to the memory of the girl, and he makes futile inquiries about the possibility of seeing the girl again on the return trip: it is too dark and too late for the uncle to stop again. Some Edenic overtones enrich the story, and some powerful rustic characterizations add humor to this tale. The richness of the story comes through the poetic rendering of the countryside as a backdrop for the boy's first perception of love. The story conveys something of how the young Bates himself had been influenced by his grandfather, who walked him through the Midlands and taught him how to observe. "Alexander" contains some humorous moments and, unlike Joyce's "Araby," suggests that the boy's experience, though he is disheartened by the prospect that he may never again see his heart's desire, will allow him to make it to manhood unscathed.

Bates had continued his efforts as a novelist with *Catherine Foster* (1929), published the same year as *Seven Tales and Alexander*. Two years later he published *Charlotte's Row,* which was more like a work in the naturalistic tradition of the proletarian novel. In 1931 Bates married, then moved to Little Chart, Kent, in southeast England. The next decade was to be one of his most productive. In 1932 he published *The Black Boxer,* a collection of eleven stories. Three of the best in this group are long short stories wherein a single character dominates the action. The title story presents an aging black fighter traveling with a carnival show. He is a skilled boxer who has deceived the show-manager, Sullivan, about his age and condition. Zeke, the forty-year-old black fighter, claims to be thirty-six. Sullivan, who acts as both promoter and referee, is betting on Zeke, who is badly beaten in his bout but, just as he is about to lose, madly rushes his opponent and knocks him out – partly through an illegal punch. Sullivan declares Zeke the winner, but Zeke, "tired, stupefied, and ashamed," has clearly been defeated in his long struggle with the cheap carnival life.

Another interesting story is *Mrs. Esmond's Life* (1931), in which Charlotte Esmond is sharply set in a milieu of the lower-class struggle for a place in the sun. A young widow, Charlotte lives near a theater with her daughter, Effie, and they run a cooked-meat shop that provides snacks for the players and audiences. Charlotte runs a neat shop without any real assistance from her daughter. But she feels that her stout, young Effie does not seem to be getting on in the world: reading cheap novels is how the girl generally passes her time. Charlotte's three sons had given her no such problems, and they are now all successes in America. When an old acquaintance, a draper whose wife is now dead, renews his friendship with Charlotte, she becomes full of tenderness for him. She begins to consider building a life with him.

One day at a picnic Charlotte spots Effie and the much-older draper clasped in each other's arms.

For a few weeks Charlotte is crushed, but she manages to resume her work. Eventually Effie and the draper do marry and have a child, and Charlotte continues carrying on her busy life at the sandwich shop while also tending the baby at times. A horrible accident then occurs while Charlotte is minding the baby and tending the shop at the same time: the child is scalded badly and dies.

Charlotte is left alone and near despair, although her sons wish her to come to America. She considers this, but she fears the uprooting and decides to go back to her sandwich making, for "After all, it was the will of God that what was to happen would happen, and that when it was time to change or move or die it would be soon. One knew no more."

Charlotte Esmond was written in 1929, a time of increasing economic depression in Britain, and it has an urban, industrial setting that constitutes the primary source of the heroine's struggle. It differs from most of Bates's earlier short stories, which have more rustic and outdoor settings and establish tones that are not as harsh as those found here.

By this time Bates had settled into his new home at Little Chart, begun writing a column called "Country Life" for *The Spectator,* and become a father. The 1930s were to be a most productive time for Bates, who explains to readers in the second volume of his autobiography *The Blossoming World* (1971) that at this time he came under the influence of four "new masters." Two were English: nature writer W. H. Hudson and poet Edward Thomas. The other two were American: Sherwood Anderson and Ernest Hemingway. Hudson, Bates continues in *The Blossoming World,* "enlarged my vision of the natural world." The love of the natural embodied in the works of Anderson and Thomas led Bates to accentuate common language and experience in his writing.

The title story of the collection *The Woman Who Had Imagination and Other Stories* (1934) and another called "The Waterfall" both concentrate on women caught in the frustrations of unhappy unions. In the title story a sensitive young man, Henry, is disgruntled at having to go on a picnic with the church choir. As he wanders away from the activities, he meets a beautiful young woman who seems shy and diffident, but the two are greatly attracted to each other. The young man accidentally learns that she is unhappily married to a much older man who is an invalid, but late that night Henry, heading home, still feels "a sense of morning in the air in spite of the stars, the silence and the darkness."

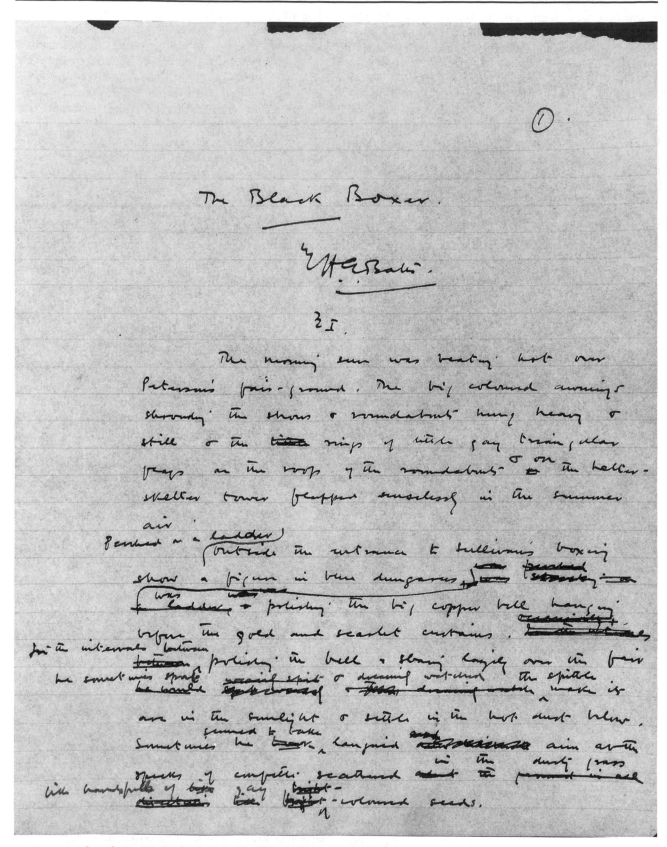

First page from the manuscript for the title story of Bates's 1932 collection (Lilly Library, Indiana University; by permission of the Estate of H. E. Bates)

The Waterfall focuses on Rose Vaughan, the forty-year-old daughter of a minister who habitually manifests most of the failings that Bates sees in contemporary religious figures: Minister Vaughan has brought up his daughter to be an austere, rather frigid person. Soon after his death Rose suddenly receives a marriage proposal from Abraham Edwards, a fellow parishioner whom she accepts — but only with a sense of duty, as she has been brought up to do. There is no love on either side in the arid marriage. Rose suggests to her husband, Abraham (a much older person than she and of a pompous nature), that to her dead father's memory it would be appropriate for the villagers to improve the waterfall, which is a point of scenic beauty as well as a functional part of the town's water system. Abraham is a pillar of the community and agrees to head the project. He hires Mr. Phillips as his engineer.

Phillips is a much younger man, outgoing and ebullient. He draws Rose into his more active lifestyle with his good-natured humor and banter. Rose is caught between her desire to join in the laughter and good times and her self-consciousness and rigid religious upbringing. In the final sequence of the story we understand that, although she is equally captivated and repelled by the engineer, when he leaves town there will be no further blossoming of Rose.

Cut and Come Again (1935), which contained fourteen stories, appeared the next year. Two stories, "The Mill" and "The Station," are the most memorable from this volume. The first, which has received the greater praise from Bates's readers, is the story of Alice Hartop, young daughter of a harsh farmer who forces her to hire out to the neighboring Holland family. There she is further victimized by Fred, the man of the house, whose wife needs Alice's help. Alice, cowering in her virtual slave status, submits to the man's sexual advances and becomes pregnant — only to be dismissed ultimately with no consideration (except for some sympathy from the man's son) and told to go back to her parents. The story ends as she reenters her own home, with the signs of labor pains beginning after her long walk back: "She did not move. Her face was flat and blank and her body static. It was only her eyes that registered the suddenness and depths of her emotions. They began to fill with tears. It was as though they had come to life at last."

The other story, "The Station," gives a similar naturalistic/realistic treatment of sexuality. The title of the story refers to a remote gas station whose only attendant is the wife of the owner. She is a woman whose attractiveness is heralded at the beginning of the story by the remarks of an older truck driver. After dinner a younger truck driver soon discovers the nature of her attractiveness when, inviting him to pick some fruit to take with him, the woman lures him into a plum orchard. Her obvious efforts at seduction actually repel the young man. The character of the woman, who is known to keep the station open at late hours, adds a decidedly strange aura to the story.

The title story, "Cut and Come Again," is a vignette that beautifully and clearly presents a mood, this time between a young married couple undergoing some unnamed but painful problems. The man is cutting remnant hay at the edge of the field. She has come to talk about their common problem, but their dialogue does not indicate any change in the situation. Will there be a happy ending? As the girl leaves, Bates's narrative merely concludes that "even then he would cease his attack on the hedge and still look after her, unsure about it all, lost in a conflict of doubt and tenderness and some inexpressible pain."

Before the end of the 1930s Bates produced three more collections of short stories: *Something Short and Sweet* (1937), *My Uncle Silas* (1939), and *The Flying Goat* (1939). The first two generally sustained the quality of the previous volumes; the latter, by common judgments, did not. Perhaps the weaknesses of *The Flying Goat* should not be much of a surprise, for Bates's production was extremely prodigious. His family was also increasing, and he gave much of his time to the three children. In 1938 he had gone to America for the first time to consult with the *Atlantic Monthly* about an American edition of his popular novel *Spella Ho* (1938). The prospect of war for Britain was growing, and Bates, though despising the idea of war, played his part in early antiwar efforts even while keeping up with his fiction writing.

The distinct comedy of the Uncle Silas stories constitutes some change of pace from the naturalism of the previous stories. Several of the stories in this volume already had been published separately in earlier collections and had been well received. Bates's preface to the 1939 collection recalls Silas as "this happy, lusty and devilished character," and Silas is all of that. Bates's own uncle, Joseph Betts, was the real-life model for Silas. Betts had given up the manufacture of shoes and bought a small farm in the country, and Bates used to pay him frequent Sunday visits. If Betts supplied some of what appears in Uncle Silas, however, there is no doubt that behind the fictional Silas's nonconformity, especially his anti-Puritan mores, stands the author him-

THE WOMAN
WHO HAD
IMAGINATION

fourteen stories by

H. E. BATES

*Dust jacket for Bates's 1934 collection of stories, published
during his most productive decade as a short-fiction writer
(courtesy of the Lilly Library, Indiana University)*

self at a short distance. Bates says: "Certainly there
was no strain of the Puritan in my Uncle Silas, who
got gloriously and regularly drunk. He loved food
and the ladies and good company, was not afraid to
wear a huge and flamboyant buttonhole, told lies,
got the better of his fellow-man whenever the
chance offered itself, used a scythe like an angel,
was a wonderful gardener, took the local lord's
pheasants, and yet succeeded in remaining an honest, genuine and lovable character." In 1957 a second collection of the Uncle Silas tales, *Sugar for the
Horse,* was published.

Dean R. Baldwin, Bates's biographer-critic,
points out that in the Silas story "The Lily" Bates
first begins to use Silas as an ironic narrator, a
major development from his usual third-person narration. The Silas stories are usually quite brief, four
or five pages long, with the voice of Silas recounting
events and dramatizing them via his colorful imagination. Toward the end of his career Bates also pro-

duced a successful comic series of short novels with
the character of Pop Larkin, a figure who shares
some of the humorous traits of Uncle Silas.

With England at war with Germany in October 1941, Bates, partly through the influence of
Graham Greene, found his way into the public relations division of the RAF. It was the first time a
story writer was ever commissioned in order to continue his writing within the military. It was a successful experiment, for within two years Bates produced two volumes of stories for the RAF: *The
Greatest People in the World and Other Stories* (1942)
and *How Sleep the Brave and Other Stories* (1943).
These he wrote under the pseudonym of "Flying
Officer X," but the British public soon was aware of
the author's real identity, and Bates's reputation
began to grow. The stories are very brief, like the
Silas stories. Under a thin fictional veneer they present clearly the life and times of the military personnel, and Bates's interest in the human nature of
these men and women prevents him from becoming
a mere propagandist for the war effort.

Bates's ill health at this time was part of the
reason that his short-story production did not
match his earlier record. An abdominal pain hampered his activity for several years, but this did not
prevent his writing in 1941 *The Modern Short Story,* a
fine and insightful book on a subject close to the
writer's heart. In his 1972 preface to the later edition of this book Bates, looking back on developments in fiction and in drama, called the writing of
the 1950s and 1960s in both Britain and America
"even darker" than that of the tragic war years
themselves. He was principally objecting to "A new
generation of writers [who] sprang up with no other
purpose than to tell all, revolting or revoltingly silly
though it might be."

A book that brought Bates even more prominence in this wartime period was the novel *Fair
Stood the Wind for France* (1944). His RAF assignments had occasionally taken him to France and
eventually to the Far East, and his novel follows the
efforts of John Franklin, an English pilot, to return
to his home base in England. The plot involves a series of hazardous escapes mainly through the
French underground, where he finds an ally and a
true love in the person of Françoise, a woman who
brings a distinct religious overtone, and thereby additional strength, to the novel.

Following his demobilization in 1945 Bates
wrote in the next four years three novels, all growing out of his former assignment by the British air
ministry to write (especially for American readers)
accounts of the struggle in Burma, where the Japa-

nese had gained a stronghold. With his feel for the countryside of France, Bates had already written ably in *Fair Stood the Wind for France,* and he demonstrates in the three Burmese novels – *The Purple Plain* (1947), *The Jacaranda Tree* (1949), and *The Scarlet Sword* (1950) – that he was equally effective in handling Far East landscapes and people. Joseph Conrad, Rudyard Kipling, and W. Somerset Maugham had preceded him in writing accounts of life in Far Eastern outposts, and Bates had read all of these writers. Bates's Far Eastern novels and short stories also have realistic settings and engage the reader's interest in the lives of those in these countries.

In *The Scarlet Sword,* for example, Bates recounts an attack on a Burmese mission and its hospital, which is being run by two Catholic priests, Father Simpson and Father Angstey. Death and violence appear frequently in this novel, yet despite Bates's powerful bias against institutional Christianity, he never loses sight of the presence of common humanity – natives, British nurses, and workers, as well as the Catholic priests. His outlook on life is here shown to be one ripened by his wartime experiences to include a greater understanding of man's fate, a greater willingness to see beyond the social inequities than Bates had earlier felt. In a certain sense his enlistment as a writer in the British military service had become a kind of university for him, since he may have lacked the kind of camaraderie, social as well as intellectual, that other authors normally acquire via their university friendships.

Dennis Vannatta, a discerning critic of Bates, speaks of the general quality of his later short fiction: "the short stories in the 1950s and 1960s mark a return to the high standards and the methods of the prewar years. Indeed *Colonel Julian and Other Stories* (1951), *The Daffodil Sky* (1955), and *The Enchantress and Other Stories* (1961) warrant comparison with Bates' finest collections."

Colonel Julian and Other Stories exhibits many stories set in countries other than England, stories frequently dealing with war and postwar issues. His themes are often directed toward peoples' struggles with a changing world. In "The Frontier," one of the stories from the Colonel Julian collection, the main character, Davis, has been an English tea grower and manufacturer in postwar Calcutta for the past twenty years. Although his tea plantation in the north is situated amid some lovely mountain scenery, he is a man filled with boredom. Although he enjoys remembering the faces of the nurses that he viewed during the last days of the war, there really has been no woman of any significance in his life. And the recent postcolonial uprisings of the Indian factions, with their "Quit India" slogans, have increased his weariness.

He aids and befriends a young British nurse as he is getting on a train heading north to the cooler climate of his mountain retreat and tea plantation. There has been a rape and murder in his plantation community, and Davis is going to spend his weekend helping to search for the criminal. Davis invites the nurse, Blake, to be his guest. She is attractive but appears to have no more zest for life than Davis himself. She does, however, show interest whenever the hunt for the criminal is mentioned, and she desires to participate. Davis is attracted to her, eyes her repeatedly, and soon makes some weak efforts to seduce her. The girl at moments appears to be willing. But Bates uses these maneuvers to underscore the emptiness of the man. The next day in the hunt Davis, tired, sits down by a river and comes within the sights of the escapee's rifle. Suddenly shot and rendered unable to speak, Davis dies soon after in Blake's arms: "All the life of his body, borne on a great torrent of blood, was flowing back to his head, choking with hideous congestion his sight and breath. . . . And when she looked back at his eyes she saw that all sight of sky, the mountains, and the haze that hid the further mountains had been extinguished too."

"The Frontier" is an effective, tightly constructed fifteen-page story. The vividly rendered setting of the mountainous Dooar region of India and the beauty of the high mountain of Kanchenjunga are effective as symbols of what was lacking in the life of the British tea grower, and the story memorably presents Bates's views of postcolonial world tensions.

Publication of Bates's short fiction continued – even posthumously, with *The Yellow Meads of Asphodel* (1976) – but the narrative appeal of the late collections diminishes. His longer works of fiction, the novellas, do not display this tapering off, however. In his autobiography Bates wrote that he became more enamored of the novella than of the short story while writing *The Cruise of the Breadwinner* (1946), and he claimed that he was influenced largely by Stephen Crane's *The Red Badge of Courage* (1895), although critic James Agate compared Bates's novella to Joseph Conrad's *Typhoon* (1903). Setting this novella in World War II times, Bates presents an old sea captain and a mere boy battling the elements and enemy planes that strafe their ramshackle fishing boat.

When Bates resolved to give more attention to writing the novella, he had a difficult task convincing his publishers of the marketability of the novella, but *The Nature of Love: Three Short Novels* (1953) sold exceptionally well. It was dedicated to Maugham, whose craftsmanship Bates still admired, although he saw Maugham as not so much a cynic as a sentimentalist – a derogation that cannot be fairly applied to Bates himself. The three stories – "Dulcima," "The Grass God," and "The Delicate Nature" – all center on amorous pursuits that end harshly or in disaster. In the first instance a homely, poor, and extremely fat girl raised without any real love takes up with her stage manager. When she tries to escape his lust and pursue another lover, the manager slays the rival. In "The Grass God" a wealthy man has a secret affair with a younger lady, who sees through the lust of their summer romance and rejects her "lover" at the end. "The Delicate Nature" is set in Malaysia, where the central figure is a plantation owner who has brought his bride from England to the Far East. Here the action turns on the first-person narrator, Simpson, an assistant to owner Malan, who becomes infatuated with Vera, the owner's wife. After a full affair Simpson is summarily and callously rejected by Vera. All three novellas thus examine ironies of unfulfilled love. In some respects these stories do reflect a Maugham-like cynicism, but they are related with more straightforwardness than one generally associates with the writing of Maugham.

The next series of novellas, *Death of a Huntsman: Four Short Novels,* came four years later in 1957. It included "The Death of a Huntsman," one of Bates's best-regarded novellas, which examines the tension between Harry Barnfield's love for both a mother (an old friend) and for the lady's beautiful young daughter. Harry, already married to an invalid, cannot cope with this situation, and his problem is solved by his sudden and violent death. The two other novellas in this collection, "Night Train to the West" and "Summer in Salandar," are also love stories that have unhappy endings, and in both of these the plotting, characterizations, and denouements reveal how Bates was still developing his talents as a writer of novellas.

Bates's later collections of novellas included *An Aspidistra in Babylon: Four Novellas* (1960), *The Golden Oriole: Five Novellas* (1962), and *The Four Beauties: Four Novellas* (1968). In these he continued to hold his readers by his tightly constructed plots. While most of his stories center on the characters' love interests, an aura of bitterness appears even though they are cast in a comic mode.

Bates published his novella *The Triple Echo* (1970) by itself. He tells us in the last volume of his autobiography, *The World in Ripeness* (1972) that he had worked intermittently on this story for twenty-five years without getting the handle on it until much later. He explains that when he learned that he should have been working with only two main characters instead of three, he succeeded at last in telling this story of an AWOL British soldier who is befriended by a Mrs. Charlesworth, the lonesome wife of a prisoner of war in Japan. Bates held the story to be one of his best novellas, but one can argue that it remains flawed by both its repetitiousness and the inconsistencies in both of its main characters. The story seems drawn out unnecessarily, and the love affair between Mrs. Charlesworth and Barton, the young soldier, strains credibility – especially in the woman's efforts to conceal the soldier and in Barton's disguise and actions as Mrs. Charlesworth's sister. The extreme violence of the story's ending is tragic, but the hide-and-seek game with the military police that continues over an extended time comes across as too weak for the circumstances.

Bates also continued to write novels in his later years, even though the novella had become his favorite form. Still one of the best-regarded of all his novels is *Love For Lydia* (1952), the popularity of which has been enhanced by its television presentations in Britain and America after Bates's death in 1974. But toward the latter part of his career Bates began a series of short novels that were to become his most successful, or most popular, fictional works – and which centered on the character of Pop Larkin. These included *The Darling Buds of May* (1958), *A Breath of French Air* (1959), *When the Green Woods Laugh* (1960), *Oh! To Be In England* (1963), and *A Little of What You Fancy* (1970). The reason for this success is their rollicking comic spirit. The whole Larkin family revels in the good things of the earth. Pop is a freelance junkdealer and full-time fortune hunter who never lets anything disagreeable interfere with life's pleasures. The Larkins' love of eating, drinking, and sex is infectious among their friends and neighbors.

In their first adventure in *The Darling Buds of May* Mr. Charlton, a tax collector, comes to check on Pop's failure to file his returns. The eldest of the five Larkin daughters, Mariette, has just informed her mother that she is pregnant and does not know the name of the father, and all the Larkins join forces to ensnare Mr. Charlton as the proper object, a husband for Mariette. They inveigle him to stay for dinner and then the weekend – by which time he has fallen for Mariette, abandoned his arid work as collector, and become Pop's ally and expert on how to beat the tax laws. This robust, ribald comic action is best seen as a Batesian critique of Cold War England, a mode of countering all that he felt was pejorative and artificial in governmental red tape and puritanical pomp in the British makeup. That Pop had never taken time to bother getting married to his mate, or in getting his children baptized, is another indication of Bates's general attitude toward institutional religion. Ma Larkin approves of all of Pop's actions, and when asked why she had never insisted on a marriage, she answers that, after all, she might have lost Pop if she had.

In all this Herbert Bates was giving full rein, for the first time in his writing, to a genuinely comic talent and spirit. These Larkin stories are crowded with good fun and frolic. Pop Larkin is akin to the earlier and also successful Uncle Silas, a character Bates enjoyed and returned to throughout his writing, claiming in *The World in Ripeness* that "The only things I don't share with Pop are a business ability to sell junk at a profit of three hundred and more per cent or to avoid the payment of income tax."

Bates did have an ability to carve for himself a niche among English short-fiction artists of the twentieth century, and he managed this career essentially on his own, without the traditional university background. His natural love of the land, its vegetation, and its flowers is joined with his interest in and love for the ordinary folk of English small towns and countryside that enrich his tales of love, human weakness, and travail. Baldwin, Bates's biographer and critic, offers this sympathetic assessment of the author's work in "Atmosphere in the Stories of H. E. Bates": "Complexities of emotion rather than of plot of character are his trademark, and he almost never ventures into political commentary, social criticism or abstract ideas. The interaction of people with one another and with their immediate environment are the focus of interest. Yet Bates' stories have intricate structure and a subtle texture that makes them curiously powerful and resonant."

"Boy Blue" was a favorite name given Bates by some of his fellow townsmen in Rushden. This epithet, borrowed from the nursery rhyme, recalls the distinctive light blue color of the man's eyes. It is somehow an appropriate one for a writer whose stories still carry the power to captivate his readers.

Bibliography:

Peter Eads, *H. E. Bates: A Bibliographical Study* (Winchester, Hampshire: St. Paul's Bibliographies, 1990).

Biography:

Dean R. Baldwin, *H. E. Bates: A Literary Life* (Selinsgrove, Pa.: Susquehanna University Press, 1987).

References:

Walter Allen, *The Short Story in English* (New York: Oxford University Press, 1981), pp. 260–264;

Dean R. Baldwin, "Atmosphere in the Stories of H. E. Bates," *Studies in Short Fiction,* 21 (Summer 1984): 215–222;

T. O. Beachcroft, *The Modest Art* (London: Oxford University Press, 1968), pp. 185–188;

Hector Bolitho, "A Note on Bernard Shaw and H. E. Bates," *Texas Quarterly,* 11 (Spring 1968): 100–112;

William Frierson, *The English Novel in Transition, 1885–1940* (New York: Cooper Square Publishers, 1965), pp. 283, 306–308, 320–321;

David Garnett, *Great Friends: Portraits of Seventeen Writers* (New York: Atheneum, 1980), pp. 204–209;

James Gindin, "A. E. Coppard and H. E. Bates," in *The English Short Story, 1945–1980,* edited by Joseph M. Flora (Boston: Twayne, 1985), pp. 113–141;

Dennis Vannatta, *H. E. Bates* (Boston: Twayne, 1983).

Papers:

Most of H. E. Bates's manuscripts and letters are the property of the Harry Ransom Humanities Research Center of the University of Texas at Austin.

Stella Benson

(6 January 1892 – 6 December 1933)

George M. Johnson
University College of the Cariboo

See also the Benson entry in *DLB 36: British Novelists, 1890–1929: Modernists.*

BOOKS: *I Pose* (London: Macmillan, 1915; New York: Macmillan, 1916);

This Is the End (London: Macmillan, 1917);

Twenty (London: Macmillan, 1918; New York: Macmillan, 1918);

Living Alone (London: Macmillan, 1919);

Kwan-Yin (San Francisco: Grabhorn Press, 1922);

The Poor Man (London: Macmillan, 1922; New York: Macmillan, 1923);

Pipers and a Dancer (London: Macmillan, 1924; New York: Macmillan, 1924);

The Little World (London: Macmillan, 1925; New York: Macmillan, 1925);

The Awakening: A Fantasy (San Francisco: Lantern Press, 1925);

Goodbye, Stranger (London: Macmillan, 1926; New York: Macmillan, 1926);

The Man Who Missed the 'Bus: A Story (London: Elkin Mathews & Marrot, 1928);

Worlds Within Worlds (London: Macmillan, 1928; New York & London: Harper, 1929);

The Far-Away Bride (New York & London: Harper, 1930); republished as *Tobit Transplanted* (London: Macmillan, 1931);

Hope Against Hope, and Other Stories (London: Macmillan, 1931);

Christmas Formula and Other Stories (London: Joiner & Steele, 1932);

Pull Devil, Pull Baker, by Benson and Count Nicolas de Toulouse Lautrec de Savine (New York: Harper / London: Macmillan, 1933);

Mundos: An Unfinished Novel (London: Macmillan, 1935);

Poems (London: Macmillan, 1935);

Collected Short Stories (London: Macmillan, 1936).

SELECTED PERIODICAL PUBLICATIONS – UNCOLLECTED:

FICTION

"A Dream," *Saturday Review of Literature,* 6 (19 April 1930): 946;

"Two Ghosts," *Harper's Monthly Magazine,* 161 (August 1930): 371–372;

"Search for Mr. Loo," *Harper's Monthly Magazine,* 162 (May 1931): 653–659;

"Destination," *Harper's Monthly Magazine,* 164 (December 1931): 23–28;

"The Prank," *Scholastic,* 31 (8 January 1938): 3–4.

NONFICTION

"Another Tyranny," *Bookman,* 48 (January 1919): 640–643;

"Freudian America," *Bookman,* 49 (May 1919): 304–305;

"Bags and Barrows," *Dial,* 67 (12 July 1919): 11–14;

"Little Back Room," *Dial,* 67 (4 October 1919): 291–294;

"Hunting Worlds," *Bookman,* 53 (June 1921): 344–345;

"Lines Written in a Temper," *Saturday Review of Literature,* 3 (25 September 1926): 134–135;

"Escape from Adventure," *Fortnightly Review,* new series 123 (February 1928): 277–282;

"Eleuthera," *Saturday Review of Literature,* 5 (4 May 1929): 974;

"Alarums and Excursions," *Fortnightly Review,* new series 128 (November 1930): 625–634;

"Watching Lips Moving," *Saturday Review of Literature,* 7 (20 June 1931): 910;

"Reflections in a Mirror," *Saturday Review of Literature,* 8 (15 August 1931): 54;

"The Ignoramus as Gardener in the Far East," *Fortnightly Review,* new series 130 (October 1931): 478–481;

"News from the Seat of War," *New Yorker,* 8 (2 April 1932): 34–40;

"Den-Fil – Useful Knowledge," *Saturday Review of Literature,* 8 (28 May 1932): 753–754;

"The Old Prince," *New Yorker,* 8 (15 October 1932): 18–20;

"Firefly to Steer By," *Harper's Monthly Magazine,* 166 (December 1932): 122–124;

"Wild Pygmies Afloat," *Harper's Monthly Magazine,* 166 (May 1933): 735–739;

"Observations on Canine Blue Blood," *Harper's Monthly Magazine,* 167 (August 1933): 375–378;

"More Dreams," *Saturday Review of Literature,* 10 (16 December 1933): 354;

"Detour in Tonkin," *Fortnightly Review,* new series; 135 (January 1934): 77–85;

"Blaming the Shrew," *Saturday Review of Literature,* 11 (1 September 1934): 83.

Stella Benson at Arosa, Switzerland, early in 1911

Stella Benson lived a life of travel and adventure despite chronic ill health and bouts of depression. Her seven novels, for which she is best known, reflect her extensive travels in their meticulously and delightfully described exotic settings and her insight into ways of thinking in foreign cultures, and these led Geoffrey West to claim that "Stella Benson has cultivated the world; she is the true novelist of (in Mr. Wells's word) cosmocracy, equally at home in every continent and with people of whatever colour or creed." Nevertheless, she remained staunchly English in her outlook, one of several paradoxes in her life and writing. She frequently satirized various aspects of foreign cultures – particularly American, though she was no easier on the English colonial mentality. After writing an acerbic article about Hong Kong near the end of her life, she stated, "I have never dreamed that there was any danger in laughing at English people, so safe was I in the knowledge that I *am* English, and that fundamentally I love Englishness." Much of the time that she lived abroad, particularly in Asia, was owing to circumstances beyond her control, and she did not allow herself to be tied slavishly to the settings that she described so well. Notably in her early fiction she cleverly blended fantasy and reality, and this blend also appears in several of her twenty-odd short stories.

Benson's novels and stories also reflect her travails as a twentieth-century woman: supporting female suffrage, living in a hostile colonial setting, and witnessing the tragedy of World War I. Some of her short stories in particular seem modern in their depictions of individuals lost, isolated, and alienated in strange and frightening situations. She shares with Virginia Woolf, whom she knew and admired above all other contemporary English novelists, a certain wit and whimsicality in treating these circumstances, but unlike Woolf's stories, Benson's present no moments of being, however fleeting, when characters achieve communion with one another or at least heightened perceptions of themselves. Both writers were highly conscious in their craft and seemed to be born writers. Katherine Mansfield, another contemporary, wrote in a review of Benson's third novel, *Living Alone* (1919), that "We hardly dare to use the thumb-marked phrase, 'a born writer'; but if it means anything Miss Stella Benson is one. She seems to write . . . like a child gathering flowers."

Benson was certainly born into circumstances offering inspiration to a potential young author. Her paternal grandmother was related to Samuel Pepys, a connection cherished by Stella and which may have helped motivate her to keep a diary as a child. Two sisters of her mother, Caroline Essex Cholmondeley, were writers. Hester Cholmondeley wrote obsessively, leaving a 222,000-word diary as well as stories, essays, and a biographical survey of great nineteenth-century figures by the time she died at age twenty-two. Mary authored eleven novels, the most controversial of which, *Red Pottage* (1899), exposed complacency in the clergy.

However, other less favorable features of Stella Benson's early family life also shaped her artistic vision. Born 6 January 1892 at Lutwyche Hall, Shropshire, Stella was the third child of Ralph Beaumont Benson and Caroline Essex Benson, who had

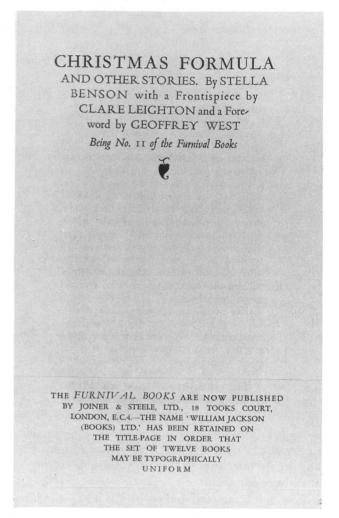

CHRISTMAS FORMULA
AND OTHER STORIES. By STELLA
BENSON with a Frontispiece by
CLARE LEIGHTON and a Fore-
word by GEOFFREY WEST

Being No. 11 of the Furnival Books

THE *FURNIVAL BOOKS* ARE NOW PUBLISHED
BY JOINER & STEELE, LTD., 18 TOOKS COURT,
LONDON, E.C.4.—THE NAME 'WILLIAM JACKSON
(BOOKS) LTD.' HAS BEEN RETAINED ON
THE TITLE-PAGE IN ORDER THAT
THE SET OF TWELVE BOOKS
MAY BE TYPOGRAPHICALLY
UNIFORM

Frontispiece and title page for Benson's 1932 collection of stories, published in a limited edition of 550 copies

been married in 1886. The heir of a nouveau riche family, Ralph was clever and good-looking. As a passionate note about Stella reveals, he appears to have formed a close attachment to his only surviving daughter, "the first bloom of [his] winter rose." However, he could be a violent disciplinarian, was often absent from the home, and was remembered as a womanizer. Not until she was eighteen years old did Stella learn from her mother the reason for his "irritable and eccentric," "unapproachable and unaccountable" behavior – alcoholism. Somewhat strangely, he abhorred being touched, a trait that Stella also demonstrated throughout her adult life.

Stella's mother descended from the ancient landed Essex family, numbering marquesses and earls among its members. She appears to have been quite concerned about her daughter's chronic bronchial problems and was perhaps overprotective of her. Whereas Stella associated her father and his family with the impulsive, "egotistical," and "cold-hearted," she identified her mother and her family with tradition, duty, and prudence. Caroline Benson coped with the "dreadful" years in which her marriage disintegrated by moving about to places (such as France) more congenial to Stella's health, by living with relatives, and by hiring a succession of nannies. Stella's older brother George recalled the "insane cruelty" of one of these caretakers and claimed that it contributed to the early death of their sister, Catherine Maia, at age nine in 1899. Her death profoundly affected Stella, who became even more isolated and lonely than her illnesses had hitherto made her. In the year following her sister's death Stella greeted one governess by saying, "I am young, but I have had a great deal of sorrow in my life."

She seems to have responded in part by absenting herself mentally during play and by writing.

In 1899 she contributed to a children's magazine, *St. Nicholas,* and won silver and gold medals for stories and poems; in 1901 she began a diary that she continued keeping until her death. A passage from a collection of her essays, *Worlds Within Worlds* (1928), suggests the value she found in her diary: "Diaries are like dreams, an inward consolation to the outwardly humiliated." Attempts to educate her did not fare as well as her diary, for they always ended "in illness and great nervous unhappiness," and Stella later wrote of her childhood that she "hope[d] never to be so unhappy again, or so unlovable, or so morbid." In 1921, when she admitted after having read a book on psychoanalysis that "I am thwarted in my sexual side," she surmised that the root lay in her childhood. Her mother reflected on those days by rather ambiguously saying that Stella had been "ill-used." Given the details of her father's impulsive and inconsistent behavior and Stella's haphazard exposure to a series of governesses, one cannot help but wonder whether she had been in some way abused. Certainly, as biographer Joy Grant claims, Stella throughout her life felt "acute sympathetic pain" in the presence of any distress or loss experienced by another human or animal.

Sent to a private school in 1906, she craved acceptance; on her holidays she thought of "writing a novel just for practice. I think I have the plot, which is Egyptian in the time of the tenth plague." Stella was again plagued by ill health, preventing her from returning to school and causing her to submit to the "Same old lonely lessons again" from yet another governess. From 1907 to 1911 she suffered from influenza and from severe menstrual pain, started to lose her hearing, and succumbed to chronic pleurisy and headaches. She had several brief and upsetting meetings with her father, whose mental health was deteriorating. On one occasion in 1908 Stella wrote that "he knawed his hands and kept saying, 'Maiden, maiden-a-grown-up-maiden.'" Stella pitied her abandoned mother, but the tension between them had led to Stella's being shipped off in 1910 to study music, French, and German at a girls' school in Freiburg, Germany. When her health broke after a month of near-hysterical excitement, she wrote that "I can't bear going back to living alone with Mother as always." Nevertheless she did not have much choice and was whisked away to Arosa in Switzerland, where she spent seventeen months – "the happiest in my life," she wrote. In the early summer of 1911 she returned to England, and then in October moved again to Chernex, near Montreux, Switzerland. In that month they learned of her father's death of a brain hemorrhage.

During these difficult years Stella found consolation in her dog Pepper and in a secret, "imaginary world filled with imaginary people," one that could sometimes frighteningly overtake the real world, as she realized in a 1908 diary entry: "my dream people are getting so real that they are mixing up with real people in an extraordinary way.... I don't think I or anybody would have believed what company thought people are, and how they drive away loneliness.... I have never met a real person who would give me half as much comfort." She also kept on writing – her diary, poetry, and a novel. Written between August 1910 and March 1911, this novel provided relief since it provided an outlet for the thought-people. Her reading during the period included Thomas Carlyle's *The French Revolution* (1837), Jane Austen, Elizabeth Cleghorn Gaskell, Rudyard Kipling, and Dinah Maria Craik.

Stella began 1912 on a more social note, traveling in Switzerland and the south of France and flirting with young men along the way. However, illness overtook her late in the year and persisted into 1913. Her frustration at her condition, along with a developing interest in the suffragette movement, made her determined to become independent. After a painful sinus operation at Lausanne she convalesced with her mother in Jamaica during the winter of 1913–1914. Here she gathered material for her first published novel, *I Pose* (1915).

In May 1914, soon after her return from Jamaica, she embarked on her "new" life by herself in London, despite opposition from her mother. Initially she socialized and worked in the "Literary Department" of the disorganized Women Writers' Suffrage League, switching to the United Suffragists in the same year. After World War I broke out in August, she volunteered to work with the Women's Emergency Corps and was sent to Hoxton in the dangerous cockney East End of London to work for the Charity Organization Society (COS), later called the Salvation Army. Checking on potential charity cases fulfilled her sense of duty and gave her independence, but she disliked the self-righteous attitude and some of the methods of the organization, as revealed in the satire she made of it in her third novel, *Living Alone* (1919). Her new life also included attentions from Nigel Benbough, two years her junior, whom she had met in 1913. Partly owing to the frenzy of wartime, Stella agreed to a one-year engagement, but she felt quite ambivalent, as a diary entry makes clear: "In theory I am awfully fond of Nigel, and thrill a little when I touch him by mistake, but when he touches me on purpose, I hate it, my hand still feels as if blushing furiously where he kissed it. Obviously I am born to be a lone literary woman as close proximity horrifies me so." After two months she broke the engagement and immediately suffered an attack of muscular rheumatism. Nevertheless, she soon returned to her charity work, branching off on her own by helping a one-legged woman set up a business making paper bags.

At the end of August 1915 her first novel, *I Pose,* had been accepted by Macmillan, publisher of her Aunt Mary's novels. In a lively and epigrammatic style it traces the adventures of an unnamed militant suffragette and a gardener. At the denouement Benson radically subverts the traditional closure of romance in marriage by having her heroine defiantly hurl a bomb at a church altar. Gratified by the novel's financial success (it netted her sixty pounds) and by her public recognition, Benson penned her first of many journalistic pieces, "a whimsical piece about London buses" for the *Pall Mall Gazette,* while recuperating from yet another illness.

In 1916 she continued her charity work. Although she loved the crowds, noise, and excitement of wartime London, she periodically escaped to the countryside to visit friends and relatives or to be alone. She spent July 1916 in Cornwall, where she worked on her next novel, *This Is the End* (1917). Benson finished the war years by leaving the COS, working as a gardener in Berkshire for the war effort, and deciding (despite opposition from her mother) to travel to California on the pretext that the climate there would benefit her lungs. After arriving in New York in July 1918, she visited Radnor, Pennsylvania, and then Chicago, where Harriet Monroe, editor of *Poetry,* described her as "a weird and eerie little creature, frail in body but possessed of a keen mind, a roving imagination, and an indomitable will." She arrived in Berkeley just before Christmas and embarked on some of the happiest but also most intense months of her life with her new friends Bertha Pope, the poet-playwright Witter Bynner, and others. Eventually, the fast-paced, bohemian lifestyle ended when she verged on nervous breakdown.

In California she worked at a succession of jobs, including one as a reader for the University of California Press, and she continued to work on a novel, *Living Alone,* begun in 1917 and set in wartime London. By December 1919 Stella was feeling quite alienated by the vulgarity of America and decided to travel to Hong Kong by way of Honolulu and Japan. After a term teaching at an Anglican boys' school in Hong Kong, she secured a position at a medical institute in Peking.

In China, where she would spend much of the rest of her life, she met James "Shaemus" Carew O'Gorman Anderson, employed by the Imperial Chinese Customs Service. She married him in London exactly one year after their meeting, despite his initial entanglement with another woman and an intervening separation when she returned to England via India. Making a daring honeymoon journey from New York to California in a Model T Ford affectionately named Stephanie, Stella all the while worked on her novel, *The Poor Man* (1922), a satiric treatment of her first stay in California.

In Yunnan and then Mengtsz, where the couple soon resumed their residence in China, any recognition of Stella's talent was welcome, since she typically felt unappreciated by and alienated from the unimaginative, narrow-minded administrators who made up their social life there. To make matters worse, she felt victimized by gossip because she failed to produce a baby — ironically owing to Shaemus's recurring syphilis. Though "no longer in the slightest degree in love with him," she felt a compassionate understanding of him, which she successfully transformed into the character of Jacob in her next novel, *Pipers and a Dancer* (1924). Other experiences during her travels she shaped into articles published by various periodicals, including *The Nation and Athenaeum* and the New York *Bookman,* and collected in two well-received volumes, *The Little World* (1925) and *Worlds Within Worlds.*

Despite the satisfaction of producing another novel and of experiencing the adventures described in her articles, Stella suffered intermittently from depression during these years. One such period beginning in May 1924 did not abate when the couple heard in March 1925 that Shaemus was to be posted in Shanghai, a city both detested. The order coincided with Stella's completion of what was to be one of her better novels, *Goodbye, Stranger* (1926), "a story of exile and frustration, an angry story in which the satirist and the victim are one," in biographer R. Ellis Roberts's words. But before its appearance Benson's first short story was published in book form, *The Awakening: A Fantasy* (1925), a work that employs fantasy for a satiric end. A fallen god traces the decline of the gods as the grandeur of their creations has shrunk into cleverness and ingenuity because of their competitiveness. The creation of man has been "the most fatal step in our slow suicide" and occasioned division among the gods. The young narrator god consequently flees west to develop his dream of democracy. Key to the plan is the birth of a man who could be both Man and

God. At the close the narrator recounts his near victory when he learns of the birth of such a one in Bethlehem and assumes it to be Bethlehem, Pennsylvania – only to discover that the birth has occurred in the middle-eastern Bethlehem under his bitter rival's star. A tone of lament underlies this highly imaginative tale.

Instead of remaining with Shaemus at his new post in Shanghai, Stella decided to return to England for six months via California and the Bahamas, where she visited her brother George. On the ship she befriended a colleague of Sigmund Freud, the Viennese psychiatrist Willi Gutmann, who warned her not to undergo psychoanalysis or she would "certainly lose her husband, probably her art, and perhaps her life." In London by July 1925 she increased her circle of literary friends by meeting Virginia and Leonard Woolf, Sydney Schiff ("Stephen Hudson"), Naomi Mitchison, Winifred Holtby, and Vera Brittain. In less than two months Benson returned to Lung Ching Tsun, Manchuria, via Canada. She found the isolated town "horrible" but made the best of it, spending her time gardening, learning Russian, and dabbling in photography. In late November 1926 she got away again, this time to San Francisco, where she met the critic I. A. Richards and Hugh Walpole. Shaemus wrote to her of his difficulties in being celibate during her long absences, and with reservations Stella gave him permission to take "a proxy wife." However, by the end of March 1927 she was back with Shaemus, disturbed by the fact that he had been making love to a Russian woman during the winter.

Despite marital difficulties, during this stay Stella discovered the idea for her most widely acclaimed novel, *The Far-Away Bride* (1930; published in Great Britain as *Tobit Transplanted* in 1931), through her reading of Tobit's story in the Apocrypha, and she continued to write articles and short stories. One article, published as "Storm in a Manchurian Teacup" by *The Nation and Athenaeum* in 1927, got her into trouble with Japanese diplomatic officials because of its critical description of Japanese resistance to a perfectly legal Chinese tax.

Luckily Shaemus's stint in Manchuria ended soon after, and by 27 November 1927 the couple settled into a flat in South Kensington. Stella spent most of the next two years in a whirlwind of social and familial activity in England. At a tea party held in her honor by literary agent Curtis Brown she met novelists May Sinclair, William Gerhardie, and Rose Macaulay. Vita Sackville-West, Aldous Huxley, H. G. Wells, Ella Hepworth-Dixon, Michael

Arlen, G. B. Shaw, and Walter de la Mare also were introduced to her and were scrutinized in her diary. For instance, she surprisingly found Wells "rather easy to get on with and not the traditional lady-killer at all – rumple-haired and schoolboylike and with a high falsetto voice." Amid squabbles with Shaemus, Stella fell in love with an explorer named Bill Bickerton, a character who apparently looked like Ernest Hemingway but in other ways recalled Shaw's Hector Hushabye (*Heartbreak House,* 1919). Stella entertained fantasies of having his baby, was rejected by him, and later saw her "Bill-craving" as a last hope before middle age. Shaemus meanwhile pursued a mutual friend, Lady Eileen Orde, a painter, while vacationing with Stella and the Ordes in July in Antibes on the Riviera. Back in London in the fall they were swept up in the maelstrom of bohemian parties, some featuring what Stella called "Bloomsbury intersexuals."

Just before Christmas Benson had a short story, *The Man Who Missed the 'Bus* (1928), published in a special autographed edition of 530 copies. In this eerie fantasy Mr. Robinson, a virgin without friends, loses the capacity to communicate with other human beings or even to see their faces. He attempts to escape the resort town he is visiting but misses the bus and is forced to take comfort in observing the movements of animals, including dogs and mice, not burdened with self-consciousness. When he finally catches the bus, it seems as if it were the bus to the beyond and as if Mr. Robinson is already dead. He is one of Benson's typically isolated protagonists whose valuing things more than people has left him with an unlived life, and he thus faintly resembles Henry James's similarly afflicted characters.

The year 1929 began badly for Benson with illness and marital disputes. However, by 11 February she was visiting Eleuthera in the Bahamas once again, where her brother George owned a development company. She returned to England in March to see Shaemus off by ship to his next post at Nanning, in south China. In his absence she worked on *The Far-Away Bride* and wrote to Shaemus, "I insist on being a writer first and a wife second: a man artist would insist and I insist." By October she had joined Shaemus in Nanning, where she had "no less than ten servants." She liked the place, despite the imminent threat of war, and in this climate finished *The Far-Away Bride,* a work that develops the theme that most obsessed her – that of loss of identity and resulting isolation – in tracing the plight of the White Russians exiled in Manchuria. This carefully crafted novel with its range of characters

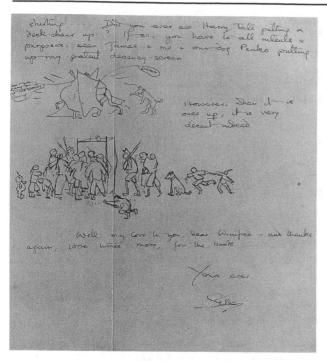

Page from a 1933 letter by Benson, in Pakhoi, China, to Winifred Holtby – illustrating the setting up of a makeshift "decency-screen" as a bathing tent on local beaches (from R. Ellis Roberts, Portrait of Stella Benson, *1939)*

garnered Benson both the A. C. Benson silver medal for "services to literature" and, more important to her, the French Femina-Vie Heureuse prize in 1932.

During her brief stay in Nanning, Stella also wrote short stories, including one of her best, "The Desert Islander," later collected in *Hope against Hope and Other Stories* (1931). It fictionalizes "a gallant, vain attempt" by Shaemus to get one of their few remaining colleagues, a Swede afflicted by syphilis, to a hospital through the fighting converging on their town. In the story a Russian deserter with an infected leg receives help from a bland Englishman mindlessly devoted to duty, his ingrained code of ethics. Most reader sympathy lies with the fiercely independent Russian – until the Englishman is hit by a stray bullet and the Russian feels relief because his shame will die with his "friend." In another – "A Dream," first published in the *Saturday Review of Literature* in April 1930 – the protagonist, Mrs. Wander, is even more completely isolated than is "the man who missed the bus" in the earlier story of that title. While anesthetized, Mrs. Wander crosses a valley and is comforted in the arms of an old nanny, only to realize finally that she, as well as the nanny, is dead. In its treatment of a beyond-death experience, the story is typical of the age.

By April 1930 the threat of a Cantonese attack caused the British consul to order the Bensons to leave Nanning, and they escaped by boat. Shaemus's next posting was to Hong Kong, not looked on favorably by Stella because of its provincial attitudes. There a prematurely aging Stella became preoccupied with the imagery of bones, a preoccupation derived partly from a poem by A. E. Housman called "The Immortal Part" (1896). For Benson bones symbolized the stripping away of pretense, and with this idea she began her next novel with the working title "The Bones," later evolving into what was finally published as *Mundos: An Unfinished Novel* (1935). However, she provided no more biting satire on pretense and uniform thinking than in her short story "Tchotl," also written around this time and first collected in *Christmas Formula and Other Stories* (1932). Nielson, an American and the only foreigner in Lao-pao, seizes on the arrival of an English-speaking Chinaman to expound some of his "Ideals." These have been indelibly imprinted in him from his hometown of Jenkinsville, Minnesota, one of innumerable American towns where "Democratic education is an incurable affliction; it informs once and for all." Tchotl, "the real World Language" using only single syllables, has also originated there, and Nielson proceeds to sell the textbook to the ironically idealistic Chin Yu-ting, who enthuses, "To soar over all the barriers of language at one jumping. To be so conveniently in touch with the universe – this would be well worth five dollars gold." When Nielson discovers in the day's mail that the World Language has been a flop, he hesitates for only the briefest moment before realizing that "his duty was loyalty to the Successful Deal." Nielson and his compatriots are laughingly condemned for their big talk, big deals, and materialism.

In "Two Ghosts," a story published in *Harper's Monthly Magazine* in August 1930, Benson portrays a power struggle between two English people who have spent the first year of their marriage in south China. They argue over their memory of a third person there until a reading of the woman's diary causes the woman to realize that "we've been remembering a ghost – two ghosts – the ghosts of the people we tried to be, William, when it still seemed worth while to us to try to please each other."

Toward the end of 1931 Benson published another limited edition of stories, *Hope Against Hope and Other Stories*. "Hope Against Hope" deals movingly with the complete failure of communication between a confirmed bachelor, Ward Clark, and his nurse, Miss Hope. Readers are privy to Clark's increasing irritation with Nurse Hope's attempts to cheer and interest him. He refuses to see her as an intelligent and imaginative individual and instead stereotypes her as an over-thirty spinster. Miss Hope makes the best of her situation by engaging a fifty-year-old schoolmaster in conversation while Clark flirts with the man's nineteen-year-old daughter. Following the departure of the schoolmaster and his daughter, Miss Hope disappears, but she turns up again in the arms of fishermen who have rescued her from her suicidal attempt at drowning. As all Clark can feel is exasperation, he shrinks even further in the reader's estimation. Benson underlines her theme in the modern-sounding despair of Hope's concluding lines: "Oh – how far away – how far away – men and women are from each other. . . ."

That theme was driven home for Benson late in 1931 during her work on a committee investigating the "international traffic" of prostitutes in Hong Kong. She visited brothels and was shocked and angered by the suffering she saw, including that of a sixteen-year-old lifelong prostitute whose eyes and nose had been "almost eaten away" with syphilis. She channeled her outrage into a report for the League of Nations.

In January 1932 Benson embarked again for England, spending a month en route with friends in California. Owing to the success of *Tobit Transplanted,* she found herself a literary celebrity in London. At a 4 May reception she accepted the Femina-Vie Heureuse prize from Harold Nicholson, with Rebecca West, G. B. Stern, and E. M. Forster in the audience. She was also answering fan mail of forty or fifty letters a day. This success enabled her to fulfill a longing for a house in London, and on 18 June she moved into a semidetached villa in Kensington. There she entertained extensively, one of her more noteworthy guests being Wyndham Lewis, who drew an austere portrait of her. She also renewed what was becoming a friendship with Virginia Woolf, whose novel *The Waves* (1931) she had read four times in succession. The summer passed all too quickly, and by 25 August she was off to China to rejoin Shaemus, who had been posted to the island of Hoi-How off the coast of Hong Kong. Ellis Roberts, one of her few friends remaining in London in August, wrote of her parting that "I had never known Stella so depressed about a decision as she was about this one to return to China. . . . I knew she felt that, if she went on the 26th of August, she would not see England again."

To make matters worse, Stella had written a satiric piece on Hong Kong and on arriving there found herself verbally attacked until she and Shaemus escaped to Hoi-How at the beginning of October. From there they moved to the more palatable Pakhoi. During her stay a third limited edition of stories, *Christmas Formula and Other Stories,* was published. The title story, set in a horrific future, is comparable to that of Aldous Huxley's novel *Brave New World* (1932), in that genuine feeling has been replaced by empty formulas with faint connections to various traditions. The protagonist arrives in London, now district S.E. 416 of New York, from Tibet – the only independent state outside the jurisdiction of the United World government. He sentimentally listens to church bells but is informed that they are the sounds of the wireless and that churches have nothing to do with Christmas. After receiving "Mother's Kiss," from an anonymous woman who squirts him with "Mother's Tear of Joy Certified 100 per cent," he submits to a series of meaningless, impersonal "customs" before retreating in isolation to his ship and the old world. The tale is her most biting satire on mindless following of convention and on the potential impact of cheap American culture on the world.

Early in 1933 she published a very different kind of collection – her "folly," *Pull Devil, Pull Baker.* In it she gathered the stories of "Count Nicolas de Toulouse Lautrec de Savine, KM, Knight of St. Vladimir Cross, St. Anna, etc., etc.," an incorrigible old liar whom she had met in Hong Kong in 1931 and taken pity on. Some of his stories present his memory of himself as "the Don Juan of our Days" who had spent two million rubles on women, but Benson's commentary undercuts these preposterous tales. Only one of her commentaries-cum-short-stories, "The Man Who Fell in Love with the Co-Operative Stores," is reprinted in her *Collected Short Stories* (1936). In this lighthearted tale's touch of absurdity she exposes the commodity-based approach to love of an aging Don Juan, but there is an underlying cynicism in the repeated lines, "I know now, of course, that there is no such thing as love."

The Bensons concluded the round of launch parties at Pakhoi with a six-week tour of the Dutch East Indies in July. Despite intermittent illness, Stella was off again with Shaemus in November – this time to Hongay, where she contracted pneumonia and died on 6 December 1933. Hearing of her death, Virginia Woolf wrote, "How mournful the afternoon seems. . . . A very fine steady mind: much suffering; suppressed. . . . A curious feeling: when a writer like S. B. dies, that one's response is diminished; Here and Now won't be lit up by her: it's life lessened."

Her life having been cut off so abruptly, it is not surprising that several of her works, including collections of her poems, short stories, and an unfinished novel, were published posthumously. About the novel, *Mundos,* L. P. Hartley wrote that "[Stella Benson's] talent never found more brilliant expression than in the haunting, disturbing cadences of her swan song," and her *Collected Short Stories* contained several significant stories. "Submarine" vividly captures the fear of revenge felt by a woman who, while diving with her uncomprehending husband, senses that the man in charge of the raft above may be one who has vowed revenge after the couple has dismissed his crooked mother, their former housekeeper. In "On the Contrary" an obnoxious Englishman fond of disagreement and of his own voice unnecessarily leads his temporarily stranded shipmates into a costly near disaster before being outrageously hailed by the "flock" as a hero. Benson likely derived this character from her experience of male administrators, for to Virginia Woolf she had written: "The keynote of China, I have decided, is a *Booming*; a male voice Booming in a female ear, booming instruction almost always incorrect, or Booming boasts."

"Story Coldly Told" focuses on the responses of several white people kidnapped by native Gildi brigands "tired of foreign influence" in a remote imaginary country. With hilarious results the vice-consul, Scrobham, "a skinful of illusions," romanticizes the Gildi "gentlemen" and applies a moral code that is meaningless to them. Miss Sims, a missionary, is even more completely uninformed about this society and preaches on the sinfulness of brigandage. She manages to convert several of the brigands, however, who then murder their leader, Rak Mandi, as a sign of their newfound belief in the religion of love. Only the narrator sees the irony of this situation and extends enough concern for the Rak to make his dying moments more comfortable. This story conveys humorously and powerfully one's feelings of a lack of control and the haphazardness of experience when various ideologies and codes of behavior meet.

All in all Benson's works in *Collected Short Stories* are well crafted, even though a few suffer from being too "clever." One of several favorable reviews stated that "To read the stories of Stella Benson is to regret again that she has gone. Scarcely anyone to-day uses the impish humour that was hers or aims such wicked wit. Yet we are conscious of tenderness that we are almost ashamed of discerning; as though it were an indiscretion." Among contemporary critics Geoffrey West offered the highest praise and clearest summary of her work when he wrote that "She is, beyond doubt, one of the most scrupulous and accomplished, as she is one of the wittiest and — in her own microcosmic way — one of the wisest writers of our day. She offers, in her dozen volumes, a treasure-cave of delights for repeated exploration." Despite such accolades and her very modern ironic, sometimes bitter perspective that one might expect to have aroused continuing interest in her work, her oeuvre has been almost completely neglected and deserves reappraisal.

Letters:

Some Letters of Stella Benson 1928–1933, edited by Cecil Clarabut (Hong Kong: Libra Press, 1978);

Naomi Mitchison, *You May Well Ask: A Memoir, 1920–1940* (London: Gollancz, 1979);

"Stella Benson: Letters to Laura Hutton 1915–1919," edited by William Brandon, *Massachusetts Review,* 25 (Summer 1984): 225–246.

Bibliography:

J. Gawsworth, *Ten Contemporaries: Notes toward Their Definitive Bibliography* (London: Joiner & Steele, 1933).

Biographies:

R. Ellis Roberts, *Portrait of Stella Benson* (London: Macmillan, 1939);

Joy Grant, *Stella Benson: A Biography* (London: Macmillan, 1987).

References:

Georgina Battiscombe, "Stella Benson," *Nineteenth Century and After,* 141 (May 1947): 208–216;

R. Meredith Bedell, *Stella Benson* (Boston: Twayne, 1983);

Phyllis Bottome, *Stella Benson* (San Francisco: Grabhorn Press, 1934);

Vera Brittain, *Testament of Friendship* (London: Macmillan, 1942);

Joseph A. Collins, "Two Lesser Literary Ladies of London: Stella Benson and Virginia Woolf," in his *The Doctor Looks at Literature: Psychological Studies of Life and Letters* (New York: Doran, 1923);

Doris Estcourt, "Stella Benson," *Bookman* (London), 82 (May 1932): 103–104;

Reginald Brimley Johnson, "Stella Benson," in his *Some Contemporary Novelists (Women)* (Freeport, N.Y.: Books for Libraries Press, 1970), pp. 163–174;

Stuart P. B. Mais, "Stella Benson," in his *Some Modern Authors* (London: Richards, 1923), pp. 32–38;

W. H. Mellers, "Fairies in Bloomsbohemia," *Scrutiny,* 8 (September 1939): 221–225;

Christopher Morley, "Stella Benson," *Saturday Review of Literature* (16 December 1933): 354;

Siegfried Steinbeck, *Der ausgesetzte Mensch: zum Leben und Werk von Stella Benson 1892–1933* (Bern: Francke, 1959).

Papers:

Benson's diaries are held at the University of Cambridge Library. Benson's letters are deposited at the following institutions: Harry Ransom Humanities Research Center, University of Texas at Austin; Harvard University Library; Joseph Regenstein Library, University of Chicago; Brotherton Library, University of Leeds; Harold Cohen Library, University of Liverpool; British Museum Library; Berg Collection, New York Public Library; Research Libraries, New York Public Library; Mills College Library, Oakland; and Library of Congress.

John Davys Beresford
(7 March 1873 – 2 February 1947)

George M. Johnson
University College of the Cariboo

BOOKS: *The Early History of Jacob Stahl* (London: Sidgwick & Jackson, 1911; Boston: Little, Brown / New York: Doran, 1911);

The Hampdenshire Wonder (London: Sidgwick & Jackson, 1911; London: Collins, 1911); republished as *The Wonder* (New York: Doran, 1917);

A Candidate for Truth (London: Sidgwick & Jackson, 1912; Boston: Little, Brown / New York: Doran, 1912);

Goslings (London: Heinemann, 1913); republished as *A World of Women* (New York: Macaulay, 1913);

The House in Demetrius Road (London: Heinemann, 1914; New York: Doran, 1914);

The Compleat Angler: A Duologue, by Beresford and Arthur Scott Craven (London: French, 1915);

H. G. Wells (London: Nisbet, 1915; New York: Holt, 1915);

The Invisible Event (London: Sidgwick & Jackson, 1915; New York: Doran, 1915);

The Mountains of the Moon (London & New York: Cassell, 1915);

Poems by Two Brothers, by Beresford and Richard Beresford (London: Macdonald, 1915);

These Lynnekers (London & New York: Cassell, 1916; New York: Doran, 1916);

House-mates (London & New York: Cassell, 1917; New York: Doran, 1917);

W. E. Ford: A Biography, by Beresford and Kenneth Richmond (London: Collins, 1917; New York: Doran, 1917);

Nineteen Impressions (London: Sidgwick & Jackson, 1918);

God's Counterpoint (London: Collins, 1918; New York: Doran, 1918);

The Jervaise Comedy (London: Collins, 1919; New York: Macmillan, 1919);

An Imperfect Mother (London: Collins, 1920; New York: Macmillan, 1920);

Revolution: A Novel (London: Collins, 1921); republished as *Revolution: A Story of the Near Future in England* (New York & London: Putnam, 1921);

Signs and Wonders (Waltham St. Lawrence, Berkshire: Golden Cockerel Press, 1921; New York: Putnam, 1921);

The Prisoners of Hartling (London: Collins, 1922; New York: Macmillan, 1922);

Taken from Life, by Beresford and E. O. Hoppé (London: Collins, 1922);

The Imperturbable Duchess, and Other Stories (London: Collins, 1923);

Love's Pilgrim (London: Collins, 1923; Indianapolis: Bobbs-Merrill, 1923);

Unity (London: Collins, 1924; Indianapolis: Bobbs-Merrill, 1924);

The Monkey Puzzle (London: Collins, 1925; Indianapolis: Bobbs-Merrill, 1925);

That Kind of Man (London: Collins, 1926); republished as *Almost Pagan* (Indianapolis: Bobbs-Merrill, 1926);

The Decoy (London: Collins, 1927);

The Tapestry (London: Collins, 1927; Indianapolis: Bobbs-Merrill, 1927);

The Instrument of Destiny: A Detective Story (London: Collins, 1928; Indianapolis: Bobbs-Merrill, 1928);

All or Nothing (London: Collins, 1928; Indianapolis: Bobbs-Merrill, 1928);

Writing Aloud (London: Collins, 1928);

The Meeting Place, and Other Stories (London: Faber & Faber, 1929);

Real People (London: Collins, 1929);

Love's Illusion (London: Collins, 1930; New York: Dutton / New York: Viking, 1930);

Seven, Bobsworth (London: Faber & Faber, 1930);

An Innocent Criminal (London: Collins, 1931; New York: Dutton, 1931);

The Old People (London: Collins, 1931; New York: Dutton, 1932);

The Middle Generation (London: Collins, 1931; New York: Dutton, 1933);

The Next Generation (London: Benn, 1932);

The Inheritor (London: Benn, 1933);

The Camberwell Miracle (London: Heinemann, 1933);

The Young People (London: Collins, 1933; New York: Dutton, 1934);

The Case for Faith-Healing (London: Allen & Unwin, 1934);

Peckover (London: Heinemann, 1934; New York: Dutton, 1935);

On a Huge Hill (London & Toronto: Heinemann, 1935);

Blackthorn Winter, and Other Stories (London: Hutchinson, 1936);

The Faithful Lovers (London: Hutchinson, 1936; New York: Furman, 1936);

Cleo (London: Hutchinson, 1937);

Unfinished Road (London: Hutchinson, 1937);

What I Believe (London: Heinemann, 1938);

Strange Rival (London: Hutchinson, 1939);

Snell's Folly (London: Hutchinson, 1939);

The Idea of God (London: Clarke, 1940);

Quiet Corner (London: Hutchinson, 1940);

What Dreams May Come (London & Melbourne: Hutchinson, 1941);

A Common Enemy (London & New York: Hutchinson, 1942);

The Benefactor (London: Hutchinson, 1943);

If This Were True (London: Hutchinson, 1943);

The Long View (London: Hutchinson, 1943);

Men in the Same Boat, by Beresford and Esmé Wynne-Tyson (London: Hutchinson, 1943);

The Riddle of the Tower, by Beresford and Wynne-Tyson (London: Hutchinson, 1944);

The Prisoner (London: Hutchinson, 1946);

The Gift, by Beresford and Wynne-Tyson (London: Hutchinson, 1947).

PLAY PRODUCTIONS: *The Compleat Angler: A Duologue,* by Beresford and Arthur Scott Craven, Manchester, Hippodrome, 29 June 1914; London, Coliseum, 13 July 1914;

Howard and Son, by Beresford and Kenneth Richmond, London Coliseum, 14 August 1916.

OTHER: Dorothy Richardson, *Pointed Roofs,* introduction by Beresford (London: Duckworth, 1915);

The Perfect Machine, by Beresford and Arthur Scott Craven, English Review, 26 (May 1918): 393–408;

"My Religion," in *My Religion: Essays by Arnold Bennett, Hugh Walpole, R. West, J. D. Beresford, and Others* (London: Hutchinson, 1925; New York: Appleton, 1926), pp. 55–61;

"Experiment in the Novel," in City Literary Institute, *Tradition and Experiment in Present-Day Literature: Addresses Delivered at the City Literary Institute by R. H. Mottram, Beresford, and Others* (London: Oxford University Press, 1929): 23–53;

"Human Relations," in *The Root of the Matter: Essays by Beresford and Others,* by H. R. L. Sheppard (London: Cassell, 1937), pp. 4–47;

Esmé Wynne-Tyson, *The Unity of Being,* introduction by Beresford (London: Dakers, 1949).

SELECTED PERIODICAL PUBLICATIONS – UNCOLLECTED:
FICTION
"The Paper-Seller," *Academy,* 25 January 1902: 99;

"A 'Things Seen,' " *Academy,* 31 May 1902, p. 563;

"A Test of Friendship," *Westminster Gazette,* 10 June 1908, p. 2;

"Miranda. VI. On Idealism," *Westminster Gazette,* 11 July 1908, p. 2;

"Vision," *Westminster Gazette,* 15 June 1912, p. 2;

"Management," *Westminster Gazette,* 10 May 1913, p. 2;

"Pipes. A Study in British Endurance," *Westminster Gazette,* 16 February 1918, pp. 1–2;

The Perfect Machine, by Beresford and Arthur Scott Craven, *English Review* 26 (May 1918): 393–408;

"The Old Champion," *Manchester Guardian,* 2 October 1927, p. 20;

"The Expert," *Manchester Guardian,* 3 November 1927, p. 18;

"The Hairdresser," *Manchester Guardian,* 15 November 1927, p. 22;

"An American in Paradise," *Manchester Guardian,* 22 November 1927, p. 20;

"Master and Servant," *Manchester Guardian,* 29 November 1927, p. 20;

"Undesirable Knowledge," *Manchester Guardian,* 12 December 1927, p. 16;

"The Peasant," *Manchester Guardian,* 27 January 1928, p. 20;

"The Pricked Balloon," *Manchester Guardian,* 26 March 1928, p. 16;

"J's Education," *Manchester Guardian,* 12 April 1928, p. 16;

"The Parasite," *Manchester Guardian,* 25 June 1928, p. 18;

"Artificial Sunlight," *Manchester Guardian,* 4 July 1928, p. 30;

"Betterment," *Manchester Guardian,* 12 March 1930, p. 22;

"High Time," *Manchester Guardian,* 7 March 1934, p. 18;

"The Way Home," *Manchester Guardian,* 11 August 1936, p. 18;

"Washing-Up," *Manchester Guardian,* 9 November 1936, p. 16;

"Parachutist," by Beresford and Esmé Wynne-Tyson, *Manchester Guardian,* 23 July 1940, p. 10;

"The Parting," by Beresford and Wynne-Tyson, *Manchester Guardian,* 20 December 1940, p. 10;

"The Maginot Line," *Christian Science Monitor,* 8 May 1941, p. 22;

"The Worrit," by Beresford and Wynne-Tyson, *Manchester Guardian,* 11 June 1941, p. 4;

"Here and There," by Beresford and Wynne-Tyson, *Manchester Guardian,* 13 October 1941, p. 4;

"From a Height," *Christian Science Monitor,* 25 February 1942, p. 20;

"The Swollen-Headed Ghost," by Beresford and Wynne-Tyson, *Manchester Guardian,* 27 November 1942, p. 4;

"Waters of Lethe," by Beresford and Wynne-Tyson, *Manchester Guardian,* 4 March 1943, p. 4;

"Top of the Hill," by Beresford and Wynne-Tyson, *Manchester Guardian,* 11 June 1943, p. 4;

"This Desirable Property," by Beresford and Wynne-Tyson, *Manchester Guardian,* 8 March 1944, p. 4;

"Other Corners," by Beresford and Wynne-Tyson, *Woman's Magazine,* September 1945, pp. 17–19.

NONFICTION

"The Reading Competition," *Punch,* 4 March 1908, p. 1171;

"On Ghosts," (London) *Times,* 2 January 1914, p. 3b;

"Mr. Maartens and the Realists," *Westminster Gazette,* 30 May 1914, p. 2;

"The 'Maltruist,' " *Westminster Gazette,* 6 January 1917, pp. 1–2;

"Average Man," *Westminster Gazette,* 26 July 1918, pp. 1–2;

"A New Form of Matter," *Harper's,* 138 (May 1919): 803–810;

"Psychoanalysis and the Novel," *London Mercury,* 2 (1919–1920): 426–434;

"The Crux of Psychical Research, Part I," *Westminster Gazette,* 6 March 1920, p. 8;

"The Crux of Psychical Research, Part II," *Westminster Gazette,* 13 March 1920, p. 8;

"More New Facts in Psychical Research," *Harper's,* 144 (March 1922): 475–482;

"Successors of Charles Dickens," *Nation and Athenæum,* 34 (29 December 1923): 487–488;

"Common-Sense of the Book Trade," *Nation and Athenæum,* 35 (27 September 1924): 775–776;

"Unpleasant Fiction," *Bookman* (London), 68 (April 1925): 11;

"What Literary Men Believe in Religion," *Literary Digest,* 87 (31 October 1925): 24–25;

"Le déclin de l'influence de la psycho-analyses sur le roman anglais," by Beresford, translated by M. Vernon, *Mercure de France,* 190 (1 September 1926): 257–266;

"Experience," *Manchester Guardian,* 30 December 1927, p. 16;

"The Work of Henry Williamson," *Bookman* (London), 73 (January 1928): 207–208;

"The Plane Trees," *Nation and Athenæum,* 42 (4 February 1928): 682;

"New Books That Ought to Be Better Known," *Bookman* (London) 75 (December 1928): 166;

"The Mysterious in Real Life," *Bookman* (London), 77 (December 1929): 177;

"From London," *Aryan Path,* 1 (January 1930): 46–50;

"The Tendency of National Policy," *Aryan Path,* 1 (February 1930): 111–114;

"Towards a Universal Religion," *Aryan Path,* 1 (March 1930): 148–152;

"Art and Religion," *Aryan Path,* 1 (April 1930): 254–257;

"From London," *Aryan Path,* 1 (May 1930): 331–334;

"The Tendency of Recent Fiction," *Bookman* (London), 78 (May 1930): 107–108;

"On Exorcising Evil," *Aryan Path,* 1 (June 1930): 389–392;

"Science and Religion," *Aryan Path,* 1 (July 1930): 460–463;

"Looking Towards 1975," *Aryan Path,* 1 (August 1930): 495–499;

"The Colour Line," *Aryan Path,* 1 (September 1930): 566–569;

"The Soul's Dark Cottage," *Nation and Athenæum,* 48 (4 October 1930): 13–15;

"Personal and Impersonal Methods," *Aryan Path,* 1 (October 1930): 652–656;

"The Road to Knowledge," *Saturday Review,* 150 (8 November 1930): 586–587;

"Personal and Impersonal Methods," *Aryan Path,* 1 (November 1930): 741–744;

"Utopias," *Aryan Path,* 1 (December 1930): 800–803;

"Stones for Bread," *Aryan Path,* 2 (January 1931): 47–51;

"Synthesis," *Aryan Path*, 2 (February 1931): 115–119;

"God and His Shadow," *Aryan Path*, 2 (March 1931): 207–211;

"The Discovery of the Self: An Essay in Religious Experience," *Aryan Path*, 2 (March 1931): 131–136;

"The Discovery of the Self: An Essay in Religious Experience," *Aryan Path*, 2 (April 1931): 237–243;

"The Discovery of the Self: An Essay in Religious Experience," *Aryan Path*, 2 (May 1931): 390–394;

"The Gift of Love," *Aryan Path*, 2 (June 1931): 375–379;

"The Chaos of Modern Psychology," *Aryan Path*, 2 (June 1931): 399–403;

"The Phenomena of Spiritualism," *Aryan Path*, 2 (July 1931): 460–465;

"Indian Art: Exhibition in London," *Aryan Path*, 2 (August 1931): 560–564;

"The Appearance of Dogma," *Aryan Path*, 2 (September 1931): 595–600;

"The Moral Aspect of Reincarnation," *Aryan Path*, 2 (October 1931): 679–683;

"Automatism – I. Natural Impulse and Free Will," *Aryan Path*, 2 (November 1931): 766–770;

"Automatism – II. Two Ways to Realization," *Aryan Path*, 2 (December 1931): 836–841;

"Unemployment: Past Karma and Future Hope," *Aryan Path*, 3 (January 1932): 37–40;

"God and His Shadow," *Aryan Path*, 3 (March 1932): 107–111;

"An Impractical Philosophy," *Aryan Path*, 3 (May 1932): 342–347;

"The Chaos of Modern Psychology," *Aryan Path*, 3 (June 1932): 399–403;

"The Development of Consciousness," *Aryan Path*, 3 (July 1932): 486–490;

"Old Thames," *Spectator*, 149 (23 July 1932): 105–106;

"Determination and Free Will," *Aryan Path*, 3 (August 1932): 540–544;

"Supping with the Poets," *Spectator*, 149 (27 August 1932): 256–257;

"The Evolution of Religion," *Aryan Path*, 3 (September 1932): 632–636;

"Tranquility," *Spectator*, 149 (17 September 1932): 337–338;

"John Bunyan and Women," *Spectator*, 149 (22 October 1932): 532;

"Philosophy and Mysticism," *Aryan Path*, 3 (November 1932): 766–770;

"Reflections on Bacon," *Spectator*, 149 (25 November 1932): 748–749;

"The Problem of Consciousness," *Aryan Path*, 3 (December 1932): 816–820;

"Throcking," *Spectator*, 150 (6 January 1933): 10–11;

"Evolution," *Aryan Path*, 4 (January 1933): 22–26;

"Nature Is Alive: Human Ego Is Supreme," *Aryan Path*, 4 (January 1933): 408–412;

"D. H. Lawrence: The Man of Kama-Manas," *Aryan Path*, 4 (February 1933): 93–95;

"The First Article of Belief," *Aryan Path*, 4 (March 1933): 176–179;

"The Next Step Forward," *Aryan Path*, 4 (May 1933): 294–298;

"Equality," *Aryan Path*, 4 (July 1933): 474–478;

"Old and New England," *Spectator*, 151 (25 August 1933): 246–247;

"Man and His God," *Aryan Path*, 4 (September 1933): 602–606;

"Evolution and Redemption," *Aryan Path*, 4 (October 1933): 689–692;

"The Sin of Retaliation," *Aryan Path*, 4 (December 1933): 802–805;

"A Letter from London," *Aryan Path*, 5 (February 1934): 119–122;

"I – Influence of Indian Thought," *Aryan Path*, 5 (April 1934): 241–245;

"The Artist and the World Today," *Bookman* (London), 86 (May 1934): 94;

"A Letter from London," *Aryan Path*, 5 (August 1934): 537–542;

"Will and Wish," *Aryan Path*, 5 (October 1934): 629–633;

"The Philosophy of A. N. Whitehead," *Aryan Path*, 5 (November 1934): 683–687;

"A Reasonable Doctrine But – !," *Aryan Path*, 6 (March 1935): 130–134;

"On Teaching," *Aryan Path*, 6 (April 1935): 235–239;

"The Faculty of Research: A Staff But Not a Sign Post," *Aryan Path*, 6 (September 1935): 547–551;

"The Heresy of Separateness," *Aryan Path*, 7 (January 1936): 25–28;

"The World Is One: Western Religion and Internationalism," *Aryan Path*, 7 (February 1936): 82–86;

"The Storehouse of Memory," *Aryan Path*, 7 (June 1936): 264–268;

"The One in the Many," *Aryan Path*, 7 (September 1936): 421–425;

"New Books and Old – Reviews," *Aryan Path*, 7 (October 1936): 481;

"New Books and Old – Reviews," *Aryan Path,* 7 (November 1936): 532–533;

"The Phenomena of Jesus – I. – Temptation of Jesus," *Aryan Path,* 7 (December 1936): 539–542;

"Christian Asceticism," *Aryan Path,* 8 (July 1937): 324–328;

"New Books and Old – Reviews," *Aryan Path,* 8 (September 1937): 431–432;

"The Reproof of Righteousness," *Aryan Path,* 8 (December 1937): 571–574;

"The Author's Dream," *Manchester Guardian,* 7 June 1938, p. 18;

"The Law of Love," *Aryan Path,* 9 (September 1938): 442–444;

"The Future of Religion: I. The Inevitability of a World-Religion," *Aryan Path,* 9 (November 1938): 535–538;

"The Coming of the Forerunners," *Aryan Path,* 9 (December 1938): 596–601;

"New Books and Old – Reviews," *Aryan Path,* 10 (February 1939): 114–115;

"Ways of Knowledge," *Aryan Path,* 10 (June 1939): 304–307;

"The Meeting Place of East and West," *Aryan Path,* 10 (July 1939): 355–359;

"Political Thought," *Aryan Path,* 10 (August 1939): 403;

"Indian Nationalism," *Aryan Path,* 10 (November, 1939): 546–548;

"New Books and Old – Reviews," *Aryan Path,* 11 (July 1940): 368–369;

"Recent Developments in Spiritualism," *Aryan Path,* 13 (April 1942): 160–164;

"The Nature of Man," *Aryan Path,* 13 (July 1942): 317–319;

"Max Plowman," *Aryan Path,* 14 (August 1943): 367–368;

"Needed: A Living Faith," *Aryan Path,* 14 (November 1943): 512–514;

"The Federation of the World," *Aryan Path,* 15 (January 1944): 14–19;

"Moral Theology of Today," *Aryan Path,* 15 (May 1944): 220–221;

"Man and the State," *Aryan Path,* 15 (July 1944): 305–309;

"Towards Totalitarianism," *Aryan Path,* 15 (November 1944): 431–432;

"New Books and Old – Reviews," *Aryan Path,* 16 (April 1945): 147;

"Telepathy," *Aryan Path,* 16 (August 1945): 301–303;

"The Demand for Justice," *Aryan Path,* 17 (May 1946): 184–186;

"New Books and Old – Reviewers," *Aryan Path,* 17 (July 1946): 275–276;

"A Statement of Belief," *Aryan Path,* 17 (October 1946): 369–373;

"Wisdom as Old as Thinking Man," *Aryan Path,* 18 (April 1947): 178–180.

John Davys Beresford was a restless and passionate seeker of truth whose quest led him to explore a range of ideas from materialism and realism to psychic research, psychoanalysis, Eastern mysticism, and Christian Science. An underlying idealism informs his writing in all of the genres that he experimented with, including the realistic, fantasy, psychological, and mystical novel; short stories of these types; and essays and reviews on literary, psychological, philosophical, and mystical topics. In a stream-of-consciousness passage from *Writing Aloud* (1928), he asserted that he had "but a single theme, the re-education of human beings."

He found an audience for this concern in 1911 with his first two novels, one realistic and one fantasy, and reviewers quickly tagged him as one of the most promising of the younger generation of Georgian novelists. His Jacob Stahl trilogy (*The Early History of Jacob Stahl* [1911], *A Candidate for Truth* [1912], and *The Invisible Event* [1915]) established his reputation as a solid realistic novelist. He built on this foundation with early forays into the psychoanalytic novel and *roman à thèse* with *God's Counterpoint* (1918) and *Revolution: A Novel* (1921), respectively.

By the 1920s Virginia Woolf could record in her *Diary* (1978) her pleasure at being offered a chance to review *Revolution,* and the critic Abel Chevalley could argue in 1924 that of a group including D. H. Lawrence, Frank Swinnerton, and Hugh Walpole, Beresford was "[t]he one most equally endowed with that *intelligence* and that *imagination* of life which make good writers of fiction." However, from the late 1920s to his death, increasing financial necessity forced him to churn out novels and reviews frequently lacking the inspiration and quality of his earlier work. Though virtually ignored since his death, Beresford deserves a place in the history of the Georgian period and of the novel for his thematic innovations, notably his treatment of "unpleasant" topics of human pathology that drew on his extensive knowledge of psychology.

Beresford's short stories have perhaps more unjustly suffered a neglect similar to that of the novels, since the stories commonly capture an inspired moment and reflect the pleasure that he found in writing them because they did not require the endurance of novel writing. Beresford divided his sto-

J. D. Beresford, with Esmé Wynne-Tyson in 1941 (courtesy of Jon Wynne-Tyson)

ries into those conventional, sentimental tales written for commercial purposes and those written to amuse himself, but one can identify quite a range — from brief whimsical contes to romance, mystery, and psychic stories, many containing rare psychological and spiritual insight.

Beresford did not develop straightforwardly as a writer. He was born on 7 March 1873 in Castor, Northamptonshire, as the second son of an evangelical couple, the Reverend John James Beresford, a Church of England minister, and Adelaide Elizabeth Morgan. At three and a half years old he suffered a trauma that significantly altered his life. His nurse neglected to change his clothes after he got wet during a carriage ride, and he succumbed to infantile paralysis, causing permanent lameness. He conveys the powerful emotion that event left when he asserts in his autobiography, "The name of that nurse had a place in my youth among the outstanding criminals of the century." The event changed the family dynamic in that his mother, estranged from her husband (who was fourteen years older than she), invested her affection in her needy second son, J. D. His father, proud of J. D.'s older brother, viewed his second son's affliction as an embarrassment and consequently neglected the boy's education.

Nevertheless, J. D. wrote that his lameness helped to decide his career; J. D.'s son Tristram went further by claiming that the disability was the making of him, spurring him to overcome obstacles.

Beresford recalled that his "education was a very haphazard affair." From the ages of eight to twelve he did attend various schools at Peterborough, a public school at Oundle, for a year; a boarding school in Norfolk; and the Peterborough King's School until he reached age sixteen, but he had no particular ambitions and learned nothing that fitted him for any profession. Occasionally he was the "butt for bullying," and he remembered being called "Miss Beresford," "being tied to an apple tree in the playground and being pelted with chestnuts." Nevertheless, he did begin writing fiction at school, perhaps as a way of imaginatively creating a world in which he was not "defective." Mostly he was educated informally, from the time his mother read Dickens to him to the years of his youth — when he energetically used the Peterborough public library to obtain William Harrison Ainsworth's books among such others as Samuel Richardson's *Pamela* (1740–1741) and works by Charles Kingsley.

At age sixteen Beresford, who knew that he did not want to go into the church, proposed becoming an engineer – a proposal rejected by his father, who believed Beresford's disability would make it impossible. Instead the Reverend Mr. Beresford suggested architecture, which was accepted by the lackadaisical boy. He was articled first with the local diocesan surveyor and then in Gray's Inn, London.

London opened up a new world for the sheltered youth, who succumbed to "the magic of its theatres and music halls." Though he lived briefly with his brother and then with a cousin, he soon adopted a transient, boardinghouse life during which he met G. F. Rogers, who started Beresford "on the road of independent thinking and self-education." An out-physician at the London Hospital, Rogers questioned Beresford's fundamentalist faith and helped him throw off "those shackles of orthodoxy . . . in a single evening." Beresford became a convinced evolutionist, and one wonders how this was received at the rectory, where he spent a long summer in 1895.

Back in London in September, Beresford reluctantly began working as a draftsman for architect Edwin T. Hall. During "eight years of slavery" there he seems mainly to have been exposed to various expletives, and he finally realized that the career had no future. As an escape he continued to educate himself during this period, reading scientists and philosophers such as Samuel Laing and Charles Darwin on Saturday afternoons at the British Library and fiction such as H. G. Wells's *The Wheels of Chance* (1896) from Mudie's lending library. By the summer of 1901 Beresford was making "spasmodic efforts to write short stories." Despite being hampered by a "habit of self-deprecation," his efforts paid off when he won a one-guinea prize for "the best portrait of a street character," a piece titled "The Paper-Seller" in the journal *Academy,* to which he then apparently contributed fairly regularly. A second mentor, Arthur Scaife, provided Beresford with a sociological education from 1902. Beresford reached another juncture when in 1903 he read the Cambridge-educated psychic researcher Frederic W. H. Myers's *Human Personality and Its Survival of Bodily Death* (1903), "a book of modern wonders that gave my mind a new twist," he later claimed. Myers's descriptions of the subliminal self and multiple personalities sparked Beresford's fascination with abnormal psychology and led him gradually "to abandon the realist for the idealist position."

Not only did Beresford begin writing in earnest in 1901, but he also met his future wife, Linda Lawrence, at a party. Though Beresford from ages eighteen to twenty-five had had a "passionate secret love-affair" about which he preferred to say too little rather than too much, his life was "singularly lacking in feminine society" during this time. Mrs. Lawrence, a former actress, had married an actor who deserted her, and thus various obstacles presented themselves before the new couple could get married, which they did on 28 November 1903. Her contacts led to Beresford's writing a play submitted to Beerbohm Tree but never staged. Beresford also completed a novel, but it received a similar fate and was never published. To make matters worse, Linda suffered a miscarriage several months after their honeymoon.

Beresford had escaped the slavery of office routine by becoming an agent with the New York Life Insurance Company just before marrying. After some initial success he failed at this occupation before landing a position as editor of the bookseller W. H. Smith's first annual, which appeared in 1906. Thereafter he wrote advertising copy for Smith and then for S. H. Benson, eventually transforming his experiences with these firms into his novel *A Candidate for Truth.*

During Christmas 1905 Beresford began collaborating on plays with Arthur Harvey-James (stage name Scott Craven), who had been introduced to Beresford by his wife and who became Beresford's closest male friend. At least one of these plays, *The Compleat Angler: A Duologue,* was produced. After Beresford lost his job with Benson's, he increased his writing efforts – doing unpaid reviewing for a monthly, *The Literary World,* and producing three more novels by 1907.

About this time Beresford's marriage began to crumble under the pressures of financial distress and his wife's infidelity, and he willingly consented to a divorce, although it took some time to obtain. In the midst of this personal crisis Beresford's literary fortunes finally began to change: in March 1908 he published a light satiric essay in *Punch* and, more important, was added to the review staff of the *Westminster Gazette* shortly thereafter. In the latter periodical, described by Beresford as "the most scholarly and literary of all the London evening papers," he published his first short stories, including "A Test of Friendship" in June 1908, and "Miranda. VI. On Idealism" in July 1908. According to Beresford's biographer Helmut Gerber, "All these stories favour an idealistic attitude, all have a subdued humorous tone, all have a touch of sentiment or pathos, and all use the stylistic techniques we label realistic."

During 1908 Beresford also began writing *The Early History of Jacob Stahl,* a realistic bildungsroman tempered by idealism and giving some attention to subconscious motivation, though this first novel was not published until 1911. Reviewers lauded it, along with the two other volumes of the trilogy – *A Candidate For Truth* and *The Invisible Event* – as a psychological masterpiece placing him in the forefront of modern novelists. In 1911 Beresford demonstrated his versatility by publishing another novel, *The Hampdenshire Wonder,* a speculative narrative about a child genius whose stupendous intellect enables him to make sense of the phenomena of life from his own observation before he devours the accumulated knowledge of civilization, most of which he rejects. The first novel to consider seriously the consequences of an individual's attaining a higher evolutionary stage than his contemporaries, it earned the praise of readers like Bernard Shaw and has since become an influential classic of scientific romance.

These early successes drew Beresford from the fringe into neo-Georgian literary circles, though he was never as well connected as a Virginia Woolf or a Bertrand Russell. Beresford and Hugh Walpole reviewed each other's novels and developed a cautious friendship later hampered by differences in aim and literary method. Beresford had also admired H. G. Wells's literary method as early as 1903 and finally got a chance to meet him at the Savile Club in 1913. Though the young writer sympathized with Wells's "social ideals and propaganda," he could not admire Wells's materialism or his opposition to religious ideas. Nevertheless, in *H. G. Wells* (1915), Beresford wrote the first appreciative monograph on Wells, characterized him as A. B. Ellis in his novel *The Invisible Event,* and maintained his friendship with Wells and his wife, Jane, while in France in the 1920s. Beresford found more in common spiritually and psychologically with Katherine Mansfield and Walter de la Mare, whom he had come to know in 1911, as all three reviewed for the *Westminster Gazette.* Both Beresford and Mansfield became interested in theosophy through A. R. Orage, editor of the *New Age,* and in 1922 the two attended classes together on the theosophical teachings of Ouspensky. De la Mare became Beresford's closest friend after Craven was killed in the war in 1917. The two mutually influenced each other, Beresford dedicating to him *Signs and Wonders* (1921), a volume of whimsical short stories in the manner of de la Mare.

Beresford's life took another turn at this time when he met Beatrice "Trissie" Roskams at his boardinghouse on Fellowes Road. The relationship that developed was based on mutual need but was unequal in other ways. Beresford attempted to change her rather conventional opinions and implored her to join him in Penzance, North Cornwall, where he retreated to dream and to write. After initially breaking her promise to do so, she eventually subdued her conscience and joined him, until they married in May 1913. The first of their four children, Tristram, was born in 1914. The couple lived mainly in the wilds of Cornwall until late in 1916, when they moved to London for the birth of their second son, Aden.

Visitors to the retreat included Walpole, Mansfield, John Middleton Murry, Dorothy M. Richardson, and D. H. Lawrence. Beresford had come to know Richardson, the most frequent visitor, when she worked as part-time secretary to a dentist on Wimpole Street, and he quickly developed a rapport with her. He acted as her literary adviser, reading the manuscript of her Pilgrimage (1938) series and contributing an appreciative introduction. With Lawrence, whom he had met and seen frequently over the winter of 1915–1916, Beresford played the role of father. Though Beresford liked Lawrence, whom he saw in theosophical terms as a young soul, he also claimed that Lawrence's "obsession with sex bored me." Beresford helped emancipate Lawrence and Freda von Richthofen Weekley by lending them his Cornish house at Portcothan during that same winter, and in 1919 by helping Lawrence procure a grant from the Royal Literary Fund.

During the second decade of the century Beresford also became friends with Naomi Royde Smith, who taught him about the misuse of English; May Sinclair, whom he initially worshipped as a "high-priestess" of literature; and Kenneth Richmond, a writer on education with whom Beresford shared an interest in the Society For Psychical Research and collaborated in writing a biography, *W. E. Ford* (1917). Another friend, M. David Eder, had introduced Beresford to psychoanalysis in 1912 and was one of the first supporters of Sigmund Freud in Britain. Though initially attracted to Freud, whom Beresford read from the perspective of psychic research, he later rejected the emphasis on sexual preoccupation in Freudian theory and moved closer to Carl Jung's position, as did Eder.

By 1918 Beresford had established himself with nine well-reviewed novels and short stories placed in such prestigious periodicals as the *English Review, The Seven Arts,* Middleton Murry's short-lived magazines *Rhythm* and *The Blue Review,* and of course the *Westminster Gazette.* He decided to collect the best of these stories for publication that year under the title *Nineteen Impressions.* The volume demonstrates clearly Beresford's interest in philosophical idealism, particularly in Henri Bergson's idea (used as an epigraph to one of the tales) that "There is neither time nor even succession in space," psychic research, and psychoanalysis. In an introduction written as a response to friends' requests for explanations of several stories, Beresford suggests that the "impressions" of the title refer to moments of awareness of "something bright beyond, something that shines." He hopes that these stories will provide an "instant's separation" from the sensations of physical life and claims two motives: to display "the movement of modern life in an ordinary setting" and hesitatingly to suggest "the essential reality behind every expression." Many of these symbolic stories deal with uncanny or transcendental experiences in which fate plays a role and time collapses, leading to a new perspective on the world.

The opening story, however, seems to present an allegory for a materialist's view of the world through a visit to "Cut-Throat Farm," the title of the piece, in what appears to the narrator to be "The Valley of the Shadow of Death." His horror intensifies as one by one the starving animals disappear, victims of the knife of the predatory farmer who sizes up the narrator at the close. The following story, "The Power O' Money," takes another stab at the materialist's view by suggesting that those possessed by hopes in the material world are victims of an illusion. Tenant Joe Baker pathetically lives by the belief that he will eventually receive the five pounds per year promised to him by an agent who has a sign advertising "The Imperial Palace Hotel" placed on Baker's property. Years later Baker finally discovers that the hotel was never completed and the company has gone bankrupt long before, and he is taken to the workhouse as "one insignificant victim of frenzied finance."

One of the best uncanny tales, "The Criminal," concerns two reporters' attempts to satisfy their curiosities about the appearance of "the arch-criminal, the very creator of crime," who has been brought to an on-camera trial in order to simulate fairness. Since both reporters have adopted the principle of the open mind, they remain outsiders who do not join in the "great cry for revenge" voiced by "the whole civilisation of Christendom." Everyone else has an interest in executing the criminal, who has caused universal suffering. That characterization of the arch-criminal, along with the charge that the number of deaths for which he is responsible is incalculable, suggests that he represents the evil within all or within the collective unconscious. This possibility is strengthened when the reporters obtain strongly conflicting reports of his appearance from those who are admitted to the trial. The two reporters persist until one is finally admitted and secretly takes photographs. Beresford invokes the supernatural when the two discover that no trace of the criminal appears in the pictures, although the surroundings appear perfectly on the film.

Beresford rather harshly commented on the tale in a letter to Sir Edward Howard Marsh (14 February 1918):

> The Criminal was an abortive attempt to pose the suggestion that crime was a figment of the imagination, and that the arch criminal merely presented some force antagonistic to our own tendencies, and hence that we see him as the negation of some pet ideal of our own. I had not read a word of psychoanalysis, when I wrote it, but I see now, that many of Jung's theories are implicit in my idea.

However, he defended it against the charge made by J. K. Prothero in "The New Age" that he had plagiarized Rudyard Kipling's "The End of the Passage." Beresford claimed that "No two stories could have been less like one another, but in each of them a photographic camera had played some part."

"Flaws in the Time Scheme," a series of three stories following "The Criminal," deals more didactically with the effects of psychic phenomena. In the first, "An Effect of Reincarnation," a skeptical narrator gives offhand advice to a friend, Tommy Birch, to join the Theosophical Society to discover his past reincarnations. After Birch does so and reveals that he has been a martyr during the English Renaissance, his friends dismiss him, especially when he decides to become a lay missionary in China. Another friend remarks that "it wasn't in the scheme of things that he would be killed twice for the same offence," and the detail that Birch is not killed during a mass slaughter at an uprising is presented without comment. In "A Case of Prevision," Jessop hallucinates about a landslide while walking with his friend Galt along the Cornish coast. Galt attempts to cure him by using posthypnotic suggestion but later reads of a cliff accident in which Jessop has perished. In the less-didactic "The Late Occupier" the narrator listens to a house agent's monologue and is struck by repetition of the word "occupier." He slips out of time and experiences the tale of a man obsessed with occupying the house after his wife has died and he no longer can pay the bills. The narrator images the unfortunate end of the man before returning to the present and abruptly leaving the affronted house agent. A note explains that the story is a draft of "The Lost Suburb," presented later in the collection. In that version the narrator becomes obsessed with finding the house because of an "unplaced memory," a moment of unity with life experienced when he has viewed the building in childhood, although he later believes that he has an older association with the place. The dimension of memory and time passing adds to the depth of mystery in the piece. In "Force Majeure" place similarly exerts an obsessive influence. In this case the protagonist's chambers have a sinister impact, causing the protagonist to defenestrate his dead lover's dog and then to jump from the window himself after sounds of the lover and the dog persist.

Several other stories imbue place with a larger, even symbolic significance. In "The Little Town" the narrator visits St. Erth, Cornwall, where he feels the presence of "unseen creatures" before he attends a crude puppet show at the Kosmos Theatre. Obsessed by the ineptitude of the operator, the narrator confronts him — only to find a serene and wise old man with no visible connection to the "tottering figures" below. The piece may well be an allegory of God's relation to mankind but is not limited to this interpretation. "The Empty Theatre" focuses on a narrator "shut in to a little world" as he sits on the parade at a holiday resort watching a storm approach. As he slips out of time he hears the voice of an actor who recounts a feeling of having lost his audience and finding himself exposed in "a great theatre." After the storm rages and passes and the narrator finds himself "alone in a deserted world," the possibility arises that the performance described has been another chilling allegory of God's relation to His creation.

"Powers of the Air" also features a storm, though in a less distinct setting. An older person attempts to warn an unseeing youth of "the forces that have power in the black time," but the arrogant young man, ignoring him and braving the elements, returns filled with exhilaration and new knowledge. If this story of 1915 reflects the mood of at least the early war years, "Lost in the Fog" (1916), placed at the end of the volume, may represent a more defined allegory of the conflict. In attempting to escape the London fog the narrator leaves by train but takes the wrong line and ends up in a village where a mortal feud is taking place between the Turtons and the Franks. After he wonders whether he should help, he finds relief in returning to the world he *knew* but closes with the pointed questions, "Is it conceivable that out there in the little unknown village — for ever lost to me in a world of

THE
IMPERTURBABLE
DUCHESS
AND OTHER STORIES
by
J. D. BERESFORD

LONDON: 48 PALL MALL
W. COLLINS SONS & CO. LTD.
GLASGOW MELBOURNE AUCKLAND

Title page for Beresford's third collection of stories, for which he wrote a foreword about his experiments with fictional technique (courtesy of the Lilly Library, Indiana University)

white mist — men are fighting and killing each other? Surely it cannot be true?" Beresford's transformation of the conflict of nations into a local conflict effectively makes the horror more real and immediate.

Another group of stories focuses more precisely on individuals whose visions often expand or alter because they escape from time or because time collapses. In "The Escape" a man beset by trivial worries has an out-of-body experience in which he views the vast panorama of the Earth and its position in the universe. Afterward he attains peace, and daily routine seems insignificant. "The Ashes of Last Night's Fire" contrasts an early moment of exaltation and intense material ambition in a man's life with a later period of comfort and oblivion. "The Misanthrope" presents a bleaker view of humanity, as the narrator discovers that William Copley has become a misanthrope because he has the ability to see the defects of individuals, including the narrator, when he looks back over his shoulder at them. By contrast, "The Instrument of Destiny" offers promise for the future. Adrian knows that he will be the instrument of destiny and, just as "the fog of his material life began to thicken," his vision contracts "into an urgent desire for expression" that he finds through a sexual encounter, after which he is abruptly killed. However, a child is born of that moment of ecstasy "and he may be the saviour of mankind, or at least a link in the long, long chain of man's transcending destiny." "The Man in the Machine" refers to the protagonist of this tale, who barely escapes death from a fall. Under the influence of morphine he enters the "Great Hall" of his vision and experiences the body as machine in which the man at the controls seems "hopelessly distant."

Two other brief tales deal with vision over generations. "The Great Tradition" centers on a legend of marmalade-making and deflates the sacredness with which some traditions are held. "The Contemporaries" climaxes with a moment of unspoken communion between the youngest and oldest at a gathering of five generations.

Many of these cryptic contes effectively create uncanny, otherworldly atmospheres and provoke ontological questioning. The ambiguity of situation and philosophical dimensions give these stories a rich texture marred only occasionally by didacticism. The reviewer for the 31 January 1918 *Times Literary Supplement* judged that "they are, on the whole, very successful adventures in the uncanny. A few may be rather too mechanical to be convincing and too trivial to be interesting; but most of them one reads eagerly, convinced, and, to a certain degree, thrilled. They do convey genuine impressions of strange flights of the mind (as we may for convenience term it) into the past, into the future, and more especially, under the surface of appearances."

Beresford continued his experimentation and preoccupation with altered perspectives and psychic phenomena in his second volume of stories, *Signs and Wonders* – the third volume published by the Golden Cockerel Press, and now a collector's item. A brief prologue, "The Appearance of Man," sets the tone by placing a mundane conversation between a woman and two men against the backdrop of images depicting the passing of time from the beginning to the end of the world. The ironic reiteration of the statement "The world's a very small place" implies the blinkered vision of mankind and plays with the idea that all time can happen in an in-

stant. In the title story of the volume the narrator has a transcendental experience and sees a procession of "signs and wonders" across the sky before he returns to reflect on humanity's preoccupation with "the miserable importance of their instant lives." In "The Cage" while riding the tube the narrator envisions an encounter between himself and a primitive man. He benevolently reveals to the primate the distant future and the escape from the cage that the imagination may offer, but the primate recoils in terror at the glimpse of commuters reading, "staring so intently and incomprehensibly at those amazing little black-dotted white sheets." The disturbed narrator is left wondering whether "the distant future might not seem equally unendurable to me?" In "Enlargement" the narrator escapes from a modern cage, the air-raid shelter, and feels liberated as he approaches the Cleopatra's Needle monument in London. Beresford vividly creates the atmosphere of the deafening bombardment, but even more shocking is the vision of a procession of elephants that causes the narrator to feel that "he had pierced the veil of the commonplace." Later his landlady reduces the experience to a comic sight when she reports that elephants had escaped from the " 'Ippodrome."

Several subsequent stories deal with various spiritual and psychological types of characters, occasionally with too much didacticism. "The Perfect Smile" traces the development of Douglas Owen's gift of smiling to avoid punishment. After committing murder he resorts to his gift once again during his sentencing, but it fails him: the hideous grimace replacing it reveals his soul and foreshadows his deliverance at long last to the devil. "The Hidden Beast" tells of a man attracted more to the wild in man than to the restrained. One of Beresford's many outsider figures, he arouses the suspicion of townspeople who hear the screaming of a beast from his house at night and who search his house in vain during the day. The narrator realizes that the beast lies within the man, who strikes out for the wild at the close of the tale. "The Barrage: A Study in Extroversion" and "The Introvert" deal too didactically with those psychoanalytic types, though it is interesting that Beresford presents the latter more favorably, especially as these types make up the majority of his protagonists in his novels. "The Barrier" similarly examines a type, the glutton, whose spirit is imprisoned by his indulgence in physical satisfactions.

Most of the remaining stories deal with visions of the future or of the immediate past, specifically the trauma of World War I. "The Convert" treats a subject similar to Beresford's novel *Revolution* – the possibility of revolution in England – but from the viewpoint of a detached historian whose reputation has been based on his claim that the "English temper" would never permit revolution. On the night of the outbreak a young woman confronts him with the fact that he has been responsible for it and converts him to becoming an adviser to the rebel "Youth League." The consciously Wellsian tale "A Negligible Experiment" presents an apocalyptic vision of the future, a cosmic collision in which the earth and its inhabitants appear to be a negligible experiment, and this view is ironically underlined by the framing device of a young sculptor's futile attempt to model man in plasticine. In a variation of the Orpheus legend, "The Miracle" presents a wife who reclaims her comatose, shell-shocked husband through an out-of-body vision. In "Young Strickland's Career" Strickland obsesses about the future of his son until he views in a crystal ball a live scarecrow digging turnips. This fragment of his past transforms into horrific reality when he searches for his son on a battlefield in France after the war. "A Difference of Temperament" contrasts the boastfulness of an adventurer in business with the reservation of his longtime associate, who has lost his arm in the war. "Reference Wanted!" presents the story of a possibly shell-shocked man who claims to have been caught plagiarizing the works of European writers; at the close the narrator has the impression that he has heard *this* story somewhere before. "As the Crow Flies" focuses on a work of that title supposedly written by novelist George Wallace but never found by his publisher after Wallace dies in the Boer War. Ironically the reputation of the unwritten book outlives him.

The collection closes with the longer story, "The Night of Creation," based on a weekend at H. G. Wells's home in Easton Glebe and presented in the form of a Society For Psychical Research case. Despite a pedantic opening, Beresford manages to develop dramatic tension through two characters – a skeptic and rationalist, Harrison, and a psychic researcher, Vernon. After the apparition of a woman in white appears in the garden during a house party, Harrison sets out to show that it was Phyllis Messenger, rejected by her lover and suicidal, who had appeared in a trance state. Harrison triumphs over Vernon, but an anomalous piece of evidence that he suppresses bothers him and leads to the shock of discovery that the woman in white was Phyllis's friend who had committed suicide several weeks earlier.

Signs and Wonders develops Beresford's dual interest in psychological states and in signs "of the coming of the new age – the age of the Spirit" in speculative stories most compelling when not overtly didactic. Despite appearing in an edition limited to fifteen hundred copies, the volume was generally well received, as critics recognized Beresford's talent for presenting a "sudden flash of the unexpected." At least one modern critic, Brian Stableford, has rediscovered Beresford's talent, as he claims that in Beresford's first two volumes "The vignettes are ahead of their time in their methods and preoccupations. They are surreal and oblique, playing with time and space in a manner that was not to become fashionable for many years. Their interest in psychological theory and in the peculiarities of man's existential predicament was virtually unprecedented in English fiction, though not in Russian or French short stories."

From 1918 Beresford had been literary adviser to Collins, the firm that had published his psychoanalytic novels, notably *God's Counterpoint* and *An Imperfect Mother* (1920). These were among the first of this subgenre in England, and in 1923 Beresford published with Collins his third collection of stories, *The Imperturbable Duchess*. He signals a change of tone in the preface titled "Author's Advice," as he describes for young writers aspiring to financial success the economics of writing. With some bitterness he recounts how he had begun with an obsession for originality in subject and treatment in his contes but was forced to abandon them since they did not pay. Instead he turned to the "writing of short stories that meant nothing." The title story, dating from 1913, and "Reparation" represent his original aims, whereas the others deliberately avoid obscurity and are written in the condensed and polished style necessary for commercial success. Though the volume does vary more in quality than earlier ones, Beresford was perhaps being too hard on himself, for the collection does cohere around significant themes. Most of the stories feature alienated or obsessed outsider figures and probe the intervention of fate in their lives, occasionally through uncanny circumstances.

"The Grand Style" develops the dilemma outlined in the preface, for it features an artist who scorns to please but who, after viewing a vile dramatic performance by a worn-out troupe, nearly succumbs to the persuasions of a commercially minded theater manager to write him an "art" play. The poet is impressed that the actors perform with nothing to gain until fate intervenes and he learns from one of them that they were playing up to the manager. "The Whole Truth" similarly employs a story about the theater to comment on the relationship between art and life. Playwright Roger Cartwright discovers poverty-stricken actress Barbara Lake about to commit suicide. He takes her in and transcribes her story into a successful stage play in which she plays herself. Believing that he has discovered romance in the hard reality of life, he proposes to Miss Lake, only to discover "the whole truth" – that she has a longtime love with whom she plans to reunite in Canada. Life outdoes art in the title story as well, one of the best in the collection and one of several focusing on unusual relationships.

Class-conscious writer Cunningham Black affronts "the Imperturbable Duchess" Valetta, duchess of Tottenham, on a train – only to discover that they are both guests at the same weekend house party. He seizes the opportunity to humiliate the ignorant but dignified Valetta but is not entirely successful until he vindictively transforms their contretemps into a short story, a play, a novel, and a series of short stories, which successively move further from the truth. Having fulfilled his obsession "to prove that cleverness was more than the air of the aristocrat," he attempts to make amends to the by-now infamous and exiled duchess, whose single dignified comment – "insufferable" – exposes the gulf between social classes once again.

"The Successful Marriage" treats class differences from the opposite perspective. In it a shabby narrator exposes the prejudice and snobbery of an aristocrat by recounting to him the tale of a successful "mixed" marriage between a carpenter and the daughter of an earl before the story neatly reveals the narrator's identity as the suitor of the aristocrat's daughter. In "The Awakening" the atypical feature of the relationship portrayed is age difference. Arthur Gannett, an unadventurous Cornish merchant, adopts a nine-year-old Italian girl shipwrecked off the coast of his village and raises her as his daughter. Beresford shows that fate has been responsible for her arrival, and fate determines her career choice as an actress and her seduction in London by an actor. This news shakes Arthur out of his complacency, and he determines to murder her seducer. When this seducer fatefully dies of fright, Arthur is thus enabled to act on his submerged desire for her. "The Sentimentalists" deals less conventionally with awakening desire. A depressed doctor with a nonentity of a wife develops an attraction for a delicate patient with an alcoholic husband. Fate intervenes at predictably regular intervals to dispatch both spouses, but readers' expectations are subverted and desire is deferred permanently when the couple eventually realize that their unspoken desires had "bled internally, and the life had gone from them."

"The Looking-Glass" explores an almost uncanny relationship between Rachel Deane and her elderly aunt of the same name. On visiting the aunt, Rachel realizes that she resembles her, even down to her facial expressions, but is shocked when she discovers that she has become a mirror for her aunt, who maintains her youth through the strength of her obsession with her resemblance to her niece. Once that idea is shattered by a glance in a mirror, the aunt withers and quickly dies.

Beresford probes other types of obsessions in the remaining stories. In "The Deserter," written in 1914, a soldier obsessed with deserting ironically encounters a Frenchman spying for the Germans. This nets him a promotion, though he recognizes in the Frenchman the same cowardly impulse that he attributes to temporary insanity in himself. In "Paul Hickson's Return to the Wild" the protagonist's obsession with a holiday turns to resentment against authority when his holiday is canceled because of a heat wave that afflicts his coworkers. This tale of the office worker who snaps, transgresses, and becomes a fugitive in the wilds seems quite modern, though the denouement is perhaps too neat. Both "Expiation" and "Reparation" deal with resolving guilt complexes. In "Expiation" the guilt arises out of the still-topical issue of euthanasia. In "Reparation," the stronger of the two stories, Angus Whitely undertakes an amazing odyssey to fulfill the dying wish of his boss to make reparation to a young woman whom the boss believes he has impregnated. After ceasing the quest and then continuing because he feels haunted, Whitely finally catches up with the ungrateful woman – only to find that she has not been ruined, though she takes the gift of diamonds anyway. "No Defence" employs more supernaturalism when a crime of passion is repeated in a haunted house, although evidence of supernatural interference cannot be introduced in the subsequent divorce proceedings.

Though less experimental than his first two volumes, *The Imperturbable Duchess* contains some subtle emotional and psychological analysis, as one reviewer noted, as well as several stories with unexpected and refreshing endings. The publication of this volume corresponded with a personal crisis partly touched off by the antagonism of Beresford's wife to his studies with the Ouspensky group and exacerbated by the perversion of his literary judgment: Beresford had for five years been forced to deal with approximately forty manuscripts a week for his publisher Collins. In autumn of 1923 he consequently decided to take his family to France, a move made possible through the sale of a novel, *Unity* (1924), to a woman's magazine for five hundred pounds. During their four-year sojourn in France the family moved frequently, but Beresford was consistently charmed by the French and exhilarated by the climate. Unfortunately he did not manage to capture this feeling of release in his novels, which continued to probe abnormal psychology and moral dilemmas with more didacticism.

Near the end of their stay in France, Trissie, at age forty-six, gave birth to their daughter Elisabeth, who has become a popular children's writer. When the family returned to England in September of 1927, the rift between Beresford and his conventional wife had widened. His financial situation had become more precarious, and this necessitated increased production. Beresford's frustration is captured in his "Conclusion" appearing in his next volume of short stories, *The Meeting Place, and Other Stories,* published by Faber and Faber in 1929.

In the "Conclusion" Beresford reiterates his criticism of the control exerted by American magazines in their demands for sentimental and romantic conventions. He also reveals the boredom that he had to overcome in trying to address the average man or woman and the immense labor involved in constructing such artificial tales. As in previous volumes, the stories can be divided into two groups — those written for the market, and those shorter pieces written to indulge his own taste. In most, Beresford remains preoccupied with encounters or moments at which "the hand of God" enters: "You may call it Fate, Luck, Coincidence, anything you like, but I sometimes wonder if they are not just different names for the same thing," claims one of his narrators.

By far the most striking are those speculative and quizzical tales reminiscent of his first two volumes. In "The Man Who Hated Flies" a scientist eliminates flies as well as, inadvertently, other crucial insect species. Ironically his son discovers an immune fly that restores the balance, and the story offers a wry commentary on tampering with Providence. In "The Wind and Mr. Tittler" a timid, orderly, and thoroughly conventional man is "carried away into the depths of space with all the other rubbish" by an unnatural wind. "The Marionettes" presents an allegory of the inception of creation reminiscent of "The Little Town." Wallace Edgar undergoes a spiritual rebirth when he believes that he cannot be seen in a mirror, which is really a real-

J. D. BERESFORD

THE
MEETING
PLACE
AND OTHER STORIES

J. D. BERESFORD

Dust jacket for Beresford's 1929 collection of stories, to which he added a closing essay denouncing the influence that American magazine publishers exercised on short-fiction writers (courtesy of the Lilly Library, Indiana University)

istic painting, in "The Devil's Own Luck." In "Common Humanity" two doctors experiment for the good of humanity on a drunken specimen "of common humanity." They are oblivious to the man's formerly powerful status as adviser to an emperor, as revealed through his dreams. "The Trap Without a Bait" offers a mocking indictment of the middle class by portraying a visit to a materially perfect but empty town symbolic of the artificiality and soullessness of this class, which is created on paper and maintained by belief. In the ambiguous "Illusion," during a prodigal party at the Pandemonium Stanley has a vision of an endless procession of unemployed surging forward to overwhelm the wasters. In "The Summary" a novelist asked to write out the whole truth at Judgment Day finds he has learned nothing on the subject during his lifetime.

The bitterness of this allegory does not carry into a smaller cluster of stories that might be termed psychological mysteries or thrillers. These include "Ways of Escape," presenting a wife's perspective on her convicted husband's foiled escape; "The Artificial Mole"; "The Clever Mr. Fall," resembling "The Imperturbable Duchess" in its portrayal of class conflict; and "The Last Tenants," which develops a novelist's uncanny attraction to an unknown woman with similar tastes in books. These longer stories feature most of the conventions of this genre, notably the twist at the close.

Another group of tales probes the psychology of various unusual relationships. Both "The Meeting Place" and "Laughter and Tears" deal with the meeting place between one's dreams and one's life, between fiction and reality, and lead to revelations of love between novelists. In "The Air of Paris" a character with an uneventful life has a rather comic encounter with a passionate Frenchwoman, and this leads to a new resolve. "Verity" recalls "The Sentimentalists" in that a long-standing attraction does not come to fruition. In "Love of Youth" a mother at a timeless moment falls in love with the suitor of her daughter, whereas in "The Indomitable Mrs. Garthorne" a mother attempts to block the marriage of her son to her former husband's adopted daughter.

"The Hands of Serge David" falls between this type of story and a final set focusing on extraordinary individuals. It depicts how a musician overcomes a psychological block with the aid of a woman who forces back into his consciousness the memory of a trauma that she caused, and the couple marries after this revelation. "The Gambler" tells an amazing tale of a turn of fortune for the title character, while the narrator of "The Champion" tells what turns out to be an unreliable tale of how an accident ended his brilliant billiards career. In "Tops and Bottoms" a grocer amusingly proves his tenuous connection with the "'ighest in the land," and in "Professional Pride" a burglar tells how he turned himself in to thwart his victim's insurance scam.

Though the reviewer in *Punch* admired Beresford's range in this collection, fewer of these tales show the inspiration of earlier volumes, a trend that unfortunately continues in Beresford's final volume, *Blackthorn Winter, and Other Stories* (1936). In a preface more cynical than earlier ones, Beresford states that instead of trying to trick readers by interspersing "unpalatable" with sentimental magazine-market stories, he has separated them honestly. Most of the first sixteen stories are relatively conventional and lightweight, although many

are linked by a theme of mistaken identities and deceptive appearances. The title story is representative in that it shows how a young woman's fantasies about a novelist nearly lead to her deception by another writer with a similar name — until she is romantically saved by the actual novelist, who writes under a pseudonym. "Allied Interests," "The Lift," "Love is Blind," "Two Romantics," "A Scrap of Paper" and, most notably, "The Two Sirens" similarly depict initial misperceptions or mysteries leading to love relationships. "Reality" convincingly conveys a vain young woman's awakening to love brought about by her reluctant participation in a poor family's crisis. Beresford deftly handles the image of "The Open Door" in a story of that title that shows the transformation of a relationship between a peevish, spoiled wife and her long-suffering husband. "With Modern Effects" deals with another kind of transformation, as a family overcomes conflicts and feels the Christmas spirit despite the children's obsessions with the modern material trappings of that season. "Ailing Mary" perhaps reveals something of Beresford's feelings about magazine editors: it features an arrogant editor who is humbled by the failure of the car that he has boasted about. "The Other Way" vaguely recalls stories such as "The Hidden Beast" that deal with the animal nature of man, but in this one the two conflicting characters transcend their brute instincts. Beresford closes this section with two mysteries, "The Coincidence" and "The Beck Lodge Case," the latter of which is far more compelling. One of his rare forays into the world of politics and espionage appears in "Number 10," based on an actual incident in which the publication of a letter allegedly from Communist Grigori Zinoviev to British Communists led to the defeat of the Labour government in 1924.

In the remaining twelve contes Beresford sketches a range of incidents from the trivial and humorous to the significant, all of which have a transforming quality about them. In "The Bitter Look," for instance, a personable pig's penetrating stare before being slaughtered mortally affects its owner. The transformation in "Dreams, Idle Dreams," brings about a state of disillusionment and confusion, whereas in "Authority" a nonentity at a party suddenly takes charge during a medical crisis. "The Irrational Quantity," the narrator's encounter in the bathtub with a fanciful figure, the Root of Minus One who is the victim of mathematical imprecision, is the most playfully imaginative of these. By far the most intriguing and probably revealing is "A Feat of Alchemy," in which the narrator throws a broad selection of novels into a cauldron and boils them down until only the following contents remain: "1. A few really beautiful crystals of idealism; 2. Some crystals — feathery things — of romance; 3. A lot of grey powder, slightly bitter, which must have been realism; 4. Some unanalysable stuff, probably humour; 5. Two or three handfuls of detritus — the bulk of the residue — very light in weight and almost colourless, which I judged to be practically worthless." This allegory can be read as Beresford's rather bitter commentary on his profession or as his critical assessment of what his own contribution, under pressures from publishers and demands of popular-market readers, has been. If the latter, then his assessment is surely too severe. Though this volume did not receive as much attention as earlier ones, a March 1936 reviewer for the *Times Literary Supplement* astutely observed that Beresford's "sincerity and humanity" redeem the commercial stories and that the "tonic effect of satire and sly fun-poking [of the sketches] is very salutary."

Approximately two years after this volume of transformations was published, Beresford underwent his own when he encountered Esmé Wynne-Tyson in Brighton, where he had moved his family in 1931. A childhood friend of actor/dramatist Noel Coward and a former actress, novelist, and journalist, Wynne-Tyson described the Beresford whom she met as having been ground down by a routine of writing for profit about subjects that did not really interest him. He would have preferred continuing to write about metaphysics and faith healing — the latter having been the subject of his successful novel *The Camberwell Miracle* (1933) and a monograph, *The Case for Faith-Healing* (1934) — but had been blocked by opposition from his religiously orthodox wife. Wynne-Tyson lent him Mary Baker Eddy's *Science and Health* (1875), and through discussions with him renewed his passion for seeking truth. He developed an inner conviction of the power of faith healing, overcame periodic bouts of neuralgia, became a vegetarian, and generally became more spiritually integrated. As his spiritual affinity with Wynne-Tyson increased, they became determined to communicate "the truth to all who may desire to know."

In order to find the peace necessary for collaboration, Beresford moved out of his household and into a service flat in May 1939. In four months the two completed their first novel together, *Strange Rival* (1939), though it was published only under Beresford's name for financial reasons. Wynne-Tyson, who had separated from her husband in 1930, and Beresford thereafter maintained a pla-

tonic relationship while living in a series of hotels and vegetarian guest houses mainly in the West Country. The collaboration proved both spiritually and financially fruitful, as in the ensuing eight years Beresford averaged two books a year as well as short stories, sketches, articles, and reviews published principally in such periodicals as the *Aryan Path, Manchester Guardian, Christian Science Monitor,* and *Times Literary Supplement.*

The Prisoner (1946), a final novel written without collaboration with Wynne-Tyson and containing some apparently autobiographical elements, seems to have provided some catharsis for Beresford. Wynne-Tyson noticed that Beresford had begun to tire while writing the last part of their final collaboration, *The Gift* (1947), but he had persisted. He then nearly completed an autobiography, never published because of his wife's opposition, before he died on 2 February 1947.

Those who knew Beresford comment most frequently on his gentleness, tolerance, kindness, and compassion, though he also possessed a vigorous sense of humor. He had maintained his pacifist stance throughout World War II, achieved a degree of disengagement from things visible, and never became fixed or thereby limited in his thinking about any of the creeds or isms that he had examined. To his death he had continued to quest for truth about ultimate questions. Wynne-Tyson adds that "His spiritual understanding brought J. D. wholeness, happiness, and peace of mind."

His best stories reflect these values in their sensitivity to the unseen and in their penetrating psychological insight, and they are marred only occasionally by didacticism. Many of his finest stories were written early in his career, before financial pressures forced him to resort to the formulaic writing condemned in the bitter tones of his introductions to later volumes. Critic Brian Stableford captures the potential of these early and innovative tales in his claim that "it is probable that modern readers, familiar with the fiction of Jorge Luis Borges and Italo Calvino as well as the surreal fantasies of Nikolai Gogol and Franz Kafka, would find more in these stories than contemporary readers could have." Beresford's concern with presenting various kinds of awakenings, from sentimental to speculative, make these stories seem today just as relevant and necessary as when they were written.

Bibliography:

Helmut E. Gerber, "J. D. Beresford: A Bibliography," *Bulletin of Bibliography,* 21 (January–April 1956): 201–204.

References:

A. St. John Adcock, "John Davys Beresford," in his *Gods of Modern Grub Street* (London: Sampson Low, Marston, 1923), pp. 33–39;

Abel Chevalley, "J. D. Beresford," in his *The Modern English Novel* (New York: Haskell, 1973), pp. 228–235;

Helmut E. Gerber, "J. D. Beresford: The Freudian Element," *Literature and Psychology,* 6 (August 1956): 78–86;

Gerald Gould, *The English Novel of To-Day* (New York: Books for Libraries Press, 1971);

R. Hoops, *Der Einfluss der Psychoanalyse auf die Englische Literatur* (Heidelburg: Carl Winters Universitatsbuchhandlung, 1934);

Edward A. Hungerford, "Mrs. Woolf, Freud, and J. D. Beresford," *Literature and Psychology,* 3 (August 1955): 49–51;

Reginald Brimley Johnson, "J. D. Beresford," in his *Some Contemporary Novelists (Men)* (Freeport, N.Y.: Books for Libraries Press, 1970), pp. 97–119;

Brian Stableford, *"The Hampdenshire Wonder,"* in *Survey of Science Fiction,* volume 2, edited by Frank W. Magill (Salem: Englewood, 1979), pp. 945–949;

Stableford, "J. D. Beresford 1873–1947," in *Supernatural Fiction Writers: Fantasy and Horror,* volume 1, edited by E. F. Bleiler (New York: Scribners, 1985), pp. 457–461;

Frank Swinnerton, "Oliver Onions and J. D. Beresford," in his *The Georgian Literary Scene 1910–1935* (New York: Farrar, Straus, 1935), pp. 238–241.

Papers:
Jon Wynne-Tyson possesses the main collection of Beresford's typescripts, diaries, and other papers. There are also letters of Beresford in the collections of the National Library of Wales, the British Library, the University of Reading, and the New York Public Library.

Elizabeth Bowen

(7 June 1899 – 22 February 1973)

Laurel Smith
Vincennes University

See also the Bowen entry in *DLB 15: British Novelists, 1930–1959, Part 1.*

BOOKS: *Encounters: Stories* (London: Sidgwick & Jackson, 1923; New York: Boni & Liveright, 1923); republished as *Encounters: Early Stories* (London: Sidgwick & Jackson, 1949);

Ann Lee's and Other Stories (London: Sidgwick & Jackson, 1926; New York: Boni & Liveright, 1926);

The Hotel (London: Constable, 1927; New York: Dial, 1928);

The Last September (London: Constable, 1929; New York: Dial, 1929);

Joining Charles and Other Stories (London: Constable, 1929; New York: Dial, 1929);

Friends and Relations: A Novel (London: Constable, 1931); republished as *Friends and Relations* (New York: Dial, 1931);

To the North (London: Gollancz, 1932; New York: Knopf, 1933);

The Cat Jumps and Other Stories (London: Gollancz, 1934);

The House in Paris (London: Gollancz, 1935; New York: Knopf, 1936);

The Death of the Heart (London: Gollancz, 1938; New York: Knopf, 1939);

Look at All Those Roses: Short Stories (London: Gollancz, 1941; New York: Knopf, 1941);

English Novelists (London: Collins, 1942; New York: Hastings House, 1942);

Bowen's Court (London: Longmans, Green, 1942; New York: Knopf, 1942);

Seven Winters (Dublin: Cuala Press, 1942); republished as *Seven Winters: Memories of a Dublin Childhood* (London & New York: Longmans, Green, 1943);

The Demon Lover, and Other Stories (London: Cape, 1945); republished as *Ivy Gripped the Steps, and Other Stories* (New York: Knopf, 1946);

Elizabeth Bowen

Anthony Trollope: A New Judgement (London, New York & Toronto: Oxford University Press, 1946);

Selected Stories (London & Dublin: Maurice Fridberg, 1946);

Why Do I Write? An Exchange of Views Between Elizabeth Bowen, Graham Green, & V. S. Pritchett (London: Marshall, 1948; Folcroft, Pa.: Folcroft, 1969);

The Heat of the Day (London: Cape, 1949; New York: Knopf, 1949);

Collected Impressions (London & New York: Longmans, Green, 1950; New York: Knopf, 1950);

Early Stories (New York: Knopf, 1951) – comprises *Encounters* and *Ann Lee's and Other Stories*;

The Shelbourne: A Centre in Dublin Life for More Than a Century (London: Harrap, 1951); republished as *The Shelbourne Hotel* (New York: Knopf, 1951);

A World of Love (London: Cape, 1955; New York: Knopf, 1955);

Stories by Elizabeth Bowen (New York: Vintage, 1959);

A Time in Rome (London: Longmans, Green, 1960; New York: Knopf, 1960);

Afterthought: Pieces about Writing (London: Longmans, Green, 1962; New York: Knopf, 1964);

Seven Winters: Memories of a Dublin Childhood & Afterthought: Pieces about Writing (New York: Knopf, 1962);

The Little Girls (London: Cape, 1964; New York: Knopf, 1964);

A Day in the Dark and Other Stories (London: Cape, 1965; New York: Knopf, 1965);

The Good Tiger (New York: Knopf, 1965);

Eva Trout; or, Changing Scenes (New York: Knopf, 1968; London: Cape, 1969);

Nativity Play (Chicago: Dramatic Publishing, 1974);

Pictures and Conversations (New York: Knopf, 1975);

Irish Stories (Dublin: Poolbeg Press, 1978).

Collections: *The Collected Stories of Elizabeth Bowen,* introduction by Angus Wilson (New York: Knopf, 1981);

The Mulberry Tree: Writings of Elizabeth Bowen, edited by Hermione Lee (San Diego: Harcourt Brace Jovanovich, 1987).

OTHER: *The Faber Book of Modern Stories,* edited, with an introduction, by Bowen (London: Faber & Faber, 1937);

How I Write My Novels, by Elizabeth Bowen [and Others], compiled by John Irwin (London: Spearman, 1948);

Anthony Trollope, *Doctor Thorne,* introduction by Bowen (Boston: Houghton Mifflin, 1959);

Virginia Woolf, *Orlando: A Biography,* afterword by Bowen (New York: New American Library, 1960).

Though not a literary giant of the stature of James Joyce or Virginia Woolf, Elizabeth Bowen is an important twentieth-century literary figure whose fiction has been well received. In presenting the complex truths of human relationships that are her central concerns, that fiction typically attends carefully to realistic details of both character and place. Indeed, in her best stories as well as in her novels Bowen unobtrusively steers readers through the geography of motives and interactions on which human identity and human character depend.

Elizabeth Bowen was born 7 June 1899 in Dublin, but her family home was Bowen's Court, near Kildorrey, County Cork, Ireland. Since the eighteenth century this ancestral home, built by the third Henry Bowen, had been the place that Elizabeth Bowen claimed had "made all the succeeding Bowens." The family can be traced to Welsh, not English, forebears, but critics and biographers have considered her heritage, as did Bowen herself, "classic Anglo-Irish." This heritage was inherently paradoxical: having both Dublin and rural residences, the family lived in a country house yet was separated from the indigenous people by politics and religion. Such families were steadfastly connected to Ireland yet also steeped in the narrower cultural traditions of their particular families. Their lives, according to Bowen, were "singular, independent and secretive." The psychological closeness that pervades the best of Bowen's fiction recalls the condition of Anglo-Irish society during her childhood.

Elizabeth was the only child of Henry Cole Bowen and Florence Colley Brown, whom Victoria Glendinning calls two "vague and dreamy people," and thus Bowen added the independence of being an only child to that of living an isolated country life. As a small child Bowen divided her residency between 15 Herbert Place, Dublin, and Bowen's Court. This pattern altered in 1905 when Henry Bowen became more and more withdrawn, eventually suffering a nervous breakdown. His wife was not prepared to deal with this change by herself, so she and Elizabeth began living near cousins in southern England. Glendinning reports that Elizabeth saw these years as a time of "not noticing" harsh problems. She began to insulate herself from stress by paying close attention to place and to her childhood world; she found great solace in imagination. She also developed the stammer that persisted through her adulthood. Biographer Glendinning notes that a rich friend of Bowen once arranged for her stammer to be treated by an Austrian psychiatrist, who "laid bare before her his own personal anguishes, both private and professional." Elizabeth was "fascinated" by his disclosure but revealed nothing about herself — and consequently retained her stammer.

By the time Elizabeth was twelve Henry Bowen was recovering, preparing to reunite his family and resume his law practice. Unfortunately, Mrs. Bowen had been diagnosed with cancer and died when Elizabeth was thirteen, so from this time Elizabeth's upbringing was directed by her maternal aunts. They arranged for her to attend Downe House, a boarding school in Kent, from 1914 to

1917. The school, which Elizabeth enjoyed, had been Charles Darwin's residence; his study was the common room. When Elizabeth left the school to begin her adult life, her father had remarried and her main interests had shifted to England.

Even during her adolescence Elizabeth Bowen had thought that she would become an artist, and at age twenty she attended the London County Council School of Art for two terms in pursuit of this goal. She had also done much creative writing at Downe House, so she had been writing short stories even before she began art school. Writing was finally her dominant calling, but Bowen brought her awareness of visual arts into her vocation: she subsequently remarked years later that "often when I write I am trying to make words do the work of line and colour. I have the painter's sensitivity to light. Much (and perhaps the best) of my writing is verbal painting." Finding a first publisher took more than sensitivity and talent, however.

Bowen's first literary patron was Rose Macauley, who had been at Oxford with Downe House headmistress Olive Willis. By the early 1920s Macauley was an established critic and novelist who encouraged Bowen and introduced her to Naomi Royde-Smith, editor of the *Westminster Gazette.* Bowen's first published story appeared in this journal, and through Macauley and Royde-Smith, Bowen's circle of literary acquaintances expanded to include Edith Sitwell, Walter de la Mare, and Aldous Huxley. Although Bowen was not a member of the Bloomsbury group, she and Virginia Woolf did become friends. After her marriage Bowen was accepted into an Oxford intellectual circle that included David Cecil, Maurice Bowra, Cyril Connolly, Evelyn Waugh, Isaiah Berlin, Anthony Powell, and other major literary figures of the time.

In 1923 Bowen's first book, *Encounters: Stories,* was published by Sidgwick and Jackson. The value of a young person's perspective, one that Bowen would use repeatedly, can be seen in many of these stories. Adults become especially unsympathetic when they are self-indulgent, incapable of seeing with the cleaner, and sometimes more cruel, eyes of the young. An autobiographical story in this collection, "Coming Home," reflects some of the feelings and frustrations of the young Elizabeth, who had been sent away while her mother lay dying. In this story young Rosalind is disappointed to return from school and find her mother, "Darlingest," away. From disappointment Rosalind begins to feel worry and guilt that perhaps *she* is somehow responsible if something has happened to her mother. Once Darlingest safely returns, however, Rosalind sulks.

Elizabeth Bowen at the age of six

When she later seeks forgiveness for her childish behavior, Rosalind must face the sad truth that Darlingest is more important to her than Rosalind is to her mother.

Her first book having been published, Elizabeth Bowen married Alan Charles Cameron in 1923. They had met in Oxford, where Elizabeth's cousin and lifelong friend Audrey Fiennes was living with her widowed mother. Cameron had attended Oxford, fought in World War I, and in the early part of their marriage seemed the dominant spouse. As Elizabeth was just launching her career, Alan did much to make her more sophisticated. Cameron began his own career as an Oxford schoolmaster, and his financial security as a civil servant in education eventually enabled Elizabeth to begin modernizing Bowen's Court when she inherited the ancestral home from her father in 1930.

During the first two years of their marriage, Elizabeth and Alan lived at Kingsthorpe, Northampton, where he was assistant secretary for education for Northamptonshire. There Bowen produced two more books, *Ann Lee's and Other Stories* (1926) and *The Hotel* (1927), the latter being her first novel. The title story of *Ann Lee's* had been first published in an abridged version by John Strachey in the *Spectator.* By this time Bowen had an agent, Curtis Brown. Her stories, however, were still largely rejected. In retrospect Bowen recognized that editors may have thought she had incorporated too much experimental

Bowen's Court, the family estate in County Cork, Ireland

"atmosphere" and lost an earlier freshness. Many of these stories, she noted, represent "questions asked" and reflect a stylistic tension born of Bowen's looking back and transforming her own experience into fiction.

Alan Cameron became secretary of education for the city of Oxford in 1925, and there Elizabeth Bowen gained acceptance in a society that did not often accept outsiders. Part of her success can be attributed to the fact that she was a legitimate writer with work in print, but her strong personality and many qualities as both a hostess and a friend ensured her success. Cameron was the one socially outside these Oxford intelligentsia, but he did not begrudge his wife's success, as the two loved and depended on each other. Bowen may have been the famous wife, but she was always formally introduced as Mrs. Cameron at social events.

Following publication of her second novel, *The Last September* (1929), Bowen's other writing

during her years at Oxford included two collections of short fiction, *Joining Charles and Other Stories* (1929) and *The Cat Jumps and Other Stories* (1934). By the time the second of these appeared, Bowen's audience was firmly established: the fifteen hundred first-edition copies sold out immediately. "The Cat Jumps" is an interesting story that presents Bowen's deft handling of the supernatural. "Her Table Spread," also included in the 1934 collection, features the "abnormal" Valeria Cuffe, a statuesque young heiress who is still "detained in childhood," sees herself as a princess, and wraps herself in fantasies about her possible princes. Unfortunately, her life on an isolated estate offers her few interests other than her search for the perfect suitor, a search that eventually sends her into the evening rain toward a navy destroyer anchored offshore. There is no landing party to join her for dinner, and Mr. Alban, the dinner guest who might have been a match, feels regret and dismay along with a stirring of passion for the girl in ruined red satin who comes home in the rain. The physical and emotional atmosphere of "Her Table Spread" is rich in its suggestion of social tension that is a psychological tension as well.

Another landscape that reflects emotional stress and the power of situation or place appears in "The Disinherited." Davina Archworth has brought her new friend, Marianne Harvey, to the shut-up home of Lord Thingummy for a gathering of an odd group of people without money or real profession or place. Oliver, the would-be lover of Davina, is "an enemy of society, having been led to expect what he did not get." Marianne has her married life with her husband, Matthew, but she too seems out of place in the company of these people, and even her husband senses something wrong when they are home together the next day. Prothero, the chauffeur of Davina's aunt, has literally gotten away with murder, but he too is disinherited, and he spends his nights writing to his murdered wife and burning the letters. The repercussions of failed expectations follow everyone in this Bowen tale.

Bowen had also published three more novels by 1935 – *Friends and Relations* (1931), *To the North* (1932), and *The House in Paris* (1935) – and in that year Cameron and Bowen moved to 2 Clarence Terrace, Regent's Park, London, when he was appointed secretary to the Central Council of School Broadcasting at the BBC. This move, like the move to Oxford, enhanced Elizabeth's career. By this time she was writing reviews for the *Tatler* in addition to her regular writing of fiction, and in 1938 she published *The Death of the Heart,* a novel that many readers have considered her best and that continues to receive critical praise for its psychological realism and technical achievement.

Look at All Those Roses: Short Stories (1941), a collection of works written in the same period as *The Death of the Heart,* contains two important stories that focus on children. In "The Easter Egg Party" Eunice and Isabelle Evers are contented spinsters, "Amazons in homespuns" who wish to "restore childhood" to young Hermione. But Hermione already possesses a mixed identity of childishness and maturity, and the country idyll planned by the two middle-aged sisters becomes disturbing for all three. The Easter-egg party that delights the country children only alienates the unattractive Hermione, who demands to return to her own world, with all its scandal and lost innocence. This story voices Bowen's demand for honesty and her apprehensions about the self-delusive folly of seeking to pro-

tect others from corruption or somehow keep them innocent. Hermione shows the sisters the reality that Eden is not, in fact, made to order for anyone.

In "Tears, Idle Tears" seven-year-old Frederick Dickinson seems to have no reason to burst into tears and embarrass his elegant, widowed mother. Yet this behavior is not unusual for Frederick, as he and his mother walk in Regent's Park. His crying, another consequence of lost innocence, dates from his father's death when the boy was two years old. At that time his mother had saved all her sobs to pour onto his baby cot, where the boy had silently awakened without fully knowing the reason for her grief. Now touching her fox fur lightly and appearing as "a lovely mother to have," his mother seems more like an ornament than a person in Bowen's descriptions. Her perfect world is just as false as that of the sisters in "The Easter Egg Party." Meanwhile Frederick meets a girl in the park who is not appalled by him and who mentions another boy, George, who has the same senseless crying affliction. This disclosure represents hope of salvation, and when Frederick looks back on this day, he remembers "a sense of lonely shame being gone" – even as he completely forgets the story about George.

The title story from *Look at All Those Roses* also features a young character, Josephine, as well as Lou, a young woman whose love affair is faltering. Lou and Edward experience car trouble after a weekend away from London; when Edward seeks help, Lou is left in the home of Mrs. Mather and her daughter Josephine, who is confined to an invalid's carriage. The atmosphere is almost sirenlike, as Lou lulls herself into thinking that Edward – like the runaway husband and father Mr. Mather – will not be coming back anymore. In fact, Lou begins to think that staying with the Mathers would be preferable: "No wonder I've been tired," she says, "only half getting what I don't really want. Now I want nothing." But Edward does return; Lou leaves, and the status of the affair remains vague. Both the reality and the humanity of the vagueness mark Bowen's art.

The complexity of a love affair and the ways in which others are touched by it are scrutinized in "Summer Night." Robinson feels perfectly free to entertain Emma, a married woman, at his country house, but this freedom does not guarantee happiness or true love. The visit of Justin and his deaf sister Queenie before Emma arrives faintly suggests other possibilities: that Robinson might find greater satisfaction in traditionally courting Queenie, or that making a home for his absent sons might drive

Bowen in the dining room at Bowen's Court

away boredom more effectively. And Emma's husband, the Major, does not deserve his wife's temporary desertion when he is left with Aunt Fran and the children. Only Queenie, in her world of silence and memory, seems truly satisfied. Even her brother Justin feels betrayed enough to write Robinson a wild letter before he goes to bed. In these stories Bowen does not dwell on madness or frantic eros: men and women are too easily bored, or simply restless, even in their passions.

World War II dominated much of Bowen's life in London and the writing she produced during this period. While Cameron joined the Home Guard, supervising the defense of the Broadcasting House during the raids, Bowen became an Air Raid Precautions warden. The war also became an important backdrop for her novel *The Heat of the Day* (1949) and for her short fiction written during the early 1940s and collected as *The Demon Lover, and Other Stories* (1945).

In his introduction to *The Collected Stories of Elizabeth Bowen* Angus Wilson notes that her stories

may be some of the best records any future generation will have of London during the war and of the psychological violence and tenderness that the war evoked. Through the stories in *The Demon Lover, and Other Stories* readers may also gain an appreciation for Bowen's ghosts — spirits that are rarely malign but that seem to elucidate the "real" world. In "The Happy Autumn Fields" Mary prefers to dwell in a past peopled by ghosts inspired by letters that are more real than her own bombed house. London exists as its own moonlit ghost in "Mysterious Kor," a story that superbly displays Bowen's painting with words and also shows the threads of feeling that may become entangled in times of war. And the title story, "The Demon Lover," introduces the ghost or "demon" born of one woman's fickle nature.

There are other demons in the stories from this collection. In "Songs My Father Sang Me" a woman is haunted as much by her memory of the girl she had been with her father as by that of the long-absent father himself. In a conversation with her lover, the nameless woman recalls her mother's aspiration for good appearances and "middle class-dom" while her father remained a romantic who could not, and finally would not, be a traveling salesman. Her father's inability to finish any song he started was akin to his inability to get beyond his youth in World War I. These songs for another age, for love itself, are melodies in the end voiced by the daughter, herself thwarted in love. "The Inherited Clock" depicts another kind of haunting past when Clara inherits her rich Cousin Rosanna's clock. Clara and her fellow heir, her cousin Paul, have always known about Rosanna's will and their equal shares of her fortune. Neither Paul with his fickle nature nor Clara with her steadfast and hopeless love for a married man are likely to find that their inheritances improve their lives. Yet Paul is determined to have the skeleton clock, and Clara, though she loathes it, is unwilling to hand it over. Finally, when Paul recounts their stopping the clock as children, an incident that Rosanna had never discovered, other truths come to light. Rosanna's disdain, not affection, have directed this "gift" to Clara, and once that memory is recovered, Clara is changed. Thus truth, not love or money, is the real force that moves people.

Bowen's short fiction reiterates those themes found in her novels. Some critics find that the short story seems an even more appropriate form than the novel for Bowen's psychological portraits and powerful sense of the period. The tight structure of the stories, comparable to that in the finely wrought stories of Henry James, allows Bowen to maintain control and to reveal, not state, those values and insights that present the truth of human feeling. In "Ivy Gripped the Steps" the hero returns to an abandoned house he knew from childhood on the south coast of England, accessible now just after D day. The power of place holds him, because he is still crushed by the memory of himself as a boy, often a visitor here, in love with a beautiful older woman who saw him only as a charming diversion. The perception and the power of childhood, the intricacies of history and place, and the poignant forces of love are familiar Bowen themes that are masterfully handled in this single story.

After the war Bowen's novels, short stories, and essays continued to appear along with reflections on her childhood and other memoirs. Of particular importance is *The Heat of the Day,* generally considered to be Bowen's last major novel, which she intended to be a retrospective, blending public record with personal recollection. Although three more novels were to follow this — *A World of Love*

(1955), *The Little Girls* (1964), and *Eva Trout; or, Changing Scenes* (1968) — none of these demonstrates the mastery of Bowen's best fiction.

Bowen and Cameron had alternated between living in England and living at Bowen's Court throughout their marriage, but in 1952 the couple decided to live at Bowen's Court permanently. Unfortunately Cameron was seriously ill and died that same year. Following her husband's death Bowen remained at the family home until 1959, when she decided to sell Bowen's Court and return to England. Bowen, however much she was writing, remained an active traveler. From 1950 until her final illness she spent part of every year in the United States, where she visited campuses, lectured, and worked as a writer in residence. Glendinning states that the United States became as important to Bowen as Ireland, England, France, or Italy. When she returned from her travels, Bowen came home to Old Headington and later to Hythe in Kent, the place where her mother had died. Troubled by respiratory problems in the latter part of her life, she died of lung cancer on 22 February 1973 at Hythe.

Bowen was an energetic individual, a prolific writer, and a diligent woman of letters. A famous Bowen phrase from *The House in Paris* relates her philosophy of living: she feared having "a life to let." Bowen's lifestyle certainly precluded such an existence. During her career she had produced a new book almost every year, from fiction to history, autobiography, or criticism. She wrote essays and reviews for the *New Statesman and Nation,* the *Tatler,* the *Spectator,* the *Cornhill Magazine,* the *Saturday Review of Literature,* the *New Republic,* the *New York Times Magazine,* and *Harpers.* In the late 1950s she became associate editor of *London Magazine* after having been a contributor to this journal as well. But her life was not confined to writing and publishing. She entertained extensively in England and at Bowen's Court, and she moved beyond English and Irish literary circles to lecture in the United States, Canada, and Europe — and to be featured on radio and television.

As a strong woman who knew success in her lifetime and whose work has maintained a steady appreciation since her death, Bowen is a writer whose best short fiction, particularly that from the 1930s and 1940s, has confirmed critical regard for her as an important figure in English literature. Although the tight structure, the significant patterns, the impressionistic perception, and the psychological realism that may distinguish her writing have attracted the attention of some feminist scholars, Bowen was conscious of her literary success as something that she earned in an intellectual and literary milieu that was both male and female. Her themes are diverse and often uncomfortable, from incest and homosexuality to the absurdities of love and unpopular politics. Bowen appreciated independence on many levels, especially as an artist, but for her the heritage of that independence went beyond feminism.

Bibliography:

J'nan M. Sellery, *Elizabeth Bowen: A Descriptive Bibliography* (Austin: University of Texas Press, 1977).

Biography:

Victoria Glendinning, *Elizabeth Bowen* (New York: Knopf, 1977).

References:

Alan E. Austin, *Elizabeth Bowen* (New York: Twayne, 1971);

Harriet Blodgett, *Patterns of Reality: Elizabeth Bowen's Novels* (The Hague: Mouton, 1975);

Harriet Chessman, "Women and Language in the Fiction of Elizabeth Bowen," *Twentieth Century Literature,* 29 (Spring 1983): 69–85;

Janet Egleson Dunleavy, "Mary Lavin, Elizabeth Bowen, and a New Generation: The Irish Short Story at Midcentury," in *The Irish Short Story: A Critical History,* edited by James Kilroy (Boston: Twayne, 1984), pp. 145–168;

Edwin Kenny, *Elizabeth Bowen* (Lewisburg, Pa.: Bucknell University Press, 1975);

Siobhán Kilfeather, "Elizabeth Bowen;" in *British Writers: Supplement II,* edited by George Stade (New York: Scribners, 1992), pp. 77–96;

Hermione Lee, *Elizabeth Bowen: An Estimation* (London: Vision, 1981);

Seán O'Faoláin, "Elizabeth Bowen: Romance Does Not Pay," in his *The Vanishing Hero: Studies in Novelists of the Twenties* (London: Eyre & Spottiswoode, 1956), pp. 146–169;

Walter Sullivan, "A Sense of Place: Elizabeth Bowen and the Landscape of the Heart," *Sewanee Review,* 84 (Winter 1976): 142–149.

Papers:

Manuscripts and letters to and from Elizabeth Bowen are in the Harry Ransom Humanities Research Center, University of Texas at Austin; letters written by Elizabeth Bowen are in the Berg Collection of the New York Public Library.

A. E. Coppard
(4 January 1878 – 13 January 1957)

Frank Edmund Smith
William Rainey Harper College

BOOKS: *Adam & Eve & Pinch Me: Tales* (Waltham Saint Lawrence, Berkshire: Golden Cockerel Press, 1921); republished, also containing stories from *Clorinda Walks in Heaven* (New York: Knopf, 1922);

Clorinda Walks in Heaven (Waltham Saint Lawrence, Berkshire: Golden Cockerel Press, 1922);

Hips & Haws: Poems (Waltham Saint Lawrence, Berkshire: Golden Cockerel Press, 1922);

The Black Dog, and Other Stories (London: Cape, 1923; New York: Knopf, 1923); republished as *The Black Dog: Tales* (London: Cape, 1950);

Fishmonger's Fiddle: Tales (London: Cape, 1925; New York: Knopf, 1925);

The Field of Mustard: Tales (London: Cape, 1926; New York: Knopf, 1927);

Pelagea, and Other Poems (Waltham Saint Lawrence, Berkshire: Golden Cockerel Press, 1926);

Yokohama Garland, and Other Poems (Philadelphia: Centaur Press, 1926);

Count Stefan (Waltham Saint Lawrence, Berkshire: Golden Cockerel Press, 1928);

Silver Circus: Tales (London: Cape, 1928; New York: Knopf, 1929);

The Collected Poems of A. E. Coppard (London: Cape, 1928; New York: Knopf, 1928);

The Higgler (Chelsea, N.Y.: Chocorua Press, 1930);

Pink Furniture: A Tale for Lovely Children with Noble Natures (London: Cape, 1930; New York: Cape & H. Smith, 1930);

The Man from Kilsheelan: A Tale (London: William Jackson, 1930);

The Hundredth Story of A. E. Coppard (Waltham Saint Lawrence, Berkshire: Golden Cockerel Press, 1931);

Fares Please! An Omnibus (London: Cape, 1931) — comprises *The Black Dog and Other Stories, The Field of Mustard: Tales,* and *Silver Circus: Tales*;

Easter Day (London: Ulysses Bookshop, 1931);

Nixey's Harlequin: Tales (London: Cape, 1931; New York: Knopf, 1932);

Cheefoo (Croton Falls, N.Y.: Spiral, 1932);

A. E. Coppard (courtesy of the Lilly Library, Indiana University)

Crotty Shinkwin: A Tale of the Strange Adventure That Befell a Butcher of County Clare. The Beauty Spot: A Tale Concerning the Chilterns (Waltham Saint Lawrence, Berkshire: Golden Cockerel Press, 1932);

Rummy: That Noble Game Expounded in Prose, Poetry, Diagram, and Engraving, . . . with an Account of Certain Diversions into the Mountain Fastnesses of Cork and Kerry (Waltham Saint Lawrence, Berkshire: Golden Cockerel Press, 1932; Boston & New York: Houghton Mifflin, 1933);

Dunky Fitlow: Tales (London: Cape, 1933);

Ring the Bells of Heaven (London: White Owl, 1933);

Emergency Exit (New York: Random House, 1934);

Good Samaritans (New York: Spiral, 1934);

The Fairies Return; or, New Tales for Old, by Coppard and others (London: Myers, 1934);

Polly Oliver: Tales (London: Cape, 1935);

Cherry Ripe: Poems (Windham, Conn.: Hawthorne House, 1935; Chepstow: Tintern, 1935);

The Ninepenny Flute: Twenty-One Tales (London: Macmillan, 1937);

Tapster's Tapestry (London: Golden Cockerel Press, 1938);

You Never Know, Do You? and Other Tales (London: Methuen, 1939);

Ugly Anna, and Other Tales (London: Methuen, 1944);

Selected Tales, from His Twelve Volumes Published between the Wars (London: Cape, 1946);

Fearful Pleasures (Sauk City, Wis.: Arkham House, 1946; London & New York: Peter Nevill, 1951);

Dark-Eyed Lady: Fourteen Tales (London: Methuen, 1947);

The Collected Tales of A. E. Coppard (New York: Knopf, 1948);

Lucy in Her Pink Jacket (London & New York: Peter Nevill, 1954);

It's Me, O Lord! (London: Methuen, 1957).

OTHER: Robert Burns, *Songs from Robert Burns,* edited by Coppard (Waltham Saint Lawrence, Berkshire: Golden Cockerel Press, 1925).

SELECTED PERIODICAL PUBLICATIONS – UNCOLLECTED: "Review of *Short Story Writing for Profit* by Michael Joseph," *Spectator,* 132 (12 January 1924): 56;

"American Short Story," *Manchester Guardian,* 20 November 1925, p. 5;

"The Craft of the Short Story: Lessons from the Folk Tale," *T. P.'s and Cassell's Weekly,* 9 (28 January 1928): 481;

"British Short Story," *Manchester Guardian,* 22 November 1929, p. 7;

"On First Getting into Print," *Colophon,* part 6, no. 9, May 1931;

"The Short Story," *Writer,* 4, no. 4 (October 1949): 7–9.

On All Fool's Day 1919 Alfred Edgar Coppard left his job as a clerk-cost accountant at the Eagle Ironworks in Oxford to live alone in a cottage at Shepards Pit, where he began to re-create himself as A. E. Coppard, author. Although the most dramatic, this was not the first of his transformations, nor was it the last time he gave himself a new name to express his new identity. He was forty-one years old. He had written about a dozen short stories since 1912 and had finally published six in late 1918, and he was now prepared to make fifty pounds in savings sustain him until he gained the literary recognition that he craved.

He stayed at Shepards Pit for three years, living mostly on raw vegetables and writing much poetry and several more short stories. His first collection of short stories had been turned down by such publishers as Methuen, Macmillan, Constable, and Chatto and Windus before Harold Taylor inquired if Coppard might have a manuscript to inaugurate Taylor's newly formed communal enterprise, the Golden Cockerel Press. Five hundred and fifty first-edition copies of *Adam & Eve & Pinch Me: Tales* were published on All Fool's Day 1921, and these were followed by two more Golden Cockerel editions. In 1922 Knopf brought out an edition in the United States, and Coppard published another collection of tales – *Clorinda Walks in Heaven* – and a collection of poetry, *Hips & Haws: Poems,* with the Golden Cockerel Press. He had arrived as an author.

Coppard, the eldest son of George and Emily Southwell Coppard, a tailor and a housemaid respectively, was born in Folkstone, Kent. After his father deserted the family in 1884, his mother and her four children moved to Brighton. George rejoined his family at Brighton but died of tuberculosis when "Alfie" was nine, so his mother supported the family with work as a presser and with parish relief. Coppard's formal education soon ended when, supposedly because of poor health, he was taken out of school and apprenticed to a paraffin oil vendor. He was later sent to live with relatives in London, where he worked as an errand boy in a tailor shop and as a messenger for the Reuters news agency. In 1892 his mother agreed to let him return home, and he began a series of office jobs at local businesses and manufacturing firms that eventually led him to the city of Oxford.

Coppard never forgot his early years; as an adult he talked endlessly about the privation of his childhood. He felt the shame of poverty, but he felt superior for having been poor. He pursued money, but he proudly devalued it. Fellow author Frank O'Connor writes about Coppard's "unearned income complex," an ambivalence about money that surfaced continually through his life and work. Coppard complained that books that had earned him very little commanded high prices from collectors on the used-book market, especially if he had signed the copies. His father had been a socialist, and Coppard was certainly a socialist sympathizer who worked hard to make himself socially and economically respectable. Being from the working class, he was fascinated with the earthy vulgarity of foundry laborers at the Brighton Works, but as an office worker he was sensitive, high-minded. He went with them on their whoring escapades at the seafront, but his romantic view of women kept him from trafficking with the "bawds" and so, although he accompanied his fellow workers, Coppard did not share in their pleasures. Embarrassed by his lack of formal education, he nonetheless felt superior because of his personal reading. His fiction came to embrace and portray common people, ordinary "vulgar" folk, and he insisted on calling his short stories "tales" because he saw them as an evolution of the oral folk tradition.

During his years of working for a living before becoming a writer, he had always striven to make something of himself. At fifteen he took up professional sprinting and competed successfully for a dozen years. This early interest in athletics evolved through his twenties and thirties into a variety of physical pursuits including boxing, dog training, swimming, shooting, soccer, and marathon hiking, the last two interests becoming lifelong passions. More significantly, on a winter night when he was seventeen he stopped under the shelter of a second-hand bookseller's awning and read the poem that changed his life – John Keats's "La Belle Dame Sans Merci" (1820), shaping for him a magical view of language and women. The other major sources of his literary awakening included Thomas Hardy's *Life's Little Ironies* (1894), which made him determined to write short stories, and the combined influences of American poet Walt Whitman's *Leaves of Grass* (1855) and the poems of Robert Bridges. As Coppard recalls in his autobiography, *It's Me, O Lord!* (1957), Bridges's poetry "altered my stance towards pretty well everything, not merely to the art I was groping for but to life and its thought surrounding me."

He became a compulsive reader; the money he won by racing went to buy books. Thomas O. Beachcroft points out that Coppard read and pondered innumerable literary works that well-educated people know only by reputation: Chaucer's poetry, John Milton's *Paradise Lost* (1667), Charles Darwin's *On the Origin of Species by Means of Natural Selection* (1859), the Hindu Rig-Veda and Upanishads, and works of Shakespeare, for example. As a young man Coppard was proud of reading all of everything, the longer the better. He claimed to be the only person alive to have finished all of poet Samuel Butler's *Hudibras* (1663–1664, 1678). He became something of a tyrant, demanding complete silence

Coppard on a Brighton racecourse in 1901, during his eighth year as a professional sprinter

from his mother and sisters while he read, and he later described the effect of all this untutored reading as making him "undisciplined, self-willed, opinionated, and intolerant," especially about anyone else's literary opinions. He called Robert Browning's *The Ring and the Book* (1868–1869) "the most beautiful long poem ever written," reading it over and over literally until the end of his life. In his autobiographical writing Coppard regrets that during all his youth and early adulthood, he knew no one with whom he could discuss books. He felt isolated and lonely but also smug and superior — attitudes that would later appear in his life and in some of his writing. Yet he was always cheerful and enthusiastically social. He loved workingmen's taverns (often the settings for his tales), where he argued hotly for his literary and political opinions before regularly breaking into laughter at the absurdity of his own positions.

By 1902 he began to enter and win annual essay competitions. In 1905 he married Lily Anne Richards, who had encouraged his literary interests and even set topics for him to write about. But it was not until they moved to Oxford, when he was twenty-nine years old, that he began to have literary ambitions. As O'Connor notes, "He loved Oxford as Newman and Arnold loved it, but he went there as a clerk, not a student." He attended lectures and concerts, became involved in literary groups, read in the Radcliffe Camera, and followed student social and athletic events. For the first time he was living among people who valued the written word. He became aware of how truly ignorant he was, but he also came to recognize his strengths. The undergraduates and dons of Oxford who befriended him gave his mind its first real test, and, although he sometimes cringed at his own ignorance, he also felt smugly superior to them because of the depth of his self-education. He had read far more English literature than the young men who so casually displayed their intelligence, and he fervently debated them about literary traditions. But they could read in other languages, and they wrote poetry.

He had been competing in sports for much of his life; living in Oxford, he became determined to compete at writing. Reading had nourished his mind, yet, he said, it had made him passive. Oxford shook him out of the "lullaby." He writes in his autobiography that "here were all these boys, boys! with their poems and tales already in being . . . some even in real books. Straightway I was fired, though not by any more worthy muse than the spirit of rivalry." Lily Anne moved the Coppards to a cottage at Combe so that Alf, as he was then called, could escape all the clubs and activities that distracted him. At the age of thirty-four he produced his first story, a twelve-thousand-word piece called "Fleet" that was rejected by the *English Review* for being too long. During this same period he wrote "Piffingcap" and "Clorinda Walks in Heaven." The Coppards moved back to Oxford during World War I, from which he was deferred because his employment at the ironworks was part of the war effort. During these years he wrote some of his finest tales – "Weep Not, My Wanton," "Dusky Ruth," "Arabesque: The Mouse," and "Adam and Eve and Pinch Me." Toward the end of this period he wrote "Marching to Zion," based on a walking trip he had taken.

He began to get poetry published in *The Egoist* and the *Nation* in 1917. But Coppard dates his beginning as an author from July 1918, when *Pearson's Magazine* published "Piffingcap" and paid him for it. Soon the *Saturday Westminster Gazette* and the *English Review* published two more stories, and the *Manchester Guardian* and *Saturday Westminster* published "Mr. Lightfoot in the Green Isle" serially in 1918 and 1919. Coppard had met E. J. O'Brien in Oxford and gathered that O'Brien already had a formidable reputation at promoting the short story, but he refused to solicit aid. He had come so far without tutors or formal education, and he felt that he had to succeed entirely on his own merits, without a patron: "It was excruciatingly important to me that my writing

should be judged, not boosted." O'Brien did not promote Coppard's early career but did later include him in his annual anthology, *The Best British Short Stories,* from 1922 to 1928 – and even dedicated the 1924 edition to him. In 1919, however, the aspiring and determined Coppard quit his job and moved alone to the cottage at Shepard's Pit, Bayswater, Headington.

His first collection was well received, though it made the author little money. The *Times Literary Supplement* review of *Adam & Eve & Pinch Me: Tales* credits Anton Chekhov, Guy de Maupassant, and Irish writers for their influence on Coppard's stories. This was the first instance of a long record of reviewers and commentators misreading his work or misrepresenting his life. He had read de Maupassant in 1903 but had not read Chekhov, whose work he came to know well, until most of the *Adam & Eve & Pinch Me* stories were completed. The Irish influence came from Coppard's incredible gift of observation. He had taken his first walking tour of Ireland in 1915 and another soon after. He had the professional writer's habit of carrying notebooks with him and of recording names of people and places, descriptions of scenes, and long dialogues that he overheard, especially in pubs. This reputation for imitating Irish writers persisted, as did another accusation that he was trying too hard and straining for effect. Probably his reputation as a writer of fantasy and supernatural fiction began with the title story of this first volume, a tale about a man who has an out-of-body experience in an Edenlike garden. Yet of more than two hundred stories by Coppard, only about four dozen fit into this broad category.

Coppard was always a self-conscious writer, not the natural or primitive one that some came to see and that he sometimes pretended to be. His writing in these early stories is not forced, although that would come later when he began to imitate himself. His prose has a lyric feel, and the *London Mercury* review recognized that. *Poetic* came to be the word used most often, and most accurately, to describe the form and effect of his short stories. If any single demonstration is wanted to prove that Coppard is not a simple storyteller, "Arabesque: The Mouse" provides that evidence. Conscious artistry is clear in this ornate, interwoven pattern of motifs on the figure of a mouse. So elaborate is its construction that its most remarkable feature is that, when read, it does not appear contrived. The narrative unfolds through two simultaneous actions that mirror each other. Alternately repelled and delighted by what he sees, a man sits in a lonely room watching the antics of a mouse. The setting and the mouse trigger memories of his mother and of a girl, but this revelry collapses with the sound of a mousetrap. The man throws the mutilated mouse out the window and resets the trap. Though the overt events are limited, they resonate with a dark, brooding tone that transforms the interior action into a kind of psychological horror story.

The opening is almost farcical in its extremes. A man named Filip sits "reading Russian novels until he thought he was mad" in a room smelling of "dried apples and mice." He begins to watch the mouse and then he goes to the cupboard to inspect the baited trap. He recoils at its meanness. He decides to throw it in the fire but changes his mind because the house swarms with mice, and he replaces it with the thought, "I hope that little beastie won't go and do anything foolish." He remembers his mother's death after she was run down by a cart that crushed her hands. The trauma has fixed his temperament as one of mixed horror and morbid fascination at brutality in himself and others. Filip has grown into a man of generosity and rebellion, a social-moral reformer who shouts about "Justice and Sin" and who has sought the companionship of "melodious-minded men" and "fair unambiguous women" until continued rebuffs have made him timid and misanthropic. He has once known such a woman – Cassia, whose "eyes were full of starry inquiry like the eyes of a mouse." Their one evening together at a village festival had made him hope for a perfect love, but, when he took her home, he heard footsteps behind her front door and the clack of a bolt.

With a "snap" the narrative turns from the man's memories to the present. The trap has gone off, amputating the mouse's forefeet. Cut off from nature and man, Filip cannot act. Should he crush the mouse? Throw it in the fire? In either case he would have to experience the death of the mouse. He will not chance any more involvement with life, so he tosses it out the window, sits for ten minutes in shame, and then runs down the stairs "searching long and vainly for the little philosopher." Finally, he returns to the room and resets the trap – a device that, like Filip, can only react. Melancholia has become his prevailing temperament: "his griefs were half deliberate, his despairs half unreal." Throughout the presentation of events at the immediate moment and in two flashbacks connected by a tightly written commentary, transforming motifs of deaths, hearts, hands, eyes, apples, and mice twist and weave to shape the reader's recognition of Filip's alienation and impotence.

In 1922 Coppard was back at Oxford to read his tales and lecture on Chekhov and de Maupassant. He had proved himself. His second book, *Clorinda Walks in Heaven,* was published to enthusiastic reviews: the *Times Literary Supplement* suggested that the fiction went beyond mere narrative to evoke deep response. Coppard's landlord wanted the cottage for another purpose, so Lily Anne found a cottage at Chinoor in the Chilterns. He moved there for a year before leaving her, apparently for good, and isolating himself in a hut at Little Poynatts, where he lived until 1927. He continued to write, and he also took up with a series of women. One of them was Gay Taylor, the wife of his publisher, Harold Taylor, who was by then dying of cancer.

Much of Coppard's life during this period can be deduced from a series of autobiographical stories about his fictional character named Johnny Flynn and, to a lesser extent, from a biographical novel by Gay Taylor. Coppard dedicated *Clorinda Walks in Heaven* "To Mrs. Flynn," by which he meant his mother, and he began to refer to himself as Flynn and to encourage his friends to do so as well. "The Presser," "The Cherry Tree," "Pedestrian Fancy," and "Pomona's Babe" recount with some accuracy events from Coppard's childhood and adolescence. In *It's Me, O Lord!* Coppard confirms the autobiographical bases of these stories, but he also cautions readers to be wary about apparent truths in his autobiography. He regularly referred to himself as a "fiction-monger," someone not to be trusted about truth or fiction. Through these stories runs the paradoxical theme that appears repeatedly in Coppard's fiction and life – his shame at being common and his pride at being poor, lower class, and literary.

"My Hundredth Tale" recounts Johnny Flynn's boyhood and career as a writer. He lives alone in a hut, consumed with his own awareness. He has affairs with three women, the first two of whom are too vulgar for him; the last, a real lady, finds him too vulgar for her. Gay Taylor's *No Goodness in the Worm* (1930) is set in a similar hut where Valentine Spens (Taylor) meets furniture maker Francis Merryweather (Coppard), who delivers her from a "half-infantile, half-sexed life." Eventually she finds him merely clever, obsessed with himself, and impudent. He confuses fact and fiction. She leaves him and attempts suicide after he impregnates her best friend. This novel at least accurately portrays Coppard's appearance and mannerisms.

The Black Dog, and Other Stories, dedicated "To Gay," appeared in 1923. Reviewers had begun to

the interior ~~surface~~ a walls, lovelier than dreamed-of pictures. The heads ~~Faces~~ of mothers & old dames were also imaged ~~figured~~ there, recognizable in their black shadows; & little children held up their hands between window & wall to make five-fingered shapes upon the golden screen. ~~When he was climbed up to the further end of the moor it was like driving into an~~ To drive on the moor then was to drive into blasts more dire, and darkness began to fall, & bitter cold it was. There were no birds to be seen, neither beast nor man. The moor was empty of everything except sound & a marvel of dying light & Harvey Witlow of Dinnop with a sour old nag driving from end to end of it. At Prattle Corner dusk was already abroad: there was just one shaft of light that broached a sharp-angled stack in the rickyard, an ark of darkness, along whose top gads & wooden fins & tilted straws were miraculously fringed in ~~fir~~ the last glare. Hitching his nag to the palings he knocked at the door, & knew in the gloom it was Mary who opened it & stood peering forth at him

"Good evening" he said, touching his hat.

"Oh!" the girl uttered a cry "Higgler! What do you come for?" It was the longest sentence she had ever spoken to him; a sad frightened voice

"I thought" he began "I'd call — & see Mrs S—— I wondered . . . . . "

"Mother's dead" said the girl. She drew the door further back, as if inviting him, & he entered. The door was shut behind him, & they were alone, in darkness, together. The girl was deeply grieving. Trembling, he asked the question: "What is it you tell me, Mary?"

Page from the manuscript for Coppard's best-known story, "The Higgler" (courtesy of the Lilly Library, Indiana University)

type Coppard as a literary bucolic, but the *Times Literary Supplement* review was especially perceptive about his materials and structures. It noted accurately that he does not sentimentalize or idealize the country. Coppard was coming to be regarded as one of the major fiction writers of the postwar period. Striking evidence of this was editor Ford Madox Ford's plan to feature him in Ford's new literary magazine, the *Transatlantic Review,* and a 1923 prospectus for the journal ranks Coppard with James Joyce, E. E. Cummings, Ezra Pound, and T. S. Eliot. Coppard supplied copy for three numbers, including that of May 1924, which published one of his major stories, "The Higgler." This tale concerns Coppard's most important subject matter – the human condition. From birth to death poor men and women experience unfulfilled, bittersweet longings for things they cannot have. Captives of time and change, they can neither control nor escape their fates.

"The Higgler" is Coppard's best-known and perhaps most representative tale. The narrative line, as in most Coppard stories, is simple. In an attempt to expand his failing business Harvey Witlow, the higgler, travels across Shag Moor to the Sadgrove farm. Mrs. Sadgrove sells him scores of eggs and dozens of chickens, and he soon contracts with her to buy other produce of her farm. Harvey is struck with Mary Sadgrove – a lovely, educated, shy, quiet girl. After repeated visits, partially business and partially personal, Mrs. Sadgrove offers Harvey the girl and the farm, worth £3,000. Harvey, weighing his perceived worth against the girl's apparent value, decides that he is being ensnared or ridiculed, and he quickly marries another – the coarse, unsympathetic Sophy Daws. Months later, his business once again failing, he returns to the Sadgrove farm to ask for a loan. He finds Mary alone, helplessly trying to lay out the body of her dead mother. Helping her complete the task, he learns to his dismay that the marriage had been her idea, that she had loved him but had been too shy to ask for herself. The higgler's foolish suspicions have cost him a beautiful woman and a prosperous life.

"The Higgler" contains some of Coppard's most evocative writing, as he was using words with great care and precision in developing themes through animal imagery and contrasting natural settings. Coppard loved to collect and use outrageous names: Harvey Witlow is "shrewd," "crafty," and "cunning" – but not wise. Mary Sadgrove lives quietly by Prattle Corner. Tropes of desolation and loss, violence and death establish a mood that shifts from light to dark: "The furze was always green and growing, and, taking no account of seasons, often golden. Here in summer solitude lounged and snoozed; at other times, as now, it shivered and looked sinister." Harvey has become accustomed to seeing life fatalistically. Like many of Coppard's male characters, the higgler, though not unkind or incompetent, is insensitive to the hopeful, intuitive, feminine qualities of nature.

After the *Transatlantic Review* had failed, Ford, who called Coppard "the White Hope of British Literature," continued to promote him through Ford's own writing. However, it seems likely that Ford was taken as much by Coppard's personality and dramatic physical appearance as by his writing. Ford and others remarked on Coppard's dark skin, black hair, and hawklike nose. His physical ease and athleticism must have set him apart from drawing-room writers.

By 1925 his reputation had become significant enough to ensure his inclusion in *The Borzoi,* Knopf's record of ten years of publishing. *Fishmonger's Fiddle: Tales* (1925), dedicated "To Gay," was published the same year and received even greater praise and more careful reading than his earlier work. The *Times Literary Supplement* said that his writing "suggests . . . the old Dutch painters" in its color and concrete detail. He was sought as a writer of opinion pieces and as a subject for interviews and portraits in magazines.

His impact on the English short story was so sudden that he was constantly referred to as a "young" writer, though he was nearly in his fifties. His emergence, seemingly from nowhere, has often been commented on. Ford Madox Ford wrote in 1927, "It is impossible to say whence Mr. Coppard can derive. . . . [S]uddenly he wrote stories – and much as was the case with Conrad, suddenly found himself famous in England." H. E. Bates, who credited Coppard with influencing his own beginnings as a short-story writer and who later became the closest thing Coppard had to a literary enemy, wrote in 1941 that, because Coppard had waited so long in life before beginning to write, his first work shows a maturity uncommon to the beginning writer: "Coppard's first window display, in fact, was like a show of well-made, bright coloured handicraft: strong in texture, bold and fanciful in design, carefully finished."

Through the rest of the 1920s he was regularly mentioned as one of the most important writers of his time. Like many writers of that period, Coppard was aware of what he was doing. He knew that he was creating a form, knew that the short story, with its own structuring devices, was a different genre from the novel. He saw his work as part of a literary tradition, and the sophistication of his techniques still impresses modern readers. Although little happens in most of his best stories, they develop through elaborate systems of interwoven and supportive tropes. He plays with words and stretches syntax to get effects both serious and comic. He uses comedy to look at pain, and he charges his tales with sexual tension artfully disguised in metaphor.

He created and developed the interlude — an apparently digressive, often comic narrative event that colors, comments on, or counterpoints the story proper. Although they do not occur in all his fictions, they serve as a kind of stylistic watermark. The interlude provides a break in the action and takes the form of a dialogue overheard — usually by the main characters, though sometimes by the narrative persona who directs the reader away from the central narrative. Typically the dialogue is between two or more rustics who discourse comically on the weather, poaching, farming, or places visited. These interludes perform at least two functions: they add touches of realism that flesh out the tale, and they enhance its voice, supplying part of the sound of the tale being told — with all its irrelevancies and digressions. In effect they disguise some of Coppard's sophisticated literary qualities and take the short story back to its vulgar roots.

Sometimes the interludes do more. The ludicrous interlude in "Fishmonger's Fiddle" provides an interpretive key to the story. Maxie, a timid woman married but abandoned, goes on an outing with Blackburne, who loves her. They stop at an inn where the action turns to an elegantly dressed man who winks at her and sings a silly song: "Oh, the Queen of Poland is my queen / And I'm her salamander." Fearing hellfire, Maxie refuses Blackburne's request that they live together. But at the end of the story she fantasizes a future with him as the song, which represents freedom from convention, perseveres in her mind. Interludes function similarly in "The Presser," "The Higgler," and "Alice Brady."

Frank O'Connor has said that in Coppard's early books the reader feels that the form of the short story is being handled in a new way. Unlike other writers who settle into one convention that appeals to them, Coppard "never settles for . . . any convention other than his own need to grip the reader by the lapel and make him listen. . . . [H]is formal range is remarkable — greater I should say than that of any other storyteller." Coppard's command of forms that control the inner structure of a work was far-reaching and sure. "The Little Mis-

tress," for instance, is shaped in a literal movement that begins outside the Harper home, moves the reader inside the home, and, gradually and figuratively, creates a new view of the character's psychology. A second level of action supports this revelation, in which characters are mirrored literally and figuratively. Coppard loved to play with parallel and antithetical language and forms.

"Simple Simon" unfolds on both these levels: "The sun never was clear in the forest, but the fogs that rose in its unshaken shade were neither sweet nor sour. Lonely was Simon, for he had given up all the sweet of the world and had received none of the sweet of heaven." Simon goes to heaven and finds there a house in the forest that, except for its perfection, duplicates his own broken home on earth. In "Pomona's Babe," like the other Johnny Flynn stories, the characterization creates a person whose idealizing of the world through literature leads first to escape and then to romantic impotence. This story develops through repeated patterns of aborted attempts by the youthful Johnny to leave the world of books long enough to engage the world around him. Although he wishes to act decisively, insisting that his sister, Pomona, will have her baby at home and even planning to murder the man who has impregnated her, in fact he would rather fantasize than act. So his mother makes and acts on the decisions, sending her daughter to the workhouse and confronting Pomona's lover while Johnny watches from the shadows.

In 1926 Coppard met a young South African medical student, Winifred De Kok, who began to visit him in his hut and eventually became his second wife. She introduced him to the analyst Wilhelm Steckel, who told him the story that came to be "Silver Circus." *The Field of Mustard: Tales* (1926), dedicated "To Wynne," has been characterized as woodcuts seen from the viewpoint of a poet. C. Henry Warren, reviewing the collection in the January 1927 *Bookman,* labels Coppard one of the "recognized masters of the short story" and links him with the crafting of a new vision of the short-story genre. The title story is Coppard's masterpiece, one of the finest examples of lyric short fiction produced by any writer.

The story opens on "three sere disvirgined women" collecting firewood in the Black Wood on a windy November afternoon. Color, odor, and texture are important ingredients of the story, a pastoral in the form of an eclogue. The interweaving of light and dark casts a bleak spell on the action. "Hoar" is the white of age, while the yellow of the mustard suggests withering and death. The only green is that of a "briar," a contradictory figure that reinforces the preceding oxymoron "sweet ruin." The women are pulling "dead branches" from trees and stacking them in bundles. Age has overtaken the three women, and death is not far behind. They wear clothing of "dull blue" and "grey," and the wind tousles their "gaunt locks." Dinah Lock, the dominant character, has grown enormously fat, while Rose Olliver's and Amy Hardwick's bodies show the unmistakable signs of aging. They meet an old hedger who tells them the time "by his ancient watch," the relic of an old war.

Dinah and Rose carry their bundles of kindling back through the field of mustard and sit down to wait for Amy. They begin to talk. The descriptions and dialogue that follow convey the women's sense of despair and loss, a loss that the reader shares as a party to the human condition. Sentenced to a brief journey that begins at the cradle and ends at the grave, humans are prisoners of rotting time, and time is bankrupt because the Garden is forever lost. The Golden Age has gone sour. Youth and its promise of love and fruition have gone to ruin – indeed, are never anything more than vain desires. Their talk turns to friendship and love and death. "Oh God, cradle and grave is all there is for we," says Dinah. And later, "I like you, Rose; I wish you was a man." This and other sexually ambiguous references compound the sense that life is empty and meaningless. Dinah and Rose continue to share thoughts about their lost hopes, although the narrator notes that Dinah's "corpulence dispossessed her of tragedy." Rose, who is childless, envies Dinah for being the mother of four children, but Dinah maintains that her "family's a torment." Even her husband is a loss to her: he has been "no man at all since he was ill." Rose snaps off a sprig of mustard flower, places the bloom partly in her mouth, and moves it in and out of her mouth.

For woman, who flowers for a brief while and then fades, the loss of time is particularly cruel. Her womb may figuratively afford some means to reach out to the future, but that future promises her children nothing more than she has received – disappointment and death. Dinah lies down next to Rose and begins to reminisce about Rufus Blackthorn, the former gamekeeper with whom she has had a love affair. The two women talk about him, each lost in her own memories, until each realizes that the other has been his lover – and their romantic recollections decay into bitter denunciation: "We was all cheap to him," one remarks. Now even memory has turned sour. Amy catches up to them, and the three continue toward home. Rose still en-

vies Dinah's children, but Dinah tells her, "Ain't you got a fire of your own indoors? . . . Well, why don't you sit by it then!" To grieve for loss is foolishness; even to remember it is unwise. The world is a place of aimless tragedies and certain snares. Yet something remains, a shared sorrow: "The wind hustled the two women close together, and as they stumbled under their burdens Dinah Lock stretched out a hand and touched the other woman's arm." The narrative concludes, "the lovely earth seemed to sigh in grief at some calamity all unknown to men." Having lost the Garden, all the loveliness of the earth is but a soured image dully reflected in a yellowed mirror.

This story epitomizes Coppard's tales about the secret life of women. O'Connor has remarked on this, and it would be impossible to read much of Coppard without noticing it. His awareness of women's inner lives can be astonishing, even when focused through a male perspective, as he does in "The Watercress Girl." Often his stories, such as "The Higgler" or "The Black Dog," focus on a man who is mystified, puzzled, or confused by a woman. Yet the narrative never leaves any sense that the woman is being confusing. Instead, the implication is of a rich, hidden life; an elemental sexuality; or, perhaps, a deep sorrow inherent in women – a pain unknowable to men, who in these tales are blocked from understanding by their own attitudes of self-importance, suspicion, or priggishness.

Another of Coppard's most representative stories, "The Old Venerable," also appeared in *The Field of Mustard*. Its depiction of hopeful poverty ground down by cruelty and fate reveals the depth of Coppard's concern with injustice and his skill at incorporating social issues into fiction. Old Dick, seventy years old and crippled but cheery and honest, resides in a tent shanty in the woods and "prime[s] his starved heart with hope." The object of his dreams is a donkey that could double or triple the amount of work he can do and thereby "make him a rich man." When a litter of pedigreed retrievers is born on a nearby estate, he begs the head keeper for the runt that is about to be killed. Under his care Sossy thrives and becomes a first-class bird dog. He could sell the bitch for a donkey, but he arranges instead to breed her on the sly to an outstanding retriever. As he waits for the pups to be born, he computes their value and reckons that he can buy a horse and cart and can perhaps even attract a wife.

Then a new gamekeeper appears and orders him out of the woods. Old Dick exchanges ugly words with the young man, and, after Sossy's pups are born, the keeper shoots the bitch. Without nourishment the pups begin to die. In the powerful conclusion the old man drowns the rest, one at a time: " 'There's your donkey,' he gurgled, '. . . And there. . . goes your cob and your cart and. . . the old gal.' " Conveying Old Dick's despair in powerful and immediate terms, Coppard's extraordinary language puts the reader in contact with stark emotions.

With *The Field of Mustard* stories Coppard reached the height of his powers. Although he wrote many more fine tales, they began to get lost in the volume of his production, many of them cranked-out imitations of earlier tales. His obsession with theme and cleverness overwhelmed the delicate formal structures at which he was so skilled. Also as he moved up in society he attempted more and more stories about middle- and upper-class people, whom he had never understood, and these stories sound false.

The Coppards moved to London in 1927, and the following year saw the publication of *The Collected Poems of A. E. Coppard, Silver Circus: Tales,* and *Count Stefan,* this last of which was the first of his tales and poems published individually for collectors. A review of *Silver Circus: Tales* by *The Evening News* misreads the book by arguing that Coppard should stick to writing rural tales and by praising "The Presser." Coppard angrily responded that that story was set in the slums of London.

Coppard and Winifred married in 1931 and in 1933 moved to Walberswick, Suffolk, where he began to make himself known as "The Warden of Walberswick." The greatest number of Coppard publications and recognitions came during 1930–1935. He published *Fares Please! An Omnibus* (1931), a collection of stories from three earlier books, and *Nixey's Harlequin: Tales* (1931), *Dunky Fitlow: Tales* (1933), and *Polly Oliver: Tales* (1935). Jacob Schwartz compiled a bibliography of his work to date (1931), and Gilbert Fabes published a list of Coppard's first editions (1933). This last had become necessary because Coppard's work, which had always been published in small editions, was rare and therefore valuable to collectors. Coppard was furious that collectors, whom he felt did not read anyway, were making more on his books than he had. A particularly bitter experience was occasioned by a pirated edition of *The Higgler* (1930), published in New York for sixty-five dollars a copy and each with a page of the original manuscript in Coppard's hand. He decided to cash in on the market, and with support from patrons he began to publish illustrated limited editions consisting of one or two poems and tales,

including *The Man from Kilsheelan: A Tale* (1930), *The Hundredth Story of A. E. Coppard* (1931), *Crotty Shinkwin: A Tale of the Strange Adventure That Befell a Butcher of County Clare. The Beauty Spot: A Tale Concerning the Chilterns* (1932), and *Ring the Bells of Heaven* (1933).

A *Times Literary Supplement* review of *The Ninepenny Flute: Twenty-One Tales* (1937) recognizes Coppard's decline as "an impulse towards caricature." In 1938 the Coppards moved to Duton Hill, Dunmow, Essex, where he remained for the rest of his life. He continued to play soccer enthusiastically and to take long walking trips. He also continued to publish, producing *You Never Know, Do You? and Other Tales* (1939); *Ugly Anna, and Other Tales* (1944); *Selected Tales, from His Twelve Volumes Published between the Wars* (1946); a collection of supernatural tales, *Fearful Pleasures* (1946); *Dark-Eyed Lady: Fourteen Tales* (1947); and *Lucy in Her Pink Jacket* (1954), this last of which was not even reviewed by the *Times*. Knopf published *The Collected Tales of A. E. Coppard,* more accurately a collection of selected tales, in 1948, and this led to Coppard's most significant financial reward and literary tribute. Earl E. Fisk of Green Bay, Wisconsin, a reader who had collected and supported Coppard's work since the 1920s, organized a successful letter-writing campaign by authors such as Eudora Welty, Rebecca West, Elizabeth Bowen, Gerald Bullett, Robert Frost, and Carl Sandburg to get *The Collected Tales* selected for promotion and distribution by the Book-of-the-Month Club. It was offered as a dividend book in 1951, and this earned Coppard the largest single sum of his career. Most of the money he quickly spent or gave away to socialist causes.

In 1955 Methuen convinced Coppard to write an autobiography, which he titled *It's Me, O Lord!* from the spiritual he loved to hear sung by Paul Robeson. Regardless of the title of the autobiography and the continual references to God that appear throughout his writing, Coppard was a confirmed atheist to the end. He sent off the corrected proofs the day before he entered a London hospital for the last time, taking with him his copy of Robert Browning's *The Ring and the Book.* Despite good reviews, sales of his autobiography were poor; Winifred received only about £300. The *Times* review of the autobiography misrepresented Coppard's tales as being loving comedies about the upper classes. After a lifetime of arguing about his work being misread, Coppard lost at the end.

He had already expressed in *It's Me, O Lord!* his wish to have no "headstone or tomby memorial," which he compared to "an advertisement that has lost its function." Consequently, and somewhat ironically, a silver sacristy lamp bearing his name and dates was hung in the chapel of Blessed John Ball, priest and martyr, in the lovely fifteenth-century Church of St. John the Baptist in Thaxted, Essex, a few miles from Coppard's last home in Dunmow. John Ball, one of the leaders of Wat Tyler's revolt in 1381, had been a socialist remembered for the rallying cry found in the chapel: "Good people, things will never go well in England so long as goods be not in common."

Coppard wrote a handful of the best short stories in the English language and a wonderfully engaging autobiography. He contributed significantly to the movement of the short story from being a truncated novel to acquiring its own form. However, because he was determined to make a living as a writer, he wrote far too much. That and the facts that he was a loner, belonging to no groups or circles that would have advanced his reputation; that he began his career so late and wrote about a time that was rapidly disappearing; and that he wrote in a genre that until recently has had little respect or commercial success all contribute to his meager reputation.

Interviews:

Louise Morgan, "A. E. Coppard on How to Write Short Stories," *Everyman*, 4 (22 January 1931): 793–795;

Morgan, *Writers at Work* (London: Chatto & Windus, 1931);

Ashley Sampson, "Mr. A. E. Coppard on Current Literature," *John O'London's Weekly*, 32 (1 December 1934): 356.

Bibliographies:

Jacob Schwartz, *The Writings of Alfred Edgar Coppard: A Bibliography*, with foreword and notes by Coppard (London: Ulysses Bookshop, 1931; Norwood, Penn.: Norwood, 1977);

Gilbert H. Fabes, *The First Editions of A. E. Coppard, A. P. Herbert, and Charles Morgan* (London: Myers, 1933).

References:

H. E. Bates, *The Modern Short Story: A Critical Survey* (London: T. Nelson, 1941; Boston: The Writer, 1961);

Thomas O. Beachcroft, *The English Short Story*, volume 2 (London: Longmans, Green, 1964);

Beachcroft, *The Modest Art: A Survey of the Short Story in English* (London: Oxford University Press, 1968);

Dorothy Brewster and Angus Burrell, *Modern Fiction* (New York: Columbia University Press, 1926);

Gerald William Bullett, *Modern English Fiction: A Personal View* (London: H. Jenkins, 1926);

Lily Anne Coppard, *The Orange Court* (London: Cape, 1929);

Winifred Mary De Kok, *New Babes for Old: A Book for Parents* (London: Gollancz, 1932);

James Gindin, "A. E. Coppard and H. E. Bates," in *The English Short Story, 1880–1945: A Critical History*, edited by Joseph M. Flora (Boston: Twayne, 1985), pp. 113–141;

Adrian H. Jaffe and Virgil Scott, eds., *Studies in the Short Story* (New York: Dryden Press, 1954);

A. Jehin, *Remarks on the Style of A. E. Coppard*, English Pamphlet Series, no. 8 (Buenos Aires: Argentine Association of English Culture, 1944);

M. Lyster, "The Short Stories of A. E. Coppard," *Irish Statesman*, 8 (2 July 1927): 399;

Russell Charles MacDonald, "A. E. Coppard: A Critical Study of His Short Stories," dissertation, University of Pennsylvania, 1961;

Frank O'Connor, *The Lonely Voice: A Study of the Short Story* (Cleveland: World, 1963);

George Brandon Saul, "A. E. Coppard: His Life and Poetry to the Publication of the 'Bibliography,'" dissertation, University of Pennsylvania, 1932;

Frank Edmund Smith, "A. E. Coppard," in *Supernatural Fiction Writers: Fantasy and Horror*, volume 2, edited by Everett Franklin Bleiler (New York: Scribners, 1985), pp. 523–528;

Smith, *Flynn: A Study of A. E. Coppard and His Short Fiction*, dissertation, Loyola University of Chicago, 1973;

Gay Taylor, *No Goodness in the Worm* (London: Gollancz, 1930);

C. Henry Warren, "The Modern Short Story," *Bookman*, 71 (January 1927): 236; 74 (February 1929): 294; 85 (April 1933): 8–11.

Papers:

The bulk of Coppard's papers and correspondence is at the Harry Ransom Humanities Research Center at the University of Texas at Austin. Additional papers, especially correspondence, are located at Syracuse University, Stanford University, and Yale University.

Walter de la Mare

(25 April 1873 – 22 June 1956)

Lana Hartman Landon
Bethany College

See also the de la Mare entries in *DLB 19: British Poets, 1880–1914* and *DLB 153: Late-Victorian and Edwardian British Novelists, First Series.*

BOOKS: *Songs of Childhood,* as Walter Ramal (London, New York & Bombay: Longmans, Green, 1902);

Henry Brocken: His Travels and Adventures in the Rich, Strange, Scarce-Imaginable Regions of Romance (London: Murray, 1904; New York: Knopf, 1924);

Poems (London: Murray, 1906);

The Return (London: Arnold, 1910; New York & London: Putnam, 1911; revised, London: Collins, 1922; revised, London: Faber & Faber, 1945);

The Three Mulla-Mulgars (London: Duckworth, 1910; New York: Knopf, 1919); republished as *The Three Royal Monkeys; or, The Three Mulla-Mulgars* (London: Faber & Faber, 1935); republished as *The Three Royal Monkeys* (New York: Knopf, 1948);

The Listeners, and Other Poems (London: Constable, 1912; New York: Holt, 1916);

Peacock Pie: A Book of Rhymes (London: Constable, 1913; New York: Holt, 1917);

The Sunken Garden, and Other Poems (London: Beaumont, 1917); republished as *The Sunken Garden, and Other Verses* ([Birmingham]: Birmingham School of Printing, 1931);

Motley, and Other Poems (London: Constable, 1918; New York: Holt, 1918);

Flora (London: Heinemann, 1919);

Rupert Brooke and the Intellectual Imagination: A Lecture (London: Sidgwick & Jackson, 1919; New York: Harcourt, Brace & Rowe, 1920);

Poems, 1901 to 1918, 2 volumes (London: Constable, 1920); republished as *Collected Poems, 1901–1918* (New York: Holt, 1920);

Story and Rhyme (London & Toronto: Dent / New York: Dutton, 1921);

Walter de la Mare

Memoirs of a Midget (London, Glasgow, Melbourne & Auckland: Collins, 1921; New York: Knopf, 1922);

Crossings: A Fairy Play, music by C. Armstrong Gibbs (London: Beaumont, 1921; New York: Knopf, 1923);

The Veil, and Other Poems (London, Bombay & Sydney: Constable, 1921; New York: Holt, 1922);

Down-Adown-Derry: A Book of Fairy Poems (London: Constable, 1922; New York: Holt, 1922);

Lispet, Lispett and Vaine (London: Morland, 1923);

Thus Her Tale: A Poem (Edinburgh: Porpoise, 1923);

The Riddle, and Other Stories (London: Selwyn & Blount, 1923); republished as *The Riddle, and Other Tales* (New York: Knopf, 1923);

A Ballad of Christmas (London: Selwyn & Blount, 1924);

Ding Dong Bell (London: Selwyn & Blount, 1924; New York: Knopf, 1924);

Broomsticks, and Other Tales (London: Constable, 1925; New York: Knopf, 1925);

Miss Jemima (Oxford: Blackwell, 1925; Poughkeepsie, N.Y.: Artists & Writers Guild, 1935);

The Connoisseur, and Other Stories (London, Glasgow, Sydney & Auckland: Collins, 1926; New York: Knopf, 1926);

St. Andrews: Two Poems, by de la Mare and Rudyard Kipling (London: A. & C. Black, 1926);

Selected Poems (New York: Holt, 1927);

Old Joe (Oxford: Blackwell, 1927);

Stuff and Nonsense, and So On (London: Constable, 1927; New York: Holt, 1927);

Told Again: Traditional Tales (Oxford: Blackwell, 1927); republished as *Told Again: Old Tales Told Again* (New York: Knopf, 1927) – republished as volumes 1 and 2 of *Readings: Traditional Tales* (Oxford: Blackwell, 1928);

Alone (London: Faber & Gwyer, 1927);

Lucy (Oxford: Blackwell, 1927);

At First Sight: A Novel (New York: Crosby Gaige, 1928);

Self to Self (London: Faber & Gwyer, 1928);

The Captive, and Other Poems (New York: Bowling Green, 1928);

A Snowdrop (London: Faber & Faber, 1929);

Stories from the Bible (London: Faber & Gwyer, 1929; New York: Cosmopolitan, 1929);

Desert Islands and Robinson Crusoe (London: Faber & Faber / New York: Fountain, 1930);

News (London: Faber & Faber, 1930);

Poems for Children (London: Constable, 1930; New York: Holt, 1930);

On the Edge: Short Stories (London: Faber & Faber, 1930); republished as *On the Edge* (New York: Knopf, 1931);

Two Poems ([London?]: Privately printed, 1931);

Seven Short Stories (London: Faber & Faber, 1931);

To Lucy (London: Faber & Faber, 1931);

The Printing of Poetry (Cambridge: Cambridge University Press, 1931);

The Dutch Cheese (New York: Knopf, 1931);

Lewis Carroll (London: Faber & Faber, 1932);

The Fleeting, and Other Poems (London: Constable, 1933; New York: Knopf, 1933);

The Lord Fish (London: Faber & Faber, 1933);

The Walter de la Mare Omnibus (London: Collins, 1933);

A Froward Child (London: Faber & Faber, 1934);

Poetry in Prose (London: Milford, 1935; New York: Oxford University Press, 1937);

Poems, 1919 to 1934 (London: Constable, 1935; New York: Holt, 1936);

The Nap, and Other Stories (London & Edinburgh: Nelson, 1936);

The Wind Blows Over (London: Faber & Faber, 1936; New York: Macmillan, 1936);

This Year: Next Year (London: Faber & Faber, 1937; New York: Holt, 1937);

Stories, Essays and Poems, edited by Mildred M. Bozman (London: Dent, 1938);

An Introduction to Everyman (London: Dent, 1938);

Memory, and Other Poems (London: Constable, 1938; New York: Holt, 1938);

Two Poems by Walter de la Mare and – but! – Arthur Rogers (Newcastle: Privately printed, 1938);

Haunted (London: Linden, 1939);

Pleasures and Speculations (London: Faber & Faber, 1940);

Collected Poems (New York: Holt, 1941; London: Faber & Faber, 1942);

The Picnic, and Other Stories (London: Faber & Faber, 1941);

Bells & Grass: A Book of Rhymes (London: Faber & Faber, 1941); republished as *Bells and Grass* (New York: Viking, 1942);

Mr. Bumps and His Monkey (Chicago & Philadelphia: Winston, 1942);

Time Passes, and Other Poems (London: Faber & Faber, 1942);

The Old Lion, and Other Stories (London: Faber & Faber, 1942);

Best Stories (London: Faber & Faber, 1942);

The Magic Jacket, and Other Stories (London: Faber & Faber, 1943); republished as *The Magic Jacket* (New York: Knopf, 1962);

Collected Rhymes & Verses (London: Faber & Faber, 1944); republished as *Rhymes and Verses: Collected Poems for Children* (New York: Holt, 1947);

The Scarecrow, and Other Stories (London: Faber & Faber, 1945);

The Burning-Glass, and Other Poems (London: Faber & Faber, 1945); republished as *The Burning-Glass and Other Poems, Including The Traveller* (New York: Viking, 1945);

The Dutch Cheese and Other Stories (London: Faber & Faber, 1946);

The Traveller (London: Faber & Faber, 1946);

Collected Stories for Children (London: Faber & Faber, 1947);

The Collected Tales, edited by Edward Wagenknecht (New York: Knopf, 1950);

Inward Companion: Poems (London: Faber & Faber, 1950);

Winged Chariot (London: Faber & Faber, 1951); republished in two volumes as *Winged Chariot, and Other Poems* (New York: Viking, 1951), with volume 2 comprising *Inward Companion;*

Selected Stories and Verses (Harmondsworth: Penguin, 1952);

Private View (London: Faber & Faber, 1953);

O Lovely England, and Other Poems (London: Faber & Faber, 1953; New York: Viking, 1956);

The Winnowing Dream (London: Faber & Faber, 1954);

Selected Poems, edited by R. N. Green-Armytage (London: Faber & Faber, 1954);

A Beginning, and Other Stories (London: Faber & Faber, 1955);

Walter de la Mare: A Selection from His Writings, edited by Kenneth Hopkins (London: Faber & Faber, 1956);

Ghost Stories (London: Folio Society, 1960);

A Penny a Day (New York: Knopf, 1960);

A Choice of de la Mare's Verse, edited by W. H. Auden (London: Faber & Faber, 1963);

Complete Poems (London: Faber & Faber, 1969; New York: Knopf, 1970).

OTHER: Philip Edward Thomas, *Collected Poems,* foreword by de la Mare (London: Selwyn & Blount, 1920);

Come Hither: A Collection of Rhymes and Poems for the Young of All Ages, edited by de la Mare (London: Constable, 1923; New York: Knopf, 1923);

Readings: Traditional Tales, compiled by de la Mare and Thomas Quayle, 6 volumes (Oxford: Blackwell, 1925–1928); 1 volume (New York: Knopf, 1927);

William Shakespeare, *The Shakespeare Songs,* edited by Tucker Brooke, introduction by de la Mare (London: Dent, 1929);

Christina Rossetti, *Poems,* edited, with an introduction, by de la Mare (Newtown: Gregynog Press, 1930);

The Eighteen-Eighties: Essays by Fellows of the Royal Society of Literature, edited by de la Mare (Cambridge: Cambridge University Press, 1930);

They Walk Again: An Anthology of Ghost Stories, edited by Colin de la Mare, introduction by Walter de la Mare (London: Faber & Faber, 1931);

Tom Tiddler's Ground: A Book of Poetry for the Junior and Middle Schools, edited by de la Mare (London & Glasgow: Collins' Clear-Type Press, 1931); republished as *Tom Tiddler's Ground: A Book of Poetry for Children* (London: Collins, 1932; New York: Knopf, 1962);

Charles Dickens, *The Cricket on the Hearth,* introduction by de la Mare ([London]: Golden Cockerel, 1933);

Early One Morning in the Spring: Chapters on Children and on Childhood As It Is Revealed in Particular in Early Memories and in Early Writings, edited, with commentary, by de la Mare (London: Faber & Faber, 1935; New York: Macmillan, 1935);

William Shakespeare, *A Midsummer Night's Dream,* edited by C. Aldred, introduction by de la Mare (London: Macmillan, 1935);

Behold, This Dreamer, edited, with commentary, by de la Mare (London: Faber & Faber, 1939; New York: Knopf, 1939);

Animal Stories, edited and adapted by de la Mare (London: Faber & Faber, 1939; New York: Scribners, 1940);

Love, edited, with an introduction, by de la Mare (London: Faber & Faber, 1943; New York: Morrow, 1946);

Nursery Rhymes for Certain Times, edited by Roger E. Ingpen, introduction by de la Mare (London: Faber & Faber, 1946);

Jean Baptiste Siméon, *Chardin (1699–1779),* introduction and notes by de la Mare (London: Faber & Faber, 1948);

Arthur Shepherd, *The Fiddlers,* words by de la Mare (South Hadley, Mass.: Valley Music, 1948);

Robin Humphrey Milford, *This Year: Next Year, A Song Cycle for Two-Part Choir (S.S.) and Piano,* words by de la Mare (London: Oxford University Press, 1948);

William B. Wordsworth, *Four Songs for High Voice with Pianoforte Accompaniment,* words by de la Mare and Robert Bridges (London: Lengnick, 1948);

Cecil Armstrong Gibbs, *In a Dream's Beguiling: Suite for Mezzo-Soprano Solo, or Semichorus, Women's Choir, S.S.A., String Orchestra, and Pianoforte,* words by de la Mare (London: Boosey, 1951).

Walter de la Mare is remembered primarily for his stories and poems for children rather than for his writing for adults. In his own day he was compared to William Blake, Samuel Taylor Coleridge, Nathaniel Hawthorne, and Edgar Allan Poe, but time has not been especially kind to him. Even his stories for children have declined in popularity, and his reputation as a writer for adults has diminished as his work has gone out of print and disappeared from anthologies. In 1924 it was possible for R. L. Megroz, in his biographical and critical study of de la Mare, to assert that "he has produced a body of work which ranks him among the poets we are pleased to call immortal." Even so, in the past twenty years only a handful of articles and dissertations have been written on him, and the majority of those concern his writing for children.

In 1947 John Atkins prophesied that "Mr. de la Mare's fame will ultimately rest on his magnificent stories and two very interesting novels, not on his accomplished but minor verse." Atkins was correct to recognize that the fiction writer was superior to the poet, but de la Mare's particular kind of short story, grounded in mood and psychological horror, has become so common in our time that the popularity of such contemporary stories has superseded that of de la Mare's antecedent stories. Yet the influence of de la Mare has not disappeared entirely, for like a character in many of his stories, it can be seen in the work of authors whose characters inhabit what is now called a "dreamscape." Modern readers of psychological fantasy who are familiar with the work of writers such as Ray Bradbury, Shirley Jackson, and even Angela Carter are quick to feel at home with de la Mare's characters and situations. His lyricism influenced a strain of popular literature that now remembers him only dimly, if at all. De la Mare himself said, "Our whole perception depends on our body, so when we die we lose not only our bodies but our whole apparatus of thought: we leave two vacua. So everyone should try to write something, so that some of his thought may be left." In his own case, de la Mare's thought has outlived his reputation.

Walter John de la Mare, often known as W. J., was born on 25 April 1873 in Charlton, Kent. His father, James, a church warden, was already sixty-two when his sixth child, Walter, was born. The de la Mares were of Huguenot descent, and Walter's mother, Lucy Sophia Browning, was the daughter of Dr. Colin Arrot Browning, a naval surgeon of Scottish descent and a distant relative of the poet Robert Browning. James de la Mare died four years after Walter was born, and the family moved to London. Although W. J. was very young when his father died, he became more attached to his father through memory as he grew older. W. J. understood that memory is less reportage than imagination: "How near to you are people in your imagination, for example, someone who had died? Do they

exist in space at all?" These questions provide the starting points for many of the mature de la Mare's best stories.

A good student, de la Mare was educated at the Choir School of St. Paul's Cathedral in London. There he founded and edited the *Choristers' Journal*, for which he wrote the greater part of its contents. What is perhaps most important about his beginnings as an author in the *Journal* is that he wrote for an audience of which he was a part, an audience that he knew intimately. In his later adult writings de la Mare's tone is most often confiding, and he frequently employs the device of letting his readers listen in on a story as it is told from one person to another — sometimes total strangers who have met in a tea shop or pub, other times friends of long standing. An implied intimacy with the audience is one of the hallmarks of de la Mare's short stories.

When he was seventeen years old, de la Mare left school at Easter and became a bookkeeper in the city offices of the Anglo-American Oil Company. He stayed with his job for eighteen years, during which he wrote stories and poems in his spare time. While working at Anglo-American Oil he published stories in such magazines as *The Cornhill, The Pall Mall Gazette, Black and White,* and *The Sketch.* "Kismet," his first published story, appeared in *Sketch* in 1895 and like all of his early stories was published under the pseudonym "Walter Ramal," the surname a loose anagram of his own.

"In the Forest" appeared in *Black and White* in 1904, and it is perhaps his most disturbing story, one about a small peasant family in the forest during wartime. The war and the location are left undefined, but, as in a nightmare, all that happens is credible within the story itself, yet horrifying at any distance beyond that of the child who is at the center of the story. This child is among the earliest incarnations of de la Mare's unusual view of childhood. In his lecture later published as *Rupert Brooke and the Intellectual Imagination* (1919) de la Mare asked, "What are the salient characteristics of childhood? Children, it will be agreed, live in a world peculiarly their own, so much so that it is doubtful if the adult can do more than very fleetingly reoccupy that far-away consciousness. There is, however, no doubt that the world of the grown-up is to children an inexhaustible astonishment and despair. They brood on us." His characters, especially his child characters, seem to be in dreamscapes of their own imagining, and the reader often feels as if he has wandered into someone else's dream by mistake.

De la Mare creates his most memorable child characters from equal parts of original sin and Platonic idealism. That is, these characters are capable of a mature evil while at the same time closer to the truth that somehow precedes human existence, a truth from which they become distanced as they age. In his *Walter de la Mare: An Exploration* Atkins has described de la Mare's philosophy of childhood and maturity this way:

> Confining [de la Mare's] philosophy to a single lifetime one is aware of a circle, beginning with childhood and ending with old age, but where the end and the beginning are the same point. It is the Platonic theory of historical cycles applied to the life-span. The age of childhood is one of dimly remembered mystery; at about the age of eighteen, when the world forces itself upon the individual in its crudest form, mystery is dissipated and replaced by reality; reality holds sway until the world looks upon the individual increasingly as a liability; there is a gradual return to mystery, which one feels is akin to the first state in more respects than a common opposition to reality.... The process, seen from his viewpoint, is Appearance – Disappearance – Reappearance. Reappearance is a recurring form of Appearance, the two are one. This is expressed in his stories by the close links that exist between children and old people, while the middle-aged are either unaware that such links exist or cannot understand them when they are aware.

The children in de la Mare's stories appear not so much knowledgeable as knowing, not so much morally bad as instinctively evil. "In the Forest" is told from the child's point of view, in a child's voice and with a child's concerns. The selfishness of the child in the story results in the death of his infant sibling:

> "I think I should *like* to go fishing, mother," I said, "and I promise you shall have the biggest I catch."
>
> But she kept on persisting that the baby was too ill to wait, that it was very queer, and that I must go for the doctor in the village. It wasn't so very far, she said, and I could fish to-morrow.
>
> "But it *is* far," I told her; "and it doesn't look so very bad; and it might be windy and cold to-morrow. It's only crying," I said. And I ran out before she could catch me.

The boy simply refuses to go for help. His refusal is comprehensible only in a context that acknowledges how far from altruism is human instinct.

In *The Fine Art of Reading and Other Literary Studies* Lord David Cecil discusses de la Mare's fictional universe:

> For all its apparent homeliness, it is a place of mystery and danger. The magic he evokes is not a comfortable magic. It disquiets the spirit as the supernatural would, if we came across it in real life. Even when it is benevo-

lent, it is convincingly genuine, and, as such, disturbing to the sense of security. When it is evil, it has the immediate inexplicable horror of nightmare. Nightmare is the right word. For a nightmare is a dream. And, after all, the most typical characteristic of these stories is their dreamlike quality. They are as enigmatic as dreams; they have also a dream's vivid, intimate intensity.

In these respects de la Mare is often compared to Hawthorne as well as to Poe, and "In the Forest" provides a portrait of a child version of Herman Melville's title character in the short story "Bartleby the Scrivener" (1856), a figure paralyzed by equal parts selfishness and fear. De la Mare's story never makes explicit the child's fear, which must be present after his father leaves the family alone and unprotected when he goes off to war. The child narrator frankly admits, "I was glad my father was gone away, because now I could do just as I pleased." He can acknowledge his fear only indirectly, as when he says, "I asked mother how long he would be away. She said she could not tell. And I wondered how they would carry back his body if he was killed in the war." "In the Forest" is the nightmare of a child expected to behave as an adult in a hostile world. When his mother goes to make burial arrangements for the deceased infant, the boy's father returns, mortally wounded and crawling across the threshold of his home to die. The father has been killed as a result of adult actions no less selfish and instinctive than those of the child narrator. De la Mare leaves his reader to ponder that we are all "In the Forest."

Forrest Reid finds another early story, "A Mote," to be interesting in relation to de la Mare's later work: "The choice of a respectable suburban background was exactly right . . . it is wonderfully effective, partly because of the contrast it affords, and partly because the marvellous, or the merely horrible, becomes much more authentic when it happens, as secretly we should like it to happen, next door."

"The Village of Old Age" appeared in September 1896 and "The Moon's Miracle" in April 1897. In "The Moon's Miracle" de la Mare introduces the Count, a character who figures in two later stories, "The Count's Courtship" and "The Almond Tree," both published in *The English Review* in 1909. The Count functions as both narrator and character in these stories. While "The Count's Courtship" is a melodramatic tale of sacrifice for love as well as pride, "The Almond Tree" is much more characteristic of de la Mare's work.

"The Almond Tree" is one of de la Mare's finest stories, because it captures the moral horror in the everyday while viewing that horror through the eyes of a child narrator, the young Count. The impact of the story relies on its child narrator, and for that reason it is often favorably compared to *What Maisie Knew* (1897) by Henry James. James's name often appears in discussions of de la Mare, because both writers were willing to acknowledge that children know the moral horror that surrounds them, and they often conform to it. "The Almond Tree," like de la Mare's later story "Physic," is a powerful study of adult unfaithfulness and jealousy. The children in both stories are aware of the powerful tensions between their parents as well as the pain their mothers feel because of their fathers' unfaithfulness.

In "The Almond Tree" Nicholas adds to his mother's pain, for he is also unfaithful to her by going with his father to see Miss Grey. His unfaithfulness is compounded when Nicholas finds that he likes her and enjoys her company. He seems to understand his father's feeling for her. When Nicholas finds his father's dead body, we are given a clear and uncompromising look into the young boy's mind:

> I felt no sorrow, but stood beside the body, regarding it only with deep wonder and a kind of earnest curiosity, yet perhaps with a remote pity, too, that he could not see me in the beautiful morning. His gray hand lay arched in the snow, his darkened face, on which showed a smear of dried blood, was turned away a little as if out of the oblique sunshine. I understood that he was dead, was already loosely speculating on what changes it would make; how I should spend my time; what would happen in the house now that he was gone, his influence, his authority, his discord. I remembered, too, that I was alone, was master of this immense secret, that I must go home sedately, as if it were Sunday, and in a low voice tell my mother, concealing any exultation I might feel in the office.

This passage demonstrates how acutely de la Mare understood the child as an amalgam of curiosity, speculation, narcissism, and self-absorption. Nicholas, like the boy of "In the Forest," is presented as a complete being with a child's mind and emotions, not *childlike* ones. The Count disappears as the intermediary narrator, and we are allowed to look directly into the child's mind and heart; we look directly at what we were as children, not at what we wish to have been.

Reid has suggested that de la Mare's making Nicholas the young Count serves no artistic purpose other than to link stories arbitrarily, but it is a case of de la Mare using one of his favorite devices to set the tale at two removes from the reader: the Count's story is told to the narrator of the story,

Dust jacket from the first of five short-story collections de la Mare published during World War II

and the readers are at another remove. In addition, as Reid points out, "we do not get the little boy's impressions directly, but only the Count's memory of them brought out in conversation, and he has to remember." The distancing technique is so common in de la Mare's work that his artistic method seems calculated to work toward a particular effect. Either the distancing is to serve as a cushion between the intense feelings expressed in and by the story, or de la Mare is modeling for his readers the proper attitude they should assume. In many of his stories the character who appears as the listener expresses disbelief yet listens on and, in the end, believes. Often de la Mare's characters, like those in Samuel Taylor Coleridge's "The Rime of the Ancient Mariner" (1798), are trapped by someone who foists upon them a story told with the same compulsion and desperation as Coleridge's title character displays. De la Mare is interested not only in the stories these Ancient Mariners tell, but in the reactions of the Wedding-Guest listeners as well. Those auditors (and by analogy his readers) find these stories both compelling and repellent at the same time.

De la Mare is an allusive writer; he expects his readers to have read widely in British literature, especially the works of Shakespeare. His use of the Count in more than one story creates a texture of allusion within his own work. While many of his stories rely on the same narrative techniques and central themes, it is not the result of a lack of imagination so much as an artistic preoccupation with the potential for evil in human beings. Most of his stories center on this sinister potential that resides in the most unlikely people all along. Before Hannah Arendt coined the phrase "the banality of evil," de la Mare explored through his characters the depth of evil in the quotidian. His stories reveal the truth that for many people life is frequently unsatisfying, disappointing, and even overrated.

The mind of a young boy is complex terrain that de la Mare surveys in many of his stories. Among the most disturbing is "The Trumpet." While not a tale of the supernatural, it explores a dark side of the child's mind as well as the relationship between boys of unequal social status. De la Mare does not dwell on the British class system, but it is an important component of many of his stories. "The Trumpet" takes place in a church, typically one of de la Mare's favorite settings. In this story two boys, Philip and Dick, are prompted by a mixture of mischief and adventure to steal into a church late at night. Dick is the illegitimate child of a woman in the village; Philip is the rector's son. They represent different social classes as well as different religious orientations. Dick is a chorister — emotional, quick to feel, and impetuous. Philip's religious response is intellectual; he thinks about angels and searches the Bible to find out about them. Dick responds with his heart; Philip, the craftier of the two, responds with his mind.

Philip is fascinated with a statue of an angel blowing on a trumpet in the sanctuary of the church. For many hours and through many church services he has sat contemplating the angel and the power of the trumpet. He recognizes that the angel has been captured in the midst of an action, between intention and accomplishment. However, Philip imagines that if only one were to blow into the trumpet, he could bring on the Day of Judgment. At Philip's instigation the more daring and reckless Dick climbs up on the angel to blow through the trumpet. Philip is upset because he feels that it is *his* right to blow into the trumpet, even though he is the one responsible for planting the

idea in his companion's head in the first place. When Dick falls and dies in the attempt, the trumpet is not blown but broken — and the loss that Philip feels is more of his dream than of his companion.

The story thus provides an uncompromising, unsentimental view of the world of children. De la Mare selected two epigraphs to adorn it: the first reads, "For Brutus, as you know, was Caesar's angel . . . " and the latter, "And he said . . . Am I my brother's keeper?" Both epigraphs point the story's theme of betrayal, even within the closest relationships. The story makes clear that Philip will grow to be like his father, a man without compassion in his life. Because Philip's father is a rector, he represents the limitations of the church, both as a source of love and as a source of imagination and inspiration. Philip takes the Bible seriously but responds to it intellectually and aesthetically. That response dies with the breaking of the trumpet. If the story is, as de la Mare titled it, "The Trumpet," it calls the church and society, as well as Philip, to judgment.

De la Mare referred to Jonathan Swift's *Gulliver's Travels* (1726) as his first "rememorable book," and its influence on his own first book-length work, *Henry Brocken: His Travels and Adventures in the Rich, Strange, Scarce-Imaginable Regions of Romance* (1904) is obvious. Having been written in manuscript on the notepaper of the Anglo-American Oil Company, the published work relies on the readers' knowledge of British literature and their interest in the changes de la Mare rings on works in the tradition. Both de la Mare's name and his pseudonym appeared on the title page of *Henry Brocken,* but after its publication de la Mare dropped his pseudonym.

In 1899 he married Constance Elfrida Ingpen, and they had four children: Dick, Florence, Jenny, and Colin. His best children's stories were written for, and read aloud to, his own children. However, children are prominent characters in his short stories for adults, and as such these characters are based on a more intimate knowledge of childhood than a parent gains in simply observing his offspring. De la Mare imagined his children from the inside out, and he did not idealize them.

He left the oil company in 1908, when he was granted a Civil List pension of £100 a year so that he could devote himself to his writing, which included a wide range of styles and genres. He wrote original children's stories and his own versions of stories from Jacob and Wilhelm Grimm, Aesop, Charles Perrault, English folklore, and the Bible.

He became perhaps most famous for his poetry for children, and in addition to writing his own verses, he prepared anthologies of poetry for children by other writers. He wrote novels for both children and adults, numerous book reviews and essays, and one drama, *Crossings: A Fairy Play* (1921). De la Mare lived in England all his life, but he visited the United States in 1916 to accept the Howland Memorial Prize on behalf of his friend and fellow poet Rupert Brooke, who had died the previous year.

"The Almond Tree" was collected with fourteen other stories, including "The Count's Courtship," published in *The Riddle, and Other Stories* in 1923. The stories in that volume include two others among his better known: "Miss Duveen" and "Seaton's Aunt." The title characters of these two establish the range of de la Mare's female figures. A few of his characters are little girls, but, as Reid explains, "the little girls . . . seem lured from a remoter world by spells of love and tenderness. They trail clouds of glory the boys have lost; they are the author's darlings, but they are presented far less intimately."

In "The Almond Tree," "Cape Race," and "The Wharf" de la Mare describes quite movingly the married woman, her predicaments, and her struggles — chief of which is to stay sane in the face of the horrible sameness of married life. Miss Duveen represents de la Mare's women characters who, married or not, have lost their struggles for sanity. Believing that children will understand their situation best of all, these women naturally gravitate toward children. As a story "Miss Duveen" demonstrates the elegance of de la Mare's narrative touch, for he ever so carefully guides the reader to realize that the horror is not in Miss Duveen's being unjustly considered insane, but rather that she need not have become so. The horror that readers feel is enhanced by their realizing that — like the child, Arthur, in the story — they wish for Miss Duveen to go away. Her presence is too painful. Her gradual diminution in the story mimics the gradual loss of her sanity. No more than this child, or the adult Arthur who remembers Miss Duveen, do readers wish to be responsible for her.

Seaton's aunt in the story of the same name is the most truly evil of de la Mare's characters. We see her through the eyes of her nephew and his school friend, the narrator. She is a kind of emotional vampire, and the story would be chilling even without the supernatural ending. The impact of the story requires our identification not with Seaton but with the narrator who, as a child so often does, has fallen into a relationship with another child whom

he does not like. Also in a childlike way the narrator sees that Seaton is in an unhealthy situation, even if the narrator is reluctant to recognize the evil that Seaton attributes to his aunt. Later, as an adult, the narrator discovers that Seaton was right — that the aunt is truly and thoroughly evil. The power of the story comes not so much from its supernatural dimension but from the reality that undergirds the narrative: children are confronted by evil and are powerless, realizing only in adulthood what it was that they had confronted and realizing that something should have been done. "Seaton's Aunt" is an exploration of guilt as well as horror, and that is the greatest source of its power. All of de la Mare's more-successful supernatural stories are tethered to psychological and spiritual realities.

Among de la Mare's stories of the supernatural "The Riddle" has an honored place. It is a fable more than a short story, and it relies on the folktale and fairy-tale traditions for its structure and matter-of-fact tone. The story begins, in proper fairy-tale style, "So these seven children, Ann, and Matilda, James, William and Henry, Harriet and Dorothea, came to live with their grandmother." Their grandmother welcomes them warmly, gives each a present, and promises that she will interfere in their lives very little. (De la Mare implies repeatedly in his stories that children wish to be left alone most of all.) The grandmother gives them only one warning: that "there is only one thing, just one, I would have you remember. In the large spare bedroom that looks out on the slate roof there stands in the corner an old oak chest; ay, older than I, my dears, a great deal older; older than my grandmother. Play anywhere else in the house, but not there."

One by one the children disobey her, as each child eventually climbs into the coffinlike chest and is heard from no more. Unlike modern versions of fairy tales in which children are always rescued in the end, these children are not. At the conclusion of the story the grandmother climbs the stairs, peers into the room with the chest, and "gossiping fitfully, inarticulately, with herself, the old lady went down again to her window-seat." What is "The Riddle" signaled by the title? Is it that in life we are children who disobey and disappear, are poorly watched over, and are never missed? Why does death draw the living toward it with a gravity of inevitability? Death is, if not always at the center, certainly at the circumference of de la Mare's work.

Ding Dong Bell (1924) is described in a publisher's advertisement as "three delightful fantasies interspersed with original verse." Certainly that is probably as accurate a description as is possible for a difficult work. The three stories in the volume – "Lichen," "Benighted," and "Winter" – all concern the reading of epitaphs in graveyards. The narrator and the situation are different in each, but each serves as a vehicle for interpreting the epitaphs de la Mare has written. One hesitates to call these pieces stories, for they lack the movement and plot of the traditional short story, even those of the typical de la Mare story. As a group they provide the reader significant matter for contemplation, matter ranging from the epitaphs themselves to the relationship between the pieces and their titles. *Ding Dong Bell* is a threefold meditation on mortality.

In classifying de la Mare's stories, Reid finds six tales of the supernatural: "Seaton's Aunt," "Out of the Deep," "All Hallows," "The Green Room," "A Recluse," and "Miss Jemima." While these do rely more on the supernatural than other de la Mare stories, in general all of his work displays philosophical and metaphysical, if not supernatural, concerns, and a consistent texture of the unusual, a constant threat of unreality, runs through all his adult fiction. *At First Sight: A Novel* (1928), a story about a young man who cannot see the world in full because he cannot lift up his eyes, is among de la Mare's most compelling narratives, one of the few that has a love story at its center. In this story he discusses explicitly a theme implicit in all his fiction: the limits of the physical sense of sight in contrast to the richness of an inner vision.

In "The Ideal Craftsman," arguably his best story, the reader must confront a young child who has come upon a murder scene and proceeds to take the situation in hand. The child undertakes his foray as a military expedition, an adventure behind enemy lines. Both the reader and the child gradually realize that a murder has been committed, that the fatal woman scorned is present, and that there is a corpse. The child has hated the victim, the butler, and when confronted with the hysterical woman who confesses to the murder, the child sets to exonerating her. Based on his reading, the child creates a suicide scene down to the finest detail. He is the ideal craftsman, but when he has completed the tableau and perfected it, he at last responds to the horror. The reader is forced to realize that what finally moves the child is not the murder or the corpse, but his own callous detachment and his fear of being alone. Is de la Mare distinguishing here between the detachment of the craftsman and the involvement of the artist? De la Mare regarded "a true craftsman delighting in his job" as the "finest thing any man can be." Certainly he is commenting upon the power of mimesis to purge pity and fear. What is

best in the story is de la Mare's indirect acknowledgment of his own craftsmanship. The reader finishes the story knowing that if these events were to happen, they would indeed happen *just this way*.

One of de la Mare's lighter stories, though not a lesser story by any means, is "The Nap," published in 1926 and displaying the influence of Charles Dickens. The story centers on a family man and his simple desire to have some time for himself amid the constant hubbub of his family and work. He sets aside the precious time for an illicit nap, but sleeping is not really his desire. His longing is for a contemplative space in his life, a time for reflection, for attending to his inner voices. The beauty and poignancy of the story is that, even though his requirements are so modest, he does not truly get the solitude he seeks. What is most brilliant about the story is how de la Mare unfolds the character gently and slowly through his own speech and actions. While the story is perceptive in featuring a male character and his need of relief from the demands of family, it is not a sentimental story. It is Dickensian in that we feel de la Mare's affection for his character, an affection we come to share. J. B. Priestley suggested that "this world of Mr. de la Mare's is, as it were, the other half of the Dickens' world, the poetical, mysterious, aristocratic half that Dickens, with his eyes fixed on the democratic, humorous, melodramatic elements, never gave us." "The Nap" perhaps seems most Dickensian, then, because it is set in the world of the middle class, not the aristocracy.

"The Revenant," while not one of de la Mare's most famous stories, suggests how he may have felt about comparisons between his writing and that of Edgar Allan Poe. The narrator of the story is a lecturer who is giving a public lecture about Poe's writing. The first portion of the story gives an interesting glimpse into the mind of the lecturer presenting a lecture he has given frequently before. He is aware of his audience, gauging its response and monitoring his performance, when a latecomer slips into the lecture hall. It is immediately obvious to the reader that this latecomer is Edgar Allen Poe himself, come from the grave to hear what is being said about his work. The revenant and the lecturer have a colloquy alone together after the lecture.

Even though there is a "ghost" of sorts in the story, the true terror is that which any lecturer would feel when unexpectedly confronted in the flesh by the subject of his lecture. The narrator of the story slowly declines in stature throughout and becomes a very pale and dull character indeed when

Walter de la Mare (photograph by Mark Gerson)

seen alongside even the ghost of Poe. Perhaps de la Mare is suggesting, with tongue in cheek, that Poe is *sui generis*, and that while we do not even understand his work, we should not presume to compare it to other pale imitations. As John Atkins has suggested, the message of "The Revenant" for readers of Poe is, "For God's sake stop referring to his sexual affairs and his liking for strong drink when you discuss the poet Poe; his poetry comes from something you can't see or hear or drink, from something so far inside him that no surgeon could cut it out." "The Revenant" is an *hommage* – and an honest one.

Atkins also most clearly describes the unusual beauty of de la Mare's prose style, which

is often poetry of a high order, and he constantly stumbles (the poetic process is to that extent haphazard) across brilliantly provocative transcriptions of commonplace words, things and ideas. The definition of a map as "a cabalistic picture in the flat" has no *meaning* in the ordinary sense, but poetically it is a storehouse of aesthetic and arcane significance. On the other hand, a vulgar plant such as a sunflower is translated into the

equally vulgar and vulgarly intellectualised "Van Gogh tea tray."

From "In the Forest" comes one of de la Mare's most elegant images: "The baby was asleep too, but it scarcely seemed to be really breathing – it was like a moth fluttering on a pin." The compactness of de la Mare's image, its compression of frailty and violence, make it so striking and so apropos.

In 1943 de la Mare's wife, Constance, died, and his career moved into a period of reaping what his writing had sown. In this final period of his career de la Mare was a celebrated and much honored author. He received numerous awards, including the Carnegie Medal of the Library Association, and in 1948 was named Companion of Honour by King George VI. He received honorary degrees from several universities, and in 1953, at the age of eighty, he was awarded the Order of Merit.

In 1954 de la Mare fell and suffered a slight injury to his brain. While limited in his activities, he still wrote and spent time contemplating the limits of consciousness, long a preoccupation with him.

On 22 June 1956 he died at Wickenham, Middlesex; he was buried in the crypt of St. Paul's Cathedral. His friend and bibliographer, Leonard Clark, wrote that de la Mare died as "a child of mature years."

For the reader of de la Mare's stories the "child of mature years" is a constant companion – as author, narrator, and character. Rather than as a mature person with the child alive within him, the child of mature years in de la Mare's stories is a child who has lived little but knows much. Welsh author Dylan Thomas wrote that de la Mare's subject was always "the imminence of spiritual danger," and he provided an eloquent and accurate summary of de la Mare's career when he wrote that "he has written long and short stories, for children, about children, for grown men and dead men, for the unborn, for a livelihood, for nothing, for the best reward, through innocence and with wide and deep skill, for pleasure, for fun, from suffering, and for himself."

Bibliographies:

Leonard Clark, "A Handlist of the Writings in Book Form (1902–53) of Walter de la Mare," *Studies in Bibliography,* 6 (1954): 197–217;

Edward Wagenknecht, "A List of Walter de la Mare's Contributions to the London *Times Literary Supplement,*" *Boston University Studies in English,* 1 (Winter 1955): 243–255;

Clark, "Addendum: A Checklist of Walter de la Mare," *Studies in Bibliography,* 8 (1956): 269–270;

Clark, *Walter de la Mare: A Checklist* (London: Cambridge University Press, 1956).

Biography:

Theresa Whistler, *Imagination of the Heart: The Life of Walter de la Mare* (London: Duckworth, 1994).

References:

John Aldard, "Did Walter de la Mare Stay Out of the Wind?," *Anglia,* 90 (1972): 355–360;

John Atkins, *Walter de la Mare: An Exploration* (London: Temple, 1947);

Owen Barfield, "Poetry in Walter de la Mare," *Denver Quarterly,* 8 (Autumn 1973): 69–81;

W. R. Bett, ed., *Tribute to Walter de la Mare on His Seventy-Fifth Birthday* (London: Faber & Faber, 1948);

Russell Brain, *Tea with Walter de la Mare* (London: Faber & Faber, 1957);

Rica Brenner, *Ten Modern Poets* (New York: Harcourt, Brace, 1930);

Lord David Cecil, "The Prose Tales of Walter de la Mare," in his *The Fine Art of Reading and Other Literary Studies* (New York: Bobbs-Merrill, 1957), pp. 219–232;

G. K. Chesterton, "Walter de la Mare," *Fortnightly Review,* new series 132 (July 1932): 47–53;

Harold Child, "Mr. De la Mare's World (1942)," *Essays and Reflections* (London: Cambridge University Press, 1948), pp. 20–29;

H. Coombes, "Hardy, de la Mare and Edward Thomas," *The Pelican Guide to English Literature: The Modern Age,* by Boris Ford, volume 7 (London: Penguin, 1961), pp. 138–153;

Henry Charles Duffin, *Walter de la Mare: A Study of His Poetry* (London: Sidgwick & Jackson, 1949);

N. J. Endicott, "Walter de la Mare, 1873–1956," *University of Toronto Quarterly,* 26 (January 1957): 109–121;

Boris Ford, "The Rest Was Silence: de la Mare's Last Interview," *Encounter,* 7 (September 1956): 38–46;

John Freeman, *English Portraits and Essays* (London: Hodder & Stoughton, 1924);

Horace Gregory, "The Nocturnal Traveller: de la Mare," *Poetry,* 80 (July 1952): 213–232;

Geoffrey Grigson, "Walter the Rhymer: the Poetic Style of de la Mare," *Times Literary Supplement,* 12 March 1970, pp. 281–282;

Kenneth Hopkins, *Walter de la Mare* (London: Longmans, Green, 1953);

F. R. Leavis, *New Bearings in English Poetry* (London: Chatto & Windus, 1950);

D. R. McCrosson, *Walter de la Mare* (New York: Twayne, 1966);

R. L. Megroz, *Walter de la Mare: A Biographical and Critical Study* (London: Hodder & Stoughton, 1924);

Edwin Muir, *The Present Age From 1914* (London: Cresset, 1939);

J. Middleton Murry, "The Poetry of de la Mare," in his *Countries of the Mind* (London: Collins, 1922), pp. 127–142;

David Perkins, *A History of Modern Poetry,* volume 1 (Cambridge, Mass.: Harvard University Press, 1976), pp. 179–191;

Hermann Peschmann, "The Poetry of Walter de la Mare," *English,* 11 (Spring 1957): 129–133;

"A Poet of Two Worlds: The Imagery of Mr. de la Mare," *Times Literary Supplement,* 1 August 1936, pp. 621–622;

John Press, "The Poetry of Walter de la Mare," *Ariel: A Review of International English Literature,* 1, no. 4 (1970): 29–38;

J. B. Priestley, "Mr. De la Mare," in his *Figures in Modern Literature* (London: John Lane/Bodley Head, 1924), pp. 31–54;

Forrest Reid, *Walter de la Mare: A Critical Study* (London: Faber & Faber, 1929);

I. A. Richards, *Science and Poetry* (London: Kegan Paul, Trench & Trübner, 1926);

Richards, "Walter de la Mare: a Reconsideration," *New Republic,* 174 (31 January 1976): 31–33;

Vita Sackville-West, "Walter de la Mare and *The Traveller,*" *Proceedings of the British Academy,* 39 (1953): 23–36;

Edward Shanks, *First Essays in Literature* (London: Collins, 1923);

Stuart Sherman, "Walter de la Mare," in his *The Main Stream* (New York: Scribners, 1927), pp. 196–203;

Frank Swinnerton, "Three Rogue Poets," in his *Figures in the Foreground* (London: Hutchinson, 1963), pp. 203–206;

Dylan Thomas, "Walter de la Mare as a Prose Writer," in his *Quite Early One Morning* (New York: New Directions, 1954), pp. 149–155;

William Walsh, "The Child in the Poetry of Walter de la Mare," in his *The Use of Imagination* (London: Chatto & Windus, 1959), pp. 174–182;

Charles Williams, *Poetry at Present* (London: Oxford University Press, 1930), pp. 83–95.

Papers:
De la Mare's manuscripts and correspondence are collected at Temple University Libraries, Rare Book Department; the University of Chicago Library; and King's College, Cambridge.

Caradoc Evans
(31 December 1878 – 11 January 1945)

John Harris
University of Wales, Aberystwyth

BOOKS: *My People: Stories of the Peasantry of West Wales* (London: Andrew Melrose, 1915; New York: Duffield, 1917);

Capel Sion (London: Andrew Melrose, 1916; New York: Boni & Liveright, 1918);

My Neighbours (London: Andrew Melrose, 1919; enlarged as *My Neighbors: Stories of the Welsh People* (New York: Harcourt, Brace & Howe, 1920);

Taffy: A Play of Welsh Village Life in Three Acts (London & New York: Andrew Melrose, 1924);

Nothing to Pay (London: Faber & Faber, 1930; revised edition, New York: Norton, 1930);

Wasps (London: Rich & Cowan, 1933);

This Way to Heaven (London: Rich & Cowan, 1934);

Pilgrims in a Foreign Land (London: Andrew Dakers, 1942);

Morgan Bible (London: Andrew Dakers, 1943);

The Earth Gives All and Takes All (London: Andrew Dakers, 1946);

Mother's Marvel (London: Andrew Dakers, 1949);

Fury Never Leaves Us: A Miscellany of Caradoc Evans, edited by John Harris (Bridgend, Mid Glamorgan: Poetry Wales Press, 1985; Chester Springs, Penn.: Dufour Editions, 1985);

Selected Stories, edited by Harris (Manchester: Carcanet, 1993).

SELECTED PERIODICAL PUBLICATIONS – UNCOLLECTED:

FICTION

"The Coffin," *Illustrated Review,* 1 (July 1923): 85–87;

"The Star Turn," "On the Morning," and "The Convict's Christmas," in "Three Early Stories by Caradoc Evans," edited by Trevor Williams, *Anglo-Welsh Review,* 19 (Spring 1971): 129–137;

"Sweets for a Sinner," "Rock of Ages: A Love Story," and an untitled story, in "Three Unpublished Stories by Caradoc Evans," edited by Williams, *Anglo-Welsh Review,* 20 (Autumn 1971): 82–98;

Caradoc Evans, late 1920s

"'Wisdom': An Unpublished Story," *Planet,* 90 (December 1991–January 1992): 38–43.

NONFICTION

"Advice to Young Authors," *Writer,* 37 (April 1925): 165–166;

"Caradoc Evans' Journal, 1939–44," *Welsh Review,* 4 (June 1945): 104–111;

"Caradoc Evans' Journal, 1939–44," *Welsh Review,* 4 (September 1945): 201–208.

Caradoc Evans can be counted among the handful of significant writers whose reputations rest substantially on their short stories. He published five collections, three at the beginning and two near the close of a writing career marked at both ends by world war. His whole life as author was one continuous battle – with books suppressed, a play howled down, his portrait slashed across the throat while on public display. Evans had exploded the myth of rural Wales by uncovering lust and violence, cruelty and cunning, beneath the veneer of religion. To this disturbingly original material he brought great gifts as a storyteller – a command of suspense, a staggering economy and directness, and a modernist daring with language. From the outset, too, he moved confidently beyond naturalism into scalding fantasy and black comedy of the grotesque. And if the label "realist" sits uncomfortably on him, so does that of "satirist," for his best writing has a drama and pathos not usually associated with satire. This literary audacity, allied to a courageously dissident stand, attracted poet Dylan Thomas and his generation of English-language writers in Wales, writers for whom Caradoc Evans became the founding father of "Anglo-Welsh" literature.

In one striking paragraph from the 7 April 1916 *Ideas,* a journal which Evans came to edit, he recalled the landscape of his youth:

> Sometimes I think man's labour is to dig and trim the soil, and sometimes I crave for the peace of the country. But soon I awake, and I remember things: badly-paid farm labourers; stunted, pale-faced children, whose bodies are starved and whose intellect is stifled at the hands of the village school-master; sexless women whose blood has been robbed by the soil; little villages hidden in valleys and reeking with malice.

Such alienation is startling, particularly in a son of rural Wales, but out of this background, from an imagination vitalized by the experiences of childhood, came the writing. Both Evans's parents were from families of substance. His father, William Evans, became on marriage the tenant farmer of Pantycroi, a thirty-five-acre holding on the Carmarthen bank of the river Teifi. His bride, Mary Powell, was daughter of an influential landowning family in nearby Rhydlewis, Cardigan. The Evanses were church people while the Powells, like the bulk of farmers and cottagers, were Nonconformists. Though politics might deepen the divide, such "mixed" marriages were not frowned upon – provided that, as here, the families were socially matched. But this union outraged Mary's father, particularly after his son-in-law (then in training as an auctioneer) had become involved with the sale of a neighboring farm whose tenant had been evicted for defying, in the 1868 parlia-

mentary election, the wishes of his Tory-Anglican landlord. Families thus dispossessed became martyrs to Liberal-Nonconformity, and so great was sympathy for them that local auctioneers withheld their services. As wife to such a man, Mary Evans came to forfeit any share of her father's will and thereby condemned herself to poverty – for by 1882 her thirty-two-year-old husband had died of pneumonia. In their troubled years together the Evanses produced five children, the fourth, David Caradoc, being born at Pantycroi on New Year's Eve 1878. He was registered simply as "David," but by the time of his school years "Caradoc" (or "Caradog") had been added, the unusual forename that came to identify him to the whole of his nation.

Now a widow, Mary Evans and her children settled in her native village to work a nine-acre smallholding. These early years are important, for Evans experienced his community as a child, and on leaving school he left the locality, never again to live there. Ten years of primary education are dismissed in *Who's Who* references to "Rhydlewis (Cardiganshire) Board School, which he left untaught," and the subject of school unfailingly aroused his contempt: in his fiction "schoolins," or schoolteachers, are always creatures of ridicule. The deeper charge, from one who had endured a "payment by results" regime in which school grants and the headmaster's salary were tied to the success of students in examinations, was of facts mindlessly crammed, intellect and imagination unstirred, no kindling of interest in the natural world. "The Talent Thou Gavest," an early story in *My People: Stories of the Peasantry of West Wales* (1915), reflects on Eben, the lad who leaves school to tend sheep on the moor: "His life was lonely; books were closed against him, because he had not been taught to read; and the sense of the beautiful or the curious in Nature is slow to awake in the mind of the Welsh peasant." Evans said as much of himself. He could not, he confessed, tell one tree from another, nor one bird – who in his farming community would give you a penny for such knowledge? – and this conditioning meant that never could he sentimentalize the natural world or invest it with high significance, a disposition that differentiates him from the tradition of writing about the countryside, in Wales as elsewhere.

Besides school Caradoc attended Capel Hawen, the village Congregationalist chapel presided over by the Reverend David Adams, a man who, as Evans recalled, "might have been Hitler's schoolin." Evans remembers the boyish terror that drove him into the hedge, out of sight, sooner than

Evans's boyhood home — Lanlas Uchaf, Rhydlewis, in Cardigan, Wales

meet "our ruler" on the road. The minister who had baptized him gained the dimensions of a Blakean priest: "He stalks over the land like an evil spirit; his garments typify the blackness of a nation in travail, and in the light of his eyes there is no redemption." The minister and schoolmaster shaped community opinion between them, Adams in particular denouncing "going to fairs, dablenning [taking alcohol], going to church, voting for a Tory, courting in or out of bed." Pulpit admonitions against sex, drink, and entertainment are predictable; less so the political message, but Evans reiterates the charge: "Mr. David Adams made the people think as he thought and vote as he willed them to," and it is this theocratic dimension in Welsh life that the writer came so deeply to resist. Village elders walked with God, Caradoc's own headmaster explaining in a local newspaper how "Providence interfered in 1866 to send me and not Mr. Adams to Rhydlewis, and the same Divine Power made me, indirectly, the means of bringing him to Hawen as minister of the Gospel. No, my friends, such things are not 'accidents.' "

Caradoc the schoolboy was comfortable enough to have been appointed monitor, one responsible for some teaching of juniors, and would surely have proceeded to secondary school had help from his mother's brother, medical doctor Joshua Powell, been forthcoming. It was not, and the boy therefore was forced to find work while Uncle Joshua accumulated money and reputation. Through Joshua Powell, Evans came to learn how a chasm between preaching and practice rarely harmed community leaders; on the contrary, material advancement ensured a public standing. "That is the way of the earth," Evans wrote in the 1916 *Ideas*. "If you struggle to put by a few pounds, you are called a miser. But put by thousands, and people will black your boots and whitewash your character." Evans also reflected that "what we gather in our youth we commonly carry into our graves." The baggage of Rhydlewis he bore to the end: his loss of a father against whom there was such obloquy, the helplessness of his mother before an uncle he judged rapacious and hypocritical, the disappointments of school, and the terrorism of the chapel.

Within his own family he learned the facts of political and sectarian strife, of public esteem and social standing, and the unpardonable sin of poverty. The triumphalism of the rich and the sense of poverty as a social disease – these things endured beyond all other legacies of childhood.

In February 1893 Caradoc moved to Carmarthen as a fourteen-year-old apprentice draper. Drapery was a respectable profession, and as his grandmother pointed out, a draper, unlike a farmer, doesn't get wet. For a decade or so in South Wales and London Evans avoided the rain while selling things across the counter – and loathing his work. Whatever their middle-class pretensions, shop assistants lived like slaves – hedged round by petty rules that were hung like religious texts on bedroom walls – for these were the years of "living-in." But there was life beyond the counter in theater visits and books from the public library. Reading also meant a daily newspaper, which came to represent the disputatious, liberating city for him. At Cardiff the *Western Mail* provided this much-needed platform for cultural debate in turn-of-the-century Wales. In the evenings, after twelve hours of shop duty, he would wander to the nearby newspaper offices, there to smell the ink and listen to the music of the rotary machines. While on the drapery treadmill in London, Evans enrolled in an evening composition class at the Working Men's College, and in 1906, following publication of two of his weekly sketches (some written on the paper overlaps of boxes), he finally abandoned shop work and drifted into journalism. A year later he felt secure enough to marry Rose Jesse Sewell, "the prettiest girl in London," as he told his anxious mother.

His intellectual world was likewise changing. Evans became a Christian socialist with a regard for secularists such as G. W. Foote, whose anticlerical fusillades made him a compelling speaker. There were periodicals, too: he wrote that the literary *T. P.'s Weekly* "exercised my brain and heated my imagination" through its presentation of work by Thomas Hardy, Arthur Morrison, and French and Russian writers, especially Leo Tolstoy – "the perfect story-teller." He read Robert Blatchford's socialist *Clarion,* marrying politics and literature, and *Reynold's Weekly* – the badge of emancipated radicalism for Mr. Doran in James Joyce's *Dubliners* and the first paper to publish Caradoc Evans.

After a hesitant start Evans flourished in journalism, joining *Ideas,* a Hulton popular weekly, and following Edgar Wallace into its editorial chair. His years as editor of *Ideas* from 1915 to 1917 were the most productive of his life. A married man commuting from East Sheen, he ran a magazine with a readership of two hundred thousand and at the same time published the stories that were to make his literary reputation. Writer Thomas Burke thought that a post on *Ideas* ill became the author of *My People,* but that was not how Evans saw it. He provocatively identified himself with journalism and claimed that no novelist he knew could hold down a newspaper job for a week. The remark has a class edge, insomuch as Fleet Street welcomed self-made men from unpromising backgrounds, whereas few highbrow novelists had any proletarian sympathies or any outward regard for journalism. Evans insisted that if novelists were ignored, it was because they could not write, whereas newspapers "miss no points and waste no words" and were as free from padding as the Bible: "Where would the fame of God be were it not for the group of King James men who compiled the masterpiece of journalism, the Bible? I do not believe the same hands wrote that fawning preface to James. Any minister of religion could have done it as well." Campaigning journalism did not fawn, and Evans celebrated the journalistic roots of fiction. Like Emile Zola, he dubbed himself a reporter or simple photographer, and when *My People* ran into legal trouble it is revealing that he turned to H. G. Wells for support and that the two praised each other as honest commentators writing from experience.

It is noticeable, too, how little Evans's early career resembles the conventional author's: he wrote just a handful of reviews and ad hoc pieces. For a man with a full-time job composing short stories was easier than writing novels, and Evans enjoyed the freedom of the nonprofessional writer to pursue a genre offering scant financial reward. Even so, by publishing comparatively few of his stories in the periodicals (which is where short-story writers made their money), he passed over opportunities for extra income. The stories he *did* publish separately were well targeted – in the *English Review,* a prestigious cultural monthly; in the *Westminster Gazette,* with its wide parliamentary circulation; and in the Chestertons' *New Witness,* hot on political corruption especially surrounding Lloyd George.

For all his populist avowals Evans's first showing in the *English Review* (April 1915) placed him in the camp of literary fiction, at least for English critics. The Welsh response was different, and with the appearance of "Two Welsh Studies" ("A Father in Sion" and "Be This Her Memorial") Evans was under fire and defending himself in four local newspapers: a fine polemicist, he was repeatedly to clash with opponents, mostly in the *Western Mail.*

In November 1915 came *My People,* a striking first collection published by Andrew Melrose. A Presbyterian with a background in the Sunday School League, Melrose had worked with George Douglas Brown, whose counterblast to the tender pieties of Scottish Kailyard fiction in such work as *The House with the Green Shutters* (1901) gave the publisher a line on *My People.* Melrose accepted the collection but with safeguards. A jacket was to explain that the book, though "not meat for babes," was justified on grounds of realism and the author's reforming intention. In the ensuing uproar Melrose supported Evans by alerting the Society of Authors to police harassment of Welsh booksellers and stressing the warning he had given. Melrose detested negative publicity, but whatever his private misgivings might have been, he launched a second controversial collection, *Capel Sion* (1916), and remained Evans's publisher until the firm disappeared in a takeover.

Evans's creative release can be explained in terms of an inner emotional pressure as well as a confidence and conviction strengthened by the external circumstances of 1914. As he later informed the London Writer Circle, "I like stories that are gloomy, morose and bitter, for I feel the author is chronicling the horrid sins of his enemies. An angry man is nearer himself than a happy man." Passionate anger can provide artistic motive and, if the venom is controlled, can produce explosive prose. For years Evans had been pondering his childhood in Rhydlewis and gathering incidents from life in the neighborhood: these savage, highly personal events seemed to confirm that the worst things done to Welshmen were done by other Welshmen, mostly in the name of religion. In Wales as elsewhere conditions of war deepened the social class divisions, as already-dominant farmers displayed sinister new powers in manning the military tribunals and threatening to release for service farm laborers bold enough to question wages or join a union. The big farmers, regularly the chapel elders, grew prosperous also, as Evans noted: "[I]n all wars the idealist fights for an imagined golden land, while the practical man gathers a golden harvest at home." Behind the inequalities Evans discerned an abiding moral deformity, the symptom of decayed religion, now a mix of anthropomorphism, superstition, and oily hypocrisy. Institutionalized religion had become a potent, repressive force instilling mental obedience and legitimizing injustice. "The

modern saint," Evans satirically observed, "expounds his gospel of love and sacrifice at the banquet table and he is at his best in a prayer meeting of millionaires." Theocratic Wales, whose ministers served the strong in the community, focused a condition of the times, while the Great War, far from shattering any meliorist illusions, bolstered Evans's convictions that strife was a natural state, that the injustices of the world are part of the world. As he noted in the 6 April 1917 pages of *Ideas,*

> We shall never have universal peace. At what time we shall not be fighting against a foreign enemy, we shall be fighting against our brothers and neighbours. Men will not cease to covet that which is not theirs, howsoever loudly they will cry forth their honesty. The humble shall serve the boastful; the rich shall be as gods, and they shall do no wrong, for the laws will be in their keeping.

This dark philosophy finds compelling expression in Evans's first two collections. Avarice and brutality, family violence, religious sensualism and religious control – these were not the qualities associated with rural Wales, a landscape known (if at all to English readers) through the sky-blue optimism of Allen Raine, the popular romantic novelist. Equally arresting was Evans's linguistic medium, alien yet intelligible, an amalgam of biblical phrasing, translation from the Welsh (or aggressive mistranslation), and distorted English syntax. As Evans felt, "In the rendering of idiom you must create atmosphere. If the Bible or Tolstoy were done into straight English none of us would get nearer the life and conditions with which these authors deal." To present his world in "straight English" was impossible; new content meant new expression, and this refashioning of language came perhaps more readily to a native Welsh speaker. "Foreigners write good English because they do not know English," Evans jotted in his notebook; the language used should be free of built-in notions of propriety.

In another memorable comment he allies the Bible and Marie Lloyd as literary exemplars and explains how his music-hall favorite "tells a story not by what she says but by what she says not." The technique goes to the heart of Evans's approach: letting the audience fill in the blanks and suppressing the authorial voice-over. It results in stories shorter than most – Evans aimed at around twenty-five hundred words – but ones that gain strength from being in various degrees interrelated when gathered together in book form. This cohesiveness, derived from placing events in a tight geographical framework with linking characters and action, recalls stories of closed rural communities by French and Russian writers he admired.

Evans's Manteg locale is irremediably religious, a condition established on the first page of *My People:* "Dear people, on my way to Sion I asked God what He meant. . . ." Here men talk with God; but only men do, and only some men. "Think you the Big Man chooses you before me and the Respected Bryn-Bevan to be His mouthpiece?" asks Sadrach, wealthy farmer and chapel elder, of one of his laborers. Conversations with God are homely requests for help in some commercial transaction or for advice when one of the faithful faces a spot of bother, as does Evan Rhiw ("Lamentations"), drawn into incest with his daughter Matilda. The minister reports to the flock on his chat with the Almighty:

> Boys, boys, glad was the Big Man that I spoke to Him. Do you know what He said? "Large thanks, Bern bach. Religious are you to remind me of the sin of Evan Rhiw. The man has a clean heart, and an adder in his house." "Big Man, don't you vex me" I said. "Whisper you me the name of the adder." The Big Man said, "Matilda. Evan may sin again, grievously, but I will restore him to Capel Sion, and I will bless him abundantly, for his freewill offerings to my Temple are generous." Little boys, He went back to Heaven in a cloud, and the cloud was no bigger than the flat of this old hand.

You win with God. As material prosperity is a sign of God's favor, so poverty reveals an individual moral failing. This Calvinistic message is written across Manteg in the prosperous farms of chapel deacons and in the marginal moorland, home to outcasts such as Simon and Beca in "The Way of the Earth."

> The land attached to Penrhos was changed from sterile moorland into a fertile garden by Simon and Beca. Great toil went to the taming of these ten acres of heather into the most fruitful soil in the district. Sometimes now Simon drags himself out into the open and complains when he sees his garden; and he calls Beca to look how the fields are going back to heatherland. And Beca will rise from her chair and feel her way past the bed which stands against the wooden partition, and as she touches with her right hand the ashen post that holds up the forehead of the house she knows she is facing the fields, and she too will groan, for her strength and pride are mixed with the soil.
> "Sober serious, little Simon," she says, "this is the way of the earth, man bach."
> But she means that it is the way of mortal flesh.

The way of the earth is the way of mortal flesh. Nature to Caradoc Evans offers no redemptive wis-

dom. His landscape is never described; it evolves from the stories. It is also a largely childless landscape, so that childhood-and-countryside escapism was never possible for him, as it was for so many Welsh writers.

In Manteg religion furnishes an exploitable moral vocabulary. "Be you religious," is the advice to Lissi, a workhouse girl with nerve enough to court a minister's son in "The Redeemer." *Religious, Christian,* and *respectable* are the coveted seals of approval – above all, *respectable.* "Shed God and you shed nothing, shed respectability and you shed all," as Evans remarked outside his fiction. His men are "talkists," using language to bend community opinion or for ponderous self-justification, and they define themselves by what they say, as does Evan Rhos in "Redemption," the opening story of *Capel Sion:*

> His manner was humble; on the Sabbath his face was habited in a religious smile and his lips framed the words "Big Man" or "White Jesus bach." Once in the Seiat the Ruler of the Pulpit said to him: "Evan Rhos, man, mouth your experience." He answered: "Not saintly enough is my voice to be raised." Of him this was spoken: "He breathes to the Big Man."
> A woman came to labour in his house and on his land. Her name was Hannah Harelip, and she was from the House of the Poor in Castellybryn. She was aspiring and covetous, and because Evan would not let her be mistress over all that was his, she oppressed him with the burden of her sin. But the Big Man freed Evan and joined him and Jane Pant in marriage.

This fundamentalist reading tells hardest against women, and Manteg is a remorselessly patriarchal society. "The old veil females wear divides them from the face of the Big Man." God is likewise "the Great Male," "the Big Husband at the far end of the Light" who ordains the role of a wife: "an angel ministering to me and my children," as Joshua Llanwen explains in *My People.* In an agricultural community a wife's laboring capacity guarantees a productive farm, a point rammed home by Deio to his wavering son, Tomos, in "A Heifer Without Blemish": "You need a woman to look after the land, and the cattle, and your milk man. And after you."

Evans's stories often concern the search for a suitable partner, and in the attendant maneuverings women play their parts, this being the one way they can elevate themselves. The consequences are usually dire (murder, madness, abandonment), although in "A Father in Sion" Martha succeeds and the stranger woman at Danyrefail comes to control the farm and Sadrach too. Martha, Sadrach's "gift from the Big Man," supplants his older wife, Achsah: if men want women as workhorses, they also want them sexually, even though sex is evil. When men fall, they urge secrecy, which makes sex a weapon for women to achieve their goals. Even the workhouse girl Lissi sees this. Evans was drawn to rebellious younger women whose heightened physical awareness makes them dangerous in Sion — the greatest challenges to the ways in which men see themselves. In "Greater Than Love" Esther visits the seaside with a party that includes Sam, her possessive, unlovely village suitor, but there she meets Hws Morris, a trainee minister who seduces her in a cave. Sam overhears their subsequent conversation:

"Don't you send me away now. Let me stay with you."

The man answered: "Shut your throat, you temptress. For why did you flaunt your body before my religious eyes?"

"Did you not make fair speeches to me?" said Esther.

"Terrible is your sin," said the man. "Turn away from me. Little Big Man bach, forgive me for eating of the wench's fruit."

Sam came up to them by stealth.

"Out of your head you must be, boy bach, to make sin with Esther," he said.

Hws Morris looked into Sam's face, and a horrid fear struck him, and he ran: and Sam opened his knife and running after him, caught him and killed him. He had difficulty in drawing away the blade, because it had entered into the man's skull. Then he returned to the place where Esther was, and her he killed also.

Not all of Evans's women are thus obliterated. In "The Devil in Eden" Dinah appears as his New Woman — intelligent, watchful, sexually alive, firm in the faith. But the images that abide are those of women victimized in stories of mythic dimensions: Nanni as suffering Wales, duped by a salesman and sacrificing herself in a rat-infested cottage ("Be This Her Memorial"); Achsah, imprisoned in a loft and exercised at night under a cow's halter ("A Father in Sion"); Matilda, a victim of incest who is driven in shame to a local asylum ("Lamentations"):

The men of the neighbourhood laid rabbit traps on the floor of the fields, and one trap caught the foot of Matilda, and she was delivered into Evan's hands. Having clothed her, he took a long rope, the length and thickness that is used to keep a load of hay intact, and one end of the rope he fastened round her right wrist and one end round the left wrist. In this wise he drove her before him, in the manner in which a colt is driven, to the madhouse of the three shires, which is in the town of Carmarthen, and the distance from Manteg to Carmarthen is twenty-four miles.

The appearance of *My People* prompted more than ninety newspaper and literary reviews. The book's fidelity to Welsh rural life was variously confirmed and denied, though for many English critics truthfulness mattered less than artistic conviction. "Not one [story] offends," wrote John Middleton Murray, "because beneath them all is the convincing passion of the thing deeply felt or keenly seen. One never has any tremour of apprehension concerning the writer's vision, or any suspicion that he himself has evoked the ugliness which he portrays." Flattering comparisons were evoked — to Maksim Gorky, Emile Zola, John Millington Synge, George Douglas Brown — as Evans's work was praised for "the most poignant satire since Swift" and for "the impassioned austerity of Greek drama," but what impressed most was the book's originality, a maturity and finish remarkable in an unknown author. And the style seemed so un-Celtic in its reticence, narrative simplicity, and implacable neutrality. "He does not gloat or pry," said Norman Douglas; "He conveys, rather, a sense of elemental things — the coldness, the indifference of rocks and waters. He moves above his subject."

Austere, detached, uncondemning were not words that rushed to the minds of Welsh reviewers. To them *My People* stank of treachery: Evans had sold himself for English gold. The royal pronouncement of the *Western Mail* was crushing: "We take leave to say that there is not a Welshman living of any literary note who will commend the narrative, and not a critic of any standing who will dare sign his name to an approving estimate of *My People*," and its judgment was widely reiterated with charges that the book was "artistically and ethically repulsive," "pornography," and "a farrago of filth and debased verbal coinage." Before or since its appearance, no book in Wales has stirred up such controversy. For Evans the abuse exemplified the Christian charity of his critics, while attempts to suppress the book belied their vaunted love of liberty. In January 1916 the police raided Cardiff bookshops, and Chief Constable David Williams claimed, "I was for twenty years at Scotland Yard, and I read most of the suppressed books, and 'My People' is the worst book I've ever read." Liberal-Nonconformity was hitting back and, Evans judged, at the highest level, for behind police intimidation he saw the hand of Lloyd George.

As for those hysterical attacks upon him, Evans insisted,

The leaders of Welsh nonconformity are uneasy that word of their tyranny will get into England. They and their Members of Parliament have lied to the English how the heart of rural Wales is very beautiful, the pastors are fathers in Sion, and the peasants have neither spot nor blemish.

The analysis hit the mark, and there were signs that even the English were awakening to a Welshman's particular worth – and that was why those of his countrymen brave enough to concede that Caradoc Evans had a point still condemned him for sounding off outside the family and in an international language. The reality of Wales could never be known; what mattered was its projection in a widely circulating work of fiction. Thus, after praise from reviewers such as H. L. Mencken, the Welsh-American reaction was ferocious, for Mencken saw in Caradoc Evans the fundamentalist habits of the American South laid bare: there too barbarism and booming piety went hand in hand. Mencken, who offered to supply the Young Men's Christian Association with a hundred copies of *Capel Sion,* believed that the author had somehow worked into the portrayals of his characters a sense of their own helplessness, and that by suppressing all objective comment on their actions, Evans was developing a new form in fiction. "The discreet," Mencken concluded, "will keep an eye open for what he does hereafter."

What Evans began to do was to extend his outlets by placing new stories in the *Westminster Gazette,* an influential London evening paper whose literary editor, Naomi Royde-Smith, had detected in him the makings of "a very great writer." Somewhat puzzlingly, a single story went to *Everyman,* the political weekly that had pronounced Joyce's *A Portrait of the Artist as Young Man* (1914–1915) "astonishingly powerful and extraordinarily dirty" and had opined that "Mr. James Joyce is an Irish edition of Mr. Caradoc Evans."

Evans's third collection, *My Neighbours,* ensued, its title page dated 1919 although it was published in March 1920. The delay resulted from Melrose's disquiet over two stories that Evans had submitted (and that Melrose ultimately rejected on grounds of taste) and from some last-minute cancellations in passages deemed potentially libelous. *My Neighbours* put under the microscope the London Welsh, national exemplars like Ben Lloyd making their way at the heart of the commercial kingdom. Satire needs specific targets, and behind Evans's charismatic preacher-politician loomed the most celebrated of all Welshmen, David Lloyd George, the Criccieth solicitor who had risen to become prime minister. Powerful reactions to Lloyd George in-

The photograph of Evans published as the frontispiece to the sixth edition (1919) of his first collection of stories, My People

form "According to the Pattern" and "For Better," where Ben Lloyd's ruthless vanity, his lust for riches and for women, the paranoia and obsessive political intriguing, are all on display. In a memorable final image the proclaimed Welsh leader bends a knee before the English monarch. Ben's nationalist avowals are mere political expediency, as is his early radicalism. He becomes the bosses' man, promising a servile labor force tamed by religious education. The key to his makeup is the community that bred him, its values chillingly conveyed in a single sentence on Ben's father, whose marriage had brought him much wealth and seven daughters: "Even if Abel had land, money and honour, his vessel of contentment was not filled until his wife went into her deathbed and gave him a son."

Though vibrating with political animus, the Ben Lloyd stories do not mark Evans as a socialist or even a working-class writer. His regard for the poor does not deflect his vision; he can summon up no heroes among them, nor convey any sense of their final victory, for "There is no man too holy to carry a rich man's colour." All have sinned and fallen short of the glory. Perhaps surprisingly, the perspective grants Ben the comic richness that Evans's chapel rulers display in their verbal gusto and eye for the main chance. The Bens and Bern-Davydds of this world are prodigiously inventive, in word and deed, and their creator feeds this energy. In "The Two Apostles" Ben, almost a hero-villain, talks his way out of hell through bypassing the divine rigmarole for judging individual worth. Elsewhere in *My Neighbours*, "Joseph's House" is outstanding: its autobiographical basis intensifies the emotion as Evans for the first time explores his drapery background, the genteel refuge for sickly lads that proves to be their death trap. The abuse of shop assistants, their codes of survival, and the physical decay mirroring a spiritual regression all foreshadow *Nothing to Pay* (1930), Evans's fine first novel. Reviews of *My Neighbours,* gave Melrose good advertising copy, as the volume was praised for being "clever, arresting and violently individual" and for displaying a "masterly use of dialogue" and a "subdued irony and false simplicity [that were] delightful." As with *My People* and *Capel Sion,* an American edition followed, this one prefaced by a specially prepared essay on "The Welsh People." Again Mencken stressed its pertinence: "the religious thought of the South is almost precisely identical with the religious thought of Wales."

The 1920s proved fallow years for Evans the writer, though as a journalist he prospered. Following his abrupt dismissal from *Ideas* (for having exposed a Mayfair sex-and-spies scandal), he joined the *Daily Mirror* as one of a half dozen well-paid subeditors. Subbing on the paper bonded Evans to Fleet Street, and from these years (1917–1923) came snapshots of him in the company of journalists. One of them, Edward Wright, pinpoints an essential un-Englishness about Evans: "Tall, gaunt of face, with high cheek bones and eyes usually half closed, Mr. Caradoc Evans looks a strange kind of alien, and is what he looks. D. G. Rossetti and Joseph Conrad show scarcely a more foreign cast of mind." Evans's countryman Augustus John felt at home with him and came to appreciate the strength and motive behind the stories. Comparing Evans with Dylan Thomas as interpreters of Welsh life, he judged Evans the "far more conscientious historian." And for John the older writer was a true patriot: "like God, he chastised those he loved." The notion was hard to accept, particularly for the Welsh; journalist Sewell Stokes proclaimed Evans "the best-hated

man in Wales," and when this label stuck, the recipient came to wear it with pride.

Stokes was writing in 1924, in the aftermath of "Taffy," Evans's only play: its London matinee premiere in 1923 had proven to be a triumphantly violent affair. The play was salvaged from material originally written as a novel, something of a career requirement for Evans by now. "Write a novel" he had advised an apprentice author. "If it is any good at all it will give you a position and enhance the price of your stories." The "Taffy" material brought a broader, more relaxed treatment of village life. The play is a love story centered on Marged, daughter of a dissident chapel elder, and Spurgeon Evans, an ambitious young minister seeking Sion's pulpit. They become partners both in romance and in their determination for reform. Sion must be cleansed, and as it was built, so it can be remade – by love, by a rededicated Spurgeon made whole in marriage (the other harnessing institution under scrutiny in this play). Marged extends Evans's conception of Welsh womanhood: perceptive, shrewd, and sensual, she prefigures the type who will gain the victories in the later fiction.

For the matinee performance (26 February 1923) Edith Evans, the jewel of a glittering occasion, played Marged. James Agate covered events for the *Saturday Review,* and he had plenty to report, both on and off the stage. H. G. Wells attended, as did Mary Webb and Augustus John; in the stalls sat Mrs. Lloyd George, a little in front of Margot Asquith. Above them a group of Welsh students, determined to make their protest, packed the gallery. As the curtain rose on the whitewashed walls of Capel Sion a rumpus broke out and each of the play's three acts ended in a chorus of catcalls. After a single theatrical performance Evans awoke to find himself famous. The *English Review* thought "Taffy" "so brilliant a spate of satire, wit, fun, and human analysis," while the *Observer,* invoking comparisons with Irish dramatist John Millington Synge, believed that now Wales had found "a dramatist of uncommon power who may easily become its genius." But Evans wrote no more plays; indeed, he produced little of consequence for the remainder of the decade, though opportunities arose in national journalism and he enjoyed some success as a public speaker. It was proof that nothing puts an author on the map more readily than a novel, except perhaps a play.

Professionally Evans was once more on the move, joining (as he put it) the "alcoholic stylists" and "men of the glowing pad" in literary journalism. In 1923 T. P. O'Connor appointed him acting editor of *T. P.'s Weekly,* the revived middlebrow periodical he had first encountered as a shop assistant and that now also employed the Irish poet Austin Clarke. Evans's den at Ludgate Hill held a plain table flanked by two hard chairs and a cupboard of review books. One contributor recalled him sitting in a bright yellow shirt on a chilly November morning, windows wide open and the coal fire almost dead: "He had shaggy grey-black goat's hair and violent features and the eyes of a squirrel." Evans enjoyed Fleet Street camaraderie and the steady lunchtime drinking, and through contacts there he came to place the new novel he was engaged upon. Frank Morley, the American director of Faber and Faber, accepted *Nothing to Pay* in its unfinished state, with a reasonable £175 advance.

In this Swiftian fable of the drapery underworld at the turn of the century, a miserly antihero, Amos Morgan, journeys into the heart of lower-middle-class darkness. Hard work, cold opportunism, and the obliteration of all sentiment and self-respect are his weapons — these and the protective shield of money. Wells, onetime draper himself, commended its "brutal thoroughness," although realism, critics outside Wales agreed, was not this novel's mode. "It is a fantasy — a fantasy of evil," said the *National Review.* "Mr. Evans is no more a realist than Mr. T. F. Powys," wrote V. S. Pritchett in the *Spectator;* "One accepts neither Mr. Powys on Dorsetshire nor Mr. Evans on Wales. . . . [T]here is a wild sardonic humour about Mr. Evans's hatred, something which whips the narrative off realism's earth." *Nothing to Pay* achieved a modest commercial success, managing a second Faber edition and a somewhat revised American edition. A plan to reprint the short-story collections in uniform Faber format was mooted, but sooner than accept what he deemed "riotously inadequate" terms, Evans severed links with his publishers. The action understandably pained him: "Goodness knows I never wanted to wander away from Faber and Faber" begins his last letter on the subject.

Elsewhere his life was in disarray. He was suddenly out of a job, as a circulation of seventy-two thousand had failed to save *T.P.'s Weekly* from closure in November 1929. Times were difficult on Fleet Street, and Evans's chances of a post in literary journalism must have been slim. He had a year's gratuity to live on and had met a woman who firmly believed that his future lay outside London. A year earlier Marguerite Barczinsky, a romantic novelist with a complicated past, had walked into Evans's office about a piece she had written, and almost immediately she and the editor began a tem-

pestuous affair. The relationship seemed improbable, for little in background, temperament, or opinion united them. Daughter of an Indian army officer, striking in appearance and dress, and careless of money (a chauffeur was one of life's necessities), Marguerite was a person of ready emotions and was naturally drawn to the mystical ("the sentimentalist," Caradoc called her). In politics she was flamboyantly Tory, and as an author, too, she was the opposite of Caradoc, as she published up to four novels a year under the pen names Countess Barcynska and Oliver Sandys. But her respect for the writer's calling was absolute, and Evans's genius she never doubted. It could best be served, so she thought, by his giving up London and its distractions, and this inevitably meant giving up Rose — the straightforward, unaffected woman he had married twenty years before. How, asked Marguerite, could a Cockney sparrow follow a Welsh eagle in its flight? All at once Evans turned his back on a wife and home, his circle of friends, his publisher, and any prospect of employment in the business that had sustained him. He would attempt to live as a full-time writer.

On the surface the change seemed justified. Married to Marguerite in 1933 and living with her and her son by a previous marriage (first in Gloucestershire, then in Wales), Evans completed three novels: *Wasps* (1933), This Way to Heaven (1934), and *Mother's Marvel* (1949). Problems beset them. A threat of libel action frightened Hurst and Blackett off *Wasps,* leaving the newly established firm of Rich and Cowan to publish a doctored version. *Mother's Marvel* was also rejected, under circumstances not altogether clear (it eventually appeared in 1949). In the light of *Nothing to Pay* these novels are disappointing. *Wasps,* the story of a clergyman's widow moving by "sober harlotry" toward another Marriage Mint, is certainly the best of them: a somewhat top-heavy frolic, its extravagant ideas and situations strapped to a mechanical plot. Evans lacked the novelist's architectonic command, his reading of life perhaps too narrow for the larger enterprise. The stylistic preoccupations now become obtrusive. Aphorisms stud the page — "An adulterous man has no honour for the woman he takes in adultery"; "The longer is one's life the closer one clings to it, be the cost another's life"; "She who has no place on a man's gravestone has none in his will" — as though compacted wisdom and finality of expression obviate the need for convincing narrative. It was an abandonment of the approach that had distinguished Evans as short-story writer. *Wasps* gained some good reviews ("exhilarating, extremely amusing, almost libellously provocative, totally mad, and altogether delightful" enthused *Time and Tide*), but *This Way to Heaven* proved a critical disaster. For the moment Evans had lost his passionate relationship with subject matter, or the artistic means of focusing it.

Once more the writing dried up as Evans entered a phase of increasing mental and emotional turbulence, seemingly related to the move from London. His surrendering the chance of paid employment had been against his instincts (and repeated advice to others). He missed the companionship. He missed the money. He stood no chance of living by his fiction and lacked the temperament and facility to work at hack journalism. The brutal fact was that having left with Marguerite he would henceforth remain a kept man, a position deeply injurious to his identity and self-respect. Life at Aberystwyth became more intolerable. He lived as author, inhabiting the study of an imposing town house yet publishing almost nothing. In England the later novels had detracted from his earlier achievements, which themselves were out of print. In Wales he had not much literary reputation to lose, though as a personality he continued to fascinate. Controversy clung round him. His portrait, mutilated while on display at a London revival of "Taffy," was refused by two Welsh galleries; the National Eisteddfod withdrew an invitation to adjudicate, and the BBC declined a commissioned talk on seeing his proposed script. The Caradoc Evans legend was growing.

In 1937 the family left for England, settling in Broadstairs, Kent, where Evans entered a new creative phase. He set about some short stories, the first in twenty years. "I only see bits of them," complained Marguerite, "he likes to hug his work like a dog his bone." In the unsettled summer of 1939 she revived the repertory company that had occupied her in Wales, but the outbreak of war cut short all theatricals. The Evanses retreated to safe, familiar Aberystwyth, coming to occupy a drafty hillside house outside the town. Outwardly impressing by his graciousness and sociability, Evans inwardly exercised his *Who's Who* pastime of "beholding the mote that is in my brother's eye." The local farmers were war profiteers, slave-driving their wives, starving their dogs, and ill-treating young evacuees. And as ever, "pale weak children [are] denied the fruits of the earth by money-grubbing parents." Wartime Aberystwyth repeated the Cardigan of Caradoc's boyhood by providing material for fiction, as this entry from his journal confirms:

Some time ago I bought a pint of beer at a public house round here. As I was preparing to depart, the bright-eyed, skinnyish, yellow-faced woman of the place said to me: "Come to the cellar and I'll show you where my dog died. Oh, he was a fighter, he was!" She lit a candle and I followed her. In the grey-hued cellar she said: "We found the old dog here on the morning of my husband's funeral. Dead. There was one wreath too many for my husband's coffin and so I laid it on the body of my dog." "And," I asked, "whose wreath was that you cast away so lightly?" She answered: "Mine."

The war years darkened his moods, often to black despair. "Deep down," wrote Marguerite, "I can hear the volcano rumbling and I can see the glow of the fire." For Evans "the only real thing is the light of hell running in streams." His journal confessed, "I am too much for her, I am too much for myself." Such praise as came his way he took guardedly. What use was recognition now, after years of vilification and misunderstanding? But he continued writing, publishing *Pilgrims in a Foreign Land* in 1942. The collection was the first offering of Evans's last phase, one that incorporated elements of the folktale and the supernatural within a consciously more poetic idiom. Behind the fantasy of the stories lie the same grim truths of conflict and survival. Evans's economically dominant men remain "talkists," lost in language and prey to obsession, unwilling to recognize what stares them in the face. The women, still social victims, are as individuals more potent: emotionally alive, pragmatic, and intuitive, they occupy every dimension, the sexual in particular. Now the often-bloody victories are theirs: Pilgrim is beheaded in a manner suggestive of castration in "Your Sin Will Find You Out"; Katrin gains her child and a husbandless farm in "Changeable as a Woman with Child"; Miss Fach wins her disreputable pig keeper and maintains her unspoken precept — "Cash is never dirty" — in "A Widow with a Full Purse."

Pilgrims in a Foreign Land and the novella *Morgan Bible* (1943) did something to revive Evans's reputation. The *Observer* invoked comparisons with the work of Ivy Compton-Burnett, "with whose hermetic world of desperate family life his own Welsh people . . . discover an unexpected kinship. Like her, he creates a life even more dreadful than reality, and into his crabbed elliptical prose he breathes a peculiar heat of excitement."

In late 1943 Evans's health began to give way. He did little to preserve it, working beneath a portrait of Dickens in his icy room, moving straight from a hot bath into the cold outdoors, and walking coatless for miles in wind and rain. Pneumonia left him groggy for months. "He feels so weak and his heart troubles him," Marguerite reported. "He's been so frightfully energetic all his life — just a volcano in constant eruption – and now the calm puzzles him." His heart put him in the hospital at the beginning of 1945, soon after his sixty-sixth birthday, and on 11 January he died. He was buried at the top of a high, sloping cemetery above his house near Aberystwyth (the aptly-named Brynawelon, "hill of breezes"). For the simple headstone Marguerite chose an epitaph Caradoc himself had composed some twenty years previously: "Bury me lightly so that the small rain may reach my face and the fluttering of the butterfly shall not escape my ear." She gathered up the last seven stories, which were published in 1946 as *The Earth Gives All and Takes All.*

In his posthumously published collection the vision is tempered: "Two things are a farmer's delight, a horse who is glad to see him and a piecess of clay [i.e., a woman] to warm." These goals are achieved in "Oldest Brother," where Bensha, his wife, and horse contentedly work their mountain acres. In a caravan nearby lives Bensha's mother, whose protecting love has not always encompassed another woman. Seemingly there can be reconciliation on a Welsh hillside farm. In the title story, set on the eve of World War II, Evans approaches classic terrain with undiminished verve:

> Silah schoolen was a tidy bundle and she was dressed as if every day was a Sunday. She was not tall or short, fat or thin; her cheek-bones were high and her lips were wide and her top teeth swelled from her mouth in a showy white arch.
>
> The farmer came to the threshold of the schoolhouse.
>
> "Hoi-hoi," he said. "Stop the learning and come you here."
>
> Silah came to him.
>
> "Hear I do you are for auction," he said.
>
> "Who is the bidder?" asked Silah, pretending she did not know.
>
> "A farmwr well to do."
>
> "What is the bid of the farmwr well to do?"
>
> "Forty acres and livestock, dresser and coffer and press and settle and tables and chairs."
>
> "A man with no bed needs no wife."
>
> "Forget I did. A bed there is."

This is again a story of partners maneuvering for advantage in marriage and in work, but its ending implies that men and women may come together, if along different paths. The farmer's wisdom, like chapel mouthings, is as dry dust in a loft. Ianto, meanwhile, is a pillar of good earth who, with Silah, "caressed and kneaded the earth and they poured their water upon its backward places." The last antiphonal exchange, set in a stable and moving around marriage and birth, fuses the

Evans's grave in Horeb Cemetery, near Aberystwyth. Evans wrote the epitaph for the headstone.

human and natural worlds with the religious in a manner unexpected of Caradoc Evans. Austin Clarke thought that the later stories were profoundly original achievements, proverbial in intensity and veined with "a wild, harsh, unlovely poetry." Good though they are, the blurring of narrative line suggests an author less at ease in his intentions. Evans is best on the attack, pressing the truth of his convictions.

The *Western Mail* leader on Evans's death put the majority view in Wales:

> As a Welshman Evans's disservice lay not in the fact that he deliberately caricatured his fellow countrymen, but that he unintentionally and indirectly set an example to a rising school of Welsh writers in English, who instead of looking around, prefer, as it were, to bend and peer under stones.

Evans's influence on later Anglo-Welsh writers, many of whom have pursued the short story, has been palpable and acknowledged. The most celebrated of them, Dylan Thomas, spoke in 1934 of his own "uninterrupted praise" for Evans in London literary circles. For Keidrych Rhys, founder of *Wales,* "the militant journal of the Welsh literary renaissance" (1937–1939), the author of *My People* was a pioneer in every sense, the writer who had achieved the first great expression in English of "the life and ways of thinking of a nation hitherto without expression in the outside world." Gwyn Jones, editor of the *Welsh Review,* marked the twofold significance of Caradoc Evans for a later generation of writers: the first, he found in "the high excellence of his best work, and the second what I might call his work of liberation. . . . [B]efore most of us set pen to paper he had fought savagely against the philistinism, Welsh provincialism, and the hopelessly inhibited standards of what little Anglo-Welsh literature there was." Evans signaled the arrival of a new literature "in the best possible way, with the maximum of offence and the maximum of effect." But the offense and the effect alienated Evans utterly from Welsh-speaking Wales. His assault on Nonconformity cut across the emotional roots of nationhood, and his reception in England blackened the crime. *My People,* it was thought, pandered to a taste in Celtic caricature through providing colorful bits and pieces, never the complex whole. This notion is a persistent one of Evans and other prominent Anglo-Welsh authors dancing to alien tunes.

Evans has enjoyed a partial rehabilitation, as his work is back in print (some of it under a Welsh imprint), and critical studies are forthcoming on Evans's intentions and contemporary reception, his artistic methods, and his controlling beliefs. "At best," he concluded, "we are very imperfect, in a very imperfect world." Welsh imperfections are universal ones — social exploitation, ideological validation of injustice, and unshakable money worship. Caradoc Evans treats lapsed humanity in a manner wholly his own. Once read, he is not easily forgotten.

Bibliography:

John Harris, "Caradoc Evans," in his *A Bibliographical Guide to Twenty-Four Modern Anglo-Welsh Writers* (Cardiff: University of Wales Press, 1994), pp. 69–78.

Biographies:

Oliver Sandys, *Caradoc Evans* (London: Hurst & Blackett, 1946);

John Harris, "Caradoc Evans, 1878–1945: A Biographical Introduction," in his *Fury Never Leaves Us: a Miscellany of Caradoc Evans* (Bridgend, Mid Glamorgan: Poetry Wales Press, 1985), pp. 9–45.

References:

Simon Baker, "Caradoc Evans's 'A Father in Sion' and Contemporary Critical Theory," *New Welsh Review,* 11 (Winter 1990–1991): 46–50;

John Davies and John Harris, "Caradoc Evans and the Forcers of Conscience: A Reading of 'A Father in Sion,'" *Anglo-Welsh Review,* 81 (1985): 79–89;

Harris, "The Devil in Eden: Caradoc Evans and His Wales," *New Welsh Review,* 19 (Winter 1992–1993): 10–18;

Glyn Jones, "Caradoc Evans," in his *The Dragon Has Two Tongues: Essays on Anglo-Welsh Writers and Writing* (London: Dent, 1968), pp. 64–80;

Gwyn Jones, "A Mighty Man in Sion: Caradoc Evans, 1878–1945," in his *Background to Dylan Thomas and Other Explorations* (Oxford & New York: Oxford University Press, 1992), pp. 72–88;

Mary Jones, "The Satire of Caradoc Evans," *Anglo-Welsh Review,* 72 (1982): 58–65;

D. Z. Phillips, "Distorting the Truth (Caradoc Evans)," in his *From Fantasy to Faith: The Philosophy of Religion and Twentieth-Century Literature* (London: Macmillan, 1991), pp. 84–94;

W. J. Rees, "Caradoc Evans and D. J. Williams: A Problem in Literary Sociology," *Planet,* 81 (June–July 1990): 69–80;

M. Wynn Thomas, "*My People* and the Revenge of the Novel," *New Welsh Review,* 1 (Summer 1988): 17–22;

Trevor L. Williams, *Caradoc Evans* (Cardiff: University of Wales Press, 1970).

Papers:

The National Library of Wales, Aberystwyth, has a substantial Caradoc Evans archive.

Ford Madox Ford

(17 December 1873 – 26 June 1939)

Mary S. Millar
Kingston, Ontario

See also the Ford entries in *DLB 34: British Novelists, 1890–1929: Traditionalists* and *DLB 98: Modern British Essayists, First Series.*

BOOKS: *The Brown Owl: A Fairy Story,* as Ford Madox Hueffer (London: Unwin, 1891; New York: Stokes, 1891);

The Feather, as Hueffer (London: Unwin, 1892; New York: Cassell, 1892);

The Shifting of the Fire, as Hueffer (London: Unwin, 1892; New York: Putnam, 1892);

The Questions at the Well with Sundry Other Verses for Notes of Music, as Fenil Haig (London: Digby, Long, 1893);

The Queen Who Flew, as Hueffer (London: Bliss, Sands & Foster, 1894);

Ford Madox Brown: A Record of His Life and Work, as Hueffer (London & New York: Longmans, Green, 1896);

Poems for Pictures and for Notes of Music, as Hueffer (London: MacQueen, 1900);

The Cinque Ports: A Historical and Descriptive Record, as Hueffer (Edinburgh & London: Blackwood, 1900);

The Inheritors: An Extravagant Story, by Hueffer and Joseph Conrad (New York: McClure, Phillips, 1901; London: Heinemann, 1901);

Rossetti: A Critical Essay on His Art, as Hueffer (London: Duckworth / New York: Dutton, 1902);

Romance: A Novel, by Hueffer and Conrad (London: Smith, Elder, 1903; New York: McClure, Phillips, 1904);

The Face of the Night: A Second Series of Poems for Pictures, as Hueffer (London: MacQueen, 1904);

The Soul of London: A Survey of a Modern City, as Hueffer (London: Rivers, 1905); republished in *England and the English: An Interpretation* (New York: McClure, Phillips, 1907);

The Benefactor: A Tale of a Small Circle, as Hueffer (London: Brown, Langham, 1905);

Ford Madox Ford

Hans Holbein the Younger: A Critical Monograph, as Hueffer (London: Duckworth / New York: Dutton, 1905);

The Fifth Queen: And How She Came to Court, as Hueffer (London: Rivers, 1906);

The Heart of the Country: A Survey of a Modern Land, as Hueffer (London: Rivers, 1906); republished in *England and the English: An Interpretation* (New York: McClure, Phillips, 1907);

Christina's Fairy Book, as Hueffer (London: Rivers, 1906);

Privy Seal: His Last Venture, as Hueffer (London: Rivers, 1907);

From Inland and Other Poems, as Hueffer (London: Rivers, 1907);

An English Girl: A Romance, as Hueffer (London: Methuen, 1907);

The Pre-Raphaelite Brotherhood: A Critical Monograph, as Hueffer (London: Duckworth / New York: Dutton, 1907);

The Spirit of the People: An Analysis of the English Mind, as Hueffer (London: Rivers, 1907); republished in *England and the English: An Interpretation* (New York: McClure, Phillips, 1907);

England and the English: An Interpretation, as Hueffer (New York: McClure, Phillips, 1907);

The Fifth Queen Crowned: A Romance, as Hueffer (London: Nash, 1908);

Mr. Apollo: A Just Possible Story, as Hueffer (London: Methuen, 1908);

The "Half Moon": A Romance of the Old World and the New, as Hueffer (London: Nash, 1909; Garden City, N.Y.: Doubleday, 1909);

A Call: The Tale of Two Passions, as Hueffer (London: Chatto & Windus, 1910);

Songs from London, as Hueffer (London: Elkin Mathews, 1910);

The Portrait, as Hueffer (London: Methuen, 1910);

The Simple Life Limited, as Daniel Chaucer (London & New York: John Lane, 1911);

Ancient Lights and Certain New Reflections, Being the Memories of a Young Man, as Hueffer (London: Chapman & Hall, 1911); republished as *Memories and Impressions: A Study in Atmospheres* (New York: Harper, 1911);

Ladies Whose Bright Eyes: A Romance, as Hueffer (London: Constable, 1911; New York: Baker Taylor, 1911; revised edition, Philadelphia: Lippincott, 1935);

The Critical Attitude, as Hueffer (London: Duckworth, 1911);

High Germany: Eleven Sets of Verse, as Hueffer (London: Duckworth, 1911);

The Panel: A Sheer Comedy, as Hueffer (London: Constable, 1912); revised and enlarged as *Ring for Nancy: A Sheer Comedy* (Indianapolis: Bobbs-Merrill, 1913);

The New Humpty-Dumpty, as Daniel Chaucer (London & New York: John Lane, 1912);

The Monstrous Regiment of Women, as Hueffer (London: Minerva, 1913);

Mr. Fleight, as Hueffer (London: Latimer, 1913);

The Desirable Alien, by Hueffer and Violet Hunt (London: Chatto & Windus, 1913);

The Young Lovell: A Romance, as Hueffer (London: Chatto & Windus, 1913);

Collected Poems, as Hueffer (London: Goschen, 1913);

Henry James: A Critical Study, as Hueffer (London: Secker, 1914; New York: Boni, 1915);

Antwerp, as Hueffer (London: Poetry Bookshop, 1915);

The Good Soldier: A Tale of Passion, as Hueffer (London & New York: John Lane, 1915);

When Blood Is Their Argument: An Analysis of Prussian Culture, as Hueffer (London & New York: Hodder & Stoughton, 1915);

Between St. Dennis and St. George: A Sketch of Three Civilisations, as Hueffer (London & New York: Hodder & Stoughton, 1915);

Zeppelin Nights: A London Entertainment, by Hueffer and Hunt (London & New York: John Lane, 1915);

On Heaven, and Poems Written on Active Service, as Hueffer (London & New York: John Lane, 1918);

A House, as Hueffer (London: Poetry Bookshop, 1921);

Thus to Revisit: Some Reminiscences, as Hueffer (London: Chapman & Hall, 1921; New York: Dutton, 1921);

The Marsden Case: A Romance (London: Duckworth, 1923);

Women & Men (Paris: Three Mountains Press, 1923);

Mister Bosphorus and the Muses, or A Short History of Poetry in Britain: Variety Entertainment in Four Acts (London: Duckworth, 1923);

Some Do Not . . . : A Novel (London: Duckworth, 1924; New York: Seltzer, 1924);

The Nature of a Crime, by Ford and Joseph Conrad (London: Duckworth, 1924; Garden City, N.Y.: Doubleday, 1924);

Joseph Conrad: A Personal Remembrance (London: Duckworth, 1924; Boston: Little, Brown, 1924);

No More Parades: A Novel (London: Duckworth, 1925; New York: Boni, 1925);

A Mirror to France (London: Duckworth, 1926; New York: Boni, 1926);

A Man Could Stand Up − : A Novel (London: Duckworth, 1926; New York: Boni, 1926);

New Poems (New York: Rudge, 1927);

New York Is Not America (London: Duckworth, 1927; New York: Boni, 1927);

New York Essays (New York: Rudge, 1927);

The Last Post: A Novel (New York: Literary Guild, 1928); republished as *Last Post* (London: Duckworth, 1928);

A Little Less Than Gods: A Romance (London: Duckworth, 1928; New York: Viking, 1928);

The English Novel: From the Earliest Days to the Death of Joseph Conrad (Philadelphia: Lippincott, 1929; London: Constable, 1930);

No Enemy: A Tale of Reconstruction (New York: Macaulay, 1929);

Return to Yesterday: Reminiscences, 1894–1914 (London: Gollancz, 1931; New York: Liveright, 1932);

When the Wicked Man (New York: Liveright, 1931; London: Cape, 1932);

The Rash Act: A Novel (New York: Long & Smith, 1933; London: Cape, 1933);

It Was the Nightingale (Philadelphia: Lippincott, 1933; London: Heinemann, 1934);

Henry for Hugh: A Novel (Philadelphia: Lippincott, 1934);

Provence from Minstrels to the Machine (Philadelphia: Lippincott, 1935; London: Allen & Unwin, 1938);

Vive Le Roy: A Novel (Philadelphia: Lippincott, 1936; London: Allen & Unwin, 1937);

Collected Poems (New York: Oxford University Press, 1936);

Great Trade Route (New York & Toronto: Oxford University Press, 1937; London: Allen & Unwin, 1937);

Portraits from Life (Boston & New York: Houghton Mifflin, 1937); republished as *Mightier than the Sword: Memories and Criticisms* (London: Allen & Unwin, 1938);

The March of Literature from Confucius' Day to Our Own (New York: Dial, 1938); republished as *The March of Literature, from Confucius to Modern Times* (London: Allen & Unwin, 1939);

Parade's End (New York: Knopf, 1950) – comprises *Some Do Not*, *No More Parades*, *A Man Could Stand Up –*, and *The Last Post;*

A History of Our Own Times (Bloomington: Indiana University Press, 1988; Manchester: Carcanet, 1989).

Collections: *The Bodley Head Ford Madox Ford*, 5 volumes (London: Bodley Head, 1962–1971);

Critical Writings of Ford Madox Ford, edited by Frank MacShane (Lincoln: University of Nebraska Press, 1964);

The Presence of Ford Madox Ford, edited by Sondra J. Stang (Philadelphia: University of Pennsylvania Press, 1981);

The Ford Madox Ford Reader, edited by Sondra J. Stang (Manchester: Carcanet, 1986; New York: Ecco, 1987).

SELECTED PERIODICAL PUBLICATIONS – UNCOLLECTED: "The Baron," *Macmillan's Magazine*, 87 (February 1903): 304–320;

"The Difference," *Cornhill Magazine*, 15 (August 1903): 276–288;

"The Old Conflict," *Macmillan's Magazine*, 89 (December 1903): 120–131;

"On the Edge," *Bystander*, 11 (11 July 1906): 81–84;

"Below the Stairs," *Bystander*, 11 (15 August 1906): 337–342;

"The Rendezvous," *Bystander Christmas Supplement*, 16 (11 December 1907): 3–7;

"A Saviour," *Country Life*, 22 (21 December 1907): 904–907;

"The Individualist," *Saturday Review*, 105 (9 May 1908): 591–592;

"4692 Padd," *Bystander Christmas Supplement*, 20 (9 December 1908): 3–7;

"A Silence," *Bystander*, 24 (29 December 1909): 681–684;

"Fathead," *Tramp*, 1 (March 1910): 107–115; (May 1910): 216–223; (June–July 1910): 315–324;

"What Happened at Eleven Forty-five," *Throne*, 5 (25 October 1911): 142–143;

"The Case of James Lurgan," *Bystander*, 32 (6 December 1911): 535–545;

"The Incorruptible," *Throne and Country*, 5 (13 December 1911): 422–425;

"The Medium's End," *Bystander*, 33 (13 March 1912): 551–554;

"The Fun of Genius," *English Review*, 13 (December 1912): 52–63;

"The Scaremonger," *Bystander*, 44 (25 November 1914): 273–276;

"Fun! – It's Heaven," *Bystander*, 48 (24 November 1915): 327–330;

"A Mascot," *London Mercury*, 18 (December 1927): 133–146; republished as "The Romantic Detective," *Yale Review*, 17 (April 1928): 517–537;

"The Miracle," *Yale Review*, 18 (Winter 1928): 320–331.

OTHER: "Riesenberg," in *Great Short Stories of Detection, Mystery and Horror*, second series, edited by Dorothy L. Sayers (London: Gollancz, 1931).

On 21 April 1930 Ford Madox Ford humorously replied to a request for a piece of short fiction: "Alas, though modesty is foreign to my nature I know that I cannot do certain things; the understanding of the Higher Mathematics is one; swimming under water another. But great as is my inca-

Ford with Violet Hunt (left), Rebecca West, and West's child by H. G. Wells, Anthony West

pacity in those sports it is as nothing to my inability to write a short story. Had I ever been able to I should today be a rich man. But I can't."

His self-deprecation is misleading. Beside his major achievements in other genres — novels, poetry, essays, criticism, memoirs, social history — Ford's short stories have simply never received the attention they deserve. He wrote more than seventy stories, at least half of which were published in his lifetime — in *Christina's Fairy Book* (1906) and *Zeppelin Nights: A London Entertainment* (1915), as well as in various periodicals. The unpublished stories include juvenilia and fragments; not all are of high quality, but none is without biographical or stylistic interest. Ford's short fiction spans his entire career from 1889 to the 1930s and provides valuable parallels (and sometimes contrasts) to the stages of his development as a writer of fiction. His stories show the influence of his literary models — Guy de Maupassant, Henry James, H. G. Wells, and Rud-

yard Kipling — but they also demonstrate how well and how early he subsumed these presences into a voice that was confidently his own. In his stories he worked toward the themes of his great novels, *The Good Soldier: A Tale of Passion* (1915) and the war tetralogy *Parade's End* (1950), which depict the rot at the heart of the Victorian and Edwardian society that finally disintegrated with World War I.

His theories of fictional narrative, the literary impressionism that renders events as they are perceived by the mind, were modeled on European realism, but it is notable that the specific examples in his criticism are often from short fiction — from short works of such masters as Ivan Turgenev, Anton Chekhov, or de Maupassant — rather than from long fiction. In practice he frequently experimented with literary techniques in short stories before incorporating them into a full-length novel. His success with the first-person narrator in *The Good Soldier,* for example, came only after practice in a dozen pieces of short fiction. Similarly, in *The Good Soldier* his authoritative use of time shift as arranged by memory resulted from frequent trials in short stories. The modernist methods of the four novels of *Parade's End,* in which the narrative is shaped by the subjective reactions of the experiencing psyche, were also first tried out in short stories. The stories, too, are often recognizably autobiographical and can cast interesting sidelights on important episodes in his life.

Ford was born Ford Hermann Hueffer on 17 December 1873 in Merton, Surrey, into an artistic and intellectual family. His father, Francis Hueffer, was an editor and writer with special interests in Richard Wagner and Arthur Schopenhauer, and from 1879 he was music critic of the *Times*. Ford's mother, Catherine, was an artist and daughter of another, the Pre-Raphaelite painter Ford Madox Brown; her sister, Lucy, was married to William Rossetti, brother of another Pre-Raphaelite, Dante Gabriel Rossetti, and of the poet Christina Rossetti. When Francis Hueffer died at the age of forty-three in 1889, his widow and children lived with the Browns and the Rossettis, and Brown's influence shaped Ford's early career and gave him his sense of art as vocation. His first book, *The Brown Owl: A Fairy Story* (1891), was illustrated by his grandfather and published through that older artist's influence when Ford was only eighteen. His sixth book, *Ford Madox Brown* (1896), is a 450-page biography of his grandfather, and his reminiscences of Brown and his circle appeared throughout his life, from *Ancient Lights and Certain New Reflections, Being the Memories of a Young Man* (1911) to *Portraits from Life* (1937). The boy was educated at schools in Kent and London and never went to a university, but his background made him unusually cultured — skilled and knowledgeable in painting and music (he considered becoming a composer), fluent in several languages, and exceptionally well-read.

His earliest surviving short story is a fairy tale written for his younger sister, Juliet, and showing a strength and subtlety surprising for a writer of sixteen. "Princess Goldenhair" (unpublished, 1889) was written for the first Christmas after Francis Hueffer's death, when Juliet, at the home of William Rossetti, was separated from her family at the Browns'. Its plot has elements of "Rapunzel," "The Frog Prince," and Lewis Carroll's *Alice's Adventures in Wonderland* (1865), but its theme is personal — Goldenhair/Juliet's realization of her ability to triumph over sorrow, despair, and death. She accidentally causes the death of a dwarfish suitor, only to find that he was really the handsome prince she had

desired. She runs away, almost drowns in a lake of her own tears, but discovers that her golden hair makes a raft on which she can float safely to land. Subsequently she defeats a witch (as overpowering as Mrs. Rossetti), subdues an underworld demon who roars like the printing press in the Rossettis' basement, resurrects her prince, and triumphantly returns home with him. The tone of the story is humorous and ironic; its characters (the urbane demon, the rather ineffectual prince, and the resourceful princess) are well drawn, and the story's kindness and personal application are unmistakable.

By December 1890 Ford had left school but was still living at his grandfather's and trying various kinds of writing, including another fairy tale, *The Feather* (1892), and his first novel, *The Shifting of the Fire* (1892). He was also courting his future wife, Elsie Martindale. The unpublished story fragments "Bodurdoe and Gunter" and "The Tribulations of Tolputt" (1892–1893?) are set on the Kent coast where he visited Elsie, and though the subject matter is romantic, their narratives have a social and psychological realism. Prosaic Englishmen (a curate and a bank clerk, respectively) are swept into involvement with strong-minded, passionate women — as are later heroes in *The Inheritors: An Extravagant Story* (1901), *The "Half Moon: A Romance of the Old World and New"* (1909), or *The Young Lovell: A Romance* (1913). "Elspeth" (1891) is the story of an old sailor's daughter in love with a struggling poet who is disconcertingly willing to forget her for the socially approved marriage his mother wants. Eventually Ford saves Elspeth by turning the poet's defection into an implausible dream sequence and marrying the two. The story, however, makes a genuine attempt at rendering point of view, and Ford's realizations of the Kent landscape, local people, and dialect look forward to the more accomplished methods of *The Heart of the Country: A Survey of a Modern Land* (1906).

The ambivalence of these heroes toward marriage is reflected in unsteady shifts of tone, perhaps as much because of artistic inexperience as Ford's own feelings as he approached marriage. Yet shortly after publishing another fairy tale, *The Queen Who Flew* (1894), he married Elsie and set up a succession of frugal households near Romney Marsh in Kent. With an income of two pounds a week he embarked, from necessity as much as from a sense of vocation, on a serious writing career. Here his two daughters, Christina and Katharine, were born in 1897 and 1900, respectively, and he began (or possibly continued) an affair with his wife's sister, Mary Martindale. In one of his most cynical stories,

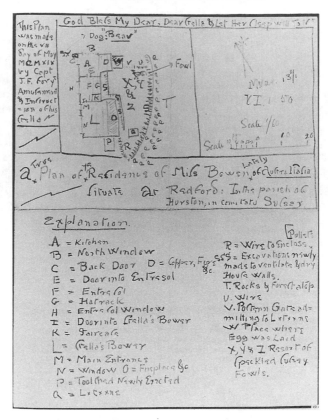

*Page from an 8 May 1919 letter to Stella Bowen, in which
Ford sketched plans for a house he hoped to share with her
(Olin Library, Cornell University; © 1992 by
Janice Biala and Julian Loewe)*

the unpublished "Idyllic Courtship of Coytmore" (1893?), a young London dilettante vacillates about a career in the arts as he does between two virtually identical sisters. He decides to become a writer and proposes to one of the sisters, but his choices of wife and career are comically arbitrary: the story refuses to reveal which sister he has married.

In Kent, Ford became part of a literary coterie which included Henry James, Joseph Conrad, Stephen Crane, and H. G. Wells, and he and Conrad developed their theories of literary impressionism both in their three collaborations – *The Inheritors*, *Romance* (1903), and *The Nature of a Crime* (serialized in 1909; published in 1924) – and separately in their long and short fiction. An unpublished fragment, "The Goose Girl" (1897–1898?), seems to touch on Ford's intertwined problems of love and art at this time. It is not the familiar fable from the Grimm brothers but a disillusioned account of a beautiful red-haired Delilah (possibly modeled on Mary Martindale), the poet she enthralls, and, in an early development of a major Ford theme, the de-

structive effects of passion on truth and integrity. The enchantress and her song represent beguiling fantasy, but Ford seems to have intended that the poet, whose own song faithfully reflects nature, ultimately escape her spell. Artistic truth was a principle he had embraced in assessing his grandfather's work in *Ford Madox Brown*, for the artist is obliged to give, as he later put it in "On Impressionism" (1913), "the fruits of his own observations and the fruits of his own observations alone."

In "The Other" (1898?), one of the stories he wrote for his children and Joseph Conrad's son, Borys, Ford uses his daughter Christina's first words to show how determinedly a child chooses the real world. The story's technique is subtle, looking forward to narrative methods Ford developed in his later work and representing the infant through dialogue, point of view, and a minimum of authorial voice. "The Other" of the title is nominally a spirit who grieves as the child irrevocably enters the human world and leaves behind its prenatal, visionary existence; but it is also recognizably a parent who sees the maturing process of his child as one of separation from himself, and this makes the story effective and touching.

The story seems, however, to have remained unpublished in Ford's lifetime, appearing in 1981 in Sondra J. Stang's *The Presence of Ford Madox Ford* while others perhaps more suitable for a popular market were published much earlier in *Christina's Fairy Book*. In these stories conventional moral prescription, such as the good boy/bad boy opposition in "Bingel and Bengel," replaces the successful mingling of fantasy with reality, and they contrast disappointingly with the energy and imagination of "Princess Goldenhair" or the elegiac appeal of the "The Other."

Christina's Fairy Book did, however, make twenty pounds for Ford, though he thought it low. (One story fragment begins with a writer about to commit suicide because he has received only twenty pounds for a book which took years to write.) In fact Ford's short stories were almost always written for economic reasons. His entire life was spent on the verge of poverty, and magazine payments, if not high, were usually more prompt than those of book agents or publishers. The financial crises of Ford's life often closely correlate with his writing of short stories.

It is no coincidence that his first stories to appear in periodicals – "The Baron," "The Difference," and "The Old Conflict" – did so in 1903, after a disappointing advance for *Romance*. All three stories, however, appeared in magazines of high quality – *Macmillan's* and *Cornhill* – and they indicate his development, both in subject and language, away from the fairy tale. In part this resulted from his reading of de Maupassant, one of the two writers (the other was Gustave Flaubert) on whom he and Conrad modeled themselves as they struggled with *The Inheritors* and *Romance*. Ford had written the preface for his wife's 1903 book of translations from de Maupassant, and his story "A Mother" (unpublished, 1902–1903) is obviously inspired by de Maupassant's "Mère Sauvage." With a shift of setting from the Franco-Prussian War of de Maupassant's story to Kent in the Napoleonic era, "A Mother" actually expands on material briefly mentioned in Ford's Kent history, *The Cinque Ports: A Historical and Descriptive Record* (1900). Ford's Mrs. Swaffer is as indomitable a mother as de Maupassant's, but in this story Ford was, as he wrote to his agent J. B. Pinker in January 1903, not merely recapitulating another writer's brand of realism but experimenting in "virtuosity" – that is, in establishing his own voice. Thus he leads up to but deliberately avoids

the grimness of de Maupassant's ending, in which the farm is destroyed and everyone dies. The turn of Ford's story is characteristically anticlimactic: Mrs. Swaffer's son lives. Despite his pathological shyness with decent women – a foreshadowing of Edward Ashburnham in *The Good Soldier: A Tale of Passion* (1915) – he wins his sweetheart and becomes a gentleman, while Mrs. Swaffer (a little like Leonora Ashburnham) doggedly makes the farm pay.

All the stories published in 1903 show some influence of de Maupassant – the crispness of his openings and the capacity of his first paragraphs to encapsulate the stories. Narrator Willie Temple of "The Baron," however, derives from James rather than de Maupassant: he is an innocent abroad, so infatuated with his beautiful German cousin that he arranges for her mad father to speak at a scientific meeting in England. The tender nostalgia of his tone is like that of John Kemp in *Romance,* but as a narrator Temple is closer to Dowell of *The Good Soldier,* particularly in his failure to see what everyone else sees. The climactic scene, in which the professor is barely prevented from revealing his madness in the Manchester lecture hall, in this respect anticipates the great protest scene in *The Good Soldier,* which similarly depends for its tension on the narrator's ignorance of strong passions beneath a civilized surface.

Narrative point of view is also crucial to "The Difference," an ambitious story in which the melodramatic plot – of a young woman who repeatedly sacrifices herself in love – matters less than its sardonic commentary interwoven between an Englishman and a Spaniard. Ford is here moving toward the juxtaposed perspectives of *The Good Soldier,* where, as in "The Difference," behavior prompted by passion can be seen as highly romantic or hopelessly foolish. "The Old Conflict," a rambling, whimsical German story about a rivalry between court musicians, is less successful. Its antique air has charm, and it is full of the constant surprises Ford admired in de Maupassant, but the style depends too heavily on Anglicizing German idiom and is far from the easy colloquial language his own theories advocated.

By 1906, however, his stories were showing new control and sophistication. After a serious breakdown in 1904 that was followed by a burst of creativity, Ford received at last the critical praise he craved – for the social essays in *The Soul of London: A Survey of a Modern City* (1905) and his Tudor romance, *The Fifth Queen: And How She Came to Court* (1906). His working life was now based in London, and he found a steady market for the next few years in the *Bystander*. This had begun as a society paper but, edited by Comyns Beaumont, by then published such writers of stature as Mark Twain, G. K. Chesterton, W. Somerset Maugham, and Violet Hunt. "On the Edge" and "Below the Stairs" are short, stylish stories on the great Ford themes of infidelity and honor. With these stories he began to achieve what in *Joseph Conrad: A Personal Remembrance* (1924) he called the true short story, "a matter of two or three pages of minutely condensed words, ending with a smack . . . what the French call a *coup de canon*." The length specifications of the *Bystander* (fifteen hundred to thirty-five hundred words – account in part for the new compression, but Ford now had the power to present a subject obliquely, through suggestion rather than statement or description. The tacit undercurrents of feeling that run through "On the Edge," a story of unhappy marriage in upper-class English society, create an atmosphere very like that of *The Good Soldier*. In the short story, even more than in the novel, Ford's penchant for the mot juste establishes context: the phrase *bonded business* in this story applies to business practice and to the social rules that limit personal freedom. Most important, here Ford employs – tactfully and successfully – a first-person narrator whose perception of events is affected by a degree of involvement with the woman saved from adultery. "Below the Stairs" is equally successful in reproducing the thought processes of a man about to be shot by an irate husband. Ford had experimented with time shifts in earlier novels, such as *The Benefactor: A Tale of a Small Circle* (1905) and *The Fifth Queen*, but not as the essential structural component that it becomes in "Below the Stairs." It is here completely natural and assured, particularly in the subjective drawing out of the moment in the mind and memory of the guilty man. The narrative fluidity and complexity anticipate the developed handling of time in *Parade's End*.

The accomplishment of these stories far exceeds the purely practical reasons which, as usual, made their production necessary – in this case, fares for the Ford's trip to the United States in the summer of 1906. Likewise, the two stories of 1907, "The Rendezvous" (another Ford rendering of a de Maupassant story) and "A Saviour," were prompted by expenses from Elsie Hueffer's illness in September and took advantage of the Christmas magazine market. A publisher's initial rejection of *The "Half Moon"* on 30 April 1908 coincides remarkably with publication of "The Individualist" in the *Saturday Review* on 9 May. One of Ford's best stories, "4692 Padd," appeared in the same month as the first

number of his own literary magazine, the *English Review*, which he partially financed. Its plot, concerning an anonymous telephone call to a man about town seen escorting another man's wife, was possibly inspired by a telegram intercepted by Elsie during Ford's affair with Mary Martindale. It later became the pivotal episode of *A Call: The Tale of Two Passions* (1910), but comparison of the two versions shows that, at this point in his literary development, Ford was much more in control of his material in the short form than in the long. *A Call* attempts to be what, five years later, *The Good Soldier* is – a peeling of the layers of social decorum that conceals furious passions and destructive conflicts; but *A Call* is ultimately too dependent on its Jamesian models to be the direct portrayal Ford wanted. "4692 Padd," on the other hand, has the tautness and focus that *A Call* lacks. Three characters – Dudley Leicester; Etta Hudson; and Grimshaw, the narrator – make up a central triangle, while a fourth, Frodsham, the listener, proves to have a philandering secret of his own. The story's fairly conventional structure – a third-person frame enclosing a first-person narration – allows flexibility in point of view through the episode and ensures continued interplay between a surface of controlling social propriety and an underlying ferment of sexual liaison and feelings strained beyond breakdown. There is economy and momentum, and the final revelation that Grimshaw himself was the anonymous caller who drove Leicester to madness is a genuine surprise that forces readers to reevaluate all that has gone before.

Ford's pattern of writing stories to resolve immediate financial needs continued. After Ford and Elsie separated in 1909, his first support payment on 8 December was followed closely by publication in the *Bystander* his only story of that year, "A Silence," on 29 December. (The magazine's usual payment of three guineas almost matched the support payment of £3 10s.) Ford was then involved with writer Violet Hunt but was refused a divorce by Elsie, and once again he drew on his life for his fiction. In "A Silence" a man whose beloved has died commits suicide while his obdurate wife berates him. Ford's story echoes a parallel episode in Hunt's *White Rose of Weary Leaf* (1908), and she also wrote a further variant in "The Prayer" (1911).

In his vicissitudes, Ford's literary associates often helped him to publish stories. As editor (1908–1909) of the *English Review*, he discovered and published the fiction of others (notably D. H. Lawrence); he also serialized in 1909 his own subsequently published novels *A Call* and *The Nature of a*

Crime, this latter a collaboration with Conrad. Ford's only short stories to appear in the *English Review,* "Riesenberg" (1911) and "The Fun of Genius" (1912), however, were published some time after a new proprietor had abruptly dismissed him at the end of 1909. Douglas Goldring, Ford's assistant at *The English Review,* then started a short-lived magazine, the *Tramp,* and published three of Ford's pieces perhaps best described as antidetective stories rewritten from earlier versions under the unpromising general title "Fathead" (1910). Unable to pay Ford at the time, Goldring later arranged (after he had become head of Max Goschen publishers) to bring out Ford's *Collected Poems* (1913) as compensation for the thirty pounds he still owed the author. Two other stories, "What Happened at Eleven Forty-five" and "The Incorruptible," both appeared in 1911 in another rather pretentious periodical, *Throne,* through Ford's earlier publishing connection with its editor, Comyns Beaumont, and business manager Rene Byles. Unfortunately references this magazine made to Violet Hunt as "Mrs. Hueffer" led to a successful lawsuit by Elsie Hueffer in 1913, a suit that ruined *Throne.*

Ford's relationship with Hunt, however, had valuable effects on his fiction, particularly from her sense of the macabre and the darkly ironic. His own fondness for fantasy still existed – as it had in, for example, *Mr. Apollo: A Just Possible Story* (1908) – but his four stories of 1911 and his first of 1912 are ghost stories, a popular genre of the time and one in which Hunt excelled. "The Case of James Lurgan" (1911) does not take itself seriously. In a tone verging on the flippant, it combines a murder mystery, a buried body, and two cousins named Holmes into an experience finally explained as telepathy, a phenomenon in which Hunt, like many of her contemporaries, had a firm belief. "The Incorruptible," a short story about a spectral dog and a comic burglar, was prompted by the poisoning of Hunt's dog. Later, after Ford had left Hunt, he expanded it into a powerful episode in *No More Parades* (1925), in which Tietjens's malevolent wife Sylvia (modeled in part on Hunt) flays a poisoned bulldog as substitute for her husband. In the intervening fourteen years Ford's narrative focus shifted from one centered on recounting events themselves to one dramatically presenting interior perceptions of those events. "The Incorruptible" depends for its effect on an event perceived as genuinely supernatural, and its story is mediated by an elderly narrator who wants to avoid disturbing his genteel after-dinner audience. In *No More Parades* Ford conveys the full horror of the dog's death through directly rendering

Sylvia's thought processes, making it infinitely more shocking.

"What Happened at Eleven Forty-five" and "The Medium's End" (1912) are slighter stories, though still interesting as exercises in first-person narration. The first is a psychological epilogue about the abrupt end of a German tramp first described in *The Heart of the Country.* As in *The Good Soldier,* Ford uses a narrator to emphasize the impossibility of ever knowing another's motivations. "The Medium's End" is about the then-current fad for spiritualism and the grasping materialism that saw it as a source of profit. A narrator describes the characters, wealthy and unscrupulous, who witness the unexpected success of a London séance, and the method allows the reader, through the narrator's tone, to share his feelings about the action. The curious flatness of the story's surface is in fact the guarded response of a man deeply embarrassed at his culpable involvement in bizarre and incredible events seven years before. Such deliberate incongruity of tone would three years later be a crucial part of Ford's characterization of Dowell, the narrator of *The Good Soldier.*

The longest of the supernatural stories, "Riesenberg," probably originated, as did *The Desirable Alien* (1913), during Ford's and Hunt's 1910 residence in Germany as part of Ford's plan to obtain a German divorce from Elsie. Undertones of war could already be heard, and Ford's story of spa patients psychologically damaged by war anticipates his war novels. The patients gathered at the spa are, like the upper-class characters at Nauheim in *The Good Soldier,* "the best people" – whose inner worlds have been shattered into madness and hallucination. Their therapy takes them, bombarded by rocky missiles, up moving mountainsides that are actually huge supernatural beings at play. The irony of Ford's plot is like the premise of Joseph Heller's later war novel, *Catch-22* (1961): the "cure" forces the patients to recognize that reality is even more insane than their hallucinations. The Brobdingnagian landscape, surreal and nightmarish, produces a vertiginous helplessness that also characterizes the landscape of war in *Parade's End.*

The first stories written after the outbreak of war in 1914 focus on civilian reactions. "The Scaremonger" (1914) presented a portrait of Edward Heron Allen, a Sussex neighbor who had expressed fears about German invasion. It vividly portrays the abject terror of "the Squire," and Allen's resentment had an immediate consequence: local authorities ordered Ford (who still had his German surname) to leave the district. Ironically Ford was at this same

James Joyce, Ezra Pound, John Quinn, and Ford Madox Ford in Paris, 1923. Quinn, an American lawyer, was the chief financial backer for the Transatlantic Review.

time between October and December 1914 publishing official anti-German propaganda in the serialized version of *When Blood Is Their Argument: An Analysis of Prussian Culture* (1915). "The Scaremonger" is more, however, than the vindictive personal satire that Allen thought it to be. At about the same time Ford was working, in his long war poem "Antwerp" (1915), on the need to find new, effective ways of expressing the war's unprecedented impact on personal feelings. "The Scaremonger" is a study in such feelings so strong as to overwhelm old inhibitions and embarrass observers. Yet it also justifies the feelings: the Squire sees further into coming events than do his contemptuous hearers, and his death on the beach at enemy hands is proof of his insight. Serapion, the Ford-figure and storyteller of the collection comprising *Zeppelin Nights,* finds in his audience a similar disbelief about the seriousness of the war. *Zeppelin Nights* is modeled on Giovanni Boccaccio's *Decameron* and its parallel group of merrymakers and storytellers seeking to forget the approach of the Black Death. Ford had published all twenty-four of these historical vignettes some years before (1908–1913), but the new framework's link-

ing passages (probably by Hunt, though the sentiments are Ford's) juxtapose old wars, individual commitment, and the present approaching doom. With Ford's added final chapter on the value of patriotic emotion, they shape the book toward its climax – Serapion/Ford's enlistment (in July 1915) in the army, though Ford was overage, unfit, and too valuable to lose.

His regiment did not immediately depart for France, and his next story, "Fun! – It's Heaven" (1915), still concerns noncombatants: a young girl whose idea of "fun" is a teashop and a band until her fiancé is killed in action. The germ for the story is the epilogue to chapter five of *Zeppelin Nights* coupled with the "working heaven" in his poem "On Heaven." Its technical premise, however, is that of his preface to *Collected Poems* (1913) – the belief that current, colloquial language is a valid means of literary expression. The skill of this three-page story lies in Ford's ability gradually to charge with meaning the clichéd *heaven* of the title, to transform it from popular meaningless slang to a phrase loaded with implications in a context of war and death. Like his war poetry, the story focuses on the pity of war, not its glory, and balances the pathos with an enlivening humor. The pity culminates in the girl's intention to enter a convent, perhaps a glance at the similar decision that Ford's daughter Christina would make in 1916.

Ford wrote at least five more war stories drawn from his own military experience. The best of these, the unpublished "The Colonel's Shoes" (1917–1919), develops themes also found in *Parade's End,* notably the "tiredness" of the combatants and the ignorance of those at home about the combatants' mental and emotional strain. It has elements of the ghost story, in the miraculous replacement of an exhausted colonel by the ghost of his nephew, and of the "doubles" concept developed in later novels – *When the Wicked Man* (1931), *The Rash Act* (1933), and *Henry for Hugh* (1934). The Colonel is an early version of Tietjens, from his enormous hands to his unceasing care for his men: his exhaustion, like Tietjens's, is because of his refusal to delegate responsibility.

The time of its writing was too early, however, for the subject to be received well. The story was rejected as nothing more than a war story in 1920, a time when most readers wanted to forget the war, and some years before the wave of literary efforts to describe it. Later stories, with a postwar setting, still deal with good people and problems of honor, but they introduce characters affected by war, such as the gassed general in "Pearls" (1930s?) or the shell-shocked soldier, Price, in "Enigma" (unpublished, 1920–1922). "Enigma" was Ford's first story written after he had changed his name in 1919, and it reflects his rural retirement after the war with the painter Stella Bowen and their young daughter, Julie. The mysterious man in "Enigma" who stares over the hedge at the farming couple, as well as their hurried and mysterious departure, may be associated with Violet Hunt's spying on Ford and Bowen in the summer of 1920. As in many episodes of *Parade's End,* Ford reverses the chronological sequence of events, beginning with Price's reactions to the departure and going on to what led up to it. This narrative method, thanks in large part to Ford himself, is now common, but it would have puzzled readers in 1920 and may explain why "Enigma" was never published.

"Nightmare" (unpublished, 1920s), set in New York, again dramatizes ignorance about the war in a bank clerk's wife who refuses to believe in his wartime heroism. "The Miracle" (1928) recalls the supernatural element of "The Colonel's Shoes" with a spiritual intervention that saves a young officer so that he can become a brilliant research scientist in the postwar world. Perhaps Ford's reversion here to the familiar narrative structure made this story more salable. Its present-day frame, however, is unconvincing; the young soldier's psychological reactions – fear, anxiety, horror, relief – in the re-created war episode are vivid and real.

By 1928, in spite of the critical success of the novels later combined in *Parade's End,* Ford was dividing his time between France and the United States in attempts to deal with publishers and find new markets. He had also begun a new relationship with an American, René Wright, the "René Katherine Clarissa David" to whom he dedicated *A Little Less Than Gods* (1928). He and Bowen parted amicably; Wright obtained a divorce from her husband, but Elsie Hueffer again refused to divorce Ford. Wright would not live with him without marriage, a situation that is probably the basis for the baffled relationship of Joseph Notterdam and Henrietta Faukner Felise in *When the Wicked Man.* Most of the unpublished "Honoria Mary Lalage" (1928?) reflects aspects of Ford's life, especially the realization by the aging rake, St. Aubyn, of the gulf in understanding between him and the younger generation. He makes, in fact, the common error of confusing their sexual freedom with his own sexual depravity. His horror at the heroine's supposed immorality reveals his double standard, but then, in an ironic turn, so does her assumption that, while she was in a faint, he must have seduced her. After both of them are undeceived, she at once arranges for a proper marriage.

The story is told in the third person, but its tone is that of a man who feels lonely, hurt, and unjustly denigrated. St. Aubyn has been publicly vilified for plagiarism about his contribution to the discoveries of a great antiquarian whose friendship St. Aubyn has subsequently lost. Translated into the field of archaeology, this situation fictionalizes the furious denials by Jessie Conrad and others, after Ford's loving reminiscences in *Joseph Conrad,* that Ford had played any significant role in either the literary collaborations or other parts of Conrad's life.

With the exception of "A Mascot" (1927) and "The Miracle," none of Ford's short stories written during the 1920s and 1930s were published. In part this can be ascribed to their innovative techniques. Ford as an editor published modernist writers such as James Joyce and Ernest Hemingway in the *Transatlantic Review* (January–December 1924), but commercial magazines were not so ready to accept his own short fiction. The method of "Honoria Mary Lalage," for example, is abrupt and disjunctive, impressionism developed into pointillism; its chronology is shifting rather than sequential, the motivation of its characters revealed in snatches of dialogue rather than in exposition, the comedy subtle and ironic, depending on misunderstanding rather than rapport. Ford's last stories were possibly attempts at a more popular appeal in an American market, but if so, they did not succeed. "Museeums" (1930s) is a peculiar, indeterminate story with alternative endings about two American lady curators. Displaying an excruciating lack of an ear for American slang, "Last Nickels" (1930s) deals with a female writer afflicted by writer's block. Updated from the Fathead stories, "Podmore's Brother" is a ponderous attempt at detective fiction, interesting only for its deliberate undercutting of all the rules of the detective story.

By this time Ford was applying his narrative methods to the writing of histories – personal, literary, geographic, and political – rather than to fiction, and his health, after a heart attack in 1930, was failing. With his last partner, the painter Janice Biala, he traveled frequently between France, England, and the United States and from 1937 to 1939 was writer in residence at Olivet College, Michigan, which in 1938 awarded him his only degree, an honorary doctorate of literature. He died at Deauville, France, on 26 June 1939.

Ford's major contributions to modern literature were his introduction of principles of European realism into his own writing, his literary impressionism as a reflection of psychological perception, his insistence on simple colloquial language, and his focus on characters and situations that faithfully mirrored the complexities of the contemporary world. His literary reputation, after some initial hostility and neglect, is now secure. *The Good Soldier* and *Parade's End* are regarded as modern classics, and critical reassessment in the last decade has recognized the significance of his poetry, travel writing, essays, and literary criticism. Rediscovery of his short fiction has been more delayed but is inevitable. In his short stories he initiated and frequently fulfilled his prime aim as a writer – which was, as he wrote in "Impressionism and Poetry" (1913), "to register my own times in terms of my own time."

Letters:

Letters of Ford Madox Ford, edited by Richard M. Ludwig (Princeton: Princeton University Press, 1965);

Pound/Ford: The Story of a Literary Friendship, edited by Brita Lindberg-Seyersted (New York: New Directions, 1982);

The Ford Madox Ford Reader, edited by Sondra J. Stang (Manchester: Carcanet, 1986; New York: Ecco, 1986), pp. 465–512;

Janis and Richard Londraville, "A Portrait of Ford Madox Ford: Unpublished Letters from the Ford-Foster Friendship," *English Literature in Transition 1880-1920,* 33, no. 2 (1990): 181–207.

Bibliographies:

David Dow Harvey, *Ford Madox Ford 1873–1939: A Bibliography of Works and Criticism* (Princeton: Princeton University Press, 1962);

Linda Tamkin, "A Secondary Source Bibliography on Ford Madox Ford, 1962–1979," *Bulletin of Bibliography,* 38 (January–March 1981): 20–25;

Rita Malenczyk, "A Secondary Source Bibliography on Ford Madox Ford, 1979–1985," *Antaeus,* 56 (1986): 231–244;

Michael Longrie, "A Secondary Source Bibliography on Ford Madox Ford, 1985–1988," *Contemporary Literature,* 30 (Summer 1989): 328–333.

Biographies:

Douglas Goldring, *The Last Pre-Raphaelite* (London: MacDonald, 1948); republished as *Trained for Genius* (New York: Dutton, 1949);

Frank MacShane, *The Life and Work of Ford Madox Ford* (New York: Horizon, 1965);

Arthur Mizener, *The Saddest Story: A Biography of Ford Madox Ford* (New York: World, 1971);

Thomas C. Moser, *The Life in the Fiction of Ford Madox Ford* (Princeton: Princeton University Press, 1980);

Alan Judd, *Ford Madox Ford* (London: Collins, 1990; Cambridge, Mass.: Harvard University Press, 1991).

References:

Stella Bowen, *Drawn from Life* (London: Collins, 1941);

Malcolm Bradbury, "Virginia Woolf and Ford Madox Ford: Two Styles of Modernity," in his *Possibilities: Essays on the State of the Novel* (London: Oxford University Press, 1973), pp. 121–139;

Raymond Brebach, *Joseph Conrad, Ford Madox Ford and the Making of Romance* (Ann Arbor: UMI Research Press, 1985);

Richard A. Cassell, *Ford Madox Ford: A Study of His Novels* (Baltimore: Johns Hopkins University Press, 1961);

Cassell, ed., *Ford Madox Ford: Modern Judgements* (London: Macmillan, 1972);

Contemporary Literature, 30, no. 2 (1989): 167–334;

Nicholas Delbanco, *Group Portrait* (New York: Morrow, 1982);

Avrom Fleishman, "The Genre of *The Good Soldier:* Ford's Comic Mastery," in *British Novelists Since 1900,* edited by Jack I. Biles (New York: AMS Press, 1987), pp. 41–53;

Douglas Goldring, *South Lodge: Reminiscences of Violet Hunt, Ford Madox Ford and the "English Review" Circle* (London: Constable, 1943);

Ambrose Gordon, *The Invisible Tent: The War Novels of Ford Madox Ford* (Austin: University of Texas Press, 1964);

Robert Green, *Ford Madox Ford: Prose and Politics* (Cambridge: Cambridge University Press, 1981);

Joan Hardwick, *An Immodest Violet: The Life of Violet Hunt* (London: Deutsch, 1990);

Violet Hunt, *The Flurried Years* (London: Hurst, 1926); republished as *I Have This to Say* (New York: Boni, 1926);

R. W. Lid, *Ford Madox Ford: The Essence of His Art* (Berkeley: University of California Press, 1964);

Frank MacShane, *Ford Madox Ford: The Critical Heritage* (London & Boston: Routledge, 1972);

John A. Meixner, *Ford Madox Ford's Novels: A Critical Study* (Minneapolis: University of Minnesota Press, 1962);

John Hope Morey, *Joseph Conrad and Ford Madox Ford: A Study in Collaboration* (Ithaca, N.Y.: Cornell University Press, 1960);

Bernard J. Poli, *Ford Madox Ford and the Transatlantic Review* (Syracuse, N.Y.: Syracuse University Press, 1967);

Robert Secor and Marie Secor, eds., *The Return of the Good Soldier: Ford Madox Ford and Violet Hunt's 1917 Diary* (Victoria, B.C.: University of Victoria Press, 1983);

Juliet Soskice, *Chapters from Childhood* (London: Selwyn, 1921);

Sondra J. Stang, *Ford Madox Ford* (New York: Ungar, 1977);

Stang, ed., *The Presence of Ford Madox Ford* (Philadelphia: University of Pennsylvania Press, 1981);

Paul L. Wiley, *Novelist of Three Worlds* (Syracuse, N.Y.: Syracuse University Press, 1962).

Papers:

The most comprehensive collection is the Ford Collection, Olin Library, Cornell University. This includes the papers of Katharine Lamb (Ford's daughter), Violet Hunt, Stella Bowen, and Julia Loewe (Ford's daughter), and Janice Biala Brustlein. Other manuscripts are held by the University of Chicago Library; the Columbia University Library; the Huntington Library; the New York Public Library; the Northwestern University Library; the Penn State University Library; the Princeton University Library; the State University of New York at Buffalo Library; the Harry Ransom Humanities Research Center, University of Texas at Austin; and the Yale University Library.

E. M. Forster

(1 January 1879 – 7 June 1970)

Carroll Viera
Tennessee Tech University

See also the Forster entries in *DLB 34: British Novelists, 1890–1929: Traditionalists*; *DLB 98: Modern British Essayists, First Series*; and *DS 10: The Bloomsbury Group*.

BOOKS: *Where Angels Fear to Tread* (Edinburgh & London: Blackwood, 1905; New York: Knopf, 1920);

The Longest Journey (Edinburgh & London: Blackwood, 1907; New York: Knopf, 1922);

A Room with a View (London: Arnold, 1908; New York & London: Putnam, 1911);

Howards End (London: Arnold, 1910; New York: Putnam, 1910);

The Celestial Omnibus, and Other Stories (London: Sidgwick & Jackson, 1911; New York: Knopf, 1923);

The Story of the Siren (Richmond, Surrey: Hogarth Press, 1920);

The Government of Egypt: Recommendations by a Committee of the International Section of the Labour Research Department, with Notes on Egypt (London: Labour Research Department, 1921);

Alexandria: A History and a Guide (Alexandria: Whitehead Morris, 1922; Garden City, N.Y.: Doubleday Anchor, 1961);

Pharos and Pharillon (Richmond, Surrey: Hogarth Press, 1923; New York: Knopf, 1923);

A Passage to India (London: Arnold, 1924; New York: Harcourt, Brace, 1924);

Anonymity: An Enquiry (London: Hogarth Press, 1925);

Aspects of the Novel (London: Arnold, 1927; New York: Harcourt, Brace, 1927);

The Eternal Moment, and Other Stories (London: Sidgwick & Jackson, 1928; New York: Harcourt, Brace, 1928);

A Letter to Madam Blanchard (London: Hogarth Press, 1931); New York: Harcourt, Brace, 1932);

Sinclair Lewis Interprets America (Cambridge, Mass.: Harvard University Press, 1932);

E. M. Forster, 1950

Goldsworthy Lowes Dickinson (London: Arnold, 1934; New York: Harcourt, Brace, 1934);

Abinger Harvest (London: Arnold, 1936; New York: Harcourt, Brace, 1936);

Reading as Usual (Tottenham, U.K., 1939);

What I Believe (London: Hogarth Press, 1939);

Nordic Twilight (London: Macmillan, 1940);

England's Pleasant Land: A Pageant Play (London: Hogarth Press, 1940);

Virginia Woolf: The Rede Lecture (Cambridge: Cambridge University Press, 1942); republished as *Virginia Woolf* (New York: Harcourt, Brace, 1942);

The Development of English Prose between 1918 and 1939 (Glasgow: Jackson, 1945);

The Collected Tales of E. M. Forster (New York: Knopf, 1947); republished as *Collected Short Stories of E. M. Forster* (London: Sidgwick & Jackson, 1948);

Two Cheers for Democracy (London: Arnold, 1951; New York: Harcourt, Brace, 1951);

Desmond MacCarthy (N.p.: Mill House, 1952);

The Hill of Devi: Being Letters from Dewas State Senior (London: Arnold, 1953; New York: Harcourt, Brace, 1953);

Battersea Rise (New York: Harcourt, Brace, 1955);

Marianne Thornton, 1797–1887: A Domestic Biography (London: Arnold, 1956; New York: Harcourt, Brace, 1956);

Maurice (London: Arnold, 1971; New York: Norton, 1971);

"Albergo Empedocle," and Other Writings, edited by George H. Thomson (New York: Liveright, 1971);

The Life to Come, and Other Stories (London: Arnold, 1972); republished as *The Life to Come, and Other Short Stories* (New York: Norton, 1972);

The Manuscript of Howards End, edited by Oliver Stallybrass (London: Arnold, 1973; New York: Holmes & Meier, 1978);

The Lucy Novels: Early Sketches for A Room with a View, edited by Stallybrass (London: Arnold, 1977; New York: Holmes & Meier, 1979);

The Manuscripts of A Passage to India, edited by Stallybrass (London: Arnold, 1978; New York: Holmes & Meier, 1979);

Commonplace Book, facsimile edition (London: Scolar Press, 1978);

Arctic Summer, and Other Fiction, edited by Elizabeth Heine and Stallybrass (London: Arnold, 1980; New York: Holmes & Meier, 1981);

The Hill of Devi, and Other Indian Writings, edited by Heine (London: Arnold, 1983; New York: Holmes & Meier, 1983);

Commonplace Book, edited by Philip Gardner (Stanford: Stanford University Press, 1985).

Collection: *The Abinger Edition of E. M. Forster,* 13 volumes, edited by Oliver Stallybrass and Elizabeth Heine (London: Arnold, 1972–1984; New York: Holmes & Meier, 1972–1984).

OTHER: George Crabbe Jr., *The Life of George Crabbe,* introduction by Forster (London: Oxford University Press, 1932);

Benjamin Britten, *Billy Budd: An Opera in Four Acts,* libretto by Forster and Eric Crozier (London, New York, Toronto, Sydney, Cape Town, Buenos Aires, Paris & Bonn: Boosey & Hawkes, 1951).

Edward Morgan Forster, though best known as a novelist, also distinguished himself in other genres, including the short story. His first collection of stories as well as four of his six novels appeared between 1905 and 1911, his most prolific years as a writer of fiction. This period also included his writing of a posthumously published novel about homosexual relationships; his last novel, *A Passage to India,* was published more than a decade later in 1924, followed in 1928 by the appearance of his second collection of stories.

Though Forster's earlier novels, especially *Howards End* (1910), received favorable reviews, *A Passage to India* secured his position as a major modern writer and inspired important scholarly studies of his fiction. After completing this most acclaimed novel, Forster turned increasingly to nonfiction, though he also wrote but did not publish stories with homosexual themes. During the last two decades of his life he was often called England's greatest living novelist.

Forster was born 1 January 1879 to Edward Morgan Llewellyn Forster and Alice Whichelo Forster. His father died in October of the following year, and Forster's childhood was dominated by his mother, with whom he lived for most of his life, and by his maternal grandmother. His father's sister, Marianne Thornton, also influenced him, especially through a legacy that made possible his education at King's College, Cambridge, where he matriculated in 1897. This legacy also made possible his extensive travels and provided him with a comfortable living that allowed him to write. His experience at King's contrasted with his unhappy early schooling, and he flourished in the company of dons such as Oscar Browning, Goldsworthy Lowes Dickinson, and Nathaniel Wedd. A fourth friend, a fellow student named H. O. Meredith, sponsored Forster's membership in The Apostles, a society whose distinguished membership had included such Victorian forebears as Alfred Tennyson and Arthur Henry Hallam. In addition, Meredith apparently elicited Forster's first intimations of his homosexual orientation.

After graduating in 1901, Forster traveled widely during the next twenty years. Two extended trips to Europe, the first from October 1901 to September 1902 and the second from March through August 1903, inspired his first and third novels, as well as some of his early stories – including "The Story of a Panic," which grew out of a walk near Ravello in May 1902.

Forster had begun and abandoned a novel during his university years, but in retrospect he identified "The Story of a Panic" as his first attempt at fiction. It appeared initially in the June 1904 issue of the *Independent Review,* a liberal publication founded the previous year as a forum for free discussion of the humanities and sciences. The *Church Times* called the tale foolish, but when it was reissued in Forster's first collection of short fiction, *The Celestial Omnibus, and Other Stories* (1911), the *Cambridge Review* considered the story superior to his first two novels.

As a prototype of the fiction that followed, "The Story of a Panic" merits close attention. Like much of the later fiction, it focuses on an upper-middle-class male who is jolted out of his complacency. Eustace, the adolescent protagonist, is vacationing in Ravello with relatives and their friends. When he and his companions enter the woods for a picnic, the artist in their company bemoans the absence of the Nereids, the Oreads, and Pan, and the curate concurs that "Pan is dead."

But a wind terrifies the group and sends everyone except Eustace fleeing down the hill. When his party returns to look for him, they find him lying quietly in the grass. The goat hoofprints nearby imply that he has encountered Pan, an encounter that transforms him into a celebrant of nature who runs through the woods, scampers down the path "like a goat," and kisses an old woman he meets on the road. Back in Ravello, he astounds his companions by leaping into the arms of Gennaro, a young Italian waiter.

That night the narrator hears Eustace singing and praising nature in the garden. When the boy refuses to come inside, the narrator bribes Gennaro to bring him back. Subdued and confined to his room, Eustace cries out; Gennaro rushes upstairs to him; and the two jump out the window. Eustace leaps over the garden wall, but Gennaro is mortally wounded.

Throughout his fiction Forster returns to the character types, themes, and narrative techniques of this story. His protagonists like Eustace, probably fictional representations of the young Forster himself, often suffer from apathy and isolation. As upper-middle-class philistines, they belong to a social class beset by avarice, superficiality, and arrogance. Surrounded by suffocating women, ineffectual and narrow clergymen, and pompous intellectuals, they are often exposed to a broader vision and an alternative life, the value of which eludes their acquaintances. The agent who has the potential to enlighten these characters usually comes from another culture – often Italian or Greek – or from the working class, two groups Forster romanticizes as more vital than the sterile philistines. The agent typically ignores or flaunts convention, but the precise nature of his influence on the protagonists is sometimes blurred, as it is in "The Story of a Panic," where both Pan and Gennaro affect Eustace in nebulous ways. The protagonists' crises become tests of character: such crises may transform their lives, as Eustace's does (though Forster fails to clarify the precise nature of the transformation); they may have little effect; or they may even precipitate violence, death, or destruction.

This story was one of the six chosen from ten submissions for *The Celestial Omnibus, and Other Stories*. Forster's work on these stories was mixed with work on his first four novels, which appeared in rapid succession: *Where Angels Fear to Tread* (1905), *The Longest Journey* (1907), *A Room with a View* (1908), and *Howards End*. All of this fiction elucidates Forster's favorite themes, which include the decadence, narrowness, and rigidity of the upper middle class, the vitality of the working class or foreigners, the cost of repression, the need for wholeness, and the restorative powers of nature.

When *The Celestial Omnibus, and Other Stories* was published in 1911, it was generally well received – although reviews ranged from wildly enthusiastic to unimpressed. The *Cambridge Review* (19 October 1911), for example, considered some of the tales among the "best stories of today," whereas the *Athenæum* (1 July 1911) labeled the selections "monotonous and facetious." The assessment of individual stories was equally uneven. The feature most consistently praised was Forster's use of classical myth, though a few critics found this material contrived.

The most enduring story of the collection, "The Road from Colonus," like "The Story of a Panic," had appeared in the *Independent Review* in 1904. Often acclaimed in Forster's own time, it is his only short story that continues to be frequently anthologized. For nearly a century most critics have regarded it as Forster's best short narrative.

Inspired by Forster's European tour of 1903, "The Road from Colonus" tells of an elderly Briton, Mr. Lucas, who is visiting Greece with companions who resemble those of Eustace – shallow tourists who have voiced enthusiastic platitudes over major attractions such as Athens, Delphi, and Thermopylae but who remain impervious to the beauty of Plataniste, a land of flowing streams and water gushing from a living tree. Mr. Lucas, like Eustace, is revitalized, but his salvation and dignity are stripped away when he is forced onto his mule and led away.

Home in England, Mr. Lucas becomes increasingly irritated by the sounds of running water, children, animals, and music, the very sources of his re-

Forster (second from right) in Rhodes during his 1903 cruise in the Mediterranean

newal in Greece. Months later when a parcel arrives from Athens wrapped in an old newspaper, Mr. Lucas and his daughter learn that almost immediately after they had left Plataniste, a blowdown killed the inhabitants of a little inn where Mr. Lucas had hoped to stay.

The title of the story, an allusion to Sophocles' play *Oedipus at Colonus,* provides a commentary on Mr. Lucas and his plight. In fact, one of the English tourists compares Mr. Lucas and his daughter to Oedipus and Antigone, and Plataniste to Colonus. The analogy is ironic: Oedipus travels *to* Colonus to meet release from suffering in a dignified death, but Mr. Lucas travels *from* a symbolic Colonus to suffer a slow decline in London.

The story contains many echoes of "The Story of a Panic." Again Forster portrays upper-middle-class English tourists as superficial and obtuse, and again he endows nature with regenerative potential. Here, however, his contrasts are more complex. Though the Greeks, like Gennaro, serve as foils to the English tourists, only Mr. Lucas idealizes them, and the details of the text both stress their slovenliness and place them, like

the English, apart from the natural beauty around them.

In addition, Mr. Lucas and his daughter are more fully drawn than the characters of Forster's first story. Forster presents as ironic what the daughter perceives as providential in her father's escape from death at Plataniste, but, in also portraying Mr. Lucas as childish and impractical and the inn and its inhabitants as unremarkable, he offers no alternative to the forcing of the protagonist from Plataniste. Greek drama pits fate against character, and through the complexity of this story Forster endows Mr. Lucas with tragic dimensions and raises more questions than he answers. Cruelly snatched from salvation and a merciful death, Mr. Lucas is condemned to a meaningless death-in-life, and his own role in this fate is ambiguous. Unlike Oedipus, he is forcibly taken from his Colonus and clearly cannot care for himself, but parallels between London and Plataniste may suggest that salvation does not depend upon place alone and that he is partially responsible for losing his inspiration. Or perhaps he is a pawn of fate after all, for as Mr. Lucas and his companions have played out their drama in Plataniste, an old Greek woman has sat relentlessly spinning on a balcony above them — a tacit allusion to the fates of Greek myth.

Four additional stories, all fantasies, complete Forster's first collection. Like "The Story of a Panic" and "The Road from Colonus," the earliest of these, "The Other Side of the Hedge," had also appeared in the *Independent Review* in 1904. Relying upon stock symbolism of a traveler who abandons the dusty road of conventional life for an Arcadian community, it reiterates Forster's conviction that embracing the unconventional life requires extreme effort.

Another fantasy, "Other Kingdom," which first appeared in 1909 in the *English Review,* again uses a title implicitly to contrast conventional and unconventional lives. In remaking the Daphne myth Forster transforms his vital heroine into a tree in order to protect her from her possessive, Midas-like fiancé. Another characteristic Forster indictment of the upper middle class, this story, however, is rare in its sympathetic portrait of a woman; most of Forster's women are suffocating and pretentious, perhaps unconscious permutations of the women who dominated his life.

"The Curate's Friend," previously published in *Putnam's Magazine* in 1907, shares with "Other Kingdom" a sympathetic treatment of a type of character that Forster usually excoriated, that of a clergyman. The narrator-cleric, who learns to celebrate nature through his contact with a faun, recalls Eustace. The clergyman also elliptically suggests that the faun has introduced him to homosexuality, an interpretation that a few early critics applied to Eustace's relationship with Gennaro.

"The Celestial Omnibus," one of Forster's best-known fantasies and most thoroughly anti-intellectual satires, celebrates the world of the spirit. First published in 1908 in the *Albany Review,* it follows the journey of a boy driven by Sir Thomas Browne to a world of rainbows, sunbeams, and great writers and their literary characters. The child infuriates his unimaginative father with his tale of fabulous adventures, but his father's friend joins the boy on his second journey. The adult, however, cannot imitate the boy's daring leap into the world of the imagination and plunges to his death in the rational world below the moving omnibus.

Forster's second collection of stories, *The Eternal Moment, and Other Stories,* appeared in 1928. Dedicated to T. E. Lawrence, this volume contains the last fiction Forster wrote, except for most of the surviving homosexual stories and his novel *A Passage to India.* By 1928 Forster had achieved wide recognition for *A Passage to India.* His reputation as a novelist and the excellence of his Anglo-Indian novel provided a standard against which his contemporaries inevitably measured this new collection of stories. Most critics regarded these stories as inferior to his first collection and to his most recent novels, *Howards End* and *A Passage to India.* The fact that this collection was less enthusiastically received than the previous volume of stories probably derives not only from its repetition — sometimes monotonous — of old themes but also from its position in Forster's chronology. Like the first collection, the second also evoked a diversity of critical reaction; and again almost every story was singled out by at least one critic as the best of the collection and by another as the worst. Most of Forster's contemporaries, however, preferred the title story, which had been written in 1904 and published the following year in the *Independent Review,* and later reviewers have shared such regard for it.

Another indictment of the upper middle class, "The Eternal Moment" tells of an author, Miss Raby, who returns to Vorta, a simple village that her first book has transformed into a tourist mecca overrun with commercialism. On her first visit an Italian porter had audaciously professed his love for her, an incident that had both insulted her and evoked the most intensely passionate feelings of her life. Now, twenty years later, she discovers that her handsome admirer has become an overweight, squalid, and avaricious concierge at an elegant hotel. Feeling responsible for the corruption of the village and the concierge, she tries unsuccessfully to rectify the damage by offering to adopt his youngest child. The concierge insults her once more, but she realizes that his presumptuous behavior as a boy had enlarged her vision of life.

Like "The Road from Colonus," "The Eternal Moment" is the only realistic story in a collection of fantasies, and it is also the most complex. Widely divergent views of Miss Raby's character and of her role in commercializing a peasant village demonstrate Forster's capacity for complexity in a way that his fantasies do not. Even the nature of the young porter is ambiguous, for though Miss Raby has always perceived him as genuinely passionate and sincere since his youth, her first traveling companion had perceived him as a womanizer. The perspective of her companion on her second visit is also important, for he contends that Miss Raby will try "to put right what never was right." Furthermore, the concierge is drawn in terms even less flattering than those describing the inhabitants of the inn at Plataniste in "Oedipus at Colonus." Nowhere does Forster indicate that Miss Raby has erred in rejecting his advances. In fact, in *Where Angels Fear to Tread* the disastrous marriage of a sophisticated British woman to a carefree variant of Miss Raby's porter serves as a gloss to this story that was published the same year as the novel.

Like Mr. Lucas, Miss Raby defies simple explanation. Forster berates the typical tourists, however, with his usual sneers. Conventional and shallow, they fail to appreciate the inherent beauty of Vorta, replacing the early morning bell with a dinner bell and putting an end to spontaneous peasant singing in the streets.

The other stories in Forster's second collection had all been separately published by 1920. "The Machine Stops," written in reaction to an early story by H. G. Wells and first published in 1909 in the *Oxford and Cambridge Review,* is Forster's only venture into science fiction. Despite its uncanny Orwellian prophecy of human dependence on technology and its frequent inclusion in anthologies earlier in the century, the story now seems dated.

Three additional stories in this collection, none fully successful, are set in whole or in part in an extraterrestrial dimension. "The Point of It," first published in 1911 in the *English Review* and disliked by Forster's friends, examines its protagonist's successful career, knighthood, and satisfactory if not exuberant marriage – mediocre accomplishments from Forster's perspective. The hero's equally undistinguished death, triggered indirectly by a blow to the head with a fish, sends him to hell, but he is redeemed by memories of his more passionate youth. "Mr. Andrews," which first appeared in 1911 in *The Open Window,* satirizes anthropomorphic notions of the afterlife and posits Forster's views of spirituality through a Christian and a Moslem who intercede for each other at heaven's gate and then reject the dull afterlife they have expected, choosing instead release into the world soul. "Coordination," first published as "Cooperation" in the *English Review* in 1912, attacks England's overly regimented school system, which Forster detested and had more fully denounced in his novel *The Longest Journey* (1907).

"The Story of the Siren" is an early story rejected by *Temple Bar,* according to a 4 March 1904 journal entry, and originally published by Virginia and Leonard Woolf as a Hogarth Press booklet in 1920. The narrator, whose dissertation falls into a grotto in the Mediterranean, hears a mythic tale that he claims has given him a glimpse of reality, although he reverts to a stance of self-assumed superiority to southern Europeans.

During the years that Forster published his best-known fiction, he also participated in other important activities. In 1902 he had begun teaching Latin at London's Working Men's College, and he remained associated with the college for twenty years. In 1906 he met Seyed Ross Masood, an Indian student in England whom Forster credited in *Two Cheers for Democracy* (1951) with exposing him to "new horizons and a new civilisation." Their friendship was refueled during Forster's visit to India in 1912 and 1913, an experience that intensified his awareness of class conflict and, he claimed, enlarged his own perspective. This trip also provided the impetus for *A Passage to India,* though not until after his second Indian visit in 1921 and 1922 did Forster complete this novel, his greatest work.

Forster also increased his ties with literati later known as the Bloomsbury Group, some of whom were also Cambridge Apostles. This former group, which included writers Lytton Strachey and Virginia Woolf, economist John Maynard Keynes, and art historian Roger Fry, celebrated individualism and truth and scorned convention and religion. Unlike most of the Bloomsbury writers, however, Forster was less experimental in his fictional techniques. A brief friendship also developed with D. H. Lawrence, whose letters describe Forster as "about the best of my contemporaries in England," but the friendship disintegrated in part because of dramatically differing personalities, attitudes, and sexual biases.

In addition to his literary circle, other significant associates included Edward Carpenter, a champion of homosexual rights whom Forster visited in 1913. Carpenter's companion, George Merrill, evoked Forster's unequivocal acceptance of his own homosexuality, and out of this acceptance came his posthumously published novel on homosexuality, *Maurice* (1971), almost universally regarded as a failure.

A year after World War I began, Forster went as a Red Cross volunteer to Alexandria, where he remained from November 1915 to January 1919 and where he discovered the poet Constantine Cavafy. Two books, *Alexandria: A History and a Guide* (1922) and *Pharos and Pharillon* (1923), resulted from this trip, their publications coming after Forster had returned to England in 1919 and in 1920 succeeded Siegfried Sassoon as literary editor of the *Daily Herald.* In October 1921 he returned to India as secretary to the maharajah of Dewas State senior, and letters and memories from this stay compose the bulk of *The Hill of Devi: Being Letters from Dewas State Senior* (1953). In the early 1920s he reviewed books for periodicals such as the *Nation,* the *Daily News,* and the *Athenæum,* and in 1927 he produced his *Aspects of the Novel,* which immediately became a standard work of literary criticism.

Despite his outpouring of nonfiction and the publication of *A Passage to India* in the 1920s, Forster was plagued by the failure of many attempts at writing following the publication of *Howards End* in 1910. In 1911 he began but abandoned a novel, "Arctic Summer," which was published posthumously in its yet-unfinished state as part of a collection titled *Arctic Summer, and Other Fiction* (1980). Shortly after abandoning work on this novel he also worked on two plays, "The Heart of Bosnia," which he completed but never published, and "St. Bridget," which he failed to complete. In a preface to *The Eternal Moment, and Other Stories,* he contended that his first two collections of short stories represent "all that I am likely to accomplish in a particular line."

Unquestionably Forster's homosexuality affected this pattern. In a well-known diary entry dated 16 June 1911, he complained of "Weariness of the only subject that I both can and may treat — the love of men for women & vice versa." At the same time, however, *Maurice,* which transcended these bounds, is inferior to Forster's novels of heterosexual love, as is most of his other homosexual fiction — which on 8 April 1922 he claimed to write "not to express myself but to excite myself."

These stories were initially kept secret and then shown to selected friends. Some appeared in Forster's final volume of stories, *The Life to Come, and Other Stories,* published posthumously in 1972, although Forster burned others. Only two selections in Forster's third collection of short fiction had previously appeared in print: "Albergo Empedocle," Forster's first published story that had appeared in *Temple Bar* in 1903, and the first section of "The Life to Come," which had appeared in both the *Listener* (23 December 1948) and the *New York Times Book Review* (6 February 1949). Either Forster (or his publishers) had judged the remaining materials to be inferior, or these works had dealt explicitly with homosexual relationships.

The earliest stories contain themes, character types, mythic elements, and structures that Forster had already fully explored. These include "Ansell," reminiscent of "The Story of the Siren" in its anti-intellectualism and probably composed in 1902 or 1903; "Albergo Empedocle," included among the submissions for the first collection but possibly omitted because of its homosexual overtones; "The

Purple Envelope," a tedious and confusing detective story with supernatural elements, a story that had been finished in January 1905 but rejected both by *Temple Bar* and by Sidgwick and Jackson; "The Helping Hand," a tale of plagiarism, of uncertain date (perhaps 1904 or 1905); and "The Rock," inspired by a trip to Cornwall, probably in February and March 1906.

Responses to Forster's final collection of short fiction and to its individual stories resembled the divergent responses to the earlier collections. A few reviewers found among these stories Forster's best writing. Others found the collection primarily of biographical and psychological interest, and still others argued that the collection should have remained unpublished. This divergence of opinion has persisted, but while critics dispute the value of this fiction, it comprises a body of material too sizable to ignore. Most, though not all, admirers of the stories with homosexual themes consider "The Life to Come" and "The Other Boat" to be the best.

"The Life to Come," the first of Forster's stories to deal explicitly with homosexuality, was written in 1922 and is the only one of these surviving stories written before the completion of *A Passage to India.* In this story missionary Paul Pinmay invites Vithobai, a wild young chief, to "Come to me in Christ," an invitation that results in a homosexual union followed by an ebullient reception of Christianity by Vithobai and his tribe. Overwhelmed by guilt, Pinmay retreats into his sterile religion and warns his impassioned admirer never to speak of their evening together.

Throughout the story Forster celebrates the vitality of primitivism and its corruption by the West. Industrialism follows in the wake of religion, and under the influence of colonialism a mining concessioner cheats Vithobai out of much of his land. As the forests are disappearing and disease is spreading, Vithobai is transformed from a noble savage into a "rather weedy Christian," although he retains a passion for Pinmay. Ten years after his conversion, Vithobai is dying of consumption spread by an imported laborer. When Pinmay visits him and reluctantly places his head upon Vithobai's frail body, the African strokes his hair and asks if they will find love in the life to come. Assured that they will, he stabs the missionary in order to send a messenger before him "to announce his arrival in the life to come."

While the story successfully examines the inseparable nature of religion and commerce in the colonial empire, it presents Vithobai as a vital alternative to staid colonial evangelists but then under-

Forster and T. S. Eliot in 1922 at Monk's House, the Sussex country house of Leonard and Virginia Woolf

cuts its force by suggesting that the impassioned African is ignorant and naive to the point of stupidity. While Vithobai is Forster's typical resident of another world (a Third World culture or a lower social class), he is also typical of Forster's homosexual lovers, whose casual encounters never offer a possibility for lasting relationships but mirror relationships that seem to have given little satisfaction to Forster himself.

"The Other Boat," another colonial tale, was inspired by Forster's first voyage to India, when the only Indian passenger had a cabin mate who threatened to throw him overboard. The opening pages, probably written around 1913, were published in England as "Entrance to an Unwritten Novel" and in America as "Cocoanut & Co.: Entrance to an Abandoned Novel." Forster finished the story in 1958. In it he underscores British Anglophilia, exposes the imperialists as weak (even the officers cannot withstand the heat of the Suez Canal region), and ridicules both the Christianity of a shallow clergyman and the Islam of a Lascar, who unknowingly prays with his posterior toward Mecca after the ship has rounded Arabia.

An Indian boy, Cocoanut, provides an imaginative contrast to these provincial characters and serves as a vehicle for enlightening the protagonist, Lionel, who becomes reacquainted with him years later on another boat on the Red Sea. Only after boarding the ship does Lionel learn that he must share a cabin with Cocoanut, who has secured passage for him after the cabins are fully booked. Though Lionel repulses the initial sexual pass from Cocoanut, Lionel makes the second advance, and the two soon become lovers engaged in a tempestuous affair. When Lionel finally decides to end their relationship, he strangles Cocoanut after a sexual encounter and then dives overboard. As in "The

Life to Come," the relationship between the two lovers is overshadowed by violence and superficial commitment.

The other two tales that involve homosexuality – "Dr. Woolacott" and "Arthur Snatchfold" – have frequently attracted both the admiration and the skepticism of reviewers. Forster wrote the first of these in 1927, and, considering it to be his best writing, he sent a copy soon afterward to T. E. Lawrence, who was also enthusiastic. Despite its title the story centers on Dr. Woolacott's patient, Clesant, rather than on the doctor himself. Confined to a languid existence, Clesant is redeemed by a passionate encounter with Death, who masquerades as a farm laborer; their union preserves Clesant from the living death suffered by Mr. Lucas of "The Road from Colonus" and from the partial existence that Dr. Woolacott's treatment would have allowed.

"Arthur Snatchfold," written in 1928, tells of a casual sexual encounter between Sir Richard Conway and Arthur Snatchfold, a young milkman. As a result of the encounter Snatchfold is arrested, but because he refuses to identify his partner, Conway is protected. This story of social protest against the harshness of Britain's laws against homosexuality assumes added poignancy in light of Oscar Wilde's imprisonment for homosexuality less than a decade before Forster began publishing fiction, although changing laws have also dated the story.

The most distinctive feature of the remaining stories of the collection is their attempt at pornographic humor. "What Does It Matter? A Morality," written in the 1930s, celebrates a politician's extramarital and homosexual affairs with his wife's blessing. In "The Classical Annex" the son of a prim museum curator is frozen into an eternal embrace with a male statue. "The Obelisk," written in 1939, recounts a sexual encounter with a sailor by a wife unaware that her husband is enjoying a similar encounter with the sailor's male companion, and "The Torque," possibly written in 1958, glamorizes homosexual rape and bestiality. One additional story in the collection, "Three Courses and a Dessert: Being a New and Gastronomic Version of the Old Game of Consequences," adds little to Forster's canon. A detective story with a surprise ending, this story was compiled by four authors, with Forster writing the chapter on the second course.

Forster's other collection of posthumous fiction, *Arctic Summer, and Other Fiction,* consists of portions of unfinished novels and stories of little belletristic value. Of the unfinished stories,

"Little Imber," begun in November 1961, is a science-fiction account of progeny produced from a homosexual union.

During the years Forster penned the fiction of *The Life to Come, and Other Stories* he was involved in covert relationships. Despite his early attraction to other men, however, his first full sexual encounter had not come until an episode with a soldier on the beach in 1916, followed by his first satisfactory affair the following year with Mohammed el Adl, a tram conductor in Alexandria. He later became associated with Harry Daley, a policeman who consorted with criminals; Bob Buckingham, another policeman; and other casual acquaintances among working-class homosexuals. Undoubtedly Forster's homosexuality exacerbated his anger at social and political injustice as well as his contempt for conventions, and it led to the stress his writing places on a need for wholeness and sexual fulfillment.

His public life, however, was very circumspect. He continued to write and speak, though he turned entirely to nonfiction. In 1934 he published a biography of Goldsworthy Lowes Dickinson, two years after Dickinson's death. The same year he contributed a regular column on social issues to *Time and Tide.* In the 1940s and 1950s Forster published reviews in the *Listener* and elsewhere, and in 1951 he co-authored the libretto for Benjamin Britten's opera *Billy Budd.* Forster also became noted for other activities. In 1932 he broadcast book reviews on the BBC, and in the 1930s he was also active in the National Council for Civil Liberties, for which he served as president for some years. Forster enjoyed the last twenty-five years of his life as a respected public figure, as his reputation, which had declined before the Second World War, rose again. In the 1940s he continued his BBC broadcasts on political as well as literary topics.

Aware and appreciative of innovation in literature, Forster credited Virginia Woolf and James Joyce with trying experimental forms that preserved a Victorian thoroughness in rendering character. Lesser writers, he commented in "The Early Novels of Virginia Woolf," were innovative in subject matter only: "They do good work, because everything is subject matter for the novel, nothing ought to be ruled out on the ground that it is remote or indecent. But they do not advance the novelist's art." The same charge may be levied against Forster's fiction, especially the short stories. Indeed it is no accident that his favorite author was Jane Austen, who, like Forster, exposed the foibles of drawing-room life – though with greater skill. Perhaps Forster's admiration for Austen also at least partially explains his legacy. Though admired by many modern writers – including W. H. Auden, Christopher Isherwood, and Katherine Mansfield – Forster, who focused on a society that was disappearing, has had minimal influence upon younger writers.

Following his mother's death in 1945 and the expiration of his lease in Abinger the next year, Forster resided for the rest of his life in Cambridge, where he had been appointed fellow in 1946. He also continued to travel, returning to India in 1945 and visiting the United States in 1947 and 1949 as well as Greece and Italy in the 1950s. He also published three significant books of nonfiction in that decade, *Two Cheers for Democracy, The Hill of Devi,* and *Marianne Thornton, 1797–1887* (1956). In 1960 he served as one of thirty-five expert witnesses in the obscenity trial of D. H. Lawrence's novel *Lady Chatterley's Lover,* which had been privately published in 1928 and republished in a bowdlerized version in 1932 before finally appearing in its unexpurgated form in that year of the trial. He died on 7 June 1970 following a stroke several days earlier.

Letters:

E. M. Forster's Letters to Donald Windham (Verona: Stamperia Valdonega, 1975);

Only Connect: Letters to Indian Friends, edited by Syed Hamid Husain (New Delhi: Arnold-Heinemann, 1979);

Selected Letters of E. M. Forster, 2 volumes, edited by Mary Lago and P. N. Furbank (Cambridge: Harvard University Press / London: Collins, 1983, 1985).

Interviews:

P. N. Furbank and F. J. H. Haskell, "The Art of Fiction: I, E. M. Forster," *Paris Review,* 1 (Spring 1953): 28–41;

William van O'Connor, "A Visit with E. M. Forster," *Western Review,* 1 (Spring 1955): 215–219;

Philip Toynbee, "E. M. Forster at Eighty," *Observer,* 28 December 1958, pp. 8, 10;

J. W. Lambert, "E. M. Forster at the Play," *Sunday Times,* 4 August 1963, p. 20;

J. H. Stape, ed., *E. M. Forster: Interviews and Recollections* (London: Macmillan, 1993; New York: St. Martin's Press, 1993).

Bibliographies:

Helmut E. Gerber, "E. M. Forster: An Annotated Checklist of Writing about Him," *English Literature in Transition,* 2 (Spring 1959): 4–27;

Maurice Beebe and Joseph Brogunier, "Criticism of E. M. Forster: A Selected Checklist," *Modern Fiction Studies,* 7 (Autumn 1961): 284–292;

B. J. Kirkpatrick, *A Bibliography of E. M. Forster* (London: Hart-Davis, 1965; revised, 1968);

John B. Shipley, "Additions to the E. M. Forster Bibliography," *Papers of the Bibliographical Society of America,* 60 (April–June 1966): 224–225;

Frederick P. W. McDowell, "The E. M. Forster Bibliography of Secondary Writings: Some Preliminary Observations," *English Literature in Transition,* 13, no. 2 (1970): 89–92;

McDowell, "E. M. Forster: An Annotated Secondary Bibliography," *English Literature in Transition,* 13, no. 2 (1970): 93–173;

Alfred Borello, *E. M. Forster: An Annotated Bibliography of Secondary Materials* (Metuchen, N.J.: Scarecrow Press, 1973);

McDowell, *E. M. Forster: An Annotated Bibliography of Writings about Him* (De Kalb: Northern Illinois University Press, 1976);

Paul and June Schlueter, "E. M. Forster," in their *The English Novel: Twentieth Century Criticism,* volume 2 (Athens: Ohio University Press, 1982), pp. 81–97;

Kirkpatrick, "E. M. Forster's Broadcast Talks," *Twentieth Century Literature,* 31 (Summer–Fall 1985): 329–341;

Claude J. Summers, *E. M. Forster: A Guide to Research* (New York & London: Garland, 1991);

J. H. Stape, "Further Additions to the Bibliographies of E. M. Forster and Virginia Woolf," *Notes and Queries,* new series 41 (September 1994): 373.

Biographies:

J. R. Ackerley, *E. M. Forster: A Portrait* (London: McKelvie, 1971);

P. N. Furbank, *E. M. Forster: A Life, Volume One: The Growth of a Novelist (1879–1914)* (London: Secker & Warburg, 1977); *E. M. Forster: A Life, Volume Two: Polycrates' Ring: (1914–1970)* (London: Secker & Warburg, 1978); republished as *E. M. Forster: A Life,* 1 volume (New York: Harcourt Brace Jovanovich, 1978; London: Secker & Warburg, 1979);

Francis King, *E. M. Forster and His World* (London: Thames & Hudson, 1978; New York: Scribners, 1978);

Nicola Beauman, *E. M. Forster: A Biography* (New York: Knopf, 1994).

References:

Laurence Brander, *E. M. Forster: A Critical Study* (Lewisburg, Penn.: Bucknell University Press, 1970);

John Colmer, *E. M. Forster: The Personal Voice* (London & Boston: Routledge & Kegan Paul, 1975);

Philip Gardner, *E. M. Forster: The Critical Heritage* (London: Routledge & Kegan Paul, 1973);

Judith Scherer Herz, *The Short Narratives of E. M. Forster* (London: Macmillan, 1988);

John Keith Johnstone, *The Bloomsbury Group: A Study of E. M. Forster, Lytton Strachey, Virginia Woolf, and Their Circle* (New York: Noonday, 1954);

Stephen K. Land, *Challenge and Conventionality in the Fiction of E. M. Forster* (New York: AMS, 1990);

John Sayre Martin, *E. M. Forster: The Endless Journey* (London: Cambridge University Press, 1976);

Frederick P. W. McDowell, *E. M. Forster* (New York: Twayne, 1969; revised edition, Boston: Twayne, 1982);

Norman Page, *E. M. Forster's Posthumous Fiction* (Victoria, B.C.: University of Victoria, 1977);

Barbara Rosecrance, *Forster's Narrative Vision* (Ithaca: Cornell University Press, 1982);

David Shusterman, *The Quest for Certitude* (Bloomington: Indiana University Press, 1965);

Oliver Stallybrass, ed., *Aspects of E. M. Forster* (New York: Harcourt, Brace & World, 1969);

Wilfred Stone, *The Cave and the Mountain: A Study of E. M. Forster* (Stanford: Stanford University Press, 1966);

Claude J. Summers, *E. M. Forster* (New York: Ungar, 1983);

George H. Thomson, *The Fiction of E. M. Forster* (Detroit: Wayne State University Press, 1967);

Lionel Trilling, *E. M. Forster* (Norfolk, Conn.: New Directions, 1943);

Alan Wilde, *Art and Order: A Study of E. M. Forster* (New York: New York University Press, 1964).

Papers:

The principal collection of Forster's papers is housed in the King's College Library of Cambridge University. Scripts of his BBC broadcasts are located in the Written Archives of the BBC. Additional material is at the British Library, the New York Public Library, Pierpont Morgan Library, and the Harry Ransom Humanities Research Center, University of Texas.

John Galsworthy

(14 August 1867 – 31 January 1933)

Shirley Laird
Tennessee Technological University

See also the Galsworthy entries in *DLB 10: Modern British Dramatists, 1900–1945, Part 1; DLB 34: British Novelists, 1890–1929: Traditionalists;* and *DLB 98: Modern British Essayists, First Series.*

BOOKS: *From the Four Winds,* as John Sinjohn (London: Unwin, 1897);

Jocelyn, as Sinjohn (London: Duckworth, 1898); as Galsworthy (Saint Clair Shores, Mich.: Scholarly Press, 1972);

Villa Rubein: A Novel, as Sinjohn (London: Duckworth, 1900);

A Man of Devon, as Sinjohn (Edinburgh & London: Blackwood, 1901);

The Island Pharisees (London: Heinemann, 1904);

The Man of Property (London: Heinemann, 1906; New York & London: Putnam, 1909);

The Country House (London: Heinemann, 1907; New York & London: Putnam, 1907);

A Commentary (London: Richards, 1908; New York & London: Putnam, 1908);

Fraternity (London: Heinemann, 1909; New York & London: Putnam, 1909);

Plays: The Silver Box; Joy; Strife (London: Duckworth, 1909);

A Justification of the Censorship of Plays (London: Heinemann, 1909);

Justice: A Tragedy in Four Acts (London: Duckworth, 1910; New York: Scribners, 1910);

A Motley (London: Heinemann, 1910; New York: Scribners, 1910);

The Spirit of Punishment (London: Humanitarian League, 1910);

"Gentles, Let Us Rest": Reprinted from "The Nation" (London: National Union of Women's Suffrage Societies, 1910?);

The Patrician (London: Heinemann, 1911; New York: Scribners, 1911);

The Little Dream: An Allegory in Six Scenes (London: Duckworth, 1911; New York: Scribners, 1911);

John Galsworthy

For Love of Beasts (London: Animals' Friend Society, 1912);

The Pigeon: A Fantasy in Three Acts (London: Duckworth, 1912; New York: Scribners, 1912);

Moods, Songs, and Doggerels (New York: Scribners, 1912; London: Heinemann, 1912);

The Inn of Tranquility: Studies and Essays (New York: Scribners, 1912; London: Heinemann, 1912);

The Eldest Son: A Domestic Drama in Three Acts (London: Duckworth, 1912; New York: Scribners, 1912);

The Fugitive: A Play in Four Acts (London: Duckworth, 1913; New York: Scribners, 1914);

The Dark Flower (London: Heinemann, 1913; New York: Scribners, 1913);

The Slaughter of Animals for Food (London: Royal Society for the Prevention of Cruelty to Animals/Council of Justice to Animals, 1913);

Treatment of Animals: Being a Speech Delivered at the Kensington Town Hall on December 15, 1913, at a Meeting Called to Protest against Cruelties to Performing Animals (London: Animals' Friend Society, 1913);

The Mob: A Play in Four Acts (London: Duckworth, 1914; New York: Scribners, 1914);

Memories (London: Heinemann / New York: Scribners, 1914);

Some Slings and Arrows, edited by Elsie E. Morton (London: E. Mathews, 1914);

The Little Man, and Other Satires (New York: Scribners, 1915; London: Heinemann, 1915);

A Bit o' Love: A Play in Three Acts (London: Duckworth, 1915; New York: Scribners, 1915);

The Freelands (London: Heinemann, 1915; New York: Scribners, 1915);

A Sheaf (New York: Scribners, 1916; London: Heinemann, 1916);

"Your Christmas Dinner is Served!" (London: National Committee for Relief in Belgium, 1916);

Beyond (New York: Scribners, 1917; London: Heinemann, 1917);

The Land: A Plea (London: Allen & Unwin, 1918);

Five Tales (New York: Scribners, 1918; London: Heinemann, 1918);

Another Sheaf (London: Heinemann, 1919; New York: Scribners, 1919);

The Burning Spear: Being the Experiences of Mr. John Lavender in Time of War, as A. R. P-M (London: Chatto & Windus, 1919); as Galsworthy (New York: Scribners, 1923);

Addresses in America (New York: Scribners, 1919; London: Heinemann, 1919);

Saint's Progress (New York: Scribners, 1919; London: Heinemann, 1919);

Tatterdemalion (London: Heinemann, 1920; New York: Scribners, 1920);

The Foundations: An Extravagant Play in Three Acts (London: Duckworth, 1920; New York: Scribners, 1920);

The Skin Game: A Tragi-comedy in Three Acts (London: Duckworth, 1920; New York: Scribners, 1923);

In Chancery (London: Heinemann, 1920; New York: Scribners, 1921);

Awakening (New York: Scribners, 1920; London: Heinemann, 1920);

The Bells of Peace (Cambridge: Heffer, 1921);

To Let (New York: Scribners, 1921; London: Heinemann, 1921);

Six Short Plays (London: Duckworth, 1921; New York: Scribners, 1921);

The Forsyte Saga (New York: Scribners, 1922; London: Heinemann, 1922);

A Family Man: In Three Acts (London: Duckworth, 1922; New York: Scribners, 1922);

Windows: A Comedy in Three Acts for Idealists and Others (London: Duckworth, 1922; New York: Scribners, 1923);

Loyalties: A Drama in Three Acts (London: Duckworth, 1922; New York: Scribners, 1923);

Captures (London: Heinemann, 1923; New York: Scribners, 1923);

International Thought (Cambridge: Heffer, 1923);

The Forest: A Drama in Four Acts (London: Duckworth, 1924; New York: Scribners, 1924);

On Expression (London: English Association, 1924);

Memorable Days (London: Privately printed, 1924);

The White Monkey (New York: Scribners, 1924; London: Heinemann, 1924);

The Little Man: A Farcical Morality in Three Scenes (London: Duckworth, 1924);

Abracadabra & Other Satires (London: Heinemann, 1924);

Old English: A Play in Three Acts (London: Duckworth, 1924; New York: Scribners, 1925);

Caravan: The Assembled Tales of John Galsworthy (London: Heinemann, 1925; New York: Scribners, 1925);

The Show: A Drama in Three Acts (London: Duckworth, 1925; New York: Scribners, 1925);

Is England Done? (London: Privately printed, 1925);

The Silver Spoon (London: Heinemann, 1926; New York: Scribners, 1926);

Escape: An Episodic Play in a Prologue and Two Parts (London: Duckworth, 1926; New York: Scribners, 1927);

Verses New and Old (London: Heinemann, 1926; New York: Scribners, 1926);

Castles in Spain & Other Screeds (London: Heinemann, 1927; New York: Scribners, 1927);

The Way to Prepare Peace (London: Whitefriars Press, 1927);

Two Forsyte Interludes: "A Silent Wooing" and "Passers By" (London: Heinemann, 1927; New York: Scribners, 1928);

Swan Song (New York: Scribners, 1928; London: Heinemann, 1928);

A Rambling Discourse (London: Mathews & Marrot, 1929);

Exiled: An Evolutionary Comedy in Three Acts (London: Duckworth, 1929; New York: Scribners, 1930);

A Modern Comedy (London: Heinemann, 1929; New York: Scribners, 1929);

The Roof: A Play in Seven Scenes (London: Duckworth, 1929; New York: Scribners, 1930);

Four Forsyte Stories (London: Heinemann / New York: Fountain Press, 1929);

On Forsyte 'Change (London: Heinemann, 1930; New York: Scribners, 1930);

Soames and the Flag (London: Heinemann, 1930; New York: Scribners, 1930);

Two Essays on Conrad (Cincinnati: Privately printed, 1930);

The Creation of Character in Literature (Oxford: Oxford University Press, 1931);

"Literature and Life": A Lecture Delivered April 13, 1931, at Princeton University (Princeton: Princeton University Press, 1931);

Maid in Waiting (London: Heinemann, 1931; New York: Scribners, 1931);

Worshipful Society (New York: Scribners, 1932);

Flowering Wilderness (London: Heinemann, 1932; New York: Scribners, 1932);

Candelabra: Selected Essays and Addresses (London: Heinemann, 1932; New York: Scribners, 1933);

Over the River (London: Heinemann, 1933); republished as *One More River* (New York: Scribners, 1933);

Author and Critic (New York: House of Books, 1933);

Ex Libris John Galsworthy, edited by Galsworthy and Ada Galsworthy (London: Heinemann, 1933);

End of the Chapter (New York: Scribners, 1934; London: Heinemann, 1935);

The Apple Tree (New York: Scribners, 1934);

The Collected Poems of John Galsworthy (New York: Scribners, 1934);

The Winter Garden: Four Dramatic Pieces (London: Duckworth, 1935);

Galsworthy in His Humour (London: Duckworth, 1935);

Forsytes, Pendyces, and Others (London: Heinemann, 1935; New York: Scribners, 1935);

Glimpses and Reflections (London & Toronto: Heinemann, 1937).

SELECTED PLAY PRODUCTION: *The First and the Last,* London, Aldwych Theatre, 30 May 1921.

John Galsworthy has earned an undisputed place in the history of the short story. A skillful and prolific short-story writer, he claims a place in the memories of freshmen for his much-anthologized short stories: "Quality," "The Japanese Quince," "The Apple Tree," and "A Stoic." Shortly before his death he was awarded the Nobel Prize for literature.

Galsworthy's childhood was privileged and prosperous. The second child of John Galsworthy, a London solicitor, and Blanche Bartleet, he was educated by a string of governesses until at the age of nine he was enrolled in school at Bournemouth. He was apparently happy at school, but not particularly noteworthy – a typical boy among other typical boys. Mr. Galsworthy decided that his son was to practice law, and the young man obediently, if not enthusiastically, studied for the bar. When an early love affair ended unhappily for Galsworthy, his father sent him to Canada to do some investigation for him. In 1892 Mr. Galsworthy sent his son abroad again – sailing to Australia, New Zealand, and the South Seas, where the young man gained extensive knowledge about ships and navigation. This was an important trip in other ways, for on this journey he made a good friend who became, according to Galsworthy, an important influence on his writing: Joseph Conrad, the first mate. Galsworthy enjoyed Conrad's tales immensely and immediately took a great liking to him. The two remained lifelong friends.

A year before this South Seas trip young Galsworthy had also met Ada Galsworthy, the wife of his cousin Arthur Galsworthy, at a dinner party. Having done much singing when he was in school, John Galsworthy had always had a good voice, and Ada had accompanied him in singing popular songs. After his return from the South Seas Galsworthy renewed his acquaintance with Ada and heard about her unhappy marriage to Arthur. The two were soon deeply in love. Ada, in fact, first suggested that he should write, and soon she was listening to Galsworthy's first writing efforts. Finally Arthur and Ada were divorced, and after ten long years of waiting, John and Ada were married in 1905, apparently living happily ever after.

Galsworthy admired short stories, a genre that he regarded as "one of the best of all forms of fiction; it is the magic vehicle for atmospheric drama. In this form the writer . . . comes nearest to the poet, the painter, the musician. The tale rises, swells and closes, like some movement of a symphony." Galsworthy's main concerns in his short stories are with love, hate, beauty, nature, injustice, age, poverty, and the treatment of animals. Most of his sto-

FROM THE FOUR
WINDS

BY
JOHN SINJOHN

LONDON: T. FISHER UNWIN
PATERNOSTER SQUARE, 1897

Title page for Galsworthy's first book, a collection of ten stories published under a pseudonym

ries are not tense, dramatic, or suspenseful; many are simply portraits or descriptions of moods.

It is not surprising, then, that Galsworthy began his writing career with short stories. His first book of short stories, *From the Four Winds* (1897), published under the pseudonym of John Sinjohn, was well received. Of more than forty reviews, most were enthusiastic, an encouraging start for Galsworthy's career. Yet near the end of his life in his Nobel Prize acceptance speech he referred to this collection as "that dreadful little book." He never revised these stories nor allowed the book to be republished, and he bought the remaining unsold copies. As a result the book was never republished and became valuable: in 1929 one copy was sold for $1,000 at a rare-book auction in New York. One of

the stories in the book, however, was included in a collection that Ada published in 1934 after Galsworthy's death. It is interesting because the main character is based on Joseph Conrad, Galsworthy's early acquaintance, strong supporter, and lifelong friend.

Although many collections of Galsworthy's short stories have been published, the major ones are *A Man of Devon* (1901), *A Commentary* (1908), *A Motley* (1910), *The Little Man, and Other Satires* (1915), *Five Tales* (1918), *Tatterdemalion* (1920), and *Captures* (1923). Many of his stories, sketches, and tales have been reprinted in various combinations. For example, *Abracadabra & Other Satires* (1924) contains the last five tales in *The Little Man,* and *Caravan: The Assembled Tales of John Galsworthy* (1925) collects some of his most impressive and best-known stories.

In 1901 Galsworthy published his second collection of short stories, *A Man of Devon,* the title piece of which is the least impressive of the four long stories comprising the collection. "A Man of Devon" is an epistolary tale, the letters being written by a detached observer, and Galsworthy's attempts to write dialect necessitate superhuman effort to read this story. The best in this collection is "The Salvation of Swithin Forsyte," a story about a man who — old, successful, and wealthy — is dying and contemplating his past. He recalls the girl he fell in love with many years ago but refused to marry because of his snobbery and her inadequate social graces. He had given her up but has never forgotten her and never found anyone else. Having lived a life without love, beauty, or devotion, he dies drinking champagne alone — a successful portrayal of the emptiness and waste of Forsyte's life.

"The Silence" is reminiscent of Conrad in its recounting the predicament of a sensitive and compassionate mining engineer abroad. Depressed by his job of sending men to work in unsafe conditions, surrounded by the dense jungle, and employed by uncompromising businessmen, he eventually commits suicide. Galsworthy exposes how relentlessly businessmen concerned only with profit destroy the humanity and lives of those who work for them.

"A Knight" is the tale of a chivalrous old man, a soldier who likes to talk about past glories. Long ago he fell in love, married, and then lost his wife to a younger man. When the wife dies and leaves someone else's child, the old knight nobly and responsibly strives to maintain the child. He is typical of many of Galsworthy's men who profoundly esteem and champion women, no matter what sacrifices the men have to make.

A Commentary includes twenty short, satiric sketches in which Galsworthy presents current concerns of a mechanized community to an audience of the young, rich, healthy, and privileged whom he criticizes and whose Edwardian fiscal policies he condemns. Story titles suggest Galsworthy's concern in each story: "A Lost Dog," "Old Age," "Fear," "Fashion," "Money," "Progress," "Justice," "Mother," "Child," and "Hope." Galsworthy had a kind and compassionate heart; nevertheless, his perspective is that of an affluent observer on an adventure from his plush environs to inspect and lament. On the whole the sketches are straightforward, general, and often overly sentimental.

A Motley collects twenty-eight stories written between 1899 and 1910, many of which had already appeared in journals and magazines. One of the previously unpublished stories, "A Portrait," is clearly Galsworthy's portrait of his father. In "The Consummation" Galsworthy obviously enjoys satirizing two of his friends, Conrad and Edward Garnett, both of whom had made occasional suggestions about his stories. In this somewhat autobiographical story an author, Harrison, publishes a book that receives good reviews and sells more than four hundred copies. When he then starts his next book, Harrison's friend, simply referred to as "the man of genius" (Conrad), makes suggestions about improvements. Yet when the book is finished, it sells fewer copies than the previous one. Laboring under the advice of both the man of genius and another referred to only as "the critic" (Garnett), Harrison produces still another book. Both the man of genius and the critic proclaim each of these last two books to be artistically better than their predecessors. In his final work, "The Consummation," the author eventually produces a book so artistically good that no one can bear to read it – and no one buys it.

A Motley shows development in Galsworthy's narrative proficiency, for he was learning how to pare the intricate plots of *A Man of Devon* and enlarge on the keen insights of *A Commentary*. By joining uncomplicated and plausible plots with perceptive examination of character and a more fluent and refined prose style, Galsworthy would eventually produce the masterpieces of *Five Tales*.

The Little Man contains two short plays, ten satiric sketches, and nine short stories. "Ultima Thule," the last story of *The Little Man,* illustrates Galsworthy's concern for the welfare of animals. It sentimentally portrays an aged musician who nourishes lost, homeless, hungry, and hurt animals rather than provide for himself. When he dies, one of his cherished birds also dies, falling right on his heart. The old musician is a spiritual descendant of Saint Francis of Assisi, and the account is one of Galsworthy's many memorials to soft-hearted and compassionate lovers of animals. *The Little Man* comprises a minor portion of Galsworthy's short fiction, but it anticipates the mastery of the stories in *Five Tales* and *Captures.*

In the first of these two Galsworthy reaches the peak of his expertise as a short-story writer. "A Stoic" and "The Apple Tree" from this collection are his two most frequently reprinted stories. Another beautiful story in this collection, "The Indian Summer of a Forsyte," links the first of his Forsyte novels, *The Man of Property* (1906), with the rest of those comprising the saga of this family.

"The First and the Last" is an emotional tale of betrayal and integrity, homicide and suicide. The younger brother of a prominent and remorseless lawyer has killed a man in defending a prostitute with whom the young man has been keeping company. The older brother, the lawyer, is concerned about his own prestige and attempts to help by hiding his younger brother's offense. When an innocent vagrant is convicted of the crime, the older brother happily intends to banish the young couple to Argentina, but the younger brother refuses to permit someone else to be executed for the murder he has committed. The lovers kill themselves but leave a note – which the older brother finds and keeps to himself. The two lovers have therefore died for nothing, since the vagrant gets the blame after all.

The conclusion of this tale is pathetic, as harsh and unethical men prevail. Particularly accomplished is the characterization of Wanda, the young prostitute. She is a poignant symbol of womanly defenselessness who, though a prey for abuse, preserves her integrity and is still capable of loving and caring about people. Galsworthy later rewrote this story as a successful one-act play, *The First and the Last,* a work included in *Six Short Plays* (1921).

"A Stoic" is set in Liverpool in 1905. As with "The First and the Last" and also "The Apple Tree," Galsworthy later turned this story into a play, in this instance a three-act comedy called *Old English* (1924). Again Galsworthy delineates a strong and unforgettable old man, Sylvanus Heythorp, an unprincipled, self-indulgent businessman who is the father of three children – one illegitimate, his favorite, and two legitimate. Both his wife and his mistress are dead, and as a widower he lavishes attention on the family of his now also-dead illegitimate son, for whom he grieves. His income being insufficient for him to maintain his standard

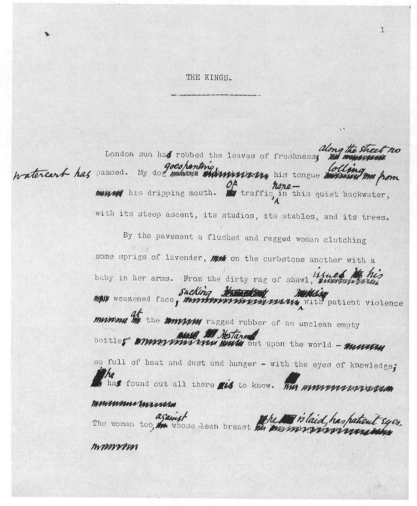

First page from the typescript for one of the twenty-eight stories and sketches collected in A Motley *(Lilly Library, Indiana University; by permission of the Estate of John Galsworthy)*

of living, Old Heythorp places himself heavily in debt to a creditor who hates him. The aged and haughty Heythorp eats a rich and elaborate last meal, goes happily to sleep, and does not awaken.

"The Apple Tree" is probably the favorite story of Galsworthy readers. The uncomplicated plot focuses on Frank Ashurst's return to the moors after an absence of more than twenty-five years. As a twenty-three-year-old student he had abandoned Megan, a seventeen-year-old Welsh girl whom he had met under an apple tree in a garden – and to whom he had proposed. His rejection of Megan has therefore symbolically betokened an offense against an edenic garden before the Fall. Ashurst, as a result, has lived an empty life whose beauty lies only in his memories of the past.

"The Juryman" is the story of Henry Bosengate, a happy and prosperous merchant who comes to realize how much he loves his wife. During World War I an army private is on trial for attempting suicide and thus robbing the king of a soldier. The private has been so unhappy in being away from his wife that he thinks his life is worthless. Sympathetic with the private, Bosengate convinces the other jurors to acquit him, and when he returns home, the merchant appreciates his own wife. The tender story suggests that most people are sympathetic and merciful and that it is possible to profit from the bad luck and misery of others in time to remember that the present is all that people have: it is important to care about people now.

Tatterdemalion includes the last of Galsworthy's war stories as well as others written after the war ended. The book is divided into two parts: "Of War-time" includes fifteen stories, and "Of Peace-time" includes eight. These stories are mediocre and do not exemplify Galsworthy at his best. Most deal with the fortunes of those at home and reveal their unrecognized heroism, loss, heartache, and patriotism. The lead sketch, "The Grey Angel," is often considered a companion to "A Portrait" in the earlier collection *A Motley,* since it seems to be a sentimentalized portrait of his mother.

In it an indomitable, aged English lady devotes herself to serving the wounded in France during the war. She is completely unselfish and regularly brings the injured French soldiers useless gifts that they esteem because of her kindness, generosity, and self-sacrifice. "Spindleberries," the first story in the second, peacetime part of the book, is a superb tale. It presents the story of two talented painters who are cousins. Alicia devotes herself to the study of beauty, lives an impoverished life, and is unconcerned about public acclaim. However, having devoted herself to beauty, she lives a rich and spiritually fulfilling life. Her cousin makes money and becomes a famous artist, yet he realizes that Alicia is a superior painter and, ultimately, a more successful person.

Captures comprises sixteen tales, the best of which is "A Feud." In this story two villagers quarrel about a dog that has been shot, their quarrel eventually resulting in the death of a son of one of the disputants. Only then does the grief-stricken father give up his hate: the price to bring peace to the two feuding families has been excessive. In "A Feud" Galsworthy illustrates that he can skillfully depict country farmers like those whom he had met through maintaining his country home. He is more successful in portraying members of village, agrarian society than he is in detailing the lives of the destitute and exploited in the metropolitan areas — with whom he had almost no connection but for whom he held much compassion.

In *Captures* Galsworthy again displays the mastery of the short story that he achieved in *Five Tales.* Galsworthy's peacetime views, however, were unlike those that he had embraced during the war. His stories became tempered, grew more romantic, and revealed a developing endurance for people's imperfections.

From *A Man of Devon* through *Captures* the themes and treatment of Galsworthy's short stories replicate those of his novels. In *The Man of Property* and *The Country House* (1907) sophisticated satires of thriving, moneyed members of society, he had reached his zenith as a novelist before World War I. *Five Tales,* which displays the height of his short-story skill, had appeared during the war. After the war had ended and Galsworthy continued the Forsyte chronicles, his interest in the short story had ebbed, and he never again demonstrated the short-story mastery he had shown in *Five Tales.*

Although Galsworthy was a skillful author in many ways, his short stories have several characteristics that make them less popular today than they had been in Galsworthy's time. His extreme sentimentality about many things, especially in his representation of women and the indigent, proves tiresome. Almost without fail his women are noble, loving, heroic, long-suffering and selfless — whether they be prostitutes, village girls, or ladies; whether they be young, middle-aged, or old; and whether they be rich or poor. Galsworthy was apparently unable to criticize women or portray them with even slight blemishes. The same is true of his depiction of male laborers, both urban and rural: most of them are unpretentious, articulate, self-abnegating, and noble. Nevertheless, Galsworthy's compassion for the poor and underprivileged was sincere, and he was one of the few to protest the unfair treatment many received from the government.

A final characteristic that may explain the diminished popularity of his short stories today is that they are mostly humorless, consistently solemn and somber. There are occasional light touches, such as in "The Consummation," but only a very few. The stories offer no escape from the serious problems of the world, for Galsworthy was determined to raise the social consciousness of his readers. His works now lie mostly unread, and, in contrast to the tremendous amount of scholarship that work produced earlier in the twentieth century, he is now the object of little attention. During his lifetime Galsworthy was much respected and esteemed, as his Nobel Prize for literature in 1932 attests. He was a prolific and talented writer admired by practically all, and his work was an important influence in the development of the short story.

Letters:

Autobiographical Letters of John Galsworthy: A Correspondence with Frank Harris, Hitherto Unpublished (New York: English Book Shop, 1933);

Letters from John Galsworthy, 1900–1932, edited by Edward Garnett (London: Cape, 1934; New York: Scribners, 1934);

Margaret Morris, *My Galsworthy Story, Including 67 Hitherto Unpublished Letters* (London: Peter Owen, 1967);

John Galsworthy's Letters to Leon Lion, edited by Asher Boldon Wilson (The Hague: Mouton, 1968).

Bibliographies:

H[arold] V. Marrot, *A Bibliography of the Works of John Galsworthy* (London: Mathews & Marrot / New York: Scribners, 1928);

Earl E. Stevens and H. Ray Stevens, *John Galsworthy: An Annotated Bibliography of Writings about Him* (De Kalb: Northern Illinois University Press, 1980).

Biographies:

H[arold] V. Marrot, *The Life and Letters of John Galsworthy* (London: Heinemann, 1935; New York: Scribners, 1936);

M. E. Reynolds, *Memories of John Galsworthy by His Sister* (London: Hale, 1936; New York: Stokes, 1937);

R. H. Mottram, *For Some We Loved: An Intimate Portrait of John and Ada Galsworthy* (London: Hutchinson, 1956);

Dudley Barker, *The Man of Principle: A View of John Galsworthy* (London: Heinemann, 1963; New York: Stein & Day, 1963);

Rudolf Sauter, *Galsworthy the Man: An Intimate Portrait* (London: Peter Owen, 1967);

Catherine Dupré, *John Galsworthy: A Biography* (London: Collins, 1976; New York: Coward, McCann & Geoghegan, 1976);

James Ginden, *The English Climate: An Excursion into a Biography of John Galsworthy* (Ann Arbor: University of Michigan Press, 1979).

References:

James Ginden, *John Galsworthy's Life and Art* (Ann Arbor: University of Michigan Press, 1987);

David Holloway, *John Galsworthy* (London: Morgan-Grampian, 1968);

Sheila Kaye-Smith, *John Galsworthy* (New York: Haskell House, 1972);

Herman Ould, *John Galsworthy* (London: Chapman & Hall, 1934);

Rudolf Sauter, *Galsworthy the Man: An Intimate Portrait* (London: Peter Owen, 1967);

Leon Schalit, *John Galsworthy: A Survey* (New York: Scribners, 1928; London: Heinemann, 1929);

J. Henry Smit, *The Short Stories of John Galsworthy* (New York: Haskell House, 1966);

Stanford Sternlicht, *John Galsworthy* (Boston: Twayne, 1987).

Papers:

The principal collection of Galsworthy memorabilia, portraits, letters, diaries, and manuscripts is in the Galsworthy Memorial Collection, established by Rudolf Sauter, Galsworthy's nephew, at the University of Birmingham in 1962. After Sauter's death much of this material was sold to an unknown buyer by surviving members of the family. Letters and manuscripts are held by the Houghton Library, Harvard University; the Bodleian Library, Oxford; and Scribners Archives, the Firestone Library, Princeton University.

Graham Greene

(2 October 1904 – 3 April 1991)

Neil Nehring
University of Texas at Austin

See also the Greene entries in *DLB 13: British Dramatists Since World War II; DLB 15: British Novelists, 1930–1959; DLB 77: British Mystery Writers, 1920–1939; DLB 100: Modern British Essayists, Second Series; CDBLB 7: Writers After World War II, 1945–1960;* *DLB Yearbook: 1985;* and *DLB Yearbook: 1991.*

BOOKS: *Babbling April* (Oxford: Blackwood, 1925);

The Man Within (London: Heinemann, 1929; Garden City, N.Y.: Doubleday, Doran, 1929);

The Name of Action (London: Heinemann, 1930; Garden City, N.Y.: Doubleday, Doran, 1931);

Rumour at Nightfall (London: Heinemann, 1931; Garden City, N.Y.: Doubleday, Doran, 1932);

Stamboul Train (London: Heinemann, 1932); republished as *Orient Express* (Garden City, N.Y.: Doubleday, Doran, 1933);

It's a Battlefield (London: Heinemann, 1934; Garden City, N.Y.: Doubleday, Doran, 1934; revised edition, London & Toronto: Heinemann, 1948);

England Made Me (London & Toronto: Heinemann, 1935; Garden City, N.Y.: Doubleday, Doran, 1935); republished as *The Shipwrecked* (New York: Viking, 1953);

The Bear Fell Free (London: Grayson & Grayson, 1935; Folcroft, Penn.: Folcroft, 1977);

The Basement Room, and Other Stories (London: Cresset, 1935);

Journey Without Maps (London & Toronto: Heinemann, 1936; Garden City, N.Y.: Doubleday, Doran, 1936);

A Gun for Sale: An Entertainment (London & Toronto: Heinemann, 1936); republished as *This Gun for Hire* (Garden City, N.Y.: Doubleday, Doran, 1936);

Brighton Rock: A Novel (London & Toronto: Heinemann, 1938); republished as *Brighton Rock: An Entertainment* (New York: Viking, 1938);

The Lawless Roads: A Mexican Journey (London & New York: Longmans, Green, 1939); republished as *Another Mexico* (New York: Viking, 1939);

The Confidential Agent: An Entertainment (London & Toronto: Heinemann, 1939; New York: Viking, 1939);

The Power and the Glory (London & Toronto: Heinemann, 1940); published simultaneously as *The Labyrinthine Ways* (New York: Viking, 1940); republished as *The Power and the Glory* (New York: Viking, 1946);

British Dramatists (London: Collins, 1942);

The Ministry of Fear: An Entertainment (London & Toronto: Heinemann, 1943; New York: Viking, 1943);

The Little Train (Norwich: Jarrold, 1946; New York: Lothrop, Lee & Shepard, 1958);

Nineteen Stories (London & Toronto: Heinemann, 1947; New York: Viking, 1949);

The Heart of the Matter (Melbourne, London & Toronto: Heinemann, 1948; New York: Viking, 1948);

Why Do I Write? An Exchange of Views between Elizabeth Bowen, Graham Greene, and V. S. Pritchett, by Greene, Elizabeth Bowen, and V. S. Pritchett (London: Marshall, 1948; Folcroft, Penn.: Folcroft, 1969);

The Third Man and The Fallen Idol (Melbourne, London & Toronto: Heinemann, 1950); abridged as *The Third Man* (New York: Viking, 1950);

The Little Fire Engine (Norwich: Jarrold, 1950); republished as *The Little Red Fire Engine* (New York: Lothrop, Lee & Shepard, 1953);

The Lost Childhood, and Other Essays (London: Eyre & Spottiswoode, 1951; New York: Viking, 1952);

The End of the Affair (Melbourne, London & Toronto: Heinemann, 1951; New York: Viking, 1951);

The Little Horse Bus (Norwich: Jarrold / London: Parrish, 1952; New York: Lothrop, Lee & Shepard, 1954);

The Living Room: A Play in Two Acts (Melbourne, London & Toronto: Heinemann, 1953; New York: Viking, 1954);

The Little Steamroller: A Story of Adventure, Mystery and Detection (London: Parrish, 1953; New York: Lothrop, Lee & Shepard, 1955);

Essais Catholiques, translated (into French) by Marcelle Sibon (Paris: Edition du Seuil, 1953);

Twenty-One Stories (London, Melbourne & Toronto: Heinemann, 1954); republished as *21 Stories* (New York: Viking, 1962);

Loser Takes All (Melbourne, London & Toronto: Heinemann, 1955; New York: Viking, 1957);

The Quiet American (Melbourne, London & Toronto: Heinemann, 1955; New York: Viking, 1956);

The Potting Shed: A Play in Three Acts (New York: Viking, 1957; London, Melbourne & Toronto: Heinemann, 1958);

Our Man in Havana: An Entertainment (London, Melbourne & Toronto: Heinemann, 1958; New York: Viking, 1958);

The Complaisant Lover: A Comedy (London, Melbourne & Toronto: Heinemann, 1959; New York: Viking, 1961);

A Visit to Morin (London: Heinemann, 1960);

A Burnt-Out Case (London, Melbourne & Toronto: Heinemann, 1961; New York: Viking, 1961);

In Search of a Character: Two African Journals (London: Bodley Head, 1961; New York: Viking, 1961);

A Sense of Reality (London: Bodley Head, 1963; New York: Viking, 1963);

The Revenge: An Autobiographical Fragment (Barnet, Hertfordshire, U.K.: Privately printed, 1963);

Carving a Statue: A Play (London: Bodley Head, 1964);

The Comedians (London: Bodley Head, 1966; New York: Viking, 1966);

May We Borrow Your Husband? And Other Comedies of the Sexual Life (London, Sydney & Toronto: Bodley Head, 1967; New York: Viking, 1967);

Modern Film Scripts: The Third Man, by Greene and Carol Reed (London: Lorrimer, 1968; New York: Simon & Schuster, 1969);

Collected Essays (London, Sydney & Toronto: Bodley Head, 1969; New York: Viking, 1969);

Travels With My Aunt: A Novel (London, Sydney & Toronto: Bodley Head, 1969; New York: Viking, 1970);

A Sort of Life (London, Sydney & Toronto: Bodley Head, 1971; New York: Simon & Schuster, 1971);

Collected Stories (London: Bodley Head/Heinemann, 1972; New York: Viking, 1973);

The Pleasure-Dome: The Collected Film Criticism 1935–40, edited by John Russell Taylor (London: Secker & Warburg, 1972); republished as *Graham Greene on Film: Collected Film Criticism, 1935–1940* (New York: Simon & Schuster, 1972);

The Honorary Consul (London, Sydney & Toronto: Bodley Head, 1973; New York: Simon & Schuster, 1973);

Lord Rochester's Monkey: Being the Life of John Wilmot, Second Earl of Rochester (London, Sydney & Toronto: Bodley Head, 1974; New York: Viking, 1974);

The Return of A. J. Raffles: An Edwardian Comedy in Three Acts Based Somewhat Loosely on E. W. Hornung's Characters in "The Amateur Cracksman" (London, Sydney & Toronto: Bodley Head, 1975; New York: Simon & Schuster, 1976);

The Human Factor (London, Sydney & Toronto: Bodley Head, 1978; New York: Simon & Schuster, 1978);

Doctor Fischer of Geneva, or the Bomb Party (London: Bodley Head, 1980; New York: Simon & Schuster, 1980);

Ways of Escape (London: Bodley Head, 1980; New York: Simon & Schuster, 1981);

Monsignor Quixote (London: Bodley Head, 1982; New York: Simon & Schuster, 1982);

J'Accuse: The Dark Side of Nice (London: Bodley Head, 1982);

Yes and No (London: Bodley Head, 1983);

Getting to Know the General: The Story of an Involvement (London: Bodley Head, 1985; New York: Simon & Schuster, 1985);

The Tenth Man (London: Bodley Head, 1985; New York: Simon & Schuster, 1985);

The Captain and the Enemy (London: Reinhardt, 1988; New York: Viking, 1988);

Yours, Etc.: Letters to the Press, 1945–1989, edited by Christopher Hawtree (London: Reinhardt, 1989; New York: Viking, 1989);

The Last Word and Other Stories (London: Reinhardt, 1990; New York: Viking, 1991);

A World of My Own: A Dream Diary (London: Reinhardt, 1992; New York: Viking, 1994).

Collections: *Three Plays* (London: Mercur, 1961);

Graham Greene: The Collected Edition, with introductions by Greene (London: Bodley Head/ Heinemann, 1970–   );

The Portable Graham Greene, edited by Philip Stratford (New York: Viking, 1973; Harmondsworth, U.K.: Penguin, 1977);

Shades of Greene: The Televised Stories of Graham Greene (London: Bodley Head/Heinemann, 1975; New York: Penguin, 1977);

Why the Epigraph? (London: Nonesuch, 1989);

Reflections (London: Reinhardt, 1990; New York: Viking, 1991).

PLAY PRODUCTIONS: *The Living Room,* London, Wyndham's Theatre, 16 April 1953;

The Potting Shed, New York, Bijou Theatre, 29 January 1957; London, Globe Theatre, 5 February 1958;

The Complaisant Lover: A Comedy, London, Globe Theatre, 18 June 1959; New York, Ethel Barrymore Theatre, 1 November 1961;

Carving a Statue, London, Haymarket Theatre, 17 September 1964; New York, Gramercy Arts Theatre, 30 April 1968;

The Return of A. J. Raffles, London, Aldwych Theatre, 4 December 1975;

Yes and No and *For Whom the Bell Chimes,* Leicester, Haymarket Studio, 20 March 1980.

MOTION PICTURES: *Twenty-One Days,* screenplay by Greene and Basil Dean, Columbia, 1937; released as *21 Days Together,* Columbia, 1940;

The Future's in the Air, commentary by Greene, Strand Film Unit, 1937;

The New Britain, commentary by Greene, Strand Film Unit, 1940;

Brighton Rock, screenplay by Greene and Terence Rattingan, Pathé, 1946; rereleased as *Young Scarface,* Mayer-Kingsley, 1952;

The Fallen Idol, screenplay by Greene, British Lion, 1948; rereleased, Selznick International, 1949;

The Third Man, screenplay by Greene, British Lion, 1949; rereleased, Selznick International, 1950;

The Stranger's Hand, screenplay by Greene and John Stafford, British Lion, 1954; rereleased, Distributors Corporation of America, 1955;

Loser Takes All, screenplay by Greene, British Lion, 1956; rereleased, Distributors Corporation of America, 1957;

Saint Joan, screenplay by Greene, adapted from George Bernard Shaw's play, United Artists, 1957;

Our Man in Havana, screenplay by Greene, Columbia, 1960;

The Comedians, screenplay by Greene, M-G-M, 1967.

OTHER: *The Old School: Essays by Divers Hands,* edited by Greene (London: Cape, 1934);

H. H. Munro, *The Best of Saki,* introduction by Greene (London: Lane, 1950; New York: Viking, 1961);

The Spy's Bedside Book: An Anthology, edited by Greene and Hugh Greene (London: Hart-Davis, 1957; New York: Carroll & Graf, 1985);

Marjorie Bowen, *The Viper of Milan: A Romance of Lombardy,* introductory note by Greene (London: Bodley Head, 1960);

Ford Madox Ford, *The Bodley Head Ford Madox Ford,* volumes 1–4, edited by Greene, with introductions in volumes 1–3 by Greene (London: Bodley Head, 1962–1963);

Victorian Detective Fiction: A Catalogue of the Collection Made by Dorothy Glover & Graham Greene, preface by Greene (London, Sydney & Toronto: Bodley Head, 1966);

An Impossible Woman: The Memoirs of Dottoressa Moor of Capri, edited, with an epilogue, by Greene (London, Sydney & Toronto: Bodley Head, 1975; New York: Viking, 1976);

Victorian Villainies, edited by Greene and Hugh Greene (Harmondsworth, U.K. & New York: Viking, 1984);

Paul Hogarth, *Graham Greene Country Visited by Paul Hogarth* (London: Pavilion, foreword and commentary by Greene, 1986).

SELECTED PERIODICAL PUBLICATIONS – UNCOLLECTED:
FICTION

"The Lieutenant Died Last," *Collier's,* 105 (29 June 1940): 9–10;

"Men at Work," *New Yorker,* 17 (25 October 1941): 50–54;

"Proof Positive," *Harper's,* 195 (October 1947): 312–314;

"A Drive in the Country," *Harper's,* 195 (November 1947): 450–457;

"The Hint of an Exploration," *Commonweal,* 49 (11 February 1949): 438–442;

"The Third Man," *American Magazine,* 147 (March 1949): 142–160;

"Church Militant," *Commonweal,* 63 (6 January 1956): 350–352;

"Dear Dr. Falkenheim," *Vogue,* 141 (1 January 1963): 100–101;

"Dream of a Strange Land," *Saturday Evening Post,* 236 (19 January 1963): 44–47;

"Beauty," *Esquire,* 59 (April 1963): 60, 142;

"The Root of All Evil," *New Statesman,* 67 (6 March 1964): 360–364; also reprinted in *Saturday Evening Post,* 237 (7 March 1964): 56–61;

"Invisible Japanese Gentlemen," *Saturday Evening Post*, 238 (20 November 1965): 60–61;

"The Blessing," *New Statesman*, 71 (25 February 1966): 254–255; also reprinted in *Harper's*, 232 (March 1966): 91–94;

"Secret," *Vogue*, 149 (1 January 1967): 94–95, 144, 151.

NONFICTION

"The Middle-Brow Film," *Fortnightly Review*, 145 (March 1936): 302–307;

"Ideas in the Cinema," *Spectator*, 159 (19 November 1937): 894–895;

"H. Sylvester," *Commonweal*, 33 (25 October 1940): 11–13;

"Self-Portrait," *Spectator*, 167 (18 July 1941): 66, 68;

"The Catholic Church's New Dogma: The Assumption of Mary," *Life*, 29 (30 October 1950): 50–52, 55–56, 58;

"Malaya, the Forgotten War," *Life*, 31 (30 July 1951): 51–54, 59–62, 65;

"The Pope Who Remains a Priest," *Life*, 31 (24 September 1951): 147–148, 151–152, 155–156, 160–162;

"The Return of Charlie Chaplin, I.: An Open Letter," *New Statesman and Nation*, 45 (27 September 1952): 344;

"Indo-China," *New Republic*, 130 (5 April 1954); 13–15;

"Last Act in Indo-China," *New Republic*, 132 (9 May 1955): 9–11; (16 May 1955): 10–12;

"The Catholic Temper in Poland," *Atlantic Monthly*, 197 (March 1956): 39–41;

"In Search of a Character," *Harper's*, 224 (January 1962): 66–74;

"Return to Cuba," *New Republic*, 149 (2 November 1963): 16–18;

"Nightmare Republic," *New Republic*, 149 (16 November 1963): 18–20;

"Reflections on the Character of Kim Philby," *Esquire*, 70 (September 1968): 110–111.

Henry Graham Greene's father, Charles, became the headmaster of Berkhamsted School in 1910 when Graham was six years old, the year of his earliest morbid memories of encounters first with a dead dog, then with a suicide who slashed his throat in full view of the boy. But in his frequent recourse to childhood and adolescence throughout his fiction and nonfiction Greene would subsequently invest his school experience with the greatest morbidity. His father's situation as headmaster set the course of Graham Greene's life not so much in an orientation to intellectual endeavor as in the profound sense of betrayal he experienced when he left

the family quarters to become a boarder in 1918. Unusually sensitive to begin with, Greene suffered prolonged if fairly mild physical and verbal torture from the affluent (or moderately affluent, in this case) barbarians for which English public schools are notorious; by 1921 he had experienced a nervous breakdown and briefly run away. The episode resulted in his being treated through psychoanalysis, a still-novel therapy in which he would retain a lifelong interest (especially in dream interpretation). Fortunately his treatment lay in the hands of the untrained but immensely empathetic – and literary – Kenneth Richmond.

The period between Greene's adolescent breakdown and his commitment to writing was a fairly short one, as he was able to adopt a literary career at the age of twenty-five. Surely one reason that his work from young adulthood to the end of the 1930s is so obsessed with childhood and adolescence is that his own youth was the primary experience he had to draw on, and he understandably sought new experience quite voraciously, taking an ill-advised trip through Liberia, for example, in 1935. Greene's brief account in *A Sort of Life* (1971) suggests that he spent nearly four years at Oxford's Balliol College (1922–1926) in a state of perpetual drunkenness and survived his oral exams through the efforts of his tutor Kenneth Bell, a former pupil and disciple of Charles Greene. Norman Sherry's biography makes it clear, however, that Graham was more enterprising than he admits – editing the literary magazine *Oxford Outlook*, reading poetry on BBC radio, publishing a book of verse titled *Babbling April* (1925), and making contacts outside the university with the likes of writer Edith Sitwell.

At the same time, darker and more daring sides manifested themselves. After visiting his family (which included three brothers and two sisters) during a vacation from Oxford in 1924, Greene became hopelessly infatuated with the governess of his sister Elisabeth. Feeling acutely frustrated as a result, by adolescent dissatisfaction with himself, Greene began playing Russian roulette, according to the essay "The Revolver in the Corner-Cupboard" (1946). Whether real or imaginary, this brief flirtation with suicide served as an antidote for his boredom, which resulted not just from the frustration and powerlessness of youth but also from the restlessness he would suffer throughout his peripatetic life and would later self-diagnose as manic depression. He also dabbled in espionage, as he visited the Ruhr zone of Germany with Claud Cockburn during the violent French occupation and later as he visited Paris during his brief membership in

Graham Greene (photograph by Graham Wood, Daily Mail*)*

the Communist Party – an affiliation that would plague him when he tried to travel through the United States during the Cold War.

Greene met his future wife, Vivien Dayrell-Browning, shortly before leaving Oxford in 1925, and he began an intense courtship that precipitated his conversion to her religion, Catholicism, a year before their marriage in 1927. He held unhappy jobs at the British American Tobacco Company and the *Nottingham Journal* before landing a subeditor's position at the *Times* of London, where he advanced steadily from 1926 until the success of his first novel in 1929, at which point he became a full-time writer. His subsequent prolificness is apparent in his publications in various genres that appeared almost annually, well into the last decade of his life. Greene also wrote film criticism for *Night and Day* and the *Spectator* in the 1930s, worked for the British Foreign Office in Sierra Leone during World War II, and subsequently assisted with many screenplays of his fiction. (*The Third Man* [1950], his most enduring effort, was a film scenario from the start.) His

unwanted if not unwarranted reputation as a Catholic novelist dated from the success of *The Heart of the Matter* (1948), after which his earlier novel *The Power and the Glory* (1940) attracted greater attention. Greene's increasingly international political enthusiasms provided the background to many of his postwar novels, from *The Quiet American* (1955), on Vietnam, to *The Human Factor* (1978), on Cold War espionage.

Until the early odds and ends in *The Last Word and Other Stories* (1990) were published near the end of Greene's life, the earliest of his collected short stories was "The End of the Party," which appeared in 1929, the same year as his first novel; it concerns a morbidly sensitive child, not surprisingly, who dies from fear of the dark. Though Greene minimizes the significance of his short fiction, stories like "The End of the Party" actually provide a clearer insight than his novels into the impact of his early unhappiness and rebellion on his work. As one might expect from a writer who concentrated on the novel, in his introduction to the collected edition of his stories he professes to "remain in this field a novelist who has happened to write short stories." For novelists, Greene writes, the short story "is often a form of escape," and he professes to re-read his short fiction with little discomfort because such escapes, or even "escapades" and "snapshots," do not "drag a whole lifetime in their wake" — as his novels do. He adds, however, that in writing short stories "the surprises might not be so far reaching as in a novel, but they [are] there all the same."

This sense of the short story and its escapades bearing "surprises" befits the significance of Greene's short fiction to an understanding of his life and work, especially his politics. In light of interviews given near the end of his life, one finds in the short stories — particularly those Greene designates as his finest — a clearer confirmation than his novels afford of the importance of anarchism, a politics of surprise, to his sensibility. The narrator of "May We Borrow Your Husband?" (1967) describes "a song Edith Piaf used to sing, 'Je ne regrette rien,'" as embracing "a phrase that . . . is always sung or spoken with defiance." The story was published just a year before the May Revolution in France, when the phrase Greene cites was spray-painted on the walls of Paris by contemporary anarchists. His "prescience" regarding international politics is often remarked upon, but not the sort of anticipation produced by this emotional kinship with young rebels in Europe (including those in England, as the discussion of "The Destructors" below indicates). Though his undergraduate political forays were mild enough (and Greene actually opposed the General Strikers in 1926, when he worked at the *Times*), they did reflect a sense of indignation on behalf of underdogs of all sorts, the strongest, most genuine element of his fiction as well as his politics. Greene was one of those lifelong rebels politicized first and foremost by the constraints and hypocrisies imposed on the adolescent and young adult, whose resulting outrage at injustice kept him forever young.

His better-known political positions seem amorphous in sum total, as most critics find, precisely because of an essentially anarchist reluctance to adhere to any doctrine: his quixotic hope for a "reasonable accord" between Catholicism and communism (most fully developed in *Monsignor Quixote,* 1982) and his unstinting opposition to U.S. foreign policy do not add up to any commonly recognized ideology. Those stances were coherent enough in his interest in Latin America, in both liberation theology and leaders such as Salvador Allende, Fidel Castro, Daniel Ortega, and Omar Torrijos. But Greene's desire after his experience in Vietnam, in the 1950s, to "go to almost any length to put my feeble twig in the spokes of American foreign policy" (as he put it in an interview with Marie-Françoise Allain) suggests that to some extent his forays into Latin America were a case of the enemy of his enemy being his friend, as Greene once admitted.

In one of the last interviews before his death, he confessed to John R. MacArthur his uncertainty over politics in general: "ever since the age of nineteen I've been on the Left, but I don't know if it means anything or whether it's just my way of thinking. I think it means being against dictatorship. And it's against the extremes of capitalism, which I think is represented by the United States." (To illustrate how diffuse Greene's politics can be, he identified the United States with the superficiality and vulgarity of the "consumer society," a complaint established in Britain by F. R. Leavis, whose elitism Greene hardly shares.) In *The Last Word and Other Stories,* however, "An Appointment with the General" (1982) indicates that his professed uncertainty has everything to do with his dislike for those who are all too certain of their politics. The French editor of a "distinguished left-wing weekly" with a "tendency towards modish politics" could not be more smug, in delivering instructions to a correspondent on her way to interview a character based on Torrijos: "'The General, I think, could be a subject in your usual style. Suitable for your brand of irony. . . . [W]e wonder whether his socialism is not rather skin-deep. He is no Marxist certainly.'"

Even if reductive treatments of Greene as a "Catholic novelist" satisfy few any longer, his nebulous ideological identifications allow Bernard Bergonzi to assert that Greene "was never an explicitly political writer" because his "idiosyncratic" Catholicism stood apart from the "Marxist model" of other writers identified with the so-called Auden generation. Yet precisely in the 1930s Greene had formed a strong friendship with the anarchist (and art critic and novelist) Herbert Read while Read was producing the work collected in *Poetry and Anarchism* (1938). In that same year Greene published *Brighton Rock,* a novel with an anarchist sensibility that his subsequent comments on the character Pinkie Brown, in *Ways of Escape* (1980), make clear: "The Others have committed worse crimes and flourish. The world is full of Others who wear the masks of success. . . . Whatever crime he may be driven to commit, the child who doesn't grow up remains the great champion of justice." The evident political basis of this antiauthoritarian sentiment is inseparable from an obsession with childhood unhappiness, with innocence and its corruption, frequently noted by critics in Greene's work. The theme of corruption appears often in the early short fiction collected in *Twenty-One Stories* (1954), especially in "The Hint of an Explanation" and "The Basement Room." The latter story was transferred to the screen by Greene in 1948 as *The Fallen Idol*, his own favorite and certainly one of the best motion-picture adaptations of his work besides *The Third Man*.

This visceral antiauthoritarianism underlies and unifies all of Greene's political positions. The politics with which it makes most sense to identify Greene, therefore, is anarchism, and he has in fact left a considerable basis for this assertion. But Sherry's biography refers only briefly to Greene's relationship with Read and makes no effort to connect Read's politics (which go entirely unmentioned) to Greene's quasi-anarchist statements cited elsewhere in the book—statements such as Greene's observation that "it has always been in the interests of the State . . . to restrict human sympathy," and thus the artist must elicit "understanding for those who lie outside the boundaries of State approval." This is a significant lapse by Sherry, who often minimizes Greene's politics. Sherry does a fine job of expressing Greene's affinities with "the downtrodden everywhere," sympathies often recorded in characters hunted by the law and embodying memories of his own youthful persecution by other students at the Berkhamsted public school, where he suffered for being the headmaster's son. But something politically stronger may be said about Greene's insistence, in *A Sort of Life,* that "I belonged on the side of the victim, not of the torturers."

That such expressions betoken an anarchist sensibility was confirmed only in the last decade or so of his life. In an early essay on Read reprinted in *Collected Essays* (1969) Greene expresses admiration for *Poetry and Anarchism* but seems tepid at best about anarchism, or Read's anarchism at least:

> Anarchism means more to him than it ever will ever mean to his readers (in spite of that vigorous and sometimes deeply moving book, *Poetry and Anarchism*) — sometimes we suspect that it means little more to him than an attempt to show his Marxist critics that he too is a political animal.

These comments were published in 1941, when Greene had just moved more completely into religious issues with *The Power and the Glory* and may have left behind some of his political preoccupations of the 1930s. At the very least, the war understandably had replaced the social inequity of the

Depression as his primary secular concern. Much later, after his extensive, renewed engagement with politics in the postwar era, Greene offered a more positive if qualified endorsement of anarchism when asked by Allain about it as a matter of express politics:

> That depends on what you mean. One of my great friends, Herbert Read, was an anarchist. For him, anarchy meant reducing a system of government to its smallest possible entity. . . . I don't think one can achieve a total elimination of centralization. In that sense I'm not an anarchist. I, like most of us, am against the abuse of power while recognizing the necessity for a minimum of power. One is always opposed to the abuses of a Franco or of a Lenin.

But near the end of his life during an interview conducted for French television by Bernard Violet, Greene was only mildly reluctant to designate himself an anarchist and declared that he had always followed the footsteps of Read in the beliefs that power must be exercised as close to the people as possible and the power of the central government reduced.

In his last days, therefore, Greene saw fit to acknowledge explicitly the anarchist tendency in his politics and work. But that tendency should have been obvious all along, especially in readings of his short fiction. In fact, the four short stories of which Greene says, in his introduction to the *Collected Stories* (1972), "I have never written anything better" — "The Destructors" and "A Chance for Mr Lever" in *Twenty-One Stories,* "Under the Garden" in *A Sense of Reality* (1963), and "Cheap in August" in *May We Borrow Your Husband?* (1967) — all provide such evidence for reading Greene as an anarchist that one wonders if he did not single them out primarily for that reason.

Anarchism is central to "The Destructors," for the story's thesis — "destruction after all is a form of creation" — is adapted from anarchist Mikhail Bakunin's famous line that "the passion for destruction is a creative passion, too!" A less conspicuous source for this heavily allegorical story may also underlie in its conception: Greene took up the subject of organized young hooligans in 1954, at the same time widespread furor first developed over the teddy-boy subculture. The only other time Greene had employed allegory in such a thoroughgoing manner was in *Brighton Rock,* his prewar championing of the young hoodlum-as-anarch. Since "The Destructors" is the only Greene fiction after World War II that recalls his interests in the 1930s, the teddy boys seem the most likely reason for Greene's

Greene (standing, third from left, beneath arrow) with his St. John's schoolmates in 1920

brief return to the subjects of youth and class in England.

The working-class teddy boys were so named because they had revived the Edwardian suit fashioned by Saville Row tailors and originally intended for upper-class young men as a nostalgic protest of the new social welfare state. The working-class teddy style had just become established in 1953, attracting notice in the English press partly as a fashion but also for its association with delinquency — most sensationally in the Clapham Common murder case of the same year. For all their execration as destructive delinquents, the teds were quite creative — not just in subverting a style aimed at their betters but also in modifying it with additions like that of the string tie derived from the riverboat gambler of Hollywood westerns who was perceived in Britain as a distinct outsider.

In "The Destructors" the Wormsley Common Gang is not at all disposed to self-destruction, unlike Greene's young male characters such as Pinkie in *Brighton Rock*. Instead, for the sake of vengeance on the owner, allegorically designated "Old Misery" and associated with the upper class, the gang

enjoys destroying a Christopher Wren–designed house, an emblem of the whole historical edifice of the English nation. The youths are no longer isolated and desperate, as in Greene's 1930s works, but an energetic collective, and the demolition of the Wren house is not condemned by Greene but is celebrated in Bakunin's terms: the gang's work is done "with the seriousness of creators — and destruction after all is a form of creation. A kind of imagination had seen this house as it had now become." Trevor, the gang's leader who possesses "an odd quality of danger," realizes that the Wren house is "beautiful." But the "word 'beautiful' [belonged to] a man wearing a top hat and a monocle, with a haw-haw accent." Given the class connotations of beauty, Trevor has little trouble persuading the others to destroy the house.

Like England during the brief age of affluence allowed by postwar rebuilding, the house sleeps while its interior is carefully demolished by economically obsolete young people. Old Misery, the house's owner and a clear allegorical voice of authority in general, wants to tell young people what they can and cannot do: "it's got to be regular. One of you asks leave and I say Yes. Sometimes I'll say No." But all the time Old Misery orders it about, the gang is busy destroying his house behind his back. The final result seems even more plausible than it would have seemed in the 1950s, in light of the collapse of the British economy during the late 1970s and early 1980s and the resulting upheavals among young people: "One moment the house had stood there with such dignity between the bomb-sites like a man in a top hat," the emblem of the upper class, "and then, bang, crash, there wasn't anything left – not anything." The gang's malevolence, Greene suggests with equanimity and even considerable delight, may lead to the destruction of England from within. "The Destructors" certainly has an air of prophecy, and Greene's prescience in this case seems intentional, as Trevor admonishes the gang: "We'd be like worms, don't you see, in an apple." Hence, in the allegory Greene's teddies compose his "Wormsley Common Gang," who aim to "make the walls fall down – *somehow.*" The gang's last words to Old Misery are quietly apocalyptic: "You wouldn't be comfortable, not in your house, you wouldn't. Not now."

"A Chance for Mr. Lever" (1936) may have been written almost two decades earlier than "The Destructors" and may derive from the miserable trek through Liberia documented in *Journey Without Maps* (1936), yet it seems perfectly consonant in a 1954 collection (*Twenty-One Stories*) headed by "The Destructors." This consonance with "The Destructors" is logical enough, because Greene had just struck up his fast friendship with Herbert Read in 1935. In *Ways of Escape* Greene records the significance of that relationship in far stronger terms than does Sherry's tepid, reductive account:

> [M]y meeting with Herbert Read was an important event in my life. He was the most gentle man I have ever known, but it was a gentleness which had been tested in the worst experience of his generation [in World War I]. . . . When you looked round for an explanation [of any subject] there he was – complete honesty born of complete experience.

Greene does not allude to anarchism, though he notes that he has emphasized personal over intellectual concerns: "when one loves a man, as I loved him, it is the small things which . . . first come to mind, before the great enduring achievements." When Greene does discuss more philosophical matters, his closing citation of Read comes closest to invoking anarchism: " 'At certain moments the individual is carried beyond his rational self, on to another ethical plane, where his actions are judged

by new standards. The impulse which moves him to irrational action I have called the sense of glory.' "

This citation, in fact, seems to be exactly the thesis Greene dramatizes in "A Chance for Mr. Lever." An aging salesman who has lost his money in the Depression and undertaken an impossible trek to sell mining equipment in Africa, Lever abandons any sense of propriety through a small, single act of fraud and abruptly finds himself set free, elevated to the new ethical plane described by Read – unethical, in the story, only by meaningless conventional standards. And regardless of whether Greene has Read's ethics specifically in mind, Lever's new-found freedom is explicitly rendered in terms of anarchism:

> The thought of the prayers he had uselessly uttered on his knees made him rebellious. . . . He was lost and he was set free. Moralities were what enabled a man to live happily and successfully with his fellows, but Mr. Lever wasn't happy and he wasn't successful. . . . Honesty is the Best Policy: he saw quite suddenly how false that was. It was an *anarchist* who sat happily over the typewriter, an anarchist who recognized nothing but one personal relationship, his affection for [his wife] Emily.
> (emphasis added)

> With the light Mr. Lever saw that Davidson was dead. "Dear, dear," he said. "Poor fellow." He spat out with the words. . . . It was like a little sediment of his conventionality. . . . Now he had said Boo to that goose.

If "A Chance for Mr. Lever" clearly derives from personal experience in evoking Greene's Liberian journey, like so much of his work its strongest personal note is really one of bitter denunciation of convention. In attempting to clarify the relation between his politics and his religion in *Ways of Escape* Greene finally concludes that even Marxist atheism is preferable to the "wasteland . . . inhabited by the pious 'suburbans,' " his only real enemies.

The blows he strikes against those suburbans in "The Destructors" and "A Chance for Mr. Lever" lie in the surprise he describes in his introduction to the collected stories. His metaphors for that surprise, "escapades" and "snapshots," seem in these stories he designated as his best to entail exemplary acts of rebelliousness, something akin to what nineteenth-century anarchists called propaganda by the deed. The phrase unfortunately came by the end of the century to refer almost exclusively to political assassination – throwing bombs in crowded cafés and so forth, ostensibly small acts in contrast to the larger habitual violence of capitalism – and such violence in the last two decades of the nineteenth century has colored the common under-

THE STAR. TUESDAY. JANUARY 18, 1921.

The Star

Telephones : 313 Central (7 lines),
6420 City (6 lines).
Telegrams: "Star, London."

WHAT WE THINK.

The Old Sham.

The Hour has come and with it the Man ! Several men, in fact. Not to put too fine a point upon it, the London Municipal Society and that fine old Roman, Lord George Hamilton. The note is struck, the standard hoisted, the flag is nailed to the mast in to-day's "Times," where we read that there is to be " no more apathy " in local government elections. A vigorous campaign against municipal waste is to be initiated this week by our old friend the London Municipal Society, the ground landlords' pet organisation. The opportunity to grind its axe on the subject of high rates is not to be missed, and the Society is going to call a " conference" and to guarantee all its candidates to support the crusade against the "twin dangers of waste and Bolshevism."

How familiar all these stage "properties" sound. There is the "reduction of debt," "municipal trading," and, of course, the limitation of rates to the lowest possible figure "compatible with efficient administration." The main causes of the increase in rates is the increase in the cost of materials and of labour. Will the London Municipal Society force the contractors to

SEA SNOW.

The Hebrides Under Their White Winter Quilts.

By "SEAMARK."

THOSE who have never slipped down coast on a bright sunny morning after a heavy snowfall only know half the story of British coastal scenery. To see it at its best one should be coming down the western run of the Sutherland coast towards Cape Wrath, or, preferably, threading the glorious maze of the Hebrides. Nominally, of course, they are islands, but in reality they are magnificent mountain tops rearing perpendicularly from the water's edge: and in the tiny channels between these vast walls there is often only room for a very small boat to make steerage way.

Dawn on the Hebrides.

A heavy snowfall softens much of the shaggy ferocity of the Hebridean crags, but even so, in their spotless white quilts they are grimly perfect. They give of their best in the early dawn when a rose pink sunrise reaches across from the horizon and tints their glaring white with the faint colours from the palette of the morn. Eunessan swims in a pool of amber half-light, at the base of its own high battlements. Iona looms solitary and desolate across the way, shadowed in grey where the sea frets its edge but burning redly at its crest as a scarlet shaft from the east bursts upon it. Staffa is on fire in the distance like a row of snow torches rising from a cold blue lake: and

THE TICK OF THE CLOCK.

A Legend.

By H. GRAHAM GREENE.

" The tree was life, and the fruit death, and the hid seed was love."—
Sir Lewis Morris.

"TICK-TOCK, tick-tock," said the old clock in the attic, and the little old servant dusted it and polished it and wound it up just as if it stood in the drawing-room down below and told the time to all the house. Really it stood in the corner of her own cobwebby bedroom, and the time it told was—well, it was anything from ten to ninety minutes out. But every day before she cleaned the silver this peculiar old woman attended to the clock, just as if she was performing a sacred ceremony.

* * *

Indeed, she meant it as a sign of her worship, for every night it seemed to be on the point of telling her something, what she did not know, and she wished by her service to persuade it to speak. But the clock only said, " Tick-tock, tick-tock."

She was so old that the children said she was a witch. They fled when they met her alone, never realising the pain they were giving to her, for she had always longed for a child to love. So the affection which she could not lavish upon them she gave to the clock, which was older, far older, than she.

* * *

104

Beginning of "The Tick of the Clock," Greene's first published story, in the 18 January 1921 issue of The Star *(London)*

standing of anarchism ever since. But propaganda by the deed originally meant more genuinely exemplary acts, such as the installation of communitarian ideals by the Paris Commune in 1871, and this more positive sense comes through in "The Destructors" and "A Chance for Mr. Lever." Greene even saves Mr. Lever at the end of the story: after suggesting throughout that Lever's situation is hopeless and in the last paragraph that he has received a fatal infection of yellow fever, Greene's last sentence suddenly returns Lever to a successful new life crisscrossing Europe.

But the "deeds" in *Twenty-One Stories* can also be quite dark and violent, as in another

story from the 1930s, "A Drive in the Country." Written in 1937, the story appears to be a dress rehearsal for *Brighton Rock,* at the end of which Pinkie attempts to lure the innocent Rose into a suicide pact on a roadtrip. The situation in "A Drive in the Country" differs in one respect, however. Greene's sympathy is fully with the male, whom the Depression has driven to a quite sincere intention to commit suicide. As this protagonist insists,

"They think I ought to get a job. When you're that age you don't realize there aren't any jobs for some of us — any more for ever.... Every year, you know, there's

134

less chances, because there are more people younger than I am." . . . There was a savagery in his manner. He took security, peace, order in his teeth and worried them.

The anarchist's girlfriend, on the other hand, decides that she likes order and security, for after she leaves the young man to his demise she feels "nothing but gladness because she had escaped from him" in order to return home, to doors bolted carefully by her father. Like Mr. Lever, the young romantic couple in the comic "When Greek Meets Greek" (1941) meets a far better end – through fraudulent ends justified by the bankruptcy of authority including their fathers, both con men: "There were bigger frauds all around them: officials of the Ministries, . . . controllers of this and that, . . . and men with the big blank faces of advertisement hoardings. . . . Their fraud was a small one by the world's standard."

Twenty-One Stories also includes a seemingly more doctrinaire political story from the mid 1930s, "Brother" (1936). The Parisian setting derives from Greene's brief visit to Paris in 1925, when he was a member of the small Oxford Communist Party, although the fictional situation is more violent than anything he encountered. John Bayley considers "Brother" an embarrassment, "almost a parody of the contemporary tale 'of social significance,' . . . with something of that almost 'camp' bravado which reminds the reader both of school stories and of the contemporary cinema." The story hinges on a petit bourgeois café owner's sudden conversion to the brotherhood of man after having been invaded first by rioters and then by policemen who have shot up his bar and killed one of the Reds. The apparent sacrifice of politics to melodrama is hardly retrograde, but perfectly in keeping with Greene's political sensibility. Sherry's biography reports that Joseph Macleod, a friend at Oxford in the 1920s, could not believe that Greene was a member of the Party: "It was a surprise beyond all words," Macleod recalled, for "Graham was more stirred and activated by individual victimisation than by class or wage exploitations." If one reads "Brother" on that individual level, the proprietor's sympathy for the dead man, the story seems much less a wooden effort to celebrate solidarity and much more in keeping with Greene's other work in the 1930s. The conclusion seems far from ludicrous, furthermore, if one considers the proprietor's anti-authoritarian fury at the police to be just as important as his sentiment: "They enter my café, he thought, they smash my windows, they order me about and think that all

is well if they pay, pay, pay. It occurred to him that these men were intruders."

The third of the stories Greene singled out, "Under the Garden" (1963), is actually a novella, and it approaches childhood with an interest more psychological than social, as it investigates a childhood dream to the point of seeming fantastic. Yet the discoveries of the narrator, Wilditch, once again involve a repudiation of authority and convention. Having been diagnosed with cancer, Wilditch returns to his childhood home Winton Hall, where he is particularly obsessed with verifying a memory of discovering treasure on the estate – on an island that turns out to be the size of a room and in the middle of a small pond. His dream of discovering treasure at the age of seven piques him, not through any interest in riches but through "the final effort of a poetic imagination that afterwards had been rigidly controlled" by family, school, and employment, as "a quality to be suppressed." But by the end of the story Wilditch discovers that the dream has in fact set the course of his nonetheless unconventional, well-traveled life and of his refusal of responsibility, and this leads him to wonder if the dream had occurred all at once or if the details had "accumulated year by year, like coral, in the sea of the unconscious around the original dream. . . . If it had not been for his dream of the tunnel and the bearded man and the hidden treasure, couldn't he have made a less restless life for himself?"

Wilditch recounts at length his meeting in the dream with an eccentric, one-legged old man named Javitt and his harelip wife, Maria, who live underground, literally and figuratively. The essence of "Under the Garden" lies in Javitt's tutoring Wilditch in the ways of "rogues," people who refuse to conform:

[O]nly when you get back to zero, to the real ugly base of things, there's a chance to start again free and independent. . . . Sometimes you find someone who wants things different, who's tired of all the plus signs [or relentless positivism and conformity] and wants to find zero, and he starts breeding away with the differences. . . .

It's the hardest thing in the world for a rogue to survive. For hundreds of years now we've been living underground and we'll have the laugh of you yet, coming up above for keeps in a dead world.

This last threat seems reminiscent of the prophetic tone of "The Destructors." Generally like that story, Javitt's instructions for a rogue's conduct are impeccably anarchic (as are his asides such as "Riots . . . purge like a dose of salts"): "Be disloyal. It's your duty to the human race. The human race

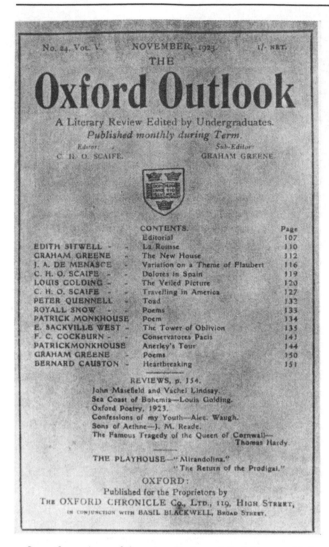

*Cover for an issue of the university journal that Greene edited
from 1923 until 1925*

needs to survive and it's the loyal man who dies first from anxiety or a bullet or overwork. [Y]ou'll have to forget all your schoolmasters try to teach you." Encouraged by Javitt to scour the world for romance, Wilditch finds that "it was as though the purpose of life had suddenly come to me. . . . 'I'll work my passage,' I said, 'before the mast.' "

The mast has indeed become "a career sacred to [Wilditch]," but he takes pride above all in having "never taken his various professions seriously: he had been loyal to no one," exactly as Javitt directed. The refusal to take seriously the demands of work, in particular, as part of a general disavowal of institutional imperatives, make Wilditch's lifelong evasion of responsibility not some character dysfunction but an admirable pursuit of freedom — freedom of the sort discovered only very late by Mr. Lever. Greene comes very close to anticipating

another Parisian slogan of May 1968 besides *je ne regrette rien: ne travaillez jamais,* or "never work."

The concluding story in *A Sense of Reality,* "A Discovery in the Woods," seems to be another allegory of childhood, but its utter disconnection from any contemporary context makes the allegory obscure to the point of fantasy — more in keeping with "Under the Garden" than with "The Destructors." "A Discovery in the Woods" and "Under the Garden" together display a much more indirect approach adopted by the aging Greene to the central theme of his prewar work, the conflict of youth and authority. "A Discovery in the Woods" in fact is much like a Franz Kafka story in giving every appearance of being allegorical without actually yielding any very certain interpretation.

To this end Greene deliberately plants false clues: for much of the story one is convinced that the children belong to a generation not long descended from that of Noah and have discovered his ark, but at the end a few letters inscribed on the wreck — "FRANCE" — prove indecipherable runes for the children and their society (an almost entirely isolated fishing village called Bottom) but are perfectly and suddenly familiar to the reader. Since the context is not so timeless as one assumed, the conclusion is even more mysterious: why do the children (like the whole of their tiny society) turn out to be misshapen dwarves who marvel at the straight-boned skeleton of a six-foot-tall man? A seven-year-old girl, Liz, keens "for a whole world lost," repeatedly asking "'Why aren't there any giants now?'"

The answer, perhaps, is that the dwarfism and deformation of the villagers and their loss of a more heroic world have everything to do with their subservience to the authority of custom and law. In order to discover the "ark," the children must violate the village's arbitrary, self-imposed boundaries — rules handed down by a tradition that no one understands. The early portions of the story clearly make much of the whole issue of violating custom:

> "There must be a reason," Liz said, "why they don't want us to go."
> "There's no reason," Pete said, "except the law."
> . . . It seemed odd to him that day how reluctant they were to take his advice. [I]f he had to choose his successor he would prefer Number Three's care-for-nothing character than the elderly inherited rules of Number One or the unadventurous reliability of Number Two.

Pete functions much like Trevor in "The Destructors," as he badgers and cajoles his "gang" into their transgressive journey, "a revolutionary proposal" founded in a "profound belief he shared with no one else" – the complaint of restless youth that "Bottom's not the world." A single early clue that all is not right with the villagers is in a description of Pete's mother, who "from some past generation inherited [an] ability to generalize, of which he and his father were quite incapable." The primary sort of generalization lost in their society, apparently, involves the ability to question authority and the law, an ability that comprises a perfectly contemporary matter.

The last of the stories Greene describes as among the best of his writing, "Cheap in August," differs from the other three in reflecting his turn to comedy in some works of the postwar period. But, as John Spurling observes, comedy too "for Greene is bound up with antagonism to conventional society." In "Cheap in August" Mary Watson, an Englishwoman married to a dull if successful American literary academic, travels to Jamaica in the interest of having an affair, but she winds up unexpectedly with an elderly, overweight American, Henry Hickslaughter, with a fear of the dark. In its hatred of Coca-Cola, television, ads for shaving cream, and fat tourists from Saint Louis, the story reveals the depth of Greene's loathing for the United States and attacks its general ethos of affluence and consumption rather than its foreign policy.

Mary's desire for freedom recalls that of characters like Mr. Lever and Wilditch: "She couldn't pretend to be a tigress in a cage, but they kept smaller creatures in cages." But this desire is diminished by her admission that, in comparison with her husband, "she was more American by choice than he was by birth." Hickslaughter eventually wins not only her pity but also some real affection, precisely because he is so atypical of Americans: "his frankness about money or rather about the lack of it . . . could almost be classed as an un-American activity. [H]e was supremely uninterested in his own doings; she was certainly discovering an America which she had not known existed." Thus, he offers a sense of adventure in spite of what he is, for he appears as "the first unsuccessful American she had ever had a drink with. . . . Nobody anywhere admitted failure or fear; they were like sins 'hushed up.' " Another story in *May We Borrow Your Husband?*, "Two Gentle People," continues Greene's vituperation of American culture, again in terms of Coca-Cola and the Time-Life publishing conglomerate in particular. Henry Greaves's shrewish wife despises Antibes because "she misses America – she will never believe that the Coca-Cola tastes the same here."

May We Borrow Your Husband?, though a collection of what the rest of the full title identifies as "comedies of the sexual life," also includes "The Root of All Evil," a story explicitly invoking anarchism. In a German village at the end of the nineteenth century, a drinking group conceals itself from one unpopular fellow, and this leads to suspicion that a secret society of anarchists is at work. The ostracized man enlists police surveillance operations involving recourse to transvestism, and the results are more farcical than those of most other pieces in Greene's oeuvre. But he has a point to make about authoritarianism, too: a policeman who balks at shaving his moustache and wearing a dress is told simply that "in the service of the law" he should abandon any scruples. More significant is the punchline to the story, which is more heavily ironic than comic. As the narrator concludes his recounting of his own father's telling of this story, the narrator recollects the ostensible moral that having secrets leads to every sin imaginable – above all, the subornation of authority:

> "Subornation of authority?"
> "Yes," he said. . . . "Men in women's clothes – the terrible sin of Sodom."
> "And what's that?" I asked with excited expectation.
> "At your age," my father said, "some things must remain secret."

Though "The Root of All Evil" appears perfectly farcical, Greene's last-second skewering of the hypocrisy of authority figures suddenly and adroitly brings into the foreground what have earlier seemed merely topical references to anarchism: " 'Anarchy is out to upset everything' " and "There had been an anarchist outrage at Schloss."

This subversiveness may reflect Greene's advancing age, in its stark contrast to his outright bitterness and rage in earlier work, but the later stories are perfectly in keeping with that vitriolic anti-authoritarianism. Another farce in *May We Borrow Your Husband?*, "Doctor Crombie," makes no political reference whatsoever; the narrator recollects a school doctor's views about sex – namely, that it causes cancer. But this is not entirely a laughing matter when one considers Greene's memory of the "abnormal fear of sexuality" that characterized the English public schools and that Greene discusses in his own essay "The Old School." He criticizes the system's authorities – implicitly including his father, as Sherry points out – for their myopia: "One is alternately amazed at the unworldly innocence of the pedagogic mind and its tortuous obscenity." These are exactly the qualities embodied in the fictional Dr. Crombie.

The episode in Greene's life that led to this conclusion was that moment in adolescence when he briefly had run away from home and school to escape torment by his fellow schoolboys. Upon Greene's return his father, perpetually anxious about the possibility of discovering homosexuality at the school, had been unable to understand Graham's account of psychological torture and general vulgarity, and he concluded that the boy was the victim of a masturbation ring. This parental myopia at a crucial moment perhaps explains why much of Greene's anti-authoritarian fiction – "A Discovery in the Woods," "A Drive in the Country," "When Greek Meets Greek" – casts paternal figures (and a maternal authority figure in "Under the Garden") as objects of derision and sources of oppression.

The most important result of Greene's adolescent breakdown, though, was his lifelong sympathy for the suffering and for the underdog, the basis of his contumacy. His early work in particular, based predominantly in "the memories of flight, rebellion and misery during those first sixteen years when the novelist is formed," enacts a revenge on his tormentors at Berkhamsted. Greene wonders in *A Sort of Life* "if I would ever have written a book had it not been for [his schoolmates], if those years of humiliation had not given me an excessive desire to prove that I was good at something." It is remarkable, says Sherry, "that a relationship between a few boys at a public school should have had such repercussions, bringing Graham Greene to . . . sympathy for the outsider [and] the hunted man (for he had felt hunted); . . . he would have a profound interest in, and compulsive love for, the down-trodden everywhere." Whatever the degree of Greene's affiliation with anarchism as an ideology, his visceral anti-authoritarianism, so keen a personal feeling, is indisputable. His ability to extend his anger on behalf of victims well beyond his own experiences (whether in terms of class or of nationality) is finally the quality that sets him apart as an artist.

Interviews:

Michael Mewshaw, "Greene in Antibes," *London Magazine,* 17 (June–July 1977): 35–45;

Karel Kyncl, "A Conversation with Graham Greene," *Index on Censorship,* 13 (June 1984): 2–6;

Charles Trueheart, "The World of Graham Greene," *Manchester Guardian Weekly,* 23 October 1988, pp. 19–20;

Marie-Françoise Allain, *Conversations with Graham Greene,* translated by Guido Waldman (New York & London: Penguin, 1991);

John R. MacArthur, "Last Word from Graham Greene," *Progressive,* June 1991, pp. 25–28.

Bibliographies:

Jerry Don Vann, *Graham Greene: A Checklist of Criticism* (Lexington: University of Kentucky Press, 1970);

Robert H. Miller, *Graham Greene: A Descriptive Catalog* (Lexington: University of Kentucky Press, 1979);

R. A. Wobbe, *Graham Greene: A Bibliography and Guide to Research* (New York & London: Garland, 1979);

A. F. Cassis, *Graham Greene: An Annotated Bibliography of Criticism* (Metuchen, N.J. & London: Scarecrow Press, 1981);

Richard Costa, "Graham Greene: A Checklist," *College Literature,* 12 (Winter 1985): 85–94;

Neil Brennan and Alan R. Radway, *A Bibliography of Graham Greene* (New York: Oxford University Press, 1990);

Alan Warren Friedman, "The Status of Graham Greene Studies," *Library Chronicle,* 20, no. 4 (1991): 37–67.

Biography:

Norman Sherry, *The Life of Graham Greene,* 2 volumes (New York: Viking, 1989, 1994).

References:

Judith Adamson, *Graham Greene and Cinema* (Norman, Okla.: Pilgrim Books, 1984);

John Atkins, "Two Views of Life: William Golding and Graham Greene," *Studies in the Literary Imagination,* 13 (Spring 1980): 81–96;

John Bayley, "Graham Greene: The Short Stories," in *Graham Greene: A Revaluation,* edited by Jeffrey Meyers (New York: St. Martin's Press, 1990), pp. 85–103;

Bernard Bergonzi, *Reading the Thirties: Texts and Contexts* (London: Macmillan, 1978);

Harold Bloom, ed., *Graham Greene* (New York: Chelsea, 1987);

A. F. Cassis, "The Dream as Literary Device in Graham Greene's Novels," *Literature and Psychology,* 24 (Spring 1974): 99–108;

Maria Couto, *Graham Greene: On the Frontier: Politics and Religion in the Novels* (New York: St. Martin's Press, 1988);

Richard Creese, "Abstracting and Recording Narration in *The Good Soldier* and *The End of the Af-*

fair," *Journal of Narrative Technique,* 16 (Winter 1986): 1–14;

A. A. DeVitis, *Graham Greene,* revised edition (Boston: Twayne, 1986);

Denis Donoghue, "Secret Sharer," *New York Review of Books,* 19 February 1981, pp. 14–18;

Terry Eagleton, *Exiles and Emigrés: Studies in Modern Literature* (New York: Schocken, 1970);

Quentin Falk, *Travels in Greeneland: The Cinema of Graham Greene* (London, Melbourne & New York: Quartet, 1984);

Georg M. A. Gaston, *The Pursuit of Salvation: A Critical Guide to the Novels of Graham Greene* (Troy, N.Y.: Whitsun, 1984);

Graham Greene, "Graham Greene at Eighty: Musings on Writing, Religion, and Politics," *World Press Review,* 31 (December 1984): 31–32;

David Leon Higdon, "Saint Catherine, Von Hugel 28714 and Graham Greene's *The End of the Affair,*" *English Studies,* 62 (January 1981): 46–52;

Samuel Hynes, ed., *Graham Greene: A Collection of Critical Essays* (Englewood Cliffs, N.J.: Prentice-Hall, 1973);

Richard Kelly, *Graham Greene* (New York: Ungar, 1984);

David J. Leigh, "Greene, Golding and the Politics of Literature," *America,* 119 (26 November 1983): 331–332;

David Lodge, *Graham Greene* (New York: Columbia University Press, 1966);

Frank D. McConnell, "Perspectives: Graham Greene," *Wilson Quarterly,* 5 (Winter 1981): 168–186;

Neil McEwan, *Graham Greene* (New York: St. Martin's Press, 1988);

Jeffrey Meyers, ed., *Graham Greene: A Revaluation* (New York: St. Martin's Press, 1990);

Robert H. Miller, *Understanding Graham Greene* (Columbia: University of South Carolina Press, 1990);

Neil Nehring, *Flowers in the Dustbin: Culture, Anarchy, and Postwar England* (Ann Arbor: University of Michigan Press, 1993);

Nehring, "Revolt into Style: Graham Greene Meets the Sex Pistols," *PMLA,* 106 (March 1991): 222–237;

Conor Cruise O'Brien, "A Funny Sort of God," *New York Review of Books,* 18 (18 October 1973): 56–58;

Paul O'Prey, *A Reader's Guide to Graham Greene* (London: Thames & Hudson, 1988);

George Orwell, "The Sanctified Sinner," in his *The Collected Essays, Journalism and Letters of George Orwell,* edited by Sonia Orwell and Ian Angus (New York: Harcourt, Brace & World, 1968);

Gene D. Phillips, S.J., *Graham Greene: The Films of His Fiction* (New York: Columbia University Teachers College Press, 1974);

Anne T. Salvatore, *Greene and Kierkegaard: The Discourse of Belief* (Tuscaloosa: University of Alabama Press, 1988);

Roger Sharrock, *Saints, Sinners and Comedians: The Novels of Graham Greene* (Notre Dame, Ind.: University of Notre Dame Press, 1984);

Marc Silverstein, "After the Fall: The World of Graham Greene's Thrillers," *Novel,* 22 (Fall 1988): 24–44;

Grahame Smith, *The Achievement of Graham Greene* (Sussex: Harvester / Totowa, N.J.: Barnes & Noble, 1986);

John Spurling, *Graham Greene* (New York: Methuen, 1983);

Philip Stratford, ed., "Introduction" to *The Portable Graham Greene* (New York: Viking, 1973), pp. vii–xiii;

Brian Thomas, *An Uncertain Fate: The Idiom of Romance in the Later Novels of Graham Greene* (Athens: University of Georgia Press, 1980);

John Updike, "The Passion of Graham Greene," *New York Review of Books,* 37 (16 August 1990): 16–17;

John Vinocur, "The Soul Searching Continues for Graham Greene," *New York Times Magazine,* 3 March 1985, p. 38;

Ronald Walker, *The Infernal Paradise: Mexico and the Modern English Novel* (Berkeley & Los Angeles: University of California Press, 1978);

Peter Wolfe, *Graham Greene: The Entertainer* (Carbondale: Southern Illinois University Press, 1972);

Wolfe, ed., *Essays in Graham Greene* (Greenwood, Fla.: Penkevill, 1987).

Papers:

The Harry Ransom Humanities Research Center, University of Texas at Austin, has manuscripts and typescripts of most of Greene's books, plus working drafts and final manuscripts of various short stories and articles, as well as much of the correspondence. There are Greene holdings at Georgetown University; Boston College; the Lilly Library, Indiana University; the Pennsylvania State University Library; the Library of Congress; and the British Library.

Violet Hunt

(28 September 1862 – 16 January 1942)

Kathryn Ledbetter
Oklahoma Baptist University

BOOKS: *The Maiden's Progress* (London: Osgood, McIlvaine, 1894);

A Hard Woman (London: Chapman & Hall, 1895);

The Way of Marriage (London: Chapman & Hall, 1896);

Unkist, Unkind! (London: Chapman & Hall, 1897);

The Human Interest (London: Methuen, 1899);

Affairs of the Heart (London: Freemantle, 1900);

The Celebrity at Home (London: Chapman & Hall, 1904);

Sooner or Later (London: Chapman & Hall, 1904);

The Cat (London: A. & C. Black, 1905);

The Workaday Woman (London: Laurie, 1906);

White Rose of Weary Leaf (London: Heinemann, 1908);

The Wife of Altamont (London: Heinemann, 1910);

The Life Story of a Cat (London: A. & C. Black, 1910);

Tales of the Uneasy (London: Heinemann, 1911);

The Doll (London: Stanley Paul, 1911);

Zeppelin Nights: A London Entertainment, by Hunt and Ford Madox Hueffer (London: Chatto & Windus, 1912);

The Governess, by Hunt and Margaret Hunt (London: Chatto & Windus, 1912);

The Desirable Alien at Home and in Germany, by Hunt and Hueffer (London: Chatto & Windus, 1913);

The Celebrity's Daughter (London: Stanley Paul, 1913);

The House of Many Mirrors (London: Stanley Paul, 1915);

Their Lives (London: Stanley Paul, 1916);

The Last Ditch (London: Stanley Paul, 1918);

Their Hearts (London: Stanley Paul, 1921);

The Tiger Skin (London: Heinemann, 1924);

More Tales of the Uneasy (London: Heinemann, 1925);

The Flurried Years (London: Hurst & Blackett, 1926); republished as *I Have This to Say: The Story of My Flurried Years* (New York: Boni & Liveright, 1926);

Violet Hunt

The Wife of Rossetti: Her Life and Death (London & New York: Lane, 1932).

OTHER: *The Great Poets Birthday Album: A Selection from the Poetical Works of Shakespeare, Wordsworth, Hood . . . ,* preface by Hunt (London: Eyre & Spottiswoode, 1892);

"The End of the Beginning," in *Dialogues of the Day,* edited by Oswald Crawfurd (London: Chapman & Hall, 1895), pp. 27–41;

Violet Hunt, the Honourable Mrs. Arthur Henniker, Lady Ridley and others, *Stories and Play*

140

Stories, three plays by Hunt (London: Chapman & Hall, 1897);

Giacomo Girolamo Casanova di Seingalt, *The Memoirs of Jacques Casanova de Seingalt,* translation by Hunt and Agnes Farley, with an introduction by Hunt, 2 volumes (London: Chapman & Hall, 1902);

Berthe Tosti, *The Heart of Ruby,* translated by Hunt (London: Chapman & Hall, 1903);

Golden String: A Day Book for Busy Men and Women, edited by Hunt and Susan, Countess of Malmesbury (London: Murray, 1912);

Margaret Hunt, *Thornicroft's Model,* preface by Violet Hunt (London: Chatto & Windus, 1912).

A lingering fascination with Violet Hunt usually concentrates on the entourage of literary friends and lovers who surrounded her brilliant, glamorous, sometimes scandalous life. Critics rarely choose to examine her voluminous contribution as a poet, journalist, and writer of short fiction and novels, probably because Hunt created her own fame as an obsessive talker, shocking Edwardian society with details about her unconventional love affairs. Indeed, Hunt's record as a strong-minded, freedom-loving feminist is impressive, and her forceful personality figured in characters of novels by W. Somerset Maugham, H. G. Wells, and Ford Madox Ford. Henry James called her his "Purple Patch" and his "Improper Person of Babylon." Oscar Wilde, who once proposed marriage to her, called Hunt "the sweetest Violet in England." She was friends with several generations of celebrities in the London literary scene at the turn of the twentieth century, but her reputation as a provocative, flirtatious socialite and mistress of novelist Ford Madox Ford often overshadows her importance as a writer.

Yet from 1894 until her death Violet Hunt published seventeen novels; three collections of short fiction; memoirs of her years with Ford and the *English Review;* a biography of Elizabeth Siddal (the wife of Pre-Raphaelite artist and poet Dante Gabriel Rossetti); two book translations; six collaborations; and poetry, essays, and reviews in several London newspapers and magazines. In her day Hunt was considered one of the most promising of a new crowd of writers; yet two recent biographies of Hunt merely repeat the accounts of her love affairs and neglect in-depth treatment of her work. If Hunt's short fiction does not rate major attention, it certainly deserves closer examination than it has usually received.

Hunt with Ford Madox Hueffer, circa 1911–1912

Isabel Violet Hunt was born at 29 Old Elvet in Durham in 1862, the eldest daughter of landscape artist Alfred William Hunt and novelist Margaret Peacock. For a short time Violet lived with Margaret's cousin Mary Peacock and her husband, John Fogg-Elliot, the local justice of the peace. The Hunt home at Elvet Hill became a center for Durham intellectuals because of Alfred Hunt's interest in the avant-garde artistic and literary group known as the Pre-Raphaelites. Alfred met the group through John Ruskin, Ford Madox Brown, and Holman Hunt, but he never considered himself a true Pre-Raphaelite. His great ambition was to be a member of the Royal Academy; his greatest failure was in the lack of attention that the Royal Academy paid to his art. Although he was an important figure in the Old Water-Colour Society, later renamed the Royal Water-Colour Society, Hunt never overcame a gloomy sense of missed opportunities that permeated his family relationships. Margaret Hunt's bitterness at her husband's disengagement from family affairs and her sharp tongue dominated the group, and she almost single-handedly maneuvered the family into a prominent social position. Violet later repeated this weak male/dominating female pattern of relationships with her own lovers.

Violet had two sisters. Venetia Margaret (usually called Venice), born 4 August 1864, was named after John Ruskin's collection of essays *The Stones of Venice* (1851–1853); Ruskin became her godfather, entrusted with her religious training. She married William Arthur Smith Benson, a designer and follower of William Morris, and had one daughter, Rosamund, who became a great favorite of Hunt until Venice refused to allow her daughter to visit. Hunt's other sister, Silvia Kingsley, was born 8 September 1865 and was named after Holman Hunt's 1851 painting, *Valentine Rescuing Sylvia from Proteus*. She married a country squire, John Walton Fogg-Elliot, in Durham and had one daughter, Amerye Margaret, born in 1891.

In 1866, when Hunt was four years old, the family moved to London, to Campden Hill in Kensington at One Tor Villas; Margaret's ambitious drive to entertain and impress London society was fulfilled in their spacious new home, an elaborate display of Victorian design, while Alfred retreated to his comfortable studio at the top of the villa. Appearances were crucially important to Mrs. Hunt, sometimes more important than the welfare of her family. A Victorian concern for propriety and living well was passed on to her daughters, but the absence of a loving father and the dominance of an angry, ambitious mother caused emotional problems that would ensure constant divisions between the girls, jealous for their share of their parents' estate. Hunt's *Their Lives* (1916) recounts a story of cruelty and competition between the three sisters that continued until their deaths.

As Margaret became famous for her novels (she published an average of one novel each year from 1873 to 1886) and Alfred's art was exhibited frequently in London, their home became a haven for writers and artists such as Robert Browning, Ruskin, John Everett Millais, and Alfred Tennyson. The Hunt girls observed Victorian intellectuals firsthand. Hunt read voraciously from her mother's library and was educated by foreign governesses. She began to write stories, imitating those of Sir Walter Scott and others. Fascinated with her mother's tales about the "White Lady," a ghost who lived in the kitchen at her childhood home, the me-

dieval Crook Hall, Hunt especially loved tales of the macabre. At the age of eleven Hunt was sent to Notting Hill and Ealing High School in Norland Square, Kensington. Although she thought she wanted to be an actress, she published poetry in *Century* magazine at the age of thirteen. After high school Hunt studied art at the Kensington Art School for three years, but her interests had long been directed toward romantic interludes; in 1879, at the age of seventeen, she met Oscar Wilde at the home of her mother's former art teacher, William Bell Scott, and she later mentioned this event as her "coming out" experience. She often visited Wilde at Thames House at 13 Salisbury Street, and he called at Tor Villa weekly, but their relationship was interrupted by Wilde's tour in America. The couple grew apart, but Hunt later loved to fantasize about what might have been had she married Wilde.

The first person to take an interest in Hunt's writing was Andrew Lang, who wrote an introduction to Margaret Hunt's 1884 translation of *Grimm's Household Tales*. Lang encouraged Violet and coached her in the writing of poetry, and he allowed her and Silvia to help with an adaptation of his tales from the Norse for *The Blue Fairy Book* (1889) and *The Red Fairy Book* (1890), two of the most popular collections of fairy tales in the Victorian period. Lang's efforts enabled her to publish her poem "The Death of the Shameful Knight" in *Longman's Magazine* in July 1883.

In 1884, when Hunt was twenty-two, she became involved in the first of many love affairs with older married men; she preferred exciting, tumultuous adventures with men her father's age to relationships with more-suitable companions, most of whom she considered boring. The pattern was set with George Boughton, a successful painter, illustrator, and writer three years younger than her father. Although Hunt's disregard for her own reputation threatened to ruin the family socially, Margaret Hunt sent Violet to Paris and hoped to avoid scandal, while Alfred escaped to his studio.

Details of Hunt's capricious flirtations and affairs are faithfully reported in her autobiographical novels, *Their Lives* and *Their Hearts* (1921), and an understanding of the destructive effects of such relationships explains much about her fiction. Sexually frustrated, independent women in these works are often at odds with men who fear their frankness. Disgusted yet excited by sensual invitation, the men usually leave Hunt's "modern" women for safer, traditionally softer women. The latter women are driven by their desperate needs for love while remaining bound to Victorian propriety. Like her female characters, Hunt was divided between her desires to be conventional and accepted in London social circles and her need to shock the respectable upper middle class. Yet her scandalous relationships with older, married men including Boughton, Oswald Crawfurd, Wells, and Ford left her syphilitic, alone, and bitter in her old age.

While her sisters were marrying and raising children, Hunt was writing articles and novels, living alone with her parents at Tor Villa, and arranging secret meetings with her married lovers. In December 1896, seven months after her father died, Hunt and her mother moved across from Tor Villa into a three-story house named South Lodge after the astronomer Sir James South, who had lived in the home earlier in the century. Although Alfred left a comfortable estate of £25,958 and Margaret's income from her novels was considerable, she insisted on frugal spending for clothing and personal items but adorned the home in elegant design. Violet raised Persian cats to give to friends, such as novelists Arnold Bennett and Thomas Hardy. South Lodge became famous as her haven for artists and writers for two decades, but after her death the plaque on its gate commemorated the site as a previous home of Ford Madox Ford, with no mention of the Hunt family.

Hunt's first short story, "A Thief in the Night," was published under the pseudonym Violet Herris in *Belgravia* magazine. At the same time she was filling her social calendar with parties and balls in 1889, she began writing for magazines published by friends in the literary community; knowing all the important names in journalism and publishing eased her path to success as a writer. In June 1890 she began a passionate affair with fifty-seven-year-old diplomat, writer, and editor Oswald Crawfurd, who wrote articles for the *Fortnightly Review,* helped launch the literary journal *Black and White,* and was appointed managing editor of Chapman and Hall publishers. Crawfurd's journal featured dialogues, stories told without the use of any narrative devices. Hunt excelled in this genre because of her ability to converse fluently at any social gathering. Her work was included in an anthology of these dialogues, *Dialogues of the Day* (1895), which was edited by Crawfurd and also featured works by Hunt's mother, Margaret, and sister Silvia.

Hunt was soon writing regular book reviews for *Black and White* and attracting admirers from other journals such as the *Pall Mall Gazette,* the *Pall Mall Budget,* the *Sketch,* and the *Illustrated London News,* all of which pleaded with her to disregard Crawfurd's jealous protection and write columns and articles for them. Her first novel, *The Maiden's Progress* (1894), was a collection of dialogues previously published in these magazines. The October 1894 issue of the *Bookman* praised this work, which it proclaimed to be "among the three or four best novels of the season," and described the new dialogue form as a "distinct advantage in the way of readableness over a stage play, and indeed, apart from the novelty of its form, its popular success is well deserved."

Crawfurd encouraged Hunt to write novels and helped her publish them by serializing *A Hard Woman* (1895) in *Chapman's Magazine;* it later sold two thousand copies. Hunt was immersed in a promising writing career, in demand by important publications and respected as a novelist of the future. She was financially independent and actively involved in a flurry of social events with the brilliant and attractive people of London, and she wrote furiously, averaging a novel a year for the next fifteen years. Her novels, often featuring weak men and strong women struggling with sexual obsessions, were reviewed positively in various journals. *The Human Interest* (1899) was a "very clever study of the quick-witted, discontented woman of to-day, whose cultivation and aspirations are much above her opportunities," according to a reviewer in the November 1899 number of the *Bookman,* and the *Athenæum* of 21 October 1899 reported the novel's strong point was its dialogue, which was "clever and vivacious; indeed, she writes better dialogue than any other woman novelist of the day."

Hunt scholars cite *Tales of the Uneasy* (1911) as her first collection of stories and always discuss *Affairs of the Heart* (1900) as a novel; however, the latter is a selection of some of her most popular short fiction published before 1900 in magazines. It contains thirteen short stories and two brief skits, or dialogues, featuring independent women involved with inconstant men. The most frequently anthologized of the group is "His Widows," a story of Miss Varney and Miss Leven — two rich, eccentric, fashionable but reclusive women who thrive on memories of their love with Robert Musgrave, who has died a decade before. Although he had been "equally indifferent" to both of them, their adoration of the man bonds them until one reveals a packet of letters that shows he favored her: the secret destroys their friendship. Hunt's familiar themes are obvious, as the women are poised against each other in a battle over a man's wavering affections. Love is a power game in which the most manipulative woman wins over a weak man's heart: the secret letters are Miss Leven's source of contentment, securing her power over Musgrave even in his musty grave. *Affairs of the Heart* received little critical attention, but it is important as a representation of the types of short fiction accepted in the magazines of Violet's generation. Her stories were short but complicated in plot, involving levels of truth about the dynamics of relationships between men and women; her subject was always a reexamination of her own position as a daring bohemian woman challenging the values of her society in her generation.

In 1902 Hunt had a brief affair with twenty-nine-year-old W. Somerset Maugham, who had just published his novel *Mrs. Craddock* and was editing the literary magazine the *Venture*. Hunt contributed to the publication from 1902 to 1904 and dedicated her most successful novel, *White Rose of Weary Leaf* (1908), to Maugham, who encouraged her to leave Chapman and Hall and submitted the work to his own publisher, William Heinemann, in 1907. Maugham later used Hunt as a model for his character Rose Waterford in *The Moon and Sixpence* (1919). Association with him widened her circle of friends to include Bennett, who was so impressed with Hunt that he created Carlotta Peel in his *Sacred and Profane Love* after her image. Maugham read Hunt's *Sooner or Later* (1904), her autobiographical novel which is dedicated to her old friend Henry James and which recounts her painful affair with Crawfurd. Maugham also supported Hunt in her battles with public opinion.

During 1906, Bram Stoker, Radclyffe Hall, Bennett, Maugham, and Wells, Hunt's lover at that time, met for bimonthly luncheons that she organized at the Writer's Club on Bruton Street. At that time Hunt was also joining the Women's Social and Political Union, led by the militant feminist Emmeline Pankhurst. Hunt held meetings at her South Lodge home and used her connections in the literary world to enlist support. Although she was never arrested (because of her position in society), she attended mass meetings in support of women's suffrage.

The most important relationship in Hunt's life began in 1909 and was with Joseph Leopold Ford Hermann Madox Hueffer, eventually known as novelist Ford Madox Ford, author of *The Good Soldier* (1915) and *Parade's End* (1924–1928) and collaborator with Joseph Conrad on three novels. Hunt and Ford shared Pre-Raphaelite backgrounds (his grandfather was the painter Ford Madox Brown)

and developed a tempestuous mutual dependency fueled by Ford's neurotic needs to be cared for and Hunt's delight in unconventional arrangements. Ford was emotionally vulnerable, and she was more than willing to rescue him. The age difference between them was uncharacteristic of Violet's pattern, for she was the older of the two: Ford was thirty-five and Violet forty-six.

The relationship led them into several scandalous plots to effect Ford's divorce from his wife, Elsie Martindale, one plot including the claim that he had married Hunt in Germany and was reclaiming his German citizenship. This plan was disastrous for both lovers, for Hunt lost whatever respectability remained in her reputation: her important social invitations disappeared, and Ford was financially and emotionally devastated by the libel suit brought by his wife as a result of his claims. Few of Hunt's former friends would visit South Lodge after the trial, and Ford was so distraught that he got a commission and left for World War I in August 1915, at the age of forty-two.

The early years of what would be Hunt's ten-year relationship with Ford marked a fruitful period that shaped the literary history of the twentieth century. Ford launched the *English Review,* a publication that he invented as a showcase for imaginative literature and that featured the work of such writers as Wells, Thomas Hardy, James, W. H. Hudson, John Galsworthy, Bennett, D. H. Lawrence, G. K. Chesterton, W. B. Yeats, Hilaire Belloc, E. M. Forster, Ezra Pound, Wyndham Lewis, George Moore, Rupert Brooke, and others during Ford's careful editorship from 1908 to 1909. Always looking for new talent, Ford eagerly read three of Hunt's stories and chose "The Coach" for the March 1909 number. Gathering rich subscribers from her crowd of influential friends, Hunt later became a reader, subeditor, and contributor for the publication.

Her collection of stories, *Tales of the Uneasy,* appeared to good reviews: the *Bookman* of May 1911 said that Hunt "knows as well as any living English writer how to write a short story" and welcomed the collection to "an already considerable reputation." The *Athenæum* of 15 April 1911 said that "her style is excellent, her grasp of her subjects sure, and her insight exceptionally clear and sane." Averaging twenty to forty pages in length, the nine tales included in the volume had been first published in magazines and journals during her first ten years of professional authorship. Remarkable for their mixture of Gothic and Edwardian styles, they represent an important stage in the development of the ghost-story genre being explored at the time by Stoker in

Dracula and Henry James in "The Turn of the Screw."

Gothic tales had been familiar to readers since the eighteenth century, but Hunt created her own type of supernatural macabre that features sensitive but independent heroines involved with men who are too weak to contribute emotionally to the relationship. The combination of ghost story and commentary on the independent woman makes Hunt's stories seem to balance precariously between two different centuries; she is at once Romantic, Victorian, and modern. Clearly autobiographical, the tales examine issues in Hunt's own life while moving swiftly through brilliant, sometimes ironic, dialogue to a shocking end. They show Hunt as a woman unsure of herself yet determined to have her way.

In "The Telegram" Hunt's portrayal of the flirtatious Alice Damer criticizes the shallow, selfish woman incapable of compassion. Alice is physically repulsed by her faithful old suitor, Everard Jenkyns, but she leads him on through years of abuse and neglect to feed her vanity. Thriving on his subservience and failing to notice his ill health, Alice waits until she feels that she is too old to attract another lover before she decides to ask Everard to marry her. By the time she invites him to dinner for the proposal, Everard is nothing more than an empty shell. Indeed, it is only his ghost who appears at dinner; as Hunt knew, life without love is no life. Alice regrets her lost opportunity now that she is faced with her own emptiness, but she does not feel responsible for Everard's fate until she confronts the damaging effects of dependency and control.

An actor is torn between two wives in "The Operation," a story first published as "A Physical Lien" in the *Fortnightly Review* (2 November 1908). The new wife, Florence, thinks she can hold on to her actor-husband by appearing selfish and inaccessible, detaching herself from his career. The divorced wife, Julia, advises Florence not to be the "ghost of a wife" as Julia had been, mothering and fussing over Joe. Yet when Julia dies, she is the woman who controls Joe, for he realizes that he has never loved Florence and becomes suicidal in his desire to join Julia in death. Hunt shows through Julia that the woman who dominates a man always wins him over, regardless of the damaging effects of such manipulation; the emotionally detached woman loses him.

This theme is repeated in "The Memoir," when Mabel, a "plain woman, well dressed," competes with the younger Cynthia Chenies for Sir Hilary Greenwell's unreliable affections. The manipulative wife Mabel wins, while the independent Cyn-

Throne   28   APRIL, 3, 1912.

The LIBRARY: *WEEK by WEEK.*
By FRANK A. MUMBY.

A Link with the Past. Messrs. Chatto and Windus have in the press a book which forms an interesting link between the modern school of fiction and that of a generation or so ago, in the waning days of the three volume novel—those good old days as they are now regarded in the book trade, though the three volume novel, be it remembered, had just as many critics in its own time as the six-shilling novel of to-day. The forthcoming book is a romance entitled "The Governess," by Mrs. Alfred Hunt, one of the popular novelists of the old days, and her daughter, Miss Violet Hunt (now Mrs. Ford Madox Hueffer) one of the successful of the modern school.

Hills and Saunders.   *Elliott and Fry.*

On the left, Mrs. Alfred Hunt, who is joint authoress with her daughter, Miss Violet Hunt (Mrs. Ford Madox Hueffer) (right), of a forthcoming novel, "The Governess," which links the modern school of fiction with the old three-volume days.

Notice in the Throne *for the last novel by Mrs. Alfred Hunt, on which her daughter Violet Hunt collaborated. Because Violet Hunt is identified as "Mrs. Ford Madox Hueffer," Elsie Hueffer, his legal wife, sued the magazine.*

thia suffers. After Sir Hilary's death Cynthia discovers that he has seen her as "overpowering" and has written letters to his wife that portray her competitor as an adoring flirt who "seems quite to enjoy saying risque things and compromising herself." Sir Hilary, who has weakly wavered between the two women, denies true devotion to either of them, but Mabel controls his life by editing his memoirs.

These stories play out Hunt's relationships with weak men who fear commitment – men such as Boughton, Crawfurd, and Ford. The ghost story sometimes yields to Hunt's favorite presentation of her type of possessive love; however, Gothic stories such as "The Coach," "The Witness," "The Barometer," and "The Tiger Skin" were popular and frequently anthologized. "The Coach," for example, appeared in two collections edited by Maugham, *Georgian Stories* (1922) and *Tellers of Tales* (1939). Here Hunt is faithful to the characteristic Gothic

meets the coach, the passengers realize the inevitability of death and the necessity of accepting it.

Hunt's stories often develop in or around haunted houses; her mother's recollections of growing up in a thirteenth-century medieval manor haunted by a ghost who lived in the kitchen had impressed her imagination. "The Blue Bonnet" takes place at an old deserted manor on a Yorkshire moor where two travelers rest. They become so fascinated with the house and its former inhabitants that one of the characters makes up a story about the family members, one that includes insanity, murder, drowning, and sexual intimidation. In "The Witness" a woman kills her lover's insane wife in a crumbling old manor house while her lover's dog witnesses the event; she later suspects the dog of telling her secret to the village. The leading characters in "The Prayer" live in a gravelike house because the wife's prayers to have her dead husband returned are answered. Her husband comes back to life as a man who stays young and handsome but is sensually impaired, nothing more than a body stranded on earth without a spirit. "The Barometer" resembles the most sentimental of nineteenth-century fiction: two children, relegated to sleep in a dilapidated barn beside the vicarage hall in the Yorkshire Wolds, are killed by lightning after experiencing a premonition.

A love for animals frequently becomes part of the plot in stories such as the macabre "The Tiger-Skin," her longest and most terrifying in *Tales of the Uneasy*. Surrounded by a house full of cats, the daughter of a cruel doctor who defends child abuse becomes a heartless beast herself. As cats howl in the night, unmentionable experiments are conducted behind the private door at the back of the house. Adopting her father's theories on eugenics, Adelaide Favarger looks for a husband to father a perfect child. After the unmarried Adelaide is impregnated by a man who feels drawn by her challenging strength but is repulsed by her cruelty, he abandons her without knowing that she is pregnant. When Adelaide sees that the baby girl is sickly, she trades it for a healthy child belonging to the maid, Gertrude, and allows her own child to starve to death in a garret at the top of the home. Like her father, Adelaide believes that a sick child deserves to die, for that is nature's way of weeding out the weak; even cats will abuse their children, she rationalizes. When her former lover returns, he feels sorry for the sickly child, but he is too weak to confront Adelaide and save the girl. The story is a fast-moving, disturbing account of abuse, a shock-

MORE TALES OF THE UNEASY

BY

VIOLET HUNT

LONDON
WILLIAM HEINEMANN, LTD.
1925

Title page for Hunt's 1925 collection of stories, for which Henry James had facetiously proposed the title "Ghost Stories of a Worldly Woman" (courtesy of the Lilly Library, Indiana University)

scenery and provincial superstition. Like Ann Radcliffe, she features individuals terrified by overpowering forces they cannot control. The wild River Firth surges and swells eerily as a "heavy and antique" coach bounces along a lonely road on a moonlit Saint John's Eve, the night when, according to old superstition, a headless coachman carries souls to their deaths. His five passengers are murderers, socialites, and working people who justify their crimes of pride, vanity, and greed during the journey. When the coach runs over a dogcart and kills two children, the passengers watch in horror but go on with their stories, secretly thrilled to see blood from the disaster. When one of the children

ing presage of attitudes from dark years that were to come in European history.

The years ahead were also dark years for Hunt. Her relationship with Ford painfully deteriorated until their breakup in 1919, and the war made her feel abandoned, angry at the discomforts and displacement of social activities. Nevertheless, she continued to write and travel extensively, collaborating with Ford on *Zeppelin Nights: A London Entertainment* (1912) and *The Desirable Alien at Home and in Germany* (1913), for the latter of which Ford wrote the preface and two chapters. Ford also wrote the preface for *The Governess* (1912), a novel begun by Margaret Hunt but finished by Violet and dedicated to the memory of her father. In 1912 she reprinted her mother's first novel, *Thornicroft's Model,* and signed a preface that she later claimed had been written by Ford. In *The Celebrity's Daughter* (1913) Hunt nourished her fantasy of marriage to Ford by dedicating the book to "My Husband"; *The House of Many Mirrors* (1915) is dedicated to Ford's former partner, Joseph Conrad.

On 1 November 1912 Margaret Hunt died from a fever at the age of eighty-two, bequeathing South Lodge to Violet. Her sisters contested the will, saying that Hunt had forced their mother into giving her the property. They had never approved of her lifestyle and did everything legally possible to prohibit her from getting the estate, but Hunt persisted and won. Her favorite niece, Rosamond, died in 1920 from measles complicated by pneumonia, and her sister Silvia died twenty days later from pneumonia and heart failure at the age of fifty-four. A few of Hunt's old friends stood by her after the sensational trial with Ford's wife: May Sinclair, Ethyl Colburn Mayne, Radclyffe Hall, Dorothy Richardson, and Rebecca West were steady friends offering comfort, but Hunt grieved the loss of her youth and felt abandoned by love, lonely at South Lodge. She kept busy by writing stories, which were eagerly accepted, as always, by London magazines.

In 1925 she published another collection of stories, *More Tales of the Uneasy.* Her preface acknowledges a debt to Henry James, an innovator in the genre of the short story, as well as to others who had contributed to her development as a writer: Wells, Bennett, and Conrad. She relates a charming history of her reading and writing experience, and she gives James the credit for naming her collection after teasing her by proposing the title "Ghost Stories of a Worldly Woman." The proposal was an appropriate suggestion.

In *More Tales of the Uneasy* Hunt experiments with the longer short story: the four tales in the col-

lection are the length of novellas. Hunt continued her ghost stories, heavily laced with familiar themes involving the "worldly" woman. Ethne Aragon in "The Night of No Weather" is only thirty years old, but her suicidal melancholia after the death of her mother leaves her empty, and she returns to society feeling "as if she were a dead person watching the ways of humanity she had so recently cast off." Her only enjoyment in life is from the memories of the many pets she has owned in the past. Just as in Hunt's own life, Ethne has fought with her family over her mother's will, but she has lost her property and has been forced to take rooms that allow no pets. Again Hunt's characters find that life without love is death in life: having committed suicide in her flat before a party, Ethne is merely a ghost.

The longest story in this collection, "Love's Last Leave," portrays the plight of women left on the home front in 1915 – abandoned in torn cities with food lines and no means of transit, their long, anxious nights filled with blackouts and emptied of parties. The story describes events in the lives of the Tremlett sisters, who clash between the traditional and the unconventional. Again Hunt emphasizes a woman's power over her man, as Aggie is determined to bring her husband, Willy, home safely from the war by willing it so. When she tells the family members of a visit from Willy during the night, they are shocked, for nobody has seen him come or leave. But Aggie says that she "just wrapped him all round in my thoughts like a cloud or a cocoon and brought him to me, safe and sound – all there was of him – all that mattered." All that matters is his soul; the body is nothing. The maid reports having heard strange voices, but the family thinks Aggie is seeing visions. Insanity, suicide, greed, and unnatural dependencies shape this gruesome story of a woman who takes her son to death with her.

The stories from *More Tales of the Uneasy* indicate a marked improvement in Hunt's technical skills. Her plots begin to balance a wider range of themes or relationships. Thus in "Love's Last Leave" one finds the story of competition between two sisters, descriptions of social life in London during the war, and an uncharacteristic portrayal of a delicate boy named Peter. The growing insanity of Aggie, one of the sisters, as she awaits the return of her husband from World War I animates these elements. The husband returns, according to Aggie, but apparently only in spirit: word of his death comes to the household late at night, at the same time that a maid hears Aggie speaking from her bedroom to a man. When Aggie later insists that her husband has appeared, everyone merely thinks that she is insane. The tragic double suicide of Aggie and Peter at the end of the story complicates and renders ambiguous the plot, but Hunt's depiction of life for women on the homefront during the war makes her mystical tale interesting.

During the 1920s Hunt decided to reveal many details of her own life: *The Flurried Years,* her memoir of the years with Ford and the *English Review,* was published in 1926 in London and New York. (The American edition, which includes an appendix of the newspaper accounts of her court cases, was titled *I Have This to Say.*) She used her diaries as a chronological guide that recreated the intensity of her feelings during these years. The memoir provides clever, witty reminiscences of famous people she met as well as of the scandals she knew. It remains is accessible today, while her novels and short stories have unfortunately disappeared. This leaves readers to appreciate the name-dropping prose that proves her wit but eclipses her imaginative talents.

As she passed through her last years Violet was ill from syphilis contracted from Oswald Crawfurd. Thin, faded, ghostly, and confused by disease, Hunt died of pneumonia at the age of seventy-nine on 16 January 1942. She was cremated and her ashes placed in her parents' grave at Brookwood Cemetery. There was no fanfare and no mourners or burial service. The "Improper Person of Babylon," who had figured in the novels of some of the best authors in the twentieth century and contributed much to the short-fiction and ghost-story genres, requested the following inscription on her tombstone: "Violet, daughter of Alfred William Hunt." The inscription has some justice, since her life was a response to the insubstantial ghost who was her father.

Biographies:

Douglas Goldring, *South Lodge: Reminiscences of Violet Hunt, Ford Madox Ford and the English Review Circle* (London: Constable, 1943);

Joan Hardwick, *An Immodest Violet: The Life of Violet Hunt* (London: Deutsch, 1990);

Barbara Belford, *Violet: The Story of the Irrepressible Violet Hunt and Her Circle of Lovers and Friends — Ford Madox Ford, H. G. Wells, Somerset Maugham, and Henry James* (New York: Simon & Schuster, 1990).

References:

Richard Aldington, "Violet Hunt," *Egoist,* 1 (1 January 1914): 17–18;

Jane E. Miller, "The Edward Naumburg, Jr., Collection of Violet Hunt," *Princeton University Library Chronicle,* 51 (Winter 1990): 210–218;

Marie Secor, "Violet Hunt, Novelist: A Reintroduction," *English Literature in Transition,* 19, no. 1 (1976): 25–34;

Marie and Robert Secor, "Violet Hunt's *Tales of the Uneasy:* Ghost Stories of a Worldly Woman," *Women & Literature,* 6 (Spring 1978): 16–27;

Robert Secor, "Henry James and Violet Hunt, the 'Improper Person of Babylon,' " *Journal of Modern Literature,* 13 (March 1986): 3–36;

Joseph Wiesenfarth, "Violet Hunt Rewrites Jane Austen: *Pride and Prejudice* (1813) and *Their Lives* (1916)," *Persuasions: Journal of the Jane Austen Society of North America,* 11 (16 December 1989): 61–65.

Papers:

A collection of unpublished papers of Margaret and Violet Hunt are in the Ford Collection at Cornell University.

Aldous Huxley

(26 July 1894 – 22 November 1963)

Sally A. Paulsell
IUPU Columbus

See also the Huxley entries in *DLB 36: British Novelists, 1890–1929: Modernists* and *DLB 100: Modern British Essayists, Second Series.*

BOOKS: *The Burning Wheel* (Oxford: Blackwell, 1916);

Jonah (Oxford: Holywell, 1917);

The Defeat of Youth, and Other Poems (Oxford: Blackwell, 1918);

Limbo (London: Chatto & Windus, 1920; New York: Doran, 1920);

Leda (London: Chatto & Windus, 1920; New York: Doran, 1920);

Crome Yellow (London: Chatto & Windus, 1921; New York: Doran, 1922);

Mortal Coils (London: Chatto & Windus, 1922; New York: Doran, 1922);

On the Margin: Notes and Essays (London: Chatto & Windus, 1923; New York: Doran, 1923);

Antic Hay (London: Chatto & Windus, 1923; New York: Doran, 1923);

Little Mexican, & Other Stories (London: Chatto & Windus, 1924); republished as *Young Archimedes, and Other Stories* (New York: Doran, 1924);

Those Barren Leaves (London: Chatto & Windus, 1925; New York: Doran, 1925);

Along the Road: Notes and Essays of a Tourist (London: Chatto & Windus, 1925; New York: Doran, 1925);

Selected Poems (Oxford: Blackwell, 1925; New York: Appleton, 1925);

Two or Three Graces, and Other Stories (London: Chatto & Windus, 1926; New York: Doran, 1926);

Jesting Pilate (London: Chatto & Windus, 1926; New York: Doran, 1926);

Essays New and Old (London: Chatto & Windus, 1926; New York: Doran, 1927);

Proper Studies (London: Chatto & Windus, 1927; Garden City, N.Y.: Doubleday, Doran, 1928);

Point Counter Point (London: Chatto & Windus, 1928; Garden City, N.Y.: Doubleday, Doran, 1928);

Arabia Infelix, and Other Poems (London: Chatto & Windus / New York: Fountain Press, 1929);

Holy Face, and Other Essays (London: Fleuron, 1929);

Do What You Will: Essays (London: Chatto & Windus, 1929; Garden City, N.Y.: Doubleday, Doran, 1929);

Brief Candles: Stories (London: Chatto & Windus, 1930; Garden City, N.Y.: Doubleday, Doran, 1930);

Vulgarity in Literature: Digressions from a Theme (London: Chatto & Windus, 1930);

Apennine (Gaylordsville, Conn.: Slide Mountain Press, 1930);

Music at Night, and Other Essays (London: Chatto & Windus, 1931; Garden City, N.Y.: Doubleday, Doran, 1931);

The World of Light: A Comedy in Three Acts (London: Chatto & Windus, 1931; Garden City, N.Y.: Doubleday, Doran, 1931);

The Cicadas, and Other Poems (London: Chatto & Windus, 1931; Garden City, N.Y.: Doubleday, Doran, 1931);

Brave New World (London: Chatto & Windus, 1932; Garden City, N.Y.: Doubleday, Doran, 1932);

Texts and Pretexts: An Anthology with Commentaries (London: Chatto & Windus, 1932; New York: Harper, 1933);

T. H. Huxley as a Man of Letters (London: Macmillan, 1932);

Beyond the Mexique Bay (London: Chatto & Windus, 1934; New York: Harper, 1934);

Eyeless in Gaza (London: Chatto & Windus, 1936; New York: Harper, 1936);

1936 . . . Peace? (London: Friends Peace Committee, 1936);

The Olive Tree, and Other Essays (London: Chatto & Windus, 1936; New York: Harper, 1937);

Aldous Huxley, circa 1950

What Are You Going to Do about It? The Case for Constructive Peace (London: Chatto & Windus, 1936; New York: Harper, 1936);

Ends and Means: An Enquiry into the Nature of Ideals and into the Methods Employed for Their Realization (London: Chatto & Windus, 1937; New York: Harper, 1937);

Stories, Essays, and Poems (London: Dent, 1937);

The Elder Peter Bruegel (New York: Wiley, 1938);

The Most Agreeable Vice (Los Angeles: Ritchie, 1938);

The Gioconda Smile (London: Chatto & Windus, 1938);

After Many a Summer (London: Chatto & Windus, 1939); republished as *After Many a Summer Dies the Swan* (New York: Harper, 1939);

Words and Their Meanings (Los Angeles: Ritchie, 1940);

Grey Eminence: A Study in Religion and Politics (London: Chatto & Windus, 1941; New York: Harper, 1941);

The Art of Seeing (New York: Harper, 1942; London: Chatto & Windus, 1943);

Time Must Have a Stop (New York: Harper, 1944; London: Chatto & Windus, 1945);

Twice Seven: Fourteen Selected Stories (London: Reprint Society, 1944);

The Perennial Philosophy (New York: Harper, 1945; London: Chatto & Windus, 1946);

Science, Liberty, and Peace (New York: Harper, 1946; London: Chatto & Windus, 1947);

Verses and a Comedy (London: Chatto & Windus, 1946);

The World of Aldous Huxley: An Omnibus of His Fiction and Non-Fiction over Three Decades, edited by Charles J. Rolo (New York: Harper, 1947);

Ape and Essence (New York: Harper, 1948; London: Chatto & Windus, 1949);

The Gioconda Smile: A Play (London: Chatto & Windus, 1948; New York: Harper, 1948);

Prisons, with the "Carceri" Etchings by G. B. Piranesi (London: Trianon, 1949; Los Angeles: Zeitlin & Ver Brugge, 1949);

Themes and Variations (London: Chatto & Windus, 1950; New York: Harper, 1950);

The Devils of Loudun (London: Chatto & Windus, 1952; New York: Harper, 1952);

Joyce, the Artificer: Two Studies of Joyce's Method, by Huxley and Stuart Gilbert (London: Chiswick, 1952);

A Day in Windsor, by Huxley and J. A. Kings (London: Britannicus Liber, 1953);

The Doors of Perception (London: Chatto & Windus, 1954; New York: Harper, 1954);

The French of Paris (New York: Harper, 1954);

The Genius and the Goddess (London: Chatto & Windus, 1955; New York: Harper, 1955);

Adonis and the Alphabet, and Other Essays (London: Chatto & Windus, 1956); republished as *Tomorrow and Tomorrow and Tomorrow, and Other Essays* (New York: Harper, 1956);

Heaven and Hell (London: Chatto & Windus, 1956; New York: Harper, 1956);

Collected Short Stories (London: Chatto & Windus, 1957; New York: Harper, 1957);

Brave New World Revisited (London: Chatto & Windus, 1958; New York: Harper, 1958);

Collected Essays (New York: Harper, 1959);

On Art and Artists, edited by Morris Philipson (London: Chatto & Windus, 1960; New York: Harper, 1960);

Island: A Novel (London: Chatto & Windus, 1962; New York: Harper, 1962);

Literature and Science (London: Chatto & Windus, 1963; New York: Harper & Row, 1963);

The Crows of Pearlblossom (New York: Random House, 1967; London: Chatto & Windus, 1968);

The Human Situation: Lectures at Santa Barbara, 1959, edited by Pierro Ferrucci (New York: Harper & Row, 1972).

Collections: *Rotunda: A Selection from the Works of Aldous Huxley* (London: Chatto & Windus, 1932);

Retrospect: An Omnibus of Aldous Huxley's Books (Garden City, N.Y.: Doubleday, Doran, 1933);

The Collected Poetry of Aldous Huxley, edited by Donald Watt (London: Chatto & Windus, 1971; New York: Harper & Row, 1971).

MOTION PICTURES: *Pride and Prejudice*, scenario by Huxley and Jane Murfin, M-G-M, 1940;

Madame Curie, treatment by Huxley, M-G-M, 1943;

Jane Eyre, scenario by Huxley, 20th Century–Fox, 1944;

A Woman's Vengeance, adaptation by Huxley from his play *The Gioconda Smile*, Universal-International, 1948.

OTHER: Thomas Humphry Ward, ed., *The English Poets: Selections with Critical Introductions*, introductions to poetry of John Davidson, Ernest Dowson, and Richard Middleton by Huxley (London: Macmillan, 1918);

Rémy de Gourmont, *A Virgin Heart: A Novel*, translated by Huxley (New York: Brown, 1921; London: Allen & Unwin, 1926);

Mrs. Frances Sheridan, *The Discovery: A Comedy in Five Acts*, introduction and stage adaptation by Huxley (London: Chatto & Windus, 1924; New York: Doran, 1925);

Claude P. J. de Crébillon, *The Opportunities of a Night*, introduction by Huxley (London: Chapman & Hall, 1925);

Benjamin R. Haydon, *The Autobiography and Memoirs of Benjamin Haydon*, introduction by Huxley (London: Davies, 1926; New York: Harcourt, Brace, 1926);

Oliver Simon and Jules Rodenberg, *Printing of Today*, introduction by Huxley (London: Davies, 1928; New York: Harper, 1928);

J. H. Burns, *A Vision of Education: Being an Imaginary Verbatim Report of the First Interplanetary Conference*, preface by Huxley (London: Williams & Norgate, 1929);

Campbell Dixon, *This Way to Paradise: A Play in Three Acts from the Novel Point Counter Point, by Aldous Huxley*, preface by Huxley (London: Chatto & Windus, 1930);

Maurice A. Pink, *A Realist Looks at Democracy*, preface by Huxley (London: Benn, 1930; New York: Stokes, 1931);

Douglas Goldering, *The Fortune*, preface by Huxley (London: Harmsworth, 1931);

The Letters of D. H. Lawrence, edited, with an introduction, by Huxley (London: Heinemann, 1932; New York: Viking, 1932);

Samuel Butler, *Erewhon*, introduction by Huxley (New York: Limited Editions Club, 1934);

Alfred H. Mendes, *Pitch Lake: A Story from Trinidad*, introduction by Huxley (London: Duckworth, 1934);

Norman Haire, *Birth-Control Methods (Contraception, Abortion, Sterilization)*, foreword by Huxley (London: Allen & Unwin, 1936);

Charlotte Wolff, *Studies in Hand-Reading*, preface by Huxley (London: Chatto & Windus, 1936; New York: Knopf, 1937);

New York Museum of Modern Art, *Posters by E. McKnight Kauffer*, foreword by Huxley (New York: Museum of Modern Art, 1937; London: Allen & Unwin, 1937);

Lawrence C. Powell, ed., *The Manuscripts of D. H. Lawrence: A Descriptive Catalog*, introduction by Huxley (Los Angeles: Ritchie, 1937);

An Encyclopedia of Pacifism, edited by Huxley (London: Chatto & Windus, 1937; New York: Harper, 1937);

Barthélemy de Ligt, *The Conquest of Violence: An Essay on War and Revolution,* introduction by Huxley (London: Routledge, 1938; New York: Dutton, 1938);

They Still Draw Pictures! A Collection of 60 Drawings Made by Spanish Children During the War, introduction by Huxley (New York: Spanish Child Welfare Association of America, 1938);

Knud Merrild, *Knud Merrild, a Poet and Two Painters: A Memoir of D. H. Lawrence,* preface by Huxley (London: Routledge, 1938; New York: Viking, 1939);

Hyacinthe Dubreuil, *A Chance for Everybody: A Liberal Basis for the Organization of Work,* foreword by Huxley (London: Chatto & Windus, 1939);

Maxim Gorky, *A Book of Short Stories,* foreword by Huxley (London: Cape, 1939; New York: Holt, 1939);

Allan A. Hunter, *White Corpuscles in Europe,* foreword by Huxley (Chicago: Willett, 1939);

Joseph Daniel Unwin, *Hopousia; or, The Sexual and Economic Foundations of a New Society,* introduction by Huxley (London: Allen & Unwin, 1940; New York: Piest, 1940);

Ashley Montagu, *Man's Most Dangerous Myth: The Fallacy of Race,* foreword by Huxley (London: Columbia University Press, 1942);

Francisco J. de Goya y Lucientes, *The Complete Etchings of Goya,* foreword by Huxley (New York: Crown, 1943; London: Wingate, 1959);

Bhagavadgita: The Song of God, introduction by Huxley (Hollywood, Cal.: Rodd, 1944; London: Phoenix House, 1947);

William Law, *Selected Mystical Writings,* foreword by Huxley (New York: Harper, 1948);

Ramakrishna, *Ramakrishna: Prophet of New India,* foreword by Huxley (New York: Harper, 1948; London: Rider, 1951);

Victor W. Von Hagen, *Frederick Catherwood,* introduction by Huxley (London & New York: Oxford University Press, 1950);

Ramakrishna, *The Gospel of Sri Ramakrishna,* foreword by Huxley (New York: Ramakrishna-Vivekananda Center, 1952);

Jiddu Krishnamurti, *The First and Last Freedom,* introduction by Huxley (New York: Harper, 1954; London: Gollancz, 1954);

Hubert Benoît, *The Supreme Doctrine: Psychological Studies in Zen Thought,* foreword by Huxley (London: Routledge & Kegan Paul, 1955; New York: Pantheon, 1955);

Frederick Mayer, *New Directions for the American University,* introduction by Huxley (Washington, D.C.: Public Affairs Press, 1957);

Alvah W. Sulloway, *Birth Control and Catholic Doctrine,* preface by Huxley (Boston: Beacon, 1959);

Danilo Dolci, *Report from Palermo,* introduction by Huxley (New York: Orion, 1959).

Among intellectuals Aldous Huxley's reputation as a novelist flourished in the 1920s. His literary accomplishments span many genres: poetry, essays, plays, journalism, historical studies, travel works, screenplays, and short stories. Like the novels, the short stories reveal contrapuntal tension within Huxley as he searched for an authentic voice — for identity and order in this grievous, chaotic world. Reflecting post–World War I disillusionment, Huxley struggled with a thoroughgoing skepticism; indeed, in his foreword to *Brave New World* (1932) he calls his earlier self a "Pyrrhonic aesthete" — one who doubts everything. His early writing, therefore, explored the truth and humor in the idea "that human beings are given free will in order to choose between insanity on the one hand and lunacy on the other." His irreverent satire can be traced largely to that brilliance that distinguished his family forebears and to several traumatic experiences in his life.

Huxley was born at Laleham near Godalming, Surrey, into an intellectually prestigious family on 26 July 1894. His struggle between skepticism and faith derived naturally from the two branches of his family. His paternal grandfather, Thomas Henry Huxley, was a man of letters, a biologist, and a proponent of Charles Darwin's theory of evolution; his maternal grandfather, Rev. Thomas Arnold, vacillated between the Anglican Church and the Roman Catholic Church. This tug between agnosticism and religious belief repeatedly manifests itself in his writing. Huxley's illustrious lineage also includes his great-grandfather, Dr. Thomas Arnold of Rugby, an educational reformer; his great-uncle, Matthew Arnold, a poet and educator; and his aunt, Mrs. Humphrey Ward, a novelist. Huxley's immediate family continued the tradition of intellectual luminaries. His father, Leonard Huxley, taught at Charterhouse before eventually joining the publishing firm of Smith, Elder, as reader and literary adviser. There he edited the *Cornhill Magazine* and wrote a biography of his father, *Life and Letters of Thomas Henry Huxley* (1900). A few years after her fourth child was born, Huxley's mother, Julia Frances Arnold Huxley, founded a girls' school at Prior's Field.

The four Huxley children lived happy lives in a stimulating household and were baptized into the Church of England despite their father's agnosticism and their mother's nonsectarian faith. Sybille Bedford,

Huxley and D. H. Lawrence in the hills near Florence, Italy, 28 October 1926 (photograph by Maria Huxley)

biographer of Aldous Huxley, writes that "like his mother Aldous possessed invisible moral authority." Huxley's brother Julian (who became a noted biologist) recognized a mystical quality in his brother's personality when they were children: from the time Aldous was five years old Julian recognized that the boy "possessed some innate superiority and moved on a different level of being from us other children."

Nevertheless, the household was not immune to tragedy. Huxley's mother died from cancer in 1908 when he was just fourteen. At sixteen while at Eton College he contracted an eye disease (keratitis punctata) that left him nearly blind for eighteen months, permanently damaged his sight, and thus ended his hopes for a scientific or medical career. In 1914 Huxley's brother Trevenen committed suicide. The horrors of a war for which Huxley was disqualified followed, but Huxley performed alternative service in the antiwar atmosphere of Garsington, the country estate of Lady Ottoline and Sir Philip Morrell. All of these events were to affect the

subjects, settings, tones, moods, and imagery of Huxley's writing.

At Balliol College, Oxford, from 1913 to 1916 Huxley excelled in his academic work and gained writing experience by editing literary journals. At nearby Garsington he met many stimulating writers and intellectuals as well as his future wife, Maria Nys – a shy young Belgian refugee staying there. During this period Huxley was also writing, publishing, and giving readings of his poetry. A favorite story emphasizing his intellectual bent concerns his reading of a new *Handy Volume of the Encyclopaedia Britannica*. He had a special box built to contain this volume, which he carried with him on his travels. Friends said they could tell which volume he was reading by his conversation – "one day it would be Alps, Andes and Apennines, and the next it would be the Himalayas and the Hippocratic Oath." In 1920, a year after Aldous's marriage to Maria, his son Matthew was born, and Huxley published his first book of short stories.

Published between 1920 and 1930, his five short-story collections cover a relatively short period of a writing career that began in 1916 with the publication of his first poetry collection, *The Burning Wheel,* and continued until 1963 when his last book, *Literature and Science,* appeared only two months before his death. Although only about sixteen hundred copies were sold of his first volume of short stories, *Limbo* (1920), his fresh voice forecasting the ironic postwar temperament attracted attention. His writing was characterized as delectable, sophisticated, fastidiously cynical, and of lasting importance.

This early volume contains six stories and a short closet play with themes closely resembling those of his first novel, *Crome Yellow* (1921), published the following year. Like his novels, Huxley's short stories are filled with eccentric people who often focus so exclusively on one idea that they lose contact with the mainstream of life. These eccentrics engage in witty dialogues without ever really understanding one another, and these satires are often set at English country-house parties. His stories also often incorporate incidents or themes that parallel his own biography. In "The Death of Lully" from this first collection, for example, a desirable woman has breast cancer, as did Huxley's mother; the disruptions of war figure prominently in stories such as "The Bookshop," "Happily Ever After," and "The Farcical History of Richard Greenow." Themes of sight, distorted sight, and insight permeate Huxley's short stories, and a suicide like that of Huxley's brother Trevenen occurs in "Eupompus Gave Splendour to Art by Numbers."

This last story presents Emberlin, a London academic who lives in an "oasis of aloofness." Having published a volume of verses in a moment of youthful folly, he spends his time buying back copies of the book and burning them. Emberlin becomes obsessed with Eupompus, a portrait artist in ancient Alexandria who abandoned this lucrative form of art because he fell in love with numbers. To Eupompus numbers suddenly appeared to be the only true reality, and he filled his paintings with thirty-three thousand black swans, an orchard of identical trees, or masses of people. His misguided followers studied these paintings by counting and recounting the objects on the canvas. This new school of "Philarithmics" reached its apex when the mad artist began a painting of "Pure Number." In a moment of "sanity" Eupompus killed two of his disciples and committed suicide before he finished this idiosyncratic, exclusive vision of ultimate reality, but Emberlin becomes a devoted Eupompian and loses himself in the insanity of numerical bliss. Wholeness eludes this fractured life, just as it does

the lives of many Huxleyan characters, including Richard Greenow.

Incompleteness and fragmentation in "The Farcical History of Richard Greenow," the longest story in *Limbo,* exist in the dual personality of Dick, a psychological hermaphrodite. Dick has failed to nurture what psychologist Carl Jung calls the anima (the feminine soul present in man), and he is left vulnerable to attacks of emotional excess. Dick's public, socially accepted personality serves as president of the Fabian Society, wins honors at Oxford, works on his Synthetic Philosophy, and joins the staff of *Weekly International*. By night Dick's personality transforms itself into Pearl Bellairs, who writes romantic novels that have enormous sales. When the war starts, Dick tries to be a reasonable voice of pacifism, but Pearl writes recruiting songs and patriotic articles. When Dick, a conscientious objector, becomes fatigued from leading an anticonscription campaign, Pearl takes over for days at a time with her prowar message, and Dick's mental stability is in jeopardy. In a moment of sanity when he realizes that he is in an insane asylum, he tries to write a last statement – which emerges half antiwar and half militaristic. These two voices in his divided self fight for dominance until Dick dies. His jailers consider his scribbled papers as the ravings of a madman.

Huxley's early fiction repeats the unhappy results of Richard Greenow's emotional neglect in many different forms. In "Happily Ever After," for instance, Guy Lambourne becomes engaged to his guardian's daughter during the first year of the war. Although they write to one another faithfully, they maintain a rational relationship rather than explore their emotions. When Guy comes home on leave, a diverse house party gathers, prefiguring those later country-house parties in *Crome Yellow* and *Those Barren Leaves* (1925). The ideas and conversation of the guests intrude, and the young couple are kept from exploring their sexual desires. Opportunity passes; Guy returns to the war, where he is killed.

Huxley's overly cerebral characters such as Emberlin, Dick, and Guy, who have neglected their social and feeling selves, embody tendencies not only of Huxley but also of Denis Stone in *Crome Yellow*. Guy, like Denis, goes into a moonlit garden with his beloved and begins to kiss the woman he loves; for once, both of these young men act on their emotions. This brief mystical moment passes, however, and they suffer from a failure of confidence. Guy remembers his one lustful encounter with a prostitute, and he pushes his fiancée away in disgust. Denis, on the other hand, boastfully offers to carry his love back to the house after she has fallen and hurt herself. When he attempts to do so, however, he staggers out of control and becomes the object of laughter. Unable to bear the shameful humiliation, Guy returns to war and death; Denis, pleading urgent family business, leaves Crome and meets a kind of spiritual death. Ironically Denis "felt as though he were making arrangements for his own funeral." This theme of divided personalities – rational thought versus unrestrained emotion – runs throughout Huxley's short stories. Wholeness eludes most of his characters, who yearn for the values found in the religion, love, and family life that are missing in postwar society.

Although Huxley's second volume of short stories, *Mortal Coils* (1922), no longer portrays the tension of wartime settings, the stories continue to present the post–World War atmosphere of decay and fragmentation. The settings also shift from England to Italy, which Huxley and his wife first visited in April 1921 before finally moving there in 1923 to live for four productive years. The dichotomy between intention and action in the characters of Guy and Denis continues to appear in Henry Hutton, the central character of Huxley's best-known story, "The Gioconda Smile." Hutton, whose invalid wife suffers from a bad heart, has secret liaisons with other women. He flirts with Janet Spence, an unmarried friend with an enigmatic gioconda smile, and he seduces Doris, a pretty but shallow young woman. Having misread Hutton's intentions and anticipating that he would marry her if he were free to do so, Janet poisons his wife – who dies one night when Hutton is with Doris. In a moment of contrition after the funeral, he resolves never to see Doris again. Even so, intention and action do not coincide; within two weeks he secretly marries Doris – and proceeds to seduce a servant girl. Like Richard Greenow, who fails in his attempt to live an unemotional, cerebral life of reason, Hutton also fails to restrain his emotional appetites. Janet's expectations do not match reality either, for Hutton has married someone else and is moving to Italy. Rejected, Janet gets her revenge by accusing Hutton of the crime, and he is convicted and executed. Only Dr. Lillard knows the sad truth. Years later when Huxley rewrote "The Gioconda Smile" as a play and as a film, Dr. Lillard becomes a mystical visionary and saves Hutton from execution.

Three other short stories in *Mortal Coils* – "The Tillotson Banquet," "Green Tunnels," and "Nuns at Luncheon" – are among Huxley's best. They all explore the unexpected twists and turns of a chaotic, hostile world that keep characters from fulfilling their goals and expectations. In "The Tillotson Banquet" Lord Badgery sponsors a subscription dinner for an aging painter whose work has been recognized as that of a genius. The ninety-seven-year-old painter, Walter Tillotson (now almost blind, palsied, and living in poverty), hopes to be restored to his prominent place in the world. The day after the banquet the art enthusiasts, still enchanted with Tillotson's art, have ironically already dismissed the artist as irrelevant and invisible. Although his art will live, Tillotson faces deprivation, decay, and death.

The major characters in "Green Tunnels" and "Nuns at Luncheon" also fail to fulfill their expectations about life, although some have moments of insight. The mixture of satire and lyricism in "Green Tunnels" surfaces in Barbara Buzzacott and Mr. Topes – a young woman and a sixty-year-old man. The Buzzacotts and the Topeses, English expatriates living in Italy to avoid British taxes, discuss art and culture endlessly. To avoid the boring adult conversation, Barbara manages to live in her imagination. She romanticizes that a young Italian marquess has noticed her and written a message in the sand for her. Her fantasy evaporates when she sees the marquess on the beach with a woman of questionable character and discovers that Mr. Topes has written the name of a poem in the sand in her honor: her youthful beauty and innocence have poetically inspired him. Having led an empty life, Mr. Topes nearly weeps because the mystical beauty of the sea, the mountains, the clouds, and the young girl have given him hope for eternity. Barbara cries because reality does not measure up to the creations of her romantic imagination. Mr. Topes and Barbara do not have the same mystical visions, but like Calamy in *Those Barren Leaves* they have at least a brief hope that life can be reassuring instead of frightening and chaotic.

In "Nuns at Luncheon" a sexual assault by her father's friend when Sister Agatha was a young girl has shattered her goals and expectations about life. At age twenty-two during World War I she has joined a religious order and become a hospital nurse ministering to wounded soldiers. Although she tries to avoid spiritual pride, the atheism of her patients challenges her, and Sister Agatha's spirits are euphoric when she converts several of those patients. While caring for another prisoner who has been hospitalized, she falls in love. Convincing herself that he has found salvation, she helps the prisoner, dressed in nun's clothing, to escape detention. Having stolen an associate sister's clothes, run away from the convent, and broken her vows, Sister

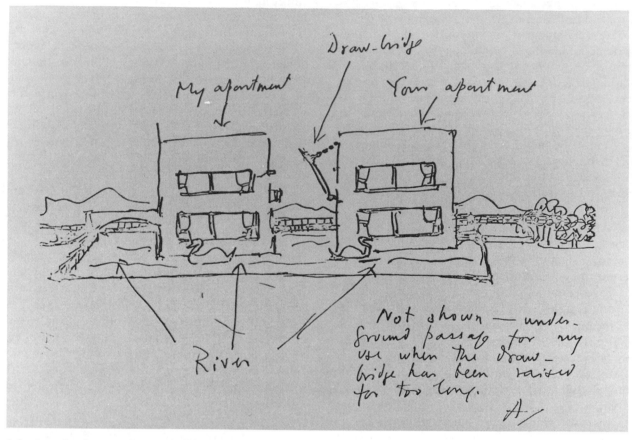

A facetious plan for a new house, which Huxley enclosed in a 29 June 1961 letter to his second wife, Laura, after a fire had destroyed their residence in the Hollywood Hills, California, on 12 May of that year (Laura Archera Huxley, This Timeless Moment: A Personal View of Aldous Huxley, *1968)*

Agatha returns to the Sisters of Charity after she has been deserted by the prisoner – who has added to her humiliation by having stolen her false teeth. The disgraced nun attends her own funeral service in the chapel. In some of Huxley's harshest irony Sister Agatha – looking like a toothless, walking corpse – returns to the hospital as a charwoman. In a world disrupted by violence and war her choices have left her, like Hutton in "The Gioconda Smile," already dead and in hell.

Huxley's collections of fiction (*Limbo, Crome Yellow,* and *Mortal Coils*) gained steadily in reputation, and in January 1923 he signed an agreement with Chatto and Windus to publish two works of fiction (one of which was to be a novel) each year for the next three years. Although this arrangement provided Huxley (a young husband and father of a two-year-old son) with a steady income and thus relieved his financial stress, it required tremendous creative discipline. Huxley felt equal to the challenge, and by November he had published his second novel, *Antic Hay* (1923), followed in May by his third book of short stories, *Little Mexican, & Other Stories* (1924).

In the six stories of *Little Mexican* satire and witty dialogue highlighting different points of view continued to undergird Huxley's search for identity and values in a harsh, disorderly world. For example, an Italian count in "Little Mexican" manipulates his son's life so that he remains trapped by family and business responsibilities while the old count lives as if he were on continual holiday. The son, old in spirit, never gets to experience the world. "Hubert and Minnie" depicts disappointing love between the title characters – Hubert because he realizes that he is not in love, at least not with this older woman, and Minnie because she faces a vast loneliness. "Fard," a term meaning a burden or an empty life, exemplifies the lives of all of the characters in this story. The maid, Sophie, labors long hours for her self-indulgent mistress, and although Sophie feels sick and dizzy, her mistress feels pity only for herself – because she has to look at her miserable, yellow-faced maid. Her mistress insists that Sophie put on rouge so that she will not look so pale and tired, but "Madame" never considers letting Sophie rest.

In "The Portrait" Mr. Bigger, an art dealer, plays a harsh trick on a customer and an artist. The customer, having just bought a large manor house, wants to furnish it appropriately with Old Masters. Mr. Bigger seizes the opportunity to sell the customer a bogus painting, for which he invents an appropriately romantic story in order to enhance the sale. The status-conscious buyer pays £680 for the so-called Venetian painting – with the stipulation that Mr. Bigger provide a typewritten copy of the story about the painting. The art dealer pays a young, aspiring painter £25 for the fraudulent Old Master. Each person experiences a different reality – both the customer and the painter leave satisfied, yet both have been cheated.

The first and last stories in *Little Mexican* have been highly praised. The first, "Uncle Spencer," is set in Belgium, the native country of Huxley's wife, and comprises almost half of the book. In its long introduction the narrator recounts spending his school holidays with his uncle in Longres. During World War I Uncle Spencer and Longres's cobbler, Monsieur Alphonse, are interned in prison camps, where all cultures and classes of people must live together. Alphonse becomes unable to tolerate confinement; he dies after making startling predictions about the war. Uncle Spencer falls in love with a fellow prisoner, Emmy Wendle, a former dance-hall girl half as old as he is. They become separated, and after the war he cannot find her. Uncle Spencer continues to believe that he will find Emmy, because Alphonse, whose other predictions have all come true, had predicted that they would marry. Huxley captures the harsh realities facing people whose lives have been disrupted by war. They no longer have orderly routines or religious and family support to sustain them.

Just as Alphonse lets himself die, a precocious peasant child in "Young Archimedes" commits suicide by throwing himself out a window. The Italian child, Guido, is a genius in music and mathematics, but he feels abandoned when his parents succumb to their landlady's pressure to take him from his family, playmates, and familiar surroundings. She forces young Guido to practice the piano long hours each day. The story ends with both the waste of a child's life in a disorderly world and a mystical affirmation of the purity of a child's extraordinary sense of reality.

Huxley continued his contractual obligations with Chatto and Windus by publishing *Those Barren Leaves,* a novel in which for the first time mystical solitude emerges as a feasible alternative to the emptiness of modern life. After completing this novel, Huxley and Maria began an eleven-month world tour that focused on Asia and undoubtedly reinforced Huxley's fascination with mystical religion. Although in his short stories Huxley had been exploring the different realities people experience in the world, his mystical idealism had been overshadowed by such personal grief as his mother's death by disease, his brother's death by suicide, his own illness causing near blindness, and the horrors of war. Huxley's persona of the skeptical "Pyrrhonic aesthete" could no longer concentrate on life's meaninglessness without struggling to overcome such personal hopelessness and despair.

Huxley's fourth book of short stories, *Two or Three Graces, and Other Stories* (1926), follows a pattern of one long novella and several shorter stories. Continuing to find loyal readers without being bestsellers, these books of short fiction helped keep Huxley solvent; *Two or Three Graces* sold two thousand hardbound copies and thirty-five hundred paperbound copies at publication. The three shorter stories – "Half-Holiday," "The Monocle," and "Fairy Godmother" – all involve lonely persons ridiculed by others. The first story begins with a mystical description of London, "a city of the imagination." But reality breaks through the imagination when two young girls reject and humiliate Peter Brett because of class differences and his unfortunate stammer. In the second story Gregory, a self-centered hypocrite, lives in a state of insecurity: he wears a monocle, a token of the position to which he aspires, but this adornment fails to make others respect him. In the third story Mrs. Escobar, the fairy godmother, "does unto others" as long as it makes her feel superior to them, and her unsuitable gifts, patronizingly given, do not produce love and affection. In each story the protagonist's romantic expectations do not fit with the harsh reality of the world.

Critics often find a strong influence from D. H. Lawrence in Huxley's novella "Two or Three Graces." Although Huxley and Lawrence had first met in 1915, the two novelists did not become close friends until they began visiting one another in Italy in 1926. Huxley certainly knew Lawrence's novels, however, and in a 23 June 1920 letter to Leonard Huxley he described Lawrence as a "slightly insane novelist, who was analysed for his complexes, dark and tufty ones, tangled in his mind." The character of Kingham, a temperamental writer in "Two or Three Graces," resembles Lawrence. In his affair with Grace Peddley, Kingham purposely provokes emotional complications in order to create tension and sexual passion. He perversely humiliates her or makes her suffer as a way of stimulating his own emotions. Weary of Grace, Kingham leaves her in a final act of cruelty. Eventually she returns to her boring husband or goes on to another affair. Huxley's satiric tale of human relationships driven by unbridled passion and deprived of any form of reason leads to *Point Counter Point* (1928), Huxley's musically structured novel in which many episodes of sexual seduction take place contrapuntally.

Huxley returned to poetry in 1929 with a short volume, *Arabia Infelix, and Other Poems*. Huxley's spiritual crises scarred these years at the end of the decade, and Huxley strove in these poems to overcome his own hopelessness and despair. Because the external world offers no consolation, Huxley increasingly tried to reach a visionary world through a struggle to diminish the human ego.

In *Brief Candles: Stories* (1930) Huxley writes about people who have overdeveloped egos that inhibit their emotional and spiritual maturity. Chawdron, in a story by that name, is enormously wealthy and ruthless in business. Emotionally he gravitates to women who control him through such kittenish and childlike behavior as baby talk and feigned, mysterious illnesses. His relationships resemble that of Jo Stoyte and his promiscuous but pious mistress in the later novel *After Many a Summer* (1939). In "The Rest Cure" Moira's grandfather spoils her and raises her as a pet. When she marries a cancer researcher, John Tarwin, their self-absorptions prevent love or sex between them. In Italy Moira has a torrid affair with a young man who takes advantage of her for her money. Pushed over the edge, she shoots herself. The children in "The Claxtons" suffer from the superior attitude of their mother, Martha Claxton, who enforces a spartan lifestyle on her family. Because she controls the money, her husband, Herbert, remains stoically in agreement; her son, Paul, becomes rebellious; her daughter, Sylvia, retreats into spiritual isolation. Huxley caricatures the private lives of family members in which the eccentric personalities of the dominant egos crush the weaker family members. Huxley no longer is amused with this pretentious spirituality.

The novella "After the Fireworks," which was written the year after publication of *Point Counter Point,* dominates these shorter stories in *Brief Candles*. The egoistic novelist Miles Fanning, an aging advocate of Lawrence's philosophy of the harmony of mind, body, and spirit expressed through passionate sexuality, reluctantly takes an eager young lover, Pamela Tarn. Trapped by his romantic sto-

ries of liberated young women, Miles and Pamela become disillusioned. Huxley wickedly satirizes and even parodies their relationship when Fanning becomes ill with a liver ailment because of his overactive sex life, and Pamela makes plans to join a younger man. The Italian fireworks display stimulates sexual desire rather than love or mystical vision. With this story Huxley began to reject Lawrence's philosophy and return to his own mystical quest.

Huxley stopped writing short stories after 1930 because, as he had written in a 29 April 1924 letter to his father, "the mere business of telling a story interests me less and less. . . . The only really and permanently absorbing things are attitudes towards life and the relation of man to the world." As he moved toward more open discussion of spirituality and idealism in a mystical unity of all things, longer fictional formats worked best for him. Nevertheless, the short stories, which illuminate his attitudes toward life in less-complex structures, will remain satiric gems.

Letters:

The Letters of Aldous Huxley, edited by Grover Smith (London: Chatto & Windus, 1969; New York: Harper & Row, 1969).

Bibliographies:

Claire John Eschelback and Joyce Lee Shober, *Aldous Huxley: A Bibliography 1916–1959* (Berkeley & Los Angeles: University of California Press, 1961; London: Cambridge University Press, 1961);

Thomas D. Clareson and Carolyn S. Andrews, "Aldous Huxley: A Bibliography 1960–1964," *Extrapolation,* 6 (December 1964): 2–21;

Dennis D. Davis, "Aldous Huxley: A Bibliography 1965–1973," *Bulletin of Bibliography,* 31 (April–June 1974): 67–70.

Biographies:

Julian Huxley, ed., *Aldous Huxley, 1894–1963: A Memorial Volume* (London: Chatto & Windus, 1965; New York: Harper & Row, 1965);

Ronald W. Clark, *The Huxleys* (London: Heinemann, 1968; New York: McGraw, 1968);

Laura Archera Huxley, *This Timeless Moment: A Personal View of Aldous Huxley* (New York: Farrar, Straus & Giroux, 1968; London: Hogarth, 1969);

Philip Thody, *Aldous Huxley: A Biographical Introduction* (London: Studio Vista, 1973);

Sybille Bedford, *Aldous Huxley: A Biography,* 2 volumes (London: Chatto & Windus, 1973–1974);

David King Dunaway, *Huxley in Hollywood* (New York: Harper & Row, 1989).

References:

John Atkins, *Aldous Huxley: A Literary Study* (London: Calder, 1956; revised edition, New York: Orion, 1968);

Milton Birnbaum, *Aldous Huxley's Quest for Values* (Knoxville: University of Tennessee Press, 1971);

Peter Bowering, *Aldous Huxley: A Study of the Major Novels* (London: Athlone Press, 1969; New York: Oxford University Press, 1969);

Peter E. Firchow, *Aldous Huxley, Satirist and Novelist* (Minneapolis: University of Minnesota Press, 1972);

Charles M. Holmes, *Aldous Huxley and the Way to Reality* (Bloomington & London: Indiana University Press, 1969);

Jerome Meckier, *Aldous Huxley: Satire and Structure* (London: Chatto & Windus, 1969; New York: Barnes & Noble, 1971);

Maria Schubert, "The Use of Irony in Aldous Huxley's Short Fiction," in *A Salzburg Miscellany: English and American Studies 1964–84,* volume 2, edited by James Hogg (Salzburg: Institut für Anglistik und Amerikanistik Universtät Salzburg, 1984);

George Woodcock, *Dawn and the Darkest Hour: A Study of Aldous Huxley* (London: Faber & Faber, 1972; New York: Viking, 1972).

James Joyce

(2 February 1882 – 13 January 1941)

Kevin J. H. Dettmar
Clemson University

See also the Joyce entries in *DLB 10: Modern British Dramatists, 1900–1945; DLB 19: British Poets, 1880–1914;* and *DLB 36: British Novelists, 1890–1929: Modernists.*

BOOKS: *Two Essays: "A Forgotten Aspect of the University Question," by F. J. C. Skeffington and "The Day of the Rabblement," by James Joyce* (Dublin: Privately printed, 1901);

Chamber Music (London: Elkin Mathews, 1907; New York: Huebsch, 1918);

Dubliners (London: Grant Richards, 1914; New York: Huebsch, 1916);

A Portrait of the Artist as a Young Man (New York: Huebsch, 1916; London: Egoist, 1917);

Exiles: A Play in Three Acts (London: Grant Richards, 1918; New York: Huebsch, 1918);

Ulysses (Paris: Shakespeare, 1922; London: Egoist, 1922; New York: Random House, 1934);

Pomes Penyeach (Paris: Shakespeare, 1927; Princeton: Sylvia Beach, 1931; London: Harmsworth, 1932);

Collected Poems (New York: Black Sun, 1936);

Finnegans Wake (London: Faber & Faber, 1939; New York: Viking, 1939);

Stephen Hero (London: Cape, 1944; New York: New Directions, 1944);

The Critical Writings of James Joyce, edited by Ellsworth Mason and Richard Ellmann (New York: Viking, 1959);

The Workshop of Dedalus: James Joyce and the Materials for "A Portrait of the Artist as a Young Man," edited by Robert Scholes and Richard M. Kain (Evanston, Ill.: Northwestern University Press, 1965);

Giacomo Joyce, edited by Ellmann (New York: Viking, 1968);

Ulysses: A Facsimile of the Manuscript, edited by Clive Driver (New York: Farrar, Straus & Giroux, 1975);

Ulysses Notebooks, edited by Phillip F. Herring (Charlottesville: University of Virginia Press, 1977);

The James Joyce Archive, 63 volumes, edited by Michael Groden, Hans Walter Gabler, David Hayman, A. Walton Litz, and Danis Rose (New York & London: Garland, 1978);

Ulysses: A Critical and Synoptic Edition, 3 volumes, edited by Gabler, Wolfhard Steppe, and Claus

Melchior (New York & London: Garland, 1984);

Ulysses, edited by Gabler, Steppe, and Melchior (New York: Random House / London: Bodley Head, 1986);

Poems and Epiphanies, edited by Ellmann and Litz (New York: Viking / London: Faber & Faber, 1990).

Rather than forging radically new means for fiction, the novels of James Joyce — *A Portrait of the Artist as a Young Man* (1916), *Ulysses* (1922), and *Finnegans Wake* (1939) — as well as his single short-story collection, *Dubliners* (1914), changed the way fiction has been written in the twentieth century by subtly refining the advances made by others. Joyce's strict narrative focus in such a story as "The Sisters" (1904), for instance, had been used by Henry James in *What Maisie Knew* (1897); his use of free indirect discourse had been suggested by Gustave Flaubert's *style indirect libre* employed so successfully in *Madame Bovary* (1856–1857). In Joyce's hands, however, such techniques became seamless, almost invisible parts of the narrative structure. What could at times seem awkward in other writers makes itself known in Joyce's texts only after repeated careful readings.

James Augustus Alyosius Joyce was born on 2 February 1882 in Rathgar, a modest borough of Dublin, Ireland. He was the eldest of what his father, John Stanislaus Joyce, estimated as "sixteen or seventeen children," ten of whom survived infancy. By the time of his birth the fortunes of his father were already declining. Stephen Dedalus, the autobiographical hero of *A Portrait of the Artist as a Young Man,* was to describe his father as "a medical student, an oarsman, a tenor, an amateur actor, a shouting politician, a small landlord, a small investor, a drinker, a good fellow, a storyteller, somebody's secretary, something in a distillery, a taxgatherer, a bankrupt and at present a praiser of his own past." The description was an apt one of Joyce's own father, as well. His mother, Mary Jane (Murray) Joyce, seems to have been precisely the kind of calming influence John Joyce sorely needed; as James Joyce's biographer Richard Ellmann puts it, if John Joyce "was the principle of chaos, she was the principle of order to which he might cling."

In the fall of 1888, at age six, Joyce was enrolled as the youngest of the boarders at Clongowes Wood College, an academically sound Jesuit boarding school outside Dublin in Salins, County Kildare. He was to live at the college, except during holidays, until June 1891. By the end of the 1890-1891 school year, however, his father's mounting financial difficulties dictated that he be withdrawn from the college. He was allowed for a time to study at home by himself, which he seems to have done conscientiously. Sometime during the fall or winter term of 1893 John Joyce finally enrolled James in the Christian Brothers' School, a considerable descent both academically and socially for the Joyces. Fortunately Father John Conmee, who had been rector at Clongowes while James had been a student there, was now the prefect of studies at an outstanding Jesuit day school, Belvedere College. Hearing of James's somewhat compromised situation, he arranged for all the Joyce boys to attend Belvedere without fees, and James began his studies there on 6 April 1893.

Joyce distinguished himself at Belvedere, and upon graduating in 1898 he matriculated at University College of the Catholic University in Dublin founded by John Henry Cardinal Newman in 1853. Again Joyce did exceptionally well. In the fall of his sophomore year he prepared a paper defending Henrik Ibsen's drama, a paper titled "Drama and Life," for presentation to the college Literary and Historical Society. The paper was suppressed, however, by the college president. Joyce protested and prevailed, but when the paper was read on 20 January 1900 it was roundly condemned by Joyce's classmates, who found the morality evidenced in Ibsen's plays reprehensible, just as the president had.

Joyce replied to his attackers' objections, apparently with little efficacy, but his was the last word. On 1 April 1900 Joyce published an essay, "Ibsen's New Drama," in the venerable *Fortnightly Review.* As Ellmann writes, "his fellow-students were dumbfounded. . . . From now on Joyce was the man who had published the article in the *Fortnightly* and his confirmation of his good opinion of himself encouraged him to stand even more aloof." Stand aloof he did, producing a diatribe essay, "The Day of the Rabblement," in 1901 that attacked the social, political, and literary climate of Ireland. In February 1902 he read another paper before the literary society, this one on James Clarence Mangan, a victim (in Joyce's view) of the provincialism that he had decried in "The Day of the Rabblement."

Joyce took his degree in October, and in November 1902 he left Ireland for Paris, aiming to fulfill his fictional Stephen Dedalus's promise to try to "fly by" the nets of nationality, language, and religion via the strategy Stephen had articulated: "silence, exile, and cunning." Joyce's announced purpose was to pursue a medical degree, but the haphazard nature of his preparations and the half-hearted manner in which he approached the medical school curriculum belied the sincerity of his devotion to this career. The medical degree seems to have been a smokescreen behind which he could hide from his parents, and perhaps even from himself, his quest "to discover," as he later wrote in *A Portrait of the Artist as a Young Man,* "the mode of life or art whereby [his] spirit could express itself in unfettered freedom."

That exile in Paris – at least the first such – was to end rather quickly in April 1903: Joyce returned hastily to be with his mother, who was suffering from liver cancer that had been misdiagnosed as cirrhosis. Her final illness was slow and painful; she died on 13 August 1903. In the fourteen months that followed, before his second (and permanent) emigration from Ireland, Joyce wrote a two-thousand-word autobiographical essay, "A Portrait of the Artist" – a tentative gesture toward his first great novel, *A Portrait of the Artist as a Young Man.* He also began "Stephen Hero," the abortive first-draft version of the autobiographical novel, and he met, made a lifetime commitment to, and made plans to elope with Nora Barnacle, the woman he would formally marry in 1931. At this time, too, he wrote his first work of short fiction, "The Sisters," which was later to be the keystone of the collection *Dubliners.*

Joyce seems to have begun writing *Dubliners* with the conscious intention of reforming the craft of fiction. Many of his early letters to his brother Stanislaus reflect his impatience with a lack of subtlety in the fiction of both his forebears and contemporaries. In November 1904, for instance, while working on an early version of the story "Clay," Joyce complained of George Moore's collection of stories *The Untilled Field* (1903):

> Damned stupid. A woman alludes to her husband in the confession-box as "Ned." Ned thinks &c! A lady who has been living for three years on the line between Bray and Dublin is told by her husband that there is a meeting in Dublin at which he must be present. She looks up the table to see the hours of the trains. This on DW and WR [the Dublin, Wicklow, and Wexford Railway] where the trains go regularly; this after three years. Isn't it rather stupid of Moore. And the punctuation! Madonna!

Joyce's influence on the modern short story is especially remarkable, for his output was so slim – just the one volume of fifteen stories called *Dubliners.* The volume began as a single story, "The Sisters," written in response to a request from Irish poet and mystic AE (George William Russell), an editor for the agricultural paper *The Irish Homestead.* Russell had seen some chapters of Joyce's unpublished novel "Stephen Hero" and had admired them; he wrote Joyce in July 1904 to request a submission for *The Irish Homestead:*

> Dear Joyce: Look at the story in this paper, The Irish Homestead. Could you write anything simple, rural?, livemaking?, pathos?, which could be inserted so as not to shock the readers. If you could furnish a short story about 1800 words suitable for insertion the editor will pay £1. It is easily earned money if you can write fluently and don't mind playing to the common understanding or liking for once in a way. You can sign it any name you like as a pseudonym.

This seems to have been all the suggestion Joyce needed; indeed, the tight format Russell dictated may have come as a welcome relief from the sprawling novel which Joyce had seemed unable to control. He must have written the story easily, for it appeared as "Our Weekly Story" in the 13 August 1904 issue of *The Irish Homestead.* "The Sisters" was revised considerably for its appearance in *Dubliners,* where it introduces the collection and introduces many motifs woven throughout the other stories of the volume.

Much of Joyce's creative credo seems to have been firmly in place before he ever seriously put pen to paper. To a greater extent than he later did with *A Portrait of the Artist as a Young Man,* Joyce attempted to articulate both his aesthetic and moral goals for *Dubliners* in letters to Stanislaus as well as in the sometimes acrimonious correspondence to his fainthearted British publisher, Grant Richards. In August 1904, fresh upon the publication of "The Sisters," Joyce wrote to his friend Constantine Curran about what he was already calling *Dubliners,* which he described as a series of ten "epicleti" – apparently his plural form of the Greek word *epiclesis,* a term that denotes the moment in the Greek Orthodox mass when the priest invokes the Spirit of God to come down and transform the elements of the Eucharist. His volume, Joyce wrote to Curran, was intended "to betray the soul of that hemiplegia or paralysis which many consider a city."

By the time Joyce offered *Dubliners* to Grant Richards – William Heinemann had already declined Joyce's invitation to consider the manuscript – the story had grown to twelve stories. The Joyce household had also grown by one, as Georgio had been born on 27 July. In his 15 October 1905 letter to Richards, Joyce underscored his moral aim in writing the collection: "I think," the letter closes, "people might be willing to pay for the special

A Painful ~~Case~~ Case

Mr James Duffy lived in Chapelizod because
he wished to be as far as possible from
the city of which he was a citizen and
because he found all the other suburbs
of Dublin mean, modern and pretentious.
He lived in an old sombre house and
from his window he could look into
the disused distillery or upwards along
the shallow river on which Dublin is
built. The lofty walls of his uncarpeted
room were free from pictures. He had
himself bought every article of furniture
in the room; a black iron bedstead,
an iron washstand, ~~too~~ three cane
chairs, a clothes rack, a coal-scuttle,
a fender and irons and a square table
on which lay a double desk. A bookcase
had been made in an alcove by means
of shelves of white wood. The bed was
clothed with white bedclothes and a
black and scarlet rug covered the foot.
A little handmirror hung above the
washstand and during the day, a
white-shaded lamp stood as the sole
ornament of the mantelpiece. The books
on the white wooden shelves were
arranged from below upwards according

First page from a draft for one of the stories in Dubliners *(The James Joyce Archive)*

odour of corruption which, I hope, floats over my stories." Owing to his sense of the ethical function of the stories, Joyce was intractable when Richards began to express concern over potentially actionable phrases and passages in the stories. For instance, Joyce insisted on using the vulgar expression *bloody* in his story "Grace," presumably because that is the word that a man like Tom Kernan would have used. In response to Richards's suggestion that he would not publish the story without changes in such language, Joyce replied: "I have written my book with considerable care, in spite of a hundred difficulties, and in accordance with what I understand to be the classical tradition of my art." Joyce closed by duly informing Richards that the collection had expanded to fourteen stories.

Joyce's battle to have *Dubliners* published raged for a full decade. In May 1906 he wrote Richards again to assert the high purpose of his sometimes-low prose: "My intention was to write a chapter of the moral history of my country and I chose Dublin for the scene because that city seemed to me the centre of paralysis. . . . I have written it for the most part in a style of scrupulous meanness and with the conviction that he is a very bold man who dares to alter in the presentment, still more to deform, whatever he has seen and heard." In Joyce's mind, the realistic language of the *Dubliners* stories was something more than an aesthetic decision — it was akin to a moral imperative. He interpreted the reluctance of the Irish people to read such prose — or even, indeed, Richards's own reluctance to publish it — as a sign of moral cowardice and hypocrisy: "It is not my fault that the odour of ashpits and old weeds and offal hangs round my stories. I seriously believe that you will retard the course of civilisation in Ireland by preventing the Irish people from having one good look at themselves in my nicely polished looking-glass."

"The Sisters" is the first of three stories in *Dubliners* that Joyce referred to as "stories of my childhood." It is told by a first-person narrator, a young boy perhaps thirteen to sixteen years old, whose identity raises many unanswered questions: what is the boy's name, for instance, and why is he living with his aunt and uncle? Many more important mysteries are suggested as he tells his tale, although the basic outlines of the story are quite simple: the boy, who has spent much of his time under the tutelage of an old priest, the Reverend James Flynn, learns that his mentor has died after a long decline. Together with his aunt, he makes a call at the house of mourning and hears vague suggestions of the old priest's mental and moral, as well as phys-

ical, corruption. As with all the *Dubliners* stories, such a bare plot summary suggests almost nothing of the story's haunting power: the story depends on no hidden secret brought to light, no surprise ending that a plot summary might betray. This is perhaps partly what Joyce had in mind when he described his technique in the stories as "a style of scrupulous meanness": as in real life, events unfold rather regularly and unremarkably.

"The Sisters" is largely a story of the initiation of a young boy into the adult world. Real-world experience collides repeatedly in the story with the boy's expectations, and that world comes to seem a different place from that which he has been led to expect. The first significant shock occurs the day after the priest's death when, after his breakfast, the boy heads down to the priest's little house and reads the card posted on his door and adorned with a black crape:

July 1st, 1895

The Rev. James Flynn
(formerly of S. Catherine's Church,
Meath Street), aged sixty-five years.

R.I.P.

Reading the card, the narrator tells us, "persuaded me that he was dead and I was disturbed to find myself at check. . . . I found it strange that neither I nor the day seemed in a mourning mood and I felt even annoyed at discovering in myself a sensation of freedom as if I had been freed from something by his death." Social decorum, of course, demands that he put on mourning dress and a mourning mood; indeed, his Romantic reading seems to have suggested to him that even the natural environment should go into some cosmic mourning, according to the logic of what John Ruskin (*Modern Painters,* 1856) called the pathetic fallacy. But the truth of the situation is that the boy feels not loss, but freedom; the forms he has been taught simply do not account for the feelings he experiences.

Nor do social forms help him deal with the banal conversation that transpires at the traditional Irish wake in the last scene of the story. The sisters of the title — James Flynn's sisters, Nannie and Eliza — serve sherry and cream crackers, and Eliza and the boy's aunt trade all the predictable, socially sanctioned clichés: "Did he . . . peacefully?" the aunt asks. Eliza replies, "O, quite peacefully, ma'am. . . . You couldn't tell when the breath went

he had finished his recitation there was a silence and then a burst of clapping: even Mr Hynes clapped. The applause continued for a little time. When it had ceased all the auditors drank from their bottles in silence. Pok! the cork flew out of Mr Hynes's bottle but Mr Hynes remained sitting on the table as if he had not heard the invitation.

— Good man, Joe! said Mr O'Connor, taking out cigarette-papers and tobacco in order to conceal his emotion—

— What d'ye think of that, Crofton? said Mr Henchy. Isn't that fine—what?—

Mr Crofton said that it was a very fine piece of writing.

Jas Joyce.
29 August 1905

Last page from a draft for "Ivy Day in the Committee Room," the Dubliners *story that Joyce liked best (The James Joyce Archive)*

out of him. He had a beautiful death, God be praised." In the face of such talk the boy just sits silently, listening to everything, and without warning the conversation turns. After a moment's silence Eliza says shrewdly: "Mind you, there was something queer coming over him latterly." These words, and those that follow, sound almost vindictive, coming suddenly from Eliza's mouth: something like genuine feeling seems again to be breaking through the thin veneer of social convention. In Eliza's case what breaks through perhaps betokens her feeling that she had been taken advantage of for years in the service of her brother, in the service ultimately of the church — for which she has perhaps paid the price of diminished possibilities of ever marrying and finding her own happiness.

"An Encounter," more specifically than "The Sisters," is based on an experience of Joyce's own childhood: a day's "miching" (playing truant) planned and executed by Joyce and his younger brother Stanislaus. "In 'An Encounter,'" as Stanislaus recounted the story,

> my brother describes a day's miching which he and I planned and carried out while we were living in North Richmond Street, and our encounters with an elderly pederast. For us he was just a "juggins." Neither of us could have any notion at the time what kind of "juggins" he was, but something funny in his speech and behaviour put us on our guard at once. We thought he might be an escaped madman. As he looked about fifty and had a military air, I nicknamed him "the captain of fifty" from a phrase I had seen somewhere in a Biblical quotation.

This incident clearly made an impression on the young writer; in a letter of 10 October 1905 Stanislaus writes of "that astonishing unravelling of the sodomite's mind" that James Joyce captures in "An Encounter," and additionally of "the sensation of terror — you were afraid he might catch you by the ankles."

The story in many ways recapitulates the theme of freedom versus socially imposed oppression that Joyce presents in "The Sisters." Its narrator has a youthful enthusiasm for stories of the Wild West, as popular literature such as *The Union Jack, Pluck,* and *The Halfpenny Marvel* stirs up his desire for freedom and adventure. By contrast, the stifling atmosphere of his Catholic school is also nicely evoked in opening pages: "when the restraining influence of the school was at a distance," the narrator reports, "I began to hunger again for wild sensations, for the escape which those chronicles of disorder alone seemed to offer me."

The narrator and two of his friends plan a day's miching, for, as the narrator recounts, "I wanted real adventures to happen to myself. But real adventures, I reflected, do not happen to people who remain at home: they must be sought abroad." The boy and his friend Mahony define *abroad* rather loosely; their great escape consists of a meeting at the Canal Bridge and an excursion to the Pigeon House, a grand total of just a few miles. Their trip is more or less uneventful, everything taking a bit longer than expected. After a light lunch the boys lie down on the bank of the River Dodder, too tired to complete their journey to the Pigeon House.

But here in a deserted field on the bank of the Dodder the boys have their "encounter" with the "old pederast" that Stanislaus Joyce described. Like the narrator, the pederast remains nameless; Mahony calls him "a queer old josser." The man's talk is friendly enough, and yet, as in Stanislaus's recollection of his real-life encounter, there is "something funny in his speech and behaviour" that puts at least the narrator "on his guard at once." The narrator and the man talk about literature; the man's taste seems to prefer Romantic poetry and prose, the verse of Thomas Moore and the novels of Sir Walter Scott and Lord Lytton. The narrator, hoping to impress the older man, pretends to have read everything he mentions. The unintended result is that a kind of bond is implicitly built between the two: "Ah, I can see you are a bookworm like myself," the man says; "'Now,' he added, pointing to Mahony who was regarding us with open eyes, 'he is different; he goes in for games.'"

The talk quickly turns from literature to love, and though the old man expresses attitudes toward love "strangely liberal in a man of his age," something about his manner rings false: "He gave me the impression," the narrator says, "that he was repeating something which he had learned by heart or that, magnetised by some words of his own speech, his mind was slowly circling round and round in the same orbit." As his monologue about young girls winds to a close, the old man excuses himself for a few minutes and walks off some distance; he is still visible, though, and Mahony, who has followed him with his eyes, exclaims: "I say! Look at what he's doing! . . . I say . . . He's a queer old josser!" The *Oxford English Dictionary* records that the word *queer* did not become synonymous with *homosexual* until the early 1920s, but that definition seems implied here; quite likely, the word had begun to take on connotations of homosexuality in spoken English and schoolboy slang before appearing in public, written contexts with this meaning. Certainly when the old josser returns from his errand – masturbation, in all likelihood – his subject has changed from little girls to little boys as new objects of his interest, and he declares that he would like to give a "rough and unruly" boy "a nice warm whipping. . . . [T]here was nothing in this world he would like so well as that." Mahony has by this time wisely left the two bookworms, and while baring his soul to the narrator in all its corruption, the old man seems to the narrator "to plead with me that I should understand him."

The sexual mystery that the "queer old josser" attempts to unfold before the boy parallels the religious mystery that Father Flynn tries to impart to his young protégé, and both men seem to their young friends to be pleading for understanding or forgiveness – Father Flynn in the protagonist's dream. Also like Father Flynn, the queer old josser of "An Encounter" embodies the paralysis that Joyce felt pervaded the Dublin of his time: both men point out quite vividly to the young protagonists the futility that their provincial environment seems to breed. As "An Encounter" ends, the protagonist is forced to call on his friend Mahony for help – really as an alibi to permit him to escape politely from the old josser. To the forms of paralysis suggested in the collection's opening story, "An Encounter" adds two further: the sexual "paralysis" of the old man, and the paralyzing force of social convention, especially of ideas of social and intellectual superiority. By arrogantly insisting on his level of culture in talking with the old man, the protagonist ironically identifies himself so closely with the man that he finally has trouble extricating himself. Better, perhaps, to admit not having read Lord Lytton than to suggest that you are a soul mate to such a character as the old josser.

"Araby," along with the closing story, "The Dead," is the most frequently anthologized of the *Dubliners* stories. This may be partly because in "Araby" Joyce's device of the epiphany – focusing the story on a dramatic moment of self-revelation, or of revelation about the nature of the world – seems particularly evident. In fact the story closes on two distinct epiphanies – the first "dramatic," promising insight into the outside world, and the second lyric, suggesting that the narrator/protagonist has gained some measure of self-knowledge by the story's close.

The opening paragraphs of "Araby" are among the most tantalizing in all of Joyce's writing. The flood of realistic details – the house that stands at the blind end of a blind street, the paper-covered books that the boy discovers in the spare room, the "wild garden behind the house" with its "central apple tree" – prods us to read beyond these surface details to another level of significance. The most useful detail is probably the reference to Scott's Romantic novel *The Abbot,* for if this young protagonist has not simply seen but actually read Scott, his penchant for old-time romance makes more sense. When he introduces the object of his affection into the story, for instance, the evidence of lush Romantic prose stylistics is palpable: "The space of sky above us was the colour of ever-changing violet and towards it the lamps of the street lifted their feeble lanterns." The girl with whom he has fallen in love is the older sister of a friend, Mangan, and so great is the boy's reticence that we never learn her name; indeed, he may never have learned it himself. She remains, throughout the story, just "Mangan's sister."

Yet the boy does know that this is the woman of his dreams – his lady fair on whose behalf he will go in quest of exotic tokens of his love at the bazaar, Araby. Beneath this hackneyed world borne of romance fiction, however, an altogether different one exists, signaled in the text by a fresher, more evocative prose style. To learn to speak and write of love from Scott is, of course, no education in writing about the desires and attractions of the flesh; and when the narrator resorts to the voice of the Romantic fiction with which he has been brought up, Mangan's sister lacks not only a name, but more significantly a body as well. But in surprising moments something else breaks through his narrative: he dares to talk of "her figure," for instance, in that first paragraph about her, and describes how "her dress swung as she moved her body and the soft rope of her hair tossed from side to side."

At last, after months of worship from afar, the silence is broken – and, as we might expect, not by the boy himself, but by his ladylove. She speaks to him and asks if he will be going to Araby; abashed, he quickly answers that he will and that since she will be unable to attend, he will bring her something. Like all true romantic knights, the boy encounters obstacles before reaching the bazaar: he must get permission and money from his aunt and uncle, and while he and his aunt await his uncle's return home, the man is out drinking. He is quite drunk, and late, when he finally returns home, but the boy insists that he must make his journey that evening, and after a late start he does arrive at the "large building which displayed the magical name."

When he enters the great hall, he can see that the bazaar has shut down for the night, but after finding his way to a still-open stall offering various curios for sale, he begins to look over the merchandise in hopes of finding something suitable for Mangan's sister. As he shops, he overhears a banal conversation – some mild flirtation – between the shopgirl and two "young gentlemen" with English accents. Something about this overheard conversation troubles the protagonist, and though we are not given a precise analysis of his thoughts through the first-person narrator, their overheard banter suggests to the boy that a romance in the real world is nothing like the romantic visions his reading has conjured for him: "O, I never said such a thing!" "O, but you did!" "O, but I didn't!" The fact that this occurs not between a romantic couple, but among a threesome reinforces the boy's growing uneasiness about the romantic dreams that he has attempted to realize in his own life.

Still disturbed by this scene, the boy lingers awhile, pretending interest in the girl's wares, and then "turned away slowly and walked down the middle of the bazaar." In a scene that is played out, with variations, by others among Joyce's autobiographical figures in *Dubliners* (James Duffy in "A Painful Case," Gabriel Conroy in "The Dead"), the protagonist has here "turned away" literally and figuratively from his moment of realization – from what Joyce in the draft novel "Stephen Hero" called the moment of "epiphany." In a paragraph meant to sum up the boy's insight, the narrator instead turns away from the implications of the insight which the boy might have attained: "Gazing up into the darkness, I saw myself as a creature driven and derided by vanity; and my eyes burned with anguish and anger."

Gazing into real darkness, of course, one finds only the image of the mind's eye; what the boy figures here as "one good look in the lookingglass" is instead a falsifying moment of re-creating himself, one in which the boy attempts to supersede, through overblown rhetoric and prose style, the reality of what his senses have tried to teach him on this night. Talking with his friend Arthur Power in Paris, Joyce remarked of Anton Chekhov's plays that "As the play ends, for a moment you think that his characters have awakened from their illusions, but as the curtain comes down you realize that they will soon be building new ones to forget the old." Though perhaps the first, the young boy of "Araby" is by no means the last of the *Dubliners* protagonists to extinguish real self-awareness in this fashion.

In "Eveline" one finds another class of Joyce's narratives, those he called "stories of adolescence,"

which are written from a third-person perspective though influenced subtly with free indirect discourse. Joyce's choice of the word *adolescence* to classify these stories is used to denote the period of entry into adulthood, rather than strictly the period of transformation to bodily maturity. Thus, Eveline Hill is a bit more than nineteen years old and is a creature of habit. As she sits at her window in the story's opening tableau and watches the world pass by outside her house, Eveline is perfectly passive: rather than smelling the curtains near her head, for instance, the text insists that "in her nostrils was the odour of dusty cretonne."

Eveline, who has the responsibility of caring for her widower father and two younger siblings, has of late taken up with an exciting young sailor named Frank; he, in turn, has proposed that she run off with him and sail to Buenos Aires. As Eveline awaits the time of her rendezvous with Frank, she thinks over the rather dreary life she would be leaving behind in narrative tones that color it with some affection: "She had hard work to keep the home together and to see that the two young children who had been left to her charge went to school regularly and got their meals regularly. It was hard work – a hard life – but now that she was about to leave it she did not find it a wholly undesirable life."

As Eveline's thoughts unfold on the page, they present the process of rationalization at work. Eveline's father is a profligate drunkard who abuses her psychologically – with the possibility of physical, perhaps even sexual, violence included: "Even now, though she was over nineteen, she sometimes felt herself in danger of her father's violence. . . . Latterly he had begun to threaten her and say what he would do to her only for her dead mother's sake. And now she had nobody to protect her." Nevertheless, as the possibility of running off with Frank begins to sound frighteningly real, Eveline evokes her father as a warm, nurturing parent: "Sometimes he could be very nice. Not long before, when she had been laid up for a day, he had read her out a ghost story and made toast for her at the fire. Another day, when their mother was alive, they had all gone to the Hill of Howth. She remembered her father putting on her mother's bonnet to make the children laugh." A more objective head might protest that two warm moments in nineteen years do not a benevolent father make, but Eveline is not evaluating the evidence objectively. Her reflections are cast in the light of what she secretly knows she wants to do – to stay.

Eveline does keep her appointment with Frank at the North Wall port; she does not, however, board the ship with him. As they walk up the gangway, Eveline freezes – in *Dubliners* this is the most vivid illustration of paralysis: "She gripped with both hands at the iron railing. . . . It was impossible. Her hands clutched the iron in frenzy. . . . She set her white face to him, passive, like a helpless animal. Her eyes gave him no sign of love or farewell or recognition." Given a chance for change, Eveline rejects it in favor of the familiar. It is important not to overstate the stakes at the story's conclusion, however, for Joyce writes not in stark black-and-white terms but in morally ambiguous shades of gray, even if his characters incline to melodrama. Eveline's father is something of a monster; but Frank, for all we know, may not be any saint. Eveline thinks, during her reverie, about the respect that being married would bring her, and yet for all the narrative tells us, Frank may never have explicitly proposed marriage. Eveline's assumption that they would, of course, marry once out of Dublin may just be a convenient fiction that she uses to salve her Catholic conscience. While Frank promises change for Eveline, there is no guarantee that her life will change for the better. In order to escape with Frank, Eveline would have to take a chance, to make a change that would invite an outcome that she could not foresee. But Eveline, like so many of the *Dubliners* characters, perceives any and every change as loss. "Everything changes," Eveline thinks early in the story; yet while she knows this with her head, her heart rejects it, and she chooses the hell she knows rather than the possible hell of the unknown.

"After the Race" is perhaps the most universally ignored of the *Dubliners* stories. Joyce called it one of "the two worst stories" in the collection – but he was certainly wrong about his estimation of the other story, "A Painful Case." "After the Race" grew out of Joyce's experience interviewing French race-car driver Henri Fournier in Paris in April 1903. Joyce's story shifts the setting to Dublin, and the central character is not Frenchman Charles Ségouin, the car's owner, but rather Jimmy Doyle, the young Irishman who has been "taken in" (in both senses of that term) by Ségouin and his friends.

The Dublin setting for the race – in which the French teams "were virtual victors," placing second and third behind the Germans – makes a rather stark backdrop for the Europeans' displays of wealth and engineering know-how. The cars coming over the hill at Inchicore are described as "ca-reering homeward and through this channel of poverty and inaction the Continent sped its wealth and industry." Joyce is unusually unsubtle in criticizing the people of Dublin in this story. In the opening paragraph, for instance, they are described as "rais[ing] the cheer of the gratefully oppressed." The Dubliners who line the streets to pay homage to "their friends, the French" are, we later discover, not so very different from Jimmy Doyle, who does not want to appear uncultured or naive – and instead pays a large price for his false sophistication.

As Ségouin's car speeds through the city, Jimmy is one of its four occupants; he has become acquainted with Ségouin during a term at Cambridge, and Ségouin has not only allowed Jimmy to keep company with him but has honored him so far as to allow Jimmy to invest some of his money in the automobile company Ségouin is about to open in Paris. "Of course, the investment was a good one," the narrative informs us; "Ségouin had managed to give the impression that it was by a favour of friendship the mite of Irish money was to be included in the capital of the concern." What Ségouin regards as a "mite," however, was to Jimmy no such thing: "Ségouin, perhaps, would not think it a great sum," Jimmy thinks, "but Jimmy who, in spite of temporary errors, was at heart the inheritor of solid instincts knew well with what difficulty it had been got together." Already, the investment was paying off handsomely: Jimmy's being allowed to ride with the other men and Ségouin's introducing Jimmy to another of the French competitors are owing in part to Jimmy's "investment" rather than to any debt of friendship, for on a personal level Ségouin appears singularly uninterested in Jimmy. Yet Jimmy feels he is receiving a good return on his investment, for "he had been seen by many of his friends that day in the company of these Continentals."

At age twenty-six Jimmy is younger than his years. Caught up in the glamour and excitement of this "fast" crowd, Jimmy allows himself to be seduced by the atmosphere of bonhomie that hangs over the evening. As the young men head out to the yacht of an American named Farley, Jimmy begins to drink perhaps more than he should, to relax perhaps more than he should, and as cards are proposed and dealt, Jimmy begins to bet perhaps more than he should, especially in his intoxicated state. A false sense of merriment pervades these last pages; via free indirect discourse, we see Jimmy bravely forcing expressions of his pleasure that he seems not to feel: "What merriment!" "What jovial fellows! What good company they were!" "What excitement!"

When the reckoning comes (and Jimmy must entrust the reckoning to others, for he "frequently mistook his cards and the other men had to calculate his I.O.U.'s for him"), Jimmy has lost heavily. Heavily enough that his investment in Ségouin's motor company has been consumed? The text is not clear on this point – because Jimmy himself is not. Much of the evidence that would be crucial for a retelling of this story from another perspective is missing, because the final scenes are narrated so narrowly, from Jimmy's perspective; but it is certainly possible to construct an alternative narrative for what facts we have, a narrative of betrayal about how a cunning Frenchman has deliberately exploited Jimmy's lack of sophistication, his desperate need to hide it, and his typically Irish intemperance. Jimmy has been had, but his desire for acceptance by these men he admires is so strong that he would rather silently allow himself to be robbed than call attention to his victimization by protesting it.

"Two Gallants," the sixth story in *Dubliners,* was thirteenth in date of composition – having been written, in fact, after Joyce had submitted a twelve-story *Dubliners* to his publisher, Grant Richards. Yet it was one of Joyce's favorites: "It is one of the most important stories in the book," Joyce wrote Richards; "I would rather sacrifice *five* of the other stories (which I could name) than this one. It is the story (after *Ivy Day in the Committee-Room*) which pleases me most." The story focuses on two Dublin "gallants," Lenehan and Corley. As the two men walk the city streets in "the warm grey evening air," Lenehan is trying hard to ingratiate himself with Corley – for some unknown reason – and Corley seems largely uninterested in Lenehan's company or attention. Lenehan is clearly what Stephen Dedalus's schoolmates at Clongowes Wood College would call Corley's "suck," or toady, for Lenehan "wore an amused listening face. . . . Little jets of wheezing laughter followed one another out of his convulsed body. His eyes, twinkling with cunning enjoyment, glanced at every moment towards his companion's face. . . . When he was quite sure that the narrative had ended he laughed noiselessly for fully half a minute. Then he said: 'Well! . . . That takes the biscuit! – . . . That takes the solitary, unique, and, if I may so call it, *recherché* biscuit!' "

Corley has apparently been telling a story about a woman whose favors he has recently enjoyed – or so he would have Lenehan think – and Lenehan is cunning enough to feed Corley's vanity ("Maybe she thinks you'll marry her," said Lenehan). One-third of the way through the story, though, Lenehan makes a remark to Corley for which no ready interpretation seems evident: " 'Well . . . tell me, Corley, I suppose you'll be able to pull it off all right, eh?' . . . 'Is she game for that?' asked Lenehan dubiously. 'You never know women.' " Exactly what Corley expects to get from "her" is unknown, and it remains so until the conclusion. Given the conversation that has transpired between the two gallants, however, a reasonable guess might be that Corley is after some sort of sexual favor and that Lenehan experiences a vicarious thrill at merely hearing the tale told.

It becomes clear that the two are walking toward an assignation with the woman Corley intends to victimize. As they approach the young woman standing on a street corner, Lenehan insists that Corley let him "have a squint at her," and Corley does so, seemingly in order to make Lenehan more jealous of his sexual prowess. Joyce's prose spares no indignity to the woman whom Lenehan sees, but she is nonetheless attractive to him: "Lenehan's eyes noted approvingly her stout short muscular body. Frank rude health glowed in her face, on her fat red cheeks and in her unabashed blue eyes. Her features were blunt. She had broad nostrils, a straggling mouth which lay open in a contented leer, and two projecting front teeth." The two men part – Corley on his rendezvous, Lenehan to kill time until "half ten," when he will rejoin his friend.

Lenehan goes into a restaurant for a cheap meal and compares unfavorably his own situation – romantic, fiscal, spiritual – with Corley's. He wonders intermittently whether Corley has successfully handled his secret mission, and Lenehan begins to worry that Corley might achieve his conquest and then "give him [Lenehan] the slip." But Corley keeps the appointment; Lenehan is at the meeting place in time to watch Corley walking the young woman back to her door. As the two approach, Lenehan notices that they are not talking, and he assumes that Corley has failed. They stop at her door, however, and talk for a few minutes before she descends the steps to her house, while Corley waits outside. After a short while, a woman – and the narrative does say "a" woman, rather than "the" woman – emerges from the house for a moment, her form hidden by Corley's, and is just as suddenly back indoors.

As Corley walks away from the house and toward Stephen's Green, Lenehan approaches his friend to learn whether or not he has been successful. Corley apparently wants nothing to do with him and will not speak to him. To Lenehan's repeated entreaties, however – "Well? he said. Did it come off? . . . Can't you tell us? he said. Did you try her?" – Corley silently answers by slowly opening his fist "to the gaze of his disciple": "A small gold coin shone in the palm." In one respect the story's central puzzle has been solved, but many more correlative puzzles are simultaneously posed. How has Corley "earned," or coerced, this money from the young woman? Why does the narrative leave unclear the identity of the woman who comes out to Corley? What does Corley see in the young woman – or, perhaps, what does she see in him – a man whose "head was large, globular and oily; it sweated in all weather; and his large round hat, set upon it sideways, looked like a bulb which had grown out of another"?

If "Two Gallants" shows that sexuality in turn-of-the-century, working-class Dublin has become a debased currency, "The Boarding House" shows the exchange value of a woman's sexuality from three viewpoints: the woman's, her lover's, and her mother's. Mrs. Mooney, having petitioned for and received a legal separation from her alcoholic husband, now runs a boardinghouse in Hardwicke Street, and the empty rooms of her home are let to young men who work in the city. "Mrs. Mooney's young men paid fifteen shillings a week for board and lodgings (beer or stout at dinner excluded)," and most of the boarders spend the weekend away. When they return on Sunday nights there is often "a reunion in Mrs. Mooney's front drawing-room," with singing and dancing. Polly Mooney, the owner's nineteen-year-old daughter, often sings at these gatherings, and her song is a rather coy production: "*I'm a . . . naughty girl. / You needn't sham: / You know I am.*"

The boarders, we learn, have taken to referring to Mrs. Mooney as "The Madame," and not without cause; after Polly has served a short stint at secretarial work, Mrs. Mooney has brought her daughter back to help at home. Mrs. Mooney's parental supervision of Polly, however, amounts to pandering: "As Polly was very lively the intention was to give her the run of the young men. Besides, young men like to feel that there is a young woman not very far away. Polly, of course, flirted with the young men but Mrs. Mooney, who was a shrewd judge, knew that the young men were only passing the time away: none of them meant business."

Bob Doran, as it turns out, does mean business; or Mrs. Mooney means to do business with him. As she is about to despair of Polly ever establishing a relationship with a suitable suitor, she notices "that something [is] going on between Polly and one of the young men." She watches the pair, and although Polly knows that she and Mr. Doran

are being watched, she does not let on. Finally, when the affair has progressed far enough that Mrs. Mooney feels certain Mr. Doran is trapped, she takes action. In order to confirm her suspicions, she has a frank discussion with Polly, a conversation made more awkward than necessary by both parties feigning ignorance of the motives and complicity of the other.

The bulk of the story plays with the anticipation of Mrs. Mooney and the anxiety of Mr. Doran as they await their showdown. As she waits, Mrs. Mooney, like a seasoned poker player, reviews her cards:

> She was sure she would win. To begin with she had all the weight of social opinion on her side: she was an outraged mother. She had allowed him to live beneath her roof, assuming that he was a man of honour, and he had simply abused her hospitality. He was thirty-four or thirty-five years of age, so that youth could not be pleaded as his excuse; nor could ignorance be his excuse since he was a man who had seen something of the world. He had simply taken advantage of Polly's youth and inexperience: that was evident. The question was: What reparation would he make?

The language of social convention, socially constructed roles, is predominant in Mrs. Mooney's thoughts. Most of her assertions are partially or wholly undercut by the narrative – her assertion, for instance, that Doran has taken advantage of Polly. But the importance of these phrases would seem to lie more in their strategic resonance than in the veracity of what they denote: an "outraged mother," for instance, has by definition been wronged and deserves compensation. Mrs. Mooney is not "in the right" in any absolute moral sense here; yet, as we listen to her thoughts while she anticipates her meeting with Bob Doran, we can see that she has one right – because she can marshal the rhetoric of moral outrage to her purpose.

As for Bob Doran, he tries vainly to console himself with equally formulaic narratives of domestic bliss, but the best he can manage is the feeble "Perhaps they could be happy together." Rather than anticipating that he will be happy ever after, Bob Doran has "a notion that he was being had." "She *was* a little vulgar," he thinks to himself; "sometimes she said *I seen* and *If I had've known*. But what would grammar matter if he really loved her?"

After these vignettes of Mrs. Mooney's and Bob Doran's thoughts, Joyce's narrative finally presents the consciousness of Polly Mooney. As her beau marches downstairs to meet with her "outraged mother," she goes "back to the bed again and

[sits] at the foot. She regard[s] the pillows for a long time and the sight of them awaken[s] in her mind secret amiable memories." Polly's head has lain on those pillows before, and the "secret amiable memories" that flood her mind are secret amorous memories. Though the story does not baldly say so, Polly has enjoyed sharing the (pre)marital bed with Bob.

When her mother calls her from downstairs, Polly rushes to the railing to answer, and only then does she "remem[ber] what she had been waiting for." According to conventions, according to the lies mother and daughter allow each other to hide behind, Polly is waiting for a proposal of marriage. The reader has seen Polly waiting on Bob's bed; the reader knows better.

"A Little Cloud" is the first of those stories that Joyce dubbed "stories of mature life." The problems exposed in these later stories are as weighty as those in Joyce's first two classes of stories, but they are less likely to be solved. Joyce strongly believed that people are all, more or less, creatures of habit — and are less likely to change as they go on living. Thus Thomas Malone "Little" Chandler, the protagonist of "A Little Cloud," lives a fairly regular and uneventful life. He flatters himself that under other, more propitious circumstances, he might have been a writer, a poet: "Could he write something original? He was not sure what idea he wished to express but the thought that a poetic moment had touched him took life within him like an infant hope. . . . He tried to weigh his soul to see if it was a poet's soul." Such musings become all the more urgent for Chandler, because on the day of the story he is to meet with an old friend, Ignatius Gallaher, who has apparently enjoyed some success as a London journalist.

When Chandler meets with Gallaher that evening in Corless's, the mighty Gallaher is something of a disappointment to both Chandler and the reader. Whether a successful journalist or not, Gallaher is certainly a blowhard. Chandler has a mind full of poetic clichés ("The English critics, perhaps, would recognise him as one of the Celtic school by reason of the melancholy tone of his poems; besides that, he would put in allusions"), and Gallaher, who lives in London and spends time on "the Continent," is full of the worst kind of condescension and "worldly" wisdom: "Damn proofs and printers, I say, for a few days. I'm deuced glad, I can tell you, to get back to the old country. Does a fellow good, a bit of a holiday. I feel a ton better since I landed again in dear dirty Dublin."

Gallaher's pretentiousness and patronizing boasting nevertheless depress Chandler, and he re-

turns home despairing of what he has accomplished in his own life. His wife, Annie, decides to run out to buy some tea, and Chandler is left to care for their infant son. In Annie's absence Chandler sizes up the material evidence of the success of their life together and finds it wanting: "He . . . glanced nervously round the room. He found something mean in the pretty furniture which he had bought for his house on the hire system. Annie had chosen it herself and it reminded him of her. It too was prim and pretty. A dull resentment against his life awoke within him." Chandler tries to escape the restraints of his provincial, middle-class life via Byronic poetry, but Byron's poetic cry is interrupted by the cry of Chandler's infant son, and Chandler is again convinced of the futility of his situation: "It was useless, useless! He was a prisoner for life."

Annie returns home to find her son crying hysterically and her husband unable to do anything to comfort him. She immediately takes her child's side: "What have you done to him?," she accuses Chandler, and then turning to the child she coos, "My little man! My little mannie! Was 'ou frightened, love?" Among his acquaintances Chandler is called "Little Chandler" because, "though he was but slightly under the average stature, he gave one the idea of being a little man." Yet for Annie, her "little man," her infant son, has replaced her husband in her affections. To be thus rejected by his wife when he has just minutes earlier been wondering whether she is worthy of his love comes as a devastating blow to Chandler. But of his final state of mind Joyce provides little to judge: Chandler "listened while the paroxysm of the child's sobbing grew less and less; and tears of remorse started to his eyes." Remorse for what he has done, or remorse for the course of life he has chosen? Such ambiguity is intentional.

"Counterparts" is among the bitterest, most hopeless of the *Dubliners* collection. The story's protagonist, Farrington, works as a copyist in a law office, and from the time he arrives in the morning until he leaves at night, Farrington transcribes copies of legal documents — or at least he is supposed to. Farrington is frustrated in his job and is inclined to satisfy his powerful thirst in local public houses rather than to carry out his scribal duties. His boss, Mr. Alleyne, is a petty tyrant, and as the story opens Farrington is being summoned to his office. There Farrington is upbraided for his tardiness in copying out a contract and is warned that if the work is not completed by the close of business that day, Mr. Alleyne will bring the matter to the attention of the other partner, Mr. Crosbie.

As Farrington returns to his desk, however, he finds that he cannot contemplate returning to his contracts without slipping out for a drink. After a quick glass of porter in a dark pub, Farrington returns to his office but can make no progress in his work. The Delacour contract that particularly plagues him is reduced to a meaningless fragment in Farrington's consciousness and is thus fittingly rendered meaningless to Joyce's reader: *"In no case shall the said Bernard Bodley be...."* Even with the threat of being fired hanging over his head, Farrington cannot bring himself to make the copy.

With Miss Delacour by his side Mr. Alleyne approaches Farrington's desk to inquire about the correspondence in the Delacour case; the folder that Farrington hands to Mr. Alleyne is incomplete, and though Farrington knows it, he denies it to his boss. As Alleyne's temper flares, he demands ironically of Farrington, " – Tell me . . . do you take me for a fool? Do you think me an utter fool?" Farrington's answer, though unpremeditated, is savage: " – I don't think, sir, . . . that that's a fair question to put to me." Alleyne is furious, not least of all because Farrington has humiliated him in front of Miss Delacour, whom Alleyne is rumored to be "sweet on," and as Farrington leaves for the day, he realizes that tomorrow he will be looking for work.

Characteristically Farrington seeks oblivion in alcohol. He pawns his watch chain and manages to spend the entire six shillings – enough to purchase perhaps seventy-two glasses of Guinness – in bars. While drinking to forget, however, he is ironically condemned to remember his indiscretion with Mr. Alleyne. When recounted to his drinking buddies, Farrington's retort comes to sound heroic, but just as Alleyne was made to look foolish in front of a woman, Farrington in the pub is ritually humiliated before a woman in whom he is interested. If he has hoped to forget his troubles or perhaps even to regain a measure of his self-respect during his time in the pubs, Farrington is bitterly disappointed. He returns home "full of smouldering anger and revengefulness. He felt humiliated and discontented; he did not even feel drunk; and he had only twopence in his pocket." Rather than conquering, Farrington has again been conquered: "He had lost his reputation as a strong man, having been defeated twice by a mere boy. His heart swelled with fury and, when he thought of the woman in the big hat who had brushed against him and said *Pardon!* his fury nearly choked him."

When he returns home, his wife has gone out to the chapel and left his young son, Tom, to heat up his father's dinner for him. Tom clearly has done nothing to deserve his father's wrath, but that wrath must be spent – and Farrington contrives an excuse to take it out on his child. " ' – I'll teach you to let the fire out!' he said, rolling up his sleeve in order to give his arm free play." The story fades out before that arm is given free play, but the reader can only assume that Tom is made to pay for his father's various humiliations during the day and evening. Thus Tom becomes his father's counterpart, suffering upon his body the emotional stripes his father has taken.

"Clay" is a deceptively complex story. This is owing largely to Joyce's willful obscurity about many of its realistic details. Maria, the story's protagonist, works at a place called the Dublin by Lamplight Laundry. What is not spelled out explicitly is that the laundry is a benevolent enterprise run by zealous Protestant women who rescue prostitutes from the streets and attempt to provide them with a more dignified way of supporting themselves. A reader might be tempted to jump to the conclusion that Maria is one of these fallen women who has been shown the error of her ways, but in fact, rather than being one of the laundry's reclamation projects, Maria seems to have been hired to work with the fallen women. The story's opening paragraphs repay careful reading, for in them one detects the linguistic presence of Maria herself, hiding behind the third-person narrative and coloring the narrative with the language of her desire. This is evident through the subtle ways in which she attempts to distance herself from the other women working at the laundry.

Maria is preparing to visit old friends, Joe Donnelly and his family, when she gets off work. The precise nature of her relationship to the Donnellys is unspecified; most likely, she had been some kind of domestic servant in the Donnelly household when Joe and his brother, Alphy, were boys. The early pages present Maria's consciousness as she prepares for her excursion. The evening, as it turns out, is filled with minor blows to Maria's sense of herself, to the narrative she tells us and tells herself about who she is. The first blow comes on her way to the Donnellys', as she stops in a cake shop to buy some sweets for the gathering. The woman behind the counter, a "stylish young lady," is quite impatient with Maria's indecision and asks her "was it a wedding-cake she wanted to buy"? At the shop girl's rudeness Maria merely blushes and smiles; she settles on a plumcake, and heads for the tram to Drumcondra.

The tram is full, but "an elderly gentleman made room for her." The description continues, "He was a stout gentleman and he wore a brown hard hat; he had a square red face and a greyish moustache." Though nothing about his dress or deportment suggests that he is a gentleman, Maria proceeds to give him a kind of promotion: "Maria thought he was a colonel-looking gentleman." In retrospect, the reader will surely return to this passage and question what might suggest that a man in civilian (indeed lower-middle-class) clothing is a colonel. The answer is nothing but the fact that Maria would like her tram conversation to be dignified by thinking that it has occurred with a man of substance, of quality. Maria knows, however, that this wish is not the truth of the situation, for she reflects as she leaves the tram "how easy it was to know a gentleman even when he had a drop taken." Maria's "gentleman," to a more cynical eye, is a shabby-genteel old drunk "making time" with Maria not because of who she is, but because he loves the sound of his own voice. It is Maria's interest, however, not to make such fine distinctions.

When she arrives at the Donnelly's Hallow Eve gathering (for a celebration of what the "colonel-looking gentleman" had told Maria that Americans call Halloween), she no longer has her plumcake. In order to assuage Maria's hurt feelings over the missing cake, it is suggested that her gentleman must have stolen it; Maria's sense of self is so fragile that she is willing to allow her gentleman to suffer such a precipitous demotion in order to cover over her error. After much drinking, mostly on the part of Joe Donnelly, the Donnelly children and their neighborhood friends persuade Maria to take part in a traditional Irish Hallows' Eve game in which the participant is blindfolded and forced to choose from plates which contain a prayer book, a ring, water, or clay. These substances symbolize various fates for the participant: the prayer book (in some versions of the game) suggests that she will enter a convent; the ring, that she will soon marry; the water, that she will make a trip across the ocean and emigrate; and the clay, that she will die.

In a passage of remarkable narrative complexity that Margot Norris calls "narration behind a blindfold," the scene that presumably gives the story its title unfolds: the game participants

> led her up to the table amid laughing and joking and she put her hand out in the air as she was told to do. She moved her hand about here and there in the air and descended on one of the saucers. She felt a soft wet substance with her fingers and was surprised that nobody spoke or took off her bandage. There was a pause

for a few seconds; and then a great deal of scuffling and whispering. Somebody said something very cross to one of the next-door girls and told her to throw it out at once: that was no play. Maria understood that it was wrong that time and so she had to do it over again: and this time she got the prayer-book.

The narrative nicely skirts the issue of whether or not Maria understands the cruelty to which she has been subjected, because at some level Maria herself seems to be filtering the perceptions that are presented in the text. Readers certainly have no other ground from which to judge; they too are blindfolded, or at least forced to wear blinders.

The story closes on a poignant scene in which Maria is asked for a song before she leaves, and after some hesitation Maria agrees to sing "I Dreamt That I Dwelt," from Irish composer Michael William Balfe's opera *The Bohemian Girl*. The title of the opera suggests that this is an ironically inappropriate part for Maria to sing, and Maria perhaps magnifies that irony by singing the first verse a second time, in place of the second verse, the lyrics of which would have underscored the loneliness of her life. Maria reads in the lachrymose response of her audience a real pity for her situation: "Joe was very much moved." The final sentence of the story seems to undercut Maria's readings of events, however, for like the "colonel-looking gentleman" on the tram who had "a drop taken," Joe is so intoxicated by the story's close that readers can no longer take his reaction at face value: "his eyes filled up so much with tears that he could not find what he was looking for and in the end he had to ask his wife to tell him where the corkscrew was."

Mr. James Duffy, the protagonist of "A Painful Case," is a creature of habit to a greater degree than any other character in *Dubliners*. Compared to Eveline Hill, for instance, Duffy has had many years to let his habits harden into rigid, inflexible patterns for living. The story introduces him metonymicly – through a careful description of his room, where nothing is out of place. Mr. Duffy "abhorred anything which betokened physical or mental disorder."

Duffy's life is also a solitary one: "He had neither companions nor friends, church nor creed. He lived his spiritual life without any communion with others, visiting his relatives at Christmas and escorting them to the cemetery when they died"; "his life rolled out evenly" and forms "an adventureless tale." Then, almost in spite of himself, adventure enters Duffy's tale in the form of Emily Sinico, a married woman about his age. Meeting her three times by accident at various cultural occasions in the city, Duffy decides to make an appointment with her and is accepted. Although Mrs. Sinico is married and has an adolescent daughter, Duffy's influence over the narrative tries to downplay the adulterous aspect of the relationship: "Neither he nor she had had any such adventure before and neither was conscious of any incongruity."

Then, suddenly, their relationship ends: "One night during which she had shown every sign of unusual excitement, Mrs. Sinico caught up his hand passionately and pressed it to her cheek." Though entangled in this relationship, Duffy has done his best to keep it one-sided and intellectual; deep down he retains the instinct of the celibate, and this outburst of Mrs. Sinico destroys his belief that their relationship might continue. In his private writings Duffy later renders the moral of his story this way: "Love between man and man is impossible because there must not be sexual intercourse and friendship between man and woman is impossible because there must be sexual intercourse." Thus doing his best not to let the Sinico affair leave any sort of mark on him, Duffy returns to the dull regularity of his life.

Joyce's story then skips four years ahead. Duffy's life once again rolls out evenly, "an adventureless tale." His one brief experiment in community having gone terribly wrong, he returns to keeping company with no one but himself. Then one evening as he is eating his supper in an inexpensive restaurant, he reads in the newspaper a narrative of Emily Sinico's death. The text of the story is fully reproduced in Joyce's story; it relates that Mrs. Sinico had been struck by a train the night before, apparently while out buying liquor. The story, as Duffy notices, is full of euphemism and circumlocution, but between its lines both the reader and Duffy realize that Mrs. Sinico's life has described a downward spiral for quite some time. Duffy, however, in his self-important moralizing about her immoral death, conveniently suppresses one important fact: while he reads of her death four years after the breakup of their affair, the newspaper reports that Mrs. Sinico's husband has testified that his wife had taken to drink only "about two years ago." Thus, while Duffy affirms his own importance in Mrs. Sinico's life by assuming that his departure has occasioned her drinking, and ultimately her death, the facts would seem to be otherwise.

Her "commonplace vulgar death" disgusts Duffy; indeed, he refers to the god who would allow such poetic justice as "Just God," and concludes that his onetime soul's companion "had been unfit to live, without any strength of purpose, and easy prey to habits, one of the wrecks on which

civilisation has been reared." The reader is struck, in working through Duffy's reaction to Mrs. Sinico's death, that there is no apparent hint of sympathy; instead, he seems to feel only betrayed, as if she has humiliated him by dying in such a degraded fashion. Uncharacteristically Duffy decides to try to shake off the specter of her death by retreating to the warm anonymity of a public house, but alcohol – surely an ironic anesthetic for Duffy to choose, in the wake of Mrs. Sinico's death – does nothing to ease his pain. As he walks back to his room Duffy does his best to erase all memory of the one emotional dissipation in his life. In one of most savage endings of any story in the volume, Duffy, having seen the ghost of his own egotism, turns from the wisdom it would communicate and instead makes the cowardly decision that it was unreal: "He began to doubt the reality of what memory told him. . . . He could not feel her near him in the darkness nor her voice touch his ear." Again, the character apprehends no epiphany here, but rather steadfastly refuses to deal with the crisis that such self-reflection should precipitate.

Critic Vivian Mercier once described Samuel Beckett's *Waiting for Godot* as a play in which nothing happens, twice; Joyce's "Ivy Day in the Committee Room" might similarly be called a story in which nothing happens, once. In a letter to his brother Joyce called it the story that pleased him most; its most striking formal characteristic is its spare, static presentation. Stephen Dedalus, in his famous aesthetics disquisition in *A Portrait of the Artist as a Young Man,* declares that proper art is static rather than kinetic, and that in the evolution of literary forms, the dramatic represents the highest, purest form of literary art. "Ivy Day in the Committee Room" impresses with its dramatic presentation and finely nuanced evocation of character through subtle differences in idiolect – but it is not a memorable, participatory story in the ways that "Araby," "Eveline," "Clay," or even "The Dead" are. It is closer to formal perfection than any other story in *Dubliners,* but for that reason it reads more like a morality play than a tale that turns the tables on its readers.

Its setting and story are easily described. The cast of characters – which is somewhat fluid, with various election-day canvassers drifting in and out during the day – are convened in a dark, cold room that serves as a political campaign headquarters. The date is significantly 6 October – the anniversary of the death of Ireland's "uncrowned king," Charles Stuart Parnell, and locally known as "Ivy Day" for the custom of wearing an ivy leaf in memory of "the Chief." The various campaign workers who appear at the committee room in Wicklow Street – Hynes, Crofton, O'Connor, Henchy, Father Keon – are poignantly aware of the significance of the date and of the way that Irish history is repeating itself as farce. None of the workers seems to care about, or even believe in, the candidate for whom they are working; most of the conversation concerns when their candidate, Richard J. Tierney, might appear with their pay or, failing that, whether some stout might not be sent to them in the interim. Politics, a matter of passion on both sides during Parnell's rise and fall, has now become simply a matter of money; even the most militantly nationalistic of the campaign workers, Henchy, is able to swallow his objections to the announced visit of the British monarch, Edward VII, because "What we want in this country . . . is capital. The King's coming here will mean an influx of money into this country. . . . It's capital we want."

Ultimately aided with a dozen bottles of stout, the conversation of the men around the dying fire is clichéd, tired, banal. Hynes has, sometime in the past, written a poem on the death of Parnell. As the story closes with the dim light from the coal fire growing dimmer, the others persuade Hynes to recite his poem as a tribute to their dead Chief. It seems clear that Joyce meant this poem as a fairly slight production, both in its diction ("Shame on the coward caitiff hands / That smote their Lord or with a kiss / Betrayed him . . . ") and sentiment ("But Erin, list, his spirit may / Rise, like the Phoenix from the flames, / When breaks the dawning day"). In a sense Parnell is being confirmed as dead through this poetic monument/mausoleum erected over his memory. Like the ivy leaf worn on the lapels of the campaign workers, an emblem that makes absolutely no difference to their daily lives, this poem verbally embraces a promise of Parnell's rebirth – yet in effect drives another nail into his coffin. As Henchy sacrilegiously puts it before rapprochement with the British monarch is suggested, "Parnell . . . is dead." Such, too, seems to be the burden of the story's final line – presented in third-person narration, rather than in direct discourse from the conservative Crofton: "Mr. Crofton said that it was a very fine piece of writing."

Unlike "Ivy Day in the Committee Room," which is a static, almost inhuman set piece, "A Mother" insists that its readers take a stand vis-à-vis the events it presents. A daughter, Kathleen Kearney, has been contracted to play accompaniment for a series of four concerts, but in fact (as the title suggests) her mother holds center stage. Mrs. Kearney (née Devlin) holds pretensions to a higher place in society than has been allowed her, and this injustice she seeks vicariously to right through her daughter. Kathleen, like her mother, is sent to the best convent schools and taught French and music; additionally she is sent to the Royal Academy of Music. On top of these gifts her mother adds yet another, shrewdly calculated to assist Kathleen in her social climb: "When the Irish Revival began to be appreciable Mrs. Kearney determined to take advantage of her daughter's name and brought an Irish teacher to the house." The pronominal slippage in this passage is intentional and indicates Mrs. Kearney's destructive characteristic: her tendency to confuse Kathleen's accomplishments, and disappointments, with her own.

The narrative of "A Mother," like those of so many other *Dubliners* stories, is subtly influenced by the cast of the protagonist's mind. Its readers hear cadences of Mrs. Kearney's speech, and her high opinion of herself, in this description of her promotional activities on behalf of the concerts: "She forgot nothing and, thanks to her, everything that was to be done was done." That last phrase, echoing John's description of the work of the Logos at the creation of the world ("All things were made by him, and without him was not anything made that was made"), sounds like Joyce's ironic deflation of Mrs. Kearney; certainly, though her voice has some role in the constitution of the narrative, that narrative is not wholly sympathetic to her or her project. Superintending both her daughter's career and her life, she embodies the stereotype of the stage mother too closely to win reader sympathy.

The conflict builds slowly, but in the closing pages it is as dynamic as anything in the collection. The narrative leaves an impression that most of the other artistes are comfortable working without formal contracts, but Mrs. Kearney has negotiated Kathleen's contract for her – one that promises payment of eight guineas for four concerts. When the concert series is not as well attended as had been hoped (owing, in Mrs. Kearney's opinion, to improper management and promotion), the decision is made to cancel the performance set for the third night and to concentrate the sponsoring organization's resources to promote the fourth and final performance on Saturday night. This immediately raises for Mrs. Kearney the question of whether or not Kathleen will be paid for all four performances. She insists, reasonably enough, that the contract obligates the committee to pay her daughter eight guineas, regardless of how many concerts are actually performed.

Mrs. Kearney, however, gets no satisfaction from Hoppy Holohan, the assistant secretary of the society with whom she had made the contract. On the night of the final performance not only is Kathleen's fee in doubt, but she has not received any part of her wages; this, for Mrs. Kearney, is just too much. She creates a stir backstage and holds up the beginning of the performance until her daughter is paid. The concert begins when Kathleen is paid only four pounds, but under Mrs. Kearney's threat that her daughter will not return after the intermission unless she is paid the rest of her fee.

Mrs. Kearney is, by most standards, behaving quite badly; none of the artists have been paid in full for their performances, and Kathleen is hardly the most distinguished of the group. But the dismissive way in which Mrs. Kearney is treated by Holohan, his boss Mr. Fitzpatrick, and the male artistes helps explain her distrustful conduct and shrillness toward these men. At the same time, since she is so easily characterized as a stage mother, all these men seem to understand that she need not be taken seriously. Both parties are thereby hardened in their prejudices.

If "Ivy Day in the Committee Room" exposes the reduction of political passion to pure financial self-interest and "A Mother" suggests that art in contemporary Dublin has become nothing more exalted than a fiscal transaction, "Grace" diagnoses modern religion as nothing but a minor branch of modern economics. The story begins quite literally with a fall, which has obvious metaphoric import: Tom Kernan, drunk and unsteady ("peloothered," Martin Cunningham calls him), pitches headfirst down the stairs into the men's room of a bar, where he is discovered semiconscious. Kernan is quickly resurrected through recourse to the substance that precipitated his downfall: "A young man in a cycling-suit cleared his way through the ring of bystanders. He knelt down promptly beside the injured man and called for water. . . . The young man washed the blood from the injured man's mouth and then called for some brandy. . . . The brandy was forced down the man's throat. In a few seconds he opened his eyes and looked about him."

Alcohol causes Kernan's fall, but it also allows him to rise. So when Kernan leaves the bar with Power, Power expresses regrets to the man in the cycling suit that "they could not have a little drink together." When Power gets Kernan home, Mrs. Kernan apologizes that she has "nothing in the house to offer" him. Power's plan for reforming Kernan is to persuade him to come on a Catholic retreat with Power and some of Kernan's other busi-

ness friends. When the three friends come to make their appeal, Mrs. Kernan produces a tray of stout for the guests (though none for her convalescent husband), and when Mr. Fogarty shows up later, he has brought Kernan a bottle of whiskey as a get-well gift.

After a long bedside conversation in which the idea of a religious retreat is "inadvertently" mentioned to Kernan, the men make their retreat, during which the conversation is remarkable primarily for its misinformation about Catholic Church history and doctrine – misinformation that helps underscore Joyce's understated, somewhat arcane humor here. Kernan's friends have emphasized that the retreat will not be hard-hitting but tailor-made for men of the world – businessmen. In an ironic twist to William Wordsworth's description of the role of the poet, the priest leading this retreat, Father Purdon, fancies himself "a man of the world speaking to his fellow-men." The short paraphrase of the father's message should be read in its entirety in order to appreciate Joyce's understated irony, but the extended metaphor that Purdon uses, that of squaring one's accounts with God, seems an especially inappropriate one to use – given the Gospel's message that Christians are unable to square their own accounts. The priest advises the retreaters to "be straight and manly with God," and if, "as might happen, there were some discrepancies" in their spiritual accounts, "to be frank and say like a man: 'Well, I have looked into my accounts. I find this wrong and this wrong. But, with God's grace, I will rectify this and this. I will set right my accounts.' " Joyce's narrative ironically is saying that religion must differ in some respects from "spiritual accounting."

The closing story of *Dubliners,* "The Dead," is justly considered the most accomplished piece in the volume. In it Joyce revisits many themes explored throughout the collection, but with the benefit of hindsight, for the story was written after the rest of the volume had been completed, indeed submitted as a finished collection to a publisher. In a 26 September 1906 letter to his brother Stanislaus, Joyce explained his motive for writing a final story for *Dubliners:* "I have not reproduced its [Dublin's] ingenious insularity and its hospitality, the latter 'virtue' so far as I can see does not exist elsewhere in Europe." Critics have often adduced this letter as evidence of Joyce's desire to close the volume with a sympathetic, "generous" portrait of his home city. To read it so, however, is to ignore the irony beneath the letter's polite surface – irony manifest, for instance, in Joyce's enclosing the word *virtue* within

F. Scott Fitzgerald's cartoon in Sylvia Beach's copy of The Great Gatsby. *Commemorating a dinner party that Beach gave to introduce Fitzgerald to Joyce, the cartoon depicts Adrienne Monnier, Lucie Chamson, André Chamson, Zelda Fitzgerald, F. Scott Fitzgerald, Joyce, and Beach (Sylvia Beach Collection, Princeton University Library).*

quotation marks. "The Dead" has provoked passionately opposing opinions in different critics, most of whom focus their disagreements on the final paragraphs of the story's closing tableau. But in any event this narrative may be read as a story that closes the volume with a perspective as bleakly ironic and hopeless as any in the collection.

"The Dead" falls conveniently into three sections, all of which present events occurring on the night of 6 December, the Feast of Epiphany in the Catholic calendar. Epiphany is the occasion for the annual dance held for all of the friends and family of the Misses Morkan. "[N]ever once," the narrative informs us in the voice of Lily, the caretaker's daughter who serves in the Morkan's home, "had it fallen flat. For years and years it had gone off in splendid style as long as anyone could remember." Gabriel Conroy is the middle-aged nephew of Kate and Julia Morkan, and, since the Misses Morkan have never married, he is the unofficial guest of honor at their annual dance. The success or failure of the dance seems to depend largely on how well Gabriel performs his duties as host – and on whether or not Freddy Malins will turn up "screwed" (drunk) at the party.

The arrival of Gabriel and his wife Gretta is eagerly anticipated by Lily and the Morkan sisters. Within an hour of his arrival, however, Gabriel suffers three "insults – to which he responds in ways that reveal the magnitude of his ego and of his insecurity. The first occurs in the cloakroom as Gabriel attempts to make small talk with Lily, the servant with whom he is on friendly, if not intimate terms. His banter is well-meaning, but it is also somewhat insensitive, depending as it does upon his superior education and social position to inquire into matters such as Lily's plans for marriage, matters that he has really no right to know. Lily's angry response upsets Gabriel, who forces a small coin, a Christmas present, on Lily, in order to buy off her anger or assuage his own sense of wrongdoing. Gabriel is not a man who deals gracefully with evidence of his own imperfections, and this is apparent in the second incident at which he takes some offense: when his aunts and Gretta amiably tease him about his solicitude for his wife. Among such an inoffensive group Gabriel should have nothing to fear, but the magnitude of his egotism is such that he cannot stand to have his character questioned, even lightheartedly, by his intimates.

A third strike against Gabriel is the one that most wounds him. After what would appear to have been a friendly discussion on the dance floor with Miss Molly Ivors, an Irish nationalist and former university classmate who questions his patriotism in writing for a newspaper opposed to independence for Ireland, Miss Ivors whispers in Gabriel's ear the taunt "West Briton." Although her remark is whispered into his ear, he feels that she has publicly humiliated him.

The second section of the story includes the holiday meal and Gabriel's long-anticipated speech, ostensibly a celebration of the Irish virtues of hospitality and generosity. In fact the speech is a mean-spirited production, for Gabriel – vainly seeking self-justification and some self-gratifying revenge on Miss Ivors, who has already left the party – intentionally talks over the heads of his auditors who comprise its intended subjects. The speech offers further evidence of Gabriel's overarching egotism.

The third section of the story follows Gabriel and Gretta as they prepare to leave the dance and return to the hotel, where they have taken a room for the night in order to avoid a long, cold trip back to Monkstown. Gretta hears a tenor singing "The Lass of Aughrim," and from her memory the song recalls a former suitor, Michael Furey, from her home in Galway. She is distracted with these memories in the hotel room, and when Gabriel (expecting to enjoy an ego-restoring romantic evening with his wife) inquires into the reason for her melancholy, he comes by degrees to understand her grieving anew for Furey, the boy about whom she says, "I think he died for me." The fact that his wife recalls this boy with such tenderness suggests, to the melodramatic imagination with which Gabriel supports his fragile ego, that "he and she had never lived together as man and wife." Instead of questioning whether Furey had died for love of Gretta rather than from tuberculosis (which the narrative seems to suggest), Gabriel simply accepts what he is told because it confirms for him what he would like to believe about himself: that he is more sinned against than sinning, undeserving of the outrageous fortune that fate has dealt him.

This, however, is only the book's ultimate example of egotistical self-deception. Gabriel transforms Gretta's words into a comforting vision of his final end:

> The time had come for him to set out on his journey westward. Yes, the newspapers were right: snow was general all over Ireland. . . . It was falling . . . upon every part of the lonely churchyard on the hill where Michael Furey lay buried. It lay thickly drifted on the crooked crosses and headstones, on the spears of the little gate, on the barren thorns. His soul swooned slowly as he heard the snow falling faintly through the universe and

faintly falling, like the descent of their last end, upon all the living and the dead.

These are perhaps the most famous, and among the most beautiful, words that Joyce ever penned. Gabriel now seems to be egotistical about his humiliation, his martyrdom. Though many critics have read in these final paragraphs a triumphant, affirmative response to the rather pessimistic view of human growth and change that the other stories of the collection present, both the logic of the collection and the intricate voice of the story's closing pages suggest otherwise. Joyce did not suddenly improve his view of the human race when he came to write "The Dead."

Letters:

Letters of James Joyce, volume 1, edited by Stuart Gilbert (New York: Viking, 1957; revised, 1965); volumes 2 and 3, edited by Richard Ellmann (New York: Viking, 1966);

Selected Letters, edited by Ellmann (New York: Viking / London: Faber & Faber, 1975).

Bibliographies:

John J. Slocum and Herbert Cahoon, *A Bibliography of James Joyce, 1882–1941* (New Haven: Yale University Press, 1953);

Alan M. Cohn, "Supplementary James Joyce Checklist," *James Joyce Quarterly* (1959–   );

Robert Scholes, *The Cornell Joyce Collection: A Catalogue* (Ithaca: Cornell University Press, 1961);

Peter Spielberg, *James Joyce's Manuscripts and Letters at the University of Buffalo: A Catalogue* (Albany: SUNY Press, 1962);

Robert H. Deming, *A Bibliography of James Joyce Studies,* second edition (Boston: G. K. Hall, 1977);

Thomas Jackson Rice, *James Joyce: A Guide to Research* (New York: Garland, 1982);

Thomas F. Staley, *An Annotated Critical Bibliography of James Joyce* (Brighton: Harvester, 1989).

Biographies:

Herbert Gorman, *James Joyce, His First Forty Years* (New York: Huebsch, 1924);

Frank Budgen, *James Joyce and the Making of "Ulysses"* (London: Grayson, 1934; revised edition, Bloomington: Indiana University Press, 1960);

Gorman, *James Joyce* (New York: Rinehart, 1940; revised, 1948);

Stanislaus Joyce, *My Brother's Keeper: James Joyce's Early Years,* edited by Richard Ellmann (New York: Viking, 1958);

Ellmann, *James Joyce* (Oxford: Oxford University Press, 1959; revised, 1982);

Constantine Curran, *James Joyce Remembered* (New York: Oxford University Press, 1968);

Chester G. Anderson, *James Joyce and His World* (London: Thames & Hudson, 1968);

Arthur Power, *Conversations with James Joyce,* edited by Clive Hart (London: Millington, 1974);

Willard Potts, ed., *Portraits of the Artist in Exile: Recollections of James Joyce by Europeans* (Seattle: University of Washington Press, 1979);

Morris Beja, *James Joyce* (Columbus: Ohio State University Press, 1993).

References:

Derek Attridge, ed., *The Cambridge Companion to James Joyce* (Cambridge: Cambridge University Press, 1990);

Morris Beja, ed., *"Dubliners" and "A Portrait of the Artist as a Young Man": A Casebook* (London: Macmillan, 1973);

Bruce Bidwell and Linda Heffer, *The Joycean Way: A Topographic Guide to "Dubliners" and "A Portrait of the Artist as a Young Man"* (Baltimore & London: Johns Hopkins University Press, 1982);

Zach R. Bowen and James F. Carens, eds., *A Companion to Joyce Studies* (Westport, Conn.: Greenwood Press, 1984);

Homer Obed Brown, *James Joyce's Early Fiction: The Biography of a Form* (Cleveland: Case Western Reserve University Press, 1972);

Don Gifford, *Joyce Annotated: Notes for "Dubliners" and "A Portrait of the Artist as a Young Man,"* second edition (Berkeley & Los Angeles: University of California Press, 1982);

Clive Hart, ed., *James Joyce's "Dubliners": Critical Essays* (London: Faber & Faber, 1969);

Phillip Herring, *Joyce's Uncertainty Principle* (Princeton: Princeton University Press, 1987);

Hugh Kenner, *Dublin's Joyce* (Bloomington: Indiana University Press, 1956);

R. B. Kershner, *Joyce, Bakhtin, and Popular Literature: Chronicles of Disorder* (Chapel Hill: University of North Carolina Press, 1989);

Harry Levin, *James Joyce* (New York: New Directions, 1941);

Colin MacCabe, *James Joyce and the Revolution of the Word* (New York: Harper & Row, 1979);

Marvin Magalaner and Richard M. Kain, *Joyce: The Man, the Work, the Reputation* (New York: New York University Press, 1956);

Frank O'Connor, *The Lonely Voice: A Study of the Short Story* (Cleveland: World, 1963);

C. H. Peake, *James Joyce: The Citizen and the Artist* (Stanford, Cal.: Stanford University Press, 1977);

William York Tindall, *A Reader's Guide to James Joyce* (New York: Farrar, Straus & Giroux, 1959);

Donald T. Torchiana, *Backgrounds for Joyce's "Dubliners"* (Boston: Allen & Unwin, 1986);

Craig Werner, *"Dubliners": A Pluralistic World* (Boston: Twayne, 1989).

Papers:

The three largest collections of Joyce materials are housed in the libraries of Cornell University, the State University of New York at Buffalo, and the National Library of Ireland (Dublin). Other important collections are at the Rosenbach Foundation, Philadelphia; the Beinecke Rare Book and Manuscript Library, Yale University; the British Library, London; the Harry Ransom Humanities Research Center, University of Texas at Austin; and the libraries of Southern Illinois University at Carbondale, the University of Kansas, and the University of Tulsa.

D. H. Lawrence

(11 September 1885 – 2 March 1930)

Brian Murray
Loyola College in Maryland

See also the Lawrence entries in *DLB 10: Modern British Dramatists, 1900–1945*; *DLB 19: British Poets, 1880–1914*; *DLB 36: British Novelists, 1890–1929: Modernists*; and *DLB 98: Modern British Essayists, First Series.*

BOOKS: *The White Peacock* (New York: Duffield, 1911; London: Heinemann, 1911);

The Trespasser (London: Duckworth, 1912; New York: Kennerley, 1912);

Love Poems, and Others (London: Duckworth, 1913; New York: Kennerley, 1913);

Sons and Lovers (London: Duckworth, 1913; New York: Kennerley, 1913);

The Widowing of Mrs. Holroyd: A Drama in Three Acts (New York: Kennerley, 1914; London: Duckworth, 1914);

The Prussian Officer, and Other Stories (London: Duckworth, 1914; New York: Huebsch, 1916);

The Rainbow (London: Methuen, 1915; expurgated, New York: Huebsch, 1915);

Twilight in Italy (London: Duckworth, 1916; New York: Huebsch, 1916);

Amores (London: Duckworth, 1916; New York: Huebsch, 1916);

Look! We Have Come Through! (London: Chatto & Windus, 1917; New York: Huebsch, 1917);

New Poems (London: Secker, 1918; New York: Huebsch, 1920);

Bay: A Book of Poems (London: Beaumont, 1919);

Touch and Go (London: Daniel, 1920; New York: Seltzer, 1920);

Women in Love (New York: Privately printed, 1920; London: Secker, 1921);

The Lost Girl (London: Secker, 1920; New York: Seltzer, 1921);

Movements in European History, as Lawrence H. Davidson (London: Oxford University Press, 1921);

Psychoanalysis and the Unconscious (New York: Seltzer, 1921; London: Secker, 1923);

D. H. Lawrence

Tortoises (New York: Seltzer, 1921);

Sea and Sardinia (New York: Seltzer, 1921; London: Secker, 1923);

Aaron's Rod (New York: Seltzer, 1922; London: Secker, 1922);

Fantasia of the Unconscious (New York: Seltzer, 1922; London: Secker, 1923);

England, My England, and Other Stories (New York: Seltzer, 1922; London: Secker, 1924);

The Ladybird, The Fox, The Captain's Doll (London: Secker, 1923); republished as *The Captain's Doll: Three Novelettes* (New York: Seltzer, 1923);

Studies in Classic American Literature (New York: Seltzer, 1923; London: Secker, 1924);

Kangaroo (London: Secker, 1923; New York: Seltzer, 1923);

Birds, Beasts and Flowers (New York: Seltzer, 1923; London: Secker, 1923);

The Boy in the Bush, by Lawrence and M. L. Skinner (London: Secker, 1924; New York: Seltzer, 1924);

St. Mawr (New York: Knopf, 1925);

St. Mawr: Together with the Princess (London: Secker, 1925);

Reflections on the Death of a Porcupine, and Other Essays (Philadelphia: Centaur Press, 1925; London: Secker, 1934);

The Plumed Serpent (Quetzalcoatl) (London: Secker, 1926; New York: Knopf, 1926);

David (London: Secker, 1926; New York: Knopf, 1926);

Sun (expurgated, London: Archer, 1926; unexpurgated, Paris: Black Sun Press, 1928);

Glad Ghosts (London: Benn, 1926);

Mornings in Mexico (London: Secker, 1927; New York: Knopf, 1927);

Rawdon's Roof (London: Mathews & Marrot, 1928);

The Woman Who Rode Away, and Other Stories (London: Secker, 1928; New York: Knopf, 1928);

Lady Chatterley's Lover (Florence: Privately printed, 1928; expurgated, London: Secker, 1932; New York: Knopf, 1932; unexpurgated, New York: Grove, 1959; Harmondsworth: Penguin, 1960);

The Collected Poems of D. H. Lawrence, 2 volumes (London: Secker, 1928; New York: Cape & Smith, 1929);

The Paintings of D. H. Lawrence (London: Mandrake Press, 1929);

Pansies (London: Secker, 1929; New York: Knopf, 1929);

My Skirmish with Jolly Roger (New York: Random House, 1929); revised as *A Propos of Lady Chatterley's Lover* (London: Mandrake Press, 1930);

Pornography and Obscenity (London: Faber & Faber, 1929; New York: Knopf, 1930);

The Escaped Cock (Paris: Black Sun Press, 1929); republished as *The Man Who Died* (London: Secker, 1931; New York: Knopf, 1931);

Nettles (London: Faber & Faber, 1930);

Assorted Articles (London: Secker, 1930; New York: Knopf, 1930);

The Virgin and the Gipsy (Florence: Orioli, 1930; London: Secker, 1930; New York: Knopf, 1930);

Love among the Haystacks & Other Pieces (London: Nonesuch Press, 1930; New York: Viking, 1933);

The Triumph of the Machine (London: Faber & Faber, 1930);

Apocalypse (Florence: Orioli, 1931; New York: Viking, 1931; London: Secker, 1932);

Etruscan Places (London: Secker, 1932; New York: Viking, 1932);

Last Poems, edited by Richard Aldington (Florence: Orioli, 1932; New York: Viking, 1933; London: Secker, 1933);

The Lovely Lady, and Other Stories (London: Secker, 1933; New York: Viking, 1933);

A Collier's Friday Night (London: Secker, 1934);

A Modern Lover (London: Secker, 1934; New York: Viking, 1934);

Phoenix: The Posthumous Papers of D. H. Lawrence, edited by Edward D. McDonald (New York: Viking, 1936; London: Heinemann, 1936);

The First Lady Chatterley (New York: Dial, 1944);

The Complete Poems of D. H. Lawrence, 2 volumes, edited by Vivian de Sola Pinto and Warren Roberts (London: Heinemann, 1964; New York: Viking, 1964);

The Complete Plays of D. H. Lawrence (London: Heinemann, 1965; New York: Viking, 1966);

Phoenix II: Uncollected, Unpublished, and Other Prose Works, edited by Roberts and Harry T. Moore (New York: Viking, 1968; London: Heinemann, 1968);

John Thomas and Lady Jane (New York: Viking, 1972; London: Heinemann, 1972);

Mr. Noon, edited by Lindeth Vasey (London & New York: Cambridge University Press, 1984).

Collection: *The Cambridge Edition of the Letters and Works of D. H. Lawrence,* 34 volumes projected, general editors James T. Boulton and Warren Roberts (Cambridge, London, New York, New Rochelle, Melbourne & Sydney: Cambridge University Press, 1980–   ).

OTHER: M. M., *Memoirs of the Foreign Legion,* introduction by Lawrence (London: Secker, 1924).

D. H. Lawrence was a brilliant and difficult man who often explored and exposed his complexities and contradictions in his published prose. Few modern writers of fiction have been as strikingly original or as controversial as Lawrence. Few have

1 AE=

The Vicar's Garden

She had been silent for some minutes. The hill from the Bay is so steep that words only brew in the mind and are not uttered until the short stretch of level lane is reached. When she began to speak I knew she had been taking a wistful look into the Future from the delightful promontory of the Present which we had gained now after so long hoping, and planning, and working.

"This" Said she "would be a perfect place for a honeymoon".

Then she blushed, and I smiled.

"You see" she said hastily "the hills and the headlands give us such a lovely, happy corner of the world to ourselves, and then there are such ——"

"Snug little nests in the cliffs" I suggested; but she was meditating a higher flight.

"Such great stretches of moor where you might fancy you were the only two in the world"

"Paradise Regained" I commented.

The comment was lost on her. She had dropped my arm and was peeping through a doorway opening in a high stone wall by the roadside. I must peep also.

First page from the earliest draft for "The Shadow in the Rose Garden," collected in The Prussian Officer *(Harry Ransom Humanities Research Center, the University of Texas at Austin; by permission of the Estate of D. H. Lawrence)*

inspired such ardent admirers and such ardent foes. In 1930 E. M. Forster suggested that Lawrence "has two publics, neither of them quite satisfactory. There is the general public, who think of him as improper and scarcely read him at all, and there is a special public, who read him, but in too narrow and fanatical a way, and think of him as a sort of god, who has come to change human nature and society." Broadly and essentially this remains true today, for Lawrence still has his disciples and his detractors. In recent years the numbers of the latter appear to have grown; for many, Lawrence's name is all but synonymous with fascism and misogyny. "Lawrence who had been perceived as a guru of sexual liberation became," as Peter Widdowson puts it, "the phallocratic oppressor of gender politics."

Of course, many readers and critics remain willing to consider Lawrence more dispassionately and to appreciate the unique nature of his work within the context of his times. Lawrence remains best known for his novels, and his stories reveal much about the aesthetic values and philosophical assumptions that inform his longer fiction. But those stories, widely studied and frequently anthologized, are interesting in their own right. They have long been admired for their subtlety, intensity, and striking individuality.

Lawrence was born in Eastwood, a mining village located within ten miles of Nottingham, and – as he would later recall – "one mile from the small stream, the Erewash, which divides Nottinghamshire from Derbyshire." Lawrence thus spent his childhood in an area that was, he wrote, "a curious cross between industrialism and the old agricultural England of Shakespeare and Milton and Fielding and George Eliot." The fabled Sherwood forest was close by. "To me, as a child and a young man," wrote Lawrence in "Nottingham and the Mining Countryside," this was "the old England of the forest and agricultural past; there were no motor-cars, the mines were, in a sense, an accident in the landscape, and Robin Hood and his merry men were not very far away."

Lawrence's father was a miner's butty – a foreman of sorts – in one of Eastwood's pits. John Arthur Lawrence had little schooling and spoke in a strong Derbyshire dialect; "his life," writes Anthony Burgess, "was work, rabbiting, odd jobs about the house, the sodality of the pub." Hot-tempered, unschooled, and robust, Lawrence's father had little in common with Lawrence's mother; the daughter of an engineer, she had been reared in a more middle-class household. As a young woman Lydia Beardsall Lawrence had taught school. She

was a staunch Congregationalist who went regularly to church and who nursed growing ambitions for "Bertie," the fourth of her five children and the youngest of her sons. She did not want her sons to become miners, nor did she want them to resemble her husband, with whom she lived in increasing discord. Lydia had, as Burgess writes, fallen for John Lawrence's "physique. He was big, muscular, bearded, and fell in his turn for her gentleness, delicacy, aura of a refined world far away from his. The gods of genetics like to work through the attraction of opposites. It was a disastrous marriage, but it produced D. H. Lawrence."

After completing his studies at Nottingham High School, the sixteen-year-old Lawrence – pushed by his mother – took a clerk's job with an area firm specializing in surgical implements and orthopedic supplies. Lawrence loathed the work and remained only three months with the firm, which he called Jordan's in Sons and Lovers (1913), his third and perhaps most autobiographical novel. Having developed pneumonia – a disease that had not long before killed one of his brothers, Ernest – Lawrence left the job. As Burgess records, a doctor who examined Lawrence warned his parents "of a tubercular condition," but Lawrence himself "always refused to accept this, preferring to speak of bronchial trouble or an exceptionally bad cold or a dose of flu."

After convalescing for several months, Lawrence began work as a pupil-teacher in Eastwood. He found little satisfaction in the job, but after two years he decided nonetheless to enroll at the Ilkeston Pupil-Teacher Centre in nearby Derbyshire. Meanwhile he continued his long and important friendship with a local girl, Jessie Chambers. She had read and admired Lawrence's early, unpublished work, and she urged him to continue writing. She also served as Lawrence's main model for Miriam Leivers in Sons and Lovers.

In 1906 Lawrence entered Nottingham University College to pursue a course of study that, after two years, would grant him a teacher's certificate – but not a bachelor of arts degree. Lawrence proved strong in his studies of French and botany – the latter subject he particularly enjoyed. As Brenda Maddox notes, Lawrence was "an intent naturalist" well before he entered college, for his father, though "barely literate," knew "the name of every animal and plant in the region of Eastwood and taught them to his youngest son on their long walks together." Maddox also suggests that Lawrence's study of college botany prompted him "to consider the philosophical implications of evolution" and contributed, in part, to his rejection of Christianity.

After completing his studies Lawrence found work at a school in Croydon, a far suburb of London. Lawrence taught twelve-year-olds, and he made few friends among his colleagues. He lacked the rigid temperament of the typical pedagogue, and not surprisingly he admitted that he hated teaching. With Jessie's continuing encouragement he kept writing, aiming always to escape the dull grind of schoolmastering for "entrance into the jungle of literature."

From Croydon, Lawrence sent his short story "Odour of Chrysanthemums" to Ford Madox Hueffer, who — as Ford Madox Ford — became known not only for such novels as *The Good Soldier* (1915) but also for his astute ability to recognize and encourage talent. Ford, as editor of the *English Review*, accepted the story, and Lawrence's literary career received its first major boost. He was never to become a literary "realist" in the strict sense of that word, and in subsequent years many of his short stories resembled fables and tales, recalling those of Nathaniel Hawthorne or A. E. Coppard far more than those of Anton Chekhov or Henry James. But at the start of his career Lawrence admired the kind of literary realism often found in the *English Review;* in fact, in one letter from that period he praised the magazine for being "finely truthful" and urged the writing of fiction that is "as near to life as possible."

"Odour of Chrysanthemums" (1911) belongs more to the realist school than much of Lawrence's later fiction. It takes place in the mining country Lawrence knew so well, and its central character, Elizabeth Bates, starts the story as a collier's wife and ends it as a collier's widow. Significantly revised for its republication in 1914, the narrative builds slowly and powerfully as Elizabeth waits anxiously for her husband, Walter, to come home after working all day in the mines. He is very late, and when he is not among the weary miners trooping past "in grey sombre groups," Elizabeth assumes that he is out getting drunk with his mates. "Never mind," she tells her daughter, "they'll bring him when he does come — like a log." But Elizabeth's anger is "tinged with fear," for of course coal mines are dangerous, and accidents are common. Elizabeth's fear is confirmed, for that day her husband is killed in the mines: "E wor smothered," as one man explains.

Walter is, in fact, carried home, still wearing his "nail pitboots" and still "naked to the waist, lying stripped for work." As the story concludes, Elizabeth and her mother-in-law wash this dead "man of handsome body": he "was blond, full-fleshed, with fine limbs." The miner's mother ad-mires his "clear and clean and white" skin and recalls his hearty laugh; she calls him "the lamb, the dear lamb." Elizabeth, for her part, faces the possibility that she never really knew her husband, despite their years of marriage and physical intimacy: he was "a stranger with whom she had been living as one flesh," and they had "met in the dark and had fought in the dark, not knowing whom they met nor whom they fought." She had "denied him what he was — she saw it now. She had refused him as himself."

"Odour of Chrysanthemums" includes images and themes that recur frequently, and more elaborately, in Lawrence's later fiction. Ever attentive to the symbolic power of flowers, Lawrence's narrative returns several times to the chrysanthemums of his title. They come to represent the fragile beauty of the world while also evoking, for Elizabeth, hard memories and lost hopes. In this story Lawrence depicts, not for the last time, the real danger and the rough dignity of life in the mines, and in his way he pays tribute to men whose lives demand comradeship and courage — even while he strongly implies that their work kills not only the body but the soul. Walter, after all, is still a youth when he begins his life of work underground; he is in several respects trapped well before his normal lifespan is complete. Certainly Lawrence's reference to the mental gulf that separates Elizabeth and Walter shows the writer's interest in exploring the tension, conflict, and lack of connection that he would long associate with relations between the sexes. With its closing references to Elizabeth's "shame" and its rather direct use of biblical imagery — for Bates, the "Lamb," is a Christ-figure of sorts — "Odour of Chrysanthemums" also shows Lawrence employing the biblical and religious imagery that his published writing continued to use.

The mature Lawrence in fact was neither a churchgoer nor a believer — at least in any orthodox sense. Owing more to Charles Darwin and Friedrich Nietzsche than to traditional Christianity, his religious views, broadly defined, were mystical and imprecise. As Maddox records, Lawrence during his college years had come to reject "not only the chapel Congregationalism of his youth but Christianity and religion altogether," and he had decided that "Life on earth was a continuous stream" and that "There was no Creator who crafted individually every slug and snail. All forms of life, man included, were just drops in 'the big shimmering sea of unorganised life we call God.' " For the most part Lawrence continued to view life and God in these terms, as he formulated a highly individualistic philosophy that stressed the importance of seizing the day, knowing beauty, and being true to one's deepest passions and desires. "My great religion," Lawrence memorably wrote, "is a belief in the blood, the flesh, as being wiser than the intellect. We can go wrong in our minds. But what our blood feels and believes and says, is always true."

But as Maddox and other critics note, the effects of Lawrence's Protestant boyhood in a small English town never vanished completely from either his life or his work. As a bright and impressionable boy Lawrence went regularly to chapel, "twice on Sundays," as Maddox records, "and often in the evenings." His knowledge of conservative Protestant theology was then deeply ingrained, an inescapable force in the way he viewed the world. In many ways, writes Maddox, Lawrence "remained a Dissenter, a passionate Puritan, with a religious outlook, an uncompromising steadfastness, an instinct for hard work, and a deep feeling for the Bible and the never-seen Holy Land." Moreover, certain rather conservative strains would always remain in Lawrence's radical view of the world. He was, for example, a firm believer in marriage and sometimes celebrated it in his longer fiction – although for Lawrence marriage always meant more than quiet security and cozy routine. "Married couples in Lawrence," observes John Carey, should not be " 'stuck together like two jujube lozenges,' " – to use Lawrence's own phrase; they should be "fiercely separate in their 'dynamic blood polarity,' like copulating birds of prey, 'two eagles in mid-air, grappling, whirling.' " Lawrence did not, moreover, extol the endless pursuit of all physical pleasure. He did not advocate hedonism, writes Maddox, "but rather a trust in the rightness of natural instinct."

"Daughters of the Vicar" (1914), another early story also revised significantly after its first publication in 1911, offers a grim view of Christianity as Lawrence believed it was practiced in the sort of provincial English environment he knew. Called "Two Marriages" in its earlier version, this story also shows Lawrence's willingness to cover a large span of time within the limited frame of a single story and to bring his narrative to a subtle but pointed close. This technique avoided many of the conventional features common to short stories of the day – features such as "skillful contrivance of some single effect, and careful preparation for the 'epiphanic' moment," as Weldon Thornton notes. The Reverend Ernest Lindley, the vicar of the title, has "no particular character" but nurses a strong sense of superiority; inevitably, Lawrence implies,

he comes to a "conscious hatred of the majority of his flock, and unconscious hatred of himself." The vicar has "dragged on" with his duties, "pale and miserable and neutral." His wife, meanwhile, obsessed with her own image, grows bitter because of her lack of real social status and her husband's low income. The vicar's children have been "born one every year; almost mechanically"; the vicar's wife has then performed "her maternal duty, which was forced upon her."

One of their daughters ends up fleeing the vicar's narrow and suffocating world; but the other, Mary, marries a dull, machinelike man – another vicar. Mary's life also proceeds "monotonously"; there "was always a weight on top of her, something that pressed down her life." When her husband becomes sick, she tends him "mechanically, as part of her duty." In this environment Christianity is no longer a vital force. It has grown mechanical, gloomy, and abstract. It is part of a social system built upon rigid and poisonous social distinctions, and it breeds paralyzing self-consciousness and petty vanity while it smothers the possibility of truer, more passionate forms of living.

Other stories in *The Prussian Officer, and Other Stories* (1914) reveal Lawrence's continuing preoccupations. In "The Shades of Spring" – first published as "The Soiled Rose" (1913) – the bookish John Addington Syson revisits Hilda Millership, the woman he had once idealized as "his young love, his nun, his Botticelli angel." He now discovers that Hilda has become the contented lover of Arthur Pilbeam, a "ruddy and well favoured" gamekeeper "taut with animal life." Hilda shows Syson the hut in the woods where, amid the skins of various animals, she and Pilbeam make love. Syson, the story suggests, had ended his relationship with Hilda only to end up uneasily married to someone else. He now realizes that he had somehow overlooked the sheer, splendid physical fact of Hilda; he "had taken her for something she was not."

At the close of the story Syson walks to the edge of the woods, where, brooding amid patches of milkwort and lousewort near the bank of a bog, he overhears the voices of Hilda and Pilbeam. Hidden and thus reduced to the role of the voyeur, Syson watches as Hilda affectionately tends Pilbeam, who has just been stung by a bee. She "picked out the sting, put her mouth to his arm, and sucked away the drop poison. As she looked at the red mark her mouth had made, and at his arm, she said, laughing: 'That is the reddest kiss you will ever have.' " Here Lawrence uses blood in a rather Nietzschean sense, equating it with sheer passion and vitality –

Lawrence and Frieda at a farmhouse, during their 1923 visit to Mexico (Harry Ransom Humanities Research Center, the University of Texas at Austin)

attacks the officer, whom he strangles in a scene that, as Lawrence describes it, also suggests rape. The Captain's toxic repressions have in effect destroyed him, and they have destroyed the orderly too: at the close of the story both are dead, their bodies lying together. The Captain's form is "white and slender, but laid rigidly at rest"; the other looks "as if every moment it must rouse into life again, so young and unused, from a slumber."

Critics have long found homoerotic undertones in "The Prussian Officer"; some suggest that it reveals Lawrence dramatizing, consciously or not, his continuing struggle with homosexual desires he would not openly express. In any event, perhaps because he grew up in a domestic war zone, Lawrence was prone to view close relationships — particularly conjugal relationships — more "in terms of struggle rather than harmony," as Jeffrey Meyers suggests. Lawrence's fiction — long and short — shows many "cruel and mutually destructive conflicts between men and women," writes Meyers, "as well as an alternative search for satisfying relationships between men."

For Lawrence the years between 1910 and 1914 — between the publication of his earliest stories and his first volume of short fiction — were especially eventful and marked profoundly the later course of his life. In 1910 his mother died, and he completed his first novel, *The White Peacock,* which was published the following year. In 1911 Lawrence met Edward Garnett, one of the most influential editors in London and a man who worked closely with such authors as Joseph Conrad and John Galsworthy, among others. For a time Garnett became one of Lawrence's most important advisers and friends. Garnett encouraged his own publisher, Duckworth, to accept Lawrence's second novel, *The Trespasser,* which appeared in the summer of 1912, and Garnett supervised the compiling and publishing, by Duckworth, of *The Prussian Officer, and Other Stories.*

In 1912 Lawrence also met Frieda Weekley, whose husband, Ernest, taught French at Nottingham University College and whose refinement and intelligence Lawrence admired. The young writer was immediately and powerfully attracted to Frieda, the German-born mother of Weekley's three children. She was also a member of the von Richtofen family and a distant cousin of the celebrated (in Britain, the notorious) World War I flying ace, the Red Baron. Frieda was vital, dramatic, sexually adventurous, and full of her own strong opinions; she was in many respects the perfect mate for Lawrence, with his low threshold for boredom and his keen need for intellectual stimulation. Well

as much of his work does. As Carey has observed, and as "The Shades of Spring" shows, "between men and women, in Lawrence's view, 'blood contact' not mental communion, was requisite."

In the title story "The Prussian Officer" — first published as "Honour and Arms" (1914) — two males contend in a war of wills. They are army men who, for Lawrence, illustrate two polar sides of human temperament and of human possibility. One of them, the Captain, is a Prussian aristocrat, both "haughty and overbearing." The other, a mere orderly, is a warm individual who appears "to have received life direct through his senses, and acted straight from instinct." The orderly's free and spontaneous way disturbs the Captain; this "blind, instinctive sureness of movement of an unhampered young animal" sends the rigid Captain into a rage. He hates "the free movement of the handsome limbs, which no military discipline could make stiff." The Captain resorts frequently to harsh and cruel bullying, to "contempt and satire," as he is in the grip of a passion he cannot reveal. The abused orderly finally loses control of his own restraint and

read, she was for Lawrence an important channel of intellectual influence, as she and other members of her family moved in an intellectual circle that included the influential German historian Werner Sombart and the psychoanalyist Otto Gross.

In fact, through what became a lifelong relationship Frieda continued to provide an important influence in Lawrence's life and work, for throughout his life he had benefited from close, steady encouragement by particular women – first from his mother, and later from Jessie Chambers. Frieda also believed in Lawrence's talents and encouraged him greatly, often in the face of severe attack. Yet she did not simply provide him with necessary emotional support, for in fact she often upset his emotional equilibrium in their volatile relationship. Frieda taxed and tested Lawrence, and from the sparks of their conflict came the impetus for much of his art.

In 1912 Frieda left Weekley and joined Lawrence in their first flight from England and into the unknown. On the Continent they met Frieda's family and visited Italy and Switzerland. Lawrence, who had loathed the dull grind of teaching school, now found himself faced with many distractions. He was, for example, almost penniless. Ernest Weekley, moreover, was wounded by Frieda's departure and was reluctant to divorce her. Frieda missed her children – and would continue doing so in the years to come. But still Lawrence kept writing. In his lifetime he made little money from his publications, but he rarely allowed poverty, marital distractions, or his failing health to deter him from getting on with his work. Lawrence, wrote Anthony Burgess, was always – whatever else – "a professional writer" who "never whined about distraction or writer's block; he got on with his trade or, to be more fanciful, went daily down into the mine of his creative unconscious."

John Worthen rightly stresses that Lawrence's actions at this stage of his life involved considerable risk and required considerable courage. "Not only did he have enormous financial problems," writes Worthen, "he had the particular problem of abandoning the role of the self-reliant professional man, able to support a wife and family, for which his upbringing and education had fitted him. And he had the very real problem of being a boy from Eastwood who moved into the metropolitan literary world."

To pay the bills, Lawrence published in various genres, producing book reviews and essays as well as poetry, novels, and stories. For Lawrence the novel would remain the most important form – one that he once called "the one bright book of life."

After several crucial revisions, Lawrence's third novel, *Sons and Lovers,* appeared in 1913. It failed initially, but its reputation grew steadily in Lawrence's lifetime. Lawrence and Frieda's circle of friends now included other writers, among them Katherine Mansfield and her husband, John Middleton Murry. Lawrence was a lively writer of personal letters – and one of the most prolific of his age. During the years he addressed many of his most animated letters to Murry, who was a talented critic but – at least in Lawrence's view – an often exasperating man. (Murry apparently provided the inspiration for several characters in Lawrence's fiction, including the doomed Marchbanks in the 1924 short story "The Last Laugh.")

Lawrence and Frieda married in the summer of 1914, and during the following years of the Great War, they were often under stress. They would be forced, for example, to leave Cornwall in 1917, when local rumors would place them at the center of a German spy ring, and in the same year Lawrence's request for a passport would be denied. But during the war years Lawrence worked on what would become two more novels, *The Rainbow* (1915) and *Women in Love* (1920). These works brought him wide notice and much criticism, and they have remained chief sources of his fame.

After the war Lawrence and Frieda left England in late 1919 for what would become a life of frequent movement and traveling. In the early 1920s they lived in both Capri and Sicily. They visited Ceylon and Australia in 1922. By the autumn of that year they had settled in Taos, New Mexico, where Mabel Dodge Luhan had established a ranch and colony designed to foster the creative arts. In 1923 Lawrence and Frieda lived briefly in Chapala, Mexico. As he traveled throughout these years, Lawrence continued to write and publish short stories, many of which were brought together in a second collection, *England, My England, and Other Stories* (1922) – a volume that contains some of his finest work in the genre, including "Tickets Please" (1919), "You Touched Me" (1920), "The Blind Man" (1920), and "The Horse Dealer's Daughter" (1922). They deal with various themes – including power and the mystery of sexuality – frequently found in Lawrence's longer fiction and his nonfiction prose.

Like many of Lawrence's stories, "You Touched Me" is rather loosely structured, involving several characters and spanning a rather wide period of time. It opens with an account of the tepid lives of the Rockley sisters, including that of Matilda, a bookish, "tall, thin, graceful, fair girl, with a rather large nose," a girl who is happy in a "quiet, melancholy way." Some years earlier her father had adopted into the family "an ordinary boy from a Charity Home," one Hadrian, who as a youth wore "a subtle, jeering look." At fifteen Hadrian leaves England for Canada, fights in the Great War, and returns to visit the Rockley household as a "self-possessed" young man. Again he wins the affection of Mr. Rockley, who is now dying.

Hadrian stirs up a swirl of emotion in the Rockley household with his "plebian energy" and his way of walking about in his "khaki trousers, collarless, his bare neck showing." The story comes to a turning point when, one night, Matilda enters Hadrian's darkened bedroom and places her "fine, delicate hand" on his face, which is "very fresh and smooth." It is inadvertent, as Matilda has assumed that she is visiting her father. She is then "shocked" and "startled" but also "entranced" by the contact and the sensation: "her right hand, which she had laid so gently on his face, on his fresh skin, ached now, as if it were really injured." Hadrian too is deeply affected: the "soft straying tenderness of her hand" has "startled something out of his soul." Hadrian decides to marry Matilda, who is appalled. But Hadrian reminds her that she has, after all, "put your hand on me" – even though the gesture was, at least consciously, a mistake. "I shan't forget it," he tells her. "If you wake a man up, he can't go to sleep again because he's told to."

"You Touched Me" concludes with Lawrence's description of Mr. Rockley urging Matilda to accept Hadrian and to kiss him; the father's tone suggests lasciviousness as well as domination. But "You Touched Me" does more than dramatize Rockley's desire to dominate his daughters. It illustrates Lawrence's assumption that deep contact between the sexes must lead to a test of powers and wills. Like much of Lawrence's fiction, it also reveals his recognition of the inescapable fact of the irrational and the erotic in everyday life. These are forces that, submerged daily, characteristically erupt in ways that shatter expectations and transform lives marked previously by routine, repression, and fear.

"The Blind Man" explores similar notions. In this story Lawrence deals, as he often does, with a triangle of characters: here, a husband, his wife, and the wife's friend. The friend, Bertie Reid, comes to visit Maurice and Isabel Pervin at their farm on a rainy November day. Maurice had been blinded in battle at Flanders and bears "a disfiguring mark on his brow." At times he is confused and depressed, but on the whole his life is still "very full and

strangely serene for the blind man, peaceful with the almost incomprehensible peace of immediate contact in darkness." He has begun to move through the world with much sensitivity and confidence, and he knows "the presence of objects before he touched them. It was a pleasure to him to rock thus through the world of things, carried on the flood in a sort of blood-presence." He finds it "a pleasure to stretch forth the hand and meet the unseen object, clasp it, and possess it in pure contact."

At first Maurice does not like Bertie, a lawyer who fears "close contact of any sort" and toward whom Maurice is friendly but aloof, chivalrous but detached. Yet Maurice comes quite literally close to Bertie when, near the close of the narrative, he runs his hand over Bertie's face, feeling its texture and shape. Bertie is made uneasy – particularly when, at the blind man's insistence, Bertie touches Maurice's scar. Maurice is moved, convinced that the two men are henceforth friends. But Bertie "could not bear it that he had been touched by the blind man, his insane reserve broken in. He was like a mollusc whose shell is broken."

"The Blind Man" reveals much about the vision that informs the whole of Lawrence's fictional world. Linda Ruth Williams, in *Sex in the Head* (1993), finds this story "an exemplary statement of Lawrence's philosophy"; it shows, among other things, his belief that what one needs to seek is something like "pre-visual bliss" – a state subduing intellect, self, and distance as it seeks a more direct connection with the world. Here "blindness is a state of grace which heals the fatal gap between self and other, a gap opened up by the conscious self's ability to see, to see the world *as* other." William concludes, "The 'unspeakable,' 'incomprehensible' self which is born of the shadowy reunion between blind self and dark otherness is Lawrence's final, authentic goal."

In "The Horse Dealer's Daughter" – another tale of connection and resurrection – Lawrence depicts Sam Fergusson, a doctor who at the story's close finds himself proposing marriage to a lonely and weary young woman, Mabel, whom he has just saved from drowning. While tending her after this rescue, Fergusson removes Mabel's "saturated, earthy-smelling clothing" and wraps her "naked in the blankets." She is a simple woman with a "bulldog" face, a woman who interprets – or more precisely senses – in the doctor's actions a passionate love he would not otherwise declare as he looks down at her "tangled wet hair," her "wild, bare, animal shoulders." The story makes it clear that Fergusson has not intended to love Mabel. Yet still he is drawn to touch her bare shoulders, and he feels not only flesh but "a flame." Fergusson declares his love to Mabel, much to his own amazement: he kisses her "on the mouth, gently, with the kiss that is an eternal pledge," and then again, "gently, passionately, with his heart's painful kiss." The story shows the disorienting nature of touch, of physical connection – but it also shows less overtly the ambivalence that often accompanies any intimate relationships, perhaps particularly romantic or sexual ones. Mabel is frightened; the doctor is confused, declaring his desire but moving "blindly" – his kisses full of pain as well as tenderness.

Lawrence makes clear that Fergusson is drawn to "the colliers and the iron-workers"; near them, his "nerves were excited and gratified." As is typical of Lawrence's fiction, reiteration emphasizes the point: Fergusson may grumble and say that "he hated the hellish hole. But as a matter of fact it excited him, the contact with the rough, strongly-feeling people was a stimulant applied direct to his nerves." Lawrence's views of the working class were – like his views on many things – ambivalent and at times hard to define. He could denounce democracy and advocate a "natural aristocracy" that should be capable of controlling the mass of men, the "monster with a million worm-like heads." But peasants and servants – people who live outside the rigid confines of the British middle or upper classes – are often linked in his fiction with the kind of keen and instinctive vitality he frequently praised. Such ambivalence remained a distinguishing feature of Lawrence's fiction: one sees it, for example, in Oliver Mellors, the gamekeeper and title character of *Lady Chatterley's Lover* (1928), a work that – because of its sexual explicitness – was immediately banned from public sale and not widely available in Britain until the early 1960s.

From the start Lawrence was such a daring writer. His references in "A Horse Dealer's Daughter" to Mabel's "wild, bare, animal shoulders" are typical of what some reviewers found shocking in Lawrence's work well before the appearance of *Lady Chatterley's Lover,* for an explicit treatment of female sexuality was far from standard fare in the popular or serious fiction of Lawrence's day. In this regard "Tickets, Please" is also worth noting. Like "Odour of Chrysanthemums," this story opens with a neatly "realistic" description of life in the English Midlands; here Lawrence recalls a "single-line tramway system" that runs past the churches, cinema, and collieries. Riding in its "green and creamy coloured" cars is "always an adventure," for they are driven by men deemed unfit for military service in

Lawrence near his Villa Mirenda residence in Italy, 1926–1927

wartime, but who "have the spirit of the devil in them." Moreover, the tram's ticket collectors are bold, flirtatious young women who "have all the sang-froid of an old non-commissioned officer." They "fear nobody – and everybody fears them." A more conventional writer of Lawrence's day might attempt to tame these girls, or at least smooth their rough edges by making them suitably subdued or moony before then setting them firmly in their places.

Lawrence, however, looks directly at the fact of their sexuality, and he suggests that in life sex and violence are frequently mixed. The central figure is Annie, a tram conductor who is also a "plump, alive little creature." She is possessive too, and in due course she decides to gain revenge on John Thomas Raynor, one of the system's inspectors and a notorious flirt. Annie wants John to be more than "a mere nocturnal presence"; she wants him in order "to take an intelligent interest in him, and to have an intelligent response." Yet John Thomas, in turn, avoids Annie and starts "enjoying pastures new." When Annie's more instinctive and passionate side starts to rise, she plots her revenge with a "half-dozen girls who knew John Thomas only too well." They trap him, tease him, and end up "pulling and tearing and beating him." Their "blood was now thoroughly up"; they become "strange, wild creatures"; their faces "were flushed, their hair wild, their eyes were all glittering strangely." They beat the young man, scratch him, rip his clothes, and leave him "quite still, with his face averted, as an animal lies when it is defeated and at the mercy of the captor." They are victorious, and they "giggle wildly" over their helpless male, who is in "a kind of trance of fear and antagonism" before the "unnatural strength and power" they show.

In "England, My England" (1915), the volume's title story, Lawrence moves from his familiar Midlands setting to depict a more upper-class figure – Egbert, who is the product of "age-long breeding" and "of course was an amateur – a born amateur." He floats along without clear ambition, his family supported primarily from money provided by the father of his wife, Winifred. As in "The Rocking-Horse Winner" (1926), money thus becomes a source of strife between husband and wife. Winifred is not obsessed with money; still, it bothers her that "she was dependent on her father for three-fourths of the money spent for herself and her children" and that her husband lives busily but without direction – as if he is driven only by the aim "to hold aloof. To do nobody any damage."

But Egbert unintentionally does damage when his six-year-old daughter falls on a sickle he has left lying in the grass. She is deeply cut and becomes feverish. Her leg is saved, but she remains crippled, walking "with iron supports to her leg, and a little crutch." In the wake of this disaster Egbert grows more distant from Winifred; she wearies of his "triumphant loneliness" and is largely unmoved when he decides to join the army and is duly sent to Flanders. There he is twice wounded and finally killed, shot in the head during a "small, unimportant action" near horse-chestnut trees and fields filled with flowers. Lawrence carefully details Egbert's death, which he depicts as the ultimate state of solitude, the "great darkness" and "the great forgetting."

Critics have often noted that the figure of Egbert appears to owe much to Percy Lucas, the brother-in-law of Viola Meynell, who was both a longtime friend of Lawrence and a member of one of Britain's leading literary families. Percy, writes Jeffrey Meyers, was "just the sort of aesthete, dilettante, and rentier who irritated Lawrence and provoked his anger." But more recently another critic, Weldon Thornton, suggests that, like many of Lawrence's stories, "England, My England" is in its way enigmatic and intricate, resembling a poem as much as a tale. It is more than a piercing attack on a particular individual, however objectionable. For Thornton, Egbert is not utterly unsympathetic, and the story's narrative voice should not be identified automatically with Lawrence's own. Thornton suggests that the narrative voice, "though not monovocal," often "speaks from the perspective of the Marshalls" – the family Egbert has entered through marriage – and it "reflects their attitude toward life." From their perspective Egbert, the aesthete, cannot hope to measure up; he senses this and begins increasingly to suffer from self-doubt. He loses his "fine, spontaneous indifference to authority and responsibility" and lives instead "in negation of his own best qualities" – a negation that leads finally to his enlistment in the army, where his death amounts to a kind of suicide. For Thornton the final pages "provide a profound and troubling account of what happens in a psyche that has lost faith in itself and turned upon itself. Egbert comes to see himself as doomed, as fated, and feels a self-punishing need to consciously observe the process of his own decline."

"England, My England" is notable for what it shows about Lawrence's evolving style and voice, for the way it shows his stories building on the clean, uncluttered style of his earlier pieces – but building with a bite. In some ways the story recalls the relaxed, somewhat repetitive and colloquial style of the spoken tale, with its reiterations and underlined assertions. With Lawrence, however, such authorial intrusions have an edge, an ironic sharpness: "What are you really going to do with a man like Egbert?" the narrator pauses to ask. "It was not that he was idle," the narrator – whoever it is – starkly continues. "He was *not* idle. He was always doing something." Still, Egbert failed "to come to grips with life" – or, as the narrator comments, "you can bring an ass to the water, but you cannot make him drink. The world was the water and Egbert was the ass. And he wasn't having any. He couldn't: he just couldn't. Since necessity did not force him to work for his bread and butter, he would not work for work's sake. You can't make the columbine flowers nod in January, nor make the cuckoo sing in England at Christmas. Why? It isn't his season. He doesn't want to. Nay, he *can't* want to."

This fable or fairy-tale quality characterizes much of Lawrence's short fiction, including "The Princess" (1925) – a story with thematic similarities to "The Woman Who Rode Away" (1925). "The

Princess" is Dollie Urquhart, a woman in her thirties who, after the death of her rather mad and possessive father, decides to see something of the world. Accompanied by her female companion, who "also was virginal," the Princess (as both her father and Lawrence's narrative call her) goes to New Mexico, to a "ranch for the rich" that "lay by a stream on the desert some four miles from the foot of the mountains, a mile away from the Indian pueblo of San Cristobal." There she mingles daily with the other guests, for she "still entertain[s] the idea of *marriage*." But the Princess finds herself "intrigued" by only one man — a strong, sullen ranch hand and guide called Domingo Romero. The two become friends — although the Princess cannot imagine marrying a man so exotically unlike herself.

Their relationship takes a sharp but not entirely surprising turn when the Princess finds herself alone with Romero in an isolated mountain cabin. She has, the story implies, wanted Romero desperately on an instinctive, unconscious level, but she has been sheltered, repressed. Moreover, somewhat like Egbert, who also feared human contact and connection, "she wanted to keep herself intact, untouched, that no one should have any power over her, or rights to her. It was a wild necessity in her that no one, particularly no man, should have any rights or power over her, that no one and nothing should possess her." But, during the mountain night, she is cold. Domingo, with his "terrible animal warmth," warms the Princess and then "possesses" her although, as the narrator notes, "She had never, never wanted to be given over to this." However, "she had *willed* that it should happen to her. And according to her will, she lay and let it happen. But she never wanted it. She never wanted to be thus assailed and handled, and mauled. She wanted to keep herself to her herself. However, she had willed it to happen, and it had happened."

In "The Woman Who Rode Away" (1925) something similar occurs. The central figure, an unnamed woman of thirty-three, has been married to a man who loves little more than "work, work, work" and who has then, in many ways, remained unwed. With her husband she moves to Mexico, where he looks after his business interests and she grows restless, bored. She becomes intrigued by the thought of Indians and their mystic and secretive ways in the surrounding hills. She is in fact "overcome by a foolish romanticism more unreal than a girl's. She felt it was her destiny to wander into the secret haunts of these timeless, mysterious, marvellous Indians of the mountains." She yearns to connect with something deeper, grander, more passionate than herself — and the life she has been living.

Alone on horseback she travels into the mountains, into the world of the Indians, being driven as if "she had no will of her own." She not only encounters Indians, but finds herself partaking in a ritual of the deepest significance to their way of life. At the story's close she is on a "fumigated" altar and is held in place by "four powerful men" as another man, older, a naked priest in "a state of barbaric ecstasy," prepares sacrificially to rip her open with a knife. His eyes "were not anxious. Black, and fixed, and as if sightless, they watched the sun, seeing beyond the sun. And in their black, empty concentration there was power, power intensely abstract and remote, but deep, deep to the heart of the earth, and the heart of the sun."

In both of these stories Lawrence presents women who enter realms not sanctioned as safe or proper by their society. Notably these characters also end up in passive roles, dominated by males, and for this and other reasons both stories disturb many contemporary readers. Janice Hubbard Harris suggests that in "The Woman Who Rode Away" Lawrence has constructed "presumably a religious and cultural fable" that can be seen on one level as a dramatization of "the shift in an individual's consciousness from a rational, scientific, industrial mind set to a more mystical, sensual understanding of reality." But the story also often reads "as a dramatization of sadomasochism." "When the woman is first captured," notes Harris, she "must crawl on her hands and knees between her erect captors as they traverse a narrow mountain ledge. When she is first brought to the gathering of the priesthood, she declines to undress. Several strong men take knives and slit her clothes, lifting them away, leaving her naked in their company." This situation is repeated; in various ceremonies, the woman "is stripped, massaged by the priests, reclothed." Additionally, notes Harris, the woman's journey "is also associated with the passing of the power from female to male," as if to say that the female "must be broken." Carey has also stressed that, for Lawrence, "besides mindlessness, the other essential in sexual relations" is that of a "male dominance" in which " 'The old dominant male,' 'the phallic wind rushing through the dark,' must arise and sweep away silly modern notions of parity between men and women. The female must find her fulfillment once more in 'glorifying the blood male.' "

Such observations are essentially true, but Lawrence was also a more complicated and contradictory thinker than perhaps most biographies and critical studies allow. Anne Fernihough illustrates this fact by noting, for example, that those who would dismiss Lawrence as a protofascist who celebrates violence in the name of his own soaring ideals also ignore the fact that he warns repeatedly "against the dangers of an unbridled idealism." Fernihough thus disagrees with Bertrand Russell's "notorious remark that Lawrence's views 'led straight to Auschwitz.'" "Auschwitz," she contends, "the apotheosis of an idealism in which the body had become utterly dispensible, would, I believe, have utterly horrified Lawrence."

Like most people, Lawrence was shaped by the habits and circumstances of his childhood environment: "to be the dominant partner" with his own wife was, as Burgess notes, "something he had inherited from the Eastwood tradition in which the breadwinner was literally called 't'master.'" Frieda's zestful willingness to fight back undoubtedly invigorated Lawrence's brief life and perhaps encouraged him to view the proverbial battle of the sexes in such stark terms for so long a time. For whatever reasons — including, perhaps, his doubt about his own sexuality — Lawrence was routinely combative in his dealings with women as well as men. Often when such others were "his social superiors," they would "have to submit," Burgess notes, "to the cycle of Laurentian amicality — ingratiating and deferential charm; bullying for a good they could not usually see; bitter rejection with the coda of satirical eternization in whatever novel" — or story — "he happened to be writing." This may explain his unfavorable portraits of such others as John Middleton Murry and Mabel Dodge Luhan.

Of course Lawrence's fiction is not obsessively violent, and it can be strikingly beautiful as well — particularly in its treatment of the natural world. T. S. Eliot, who found little to admire in Lawrence's fiction, noted in 1927 that "Mr. Lawrence has a descriptive genius second to no writer living; he can reproduce for you not only the sound, the colour and form, the light and shade, the smell, but all the finer thrills of sensation." Yet as Diana Trilling once noted, Lawrence's writing tends to lack "the quick warm touch of instinctive sympathy for his fellow-man." Indeed, in his letters Lawrence often reveals a strong misanthropic streak, as when he noted bluntly in 1928, for example, that "I curse my age, and all the people in it. I hate my fellow men most thoroughly."

Lawrence's fiction also tends to lack humor as well — and, with it, what Trilling calls that "promise of the kind of understanding that is shared in laughter." In some of Lawrence's later stories, little more than nastiness appears. In "The Woman Who Rode Away," for example, Lawrence treats icily the gullible woman who ends up on the altar of sacrifice. "The Princess" also displays a certain snideness in Lawrence's depiction of Dollie. There are gratuitous, sneering references to "the Jews" who are her guests at the ranch — people whom Dollie does not like, but to whom she finds it mildly amusing to talk. Lawrence's letters show him airing anti-Semitic attitudes even as the vilification of Jews in Europe was beginning, too frequently voicing on racial matters opinions that are stupid and morally disgusting. But then it often seems as if the later Lawrence hated everyone, regardless of race or creed. He wrote sneeringly or venomously about many nationalities or ethnic groups.

One cannot ignore the influence of disease on Lawrence's mind and his writing, for he was an intense and passionate man who lived most of his life under the sentence of death, as the tubercular condition first diagnosed in his adolescence worsened through the years. Aldous Huxley, one of Lawrence's closer friends, often suggested that Lawrence's consumption produced his later misanthropy. "I don't think one can exaggerate the importance of the disease in Lawrence," Huxley observed. Meyers, among other biographers, concurs. "Tuberculosis undoubtedly sharpened his sense of imminent extinction," Meyers writes, "but also heightened — in his late works on the resurrection theme — his appreciation of physical sensations and the beauty of the body. Most important of all, his awareness of doom gave him a terrible sense of urgency, which intensified his feelings and his powers of expression."

One senses something of the presence of the disease in "Sun" (1925), a story in which the image of fire and heat is strong and in which many of Lawrence's continuing preoccupations again appear. The story's central character, Juliet, is a married woman with a small son, a woman who discovers the simple pleasure of being naked beneath the sun. With her husband and her child she has left their home in New York for a stay in the Mediterranean. Soon after arriving here she finds a secluded area near a rocky bluff and amid cypress trees, where she removes her clothing. She "sat and offered her bosom to the sun," and the sun, "pulsing" and "alive," responds: he "faced down to her with his look of blue fire, and enveloped her breasts and her face, her throat, her tired belly, her knees, her thighs and her feet." She "could feel the sun penetrating even into her bones; nay, farther, even into her emotions and her thoughts. The dark tensions of her emotion began to give way, the cold dark clots of her thoughts began to dissolve." She begins to feel warm, to "dissolve in the sun," and she "lay half stunned with wonder at the thing that was happening to her." Part of the reason Lawrence himself had traveled widely was to find a climatic "cure" for his consumption; he was drawn to the sun, to bright warmth, and at least on one level this story reflects something of his own therapeutic response to the sensation of healing and calming heat.

But of course his description of Juliet's encounter with the sun is also replete with strong erotic connotations. He describes Juliet's "mating" with the sun, which becomes a "ritual" that brings her not only "joy" but a sense of detachment from those unable or unwilling to accept this "knowledge of the sun." Most people, Juliet realizes, are "so unelemental, so unsunned. They were so like graveyard worms." They fear death; they fear too "the natural blaze of life"; they fear the sun. They are "innerly cowed," too repressed, too unwilling to surrender, like Juliet, to that "mysterious power inside her, deeper than her known consciousness and will" that puts her "into connection with the sun" and brings forth her "true" self, her animal self that is keenly wary of "the vast cold apparatus of civilisation." Her child, who also basks daily in the sun, grows happy and golden as a result; he runs about "like a young animal absorbed in life."

In contrast to Juliet stands Maurice, her husband, a "clean-shaven, grey-faced" figure who is good, but gentle and shy. A "suppressed nervous soul," he wears a dark suit and a pale gray hat, and his hair is always sleek, "not a hair out of place." As Lawrence makes clear, the man has been caught, conditioned, repressed: "He had the gold-grey eyes of an animal that has been caught young, and reared completely in captivity." Juliet, the story shows, is herself caught and bound inextricably to Maurice, who — to his credit — shows in the end "a desperate kind of courage of his desire" when he too dares to "walk in the sun, even ridiculously." But Juliet can imagine other, more vital possibilities. She watches from a distance a peasant, a "rather fat, very broad fellow" whose "attraction was in his vitality," in his "broad, sunburnt" face. Sensing "the spark between us," Juliet is drawn to him; he has, she knows, "that wild animal faculty."

By late December 1925, when Lawrence wrote the first, less sexually explicit version of "Sun," his physical decline had grown more severe. (The second, unexpurgated version of the story was published in Paris by the Black Sun Press in 1928.) During the final five years of his life Lawrence "contin-ued his restless quest for a congenial climate and an attractive place to stay," as Meyers records. He lived in various Italian villages; in the Swiss Alps; in Bandol, on the French coast; in Venice; and near Cannes, where he died in the early spring of 1930. Still Lawrence remained intellectually and artistically active during these last years. He made a close study of Etruscan culture and art; he completed *Lady Chatterley's Lover;* he wrote "The Man Who Died," a long tale first published in two parts (the first, "The Escaped Cock," appeared in 1928). This tale was designed in part to challenge conventional attitudes regarding the nature of Christ's divinity. Jeffrey Meyers suggests that "The Man Who Died," like *Lady Chatterley's Lover,* "moves – through a reawakening of the senses – from a Christian to a pagan world and follows the cycle of the seasons through winter to triumphant spring." It is "an exemplary fable in which Christ, a man of the flesh rather than the spirit, moves from death to life."

Lawrence once described himself "as a kind of human bomb," and elsewhere as "a profoundly religious man." But many readers of both *Lady Chatterley's Lover* and such stories as "The Man Who Died" have found in them more proof of destruction than inspiration. That novel, easily Lawrence's most notorious work, was widely denounced as obscene and just as widely banned. By 1928 many in Europe and America who had never read a word of D. H. Lawrence had accepted the notion that he was the author of dirty books. Britain's *John Bull,* by then a fading middlebrow magazine, had characterized Lawrence as a man "obsessed by sex," a man with the nerve to produce a book "which we have no hesitation in describing as the most evil outpouring that has ever besmirched the literature of our country." "The sewers of French pornography," it went on to exclaim, "would be dragged in vain to find a parallel in beastliness. The creations of muddy-minded perverts, peddled in the backstreet bookstalls of Paris are prudish by comparison." As a result of this renewed notoriety, Lawrence's mail from Bandol to London was, in late 1928, intercepted and examined. During the following summer an exhibition of Lawrence's paintings – some of them showing male nudes – was raided by London police. "People," complained Lawrence in a 1927 letter, *"can't even look"* at his paintings; they "glance, and look quickly away. I wish I could paint a picture that would just *kill* every cowardly and ill-minded person that looked at it. My word, what a slaughter!"

In *Lady Chatterley's Lover,* undoubtedly the major work of Lawrence's final period, one finds situations and themes that also recur frequently in his shorter fiction. Constance Chatterley is in search of vital existence but is married to a damaged or lifeless man. That man, Clifford Chatterley, is a member of the moneyed, etiolated aristocracy. The woman finds vitality and fulfillment in a more earthy, less educated figure, the gamekeeper Mellors, who is "not afraid and not ashamed," who is "full of courage and full of life," and who teaches her much. In Constance Chatterley more than in Elizabeth Bates or Juliet in "Sun," "the shame died." Shame, explains Lawrence in *Lady Chatterley's Lover,* "is fear: the deep organic shame, the old, old physical fear which crouches in the bodily roots of us." Constance, once she has become "shameless," comes to know "her sensual self." She feels "a triumph, almost vainglory. So! That was how it was! That was life! That was how oneself really was! There was nothing left to disguise or be ashamed of. She shared her ultimate nakedness with a man, another being."

Despite these often moving exclamations and its blunt use of time-honored profanities, *Lady Chatterley's Lover* is a rather flat, formulaic book – far from Lawrence at his best. It is also more traditionally "romantic" than many readers have been led to assume, focusing as it does on the intense but exclusive union of Connie and Mellors, one woman and one man. "The married Lawrence," as Anthony Burgess insisted, "became the great sex prophet who believed in fidelity and, when circumstances enforced it, a fierce chastity." *Lady Chatterley's Lover,* he wrote, "is as much about chastity as amorous abandon." Harris suggests that, similarly, Lawrence's later short stories "are thin fare, the weary performances of a dying man." There are, however, notable exceptions – including, along with "Sun," two well-known pieces: "The Rocking-Horse Winner" (1925) and "The Man Who Loved Islands" (1926).

"The Rocking-Horse Winner" begins in a way that again suggests the style and structure of the fairy tale or fable: "There was a woman who was beautiful, who started with all the advantages, yet she had no luck." She has had "bonny" children, but she finds it difficult to love them – for "only she herself knew that at the centre of her heart was a hard little place that could not feel love, no, not for anybody." The woman's deep coldness influences the actions of her son, Paul, an acutely sensitive boy who develops an uncanny ability for betting accurately and profitably on horse races. Paul senses that his upper-class household has become short of cash, something that his mother much desires and

spends foolishly. Paul picks winning horses while riding trancelike on a rocking horse – an act that not only gets his mother's attention but also bolsters the family income. Paul thus considers himself "lucky," for in the life he has known money is what links one directly to social success. But while still in his boyhood Paul dies – done in, the story suggests, by his strange and frantic riding, by the misdirected spiritual emptiness of his quest.

"The Rocking-Horse Winner" is notable for its clear language and straightforward plot: it seems transparently simple in design and intent. Yet like many of Lawrence's stories it can be read richly on several levels, and it has been widely discussed. Meyers, for one, contends that the story (which he believes to have been inspired by Lawrence's acquaintance with Lady Cynthia Asquith and her family) portrays "upper-class financial anxiety and social pretension, modern man's mad mechanical gallop for wealth and material goods, and the destruction of a family that chooses money above affection." Meyers also points out that Paul's frantic riding on a wooden horse "becomes a substitute for maternal love – as money is for sexual love – and he makes a Faustian bargain with evil powers for forbidden knowledge." The riding also suggests "the sexual act – or a child's imitation of the act – which goes and gets nowhere." Harris also describes the story as a "satire on a society governed by a money ethic." In Paul's lonely, secret, "trancelike" actions she and other critics find an "echo" of "Lawrence's description of masturbation, physical and psychic, in his essay 'Pornography and Obscenity.'"

In this essay Lawrence implicitly defends much of his art, as he describes the impulse for pornography as growing inevitably from a post-Puritan culture in which too many people remain "repelled by the simplest and most natural stirrings of sexual feeling," a culture in which people "nearly always enjoy some unsimple and unnatural form of sex excitement, secretly." He argues here that "there's nothing wrong with sexual feelings in themselves, so long as they are straightforward and not sneaking or sly. The right sort of sex stimulus," which Lawrence finds, for example, in Boccaccio, "is invaluable to human daily life. Without it the world grows grey." Pornography, then, "isn't sex appeal or sex stimulus in art. It isn't even a deliberate intention on the part of the artist to arouse or excite sexual feelings." It is instead "the attempt to insult sex, to do dirt on it." It is an "insult to the human body" that degrades our deepest instincts by prompting the belief that "sex is dirt and dirt is sex," while also acting as "an invariable stimulant to the vice of self-abuse, onanism, masturbation, call it what you will" – in which "there is nothing but loss. There is no reciprocity. There is merely the spending away of a certain force, and no return. The body remains, in a sense, a corpse, after the act of self-abuse. There is no change, only deadening. There is what we call dead loss. And this is not the case in any act of sexual intercourse between two people. Two people may destroy one another in sex. But they cannot just produce the null effect of masturbation."

Unhindered as always by statistics and scientific studies, Lawrence speculates freely that this practice became widespread in Britain during the nineteenth century and contributed to "an increasing emptying of the real vitality and the real *being* of men, till now people are little more than shells of people." Their responses, their awareness, their activities are "dead": they are shells, "fatally self-preoccupied and incapable of either giving or taking." Enclosed within the vicious circle of the self, with no vital contacts outside, the self becomes emptier – until it is almost a nothingness.

In this context John Middleton Murry's review of *Lady Chatterley's Lover* is particularly worth noting. Murry, writing in the *Adelphi* in 1929, fairly observed that for Lawrence, ever the extremist, there are "two ultimate realities in human life: one, the absolute and utter isolation of the individual, the other, the sole real emergence from that isolation in the perfect sexual fulfillment." Certainly, Lawrence's stories show him writing frequently of characters who are pulled suddenly, dramatically, and sometimes ambivalently from tight self-enclosure after an act or event forces them to face intensely the vivid fact of another, often more vibrant person: the Other who can represent not only the power of sexual attraction but the larger mystery of human Being.

Lawrence then wrote frequently and critically in his fiction about disconnected individuals impaired by some degree of self-absorption. Yet in his letters and his fiction Lawrence's misanthropic side often gets the better of his capacity for tenderness and benevolence, and he seems at times to prefer a world utterly purged of people and filled instead with beautiful plants and strong, graceful beasts. But "The Man Who Loved Islands" criticizes this impulse to withdraw from life and thus to exist in a self-preoccupied state. Its main figure, Cathcart, "wanted an island all of his own; not necessarily to be alone on it, but to make a world of his own." This "lover of islands" aims for "insulation," for "an island," the narrator notes, "is a nest which

holds one egg, and one only. The egg is the islander himself."

Cathcart – modeled in part on Lawrence's friend, the Scottish novelist Compton Mackenzie – takes a long lease on an island "quite near at home, no palm trees nor boom of surf on the reef, nor any of that sort of thing; but a good solid dwelling-house, rather gloomy, above the landing place," and with it some whitewashed cottages and a few "rocky fields" where oats grew and "cows lay chewing." But the man is not entirely happy here, in part because his well-kept retreat eats up much of his cash; indeed, eventually, he must sell out to a company that turns the property into a "honeymoon-and-golf" resort. The man then moves to another smaller island, where he fathers a child with a servant girl, marries her, and ends up depressed. He flees, finally, to another island; here, there are bits of beauty to admire – like "one gull, a big, handsome fellow, who would walk back and forth, back and forth in front of the open door of the cabin, as if he had some mission there."

This bird is described in passing but with Lawrence's wonderful sense of detail and his typically keen appreciation of the natural world. The bird is "big, and pearl-grey, and his roundesses were as smooth and lovely as a pearl. Only the folded wings had shut black pinions, and on the closed black feathers were three very distinct dots, making a pattern." There is also a pattern to this life of "The Man Who Loved Islands," for on this third island he is pictured at last not in a private utopia, but in a storm, battered by wind and snow: "The elements! The elements! His mind repeated the word dumbly. You can't win against the elements" – a poignant phrase, written by an author losing his own battle with the natural world.

As Janice Harris notes, "The Man Who Loved Islands" documents one man's narrowing vision and his struggle to survive. Cathcart begins with an ambitious plan of making an ideal society. He fails, and he then seeks to maintain a more "manageable relationship with one other person" – and fails again. In the end he "works only at managing his own narrow needs for food, shelter, and a quiet consciousness." This story, through its fabular features, can be read in several ways. It appears to mock Cathcart's egoism even as it admires his drive to live on his own terms. It suggests that the man who seeks to build a world of his own, who lives outside the mainstream, is engaged invariably in a difficult – and perhaps foolhardy – task. For Harris, Cathcart's "islanding" – his "foolish attempt to immunize himself and his thinking against all opposing energies" – results in his "sin and stupidity." The "target of satire" in this piece is, she believes, "any mode of knowing that attempts to separate knowledge and inquiry from opposition and change."

"The Man Who Loved Islands" is the work of a writer still young but doomed. On the whole Lawrence's later stories are not as satisfying as those written earlier in his career. They are "sometimes too symbolically wrought to seem other than obsessional," as Alastair Niven observes, but still "we seldom feel that Lawrence repeats himself" in these pieces, for "even when the themes are familiar the imaginative form they take is usually unique." Niven stresses that, as a stylist, Lawrence always went brilliantly his own way. Although he knew Katherine Mansfield, for example, Lawrence

never imitated her style. Nor did he borrow from the classic continental short-story writers. He found a voice so uniquely his own that one can open almost any page of one of his tales and recognize it as distinctively Lawrentian. Urgent prose, with carefully placed emphases and recurring key words; background detail fully creating the intended world yet corresponding to the emotional nature of the protagonists; private moods evoking public themes and metaphysics. It does not always work, but when it does, in a naturalistic tale such as "Odour of Chrysanthemums" or in a ritualistic piece such as "The Woman Who Rode Away," we see in Lawrence a complete master of the shorter narrative.

In his 1930 lecture on Lawrence, E. M. Forster observed that Lawrence's "dislike of civilization was not a pose, as it is with many writers. He hated it fundamentally, because it has made human beings conscious, and society mechanical. Like Blake and other mystics, he condemns the intellect with its barren chains of reasoning and its dead weights of information." What does he approve of? "Well," writes Forster, "the very word 'approve' would make him hiss with rage, it is so smooth and smug, but he is certainly seeking the forgotten wisdom, as he called it; he would like instinct to re-arise and connect men by ways now dissused." But as Diana Trilling has added, Lawrence "is not at all against the intellect as such, but only against what he sees as perverted uses of the intellect." Certainly Lawrence did not celebrate "savage-worship" or "child-worship." In fact, argues Trilling, "Lawrence himself is clear and insistent that the only condition for sexuality is full maturity" – a rare quality: "Far from making a cult of childhood, he attacks most of the activities of mankind for their infantilism." He does, however, "make a cult" of manhood; "just as his hatred of the will is the negative program forged

in his childhood experience, so the phallic quest is the positive program. It is man in the full assurance of his sexual self that Lawrence sets up for worship." Certainly as such stories as "The Princess" show, "the dark god" of Lawrence's "mystical universe" is, as Trilling suggests, "the phallic god, and he is certain that when Christianity raised, in place of the dark gods of our blood, the God of light, it conspired at the death of life."

John Carey feels that Lawrence, who "professed to distrust thought, and said that ideas were the dead leaves thrown off from a living tree," nonetheless "had a set of passions and hatreds that he turned into beliefs" – and these, Carey believes, are clear enough. They include, among other things, a belief not only in "male dominance" but in "the blood, the flesh, as being wiser than the intellect." For Lawrence, "mankind is divided into natural aristocrats and natural slaves," and he is suspicious of "benevolence and pity," for these " 'destroy the man in a man.' " Both the stories and novels also show a kind of fevered anti-intellectualism at work: in *Lady Chatterley's Lover,* Carey notes, Mellors pointedly suggests that the masses "should not be taught to think; and Lawrence, too, argues that mental consciousness is 'a catastrophe' for most people. All schools should be closed at once, he advises, and no child should learn to read unless it has enough enthusiasm to teach itself."

Carey rightly concludes that those who find Lawrence's thought disturbing, offensive, or even "satanic" at least "do him the courtesy of treating it as real thought. Much more reprehensible are the well-meaning dilutions offered by his defenders: the pretence that he really was a decent, moderate sort of fellow, almost a Christian, and the argument that the thought cannot be separated from the 'art' in which it occurs." Only in Lawrence's books, in his novels and short stories, writes Carey, "the thought is alive. Extracted, schematized, it loses its shifting, paradoxical quality: the luminous visual and verbal power marshalled to attack the visual and verbal; the intellect deriding the intellect; the sensitivity and callousness fused together. It loses, too, its personality, its human smell – and this is a vital consideration, for it is the final paradox of Lawrence's thought that, separated from his warm, intense, wonderfully articulate being, it becomes the philosophy of any thug or moron."

Letters:

The Letters of D. H. Lawrence, edited by James T. Boulton, 7 volumes (Cambridge: Cambridge University Press, 1979–1994).

Bibliography:

John E. Stoll, *D. H. Lawrence: A Bibliography, 1911–1975* (New York: Whitson, 1977).

Biographies:

John Worthen, *D. H. Lawrence: A Literary Life* (London: Macmillan, 1989);

Jeffrey Meyers, *D. H. Lawrence: A Biography* (New York: Knopf, 1990);

Worthen, *D. H. Lawrence: The Early Years, 1885–1912* (Cambridge: Cambridge University Press, 1991);

Brenda Maddox, *D. H. Lawrence: The Story of a Marriage* (New York: Simon & Schuster, 1994).

References:

George J. Becker, *D. H. Lawrence* (New York: Ungar, 1980);

Michael Black, *D. H. Lawrence: The Early Fiction* (New York: Macmillan, 1986);

Anthony Burgess, *Flame Into Being* (New York: Arbor House, 1985);

John Carey, *The Intellectuals and the Masses* (New York: St. Martin's Press, 1992);

R. P. Draper, ed., *D. H. Lawrence: The Critical Heritage* (London & New York: Routledge & Kegan Paul, 1970);

Anne Fernihough, *D. H. Lawrence: Aesthetics and Ideology* (Oxford: Clarendon Press, 1993);

Janice Hubbard Harris, *The Short Fiction of D. H. Lawrence* (New Brunswick, N.J.: Rutgers University Press, 1984);

Haruhide Mori, ed., *A Conversation on D. H. Lawrence* (Los Angeles: Friends of the UCLA Library, 1974);

Alastair Niven, *D. H. Lawrence: The Writer and His Work* (Essex: Longman, 1980);

Stephen Spender, ed., *D. H. Lawrence: Novelist, Poet, Prophet* (New York: Harper & Row, 1973);

Weldon Thornton, *D. H. Lawrence: A Study of the Short Fiction* (New York: Twayne, 1993);

Diana Trilling, "Editor's Introduction," in her *The Portable D. H. Lawrence* (New York: Viking, 1947);

Peter Widdowson, ed., *D. H. Lawrence* (London & New York: Longman, 1992);

Linda Ruth Williams, *Sex in the Head: Visions of Femininity and Film in D. H. Lawrence* (New York: Harvestor Wheatsheaf, 1993).

Alun Lewis

(1 July 1915 – 5 March 1944)

Alexander Malcolm Forbes
University College of the Cariboo

See also the Lewis entry in *DLB 20: Victorian Novelists Before 1885.*

BOOKS: *Raiders' Dawn and Other Poems* (London: Allen & Unwin, 1942; New York: Macmillan, 1942);

The Last Inspection (London: Allen & Unwin, 1942; New York: Macmillan, 1943);

Ha! Ha! Among the Trumpets: Poems in Transit (London: Allen & Unwin, 1945);

Letters from India (Cardiff: Penmark Press, 1946);

In the Green Tree (London: Allen & Unwin, 1948).

Collections:

Alun Lewis: Selected Poetry and Prose, edited by Ian Hamilton (London: Allen & Unwin, 1966);

Alun Lewis: A Miscellany of His Writings, edited by John Pikoulis (Bridgend: Poetry Wales, 1982);

Alun Lewis: Collected Stories, edited by Cary Archard (Bridgend: Seren, 1990).

Alun Lewis

Although Alun Lewis has been acknowledged one of the most significant poets of World War II, he was also a masterful writer of short stories. A. L. Rowse considered the stories in *The Last Inspection* (1942) "the finest" to "come out of the war," and some have thought the stories to be Lewis's supreme achievement. Walter Allen, for example, writing in the *New Statesman,* remarked that they represent "an altogether higher level than any other English writing inspired by the war." While Lewis's stories are by no means limited to the subject of war, the war stories would, by themselves, make him an important writer of his time.

Lewis was born 1 July 1915 in Cwmaman, in the coal-mining region of south Wales, to T. J. "Tom" Lewis and Gwladys Elizabeth Lewis. Soon after the birth of a second son, Glyn, Tom left a teaching position to enlist, and the family moved to Yorkshire. They returned to Cwmaman after he was wounded in 1918, and they then moved to Glynhafod, where Alun began school in 1920 – be-

tween the births of another son, Huw, and a daughter, Mair. Holidays were spent at Penbryn.

Lewis began to attend Cowbridge grammar school in 1926. Although unhappy there, he found in the school journal, the *Bovian,* his first literary outlet, and he published there his first stories and a childhood reminiscence. The stories present remarkably mature anticipations of his later fiction.

In "The Return of Dick Turpin" (1929) the famous highwayman returns from the dead and attempts to resume his occupation, only to encounter a mechanized world. Defeated, he returns to the grave – an early representation of a recurrent theme in Lewis's fiction, the isolation of the individual in a world hostile to human aspirations. "The Death of Monga" (1930) recounts another defeat, one in which nature proves destructive and predatory, as birds are killed during migration and only one, Monga, is left to die at human hands.

"The Tale of a Dwarf" (1931) describes another isolated individual destroyed by the world. The ironically named Felix, a dwarf, is abducted and displayed in carnivals, where he dies while attempting to escape. He is Lewis's first psychologically complex character: on display, he is "a creature of angles," rocking to and fro while "beating a ceaseless echoing tattoo" on "unseen floorboards."

"Memories of Childhood" (1931) shows that Lewis as a child sought in the imagination those ideals he could not find in the world. To Lewis nature's beauty is associated with a mysterious radiance, although he knows that nature can also be predatory. "The End of the Hunt" (1931) recognizes that natural predation can be vengeful, as a hound pursues a fox that once had injured it. When the two kill each other, it becomes clear that, to Lewis, the radiance associated with nature is not necessarily to be found *in* nature, but in something *suggested* by one's perception of nature. Although Lewis had not yet read Richard Jefferies's "Story of My Heart," the work he would later term "the nearest expression" to his own thought, both his autobiographical sketch and "The End of the Hunt" show that his view of nature anticipated that which he would discover in Jefferies.

"They Say There's a Boat on the River" (1932) differentiates between ideal beauty and imperfect, worldly beauty. This Tennysonian fable cautions against any uncritical surrender to beauty, much as "The Death of Monga" and "The End of the Hunt" caution against seeing only a bright side of nature. When a vessel arrives upon the shores of Lotus Land, the crew members ignore the advice of their goddess, the Queen of Beauty, and bring the voyage to an unhappy conclusion by eating the deceptively beautiful lotus flowers.

In the fall of 1932 Lewis left to major in history at the University College of Wales at Aberystwyth. In 1934 he contributed "If Such Be Nature's Holy Plan" and "The Whirligig of Fate" to the student journal, the *Dragon.*

In the first story an unnamed farmer, sensing a personal malice against himself, quarrels with nature. His daughter Millie adopts a more balanced view: while agreeing with Alfred Tennyson that nature is "red in tooth and claw," she nevertheless feels that "Nature will right things." Before the story concludes, however, her father comes to feel the "vital urge" of nature and recognizes that genuine happiness can emerge from suffering and sacrifice, for through them "new life" begins. For the

first time Lewis combines in a single story his sense of the destructiveness of nature and his conviction of its ultimately positive guidance.

In "The Whirligig of Fate" the Cardigan setting provides Lewis with his first opportunity to write a distinctively Welsh story, one in which human decisions yield to the deeper powers of nature. To avenge himself after his parson has acquired a motorcar, one which makes his horse-and-buggy services superfluous, sexton Isaac Bowen deflates the car's tires the night before the parson is to preach in Llanglas, a few miles away. When the parson requests the horse and buggy, Bowen accommodates him but does everything possible to delay him further. During the journey the horse stops to eat deadly nightshade, and the sexton's vengeance returns upon him, as the horse dies. Bowen's attempt to revive his horse is caught up in the natural cycles that comprise the "whirligig of fate."

Lewis graduated in 1935 and in September went to Manchester University. There he obtained a master's degree in medieval history in 1937, but he became disillusioned with scholarly research. He continued writing stories, however, and again published them in a student journal: "The Monk's Tale," "Chestnuts," and "The Wedding Breakfast" all appeared in the *Serpent* in 1936. That summer Lewis also wrote "Interruption," first published in *English Story,* a collection of new stories annually published in London by Collins. The story was later reprinted in the only collection of his stories to appear in his lifetime, *The Last Inspection.*

In "The Monk's Tale" Brother Wilfred recounts his meeting fifty years earlier with a minstrel. While the Monk of Chaucer's *Canterbury Tales* (circa 1387) is attracted to the freedoms of hunting, Lewis's Brother Wilfred is drawn to the memory of the freely wandering minstrel; while Chaucer's Monk recounts the tragic downfalls of the famous, Brother Wilfred details the laments of Hakon, the minstrel, for all human sufferers. After many journeys the thought of human suffering becomes too much for Hakon, and he invites the demons of evil to enter into himself so that they might cease to plague others. Unlike the swine in Luke 8:33, however, Hakon does not die; instead, he begins to torment people – until a meeting with the sister of one of his victims reawakens his compassion.

"Chestnuts" explores the light and the dark sides of nature. Set in a boarding school, the story contrasts one student, Bristow, who shares Lewis's aspirations to be a poet, with another student, Mottram. Bristow is an introspective reader of Keats and Shelley, but Mottram is the opposite: unresponsive to literature, extroverted, and boastful about his supposed sexual exploits. Bristow, who recently has begun a platonic relationship with a young woman, finds himself at first repelled by, but then drawn into, Mottram's accounts. The story fictionally reflects the influence of D. H. Lawrence on Lewis, as it explores the connection between an emergent imaginative awareness and emergent sexual awareness. Lewis then redraws the connection in "Interruption," a story in which three children become aware of death at the same time that they become aware of sexuality.

"The Wedding Breakfast" satirizes commercial life and its posturings. Although pretentious, the wedding breakfast of Menna Merriman and Albert Groves is a shabby affair conducted in the kitchen behind her father's shop. Neglected by everyone during the breakfast is Menna's sister, Martha, who, like her biblical predecessor, is busy with serving. Unlike her biblical predecessor, however, she is more perceptive than her sister and the others around her, for she proves to be the only one who is responsive to nature.

In May 1937 Lewis visited a retreat in France, but the visit only deepened the unhappiness he had begun to feel in Manchester. He returned to Aberystwyth to work for a teacher's diploma and spent the next months as a student teacher in Dolgellau before he obtained his diploma the following year. Lewis's return to Wales was marked by the appearance in the *Dragon* of two stories with Welsh settings.

"Attitude," like "The Monk's Tale," reflects Lewis's training as a medievalist. But here the training itself is the focus, as the academic world is shown to be inimical to all that is natural. The protagonist, Frieda Thomas, shares many similarities with Lewis: she is Welsh, has studied medieval history at Manchester, and has written poetry – only to find her creative life stifled. Her marriage to the historian Peter Topaypaul only deepens her unhappiness, for he is unsympathetic both to her and to nature, the source of her strength. When he becomes ill, she takes him to her native valley so that he, and their marriage, might be restored through contact with nature. The return proves life-restoring to her, but it fails to rescue him.

In "Squibs for the Guy" Lewis turns to serious problems of contemporary Welsh society. As the children of unemployed Mr. Gummer stuff a mannequin in preparation for setting it on fire, Gummer's landlord appears and demands to be paid the rent that Gummer owes. After the landlord departs,

Gummer decides to light the "guy" immediately: to him it has become an effigy of the landlord.

Unemployed, Lewis spent the summer of 1938 writing an article based upon his graduate research, one that was eventually published in the *English Historical Review* in 1939. At the end of the summer he traveled through Normandy.

In the fall Lewis found employment as a teacher at the Lewis School in Pengam. The *Manchester Guardian* published "Picnic," later included in *The Last Inspection,* at this time and published two more stories, "Cardinali Crisis" and "The Poetry Lesson," the next year.

The first story displays Lewis's gift for domestic satire manifested in "The Wedding Breakfast," although here the colors are darker. When her father is sent to prison, Marion goes to live with her Aunt Flora and Uncle Hubert, where she suffers countless assaults upon her sensitive nature. The assaults reach a climax during a seaside picnic. Only within sight of the sea, and in the natural empathy of Norah (a friend of Flora's self-important nephew Leonard), does Marion receive the comfort denied her by social pretension.

"Cardinali Crisis" argues against the prejudices engendered by the deepening European crisis by insisting upon the distinction between individuals and the political states from which they come. Antonio Cardinali, who has long served Welsh miners in his coffee shop, becomes the object of the colliers' jests when Benito Mussolini intervenes in Spain. When Cardinali is called to the Italian consulate for possible conscription, however, it becomes clear that he not only has nothing to do with Mussolini, but also wants nothing to do with the Italian army.

"The Poetry Lesson" is semi-autobiographical. The story of a teacher, it appears to capture something of Lewis's own experiences and suggests his evident goals as a teacher. The teacher overcomes his students' inattention by reading them a poem that touches something deep within them.

Early in 1939 Lewis wrote "The Housekeeper," a Lawrencian story that would appear in *The Last Inspection.* Like "Squibs for the Guy," it examines the poverty of a Welsh family and details the entrapment felt by a woman, Myfanwy, when her husband, Penry, is left unemployed by the closure of his mine. She hopes that education might free her son Jackie, her "little husband."

In the spring of 1939 Lewis made a bicycle tour of Somerset. An account of it from the journal he long kept was published posthumously as "English Weekend" in a 1979 issue of the *Anglo-Welsh*

Review. It includes a significant statement by Lewis about his art and his philosophy: what he wishes, he writes, is to seize life with an intuitive immediacy, even though life is a process and everything leads to something else. Everything happens, in fact, *through* something. Lewis's concern for natural and social processes, throughout his fiction, reflects this perception.

In May, Lewis met his future wife, Gweno Ellis, and during a summer at Penbryn he published "The Testimonial" in the *Ludovican,* the Lewis School magazine. He also wrote "Rain," yet another story unpublished until its inclusion in *Alun Lewis: A Miscellany of His Writings* (1982). The first is a satire of academic life. In Professor Adderby, who has utterly forgotten both his students and the world, the story attacks the effects of an unnatural existence. The second story juxtaposes birth with death, indirectly identifying each with the other. After his wife has given birth, a man leaves his cottage, only to hear a scream. Finding a trapped rabbit, he kills it to relieve it from suffering. As the man returns home, a mare bolts, sensing traces of death upon the new parent.

Throughout the autumn of 1939 Lewis was torn between a desire to serve in the war that had erupted and a reluctance to kill. In the meantime he continued to teach and to write, publishing in the *Welsh Review* another story, "The Wanderers," which was eventually included in *The Last Inspection.*

Like many of Lewis's later stories, this Lawrencian tale is divided into three parts. In the first section the unnamed Welsh wife of a gypsy discovers her husband's infidelity, and this prompts her to have an affair with an itinerant onion seller. In the second part Micah, the couple's son, discloses this affair to his father. When the onion seller leaves, the mother follows him to Cardigan, only to reverse her decision in the concluding section when she realizes that she must protect her son, now left alone with his brutal father.

In March 1940 Lewis registered in the reserves, as a way of serving in the war without killing. In May, however, he revised his decision and registered for active service. He was sent to the Railway Training Center at Longmoor, Hampshire, and his experiences there shaped a story, "Lance-Jack," which was published later that year in *Life and Letters Today* and subsequently included in *The Last Inspection.* The story is an experiment that combines nonfiction with fiction, the essay with narrative.

The first part is overtly autobiographical, a reflective essay that analyzes how the army introduces soldiers to a new way of life. The soldier becomes detached, but through the detachment a new opportunity emerges as the individual, unencumbered by old forms and places, is freed to pursue the highest ends. In the second part Lewis turns to historical fiction, entering imaginatively into the thoughts of a German soldier and showing how he feels the kind of detachment described — although in fighting for an unjust cause, the German soldier pursues ignoble ends. The third part returns to autobiography and self-reflection, in which Lewis's own Hardyesque loneliness (like that which the narrative discerns in such characters as Tess Durbeyfield and Jude Fawley) is revealed. Although no connection is explicitly drawn between the second part and the third, it is clear that a new appreciation of the relative democracy of the British army has been prompted by the imaginative excursion into the mind of the German soldier.

Lewis was then transferred to a Royal Engineers battalion at Bordon and sent for training to another battalion near Longmoor. Here he concentrated on his poetry. Influenced by William Butler Yeats, he was even more strongly influenced by the poet with whom he had come to identify himself, Edward Thomas. Lewis visited Thomas's house in October, a visit prompting Lewis to write his most famous poem, "All day it has rained," which *Horizon* published in 1941 together with a review of Thomas's poems by Lewis. The review reveals the kinship that Lewis felt with Thomas, a World War I soldier-poet who had also suffered from a "dark and divided personality" that Lewis saw as similar to his own. At the same time Lewis sought in his own writing, prose as well as verse, what he found in Thomas's: the ability to express "the most complex and mysterious moods," to "convey a tremendous reality" of "place and time and mind" in a style that unites "strength, simplicity and a natural delicacy."

Shortly before the end of the year Lewis wrote "The Farewell Binge," another narrative eventually included in *The Last Inspection.* The story describes how Mack, one soldier at a bar, freely accepts drinks from his comrades but then refuses to buy drinks for them in return when he is confronted. Dick, the soldier who confronts him, believes that the one hope for humanity lies in friendship, and Mack's failure to pass this small but crucial test leaves Dick pessimistic.

Posted to railway duty at Longmoor, Lewis wrote the story that, after its springtime publication in *Horizon,* became the title story of *The Last Inspection.* He also wrote "They Came," another narrative

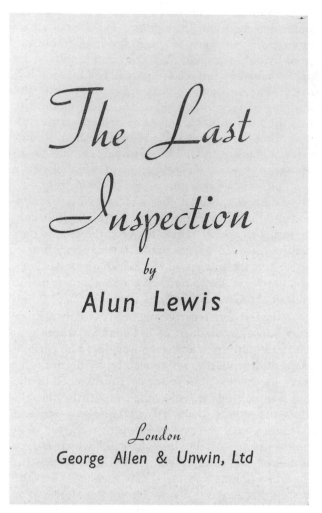

The Last Inspection

by

Alun Lewis

London
George Allen & Unwin, Ltd

Title page for Lewis's first collection of short fiction (courtesy of the Lilly Library, Indiana University). By the end of 1943 thirty-five hundred copies had been sold.

that was published in the collection *English Story* and won the Edward J. O'Brien Prize for short fiction in 1941.

"The Last Inspection" is a satire. The general in charge of completing a railway line plans an inspection; the line is incomplete, however, and the inspection turns into an officers' lunch. When the lunch train returns to its shed, a telegram informs the engineer, Fred Tube, that his family has been bombed in London. The suffering of British civilians in a war ignored by officers of the home forces became a frequent target of Lewis's satire.

Civilian suffering is vividly described in the second story, "They Came." A Welsh soldier, Taffy, returns from home leave and recounts the death of his wife in a horrifying air raid. Taffy's mate Nobby reassures him that Taffy and his wife now "belong to each other for keeps," as through

this assurance the story affirms love to be the one thing that truly survives war.

During the spring Lewis proposed to publish a series of inexpensive broadsheets, each to reproduce a Welsh poem accompanied by a woodcut. The Caseg Broadsheets, which would appear for the next year, did much to popularize Welsh literature, although their publication had to be discontinued when production costs became too high. In the spring Lewis was again transferred – first to Heysham, Lancashire, for an officers' training course and then to an infantry training center in Gloucester.

On 5 July 1941 Lewis and Gweno Ellis married. Upon his return to Heysham, Lewis prepared his first collection of poems for publication, but he also found time to write one story, "The Prisoners." First published in *The Last Inspection,* it addresses how war and army life deaden instinct by burying it in brutality or apathy. Conversations of military prisoners are recorded as confirmations of that effect.

Following a leave in November Lewis was posted as a subaltern to the South Wales Borderers in Suffolk. A deepening sense of the injustices of army life grew upon him, and this sense is reflected in a story, "Private Jones," written early in 1942 and later included in *The Last Inspection.* Like the protagonists of Lewis's earliest stories, the illiterate Welsh laborer Siencyn Jones is baffled by the new environment in which he finds himself. Lewis traces Jones's mishaps, which reveal a potentially excellent soldier beneath a baffled one. The potential, predictably, is not seen by the officers, and only another private, Daniel Evans, perceives Jones's worth.

In February 1942 Allen and Unwin agreed to publish a collection of Lewis's stories, and in March his first collection of poems, *Raiders' Dawn and Other Poems,* appeared – and received excellent reviews. Later that spring Lewis was transferred to a battle school at Aldeburgh, where he wrote four more stories included in *The Last Inspection:* "It's a Long Way to Go," "Acting-Captain," "The Children," and "Cold Spell."

The first section of "It's a Long Way to Go" is a variation of "The Last Inspection," as it displays the discontent of 2d. Lt. David Greening with the inactivity of the home forces and discloses his awareness of civilian suffering. The second section moves beyond satire of the military to enunciate a belief that is apparently as much Lewis's as Greening's: during a final inspection before posting to India, Greening learns that a pilot has been downed. As he returns to Wales for his embarkation leave, the empathy he feels for the pilot prompts him to recognize "Some vast thing, something universal," working "tirelessly for good." In the final section Greening at home finds in the moon a symbol for his optimism that something works mysteriously through nature toward good.

"Acting-Captain" satirizes the management of the home forces in its account of the cruelties that acting Capt. Hector Cochrane inflicts upon Eva Barthgate, a woman he has been seeing, as well as upon two of his men – Curly Norris, a classicist denied promotion because of a stoop, and Taffy Thomas, a Welsh soldier who wants to join the Commandos in order to do something for the war. The story concludes with Thomas's return home to Swansea, where he witnesses his wife's death in an air raid.

Fiction and history blend throughout "The Children." The first section retells the story of Hansel and Gretel in such a way as to suggest that they are actual children living in a time of war. The second section shows them lost in the forest, where they are imprisoned in a house of nightmares by the witch of war; Hansel, now a soldier, must struggle to separate dream from reality, but the reality of Gretel's love finally frees him – as the soldier that he has become dies. In the third section the pair emerge, having grown through the nightmares of adulthood and come out of the wood as children – children who have successfully overcome the witch.

"Cold Spell" is a retelling of "The Children," with Hansel and Gretel replaced by a nameless flight sergeant and Gracie. Despite his feelings for Gracie, the flight sergeant's responses are frozen: he is more in love with his work than with her. The couple is compared to "Hansel and Gretel in the wood," their frozen emotion a correlative for the witch's prison. Whereas Gretel's love released Hansel in "The Children," however, the experience of a comrade's death releases the sergeant from his attachment to war and frees him to respond to Gracie's love.

In June Lewis was transferred to Dorset, where he reread a favorite author, E. M. Forster, and visited the homes of two other writers who had influenced him, Thomas Hardy and T. E. Lawrence. Lawrence had become a second Edward Thomas to Lewis by this time, and the visit to Lawrence's home produced another story for *The Last Inspection:* "Dusty Hermitage," which recounts a fictional soldier's visit to the home. A woman who cares for the home, and who had once loved Lawrence, sees in the soldier a striking resemblance to Lawrence.

Adding a final four stories to those he had already completed, Lewis finished his selection of stories for *The Last Inspection* by the end of the summer. "Flick" analyzes some of the reasons for the inefficiency of the army, as it brings together the speaker, an officer who has never seen combat, and Pvt. F. L. C. Wilson. Although the private has been cited for heroism, he has refused a commission and prefers to remain in the ranks – in order to accomplish something. Flick alters the officer's conception of rank and his view of the army. In return the officer deepens Flick's understanding of the war by enlarging the practical man's imagination. In the friendship of the two, a friendship against all rules of rank, Lewis displays the possibility of uniting practical commitment with imagination.

"Almost a Gentleman" examines the life of a soldier who, unlike Flick, actively seeks a commission, only to be denied one. The story of Burton, who is Jewish, raises the possibility that anti-Semitism was a serious problem in the army. "The Lapse" turns to civilian life and records the attempt of a man, stifled by routine, to do something extraordinary. After years of riding from work on the same train, with the same passengers, the man startles everyone by getting off at the wrong station – a deliberate decision, for he wishes to follow a fellow passenger whose life has aroused his curiosity. When the guard reprimands him for his apparent mistake, he returns to the train. "Ballerina" brings army and civilian life together in the meeting between a soldier and a young woman. In the verbal dance that follows, the soldier discovers that she is married to a soldier overseas.

Soon after returning to the Borderers in Southend, Lewis sailed for India on 29 October 1942, arriving there on 19 November. En route he listened to a soldier's description of a kibbutz he had visited while serving in the Middle East, and this soldier's account was incorporated in "The Orange Grove," a story included in Lewis's second collection of short fiction, *In the Green Tree* (1948). From Bombay Lewis traveled to Nira, and in January an accidental injury led to his hospitalization in Poona, where he spent the next six weeks. These experiences shaped two stories, "The Earth Is a Syllable" and "Ward 'O'3(b)," also included in his second collection.

The first is an impressionistic account of the last hours of a wounded officer dying in Burma. The officer, who resembles Lewis himself, had always known that he would die if sent to Burma. In reviewing his life, he perceives that his most important conflicts have been inner and that life is a matter of small syllables, "simply whether to say Yes or No to a thing." Mistakenly believing, in his illness, that his wife is present, he stumbles from an ambulance in which he has been lying – his action a small and affirmative syllable of response to love.

The second story is a study in contrasts, as four different soldiers recuperate in an Indian military hospital where they await the decision of a medical board about their fate. The two whose hopes are most strongly linked to army decisions are disappointed: Captain Brownlow-Grace, a career officer who wants to return to active service, is discharged; Lieutenant Moncrieff, who wants to be discharged, must continue to serve. Lieutenant-Quartermaster Withers also seeks to be discharged, but his wish is less intense than Moncrieff's, and he is granted it – whereupon he has second thoughts.

The only one whose fate remains unknown at the end of the story is the one indifferent to it. Lieutenant Weston's interests and conflicts are inner, as they are for the officer in "The Earth is a Syllable." Like that officer, Weston is concerned with love: a woman he loves has married another man, and Weston must win his inner battle. By the end of the story he appears to have done so, for he becomes convinced that love survives and is worth living for, whatever obstacles it encounters through any specific attempt to reach out to another. When Weston dips his hand into a pool, the circles that are produced ripple outward, encounter the barrier of the edge of the pool, and then turn inward. In the pool, Weston sees himself; in the circles, the love that survives by turning inward when it encounters the obstacles of the world.

The Last Inspection, which was actually published in February 1943 rather than in 1942, as the publication date in the volume indicates, appeared while Lewis was hospitalized. The collection received positive reviews in prominent journals such as *Punch,* and its first edition sold out within four weeks; a total of thirty-five hundred copies were sold during the year. Upon his release from the hospital Lewis returned to Nira, where he was appointed an intelligence officer. His battalion was soon relocated to Lake Kharakvasla, and other moves followed. A journey at this time meshed in Lewis's imagination with the story of the kibbutz that he had heard en route to India, and this resulted in the writing of "The Orange Grove."

In this story, after the murder of his driver in the Indian countryside, Staff-Captain Beale is forced to drive with the corpse. As he drives, he quickly loses his senses of both time and place. The driver had long been a possessive man, but he had once confessed to Beale a wish to live upon one of the collectives he had observed during his Middle Eastern service. The orange groves of the farmers had come to symbolize for him a life superior to anything he had known.

Caring for the driver's body leads Beale unexpectedly to realize in his own life what the driver had wished for but never found. Beale develops a profound respect for the body and enlists the aid of a group of Gypsies to help him carry it when his truck is mired in a river. He enters into their collective life as he joins their wanderings, which are determined neither by map nor clock but by genuinely human needs: the search for pasture and water. In every sense Beale experiences the possibility of moving beyond time, space, and isolation.

Lewis's battalion returned to Lake Kharakvasla at the end of July, and he was then sent to Karachi to attend a military intelligence school. Upon graduation he was offered a captaincy but refused it: he apparently sensed, as his stories imply, that opportunities for action would be diminished by promotion. After rejoining his battalion at Lake Kharakvasla, where he suffered an especially long and serious bout of depression, Lewis was forced in November to return to the hospital at Poona for treatment of malaria. After being discharged from the hospital he went back to Poona at the beginning of December for a reunion with his brother Glyn, a reunion that would shape another story, "The Reunion," in his second collection of short fiction.

Violence surrounds the fictional transformation of the reunion, as Eric, who has been wounded in Burma, meets his brother Vincent. Narrative point of view shifts repeatedly to show the differences between experience and inexperience. Eric carries into the reunion the deadening effects of army life and the trauma of the engagement in which he has killed a soldier who had wounded him. At the end of the visit Eric's flashbacks prompt him to respond fiercely to a noisy party in an adjacent room. Whether his response is actual or only imagined is impossible for the reader to determine, however, as the surrealistic conclusion re-creates ambiguously Eric's violent act of self-preservation in Burma.

In January 1944 Lewis completed the revision of his second collection of poems, *Ha! Ha! Among the Trumpets: Poems in Transit* (1945). The following month he left with his battalion for Burma, and there he volunteered to join a patrol in the Goppe Pass, where a shot from his own pistol killed him on

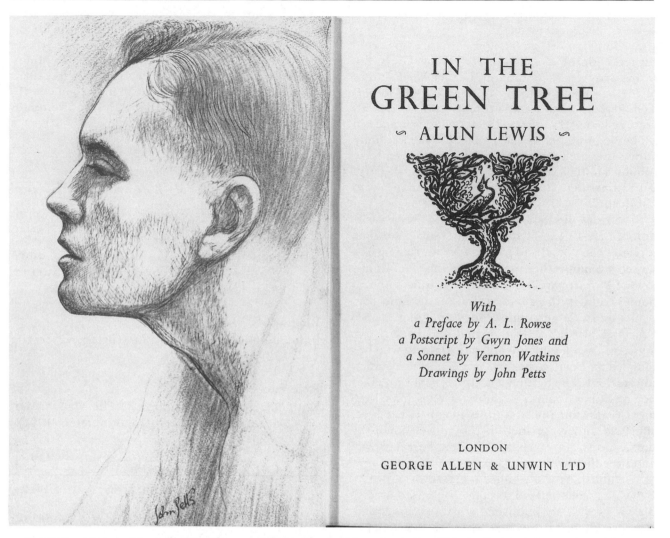

IN THE
GREEN TREE

❧ ALUN LEWIS ❧

With
a Preface by A. L. Rowse
a Postscript by Gwyn Jones and
a Sonnet by Vernon Watkins
Drawings by John Petts

LONDON
GEORGE ALLEN & UNWIN LTD

Frontispiece portrait of Lewis by John Petts and title page from Lewis's posthumously published collection of short stories and letters (courtesy of the Lilly Library, Indiana University)

5 March. The wound was judged accidental by the inquiry that followed, although many fellow soldiers, aware of Lewis's frequent struggles with depression, were convinced that it had not been.

In 1948 Allen and Unwin published *In the Green Tree,* a collection that also contains two additional stories – "Night Journey," an impressionistic account of the passengers who take a night train across wartime England, and "The Raid," an attack upon British imperial policies. Ordered to arrest a man suspected of killing British troops, Selden marches his platoon to a village where an informer discloses the wanted man's hideout. When the man is arrested, he is asked why he killed the troops: "For my country," he responds; "Everybody says that," is the retort.

A collected edition of Lewis's stories did not appear until 1990, but when it did, its editor, Cary Archard, included six previously unpublished stories in the volume, *Alun Lewis: Collected Stories.* "And At My Departing" offers an account of the last days of a Miss Brook. Throughout the story the reader is made to question the reliability of the account, and its ambiguity ensures that the story cannot be dismissed. "Duration" shows the power of nature to console a soldier separated from the woman he loves. The soldier sees, in a simple row of pigeons, a natural testimony to the endurance of love.

"'It was very warm and welcome'" illustrates how easily the fragile economy of a Welsh collier's family can be overturned. When Mr. Jenkins's daughter, Doris, becomes pregnant by Ben James, the son and heir of the local grocer, James insists that he will marry her only if a large dowry is provided. Jenkins capitulates, and the family, unprepared for its confrontation with commercial ruthlessness, is virtually ruined.

"Impasse" is an allegorical story also concerned with the effects of greed. When Gwyn Edwards acquires a greyhound, Beauty, the fortunes of the boy's entire family tumble. Gwyn's father, Ted, neglects his work as a cobbler in the Welsh village, as he enters the dog in races and is funded in his betting by a bookie, Ben Lake. Gwyn reluctantly allows the dog to compete, but he balks when Lake proposes to fix a race: Beauty is to lose and Ted will bet against her. Gwyn can find no solution but to kill Beauty.

" 'Enid didn't know what to do' " is a variation of Lewis's earlier story, "Chestnuts": this time it relates the sexual and imaginative awakening of a young woman rather than of a young man. Enid's love of Mozart parallels the earlier Bristow's love of poetry, and in the character of Bessie, Enid confronts a female version of Mottram. "Alexander's Feast" is also about the sexual and imaginative awakening of a young woman. Elizabeth, who has long led an isolated life, makes a deliberate decision to seek love. She befriends a young man who takes her to hear a famous organist. Feeling herself almost ready, for the first time, to experience love, she falls under the spell of the music. When the music stops, however, she suddenly breaks away and flees the theater in fear.

Publishing these hitherto-unknown stories by Lewis in a collected edition that also makes accessible his previously published stories should stimulate new interest in a writer whose short fiction has for many years been unjustly neglected. The range of Lewis's stories is far more extensive than might be thought by those who knew him only through his reputation as a war writer. The stories about war often prove to be stories about civilian life no less than military, and those about civilian life explore many forms of economic and social conflict. The stories examine individuals as well as societies, military or civilian, and examine them not only in their frequently ironic social relationships but also in their solitude, their isolation. The stories make frequent and significant contributions to the literature of nature, which they treat not only as an object of description but also as a subject for philosophical reflection. Through his stories no less than through his poems Lewis made an important contribution to Anglo-Welsh literature in the twentieth century.

Letters:
Letters from India (Cardiff: Penmark, 1946);
Alun Lewis: Letters to My Wife, edited by Gweno Lewis (Bridgend: Seren, 1989).

Bibliography:
John Stuart Williams, "Alun Lewis: A Select Bibliography," *Anglo-Welsh Review,* 16 (Spring 1967): 13–15.

Biography:
John Pikoulis, *Alun Lewis: A Life* (Bridgend: Seren, 1991).

References:
Kathleen Devine, "Alun Lewis: The Manchester Stories," *New Welsh Review,* 4 (Summer 1991): 24–29;
Devine, "Alun Lewis's 'Almost a Gentleman,'" *Anglo-Welsh Review,* 67 (1980): 79–84;
Alun John, *Alun Lewis* (Cardiff: University of Wales Press, 1970);
Gwyn Jones, "Postscript by Gwyn Jones," *In the Green Tree,* by Lewis (London: Allen & Unwin, 1948), pp. 137–141;
John Pikoulis, "Alun Lewis and Edward Thomas," *Critical Quarterly,* 23 (Winter 1981): 25–44;
A. L. Rowse, "Preface by A. L. Rowse," in *In the Green Tree,* by Lewis (London: Allen & Unwin, 1948), pp. 7–14;
John Stuart Williams, "The Short Stories of Alun Lewis," *Anglo-Welsh Review,* 14 (Winter 1964–1965): 16–25.

Katherine Mansfield

(14 October 1888 – 9 January 1923)

James Gindin
University of Michigan

BOOKS: *In a German Pension* (London: Stephen Swift, 1911; New York: Knopf, 1926);

Prelude (Richmond, U.K.: Hogarth, 1918); republished, in expanded original version, as *The Aloe* (New York: Knopf, 1930; London: Constable, 1930);

Je ne parle pas français (Hampstead: Heron, 1919);

Bliss and Other Stories (London: Constable, 1920; New York: Knopf, 1920);

The Garden Party, and Other Stories (London: Constable, 1922; New York: Knopf, 1922);

The Doves' Nest, and Other Stories, edited by J. M. Murry (London: Constable, 1923; New York: Knopf, 1923);

Poems, edited by Murry (London: Constable, 1923; New York: Knopf, 1924);

Something Childish, and Other Stories, edited by Murry (London: Constable, 1924); republished as *The Little Girl, and Other Stories* (New York: Knopf, 1924);

The Journal of Katherine Mansfield, edited by Murry (London: Constable, 1927; New York: Knopf, 1927);

Novels and Novelists, edited by Murry (London: Constable, 1930; New York: Knopf, 1930);

Stories by Katherine Mansfield (New York: Knopf, 1930);

A Fairy Story (Stanford: Stanford University Library, 1932);

The Short Stories of Katherine Mansfield, edited by Murry (New York: Knopf, 1937);

To Stanislaw Wyspianski (London: Privately printed for B. Rota by the Favil Press, 1938);

The Scrapbook of Katherine Mansfield, edited by Murry (London: Constable, 1939; New York: Knopf, 1939);

Collected Stories of Katherine Mansfield (London: Constable, 1945);

The Journal of Katherine Mansfield, "Definitive Edition," edited by Murry (London: Constable, 1954);

Katherine Mansfield

Undiscovered Country: The New Zealand Stories of Katherine Mansfield, edited by Ian Gordon (London: Longman, 1974);

Katherine Mansfield: Publications in Australia, 1907–09, edited by Jean E. Stone (Sydney: Wentworth Books, 1977);

The Urewera Notebook, edited by Gordon (Oxford & New York: Oxford University Press, 1978);

The Stories of Katherine Mansfield, edited by Antony Alpers (Oxford & New York: Oxford University Press, 1984);

The Candle Fairy: Stories, Fairy Tales & Verse for Children, edited by Alister Taylor (Auckland: Alister Taylor, 1992).

OTHER: Maxim Gorki, *Reminiscences of Leonid Andreyev,* translated by Mansfield and S. S. Koteliansky (New York: C. Gaige, 1928; London: Heinemann, 1931);

Maxim Gorky, *Reminiscences of Tolstoy, Chekhov, and Andreev,* translated by Mansfield, Koteliansky, and Leonard Woolf (London: Hogarth Press, 1934; New York: Howard Fertig, 1995).

Even before she died at the age of thirty-four Katherine Mansfield had achieved a reputation as one of the most talented writers of the modern short story in English. From 1910 publications in periodicals like the *New Age* through the five volumes of stories published before her death, Mansfield was recognized as innovative, accessible, and psychologically acute, one of the pioneers of the avant-garde in the creation of the short story. Her language was clear and precise; her emotion and reaction to experience carefully distilled and resonant. Her use of image and symbol were sharp, suggestive, and new without seeming forced or written to some preconceived formula. Her themes were various: the difficulties and ambivalences of families and sexuality, the fragility and vulnerability of relationships, the complexities and insensitivities of the rising middle classes, the social consequences of war, and overwhelmingly the attempt to extract whatever beauty and vitality one can from mundane and increasingly difficult experience.

The growing avant-garde of the second and third decades of the twentieth century admired her unique insight. Virginia Woolf – who alternately disapproved of and envied Mansfield's wider and more amorphous sexual, economic, and social experience and who was both her principal rival and close friend in a shifting, difficult, intense, and communicative relationship – always respected and learned from Mansfield's writing. When she heard that Mansfield had died, Woolf wrote in her diary: "I was jealous of her writing – the only writing I have ever been jealous of." Mansfield's fiction has been increasingly respected throughout the years, the quality of her thought and writing praised as further stories, journals, scrapbooks, and letters have been posthumously published. Although reminiscences, particularly those of John Middleton

Murry, the husband who survived her, have sometimes tended to sanctify her, healthy reactions against sanctity have questioned the reputations of Murry and others; they have questioned not at all Mansfield's fiction or her role as a significant and seminal modernist. The variety and brevity of the fiction, its accessibility as well as its length, have enabled Mansfield to reach an expanding audience throughout the century.

Mansfield was born as Kathleen Mansfield Beauchamp in Wellington, New Zealand, on 14 October 1888, the third daughter in a commercially and socially expansive family. Her father, Harold Beauchamp, had been born in the gold-prospecting fields of Australia, had immigrated to New Zealand, and had become a noteworthy success in insurance, company directorships, and finally the Bank of New Zealand (he was knighted just a few days before his talented daughter died). Her mother, Annie Burnell Dyer Beauchamp, had also been born in Australia and had immigrated when her father was sent to New Zealand to start a branch of an Australian insurance firm. Both parents were only one generation removed from the English immigrants who still referred to Great Britain as home.

When Kathleen was just one year old her parents went to England, her pregnant mother returning in six months. The child, a fourth daughter, developed infantile cholera and died within three months. A fifth daughter was soon born and then, finally, the son and last child, Leslie (often called Boy), whom everyone idolized. Her birth-order position in the family, her childhood pudginess, and the fact that she wore glasses left Kathleen feeling ignored or neglected, although she was close to her maternal grandmother. This grandparent, with two of her own unmarried daughters, lived with the Beauchamps in increasingly large and comfortable houses, first in Karori, a country district outside the city, and then in the luxurious setting of Tinakori Road, Wellington – the house depicted in one of Katherine Mansfield's best-known stories, "The Garden Party." In the later stories that deal with Mansfield's childhood in New Zealand, the father is always vigorous and successful, yet emotionally dependent on the devotion of the wife and children around him. The mother is quiet, more tense and socially conventional, sometimes ill, always eager to please her husband but often remote from or indifferent to her daughters.

In 1898 the Beauchamp parents visited England and stayed for a time with Harold's even more successful cousin who had returned from Australia to establish his family in a country house in

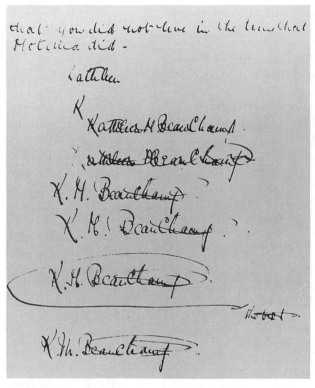

*A list of pen names Kathleen Mansfield Beauchamp considered in
1903, before deciding to use the name Katherine Mansfield
(Alexander Turnbull Library, Wellington, New Zealand)*

Kent. The cousin's daughter, May, had just married the German count von Arnim and written *Elizabeth and Her German Garden,* which reached its twenty-second edition in England by May 1899. Whether or not the Beauchamp parents brought a copy of the book back to New Zealand, family legend dates Kathleen's determination to become a writer from that point. Yet her tales in school newspapers, her writing of and performances in plays, and her composition of poems were visible even earlier. Teachers at her private school recalled Kathleen as a "surly sort of girl" and "imaginative to the point of untruth," or "shabby and inky" and inquisitive about her teachers' views on free love. She wrote most of and edited the school's first magazine.

In January 1903 the whole family visited England, this time leaving the three oldest girls at Queen's College in Harley Street, a small school that specialized in the arts and languages, allowed its young women students considerable freedom for the time, and had room for about forty boarders. Kass or Katherine (as she was now usually called — the name Kathleen had been abandoned) continued music lessons, went to concerts and the theater, edited the college magazine, read, and wrote. John

Middleton Murry, in his preface to the posthumously published complete edition of her short stories, wrote that, in addition to her dedication to the cello, these Queen's College years brought her "the beginning of intellectual freedom through an admiration of Oscar Wilde and the English 'decadents.' " Recalling her enthusiasm for Wilde in her later journal entry for May 1908, Mansfield wrote that she was now "growing capable of seeing a wider vision — a little Oscar, a little Symons, a little Dolf Wyllarde – Ibsen, Tolstoi, Elizabeth Robins, Shaw, D'Annunzio, Meredith." In 1906 the Beauchamp parents returned to collect the girls, and, after a summer of travel, the family boarded ship to return to New Zealand a few days after Mansfield's eighteenth birthday (she had begun to use the name Mansfield more frequently — it was her middle name as well as her favorite grandmother's maiden name).

The three girls were expected to excel at the parties and receptions of thriving Wellington and to find suitable husbands. Yet even on board the ship Katherine was uneasy and rebellious. What survives of her journal from the voyage in November 1906 has passages in which "a sense of unutterable loneliness pervaded my spirit. I knew this sea was eternal. I was eternal." At the same time she was fascinated by the members of the cricket team who were also passengers, "the whole octave of the sex," particularly one with "a low, full, strangely exciting voice . . . [and whose] face is clean cut, like the face of a statue, his mouth absolutely Grecian. . . . When I am with him a preposterous desire seizes me, I want to be badly hurt by him. I should like to be strangled by his firm hands." She found both her parents interfering and impossible:

> They are worse than I had even expected. They are prying and curious, they are watchful and they discuss only the food. They quarrel between themselves in a hopelessly vulgar fashion. My father spoke of my returning as damned rot, said look here, he wouldn't have me fooling around in dark corners with fellows. His hands, covered with long sand hair, are absolutely cruel hands. . . . *She* is constantly suspicious, constantly overbearingly tyrannous. I watch him walking all the deck, his full hideous speckled trousers. . . . [S]he is . . . easily upset. Tells him what he must and must not do . . . looks constantly uneasy. I shall never be able to live at home. I can plainly see that. For more than a quarter of an hour they are quite unbearable, and so absolutely my mental inferiors. What is going to happen in the future? I am full of restless wonder but I have none of that glorious expectancy that I used to have so much.

The "glorious expectancy" – its loss, its occasional tenuous resurrection, its desperate attempts to reclaim life – is the theme of many of her later stories set in New Zealand.

Back in Wellington Katherine found what artistic community she could. She studied the cello with Thomas Trowell, whose twin sons had followed the Beauchamp daughters to London to study music. She went on a monthlong camping trip to Maori settlements on the North Island, and her journal is full of colorful descriptions of flowers, bush, weather, and people. She became close to a slightly older artist named Edith Kathleen Bendall, and they planned a children's book, with poems by Katherine and drawings by Edith. They also went on excursions to the rocks and bays around Wellington, Katherine recording in her journal sexual attraction and consolation, although Edith in later years was reluctant to describe the relationship in such erotic terms. From the testimony of her letters and journals as well as other people, Katherine had probably had earlier sexual experience with both men and women in England: she had written a clearly lesbian story, "Leves Amores" (reprinted in an appendix to Claire Tomalin's biography of Mansfield), and sent a copy of it to a friend back in England. In later years Mansfield talked of her relationship with Edith Bendall as significant, and she used K. Bendall as one of her pseudonyms for the stories she began to circulate.

She wrote four stories published in successive months in late 1907 in the Melbourne periodical *Native Companion*. On 23 September 1907 she wrote the editor that she was poor, obscure, "with a rapacious appetite for everything and principles as light as my purse." As she said frequently, she longed to go back to London. She tried on poses as frequently as she gave different signatures to essays, letters, and stories. She used the pseudonyms Julian Mark (for one of the stories published in *Native Companion*), K. Bendall, Matilda Berry, as well as, most frequently, the Katherine Mansfield that she later used exclusively. For personal friends and family she was Kass, Katherine, Katie, Catherine (this spelling apparently had religious significance for her), Katharina, Katerina, Kissienka, or K. X. – before she became Whig or Tig for Murry. Finally in July 1908, after what apparently had been many strained discussions, she secured her parents' permission and an allowance to return to London to live.

Her next three or four years, mostly in the midst of bohemian life in London, were described by Murry as "tumultuous existence," many parts of which "remain obscure." She later destroyed most of her diaries and journal from 1906 to 1912, leaving Murry "no doubt whatever that the once ardent disciple of the doctrine of living dangerously came eventually to regard much of her eagerly sought experience . . . as waste – destruction too." She had earlier thought herself in love with one of the Trowell twins, Arnold, generally regarded as the more talented musician. But in London, still taking lessons from the father and close to the immigrant Trowell family, she became more attached to the other twin, Garnet. The Trowell parents thought them too young to marry, and Katherine was no longer welcome in the house. She went to join Garnet in Liverpool and Glasgow – perhaps in Hull as well – where he had a job in the orchestra of the touring Moody–Manners Opera Company. Biographers differ about where missing parts of her journal might reveal she was at various times, but at some point Katherine became pregnant with Garnet's child. Either afterward, or perhaps just shortly before (as Mansfield's principal biographer, Antony Alpers, believes is more plausible), Mansfield suddenly married a man named George Bowden whom she had met at musical parties and known for three weeks. They married at the Paddington Register office on 2 March 1909, Katherine

Mansfield and John Middleton Murry in 1913 (Mrs. Mary Middleton Murry Collection, Alexander Turnbull Library, Wellington, New Zealand)

dressed all in black. Bowden later recalled that "she looked like Oscar Wilde." After the ceremony they went to the theater and a hotel suite they had engaged and had dinner. Katherine suddenly left well before the night was over. She later said that "she couldn't bear the pink satin bedspread at the hotel, or the lampshade with pink tassels." She joined Garnet Trowell in Glasgow about a week later.

Meanwhile, alerted to Katherine's erratic sexual behavior (and apparently aware that some of her relationships were with women), Katherine's mother set off for England. The journey took about seven weeks, and she arrived in London on 27 May 1909. Whether or not she knew that Katherine was pregnant is uncertain, but she reported that she thought it necessary to separate Katherine from her closest female friend, Ida Baker. Annie Beauchamp talked of putting her errant daughter in a convent, but she placed her in an expensive hotel in Bad Wörishofen, a Bavarian spa, and then in a less expensive pension. Annie left in time to board a ship leaving England for New Zealand by 10 June, and, alone, Katherine apparently had a miscarriage in late June. When Annie reached Wellington, she cut Katherine out of her will.

After Katherine returned to London, her life of sudden and random alliances resumed for more than two years. The best source for these years is Baker, her intensely loyal and dedicated friend ever since school days at Queen's College. Baker worshiped Katherine – stayed with her when Katherine so wished and left when Katherine so wished. Her only purpose, she often said, was to "serve" Katherine, to stay "staunchly" by her side whenever she

could. Baker saw more of her, and lived with her more often, than did anyone else from late 1908 until late 1911, years in which Baker's memoirs report that Katherine, although dedicated to her writing, was also "wilful, emotionally voracious, and undisciplined in the sense that she had not yet been schooled to the knowledge that self-assertion bears results, results not always readily controlled." After Katherine's return from Germany, Baker stayed with her almost constantly, "guarded [her] through illness and convalescence, . . . participated in the final break with Mr. Bowden, [and] shared the progress of a second love affair (which again resulted in a doomed pregnancy)." The illness was apparently gonorrhea; the operation, one for "peritonitis" connected with the gonorrhea. It was the second pregnancy terminated either by another miscarriage or by abortion.

In the midst of her physical and emotional turbulence Mansfield wrote constantly. In 1910 A. R. Orage, the editor of *New Age,* then perhaps the most noteworthy avant-garde journal of literature, politics, and art, accepted some of her work, and she began to contribute stories and sketches regularly. She wrote letters to the editor describing London street life, one letter like a prose poem full of the colors of "pilgrims straining forward to Nowhere." She joined with Beatrice Hastings (Orage's mistress) to write short parodies of more-established authors (whose work *New Age* often published) such as G. K. Chesterton, Arnold Bennett, Eden Phillpotts, and H. G. Wells. She tried different styles and tones: rhapsodic descriptions of the unusual, caustic satire, careful probings of relationships for the existence or absence of "soul."

One of her earliest pieces, "The Tiredness of Rosabel," first written in 1908, is the fantasy of a young milliner's assistant on her bus ride home after a hard day's work trying to please snobbish and exacting customers. The rain blurs most of what she sees, but at moments "light striking on the panes turned their dullness to opal and silver, and the jewellers' shops seen through this were fairy palaces." At the same time the young woman "would have sacrificed her soul for a good dinner," and she recoils from the "sickening smell of warm humanity" that the crowded bus exudes. As Mansfield presents the confined, sodden details of the woman's experience back at her fourth-floor walk-up flat beyond Earl's Court, the young milliner focuses on the distances of her fantasy; the lights, color, and excitement generated by her clientele; and the elegant hats that she sells. The fantasy develops into the wealthy, attractive young man replacing his snobbish fiancée with her and announcing their engagement in the *Court Circular* before the wedding at St. George's, Hanover Square. After the wedding "they motored down to Harry's old ancestral home for the honeymoon; the peasants in the village curtseyed as they passed." The fantasy is predictable, but the story works well through the language, the details, and the carefully constructed point of view that presents so immediately and directly the stereotypes of her imagination in contrast to her clear observations.

Much of Mansfield's early work is in the form of the sketch, highly popular in the journals of the time, in which a segment of life, like the shop girl's perspective, is described, but neither plot nor theme is developed sufficiently to warrant designating the work a story. Her first volume, *In a German Pension* (1911), consisted primarily of sketches, many of which she had written from her life in Bad Wörishofen in 1909. Generally presenting the Germans from the point of view of a quiet, observant young English woman, the sketches satirize Germans mercilessly, depicting them as crude, gross, pompous, self-satisfied. Some, like "The Baron," concentrate on German snobberies: the titled man at the resort will speak to no one except the young English tourist — to whom he confesses that he never speaks to anyone so that he can order double portions of food and elicit no comment. Others, like "The Luft Bad," mock the trivial and excessive Germanic concern with digestion and appearance among the ladies in the spa. Although the English narrator turns some of the mockery on herself, even more is directed toward the man in the "luft bad" next door who "buries himself up to the armpits in mud and refuses to believe in the Trinity." Another satire, "A Birthday," depicts a difficult childbirth from the point of view of a swinish father who in the midst of his wife's pain can think only of himself. A few of the sketches combine the usual German grossness (and related obsessions with food and soul) with pompous German assurance that the English need not fear invasion. In "Germans at Meat" one fat consumer named Herr Rat tells the English tourist that "You have got no army at all — a few little boys with their veins full of nicotine poisoning." An equally gross but more soulful German reassures the tourist: "Don't be afraid. . . . We don't want England. If we did we would have had her long ago."

Although there is no evidence in her letters or writing that Mansfield shared the invasion scare of 1910 and 1911 that provided the subject of popular plays and Kiplingesque adventure tales, some of the reviews welcomed her treatment of Germans more than her craft. One said that she wrote about Germans extremely well but "dwelt a little too insistently on the grossness or coarseness, which is undeniable." Others praised her "malicious accuracy," and only a few, Beatrice Hastings among them, thought her work marred by occasional sentimentality. Mansfield herself was apparently ambivalent about responses to the political implications of the treatment of Germans in her fiction. She hoped in 1914 that war could be avoided, but when it began she was both crushed and conventionally patriotic. After describing a darkened, sad, excited London in a September 1914 letter to a friend in New Zealand, Mansfield concluded that "Although in many ways these are dark and depressing days, still they are brightened by the display of real and splendid courage on the part of all the people. The fact that England is fighting for something beyond mere worldly gain and power seems to have a real moral effect upon the people, and they are become more brave and more generous than one could have believed in days of peace." Her letters to her parents echo the same thoughts, although one blames the Prussians rather than "those simple warm-hearted bavarians." As the war continued and Mansfield was horrified by deaths of those she knew well and by jingoism of any sort, she seemed to reject her volume of German sketches entirely. She did not want it reprinted during the war, nor even after the war was over — when she thought the stories might still be read as easy propaganda. She questioned the propitiousness of publishing the volume for an American audience in May 1922 by saying that she thought the book a "most inferior . . . youthful extravagance of expression and youthful disgust."

Not all of *In a German Pension,* however, is inferior or an expression of youthful disgust. Parts of some sketches and early stories reveal many of the narrative skills and psychological complexities of Mansfield's mature fiction. One of the most interesting of the stories is "The Modern Soul," which begins with a stereotype of the pompous German music professor explaining to the young English narrator why he incessantly eats cherries: "There is nothing like cherries for producing free saliva after trombone playing, especially after Grieg's 'Ich Liebe Dich.' " His cherry-eating is connected with a consuming desire for women, and he soon introduces the narrator to the object of his current interest, a young German actress who travels the spa-concert circuit with her mother. The two older Germans, the professor and the actress's mother, talk incessantly of food and soul. They agree that the English are "fish-blooded," cold and without soul, or that "England is merely an island of beef flesh swimming in a warm gulf stream of gravy."

As the story develops, the actress, called "the modern soul," confides to the narrator that she is "furiously Sapphic" – more interested in the narrator than in the loathsome professor. But she is also attached to her mother and cannot think of leaving her. The narrator, attempting to be helpful, suggests that the actress have her mother and the professor marry, which would allow all to continue the artistic tour and leave the actress free to follow her own attractions. The actress, a "soul" less modern than manipulating, is appalled and stages her own fainting spell, which leads to a comic conclusion suggesting that the actress will marry the professor after all and keep him as her "pillow," as the security of her respectability, while he may continue to bluster and consume cherries. The "modern soul" is posture and hypocrisy; the varieties of sexual attraction are puzzles and complexities that human beings cannot handle.

Bisexual themes and the complexity of human emotion characterize other early stories. "Bain Turc," a satire apparently not written until 1913, is set in a German Turkish bath. The conflict it depicts between openly lesbian women and those who can talk only of food and men is obvious to the reader, though it is less so to some of the characters not conscious of the implications of their words. This story seems like the most flat and caustic of Mansfield's early satiric sketches. More skillfully done and complex is "New Dresses," written in 1910 although not published until 1912. The first of Mansfield's stories to model her own family circumstances in New Zealand, "New Dresses" adopts the

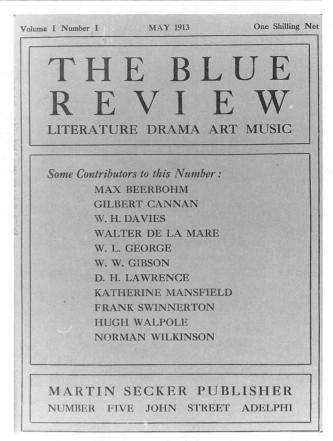

Cover for the first issue of the short-lived magazine that Mansfield and John Middleton Murry edited

point of view of the dissident, sloppy, tomboyish daughter ignored by both the remote, conventional mother who seems to care more for her children's clothes than for her children and by the boastful, ungenerous, egotistical father whose attention centers on his youngest child, the only boy. "New Dresses" excoriates both parents, and the dissident child is rescued only by the grandmother and a close family friend, the doctor – surrogate parents who are without much power but are given understanding that the parents lack. Yet the dissident girl's insight into the ways in which she deliberately provokes her parents and into her own jealousy of her younger brother removes from the story the easy self-pity its situation might generate.

A different geographical and social New Zealand background distinguishes another early story, "The Woman at the Store" (1911). This story is set in the blistering heat of the desert where the narrator describes how "the sky was of slate colour, and the sound of the larks reminded me of slate pencils scraping over its surface. There was nothing to be seen but wave after wave of tussock grass, patched

JE NE PARLE PAS FRANCAIS
by
KATHERINE MANSFIELD

THE HERON PRESS : HAMPSTEAD
MCMXIX

Title page for John Middleton Murry's copy of the 1919 limited edition of a short story by Mansfield (courtesy of Special Collections, Thomas Cooper Library, University of South Carolina)

carriages) reveals to the travelers that she has finally shot and killed her husband, the psychological explosions of identity and contrast match the primitivism and power of the isolated setting. It is a Lawrencian story written more than a year before Mansfield met D. H. Lawrence.

Perhaps something central about Mansfield's emotions in the difficult, unstable, defiant, lonely, searching years from 1908 to the end of 1911 is visible in "The Little Governess," which was apparently written shortly before its publication in early 1915 (by that time almost all that Mansfield wrote would be published immediately in one periodical or another). The childlike fantasy begins with a young Englishwoman on her first trip alone to the Continent, where she is to meet in Munich the employer who has arranged to hire her as a governess in Augsburg. Warned about Continental impropriety and perfidy, she is frightened on the trip, mistrusts everyone, and refuses to acknowledge porters, eat food on the train, or tip bellboys at the hotel. When a polite old gentleman enters her carriage on the train, she is aware that he might be thinking "how tragic for a little governess to possess hair that made one think of tangerines and marigolds, of apricots and tortoise-shell cats and champagne." This is, of course, what she really hopes he is thinking, and she chooses to treat this fantasy as innocent and protective.

She allows him to buy her strawberries, which she enjoys as the juice runs down her fingers. When they reach Munich early in the morning, she goes to the hotel where her employer is to meet her late in the afternoon; she intends to stay in her room until then. But the old gentleman, whom she still thinks of as a "fairy god-father," arrives and persuades her that he might innocently show her the town for just an hour or two. The tour stretches through "white sausages" with beer at eleven, lunch, and late afternoon ices, each entailing more physical proximity, until he takes her to his flat. What is remarkable about the story is the flexibility of the governess's consciousness throughout the tour. She simultaneously seems to believe in the innocence of the city that her protective godfather is showing her — and to want him to violate her innocence, as she understands the sexuality of all the signs. She is conscious of time in the distance and of her need to return to the hotel, yet she nonetheless tells her godfather that her watch has stopped because she forgot to wind it on the journey — and he suggests just one further excursion or treat.

When his delicacy changes in his flat to direct sexual assault, she breaks free and returns to her

with purple orchids and manuka bushes covered with thick spider webs." The narrator is traveling with two men, one of whom knows of an isolated store where the woman owner, if her husband is away, might sleep with a passing traveler. They find the store, but they are unprepared for the complex emotions they encounter: sexual attraction, rage at the men who use and then abandon women, violent hostility within and outside the sexuality, and resentments of the isolated outback woman reflected in the middle-class traveling woman. Although the conclusion is melodramatic, when the almost-mute child of the outback woman (who has had four mis-

hotel through the crowded streets "full of old men with twitching knees." Of course, she is too late: her employer had waited for a time, had been told that the governess had gone out with a man and left no message, and he has gone away. The story ends with the governess alone and desolate, her knowledge of herself no consolation for her emptiness and estrangement.

The sense of estrangement, of a loneliness sometimes desperate, and the intense desires for varying connections seemed to dominate both Mansfield's emotions and her prose at least until she met John Middleton Murry in December 1911. Her loneliness and estrangements were personal, social, cultural, and national: the colonial in England, the posturing Englishwoman on the Continent, the new middle-class colonial trying to be part of Bohemian London, the rebellious observer still dependent on the grudged parental allowance. She always felt herself to be the outsider — sometimes hating it, often welcoming it. In New Zealand, she longed for England; in England, she longed for the Continent, often further east than she had ever been.

The meeting with Murry in late 1911 stabilized Mansfield's life to some extent, but not completely. She still moved from one flat or house to another every few months — sometimes with Murry, sometimes without him. As late as January 1917 Mansfield, well known as a writer, had to write Ottoline Morrell for a financial reference in order to rent a flat. And affairs with both Murry and Baker as well as with other men and women continued, although with less frequency than in earlier years. But a major change was the focus on magazines and an engagement in London literary life in the years just before the First World War. Murry had thought of himself as an editor and critic, an organizer of the arts, and while still an undergraduate, he had joined Michael Sadleir and J. D. Fergusson, a Scottish painter living in Paris, in starting a little magazine called *Rhythm*. Mansfield, after a dispute with Orage, had sent *Rhythm* a story that soon led to her meeting Murry. She persuaded him to leave Oxford and move in with her — both of them to write, to engage in literary controversy, to maintain contact with other writers, and to edit the magazine.

Rhythm gathered considerable talent but lost its financial backing, and Murry and Mansfield then reorganized it as the *Blue Review*, but that lasted only three issues. They did, however, meet other writers and succeeded in becoming part of literary London. D. H. Lawrence, for example, stopped at the office of the *Blue Review* to submit work, and

Murry, Mansfield, Lawrence, and Frieda Weekley soon became close. These proved to be a volatile set of relationships that kept changing, waxing and waning among the four for the rest of their lives.

One of the principal beliefs that Mansfield, Murry, and Lawrence shared was a conviction about the singular importance of Russian literature. On the evening that Mansfield and Murry met, Murry later recorded, he was impressed by the assurance with which she spoke about the superiority of German to English translations of the Russian. Yet for some time, Mansfield was hesitant about including Fyodor Dostoyevsky in the Russian canon, although his fiction was beginning to be translated into English around 1910. From the evidence in her journal, Mansfield began finding herself in Anton Chekhov in early 1914. By August of the same year, she no longer cared for Ivan Turgenev, the staple of an older English interest taken in the Russian, for example, by Henry James. "I simply cannot believe," Mansfield wrote, "that there was a time I cared about Turgenev. Such a poseur! Such a hypocrite!" In February 1915 she still disliked *Crime and Punishment*, which she thought was "very bad."

Murry, however, had already begun long conversations about Dostoyevsky with Lawrence and other friends like the Gordon Campbells. In trying to define his own critical position, Murry felt himself an "instrument" of Dostoyevsky and felt that his absorption in Dostoyevsky might lead him into forms of heightened self-consciousness. Mansfield was at first skeptical about the implicit mysticism, "a 'passionate' admiration for that which has no reality at all." Murry, however, was known as an advocate of all things Russian, and he was offered a job at the British Embassy Library in Saint Petersburg in June 1914 before being commissioned by publisher Martin Secker to write a critical book on Dostoyevsky. Talk and argument with the Lawrences and the Campbells continued, as well as indulging in what were called "Dostoyevsky nights," apparently long sessions of drink, mutual self-analysis, and strong "displays of emotion." Mansfield was converted to Dostoyevsky, at least so far that by February 1916 she wrote that Murry's book, which was about to be published, was "really brilliant."

During 1912, 1913, and 1914 Murry and Mansfield lived together on and off for months at a time. They wrote often about their mutual desire to marry, find a quiet place in the country, write, and start a family, but increasingly these statements looked like myth through which each sustained illusions of the other. They could not marry legally because Mansfield was still married to George

Katherine Mansfield

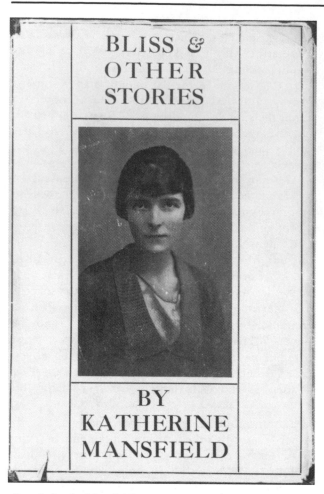

Dust jacket for Mansfield's 1920 collection (courtesy of the Lilly Library, Indiana University). "Bliss" is one of Mansfield's most frequently anthologized short stories.

Bowden, and though they often talked of her divorce and remarriage, they did not marry until 3 May 1918. At times Mansfield wrote as if she wanted only Murry and yet was disappointed with his inadequacies; at times, she wrote as if she could not stand him and claimed that she wanted to separate permanently from him in late 1914. All evidence indicates that their relationship was never very passionate, and Murry, writing much later, maintained that he had never known sexual fulfillment until his fourth marriage, when he was in his late fifties. Mansfield was seriously ill throughout their relationship together, and her letters seem to reveal that she experienced more passion with others than she could sustain with Murry. Critics have sometimes explained the childlike quality of Murry's and Mansfield's love for each other as compensation for their unhappy childhoods, but they also acknowledge that both had experienced earlier ravaging, much less childlike sexual relationships and

had sought a simpler, more innocent sexuality with each other.

So much of Mansfield's energy went into assuaging illness, becoming a part of literary London, and trying to find a way of living that could fit her fantasies and enable her to write that these years during which she was acquiring recognition are among her least productive. She still wrote satires, sketches, articles, and critiques, but her fiction seemed not to advance far. In all of 1913, for example, she published only "Something Childish But Very Natural," a long fantasy of a young suburban couple who meet frequently on a train and develop their plan for perfect love in a country cottage. The seventeen-year-old Edna, entranced by the idea of love but afraid that any physical contact will shatter her romantic dream, fails to arrive at the cottage where she and Henry, her eighteen-year-old platonic lover, plan to live out their dream. She instead sends him a note, the contents of which are undisclosed but which leave Henry immobolized and defeated. Both are curiously passive figures, as if they have always known that living out their fantasy will be impossible.

In many ways Mansfield, despite the conventionally patriotic statements she occasionally made, seemed almost to ignore the First World War for its first six months — and to try to live as fully as possible in accustomed patterns. But the denial was impossible to maintain, especially as news of the deaths of friends like the sculptor Henri Gaudier-Brzeska began to reach them. Murry was rejected for service because doctors incorrectly thought that he might have tuberculosis. The war was inevitably central to everyone's consciousness. In January 1915 Mansfield's journal recorded that she was trying to write in the midst of constant turmoil and interruption. She had for more than a month thought herself in love with Francis Carco, a French writer serving in the army on the Western Front. She also reported nights of reconciliation with Murry (which she then felt guilty about) and constant visits and letters from the Lawrences, filled with their own anguish, indecision, and plans. Worse than all these, however, was the war, of which Mansfield wrote, "I have simply felt it closing in on me and my unhappy love, and all to no purpose."

Encouraged by Lawrence and given money by her brother, Leslie, who had come to England to join the armed forces, Mansfield went to France to find Carco in what was called the "Zone of the Armies." Telling lies to officials and using whatever charms or excuses were required, as she chronicled in her story "An Indiscreet Journey," Mansfield worked her way into this area, where she spent four days with Carco in lodgings at the front. The affair was disillusioning, and she returned alone to Carco's flat in Paris, where she wrote steadily and seriously. During the next few months she spent time alternating between reconciling with Murry in London and writing in Paris. In her journal Mansfield's passages of longing for Carco seemed to be replaced by quotations from Chekhov.

She developed a new confidence in her writing, in the control she could manifest through her clear and distant observations of others and herself. In June 1915 Mansfield and Murry settled in Acacia Road, Saint John's Wood, where she felt more certain than ever that she had found the calm locus she needed for her work. While her brother's unit was training for service in France, she spent much of the summer in long conversations with him about their family and early days in New Zealand. Although she had seen little of him in recent years, she now regarded him as the most discerning and sympathetic member of the family, the one with whom she shared most. Little more than two weeks after he landed in France, however, Leslie was killed, "blown to bits" on 7 October 1915 while demonstrating to his men how to lob a hand grenade. Mansfield was desolate, filling her journal with long passages addressed to Leslie: "I've got things to do for both of us, and then I will come as quickly as I can. Dearest heart, I know you are there, and I live with you, and I will write for you. . . . [W]hen I leave this house and this place it will be with you, and I will never even for the shortest space of time be away from you again. You know I can never be Jack's lover again. You have me. You're in my flesh as well as my soul. I give Jack my 'surplus' love, but to you I hold and to you I give my deepest love. Jack is no more than . . . anybody might be."

Mansfield knew that she could no longer live in the house on Acacia Road, and in November she and Murry traveled to the south of France, then still relatively untouched by the war. When he had settled Mansfield in Bandol in early December, Murry returned to his magazine work in London. In Bandol during the next four months Mansfield began writing the intense, apparently casual but deeply painful fiction that transformed her career. She started work on *The Aloe* (1930), begun as her first attempt at a full-length novel and set in the framework of her growing up in New Zealand, a work drawing on those long conversations with her brother the previous summer. Murry, in his introduction to the 1937 complete edition of her stories, wrote of her "turn back toward her early childhood

as a life which had existed apart from, and uncontaminated by, the mechanical civilization which had produced the war." To some extent this was true, but *The Aloe* also permitted her to explore the consciousness of her many characters and family members, to connect their pasts with their presents in ways that revealed the antagonisms, alliances, and jealousies that propelled both the family and the society. The consciousness, far from innocent, was represented in the aloe, the large bushlike tree known initially as African trees in the center of the "spread tangled garden," divided between the bewildering tall trees and "strange bushes" that suggest the father – and the "box borders" with a profusion of flowers that suggest the mother.

In the fiction the aloe is the "fat swelling plant with its cruel leaves and fleshy stem" that magnificently clings with "claws" to the ground and flowers only once every hundred years. For the young members of the family the aloe is sinister and uncontrollable but also a part of them. *The Aloe* was not published at the time (Murry published the original version in 1930) but, revised and compressed in the summer of 1917, appeared as *Prelude,* the second publication of Virginia and Leonard Woolf's Hogarth Press in 1918. *Prelude,* which presents family conflicts and alliances more subtly through varieties of floral description than *The Aloe* does, represents the Beauchamps' move to Karori, the large house in the countryside, in 1893.

The story is seen through the perspective of Kezia, the younger daughter who feels loved by her grandmother rather than her mother. The father loves the country – the birds, the grasses, the opportunity to explore the wilds and to exercise – even though he must take a long trip to Wellington to work every day. The mother, constantly tired and attempting to escape or avoid the emotional demands placed on her, both loves and hates her husband. The spinster aunt feels isolated and deprived of her chances in the country to which they have moved. The daughters, full of rivalry, are described through the games they play, their dreams, and the flowers and bush depicted in naturalistically accurate detail. Some of what they see is cruel and violent, like the beheading of a duck. Mansfield acknowledged that she had developed some of her extraordinary ability to describe nature, to make accounts simultaneously naturalistic and symbolic, from Lawrence. Their accounts of the forms of nature they had mutually observed, reflected upon, and discussed had comprised much of their conversations.

The story moves simultaneously toward the aloe tree and the wife's longing – despite her fatigue as well as her attractions and repulsions for her husband – to hand him her last "little packet" of feeling that he has always most wanted. At times she feels resigned and wonders, "What am I guarding myself for so preciously? I shall go on having children and Stanley will go on making money and the children and the gardens will grow bigger and bigger, with whole fleets of aloes in them for me to choose from." The story suggests without underlining that the possible flowering of the aloe next year may represent the birth of the son, the purpose of Stanley's family. Mansfield, with her skillful naturalistic inconclusiveness, turns the final scene to the spinster aunt, who is thus further isolated in her superficial conventionality.

Conceived at the same time although not written or published for some years, "At the Bay" continues the story begun in *Prelude*. Constructed, as is *Prelude,* through quick movements from one scene to another and from the perspectives of different characters, "At the Bay" focuses on the beach and houses on the other side of Karori from Wellington and begins with the early-morning swim of the father, Stanley, before the daily rituals of obeisance from his family as he sets off for work in Wellington. He and the others lavish their devotion on the Boy, who is now three or four years old. The mother still loves and resents her husband, focuses her attention on her son, and ignores her daughters. In this story Mansfield does more with servants and neighbors, and this gives the whole colony social meaning as part of Wellington's rapidly rising bourgeoisie. The spinster aunt is developed much further: she is attracted to a childless woman whom she sees frequently on the beach, yet she is finally frightened when she recognizes that the childless woman's satires of local families cloak a lesbian overture. The spinster aunt desperately wants a male lover, though not the lesbian woman's philandering husband. Like the spinster aunt, the mother is seen more sympathetically than in the earlier story, and this is doubtless attributable to its date of composition: Annie Beauchamp's weak heart gave out in 1918 (she was only fifty-four), by which time, Ida Baker reports, Katherine had come to feel that her sensitive, too conventional, "fastidious" mother really understood and cared for her more than did her more intelligent, parsimonious, "controlling" father. Mansfield's increased ranges of sympathy and social concern have led some critics to find "At the Bay" the better story – in fact, her very best. Other critics feel that nothing, not even fine passages about the power and mystery of the sea, can match the descriptions of plants, birds, flowers, and natural phenomena in *Prelude*. Both of these long stories, the closest Mansfield came to writing a novel, are among her most considerable achievements.

Mansfield left Bandol in the spring of 1916 to join Murry and the Lawrences in renting adjoining cottages in Cornwall. Given the volatility and the rapid oscillations between love and hate among the four, such an arrangement clearly could not work for long. Yet letters, biographies, and a reading of the fiction provide evidence of the constant intellectual interchange in the focus on nature and natural description, the interest in psychology, and the incessant reappraisal of the dynamics of relationships. They also, particularly in 1916, shared interests in Russian literature and in what one could learn from Chekhov and Dostoyevsky. Murry was finishing his book on Dostoyevsky, and Mansfield's journal for March 1916 contains pages of elaborate notes on three Dostoyevsky novels she was then appreciatively reading. In the midst of the difficult weeks in Cornwall, Mansfield continued to work, though this became more difficult when the foursome split up and Murry and Mansfield, with little money, wandered from one friend to another – sometimes together, sometimes separately.

They were frequent guests at Garsington, Ottoline Morrell's sanctuary for writers and intellectuals, where they became parts of those entangling alliances and separations: Mansfield, for example, had a short and apparently unsatisfactory affair with Bertrand Russell. Ida Baker also reentered Katherine's life in 1916. In March 1914 she had gone to Rhodesia, where her father was in the colonial service, to rejoin her family. In September 1916 she had returned to England, partly bored by life in Rhodesia and partly missing Katherine, although the two had corresponded warmly and regularly. Wanting to help in the war in England, Baker trained as a machinist and worked at an airplane factory in Putney, always ready to move in with or serve Katherine whenever required. The fiction, prolific and often brilliant throughout 1917 and 1918, concentrates on the vagaries, uncertainties, and pain of human relationships. Often dependent on psychologically revealing monologue even in tales as slight as "The Black Cap," a comedy of mismanaged adultery, the fiction of the period grows increasingly complex and intricate in its study of relationships.

Many of the best stories of this period use, more or less explicitly, Mansfield's bisexual sensibilities. "Bliss," for example, one of her most appreciated stories, begins with an ecstatic young woman preparing to give a dinner party, almost a social rite, as she exults in her baby, her husband, and her guests. Her ecstasy is innocent: she thinks of her relationship with her husband as that of "good pals" and anticipates what might be their first night of passion after the dinner party. She sees her baby daughter as a prize and is jealous of the necessary nursemaid; she loves her other trophy, the enigmatic and attractive Miss Fulton, her social "find" to be set as the "fullest, richest bloom" among the satirized stereotypes of the avant-garde – the artistic couple who both dress, look, and act like chattering monkeys; the frightened and pretentious poet who sees himself driving "through Eternity in a *timeless* taxi." The innocence is most manifestly represented in the "lovely pear tree" outside the window, "its wide open blossoms as a symbol of her own life," a symbol that the hostess, Bertha, first focuses on herself and then shows to Miss Fulton, depicted as a goddess of the moon about to touch the blossoms of the tree as a sign of their intimacy.

The pear tree, although it has been read as a lesbian symbol, appears in Mansfield's journal as a tree that signified to both her and her brother the innocence of their New Zealand childhoods. The story subtly develops the sexuality of Bertha's ambivalent attractions and sustains an ambiguity about her consciousness of her implicit feelings. But Bertha's consciousness is painfully exposed and her innocence destroyed when she sees unmistakable signs of a sexual affair between her husband and Miss Fulton. She feels doubly betrayed – the victim, not the apex, of a sexual triangle. In developing her themes so subtly and resonantly, Mansfield achieves a story of considerably compressed effectiveness. Some critics have followed Murry in thinking the story a "sophisticated failure" in which "the discordant combination of caricature with emotional pathos" helps create the failure. But most critics regard the combination of "caricature with emotional pathos" as part of the point: Bertha is in some ways as silly as the fashionable chattering monkeys; the posturing poet is as betrayed by the fashionable ambivalences of feeling as Bertha is. The line between the posturing and the genuine wavers in a world in which characters are so uncertain and changeable about what they feel, and both honest emotion and the bliss of expectation are invariably betrayed.

Other stories of this period are equally fine, whether extended to chronicle the segment of a life or compressed in a short single scene. *Je ne parle pas français* (1919) is an extended account of the rather pedestrian male narrator's experience on the fringes of the literary life in Paris. Fashionably disillu-

sioned, he begins in a dirty Paris café with the assertion, "I don't believe in the human soul," and quotes his own literary and cultural images self-consciously as echoes of J. Alfred Prufrock's "dying fall." He envies his more ebullient, successful friend, an English writer who travels back and forth between Paris and London. Signs of the narrator's homosexual attraction are clear but are never taken up, as if the Englishman is toying with the feelings of the French writer. On one visit the Englishman brings a woman, a passive beauty called Mouse, with whom he says he is eloping. The three begin a painful series of symbolic connections and rejections, the narrator dwelling on his long-ago seduction by an African laundress, an affair that has impaired his ability to love.

Suddenly the Englishman abandons Mouse, leaving her stranded and still unmarried in Paris, as if she is his legacy to the narrator. But the narrator, as if in revenge toward the Englishman for abandoning him, never takes up the expected gentlemanly rescue, though that is clearly invited. This story, one of Mansfield's most grim, focuses on the woman entirely betrayed by the male homosexual emotion that can center only on the self or other men, the woman as a pawn in complex interplays of male power, attraction, narcissism, and control. The story is replete with similarities to Dostoyevsky's *Notes from the Underground* (1864), particularly the section called "the Mousehole," although Dostoyevsky's mouse character is male.

Compressed into a single scene in a restaurant, "A Dill Pickle" relates the encounter of a couple accidentally meeting again six years after their affair ended, and like many of the stories, it uses attraction to food, particularly fruit, to suggest sexual attraction. Here the woman first recognizes the man by his "special" way of peeling an orange, as he often interrupts her talk to peel fruit or inquire about what she may or may not want to order. She is attracted to him again – to his talk, his obvious prosperity, his travels, especially to Russia, which "was all that we had imagined." She is almost ready to succumb to him again when, with world-weariness and false castigation of both of them, he asserts that their affair would have lasted had they both not been "such egoists, so self-engrossed, so wrapped up in ourselves that we hadn't a corner in our hearts for anybody else. Do you know . . . I began studying a Mind System when I was in Russia. . . ." By the time his voice reaches Russia, she is gone. Mansfield needs no comment to convey that the self-engrossment is entirely his, the sensual approach to fruit not a suggestion of sexual attraction but the opposite, an avoidance of heterosexual contact. As a concluding line Mansfield adds his plea to the waitress that he not be charged for the cream that she did not touch, a line that makes his self-engrossment vulgar and materialistic as well as empty. Mansfield never wrote more skillfully about various betrayals of human emotion and sexuality than she did in these stories of 1917 and early 1918 when she was at Bandol.

A combination of wartime shortages and the increasing difficulty of civilian travel made Bandol in early 1918 very different from the paradise untouched by war that it had seemed to Mansfield two years earlier. In December 1917 a doctor had discovered her active tuberculosis and prescribed winters in the Mediterranean climate. Shortly after the exhausting journey through war-torn France she suffered her first lung hemorrhage. Baker came to Bandol to care for her, and, although Mansfield resented her dependence on Baker, she also managed to write with fervor and skill during the next few months. This is also the period in which ambivalence and mutual influence between Mansfield and Virginia Woolf were at their strongest, the time when *Prelude* was being published. Mansfield and Woolf had met in late 1916 when Mansfield was visiting Garsington frequently and coming to know Bloomsbury. She had little respect for what she saw as the delicacy of most Bloomsbury sensibilities, and after reading *Howard's End* (1910) she wrote in her journal in May 1917, "E. M. Forster never gets any further than warming the teapot. He's a rare fine hand at that. Feel this teapot. Is it not beautifully warm? Yes, but there ain't going to be no tea. . . . And I can never be perfectly certain whether Helen was got with child by Leonard Bast or by his fatal forgotten umbrella. All things considered, I think it must have been the umbrella."

Mansfield's judgments of Woolf and Woolf's work were much more complicated. Their relationship developed slowly through many visits and long talks during much of 1917. They were entranced with each other's writing, yet wary. As late as October 1917, when she already thought so highly of *Prelude* that she offered to print it, Woolf was still sufficiently snobbish and censorious about Mansfield's past to record in her own diary her first impression of Katherine: "she stinks like a – well civet cat that had taken to street walking. In truth, I'm a little shocked by her commonness at first sight; lines so hard & cheap. However, when this diminishes, she is so intelligent & inscrutable that she repays friendship." Mansfield did not let the social gulf between them cloud her perception. In July 1917 she wrote Ottoline Morrell, "I do like her tremendously. . . . I felt then for the first time the strange, trembling, glinting quality of her mind – and quite for the first time she seemed to me to be one of those Dostoievsky women whose 'innocence' has been hurt." The more they talked of writing and of each other's work through late 1917, the closer they became.

After a visit in August Mansfield wrote Woolf,

[D]on't let THEM ever persuade you that I spend any of my precious time swapping hats or committing adultery – I'm far too arrogant & proud. However, let them think what they like. Theres a most wonderful greengage light on the tree outside and little white clouds bobbing over the sky like rabbits. . . . Yes, your Flower Bed is *very* good. There's a still, quivering, changing light over it all and a sense of those couples dissolving in the bright air which fascinates me.

Mansfield was referring to Woolf's experiments with simultaneously descriptive and symbolic prose in *Kew Gardens* (not published until 1919), a form of prose that Woolf thought she had, in part, learned from Mansfield's *Prelude*. Influence was mutual: as Vincent O'Sullivan, the critic and editor of Mansfield's collected letters, has shown, Mansfield developed from Woolf a capacity to describe moments of intense perception, "that condition of standing outside of things, yet being more intensely in them." O'Sullivan illustrates this double stance in Mansfield's story "The Flower," in which an ill woman visiting a seedy doctor can listen to his false reassurances delivered to relieve her self-pitying, emotionally solipsistic husband. As she does so, the woman can also discern a moment of revelation created by the details of the room and the flowers, a moment that is both one "of spontaneous elation" and a recognition of the illness she will never overcome. No other writers of the time could match Mansfield's or Woolf's capacity to convey the simultaneity of multiple and searching human perceptions.

After the diagnosis of tuberculosis in late 1917 Mansfield's compounded illnesses became increasingly debilitating. Alpers reports that on her thirtieth birthday in 1918 two eminent London tuberculosis specialists examined her separately and agreed that she should enter a sanatorium. Otherwise, they insisted, her life expectancy was "four years at the outside." She refused to enter the sanatorium, and at the end of 1918 she learned from another doctor whom she consulted about her illnesses that what she had regarded as "rheumatism" was a residual gonococcal infection that had long since rendered

Dorothy Brett, Katherine Mansfield, and Ida Baker in 1921 (Alexander Turnbull Library, Wellington, New Zealand)

conception of a child improbable and had seriously affected her heart.

Although she often could read or write for only a few hours a day, Mansfield worked as much as she could in defiance of the predictions. She helped Murry with his editing and wrote reviews. Along with her (and Lawrence's) old friend S. S. Koteliansky she began in early 1919 a project to translate all of Chekhov's letters into English. As she wrote to Woolf in May 1919, one letter that she published in the *Athenæum* she regarded as crucial for her writing — a letter in which Chekhov had asserted that "what the writer does is not so much to *solve* the question but to *put* the question. There must be the question put. That seems to me a very

nice dividing line between the true & the false writer." She never finished the edition (which Koteliansky completed and published with Philip Tomlinson in 1925), nor did she come close to the original aim of publishing her edition before that which Constance Garnett published in 1920.

Mansfield thought Garnett's translations, by far the best-known translations from Russian into English from 1908 or 1909 on, were inadequate — especially those of Chekhov: "She seems to take the nerve out of Tchekhov before she starts working on him," Mansfield wrote, "like the dentist takes the nerve from a tooth." More than ever Mansfield's letters and journals of her last years are crowded with references to Dostoyevsky and Chekhov.

Those to Dostoyevsky focus on his recognitions of consciousness, his extraordinary capacity to depict the agonies of the human soul. But Mansfield felt that Chekhov knew as well as Dostoyevsky the agonies of consciousness, and he retained a capacity to respond to the outside world; he acknowledged a need to write and live simultaneously with one's recognitions, as her letters insisted: "externally & during the day one smiles and chats & says one has had a pretty rotten time, perhaps – but God! God! Tchekhov would understand: Dostoyevsky wouldn't." She often quoted Chekhov as the oracle about both writing and life, and she prominently placed, in her journal for February 1921, his statement: "They say philosophers and the truly wise are indifferent. It is false: indifference is the paralysis of the soul; it is premature death."

She came to identify personally with Chekhov – both were tubercular; both attuned to the casual coexistence of violently different inner and outer worlds; both dependent on others although painfully and resolutely alone. As she felt increasingly that her ailments were as much of the soul as of the body, she wrote Koteliansky that, although she would try to get well in any way she could, "If I *do* die perhaps there will be a small private heaven for consumptives only. In that case I shall see Tchekhov."

Most of Mansfield's waning energy went into her stories. Ida Baker, with whom she lived for much of late 1920 and 1921, records two periods of astonishing and feverish activity dedicated to fiction, one at Menton from October through mid December 1920 and the other at Montana-sur-Sierre in the French Alps from July through November 1921. Murry still visited her often, and she wrote him constantly, although in early 1921 she was angry at him because he had not told her about his affair with Princess Bibesco in London. Although Mansfield was no longer interested in sex, she could still be jealous and required the alternating devotions of both Murry and Baker. In her own way Mansfield memorialized both of them. Baker is characterized as one of two sisters in "The Daughters of the Late Colonel," a long tale of two middle-aged women who have devoted their whole lives to a tyrannical father. After his death they still cannot believe that he is gone and refer all their actions and decisions to what he would have wanted. Through this potentially comic framework, Mansfield shows brilliantly the sufferings and deprivations of two women who, emotionally, have not lived at all.

A late portrait of Murry is visible in "The Man Without a Temperament," written just slightly earlier. Set at a holiday resort in the south of France, the story poses familiar and satiric stereotypes of European vacationers against an invalid woman (whom two years at the resort will either cure or kill) and her apparently calm, gentle, protective husband. The story works through the compression and force of its imagery. The invalid woman, as she strolls through the garden, sees that "out of the thick, fleshy leaves of a cactus there rose an aloe stem loaded with pale flowers that looked as though they had been cut out of butter; . . . over a bed of scarlet waxen flowers some big black insects 'zoom-zoomed'; a great, gaudy creeper, orange splashed with jet, sprawled against the wall." Such images contrast with those of early snow, moonlight, and small wild flowers that the woman recalls in flashback scenes of earlier days in London. The wild floral imagery all signifies decay and over-ripeness, the woman's sense of the victory of disease and of her impending death. Even the undiscerning vacationers around begin to notice something sterile in the husband's overprotectiveness, his calm measurements of routine, and the antiseptic quality of his politeness. All forms of description, nature, and character convey the woman's knowledge that just as she shows signs of physical decay, her husband represents the decay or absence of emotion, of relationship. The story reaches a frightening climax at night in the bedroom, done in antiseptic cold white. The two are asleep, but the sound of a mosquito trapped in the netting of her bed awakens the husband. He gets out of bed and kills the mosquito. Then as he leans over protectively and kisses her gently, he whispers, "Rot!" The rot is in her health, their marriage, and the emptiness of his emotional life – equivalent deaths.

Other effective late stories, like "The Singing Lesson" and "Her First Ball," quickly and rhythmically recount emotional resurrection after disillusioning circumstance. Although simple in outline and situation, these stories carry force in their compressed presentation of the determination of the young central characters to hold on to pleasure. Social issues are more visible than ever in some of the later fiction. In "A Cup of Tea" a young London wife forgoes buying an expensive antique box out of social guilt and brings home a pretty young beggar-woman for tea instead. She regards her encounter with the beggar as talismanic, "like something out of a novel by Dostoyevsky, this meeting in the dusk." But when her husband returns and finds the beggar-woman "astonishingly pretty," the wife forgoes her social concern and manipulates her husband into promising to give her the money for the expensive antique box, an artifact of class.

The long last version of the New Zealand family, "The Garden Party," significantly adds social dimensions to an understanding of family rivalries and dynamics. Here, in one of Mansfield's best-known and most frequently reprinted stories, Laura recognizes from the beginning the sensitivity of the workmen who come to put up the tent for the party. Her shock at hearing of the death of another workman, a carter who lives just a street away, propels Laura into wanting to stop the garden party. Her conventional family, thinking Laura's concern is as "extravagant" as she feels their insistence on having the party is, prevails – and the party continues. But when she visits the family of the dead man and brings them useless leftovers from the party, she understands the pains and identities across unbridgeable social gulfs, the "extravagant" human connections.

The irresolvable suspension of human emotion between self and otherness adds to the recognition of irremediable class distinctions, a social concern in one of Mansfield's most deeply Chekhovian stories. In tone and treatment some of the late stories move into more twentieth-century forms of social satire. In "Marriage à la Mode" Mansfield follows an earnest, hard-working young man as he collects fruit for his children and rushes to make the train for the country retreat he has established so selflessly. When he arrives he finds his wife and her pretentious, artsy friends so immersed in their trivial social activities that they scarcely have time to notice him. They are condescending spongers in a satire that, though more understated and less outrageous than the fiction of Evelyn Waugh, is just as astringent about the new social order that both replaces and feeds on the world of the Edwardian bourgeoisie.

Apparently Mansfield's last completed story, "The Fly" was finished in February 1922 and operates almost entirely through metaphor. Two old men in the city refer to their sons, killed in the war. One, the more feeble, is cared for by his daughters and mourns only when alone. He becomes absorbed in watching a fly that has fallen into the inkpot. After he flicks the fly out and onto a piece of blotting paper, he watches with fascination as the fly attempts to shake its limbs free of the large drop of ink. The old man deliberately repeats the process, admiring and torturing the fly with successive ink blots until the fly is dead. The story has drawn more explication than has any other, and it has been read as a metaphor of the torture of the youn-

ger generation by the war, as a figurative tableau of capitalistic exploitation of struggling life, as an emblem of Mansfield's vigorous and successful father who long outlived both his only son and his artist daughter, or as an echo of a Chekhov story in which a poor office clerk tortures a cockroach in futile rebellion against his boss. None of these readings, of course, contradicts others, yet the image of the determined fly in what is finally always a futile struggle to free itself of viscous circumstance can stand as an image of both Mansfield's life and the tensions of her achievements in fiction.

For in her last year she became interested in signs of the Russian "soul" being incorporated therapeutically into western European culture. She sought first the treatment of a Dr. Manoukhin, which used "cosmic anatomy" and doctrines of the occult. She failed to develop that faith, and she then joined the emigré Greek, then Russian, George Gurdjieff at the Institute for the Harmonious Development of Man, which he established at Fontainebleau, a community he established to follow his teachings. Less than three months after she entered his Institute, she died of a massive tubercular hemorrhage.

But with the publication of highly praised volumes of her short stories in December 1920 and February 1922, Mansfield's reputation as a writer of brilliantly compressed short fiction had been well established by the time of her death. Later collections of short stories in 1923 and in 1924 sustained her reputation, as well as publication of her *Poems* (1923), of *The Journal of Katherine Mansfield* (1927, with the definitive edition published in 1954), of a selection from her letters (1928), and the fullest possible collection of her stories in 1937. All these, as well as later editions of her "scrapbooks" and further letters, were edited by Murry. The scraps and pieces in which she left both literary and personal material, as well as what was often a virtually illegible handwriting, made publication slow and difficult. New material and further letters have surfaced during the years, enough that Alpers, having published the most comprehensive biography of Mansfield possible in 1953, could justify completely rewriting and publishing a more informed biography in 1980. The full, collected letters edited by Vincent O'Sullivan and Margaret Scott have taken longer to complete – the third of a projected four volumes appeared in 1993.

Murry, as editor of Mansfield's work, was scrupulous in printing what he thought he could and throwing nothing away. He preserved both what he felt he could not print (more often because it might be damaging to Mansfield than because it might damage his own reputation) and what Mansfield had asked him to destroy. His own attempts to manipulate reception of Mansfield and sanctify everything about her, however, was another matter. He was elaborate, pretentious, full of self-pity for the ways in which his service for Mansfield altered and impeded his own career, and he was often dogmatically moralistic about Mansfield's virtues in ways that she had not been. In his introduction to the 1930 American edition of *Stories by Katherine Mansfield,* for example, he insisted that the "essential" quality of her work was "a kind of *purity,*" not only one of style or vision but of her whole life, her absolute fidelity "to some spirit of truth which she served."

Yet despite such sanctified pomposities, the high critical estimate in which Mansfield's work is held has never substantially changed but has only broadened and expanded through the years with the discovery of further materials and information. Even the grounds on which she has been considered and praised have not substantially altered: the remarkable capacity to describe flowers, plants, and animals in ways that are simultaneously naturalistic and symbolic; the astringent satire of character that also shows a penetrating understanding; the depiction of the complexity of human relationships, particularly overt and covert sexual relationships; the Chekhovian qualities; the themes that insist on the contemporary, on using the past to establish connections to the immediate and the present. Above all, Mansfield has consistently been praised for the compression and understatement of her prose, for her capacity to pack complex emotion and thought into the deceptively simple and direct outlines of her stories. Her work has for many years been seen as a model of the specifically modern short story in English and of the changes in literary focus it represents.

Letters:

The Letters of Katherine Mansfield, edited by J. M. Murry (2 volumes, London: Constable, 1928; 1 volume, New York: Knopf, 1929);

Katherine Mansfield's Letters to John Middleton Murry, 1913–1922, edited by Murry (London: Constable / New York: Knopf, 1951);

The Collected Letters of Katherine Mansfield, edited by Vincent O'Sullivan and Margaret Scott, 3 volumes (Oxford: Clarendon Press, 1984, 1987, 1993–).

Bibliographies:

Ruth Elvish Mantz, *The Critical Bibliography of Katherine Mansfield* (London: Constable, 1931);

B. J. Kirkpatrick, *A Bibliography of Katherine Mansfield* (Oxford: Clarendon Press, 1989).

Biographies:

Ruth Elvish Mantz and J. M. Murry, *The Life of Katherine Mansfield* (London: Constable, 1933);

Murry, *Between Two Worlds* (London: Cape, 1935; New York: Messner, 1936);

Antony Alpers, *Katherine Mansfield: A Biography* (London: Cape, 1953);

Ida Baker, *Katherine Mansfield: The Memories of L. M.* (London: M. Joseph, 1971);

Jeffrey Meyers, *Katherine Mansfield: A Biography* (London: Hamish Hamilton, 1978);

John Carswell, *Lives and Letters: A. R. Orage, Katherine Mansfield, Beatrice Hastings, John Middleton Murry, S. S. Koteliansky, 1906–1957* (London: Faber & Faber, 1978);

Alpers, *The Life of Katherine Mansfield* (London: Cape, 1980; New York: Viking, 1980);

Claire Tomalin, *Katherine Mansfield: A Secret Life* (London & New York: Viking, 1987).

References:

Sylvia Berkman, *Katherine Mansfield: A Critical Study* (New Haven: Yale University Press, 1951);

Elizabeth Bowen, "A Living Writer," *Cornhill Magazine,* 1010 (Winter 1956–1957): 121–134;

C. A. Hankin, *Katherine Mansfield and her Confessional Stories* (New York: St. Martin's Press, 1983);

Marvin Magalaner, *The Fiction of Katherine Mansfield* (Carbondale, Ill.: Southern Illinois University Press, 1971);

Vincent O'Sullivan, *Katherine Mansfield's New Zealand* (Auckland: Golden Press, 1974);

O'Sullivan, "The Magnetic Chain: Notes and Approaches to K. M.," *Landfall: The New Zealand Quarterly,* 114 (June 1975): 95–131;

Elisabeth Schneider, "Katherine Mansfield and Chekhov," *Modern Language Notes,* 50 (June 1935): 394–396.

Papers:

The principal collection of Mansfield letters and manuscripts is in the Alexander Turnbull Library, now part of the National Library in Wellington, New Zealand. A few letters are in the possession of Antony Alpers and of Colin Middleton Murry, J. M. Murry's son. Substantial collections of Mansfield materials exist at the Henry W. and Albert A. Berg Collection of the New York Public Library; the British Library, London; the Mitchell Library, Sydney; the Smith College Library Rare Book Room, Northampton, Massachusetts; the Stanford University Library; the Strachey Trust, London; the Library of Sussex University; and the Harry Ransom Humanities Research Center of the University of Texas at Austin.

W. Somerset Maugham

(25 January 1874 – 16 December 1965)

Archie K. Loss
Penn State University—Erie (The Behrend College)

See also the Maugham entries in *DLB 10: Modern British Dramatists, 1900–1945*; *DLB 36: British Novelists, 1890–1929: Modernists*; *DLB 77: British Mystery Writers, 1920–1939*; and *DLB 100: Modern British Essayists, Second Series.*

BOOKS: *Liza of Lambeth* (London: Unwin, 1897; revised, 1904; New York: Doran, [1921]);

The Making of a Saint (London: Unwin, 1898; Boston: Page, 1898);

Orientations (London: Unwin, 1899);

The Hero (London: Hutchinson, 1901);

Mrs. Craddock (London: Heinemann, 1902; revised, 1955; New York: Doran, 1920);

A Man of Honour: A Play in Four Acts (London: Chapman & Hall, 1903); republished as *A Man of Honour: A Tragedy in Four Acts* (Chicago: Dramatic Publishing, [1903]);

The Merry-Go-Round (London: Heinemann, 1904);

The Land of the Blessed Virgin: Sketches and Impressions in Andalusia (London: Heinemann, 1905; New York: Knopf, 1920); republished as *Andalusia: Sketches and Impressions* (New York: Knopf, 1920);

The Bishop's Apron: A Study in the Origins of a Great Family (London: Chapman & Hall, 1906);

The Explorer (London: Heinemann, 1908 [i.e., 1907]; New York: Baker & Taylor, 1909);

The Magician (London: Heinemann, 1908; New York: Duffield, 1909);

Lady Frederick: A Comedy in Three Acts (London: Heinemann, 1912 [i.e., 1911]; Chicago: Dramatic Publishing, 1912?);

Jack Straw: A Farce in Three Acts (London: Heinemann, 1912 [i.e., 1911]; Chicago: Dramatic Publishing, 1912);

Mrs. Dot: A Farce in Three Acts (London: Heinemann, 1912; Chicago: Dramatic Publishing, 1912);

Penelope: A Comedy in Three Acts (London: Heinemann, 1912; Chicago: Dramatic Publishing, 1912);

W. Somerset Maugham (photograph by Mark Gerson)

The Explorer: A Melodrama in Four Acts (London: Heinemann, 1912; Chicago: Dramatic Publishing, 1912);

The Tenth Man: A Tragic Comedy in Three Acts (London: Heinemann, 1913; Chicago: Dramatic Publishing, 1913);

Landed Gentry: A Comedy in Four Acts (London: Heinemann, 1913; Chicago: Dramatic Publishing, 1913);

The Land of Promise: A Comedy in Four Acts (London: Bickers, 1913);

Smith: A Comedy in Four Acts (London: Heinemann, 1913; Chicago: Dramatic Publishing, [1913?]);

Of Human Bondage (London: Heinemann, 1915; New York: Doran, 1915);

The Moon and Sixpence (London: Heinemann, 1919; New York: Doran, 1919);

The Unknown: A Play in Three Acts (London: Heinemann, 1920; New York: Doran, 1920);

The Circle: A Comedy in Three Acts (London: Heinemann, 1921; New York: Doran, [1921]);

The Trembling of a Leaf: Little Stories of the South Sea Islands (New York: Doran, 1921; London: Heinemann, 1921); republished as *Sadie Thompson, and Other Stories of the South Sea Islands* (London: Readers Library, [1928]);

Caesar's Wife: A Comedy in Three Acts (London: Heinemann, 1922; New York: Doran, 1923);

East of Suez: A Play in Seven Scenes (London: Heinemann, 1922; New York: Doran, 1922);

The Land of Promise: A Comedy in Four Acts (London: Heinemann, 1922; New York: Doran, 1923);

On a Chinese Screen (London: Heinemann, 1922; New York: Doran, 1922);

Our Betters: A Comedy in Three Acts (London: Heinemann, 1923; New York: Doran, 1923);

The Unattainable: A Farce in Three Acts (London: Heinemann, 1923);

Home and Beauty: A Farce in Three Acts (London: Heinemann, 1923);

Loaves and Fishes: A Comedy in Four Acts (London: Heinemann, 1924);

The Letter: A Play in Three Acts (New York: Doran, [1925]; London: Heinemann, [1927]);

The Painted Veil (London: Heinemann, 1925; New York: Doran, 1925);

The Casuarina Tree: Six Stories (London: Heinemann, 1926; New York: Doran, 1926); republished as *The Letter: Stories of Crime* (London & Glasgow: Collins, 1930);

The Constant Wife: A Comedy in Three Acts (New York: Doran, [1927]; London: Heinemann, 1927);

Ashenden: or, The British Agent (London: Heinemann, 1928; Garden City, N.Y.: Doubleday, Doran, 1928);

The Sacred Flame: A Play in Three Acts (Garden City, N.Y.: Doubleday, Doran, 1928; London: Heinemann, 1929);

The Bread-Winner: A Comedy in One Act (London: Heinemann, [1930]); republished as *The Breadwinner: A Comedy* (Garden City, N.Y.: Doubleday, Doran, 1931);

The Gentleman in the Parlour: A Record of a Journey from Rangoon to Haiphong (London: Heinemann, [1930]; Garden City, N.Y.: Doubleday, Doran, 1930);

Cakes and Ale: or, The Skeleton in the Cupboard (London: Heinemann, 1930; Garden City, N.Y.: Doubleday, Doran, 1930);

Six Stories Written in the First Person Singular (Garden City, N.Y.: Doubleday, Doran, 1931; London: Heinemann, 1931);

The Book-Bag (Florence, Italy: Orioli, 1932);

The Narrow Corner (London: Heinemann, 1932; Garden City, N.Y.: Doubleday, Doran, 1932);

For Services Rendered: A Play in Three Acts (London: Heinemann, 1932; Garden City, N.Y.: Doubleday, Doran, 1933);

Ah King (Garden City, N.Y.: Doubleday, Doran, 1933); republished as *Ah King: Six Stories* (London: Heinemann, [1933]);

Sheppey: A Play in Three Acts (London: Heinemann, 1933);

Don Fernando; or, Variations on Some Spanish Themes (London & Toronto: Heinemann, [1935]; Garden City, N.Y.: Doubleday, Doran, 1935; revised edition, Melbourne, London & Toronto: Heinemann, 1950);

My South Sea Island (Chicago: Abramson, 1936);

Cosmopolitans: Very Short Stories (London & Toronto: Heinemann, 1936); republished as *Cosmopolitans* (Garden City, N.Y.: Doubleday, Doran, 1936);

Theatre: A Novel (Garden City, N.Y.: Doubleday, Doran, 1937; London & Toronto: Heinemann, 1937);

The Summing Up (London & Toronto: Heinemann, 1938; Garden City, N.Y.: Doubleday, Doran, 1938);

Princess September and the Nightingale (London & New York: Oxford University Press, 1939);

Christmas Holiday (London & Toronto: Heinemann, [1939]; Garden City, N.Y.: Doubleday, Doran, 1939);

France at War (London: Heinemann, 1940; New York: Doubleday, Doran, 1940);

Books and You (London & Toronto: Heinemann, 1940; New York: Doubleday, Doran, 1940);

The Mixture As Before (London & Toronto: Heinemann, 1940; New York: Doubleday, Doran, 1940);

Up at the Villa (New York: Doubleday, Doran, 1941; London & Toronto: Heinemann, 1941);

Strictly Personal (Garden City, N.Y.: Doubleday, Doran, 1941; London & Toronto: Heinemann, 1942);

The Outstation: A Story, edited by Max Moser (Bern, Switzerland: Francke, [1942]);

The Hour Before the Dawn: A Novel (Garden City, N.Y.: Doubleday, Doran, 1942; Sydney & London: Angus & Robertson, 1945);

The Unconquered (New York: House of Books, 1944);

The Razor's Edge: A Novel (Garden City, N.Y.: Doubleday, Doran, 1944; London & Toronto: Heinemann, 1944);

Then and Now: A Novel (London & Toronto: Heinemann, 1946; Garden City, N.Y.: Doubleday, 1946); republished as *Fools and Their Folly* (New York: Avon, [1949]);

Creatures of Circumstance (London & Toronto: Heinemann, 1947; Garden City, N.Y.: Doubleday, 1947);

Catalina: A Romance (London: Heinemann, 1948; Garden City, N.Y.: Doubleday, 1948);

Here and There: Short Stories (Melbourne, London & Toronto: Heinemann, 1948);

Great Novelists and Their Novels: Essays on the Ten Greatest Novels of the World and the Men and Women Who Wrote Them (Philadelphia & Toronto: Winston, 1948); revised and enlarged as *Ten Novels and Their Authors* (London: Heinemann, 1954); republished as *The Art of Fiction: An Introduction to Ten Novels and Their Authors* (Garden City, N.Y.: Doubleday, 1955);

A Writer's Notebook (London: Heinemann, 1949; Garden City, N.Y.: Doubleday, 1949);

The Writer's Point of View (London: Cambridge University Press, 1951);

The World Over: Stories of Manifold Places and People (Garden City, N.Y.: Doubleday, 1952);

The Constant Wife: A Comedy in Three Acts (Garden City, N.Y.: Doubleday, 1952);

Encore: Original Stories by W. Somerset Maugham, Screenplays by T. E. B. Clarke, Arthur Macrae, Eric Ambler (Garden City, N.Y.: Doubleday, 1952);

The Vagrant Mood: Six Essays (London: Heinemann, 1952; Garden City, N.Y.: Doubleday, 1953);

Selected Novels, 3 volumes (London: Heinemann, 1953);

The Partial View (London: Heinemann, [1954]) – comprises *The Summing Up* and *A Writer's Notebook*;

The Magician: A Novel, Together with A Fragment of Autobiography (London: Heinemann, 1956); republished as *The Magician: Together with A Fragment of Autobiography* (Garden City, N.Y.: Doubleday, 1957);

Points of View (London: Heinemann, 1958; Garden City, N.Y.: Doubleday, 1959);

Purely for My Pleasure (London: Heinemann, 1962; Garden City, N.Y.: Doubleday, 1962);

Selected Prefaces and Introductions of W. Somerset Maugham (Garden City, N.Y.: Doubleday, 1963).

Collections: *The Collected Plays,* 3 volumes (London: Heinemann, 1931);

The Collected Edition of the Works of W. Somerset Maugham, 35 volumes (London: Heinemann, 1931–1969);

Altogether: Being the Collected Stories of W. Somerset Maugham (London: Heinemann, 1934); republished as *East and West: The Collected Short Stories of W. Somerset Maugham* (Garden City, N.Y.: Doubleday, Doran, 1934);

The Complete Short Stories of W. Somerset Maugham (3 volumes, London: Heinemann, 1951; 2 volumes, Garden City, N.Y.: Doubleday, 1952);

The Works of W. Somerset Maugham, 45 volumes (New York: Arno, 1977).

OTHER: *The Traveller's Library,* compiled, with an introduction, by Maugham (Garden City, N.Y.: Doubleday, Doran, 1933); republished as *Fifty Modern English Writers* (Garden City, N.Y.: Doubleday, Doran, 1933);

Tellers of Tales: 100 Short Stories from the United States, England, France, Russia and Germany, compiled, with an introduction, by Maugham (New York: Doubleday, Doran, 1939); republished as *The Greatest Stories of All Times: Tellers of Tales* (Garden City, N.Y.: Garden City Publishing, 1943);

Great Modern Reading: W. Somerset Maugham's Introduction to Modern English and American Literature, compiled by Maugham (Garden City, N.Y.: Doubleday, 1943);

Charles Dickens, *David Copperfield,* edited by Maugham (Philadelphia: Winston, 1948);

Henry Fielding, *The History of Tom Jones, A Foundling,* edited by Maugham (Philadelphia: Winston, 1948);

Jane Austen, *Pride and Prejudice,* edited by Maugham (Philadelphia: Winston, 1949);

Honoré de Balzac, *Old Man Goriot,* edited by Maugham (Philadelphia: Winston, 1949);

Marie Henri Beyle, *The Red and the Black,* edited by Maugham (Philadelphia: Winston, 1949);

Emily Brontë, *Wuthering Heights,* edited by Maugham (Philadelphia: Winston, 1949);

Fyodor Mikhaylovich Dostoyevsky, *The Brothers Karamazov,* edited by Maugham (Philadelphia: Winston, 1949);

Gustave Flaubert, *Madame Bovary,* edited by Maugham (Philadelphia: Winston, 1949);

Rudyard Kipling, *A Choice of Kipling's Prose,* compiled, with an introduction, by Maugham (London: Macmillan, 1952);

Raymond Mander and Joe Mitchenson, *The Artist and the Theatre: The Story of the Paintings Collected and Presented to the National Theatre by W. Somerset Maugham,* with an introduction by Maugham (London: Heinemann, 1955).

PLAY PRODUCTIONS: *Schiffbrüchig,* Berlin, Schall and Rauch, 3 January 1902;

A Man of Honour: A Tragedy in Four Acts, London, Imperial Theatre, 22 February 1903;

Mademoiselle Zampa, London, Avenue Theatre, 18 February 1904;

Lady Frederick: A Comedy in Three Acts, London, Royal Court Theatre, 26 October 1907;

Jack Straw: A Farce in Three Acts, London, Vaudeville Theatre, 26 March 1908;

Mrs. Dot: A Farce in Three Acts, London, Comedy Theatre, 27 April 1908;

The Explorer: A Melodrama in Four Acts, London, Lyric Theatre, 13 June 1908; revised production, London, Lyric Theatre, 19 May 1909;

Penelope: A Comedy in Three Acts, London, Comedy Theatre, 9 January 1909;

The Noble Spaniard, adapted from Ernest Grenet-Dancourt's *Les Gaités du veuvage,* London, New Royalty Theatre, 20 March 1909;

Smith: A Comedy in Four Acts, London, Comedy Theatre, 30 September 1909;

The Tenth Man: A Tragic Comedy in Three Acts, London, Globe Theatre, 24 February 1910;

Grace, London, Duke of York's Theatre, 15 October 1910;

Loaves and Fishes: A Comedy in Four Acts, London, Duke of York's Theatre, 24 February 1911;

The Perfect Gentleman, adapted from Molière's *Le Bourgeois Gentilhomme,* London, His Majesty's Theatre, 27 May 1913;

The Land of Promise: A Comedy in Four Acts, New York, Lyceum Theater, 25 December 1913; London, Duke of York's Theatre, 26 February 1914;

Caroline, London, New Theatre, 8 February 1916;

Our Betters: A Comedy in Three Acts, New York, Hudson Theater, 12 March 1917; London, Globe Theatre, 12 September 1923;

Love in a Cottage, London, Globe Theatre, 26 January 1918;

Caesar's Wife: A Comedy in Three Acts, London, Royalty Theatre, 27 March 1919;

Home and Beauty, Atlantic City, N.J., Globe Theater, 4 August 1919; London, Playhouse, 30 August 1919; produced again as *Too Many Husbands,* New York, Booth Theater, 8 October 1919;

The Unknown: A Play in Three Acts, London, Aldwych Theatre, 9 August 1920;

The Circle: A Comedy in Three Acts, London, Haymarket Theatre, 3 March 1921;

East of Suez: A Play in Seven Scenes, London, His Majesty's Theatre, 2 September 1922;

The Camel's Back, New York, Vanderbilt Theater, 13 November 1923; London, Playhouse, 31 January 1924;

The Constant Wife: A Comedy in Thee Acts, New York, Maxine Elliot's Theater, 29 November 1926; London, Strand Theatre, 6 April 1927;

The Letter: A Play in Three Acts, London, Playhouse, 24 February 1927;

The Sacred Flame: A Play in Three Acts, New York, Henry Miller's Theater, 19 November 1928; London, Playhouse, 8 February 1929;

The Breadwinner: A Comedy in One Act, London, Vaudeville Theatre, 30 September 1930;

For Services Rendered: A Play in Three Acts, London, Globe Theatre, 1 November 1932;

The Mask and the Face, adapted from Luigi Chiarelli's *La Maschere e il volto,* New York, Fifty-Second Street Theater, 8 May 1933;

Sheppey: A Play in Three Acts, London, Wyndham's Theatre, 14 September 1933.

The most important events in the life of William Somerset Maugham were those over which he had no control. Like one of the characters in his fiction or drama, Maugham was dealt an imperfect hand. Certain facts shaped the course of his life as a child and as an adult — the death of his mother when he was barely eight years old; the death of his father two years later; his adoption by a childless uncle and aunt; his stammer, which made ordinary communication difficult; and his homosexuality. The first he could never overcome; the last he could never forget. All decisively influenced the direction of his life.

Perhaps most important of all was the fact that he was born in Paris on 25 January 1874, the fourth son of an English lawyer who handled the affairs of the British embassy. France was to become the place where he spent most of his life — as did his father and his mother, who had grown up there. One reason he wrote so much about exiles was that, in a literal sense, he was an exile: an Englishman born in a foreign country, one whose language became the first he was to know and whose culture became fundamental to his adult life. Exile largely explains his own peripatetic life, as Maugham deliberately set out to see as much of the world as he could, seeking material to write about in short stories, novels, and plays. The subject matter most associated with his name became the life of British colonials in the East, which he knew firsthand from his travels. His travels were also an escape from a style of life that he could not always accommodate.

His first trip across the sea, however, was not an escape so much as a forced departure. After a happy infancy and early childhood in a family that had lived comfortably, even somewhat extravagantly, in France, Maugham crossed the English Channel to a different sort of life after the death of his mother and father. The death of his mother was undoubtedly the most significant event of his childhood, as for years afterward he could not write about it without strongly conveying the sense of pain it had caused him.

Maugham's Uncle Henry, to whom young Maugham's care was entrusted, was vicar of the parish of All Saints in Whitstable, Kent, a seaside town. Life with the vicar and his German-born wife, Sophie, was stable and secure; the house had great charm, and the town of Whitstable was in most respects a pleasant community in which to grow up. The lifestyle of a vicar in such a parish was not grand, but it was not excessively poor either. There was always food to eat and a servant to help with the cooking; there was also no question about sending young Willie off to school. Perhaps the problem at Whitstable was that the vicar and his wife were childless; Willie came into their lives long after they had decided, or had let God decide, that they would not have children. Willie's aunt cared for him, but the vicar was her primary concern.

Cut off from the culture in which he had grown up, and separated from the nurse to whom he had been much attached before being left parentless, Willie drew into himself. He began to read copiously from his uncle's library (one of the best features of the house), developing a habit that was to last for a lifetime. Wherever Maugham traveled in his later years, he took with him a plentiful supply of books.

When it was time for Willie to go away to school, it was only natural for his uncle to choose a school that would prepare him to enter the church. There was no better course for a boy with little income yet of a genteel class. King's School in Canterbury was affiliated with the Church of England and was popular with its clergy. Willie entered there in May 1885; it was to be one of the most miserable experiences of his life.

There Maugham endured so many of the events common to the school experiences of other writers of his generation that he seems to have followed a formula: he had a bad stammer that other boys liked to imitate; he was extremely shy; he was not good at games. In addition, to his detriment with the masters at the school, he was an uneven student – not indifferent, certainly not unintelligent, but inconsistent. He had great trouble making friends, and when he did manage to make them, he became so possessive that he choked off the relationship before it could develop.

It is also probable that at King's School Maugham first realized his homosexuality. The English public school has always been viewed both as a place where the future leaders of England are cultivated and as a hotbed of homoeroticism. Maugham's personal experiences were probably closer to those described in Evelyn Waugh's *Decline and Fall* (1928) than to those in James Hilton's *Goodbye Mr. Chips* (1934). Whether he were in school or not, however, his homosexuality would undoubtedly have emerged; the presence of comely adolescent boys merely precipitated what was for him a natural sexual urge. However unexceptional, Maugham's homosexuality was bound to be frustrating at school since it likely remained unexpressed.

With an assertion of the same will that was ultimately to lead him to declare that he was a writer, Maugham eventually determined that he would not stay on at King's. Some of his independence derived from the fact that his father's bequest, meager though it was, provided for his keep, but young Maugham had a single-mindedness that was to remain one of his strongest positive qualities. His uncle was not happy with Maugham's decision to leave the school, but Maugham had made up his mind. After recuperating from a bout of pleurisy in the south of France, he decided to go to Germany to attend the University of Heidelberg. The pattern of exile asserted itself for the first time in adolescent Maugham, who traveled in this instance to the country where his aunt Sophie had been born.

His experiences at Heidelberg were valuable to Maugham in several respects, but probably the most important personal experience of the trip was his first homosexual affair – with the English aesthete Ellingham Brooks, later fictionalized as the character Hayward in Maugham's novel *Of Human Bondage* (1915). With this experience Maugham acknowledged his homosexuality; all of the repressed longings of school days found expression, however briefly, in this affair with a dilettante who was able to perceive beauty in the work of others but not to express it in his own. Maugham's first exposure to the German philosopher Arthur Schopenhauer and Norwegian playwright Henrik Ibsen perhaps had more enduring effects, though his dislike of German life led to an aversion to that country that lasted for the rest of his life.

Back in England after the experience of Heidelberg and seeking some profession, Maugham eventually decided on medical school and enrolled at St. Thomas's Hospital in London. His choice, however, represented another paradox in his life, for he entered medical studies knowing that he really wanted to be a writer. The study of medicine, Maugham decided, would be a form of insurance: if writing failed, medicine would always be there to provide a living. His practical side never showed itself more plainly.

In the same year that he passed his medical exams he brought out with some success his first novel, *Liza of Lambeth* (1897), thus satisfying the agreement he had made with himself. Although licensed to practice medicine, Maugham decided, on the strength of one modest success as a novelist, that he would practice writing instead. He approached writing in the same spirit that he had approached a medical career: it was for him a choice of profession. If he had known how difficult it would prove to establish himself firmly, perhaps he would have chosen differently.

As a novelist and short-story writer he faltered for the next few years. He lacked appropriate subject matter on which to exercise his skills, and none of his fiction had much success. At the same time, however, he was beginning to experiment with the form that made his reputation – drama. That experimentation finally bore fruit in 1907, when his play *Lady Frederick* became a comedy hit. By the middle of 1908 he had four plays running at the same time in the West End, and Maugham was to become one of the most successful playwrights in the history of British drama.

In 1911 Maugham first met Syrie Barnardo Wellcome, the daughter of a founder of Victorian homes for foundlings and the unhappy wife of a man much older than she. Maugham felt drawn to her, but until she could get a divorce from her husband, the relationship seemed unpromising. Eventually, however, she became pregnant by Maugham and gave birth to their daughter, Liza, in 1915 – by which time Wellcome had secured her divorce and was able to marry Maugham. His motives in marrying her by then had less to do with real affection than with what he considered appropriate behavior

under the circumstances of her pregnancy, and, not surprising, their marriage in 1917 would finally end in divorce – for which she would file in 1927. By then Maugham's years of success would enable him to settle upon her a substantial income when their divorce became final in 1929.

Despite his growing success as a playwright as the first decade of the twentieth century closed, Maugham's artistic interest was returning to the form with which he had started his writing career. Putting aside his theatrical commitments, he began to examine a subject he had tried to treat before but had done so with no success: an account of the growth and development of a young man like himself, orphaned at an early age and forced to live with a childless uncle and aunt. It was a difficult and time-consuming subject for Maugham to deal with, but the result was his finest achievement, *Of Human Bondage,* which first appeared in 1915 to a world much preoccupied by other, larger events. In August 1914 World War I had begun.

It may seem somewhat out of character for Maugham, a successful writer, afflicted with a terrible shyness, to volunteer for the ambulance service in France, but the gesture illustrates his desire for respectability and public approval. Many writers and artists felt powerfully drawn by the conflict, not only in England but also in Europe and the United States, and Maugham showed considerable courage in the Red Cross work he did early in the war. During his year in the trenches he also found the opportunity to meet the man with whom he was to spend much of the rest of his life, an American named Gerald Haxton, who was to be his secretary and companion.

Following Maugham's tour of duty in France, his Red Cross unit disbanded and its members scattered. He and Haxton parted for a time – Haxton returning to the United States with vague hopes of finding a job there, Maugham moving on to Rome with plans to resume his career as a playwright. There his fluency with languages and his powers of meticulous observation made Maugham, in the eyes of the British Intelligence Service, an attractive recruit for espionage operations that the agency planned to conduct in Switzerland. He agreed to serve, and his experiences in places such as Lucerne and Geneva – and later in Petrograd, Russia, where he was to accept a second assignment as a secret agent in the few months before the Russian Revolution of 1917 – proved valuable for the short stories later collected in *Ashenden: or, The British Agent* (1928). But when Maugham first developed symptoms of tuberculosis during his Switzerland assignment, the agency released him from further espionage duties there, and he returned to London. There he made plans for his first long journey to Tahiti and the Far East – a trip that, again with Haxton as his companion, provided Maugham with a rich store of experiences and characters for stories later published in *The Trembling of a Leaf: Little Stories of the South Sea Islands* (1921).

Maugham did not begin to write short fiction seriously until he had established his reputation as a dramatist and novelist. All but a few of his stories were published in *Cosmopolitan,* a popular monthly whose editor, Ray Long, gave Maugham considerable leeway in both subject matter and length. "Sometimes the stories were cut," Maugham remarks in one of his prefaces, "but I was never asked to make the smallest alteration to suit . . . the taste of the readers." Yet Maugham aimed his short fiction, like most of his work, at a broad audience, and this fact, more than the liberties granted by a particular editor or magazine, dictated much of its subject matter, form, and tone.

A group of stories not included in his collected short stories had appeared in 1899 under the title *Orientations,* and with the story "Rain" Maugham recommenced the writing of short fiction in 1919. "Rain" has become his most famous work of short fiction, anthologized many times and adapted to the stage in a production starring Jeanne Eagels and to motion pictures several times. In many ways it typifies what Maugham was to do in the form; for that reason, in addition to its popularity, it deserves close attention.

On a trip from Honolulu to Pago Pago in 1916 Maugham characteristically took notes on his fellow passengers. One was of a woman about twenty-seven years old, reputedly a prostitute who had just escaped a major raid on the red-light district of Honolulu. Two others were a medical missionary from the Gilbert Islands and his wife. The latter, Maugham said, "spoke of the depravity of the natives in a voice which nothing could hush." After noting the physical appearance of this group, Maugham sketched the following plot:

> A prostitute, flying from Honolulu after a raid, lands at Pago Pago. There lands also a missionary and his wife. Also the narrator. All are obliged to stay there owing to an outbreak of measles. The missionary finding out her profession persecutes her. He reduces her to misery, shame, and repentance, he has no mercy on her. He induces the governor to order her return to Honolulu. One morning he is found with his throat cut by his own hand and she is once more radiant and self-possessed. She looks at men and scornfully exclaims: dirty pigs.

Several things are notable in this sketch. One is how closely the story, as finally written, conforms to Maugham's notes: with little adumbration, this short paragraph could serve as an abstract of the finished tale. Indeed Maugham has already conceived the ending of the story before beginning to write it, for this is how the published version concludes: "You men! You filthy, dirty pigs! You're all the same, all of you. Pigs! Pigs!" Such emphasis on the final speech is not surprising in the work of someone who had made a success of writing drama, and it is typical of many of Maugham's short stories.

A final point, equally important to note, concerns the narrative technique. To serve as the narrator referred to in the plot sketch, Maugham creates the character of Doctor Macphail, who is traveling with his wife to Apia, where he is to spend the next year. Like Maugham, he is a physician. Like Maugham also, he has just returned from wartime duty at the front, but with "a wound that had taken longer to heal than it should." The Scotsman Macphail and his wife become acquainted with the Reverend Davidson and his wife, who are Americans. Though not, strictly speaking, a narrator, Doctor Macphail provides such a perspective.

In "Rain" Maugham does not so much tell the story of the evolving relationship between the Reverend Davidson and the prostitute, Sadie Thompson, as tell *about* it. Doctor Macphail becomes the filter through which the events of the story are sifted; his comments determine the reader's sense of what is happening. When he finally tries to act on Sadie's behalf, he is showing the kind of charity that Davidson should show, and, when Sadie utters her famous final line, only Doctor Macphail fully understands what she means.

This strategy has a distancing effect, partly for the sake of irony but also, it seems, to make direct treatment of the subject of the story unnecessary. As a result, the reader adopts the emotional disposition of the doctor; the main events of the story are happening somewhere else, and Macphail's judgments are the ticket of admission. One way or another, this approach to storytelling characterizes much of Maugham's short fiction.

This is not to suggest that Maugham adopts characteristically modern techniques of distancing or indirection. In fact, in his preface to the first volume of the collected short stories he questions the effectiveness of such techniques. Taking as his target the short stories of Anton Chekhov, then especially popular, he remarks: "If a short story is a piece of prose dealing with more or less imaginary

Page from the manuscript for Maugham's best-known short story

persons no one wrote better short stories than Chekhov. If, however, as some think, it should be the representation of an action, complete in itself and of a certain limited length, he leaves something to be desired."

Maugham's models in short fiction are of a different kind, and this separates him from many of the mainstream short-fiction writers of this century.

The French writer Guy de Maupassant in particular served Maugham as an example of what could be achieved in the genre. While acknowledging de Maupassant's many shortcomings as an artist, including superficiality of character development, Maugham's preface to his *Complete Short Stories* (1951) goes on to note what makes de Maupassant a good writer of short fiction:

Maupassant's stories are good stories. The anecdote is interesting apart from the narration so that it would gain attention if it were told over the dinner table; and that seems to me a very great merit indeed. . . . These stories have a beginning, a middle and an end. They do not wander along an uncertain line so that you cannot see whither they are leading, but follow without hesitation, from exposition to climax, a bold and vigorous curve.

This description sums up the qualities Maugham sought to incorporate in his own stories: a story "told," frequently in the first person, and not an experience re-created; a clear plot line, following what was then the usual strategy of popular drama and short fiction; and a decisive climax that, if successfully done, seems to be somehow inevitable.

While Maugham is as quick to praise what he likes in Chekhov – "concision," "the intimate feeling of a place," and characters "with a strange and unearthly life" – his own work is clearly in another mold. In stories like "Rain" the results can be quite satisfying; in less engaging stories Maugham's criticism of de Maupassant – "a simplification of character which is effective enough in a short story, but on reflection leaves you unconvinced" – applies all too well to his own work.

Most of the stories of the 1920s – those collected in *The Trembling of a Leaf* and *The Casuarina Tree* (1926) – are set in the Far East (specifically in Malaysia) or in the South Pacific. In the literature of British colonialism Maugham's Eastern stories fall chronologically after those of Rudyard Kipling and Joseph Conrad (writers whose careers had both effectively ended by the beginning of the 1920s) and before those of George Orwell, Evelyn Waugh, and Graham Greene. They are contemporaneous with E. M. Forster's *Passage to India* (1924), which, while not short fiction, provides an illuminating comparison with what Maugham was writing.

While Maugham's work lacks the moral complexity of Forster's, the two share skepticism about the white presence in the Eastern Hemisphere. In many stories Maugham depicts white characters who have crossed the line separating their world from that of the natives and found their new existence more satisfying than their old. In this there is some of the same appreciation of Eastern culture shown in Forster's novel through the character of Fielding, who befriends Aziz and becomes involved in his ensuing difficulties. Thus the title character of Maugham's story "The Fall of Edward Barnard" goes to Tahiti with the idea of making a fortune and ends up marrying a native woman and staying in the islands for the rest of his life. This story reiterates a theme of the novel *The Moon and Sixpence*

(1919), also set partly in Tahiti, and its American characters and Chicago setting of the frame story anticipate Maugham's last major novel, *The Razor's Edge* (1944). Similarly in "Red" an American sailor falls in love with a woman on a South Sea island, only to have their idyll interrupted by his being shanghaied into service on a merchant ship. After many years he returns for a nostalgic glimpse at the place where they had lived, and he finds his lover an old woman who does not recognize him. Sympathy for native life and customs is also expressed in "Rain," where the sanctimoniousness of the Davidsons is contrasted with the more accepting view of Doctor Macphail.

At the same time, however, Maugham's characters are not attracted to native life as a result of moral conviction like Forster's Fielding, but rather from a fuzzy romanticism – the "exotic East" of the popular imagination. In no way do Maugham's characters seriously question the system of class and caste operating in their colonial outstations. Thus, in "The Force of Circumstance," a woman rejects her husband because he refuses to use force to put a group of rebellious natives in their place, and in "The Outstation" a colonial officer ameliorates the punishment of a native servant who has killed his assistant, but he does so mainly to have the servant more fully in his power and to perpetuate his own white influence. Maugham's stories suggest that colonialism, while often not for the betterment of indigenous peoples, has about it the same inevitability as the fates of many of his characters: it is in the nature of things that some people should be subjugated to the will of others. Nowhere does one sense, as in Forster, the more liberal view that colonialism is wrong by its very nature and does as much moral damage to its agents as to its subjects. In Maugham's fiction evil is inherent in human behavior, and the circumstances of colonialism only encourage what is already there.

Thus many of his stories, deprived of their exotic settings, would turn out much the same. Perhaps the best example of this is "The Letter." Based on an actual murder in Malaya in 1911 and later dramatized by Maugham and made into a popular motion picture, "The Letter" tells of a crime of passion in which the wife of an English colonial shoots the man with whom she has been having an affair because she finds he has deserted her for his former lover, a Chinese woman. On the surface, the woman's racism and the colonial setting seem central to the story, but in fact it has a melodramatic plot that could take any setting and turn out essentially the same.

Dust jacket for Maugham's 1928 collection of short stories about a British spy (courtesy of Otto Penzler)

Generally Maugham's view of human nature is fixed. In story after story, characters either act according to selfish needs or are done in by the selfish needs of others. Circumstances dictate action more than human will, but when a contest of wills does occur, evil triumphs as often as good. "I think what has struck me most in human beings," Maugham asserted in *The Summing Up* (1938), "is their lack of consistency. I have never seen people all of a piece. It has amazed me that the most incongruous traits should exist in the same person and for all that yield a plausible harmony." On the whole, Maugham's characters place personal interest higher than anything else in their priorities.

This view of human nature may account for one of Maugham's favorite narrative devices – the use of the first-person narrator, frequently a persona of the author who describes but is not always directly involved in the events of the story. This de-

vice permits Maugham to view his characters at a distance and with a tone that suggests detachment as the only possible response to the human comedy. In "The Alien Corn," for example, the narrator is a novelist and playwright whose relationship to the central characters – a group of wealthy English Jews with social aspirations – is one of guest to hosts: he has spent time with them for dinner or the weekend and has observed, or overheard, the events with which the story deals. This device leads to some ironies, but also to a sense that the events described are not *his:* they are seen at a distance, and the narrator's credibility determines theirs.

One group of stories not written with first-person narration deserves particular mention – the group collected under the title *Ashenden,* the volume in which Maugham fictionalized his experiences as a secret agent during World War I. Together the stories have sufficient unity of tone and purpose to amount to a novel.

Ashenden, their central character, is the opposite of the conventional spy. That image – nurtured in fiction of Maugham's day by such popular authors as E. Phillips Oppenheim, John Buchan, and Anthony Hope – required the spy to be a dashing, romantic figure: handsome, cosmopolitan, ready to serve the ladies as readily as he serves his country. Such spies and adventurers are latter-day versions of Alexandre Dumas's Count of Monte Cristo and predecessors of Ian Fleming's popular James Bond.

The Ashenden of Maugham's stories, on the other hand, is reserved, stoic, unromantic; his work as a spy is dull, repetitive, even meaningless. He seems to have been chosen for his task because, whatever talent he has as a writer, he does not know much about espionage and is not likely to wish to distinguish himself by unusual tactics or foolish behavior. In short, he is more acted upon than active; he lets events (or superiors) dictate his moves rather than attempting to dictate events for himself; and he deliberately avoids romantic contacts that might vitiate his sense of responsibility. He is the unheroic hero – not a hero at all, but an observer chosen for his task because of his powers of observation and his distance from others. In this he anticipates characters in the spy novels of Graham Greene and John le Carré, characters who seem to exist outside the realm of conventional morality.

One of the best features of the stories of the *Ashenden* group is their understated style, which matches in tone and syntax the character of their antihero. This is Maugham at his best, as in the final story of the group, "Mr. Harrington's Washing," set in revolutionary Russia:

> Anastasia Alexandrovna touched Ashenden's arm to draw his attention; sitting on the pavement, her head bent right down to her lap, was a woman and she was dead. A little way on two men had fallen together. They were dead too. The wounded, one supposed, had managed to drag themselves away or their friends had carried them. Then they found Mr. Harrington. His derby had rolled in the gutter. He lay on his face, in a pool of blood, his bald head, with its prominent bones, very white; his neat black coat smeared and muddy. But his hand was clenched tight on the parcel that contained four shirts, two union suits, a pair of pajamas, and four collars. Mr. Harrington had not let his washing go.

In 1926 Maugham bought a rather strangely designed house on the French Riviera, had it done over, and called it the Villa Mauresque. Here, with his art collection and in an environment that he completely controlled, Maugham led what appeared to be an idyllic life. He wrote every day from 9:00 to 12:45, had the substantial lunch of the Mediterranean countries, napped and exercised in the afternoon, had friends in for dinner, and often finished the evening with a game of bridge or, if guests were not present, a good detective novel.

The guest list at the Villa Mauresque included well-known artists and writers as well as many members of the peerage. The Duke and Duchess of Windsor were probably the biggest names in the last category to visit there, but Maugham's acquaintance with titled people increased with his wealth and reputation. He came to epitomize the writer as gentleman.

The fall of France in 1940 ended the easy life at the Villa Mauresque, though Maugham was able to pursue it elsewhere. He had survived the Great Depression with his fortune intact, but when the Nazis swept through France in the spring of 1940 he along with countless others who lived on the Riviera had to flee. Although he had given up writing for the theater by 1933, he had published numerous works of fiction, including the novel *Cakes and Ale: or, The Skeleton in the Cupboard* (1930). He had also published a volume of reminiscences and essays that he called *The Summing Up,* the first of many such works he was to produce in his later years.

His life during World War II was largely provided for him by his American publisher, Nelson Doubleday. Maugham came to the United States to make a speaking tour on behalf of the British war effort, but he stayed for the duration. He lived in a house built for him on Doubleday's South Carolina plantation, where he finished work on his last major novel, *The Razor's Edge.* Other British citizens who lived in the United States during the war — for instance, those in the British motion picture industry in Hollywood — were criticized for deserting the home front in a time of crisis. Maugham had not lived on the home front for so many years that such criticism could scarcely be leveled at him. Living in the United States was merely another form of exile for the aging Maugham, part of the pattern of his life.

The period after the war, as Maugham grew into old age, represented a time of declining artistic powers, if not of reputation. He took another companion, Alan Searle, who ministered to his needs in the years after Gerald Haxton died in 1944. He moved back to France, restoring the Villa Mauresque almost to its prewar splendor, but became involved with his daughter and her family in litigation about the rights to his art collection, originally intended as Liza's inheritance. Maugham ended his days estranged from virtually everyone he knew. Never entirely happy in his youth or middle age, he grew less happy with age. Reduced to incoherence and near madness at the end, Maugham's exile was complete.

In spite of or perhaps because of his success, Maugham's work has had detractors. Other authors earned less money but more praise, and this led him to adopt a somewhat defensive tone in his later years, as if to say that it did not matter to him what anyone thought: he had done his best, and the world would have to judge him accordingly.

Preeminent among his detractors was American critic Edmund Wilson, who, in a celebrated review of the late 1940s, declared unequivocally that he thought Maugham's short fiction second-rate: "These [short] stories are magazine commodities . . . on about the same level as Sherlock Holmes; but Sherlock Holmes has more literary dignity precisely because it is less pretentious." Wilson concluded that "Mr. Maugham makes play with . . . serious themes, but his work is full of bogus motivations that are needed to turn out the monthly trick. He is for our day . . . what Bulwer-Lytton was for Dickens's: a half-trashy novelist, who writes badly, but is patronized by half-serious readers, who do not care much about writing."

Despite such negative judgments, Maugham's popularity extended into his last years. In 1950, for example, at the beginning of his last productive decade as an author, Maugham was ranked twelfth in a list of the world's best authors compiled by author and editor Whit Burnett. Considering that those polled included authors, editors, book reviewers, United States P.E.N. Club members, bookstore personnel, and miscellaneous public figures, Maugham's standing (with 427 votes) is some indication of how strong his reputation was. (By comparison, Bernard Shaw, who placed first in the list, garnered 539 votes; only one other English author, Aldous Huxley, had more votes than Maugham.) One poll, done with a limited clientele and recorded in one anthology, may prove little, but the people surveyed make an impressive list, and the results reveal much about Maugham's standing before the English-speaking audiences of midcentury.

Voices of two authors who can claim considerable achievement in fiction, short as well as long, provide a counterbalance to Edmund Wilson's. Evelyn Waugh, not always so charitable to other authors, praised Maugham as "the only living studio-master with whom one can study with profit," and Angus Wilson, in the 1967 preface to a volume of Maugham's *Cakes and Ale and Twelve Short Stories,* observed acutely:

> No author has more cleverly converted his defects into assets, not only by his assumption of the classic and stoic framework of life (through which the lost romantic is only occasionally allowed yearningly to peer), but far more by the perfection of his craft, imposing upon his carefully limited material an even more rigorous form, and then becoming so completely master of this highly artificial technique that his stories appear to flow with the ease and simplicity of ordinary, everyday muddled life.

To some his short fiction may seem artificial. Equally objectionable to many is what they perceive as racism in the blandness of his colonial view and his tendency to use epithets such as *oriental* and *Jewish.* Another serious charge against Maugham is sexism, for women in Maugham's fiction all too frequently are either the passive recipients of men's physical needs and desires or the chief antagonists to their satisfaction. At best he can be accused of old-fashioned views of gender; at his worst, of misogyny.

At the same time, Maugham's short fiction can give the pleasure of a well-crafted story with a sure sense of direction, much in the manner of a mystery or detective tale. In fact, it is regrettable that Maugham never pursued further the genre he mined in *Ashenden.* Nonetheless, with virtually all of his work still in print and some of it standard fare in college literature courses, he is likely to be with us for some time – a popular writer with a serious in-

tent that frequently lifts his work from the commercial genres of his day into the house of literature.

Bibliographies:

Raymond Manders and Joe Mitchenson, *Theatrical Companion to Maugham: A Pictorial Record of the First Performances of the Plays of W. Somerset Maugham* (London: Rockliff, 1955);

W. H. Henry Jr., *A French Bibliography of W. Somerset Maugham* (Charlottesville: Bibliographical Society of the University of Virginia, 1967);

Charles Sanders and others, *W. Somerset Maugham: An Annotated Bibliography of Writings About Him* (De Kalb: Northern Illinois University Press, 1970);

Raymond Toole Stott, *A Bibliography of the Works of W. Somerset Maugham* (London: Kaye & Ward, 1973).

Biographies:

Karl G. Pfeiffer, *W. Somerset Maugham: A Candid Portrait* (New York: Norton, 1959);

Wilmon Menard, *The Two Worlds of Somerset Maugham* (Los Angeles: Sherbourne Press, 1965);

Garson Kanin, *Remembering Mr. Maugham* (London: Hamish Hamilton, 1966; New York: Atheneum, 1966);

Robin Maugham, *Somerset and All the Maughams* (London: Longmans/Heinemann, 1966);

Beverly Nichols, *A Base of Human Bondage* (London: Secker & Warburg, 1966);

Joseph Dobrinsky, *La Jeunesse de Somerset Maugham (1874–1903)* (Paris: Didier, 1976);

Frederic Raphael, *W. Somerset Maugham and His World* (New York: Scribners, 1976);

Anthony Curtis, *Somerset Maugham* (New York: Macmillan, 1977);

Robin Maugham, *Conversations with Willie: Recollections of W. Somerset Maugham* (New York: Simon & Schuster, 1978);

Ted Morgan, *Maugham* (New York: Simon & Schuster, 1980);

Robert Lorin Calder, *Willie: The Life of W. Somerset Maugham* (London: Heinemann, 1989).

References:

Stanley Archer, *W. Somerset Maugham: A Study of the Short Fiction* (Boston: Twayne, 1993);

Ronald E. Barnes, *The Dramatic Comedy of William Somerset Maugham* (The Hague & Paris: Mouton, 1968);

Laurence Brander, *Somerset Maugham: A Guide* (Edinburgh: Oliver & Boyd, 1963);

Ivor Brown, *W. Somerset Maugham* (London: International Textbook, 1970);

Robert Lorin Calder, *W. Somerset Maugham and the Quest for Freedom* (London: Heinemann, 1972);

Richard A. Cordell, *Somerset Maugham, A Writer for All Seasons: A Biographical and Critical Study,* revised edition (Bloomington & London: Indiana University Press, 1969);

Anthony Curtis, *The Pattern of Maugham* (New York: Taplinger, 1974);

Klaus W. Jonas, *The Maugham Enigma* (New York: Citadel Press, 1954);

Jonas, *The World of Somerset Maugham* (New York: British Book Centre, 1959);

Archie K. Loss, *Of Human Bondage: Coming of Age in the Novel* (Boston: Twayne, 1990);

Loss, *W. Somerset Maugham* (New York: Crossroads-Ungar, 1987);

M. K. Naik, *W. Somerset Maugham* (Norman: University of Oklahoma Press, 1966).

Papers:

Maugham's papers are archived at the Yale University Library as well as among the holdings of the Harry Ransom Humanities Research Center, University of Texas at Austin; the Berg Collection, New York Public Library; the Lilly Library, Indiana University; Stanford University; the Houghton Library, Harvard University; the Fales Collection, New York University; the Butler Library, Columbia University; the Olin Library, Cornell University; Beaverbrook Papers, House of Lords Records Office, London; and the University of Arkansas Library.

H. H. Munro (Saki)
(18 December 1870 – 14 November 1916)

Alexander Malcolm Forbes
University College of the Cariboo

See also the Munro entry in *DLB 34: British Novelists, 1890–1929: Traditionalists.*

BOOKS: *The Rise of the Russian Empire* (London: Richards, 1900; Boston: L. C. Page, 1901);

The Westminster Alice (London: Westminster Gazette, 1902; New York: Viking, 1929);

Reginald (London: Methuen, 1904; New York: McBride, 1921);

Reginald in Russia, and Other Sketches (London: Methuen, 1910; New York: John Lane, 1921);

The Chronicles of Clovis (London: John Lane, 1911; New York: John Lane, 1912);

The Unbearable Bassington (London & New York: John Lane, 1912);

When William Came: A Story of London Under the Hohenzollerns (London & New York: John Lane, 1914);

Beasts and Super-Beasts (London & New York: John Lane, 1914);

The Toys of Peace, and Other Papers (London & New York: John Lane, 1919);

Reginald, and Reginald in Russia (London: John Lane/Bodley Head, 1921; New York: Viking, 1929);

The Square Egg, and Other Sketches, with Three Plays (London: John Lane, 1924; New York: Viking, 1929).

Collections: *The Works of Saki,* 8 volumes (London: John Lane/Bodley Head, 1926–1927; New York: Viking, 1927–1929);

The Short Stories of Saki (H. H. Munro) Complete (New York: Viking, 1930); republished as *The Complete Short Stories of Saki (H. H. Munro)* (New York: Halcyon House, 1939);

The Novels and Plays of Saki (H. H. Munro) Complete in One Volume (New York: Viking, 1933; London: John Lane, 1933);

The Complete Saki (New York: Doubleday, 1976; London: Penguin, 1982);

H. H. Munro (photograph by E. O. Hoppé)

The Complete Works of Saki (London: Bodley Head, 1980).

Hector Hugh Munro (Saki) expanded the possibilities of the short story by infusing it with the interests and techniques of the comedy of manners. In

240

so doing, Munro produced satiric narratives remembered for their epigrammatic wit, narrative economy, and logically developed surprise endings. He transmitted the traditions of Oscar Wilde and his predecessors to P. G. Wodehouse, Evelyn Waugh, and Noel Coward, while he earned the interest of many other writers such as Graham Greene, G. K. Chesterton, and A. A. Milne.

Born 18 December 1870 in Akyab, Burma, to Charles Augustus and Mary Frances Munro, the boy was taken to England with his brother and sister in 1873, after their mother's death, to be raised by two aunts at Pilton, in North Devon. The children accompanied their father on many extended visits to the Continent when he retired from the army in 1888, and Munro followed his father's example by going to Burma in 1893 as an officer of police. When he contracted malaria, Munro returned to England the following year and convalesced in Devonshire until he left for London in 1896 to attempt a living as a writer.

Munro's first important publication was a history of Russia. Published in 1900 to mixed reviews, *The Rise of the Russian Empire* was neither a financial nor a critical success. While working on this history, however, Munro published a short story, "Dogged," in the February 1899 issue of *St. Paul's,* a story that has never been republished despite its anticipation of the ironic reversals and awkward animals of Munro's later fiction. In the story Artemus Gibbon (Munro was still a historian) acquires a dog that drives away his friends and secures his eviction.

A second attempt at fiction in 1900 was successful. A collaboration with political cartoonist Francis Carruthers Gould produced "Alice in Westminster," a series of satires in which Carruthers' caricatures were accompanied by Munro's prose. Although Munro was a Tory, the Tory government's inept handling of the Boer War was the main target. The series as a whole was an imitation in the eighteenth-century sense: an application of an earlier literary model to contemporary life. The model was Lewis Carroll's *Alice's Adventures in Wonderland* (1865), and the series was published in the Liberal-leaning *Westminster Gazette.* It proved popular and was republished as a collection, *The Westminster Alice,* in 1902. A subsequent collaboration with Gould in 1902 proved less successful: this was an imitation of Rudyard Kipling's *Just So Stories* (1902) entitled the "Not So Stories," which was subsequently retitled "The Political Jungle-Book" while the series was still running in the *Westminster Gazette.*

In the Alice series Munro used the pen name "Saki" for the first time. In her "Biography of Saki" Ethel Munro confirms that her brother adopted the name from the cupbearer of the gods in Edward Fitzgerald's *The Rubáiyát of Omar Khayyám* (1859) a character who pours out the transient bubbles of life much as Munro would pour out his brief satires on the passing world. He later employed the poem for political satire in two other imitations — both published in 1901 and both signed "Saki" — and he referred to it in his stories.

Munro's appointment in 1902 as foreign correspondent for the Tory *Morning Post* formally began his career as a journalist, although the *Westminster Gazette* published his first series of short stories in the following year. These *Reginald* stories appeared throughout 1903 and were well received by critics: they proved to be the most well received, in fact, of Munro's stories. They were also of sufficient, if modest, popular success to be collected in a single volume by Methuen in 1904 and were republished three times during Munro's lifetime.

The characteristics that define "Saki" are all present in these stories. In "Reginald" the protagonist displays the wit that makes him a useful tool for satirizing staid pretension and the aestheticism that makes him an affectionate object of satire himself. The anonymous narrator is also an aesthete, but one sufficiently restrained to serve as a foil to his friend's verbal misbehavior at a garden party. The narrator all but disappears in "Reginald on Christmas Presents" — a story in which Reginald defines the necessities of life (liqueurs figure prominently) — only to reappear in "Reginald on the Academy" as "the Other." To Reginald, the Royal Academy is a failure, but one partly redeemed by its exhibit of bad pictures whenever its legitimately social function collapses.

"Reginald at the Theatre," a multileveled satiric dialogue, is important for understanding Munro. Testifying to the ultimately dramatic origins of these stories, extended dialogues appear throughout his fiction and often comprise the stories themselves. Reginald's interlocuter, "the Duchess," a self-indulgent aristocrat who prides herself for her ethics, is a type — but she is also an individual, as are Munro's other types. She is not a personification of pure greed, and nothing in the story suggests that her enjoyments are to be dismissed outright, but only insofar as they blind her to self-contradiction. The story satirizes a world dominated by market values, as Reginald identifies the horrors of poverty just "down the Embankment": "where everything is based on competition," there must be "a debit as well as a credit account." Munro's satire shows him to be in the tradition of the eighteenth-century Tory

Illustration by Francis Carruthers Gould for "Alice in a Fog,"
one of the political satires Munro contributed to a series collected
as The Westminster Alice *(Westminster Gazette)*

satirists, for whom raw commercialism was a target. Like Swift, however, Munro despairs of reform, and in later stories this despair turns satirically toward idealistic schemes of reform: the poor must be fed, but if they *are* to be fed, "something else" must be "fed upon."

"Reginald's Peace Poem" extends aesthetic satire by ridiculing weak contemporary poetry, but it also reinforces a perception that human nature is fundamentally predatory. Its satire on pacifism does not suggest a desire for war, but it suggests that certain human elements are intractable and must be recognized as such. In "Reginald's Choir Treat," however, satire again becomes playful, as Reginald's mischievous nature, rather than human nature in general, becomes the subject.

Needless worries and the faults of British education are examined in "Reginald on Worries," and the social conventions of house parties are dissected in "Reginald on House Parties." In "Reginald at the Carlton" the Duchess and Reginald renew their conversation, in which hors d'oeuvres become a metaphor for the neglected op-portunities of childhood: later, one wishes one had eaten more.

"Reginald on Besetting Sins: The Woman Who Told the Truth" is a double-edged satire both on a world unprepared to hear the truth and on the indiscretion of telling it openly in such a world. "Reginald's Drama" extends literary satire to include contemporary drama, while "Reginald on Tariffs" argues for import duties on items in bad taste, and bounties to encourage the exporting of citizens who take life seriously. Reginald does not wish to be exported, as confirmed by "Reginald's Christmas Revel," in which he recounts a practical joke played upon a fellow houseguest.

Reginald offers the Duchess an even more decadent poem than she has requested in "Reginald's Rubaiyat," and, in "The Innocence of Reginald," he terrifies his friends with the suggestion that he might have composed his memoirs. Once again the world is not prepared to hear the truth.

As the Reginald stories were appearing and during the years immediately following, Munro continued his work as a correspondent reporting from Macedonia, the Balkans, Austria, Poland, and Russia – in the last of which assignments he witnessed Bloody Sunday while in Saint Petersburg (22 January 1905). His dispatches predicted an enlargement of Balkan conflict, and his experiences made him acutely aware that national independence was something easily lost. In his later novel *When William Came: A Story of London Under the Hohenzollerns* (1914), Munro warned Britain that it could face occupation by Germany and called for a greater national seriousness. This was a logical extension of a related call for greater personal seriousness that his preceding novel, *The Unbearable Bassington* (1912), had offered in its critical reexamination of the lives of England's Reginalds.

In 1906 the *Morning Post* reassigned Munro to Paris, where he reported on both cultural and political events. The death of his father in 1907 prompted a brief return to England, but Munro returned permanently to Britain in 1908 when he left the *Morning Post* to devote himself to fiction. Munro settled in London, maintained a cottage in Surrey, and from 1909 until 1914 published stories in the *Westminster Gazette,* the *Morning Post,* and the Tory *Bystander.* Three collections of these stories appeared during Munro's lifetime: *Reginald in Russia, and Other Sketches* (1910), *The Chronicles of Clovis* (1911), and *Beasts and Super-Beasts* (1914).

Reginald in Russia is widely considered to be less successful, artistically, than its predecessor: macabre and supernatural subjects are introduced, and these prevent Munro from writing the kind of satire in which he excelled, although the new subjects extend the range of his fiction. The title story draws on Munro's Russian experiences to satirize a Russian princess who indulges in socialist views. As in "Reginald at the Theatre" the satire is directed less against worldly pleasures (although excesses do receive a critical glance) than against the hypocrisy of espousing socialist doctrines while reaping the benefits of privilege. Despite the title of the collection, neither Reginald nor Russia appear in the other "Sketches."

With "The Reticence of Lady Anne" Munro's fiction takes a new turn, introducing the macabre and reducing satire to insignificance. When Egbert speaks to his wife, Lady Anne, he receives no response, and the reader learns that Egbert has been addressing a corpse. Another corpse appears in "The Lost Sanjak," a case of mistaken identity in which a man is convicted for his own murder. Munro concludes, however, with an extraordinary shift into satire by showing how the man is unable to prove his identity because of the speciousness of contemporary education: the man lacks any specialized knowledge that might prove who he is.

In its account of the shopping habits of wealthy women, "The Sex That Doesn't Shop" recalls the stories of *Reginald,* but in "The Blood-Feud of Toad-Water: A West-Country Epic" Munro begins to draw upon his knowledge of the West Country to engage in mock-heroic satire of long-standing country feuds.

New satiric targets, the suffragettes, emerge in "A Young Turkish Catastrophe." Although a later story such as "The Gala Programme" suggests that Munro ultimately objects to the suffragettes' willingness to engage in disorderly conduct rather than to calls for womens' rights, "A Young Turkish Catastrophe" does nothing to rescue Munro from the charge of being insensitive to those rights.

An unexpected affinity to Thomas Hardy is displayed in "Judkin of the Parcels," as the narrator meditates on the "tedious cheerfulness" of a man who had once known a life better than his present existence, as the man repeatedly carries parcels about a muddy land. In "Gabriel-Ernest," the story of a werewolf, the supernatural enters Munro's fiction for the first time.

The remaining stories return to the satiric traditions of the comedy of manners and strike various targets: meanness, in "The Saint and the Goblin" and "The Soul of Laploshka"; the rituals of foxhunting, in "The Bag"; house parties, in "The Strategist"; and love triangles, in "Cross Currents."

"The Baker's Dozen" is a one-act play that demonstrates how much importance lies in a name, as is also evident in "The Mouse."

With *The Chronicles of Clovis* Munro began an association with a new publisher. John Lane had cofounded The Bodley Head and under its imprint had published the *Yellow Book,* a journal with which Max Beerbohm and Aubrey Beardsley had been associated. Through Lane, accordingly, a new connection between Munro and the 1890s was effected, although the modest yet respectable sales of *Reginald in Russia, and Other Sketches* had prompted Munro's decision to change publishers.

Sales of *The Chronicles of Clovis* were again only modest, despite good reviews. The collection did, however, mark the first appearance of Munro's fiction in the United States, through a 1912 republication. (Only the earlier history, *The Rise of the Russian Empire,* had been republished in the United States in 1901.) The collection sold fourteen thousand copies and was for awhile the most successful of Munro's collections published in America. Viking eventually republished all of Munro's collections, but the sixty-six thousand copies sold of *The Works of Saki* (1927–1929) surpassed them all.

Although many of the stories in *The Chronicles of Clovis* recall *Reginald* (with Reginald replaced by Clovis Sangrail and the Duchess by a Baroness), the darker shades of *Reginald in Russia* are also deepened. In "Esmé," for example, satire is wedded to the macabre to produce one of Munro's stranger fictions. What begins as a foxhunt deteriorates when the hounds corner a hyena that intimidates the hounds, befriends the Baroness and a fellow hunter, and then devours a child before being killed by a passing motorist. The motorist, believing that he has killed a pet dog, sends the Baroness a brooch inscribed with the hyena's name.

The next stories are more traditionally satiric. Clovis accommodates his own needs by arranging his mother's remarriage in "The Match-Maker"; a cat, taught to speak, tells unwelcome truths in "Tobermory." (A variation on both "Reginald on Besetting Sins" and "The Innocence of Reginald," this story marks the first appearance of the "depraved" Bertie van Tahn as a supporting character.) A desire for reputation leaves the protagonist vulnerable to blackmail in "Mrs. Packletide's Tiger," and the practical joke becomes a central narrative device in "The Stampeding of Lady Bastable."

Surrealism appears in Munro's "The Background," the story of a man whose tattoo is declared to be state property, an event causing much inconvenience. "Herman the Irascible – A Story of the Great Weep," however, is more traditional. Reminiscent of the first book of Jonathan Swift's *Gulliver's Travels* (1726), it is the story of a German monarch who unexpectedly finds himself on the British throne – although the suffragettes, rather than Whig policies, become the objects of Tory satire. "The Unrest-Cure" recounts a horrible plan by Clovis to reinvigorate the Huddle family.

Fiction becomes metafiction in "The Jesting of Arlington Stringham," a humorous story about the construction (and misconstruction) of humor, and the macabre reappears in "Sredni Vashtar" when a boy, Conradin, employs his ferret to exact a Gothic revenge on an oppressive guardian, Mrs. De Ropp. Ethel Munro's biography of her brother sees the source for Mrs. De Ropp, as well as for the many other oppressive aunts and guardians who appear in Munro's stories, to be one of the aunts to whom the Munro children had been entrusted. In defending Munro's work against charges of cruelty, Ethel Munro suggests that the portraits should be seen as imaginative re-creations, as the projections of much-provoked children, rather than as endorsements of actual cruelty.

Gentle social satire returns with the practical jokes of "Adrian: A Chapter in Acclimatization," a variation on "Reginald's Christmas Revel." "The Chaplet" details the consequences of playing music at meals, and "The Quest" satirizes well-intended but disastrous kindnesses. "Wratislav" is the story of an indiscrete young man's timely escape to Mexico from central Europe.

"The Easter Egg" is also set in central Europe, and Munro introduces an antihero in Lester Slaggby, whose foiling of an assassination attempt is the one courageous act of his life. Another antihero is introduced in "Filboid Studge, the Story of a Mouse That Helped." This story resembles but does not become a familiar animal fable: a little person helps a lion of commerce, but goes unrewarded.

"The Music on the Hill" marks the first appearance of the supernatural in *The Chronicles of Clovis.* Set in the mythologically rich Devon country, the story rewrites the myth of Actaeon, as the ironically named Sylvia is killed by a stag, rather than transformed into one, for the offense she has committed against Pan, rather than against Diana.

Three dialogues between Clovis and the Baroness follow. "The Story of St. Vespaluus" depicts the pretended conversion of Vespaluus to Christianity: his name betrays the fact that his supposed Pauline conversion is but a suffix attached to an older Roman paganism. "The Way to the Dairy" records how a plot to exclude a relative from the good

opinion of a wealthy aunt backfires, and "The Peace Offering" similarly recounts a failed plan to reconcile a divided community through the presentation of an amateur theatrical.

The remaining stories are variations on earlier ones. "The Peace of Mowsle Barton" echoes "The Music on the Hill," as the supernatural intrusion of two apparent witches unsettles the rustic quiet. "The Talking-Out of Tarrington" permits Clovis to display the verbal wit of Reginald in demolishing a social climber. "The Hounds of Fate" evokes "The Lost Sanjak" in another story of mistaken identity that costs an innocent life. "The Recessional" is a variation on "Reginald's Peace Poem," with Clovis replacing Reginald and a coronation ode replacing the peace poem. The story is noteworthy for providing the first unambiguous suggestion of Munro's own homosexuality, about which little is known.

Multiple reversals occur in "A Matter of Sentiment," and these ensure ironies similar to those of "The Way to the Dairy." Additional reversals occur when, in "The Secret Sin of Septimus Brope," a scholar proves to be the composer of popular songs. "Ministers of Grace" combines the political satire of Munro's Westminster Alice series with incidents involving mistaken identity and pessimism about reform, as politicians are replaced by angels who come to be mistaken for them: when partisan violence is replaced by honest benevolence in society, a resistant populace proves hostile. The final story, "The Remoulding of Groby Lington," continues the story "Dogged" by showing the profound effects of pets upon their owners. Here the man undergoes a sequence of metamorphoses into likenesses of his various pets.

Between *The Chronicles of Clovis* and *Beasts and Super-Beasts* Munro published his two novels, *The Unbearable Bassington* and *When William Came: A Story of London Under the Hohenzollerns.* Munro also worked with Charles Maude on *The Watched Pot.* Maude shortened this comedy of manners, Munro's one full-length play, and helped make it suitable for the stage. With Maude's revisions, the play was published in *The Square Egg, and Other Sketches, with Three Plays* (1924). In the summer and fall of 1912 Munro contributed occasional pieces of satiric journalism to the *Bystander,* and in 1913 he attempted a second Alice series by collaborating with another artist identified only as "Pat." Munro supplied verses for this collaborator's satiric cartoons on Prime Minister Herbert Asquith and Chancellor of the Exchequer David Lloyd George. An unsuccessful enterprise, the series commenced in the *Bystander* in

March, moved to the Tory *Daily Express* in April, and expired in May.

During this period Munro also published six stories not reprinted in any collections until A. J. Langguth collected them in an appendix in *Saki: A Life of Hector Hugh Munro, with Six Short Stories Never before Collected* (1891). Two of these stories are mirror images of one another. "The Pond" (*Bystander*, 21 February 1912) concerns a morbid woman who contemplates committing suicide by drowning herself in a pond – only to discover, when she has overcome all her suicidal inclinations but falls into it later, that the pond is less than two inches deep. "The Holy War" (*Morning Post*, 6 May 1913) similarly presents the drowning of a woman who had fought to improve her husband's West Country estate – and who achieves her wish, as her unhappy husband sees it, only through her mishap. The remaining four stories return to more-familiar fictional situations: "The Almanack" (*Morning Post*, 17 June 1913) recounts Clovis's attempt to ensure that a prediction published in a friend's almanac comes true; "A Housing Problem: The Solution of an Insoluble Dilemma" (*Bystander*, 9 July 1913) offers an ironic solution to the disputes between two houseguests; "A Sacrifice to Necessity" (*Bystander*, 15 October 1913) creates in Beryl Pevenly, who pays a gambling debt by arranging her mother's remarriage, a worthy successor to the role played by Clovis in "The Match-Maker"; "A Shot in the Dark" (*Bystander*, 3 December 1913) displays a politician in the act of outwitting himself.

Before the publication of *Beasts and Super-Beasts* animals made frequent but often dark appearances in Munro's stories. Yet with this collection Munro's strong love for animals and his whimsical humor largely precluded presentations of their sinister associations.

Illustrative of this new approach to animals are the first two stories, "The She-Wolf" and "Laura." While the supernatural was significant in stories such as "Gabriel Ernest," any suggestions of the supernatural are exploded in the first story when Clovis terrifies Leonard Bilsiter by employing a wolf to play a practical joke, to convince Bilsiter that he actually possesses the magical powers he claims to have. The second story, in which a woman wishes to be reincarnated as an otter, likewise treats the supernatural playfully.

"The Boar-Pig" and "The Brogue" derive their humor from the large animals that appear in them. The merely supporting role of the fowl in "The Hen," however, enhances the dramatic irony achieved by Clovis's use of a servant in a practical

joke that comprises a variation on "The Stampeding of Lady Bastable."

Ghosts replace animals in "The Open Window," a story that presents a version of "The Unrest-Cure," but no supernaturalism enters the story, for the ghosts prove to be fictional suggestions delivered to the receptive mind of Framton Nuttel. Similarly, the only ghosts in "The Treasure-Ship" are the ghosts of the past, as the Duchess of Dulverton inadvertently becomes a treasure ship to her nephew, who blackmails her with what he finds in a sunken boat.

"The Cobweb" is the story of a metaphorical netting, the cobweb of the past that traps a young couple who attempt to live in the present. In their blundering ways animals appear, in "The Lull," as instruments of a practical joke designed to divert a young politician from spending too much time preparing his speeches. Animals disappeared temporarily from Munro's stories in this volume, however, as he resumed his political satire. "The Unkindest Blow" is a Tory satire upon both strikes and journalistic profiting from sensational stories; "The Romancers" is another on panhandlers who would rather "undergo hours of humiliating tale-spinning and rebuff " than work. The storywriter is at least partially implicated in the satire of "The Romancers," however, as the narrator counters with a tale of his own: the cadger is left unsatisfied, but "two of a trade never agree."

"The Schartz-Metterklume Method" generates dramatic irony through a case of mistaken identity, while "The Seventh Pullet," like "The Open Window," is constructed around tall tales – this time involving animals instead of ghosts. The story retells that of the boy who cried wolf – with pullets replacing wolves in the narrative.

Other stories develop already-familiar patterns. "The Blind Spot" comes closest in the collection to recapturing the flavor of *Reginald* in its account of an epicurean who employs "a common murderer" simply because that murderer is "a very uncommon cook." "Dusk" is a version of "The Romancers," although this time the panhandler proves successful. In "A Touch of Realism" the tall tales dramatized in charades have disastrous consequences when the players carry them to literal ends.

When Munro's characters attempt to write poetry, they usually compose doggerel, as in "Reginald's Peace Poem." Doggerel can be unexpectedly successful, however, especially if it has something to do with dogs – and is chanted in the music hall, as it is in "Cousin Teresa." The fashion of editing newspapers from foreign capitals can also be unexpect-

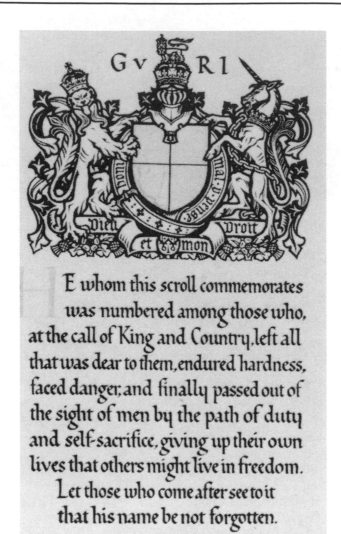

Memorial scroll sent to Munro's family by King George V

edly successful, as "The Yarkand Manner" demonstrates when the editorial staff of a paper is kidnapped while abroad. An office boy continues to publish the paper and increases its sales by writing articles himself.

In "The Byzantine Omelette" Munro returns to earlier satire of aristocratic socialists and suggests that the contradictory demands of labor unions can produce the unhappy paradox of a social omelette and no dinner, all at once. (In its hungry conclusion the story offers a new version of "The Unkindest Blow.") In "The Feast of Nemesis," Clovis's behavior recalls that of Reginald when the former proposes a new public institution: a day reserved for "primitive school-boy vengeance." In "The Dreamer" satire on the marketplace resumes, as a boy's dreams prove anything but poetic.

Tall tales delivered for benevolent purposes shape both "The Quince Tree" and "The Forbidden Buzzards," but in "The Stake" a young man tells a tall tale that permits him to gamble although he has no money. (The story is a variation of "A Sacrifice to Necessity.") In "Clovis on Parental Responsibilities" the tall tale is displaced by witty retort in a psychological combat between Clovis and a mother who contradicts his desires by wishing him to meet her offspring. Mistaken identity becomes forgotten identity in "A Holiday Task," when a bashful young man, Kenelm Jerton, is drawn into helping a stranger, beset by memory loss, to reestablish her own identity.

In "The Stalled Ox" the appearance of the ox in a neighbor's garden provides a painter, Eshley, with new surrealistic opportunities – and Munro with an opportunity to resume satire of the Royal Academy. Animals are also prominent in "The Story-Teller," in which reversing the traditional patterns of childrens' stories involving wolves discomposes an aunt but delights her nephew and nieces.

Like "The Story-Teller," "A Defensive Diamond" is both a story about storytelling and a variation on "The Romancers." While animals play important roles in the tall tales of "A Defensive Diamond," they also do so in domestic narratives, as "The Elk" illustrates when Mrs. Thropplestance's matrimonial intentions for her grandson are ruined by the intervention of her pet.

"Down Pens" follows "The Feast of Nemesis" in proposing a change in social conventions: an end to letters of thanks for unwanted gifts. In "The Name-Day" what appear to be wolves prove to be dogs, as one passenger on an abandoned railway car avariciously takes advantage of another. In "The Lumber-Room" a less literal-minded version of the Conradin from "Shredni Vashtar" imagines the revenge that animals might exact upon his surrogate aunt.

Although there are no animals in "Fur," a young woman exacts beastly revenge upon a former friend, one who has also proven herself to be a beast by refusing to reciprocate to a plea for assistance. In "The Philanthropist and the Happy Cat" (a version of "The Remoulding of Groby Lington"), philanthropy yields to the law of the jungle, and in the final story, "On Approval," the narrative patterns of "The Stalled Ox" are reversed: where a newfound success greeted Eshley's animal surrealism in that story, another surrealist painter of animals, Knopfschrank, fails miserably until a misunderstanding rescues finances in "On Approval."

By the time *Beasts and Super-Beasts* was published, Munro had resumed work as a journalist, covering the spring session of Parliament for the Tory *Outlook* and contributing political reviews to the *Bystander.* Two months after *Beasts and Super-Beasts* appeared, Britain delivered its ultimatum to Germany (3 August 1914), and Munro, despite his age, was one of the first to enlist for military service. "Hector told a friend," Ethel Munro recalled in her biography of her brother, "that, having written *When William Came,* he ought to go half-way to meet him." Munro joined the cavalry but subsequently transferred to the infantry, and he twice refused offers of a commission that would have delayed his active service by requiring a period of retraining.

Munro first saw combat in the trenches of France in November 1915, and in May 1916 he participated in the first battle of Vimy Ridge. He visited England while on leave in June 1916 and then returned to France, where he distinguished himself for extraordinary bravery at Delville Wood: under the heaviest fire, with senior officers killed or separated from their scattered troops, Munro successfully organized and led a new combat section. All first-hand accounts concur that as a soldier Munro displayed the qualities for which his friends had most deeply admired him in civilian life: selflessness, sincerity, and a strong sense of honor. A recurrence of malaria led to Munro's hospitalization at Rouen in October. Before being fully recovered, however, he voluntarily rejoined his battalion for its attack on Beaumont Hamel, where he was killed by a sniper on 14 November 1916.

During those last two years, however, Munro wrote many articles about army life for the Twenty-second Battalion's *Fortnightly Gazette.* One of these was reprinted in the *Bystander,* and he contributed three further stories from the front: "For the Duration of the War," "The Square Egg," and "Birds on the Western Front." Along with earlier stories that had also appeared in the *Post,* the *Gazette,* and the *Bystander,* these three stories (published in the *Morning Post* and the *Westminster Gazette*) were republished in two posthumous collections.

In the first of these collections, *The Toys of Peace, and Other Papers* (1919) the title story underscores Munro's conviction that human nature is neither benevolent nor easily susceptible to change: Harvey Bope's attempt to interest his nephews in peace toys fails when the children quickly turn them into war toys — an outcome foreshadowed by suggestions in "The Story-Teller." Here, however, Munro makes more clear than ever that he is sensitive to the hopes that underlie idealism. The problem, as Bope observes, is that "we have begun too late."

The next three stories provide less serious satire: "Louise," the story of an absent-minded woman who thinks she has misplaced a niece; "Tea," a satire on the conventions of afternoon tea; and "The Disappearance of Crispina Umberleigh," an account of the welcome disappearance of a tyrannical aunt. "The Wolves of Cernogratz" marks a return to the uncanny, as wolves howl at the death of a von Cernogratz character in the ancestral castle. Domestic deception proves ludicrous in "Louis," as do unwelcome guests in "The Guests." A dark tale follows in "The Penance," about the cruelties of adults and children to each other.

Humor reappears in the next four stories. The pushy Smithly-Dubbs receive their just edibles in

"The Phantom Luncheon," and "A Bread and Butter Miss" shows Bertie van Tahn placing bets on the basis of a friend's dreams. In "Bertie's Christmas Eve" the members of Bertie Steffink's family have been preparing to send him away for his own good, but the practical joke that he plays on them provides a dramatically fitting response to their attempts. Wit is also prominent in "Forewarned," which demonstrates that romantic novels and political editorials are fictions of merely opposite types.

In an approximation to parable that is rare for Munro, "The Interlopers" becomes one of his most idealistic and paradoxically pessimistic stories. When two men who have maintained an ancestral feud are both pinned beneath a tree, they realize the folly of their dispute and recognize the benefits of peace – only at the precise moment when wolves appear. False stories sell groceries in "Quail Seed," much as they sell newspapers in "The Yarkand Manner." Governments sell themselves in "Canossa," and political satire continues with attacks on suffragettes in "The Threat." The wisdom of defusing domestic discord by uniting opposition against a single target is suggested in "Excepting Mrs. Pentherby," and "Mark" displays ironic similarities between an encyclopedia salesman and a popular novelist. In a satire of supernaturalism similar to that in "The She-Wolf," "The Hedgehog" undermines ghost stories by offering one.

"The Mappined Life" is an unusual Munro story in its recording of genuinely deep emotion. While Mappin terraces provide zoo animals with a spacious habitat, the animals are probably not fooled into thinking themselves at liberty, as James Gurtleberry's niece points out. But human beings employ "superior powers of self-deception" to convince themselves that their own "unreal, stupid little lives" on their Mappin terraces leave them "untrammelled men and women leading a reasonable existence in a reasonable sphere." The key to such self-deception lies in a "lack of initiative" that deprives life of "real and eventful existence" and leaves it "conventional make-believe."

"Fate," about the desperate expedients of a gambler, recalls "The Stake," while "The Bull" is a thought-provoking story that revisits Plato in describing the anger of a farmer toward his half-brother when he discovers that relative to have earned more for his painting of a bull than the farmer himself can receive for raising an actual one.

While "The Toys of Peace" depicted the predilection of children for war toys, "Morlvera" suggests children's preferences for natural rather than highly artificial toys, although the "gilded depravity" of one doll proves irresistible to childish imagination. In "Shock Tactics" Bertie Heasant appears along with a returning Clovis, who engages in practical jokes against Bertie's mother. "The Seven Cream Jugs" and "The Occasional Garden" also demonstrate Munro's wit, the first story detailing an embarrassing case of mistaken identity and the second recounting the dilemmas of a hostess whose garden requires immediate assistance.

"The Sheep" is a story of Rupert and his prospective brother-in-law, "the Sheep," who proves infuriatingly self-satisfied about his own ineptitude. When a guard dog prevents Rupert from rescuing "the Sheep," who has literally fallen through thin ice on which he has been figuratively skating for some time, the dog becomes Rupert's favorite pet.

Both "The Oversight" and "Hyacinth" illustrate the readiness of human affairs to be overturned. In the first, careful plans for a house party fail to anticipate all possible sources of conflict; in the second, a child's vengeance disrupts an election. "The Image of the Lost Soul" is also a record of reversal, but a humorless one. Stone figures are personified here, as they had been in "The Saint and the Goblin," but the sentimentality of the story makes it different from any other by Munro – a difference that might be explained by the early date of its composition – in 1891. In this story the figure of the lost soul loses some of its sorrow when a songbird makes a nesting place of it. When the bird is subsequently caught, however, the figure is deprived of its companion and topples to the ground.

The next two stories are set in the Balkans and were written during the Balkan wars (1912–1913) to which they refer. "The Purple of the Balkan Kings" comes close to being simple political editorial in praise of independence for the Balkan States; "The Cupboard of the Yesterdays," in contrast, is perhaps the most formally complex of Munro's stories. It is structured as a dialogue in which "hopelessly divergent" positions are maintained by the two speakers, "the Wanderer" and "the Merchant."

The narrative generates irony, self-contradiction, and ambivalence in an anticipation of later twentieth-century fiction. The Wanderer discomposes the Merchant by acknowledging the attractiveness of war, describing the Balkans as "the last surviving shred of happy hunting-ground" for "passions that are fast becoming atrophied" and as an area still open to those who want "a life of boot and saddle and licence to kill and be killed." The story confirms the irony of the Wanderer's position by invoking the judgment of the Merchant against it, but merchants are never sincere or perceptive in Munro, however well spoken they may appear, and the Wanderer concludes his rhapsody by observing that "War is a wickedly destructive thing." The Wanderer is candid about the contradictions of his positions, and his candor prompts the Merchant to offer an insincere reversal of his own position – in an admission that the Wanderer promptly ignores. The "Wanderer was not in the mood to admit anything," and "He rose impatiently and walked to where the tape-machine was busy with the news from Adrianople."

The final story, "For the Duration of the War," is deeply self-reflexive, bringing Munro the writer and Munro the soldier into its narrative – although its account of the rural exile of a rector and his wife might appear to have little to do with Munro or with the warfront, where it was written. The rector perpetrates a literary forgery by passing off his own verses as those of a forgotten Persian poet, one who strongly resembles Omar Khayyám. The Persian writer's work is marked by a "comfortable, even-tempered satire and philosophy, disclosing a mockery that did not trouble to be bitter, a joy in life that was not passionate to the verge of being troublesome" – an accurate description of Omar's poetry, but also of much of Munro's own prose. That Munro is writing about himself as well as Omar here is confirmed by the specific topics of the verses, which are precisely those with which Munro was concerned at the front: false expectations of peace, active participation in war, and confrontation with death.

The second posthumous collection of stories, *The Square Egg, and Other Sketches, with Three Plays* (1924), opens where *The Toys of Peace, and Other Papers* closed – with writings from the front. If references to the war were indirect in "For the Duration of the War," "The Square Egg (A Badger's-Eye View of the War Mud in the Trenches)" presents Munro's attempt to treat the war directly. The attempt offers extended physical description of a kind never before seen in Munro's short stories:

> [W]hen you stand deep in mud, lean against mud, grasp mud-slimed objects with mud-caked fingers, wink mud away from your eyes, and shake it out of your ears, bite muddy biscuits with muddy teeth, then at least you are in a position to understand thoroughly what if feels like to wallow.

Even at the front, though, this speaker will meet a professional "romancer" of the sort encountered in "The Romancers."

The movement toward description, the last major development in Munro's fiction, intensifies in "Birds on the Western Front." Description dominates the narrative, although a story emerges: a story of the lives of birds, no less than human beings, caught in war. Munro had studied birds all his life, and the story should ensure Munro a place among the memorable writers on birds – just as this story, along with "The Square Egg," should ensure him a place among the important writers on World War I. The story not only displays a thorough knowledge of ornithology but takes birdwatching where it had rarely, if ever, gone: to the battlefield. The natural description of an unnatural landscape places descriptive irony at the service of a new-found, genuinely poetic lyricism.

Two political satires follow. "The Gala Programme: An Unrecorded Episode in Roman History" targets the suffragettes once again, faulting them explicitly for their disruptions; "The Infernal Parliament" shows hell's parliament to be thoroughly British.

Anticipations of Munro's turn toward extended description appear in both "The Achievement of the Cat" and "The Old Town of Pskoff." In the first, cats prove to be animal counterparts to "the Wanderer," creatures able to find a place in civilization while preserving a primitive instinct for battle. In the second, Munro uses impressionist description as a basis for a historical argument that medieval Russia still survives, if only in isolated communities.

"Clovis on the Alleged Romance of Business" mounts a final attack upon commerce, an attack that sees commerce as deadening to the imagination. The final story, "The Comments of Moung Ka," takes Munro back to Burma and a criticism of the undemocratic practices of the British government.

Epigrammatic wit, a strong dramatic sense, and a satiric concern with the ironies of social life mark Munro's stories, in which the traditions of the comedy of manners make dialogues of central importance. If Munro invests his short stories with the comedy of manners, however, the stories extend the range of this comedy by making the imaginations of children a frequent subject and by seeing in adults the often self-contradictory traces of the child. In turning to the uncanny, Munro at times moved beyond satire altogether – though even then he often returned to irony and further extended the comedy of manners by turning the supernatural and the animal into subjects of a social wit. The descriptive developments in Munro's later fiction likewise accommodate a pervasive sense of the ironies of human life – even if a lyrical voice emerges briefly, at the end, from the battlefield.

Stories such as "Sredni Vashtar" and "The Open Window" continue to appear in anthologies, where they have long been included, and many of Munro's stories have been dramatized and presented on television in Great Britain and North America. Editions of his works, both collected and selected, remain available. Although scholarly attention to Munro has diminished, he retains today a significant, if limited, audience.

Bibliographies:

Robert Drake, "Saki: Some Problems and a Bibliography," *English Literature in Transition,* 5, no. 1 (1962): 6–26;

H. E. Gerber and Philip Armato, "H. H. Munro ('Saki')," *English Literature in Transition,* 11, no. 1 (1968): 54–55;

Mary Ellen Quint, "H. H. Munro (Saki)," *English Literature in Transition,* 18, no. 1 (1975): 70.

Biographies:

Ethel M. Munro, "Biography of Saki," in *The Square Egg, and Other Sketches, with Three Plays,* by H. H. Munro (London: Bodley Head, 1924);

Charles H. Gillen, *H. H. Munro (Saki)* (New York: Twayne, 1969);

A. J. Langguth, *Saki: A Life of Hector Hugh Munro, with Six Short Stories Never before Collected* (London: Hamish Hamilton, 1981).

References:

Miriam Quen Cheikin, "Saki: Practical Jokes as a Clue to Comedy," *English Literature in Transition,* 21, no. 2 (1978): 121–133;

G. K. Chesterton, "Introduction," in *The Toys of Peace, and Other Papers,* by Munro (London: Bodley Head, 1926);

Noel Coward, "Introduction by Noel Coward," in *The Complete Works of Saki,* by Munro (Garden City, N.Y.: Doubleday, 1976; London: Penguin, 1982), pp. xi–xiv;

Robert Drake, "Saki's Ironic Stories," *Texas Studies in Literature and Language,* 5 (Autumn 1963): 374–388;

Graham Greene, "Introduction," in *The Best of Saki,* by Munro (London: Bodley Head, 1950), pp. v–xi;

A. A. Milne, "Introduction," in *The Chronicles of Clovis,* by Munro (London: Bodley Head, 1926), pp. ix–xiii;

Harold Orel, "H. H. Munro and the Sense of a Failed Community," *Modern British Literature,* 4 (Spring 1979): 87–96;

G. J. Spears, *The Satire of Saki* (New York: Exposition Press, 1963);

Philip Stevick, "Saki's Beasts," *English Literature in Transition,* 9, no. 1 (1966): 33–37.

Frank O'Connor
(Michael O'Donovan)
(17 September 1903 – 10 March 1966)

Michael Steinman
Nassau Community College, State University of New York

BOOKS: *Guests of the Nation* (New York & London: Macmillan, 1931);

The Saint and Mary Kate (New York & London: Macmillan, 1932);

Bones of Contention, and Other Stories (London & New York: Macmillan, 1936);

Three Old Brothers, and Other Poems (London & New York: Nelson, 1936);

The Big Fellow: A Life of Michael Collins (London: Nelson, 1937); republished as *Death in Dublin: Michael Collins and the Irish Revolution* (Garden City, N.Y.: Doubleday, Doran, 1937);

Dutch Interior (London: Macmillan, 1940; New York: Knopf, 1940);

Three Tales (Dublin: Cuala, 1941);

A Picture Book (Dublin: Cuala, 1943);

Crab Apple Jelly: Stories and Tales (London & New York: Macmillan, 1944);

Towards an Appreciation of Literature (Dublin: Metropolitan, 1945);

Selected Stories (Dublin: Fridberg, 1946);

The Art of the Theatre (London & Dublin: Fridberg, 1947);

The Common Chord: Stories and Tales (London: Macmillan, 1947; New York: Knopf, 1948);

Irish Miles (London: Macmillan, 1947);

The Road to Stratford (London: Methuen, 1948); revised and enlarged as *Shakespeare's Progress* (Cleveland: World, 1960);

Leinster, Munster, and Connaught (London: Hale, 1950);

Traveller's Samples: Stories and Tales (London: Macmillan, 1951; New York: Knopf, 1951);

The Stories of Frank O'Connor (New York: Knopf, 1952; London: Hamish Hamilton, 1953);

More Stories (New York: Knopf, 1954);

The Mirror in the Roadway: A Study of the Modern Novel (New York: Knopf, 1956; London: Hamish Hamilton, 1957);

Stories by Frank O'Connor (New York: Vintage, 1956);

Frank O'Connor in the late 1950s

Domestic Relations: Short Stories (London: Hamish Hamilton, 1957); republished as *Domestic Relations: Stories* (New York: Knopf, 1957);

An Only Child (London: Macmillan, 1961; New York: Knopf, 1961);

The Lonely Voice: A Study of the Short Story (Cleveland: World, 1962);

Collection Two (London: Macmillan, 1964);

The Backward Look: A Survey of Irish Literature (London: Macmillan, 1967); republished as *A Short History of Irish Literature: A Backward Look* (New York: Putnam, 1967);

My Father's Son (London: Macmillan, 1968; New York: Knopf, 1969);

Collection Three (London: Macmillan, 1969); republished as *A Set of Variations* (New York: Knopf, 1969);

Collected Stories, edited by Richard Ellmann (New York: Knopf, 1981);

The Cornet Player Who Betrayed Ireland, edited by Harriet Sheehy (Dublin: Poolbeg, 1981);

A Frank O'Connor Reader, edited by Michael Steinman (Syracuse, N.Y.: Syracuse University Press, 1994).

PLAY PRODUCTIONS: *In the Train,* co-authored by O'Connor and Hugh Hunt, Dublin, Abbey Theatre, 31 May 1937;

The Invincibles, co-authored by O'Connor and Hunt, Dublin, Abbey Theatre, 18 October 1937;

Moses' Rock, co-authored by O'Connor and Hunt, Dublin, Abbey Theatre, 23 February 1938;

Time's Pocket, Dublin, Abbey Theatre, 26 December 1938;

The Statue's Daughter, Dublin, Gate Theatre, 8 December 1941.

OTHER: *The Wild Bird's Nest: Poems from the Irish,* translated by O'Connor (Dublin: Cuala, 1932);

Lords and Commons, translated by O'Connor (Dublin: Cuala, 1938);

The Fountain of Magic, translated by O'Connor (London: Macmillan, 1939);

A Lament for Art O'Leary, translated by O'Connor (Dublin: Cuala, 1940);

Eric Cross, *The Tailor and Ansty,* introduction by O'Connor (London: Chapman & Hall, 1942);

Selected Poems, translated by Nigel Heseltine, preface by O'Connor (Dublin: Cuala, 1944); republished as *Twenty-Five Poems* (Banbury: Piers, 1968);

Brian Merriman, *The Midnight Court,* translated by O'Connor (London & Dublin: Fridberg, 1945);

Kings, Lords & Commons, translated and edited by O'Connor (New York: Knopf, 1959; London: Macmillan, 1961);

The Little Monasteries, translated by O'Connor (Dublin: Dolmen, 1963; London & New York: Oxford University Press, 1963);

A Golden Treasury of Irish Poetry, A.D. 600–1200, edited, translated, and introduced by O'Connor and David Greene (London: Macmillan, 1967).

SELECTED PERIODICAL PUBLICATIONS –
UNCOLLECTED: "A Boy in Prison," *Life and Letters,* 10 (August 1934): 525–535;

"Two Friends – Yeats and A. E.," *Yale Review,* 29 (September 1939): 60–88;

"An Irishman Looks at England," *Listener,* 25 (2 January 1941): 20–21;

"The Future of Irish Literature," *Horizon,* 5 (January 1942): 55–63;

"James Joyce: A Post-Mortem," *Bell,* 5 (5 February 1942): 363–375;

"At the Microphone," *Bell,* 2 (March 1942): 415–419;

"W. B. Yeats," *Sunday Independent* (Dublin), 12 September 1948, p. 4;

"Ireland," *Holiday,* 6 (December 1949): 34–65;

"And It's a Lonely, Personal Art," *New York Times Book Review,* 12 April 1953, pp. 1, 34;

"For a Two-Hundredth Birthday," *Harper's Bazaar,* 90 (January 1956): 94–95, 159;

"A Good Short Story Must Be News," *New York Times Book Review,* 10 June 1956, pp. 1, 20;

"Adventures in Translation," *Listener,* 175 (25 January 1962): 175, 178;

"Quarrelling with Yeats: A Friendly Recollection," *Esquire,* 62 (December 1964): 157, 221, 224–225, 232;

" 'Willie [Yeats] is So Silly,' " *Vogue,* 145 (1 March 1965): 122, 189–191, 193–195.

Frank O'Connor (the pseudonym of Michael O'Donovan) wrote some of the finest short fiction of this century. Although now only some of his two hundred stories are well-known, during his lifetime he had an international audience who agreed with William Butler Yeats that "O'Connor is doing for Ireland what Chekhov did for Russia." Collections of his stories appeared regularly; he published in the *The New Yorker* and *Harper's Bazaar,* and his work was translated into Danish and German. His poignant, sensitive fiction shows him to be an enthralled student of human behavior, one who could say, "I can't imagine anything better in the world than people."

Lyrical and realistic, his fiction offers a detailed examination – whether amused, rueful, or angry – of a middle-class Catholic world. He focuses on those moments of rending stress when essential character is revealed ("An iron bar must have been bent and been seen to be bent.") – whether the stress is the Irish Troubles, the pressure of a censorious community, an ungratifying marriage, or an unsympathetic family. Characters under immense pressure are transfigured against recognizable backdrops with a few crucial props – a card game, a bottle of homemade liquor, a Sacred Heart lamp. Although they must define their indi-

Dust jacket for O'Connor's first collection of short stories, which focuses primarily on the Irish Civil War (courtesy of the Lilly Library, Indiana University)

vidualities in relation to various communities – the nation, the township, the parish, the extended family – they are always confronted by loss, loneliness, and estrangement. Their lives are shaped by yearnings they cannot verbalize, and they are exiled from what they desire. Complex and often painful, his stories depict people uprooted by forces they cannot control and do not wholly comprehend.

Although his fiction is "domestic," taking place in kitchens, bedrooms, and living rooms, it describes startling disorientations as familiar, comfortable reality cracks open to reveal abysses beneath. Passions are strong, whether expressed or suppressed. Much of his work concentrates on conflicts within the family and between families, conflicts over marriage, religion, ethics, work, individuality, love, and loyalties. The conflict between personal morality and a depersonalized, rigid law echoes with tragic consequences in many stories, where an

individual may feel stifled by a repressive institution, unreasoning and inflexible. Although his themes are intricate and his characters driven by conflicting motives, the surface of his fiction is so deceptively simple that some may misread it as wholly simple – yet they, like the characters, are transformed by the experience.

O'Connor's biography is complicated by sources not easily unified. His two volumes of autobiography, *An Only Child* (1961) and *My Father's Son* (1968), focus on his childhood and adolescence and conclude in 1939, when he chose to devote himself full time to writing. His depictions of his childhood are memorable, as are his encounters with remarkable people – from eccentric neighbors to Yeats, AE (George William Russell), Daniel Corkery, and Lennox Robinson. Because much of his fiction emerged from his youth, his autobiography is invaluable: it includes the facts that, transfigured,

253

later became "The Face of Evil" and "Old Fellows," for example. Yet O'Connor himself, because of modesty or reticence, seems a shadowy figure in these autobiographies, with thirty years of his adult life unacknowledged. James Matthews's detailed 1983 biography, *Voices,* reexamines the early years and shows O'Connor in roles previously hidden — as husband, parent, lover, teacher. However, Matthews's interpretations of character and behavior are consistently unsympathetic. Thus, readers must approach these texts creatively, balancing them with Maurice Sheehy's 1969 *Michael/Frank: Studies on Frank O'Connor,* which collects affectionate and perceptive essays by William Maxwell, Thomas Flanagan, Wallace Stegner, and Richard Ellmann.

An only child, Michael O'Donovan was born into poverty in Cork in 1903 and remembered Blarney Lane, which "begins at the foot of Shandon Street near the river-bank, in sordidness, and ascends the hill to something like squalor." His father, Mick, a former soldier who played "the big drum" in a brass band, was intermittently employed as a laborer when sober. His alcoholism depleted the family's resources and victimized his wife and child: when drunk, Mick would brandish his razor, and once, when O'Connor was an infant, he threw them both out in the snow in their nightclothes. O'Connor's mother, Minnie, to whom the boy was devoted, worked as a maid and cleaning woman to support the family: had she become sick, O'Connor said in 1960, he would have starved. His formal education was constricted and uninspiring, except for one brief period when Corkery, writer and critic, was his teacher. By the age of thirteen or fourteen young O'Connor looked for a trade — not for economic survival alone, but because his teachers were convinced that he was unteachable. While he was a messenger boy for the railway, what he recalled as his "first wretched effort at composition" was published in a children's paper, although he liked to tell later interviewers that at the age of twelve he had put together a collected edition of his works.

During the Irish Troubles he was "involved in most of the activities of that imaginative revolution — at a considerable distance, of course, because I was too young." Yet distance did not prevent him from joining the Volunteers and, during the Civil War that followed, from joining the Republican side of the conflict, eventually being captured by Free State soldiers and imprisoned in an internment camp that he described in "A Boy in Prison." On his release he "became a librarian, which was at that particular moment the one job I could get without paper qual-

ifications." He began in Sligo and Wicklow, eventually becoming head of the Cork County library and then organizing the Pembroke library in Dublin. This enabled him to write, and he remained a librarian for a decade. He knew well that he could not simultaneously be an outspoken writer and an Irish civil servant, so he adopted the pseudonym Frank O'Connor, combining his middle name and his mother's maiden name.

In his twenties he became active in Irish literary circles. There he met AE, who published his first fiction, translations from the Irish, and essays in the *Irish Statesman,* and who in 1929 praised him by insisting that "there will be a biographer for Frank O'Connor." On a youthful pilgrimage to Paris that year he met James Joyce, about whom he later recalled that

> I ... liked him a lot, though I was disturbed by the remark he made when I was leaving. . . . I had admired an old print of the city of Cork in a peculiar frame and, touching the frame, asked "What's that?" "Cork," said Joyce. "I know that," I said. "but what's the frame?" "Cork," replied Joyce. "I had great difficulty in getting a French frame maker to make it."

Although fascinated by Joyce's sensitive evocation of another Irish childhood and widening innovations in his writing, O'Connor preferred his own re-creations of nineteenth-century realism, owing allegiance more to Anton Chekhov, Gustave Flaubert, and Ivan Turgenev than to the British modernism of the 1920s and 1930s. Crucial to O'Connor's work and conception of himself as an artist was a mutually gratifying relationship with Yeats, who encouraged him by publishing his translations and early stories in Cuala editions, and, in 1935, by making him a director of Dublin's strife-torn Abbey Theatre. Yeats was inspired by O'Connor's translations from the Irish and buoyed by the younger man's affection. One result of their friendship is that O'Connor, admiring the older artist but not being afraid to describe him as a "bully" when it was warranted, wrote candidly and vividly about Yeats.

In 1931 O'Connor published his first volume of stories, *Guests of the Nation,* and in 1932 his first novel, *The Saint and Mary Kate,* both works which he later assessed harshly: "I still considered myself a poet, and had little notion of how to write a story and none at all of how to write a novel, so they were produced in hysterical fits of enthusiasm, followed by similar fits of despondency, good passages alternating with bad, till I can no longer read them." The early stories are better than this assessment would indicate, although his first novel and its 1940 successor, *Dutch Interior,* are memorable now for the way they suggest that more-effective stories might have been written from the same materials. These early works received good reviews, although James Stern suggested in the *New Republic* that *Dutch Interior* was more a superior play than a novel.

His first book, collecting stories written between 1924 and 1930 and focused primarily on the Irish Civil War, bears the title of the widely anthologized "Guests of the Nation," which drew on his experiences as a young rebel. The collection received enthusiastic notice, the most fervent being that of L. A. G. Strong in the *Spectator:* "*Guests of the Nation* puts its author at once among the finest living writers of the short story." O'Connor spoke subsequently of its genesis in a 1962 talk, "Interior Voices":

> One day, when I was sitting on my bed in an Irish internment camp ... I overheard a group of country boys talking about two English soldiers whom they had held as hostages and who soon got to know the countryside better than their guards. It was obvious from the conversation that the two English boys had won the affection and understanding of our own fellows, though it wasn't the understanding of soldiers who find that they have so much in common, but the understanding of two conflicting ways of life which must either fight or be friends.

This title story opposes the cold ideology of Jeremiah Donovan, the older Irish soldier who puts duty first, to the feelings of the young soldiers like Bonaparte and Noble and their English hostages, Hawkins and Belcher — all of whom value friendship and loyalty between chums and pals. The Irish soldiers are forced to shoot the hostages with whom they have become friends, but Bonaparte, the narrator, knows that his helpless complicity is spiritual suicide: "It is so strange," he says,

> what you feel at such moments, and not to be written afterwards. Noble says he felt he seen everything ten times as big, perceiving nothing around him but the little patch of black bog with the two Englishmen stiffening into it; but with me it was the other way, as though the patch of bog where the two Englishmen were was a thousand miles away from me, and even Noble mumbling just behind me and the old woman and the birds and the bloody stars were all far away, and I was somehow very small and very lonely. And anything that ever happened to me I never felt the same about again.

That irreversible bending of an iron bar — which O'Connor said was derived from Nikolay Gogol's "The Overcoat" — defined the focus of the

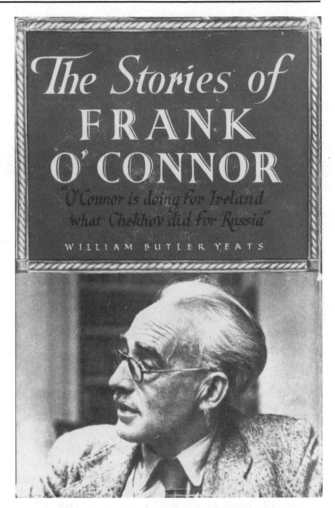

Dust jacket for O'Connor's first retrospective collection of short stories (courtesy of the Lilly Library, Indiana University)

short story for him: a small group of characters passing through a transfiguring experience with lasting emotional repercussions. "Guests of the Nation" was a story other writers envied — their admiration for it can be assessed in the number of times it has been borrowed by others — and it overshadows most of the other stories in the book except "Procession of Life," which anticipates O'Connor's explorations of the tensions between adolescents and the family.

For O'Connor, assembling a collection was an opportunity to create and re-create, as his widow Harriet Sheehy describes in her introduction to *Collection Three* (1969):

> When there were enough stories to form a new collection he didn't start trying to choose between the many extant versions of them — he simply sat down and prepared to rewrite every story.... That particular rewriting was directed towards a definite aim — which was to

255

give a book of stories the feeling of being a unity rather than a grab bag. He believed that stories – if arranged in an "ideal ambience" – could strengthen and illuminate each other. This unity was only partly preconceived, he continued to create it as he went along. He never wrote a story specifically to fit into a gap in a book – nor did he change names or locations to give superficial unity.

He was an obsessive reviser or "tinkerer," rarely satisfied with his own work; his highest self-praise, she remembers, was "Mind you, that's not a bad story." Diligent, "endless" revisions made it an unusual occurrence when a story such as "The Man of the World" was finished in three months, and given his faith in rewriting, the size of his published output is remarkable. He described his "eccentricity" in the introduction to the 1964 *Collection Two*:

> "Forgery" is how an eminent Irish writer [Seán O'Faoláin] has described this method of editing one's own work, but "forgery" is not a term of literary criticism, and is, I think, an unnecessarily harsh one to describe what at worst is a harmless eccentricity. Literature is not an aspect of banking. It is true that a number of my stories have been re-written a score of times – some as many as fifty times – and re-written again and again after publication. My wife has collected copies of "The Little Mother" she has found in the waste-paper basket, but has lost count of her total, which is distributed over three countries and ten years. This is a great annoyance to some of my friends, particularly my publishers and editors, who would prefer me to write new stories instead.... [S]imply as a forger I must be the greatest failure who ever lived because I forge only cheques that have already been cashed and spent.

The seventeen extant versions of "The Little Mother" prove that this final claim was not hyperbole. He was committed to his creative process, which began with a four-line theme presenting the "kernel" of the story in algebraic bareness and moved through multiple versions, experimenting with point of view, language, expansion, and compression until he was momentarily satisfied.

His second collection, *Bones of Contention, and Other Stories* (1936), explores familiar peacetime territory: the kitchen and bedroom, the lane, the tram, the church, the brass band, the pub. Its stories display an intuitive mastery of voices that he modestly ascribed to his weak visual imagination that left him "all the time trying to hear in my head, how people word things – because everybody speaks an entirely different language." Otis Ferguson praised this mastery of voices in the *New Republic* (3 June 1936) in terms that characterize O'Connor's best work: "Whatever the setting and whoever the people, it all boils down to the fact that O'Connor belongs to

literature by virtue of having the seasoned heart and mind (by which we mean a good man) together with the certain craft of hand and eye, by which we mean a fine writer."

"In the Train" opposes the country and the city, old and new codes of honor, in depicting the relations between Helena Maguire, who has poisoned her elderly, miserly husband, and the townspeople of provincial Farranchreesht, who perjure themselves for her at her trial in the alien modern world. In *The Short Story* Seán O'Faoláin admired O'Connor's technique and his ability to avoid the clichés of courtroom fiction: "He takes the story long after its obvious climax; he shows us the acquitted woman, the Guards, and the witnesses, all *coming back* in the train to their home. But within that general setting with what subtlety the camera approaches, one might almost say coyly approaches, the central figure. We get glimpses of her through the minds of almost everybody else before at last the camera slews full face on to the woman the story is about."

"The Majesty of the Law" again dramatizes a battle, fought in whispers, between tradition and the modern world. Old Dan Bride, having cracked his neighbor's skull in an argument, refuses to pay the fine but chooses to uphold his honor in jail. He ruminates aloud how "nothing would give him more gratification than for me to pay. But I'll punish him. I'll lie on bare boards for him. I'll suffer for him, sergeant, till he won't be able to rise his head, nor any of his children after him, for the suffering he put on me." *Bones of Contention* is also distinguished by the bittersweet comedy of a Cork brass band torn between its devotion to music and to liquor in "Orpheus and his Lute" and by O'Connor's satire of the endless talk about national problems and the national character instead of redemptive action in "What's Wrong With the Country?" "Michael's Wife," which poses unanswerable questions, is best described by O'Connor's comments on its genesis in "One Man's Way":

> Once when my father and I were staying in a little seaside place in County Cork we got into conversation with a farmer whose son had emigrated [*sic*] to America. There he had married a North of Ireland girl, and soon after she fell very ill and was advised to go home and recuperate. Before she went to her own family she spent six weeks with her husband's family in County Cork, and they all fell in love with her. It was only when she had left that they discovered from friends in America that their son had been dead before she left America at all....

"Now, why would she do a thing like that to us?" the old farmer asked, and for years I asked myself the same question.

In the late 1930s O'Connor – a public figure at the Abbey Theatre – was praised in Ireland, Great Britain, and the United States; involved in the founding of the influential journal *The Bell*; and invited to broadcast regularly on the BBC and Radio Éireann. The 1940s were difficult times for him, beginning with the severe reaction of the Irish government to his 1942 *Horizon* article, "The Future of Irish Literature," which criticized "illiterate censorships," the decline of Ireland after the Revolution into the "sectarian, utilitarian (the two nearly always go together), vulgar and provincial," and even "the emptiness and horror of Irish life" as inescapable impediments for writers. For attacking repression and censorship, he became their victim: he was not permitted to broadcast in Ireland or England or to leave the country; he could write for newspapers only under another pseudonym, "Ben Mayo."

Much of this frustration is not evident, however, in the 1944 *Crab Apple Jelly: Stories and Tales,* applauded by Kate O'Brien in the *Spectator:* "It is impossible to read Mr. O'Connor's dialogue without delight; he uses a local Anglo-Irish *patois* with close fidelity indeed, but he so infuses each phrase with the character of the speaker, and rifts it so deep with the lyricism and wild humour of his own mind that it becomes a very rich, poetic medium, charged with greatness." This collection offers stories that remarkably transfigure the incidents of his childhood. Among them are "Old Fellows," in which the child-narrator recalls being obligated to accompany his quickly intoxicated father on a weekend outing and to spend most of the day waiting outside pubs for his father to emerge, and "The Long Road to Ummera," which describes the insistence of his paternal grandmother to be buried in her hometown cemetery.

The collection's most affecting tales are the dissimilar "The Bridal Night" and "The Luceys." The first, evoking the power of love to create and destroy human loneliness, takes place in a strikingly remote landscape where the narrator casually asks an elderly woman about her children and is told the wrenching tale of the madness of her son, Denis, locked in a Cork asylum for the past twelve years because of his unrequited love for Winnie Regan, a teacher and middle-class town girl. When Denis's desperate passion has exploded so violently that the neighbors must tie him up in bed, they ask Winnie

to come to the cottage and quiet him. He begs her to join him in bed, and, above the protests of his mother, Winnie agrees. As the old woman recalls,

> He was whispering into her ear the sort of foolish things boys do be saying at that age, and then we heard no more, only the pair of them breathing. I went to the room door and looked in. He was lying with his arm about her and his head on her bosom, sleeping like a child, sleeping like he slept in his good days with no worry at all on his poor face. She did not look at me and I did not speak to her. My heart was too full. God help us, it was an old song of my father's that was going through my head: "Lonely Rock is the one wife my children will know."

In the morning she assures Denis that she will come back for him; when the police take him away, Denis says only, "Mother, tell Winnie I'll be expecting her." At the end the mother says that no one ever spoke ill of Winnie, and the narrator closes with an image of the union of landscape and spirit: "Darkness had fallen over the Atlantic, blank grey to its farthest reaches." While "Bridal Night" thus balances passion, solace, charity, and loneliness, "The Luceys" presents affection, loyalties, and stubbornness by depicting a family in a small town where secrets are impossible and gossip inevitable. O'Connor called it his favorite because of his struggle in writing it, a story of pride that divides two brothers and their families and leaves one brother on his deathbed, hoping the other will come and forgive him before he dies. The plot is simple but movingly embellished by O'Connor's deep feeling for the world of a small town and its unspoken expectations.

In 1945 O'Connor published "News for the Church" in the *New Yorker* and began a twenty-year relationship with the magazine, one that brought his mature work to its widest audience. It also enabled him to work with William Maxwell, its fiction editor and a gifted writer who became his devoted friend. "News for the Church" also was published two years later in *The Common Chord: Stories and Tales,* where a greater openness about sexuality appeared – and won tartly negative comments for O'Connor in Catholic journals. He was not attempting to keep up with the times or to write for an audience, but to write of a variety of adult situations. Many of his stories, early and late, deal with romantic love and marriage (a favorite working title for drafts was "First Love"), but sexuality had been rarely stated. "News for the Church" takes readers inside the confessional to hear a nineteen-year-old girl half proudly tell the priest that she has "had car-

O'Connor with Robert Frost (left) in Ripton, Vermont, 1952

nal intercourse with a man" – and to hear the outraged reaction of the priest. Although some have read the story as an expression of rage at the repressive power of the Irish clergy, Father Cassidy is no monochromatic enemy of the life force.

In "The Custom of the Country" a local girl falls in love with and has a baby by an Englishman who has a wife and two children. In "The Holy Door" the protagonist, a respected store owner, is miserable because he and his wife cannot have children. This situation is then complicated by his affair with the maid, one resulting in the maid's pregnancy, his wife's eventual death, and his second marriage to the woman he had loved from the start, the one who had originally refused to marry him. All of this is enacted against the backdrop of a very moral town, hungry for every detail. That censorious Irish community was the reality that surrounded O'Connor: his translation of Bryan Merriman's vigorously bawdy poem *The Midnight Court* (1945) was banned as indecent in 1946, as

were O'Connor's own *The Common Chord: Stories and Tales* in 1947 and *Traveller's Samples: Stories and Tales* in 1951. "Judas," a more typical story included in *Crab Apple Jelly,* sensitively delineates the emotional tensions in the body and spirit of its adolescent narrator Jerry Moynihan, who is enraptured by his first love, Kitty Doherty, but at the same time pained by his disloyalty to his widowed mother, who adores him and is silently jealous of Kitty. Fortunately Jerry is able to reconcile in part the two kinds of love, but the title signals the feelings of betrayal that torment him.

Traveller's Samples: Stories and Tales displays four famous examples of the type of story O'Connor is best known for, stories reflecting his childhood – a boy's-eye view of the universe in which the boy and his affectionate but often puzzled mother are allied against an ominous world most often personified by an unsympathetic father: "First Confession," "The Man of the House," "The Drunkard," and "The Thief" (the last rewritten and republished as "Christmas Morning"). In these O'Connor emerges as a gifted psychologist reinterpreting the emotionally charged stresses within families, between parents and children and between siblings. He chooses the perspective of a precocious young boy whose overconfidence in his understanding, although he cannot recognize this, is usually comic.

Terrified of his first confession in the first story, Jackie must reveal that he has planned to kill his grandmother, that he has been driven to it by her country table manners and unfairness to him. The priest is astonishingly sympathetic, and, while making it clear that murder is not advisable, he humanely allows Jackie to endure the experience of confession without being burdened by guilt. In "The Man of the House" the young boy must get his sick mother her medicine; unduly proud of his ability to accomplish such a task, he fails at it but is forgiven. In "The Drunkard" a boy secretly drinks his father's pint of porter when they are on an outing. He gets drunk and sick, and this shames his father, who must remain uncharacteristically sober. In "The Thief," a darker story, the rougher older brother switches his younger brother's toy at Christmas with his own and hopes that no one will know, but his maneuver ends in disillusionment as he finds that there is no saving illusion of Santa Claus, nothing but poverty and misery. These stories demonstrate O'Connor's affection for his subjects: to him, the writer's task was to celebrate human nature, so his youthful characters can be saved from their naiveté and the wrong choices they make. Even when they are pompous or foolish, he refuses to condescend to them in comedy: when we laugh at their limitations, we recognize ourselves in his pages.

In March 1952, having been for a decade the victim of an official disapproval that Larry Morrow called "reeking unpopularity" in *The Bell*, O'Connor left Ireland for America, where he had been invited to teach Irish literature and an advanced writing seminar at Northwestern and Harvard in the spring and summer. In 1961 at the invitation of Wallace Stegner he taught at Stanford, where Larry McMurtry and Ken Kesey were among his students. In his last years he also taught in Ireland at Trinity, the only institution to grant him an honorary degree. Students found him an enthralling teacher even when they disagreed with his approach to literature and with his faith in "the way" to write a story.

During 1952 he assembled his first retrospective collection of his finest work, *The Stories of Frank O'Connor,* which Horace Reynolds called "a new landmark in Anglo-Irish fiction." Followed in 1954 by an equally well-received companion volume, *More Stories,* these two books contain almost sixty stories covering those published from the time of "Guests of the Nation," starkly revised, to his most current work. This 1952 collection began with his most-anthologized story, "My Oedipus Complex," the apotheosis of the wise-child stories of *Traveller's Samples*. It is marvelously constructed, with the "big bed" of the parents as its center, and his command of the nuances of the spoken voice is exceptional throughout. Here the five-year-old Larry speaks with the seriousness he feels appropriate to himself:

> I always woke with the first light and, with all the responsibilities of the previous day melted, feeling myself rather like the sun, ready to illumine and rejoice. Life never seemed so simple and clear and full of possibilities as then. I put my feet out from under the clothes – I called them Mrs. Left and Mrs. Right – and invented dramatic situations for them in which they discussed the problems of the day. At least Mrs. Right did; she was very demonstrative, but I hadn't the same control of Mrs. Left, so she mostly contented herself with nodding agreement.

The singularity of this narrative springs from its alchemical mixture of language and voices: the urbane recollections of the adult narrator, in retrospect, "ready to illumine and rejoice," seamlessly combined with the sensibility and perspective of a five-year-old who invents animated dialogues for Mrs. Left and Mrs. Right. Readers are simultaneously aware of both kinds of discourse and their accompanying emotions, and neither seems false. Even the plot, potentially sentimental, is made new by O'Connor's insistence on writing as though its events had never happened before: Larry's jealousy of the new baby, soon supplanted by Father's jealousy of the new baby and their surprisingly affectionate alliance as they, both exiled from Mummy's bed, must adapt to the situation and find a place to sleep. As Larry gets Father "gingerly" to put his arm around him and assesses the result ("He was very bony but better than nothing."), the momentary peace is solidified by Father's gesture: "At Christmas he went out of his way to buy me a really nice model railway." "My Oedipus Complex," however, contributed to the paradox of O'Connor's reputation: those who know none of his other stories think of his fiction as limited to a world of precocious children, one where no dilemma is serious or irreparable.

More Stories, his second retrospective collection, was notable for "The Mad Lomasneys" and

"Lonely Rock," atypical love stories. The first, resembling "The Little Mother," takes its characters from childhood to early adulthood, with love relationships of all sorts being the common threads. In it O'Connor commemorates the human propensity for making the wrong choices with the best intentions, as the couple who seem meant for each other since childhood end up married to others – for perhaps unimportant but irreversible reasons. "Lonely Rock," with its autobiographical basis, is an anomaly: even though O'Connor had written of adulterous love ten years before, nothing approaches this story, which is set in wartime England. Jack Courtenay, married to Sylvia, is given to casual philandering, which both she and the narrator, Jack's friend Phil, know of. Sylvia pretends to be indifferent toward it or even encouraging; Phil disapproves of it. Their household is completed by his mother, Mrs. Courtenay (an affectionate re-creation of Minnie O'Donovan), good-natured and ostensibly trapped in provincial pieties. When Margaret, Jack's latest love, becomes pregnant, loses her job, and will neither give up her baby nor renounce Jack, she and her ill baby move in with the Courtenays – with Sylvia's consent and knowledge of the affair – but the fact that Jack is the father of the child is kept from Mrs. Courtenay, who is told that Margaret is a widow.

The story focuses on subtle shifts of allegiance and emotion: Phil must consider Jack's behavior to Sylvia and to Margaret; Margaret and Sylvia become allied and even exclude Jack; and Mrs. Courtenay becomes fiercely attached to the infant Teddy. All of these shifts are recorded by Phil, who is uncomfortable with the situation yet condemns none of the participants. After several months Margaret and Teddy move to more secure lodgings, but Mrs. Courtenay is heartbroken and confides to Phil that she had known instinctively that Jack was the baby's father. This shocks Phil, who had complacently assumed that the old woman was old-fashioned, simplistically pious: "It was then," he says, that "the real poignancy of the situation struck me. I had seen it only as the tragedy of Jack and Sylvia and Margaret, but what was their loneliness to that of the old woman, to whom tragedy presented itself as in a foreign tongue?"

Domestic Relations: Short Stories (1957), a collection of recent stories, reminded Denis Johnston of James Joyce's *Dubliners* (1914), although Johnston said that O'Connor's "sense of form and discipline" surpassed Joyce's, and he suggested that some of the stories in the collection were beyond Joyce's powers. This collection also returned to the thematic format of earlier collections: O'Connor had envisioned a companion volume that was to be titled "Public Relations"; another such volume, "The Collar," devoted to priests; another about children and with the punning title, "Small Ones"; and "The Little Town: Scenes of Provincial Life." The scope of *Domestic Relations* is roughly chronological, from stories of a preschool boy to adolescent romances, failed romances between mature individuals, and marital relationships which end with the death of a partner – as in "Expectation of Life," the story O'Connor wrote to "tease" his younger wife. The collection begins with six loosely connected stories about Larry Delaney, stories that take him from being a mother's boy of five to being a seventeen-year-old brigade quartermaster in the Volunteers. In these Larry must deal with emotional issues, personal and philosophical: as a child in "The Genius" he tries to find the truth about "where babies come from," falls in love with an older girl, and reconsiders his relationship with Mother. In "The Study of History" he reinvents himself, imagining the identity he would have had as the child of Father and the woman whom Father might have married, and he makes his theorizing tangible by visiting her house and introducing himself to her. In "The Duke's Children" the idea of creating another, more satisfying self is continued into adolescence, with limited success. In "Daydreams" he acts impulsively and chivalrously to aid a prostitute whose pimp has stolen her money, but he must then face the distance between his imagined nobility and real motives.

Of these stories "The Man of the World" is the most intriguing in its deceptive simplicity and its effects on the reader. Larry is here a young adolescent, self-conscious and anxious about himself and about women. He falls under the spell of Jimmy Leary, a year older but "knowing" and "sophisticated" and who, when Jimmy's parents are away, invites Larry to visit so that they can spy on the young married couple next door – a couple who, Jimmy says, does "everything." The invitation fills Larry with ambivalence: he wants desperately to be like Jimmy and to know all, but he fears the consequences. When the couple returns home, gets undressed in a quick and modest way, and then surprises Larry by beginning their nightly prayers, he is consumed by self-loathing, for their behavior is a reproach to his own, and, like Bonaparte in "Guests of the Nation," he cannot escape through prayer and is transfigured by the scene: "[B]eyond us watching the young couple from ambush, I had felt someone else watching us, so that at once we ceased to be the observers and became the observed. And the observed in such a humiliating position that nothing I could imagine our victims doing would have been so degrading." Jimmy, however, has the story's last word, which shows how little he has understood of what this incident has shown Larry: "'Sometimes, of course, it's better than that,' Jimmy's drowsy voice said from the darkness. 'You shouldn't judge it by tonight.'" The story goes beyond this seriocomic mix of gawky adolescence and self-accusation: readers trust and empathize with Larry and then must confront their own eagerness to follow him. O'Connor told Anthony Whittier in a 1957 *Paris Review* interview that his fiction is always "dragging the reader in, making the reader a part of the story.... You're saying all the time, 'This story is about you — *de te fabula*,'" and "The Man of the World" dramatically exemplifies this.

When O'Connor lectured at Stanford, Wallace Stegner urged him to publish his theories about the short story and his observations about its greatest writers; the resulting book, *The Lonely Voice: A Study of the Short Story* (1962) may appear to say more of O'Connor than of his subjects, but both are fascinating. He states that the short story "has never had a hero" but "has instead a submerged population group — a bad phrase which I have had to use for want of a better." That group at any given time includes "tramps, artists, lonely idealists, dreamers, and spoiled priests." Their identity, formed by "material squalor" and spiritual aridity, results in a form that concentrates on "this sense of outlawed figures wandering about the fringes of society" and is characterized by "an intense awareness of human loneliness." He defines the short story in relation to the folktale or anecdote, the novel, the conte or nouvelle, and considers the works of such major and such lesser-known writers as Nikolai Leskov, Anton Chekhov, Ivan Turgenev, Sherwood Anderson, Ernest Hemingway, Edith Somerville and Martin Ross, A. E. Coppard, J. D. Salinger, Joyce, Guy de Maupassant, Rudyard Kipling, Katherine Mansfield, D. H. Lawrence, Isaac Babel, Mary Lavin, and George Moore. His literary criticism may make a reader sit bolt upright at the audacity of some proposition made as if its veracity were obvious, but his experience gave O'Connor undeniable credibility, and his compelling prose makes readers reexamine their own preconceptions.

The Lonely Voice was no anomaly, as his forty years of essays and articles show. When a story or translation proved recalcitrant, he would write with conviction and knowledge on Irish history, politics, archaeology, and culture — on current fiction and theater, dream interpretation, John F. Kennedy, William Shakespeare, Roger Casement, Michael Collins, Lavin, Marcel Proust, Virginia Woolf, Arthur Miller, Jean Anouilh, Anthony Trollope, Bernard Shaw, Jonathan Swift, Charles Dickens, Thomas Hardy, Gustave Flaubert, Jane Austen, Chekhov, John Millington Synge, Sean O'Casey, AE (George William Russell), Yeats, or James Joyce.

Collection Two was the British version of the 1954 *More Stories,* a collection O'Connor had been dissatisfied with; he therefore revised it extensively for *Collection Two,* the last he assembled before his death. Harriet Sheehy was responsible for three collections of memorable yet lesser-known stories. His later work, although less known to a reading public that did not see it in the *New Yorker,* is deeper and more melancholy than his earlier work in exploring complicated relations between adults. It is not gloomy, but the solutions accessible to children in his stories are won only through loss or are entirely unattainable. *Collection Three* (slightly revised in its American republication as *A Set of Variations*) offers ambitious stories that question conventional assumptions about marriage and marital loyalties. One bittersweet story, "The Impossible Marriage," depicts two Cork children who fall in love but cannot abandon their widowed mothers — so they marry and, to the astonishment of their neighbors, the two continue to live happily as dutiful children in their respective homes. A darker story, "The Cheat," examines a marriage in which the husband, an atheist who was born a Catholic, marries a Protestant. When she begins secretly taking instruction, he is heartbroken at what he perceives as betrayal.

Conventions of parenthood are similarly rewritten in "A Set of Variations on a Borrowed Theme," when the foster children whom sixty-year-old Kate Mahoney takes in become far more real as family members than her own children. "Music When Soft Voices Die" is a striking technical departure, for it appears to be a plotless series of conversations about romance, love, sex, and morals among three women in an office, a threesome recast as if they were the string instruments in a chamber trio. Even "The Face of Evil," focused on another pious, naive young man, veers from the expected when the narrator must face the limitations of his own goodness and the inability of organized religion to save those who wander. The collection concludes with "The Teacher's Mass," "An Act of Charity," "Requiem," and "The Mass Island," heartfelt and sympathetic stories about priests under great emotional stress. In earlier stories the

O'Connor at Cashel during the 1964 filming of an Irish television series on archaeological and architectural monuments of Ireland

priests had often been the powerful voices of rigid community provincialism, but these stories display no formulaic anticlericalism.

In 1981 Harriet Sheehy assembled *The Cornet Player Who Betrayed Ireland,* a collection of previously unpublished stories written since 1926. Its title story returns to the Cork territory of "Orpheus and His Lute" but with greater emotional complications, as the child-narrator must watch his father torn by conflicting allegiances to music and politics. Given O'Connor's output and the multiple versions of his published stories, a truly "collected" single volume of his work is inconceivable, but in 1981 *Collected Stories,* introduced by O'Connor's friend Richard Ellmann, assembled one-third of his published work. Denis Donoghue spoke warmly of it in *The New York Times Book Review* (20 September 1981): "O'Connor's strength, in the best of these stories, is his generosity. Knowing what duress means, and the penury of experience available to most people, he has always wanted to do his best for them, to show the quirky doggedness practiced by people

who live on the margin." The most recent collection, *A Frank O'Connor Reader* (1994), presents works less accessible to the general reader: translations of poetry, essays, and interviews as well as fiction.

His bibliography is evidence that O'Connor was energetic, prolific, and versatile. His plays, for the most part products of his Abbey Theatre involvement, explore many themes of his fiction, especially those involving individuals caught between loyalties, and are set against backdrops of tumultuous Irish history – such as the Phoenix Park murders or the fall of nationalist leader Charles Stewart Parnell. More memorable are his translations of earlier Irish poetry, not only for the scholarship that informs them but for the energy with which he animates the originals. The emotional force of any O'Connor story permeates his translations of *The Midnight Court* and *A Lament for Art O'Leary* (1940).

Three decades after his death O'Connor's reputation is not well established – for reasons having little to do with the quality or permanence of his work. The ambivalence with which he is regarded is best characterized by his treatment in the 1991 three-volume *Field Day Anthology of Irish Writing,* edited by Seamus Deane. There he is represented by "Guests of the Nation," "The Majesty of the Law," and an apt excerpt from *An Only Child,* and he is commended by Terence Brown as being one of the most "distinguished practitioners" of the Irish short story. Yet Brown characterizes O'Connor's later work as often "conventional and formulaic" and offers this ambiguously thorny bouquet: "In about a dozen short stories he makes a claim to be considered a modern master of the form."

O'Connor has been justly categorized as the preeminent writer of Irish stories about children and small towns, but to suggest, as some have, that these were his only subjects does him no justice. Critics have found it difficult to chart his career as a steady development from youthful to mature work, as his finest pieces, in 1930 or 1965, assuredly stand on their own. He also belonged to no "school," no particular modernist or antimodernist principles or movement, and his influence is subtle, dispersed among writers who have taken his example and transformed the facts and textures of felt experiences into emotionally tangible fiction. However, it is difficult to ignore his influence in the work of writers such as William Trevor, Ita Daly, and John McGahern, who have built upon his stories their own, offering bleaker variations on his cherished themes.

Perhaps owing to the form of the short story and its original appearance in such disposable media as weekly magazines, O'Connor is also less remembered than if he had written only novels — although he is no more forgotten than his contemporaries Seán O'Faoláin and Liam O'Flaherty. Unlike them, however, he suffers the paradox of small, intense fame: the decisions of publishers to reprint the same three or four stories as representative of his work have limited his appeal. To casual readers he may also seem too simple to necessitate analysis: his work appears comprehensible on a first reading, although subsequent rereadings are consistently revealing. To some his work may appear too traditional in form and outlook, his faith in people unfashionably optimistic, his worldview insufficiently grim. Those who view O'Connor as, at best, a charming relic of the 1930s may find support in John Montague's mocking couplet — parodying the chorus of Yeats's "September 1913" — which forms the refrain of "The Siege of Mullingar, 1963": "Puritan Ireland's dead and gone, / A myth of O'Connor and O'Faoláin."

For all this, O'Connor is far from obsolete, as his concentration on the strife between individual yearnings and social constructs is undiminished by time and fashion. Although the cultural landscape of contemporary fiction will always seem more familiar to each generation of readers, O'Connor's lovers, husbands and wives, parents and children, are timeless. The elation and frustrations, the continual battles for allegiance and affection that enliven his writing, will remain.

Letters:

Michael Steinman, *The Happiness of Getting It Down Right: Letters of Frank O'Connor and William Maxwell, 1945–1966* (New York: Knopf, 1996).

Interviews:

Larry Morrow, "Meet Frank O'Connor," *Bell,* 16 (6 March 1951): 41–46;

Harvey Breit, "Talk with Frank O'Connor," *New York Times Book Review,* 24 June 1951, p. 14;

Breit, "Frank O'Connor," in his *The Writer Observed* (Cleveland: World, 1956), pp. 259–261;

Anthony Whittier, "Frank O'Connor," in *Writers at Work: The Paris Review Interviews,* edited by Malcolm Cowley (New York: Viking, 1959), pp. 161–182;

William Flynn, "Talk with the Author," *Newsweek,* 57 (13 March 1961): 98.

Bibliographies:

Gerry Brenner, "Frank O'Connor, 1903–1966: A Bibliography," *West Coast Review,* 2 (Fall 1967): 55–64;

Maurice Sheehy, "Toward a Bibliography of Frank O'Connor's Writing," in his *Michael/Frank: Studies on Frank O'Connor* (New York: Knopf, 1969), pp. 168–199.

Biography:

James Matthews, *Voices* (New York: Atheneum, 1983).

References:

Terence Brown, "Frank O'Connor," in *The Field Day Anthology of Irish Writing,* 4 volumes, edited by Seamus Deane (Derry, Northern Ireland: Field Day Publications, 1991), III: 127–128;

Alan M. Cohn and Richard F. Peterson, "Frank O'Connor on Joyce and Lawrence: An Uncollected Text," *Journal of Modern Literature,* 12 (July 1985): 211–220;

John Hildebidle, *Five Irish Writers: The Errand of Keeping Alive* (Cambridge, Mass.: Harvard University Press, 1989);

Patrick Kavanagh, "Coloured Balloons: A Study of Frank O'Connor," *Bell,* 15 (December 1947): 11–21;

Harriet O'Connor, "Listening to Frank O'Connor," *Nation,* 205 (28 August 1967): 150–151;

Seán O'Faoláin, *The Short Story* (London: Collins, 1948; New York: Devin-Adair, 1951);

O'Faoláin, "A World of Fitzies," *Times Literary Supplement,* 29 April 1977, pp. 502–503;

Maurice Sheehy, ed., *Michael/Frank: Studies on Frank O'Connor* (New York: Knopf, 1969);

Michael Steinman, *Frank O'Connor at Work* (Syracuse, N.Y.: Syracuse University Press, 1990);

Steinman, "Frank O'Connor Issue," *Twentieth Century Literature,* 36 (Fall 1990): 237–380;

Steinman, "A Frank O'Connor Theme-Book," *Irish University Review,* 22 (Autumn–Winter 1992): 242–260;

Maurice Wohlgelerntner, *Frank O'Connor: An Introduction* (New York: Columbia University Press, 1977).

Papers:

Since O'Connor believed unreservedly in revision, it is fortunate that Harriet Sheehy diligently saved the drafts and typescripts (literally rescuing them from the wastebasket) that he had thrown away. She also preserved and organized the letters, notebooks, papers, and journals that O'Connor had saved on his own. This revealing, extensive collection – its descriptive index is seventy pages long – is now the property of the University of Florida Libraries at Gainesville, Florida. It contains variant versions of many major stories, typescripts of later books – including materials for a book on dream interpretation in addition to other articles, lectures, plays, and radio and television scripts. Even more important are his notebooks and journals from 1927 to 1964, which total more than four thousand pages: the thirty-seven books contain diary entries, working drafts of stories, essays and articles, teaching notes for his courses, autobiographical sketches, "themes" of stories, and dreams he recorded.

Seán O'Faoláin

(22 February 1900 – 20 April 1991)

Richard J. Thompson
Canisius College

See also the O'Faoláin entry in *DLB 15: British Novelists, 1930–1959, Part 2.*

BOOKS: *Midsummer Night Madness and Other Stories* (London: Cape, 1932; New York: Viking, 1932);

The Life Story of Eamon De Valera (Dublin: Talbot Press, 1933);

A Nest of Simple Folk (London: Cape, 1933; New York: Viking, 1934);

Constance Markievicz; or, The Average Revolutionary: A Biography (London: Cape, 1934); revised and republished as *Constance Markievicz* (London: Sphere, 1968);

There's a Birdie in the Cage (London: Grayson, 1935);

Bird Alone (London: Cape, 1936; New York: Viking, 1936);

The Born Genius: A Short Story (Detroit: Schuman, 1936);

A Purse of Coppers: Short Stories (London: Cape, 1937; New York: Viking, 1938);

She Had to Do Something: A Comedy in Three Acts (London: Cape, 1938);

King of the Beggars: A Life of Daniel O'Connell, the Irish Liberator, in a Study of the Rise of the Modern Irish Democracy (1775–1847) (London: Nelson, 1938; New York: Viking, 1938);

De Valera (Harmondsworth: Penguin, 1939);

Come Back to Erin (London: Cape, 1940; New York: Viking, 1940);

An Irish Journey (London & New York: Longmans, Green, 1940);

The Great O'Neill: A Biography of Hugh O'Neill, Earl of Tyrone, 1550–1616 (London & New York: Longmans, Green, 1942; New York: Duell, Sloan & Pearce, 1942);

The Story of Ireland (London: Collins, 1943);

Teresa, and Other Stories (London: Cape, 1947); enlarged as *The Man Who Invented Sin, and Other Stories* (New York: Devin-Adair, 1948);

Seán O'Faoláin in 1946

The Irish (West Drayton: Penguin, 1947); republished as *The Irish: A Character Study* (New York: Devin-Adair, 1949; revised edition, London: Penguin, 1969); republished as *The Story of the Irish People* (New York: Avenel, 1982);

The Short Story (London: Collins, 1948; New York: Devin-Adair, 1951);

A Summer in Italy (London: Eyre & Spottiswoode, 1949; New York: Devin-Adair, 1950);

Newman's Way (London & New York: Longmans, Green, 1952); republished as *Newman's Way: The Odyssey of John Henry Newman* (New York: Devin-Adair, 1952);

South to Sicily (London: Collins, 1953); republished as *An Autumn in Italy* (New York: Devin-Adair, 1953);

The Vanishing Hero: Studies in Novelists of the Twenties (London: Eyre & Spottiswoode, 1956; Boston: Little, Brown, 1957); republished as *The Vanishing Hero: Studies of the Hero in the Modern Novel* (New York: Grosset & Dunlap, 1957);

Finest Stories (Boston: Little, Brown, 1957); republished as *The Stories of Seán O'Faoláin* (London: Hart-Davis, 1958); republished as *Fin-*

est Stories of Seán O'Faoláin (New York: Bantam, 1959);

I Remember! I Remember! Stories (Boston: Little, Brown, 1961; London: Hart-Davis, 1962);

Vive Moi! An Autobiography (Boston: Little, Brown, 1964; London: Hart-Davis, 1965);

The Heat of the Sun: Stories and Tales (London: Hart-Davis, 1966; Boston: Little, Brown, 1966);

The Talking Trees, and Other Stories (Boston: Little, Brown, 1970; London: Cape, 1971);

Foreign Affairs, and Other Stories (London: Constable, 1976; Boston: Little, Brown, 1976);

Selected Stories of Seán O'Faoláin (London: Constable, 1978; Boston: Little, Brown, 1978);

And Again? (London: Constable, 1979);

The Collected Stories (London: Constable, 1980; Boston: Little, Brown, 1983).

PLAY PRODUCTION: *She Had to Do Something: A Comedy in Three Acts,* Dublin, Abbey Theatre, 27 December 1937.

RADIO SCRIPT: BBC Third Programme, *The Train to Banbury,* 4 March 1947.

OTHER: Thomas Moore, *Lyrics and Satires from Tom Moore,* edited by O'Faoláin (Dublin: Cuala, 1929);

"Dickens and Thackeray," in *English Novelists: A Survey of the Novel by Twenty Contemporary Novelists,* edited by Derek Verschoyle (New York: Harcourt, Brace, 1936), pp. 141–151;

Theobald Wolfe Tone, *The Autobiography of Theobald Wolfe Tone,* abridged and edited by O'Faoláin (London: Nelson, 1937);

The Silver Branch: A Collection of the Best Old Irish Lyrics, Variously Translated, edited by O'Faoláin (London: Cape, 1938; New York: Viking, 1938);

Samuel Lover, *Adventures of Handy Andy,* edited, with a foreword, by O'Faoláin (Dublin: Parkside, 1945);

Anonymous, *D 83222: I Did Penal Servitude,* preface by O'Faoláin (Dublin: Metropolitan, 1945);

"The Train to Banbury," in *Imaginary Conversations,* edited by Rayner Heppenstall (London: Secker & Warburg, 1948), pp. 65–80;

With the Gaels of Wexford, edited, with an introduction, by O'Faoláin (Enniscorthy, Ireland, 1955);

John O'Donoghoe, *In a Quiet Land,* foreword by O'Faoláin (London: Batsford, 1957);

Short Stories: A Study in Pleasure, edited by O'Faoláin (Boston: Little, Brown, 1961).

SELECTED PERIODICAL PUBLICATIONS – UNCOLLECTED: "Cruelty and Beauty of Words," *Virginia Quarterly Review,* 4 (April 1928): 208–225;

"Literary Provincialism," *Commonweal,* 17 (21 December 1932): 214–215;

"Autobiographical Sketch," *Wilson Library Bulletin,* 8 (March 1934): 380;

"The Emancipation of Irish Writers," *Yale Review,* 23 (March 1934): 485–503;

"Plea for a New Type of Novel," *Virginia Quarterly Review,* 10 (April 1934): 189–199;

"The Modern Novel: A Catholic Point of View," *Virginia Quarterly Review,* 11 (July 1935): 339–351;

"Revamping Ireland," *Commonweal,* 12 (30 August 1935): 417–418;

"Irish Letters: To-Day and To-Morrow," *Fortnightly Review,* 138 (September 1935): 369–371;

"The Case of Sean O'Casey," *Commonweal,* 22 (11 October 1935): 577–578;

"Pigeon-Holing the Modern Novel," *London Mercury,* 33 (December 1935): 159–164;

"The Gamut of Irish Fiction," *Saturday Review of Literature,* 14 (1 August 1936): 19–20;

"The Proletarian Novel," *London Mercury,* 35 (April 1937): 583–589;

"Written Speech," *Commonweal,* 27 (5 November 1937): 35–36;

"Don Quixote O'Flaherty," *London Mercury,* 37 (December 1937): 170–175;

"Ah, Wisha! The Irish Novel," *Virginia Quarterly Review,* 17 (Spring 1941): 265–274;

"Getting at Which Public?," *Virginia Quarterly Review,* 24 (Winter 1948): 90–95;

"The Secret of the Short Story," *UN World,* 3 (March 1949): 37–38;

"The Dilemma of Irish Letters," *Month,* 2 (December 1949): 366–379;

"Ireland After Yeats," *Bell,* 18 (Summer 1953): 37–38;

"Being an Irish Writer," *Commonweal,* 58 (10 July 1953): 339–341;

"Looking Back at Writing," *Atlantic Monthly,* 198 (December 1956): 75–76;

"Are You Writing a Short Story?," *Listener,* 59 (13 February 1958): 282–283;

"A Story and a Comment," *Irish University Review,* 1 (Spring 1970): 86–97;

"A Portrait of the Artist as an Old Man," *Irish University Review,* 6 (Spring 1976): 10–18;

"What It Feels Like to Be a Writer," *Boston Irish News,* 6 (January 1981): 1, 4.

In a busy literary life that almost spanned the twentieth century Seán O'Faoláin played successive roles as biographer, novelist, critic and literary theoretician, founder and editor of an important Irish journal, historian, and travel writer. He even wrote a play staged briefly at the Abbey Theatre in 1937 and an autobiography that covers only the first third of his life. But O'Faoláin's place in world letters is guaranteed by his short-story production, which will stand in quality beside the masters of the form from Edgar Allan Poe to Ernest Hemingway. In purely Irish terms he occupies a place of honor not just as a writer but as a literary groundbreaker, a social force, and a kind of national patriarch. As Irish writer Benedict Kiely said of O'Faoláin at the time of his countryman's death, O'Faoláin gave "great thought to the country he was living in and to the best possible way of keeping it as civilized as possible." In a national literature typified by constant expatriating writers tossed about by social and political unrest, he remains, like William Butler Yeats, a beacon of steadfastness who stood by his decision to live his life in Irish terms. At the same time his appeal, like that of Yeats, is to audiences beyond the confines of Ireland.

John Francis Whalen was born in a working-class section of Cork near the River Lee to a police constable named Denis Whalen and a mother of farmer stock, Bridget Murphy. He came of age in a radically turbulent period of Irish history and emerging nationhood, that from 1916 to 1923, which is familiarly known as "the Troubles." The struggles of his parents to make a life in the city and the early influences exerted upon the youthful John by itinerant "arteestes" and actors boarding with his family are recounted in his stories and autobiography, *Vive Moi! An Autobiography* (1964). The practical and political education that he received during his late teens preceded the formal one that came throughout his twenties. His youthful experience both as a bombmaker and publicity tout for the Irish Volunteers and Irregulars, and as a student of the Gaelic language in the mountains of western Ireland, fired his lifelong interest in Irish nationalism and republicanism and contributed to the permanent position that he adopted — that of an independent humanist standing against cultural barbarism.

In the summer of his seventeenth year at Gougane Barra in West Cork, John was awarded his Fianne for fluency in his native tongue. He Irishized his name to Seán O'Faoláin (pronounced oh-foy-lawn) and met Eileen Gould from the socially respectable suburb of Cork called Sunday's Well. She was the young woman whom he married eleven years later in Boston. Between 1917 and 1929 O'Faoláin prepared for his public life. Along with his longtime friend-to-be Frank O'Connor, he entered for the first time into the cultural life of Cork, a life then dominated by the past-worshiping author Daniel Corkery. These three form the leading figures of the so-called Cork school of Irish writers. After taking a B.A. in 1921 and an M.A. in 1924 at University College Cork, O'Faoláin was helped by George William Russell and Lennox Robinson to win a £2,500 Commonwealth Fellowship to study at a university of his choice in the United States. He chose Harvard, where he remained most happily for almost three years and received another M.A. in 1929 before going off to lecture at Boston College and other American schools.

After teaching in London until 1932, O'Faoláin returned to Ireland with Eileen to start a writing career amid the gloom of the worldwide Depression and, even worse, the reactionary cultural climate of Ireland under Prime Minister Eamon De Valera. From the 1930s until the 1980s O'Faoláin worked in a hut beside a boggy field in the southern Dublin suburb of Killiney, where he produced work at a rate of five hundred words every day — a regimen that was never, as he said, in need of an "urge" from him but was rather "just like breathing." Beginning with novels of provincial life, O'Faoláin's oeuvre established the short story as a core around which biographies of Irish heroes, works of social history, literary criticism, and corrective polemics grew up. His natural gift of a prose style that soars was over the years disciplined to do so in the service of the story — O'Faoláin learned to leaven a predilection for romance with the grit and wit of irony. As he was to remark later, "Irony is the one element that saves me from being soppy."

His adamant defense of freedom of expression appeared in the journal he founded in 1940 and edited until 1946, *The Bell,* which provided encouragement and an invigorating outlet for dozens of Irish writers to become well-known. O'Faoláin defined the journal's emancipated viewpoint in the opening issue, and he insisted on what he last wrote for the journal in 1946 — that "a parochial Ireland, bounded by its own shores, has no part in our vision of the ideal nation that will yet come out of this present dull period."

O'Faoláin's honors and awards were many in his later decades, a time when he traveled widely in Italy, the country he came to love second to Ireland. His apparently happy marriage produced two children — the eminent writer, Julia, and a son, Stephen, who became a merchant marine officer. In the early

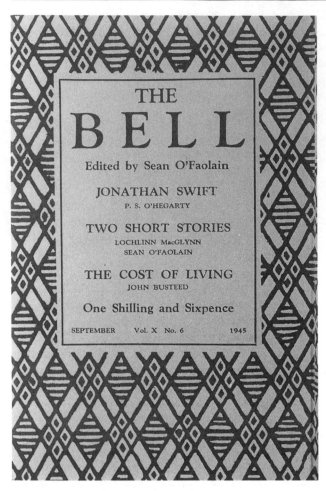

THE
BELL

Edited by Sean O'Faolain

JONATHAN SWIFT
P. S. O'HEGARTY

TWO SHORT STORIES
LOCHLINN MacGLYNN
SEAN O'FAOLAIN

THE COST OF LIVING
JOHN BUSTEED

One Shilling and Sixpence

SEPTEMBER   Vol. X No. 6   1945

Cover for an issue of the literary journal that O'Faoláin founded in 1940

1980s O'Faoláin's productivity began to dry up at the height of his reputation. Yet the critic Lawrence McCaffrey, at the time of O'Faoláin's death, described his interests as "extraordinarily cosmopolitan" and summarized the feelings of most observers when he said that "O'Faoláin functioned as the liberal conscience of the Irish nation."

The form of the modern Irish short story is often thought to have emerged during the generation before O'Faoláin's in such pioneering collections as George Moore's *The Untilled Field* (1903) and James Joyce's *Dubliners* (1914). O'Faoláin and his contemporaries inherited from such predecessors (and from others such as Corkery) a rich, dual tradition of orality, derived from the *shanachie* or village storyteller, and of literary complexity and sophistication, derived from the experiments with symbolism, psychology, and point of view tried by Continental and American story writers. Between the world wars – roughly from the emergence of a reading culture based on popular magazines until

the onset of television – the short story enjoyed its heyday, and O'Faoláin along with his contemporaries Frank O'Connor and Liam O'Flaherty was drawn by temperament and talent to the genre. In contrast to O'Connor and O'Flaherty, O'Faoláin is the Turgenev of the modern Irish story – that is, the most antiprovincial of its major practitioners after Joyce, even though his work retains its unmistakably Irish base. O'Faoláin's best Irish critic, Maurice Harmon, found in his writing a solution to the Joycean propensity for exile: "[H]is work is an interesting example of how an artist stays and faces up to home, fatherland, and church."

O'Faoláin published seven volumes of totally new stories and three collections mixing old and new ones – more than a hundred stories altogether. In them the course of his literary development runs from the provincial West Corkery of *Midsummer Night Madness and Other Stories* (1932) and *A Purse of Coppers: Short Stories* (1937) to the city in the middle volumes. He offers in the work of his maturity, which begins with *Teresa, and Other Stories* (1947), a content that is more internationally aware and less local in manner and setting, more aware of social tableaux and the comedy of manners, than that of any other Irish short-story writer. Using the city as a microcosm, O'Faoláin portrayed the preoccupations and institutions of middle-class urban society – courtship, marriage, employment and "success," adultery, and selfhood in the midst of the swarm: in short, social and domestic stability and the breaches thereof.

Titles of his successive works depict a slow widening of his career in the direction of wisdom and faith in life. The idealism and naiveté of his youth give way in *A Purse of Coppers* to a rejection of his materialistic countrymen who fumble in the greasy till. Lost innocence and an encroaching awareness of evil appear next in *Teresa,* which is followed by his own version of Marcel Proust's *Remembrance of Things Past* (1922–1931) in *I Remember! I Remember! Stories* (1961). His great themes of nostalgia, memory, and the effects of desire and random chance appear in the 1950s and 1960s, as does a new emphasis on psychological and physical passion in *The Heat of the Sun: Stories and Tales* (1966), a volume that reflects the author's developing affection for Italy. Finally *The Talking Trees, and Other Stories* (1970) and *Foreign Affairs, and Other Stories* (1976) display a culminating imaginative expansion. The talking trees of the former volume constitute the bird-filled, sacred wood of O'Faoláin's secular imagination, his point of widest empathy with his characters, while the foreignness of the latter title signals the expanding focus of his settings. In a 1957 article on O'Faoláin, John V. Kelleher observed the writer's steady maturation to the point of being "no longer distracted by Ireland" but moving with verve and humor toward an ever sharper and wider capacity for judgment.

Plot, O'Faoláin stated in the first of a series of essays on "The Craft of the Story" published in 1944 in *The Bell,* should be given a low place on the scale of technical embellishments. Instead, his stories emphasize characterization, especially that of eccentric and obsessive characters. His narrator often attenuates a story's flow by speculating on the life that is being presented; the narrator becomes a guiding conscience for the reader, with whom he effortlessly bonds. The empathy aroused by the narrative voice softens the ambiguity of many O'Faoláin plots with a tone of genial conspiratorial urbanity. Thus, conjecture and speculation abound in his stories and instill a sense of curiosity and wonder. Like Yeats, O'Faoláin likes questions more than answers and considers ambivalence the prevailing condition of sanity. As he says in the foreword to his *Finest Stories* (1957), "[A]mbivalence, once perceived, demanded a totally new approach. I have been trying to define it ever since." The ambivalence of human happiness, thwarted on the individual level by ego and solipsism and on the social level by herd instinct and taboo, is a standard theme in his stories and often lends a riddling or allegorical quality to them. Despite a penchant for indefinite narrative resolutions, O'Faoláin's stories persistently elicit sympathy for his beautifully achieved characters. As he once wrote of his characters, "Alas, if I don't love my people I always pity them." Then he added, "Damn them!"

The watershed period of O'Faoláin's literary life was his stint during World War II as founder and editor of *The Bell.* Until then O'Faoláin had cultivated a persona as a breezy aesthete and gentlemanly Man of Letters – a pipe-smoking, foulard-wearing member of the Irish Academy. He published ten diverse books between 1932 and 1939 while vying unsuccessfully for the chair of English at University College, Cork. But *The Bell* years engaged him in a lover's quarrel with Ireland, one from which he never recovered. More important, it provided the opportunity for reflection, from which came both the decision to concentrate on the short story and the ironic and knowing voice that became the stock-in-trade of his writing technique.

Collectively O'Faoláin's stories have an end-of-innocence tenor. A good example is that of "The Man Who Invented Sin," in which Old Nick as-

sumes the disarming guise of a youthful curate named *Lispeen* (Irish for frog, one of the forms assumed by the deteriorating Satan). Lispeen despoils the innocence of four vacationing postulant monks and nuns, making them feel so dirty that a lifelong pall is thrown over their innate joy. When the narrator encounters Father Lispeen twenty years later, Lispeen is "scarcely changed" except that now he cuts a Fred Astaire–like swath, flaunting "a tall silk hat and . . . a silver-headed umbrella." His rubicund face glows and shines. O'Faoláin's figure of evil declares that the four young postulants were "Such innocents! . . . Of course, I *had* to frighten them!" Hearty and beaming reassurance, Lispeen prances off – emitting a final heigh-ho as "his elongated shadow waved behind him like a tail." The dandified devil's ironic mission is not to prompt to sin those innocents whom he meets in his landlady's garden, as one might expect, but to cause them to find their joyful natures repulsive.

O'Faoláin's theme of invisible loss is matched by a concomitant one of ineradicable gain. What is gained is the boon of experience, a boon sustained through memory. "The Fur Coat" and "The End of a Good Man" illustrate the effects of memory. In the former – a popular anthology piece – a middle-aged couple who have arrived at a state of comfortable means want to announce their success to the world by garbing the wife in an expensive coat. But conscience prevents them from sinning against their lifelong habit of frugality. More than a mantle of class position, the new coat would mean that the Maguires must repudiate their foregoing lives as sacrificing patriots. In an indirect way the story shows O'Faoláin questioning the worth of his own success. The conscience that makes cowards of us all is galvanized into action by memory.

In "The End of a Good Man," Larry Dunne's racing pigeon, Brian Boru, is defeated by Michael Collins the Second. Once again the noble past is negated by opportunism, a reflexive viewpoint of O'Faoláin, who fought against Collins' Free Staters in the Irish Civil War. Larry interprets his reluctant bird, stranded on a telephone pole, in national terms: "Isn't that poor Ireland all over again? First in the race. Fast as the lightning. But he won't settle down! That bird has too much spirit – he's a high flier – and sure aren't we the same? Always up in the bloody air. Can't come down to earth." Larry kills the thing he loves most with an old Irish Republican Army (IRA) pistol, has the bird stuffed "and put in the window of his lane cabin for the world to see." Here is O'Faoláin's repeated theme of the inescapable burden of the past. Larry has become a kind of stuffed owl, as he gazes into the fire while the pigeon's eyes stare glassily out at the bloody sky, both of them grounded high-fliers.

A characteristic enthusiasm for satire infuses the typical O'Faoláin story and is transmitted in the authorial tone of a more and more detached narrator. In "Mother Matilda's Book" he mixes the warmth of felt-life with a gripping storytelling sense, showing the wicked fun that occurs when a mad old nun who is given the busywork of writing a history of her order divulges in it the shocking gossip of the convent. As one would expect from a depicter of nostalgia, there is much droll sentiment in O'Faoláin's stories, but there is little sentimentality. Writing only here and there of children (for example, in "The Talking Trees"), he invests his creations, usually at least middle-aged, with a bittersweet grace. The following three stories illustrate his typical promotion of the saving power and feeling of memory.

"The Sugawn Chair," barely three pages long, recalls the efforts of the narrator's parents years before to restore an old chair that they had acquired at the time of their marriage. The father's ineptitude as he tries to repair the seat of the chair with new rush confirms that the family's removal to the city is irreversible. That feeling of secure affection, of child for parents and of parents for one another, is perfectly and beautifully caught. In the final sentence the now-grown narrator discovers the skeleton of the chair while he is cleaning out the attic after the deaths of his parents: "As I looked at it I smelled apples, and the musk of Limerick's dust, and the turf-tang from its cottages, and the mallows among the limestone ruins, and I saw my mother and father again as they were that morning – standing over the autumn sack, their arms about one another, laughing foolishly, and madly in love again."

Aging sometimes promotes new relationships for people whose youth has faded. In "Two of a Kind," a lonely Irish merchant sailor and his neglected aunt in Brooklyn spin out wonderful lies to one another about the joys of their lives since leaving Ireland, but the lies give way to candor as their filial and maternal affection grows. The emphatic sentiment of the story centers on the couple's terrible aloneness in the midst of hordes. Like "The Sugawn Chair" it is among O'Faoláin's best heart-twisters. "In the Bosom of the Country" is likewise energized by engrossing sentiment, largely through the presence in it of three transcendentally well-drawn characters. The most interesting is the retired British army major, Frank Keene, who marries Anna Mohun six months after her alcoholic husband's death. In order to please Anna, Keene has converted to Roman Catholicism under the tutelage of the admirable local monsignor, and Frank discovers with a shock that her religion is at best vestigial and perfunctory while his has become so intense that it borders on fanaticism. The monsignor and Frank turn out to be too saintly to survive in a hazy spiritual environment that is not equal to *their* purity of spirit.

Several of O'Faoláin's best sentiment-laden stories appear in his sixth short-story volume, *The Heat of the Sun: Stories and Tales,* the title of which is taken from the moody song in William Shakespeare's *Cymbeline* (1623): "Fear no more the heat of the sun, / Nor the furious winter's rages." The stanza ends with the well-known fatalistic statement about golden lads and lasses coming to dust. Over and over O'Faoláin anatomizes the bittersweet period of life in middle age, when human passion burns not hottest but most impulsively and desperately. The topic of his best work is mature love, and one has to go to the literary pantheon – to Honoré de Balzac, Stendhal, Leo Tolstoy, and George Eliot – to locate his equals in this. In sum, O'Faoláin's usual narrative voice is that of a sentimental, ironic sensibility speculating archly upon matings and mismatings in the domestic arena.

O'Faoláin's stories habitually celebrate good food and good drink, friendship, fireplaces, and intimate conversations over brandy; and they do so without false heartiness. It is possible to see the food and drink as sublimations of sexual activity that O'Faoláin does not describe and that the short story, directed throughout its heyday at family audiences, has hardly ever described. His stories validate loyalty not only to friends but to his Irishness, a patriotism conceived in large terms and always modified ironically by an intelligent man's misgivings. It was precisely his fight against censorship and narrow nationalism during his years as editor of *The Bell* that put him outside the expatriate tradition of Irish writers of his century from George Moore and James Joyce to Sean O'Casey and Samuel Beckett. When his characters are transplanted from Ireland, they either yearn for home, as in "Two of a Kind" and "Teresa," or they actually set out to return to it, as in "Before the Day Star."

The day star, the north star, and the evening star figure regularly in O'Faoláin's stories – in "Midsummer Night Madness," "The Small Lady," "Before the Day Star," "Admiring the Scenery," "Teresa," and "Lord and Master," for instance – and they suggest, always, hope: a sense of direction subliminally detectable in the rioting skies. In fact, in the earlier stories nature is described rhapsodically and at length before yielding to O'Faoláin's greater interest in character analysis. As an impersonal biological process nature never interested O'Faoláin as it so famously did his contemporary Liam O'Flaherty. Nothing, including evil, is impersonal to O'Faoláin. It is an accurate pun to say that O'Faoláin, like O'Connor, is at his worst when dealing with evil. With the exception of "The Man Who Invented Sin," he prefers to deal with malice, overweening ambition, class-arrogance, ancestor-worship, insincerity, and infidelity in friendship and marriage – with social aberration and bad manners rather than with mortal sin, which his characters seem not to commit.

O'Faoláin himself was charged with bad literary manners early and late by Irish censors. His first book of stories was banned in 1932 mainly because it referred to a young tinker girl's "titties"; history repeated itself in 1971 when O'Faoláin won a *Playboy* magazine competition for his excellent story "Of Sanctity and Whiskey" but found that the magazine could not be imported into Ireland. Julia O'Faoláin says in "Seán at Eighty," her 1980 essay about her father, that "in the small towns of Ireland, *The Bell* was often sold from under the counter with a furtiveness usually associated with pornographic magazines."

His first two volumes, *Midsummer Night Madness* and *A Purse of Coppers,* reflect a picture of devolving Ireland in the 1920s – an angry and fragmented body politic plunging into a deep sleep. Despite his IRA activities O'Faoláin as a young writer was not interested in political proselytizing. The early books show a conservative sympathy for the old order of aristocracy and church that were under attack during the ferment of the Troubles. In the ensuing years when the country had achieved Free-State status he found that the land reforms that had been expected under the leadership of President William Thomas Cosgrave were thwarted by the shifting of an agrarian population to the towns and cities.

The seven stories of *Midsummer Night Madness* deal with the Troubles and its backdrop of land struggles – thus, O'Faoláin was looking back ten years for the material that he used in this volume, years that he had spent mainly outside the country. Two stories that typify the collection in subject matter while demonstrating his best early manner are the title story and "The Small Lady." They are both fairly long, full of an overlushness of phrase that O'Faoláin later muted. They are quite often labored in phrase and pace. Nevertheless, the title story is still extremely readable and stands as a great prelude to O'Faoláin's work.

It takes place within the great house of Old Henn, threatened with arson by the revolutionary lout Stevey Long. This edifice is clearly a symbol of the romantic Ireland that is dead or going. In the end Henn is exiled to Paris, while the narrator retains his stuffy integrity. In "The Small Lady" a monastery – a refuge for alcoholics presided over by a run-down priest – replaces the great house as an emblem of the dying social order. "The Small Lady" is the second-to-last story in the entire volume – which has, like Joyce's *Dubliners,* a pattern of organic continuity. Thus, in the final story, "The Death of Stevey Long," poetic justice exerts itself when Long, the callow villain of the opening story in the volume, is tried and executed for the murder of Mother Dale, the protagonist of the third story, "The Bombshop." The reader writhes in discomfort when the IRA buries the miserable Stevey with full military honors. But though Long is unworthy of public homage, he has actually been innocent of Mother Dale's death. O'Faoláin's social depiction of the confusion and myopia of all the political viewpoints of the period is rendered with telling ironic bemusement.

The most powerful single image of the figure of Old Henn in *Midsummer Night Madness* is of him being dragged from sleep, besotted and bedraggled, by John, the narrator, and Henn's waiting girl Gypsy. "[L]ike a picture of Don Juan in Hell," he sits up in bed framed against the fire that Stevey Long has set at the big house of the Blakes across the valley. Henn is a Titan, still at eighty years old more of a man than Stevey will ever be and a self-described "colonialist" of Irish land and women who believes his own exaggerations about the good that his ancestors and class have done for the country. He sits in a drunken stupor before the fireplace, where he resoundingly plays a British recording of Mozart's opera *Don Giovanni* (1787) and remains as unrepenting as that impious rake.

His larger-than-life quality breaks with wonder upon John, the young narrator from the city, for he has never seen a member of the ascendancy class. His response is unabashed admiration. Henn is a representative Anglo-Irishman in character and faith: old and used up, he stands in parallel with his shotgun bride, the tinker Gypsy, also a member of an ancient and disenfranchised minority that by legend descends from the Wild Geese. Henn, "in a palsy of trembling, dragging his nightshirt over his head, rump-naked, fumbling for his clothes by the pale light of the candle and the fluttering light of the burning house," sums up the plight of his class. He is a touching comedown from the old fierce Henn who once chased John's mother in his pelt when she was a girl and cut across his field. The length of O'Faoláin's first great story could be handily reduced by half, but the texture of light and dark, the sounds and smells and atmosphere of Götterdämmerung, are splendidly thick.

To save his big red house Henn acquiesces to Stevey's demand that he marry Gypsy, who is carrying a child that is probably Stevey's. To Stevey, Henn is "an English pimp": to John and the reader, he is a dissolute gentleman who befriends the coarse tinker wench when Stevey will not, just as he takes in the stunned Blakes – although "they'd rather die than come under my roof." In a summative final gesture Henn, boasting that at least "if it's a boy, 'twill keep the name alive," sweeps out of the house with Gypsy. To John – transparently John Whalen of Half Moon Street, Cork – Henn is like a "Hapsburg or a Bourbon." O'Faoláin's preference for Henn rather than Stevey is the beginning of his lifelong preference for life rather than politics, for the man committed to thinking for himself rather than the collective zealot ready only to smash things up.

The same preference is emphasized in other stories in *Midsummer Night Madness,* stories such as "The Patriot" – in which the honeymooning hero turns from the rant of the tub-thumping crusader denoted by the title and returns to his wife's arms. But O'Faoláin makes an even stronger stand for objectivity and disinterest in "The Small Lady."

The title character, Mrs. Sidney Brown, is a feminine counterpart of Old Henn. She is the wife of a British colonial officer ("Jack" – that is, John Bull) presently posted to India. Her penchant is to strip off her clothes and stand naked in the rain and moonlight, and in this state she first seduces offstage the university student, Denis, who has been assigned to guard her. To her intimates (a sizable group) the small lady is known as Bella, a name suggesting her warlike orientation and her beauty, as Denis's name suggests his latent associations with Dionysian carousing. Though she is about to be executed for having informed on six IRA men, the lady is not political but purely physical – a spectral, insatiable Lamia. In Denis's view she is Hesperus, the evening star, whose other name is Venus. After her death and Denis's escape from the pursuing IRA Tans, he comes back down to earth literally – to a valley of gaiety and rejoicing where "it was another world." Like the day star, the valley image saturates O'Faoláin's stories and represents the threatened good place of the past, a version of the Irish Tir-n'an-Og, or Land of Heart's Desire.

Bella's loss of life and divestiture of the garments of rank in "The Small Lady" correspond to Old Henn's loss of country and finery: to O'Faoláin their deaths and expulsions diminish what little the country has to offer of vividness and style. Although Denis escapes into his saving valley, what remains in the land is moribund: a decrepit monastery, mute priests, a deserted chapel, a puritanical constable (who is, in fact, Denis's father) who informs to the Tans. This and other early stories offer a country in the process of extirpating its color and definition; those qualities reappeared in O'Faoláin's stories published in the 1950s, when the modern Irish nation emerged after three decades of national grayness.

Another story which shows O'Faoláin's early misgivings about the state of Ireland is "A Broken World," which sets the tone for his second collection, *A Purse of Coppers.* This story takes place on a train heading eastward, no doubt to Dublin, and reports the opinions of an outspoken priest on his homeland and the indifference of a phlegmatic farmer to those opinions. Each departs from the train at his own stop in bad humor; the narrator is left to his musings as the train makes its final run into the snowy city. The setting of the story recalls Frank O'Connor's "In the Train," the technique of which O'Faoláin held in high regard. As in O'Connor's story the train represents process, the ongoing and interconnected action of life grinding along through time. The crabbed, "hellish" priest must, by force of nature, speak his piece on the subject of higher unity before he has to depart the scene, while the torpid farmer stumbles out of the train "exactly like an old black mongrel loping home."

Like Old Henn and Bella Brown, they are two anachronisms who have had their chance in turn, the man of the spirit and the man of the flesh, past idealism and present sloth – the first all fiery opinion, the other all watery fecklessness. They are unappealing not only to the narrator and reader but to each other, the last tired expressions of theocracy and rusticism. Just as dubious is the fate of the narrator who gets off at *his* stop, the snowy city. He meditates on "three bits of separateness, the priest, the farmer, and myself, flung off [the train] like bits of the *disjecta membra* of the wheel of life." The troubled narrator poses the question with which the grim allegory concludes: "what image . . . could warm" the people as the old religion once did, "what image of life . . . would fire and fuse us all?" The story ends with the snow covering everything and the train chugging off.

"A Broken World" conveys a sense that the fourteen stories in *A Purse of Coppers* were low tide for O'Faoláin's confidence and art. The pure depression of the story, its final jeremiad that "under that white shroud covering the whole of Ireland, life was lying broken and hardly breathing," shows the extent of O'Faoláin's emergence from the provincial influence of Daniel Corkery, whose work had warmed his early days. Instead he now reflects the jaundiced viewpoint of his new mentor, the English writer and editor Edward Garnett, toward Ireland as a place where artistic life cannot flourish. The priest's history of his mountainy parish in Wicklow where he had served when first ordained is really the history of Ireland to O'Faoláin's day – the tribes, the "foreign" names coming in, the military deployments of 1798, the perpetual subdividing of the land by the indigenous people while the baronial families married only among themselves, the emigrations, the land deserted by people gone to "live in the towns and the cities and work for wages." The gentry have been driven out or reduced to rubble, while the church and the farmers have grown disaffected with each other; the snow is general all over Ireland. Desperately, O'Faoláin asks the question that follows in the wake of Joyce's "The Dead": what hope is there for the future? O'Faoláin's tentative reply is to be found in "Admiring the Scenery." It involves the principled if unoriginal resolution of making a separate peace in one's imagination.

Clearly O'Faoláin's perplexities and despondencies during the writing of *A Purse of Coppers* are the problems of a no-longer-young writer sorting out his prospects and liabilities. The persistence of the riddle format of his work at this time suggests his tentativeness. His artistic psyche was suspended between the lush bathos of his first volume and the later smooth and worldly veneer. During the later 1930s he had recently returned from periods of living in the United States and England and fighting for a toehold as a writer in Ireland. "Admiring the Scenery," the fourth story in *A Purse of Coppers,* gives an insight into the unsettled feelings of his outlook, of being betwixt and between.

Like "A Broken World," "Admiring the Scenery" has three chief characters – a sanguine priest, a choleric "small man," and a melancholy main character named Hanafan – in addition to a phlegmatic station-porter in the background. The three are teachers who have walked into the countryside on a day off and are awaiting the train back to Newtown. As they wait, Hanafan raises the question for discussion: do ordinary people admire the scenery around them? This question leads him to the related declaration that every man lives out his own imagination of himself. The rest of the story comprises Hanafan's exemplum concerning the behavior of a stagestruck former stationmaster at this same station who fancied that he had a fine voice and who one night kept singing so ardently from the platform to the people on the arriving train that he allowed the train to pass right through the station without stopping. Thus, the stationmaster lived out his conception of himself as more than a stationmaster – as a spellbinding singer who ignores the distracting "scenery" and gives full throat to his inmost urges. So it should be, Hanafan/O'Faoláin suggests, in a country where everything is always going wrong. The preference for subjective spontaneity over social convention became the reflexive attitude of O'Faoláin stories.

But a second, more hidden story lies beneath that of the stationmaster: Hanafan himself once had a similar experience on a similar night, a night "so precious that he could not speak of it openly." On that night Hanafan was with a since-lost "friend" (no doubt a woman) to whom he recited, under the ravishing heavens, a passage from Sir Thomas Browne on the sleeplessness of lovers. Apparently Hanafan had missed his chance for love just as the stationmaster had missed the train, and they both have ended up lonely men. The story is moony and fey – too full of attitudinizing – a reflection of O'Faoláin's own confusion and turmoil, the irony of excessive self-absorption causing one to miss the train. The surface theme of spontaneity is complicated by competing themes of the danger of solipsism and the elusiveness of the muse. O'Faoláin's stories of the 1930s attest to the fineness of his voice before he had found the native song that he wished to sing.

During the next half dozen years of power and importance as editor of *The Bell,* O'Faoláin worked at a variety of literary tasks to make his living. The stories that he assembled for his third volume, *Teresa, and Other Stories,* are marked by a clear leap forward in style, by a new clarity about human character, and by the special gold of Irish writing that thereafter gilded all his stories: humor.

O'Faoláin's humor can be richly enjoyed in a story like "Teresa," in which a Mother Superior sends an immature, self-centered, and overly romantic young postulant from her order on a pilgrimage to the shrine of Sainte Thérèse Martin at Lisieux, France, in order to test the strength of her commitment to her vocation. The pampered, self-pitying child declares theatrically, "I want to be a saint!" But her models of sanctity have been gath-

O'Faoláin and Elizabeth Bowen at Bowen's Court, late 1930s

ered from motion pictures. When she stretches out-right on the floor of her cell, her panic at her discovery of an insect breaks off her meditation, and when her traveling companion, old Sister Patrick, urges her to remain in the order, she says that she cannot because there "you all eat too much." Shortly thereafter she defects for good in a tennis dress to have breakfast with her sister-in-law in London. Her crowning touch of insincerity comes two years later when she returns in material splendor for a visit to the convent with her Protestant husband, George. "You will never know what I gave up to marry you!" she assures him, as she places a cigarette between her rouged lips. George can only slink off guiltily and explain to his colleagues at work that "his wife was 'a very spiritual' woman and on occasions like this she always made him feel that he had the soul of a hog." Without preaching, O'Faoláin's satiric lance drolly penetrates the hypocrisies of Te-

resa and her surrounding characters in *Teresa, and Other Stories.*

One other story from the same collection is an O'Faoláin hallmark for its blending of satire with a new presentation, the pain of nostalgia. The blend became a familiar one in his work thereafter. "Up the Bare Stairs" is another "in the train" story, but it is done in the mature manner that culminates in "Dividends" rather than in the gnomic manner of "A Broken World": the ride from Dublin to Cork in this story, and in later ones, denotes a controlled return to the land of childhood, the realm of story. When O'Faoláin's narrator takes readers into the tunnel approaching Cork, what happens to him is like what happens to Lewis Carroll's Alice in her plunge down the rabbit hole.

On the Cork train he is mesmerized, profitably, by nostalgia, ready to penetrate his various encrustations and show his realist self. "If once the boy within us ceases to speak to the man who enfolds him," O'Faoláin later wrote in the closing lines of *Vive Moi!,* "the shape of life is broken and there is, literally, no more to be said." On this nostalgic train ride O'Faoláin's narrator meets an intriguing stranger who confides his deepest secrets to him. The personality of this character, the new baronet Francis James Nugent, is masterfully sketched in – he is a spare, wintry, graying man now taking his mother's casket home to Cork, a man whose bittersweet life has been lived spitefully. Having been humiliated years ago in school by a mercurial teacher named Brother Angelo, Nugent had been thereafter chastised by his perfectionist parents, an experience that blighted forever his opportunities for having a normal youth and has driven him to revenge himself by succeeding. He has overcompensated for his single youthful deficiency in Euclid by making himself into a robot, and in so doing he has ironically replicated the labor of his parents' whirring sewing machines.

The story is a deeply moving dissection of what pity and spite can do when they are carried to their farthest extreme. In renouncing the narrowness and poverty of his parents – in moving outward in life from the dead geranium on the landing of their flat – Sir Francis has choked off the flow of his natural affections. He lives for imaginary retaliation against people who wished him only well. As he explains, "I hated my mother and I hated my father from the day that they made me cry. They did to me the one thing that I couldn't stand up against. They did what that little cur Angelo planned they'd do. They broke my spirit with pity." The parents had silently sought their son's pity, had used it to goad him upward in the world. Now Nugent returns to Cork from London, his heart still twisted with thwarted love. Back toward the womb of pain he goes, as the train plunges into the tunnel – the water symbolizing amniotic fluid dripping from the air vents in the darkness, the narrator powerless to mitigate Nugent's self-lacerating pain.

After donning a new silk topper and black scarf, Sir Francis, belatedly vested and titled, gets off the train at the end of the story to meet his mother's people on the platform. In a most touching and ironic inversion of the birth process, the coffin containing his mother's corpse is suddenly ejected from the train's storage compartment into his fumbling grasp. Surely Nugent is wishing, too late, that his mother could see his triumphal return – he has done what she had wanted him to do. O'Faoláin demonstrates in this story a new profundity toward the

heart's devious ways, one like that conveyed by the Yeats poem "The Pity of Love" – from which O'Faoláin takes the story's epigraph: "A pity beyond all telling is hid in the heart of love." The title of the story recalls the outcast Dante, lonely in exile.

The irony and ambiguity of human emotions suffuse the stories of *The Man Who Invented Sin, and Other Stories* (1948), the enlarged American republication of *Teresa, and Other Stories.* These stories tell of the astringency inevitably at the center of the generous heart. Two lesser stories, "Unholy Living and Half Dying" and "The End of a Good Man," are good examples of this same theme, as they are of O'Faoláin's wit and intelligence. So is the quietly beautiful, mocking story "Passion" – in which six lovely lilies that are the pride and joy of the narrator's uncle are battered into the mud by a rainstorm after the uncle denies the entreaties of neighborhood mourners who want the lilies for the wake of a dead child. Owning a thing means pain, means that it owns us, as Henry David Thoreau once said. Enlightenment ignored and wisdom gained too late become staples of stories from the middle of O'Faoláin's career.

Another revealing story is "Lord and Master," which was collected in one of O'Faoláin's three retrospective volumes, *Finest Stories.* The story contains a half dozen strong character portrayals, the chief one being that of the retired schoolmaster referred to by the title, a man whose autocratic manner is at first funny, reminiscent of the bibulous pedagogue in Lynn Doyle's Ballygullion stories because, like him, Master Kennedy has taught all the townsmen and can still exert his old power of intimidation over them. Kennedy arrogantly demands that the town officials order the lake of Lord Carew drained, for its overflow dampens the foundations of the gate cottage he rents from him.

But O'Faoláin soon shows himself unsympathetic to the master's claim of his "rights." Lord Carew turns out to be selling his estate to an order of nuns; the lake will be drained and its bed put into cultivation; he has to sell the estate that his family has owned for 250 years because he is going broke and dying. Generously Carew grants Kennedy the hospitality of his manor when the latter grows suddenly ill, and then drives him around the lovely lake at nightfall on the way to the gate cottage. Kennedy has turned the town upside down for nothing: his habit of seeing the threat of Carew's power in everything is silly and mean-minded. We witness O'Faoláin's stylistic quicksilver as the two old adversaries look out over the lake from Carew's drawing room:

> Behind the haze of the fishing flies on Carew's tweed hat [Kennedy] saw an oblong sheet of water burning below its low granite coping, fiery in the sun that was sinking between a rosy scallop of clouds and the flowing hills of Villy, now as hard as jewels in the cold April air. Its long smooth glow was broken only by a row of cypresses at its far end, the reflection of whose black plumes plunged into the burning pool to spear the light again. Beneath them there were two wrestling Tritons from whose mouths two fountains rose, and crossed and fell with a soft splash. Carew watched the old man's eyes for a moment or two. They were a play of astonishment, delight, and hate. "Well, Mr. Kennedy, there's the cause of it all. And you're looking at it for, I think, the first time? And, probably, for the last time."

The "astonishment, delight, and hate" felt by the schoolmaster are only a part of the emotional mélange that O'Faoláin so faultlessly presents in this story, indeed one of his finest. As in his earliest stories, here once more is his bittersweet regret toward the diminishing fortunes of the old gentry.

In the eleven stories of his next book, *I Remember! I Remember! Stories* (1961), desire is the emotion chiefly associated with memory. The association is decidedly not the cruel one suggested by the poet T. S. Eliot, but rather one that reflects O'Faoláin's contention – argued throughout the volume – that adapting one's memories for the sake of convenience is salubrious and, in fact, essential. Otherwise, as happens to Sarah Cotter in the title story, what one remembers perfectly is "all untrue in the way that a police report is untrue, because it leaves out everything except the facts."

Sarah is plagued, and plagues her visiting sister Mary, with total recall. O'Faoláin's point is the paradoxical one that anything perfect in mankind is monstrous. Thus, "What keeps [Mary] from visiting Sarah more often is the tireless whispering of the Recording Angel's Dictaphone playing back every lightest word that has passed between the two of them since they could begin to talk." In the end Sarah's innocent perfection in eliciting details of her sister's sporadic indiscretions drives Mary to manufacture an excuse for cutting short her latest visit to Ardagh. Sarah intuits that it is the end of Mary's life-supporting visits from America – "I'll never see you again," she laments. Mary draws the curtains across the dark windows with a dramatic swish and says icily: "You'll see me lots of times. Lots and lots of times." She will not be back – everyone knows it – Sarah will go on seeing her in the relentless memory to which Mary now commits her.

In place of the Cork train tunnel O'Faoláin evokes the past in "I Remember! I Remember!" by picturing a cart passing slowly beneath the arch of the old North Gate while Mary watches and Sarah rehashes Mary's relationship with a married man: "The little cart emerged from under the arch, salmon-pink, bearing its pyramid of black peat, drawn by a tiny grey donkey. It *cric-crocked* slowly past her vision." It is a piquant figure: Mary's painful burden of memories is being trotted out by the crippled Sarah with girlish asininity. Pleasing, too, is Mary's Proustian flashback as she recalls the wood ash that was blown into the cups of wine that Joe Fenelon stole from his father's shop on Midsummer Eve years before. O'Faoláin truly has a deft feel for the fated synapses of memory.

He leads Mary to accept a dictum that she once read in Stendhal's diaries: "True feeling leaves no memory." But this rationalization will not hold up in the face of Sarah's tenacity. Slowly the reader senses that Mary is in fact guilty of the various innuendos of Sarah's casual recollections. Mary's sudden departure is much worse than any of her earlier mischiefs, for Sarah is left alone with her flawless instrument and nothing to exercise it upon – confined to a wheelchair since she was eleven, she has no past of her own. Once again O'Faoláin agitates a deeper chord of pain and hopelessness in a story that starts as a droll comedy of domestic manners.

The same process of fated randomness and its bittersweet effects is O'Faoláin's subject in the other superior story from *I Remember! I Remember!,* "A Touch of Autumn in the Air." The ambience of this story, barely ten pages long, is clearly Chekhovian and reflects the enthusiasm that O'Faoláin expresses in *Short Stories: A Study in Pleasure* (1961) for "Gooseberries," for the way that Chekhov's hero there pursues a lifelong ideal until he achieves it – only to discover that he has changed during the pursuit. As Old Daniel Cashen, successful blanket manufacturer of Roscommon, talks to the narrator, John, Cashen recalls an idyllic day sixty years ago on which he had sported among the ferns with his cousin Kitty. He and Kitty had brought the mail – two letters from Kitty's brothers – out to Kitty's father and her third brother as they were "ditching" a small meadow on the border of the family property.

While the letters had gone round, the two youngsters had flirted and frolicked. Kitty's brother Christopher, who had been a seminarian in Dublin, had written that his old girlfriend, Fanny Emphie, had entered the convent and become Sister Fidelia. She was unable to sleep well for the first few weeks, Christopher had noted, presumably because of the new-to-her traffic noises of the city. Brother Owen was doing well as pit manager of the mine near Castlecomer. Kitty playfully had made a nun's cowl from a man's handkerchief in imitation of Fanny as they had gamboled in the woods, but soon afterward she and Dan had driven home in the donkey-cart, beneath the arched trees and "the honking of wild geese called down from the north by the October moon." On the trek back, they had stopped for sweets that had the brand-name of "Conversation Lozenges," and this confection has triggered Dan's memory so many years later when he happens upon them in a candy store.

It is a simple story of an old bachelor's chance memory in the autumn of life. Yet by a combination of vivid pictorial suggestions O'Faoláin suggests Daniel Cashen's terrible sense of the deprivation of his whole adult life. For him the memory of Kitty and her relatives in the meadow is a spot of time, a moment when perfect human unity was apprehended: "It was a picture to be remembered for years: the meadow, the old man, the smoke of the distant farmhouse, patriarchal, sheltered, simple." All of life had been there that day between morning and moonlight in the river bottom, where "hundreds of streams and dykes" flowed together. Dan's own life, obviously, might have flowed along a different, better course. The paradigm of the men ditching in the primordial river, out of time, is lovingly and delicately developed by O'Faoláin. One sees that Kitty's brothers — one gone to heaven and the other to hell, but both gone from the farm in what used to be called the "Queen's County" — represent poles of possibility for the young. One sees that, when old Dan impulsively peers under the nun's cowl in the sweets-and-toys shop where his reverie starts and comes upon the old face of a total stranger, "he is as young in desire as any fledgling courtier," and one realizes that the honking geese are harbingers of winter and the passing of time, ultimately of the cold and beckoning grave.

Like Leo Tolstoy's Ivan Ilych, old Dan is a figure whose business success and belief that his life had been advancing upward has been undermined: life has gone downhill for him ever since his moment with Kitty in the meadow. His reverie confirms his insight into the littleness of his life, and he dies one week later. It is a masterfully dry yet full-bodied story, the *blanc de blanc* of the collection. O'Faoláin leaves the reader to muse over many understated images of time and loss — such as the "revolving glass doors" of the hotel that flash with "the whole movement of the universe since time began,"

or the woolen blankets that Cashen had made his refuge after the green ferns once covered him and Kitty, or the veiny ditches and streams struggling to the open sea. The story is sad, and lovely, and near perfect in its depth of feeling.

If memory is O'Faoláin's touchstone in *I Remember! I Remember!,* atmosphere is his prime concentration in the ten new stories of his next collection, *The Heat of the Sun: Stories and Tales.* The thick feel of surrounding things — of texture, weather, comforting and discomforting environments — is emphasized here. The two best stories of the collection are the title story and "Dividends." In the first Johnny Kendrick, a merchant sailor, returns to the warm wood and glass of his favorite pub south of Dublin but finds that Alfie, the bartender who had always held his group of drinking cronies together, has cancer and is in the Hospice for the Dying. The group impetuously goes around to offer comfort to the bartender's estranged wife, and, after the departure of the others, Johnny falls asleep next to her in bed. But Johnny's thoughts are all of the beautiful tease Deirdre, an unsteadfast member of the pub group who had deserted it in search of men who could give her expensive love tokens like sports cars; thus, the jilted Johnny and the bartender's widow-to-be are, to one another, substitutes for the companions they really crave in time of need.

When Johnny awakens suddenly at 5 A.M., he finds Alfie's wife sitting in Alfie's overcoat by the cold fire, instinctively sure that Alfie has died in the night. The heat of the sun — the warmth of companionship and fellow feeling now denied to Alfie — is likewise extinguished from the midst of the drinking group by Alfie's death. As Johnny goes home through the damp night, his prospects for a carefree night of pleasure now dashed, he stops to view a blackened "coal-tub" in the Coal Harbour — another reminder of his grimy nomad life — as a dawn jet soars out of Dublin above him. Amid the warm interiors of the bar scenes, the "gleam of the bottles and the wet mahogany, and the slow, floating layers of smoke," O'Faoláin gradually chips away at his protagonist's vagrant hopes and shows him forced to learn the transiency of affection, the fragility of expectation. The story has a roller-coaster structure from the boozy insulation of the pub to the deathly Coal Harbour, where everything comes to dust. This is a typical story of O'Faoláin's later period, one with a frisson of terror, of the sun burning off and of Johnny finding that he, like all mankind, is becoming like Alfie.

A particularly amusing and "O'Faoláinesque" story is "Dividends," which marks the highest quality of his work in the 1960s. Even here O'Faoláin limits his plot to a handful of essentials. The narrator's old Aunt Anna, poor all her life, sells the stock she inherits but continues every month to call on her broker, Mel Meldrum, to collect the dividends on it. The narrator, Seán, comes to Cork (through the inexorable tunnel) at the urgent request of his friend Mel and stays the weekend at Mel's regal "cottage" on the outskirts of the city. But Seán cannot make Aunt Anna see her illogic about the dividends – he can only enjoy Mel's argumentative hospitality while he observes Mel's compromising relationship with his housekeeper-typist, Sheila. The story, one of O'Faoláin's longer ones, ends with Seán's departure for Dublin after Mel states his intention to "sack" Sheila and replace her with the redoubtable Aunt Anna as his housekeeper. In gratitude Anna bequeaths her nonexistent dividends to him.

What clearly interests O'Faoláin is the moral and ethical dispute carried on by Seán and Mel. O'Faoláin spotlights with enthusiasm the dipoles and angularities of Irish belief and attitude in the contending arguments of the two old schoolmates. His real achievement in "Dividends" is in capturing with seeming ease so much dynamic character expression during one sunny weekend in June when each of his four figures reaches a major crossroads. While seeming more discursive than O'Faoláin's earlier stories, "Dividends" and the other stories in *The Heat of the Sun* are actually much tauter, tending toward Stendhal's conception of prose narrative as a "mirror being carried along a highway."

Chief among the contrasts in the story is that between the wealthy and Oxford-educated Mel, a "precise, piercing, priggish and prim" Corkonian, and the more pragmatic narrator, Seán, from Dublin. But Mel has a provincial and narrow-minded streak, the same liabilities that Seán has overcome since moving to the capital and taking on the mantle of the artist. Seán and Mel are obvious surrogates for O'Faoláin, as he mulls the disparities between his actual life and the road not taken.

Mel flaunts his substance, such as his ostentatious white Jaguar, but Ireland is not ready for such chic, as we see when his car is impeded in the middle of the city by a flock of bullocks and drovers. His sumptuous house and style are out of scale with Anna's slum flat and Sheila's cottage, and his money threatens to pervert all the characters in the story. Anna, when she sees the Turkish carpet in Mel's brokerage, splurges foolishly on a fur coat.

She begins to play the role of "a Country Lady in reduced circumstances." So too Sheila is swept beyond her power to resist by Mel, who is twice her age: he comes between her and her motorbiking boyfriend. In short, although Mel grows not to notice the human grief his wealth produces, he humiliates people with his money: Sheila and Anna, as younger and older versions of the same character, are made into Irish servants by it. At bottom, "Dividends" presents O'Faoláin's assault on modernism, egotism, vulgarity, and impersonality – a testimonial to a decent, reflective, unselfish view of life. What Seán must finally teach Mel is the right way to live, and their reencounter is the logical outcome of their schoolboy philosophical disagreements.

As Mel returns from taking Sheila home, Seán waits at Mel's cottage, where he listens to Richard Wagner's *Siegfried Idyll* – the same music that later courses through the house and awakens Seán at 2 A.M. Here the music evokes both the lovely story of Wagner's devotion to his Cosima – a December–May match like that of Mel and Sheila – and the sad romance of Brunhilde languishing in Valhalla until she is delivered by her lover's kiss. Seán says that the music "made me wish to God I was at home in bed with my wife." Ultimately Seán manages to rekindle Mel's pity, and Mel comes to believe in his own advice to his clients: a real investor knows that he must take a risk in order to accumulate dividends and not just coldly rake off fixed profits. O'Faoláin skillfully disguises the moralizing of "Dividends" beneath blankets of humorous and sophisticated prose, and Seán sums up the point: "[W]e do all the important things of life for reasons ... of which reason knows nothing – until about twenty years later."

O'Faoláin reembraced gentle preachment and worldly style in his seventh volume of stories, *The Talking Trees and Other Stories*. Of the eleven stories in the collection, "Hymeneal" is a trenchant example of its creator's later vein. It presents one of O'Faoláin's most powerful domestic dramas in which the point of the story does not emerge until the end, when Phil Doyle is asked to sort out the effects of his boss, brother-in-law, and supposed best friend, Failey Quigley, who has been killed in a car crash. Phil returns reluctantly to Dublin from rural Clare, where he has just moved with his wife, Abby, and after the funeral spends the whole night poring over Failey's intimate papers. Throughout his career as an inspector of primary schools Phil has bristled at the stupidity of all his superiors, including Failey, but his contempt for the dead man – whom he had always thought of as an "ingratiating, devious, ambitious, convivial" opportunist — slowly evaporates as Phil comes to see from the confidential documents that Failey had really been his long-time secret benefactor.

Phil grows more and more agitated at his discovery; it is pure gall for him to have to feel admiration and gratitude toward any man, especially the successful Failey. Plunging into the rainy street, he revisits his old house on the North Circular Road, the house which, as Phil discovers from Failey's effects, Failey had repurchased for him and for Abby, with whom Failey had once had a love affair. Phil returns to Failey's study chastened by the cleansing rains. He dons Failey's old dressing gown and overcoat while his own clothes dry and descends to the kitchen in the morning to sit in Failey's breakfast place, where he is doted on by Abby and Failey's widow. The marriage song of O'Faoláin's wistful title will sound over Phil and Abby's second honeymoon in their old house, one feels, and their new union will be blessed by the softening of Phil's crabby and envious nature.

"Hymeneal" is a greathearted story, though never cloying; its point is that wisdom may come belatedly as a compensation for other losses, that kindness need not be beyond our expectations, and that with age comes a richness unknown earlier in life. And O'Faoláin practices what he has preached: Phil Doyle had planned for years to write during retirement "The Book," a poisonous autobiographical exposé that would settle all of his old accounts with the fools whom he had suffered for a lifetime. Now Phil will not write "The Book"; nor did O'Faoláin, as he moved into old age, surrender his bittersweet but cheerful and compassionate outlook.

The same amused, humane outlook is maintained throughout the stories of O'Faoláin's last original collection, *Foreign Affairs, and Other Stories.* As in *The Talking Trees,* the characteristic note is sardonic — a word denoting a Sardinian plant said to produce laughter so compulsive that death results, a plant whose cousin is named woody nightshade, or (a key epithet for O'Faoláin) bittersweet. Constantly he mixes pleasure with regret, laughter with pain — never with rancor or animosity. O'Faoláin's late stories are softhearted but not softheaded, still rooted in the comedy of manners; they are more crisply cosmopolitan, more frank, sadly accepting, and worldly than his earlier ones.

Here, for instance, is the opening paragraph of the first story of *Foreign Affairs,* a boudoir comedy entitled "The Faithless Wife":

He had now been stalking his beautiful Mlle. Morphy, whose real name was Mrs. Meehawl O'Sullivan, for six weeks, and she had appeared to be so amused at every stage of the hunt, so responsive, *entrainante,* even *aquichante,* that he could already see the kill over the next horizon. At their first encounter, during the St. Patrick's Day cocktail party at the Dutch embassy, accompanied by a husband who had not a word to throw to a cat about anything except the scissors and shears that he manufactured somewhere in the West of Ireland, and who was obviously quite ill at ease and drank too much Irish whiskey, what had attracted him to her was not only her splendid Boucher figure (whence his sudden nickname for her, La Morphée), or her copper-colored hair, her lime-green Irish eyes and her seemingly poreless skin, but her calm, total and subdued elegance: the Balenciaga costume, the peacock-skin gloves, the gleaming crocodile handbag, a glimpse of tiny, lace-edged lawn handkerchief and her dry, delicate scent. He had a grateful eye and nose for such things. It was, after all, part of his job.

The "He" of the first sentence is the French diplomat Ferdinand Clichy, a histrionic lover whose headlong affair with Celia O'Sullivan comes to an end when her husband has a permanently debilitating stroke and she, out of pity, refuses to desert him. Never was O'Faoláin's characterization so sure as when the romance of the adulterous middle-aged lovers picks up momentum. Having reached the supposed candor of mature years, Celia and Ferdy actually prefer the delicious guilt of make-believe. "Your trick is to be innocence masquerading as villainy," Ferdy says to her, when he insists that she use signals such as "Three red geraniums in a row on the windowsill" to let him know that the coast is clear: "He could, she knew, have more easily checked with her by telephone, but . . . she accepted with an indulgent amusement what he obviously considered ingenious devices for increasing the voltage of passion by the trappings of conspiracy."

The whole story, as O'Faoláin structures it, is a tease, the movement of which is kept slow but pointed to the end, where the impossibility of Celia and Ferdy's affair becomes manifest to them. Then the author closes the narrative perfunctorily. O'Faoláin is instinctively not a writer to attenuate the painful implications of the lovers' breakup nor to reach for coy finales after the comedy ends. Instead, the breakup is prompted by Celia — who answers the claim of Ferdy's final letter that "You are the love of my life!" with Irish fatalism: "Don't *I* know it?"

O'Faoláin's favorite subject is in such mating of late October with late October, of Anthonys and Cleopatras in well-cut Irish tweeds. The coordinates of his prose are adjusted to the time when common sense flourishes but is troubled by passion, passion that understands mutability. Then the wary are flushed out. O'Faoláin's ultimately homespun soul always softens the incrustations that a sophisticated world tries to impose on his characters. The touchstones at the end of his writing career include a sardonic sense of life's running comedy, especially in its mating institutions; a tender feeling for the good things in life; and a penchant for late love. He gains in heart and mind from beginning to end.

Although O'Faoláin's death in 1991 received due notice in the world press, his popular reputation had by then abated – no book from him had appeared since the enormous *Collected Stories* (1980), which is now out of print. With the exception of his autobiography, no full-length work in other genres had appeared since the late 1950s. Extended critical work on O'Faoláin had also diminished by the 1980s, with the exception of Richard Bonaccorso's important book in 1987. After being included four times in the reference work *Contemporary Novelists*, he was dropped from the fifth edition of the work, and discussion of his daughter was substituted. There are few significant writers presently more deserving of serious scholarly attention than O'Faoláin, for whom we have as yet no real biography, no bibliography, collected letters, or definitive critical canon. All of these things will surely be forthcoming for a writer of his caliber.

Interviews:

Lewis Nichols, "Talk with Mr. O'Faoláin," *New York Times Book Review,* 12 May 1957, pp. 26–27;

"Talk with the Author," *Newsweek,* 59 (8 January 1962): 67;

Richard Diers, "On Writing: An Interview with Seán O'Faoláin," *Mademoiselle,* 56 (March 1963): 151, 209–215;

Julia O'Faoláin, "Seán at Eighty," *London Magazine,* 20 (June 1980): 18–28.

References:

Deborah M. Averill, "Seán O'Faoláin," in her *The Irish Short Story from George Moore to Frank O'Connor* (Washington, D.C.: University Press of America, 1982), pp. 153–224;

Richard Bonaccorso, "Irish Elegies: Three Tales of Gougane Barra," *Studies in Short Fiction,* 19 (Spring 1982): 163–167;

Bonaccorso, "Seán O'Faoláin's Foreign Affair," *Eiré-Ireland,* 16 (Summer 1981): 134–144;

Bonaccorso, *Seán O'Faoláin's Irish Vision* (Albany: State University of New York Press, 1987);

Neville Braybrooke, "Seán O'Faoláin: A Study," *Dublin Magazine,* 31 (April–June 1955): 22–27;

Hubert Butler, "*The Bell*: An Anglo-Irish View," *Irish University Review,* 6 (Spring 1976): 66–72;

Robert Cantwell, "Poet of the Irish Revolution," *New Republic,* 77 (24 January 1934): 313–314;

Malcolm Cowley, "Yeats and O'Faoláin," *New Republic,* 98 (15 February 1939): 49–50;

Gary T. Davenport, "Seán O'Faoláin's Troubles: Revolution and Provincialism in Modern Ireland," *South Atlantic Quarterly,* 75 (Summer 1976): 312–322;

Eilís Dillon, "Seán O'Faoláin and the Young Writer," *Irish University Review,* 6 (Spring 1976): 37–44;

Paul A. Doyle, *Seán O'Faoláin* (New York: Twayne, 1968);

Doyle, "Seán O'Faoláin and *The Bell,*" *Eiré-Ireland,* 1 (Fall 1966): 58–62;

Joseph Duffy, "A Broken World: The Finest Short Stories of Seán O'Faoláin," *Irish University Review,* 6 (Spring 1976): 30–36;

Richard Fallis, *The Irish Renaissance* (Syracuse, N.Y.: Syracuse University Press, 1977), pp. 228–232;

James T. Farrell, "A Harvest of O'Faoláin," *New Republic,* 136 (17 June 1957): 19–20;

James Finn, "High Standards and High Achievements," *Commonweal,* 66 (26 July 1957): 428–429;

Dermot Foley, "Monotonously Rings the Little Bell," *Irish University Review,* 6 (Spring 1976): 54–63;

Horace Gregory, "Imaginative Tales," *Saturday Review,* 40 (25 May 1957): 15–16;

Katherine Hanley, "The Short Stories of Seán O'Faoláin: Theory and Practice," *Eiré-Ireland,* 6 (Fall 1971): 3–11;

Maurice Harmon, *Seán O'Faoláin: A Critical Introduction* (Notre Dame, Ind.: University of Notre Dame Press, 1966);

Harmon, ed., "Seán O'Faoláin Special Issue," *Irish University Review,* 6 (Spring 1976);

L. V. Harrold, "The Ruined Temples of Seán O'Faoláin," *Eiré-Ireland,* 9 (Spring 1974): 115–119;

Robert H. Hopkins, "The Pastoral Mode of Seán O'Faoláin's 'The Silence of the Valley,'" *Studies in Short Fiction,* 1 (Winter 1964): 93–98;

Hilary Jenkins, "Newman's Way and O'Faoláin's Way," *Irish University Review,* 6 (Spring 1976): 87–94;

John V. Kelleher, "Loneliness Is the Key," *New York Times Book Review*, 12 May 1957, pp. 5, 23;

Kelleher, "Seán O'Faoláin," *Atlantic Monthly*, 199 (May 1957): 67–69;

Thomas E. Kennedy, "Seán O'Faoláin's 'The Silence of the Valley,'" *Critique*, 29 (Spring 1988): 188–194;

Benedict Kiely, *Modern Irish Fiction: A Critique* (Dublin: Golden Eagle Books, 1950), pp. 113–121;

James F. Kilroy, "Setting the Standards: Writers of the 1920s and 1930s," in his *The Irish Short Story: A Critical History* (Boston: Twayne, 1984), pp. 122–135;

Guy Le Moigne, "Seán O'Faoláin's Short Stories and Tales," in *The Irish Short Story*, edited by Patrick Rafroidi and Terence Brown (Atlantic Highlands, N.J.: Humanities Press, 1979), pp. 205–226;

Patrick Lynch, "O'Faoláin's Way: Pages from a Memoir," *Irish University Review*, 22 (Spring 1992): 142–150;

F. S. L. Lyons, "Seán O'Faoláin as Biographer," *Irish University Review*, 6 (Spring 1976): 95–109;

Robie Macauley, "Seán O'Faoláin, Ireland's Youngest Writer," *Irish University Review*, 6 (Spring 1976): 110–117;

Lawrence J. McCaffrey, "Seán O'Faoláin: A Tribute," *Irish Literary Supplement*, 10 (Fall 1991): 17–18;

Donal McCartney, "Seán O'Faoláin: A Nationalist Right Enough," *Irish University Review*, 6 (Spring 1976): 73–86;

Sean McMahon, "O My Youth, O My Country," *Eiré-Ireland*, 6 (Fall 1971): 145–156;

Vivian Mercier, "The Professionalism of Seán O'Faoláin," *Irish University Review*, 6 (Spring 1976): 45–53;

Julian Moynahan, "God Smiles, the Priest Beams, and the Novelist Groans," *Irish University Review*, 6 (Spring 1976): 19–29;

Donat O'Donnell (Conor Cruise O'Brien), "The Parnellism of Seán O'Faoláin," in his *Maria Cross* (New York: Oxford University Press, 1952), pp. 95–115;

Peadar O'Donnell, "The Irish Press and Seán O'Faoláin," *Bell*, 18 (Summer 1953): 5–7;

V. S. Pritchett, "O'Faoláin's Troubles," *New Statesman*, 70 (13 August 1965): 219–220;

Joseph Storey Rippier, *The Short Stories of Seán O'Faoláin: A Study in Descriptive Techniques* (New York: Barnes & Noble, 1976);

Denis Sampson, "'Admiring the Scenery': Seán O'Faoláin's Fable of the Artist," *Canadian Journal of Irish Studies*, 3 (Spring 1977): 72–79;

William Saroyan, "The Unholy Word," *Bell*, 15 (October 1947): 33–37;

Richard J. Thompson, "Seán O'Faoláin: Love's Old Sweet Song," in his *Everlasting Voices: Aspects of the Modern Irish Short Story* (Troy, N.Y.: Whitston, 1989), pp. 30–61.

Papers:

The Bancroft Library, University of California, Berkeley, has an extensive collection of O'Faoláin's letters and manuscripts.

Liam O'Flaherty

(28 August 1896 – 7 September 1984)

Paul A. Doyle
Nassau Community College (SUNY)

See also the O'Flaherty entry in *DLB 36: British Novelists, 1890–1929: Modernists* and *DLB Yearbook 1984*.

BOOKS: *Thy Neighbour's Wife* (London: Cape, 1923; New York: Boni & Liveright, 1924);

The Black Soul (London: Cape, 1924; New York: Boni & Liveright, 1925);

The Informer (London: Cape, 1925; New York: Knopf, 1925);

Civil War (London: Archer, 1925);

The Terrorist (London: Archer, 1926);

Darkness: A Tragedy in Three Acts (London: Archer, 1926);

Mr. Gilhooley (London: Cape, 1926; New York: Harcourt, Brace, 1927);

The Child of God (London: Archer, 1926);

The Life of Tim Healy (London: Cape, 1927; New York: Harcourt, Brace, 1927);

The Assassin (London: Cape, 1928; New York: Harcourt, Brace, 1928);

A Tourist's Guide to Ireland (London: Mandrake, 1929);

The House of Gold (London: Cape, 1929; New York: Harcourt, Brace, 1929);

The Return of the Brute (London: Mandrake, 1929; New York: Harcourt, Brace, 1930);

Joseph Conrad: An Appreciation (London: Lahr, 1930);

Two Years (London: Cape, 1930; New York: Harcourt, Brace, 1930);

The Puritan (London: Cape, 1931; New York: Harcourt, Brace, 1932);

The Ecstasy of Angus (London: Joiner & Steele, 1931);

A Cure for Unemployment (London: Lahr, 1931);

I Went to Russia (London: Cape, 1931; New York: Harcourt, Brace, 1931);

Skerrett (London: Gollancz, 1932; New York: Long & Smith, 1932);

The Martyr (London: Gollancz, 1933; New York: Macmillan, 1933);

Shame the Devil (London: Grayson & Grayson, 1934);

Liam O'Flaherty, 1952

Hollywood Cemetery (London: Gollancz, 1935);

Famine (London: Gollancz, 1937; New York: Random House, 1937);

Land (London: Gollancz, 1946; New York: Random House, 1946);

Insurrection (London: Gollancz, 1950; Boston: Little, Brown, 1951);

The Wilderness (Portmarnock, Ireland: Wolfhound, 1978; New York: Dodd, Mead, 1986).

Collections: *Spring Sowing* (London: Cape, 1924; New York: Knopf, 1926);

The Tent (London: Cape, 1926);

The Fairy Goose, and Two Other Stories (London: Faber & Gwyer, 1927; New York: Crosby Gaige, 1927);

Red Barbara, and Other Stories (London: Faber & Gwyer, 1928; New York: Crosby Gaige, 1928);

The Mountain Tavern, and Other Stories (London: Cape, 1929; New York: Harcourt, Brace, 1929);

The Wild Swan, and Other Stories (London: Jackson, 1932);

The Short Stories of Liam O'Flaherty (London: Cape, 1937; abridged edition, London: Digit Books, 1961); abridged and republished as *Selected Short Stories of Liam O'Flaherty* (London: New English Library, 1970); abridged and republished as *More Short Stories of Liam O'Flaherty* (London: New English Library, 1971); republished as *Liam O'Flaherty's Short Stories*, 2 volumes (London: New English Library, 1981);

Two Lovely Beasts, and Other Stories (London: Gollancz, 1948; New York: Devin-Adair, 1950);

Dúil [Desire] (Baile Átha Cliath [Dublin]: Sáirséal agus Dill, 1953);

The Stories of Liam O'Flaherty (New York: Devin-Adair, 1956);

Irish Portraits: 14 Short Stories (London: Sphere Books, 1970);

The Pedlar's Revenge, and Other Stories (Dublin: Wolfhound, 1976); republished as *Short Stories: The Pedlar's Revenge and Other Stories* (Dublin: Wolfhound, 1982);

The Test of Courage (Dublin: Wolfhound, 1977);

The Wave, and Other Stories (London: Longman, 1980).

PLAY PRODUCTION: *Dorchadas,* Dublin, 1925; privately performed in English as *Darkness,* London, studio of William Roberts, 27 April 1926.

OTHER: Alfred Lowe, *Six Cartoons,* introduction by O'Flaherty (London: W. & G. Foyle, 1930);

Heinrich Hauser, *Bitter Water,* introduction by O'Flaherty (London: Wishart, 1930); republished as *Bitter Waters,* introduction by O'Flaherty (New York: Liveright, 1930);

Rhys Davies, *The Stars, the World, and the Women,* foreword by O'Flaherty (London: Jackson, 1930);

J. C. Grant, *The Back-to-Backs,* introduction by O'Flaherty (London: Chatto & Windus, 1930).

The most significant fact regarding Liam O'Flaherty's biography and writing is that he was born on Inishmore, one of the bleak, desolate Aran Islands – an isolated, primitive, often fogbound area constantly battered by storms and storm-tossed seas off the west coast of Ireland. O'Flaherty's characters and their environment recall those described by Samuel Taylor Coleridge's "Kubla Khan": "a savage place! / . . . haunted / By woman wailing for her demon lover! / . . . with ceaseless turmoil seething, / As if this earth in fast thick pants were breathing."

Farming on the Aran Islands is difficult because much of the soil is rocky, not conducive to tilling and growth. In addition to farming many inhabitants make their livings by fishing, but the ever-present storms make this particularly precarious. The islands thus foster basic instincts and emotions, because nature there not only encourages such reactions but demands them. Certainly O'Flaherty's characters are marked by wild mood swings and often by bizarre, contradictory behavior – as was their creator's own temperament. A barbarism often seemingly untouched by any notions of manners and civility predominates in his characters, who present at times some "wild man of Borneo" features like those of figures in carnival sideshows years ago – but that are far from fraudulent or fictitious in O'Flaherty's portrayals. This wildness and instability are not only preeminent in O'Flaherty's fiction but also prevalent in his life.

A brilliant student, he was recruited for an education on the mainland, where a secondary education could be obtained for relatively little money if a student appeared to demonstrate a bent toward the priesthood. After being educated by Roman Catholic priests on the supposition that he would study for the priesthood, in 1914 he entered Holy Cross College, the Dublin diocesan seminary. He stayed there only three months, however, before leaving and enrolling in University College, Dublin, where he became active in political support for the Irish Republican rebels. O'Flaherty's life continued to follow such anti-authoritarian dispositions: while still at University College he suddenly decided to enter the Irish Guards of the British army, and he served in the infantry in France and Belgium in World War I. He was severely shell-shocked during brutal warfare against the Germans in Belgium.

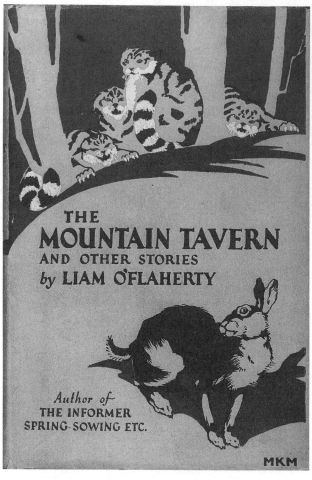

Dust jacket for O'Flaherty's 1929 collection, which includes stories about the Irish Civil War and rural Irish vignettes (courtesy of the Lilly Library, Indiana University)

Invalided out of the British army, he returned to the Aran Islands for a time of recovery but soon began a period of wide traveling to Europe, the United States, Canada, and South America. He paid his way by working as a seaman, a printer's helper, a clerk, a hotel porter, and a factory worker. His brother urged him to write about his various experiences, and O'Flaherty began to write short stories. When these early stories were rejected, however, he stopped writing almost immediately. Returning to Ireland in 1920, he became involved in the Republican struggle against the Irish Free Staters in the Civil War. O'Flaherty's sympathies went beyond republicanism, however, as he became involved in Communist political activity and helped to raise the Red flag over the Rotunda building in Dublin. He later participated in the Republican Four Courts Rebellion and was finally forced to flee to England when the Free State government sought to incarcerate him.

For a time O'Flaherty was influenced by Pyotr Kropotkin's anarchistic philosophy, but he tended to veer between Socialist and Bolshevik points of view. He later claimed that he was converted to socialism by a Scotch Socialist during his wartime service with the British army. There is certainly no doubt that O'Flaherty was throughout his career sympathetic to the poor and the rights of the workingman, even though the exact type of socialism or egalitarianism he espoused at various times is often vague.

Having arrived in England after fleeing from the Irish authorities, O'Flaherty published his first short story, "The Sniper," in a January 1923 issue of *The New Leader,* a British Socialist weekly. This narrative recounts a grim and vivid episode in the Civil War between the Irish Republicans and the Free Staters. From the rooftop of a Dublin house an unnamed sniper looks at the scene below and around him and shoots three people, including a sniper on a nearby building. The body of the other sniper falls to the street, and the protagonist, who has been wounded in the exchange of gunfire, descends to search out his company commander. Looking closely at the body of the sniper whom he has killed, he discovers that the dead man is his brother, who had chosen to serve on the other side when the war had commenced.

This initial story, set in the neighborhood of the beleaguered Four Courts, is typical of the type of narrative O'Flaherty was destined to write. Undoubtedly based at least in part on autobiographical experience, the story uses documentary details to stress the grim and deadly conflict in which one must kill or be killed. The goal is not just victory but survival, and even innocent civilians are gunned down in the vicious struggle. The horror of guerrilla warfare is powerfully and starkly conveyed.

O'Flaherty believed that he had found his true calling, and he began to write steadily. In the same year that "The Sniper" appeared, his first novel, *Thy Neighbour's Wife* (1923), was published. Set on the island of Inishmore, it describes the emotional struggles of a priest torn between his calling and the love of a woman. While the setting is convincingly presented, the characters act like primitive cave dwellers — animal-like, with very little intellection. They are violent, passionate, and constantly in torment, and the book collapses in melodrama. The highlight scene, which displays the marvelous visual gift that O'Flaherty has for describing the turbulence and influence of nature, recounts the struggles of the priest, who is boating during an especially vicious storm of the type that frequents the islands.

The following year O'Flaherty published his second novel, *The Black Soul*. In this book the protagonist undergoes constant mood changes, and primitive passions and natural instincts triumph over competing appeals of convention, respectability, and morality. The protagonist had once sought to find consolation in religion, later in anarchy, and finally in communism, but he has come to reject them all. A precursor of D. H. Lawrence's gamekeeper in *Lady Chatterley's Lover* (1928), the instinctive and animalistic protagonist of O'Flaherty's novel seduces Red John's willing wife, Mary, who is also a child of nature: "Her primitive soul was as merciless as nature itself. The tender growth of civilization had never taken root in her mind. Her love raged mightily. Like an ocean wave there was nothing within her or without her to stay its progress." The elemental forces within humans are joined by the forces of nature, especially those of the sea and wind. The novel is filled with passages of lyrical beauty describing nature, and the sea itself can proclaim, "I am the lord of nature. I heal and kill heedlessly. I drive men to a frenzy and soothe others with the same roar of my anger. I am the sadness of joy. I am the ferocity of beauty." The Lawrencian quality of such work was not accidental, for critic and editor Edward Garnett – who encouraged authors to be passionate and primitive – had been Lawrence's editor and was also serving O'Flaherty in the same capacity.

Garnett had strongly recommended that O'Flaherty write about what he knew firsthand. O'Flaherty knew the lives of farmers and fishermen on the Aran Islands and had closely observed animal life there, so Garnett urged him to focus on these materials in his stories. O'Flaherty followed the advice: his first collection of short stories, *Spring Sowing* (1924), as well as subsequent collections emphasized such documentary details – even if an episode comprised only a seemingly simple sketch of animal activity. Garnett had convinced O'Flaherty that firsthand descriptions of animals could make effective storytelling.

Animal life on the Aran Islands is not only prevalent, it is pervasive. When John Millington Synge visited the islands, he was amazed at the many varieties of birds that dominated the landscape, and he noted that the islanders became companions of the cormorants and crows. Various types of fish and farm animals were also deeply involved in the lives of the people. As parts of his subject matter in *Spring Sowing,* then, O'Flaherty set out to write sketches of animal behavior, and the collection's table of contents offers a striking number of stories devoted to animals: "The Rockfish," "The Blackbird," "Three Lambs," "The Wren's Nest," "The Black Mare," "The Wild Sow," "The Cow's Death," and "The Black Bullock."

It is amazing how O'Flaherty can make a short story or sketch from a simple episode. In "The Blackbird," for example, the description commences with the singing of a bird sitting on a stone fence as twilight breaks. The painstaking documentation of details – of time, of the surrounding natural setting and atmosphere, and of the various sensations of different animals in this drama of predator, onlookers, and prey – accumulates in a language that is simple, at times almost childlike. The narrative ultimately achieves a mesmerizing effect, creating in readers a mixed innocence and terror at the suspenseful struggle, as they wonder how the scene will conclude. The story is like a simple wood carving, so thoroughly detailed and so somber that it has a timeless quality of truth and fascination.

In "Three Lambs" twelve-year-old Michael rushes from the farmhouse before dawn, because his father has predicted that one of the sheep is soon to give birth. He observes that the sheep in question has separated from the flock, and he has difficulty finding her. The story then relates in graphic detail the separate births of three lambs: "He opened his penknife and cut the dirty wool from the sheep's udder, lest the lambs might swallow some and die." Each of the three births is recorded in a different manner, giving narrative variety as well as documentary accumulation. One thinks of cameras on a PBS television nature study, but so complete is O'Flaherty's description that even a camera view of the episode could not present it more fully and realistically.

"The Blackbird" and "Three Lambs" have happy endings, but this is frequently not the case in the animal sketches. In "The Black Mare," for example, the narrator purchases a particularly wild horse that no man seems able to ride. After bringing her back to his farm and apparently taming her, he decides to enter the mare in the local provincial horse race, because he has ridden her and witnessed her incredible speed. During the race the narrator's eagerness to win causes him to strike the mare a heavy blow, which drives her into a frenzy and makes her unstoppable. Passing the finish line as a winner, she continues to race for a fence, jumps it, and dashes on toward a large pile of boulders near the beach, where she suffers a shattering death. The rider of the horse suffers only a broken leg; his narrative conveys the wildness and the savagery of the animal with elemental fury.

O'Flaherty in the early 1930s (courtesy of the Lilly Library, Indiana University)

In "The Hook" some boys hide a sharp hook attached to a string inside a large piece of liver that they leave in view on a fence. Two seagulls fight over the meat, and when the victorious one attempts to fly away with its prize, it finds the hook embedded deeply in its mouth. As the boys rush to reel in the line, the seagull twists and struggles until finally the weak string breaks. When it returns to its nest, both the gull and its mate with herculean effort manage to dislodge the hook. The struggle of the seagull in the first instance and then the struggle of the two gulls together provide memorable episodes of raw animal nature fighting and battling for survival.

Similar narratives occur often in O'Flaherty's fiction. In "The Cow's Death" a cow is so distraught and confused when its calf is stillborn that it eventually follows the scent of the calf, which has been carried away a considerable distance and thrown over a cliff into the sea. The cow observes her calf lying on the rocks below the cliff and sees the increasing tide advancing to carry the calf into the sea. Still not realizing that the calf is dead and vainly seeking to save it, the cow jumps from the cliff.

While such description is persuasive, O'Flaherty on some occasions is not as convincing in attempting to portray the psychic workings of the animals' instincts or behavior patterns. Strained and questionable as the explanations are at times, however, they could not be rendered more plausibly by any other author. One critic has commented that in his animal sketches O'Flaherty "has written in a new way . . . as if he were not their observer, but a mystical sharer in their being."

In his later short fiction collections – *The Tent* (1926), *The Mountain Tavern, and Other Stories* (1929), and *Two Lovely Beasts, and Other Stories* (1948) – the animal sketches are continued. In "The Conger Eel" a huge eight-foot-long eel is entangled with a catch of mackerel in the nets of some fishermen. When the net is pulled aboard the boat, the fishermen attempt to kill the twisting, slithering creature, but he manages to escape over the side. In "The Wild Goat's Kid" a dog attempts to kill the goat's offspring, and a vicious fight ensues between the two animals – until one of the combatants is dead. In "The Wounded Cormorant" the injured bird is attacked and killed by a pack of its fellows. In "The Water Hen" two males fight to possess the hen, while she awaits the victor and then coyly yields to his advances. These are typical of the animal sketches, which focus on the animals rather than on humans. After a time their repetitiveness becomes obvious, and one realizes that even when they are written well, such stories can be carried only so far. The limited subject matter strains the interest of readers.

O'Flaherty's prose also presents another problem. He is capable of some lyricism and at times reaches effective poetic flights of fancy. Although negative aspects of this style can be observed especially in his lesser novels, they are magnified in several of the animal sketches. His style too often follows an essentially plain, documentary approach associated with naturalism. The prose at times overuses clichés and struggles to pick out words – as if such an effort were a tiring struggle, a rough-hewn laboring. Of course this effect fits the documentary nature of the material and the naturalistic approach to writing. To be fair, it is much more noticeable if one reads eight or ten of the animal sketches at one time. What is true of the style of Theodore Dreiser, whose work O'Flaherty admired, may be said of O'Flaherty's: for all their documentary brilliance and adeptness at handling dialogue, their styles are often flat, with a limited vocabulary and a heavy-handed, almost gnarled grasping for words.

In 1925 *The Informer,* O'Flaherty's best-known novel, was published. It won the James Tait Black Memorial Prize in England as the best novel of the year and also won a prize in France; it was especially popular in other European countries. This novel shifts its settings from the Aran Islands and the west of Ireland to the dismal slums of Dublin, and it centers on the type of material used in "The Sniper."

Irish rebel Gypo Nolan informs on a comrade, who is killed by the police. Gypo must then try to avoid retribution by the rebel group understandably infuriated by his betrayal. His attempts to avoid this fate and his encounter with the vicious Gallagher provide considerable suspense. This novel continues the grim naturalism of the animal sketches, as most of the characters evince primitive, animalistic qualities. Only the sister and the mother of the rebel whom Gypo has betrayed show any spiritual qualities.

The figure of Gallagher, who leads the revolutionary cell that must kill Gypo once they find out that he is the informer, is particularly striking, because it demonstrates the confusion in O'Flaherty's political thinking. Gallagher calls himself a "revolutionary Communist," but he appears to have little concern for the workers. He is interested only in ego satisfaction and in buoying up his own power base. His dissection by the novelist demonstrates that O'Flaherty could see deficiencies in men who professed a philosophy he claimed to admire. Yet Gallagher admits that he is not totally clear in his beliefs: in one section of the book he says, "I have no beliefs."

This change from holding the views of a "revolutionary Communist" in one sentence to holding "no beliefs" in another mirrors O'Flaherty's own varying political philosophy. At one point O'Flaherty was so attracted to communism that he went with great enthusiasm to visit Russia; he later published his impressions of this trip in 1931. After his trip he claimed that materialism and personal selfishness were just as dominant there as in other countries, but his disillusionment was never to shake completely his faith in socialism. Five years after his visit to Russia he could declare, "I believe the U.S.S.R. claims the allegiance of every civilized person in the world today."

Having already become notorious in Ireland for his socialist pronouncements, he caused further scandal when he ran off with Margaret Barrington, the wife of history professor Edmund Curtis, and married her in 1926. This union lasted only six years.

The success of *The Informer* spurred O'Flaherty to renew his zest for writing, and as the years passed he published many novels, short stories, and books of nonfiction. Novels such as *Mr. Gilhooley* (1926), *Skerrett* (1932), and especially *Famine* (1937) increased his literary reputation, and director John Ford's motion picture version of *The Informer* (1935), which won four Academy Awards, gave him even greater fame.

While he was writing his novels, O'Flaherty also continued to write short stories, which were first published in magazines and later collected in various editions. He did not cease writing animal sketches, but he began to correlate animal activities with human concerns. "The Fairy Goose" illustrates this development. The elderly Mary Wiggins had a hatching hen that died two days before the eggs were scheduled to open. When only one gosling, small and fragile, survives, she believes the gosling should be killed because of its feeble condition, but her husband persuades her to nurture it. After a few months the sickly gosling is unable to stand. Mary comes to believe that it is a fairy, so she ties colorful ribbons around its neck and sprinkles it with holy water. Eventually many of the villagers come to regard it as a sacred object, and Mary believes it has supernatural powers. Through the influence of the animal Mary attempts to cast spells, interpret dreams, and cure the illnesses of other farm animals. In exchange for her interpretations and incantations other people give her food, cloth, and similar objects. Mary and her husband also begin to sell or barter ropes of horsehair, which are supposed to be used as charms.

Finally the priest of a neighboring village hears of these activities and rides over to investigate. He is shocked by what he learns and rushes toward the goose. Mary interferes, and the priest strikes her in anger. He yanks the ribbons off the neck of the goose, ruins her special mound, and throws a stone at the creature. Threatening to report Mary Wiggins to the archbishop of the diocese, the priest denounces her activity as the devil's work and leaves. During this episode the goose has begun to hiss and to act violently for the first time in its life. To this point it had always been treated kindly by everyone, and it is understandably distressed by the new turn of events. Some of the villagers interpret the hostility of the goose as the sign of an evil spirit. When night arrives, some mischievous youths manage to coax the goose out of the Wigginses' house, and they stone it to death. When Mary discovers her dead pet, she puts a curse on the villagers and on the priest, and from that time on the villagers become quarrelsome drunkards. It is maintained that the only time when harmony had been in the community was when the goose had been honored.

"The Fairy Goose" is presented as a fable, preaching love and kindness over hate – even if the love is achieved through deception and belief in superstition or myth. Love should triumph over rigid and restrictive precepts, over thundering hellfire and damnation. The story would have been more successful if handled with more subtlety.

In "Two Lovely Beasts," another story that closely relates animal with human life, a farmer named Colm Derrane buys an attractive calf. Derrane has been charitably able to give some of the milk he produces to three neighboring families, since peasants in the west of Ireland are accustomed to help their neighbors and to share with them. Yet if Derrane raises this just-purchased calf with his own calf, his cow will not be able to give adequate milk for others who depend on the communal custom. The village and the surrounding farm area are so impoverished that no one previously has attempted to raise two yearlings.

So when Derrane buys the additional calf, the people of the area turn against him because he has broken the cooperative code, the unspoken social law in that locale: "It's too wild and barren here for any one man to stand alone. Whoever tries to stand alone and work only for his own profit becomes an enemy of all."

Yet Derrane becomes obsessed with raising his "two lovely beasts" to be champions. To reach this goal he rations milk to his own family and deprives them of the opportunity to make butter. Through violence he forces his wife to comply, and she becomes convinced that the family will "rise in the world." But even the dedication and work ethic of the family falters from diminished food and clothing. Derrane drives himself almost to starvation so that every penny can be saved. He decides to open a store in a nearby village, since shopkeepers are the only ones whose wealth increases. He prospers, and the two calves, now champion bullocks, are sold at the fair for a large profit. Derrane opens a bigger shop.

In this narrative O'Flaherty's sympathies rest with the people. Derrane has allowed selfishness and greed to dominate him. Elderly Andy Gorum, who throughout the story has denounced Derrane's individualism, continues to do so to the end, observing that most of the Irish wool and hides are being shipped overseas instead of being used to help the impoverished Irish. While Derrane and his family have prospered, they have sold out the people in that area of Ireland, perpetuated poverty in the area, and even brought new poverty to the peasants. As in "The Fairy Goose" the community's overall welfare is at stake, and the theme is that the common good should be the concern of all. Although this is obviously a significant theme, it is presented in too didactic a manner, and O'Flaherty was better served by the more objective, naturalistic approach of the animal stories than this fabular approach.

Although a reader can admire the documentary details, vividness, and focus of the animal narratives and although several critics feel that the animal sketches are the high achievement of O'Flaherty's short story production, some of his finest short fiction is produced when he probes the lives of the farmers and the fishermen on the Aran Islands and in the western part of the country. In the story "Spring Sowing" a recently married young couple take part for the first time in the annual planting. They experience the excitement of their first farming activity together, and although the work is draining and repetitive, their fresh love and the newness of their task give them much pleasure.

Yet the scene is overcast by the husband's grandfather who, bent and hobbled by years of such work, links the present with the future. When Martin and Mary Delany have done this heavy and tiring work year after year, they will no longer experience the joy and thrill that they now find in these backbreaking tasks. O'Flaherty expertly suggests the effects of time and underscores the hard and wearying life of the peasant. There is a universal union between youth and age and between the earth and humanity in general, a union that will continue long after the Delanys are laid to rest. After the initial pleasure of contact with the earth, humanity will be ground down by nature. There is a timelessness to this narrative that is vividly conveyed and deeply thought-provoking. Here is O'Flaherty at his best – using documentary details effectively and avoiding the heavy-handed didacticism that is evident in "The Fairy Goose" and "Two Lovely Beasts."

"Going Into Exile" is another superior story that echoes in the mind long after it is read. The Feeney family's two eldest children are leaving Ireland to seek work in the United States, and a party is held in the family's cabin to mark the occasion. The party, however, masks to some degree the dis-

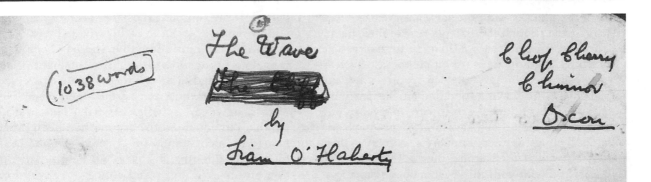

The cliff was two hundred feet high. It sloped outwards from its grassy summit, along ten feet of brown gravel, down one hundred and seventy feet of grey limestone, giant slabs piled horizontally with large slits between the slabs where seabirds nested. The outwards slope came to a round point twenty feet from the base and there the cliff sank inwards, to a distance of fifteen feet, making a dark cavern ten yards along the cliff's face and fifteen feet into the bowels of the earth. At the mouth the cavern was twenty feet high and / at the rear, the its roof touched the its floor, a flat rock that stretched from the base of the cliff to the sea, ten yards away The cavern had a black slate roof and at the rear there was a large streak of yellow gravel. The cliff was semi-circular. And at each

Page from the manuscript for the title story of the last collection published during O'Flaherty's lifetime (Lilly Library, Indiana University; by permission of the Estate of Liam O'Flaherty)

289

tress of the parents, who do not want their children to leave even though the parents realize that the departure of their children is a financial necessity. The father retreats to the barn for a time to hide his feelings, while the mother, to keep from crying, immerses herself in serving food and similar party necessities. The children – one who is twenty-one years old and the other who is nineteen – have ambivalent feelings. Understandably sad to leave their parents as well as their home, they at the same time look forward with youthful excitement and anticipation to the new adventure that lies before them. It is quite possible, as the author stresses, that the parents and children may never see each other again, since exiles frequently never return, and this melancholy prospect further adds to the mixture of sorrow and joy that pervades the party.

Here again is the type of story in which O'Flaherty excels. His description is exceedingly pictorial, and he enters the minds of the characters so that what they are thinking and feeling is convincingly revealed. The story encompasses all exiles in general – not just the Irish, who through the centuries have had to leave their native country and experience the pains of parting and the sense of permanent loss.

In "The Mountain Tavern" O'Flaherty emphasizes the tragedy of war by focusing especially on the Civil War between the Republican rebels and the Irish Free State supporters. The tavern, because of its remoteness as well as its celebratory function, always has been a symbol of comfort, solace, and refuge. Two Republican soldiers, one carrying a dying comrade through a snowstorm, expect to find security there. After a long trek they come upon the tavern and discover that it has been burned to the ground as a result of the war. Mrs. Galligan, the co-owner of the tavern, is especially bitter and denounces both fighting groups because her home and her livelihood have been destroyed in the battles: "I hate ye all," she screams, and the story ends with death, silence, and isolation. O'Flaherty persuasively dramatizes this recurring theme about war, and the ending of the story has a Hemingwayesque conclusion: "There was nothing in the whole universe again but the black ruin and the black spot where the corpse [of the Republican soldier] had lain. Night fell and snow fell, fell like soft soothing white flower petals on the black ruin and on the black spot where the corpse had lain."

While condemning the bestiality of war, O'Flaherty somewhat contradictorily professes to admire other primitive aspects of existence or at least to understand and support them. In "Red Bar-

bara," for example, Barbara Feeney, a young widow, marries a gentle and cultivated weaver. He renovates the crude hut that she has been accustomed to living in with her first husband, plants flowers, and makes their home very attractive. He is industrious and quite prosperous in his trade. None of this, however, satisfies his wife. Her first husband, an uneducated fisherman, had been savage; he had been constantly intoxicated and had beaten his wife frequently. Barbara had fought back, met him on his own level, and conceived several children by him.

Yet she is unable to conceive with her new husband – and in an area where childbearing is regarded as a duty, the neighbors grow critical and unfriendly. Joseph, the second husband, grows despondent because of Barbara's mistreatment, and he eventually passes in despair to an early grave. The wild, primitive Barbara marries a third time and becomes happy once more, although she repeatedly has to bring her new mate "staggering from the town, singing drunkenly, to her wild bed."

It is evident that O'Flaherty approves of Barbara's hostile treatment of her second husband, who links some humans with the wildness of Nature. Since Nature is often savage and destructive, it is normal for some humans to follow Nature's lead. In more than one of his stories O'Flaherty emphasizes that survival depends on humanity's harmony with Nature, even in Nature's most vicious moods. If people move too far from animal instincts (and in much of his work people are presented as nothing more than a species of animal), then they will suffer through attempting to find refuge in civilized behavior. O'Flaherty is often contradictory in both his writing and his thinking, but his more frequently expressed view links the brutal in Nature with the brutal in humanity.

Harmony with Nature is also stressed in "The Tramp," another of O'Flaherty's more successful stories. Michael Deignan and John Finnerty are paupers who live in a workhouse, where a tramp is admitted for the night. Although his appearance is disreputable, his eyes are similar to those of "a graceful wild animal." In conversation the tramp seeks to encourage Deignan and Finnerty to take to the open road. Although Deignan is only thirty-five and educated, he has never been successful in any career. The tramp has been on the road twenty-two years and has been very happy, as he tells them: "I said to myself that it was a foolish game trying to do anything in this world but sleep and eat and enjoy the sun and the earth and the sea and the rain." Deignan rejects the tramp's proposal, because he hopes to get "back to respectable life," but it is obvious that he will spend the rest of his life "to rot in idleness here with old men and useless wrecks." The tramp had originally taken to the open road after having impregnated a girl and then deserting her after her child was born. As far as O'Flaherty is concerned, the tramp is heroic, while the educated, civilized Deignan is a pathetic figure. The tramp is in unity with Nature just as Red Barbara was: as O'Flaherty often presents the issue, primitivism is not only justified but admirable.

"The Tent" presents a meeting between Carney, a former soldier, and a tinker who is accompanied by two women traveling companions. Although Carney regards himself as being on a much higher level of social refinement than the tinker, Carney is seeking employment when a rainstorm drives him to find shelter, and he asks for hospitality from the tinker and his tent-dwelling companions. The group eats together and shares a bottle of whiskey, and later Carney attempts to embrace and kiss one of the women. When the tinker sees this, he fights viciously and unfairly, and he beats Carney badly. As Carney staggers away from the tent, he sees the tinker grab the now-screaming woman to whom Carney had been attracted and take her into the shelter. It is apparent that the woman has lured Carney into this situation; she is just as primitive as the tinker. Once more the civilized man has been defeated by elemental forces close to Nature.

"The Touch" presents a similar motif. Although Kate Hernon and the impoverished Brian O'Neill are drawn to each other, she is forced by her father into a loveless marriage. It is clear from O'Flaherty's point of view that O'Neill should have carried off the willing Kate and allowed their primitive passions to thrive even at the expense of financial security. The controlling influences of civility or propriety are not for O'Flaherty: people should not intellectualize; they should trust the prompting of the blood before all else.

One might assume that because of O'Flaherty's personality and critical temperament he would be drawn to satire. As James M. Cahalan has observed, satire is prominent in *The Life of Tim Healy* (1927), *A Tourist's Guide to Ireland* (1929), and *A Cure for Unemployment* (1931); however, these are not short stories. When satire appears in his short fiction, it is usually obvious and flimsy. In "A Strange Disease," for example, a priest is satirized for emphasizing hate more than love; the more admirable figure is approved because he demonstrates love. The fact that this love is for a neighbor's wife does not disturb O'Flaherty's moral sense. In "Benedi-

camus Domino" the scene is a seminary refectory where the brothers gather and are ridiculed for various faults. For instance, Brother John is an object of such humor because he wears a hairshirt and is excessively devout, spending nights before the tabernacle in the chapel. The targets of the satire that appears in O'Flaherty's work are generally priests and storekeepers.

Some critics have found humor in some of O'Flaherty's stories, but generally only a small, scattered amount appears. Most of it involves tall tales and some slapstick. That O'Flaherty might have enjoyed some success by incorporating more humor into his work, however, can be supported by his delightful story "The Post Office," which has been collected in *The Stories of Liam O'Flaherty* (1956). In this narrative O'Flaherty is in one of his rare good moods.

Martin Conlon is postmaster in an isolated village in County Galway and runs his office in a quaint, individualistic manner. When some tourists request to send a telegram to America in Spanish, those customers who lounge about the office immediately take an interest, because it is well known that Conlon does not like to send telegrams. After attempting every possible excuse to avoid having to send this one, he is finally forced to read the telegram over the phone to the main office in Galway. The interruptions and confusions that his use of a party line entails add further merriment, as does Conlon's constant complaining about his heavy workload. This story is refreshing and genuinely good-humored; O'Flaherty was almost always too serious, grim, and hostile to let himself go in such a congenial fashion.

It should be noted that O'Flaherty also wrote some short stories in Gaelic. He had spoken Gaelic from his earliest years and at one time had worked for a Gaelic language revival. He had also hoped to organize a traveling Gaelic theater and had offered to write several plays for such a venture. He did write one play in Gaelic but received no payment. He decided to write his novels and short stories in English because of the wider readership and more satisfactory financial returns that doing so would ensure. In any event all of the stories published in Gaelic were either first published or later published in English.

After the mid 1950s O'Flaherty spent his time in retirement and in traveling. He was able to live on the royalties from *The Informer* and his short stories, which have gone through several reprintings. The facts that many of his short stories are still in print and that several critics regard them as superior to his novels attest to the significance and permanence of his work in Anglo-Irish literature.

Bibliography:

Paul A. Doyle, *Liam O'Flaherty: An Annotated Bibliography* (Troy, N.Y.: Whitston, 1971);

George Jefferson, *Liam O'Flaherty: A Descriptive Bibliography of His Works* (Dublin: Wolfhound, 1993).

References:

James M. Cahalan, *Liam O'Flaherty: A Study of the Short Fiction* (Boston: Twayne, 1991);

Paul A. Doyle, *Liam O'Flaherty* (New York: Twayne, 1971);

A. A. Kelly, *Liam O'Flaherty: The Storyteller* (London: Macmillan, 1976; New York: Harper & Row/Barnes & Noble, 1976);

Benedict Kiely, *Modern Irish Fiction* (Dublin: Golden Eagle, 1950);

Michael H. Murray, "Liam O'Flaherty and the Speaking Voice," *Studies in Short Fiction,* 5 (Winter 1968): 154–162;

James H. O'Brien, *Liam O'Flaherty* (Lewisburg, Pa.: Bucknell University Press, 1973);

Seán O'Faoláin, "Don Quixote O'Flaherty," *London Mercury,* 37 (December 1937): 170–175;

Richard J. Thompson, "The Sage Who Deep in Central Nature Dwells," *Liam O'Flaherty's Short Stories, Éire-Ireland,* 18 (Spring 1983): 80–97;

John Zneimer, *The Literary Vision of Liam O'Flaherty* (Syracuse, N.Y.: Syracuse University Press, 1970).

Papers:

An extensive collection of O'Flaherty's letters and manuscripts is at the Harry Ransom Humanities Research Center, University of Texas at Austin.

William Plomer

(10 December 1903 – 20 September 1973)

Rachael J. Lynch
University of Connecticut

See also the Plomer entry in *DLB 20: British Poets, 1914–1945.*

BOOKS: *Turbott Wolfe* (London: Hogarth Press, 1925; New York: Harcourt, Brace, 1926);

I Speak of Africa (London: Hogarth Press, 1927);

Notes for Poems (London: Hogarth Press, 1927);

The Family Tree (London: Hogarth Press, 1929);

Paper Houses (London: Hogarth Press, 1929; New York: Coward-McCann, 1929);

Sado (London: Hogarth Press, 1931); republished as *They Never Came Back* (New York: Coward-McCann, 1932);

The Case is Altered (London: Hogarth Press, 1932; New York: Farrar & Rinehart, 1932);

The Fivefold Screen (London: Hogarth Press, 1932; New York: Coward-McCann, 1932);

Cecil Rhodes (London: Davies, 1933; New York: Appleton, 1933);

The Child of Queen Victoria, and Other Stories (London: Cape, 1933);

The Invaders (London: Cape, 1934);

Ali the Lion: Ali of Tebeleni, Pasha of Jannina, 1741–1822 (London: Cape, 1936);

Visiting the Caves (London: Cape, 1936);

Selected Poems (London: Hogarth Press, 1940);

In a Bombed House, 1941: Elegy in Memory of Anthony Butts (London: Curwen Press, 1942);

Double Lives: An Autobiography (London: Cape, 1943; New York: Noonday, 1956);

The Dorking Thigh, and Other Satires (London: Cape, 1945);

Curious Relations, as William d'Arfey, with Anthony Butts (London: Cape, 1945; New York: William Sloane Associates, 1947);

Four Countries (London: Cape, 1949);

Museum Pieces (London: Cape, 1952; New York: Noonday, 1954);

Gloriana: Opera in Three Acts, libretto by Plomer (London: Boosey & Hawkes, 1953);

William Plomer in 1929 (photograph by Ker-Seymer)

A Shot in the Park (London: Cape, 1955); republished as *Borderline Ballads* (New York: Noonday, 1955);

At Home: Memoirs (London: Cape, 1958; New York: Noonday, 1958);

Collected Poems (London: Cape, 1960; enlarged, 1973);

A Choice of Ballads (London: Cape, 1960);

Conversation with My Younger Self (Ewelme [Oxfordshire: W. Plomer?], 1963);

Curlew River: A Parable for Church Performance, libretto by Plomer (London: Faber & Faber, 1964);

The Burning Fiery Furnace: Second Parable for Church Performance, libretto by Plomer (London: Faber Music, 1966);

Taste and Remember (London: Cape, 1966);

The Prodigal Son: Third Parable for Church Performance, libretto by Plomer (London: Faber Music, 1968);

A Brutal Sentimentalist and Other Stories, edited by Eiichi Sano (Toyko: Kenkyusha, 1969);

The Planes of Bedford Square (London: Bookbang, 1971);

Celebrations (London: Cape, 1972);

The Butterfly Ball and The Grasshopper's Feast (London: Cape, 1973; New York: Grossman, 1975);

Autobiography (London: Cape, 1975; New York: Taplinger, 1975);

Electric Delights, edited by Rupert Hart-Davis (London: Cape, 1978; Boston: Godine, 1978).

OTHER: Haruko Ichikawa, *Japanese Lady in Europe,* edited, with an introduction, by Plomer (London: Cape, 1937; New York: Dutton, 1937);

Robert Francis Kilvert, *Kilvert's Diary: Selections from the Diary of the Rev. Francis Kilvert,* 3 volumes, edited, with an introduction, by Plomer (London: Cape, 1938–1940); abridged as *Kilvert's Diary, 1870–1879: Selections,* 1 volume (London: Cape, 1944; New York: Macmillan, 1947); enlarged as *Kilvert's Diary: Selections from the Diary of the Rev. Francis Kilvert,* 3 volumes (London: Cape, 1961);

Herman Melville, *Selected Poems of Herman Melville,* edited by Plomer (London: Hogarth Press, 1943);

George Gissing, *A Life's Morning,* edited by Plomer (London: Home & Van Thal, 1947).

A writer of extraordinary versatility, William Plomer earned in his lifetime a reputation as a novelist, poet, writer of short and longer stories, editor, broadcaster, librettist (in collaboration with Benjamin Britten), and an indefatigable, if sometimes less than entirely forthright, autobiographer. He is most often remembered as the author of *Turbott Wolfe* (1925), a taboo-breaking book on racial relations in South Africa, the land of his birth. Begun when Plomer was nineteen and published by Leonard and Virginia Woolf's Hogarth Press before his twenty-third birthday, this remarkable first novel alone cements his reputation as a central figure of the modernist movement, and this book still attracts the attention of most of the critics currently concerned with the remarkable achievement of a man too long neglected. His more than thirty short stories, if less well-known to late-twentieth-century readers, are no less interesting.

As a close friend of two other important and like-minded South African writers, Roy Campbell and Laurens van der Post, and of many of the most stellar and influential British modernist (the Woolfs, E. M. Forster, T. S. Eliot, and others), Plomer bloomed in proximity to many of the most prominent writers of this century. The 1980s saw a resurgence of interest in Plomer: studies of his work started to appear in scholarly journals, and J. R. Doyle's 1969 critical examination was followed by a definitive biography by Peter F. Alexander. What Plomer's white South African contemporaries saw as his negrophilia – his absolute belief, as Doyle puts it, that in any and all interracial relationships "there is no question of superior and inferior – merely differences," – reveals him as significantly more egalitarian than the majority of liberal South Africans of his day, including his better-known countrywoman Olive Schreiner. His openness of mind and exceptional talents as a writer guarantee growing critical attention for Plomer at a time when postcolonial and multicultural studies are of central importance. The full extent of Plomer's remarkable achievement in several genres should again be recognized, so that this fascinating writer will be accorded the appreciation he deserves.

William Charles Franklyn Plomer, elder son of Charles and Edythe (née Waite Browne) Plomer, was born in Pietersburg, in South Africa's northern Transvaal, on 10 December 1903. Charles Plomer's position with the South African Department of Native Affairs required much traveling, and his delicate health – combined with Edythe's distaste for South Africa – encouraged them to adopt a peripatetic lifestyle. This, coupled with their desire to provide for their son the most splendid education their limited finances could buy, resulted in young William's schooling in a series of institutions in both South Africa and England. His earliest instruction was entrusted to a governess and then to his maternal aunt and uncle, Hilda and Telford Hayman, who ran a preparatory school at Spondon House, near Derby. Here he was left by his parents at the age of five, in circumstances common to the children of empire-builders: as Alexander wryly notes, "Part of the price the British Empire exacted of its white masters was the destruction of their family life." Born like William Makepeace Thackeray and Rudyard Kipling in a "distant unhealthy corner of the Empire," Plomer adapted early in his life to the trauma of separation and, according to Alexander, suffered little during this first separation at Spondon.

Young enough to be the object of special attentions and protection from his aunt, who kept him apart from his older schoolmates, he was not unhappy, though he dated his developing feelings of isolation and his adoption of the role of loner, of passive observer, from that early time. Shocked to discover her son's progressive myopia and inclined to blame her sister (who had allowed the boy to read in bright light while he had measles), his mother removed him from Spondon in 1911. After a brief further stay in England and another interlude with a governess, Edythe, William and his new brother, Peter, returned to South Africa, this time to Johannesburg. Here Plomer enjoyed the most idyllic period of his schooling while boarding as a student at the prestigious St. John's College. At this liberal institution in a location and climate he loved, William thrived. Alexander notes that "Here for the first time (and perhaps the last) he felt part of a community," and Plomer participated enthusiastically in school activities, particularly in the annual Shakespeare play. Later in his life Plomer, a homosexual who never married and took pains not to advertise his sexual orientation in his autobiographical writing, "was to derive a good deal of amusement from the thought that he had played a fairy queen in public." His family's improving finances allowed for travel in South Africa during this period – until the growing violence and threat of political chaos sent the family back to England.

During the even greater wartime chaos that awaited the Plomers on their return to Europe, William was sent first to the repressive Beechmont. With its cult of cricket, this was a school that he loathed, and he felt that it encouraged in him a later tendency toward secrecy and subversiveness. (He later associated the outgoing heterosexuality and imperialist bellicosity of his Uncle Durham, killed in the Boer War, with "the smug assumption that cricket playing was a sign of racial superiority," and he declared himself against what he saw as a tedious, incomprehensible game.) In 1917 he went on to Rugby, where, after Beechmont, he was not unhappy and where he made several lasting friends – notably Robert Birley, later headmaster of Eton and a committed opponent of what would become instituted as the policy of apartheid, and the brilliant Darcy Rutherford Gillie. What remained of his adolescence was, however, disrupted by the later years of the war. Younger Rugby students were quite aware that their barely older former classmates were being sent to the slaughter at the front. As Plomer later noted, "No child of my generation of even minimal intelligence or sensibility could have re-

Infant William Plomer, with his nurse and his father, Charles, in 1903

mained untroubled by what went on in France from 1914 onwards." He attributed his characteristic detachment – what he described as "the growing of an extra skin" and his development as "a man of reflection" rather than a "man of action" – in part to these terrible years. "The action that had been taken between 1914 and 1918," he recalled in his 1958 memoir *At Home,* "the deliberate and elaborate slaughter of man by man, was quite enough to convert a reflective child to inaction for life."

The finances of the Plomers also sustained heavy losses during the war, and the removal of William from Rugby in 1918 probably had as much to do with these losses as with the rapid deterioration of the young man's eyesight. He finished his secondary education back at St. John's in Johannesburg, where his vision improved remarkably and he distinguished himself academically, became interested in writing poetry, and considered for the first time the possibility of becoming a writer instead of a painter, his earlier ambition. He also read Marcel Proust while he was still only sixteen years old, and before leaving school he came under the influence of Edward (Teddy) Wolfe. This young Jewish painter became important to Plomer because of his artistic connections, his open homosexuality, and his admiration, both personal and erotic, for blacks. Plomer did not settle permanently into homosexual habits until his three-year sojourn in Japan, but, encouraged by Proust and Wolfe, his development in that direction was proceeding apace. After leaving public school Plomer did not continue his education, despite his father's offer of an Oxford education. Alexander suggests several convincing explanations: with a South African matriculation Plomer might well not have been accepted; money was short; and the young man did not seem to want to go. Plomer's formal education concluded, therefore, when he was seventeen, although he later claimed Japan as "my university."

The continuing changes of location throughout Plomer's early years provided an important migratory basis to his development as an artist, and in particular as a writer of short stories. He stressed the links between his life and work, saying that "everything I have written is related . . . to its originator." His stories, which draw extensively on his life experience for their material, are notable for their many settings (in South Africa, Japan, England, and to a lesser degree Greece and France), and these stories convey clearly a sense that their writer belongs, yet does not belong, to the culture portrayed. The social criticism in the stories derives much of its force from the detachment of the narrator: the Plomer narrator is frequently an alien, an outsider, a passive observer/recorder rather like Christopher Isherwood's narrator in *Goodbye to Berlin* (1939). Plomer's sense of homelessness no doubt contributed powerfully to the narrative distancing that is so much a part of his writing. He seems to have felt less alien in England than anywhere else and to have identified himself, more or less, as an Englishman, although he never appears to have felt fully "at home" anywhere – and the wry social criticism of the English stories is as detached and satiric as anything he wrote.

Plomer's parents were also potent influences on his development as a writer. To his father, Charles, he owed not only the lifestyle that engendered his feelings of isolation and detachment but also the benefits of his father's nonconformist behavior, particularly his amiable relations with and respect for the South African blacks, with whom he worked most of his life. Charles Plomer was a known negrophile who, because of his lack of regard for the color bar, was destined never to advance in his work in the Department of Native Affairs. (When Charles had first arrived in South Af-

rica in 1889, he had brought with him a letter of introduction to Cecil Rhodes, who, unsurprisingly, had no use for the young "black sheep.")

To his mother, Edythe, Plomer owed his early and lasting awareness that much of artistic and aesthetic significance was lacking in South African society, and she also encouraged her son's cultivation of the "visual appetite" so notable in his stories. Furthermore, she did not perceive herself as inherently superior to her black servants, an attitude transmitted intact to her son, and she was possessed of a capacity for calm, detached endurance that he greatly admired. Just before she died of cancer in 1939 Plomer celebrated these qualities, which he esteemed in her, in an anecdote he recounted. Upon arriving at the nursing home to visit his dying mother, Plomer found her polishing her nails. She would have done so earlier had she known he was coming, she said apologetically, but, she added "in a lightly ironical tone of voice, 'After all, one has to do one's nails.' " These words, her son notes, "were wonderfully characteristic, mingling self-mockery, calmness, courage, and a kind of disdain for the world."

Plomer's short stories, written mostly between 1926 and 1933 and reflecting a variety of international and multicultural experiences, provide a window for observing Plomer's development as a writer. They share with his novels a strong social conscience and satiric touch. *Turbott Wolfe,* for example, like several of the African stories, concerns itself with racial equality, with whites who are sadly mistaken in their beliefs that they are in any way "superior," and with love across racial barriers. The stories can also be linked profitably with his poetry through both their themes and their great sensitivity, visual acuity, and evocation of mood – what Doyle describes as a "tenderness" – common to Plomer's work in both genres. Placing his stories against his copious autobiographical writing is also particularly fascinating, because the parallel developments of the writer's life and work can be so clearly observed. As he grows firm in his hatred of notions of white superiority, so do his early stories. As his sense of humor becomes more developed, with what Doyle calls the "comic repose" replacing "the feverish seriousness of youth," his stories again reflect the change.

As one reads the short stories in chronological order one is struck by their author's development, his growing verbal, stylistic, and structural surefootedness, and also notable are a set of constants: the trademark sense of homelessness and detachment that pervades so much of what Plomer wrote, allied with a strong sense of the narrator's alienation from his or her surroundings; a trenchant social criticism relying heavily on irony, even satire, for its effect; a strong, irreverent sense of the ridiculous; a visual sharpness, an artist's touch that he called "a visual, or pictorial, imagination" (not surprising when one remembers that Plomer had initially wished to become a painter); a willingness to experiment with point of view; and finally a powerful empathy with the outsider, the underdog, the societally determined Other. Plomer's critics have linked his lifelong hatred of social hypocrisy and injustice, and his strong identification with those deemed "inferior," to his own awareness that as a homosexual he was also an outsider, a practitioner of the Unacceptable, and such a reading is supported by Plomer's own secretiveness in his autobiographies. Alexander argues convincingly that the portrayal of miscegenation in much of Plomer's fiction, particularly in *Turbott Wolfe,* disguises in the breaking of racial taboos through heterosexual love a further taboo that Plomer clearly felt unable to explore openly: homosexual love across the same racial divide. Pointing to Plomer's friend Teddy Wolfe, Alexander asks whether the title of the first novel can be coincidental.

Turbott Wolfe was soon followed by *I Speak of Africa* (1927), Plomer's first book of short stories, also published by Leonard and Virginia Woolf's Hogarth Press. The stories, like the novel, are largely drawn from Plomer's experiences from the time he finished school in 1920 until he left for Japan with Laurens van der Post in 1926. Following his decision not to attend a university, Plomer was sent by his father to learn what was for him the unlikely vocation of sheep farming. This enterprise, part of a scheme to increase the number of British settlers to counterbalance what was perceived as a serious Afrikaner threat, was doomed to failure from the beginning, not least because Plomer proved to be afraid of his charges. However, the lonely farm to which he was sent for a year as an apprentice furnished much material for fiction.

Plomer was placed with a congenial and understanding, if fiercely racist, farmer named Fred Pope, whose farm, Marsh Moor, lay about twelve miles from Molteno in the Eastern Cape. Surrounded by ruggedly impressive scenery and whites to whom, with few exceptions, he would never have dared reveal his views on racial equality, Plomer communed with the spirit of Olive Schreiner (buried less than sixty miles away) and began to work seriously on his poetry. In a bold move that revealed both his serious ambitions and his desire to connect himself with the center of current literary

consciousness, he wrote to the influential Harold Edward Monro, founder in 1913 of the Poetry Bookshop, to ask for Monro's encouragement.

As Monro apparently lost interest, this effort to connect with the literary zeitgeist failed, but Plomer persisted and on his next attempt did indeed connect. Everybody having recognized that Plomer would never make a sheep farmer, he had moved in 1922 with his family to Entumeni, on the lushly beautiful Natal coast, to run a trading post for the Zulus with his father. This enterprise proved to be successful, not least because of the genuine affection and respect that grew among father and son and their Zulu customers. Plomer's feelings at this time are revealed in a series of poems in which, as Alexander puts it, he "identified with the Zulus and wished to dissociate himself from his unattractive white neighbors," even to the extent of pretending that the poems had actually been authored *by* a Zulu. Drawing his sense of identity from the native population and finding them increasingly attractive, he also at this time began work on *Turbott Wolfe* and filed away in his imagination character types of several noble, sacrificial blacks and vicious, misguided whites who populate his African short stories.

As the novel neared completion, Plomer initiated the contact with Leonard and Virginia Woolf that led to their publishing eight consecutive Plomer manuscripts between 1925 and 1932. He also invited the South African poet Roy Campbell to lunch in Durban in June 1925, a meeting that kindled a deep and productive friendship that expanded to include Laurens van der Post, an Afrikaner journalist for the *Natal Advertiser*. In the company of these two men Plomer blossomed, sharing opinions on works in progress, articulating the antiracist agenda the three friends shared, and eventually leaving Entumeni in May 1926 at Campbell's invitation to work with him on the literary and consciousness-raising magazine *Voorslag* (Afrikaans for "whiplash"). The *Voorslag* alliance quickly crumbled, with Campbell's resignation as editor occurring two months later when the journal's management refused to allow an overt politicization of its agenda, particularly on the subject of the color bar. The friendships, however, did not, and this first adult creative period in Plomer's life ended with van der Post offering him the experience of a lifetime — a trip to Japan. Van der Post had intervened to end the mistreatment, on racial grounds, of a couple of Japanese journalists, and his kindness had led to an invitation to visit Japan by traveling as a guest aboard the steamship *Canada Maru*. Plomer's dedication to the principle of racial equality was some-

Entumeni ("the place of thorns"), Zululand – site of the trading post managed by Plomer's father in December 1922

thing in which the Japanese, recognizing that European countries saw them as inferior, were obviously interested, and when the ship's captain was told what an asset the author of *Turbott Wolfe* would be to the company's diplomatic mission, he agreed to include Plomer in the invitation. Recognizing the magnitude of the step he was taking, Plomer sailed with van der Post from Durban on 2 September 1926.

When Plomer left for Japan, his only work of short fiction to have appeared in print (in *Voorslag*) had been some of the long story "Portraits in the Nude," although he had also started work on an important story in his first collection, "Ula Masondo." Plomer sent the manuscript of *I Speak of Africa* to the Hogarth Press from Tokyo in November 1926, and when it was published in 1927, complete with an introductory attack on "that blasted heath," South Africa, and its "uncivilized white owners" whose attitude to culture he likened to "that of a dog to a lamp-post," it provoked outrage in the country that it portrayed with such venom and sadness. Alexander quotes a review in the *Cape Argue* calling the book "unpardonable" and "the final kick, so to speak, of a man who had already left the country far behind him." The volume was seen as being the work of an outsider – as in a way it was. The stories clearly betray that in the land of his birth, and certainly among whites, Plomer did not feel that he "belonged."

Plomer later said of his stories in general that "Most of my stories reflect the age by isolating some crisis caused by a change of environment or by the sudden and sometimes startling confrontation of members of different races and classes." Of the South African stories in particular he added that they "all touch more or less directly upon that conflict between white and black, which was, and is,

and is going to be the most important of all human concerns in many parts of Africa." Thematically "explosive," as Alexander puts it, and powerful in their depiction of a country in crisis and in their undermining of the notion of the color bar, the best stories in the collection command attention and respect, despite their imperfections.

The first and longest story, "Portraits in the Nude," unfolds in a series of nineteen segments, almost verbal tableaux, from which the totality of the situation may be inferred. It is not entirely successful in every respect; Doyle argues that Plomer has taken on too much raw material and that the South African Dutch *paterfamilias*, Takhaar Van Ryn, is the wrong choice as the central character. The story uses parallel narratives and symbolic suggestion to condemn the appalling behavior of white masters toward the blacks, behavior accorded the blessing of organized religion. Van Ryn witnesses without interference his sons' acts of unspeakable and unjustifiable cruelty against Shilling, their black servant who is worth no more to them than the coin for which he is named. Van Ryn, himself given to violence against his wife, becomes insane in the course of the narrative, thereby further reducing the legitimacy of the actions he condones. The narrative raises to an exalted level the black victim, whose punishment for his wife Sara's supposed insolence results largely from her refusal of Dirk Van Ryn's sexual attentions. In a segment titled "A Black Christ" (a conscious link to an early poem Plomer had called "The Black Christ"), Shilling is stripped naked, bound to a wagon wheel, and offered as what the watching Takhaar sees as "symbolic sacrifice."

In "Portraits in the Nude" – wrenching in its portrayal of white domination, violence, and evil, and powerful in its sympathy for the victims of this evil – Plomer has already identified the subject matter to which he would frequently return. The story is skilled and subtle in its parallels, powerful in its visual acuity, and at times funny, something that *Turbott Wolfe* is not. In a carefully modulated comic scene in church, the insane Takhaar shocks the congregation by confidently appearing naked among them. Simultaneously, however, this portrait of the nude fanatic prefigures that of Shilling, stripped and humiliated to take his punishment. Plomer was already learning the art of taking himself less seriously.

"Ula Masondo," the other long story in the collection, is generally acclaimed as an early masterpiece. Here Plomer concentrates, as Doyle notes, "on one character and a single idea," resulting in a poignant clarity of vision. Wrapped in a beautiful native blanket in which he is portrayed dancing like a flame in the sunlight, the black country naïf Ula leaves his home and family for the mines of Goldenville (Johannesburg). There he keeps bad company and is entirely corrupted by the values of the city. After having a near-fatal accident in the mines and seeing a vision of a bushman's cave, he does return to the country with a female companion, but he has replaced his blanket with garish, westernized clothing and shuns his family — actually pretending not to see his mother, who is driven by her grief and shame to commit suicide. Seemingly unaware of the implications of his vision or too corrupt to recover his original identity, Ula is driving his family and their values to the extinction that has been the fate of the bushmen. The plot unfolds in a manner so uncomplicated as to become at times simplistic: we are not sure, for example, just why Ula is motivated to leave home in the first place, or what the relationship between civilization and evil is. Yet from this simplicity the story of Ula Masondo derives an immense force, and the narrator is not utterly without hope. Ula has lost his spiritual center, but the narrative hints that the voice of the "phoenix of freedom" may yet rise above the oppression that enthralls it. Furthermore, the story ends on a note of deep disappointment expressed by a sympathetic, if condescending, white voice; not every white is an oppressor.

Three other stories in this first collection are singled out by critics for particular praise; when Plomer narrows his scope, he gains greater control over his subject matter. "Black Peril" presents a fascinating experiment in stream-of-consciousness narration and the simultaneous coexistence of two utterly incompatible subject realities. The center of the stream-of-consciousness is the dying Vera Corneliussen, who has apparently become overwhelmed by the taboo yet fulfilling power of her love for a black man. Like E. M. Forster, Plomer believed in the redemptive powers of connection and affection, of reaching across the artificial gulfs created by human beings to separate themselves from anything they perceive as different, threatening, or "Other." He clearly perceived the creation and obsessive maintenance of such gulfs as self-destructive folly, particularly as manifested in the South African experience. For a white minority to believe itself to be fundamentally superior and to live according to such a belief is not only folly but also impossible, and Plomer treats with unsentimental contempt those who attempt to do so. His stories, like this one written to encompass the perspectives of both Vera

and men like her husband, are most successful when they show ways in which women and their experiences (like those of all oppressed peoples — South African blacks and the English lower classes) are deliberately marginalized, sacrificed so that the preservation of a false hierarchy may be maintained. The fundamental peril, the story suggests, lies in seeing the coexistence of black and white as inherently perilous — in denying the existence, even the possibility, of a fruitful connection. For characters such as Vera's cold, isolationist, inadequate husband, George, to admit that a white woman could find fulfillment in the company and arms of a black servant, Charlie with the "electric skin," is to think the unthinkable. George is shown by Vera's comparison to be distinctly the inferior man, both in character and in physique, and it is just such inferiority that leads to the substandard thinking that perpetuates tragic divisions in South African society.

The other stories in the volume choose for their subject matter universal, rather than peculiarly South African, experiences. "Saturday, Sunday, Monday" examines the volatility of close relationships. A married farm woman, Maud, becomes threatened by the sexuality of her visiting younger sister, Lena, and the obvious currents of attraction running between Lena and Maud's husband, Piet. Although Lena pursues her own interests with a neighboring young man and presents no direct threat to Maud's marriage, Maud takes refuge from her sexual jealousy in an identity with which her sister cannot at present compete — her maternity. "Stephen Jordan's Wife" is a delicately ironic study of subjective experience and received opinion, of the gaping holes in knowing and understanding that exist even in seemingly close friendships, and of human suspiciousness and isolation. The superficial, assertive Colonel Gunn-Drummond gossips coldly to his old friend, the widower Stephen Jordan, about the elopement of Maggie Feverdew, the very woman for whom Jordan is grieving, and later Stephen aggravates, and is savagely attacked by, a pair of young lovers. "The Pensioner" also depends on ironic juxtaposition for its comment about life's uncertainty. A new retiree, a railway worker, inspires the envy of his colleagues as he contemplates his future life of leisure — only to be crushed at the crescendo of his excitement by the wheels of a train. The remaining stories — "Potted Tongue," an exaggerated account of compulsive gossiping; "The Strongest Woman in the World," who turns out to be predictably weak; and "Art and Commerce," a funny fragment about two very different audiences that both interpret the same speech as applying specifically to them – are slight in both length and impact, but all ironically detail human superficiality and lack of self-knowledge.

Working as a popular and successful teacher, first at the Tokyo School of Foreign Languages and then at an expensive private high school, Plomer was to remain in Japan for three years. He dedicated himself to learning about the country and its people from the inside, and he pursued his first serious intimate relationship with a young man named Morito Fukazawa. Plomer obviously remained more of an outsider in Japanese society than he ever had been in English surroundings, a position that tempered even his most intimate participation in Japanese society with a sense of his own distance. He was further isolated by his difficulties with the Japanese language. However, he did integrate with spectacular success in a society known for its mistrust of strangers, as he visited with Japanese friends in their homes and absorbed material that was to inform his unsentimental, critical, yet deeply sympathetic and understanding short stories about the Japanese. He had little time for the uncritically pro-Japanese bias of people like the American Lafcadio Hearn, a naturalized Japanese who, according to Plomer, had simultaneously exalted and belittled his adopted country by failing to appreciate that "it must have seemed to the interest of the Japanese to make the most of Western sentimentality about them . . . [for] behind a barrage of cherry blossoms the militarists had built up their heavy industries and plans to expand abroad."

Plomer's second book of short stories, the critically acclaimed *Paper Houses* (1929), bore the fruit of his Japanese experiences. The powerful and prophetic stories in this volume are linked to the earlier South African stories by a critique of the imperialist mentality and an unflinchingly recorded sense of impending disaster. Plomer noted in his introduction to *Four Countries* (1949) that his earlier theme of "detribalization and of transition from a village community to a great town, where an individual is apt to be exploited, recurs in the Japanese stories." Another prominent and recurring feature in these stories is the exploration of the perspective of those in subservient roles, notably women. Plomer further concerns himself in his Japanese stories with depicting and analyzing what he describes in his autobiographical volume *At Home* (1958) as the "duality, or divided nature, of the Japanese," – and of the prevailing rigid conformity of attitude that leads, as he saw it, to the annihilation of the individual response.

The first story in the collection, "Nakamura," provides visually acute details of the Japanese setting and introduces subject matter both universal and peculiarly Japanese. On observing a girl with whom he had been connected now contentedly in the company of a wrestler, Nakamura, a taxi driver, becomes consumed with sexual jealousy. Through the initial presence in his cab of a farmer unconnected with the situation, he is helped to overcome his temptation to destroy both the couple and himself in an act of suicidal revenge by driving his car over a cliff. Yet even as he relaxes, feeling that he and fate have solved his dilemma, he loses control of the vehicle and he and the passengers plunge to their deaths in a quirk of circumstance like that responsible for the death of the South African railway man in "The Pensioner."

"The Portrait of an Emperor" returns to the Japanese preoccupation with suicide, which it joins with a cynical Western examination of emperor worship. The central character, Yoshida Shojiro, kills himself because he feels guilty of dereliction of duty when a photograph of the emperor entrusted to his particular care is stolen from its shrine. After his agonizing death, his initially proud widow becomes "haunted" by her awareness that the emperor, the subject of her husband's self-annihilating veneration, is "only a man." "A Surplus Woman," set aboard a ship and concerning itself with English characters, offers in contrast a private suicide, committed for personal rather than socially prescribed reasons.

Through its main character, Tonoki, and his conversations with his English friend, Wilmington, "A Brutal Sentimentalist" is Plomer's study of what he perceived to be a duality amounting almost to what T. S. Eliot would have called a "dissociation of sensibility" in the Japanese character. Plomer was deeply disturbed by the simultaneous Japanese capacity for brutality and for sentimentality – for unthinking action at one moment and sensitive connection at another, and for placing duty, tradition, and nationality before individuality. In a searing reminiscence Tonoki recalls the childhood experience of his relative Osone, who was ordered to disembowel himself for a childish act of mischief. Only when the boy had drawn his sword to perform the act was he pardoned. Japanese nationalism is again Plomer's subject in the final story of the collection, "Mother Kamchatka: or Mr. Mainchance in Search of the Truth," a scathing comic fantasy reminiscent of Jonathan Swift's *Gulliver's Travels* (1726) in which Plomer makes fun of the Japanese flag (likened to a poached egg) and returns to his critique of emperor worship and unthinking, unquestioning nationalism.

"A Piece of Good Luck" reworks the themes of "Ula Masondo" but treats the city life of the main character, Chiye, with far greater subtlety by allowing her to exist as a strong, complex individual rather than simply as a symbol for corruption and destruction. Abused and disappointed, Chiye does survive as an intact personality, learning to survive in the teeth of adversity and adapting to an extremely difficult relocation that she and her mother initially see as a piece of luck, a chance for the betterment of a country girl. "The Sleeping Husband," projecting the perspectives of a long-suffering wife and her even more unfortunate servant through its effective first-person narration of the wife, also treats a sensitive woman's misery with delicacy and sympathy in offering an implicit critique of the Japanese attitude toward women. In "Yoka Nikki: An Eight-Day Diary" narrative via intimate revelation is again used to effect. Here Plomer's narrator writes as a diarist-traveler, consciously offering an outsider's perspective on Japan. This perspective is very much Plomer's own; the trip described was one he had taken to the island of Hokkaido and was based on his own meticulous diary of that journey.

Plomer left Japan and Fukazawa in March 1929, driven to do so by the alien aspects of Japanese culture so well portrayed in the stories, as well as by his sense of his own Englishness and by what he described as "a longing for the best of the West, in whatever form." With his return he had not lost the lessons learned in Japan, however: he recognized in the English the same imperialist tendencies, the same xenophobia, the same conformity of attitude that he had so disliked in the Japanese, and he applied to his own countrymen his signature probing – his analytical, diagnostic, almost clinical detachment. He adopted as his alter ego a character called Dr. Gruber, for whom, he explains in *At Home,* he was once mistaken, and whose importance to him is made very clear by the fact that the working title for this section of the autobiography was initially "Doctor Gruber." In the last chapter of these memoirs, under the heading "If I were Doctor Gruber," Plomer uses his alter ego's hypothetical response to his new country as a neat representation of Plomer's own sense of being essentially homeless – a migrant, simultaneously English and not English. Plomer's stories about England and the English are written very much from the perspective of this detached persona.

The sheer number of Plomer's vast, ever-expanding acquaintance after his return to England is extraordinary, and the degree of their fame even more so. From relatively modest beginnings in the Woolfs' drawing room and from the reestablishment of old friendships such as that with van der Post, the list of luminaries with whom Plomer spent his time reads like a Who's Who in literature of this century. He could claim as familiars (and these include only a few of the very grand total) E. M. Forster, T. S. Eliot, the Sitwells, Elizabeth Bowen, Christopher Isherwood, Stephen Spender, W. H. Auden, Sir Hugh Walpole, Robert Graves, Lady Ottoline Morell, Cecil Day Lewis, Rupert Hart-Davis, and Ian Fleming. What is equally extraordinary is the number of these people to whom Plomer was genuinely a friend. He possessed the gift of friendship, and his affection was clearly returned. The only Plomerian friendship known to have soured, largely as the result of Plomer's homosexuality, was that with Roy Campbell.

One of Plomer's most important and fruitful English friendships was with Anthony Butts. The "Moderately Grand Tour" taken by the two friends in 1930 and funded by Butts included Berlin, Italy, Athens, Corfu, and Paris, and it provided the experiences Plomer used for the Greek stories collected in *The Child of Queen Victoria, and Other Stories* (1933). This was Plomer's last book of entirely new stories and the volume that marked the beginning of his association with publisher Jonathan Cape, for Plomer was growing ever more uncomfortable with the poor marketing of his books by Hogarth Press. The Greek stories in the volume (which were, along with the new South African stories, reworked from material originally intended as part of a never-published autobiographical novel) are more directly concerned with homosexual experience than any of Plomer's other works of short fiction. These stories are rich in the "Local Colour" for which the last and most contemporary of them, concerned with the homosexual encounters of two young students in an exotic setting, is named. The stories are poignantly disillusioned, seemingly unable to believe that human communication is strong enough to bridge the gulfs of national and class differences and of human selfishness. Plomer's pessimism in them almost certainly stems from the abandonment he felt when his young Greek lover, Nicky, to whom he was deeply and sincerely attached, left him for another tourist with more money – and from Plomer's own uncomfortable sense of having taken advantage of the young man for the purposes of his own pleasure. The lush pleasures and illusory delights of Plomer's Greek experiences are best summed up in his own words for them: "lotos-eating."

The poignancy mingled with cynicism and mistrust that are so much a hallmark of the Greek

Plomer (left) with Roy and Mary Campbell, 1926

stories are perhaps most evident in "Nausicaa," which concerns itself with Emmanuelides, a homosexual tourist in Corfu, and his selfish use of a handsome young Greek boy. The visitor seduces the youth with empty promises to help him find Nausicaa, the missing sister whose name (suggesting the ideal femininity of the maiden who welcomed Ulysses) underlines the extent of the betrayal and, perhaps, Plomer's ambivalent feelings about his homosexual lifestyle. The narrator comments that Corfu is "haunted" by her history, but so are her visitors.

"The Crisis," set in Athens, also concerns human limitations, in this case the inability of the aptly named Fletcher B. Raper, "Newly appointed chief local executive for Greece of Study Trips in Bible Lands, Inc.," to understand anything about the land that he wishes to explain to others. Without connection one remains blind, unable to know anything. A fourth story, "The Island: An Afternoon in the Life of Costa Zappaglou," returns to the subject of male intimacy and provides a happier perspective. Based on a barely disguised autobiographical description of the magical early stages of Plomer's relationship with Nicky (and with Plomer himself appearing as Costa, the Greek tourist), this story emphasizes the satisfying closeness and power

of friendship. In an interesting link with "Folk Tale," the first Greek story in the book, Costa's sailor friend is a Klepht, connected to the past by his heritage and to the future by his transferral at the end of the story to a submarine. Set, as is "Folk Tale," in the nineteenth century, this story presents historically named characters (Nestor and Leandros) who resist the invading Albanians and Turks and join the Klephts. Through action clearly emphasizing the mythic strength and dignity of the Klephtic people, the narrative of "The Island" points symbolically to the legendary courage and endurance of the Klephts and to the human yearning for freedom. It thus reminds the reader of Plomer's early presentation of South African blacks like Shilling, who refused to surrender his dignity.

Three South African stories contain Plomer's last use of African material in his fiction and are also strongly autobiographical in being reworked, like the Greek stories, from his failed autobiographical novel; these comprise the strongest pieces of *The Child of Queen Victoria*. Here Plomer returns to his experiences at Marsh Moor and Entumeni, addressing them with the increased power and confidence of a writer who has matured since last working with a particular set of materials. The title story of the volume is narrated from the perspective of the central character, Frant (essentially Plomer himself), who moves to the Lembuland of the early stories to work at a trading post. An outsider in an alien place, Frant does make redemptive connections. The narrative points to the positive power of communication and to the danger of seeing either South African blacks or whites as stereotypes. Human beings are capable of goodness, of understanding, and of love, notwithstanding societally imposed, artificial barriers like those of race and color. Frant's attraction to the black girl Seraphina, treated with great narrative delicacy, is Plomer's testament to the human ability to cross such barriers. However, the story never succumbs to sentimentality or to wishful, idealistic thinking. Rendered literally impossible by Seraphina's drowning in a flood, the relationship Frant so desires remains in the realm of the ideal, but, as the narrative makes clear, the years of mistrust, fear, and misunderstanding have created a destructive gulf between the races that also renders the relationship impossible.

In "Down on the Farm" Plomer comes closer than at any other point in his African fiction to rendering a fulfillment of his wish for equality between black and white. This story portrays a touching and realistic, mutually affectionate and appreciative relationship between the white farmer Tom Stevens and his servant Willem. Stevens – who, as Doyle says, "treats Willem as a human being whose worth is beyond economic calculation and beyond too many easy words" – is that rare character in Plomer, "the human being who makes the reader glad he himself is human." The third South African story in this volume, "When the Sardines Came," considers relationships between the sexes rather than between races. A mature and deeply sympathetic portrayal of a childless wife's loneliness, a husband's humanity, and the triangular relationship that results when a stranger is introduced into a tired marriage, this story is set on the Natal south coast during the midwinter sardine run. This event is represented symbolically as id-producing, as invoking a carnival-like atmosphere during which normal social restraints are abandoned as everybody scrambles impulsively after the fish. The wife, Mrs. Reymond, scrambles instead after Boris, an injured fisherman whom she nurses after he has sustained a serious accident. What is remarkable about this mellow story is the husband's understanding of the situation and his decision not to interfere but to let his wife's desires, like the sardines, "run their course."

The three French contributions to *The Child of Queen Victoria,* like the Greek section, are considered by their critics to be minor when compared to Plomer's South African and Japanese short fiction, but everything in this volume is entirely readable. The French stories are marked by a detached humor reminiscent of Guy de Maupassant, whom Plomer consciously admired, and reflect on universal human experience rather than record Plomer's peculiarly French experiences. In their universality of experience they reflect the thematic widening of Plomer's short fiction as it matures, but in their relative disinterest in place they are unusual. With the exception of these stories Plomer's short fiction consistently uses, as intrinsic parts of its subject matter and themes, the perspectives and experiences of characters in particular places well-known to the author, places on which he wishes to comment.

"The Owl and the Pussy Cat" portrays a child's waiting to hear, and the child's excitement upon learning from Crofton the butler, a scandalous secret about a mysteriously elegant couple. The morbidly mysterious "A Museum Piece" is almost a ghost story, placed in the shadows of the museum and the mind and concerning a peculiar encounter between a young man in a museum and the elusive, disappearing Miss Whippington. The strongest of the three stories, "Bed Number Seventeen," is set during World War I and told from the point of

view of Victor, a young man of fifteen – as Plomer had been during the war. Victor's contact with wounded soldiers in a hospital rushes him, as his creator had been rushed during his own wartime adolescence, toward a painful maturity and understanding of human character. The differing settings and tones in these three stories point to Plomer's growing versatility and range at this time in his career.

Plomer and Butts returned from the tour that had provided so much material for *The Child of Queen Victoria* in somber moods, the results of declining Butts family finances and news of the cancer that was eventually to kill Plomer's beloved mother. From this time Plomer was to grow more established in England, where he became in 1937 a reader for publisher Jonathan Cape. At this job he excelled, despite a powerful idiosyncratic dislike of all things Canadian: he discovered talents like Derek Walcott and Ted Walker (who were published by Cape) and Sir John Betjeman and Vladimir Nabokov (who, in spite of Plomer's advice, were not). He also expanded his personal range, writing two biographies – *Cecil Rhodes* (1933) and *Ali the Lion: Ali of Tebeleni, Pasha of Jannina, 1741–1822* (1936) – and editing the wildly popular *Kilvert's Diary: Selections* (1938–1940), a series of volumes comprising the diary of a Victorian clergyman whom Plomer found most congenial. During World War II Plomer worked as a broadcaster for the BBC and, through the influence of his friend and admirer Ian Fleming, for the Naval Intelligence Division. He also produced the first volume of his autobiography, *Double Lives* (1943), in which, clearly at pains at this time in his life to define himself as an Englishman, he dwelt at great length upon his English heritage. In 1944 he first met Charles Erdmann, a Polish-German Jewish refugee and an even more displaced human being than Plomer himself; in 1946 they became companions and remained so for twenty-seven years, until Plomer's death.

After the war Plomer returned to his old job at Cape, although to his disappointment he was no longer chief reader. He renewed his friendship with van der Post and, significantly, his contacts with his Japanese friends; Plomer was a man who did more than write about the need for connection across formidable barriers. Writing about this renewed contact in *At Home: Memoirs,* he asked, "If the ties that bind individuals together are broken, what is left?"

In 1949 *Four Countries* was published, a volume of short stories consisting of reprints from his first three volumes, a powerful contribution set in Japan and written too late for inclusion in his earlier col-

Plomer (right) with W. H. Auden at the offices of the Faber and Faber publishing house, 1960 (photograph by Mark Gerson)

lections, and four previously uncollected stories set in England. This volume, the contents of which Plomer selected with pride at the end of his career as a writer of short stories, was his penultimate collection: it was followed only by *A Brutal Sentimentalist and Other Stories* (1969), consisting of works reprinted from his Japanese collection and edited by his former pupil Eiichi Sano, and yet *Four Countries* was less well received than any other book of his fiction. His English stories, like the earlier French ones and, to a lesser extent, those with a Greek setting, were generally regarded as slighter, less powerful and compelling than those set in South Africa and Japan. While it is certainly true that the English stories are lighter than his earliest work, both in subject matter and tone, they are remarkable for their mellow maturity, narrative sophistication, structural control, trenchant social satire, and humorous detailing of human foibles.

An older, more realistic Plomer no longer believed that he could change the world, but despite the tonal shift in the English stories, many of his earlier themes continued to receive attention. The engaged passion of the earliest stories, the didacticism of tone, and the strong desires to show what is wrong with the world and to make a difference were all substantially diminished. Yet Plomer remained deeply concerned with the seemingly unbridgeable gulfs separating people from different backgrounds, cultures, and perspectives, and he concentrated on poor communication between men and women and between the upper and lower classes, as well as the dangers of hiding oneself behind a wall of artificial values. He stated in the introduction to this volume that the English stories were concerned "almost inevitably, with the comedy of class distinctions." Despite the mocking urbanity of the English stories,

Plomer's portrayal of human beings living behind protective shields yet remaining morally and spiritually lost is as trenchant here as it had been in *I Speak of Africa*. Like the Indian-born William Makepeace Thackeray before him, Plomer examines English society through the skeptical, mocking, detached eyes of his outsider character, Dr. Gruber, and finds much that is worthy of his attention.

"No Ghosts" exposes — with a deft, comic touch — the illusions of the pompous and ridiculous lady novelist Mrs. de Paul-Pincus. Convinced of her superiority and cocooned (or marooned) in a cloud of sentimental illusions, she is shown to disadvantage in an encounter with the realistic, straightforward owner of Quarenden Hall, whom she mistakes for a servant because she finds him engaged in manual labor. The mocking tone of the story is not one that Mrs. de Paul-Pincus would be capable of appreciating, but even she is forced to acknowledge that at the Hall there are no ghosts.

"Ever Such a Nice Boy," though considered "slight" by its critics, addresses another theme consistent in Plomer's work: the gulf governing the master-servant relationship and that between men and women. Told from the point of view of a young female servant, this story is notable for the sympathy accorded the naive, poorly educated narrator and for what Peter Alexander praises as "a delicate, subtle study of male sexual frustration." "The Night Before the War," the best of the English stories, neatly embodies a theme of spiritual lostness in the actual lostness of a sheltered young man, as it suggests powerfully that if one is to find oneself, one must take risks, must come out from behind one's protective wall in order to engage in the redemptive process of connection. The middle-class civil servant Henry literally becomes lost, away from what he knows and where he is known: he is like Ula Masondo lost in Goldenville, Frant lost in Lembuland, and, by implication, England herself unmoored, losing her way in a pact with Hitler and tottering precariously on the brink of World War II.

Before his experiences Henry's perspectives are superficial, and to him the notion of war is slight and insubstantial. However, his maturing process is initiated by his becoming displaced, removed from his usual safe environment. As Henry sets off home after a late visit to Violet, his ailing beloved, he forgets the external symbols of his identity through which his society recognizes him for what he supposedly "is": his money, his umbrella, and the keys to his flat. With no way to prove his identity Henry spends the night as a transient in transition, temporarily displaced and denied reentry to "civilization" since he is without his societal passport. At the end of an uncomfortable and revealing night, Henry is rescued by a working-class acquaintance, the son of his cleaning woman, who lends him the money he needs to reenter a sphere from which the boy himself, because of artificial "class" distinctions, is permanently excluded. Henry has lost the illusion of safety, however, and continues his life empowered by the connections made that night; he feels "as if he had passed a difficult test." Henry's plight may be in some senses comic, but the implications of this elegant story are profound.

"A Wedding Guest" contains a superbly engineered final narrative twist, and, in its revelation that two ancient English families had ensured their continuation through the spermatic services of a handsome young butler, takes a Thackerayan swipe at the ever-diminishing vigor of the English upper classes. This effete social stratum, Plomer suggests, lacks the energy needed to reproduce itself, and without a much-needed infusion of "common" blood may rapidly cease to exist. The final narrative twist reveals that the two half-sibling children of the butler are, in ignorance of the circumstances of their births, about to marry each other. The future of the aristocracy therefore holds the promise of a total lack of self-awareness and inbreeding to the point of extinction. That the story is told by an outsider, a non–family member aware of the situation, bodes further ill for the preservation of hierarchical differences – although the teller of the story, Madam Cardoon, is the very soul of discretion.

The other story in *Four Countries* not taken from an earlier volume is "His Neighbour's Creed," set in Hiroshima and written nineteen years after *Paper Houses*. This last examination of the Japanese view of death is as grimly potent as anything Plomer wrote. Of this story Doyle comments, "it is clear that the details of the narrative were not invented to say something about the dropping of the atomic explosives on Hiroshima but that the occasion of the bombing gave the author the final insight needed in order to use the substance which he had long possessed." The narrative juxtaposes Japanese and European attitudes toward death and immortality as it contrasts contemplative Eastern acceptance of the inevitable destruction of death, tinged by a foreshadowing of the "burden" of the destruction to come to Hiroshima, with the Western view that one is remembered and can make a difference through the "repercussions" of one's actions. The seer Kurodake, grimly aware that such memorialization depends on the circumstance of the existence of somebody who can remember, urges his young visitor to leave Hiroshima so that he may die "in the customary way" and also, by implication, join East and West in his own memory of the "repercussions" of Hiroshima.

Plomer's output as a poet and novelist was significantly more substantial than his production of short stories. After the publication of *Four Countries* he continued to write in both those genres as well as to publish a second volume, and a revised edition of, his autobiography. He also gained attention as a librettist (in collaboration with Benjamin Britten) and as a radio broadcaster. A final English short story, however, written after the publication of *Four Countries,* requires commentary. In the selection of "scattered pieces" he assembled after Plomer's death and titled *Electric Delights* (1978), Rupert Hart-Davis included "A Friend of Her Father's" (as well as the very short "Miss Bourbon-Hapsburg," a good-natured swipe at a specimen of expatriate aristocracy who has become more English than the English themselves and thereby exchanged "one world of fantasy for another"). The former is a hilarious record of a Gruberian expatriate Christmas in England, a story narrated from the perspective of a young South African woman arriving in England for the first time.

Although containing an exceptionally feeble portrayal of heterosexual love (perhaps because here the relationship does not cross forbidden racial boundaries), the story captures superbly the perspective of the English expatriate, the returning colonial who finds herself to be a stranger in what she had assumed would be her own land. The narrator, a confiding young woman who has been led by her parents to believe that a country never visited is her home, finds awaiting her an alien place bearing little resemblance to her parents' idyllic reminiscences. England is gritty, not pretty, and the expected white Christmas fails to materialize. In fact the Foats, the erstwhile friends of her parents with whom she spends the holiday, are Progressives who do not even celebrate an occasion they trendily believe to be merely a fantastic superstition. Modern England is glossed by the narrator's South African frame of reference, as the gleefully trenchant satiric tone of the story reveals for what they are both her yearnings and her hosts' pretensions. "A Friend of Her Father's" may not concern itself with life and death, but it cannot be dismissed as trivial, particularly by those readers who are themselves English South African, or who number such people, expatriate or otherwise, among their acquaintances. Its perspectives on the expatriate experience ring entirely true.

The narrator does find a friend in the Foats' nephew Andrew, an orphan adoptee and therefore, like her, an outsider. The displaced couple, like Plomer and Erdmann, find companionship in each other and, significantly, plan to marry and remain in England, holding out as "Retrogs" or Retrogressives opposed to the tide of Foat-like Progressiveness.

If the nomadic Plomer can finally be said to have put down his roots anywhere, it was in England – although even there he was never very firmly planted, changing his residence frequently and accumulating little in the way of material possessions. However, after his trip abroad with Butts he left England's shores but rarely, and he returned only once, briefly, to South Africa in 1956, exactly thirty years after he had sailed for Japan. Furthermore, he did find happiness and stability after World War II in his relationship with Erdmann. His final judgments recorded in his autobiographical writing are made, with characteristic Plomerian caution, in England's favor: despite a continuing sense of existing as a detached, watchful, critical exile in his own country – a type embodied by his alter ego, Dr. Gruber – Plomer records in the closing pages of *At Home* that he has felt "no compulsion to return to Asia or Africa. More than once I have declined invitations to take up positions in Japan. . . . I know that part of me is part of Japan, but I do not yet feel that this cross-grafting process must be repeated." He continues, "As for South Africa, since the Twenties I have had no relations there except dead ones. . . . I remember Africa as a complex and violent revelation made to me when young. . . . I could not imagine living there in a state of tension that I should only find endurable if bent upon martyrdom or at least victimization."

Plomer never lost the clear-sighted relativity that so illuminates his international collection of short stories, his awareness that "to most of the human race an Englishman is a foreigner." Despite his reservations about things English and his genuine abhorrence of the imperialist mentality and the degree of xenophobia that reminded him of his time in Japan, Plomer acknowledged that his Englishness – which he defined as his sense of being connected to England, English "civilization," and English people – conferred on him a sense of personal empowerment and allowed him to become "more widely and deeply engaged – with human nature, with the past, with the arts, with the battle against the cheapening and the levelling of what is rare and diverse, and of life itself."

In the last years of his life Plomer was the gratified recipient of many honors, notably the Queen's Gold Medal for poetry in 1963 and the presidency of the Poetry Society as well as recognition as Commander of the British Empire in 1968. He died of coronary thrombosis on the night of 20 September 1973, leaving his literary estate in the hands of Rupert Hart-Davis. His contribution to South African writing was singled out for particular praise in a funeral address by his friend Laurens van der Post, who said of Plomer that "He had the singular gift of being angry in a classical sense . . . a passion that does not blur, but makes vision clearer. He became the first person writing in English in South Africa to express this anger in terms of love, and so changed the imagination of a whole age in Africa."

Biography:

Peter F. Alexander, *William Plomer: A Biography* (Oxford & New York: Oxford University Press, 1989).

References:

John R. Doyle Jr., *William Plomer* (New York: Twayne, 1969);

Marcia Leveson, ed., *Essays and Lectures* (Cape Town: David Philip, 1973);

E. R. Miner, *The Japanese Tradition in British and American Literature* (Princeton: Princeton University Press, 1958);

Martin Tucker, *Africa in Modern Literature* (New York: Ungar, 1967).

Papers:

Most of Plomer's papers are at the University of Durham, with other important collections at the Britten-Pears Museum, Aldeburgh; the Archives of Jonathan Cape Ltd., University of Reading; the Hogarth Press Archives, University of Sussex; the National English Language Museum, Grahamstown, South Africa; the National Library of New Zealand (incorporating the Alexander Turnbull Library), Wellington; the South African Library, Cape Town; and the Harry Ransom Humanities Research Center, University of Texas at Austin.

T. F. Powys

(20 December 1875 – 27 November 1953)

John David Orlet
Kaskaskia College

See also the Powys entry in *DLB 36: British Novelists, 1890–1929: Modernists.*

BOOKS: *An Interpretation of Genesis* (N.p.: Privately printed, 1907; London: Chatto & Windus, 1929; New York: Viking, 1929);

The Soliloquy of a Hermit (New York: G. Arnold Shaw, 1916); republished as *Soliloquies of a Hermit* (London: Andrew Melrose, 1918; revised, 1926);

The Left Leg (London: Chatto & Windus, 1923; New York: Knopf, 1923);

Black Bryony (London: Chatto & Windus, 1923; New York: Knopf, 1923);

Mark Only (London: Chatto & Windus, 1924; New York: Knopf, 1924);

Mr. Tasker's Gods (London: Chatto & Windus, 1925; New York: Knopf, 1925);

Mockery Gap (London: Chatto & Windus, 1925; New York: Knopf, 1925);

A Stubborn Tree (London: E. Archer, 1926);

Innocent Birds (London: Chatto & Windus, 1926; New York: Knopf, 1926);

Feed My Swine (London: E. Archer, 1926);

A Strong Girl, and The Bride: Two Stories (London: E. Archer, 1926);

What Lack I Yet? (London: E. Archer, 1927; San Francisco: Gelber, Lilienthal, 1927);

Mr. Weston's Good Wine (London: Chatto & Windus, 1927; New York: Viking, 1928);

The Rival Pastors (London: E. Archer, 1927);

The House with the Echo (London: Chatto & Windus, 1928; New York: Viking, 1928);

The Dewpond (London: Elkin Mathews & Marrot, 1928);

Fables (New York: Viking, 1929; London: Chatto & Windus, 1929); republished as *No Painted Plumage* (London: Chatto & Windus, 1934);

Christ in the Cupboard (London: E. Lahr, 1930);

The Key of the Field (London: Chiswick, 1930);

Kindness in a Corner (London: Chatto & Windus, 1930; New York: Viking, 1930);

T. F. Powys

The White Paternoster, and Other Stories (London: Chatto & Windus, 1930; New York: Viking, 1931);

Uriah on the Hill (Cambridge: Gordon Frazer, 1930);

Uncle Dottery (Bristol: Douglas Cleverdon, 1930);

The Only Penitent (London: Chatto & Windus, 1931);

When Thou Wast Naked (London: Golden Cockerel Press, 1931);

Unclay (London: Chatto & Windus, 1931; New York: Viking, 1932);

The Tithe Barn, and The Dove and the Eagle (London: K. S. Bhat, 1932);

Powys's birthplace, the rectory at Shirley in Derbyshire

The Two Thieves (London: Chatto & Windus, 1932; New York: Viking, 1933);

Captain Patch (London: Chatto & Windus, 1935);

Make Thyself Many (London: Grayson & Grayson, 1935);

Goat Green; or, The Better Gift (London: Golden Cockerel Press, 1937);

Bottle's Path, and Other Stories (London: Chatto & Windus, 1946);

God's Eyes A-Twinkle (London: Chatto & Windus, 1947);

Rosie Plum, and Other Stories, edited by F. Powys (London: Chatto & Windus, 1966);

Come and Dine, and Tadnol, edited by A. P. Riley (Hastings: R. A. Brimmell, 1967).

SELECTED PERIODICAL PUBLICATIONS – UNCOLLECTED:

FICTION

"One of the Wise," *New Leader,* 8 (15 August 1924): 9;

"Like Paradise," *Window,* 1 (July 1930): 6–12;

"The Gramophone," *Soma,* no. 4 (1933): 57–62;

"Ask and Ye Shall Receive," *Soma,* no. 5 (1934): 112–116;

"The Midnight Hour," *Everyman,* no. 22 (23 February 1934): 15–16;

"A Poor Neighbor," *Everyman,* no. 28 (18 April 1935): 730–732;

"The Race," *West Country Magazine,* no. 2 (Autumn 1946): 90–93;

"Kindness in the Country," *Courier,* 10 (June 1948): 108–112.

Though known primarily for his novels, chiefly for the allegorical *Mr. Weston's Good Wine* (1927), Theodore Francis Powys composed between 1910 and the early 1930s approximately 150 short stories principally set in the English countryside. While belonging to the rural tradition of English literature, Powys did not view life as a pastoral romp but rather, in the words of Norman Nicholson, as a Hobbesian "nightmare land halfway between Bedlam and Hell." Against a rustic backdrop Powys sought to articulate his dark vision of the human condition. The son of a country vicar, he rejected orthodox notions of Christianity while still clinging to a strong Christian morality. As a reviewer in the *Times Literary Supplement* (15 September 1932) put it, Powys was more "an inverted moralist, his hope not in everlasting life, but in everlasting death as the only sure release from the pain and cruelty of which life is woven."

Born on 20 December 1875 at Shirley in Derbyshire to the Reverend Charles Powys and Mary Cowper Johnson, T. F. Powys lived his entire life in the country. Along with his ten siblings (the novelist John Cooper Powys among them), he spent his childhood in villages in Derbyshire, Dorset, and finally Somerset, where his father served as vicar of Montecute for thirty years. After stints at two boarding schools, to which he had difficulty adjusting because they lacked the privacy he so desperately needed, he was sent at age fifteen to work on a farm in Suffolk. Not long after, he secured his own farm, called White House Farm, at Sweffling in the remote Suffolk countryside. Unsuccessful at farming, he left Sweffling to pursue a career in writing, returning in 1901 to Dorset and residing in the seaside village of Studland. In order to escape the tourists then increasingly intruding upon his privacy, he moved in 1904 to East Chaldon, where he resided until 1940.

In 1905 Powys met and married, after a brief engagement, Violet Dodds, a young woman of eighteen with whom he had little in common. She was a happy person, but Powys endured frequent bouts of severe depression, his thoughts turning occasionally to suicide, an act for which he believed himself "too

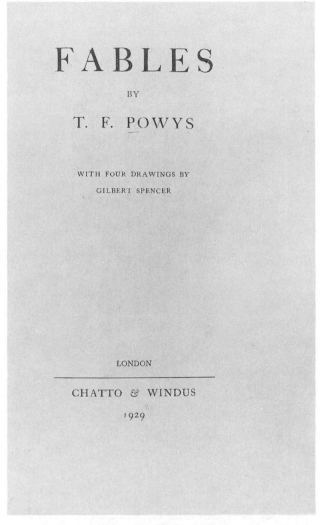

FABLES

BY

T. F. POWYS

WITH FOUR DRAWINGS BY
GILBERT SPENCER

LONDON

CHATTO & WINDUS
1929

Title page for the British edition of one of Powys's most highly regarded books, a collection of nineteen stories – all written during the seventeen months following the publication of The House with the Echo

great a coward." His inability to find publishers for his early stories, despite the help of his brother John and a family friend (and writer), Louis Wilkinson, contributed to the general fragility of his emotional state.

In 1906 and 1907 Powys's spirits improved with the birth of his first son, Charles (called "Dicky"), and the private publication of *An Interpretation of Genesis* (1907). Called by Richard P. Graves "the first important work by any member of [the Powys] family," it is a curious examination of the book of Genesis written in a purposely archaic, biblical style. It received little attention at the time and sold poorly. Between 1907 and 1916 Powys published nothing, but after a move to Beth-Car, a house on the outskirts of East Chaldon, and the

Frontispiece from Christ in the Cupboard, *the title story of which Powys described as "one of my favourite[s] of the shorter stories" (courtesy of Special Collections, Thomas Cooper Library, University of South Carolina)*

birth of his second son, Francis, in 1909, he enjoyed a period of some contentment.

His next major work, *The Soliloquy of a Hermit* (1916; republished in 1918 as *Soliloquies of a Hermit*), was written as a contribution to the never-published "Confessions by the Six Powys Brothers" – to which only John, Llewelyn, and T. F. ultimately contributed. Published in January 1916 by Arnold Shaw, then John's publisher, this work earned T. F. Powys little attention, but a reviewer in the *Dial* (2 March 1916) called him "a satirist of a different kidney" and "a companionable hermit" and concluded, "there is many a chuckle in this little book." Powys had significantly modified his style by this time, by abandoning the floridity that marked *An Interpretation of Genesis* (rife as it was with such locutions as "whereof," "thereunto," and "wouldest") for the

simplicity and lucidity of his subsequent work. His spare style, with its terse and poetic expression, recalls that of his two major influences – John Bunyan's *The Pilgrim's Progress* (1678) and the Old Testament.

Powys's first novel, *Mr. Tasker's Gods* (1925), was written in 1916 but rejected then by publisher Arnold Shaw, and subsequent novels "Amos Lear" and "Georgina, a Lady" also went unpublished. Unable to publish anything and consequently impoverished, Powys fell again into a state of grave depression from which he did not emerge until 1921, when the magazine *New Leader* agreed to publish several of his short stories. During the next five years many of these stories appeared in its pages.

With the help of writers David Garnett and Sylvia Townsend Warner, the latter of whom he met and befriended in 1922, Powys published *The Left Leg* (1923), a collection of novellas that included "The Left Leg," "Hester Dominy," and "Abraham Men." This collection explores such themes as avarice, embodied in the character of Farmer Mew; the futility of life, in "Hester Dominy"; and justice, meted out by Tinker Jar, who represents God in "The Left Leg." While sales were negligible, it was critically well received in London and led to the publication, later that same year, of his novel *Black Bryony*. It too was praised by critics.

By 1926 Powys had published four more novels – *Mark Only* (1924), *Mr. Tasker's Gods*, *Mockery Gap* (1925), and *Innocent Birds* (1926) – and had established himself, in his brother John's words, as "one of the most arresting and formidable of writers of modern fiction." But he was most highly praised for the allegorical novel *Mr. Weston's Good Wine,* unquestionably his finest work. Mr. Weston, Powys's representation of God, comes to Folly Down selling light and dark wines, symbolic of Love and Death – "always," according to William Hunter, "the two great realities" for Powys. This novel is Powys's attempt to explore the question of whether God or mankind is responsible for evil in the world.

Not until 1928, when he was fifty-three years old, did Powys publish his first collection of short stories, *The House with the Echo*. This was an uneven collection of twenty-six previously published stories set, as his novels had been, in such fictional Dorset villages as Norbury, Dodder, Madder, and Tadnol. These villages are mainly interchangeable and are peopled by an assortment of profligates, gossips, mischievous sextons, self-important squires, rapacious farmers, and corrupt or ineffectual clergymen. Criticism of Powys's work indeed often centers on his repeated use of the same characters, a repetition that critics found monotonous. Indeed, Dylan Thomas once ridiculed Powys's work by calling it a collection of "Biblical stories about old sextons called Parsnip and Dottle." His characters for the most part lack complexity and symbolize abstract qualities of good and evil; characters do not develop in his stories. His antagonists are ruthless in visiting cruelties upon their victims, who typically receive such treatment with either patient forbearance or resignation.

Noteworthy among the stories in *The House with the Echo* is "Nor Iron Bars," the story of Joseph Turvey, who found life in prison preferable to life in Norbury village. Released from jail, he finds life on the outside suffocatingly dull. And in the end, his fame for having been incarcerated now faded in his small village, he takes steps to secure his return to prison. This theme of the mundanity of existence is found elsewhere in Powys's work. "Dull Devonshire," a gentle indictment of the church, presents the epicurean Rev. Robert Herrick, one of Powys's more delightful characters, whose body is "as huge as one of the three great cider barrels that he had in his cellar." To the archdeacon who has come to remove him from his benefice for tolerating licentious behavior among the villagers of Penny Morey, the Reverend Herrick boasts gleefully, after taking a drink from his cup of cider, that "Halfpenny is far worse than we . . . ; we call ourselves good here." "Squire Duffy," a rearrangement of the parable of Lazarus and the rich man, reveals Powys's practice of adapting biblical stories to convey often unorthodox religious ideas. In this case the squire (the rich man) is condemned, not to eternal hellfire but to being continuously reminded of his shared human nature by the tombstone of a halfwit with the same name as he. The usual targets of Powys's scorn — wealthy farmers, squires, clergymen — are found in this collection.

None of Powys's short-story collections has received more praise than *Fables* (1929; republished in 1934 under the title *No Painted Plumage*), a collection of nineteen fables using animals, inanimate objects (a rope and a bucket, a hat and a post, a spittoon and a slate), and natural phenomena (waves, darkness, seaweed) as characters capable of thought and speech. Through their own interactions, their dispassionate (and often ironic) observations of human beings, or their interactions with humans, these characters reveal not facile morals but profound truths about life and death. In "Darkness and Nathaniel," one of the more notable stories, which to William Hunter "sums up the attitude" of Powys's work, the narrative develops Powys's pervasive no-

tion — that "true happiness" for mankind is death. Yet Powys, while often biting in his criticism of mankind, possesses also a genuine sympathy for human beings buffeted by the harshness of existence. "The Corpse and the Flea," a reworking of the Everyman morality play, finds Mr. Johnson, though a corpse, conscious in his coffin and awaiting the morning of his burial. He has been a pauper forsaken by all — including his own family — except a flea, for whom he has long served as host. Before the undertaker arrives, this flea declares, in the words of Christ, "I will be with you always." In the end Mr. Johnson, comforted, drifts out of consciousness.

That Powys published none of these stories individually before their publication in this volume has led critics to surmise that he saw them as a unit, not as a collection of disparate stories. Taken as a whole, *Fables* conveys what H. Coombes calls "a humane vision of life, rendered with beauty and power."

Fables was followed promptly by *The White Paternoster, and Other Stories* (1930), a collection of stories thematically similar to the rest of those in his oeuvre. "What Lack I Yet?" discusses the importance of love — or rather the damaging effects of a lack of love in one's life; "Mr. Toller's New Clothes" explores greed and treachery; and "The Baked Mole" studies cruelty — specifically the cruelty of family members toward one of their own. Included also is "Christ in the Cupboard," a story Powys considered one of his best. In this last, a variation on the parable of Lazarus and the rich man, a wealthy farmer and his family reject the importunities of Mrs. Crapper, a beggar, but grant entrance to Christ when he comes to their door. Wishing to keep him with them, they put Christ in their cupboard until such time as they need him to restore one of them to life "as He did the daughter of the Roman centurian." To their dismay, when the father lies dying and they open the cupboard door, out steps the devil exclaiming, "You hid Christ in the cupboard, . . . but your mean deeds have changed Him."

The grisly murder of his son Dicky in Africa in 1932 stunned Powys and marked the beginning of a dramatic decline in his literary output. During the subsequent five years he published only a handful of short stories and novellas, including *The Tithe Barn, and The Dove and the Eagle* (1932); *The Two Thieves* (1932, a collection of three novellas); *Make Thyself Many* (1935); *Captain Patch* (1935), a collection of mostly mediocre stories previously published; and *Goat Green; or, The Better Gift* (1937), a

Dust jacket for the first of two posthumously published collections of Powys's stories. This volume was edited by his son Francis and included some previously unpublished selections.

story republished as "The Better Gift" in the 1946 *Bottle's Path, and Other Stories*. Of these, "Jane Mollet's Box" – the story of a young girl whose act of selflessness saves from suicide the despondent pastor for whom she works as a maid – is a testament to the power of love. Ironically the atheist Vardy instructs Jane that to save Mr. Gasser (the pastor) she must show him that he is loved; Vardy tells her, "Sometimes . . . one gives away what one loves – it has been done, you know." In the end Jane explains, "it be only what I love best that will save 'ee from Hell" and gives to Mr. Gasser a box that he had given her for her fifth birthday, a box in which she has kept all that she values, and this keeps him from taking his life. "Lie Thee Down, Oddity" is the story of Mr. Cronch, a well-paid head gardener of the Honorable George Bullman. Mr. Cronch is a man whose "oddity" drives him first to quit his job and comfortable surroundings

for a ramshackle cottage on an inhospitable heath and then to perform a series of selfless acts of charity. Because his "oddity" (something akin to his conscience or his natural impulse to do what is right despite society's disapproval) will not cease troubling him, as he has repeatedly insisted that it do, Cronch finally loses his life in coming to the aid of an injured mason.

In 1933 Powys, at the age of fifty-eight, and Violet adopted a baby girl, Theodora Gay Powys, whom they called Susan. She was, according to Powys, a further reason that he gave up writing. "I am finding greater tranquility and happiness today," he told an interviewer in 1936, "in teaching [to Susan] Watt's hymns . . . than I ever found in work." And after he suffered a stroke at his home in East Chaldon in 1938, although he fully recovered, he published nothing until *Bottle's Path, and Other Stories,* a collection of eleven short stories, most of which had been published previously. Among the more successful is "The Only Penitent," in which the Reverend Hayhoe, unable to attract the villagers into his confessional, in the end absolves God – represented in the character of Tinker Jar – for being the only one, according to Powys, who needs to be forgiven for the sin of having created human beings to suffer. With its stunning and powerful denouement, this story has been hailed as Powys's finest short work. A reviewer for the *Times Literary Supplement* (27 August 1931) stated upon its first publication that it "reveals all the finer qualities of Mr. Powys's later work and therefore . . . is a story by which those new to his writings might not unfairly judge him." It is, the reviewer had concluded, a "terrible story indeed, yet with a sombre beauty which testifies to depth of feeling behind it." Of "The Dewpond," also included in this volume, another review in the *Times Literary Supplement* (15 November 1928) had asserted, "The delicate art and firm form" of this story are to be "admired for their own sake." And "The Key of the Field," which had also been published individually in 1930, had moved Hunter at that time to proclaim Powys the "greatest English short story writer."

One final collection of short stories, *Rosie Plum, and Other Stories* (1966), was published posthumously, as was *Come and Dine, and Tadnol* (1967), two previously unpublished novellas. Edited by Powys's son Francis, *Rosie Plum, and Other Stories* is a hodgepodge of stories for the most part previously published but not previously collected. Few of these stories, however, achieve the quality and the keenness of insight of Powys's *Fables* – which represents, with *Mr. Weston's Good Wine,* his highest achievement and stands as a neglected literary classic.

With the beginning of World War II Powys and his family moved inland to the village of Mappowder. There he spent his remaining days taking solitary walks in the countryside, enduring pilgrimages to his home by young writers, and – for reasons that can only be guessed at, given his heterodox religious views – attending daily services and reading the lessons at the village church. He died in 1953.

Powys never achieved more than a small but devoted readership during his lifetime, and his fiction has gone largely ignored: he was perceived by many critics as a rural writer, bound by the parochial concerns of the English countryside, and by the public as a writer blasphemous, pessimistic, and preoccupied with sex. His dark view of human nature was, however, mitigated by an ironic humor that did render his stories palatable to his readers, and despite his reputation for pessimism, Powys was widely considered a technical master, using spare plotlines, simple diction, and an intense narrative style to create powerful stories. Indeed, when he is at his best – as in *Mr. Weston's Good Wine,* in short stories such as "The Only Penitent," and in many of his fables – he is able to convey, often with great power, a vision unconstrained by topography, a vision of universal significance.

Interview:

Claude F. Luke, "Why I Have Given Up Writing," *John O' London's Weekly and Outlook,* 36 (23 October 1936): 145–146, 152.

Bibliographies:

Percy H. Muir, *Bibliographies of the First Editions of Books by Aldous Huxley and T. F. Powys* (London: Dolan, 1927; Folcroft, Penn.: Folcroft, 1969);

Peter Riley, *A Bibliography of T. F. Powys* (Hastings: Brimmell, 1967).

Biographies:

Louis Marlow [Louis Wilkinson], *Welsh Ambassadors: Powys Lives and Letters* (London: Bertram Rota, 1936);

H. Coombes, *T. F. Powys* (London: Barrie & Rockcliff, 1960);

Reginald Charles Churchill, *The Powys Brothers* (London: Longmans, Green, 1962);

Kenneth Hopkins, *The Powys Brothers: A Biographical Appreciation* (London: Phoenix House, 1967);

Richard P. Graves, *The Brothers Powys* (New York: Scribners, 1983).

References:

M. Buning, "Folly Down Revisited: Some New Light on T. F. Powys," *English Studies,* 50 (December 1969): 588–597;

Belinda Humfrey, ed., *Recollections of the Powys Brothers: Llewelyn, Theodore, and John Cowper* (London: Peter Owen, 1980);

William Hunter, *The Novels and Stories of T. F. Powys* (Cambridge: Frazer, 1930);

F. R. Leavis, "T. F. Powys," *Cambridge Review,* 51 (2 May 1930): 388–389;

Donald MacCampbell, "The Art of T. F. Powys," *Sewanee Review,* 42 (October 1934): 461–473;

Father Brocard Sewall, ed., *Theodore: Essays on T. F. Powys* (Aylesford, Kent: Saint Albert's Press, 1964);

Martin Steinmann Jr., "The Symbolism of T. F. Powys," *Critique: Studies in Modern Fiction,* 1 (Summer 1957): 49–63.

Jean Rhys

(24 August 1890 – 14 May 1979)

Frank P. Riga
Canisius College

See also the Rhys entries in *DLB 36: British Novelists, 1890–1929: Modernists* and *DLB 117: Twentieth-Century Caribbean and Black African Writers, First Series.*

BOOKS: *The Left Bank, and Other Stories* (London: Cape, 1927; New York: Harper, 1927);

Postures (London: Chatto & Windus, 1928); republished as *Quartet* (New York: Simon & Schuster, 1929);

After Leaving Mr. Mackenzie (London: Cape, 1931; New York: Knopf, 1931);

Voyage in the Dark (London: Constable, 1934; New York: Morrow, 1935);

Good Morning, Midnight (London: Constable, 1939; New York: Harper & Row, 1970);

Wide Sargasso Sea (London: Deutsch, 1966; New York: Norton, 1967);

Tigers Are Better-Looking, with a Selection from The Left Bank (London: Deutsch, 1968; New York: Harper & Row, 1974);

My Day: Three Pieces (New York: Hallman, 1975);

Sleep It Off, Lady (London: Deutsch, 1976; New York: Harper & Row, 1976);

Smile Please: An Unfinished Autobiography (London: Deutsch, 1979; New York: Harper & Row, 1980);

The Collected Short Stories, (New York & London: Norton, 1987).

OTHER: Francis Carco, *Perversity,* translated by Rhys (Chicago: Covici–Friede, 1928);

Edward de Nève (Jean Lenglet), *Barred,* translated by Rhys (London: Harmsworth, 1932).

Although Jean Rhys has been recognized as an important, if not a major, figure among twentieth-century British fiction writers, this critical evaluation came only at the end of her life, long after she had published the bulk of her work. Rhys published her first collection of short fiction, *The Left Bank, and Other Stories,* in 1927. During the next twelve years she published four novels: *Postures* (1928), *After*

Jean Rhys

Leaving Mr. Mackenzie (1931), *Voyage in the Dark* (1934), and *Good Morning, Midnight* (1939). After her fourth novel Rhys disappeared from the public eye and ceased publishing. During the next twenty-seven years she was all but forgotten.

Aside from the initial reviews, neither her novels nor her short fiction received serious critical or scholarly attention. Francis Wyndham's article written for the *Tribune,* a weekly newspaper of the British Labour Party, represented the only major attempt to focus attention on Rhys between 1939 and 1966. The article, appearing in 1950, was part of a series tellingly titled Neglected Books. So completely had Rhys vanished that by the 1950s even

314

her publishers no longer knew anything about her existence. In 1950 when actress Selma Vas Dias dramatized *Good Morning, Midnight,* she had to place a newspaper advertisement in order to find news of Rhys's whereabouts.

Only with the publication of *Wide Sargasso Sea* (1966) did Rhys begin to emerge from nearly three decades of almost complete neglect. Although British reviewers recognized this novel as an important contribution to twentieth-century fiction, she received little recognition in academic circles during the next eight years. Strong impetus for a careful consideration of Rhys's fiction was then provided by Alfred Alvarez, the English writer and critic, in a 1974 article written for *The New York Times Book Review.* Alvarez's assessment of Rhys as "the best living English novelist" proved to be a turning point, particularly in American critical reception. Since 1974 several hundred articles, many books, and a Rhys journal have attested to her growing reputation as a major twentieth-century novelist.

While her novels, particularly *Wide Sargasso Sea,* have received much critical attention, her three collections of short stories — *The Left Bank, and Other Stories; Tigers Are Better-Looking, with a Selection from The Left Bank* (1968); and *Sleep It Off, Lady* (1976) — have yet to be discussed in depth. Many critics have recognized the power, connotative richness, and imagistic resonance of her short fiction, but few have provided sustained, in-depth discussions of more than a handful of stories. Jean Rhys's short fiction thus remains a relatively unexplored but potentially fruitful area of study.

Although Rhys gave the year of her birth as 1894, her actual date of birth was 24 August 1890. She was born in the West Indies on the small British-held island of Dominica. Rhys was a Creole, a term that in the West Indies does not necessarily refer to racial or ethnic identity, but that designates those born in the colonies rather than in their countries of ethnic origin. She was a Creole of Scottish, Irish, and Welsh descent. Her family history, her place of birth, and her social, economic, and cultural positions were all to play important roles in her writings.

On her mother's side Rhys came from a long line of plantation owners whose family history dated back to the late eighteenth century, when Rhys's great grandfather, a Scotsman named James Gibson Lockhart, had emigrated to Dominica. In 1824 he acquired Geneva Estate, a twelve-hundred-acre plantation worked by 258 slaves. Rhys's mother, Minna Lockhart, was the third of six children born to Edward Lockhart and Julia Matilda

(née Woodcock). Minna was still living on the plantation when William Rees Williams, Rhys's father, who had been born in Wales in 1853 and trained as a medical doctor, emigrated from Great Britain to Dominica in 1881. He married Minna Lockhart in 1882 and moved to the port city of Roseau, where he was appointed as a medical officer. Ella Gwendoline Rees Williams, who later adopted the pen name Jean Rhys, was the fourth of five children born to the couple. She later incorporated a fictionalized version of the family history and her own childhood into *Voyage in the Dark, Wide Sargasso Sea,* and her short fiction.

Rhys lived in Dominica until the age of seventeen. Although her upper-middle-class family comprised parts of the white ruling elite in Dominica, the Williamses were by no means wealthy and were perhaps not even well-off by British standards. Rhys's oldest sister had been adopted by an aunt and uncle before Rhys was born. After her father's death Rhys was left destitute while her mother and younger sister lived in straitened circumstances. Though the family was Episcopalian, young Rhys attended a Catholic convent school, where she received a typical middle-class education for young women in the fine arts and French. At this time she began writing poetry in a small exercise book. She was, in fact, being educated to live the leisured life of a lady — one intended not for earning a living, but for marrying a member of her own class.

Rhys left Dominica for England in 1907 and entered Perse School for middle- and upper-middle-class girls. The curriculum was rigid, and for Rhys, a child from a foreign culture and unaccustomed to British codes of behavior or vigorous disciplinary measures, the school appeared as a prison run on arbitrary and incomprehensible rules. Although her achievements were uneven, she was by no means a poor student: when she sat for the Oxford and Cambridge higher certificate in Roman history, she won first prize.

In 1908 she left Perse School and entered the Academy of Dramatic Art, at the time known as Tree's School and later as the Royal Academy. According to the administrator of the academy, Rhys was a hardworking student, but her chances of success were slim because she was unwilling or unable to change her West Indian accent and adopt the upper-class British accent considered suitable for acting professionally. She left the school after two semesters in 1909, a year before her father's death. Although she wrote several pieces of short fiction at this time, these amateur efforts remained unpublished.

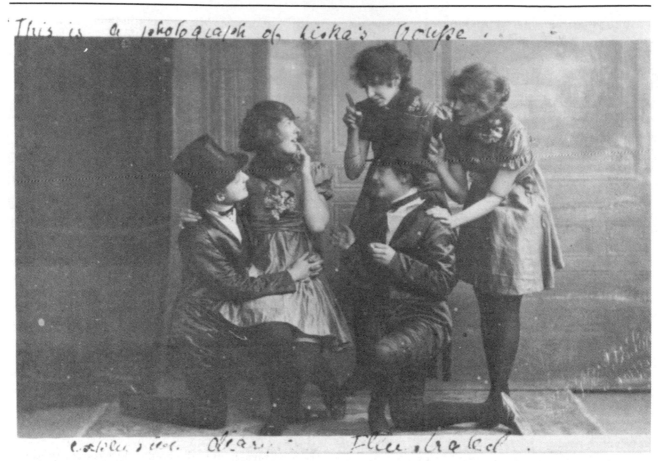

Rhys (far right), circa 1910, with Liska's Troupe, the British musical variety group with which she performed for two years

After her father's death in 1910 Rhys was penniless, but she refused to comply with her mother's request that she return to Dominica. Instead, taking the stage name of Vivien Gray, she joined a traveling musical variety troupe to earn her living as a member of a chorus line, by no means a respectable occupation for a woman of her social station and education.

Rhys had been working as a chorus girl for about a year when she had her first serious love affair – with Lancelot Smith, a wealthy gentleman banker whose interest in Rhys provided her, like other chorus girls, with a standard means of escape from the chorus line. Neither a rake nor a villain, Smith typified many Edwardian men of his social station: he was a respectable businessman in his forties who had never married but had for years maintained a series of paid liaisons with young women. A naive and inexperienced young woman who had never had a previous lover, Rhys was nineteen at the beginning of the affair, which lasted from 1910 until the fall of 1912.

When the affair ended, Rhys at first harbored thoughts of suicide. During an extended depression that followed, she entered into casual, sometimes paid relationships, one of which ended with a pregnancy in 1913. Although the child was not his and he had not seen Rhys for a year, Smith paid for an abortion and, following her difficult recovery, supported Rhys from 1913 until 1919, when she married Jean Lenglet. Shortly after her abortion in January 1914, Rhys described the experience in a series of notebooks that later became the basis for *Voyage in the Dark*. Although she preserved the notebooks carefully, she did not begin to write in earnest until a decade later.

Rhys's first husband, Jean (or John) Lenglet, had come to London in 1917, ostensibly as a reporter, but in fact he had been an agent for French intelligence since 1914. Lenglet, who claimed to come from a Dutch bourgeois family of factory owners, was fluent in several languages, including Dutch, English, German, and French – and between 1932 and 1948 he wrote several novels under the pen name Edouard de Nève. He had been married twice before, and, unknown to Rhys, he was still legally married to his second wife, whom he did not divorce until 1926, more than six years after his marriage to Rhys.

After their marriage in April 1919 Rhys and Lenglet moved to Paris. In early 1920 Rhys gave birth to a boy, who died three weeks later of pneumonia. Lenglet soon obtained a foreign service position as a secretary-interpreter in Vienna and later in Budapest, but he was also engaged in a lucrative and illegal business of black-market trading in foreign currency. The two enjoyed a brief period of wealth and ease until October 1921, when Lenglet was discovered embezzling funds and was forced to flee from Budapest with Rhys. In 1922 they were in Belgium, where their second child, Maryvonne, was born. They were poor, and Rhys had perhaps become alcoholic.

By the summer or early fall of 1924 she was again living in Paris. Having written a series of journals recounting the period in Vienna and its aftermath, she showed these to Pearl Adams, the wife of an English journalist also living in Paris. After revising and editing Rhys's journals and titling the narrative "Suzy Tells," Adams passed the manuscript to Ford Madox Ford, the well-known novelist, editor, and promoter of young writers. Ford was then publishing the *Transatlantic Review,* a short-lived journal that included the work of many Anglo-American expatriate artists and writers who frequented the Left Bank of Paris in the 1920s. He met Rhys in October 1924, and, having suggested the pen name Jean Rhys to her, he published an excerpt from "Suzy Tells," which he had renamed "Triple Sec," in the December (and final) issue of the *Transatlantic Review.* This excerpt later appeared as part of "Vienne," a novella in Rhys's first collection of short stories.

At the end of December 1924 Lenglet was arrested for misappropriating more than Fr 20,000 from a travel agency for which he had been working. In February 1925 he was sentenced to eight months in prison, and Rhys was again left destitute. Ford, who was living with Australian painter Stella Bowen, had adopted Rhys as his protégée, and sometime after Lenglet's imprisonment they invited Rhys to move in with them. As Bowen later wrote, Rhys arrived ill, desperate, and penniless, with "nothing but a cardboard suitcase and the astonishing manuscript." Ford advised her to read in French and English literature, commented on her stories, suggested cuts and stylistic changes, and attempted to introduce her to the Anglo-American crowd of expatriate writers then living in Paris.

As several of her satiric sketches indicate, she never felt drawn to literary circles, but in many ways Ford exercised a decisive and lasting influence on Rhys. He introduced her to French and English works she had not previously read and provided editorial and stylistic commentaries on her work — and perhaps most important, he convinced her that she was not just a dilettante but a serious and publishable writer. At some time (biographers disagree as to when) Rhys had become not only Ford's protégée but his lover, and following the end of her relationship with Lenglet as well as the close of her affair with Ford in 1927, Ford edited and provided an introduction (and probably the title) for Rhys's first collection of short fiction, *The Left Bank, and Other Stories.*

This is the longest of Rhys's three collections of short fiction, including twenty-two short stories ranging from the brief, one-page sketch "In the Luxembourg Gardens" to the first-person novella "Vienne." In many respects *The Left Bank* may be Rhys's seminal work, since it introduces themes and narrative strategies that reappear, albeit in modified forms, in her subsequent fiction. Although it is a first work, the collection by no means represents a beginner's first attempts at writing: it contains some of her finest, most sophisticated stories.

Like much of Rhys's fiction, the stories in *The Left Bank* can be traced, at least in part, to incidents in her life. "Villa d'Or," in which Rhys satirizes not only the wealthy with their aesthetic pretensions but also the parasitic artists (herself included) who sell their talents for lodging and comfort, derives from her experiences as a live-in ghostwriter for a wealthy American family living on the French Riviera. "Mixing Cocktails" grows out of her West Indian childhood, and the character of its protagonist as well as key themes and images are later more fully developed in *Wide Sargasso Sea.* The novella "Vienne" concerns events that parallel those of her first marriage, and it may compose one autobiographical variation among several that appear in her writing. It went through three revisions and partial publication before being collected in *The Left Bank.* Selections from "Vienne" also appeared almost verbatim, recontextualized in parts of several flashbacks, in the novella "Temps Perdi" (1969). "Vienne" demonstrates Rhys's continual reworking of autobiographical material from various perspectives.

In each reworking of her experience, Rhys viewed it from a different angle, and perhaps more than anything else these resulting variations subtly intensify and renew her development of her themes and characters. Rhys approaches her writing somewhat as an impressionist painter who paints what appears to be the same scene – Claude Monet's many versions of the Cathedral at Rouen under different conditions of light, for example – so that the reader may see the same images in a different light. Such alternative lighting recasts her experience, as her work illuminates it from a defamiliarized, ironic, and often satiric stance.

Since Ford's introductory essay to *The Left Bank,* critics have noted in Rhys's fiction the prevalence of outsiders and outcasts, many of whom view the assumptions and conventions of society from an alien viewpoint, one that allows Rhys to present an implicit critique of social norms and practices. Along with this use of character found throughout her work, Rhys creates narratorial viewpoints that are not to be fully identified with her own authorial voice. Narrators and characters may be male or female, and they may be socially, ethnically, and culturally different from Rhys herself.

In the short pieces what Ford called Rhys's "singular instinct for form" creates stories with a textural density in some cases approaching the connotative and imagistic richness of poetry. "In the Luxembourg Gardens" is a case in point. The story appears at first glance to be nothing but a fragment, scarcely more than a page long. The brevity is deceptive. With the most economical means Rhys presents a humorous and critical exploration of conventional gender roles during the sexual encounter. The sketch pictures ironically and reduces to a mere stock figure the young man sitting in the famous Parisian gardens. Neither named nor described, he is simply "a very depressed young man" who is "meditating on the faithlessness of women." Readers recognize that the young man is oblivious to the contradiction in his own behavior when he instantly forgets the faithlessness of his former partner as soon as he catches sight of a replacement. Appropriately, the replacement wears a green hat that catches his eye and serves as an ironic reminder of his now-forgotten meditation on the faithlessness of women.

As Rhys's narrator implies, so dehumanizing are the ritualized gestures of the female who appears in the garden, clearly with the purpose of picking up a male partner, that the sketch reduces her to legs, a hat, and a walk. Her walk signals her intention and evidences her complicity in the ritual by its "calculated grace." At the end of this tale the young man, his "hunting instinct" aroused, follows the young woman. Their communication is stripped to a minimum, indicating the predictability of their responses in this impersonal and yet most intimate

of relationships. They merely exchange a greeting that implies a question and its answer: "Mademoiselle. . . ." "Monsieur. . . ." The close of the sketch is not relayed by the narrator; the closing viewpoint is instead transferred to the Luxembourg Gardens, which itself sums up the transaction: "Such a waste of time . . . to be morose. Are there not always Women and Pretty Legs and Green Hats?" The ostensible background – a public park where such activities are common – has become, in an ironic turn of viewpoint, the worldly wise and jaded commentator in this reenactment of a sexual cliché.

This ironic and distanced narrative stance characterizes Rhys's approach throughout the collection. With a humorous distance maintained throughout, "Tout Montparnasse and a Lady" is also outright satire. It lampoons the cultural parochialism and the mechanical behavior of the Anglo-American expatriates who gather at a Left Bank *bal musette*. The Anglo-American crowd is portrayed ironically as "tout Montparnasse," a reference to their egocentric view of themselves as constituting the entire Bohemian quarter – to the exclusion of the Parisians themselves. Rhys satirizes these self-styled "outsiders," who pride themselves on their eccentricity and unconventionality, as moving to rhythms so fixed and predictable that they can be portrayed as a single entity. Thus, at the beginning of the sketch, "the Anglo-Saxon section of *tout Montparnasse"* is described in the singular: it "comes to dance" each week, "sits at the little tables," and toward the end of the sketch *"tout Montparnasse . . .* ordered its last drink at the bar preparatory to drifting on elsewhere."

Against this background "a romantic lady" makes several contradictory misjudgments. With an imagination shaped by her reading of George Du Maurier's *Trilby* (1894) and Francis Carco's Apache novels, she comes from America to seek thrills on the Left Bank. At first she proclaims a version of a bourgeois compromise: "she went on to explain how easy it is to be broad-minded and perfectly respectable, to combine art, passion, cleanliness, efficiency and an eye on the main chance." Later, deeper in her cups and sentimentality, she unsuccessfully seeks out another artist whom she had judged to be excessive at the opening of the story but whom she now sees as a kindred spirit. She is a successful fashion artist and he a successful portrait painter, but she is certain that he must be sad at having betrayed his youthful ideals, just as she is. Although she is made to stand out from the crowd, the romantic lady is merely a sillier version of what is satirized by the phrase *tout Montparnasse.*

Two additional stories, "A Spiritualist" and "Illusion," afford representative illustrations of Rhys's ironic play of perspectives in much of *The Left Bank*. In "A Spiritualist" a naive speaker, through a series of unwitting cues, creates an ironic countertext that undercuts his stated intention. The narrative consists of a French commandant's almost completely uninterrupted monologue. He addresses his story to a female listener, the narrator who provides an ironic foil for the commandant's words. He begins with a self-satisfied, self-pitying complaint about how unfaithful, irrational, deceptive, exhausting, and downright disappointing women are. In portraying what he believes to have been the single ideal woman in his life, however, the commandant unwittingly demonstrates not the insufficiency of women, his stated theme, but his own imperceptiveness and inflexibility in his relationships with women. His description of the perfect relationship with this former mistress is revealing: "We never quarrelled once or even argued. Never, for Madeleine gave way in everything." In praising her perfections he unconsciously demonstrates that only a passive and servile woman, willing to submit totally to his control, can fulfill his stinted view of ideal womanhood. His view exposes itself as a naive, conditioned reflex that is so internalized that the commandant has no awareness of its inherent contradictions, even absurdities.

While "A Spiritualist" treats the concept of female identity from the viewpoint of the commandant, "Illusion" explores the ambiguous responses of two women to cultural presuppositions of female desirability. While the female narrator remains empathetic toward the protagonist, an Englishwoman named Miss Bruce, she nonetheless tells the story from an increasingly ironic point of view. Miss Bruce is not a representative inhabitant of the Left Bank: she appears far too sensible, healthy, and reasonable to be part of the feverish activities that characterize the lives of the typical inhabitants of this Bohemian milieu. Although she is an artist, she does not fully participate in the Left Bank counterculture. On the contrary, in her clothing and demeanor Miss Bruce is a proper Englishwoman, apparently untouched by Left Bank unconventionalities.

Suddenly taken ill with appendicitis, Miss Bruce has been rushed to the hospital. Intending to fetch a nightgown and some extra clothing for her, the narrator enters Miss Bruce's apartment and opens the wardrobe, which is "solid," "big," and "square" – as one would expect of a conservatively dressed Englishwoman. But instead of staid cloth-

Rhys's first husband, Jean Lenglet, and their daughter, Maryvonne

ing, the narrator is astonished to discover expensive, colorful, and even fanciful gowns: "Miss Bruce's wardrobe when one opened it was a glow of colour, a riot of soft silks . . . [and] everything that one did not expect." Almost unwillingly the narrator attempts to reconstruct Miss Bruce's character and motivations. She imagines how Miss Bruce, in the confines of her room, has deconstructed her public identity as a conservative, sensible Englishwoman in order to transform herself into a seductive, erotic femme fatale.

From this point the narrative centers on the female narrator's reading of Miss Bruce's identity and on the narrator's ambivalent response to the implications of her discovery, rather than on Miss Bruce herself. Initially the dresses appear in a positive light as "jaunty," "a glow of colour," and "beautiful." But the narrator begins to see danger and temptation in the impulse that drove Miss Bruce to imitate secretly the behavior of the demimondaine. Miss Bruce has been seduced by "that perpetual hunger to be beautiful and that thirst to be loved which is the real curse of Eve." She speaks of Miss Bruce's "search for illusion" that appears "almost a vice." The narrator, too, finds herself caught in uncertainty between her own longing for this illusion, expressed in her positive description of the "smiling and graceful" dresses, and her knowledge that this fabricated identity represents an illusion, a form of seduction. Thus, when she opens the wardrobe a second time, she finds that the dresses no longer appear to be "smiling and graceful" but seem instead to be inimical: they are "slouching" and "malevolent."

Clothing, as the narrator realizes, is a lure, a seduction, and a promise for women – but it is also a trap. If female identity depends on the creation of an illusion that, in turn, depends for its success on masculine admiration and pursuit, then such an identity is fragile and ephemeral. While a few women may become powerful erotic objects, the others remain the frightened, *petites femmes* whom the narrator has observed looking worriedly into their mirrors. These others can only lose in this game of adopted identities. Miss Bruce embodies not simply a case of sexual repression or of the adoption of a male-appealing identity. She has made a conscious choice, one open to her because of her financial independence. The narrator has stressed that Miss Bruce is not beautiful but awkward, perhaps even a little ungainly. Even if she were publicly to join the game, she would be at a decided disadvantage from the outset. But the sacrifice she must make in order to retain her independence is great: despite having achieved greater autonomy, she no longer hopes to experience the passion she imagines. Her secret yielding to the temptation to dress as a desirable woman clearly reveals that she is aware of the price she pays.

Rhys criticizes sharply the gender roles that imprison the commandant, Miss Bruce, and many other characters in *The Left Bank* – roles that prevent them from having any real or deep intimacy with members of the opposite sex. In a story written years later, "Till September, Petronella," an alternative view of the fulfilling power of male-female relationships is introduced implicitly in a reference to Richard Wagner's opera *Tristan und Isolde,* in its portrayal of love as an absolute value that cuts across social barriers and conventional roles. In *The Left Bank* this ideal of love remains an implicit backdrop against which these stories of failed love are told. Rhys affirms the power and significance of love by depicting the wasteland of male-female relationships in its absence.

During a trip to London in 1926 Rhys met Leslie Tilden Smith, a literary agent to whom Ford had already sent some of the stories of *The Left Bank.* When Rhys returned to England with the manuscript of *Postures* in 1928, Tilden Smith not only placed the volume with a publisher but invited Rhys to move in permanently with him, and in

1934, a year after her divorce from Lenglet, Rhys and Tilden Smith were married. As first her lover and then her husband, Tilden Smith was cast, perhaps to an even greater extent, in the roles of caretaker, manager, and agent until his death in 1945. He protected Rhys, encouraged her, typed her manuscripts, and found publishers for her work. He cared for her during her bouts of abusive, violent behavior brought on by chronic alcoholism and recurring depressions. Mild-mannered and gentlemanly, he refused to retaliate against her for her episodes of verbal and physical violence. He borrowed money to send her on frequent writing trips to Paris, and after his father's death in 1936 he spent much of his inheritance on an extended trip to Dominica so that Rhys could revisit her former home.

The time Rhys spent with Tilden Smith between 1928 and 1940 was her most productive period. Before this she had written a series of journal-like notebooks, had published *The Left Bank,* and had written *Postures*. In the decade after 1928 she published three novels. She cut, recast, and made a creative English translation of Jean Lenglet's novel *Sous les Verrous* (1933), which she published in 1932 under the title *Barred*. She also produced the rough draft for a novel titled "Le Revenant" in 1938, but she destroyed it during one of her violent rages. Rewritten in the 1940s and 1950s, "Le Revenant" later became the basis for her masterpiece, *Wide Sargasso Sea*. Between 1935 and 1939 she also wrote drafts for more than half of the short stories that were published thirty years later in *Tigers Are Better-Looking* and *Sleep It Off, Lady.*

Her published novels of this period develop the autobiographical themes first introduced in *The Left Bank. After Leaving Mr. MacKenzie,* with its passive heroine who seems unable to help herself, was based on the aftermath of Rhys's affair with Smith. *Voyage in the Dark,* derived from material in her 1913 notebooks, includes extensive images based on memories of her childhood in Dominica and also focuses on the affair with Smith as well as her subsequent abortion. *Good Morning, Midnight,* also based on her own experiences, presents a desperate, middle-aged protagonist who, deserted by her husband and pursued by a gigolo, fails to establish any meaningful contact with others. Although much of Rhys's published work during the 1930s received relatively good reviews, *Good Morning, Midnight,* published just prior to the outbreak of World War II, was received coldly and did not sell. Its publication marked the end of a decade-long burst of creative energy that Rhys never matched again.

In 1940 Tilden Smith joined the Royal Air Force and was with Rhys only sporadically during the next five years. His constant support and care, his attentive typing of her manuscripts, and his careful nurturing of her talent were withdrawn. After his departure she almost ceased to write altogether. Her alcoholism, her violence, her obsessive dependency, and her self-destructive behavior became increasingly acute, expressing itself in bouts of deep depression, hysteria, and uncontrolled drinking. Her older brother, Edward, attempted without success to care for her while Tilden Smith was absent, and when Smith died in 1945, Rhys was once again left destitute.

At the time of her husband's death Rhys met Max Hamer, Tilden Smith's cousin, who was a trained solicitor and was acting as executor of the estate. A veteran of two world wars and more than sixty years old, he had suffered from severe shell shock and was probably as unstable as Rhys. The two were married in 1947, and their long relationship, lasting until Hamer's death in 1966, was difficult and often violent. Rhys's life continued to be marked by bouts of violent, even bizarre, public behavior and a paranoiac sense of being persecuted by her neighbors. While living with Hamer in the suburb of Beckenham from 1949 to 1950, Rhys was once taken to court for assaulting her neighbors. After spending five days in the mental ward of Holloway Prison, she was declared sane and put on probation for two years. During these same years Hamer had become involved in a shady series of money schemes initiated by his untrustworthy partners. In 1950 he was arrested, convicted of larceny, and sentenced to two years of imprisonment.

Just when these events culminated in Hamer's prison sentence and Rhys's probation in 1950, the actress Selma Vas Dias placed an advertisement in the *New Statesman,* making the first public attempt in more than a decade to locate Rhys. Vas Dias had dramatized *Good Morning, Midnight* and planned to produce it for BBC radio. Since 1939 Rhys had written little, had ceased publishing, and had dropped out of the public eye, but she responded to Vas Dias's ad.

Encouraged by a visit from Vas Dias, Rhys began once again to write. For the two years of Hamer's imprisonment near the town of Maidstone she lived alone in a small room above The Ropemaker's Arms, a pub in the town. "The Ropemaker's Diary," which she wrote during this time, consists of a series of self-accusations and responses staged in a fictional courtroom. Parts of the diary were later included in her posthumously published

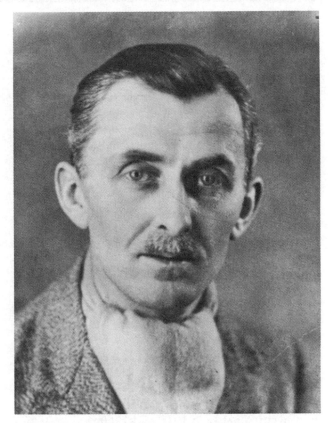

Rhys's second husband, Leslie Tilden Smith, whom she married in 1934

autobiography, *Smile Please* (1979). After Hamer's release from prison in 1952, they were utterly impoverished and fled from one place to another, as Rhys repeatedly felt that almost all of her neighbors were narrow-minded and hostile.

In 1956 Vas Dias once again contacted Rhys, who was working on "Creole," a story about her experiences in the West Indies and parts of which later became the basis for the story "Pioneers, Oh, Pioneers." Francis Wyndham also contacted Rhys in 1956 and brought her work in progress to the attention of Diana Athill, an editor for André Deutsch. In 1957 Rhys sold the option for *Wide Sargasso Sea* to Deutsch and then labored on the novel for the next nine years. During this time many literary and nonliterary people came to Rhys's aid and attempted to help her cope with poverty, illness, depression, and alcoholism as she wrote her finest novel.

Wide Sargasso Sea went through many revisions before its publication in 1966. In it Rhys used Charlotte Brontë's *Jane Eyre* (1848) as the basis for her own polemical recharacterization of Bertha Mason, the mad West Indian wife of Edward Rochester. The publication of *Wide Sargasso Sea* within months of Hamer's death in March marked a turning point in Rhys's fortunes. The novel was almost universally praised, and Rhys soon received several grants and a modest inheritance following the death of her brother, Edward. Now seventy-six years old, Rhys was recognized and no longer destitute.

In 1968 André Deutsch published Rhys's new book of short fiction, *Tigers Are Better-Looking, with a Selection from The Left Bank*. This collection was originally to be titled "The Sound of the River," and most of the stories in it had been completed by 1940. "The Sound of the River," the original title story, fictionalizes events that strongly resemble those surrounding the death of Tilden Smith. (The original volume contained two other stories, "I Spy a Stranger" and "Temps Perdi," that were eventually excluded from *Tigers Are Better-Looking* because, as Rhys agreed, they were too "sad and bitter," but a Penguin collection included both in 1969.) The new collection totaled seventeen stories, nine of them selections from *The Left Bank*. Of the eight new stories in the volume, all largely involved material Rhys had worked on between 1935 and 1945. Two stories were relatively new – "The Day They Burned the Books" and "Let Them Call It Jazz," both written between 1945 and 1968.

Most of these collected stories had been repeatedly revised. Many, like "Till September, Petronella," represent a painstaking paring down of earlier, extensive notes and rough drafts. While longer than some of the epigrammatic vignettes of *The Left Bank,* the resulting stories are no less rich and condensed, as Rhys continued to focus on themes and techniques introduced in her earlier fiction. Again she emphasized the viewpoints of those who are culturally, socially, and ethnically different. This view from outside produces a consistent, ironic disjunctiveness and distance from the norms and narrowness of mainstream society, which is seen in an unfamiliar and critical light.

In this volume Rhys concentrates on the angle of vision provided by the sick and impoverished who are unwilling or unable to adjust to society's norms. Inez Best, the protagonist of "Outside the Machine," is a penniless woman in a Paris hospital. Without means of support, she has no place to go when she must leave the hospital after her surgery. She thus lives in fear of what she sees as an insensitive, machinelike society that spits out its misfits. Waiting for her operation, she must listen to her unsympathetic wardmates as they criticize and condemn Mrs. Murphy, a neurotic patient who has out of despair attempted suicide. Inez's own situation, though it allows her to sympathize with and defend outsiders like Mrs. Murphy, nonetheless keeps her in fear: "because she was outside the machine they might come along any time with a pair of huge iron tongs and pick her up and put her on the rubbish heap, and there she would rot." A woman in the next bed sees Inez's poverty and gives her enough money to sustain her for a few days. This single act of charity mitigates this picture of a dehumanized and dehumanizing society.

In *Tigers Are Better-Looking* Rhys deals not only with outsiders who are physically and mentally different, but with those who are ethnically different. This difference makes them victims of racism and colonial oppression and excludes them from mainstream society. Set in the colony of Dominica at the turn of the century, "The Day They Burned the Books" deals with the racist colonial oppression of a mulatto woman named Mrs. Sawyer. The story is narrated from the perspective of a twelve-year-old child who, like Rhys, is a member of the white colonial elite in Dominica. Although the child reiterates the normative and biased comments of the adults of her world, she can understand only a part of their import. The resulting discrepancy between the child's account and the reader's understanding creates an ironic view of the social and racial codes prevalent in this community. Being a lower-class Englishman, Mr. Sawyer has a great reverence for his cultural heritage, as indicated by his impressive collection of books. But because he has married a pretty mulatto woman and has thus violated a social code, he is unable to rise above communal racism and treat his wife without prejudice.

Throughout their marriage Mrs. Sawyer has borne her husband's racist aspersions patiently, as if they were part of a "mysterious, obscure, sacred English joke." Yet after his death she takes her revenge, directing her long-suppressed rage against his books. This passionate book burning has wider implications than the limited exploration of one woman's rage and vengeance, for in Mrs. Sawyer's act Rhys points implicitly to the fact that his books are not the signs of a rich and living cultural heritage that is to be treasured and safeguarded. Because of the discrimination she suffered at Mr. Sawyer's hands, Mrs. Sawyer regards the books as symbols of hatred, cruelty, and oppression — a pernicious and injurious status quo.

Another story in the collection, "Let Them Call It Jazz," focuses on another colonial, one who lives in London and whose observations reveal the shortcomings of mainstream society. Though based in part on Rhys's own experience during her five days in Holloway Prison, the story is a masterpiece of dialect writing narrated by a cultural and ethnic outsider, a West Indian mulatto woman named Selina Davis. Selina's unconventional language, like her view of the world, has not been shaped according to British social and linguistic expectations. Her description of the British judicial system exposes deep biases inherent in the operation of legal standards. She is robbed of her money and is unable to find justice, because she does not know how to present an acceptable narrative to the police: the officers disbelieve her story about the theft, because she is uncertain about the precise amount of money she had and because she has acted "abnormally" in storing her money in a sock in her bed. Later she is jailed after a series of misunderstandings concerning her failure to pay a five-pound fine for drunk and disorderly behavior. The severity of the punishment stands in absurd relationship to the seriousness of the crime. In this story the misfit, who experiences an unusual case of injustice, reveals the potential injuriousness inherent in codes that fail to consider individual and cultural differences.

In 1974 Rhys signed a contract for what was to be her final collection of short fiction, and during the next two years she completed a selection of stories for *Sleep It Off, Lady*. The collection included sixteen stories, seven of which had previously appeared in various magazines. In this collection Rhys included not only the perspective of the mature woman, but also those of the child and of the elderly, thus embracing the full range of women's experience. In *Sleep It Off, Lady* the progression from childhood to old age is structured into the collection itself: the stories fall roughly into three categories corresponding to three stages in the lives of women and arranged in chronological order. The first five stories deal with childhood; the next seven stories with adulthood; and the final four with old age and death.

Rhys's delineations of female consciousness are not restricted to the private and personal, the traditional sphere of women's experience. On the contrary, the child, the demimondaine and outcast woman, and the elderly, ill, and dying who appear in Rhys's short fiction frequently provide a novel, unexpected view of life. This view from the periphery allows Rhys to present a sharply focused vision that, as in a Robert Browning monologue, sheds ironic light on wider social, cultural, historical, and psychological contexts. These wider contexts are not presented overtly but are suggested in a series of recurring cues that alert the reader to implications of which the protagonist, or even the narrator, is often unaware. Rhys's texts are thus de-

manding, since they are incomplete without the informed response of a reader acquainted with the social and historical contexts of the stories — contexts often signaled by a single detail or a single date, but also by an entire literary tradition to which Rhys's work frequently refers.

The first five stories of the collection are presented largely from the perspective of the female child who has not fully acquired or understood the normative attitudes of the adult world. The child's failure of understanding exposes the narrow sympathies and hypocrisy, even the harmfulness, of common social attitudes. The first story of the collection, "Pioneers, Oh, Pioneers," is representative of this first group. Set in the West Indies of the 1890s, it deals with an English gentleman, Mr. Ramage, who is believed to be mad and dangerous by the white colonial elite among whom he ostensibly belongs. Ramage, however, commits two serious violations of colonial codes. First, by marrying a mulatto woman of uncertain repute, he has transgressed the boundaries set not only by race and social class, but by respectability. Second, in a country where the British set themselves apart by a dress code that applies to a much colder climate, Ramage flouts this restrictive code by appearing stark naked on his isolated property in the jungle. These deviations from normative behavior lead to Ramage's exclusion from British society and eventually to his death.

The entire community maligns Ramage, and when his wife disappears, it accuses him, without evidence, of having murdered her. Only Dr. Cox, a humane and empathetic man, and his seven-year-old daughter, Rosalie, refuse to acquiesce with the attitudes of the other members of white colonial society. The sympathy of these two, and Dr. Cox's strong disapproval of what amounts to a communal witch-hunt, put into question the judgment of the entire community as it closes ranks against Ramage. Not content merely with ostracizing Ramage, members of the community wage an active campaign of innuendo and groundless accusation in which even the local newspaper plays a role. These pernicious aspersions lead to a riot on Ramage's plantation and finally to his death under mysterious circumstances. Whoever may have killed him or however he may have died, the ironic turn of events reveals that the "normal" community, which has sought to protect itself against the abnormal outsider, has proven itself more dangerous than Ramage. At the conclusion of the story even Dr. Cox reluctantly admits that Ramage was "probably a lunatic," though Dr. Cox still maintains that Ramage had been victimized. Only the child Rosalie, oblivious of adult judgments, remains loyal, and after his death she starts to write him a love letter, beginning, "My dear darling Mr. Ramage."

The conclusion points up the discrepancy between the naive view of the child, whose vision is transformed by love and empathy, and the normative, uncharitable view of adults. The latter view is embodied in the child's mother, who enters the room and finds her daughter asleep — with the unfinished letter on the table beside her. "Mrs. Cox read it, frowned, pressed her lips together, then crumpled it up and threw it out of the window." In the final lines of the story the narrator supports the child's empathy and charity. As the letter bounces off in the stiff wind, the narrator implies that the letter is a message moving toward the cemetery and Ramage's newly dug grave, "as if it knew exactly where it was going." By focusing on a member of the community who becomes the target of its malice and on the little girl who loves him unconditionally, Rhys allows social codes and the class that enforces them to reveal their latent cruelty and destructiveness.

While the first grouping of stories adopts primarily the perspective of the child, the second presents that of the young woman. Most of the narrators and protagonists of these stories are outsiders, misfits, and foreigners who do not live according to middle-class standards. "Overture and Beginners Please" is related by a young West Indian woman attending a private school in England. Feeling out of place because of her background and accent, she leaves school to join a theatrical touring company. "The Insect World" is set in London during the blitz attacks of the 1940s and plots the deterioration of a young woman's consciousness. No longer able to distinguish fact from fantasy, the protagonist Audrey views her surroundings as a surrealistic, Kafkaesque nightmare. Ironically, the fantastic vision of the half-mad Audrey seems no less real than wartime London.

"The Chevalier of the Place Blanche" has been attributed to Jean Lenglet, but Rhys certainly had a strong hand in shaping the final version, strong enough that she included it in her collection. Here a French gigolo attempts to win a beautiful but dissatisfied English painter living in Montparnasse. He needs Fr 30,000, but when she proposes the deal — she wants to study him, not make love with him — he cannot agree to the terms because she has no desire for him, only a writer's need to analyze and exploit. He cannot bring himself to submit to this "professional" humiliation.

"Before the Deluge," "On Not Shooting Sitting Birds," and "Night Out 1925" are told from the point of view of the chorus girl and demimondaine. The narrator of "Night Out 1925" unmasks the brutality and inhumanity of a wealthy and respectable Englishman by exploring his relationship to members of the Parisian demimonde, and by contrasting his view with that of his female companion — who interprets the lot of the prostitutes far differently. On this particular evening Gilbert, or "Stingy Bertie," as he is known in the quarter, takes his female companion, Suzy, to what he remembers as a lively but cheap local bar and brothel. To Gilbert's consternation the strippers and prostitutes of the shabby establishment fail to entertain him. Yet instead of questioning his own desire to be entertained by means that humiliate others, Gilbert becomes angry when the women of the place fail to sustain the illusion of energy, enjoyment, youth, and desirability that he expects to receive for his money. Instead, the entertainment he has come to see reveals itself as little more than a veneer that hides human misery, indignity, and suffering.

Throughout the story Rhys maintains an ironic distance between conflicting views. On the one hand, Suzy recognizes in these humiliated and exploited women a degraded version of herself, and she sees herself as an unwanted intruder who has come to gaze voyeuristically at them. When one of the woman looks angrily at Suzy and Gilbert from across the room, Suzy comments empathetically, "She thinks I'm here to stare and jeer. You can't blame her." On the other hand, Stingy Bertie attempts to reverse the exploiter/exploited relationship by claiming that these women exploit their clientele shamelessly. For him, they are not human beings but salable objects who owe him an evening's entertainment. When one of the prostitutes mentions her pain, Gilbert dismisses it as a mere ploy to extract money from him: "I suppose she thinks it a good idea to harp on the difficulties of her profession." He then makes a cruel and sarcastic reference to Honoré de Balzac's novel *Splendeurs et miséres des courtisanes* (1844) as he continues: "Same old miseries, no more splendors. . . . Sad isn't it." He underscores his affront by laughing.

Moved by the plight of these women and angered by Gilbert's cruelty, Suzy uses Stingy Bertie's money to pay each of the young women a handsome sum before leaving. When she informs her companion of what she has done, Gilbert wants to get rid of her, and she bids him good-bye with the same words used by the two prostitutes moments before, "A la prochaine." After he is gone, she re-

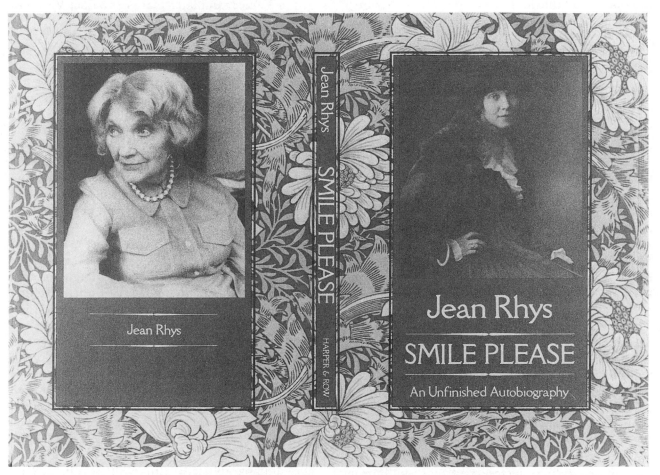

Dust jacket for the American edition of Rhys's narrative of her early life, with excerpts from the diary she kept following the death of her second husband

peats the words of Gilbert and the prostitutes: "Same old miseries. No more splendour. Not now. *Et qu'est-ce que tu veux que ça leur fasse?"* Her repetition suggests that, in her relationship to Gilbert, she sees an image of herself in the prostitutes.

The final grouping of the collection consists of four stories, all of which use the perspective of the elderly woman. In "Who Knows What's Up In the Attic" the protagonist is an older woman who decides that she will not be the "other woman" in a relationship with a married man who is younger because she cannot bear the idea of a January-May affair. The darkly pessimistic title story, "Sleep It Off, Lady," views the unsettling death of Miss Verney. An unmarried, elderly alcoholic, Miss Verney has grown fearful of death – the ultimate reality that has become overwhelming and uncontrollable in her old age – and her fear of death appears in the shape of an immense rat that haunts an old shed outside her house. At the story's end Miss Verney collapses in the shed from a heart attack and must

face the rat and the coming darkness. She calls for help, but the child who hears her assumes that she is in an alcoholic stupor and simply responds, "Sleep it off, lady." As in "Lotus," which portrays an alcoholic writer from the viewpoint of her respectable neighbors, "Sleep It Off, Lady" represents an ironic self-portrait by a writer who achieved an often-startling objectivity in her re-creation of a fictionalized self.

The final story of the collection, "I Used to Live Here Once," is a gothic tale in which a ghost horrifies herself by discovering that she is dead. Revisiting her previous home, a woman addresses two children who look straight through her. Feeling a sudden chill, the children retreat as quickly as possible, and the woman's "arms fell to her sides as she watched them running across the grass to the house. That was the first time she knew."

In "Rapunzel, Rapunzel," an analysis of the construction of female identity, Rhys addresses once more the theme she had explored fifty years previously in "Illusions," the first story of her first collection, *The Left Bank*. The title refers to the well-known Grimm brothers' fairytale "Rapunzel," which becomes the backgrounded intertext and foil for Rhys's story.

Rhys's narrator is an elderly woman recovering in a London hospital from a heart attack. An old woman in the next bed has a beautiful head of "long, silvery, white, silky" hair, which she carefully brushes for a long time each day. Her hair is a last and lovely vestige of her former identity as a beautiful, desirable woman, as the narrative suggests: "She must have taken great care of it all her life and now there it all was, intact, to comfort and reassure her that she was still herself. Even when she had it pinned up into a loose bun it fell so prettily round her face that it was difficult to think of her as an old lady." When a barber offers to trim her hair, to the horror of all those in the ward, he cuts it all off and carries it away in a plastic bag. The woman, so long accustomed to seeing her beauty and identity in terms of her hair, murmurs to herself, "Nobody will want me now." The old woman is taken violently ill and dies within a few days.

The narrator concludes with "the words repeating themselves so unreasonably in my head: 'Rapunzel, Rapunzel, let down your hair.'" In the Grimms' fairy tale Rapunzel's hair provides the connecting link between love and beauty. The attribute of beauty may have little to do with human worth in any final reckoning, and the conclusion to the Grimms' tale implies as much, but in Rhys's story the woman's hair had nonetheless remained "intact, to comfort and reassure her that she was still herself." With nothing else to stave off the consciousness of age — and of what that means in our society — the loss of her hair, the last attribute of her beauty, leads to her loss of identity and of life itself. "Rapunzel, Rapunzel" thus functions at least in part as a continuation of those probings of the nature of female identity that Rhys had begun a half century before. As in "Illusion," Rhys has here come to understand that surface qualities may in fact be superficial, but "Rapunzel, Rapunzel" gives these qualities a psychological weight that makes them almost coterminous with life itself.

Despite the sophisticated insight with which Rhys explored the nature of such social constructs, she clung to similar illusions in her own life. Once she had earned sufficient money from the sale of *Wide Sargasso Sea* and from various grants, she spent hours having her hair, her nails, and her face carefully made up — though she was never satisfied with her appearance. In 1977 she could afford to take a

trip to Venice, and later that year Selma Vas Dias died, but her estate continued to hold the rights to Rhys's work, rights that Rhys had foolishly, perhaps incompetently, signed away in 1966. Though she spent some time in a home for the elderly in 1977, Rhys was an impossible patient, and her friend Diana Melly took Rhys home to live with her. By 1978 Rhys's furious and violent behavior had taken its toll on Melly, too, and after a brief stay at a nursing home Rhys returned to her cottage at Cheriton Fitzpaine, which her brother Edward had bought for her in rural Devon in 1960. She continued to write, but her health was declining.

Since the late 1960s Rhys had been working on her unfinished autobiography, *Smile Please*. With the help of novelist David Plante she managed to work up a series of vignettes that recounted her life from her childhood in Dominica through her stint as a touring chorus girl, her first love affair and first marriage, and until the time that she showed her notebooks to Pearl Adams and began her career as a writer. The autobiography also contained several other sketches including "The Trial of Jean Rhys" — a part of the remarkable diary she had kept while her third husband was in prison and she had been living in rooms above a pub in Maidstone. Critics have claimed that by using up her autobiography in her novels, Rhys had nothing left to say and that, in fact, her novels give a truer picture of her life than her autobiographical writings. She was indeed old when she began writing *Smile Please*, and during the writing she was in ill health and often drunk. Yet the writing shows no decline in quality, and the book clearly makes one other point.

Rhys knew, instinctively perhaps, that all accounts of a life are biased by the act of narration, and however much one wishes to preserve the claim of objectivity, autobiographical writing is governed by the same principles that shape fiction. In a sense, life has no inherent shape, but art gives it one.

Despite her seeming frailty and alcohol addiction, Jean Rhys lived to be nearly ninety years old. She died on 14 May 1979.

Letters:

Jean Rhys: Letters, 1931–1966, edited by Francis Wyndham and Diana Melly (London: Deutsch, 1984); republished as *The Letters of Jean Rhys* (New York: Viking, 1984).

Bibliography:

Elgin W. Mellown, *Jean Rhys: A Descriptive and Annotated Bibliography of Works and Criticism* (New York & London: Garland, 1984).

Biography:

Carole Angier, *Jean Rhys: Life and Work* (Harmondsworth: Penguin, 1985; Boston: Little, Brown, 1991).

References:

Alfred Alvarez, "The Best Living English Novelist," *New York Times Book Review,* 17 March 1974, pp. 6–8;

Diana Athill, "Jean Rhys, and the Writing of *Wide Sargasso Sea,*" *Bookseller,* 3165 (20 August 1966): 1378–1379;

Shari Benstock, *Women of the Left Bank: Paris, 1900–1940* (Austin: University of Texas Press, 1986);

Arnold Davidson, *Jean Rhys* (New York: Ungar, 1985);

Hunter Davis, "Rip Van Rhys," *Sunday Times* (Atticus), 6 November 1966, p. 13;

Judith Kegan Gardiner, *Rhys, Stead, Lessing, and the Politics of Empathy* (Bloomington: Indiana University Press, 1989);

Coral Ann Howells, *Jean Rhys* (New York: St. Martin's Press, 1991);

Louis James, *Jean Rhys* (London: Longman, 1978);

Wally Look Lai, "The Road to Thornfield Hall: An Analysis of Jean Rhys's *Wide Sargasso Sea,*" in *New Beacon Reviews,* edited by John La Rose (London: New Beacon, 1968), pp. 38–52;

Elgin Mellown, "Character and Theme in the Novels of Jean Rhys," *Contemporary Literature,* 13 (Autumn 1972): 458–472;

Ellen Moers, *Literary Women* (Garden City, N.Y.: Doubleday, 1976);

Elaine Showalter, *A Literature of Their Own* (Princeton: Princeton University Press, 1977);

Thomas F. Staley, *Jean Rhys: A Critical Study* (London: Macmillan, 1979; Austin: University of Texas Press, 1979);

Selma Vas Dias, "In Quest of a Missing Author," *Radio Times,* 3 May 1957, p. 25;

Peter Wolfe, *Jean Rhys* (Boston: Twayne, 1980);

Francis Wyndham, "Introduction to Jean Rhys," *London Magazine,* 7 (January 1960): 15–18.

Papers:

Rhys's papers are in the McFarlin Library, University of Tulsa; the Evelyn Scott Collection, Harry Ransom Humanities Research Center, University of Texas at Austin; the British Library; and in the possession of Francis Wyndham, Rhys's literary executor.

James Stephens

(9 February 1880 or 2 February 1882 – 26 December 1950)

Thomas J. Campbell
Wheaton, Maryland

See also the Stephens entries in *DLB 19; British Poets, 1880–1914* and *DLB 153; Late Victorian and Edwardian British Novelists, First Series.*

BOOKS: *Where the Demons Grin* (Dublin: Cuala, 1908);

Insurrections (Dublin: Maunsel, 1909; New York: Macmillan, 1909);

The Lonely God and Other Poems (New York: Macmillan, 1909);

The Charwoman's Daughter (London: Macmillan, 1912); republished as *Mary, Mary* (Boston: Small, Maynard, 1912);

The Hill of Vision (New York: Macmillan, 1912; Dublin: Maunsel, 1912; abridged edition, London: Macmillan, 1922);

The Crock of Gold (London: Macmillan, 1912; Boston: Small, Maynard, 1912);

Five New Poems (London: Printed by A. T. Stevens for Flying Fame Chapbooks, 1913);

Here Are Ladies (London & New York: Macmillan, 1913);

The Demi-Gods (London & New York: Macmillan, 1914);

Songs from the Clay (London & New York: Macmillan, 1915);

The Adventures of Seumas Beg / The Rocky Road to Dublin (London: Macmillan, 1915); republished as *The Rocky Road to Dublin / The Adventures of Seumas Beg* (London & New York: Macmillan, 1915);

The Insurrection in Dublin (Dublin & London: Maunsel, 1916; New York: Macmillan, 1916);

Green Branches (Dublin & London: Maunsel, 1916; New York: Macmillan, 1916);

Hunger: A Dublin Story, as James Esse (Dublin: Candles Press, 1918);

Reincarnations (London & New York: Macmillan, 1918);

Irish Fairy Tales (London & New York: Macmillan, 1920);

James Stephens in the National Library in Dublin

Arthur Griffith: Journalist and Statesman (Dublin: Wilson, Hartnell, 1922?);

Dierdre (London & New York: Macmillan, 1923);

In the Land of Youth (London & New York: Macmillan, 1924);

Little Things and Other Poems (Freelands, Ky.: Privately printed, 1924);

A Poetry Recital (London & New York: Macmillan, 1925);

Collected Poems by James Stephens (London & New York: Macmillan, 1926); revised and enlarged edition, London & New York: Macmillan, 1954);

Etched in Moonlight (London & New York: Macmillan, 1928);

On Prose and Verse (New York: Bowling Green Press, 1928);

Optimist (Gaylordsville, Conn.: Slide Mountain, 1929);

The Outcast (London: Faber & Faber, 1929);

Julia Elizabeth: A Comedy in One Act (New York: Crosby Gaige, 1929);

Theme and Variations (New York: Fountain Press, 1930);

Strict Joy: Poems (London & New York: Macmillan, 1931);

Kings and the Moon (London & New York: Macmillan, 1938);

James Stephens: A Selection, edited by Lloyd Frankenberg (London: Macmillan, 1962); republished as *A James Stephens Reader* (New York: Macmillan, 1962);

James, Seumas and Jacques: Unpublished Writings by James Stephens, edited by Frankenberg (London & New York: Macmillan, 1964);

Desire, and Other Stories, edited by Augustine Martin (Dublin: Poolbeg, 1980);

Uncollected Prose of James Stephens, Volume 1: 1907–1915, edited by Patricia McFate (New York: St. Martin's Press, 1983).

PLAY PRODUCTION: *The Marriage of Julia Elizabeth,* Dublin, Hardwicke Street Theatre, 17 November 1911.

OTHER: Thomas MacDonagh, *The Poetical Works of Thomas MacDonagh,* edited by Stephens (London: Unwin, 1916; New York: Stokes, 1917);

"The Poets and Poetry of the Nineteenth Century," in *English Romantic Poets,* edited by Stephens, Edwin L. Beck, and Royall H. Snow (New York: American Book Company, 1933);

Victorian and Later English Poets, edited by Stephens, Beck, and Snow (New York: American Book Company, 1934);

Josef Kastein, *Jews in Germany,* preface by Stephens (London: Cresset, 1934).

James Stephens's short fiction ranks among the best written during the Irish Renaissance. At that time his work was much lauded by prominent literary figures such as AE (George William Russell) and William Butler Yeats. His capacities were such that George Moore asked him to edit some of Moore's short fiction and James Joyce considered him a worthy colleague. Prose that sounds more like speech than carefully wrought text, wry humor as well as chilling epiphanies, and a thorough fascination with Irish folklore typify Stephens's short stories. In addition to the success he enjoyed as a poet, playwright, and novelist, to some extent his achievement in early Irish short fiction ranks him among the great writers of the Irish Literary Revival.

Uncertainty clouds description of his Irish upbringing, as even the date of his birth cannot be stated precisely. Although hospital and school records suggest that he may have been born on 9 February 1880 to Francis and Charlotte Stephens of Dublin and that he was six years old when he enrolled in Meath Protestant Industry School in 1886, he gave his close friends and relatives a 2 February 1882 date and celebrated that date himself. In a BBC broadcast of 8 October 1946 Stephens related Joyce's discovery that the two authors were born "in the same country, in the same city, in the same year, in the same month, on the same day at the same hour six-o'clock in the morning of the second of February." The coincidence that Stephens shared Joyce's birth date is remarkable, yet it is a coincidence: any suggestion that Stephens was adopting Joyce's birth date to feel an affinity with him is undermined, because Stephens claimed the 1882 birth date long before he held a favorable opinion of Joyce's writing.

Details of Stephens's youth are sketchy. He was always a tiny person with "soft brown eyes [that were] lit . . . by the highest intelligence and by . . . profound, inarticulate love." Birgit Bramsbäck relates a doubtful secondhand story in which Stephens in his early teens set out alone for Belfast, only to be rescued from starvation by a woman who kindly took him in. When Stephens realized that he was actually preventing a prostitute from earning her living, he decided to leave. "A Rhinoceros, Some Ladies, and a Horse" is a similarly spurious story originally delivered by Stephens as a radio speech late in his life. It relates how Stephens lost his first job through being overly kind to an animal. Humorous characters such as a grotesque, fawning woman and a husband whose opinion of Stephens shrinks and swells throughout the story in relation to how the husband's horse and wife treat Stephens fill the short piece. The vignette includes several distinctive Stephens hallmarks: a great interest in

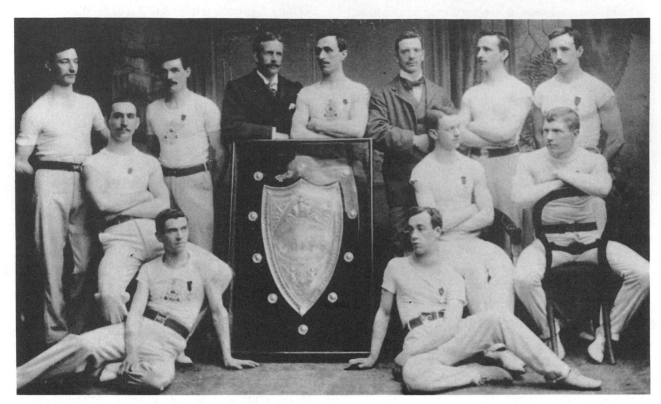

Stephens (seated on the floor, at right) as a member of the Dawson Street Gymnastic Club, which won the Irish Shield competition for Dublin in 1901

living creatures, a relish for capturing authentic lower-class speech, and indefatigable optimism and humor in the face of economic hardship. Given the playful spirit of many of Stephens's stories, it is interesting to note that one detail known about Stephens's early life is that in 1901 he competed in the Dawson Street Gymnastic Club, which won the Irish Shield.

The first hard fact known about his adult life is that between 1896 and 1912 he worked as a typist in a solicitor's office in Dublin. By 1907 Stephens had published a short story ("The Greatest Miracle") in the *United Irishman* and a poem, some articles, and a few short stories in *Sinn Fein,* a nationalist weekly (and briefly, a daily) newspaper operated by Arthur Griffith.

"The Greatest Miracle," although showing some immaturity in being derivative, has at its heart themes Stephens was later to explore more deeply in his short fiction: poverty and epiphany. In this story a policeman is transformed by a vision of a tramp, above whose wretched aspect "flickered a smile which shone with such a glorious radiance that the short red hair was transformed into the

shining aura of some immortal being, and his eyes shone like stars." In stories like "Hunger" Stephens later depicted sensitively the plight of the lower class, and in stories such as "Desire" he engrossed readers with characters who are remarkably changed by brief incidents.

Some of these early publications drew the attention of AE to Stephens, and AE had much to do with Stephens's literary output. The stories that appeared in *Sinn Fein* drew on circumstances that may be associated with events in Stephens's life: "Mrs. Jerry Gorman" concerns a man having to tell his poverty-stricken family that pride has forced him to leave his job, an incident similar to that related in "A Rhinoceros, Some Ladies, and a Horse," and "Miss Arabella Hennessy" is an anecdote involving the close relationship that develops between a boarder and his landlady. This latter story is particularly relevant to Stephens's life: he was once a boarder in a home where the husband had left his wife and daughter. Stephens accepted this woman, Millicent Josephine Kavanagh (whom he preferred to call Cynthia), as his wife in 1907, although they were not able to marry until 1919. One of Cynthia's daughters, Iris, joined James and Cynthia in their home. The newly acquired familial responsibilities added to Stephens's already full life, for by this time his literary output had such merit that he had become an accepted member of Dublin's highest circles.

During 1908 Stephens was already at work on material that was to be incorporated in his best novel and best collection of stories. *Sinn Fein* printed material that ended up in Stephens's best-known work, the novel *The Crock of Gold* (1912), and two brief pieces that were incorporated in *Here Are Ladies* (1913), an early collection of short stories. When the stories appeared in *Here Are Ladies,* the names of the characters had been removed in an effort to give the stories a more Continental appeal and to shift the emphasis of the works from character to theme. Part of Stephens's appeal is that the characters, though round and not pastiches, are usually anonymous and that the action occurs in no specific setting. "Miss Kathleen Raftery" had appeared in *Sinn Fein* on 10 October, but when reprinted in *Here Are Ladies* it was called "Three Young Wives: II." This story concerns an attractive young woman who has so many suitors that she tires of being so sought after. Suddenly she finds herself in love with a young man of no particular distinction except that of being a poet – and one who does not reciprocate her feelings. When a rich young suitor appears to woo her just when the poet is explaining his poetry to her, the poet's eyes suddenly open to the woman's charms. Thinking that she has no hopes of ever winning the poet, however, the young woman accepts the new suitor's proposal. The story ends when, with the new bride feeling cold and frightened, the poet dances at her wedding.

Stephens began a prolific period in 1909 with the publication of two books of verse, *Insurrections* and *The Lonely God and Other Poems*. He also contributed to *Sinn Fein* more than a dozen articles and short stories, many of which were later revised and collected in *The Crock of Gold* and *Here Are Ladies*. The majority of the 1909 articles were "Old Philosopher's Discourses," essays delivered through the voice of an indigent drunkard (presumably based on AE) who pontificates at the local pub. The Old Philosopher is the unifying figure of *The Crock of Gold,* but he gives a virtuoso performance as well in "There Is a Tavern in the Town," the last story of *Here Are Ladies*. This work is actually a collection of the Old Philosopher's Discourses on various subjects. "On Education"

("Tavern: IV"), for example, captures the essence of the wry humor that a description cannot:

> If a small boy, on being asked where Labrador is, replies that it is the most northerly point of the Berlin Archipelago, he may be wrong in quite a variety of ways; but even if he answered correctly he would still know just as little about the matter; while if he were to give the only proper reply to so ridiculous a conundrum, he would tell his tormentor that he did not care a rap where it was, that he had not put it there, and that he would tell his mother if the man did not leave him alone.

Whatever the topic – the absurdity of marriage, the benefits of drinking and smoking, the uselessness of inventions, or excursions to the North Pole – the Old Philosopher's lectures are delivered with a sense of humor and a belief that progress does not benefit human beings as much as some like to believe.

Another story worth mentioning from this period is "Mrs. Bernard Nagle." The title character has lost her husband's love because smallpox has left her a "husk" of the beautiful woman she once was. She begins to wish that her pregnancy will end her life so that she must no longer endure her husband's contempt. The story ends with the shocking line, "And in the night time, when the stars were hidden behind the window curtains, by the light of a lamp that fell on toiling, anxious people, in a hospital-like atmosphere of pain and clamour she did die." Biographically this story is particularly curious because it was published less than a month after the birth of the only child Cynthia and James had together, James Naoise Stephens, on 26 October 1909.

In 1910 Stephens published little in the way of fiction, but one of his most charming stories appeared in December in *Irish Homestead*. The story, called "The Unworthy Princess," focuses on a small boy who is so greatly affected by a story his mother reads him about a captive princess that he decides to sneak out of the house on a quest to slay the giant keeping her prisoner. In return for threepence and some trinkets an old three-toothed woman named Really-and-Truly tells him the location of the giant's castle. He bursts into the house and finds the beautiful princess, who has had a spell cast on her so that she appears as a stout, older woman. When the boy professes his love to the princess, she tells him that she loves another – the giant. The small boy, deeming the princess unworthy of rescue, then tells her he has "a good mind to rescue the giant from her . . . only that it was against his principles to rescue giants." Hiding from her "a mind that was tortured and a heart that had plumbed most of the depths of human suffering," the boy leaves her. Patricia McFate calls the story "a hilarious version of *Candida*." It is Stephens at his mock-heroic best.

In 1911 and 1912 Stephens was involved with other literary pursuits separate than that of short-story writing. "Mary: A Story," which later became *The Charwoman's Daughter* (1912), was appearing serially in the *Irish Review,* a literary magazine that David Houston, Thomas MacDonagh, Padraic Colum, and Stephens had founded in November 1910. Stephens's lone play, *The Marriage of Julia Elizabeth,* was being produced by the Theatre of Ireland. In October 1912 *The Crock of Gold* was published, which brought Stephens widespread recognition.

The year 1913 was a banner year for Stephens's short-story production. In January *The Nation* commissioned Stephens to write short stories, and this much influenced the direction of Stephens's work. His success with *The Crock of Gold* had enabled him to leave his position at the solicitor's office, and he left Dublin to visit Paris for a limited time, but he so enjoyed his stay that from then to the end of his life he maintained a second residence in Paris. In October *Here Are Ladies* reached the book stands. Including many fine stories that had not yet been printed in periodicals, the collection contained samples of the first modern Irish work in short fiction.

Stephens took great care in arranging the works collected in this volume. That Stephens had suggested *Triangles* as a better title for the work might be inferred from its design, for each section of *Here Are Ladies* has a tripartite structure in which a poem introduces every section. Stephens follows the poem with three related stories, often having a triune title such as "Three Heavy Husbands," and closes his presentation of these three stories with another that expands on a theme introduced by the opening poem. This structure applies to roughly the first two-thirds of the book, and Stephens filled the rest of the volume with the discourses of the Old Philosopher when his publisher asked him to expand the work before publication.

"The Threepenny-Piece" concerns a tight-fisted man named Brien O'Brien who has died. At his wake a threepenny-piece is put into his hand, and he is sent before the judge Rhadamanthus, who casts him into torment, but not before O'Brien loses his coin. Cuchulain, a seraph, finds and refuses to return it, and O'Brien raises such a ruckus that Rhadamanthus is moved to cast both him and Cuchulain back to earth, in order to be rid of them. This story, among others, perhaps set an example for Joyce in satirically approaching Celtic heroes. Patricia McFate writes that this story "serves as an exemplum of Stephens' technical ability, keen insight into human (and superhuman) nature, and wry humor." Its Irish heart made it a fine choice for Stephens to include in *The Demi-Gods* (1914) as well.

"Three Young Wives: III" concerns a woman who receives by post a suitor's proposal for her to leave her husband and run off with him. Despite her husband's aloofness toward her, when the suitor arrives she yells to him that she will not go with him and then plugs her ears so that he will not persuade her to change her mind. When her husband later returns, she is so amused by his usual callous treatment that she laughs, prompting him to slam the door on her in confusion.

"The Horses" concerns a man and an animal that moves him to reassess his life. The man and his wife have been married only shortly before the wife's "gently-repressive hand was laid upon him, and, like a startled horse, he bounded at the touch into freedom – that is, as far as the limits of the matrimonial rope would permit." The husband has accepted a life in which "one shrugs one's shoulders, settles to the collar." One day his wife sends him on an errand, and he witnesses another man beating a horse. The horse takes the beating so humbly that to the husband the horse seems to be saying, "There are no longer any meadows in the world. . . . They came in the night and took away the green meadows, and the horses do not know what to do." The husband's errands bring him to a railway station, and before he knows what he is doing he has purchased a ticket and is shrieking with laughter from a carriage, "The horses are coming again to the green meadows. Make way, make way for the great wild horses!" Martin sees the husband's wild flight as symbolizing Stephens's later "plunge . . . beyond the conventions of social realism" apparent in stories such as "Desire" and "Etched in Moonlight."

"Three Lovers Who Lost: I" is the short-story version of Stephens's play *The Marriage of Julia Elizabeth.* It concerns a young man named Mr. O'Grady, who visits Mr. and Mrs. O'Reilly to ask for the hand of their daughter, Julia Elizabeth. The young woman is out, so the parents make small talk with Mr. O'Grady while he tries to get the courage to ask them about their daughter. Mrs. O'Reilly tries unsuccessfully throughout the vignette to slice a loaf of bread for herself. Mr. O'Grady's talk continually reminds her of situations from popular songs, but when she asks her husband if the situation has a similar effect on him, Mr. O'Reilly's stock response is, "It does not, ma'm." Eventually Mr. O'Grady finds the heart to ask Julia Elizabeth's parents for her hand, but just when they give their permission to him, a letter from Julia arrives – stating that she has that day married another suitor. Mr. O'Reilly tells Mr. O'Grady to "be thankful" for his escape. Mrs. O'Reilly never gets to eat her bread.

Stephens's own assessment of his work in *Here Are Ladies* depended upon his audience. In a 16 April 1913 letter to James B. Pinker of Macmillan, Stephens stated that "it is absolutely unlike any other collection of short stories in English. I am not saying it is the best but only that it is different." And in a 13 May 1913 letter to his friend W. T. H. Howe he wrote, "I think they include some of the best writing I have ever done. One can polish a short story just like a poem." However, on 2 July of the same year, he wrote back that "There are real good things in Here Are Ladies, but it is unequal."

A review of the book by Thomas Bodkin in the *Irish Times* of 21 November 1913 asserted that "Nothing of all the items that comprise this book is makeshift or unworthy." A separate review of it by St. John G. Ervine in the April 1915 *Bookman* affirmed that it was "full of good stuff," while at the same time asserting that it lacked the Irish flavor that made Stephens's successful novels "such tasty reading." Later reception of the collection has been somewhat mixed. Martin finds the form "not very distinguished," though the volume overall is "a pleasant book to read because of the shrewdness with which its component pieces . . . are deployed." McFate calls the work "delightful" and finds Stephens's technical accomplishments in "A Glass of Beer," "The Triangle," "The Three-Penny Piece," "The Horses," and "The Blind Man" reveal his best work in the collection. She sees room for research in the arena of sexual politics with respect to "unhappy aspects of male-female relationships."

At the time of the publication of *Here Are Ladies* William Butler Yeats wrote to Stephens to tell him that *The Crock of Gold* had won the Polignac Prize, and an accompanying award of £100. Yeats presented the prize to Stephens on 28 November 1913. In a letter of 12 January 1914 to Stephen MacKenna Stephens wrote, "I was very glad to get it, for, on the day before I was notified of the prize, I had made the discovery that my total wealth in visable [*sic*] and moveable goods was, item, one wife, two babies, two cats, and fifteen shillings."

In 1914 Stephens published another novel, *The Demi-Gods,* but his greatest period of literary productivity was over. In addition, he was finding living in Paris more difficult than it had once been. His friends had him elected to the post of registrar at the National Gallery of Ireland (a sinecure given to an artist to provide income while he worked), and he returned to Ireland in July 1915. Stephens's spirits lifted when he was again with his friends AE and Stephen MacKenna.

Stephens wrote little during the next years, especially few short stories. In 1916 *The Insurrection in Dublin* was published, giving his assessment of the Easter 1916 uprising. Though Stephens was an ardent nationalist, his stance was pacifistic. A book of poetry, *Reincarnations,* appeared in 1918, and only then did another short story worthy of mention appear. Although Stephens originally wrote the piece under the pseudonym of James Esse (one of many he had), "Hunger" is perhaps his best-known story.

It tells of a housepainter's wife and her struggle to feed herself, her husband, and her three children, one of whom is crippled. An injury to her husband and the Great War intervene to make this task even more difficult. The housepainter goes to Scotland to look for work in a munitions plant in the off-season. The money he promises to send does not arrive, and his wife and children are reduced to begging. Two of the three children die before the wife learns that although her husband had found work in Scotland, he has also starved to death. In its naturalistic, dreary argument for the necessity of compassion this story is unlike others Stephens had written earlier. It was highly regarded in its time – and rightly so, according to Stephens. In a 14 July 1922 letter to Harold Loeb he wrote, "What do you mean by writing that Hunger was elected the best British Short Story for 1922? First I've heard of it. Of course its [*sic*] the best, but I dont [*sic*] expect anyone else to spot that until you and I have been very comfortably dead for about ten years."

Though his tone is tongue-in-cheek, Stephens indeed considered his earlier short-story writing successful, and other objective critics have agreed with him about "Hunger": McFate writes that it is a "relentless portrait of misery . . . conveyed with clarity and straightforwardness as objective and as crushing as a social worker's report." Martin praises its effectiveness, saying that "the stillness and desperate passivity in the adjectives [and] the implacable rhythm of the monosyllables . . . carry the central emotion which is the story's theme. . . . The story exhibits above all Stephens's remarkable instinct for narrative style."

Fantasy comprised the mode of Stephens's next major project in short fiction, after a wait of nearly six years from his 31 May 1913 letter to W. T. H. Howe, in which Stephens had written of Howe's "suggestion for a book of Irish Fairy Tales – It interests me a good deal. I would, of course, have to entirely write them and am sure I would enjoy doing so." However, as Richard Finneran put it, "Stephens did not publish any children's stories." In an inscription to the volume of tales he gave to Howe, Stephens wrote around October 1920, "It is not a book for children at all," and he added that the stories in the first part of the volume "are as good as my best work." In an 18 June 1920 letter to Sir Frederick Macmillan, Stephens wrote, "In a way I am sorry that the book must be named in this fashion, for, instead of being a collection of Fairy Tales, it is really an original book, and is, in fact, the first half of the Finn Saga, sometimes called 'the Ossian Cycle.' " In a 21 October 1920 letter he advised Henry McBride to compare the first piece, "The Story of Tuan mac Cairill," to his earlier "Desire" and to "say if 'Desire' isn't licked out of sight." He raved about the same story to Howe in a 2 February 1921 letter: "The 'Story of Tuan mac Cairill' is a collossal [sic] and terrific, and unsurpassable, top-hole story, and I shall expect to hear from you in parallel terms." Although Stephens overemphasizes the wondrous moments in *Irish Fairy Tales* (1920), Stephens's bias for this particular story was supported by Lady Gregory, who called it "extraordinarily fine."

In it, Finnian, an Abbott, decides to test a powerful non-Christian magician, Tuan mac Cairill. Finnian succeeds in converting Tuan and asks him to relate his past and repent of his sins. In disclosing his "witness of antiquity," Tuan reveals that he has lived from early postdiluvian times and was among the first people to settle in Ireland. Throughout his long life he has changed shape, becoming by turns a stag, a boar, a hawk, and a salmon and experiencing the fullness of life. Tuan's first-person description of life as a stag gives a wonderful sense of Stephens's captivating musical prose:

> Oh, loud and clear and sweet was the voice of the great stag. With what ease my lovely note went lilting. With what joy I heard the answering call. With what delight I bounded, bounded, bounded, bounded; light as a bird's plume, powerful as a storm, untiring as the sea.

Martin writes that "It is in its emphatic description of these animal sensations that Stephens's language is at its most strenuous." Finally as a salmon he is caught by Cairill, the King of Ulster, who feeds Tuan to his wife, and the queen then rebears Tuan as a boy, Tuan mac Cairill. The story ends when the Abbott affirms that Tuan will be reborn yet again in Christ. The story, though pleasant, shares none of the gripping human melodrama and likable characters with the other short stories in *Irish Fairy Tales*.

"The Birth of Bran" is such a story about a man, Fergus Fionnliath, who hates dogs so much that "when he heard that a man had drowned a litter of pups he used to visit that person and try to marry his daughter." By contrast, Fionn, Fergus's lord, loves dogs and owns three hundred of them – but especially favors two, Bran and Sceolan. Iollan Eachtach asks to marry Fionn's aunt Tuiren, whose "face was fresh as a spring morning; her voice more cheerful than the cuckoo calling from the branch that is highest in the hedge; and her form swayed like a reed and flowed like a river, so that each person thought she would surely flow to him."

Before Fionn gives his permission he makes Iollan promise to return her should she be unhappy. After the marriage Iollan's fairy lover Uct Dealv learns of Iollan's marriage and his promise. She changes Tuiren into a hound and gives her to Fergus Fionnliath, who reluctantly accepts her in the belief that she is a present from Fionn. To keep her from shivering he holds, hugs, and kisses her. The next day Fergus proclaims, "By my hand, I like that dog."

Meanwhile Fionn discovers that Tuiren has disappeared, and he demands that Iollan return her or be killed. Iollan asks Uct Dealv to reveal her, but she agrees only when Iollan promises to be hers forever. By the time Uct Dealv changes Tuiren back into human form, Tuiren has given birth to two pups, Bran and Sceolan, who are presented to Fionn. Everyone lives happily ever after. McFate calls the story "delightful," and Martin writes that it is told with "striking delicacy and humor."

Irish Fairy Tales received some favorable reviews. Ernest Boyd wrote in the *Freeman* of 9 March 1921 that "these stories are the gold transmuted from the ore of traditional material." They do not, however, live up to Stephens's tongue-in-cheek assessment:

> I feel like bragging, the first story in my Fairy Tales, "The Story of Tuan Mac Cairill," is the best short story in English . . . and further, for at this mortal minute I am just chock full of brags, the next 100 or so pages of the Fairy Tales are the best short stories in the British or any other old language.

In the same year "Desire" was published in *The Dial*. It begins with a man telling his wife how he has saved another man from being struck by a car that day. The near victim had then asked the husband what he "wished for beyond all things." The husband cannot decide, but his wife advises, "Behind everything stands desire, and you must find out your desire." The husband decides that he would like to stay forty-eight years old until he dies.

That night his wife dreams that she is on a polar expedition and, despite the temperature, does not put on her warmer clothes. In her dream she finally decides to don her warmer outfit but in the morning she awakens to find that it is missing and that the ship which she is on has landed. She loses her way in the tundra, but she wakes up in her bed before she dies in her dream. In reality she finds that she is cold, but when she moves to her husband for warmth, she discovers that his dead body is the source of the chill she feels. Appraisal of "Desire" has been thoroughly debated, but always in glowing terms. Martin sees it as a "brilliant . . . story of the erosion of domestic love" and "one of [Stephens's] bleakest and most powerful . . . comments on conjugal love and its dark alternatives." McFate views it as an epiphany story, its end recalling the conclusion of Joyce's "The Dead."

Both "Desire" and "Hunger" appeared in Stephens's second collection of short stories, *Etched in Moonlight* (1928). The title story of the collection, first published in 1923 in *Dublin Magazine,* is a dream exemplum about the relationships among a dreamer and a man and a woman. It explores issues of sexual politics and madness and is perhaps the Stephens story that shows the greatest influence of William Blake.

The narrator relates a dream in which he falls in love with a woman who decides to marry his closest friend. The narrator imprisons them in a castle, abandons them to die, and flees to self-imposed exile. Many years later he returns, only to find the couple still living. They have forgiven the narrator for his wrong, and they even introduce him to a woman who later becomes his fiancée. On the eve of the narrator's wedding the couple leads the narrator to the same castle and closes him behind the door in darkness. The narrator grapples with guilt and regret, only to be released by the couple. What has seemed to him an eternity alone has in fact been only a brief span. The couple relates that when the narrator had closed them behind the door, they had panicked — until they had realized that he had not locked the door. Initially the narrator feels a sense of well-being, but before he confesses his guilt and regret to the couple, he is horrified to watch — as if he were outside his body — as his face is hideously transformed by the wrongdoing that has gnawed at him for so long.

It is generally thought that Stephens's productivity and innovativeness ceased early in his career. With the exception of his late radio broadcasts, "Etched in Moonlight" is perhaps the last important short story that Stephens wrote: most of the other fine stories in the collection *Etched in Moonlight* had already been completed. Years later Stephens wrote in a 12 March 1928 letter to Walter H. Parker that *Etched in Moonlight* was not "a likeable book." McFate, however, finds that its prose is "hammered" and "polished" — and that its stories "provide evidence of Stephens' efforts to polish his short fiction: these are precisely cut, well-mounted gems." Yet Stephens at this time redirected his attentions to *Dierdre* (1923) — the first of two volumes of his uncompleted project of writing an Irish national epic (the other volume being the 1924 *In the Land of Youth*) — and later to his *Collected Poems by James Stephens* (1926).

In 1924 Stephens was formally recognized for his novel *Dierdre* by being awarded the medal for fiction at Dublin's Aonach Tailteann festival. After moving back to London less than a year later, Stephens toured America on the first two of what were to become many American lecture tours arranged by his friend and patron, Howe. These tours occupied most of Stephens's time throughout the years 1925–1935.

Between his tours he struck up a friendship with James Joyce, who had earlier presented his fictional Leonard Bloom of *Ulysses* [1922] overhearing in a library the disparaging comment that "James Stephens is writing some clever sketches." Although Stephens and Joyce initially had poor impressions of each other, Joyce was later so impressed by Stephens's *Dierdre* that he suggested in a 1929 letter to Harriet Weaver that, should he be unable to finish *Finnegan's Wake* (1939), Stephens would be the writer whom he wished to complete the task. Although there is some debate over Joyce's sincerity about this statement, the fact that he and Stephens discussed the issue on and off for two years should indicate Joyce's true intentions.

In 1928 *Etched in Moonlight* was published. Cyril Connolly reviewed it favorably in an issue of the *New Statesman* dated St. Patrick's Day 1928, saying that the stories "obtain a hearing which anything so well written must procure, and reveal a tragic insight into life which needs only the slightest of material to obtain its effects. . . . All the stories are good. . . . The style is lyric and precise, and admirably suited for this kind of story." However, it included no new stories worthy of discussion, and Stephens

Stephens (seated at right) with Irish tenor John Sullivan (standing) and James Joyce, in a picture Joyce said should be captioned "Three Irish Beauties"

was beginning to do what led to his great popularity — broadcasting on the BBC. His regular broadcasts began only in 1937, after the series of yearly lecture tours and his move to London in 1934. During 1937 Stephens was offered the Mark Twain medal for *Irish Fairy Tales,* but in a letter of 9 November written in his unique, mock-self-important style he refused it, saying "I deserve many medals, each as big as a barn door, & composed of massy ore enriched with diamond: but — so metaphysical am I! — I also want to know who has the right to give 'em, & what I am getting them for."

Less than two months after he refused this award, however, Stephens was in much poorer spirits. On Christmas Eve he was informed that his son, James Naoise, had been killed in an accident. The event profoundly disturbed Stephens, who never mentioned his son again. This added to a depression that Stephens was still feeling from events of 1934 and 1935, when his friends MacKenna and AE had also died.

The onset of World War II affected Stephens differently than had the Great War. Though he had been an ardent Irish nationalist, Stephens was moved by the character of the British people in coping with the blitz, and he declared himself a Brit for the duration of the fighting. During the war Stephens was given from £100 to £200 annually from the British Civil List Pension. Still he struggled to make ends meet. When his health started to fail, his friends pooled their resources to collect funds to pay for his medical expenses. And when he was offered an honorary degree in 1947 from Trinity College at Dublin University, he had first to be awarded a grant from the Royal Bounty Fund before he could afford the trip.

On 30 June 1950 Stephens gave one last radio broadcast on his childhood. Fittingly he died on St. Stephen's Day, 26 December, of that year. A 1924 assessment by Ernest Boyd in *Portraits: Real and Imaginary* praised him for being "This gnome, this elfin wit, the James Stephens of quips and fancies that bubble into laughter, of sensitive emotions that soar into prose and poetry of freshest beauty, . . . the James Stephens, above all, who has a fine soul."

Although such descriptions have furthered Stephens's reputation as "the Leprechaun of Irish literature," Boyd also wrote of him that "Kindness and humor . . . are the essence of James Stephens. . . . Pity and suffering, too, have gone into the making of him." In his short stories, which were so important to the modern beginnings of that genre in Ireland, is an account of both aspects of Stephens's nature: they describe all of life, more than does his poetry. Inside the tales is a record of life Irish and Continental; male and female; and animal, human, and superhuman.

Letters:

Letters of James Stephens, edited by Richard J. Finneran (London & New York: Macmillan, 1974).

Bibliography:

Birgit Bramsbäck, *James Stephens: A Literary and Bibliographical Study* (Dublin: Hodges, Figgis, 1959).

Biography:

Hilary Pyle, *James Stephens: His Work and an Account of His Life* (New York: Barnes & Noble, 1965).

References:

Ernest Boyd, "James Stephens," in his *Portraits: Real and Imaginary* (New York: Doran, 1924), pp. 246–254;

Augustine Martin, *James Stephens: A Critical Study* (Totowa, N.J.: Rowman & Littlefield, 1977);

Patricia McFate, *The Writings of James Stephens: Variations on a Theme of Love* (London: Macmillan, 1979).

Evelyn Waugh

(28 October 1903 – 10 April 1966)

Paul A. Doyle
Nassau Community College, State University of New York

See also the Waugh entry in *DLB 15: British Novelists, 1930–1959, Part 2.*

BOOKS: *The World to Come: A Poem in Three Cantos* (London: Privately printed, 1916);

P. R. B.: An Essay on the Pre-Raphaelite Brotherhood, 1847–1854 (London: Graham, 1926);

Rossetti: His Life and Works (London: Duckworth, 1928; New York: Dodd, Mead, 1928);

Decline and Fall (London: Chapman & Hall, 1928; Garden City, N.Y.: Doubleday, Doran, 1929);

Vile Bodies (London: Chapman & Hall, 1930; New York: Cape & Smith, 1930);

Labels: A Mediterranean Journal (London: Duckworth, 1930); republished as *A Bachelor Abroad: A Mediterranean Journal* (New York: Cape & Smith, 1930);

Remote People (London: Duckworth, 1931); republished as *They Were Still Dancing* (New York: Farrar & Rinehart, 1932);

Black Mischief (London: Chapman & Hall, 1932; New York: Farrar & Rinehart, 1932);

An Open Letter to His Eminence, the Cardinal Archbishop of Westminster (London & Tonbridge: Whitefriars, 1933);

Ninety-Two Days: The Account of a Tropical Journey Through British Guiana and Part of Brazil (London: Duckworth, 1934; New York: Farrar & Rinehart, 1934); republished as *Ninety-Two Days: A Journey in Guiana and Brazil* (London: Duckworth, 1986);

A Handful of Dust (London: Chapman & Hall, 1934; New York: Farrar & Rinehart, 1934);

Edmund Campion (London: Longmans, 1935; New York: Sheed & Ward, 1935);

Waugh in Abyssinia (London & New York: Longmans, Green, 1936);

Scoop: A Novel about Journalists (London: Chapman & Hall, 1938); republished as *Scoop* (Boston: Little, Brown, 1938);

Robbery under Law: The Mexican Object-Lesson (London: Chapman & Hall, 1939); republished as

Evelyn Waugh

Mexico: An Object Lesson (Boston: Little, Brown, 1939);

Put Out More Flags (London: Chapman & Hall, 1942; Boston: Little, Brown, 1942);

Brideshead Revisited: The Sacred and Profane Memories of Captain Charles Ryder (London: Chapman & Hall, 1945; Boston: Little, Brown, 1945; revised edition, London: Chapman & Hall, 1960);

When the Going Was Good (London: Duckworth, 1946; Boston: Little, Brown, 1946);

Scott-King's Modern Europe (London: Chapman & Hall, 1947; Boston: Little, Brown, 1949);

Wine in Peace and War (London: Saccone & Speed, 1947);

The Loved One (London: Chapman & Hall, 1948; Boston: Little, Brown, 1948);

Helena (London: Chapman & Hall, 1950; Boston: Little, Brown, 1950);

The Holy Places (London: Queen Anne Press, 1952; New York: Queen Anne Press & British Book Centre, 1953);

Men at Arms (London: Chapman & Hall, 1952; Boston: Little, Brown, 1952);

Love Among the Ruins: A Romance of the Near Future (London: Chapman & Hall, 1953);

Officers and Gentlemen (London: Chapman & Hall, 1955; Boston: Little, Brown, 1955);

The Ordeal of Gilbert Pinfold (London: Chapman & Hall, 1957; Boston: Little, Brown, 1957);

The Life of the Right Reverend Ronald Knox (London: Chapman & Hall, 1959); republished as *Monsignor Ronald Knox* (Boston: Little, Brown, 1959);

A Tourist in Africa (London: Chapman & Hall, 1960; republished as *Tourist in Africa* (Boston: Little, Brown, 1960);

Unconditional Surrender (London: Chapman & Hall, 1961); republished as *The End of the Battle* (Boston: Little, Brown, 1961);

Basil Seal Rides Again; or, The Rake's Regress (London: Chapman & Hall, 1963; Boston: Little, Brown, 1963);

A Little Learning: The First Volume of an Autobiography (London: Chapman & Hall, 1964); republished as *A Little Learning: An Autobiography, the Early Years* (Boston: Little, Brown, 1964);

Sword of Honour (London: Chapman & Hall, 1965; Boston: Little, Brown, 1966);

The Diaries and Letters of Evelyn Waugh, edited by Michael Davie (London: Weidenfeld & Nicolson, 1976; Boston: Little, Brown, 1977);

A Little Order: A Selection from the Journalism of Evelyn Waugh, edited by Donat Gallagher (London: Eyre Methuen, 1977; Boston: Little, Brown, 1981).

Collections: *Mr. Loveday's Little Outing, and Other Sad Stories* (London: Chapman & Hall, 1936; Boston: Little, Brown, 1936);

Work Suspended: Two Chapters of an Unfinished Novel (London: Chapman & Hall, 1942); enlarged as *Work Suspended, and Other Stories Written before the Second World War* (London: Chapman & Hall, 1949); enlarged and republished as *Tactical Exercise* (Boston: Little, Brown, 1954);

Charles Ryder's Schooldays, and Other Stories (Boston: Little, Brown, 1982);

The Essays, Articles and Reviews of Evelyn Waugh, edited by Donat Gallagher (Boston: Little, Brown, 1984);

Evelyn Waugh, Apprentice: The Early Writings, 1910–1927, edited by Robert Murray Davis (Norman, Okla.: Pilgrim Books, 1985).

OTHER: Francis Crease, *Thirty-Four Decorative Designs,* preface by Waugh (London: Privately printed, 1927);

Stuart Boyle and Vera Boyle, *The Rise and Fall of Mr. Prophitt,* foreword by Waugh (London: Chapman & Hall, 1938);

Christie Lawrence, *Irregular Adventure,* introduction by Waugh (London: Faber & Faber, 1947);

H. H. Munro (Saki), *The Unbearable Bassington,* introduction by Waugh (London: Eyre & Spottiswoode, 1947);

Ronald A. Knox, *A Selection from the Occasional Sermons of the Right Reverend Monsignor Ronald Arbuthnott Knox,* edited, with a preface, by Waugh (London: Dropmore, 1949);

Thomas Merton, *Elected Silence,* edited, with a foreword, by Waugh (London: Hollis & Carter, 1949);

Christopher Sykes, *Character and Situation,* introduction by Waugh (New York: Knopf, 1950);

Merton, *Waters of Silence,* edited, with a foreword, by Waugh (London: Hollis & Carter, 1950);

William Weston, *The Autobiography of an Elizabethan,* foreword by Waugh (London: Longmans, Green, 1955); republished as *An Autobiography from the Jesuit Underground* (New York: Farrar, Straus & Cudahy, 1955);

Robert Hugh Benson, *Richard Raynal, Solitary,* introduction by Waugh (Chicago: Regnery, 1956);

Lord Sudley, *William: or, More Loved Than Loving,* preface by Waugh (London: Chapman & Hall, 1956);

Knox, *A Spiritual Aeneid,* introduction by Waugh (London: Burns & Oates, 1958; New York: Sheed & Ward, 1958);

Earl of Wicklow, *Fireside Fusilier,* preface by Waugh (Dublin: Clonmore & Reynolds, 1958);

Eric Newby, *A Short Walk,* preface by Waugh (Garden City, N.Y.: Doubleday, 1959);

Hilaire Belloc, *Advice,* preface by Waugh (London: Harvill, 1960);

Knox, *Proving God: A New Apologetic,* preface by Waugh (London: The Month, 1960);

Jacqueline de Chimay, *The Life and Times of Madame Veuve Clicquot-Pousardin,* preface by Waugh (London: Curwen, 1961);

Anthony Carson, *Travels, Near and Far Out,* preface by Waugh (New York: Pantheon, 1963);

Daphne Fielding, *The Duchess of Jermyn Street: The Life and Good Times of Rosa Lewis of the Cavendish*

Hotel, preface by Waugh (London: Eyre & Spottiswoode, 1964; Boston: Little, Brown, 1964);

John Galsworthy, *The Man of Property,* preface by Waugh (Mount Vernon, N.Y.: Limited Editions, 1964);

Alfred Duggan, *Count Bohemond,* preface by Waugh (London: Faber & Faber, 1964; New York: Pantheon, 1965).

Literature must have seemed a predestined interest for Arthur Evelyn St. John Waugh, whose father, Arthur Waugh, was an author as well as head of the publishing firm of Chapman and Hall. Born in the London suburb of Hampstead on 28 October 1903, Evelyn Waugh wrote his first short story at the age of seven. Only four printed pages long and titled "The Curse of the Race," it was first published in an anthology called *Little Innocents: Childhood Reminiscences by Dame Ethyl Smith and Others* (1932). Despite its status as juvenilia, many of its features became characteristic in the mature writer's oeuvre.

The narrative focuses on a man named Rupert, about twenty-five years old, who loses £500 to a friend through a horse racing bet. Rupert decides to kill Tom, the friend to whom he owes the money, but the attempted murder fails when Rupert's sword squeaks in the dark and awakens Tom, and the intended victim and a policeman pursue Rupert. Rupert kills the policeman and the policeman's horse and takes refuge in a crowded inn – where he is forced to share a room in the dark with Tom. Despite the darkness Tom recognizes Rupert and wonders whether Rupert is again going to try to murder him or has only come to spend the night. Rupert is finally caught and hanged, and the last line of young Waugh's story reads, "I hope the story will be a leson [*sic*] to you never to bet."

The comic, the satiric, the whimsical, and the macabre – even in a story written at such an early age – show Waugh's mind as imaginative, clever, and amusing. The young man later attended Oxford University (where he was more interested in social life than in scholarship; he left without taking a degree in 1924), and there he wrote short stories for the *Oxford Broom,* the *Isis,* and the *Cherwell.* After working as a teacher and then briefly as a reporter, he published a story called "The Balance: A Yarn of the Good Old Days of Broad Trousers and High Necked Jumpers" in an anthology called *Georgian Stories, 1926.* The narrative chronicles an episode in the life of Adam Doure, a young art student whose love for Imogen Quest is thwarted when her mother

interferes. Imogen is a brainless socialite who is easily attracted and readily moves on to another boyfriend who is slovenly dressed and usually intoxicated. Adam contemplates suicide, but after conferring with his Reflection, which has an ability to speak, he chooses to live.

The narrative uses both German expressionism and cinematic techniques: various sections are given movie titles ("Everybody Loves My Baby" or "Next Morning 8:30 A.M."), and commentaries involving script directions ("Close up" and "Fade out") read as if one were watching a silent film – although most of the story is in dialogue form. Waugh used cinematic techniques in later novels, most notably *Vile Bodies* (1930). This story, then, represents a writer learning his trade and demonstrating an impressive gift for handling dialogue.

Another early short story was anthologized in *The New Decameron: The Fifth Day* (1927). Titled "The Tutor's Tale: A House of Gentlefolks," the story concerns a wealthy aristocratic family living on a remote estate. Ernest Vaughan is hired as a tutor to take the eighteen-year-old Marquess of Stayle on the grand tour. Stayle has been kept virtually secluded all his life and is controlled by his grandfather, the Duke of Vanburgh, and his two aunts. They caution Vaughan that the young man is not really insane, as reputed, but rather quite backward – and that is why they have kept him so isolated from everyone outside the ducal house.

When Vaughan and the young Marquess travel to London, Vaughan discovers that the grandfather and the aunts are the unbalanced ones, as Waugh pillories the eccentricities and weirdness of the nobility: the Duke, for example, has made "a wreath of strawberry-leaves and danced round the garden singing 'Cook's son, Dook's son, son of a belted earl,'" while the aunts are even more bizarre. A more sinister issue of financial control is implicit, since the Marquess stands to inherit the family fortune, which is to be closely guarded. After only a few days of freedom, the Marquess is forced by the family to return home, and the tutor is dismissed. In addition to being an amusing satire on the eccentricities and foibles of the rich, the story illustrates Waugh developing his art, using settings and types of characters that ultimately, as Robert Murray Davis observes, come in the novels "to be called the world of Evelyn Waugh."

Rossetti: His Life and Works (1928), Waugh's biography of Pre-Raphaelite painter and poet Dante Gabriel Rossetti, was published in the same year as *Decline and Fall,* his first novel – which was an immediate success. *Vile Bodies, A Handful of Dust*

Waugh, circa 1923, during his undergraduate years at Oxford

(1934), and other novels, travel books, and articles followed, all of which added to his literary reputation and thereby helped to ensure a market for his short fiction.

Waugh's most famous short story, "The Man Who Liked Dickens," was published in *Hearst's International combined with Cosmopolitan* in 1933. This narrative — about a naive English explorer trapped in a South American jungle and forced to read the novels of Dickens to his illiterate captor — ironically is well-known not as a short story but as the latter part of the novel *A Handful of Dust*. The Dickens story demonstrates that Waugh was not only a stylist but a master at handling ludicrous and macabre material.

Waugh's first collected volume of short fiction, consisting of pieces that he regarded as his more significant short stories, was published under the title *Mr. Loveday's Little Outing, and Other Sad Stories* (1936). The title story immediately sets the tone and displays the felicity of phrasing so typical of his work. Lord Moping "habitually threatened suicide on the occasion of [his wife's] annual garden party," and when he actually attempts suicide, his wife has

him committed to the local asylum for mental defectives. Lady Moping and her daughter Angela visit the institution and become acquainted with Mr. Loveday, an elderly inmate who is sweet, kindly, and beloved by all — and who for thirty-five years has been a popular fixture in the asylum. When he was young, he had knocked a young woman off her bicycle and strangled her. To Angela in particular Loveday seems perfectly sane, and, having a natural bent as a social reformer, she decides to do everything possible to secure his release. She visits him and asks if he would like to be free. He responds that he is quite content but wishes he could be released just for a brief outing, because "there is one thing I often wish I could do. . . . It wouldn't take long. But I do feel that if I had done it, just for a day, an afternoon even, then I would be more quiet."

After consulting legal precedents, visiting the local member of Parliament, and making other strenuous efforts on Loveday's behalf, she manages to have him freed. To the surprise of all, within two hours of his liberation he returns to the asylum and informs the doctor that he wants to stay now that he has enjoyed his holiday. Shortly thereafter the body of a strangled young lady who had been bicycling near the institution is found. Waugh thus satirically indicts sociological and psychological professors and scientific experimenters who coddle the insane and the criminal without regard for common sense and public safety. *Decline and Fall* had earlier stressed the same point when the professional sociologist and criminologist Sir Wilfred Lucas-Dockery, obsessed by theory and superficial observation and statistics, permits a preventable killing in his prison.

The plot of "Mr. Loveday's Little Outing" shows Waugh's penchant for what has come to be called "sick humor," "black humor," or even "theatre-of-the-absurd" material. Although comedy, satire, and grotesque elements are evident, a retelling of the plot does not provide an appreciation of the polished wit and style. Waugh's word choice is felicitous, and it is matched by the wryness and whimsy of the overall aura. One is reminded especially of the British comedies in which Alec Guinness starred in the 1950s — films like *Kind Hearts and Coronets, The Captain's Paradise,* and *The Lavender Hill Mob.* The plots were amusing, but the characters portrayed by Guinness added so much humor by a flick of the eyelids, a quizzical expression, a sly half-smile forming at the corner of the mouth. Waugh's prose has the same effect: it reaches what Alexander Pope's poem "An Essay on Criticism" (1711) calls "the grace beyond the reach of art." Without the grace and felicity of Waugh's style, the plot would have only a small impact.

Other stories in Waugh's first collection reinforce this conclusion. In "Bella Fleace Gave a Party" the principal character, Miss Annabel Rochfort-Doyle-Fleace, an eighty-year-old Anglo-Irish aristocrat who is the last of her family, lives in an elaborate though decaying mansion in Ireland. Having been practically a recluse for many years, she impulsively decides to give an elaborate Christmas party. She prepares the invitations, and everything is ready for a grand ball. On the night of the party the hired band is present, but no one arrives. Finally Bella Fleace, as she is called in the neighborhood, decides to eat, and the butler serves her. After the meal two couples arrive, both parvenus and uninvited. Bella refuses to receive them, and her horror at their presumption is evident. A day after the unsuccessful ball, she dies. Later her heir, a distant cousin, comes to sort out her effects and finds on her writing table the party invitations – addressed, stamped, but never mailed.

Again, while the plot is ordinary, the telling is not. Waugh works, through his style, the magic of verisimilitude, satire, and ludicrous amusement. Bella is not the sole subject of humor; a whole type of society is satirized. Her deceased brother, for example, had spent all his time creating oil paintings, his sole subject being assassinations: "his mind ran on the simple subject of assassination and before his death he had executed pictures of practically every such incident in history from Julius Caesar to General Wilson." Later, as he had been painting his own assassination, he had been shot down by some Irish rebels during the time of the Troubles.

In "Love in the Slump" the fashionable London wedding of Tom Watch and Angela Trench-Troubridge occurs, even though neither party is really in love with the other. They had been courting for some time, attending the same fashionable parties and dances, and finally marry because it is the expected thing to do. They are accidentally separated on their honeymoon and spend the whole period apart: Tom engages in drinking and sports, and Angela is involved in adultery with one of Tom's friends. It is apparent that Tom is too immature and selfish for marriage, and the frivolous, empty-headed Angela will continue to be unfaithful during the marriage.

This story, certainly influenced by Waugh's own unsuccessful first marriage, is a sardonic and cynical satire on the immorality and irresponsibility of the "upper classes." Waugh has often been ac-

CARICATURE BY THE AUTHOR OF HIS BROTHER, C. 1919

Waugh's caricature (circa 1919) of his older brother, Alec (from Evelyn Waugh, A Little Learning, *1964)*

cused of being a snob and catering to the aristocracy, but his novels and short fiction are replete with material satirizing the deficiencies of the so-called blue bloods.

In "Winner Takes All" Mrs. Kent-Cumberland constantly favors her older son, Gervase, over her younger son, Tom. Gervase is sent to a better school, given better gifts, and even given credit for a published monograph on which Tom has done all the work. After Tom has been exiled to work on a sheep farm in Australia, he eventually returns to visit England with his fiancée, the daughter of a wealthy landowner. Mrs. Kent-Cumberland realizes that Tom's fiancée, Bessie, would be the ideal rich wife whom she has sought for Gervase, and her machinations succeed in bringing this to pass: Tom is again the loser. Waugh effectively satirizes the favoritism that the English social system dictates must be shown to the eldest. Waugh, five and a half years younger than his brother Alec, may also have been thinking of the alleged privations he suffered in his own family.

"Cruise" is set on a passenger liner in the Mediterranean, where the sexual infidelity of the rich is stressed. Both older and younger generations are involved in fornication and adultery as a way of life. Although the tone is kept light and often amusing, there is again no question that the upper classes are an easy target for satire.

The sexual infidelities of the rich and their snobbery are also objects of derision in "Period Piece." Elderly Lady Amelia employs a well-bred and well-educated young woman named Miss Myers, to whom Lady Amelia reminisces about her upper-class friends – "'all people who came from anything but terrible homes,' [Lady Amelia] added with a glance at her companion; a glance as sharp and smart as a rap on the knuckles with an ivory ruler." Waugh's satire is unmistakably pointed.

As David Lodge noted, while reading Waugh one often laughs without knowing why. One often laughs or at least smiles when one may not want to. Although this response is more characteristic to the novels, where the cumulative effect is much greater, the short stories often provoke the same result. While the plot helps bring about some of the humor and furnishes the satiric foundation, it is the mot juste, the cleverness of description and phrasing, and the genius in handling dialogue that make the comedy and satire successful. Waugh's gift for recording the ludicrous and outrageous is instinctive, and the style brings pleasure.

The other short fiction in this first collection displays the same narrative qualities. There is, however, one exception – the story called "Out of Depth." Rip Van Winkle, the protagonist of this narrative, is a fashionable member of London society of the 1930s. He is a friend of Margot Metroland, Alastair Trumptington, and similar society figures who appear in some of Waugh's novels. While dining in Lady Metroland's mansion, he is introduced to a magician named Doctor Kakophilos. Van Winkle and Trumptington, who have both been drinking heavily, later stop at the doctor's home and are subjected to his magic incantations, which they regard as ridiculous: the doctor claims that he can transport people to a different period. While Alastair is sent back to the Middle Ages, Rip finds himself in a London of the twenty-fifth century.

London and its environs have become a primitive jungle, as mud and sedge dominate the landscape. The people live in huts, and Rip attempts to communicate but finds most of the language incomprehensible. Blacks make up the bulk of the population. Rip in time sees the word "Mission" painted on a simple board, and he enters a building to find a service being held by a black Dominican friar. Soon he hears the words, "Ite, missa est."

This is Waugh's only short story in which it is evident that the goal is purely didactic. Waugh had converted to Roman Catholicism in 1930, and "Out of Depth" was written as a tribute to his newfound faith. The tribute especially celebrates one feature of the faith that Waugh found most appealing: the unchanging doctrine and practices, the appeal of the permanent that this story identifies as "a shape in chaos." Rip still sees the Latin Mass being said far into the future.

The style is as readable as ever, but Waugh is not comfortable without his usual satire and humor. The message overcomes the medium. That Waugh himself realized this is indicated by the fact that he never allowed the story to be reprinted in any collections of fiction during his lifetime.

By the time this first collection appeared Waugh's life had endured some discomforting experiences. His marriage had ended in divorce, and in 1930 he had been received into the Roman Catholic Church. Following the eventual annulment of his first marriage, he married Laura Herbert in 1937, several years before the outbreak of World War II in Europe. Waugh enlisted in the Royal Marines soon after the war began, and he later served both in the commandos and with the British military liaison to Marshal Tito's partisans in Yugoslavia.

In 1949 Waugh's London publishers issued a collection called *Work Suspended, and Other Stories Written before the Second World War*. The volume had begun as a novel that Waugh had been diligently working on before the beginning of the war. The turmoil of the period and his own entry into military service prevented him from completing the book, and after the war he no longer felt the inspiration to continue it. The fragment was published in this collection along with eight short stories – seven of which had previously appeared in the *Mr. Loveday* volume. The only new story included is "An Englishman's Home."

In this narrative two schemers, brothers named Harwood-Hood, are active in a successful scam. They spread rumors in various arcadian parts of England where they have bought land in order to build an experimental industrial factory with two large chimneys and other polluting features. At a considerable profit they then plan to sell the land that they have purchased to the neighboring landowners and townspeople, who do not want the beauty and tranquillity of the countryside disturbed and overpopulated with factory workers. Many of the country dwellers have moved from the large cities or from outposts of the empire and live in pleasant retirement. Most of these older people do not own huge tracts of land; their acreage is more in the range of protagonist Beverley Metcalfe's seven acres, which he deems the proper size for a country landowner.

The rural dwellers are horrified to discover that some of the land has been sold to developers, and the distress, confusion, and contentiousness that arise skillfully satirize the latent pettiness, selfishness, and jealousies among ostensibly friendly neighbors. When a face-saving plan is agreed upon to buy the land and build a Boy Scout meeting hall, everyone finally contributes to the purchase. In the meantime Harwood-Hood and his brother use their financial profit in another part of England to maintain their large country home, which has fallen on difficult times because of increased property taxes.

The story, though laced with comic and satiric portraits, behavior, and dialogue, is much more serious than was usual for Waugh. From the overt preachiness of "Out of Depth" he learned to handle a serious theme with more lightheartedness and casualness. The narrative contains the usual quips — as in the references to "the village charwoman who dropped in twice a week to despoil their larder" and in characterizing the area as so idyllic that the "vicar found it impossible to interest them in the Left Book Club." Waugh is certainly concerned about the environment and preserving the beauty of rural England. His Harwood-Hood brothers are for some time worried that their scheme may not work in this section of the Cotswolds and hence the continued possession of their own estate may be jeopardized: "On the days when the gardens were open to the public, record crowds came to admire the topiary work. . . . Mr. Harwood-Hood's ancestors had built the house and planted the gardens in a happier time, before the days of property tax." The brothers justify their scam on the basis that a "sterner age demanded more strenuous efforts for their preservation [of their estate]." The theme is presented in such an amusing and wry manner that the message is never labored.

Work Suspended was not published in the United States until 1954, when it appeared under the title *Tactical Exercise*. This republication included a short novel, *Love Among the Ruins,* published in America for the first time, and two stories that had not appeared in the 1949 British collection: "The Curse of the Horse Race," the retitled story Waugh had written when he was seven; and the title story,

which had previously been published in a British anthology, *The Pick of Today's Short Stories* (1949).

John Verney, the husband in "Tactical Exercise," plans to kill his wife, Elizabeth, whom he has grown to hate during seven years of marriage. While on vacation they reside in an old dwelling on the edge of a cliff, and part of the fence on a balcony opening off the living room is broken. To prepare an alibi for the murder, John spreads rumors in the village bar and club that his wife sleepwalks. When he goes to the local doctor to establish his alibi further, he learns that Elizabeth has already visited the doctor to tell him of her husband's sleepwalking. In the evening he feels drugged and falls asleep: Elizabeth has drugged the one drink left in the whiskey bottle, and it is obvious that she will succeed in murdering her husband. While the story is cleverly conceived and executed, it is overly dependent on the surprise ending (in which the wife, rather than the husband, turns out to be the killer) and lacks the usual rush of narrative that so characterizes Waugh's earlier short fiction.

For financial reasons Waugh often published short stories that were later incorporated into some of his novels. Much less famous than "The Man Who Liked Dickens" but nevertheless significant is "Compassion," published in 1949. Set in Yugoslavia during the latter part of World War II, the story is based on Waugh's military experience in that country. Major Gordon is a British representative to the Joint Allied Mission to Marshal Tito's partisans. A group of 108 Jewish refugees, mainly survivors of a concentration camp located on the island of Rab, come to Gordon seeking help in leaving Yugoslavia, where they are destitute and badly treated by the Communist partisans.

Major Gordon contacts British headquarters in Italy and makes every attempt to have the refugees moved to safety. When Tito's guerrillas learn of Gordon's efforts, they have no concern for the suffering Jews, whom they extremely resent. Working with the refugees' spokesperson, Madame Kanyi, whose husband runs the powerhouse, Gordon continues his efforts, and it appears that the United Nations Relief and Rehabilitation Administration will arrange for planes to fly in and evacuate the refugees.

A fog, however, prevents the planes from landing, and Gordon is transferred back to Italy. There at Bari he continues his struggle to free the Jewish refugees from Yugoslavian control. He finally manages to have a privately supplied United Nations convoy of Ford trucks sent. Delighted that he has "done something worthwhile in this bloody war," he learns that Madame Kanyi and her husband are not among the other refugees who have arrived safely in Italy. Again Gordon goes to considerable lengths to trace and help the Kanyis, and he finally learns that they have been executed by Tito's partisans on fabricated charges – she for being friendly with Gordon, a "foreign agent," although England has done everything possible to aid Tito during the war.

This story is one of Waugh's most significant works of short fiction. Amid the satire, the story shockingly reveals the horrors and cruelties of war and of communism, and a more understanding and compassionate side of Waugh's persona is revealed. More than ten years later Waugh incorporated much of this material in his novel *Unconditional Surrender* (1961). This episode was a fitting coda to his last masterful work of fiction, the *Sword of Honour* trilogy (1965).

In 1963 a new short story, "Basil Seal Rides Again," was published in *Esquire* magazine and in a limited edition titled *Basil Seal Rides Again; or, The Rake's Regress*. The caddish Basil Seal – highborn, well-educated, and totally unprincipled but always able to land on his feet – had appeared in three of Waugh's novels. In this story he is fifty-eight years old and is in far from robust health. He and his wife go to a spa, from which he is soon discharged for violating the rules against drinking alcohol. When he learns that his daughter, Barbara, has decided to marry her completely disreputable boyfriend, he is determined to prevent what he regards as a disaster. Through a clever ruse he convinces Barbara that her boyfriend is his illegitimate son, and the suspicion of incest prevents the marriage.

There is some amusing dialogue in the story, and the prose is as faultless as ever, but the characters do not really come alive. A weary lethargy hangs over the story, and although Basil Seal has not lost his touch for skulduggery, his zest has vanished with his aging. Waugh also seems to have suffered a loss of narrative drive.

Waugh had a sudden heart attack at his home near Taunton, Somerset, and died on 10 April 1966. Sixteen years later, in 1982, his American publisher – Little, Brown – collected and published *Charles Ryder's Schooldays, and Other Stories*. Except for the addition of the title story, all of the selections in this volume are reprinted from *Mr. Loveday's Little Outing, and Other Sad Stories*. The title story in fact is not a short story but a chapter of an unfinished novel written early in Waugh's career. The publication of this chapter with the reprinting of the stories from the earlier collection was designed to take fi-

nancial advantage of the interest in Waugh and in the character of Charles Ryder that had resulted from the successful PBS Granada Television production of *Brideshead Revisited* in 1982. While a financial success, this volume added nothing new to a study of Waugh's short stories, but it did introduce him to a new generation of readers who were unfamiliar with his shorter narratives.

There is no question that Waugh was much more successful and more comfortable in writing novels than he was in writing short stories. He could develop in much more detail his urbane, satiric humor as well as his characters and plots as a novelist. Furthermore, many of the short stories were written in haste, when he was in need of money because of his impecunious spending habits. His best stories are unquestionably "Mr. Loveday's Little Outing," "Bella Fleace Gave a Party," "An Englishman's Home," and, of course, "The Man Who Liked Dickens" and "Compassion." Too many of the other stories, while always satiric and frequently comic, are less substantial. They are jeux d'esprit, notable especially for their polished style, literary grace, and classical precision.

Letters:

The Letters of Evelyn Waugh, edited by Mark Amory (London: Weidenfeld & Nicolson, 1980; New Haven: Ticknor & Fields, 1980).

Bibliographies:

"Annual Bibliography of Waugh Studies," *Evelyn Waugh Newsletter and Studies* (Autumn issue 1967–   );

Margaret Morriss and David Dooley, *Evelyn Waugh: A Reference Guide* (Boston: G. K. Hall, 1984);

Robert Murray Davis, Paul A. Doyle, Donat Gallagher, Charles E. Linck, and Winnifred Bogaards, *A Bibliography of Evelyn Waugh* (Troy, N.Y.: Whitson, 1986).

Biographies:

Christopher Sykes, *Evelyn Waugh: A Biography* (Boston: Little, Brown, 1975);

Martin Stannard, *Evelyn Waugh: The Early Years 1903–1939* (New York: Norton, 1987);

Stannard, *Evelyn Waugh: The Later Years 1939–1966* (New York: Norton, 1992).

References:

Frederick L. Beaty, *The Ironic World of Evelyn Waugh* (De Kalb: Northern Illinois University Press, 1992);

Alain Blayac, ed., *Evelyn Waugh: New Directions* (New York: St. Martin's Press, 1992);

Malcolm Bradbury, *Evelyn Waugh* (Edinburgh: Oliver & Boyd, 1964);

James F. Carens, *The Satiric Art of Evelyn Waugh* (Seattle & London: University of Washington Press, 1966);

Carens, ed., *Critical Essays of Evelyn Waugh* (Boston: G. K. Hall, 1987);

Katharyn W. Crabbe, *Evelyn Waugh* (New York: Continuum, 1988);

Robert Murray Davis, *Evelyn Waugh, Writer* (Norman, Okla.: Pilgrim Books, 1981);

Paul A. Doyle, *A Reader's Companion to the Novels and Short Stories of Evelyn Waugh* (Norman, Okla.: Pilgrim Books, 1988);

D. Paul Farr, "Waugh's Conservative Stance: Defending 'The Standards of Civilization,'" *Philological Quarterly,* 51 (April 1972): 471–484;

Martin Green, *Children of the Sun* (New York: Basic Books, 1976);

Jeffrey Heath, *The Picturesque Prison: Evelyn Waugh and His Writings* (Kingston, Ontario: McGill-Queen's University Press, 1982);

Christopher Hollis, *Evelyn Waugh* (London: Longmans, Green, 1954);

David Lodge, *Evelyn Waugh* (New York: Columbia University Press, 1971);

David Pryce-Jones, ed., *Evelyn Waugh and His World* (Boston: Little, Brown, 1973);

Frederick J. Stopp, *Evelyn Waugh, Portrait of an Artist* (London: Chapman & Hall, 1958; Boston: Little, Brown, 1958).

Papers:

An extensive collection of Waugh's manuscripts and letters as well as portions of his personal library are at the Harry Ransom Humanities Research Center, University of Texas at Austin. The Berg Collection of the New York Public Library also holds some significant materials.

P. G. Wodehouse

(15 October 1881 – 14 February 1975)

John H. Rogers
Vincennes University

See also the Wodehouse entry in *DLB 34: British Novelists, 1890–1929: Traditionalists.*

SELECTED BOOKS: *The Pothunters* (London: A. & C. Black, 1902; New York: Macmillan, 1902);

A Prefect's Uncle (London: A. & C. Black, 1903; New York: Macmillan, 1903);

Tales of St. Austin's (London: A. & C. Black, 1903);

The Gold Bat (London: A. & C. Black, 1904; New York: Macmillan, 1923);

William Tell Told Again (London: A. & C. Black, 1904; New York: Macmillan, 1904);

The Head of Kay's (London: A. & C. Black, 1905; New York: Macmillan, 1922);

Love Among the Chickens (London: Newnes, 1906; New York: Circle, 1909);

The White Feather (London: A. & C. Black, 1907; New York: Macmillan, 1922);

The Globe By the Way Book, by Wodehouse and Herbert Westbrook (London: Globe Publishing, 1908);

Not George Washington (London, Paris, New York, Toronto & Melbourne: Cassell, 1909);

The Swoop! or, How Clarence Saved England: A Tale of the Great Invasion (London: Alston Rivers, 1909);

Mike: A Public School Story (London: A. & C. Black, 1909; New York: Macmillan, 1910); chapters 30–59 republished as *Enter Psmith* (London: A. & C. Black, 1935; New York: Macmillan, 1935) and as *Mike and Psmith* (London: Jenkins, 1953); chapters 1–29 republished as *Mike at Wrykyn* (London: Jenkins, 1953);

The Intrusion of Jimmy (New York: Watt, 1910); republished as *A Gentleman of Leisure* (London: Alston Rivers, 1910);

Psmith in the City: A Sequel to Mike (London: A. & C. Black, 1910; New York: Macmillan, 1910);

The Prince and Betty (New York: Watt, 1912; London: Mills & Boon, 1912);

The Little Nugget (London: Methuen, 1913; New York: Watt, 1914);

P. G. Wodehouse and his foxhound Bill (Dulwich College)

The Man Upstairs, and Other Stories (London: Methuen, 1914);

Psmith, Journalist (London: Black, 1915; New York: Macmillan, 1915);

Something New (New York: Appleton, 1915); republished as *Something Fresh* (London: Methuen, 1915);

Uneasy Money (New York: Appleton, 1916; London: Methuen, 1917);

Piccadilly Jim (New York: Dodd, Mead, 1917; London: Jenkins, 1918);

The Man With Two Left Feet, and Other Stories (London: Methuen, 1917; enlarged, New York: A. L. Burt, 1933);

My Man Jeeves (London: Newnes, 1919);

Their Mutual Child (New York: Boni & Liveright, 1919); republished as *The Coming of Bill* (London: Jenkins, 1920);

A Damsel in Distress (New York: Doran, 1919; London: Jenkins, 1919);

The Little Warrior (New York: Doran, 1920); republished as *Jill the Reckless* (London: Jenkins, 1921);

Indiscretions of Archie (London: Jenkins, 1921; New York: Doran, 1921);

The Clicking of Cuthbert (London: Jenkins, 1922); republished as *Golf Without Tears* (New York: Doran, 1924);

Three Men and a Maid (New York: Doran, 1922); republished as *The Girl on the Boat* (London: Jenkins, 1922);

The Adventures of Sally (London: Jenkins, 1922); republished as *Mostly Sally* (New York: Doran, 1923);

The Inimitable Jeeves (London: Jenkins, 1923); republished as *Jeeves* (New York: Doran, 1923);

Leave It to Psmith (London: Jenkins, 1923; New York: Doran, 1924);

Ukridge (London: Jenkins, 1924); republished as *He Rather Enjoyed It* (New York: Doran, 1926);

Bill the Conqueror (London: Methuen, 1924; New York: Doran, 1925);

Carry On, Jeeves! (London: Jenkins, 1925; New York: Doran, 1927);

Sam the Sudden (London: Methuen, 1925); republished as *Sam in the Suburbs* (New York: Doran, 1925);

The Heart of a Goof (London: Jenkins, 1926); republished as *Divots* (New York: Doran, 1927);

The Small Bachelor (London: Methuen, 1927; New York: Doran, 1927);

Meet Mr. Mulliner (London: Jenkins, 1927; Garden City, N.Y.: Doubleday, Doran, 1928);

Money for Nothing (London: Jenkins, 1928; Garden City, N.Y.: Doubleday, Doran, 1928);

Mr. Mulliner Speaking (London: Jenkins, 1929; Garden City, N.Y.: Doubleday, Doran, 1930);

Fish Preferred (Garden City, N.Y.: Doubleday, Doran, 1929); republished as *Summer Lightning* (London: Jenkins, 1929);

Baa, Baa, Black Sheep: A Farcical Comedy in Three Acts, by Wodehouse and Ian Hay (John Hay Beith) (London & New York: French's Acting Edition, 1930);

Very Good, Jeeves (Garden City, N.Y.: Doubleday, Doran, 1930; London: Jenkins, 1930);

Big Money (Garden City, N.Y.: Doubleday, Doran, 1931; London: Jenkins, 1931);

If I Were You (Garden City, N.Y.: Doubleday, Doran, 1931; London: Jenkins, 1931);

Louder and Funnier (London: Faber & Faber, 1932);

Doctor Sally (London: Methuen, 1932);

Hot Water (London: Jenkins, 1932; Garden City, N.Y.: Doubleday, Doran, 1932);

Mulliner Nights (London: Jenkins, 1933; Garden City, N.Y.: Doubleday, Doran, 1933);

Heavy Weather (Boston: Little, Brown, 1933; London: Jenkins, 1933);

Thank You, Jeeves (London: Jenkins, 1934; Boston: Little, Brown, 1934);

Right Ho, Jeeves (London: Jenkins, 1934); republished as *Brinkley Manor* (Boston: Little, Brown, 1934);

Blandings Castle and Elsewhere (London: Jenkins, 1935); republished as *Blandings Castle* (Garden City, N.Y.: Doubleday, Doran, 1935);

The Luck of the Bodkins (London: Jenkins, 1935; revised, Boston: Little, Brown, 1936);

Young Men in Spats (London: Jenkins, 1936; revised, Garden City, N.Y.: Doubleday, Doran, 1936);

Laughing Gas (London: Jenkins, 1936; Garden City, N.Y.: Doubleday, Doran, 1936);

Anything Goes: A Musical Comedy, by Wodehouse and Guy Bolton (London: French's Acting Edition, 1936);

Lord Emsworth and Others (London: Jenkins, 1937);

The Crime Wave at Blandings (Garden City, N.Y.: Doubleday, Doran, 1937);

Summer Moonshine (Garden City, N.Y.: Doubleday, Doran, 1937; London: Jenkins, 1938);

The Code of the Woosters (Garden City, N.Y.: Doubleday, Doran, 1938; London: Jenkins, 1938);

Uncle Fred in the Springtime (Garden City, N.Y.: Doubleday, Doran, 1939; London: Jenkins, 1939);

Eggs, Beans and Crumpets (London: Jenkins, 1940; Garden City, N.Y.: Doubleday, Doran, 1940);

Quick Service (London: Jenkins, 1940; Garden City, N.Y.: Doubleday, Doran, 1940);

Money In the Bank (Garden City, N.Y.: Doubleday, Doran, 1942; London: Jenkins, 1946);

Joy in the Morning (Garden City, N.Y.: Doubleday, Doran, 1946; London: Jenkins, 1947);

Full Moon (Garden City, N.Y.: Doubleday, 1947; London: Jenkins, 1947);

Spring Fever (Garden City, N.Y.: Doubleday, 1948; London: Jenkins, 1948);

Uncle Dynamite (London: Jenkins, 1948; New York: Didier, 1948);

The Mating Season (London: Jenkins, 1949; New York: Didier, 1949);

Nothing Serious (London: Jenkins, 1950; Garden City, N.Y.: Doubleday, 1951);

The Old Reliable (London: Jenkins, 1951; Garden City, N.Y.: Doubleday, 1951);

Barmy in Wonderland (London: Jenkins, 1952); republished as *Angel Cake* (Garden City, N.Y.: Doubleday, 1952);

Pigs Have Wings (Garden City, N.Y.: Doubleday, 1952; London: Jenkins, 1952);

Ring for Jeeves (London: Jenkins, 1953); revised as *The Return of Jeeves* (New York: Simon & Schuster, 1954);

Bring on the Girls! The Improbable Story of Our Life in Musical Comedy, with Pictures to Prove It, by Wodehouse and Guy Bolton (New York: Simon & Schuster, 1953; revised, London: Jenkins, 1954);

Performing Flea (London: Jenkins, 1953); revised as *Author! Author!* (New York: Simon & Schuster, 1962);

Jeeves and the Feudal Spirit (London: Jenkins, 1954); republished as *Bertie Wooster Sees It Through* (New York: Simon & Schuster, 1955);

French Leave (London: Jenkins, 1956; New York: Simon & Schuster, 1959);

America, I Like You (New York: Simon & Schuster, 1956); revised as *Over Seventy: An Autobiography with Digressions* (London: Jenkins, 1957);

Something Fishy (London: Jenkins, 1957); republished as *The Butler Did It* (New York: Simon & Schuster, 1957);

Cocktail Time (London: Jenkins, 1958; New York: Simon & Schuster, 1958);

A Few Quick Ones (New York: Simon & Schuster, 1959; London: Jenkins, 1959);

How Right You Are, Jeeves (New York: Simon & Schuster, 1960); republished as *Jeeves in the Offing* (London: Jenkins, 1960);

The Ice in the Bedroom (New York: Simon & Schuster, 1961); republished as *Ice in the Bedroom* (London: Jenkins, 1961);

Service With a Smile (New York: Simon & Schuster, 1961; London: Jenkins, 1962);

Stiff Upper Lip, Jeeves (New York: Simon & Schuster, 1963; London: Jenkins, 1963);

Biffin's Millions (New York: Simon & Schuster, 1964); republished as *Frozen Assets* (London: Jenkins, 1964);

The Brinkmanship of Galahad Threepwood (New York: Simon & Schuster, 1965); republished as *Galahad at Blandings* (London: Jenkins, 1965);

Plum Pie (London: Jenkins, 1966; abridged, New York: Simon & Schuster, 1967);

The Purloined Paperweight (New York: Simon & Schuster, 1967); republished as *Company for Henry* (London: Jenkins, 1967);

Do Butlers Burgle Banks? (New York: Simon & Schuster, 1968; London: Jenkins, 1968);

A Pelican at Blandings (London: Jenkins, 1969); republished as *No Nudes Is Good Nudes* (New York: Simon & Schuster, 1970);

The Girl in Blue (London: Barrie & Jenkins, 1970; New York: Simon & Schuster, 1971);

Much Obliged, Jeeves (London: Barrie & Jenkins, 1971); republished as *Jeeves & the Tie That Binds* (New York: Simon & Schuster, 1971);

Pearls, Girls and Monty Bodkin (London: Barrie & Jenkins, 1972); republished as *The Plot That Thickened* (New York: Simon & Schuster, 1973);

Bachelors Anonymous (London: Barrie & Jenkins, 1973; New York: Simon & Schuster: 1974);

Aunts Aren't Gentlemen (London: Barrie & Jenkins, 1974); republished as *The Cat-Nappers* (New York: Simon & Schuster, 1975);

Quest (London: Privately printed, 1975);

Sunset at Blandings (London: Chatto & Windus, 1977; New York: Simon & Schuster, 1978).

SELECTED PLAY PRODUCTIONS: *A Gentleman of Leisure,* by Wodehouse and John Stapleton, New York, Playhouse Theater, 24 August 1911;

Hearts and Diamonds: A New Light Opera, adaptation by Wodehouse and Laurie Wylie from Ernst Marischka and Bruno Granichstaedten, *The Orlov,* London, Strand Theatre, 1 June 1926;

The Play's the Thing, New York, Henry Miller's Theatre, 3 November 1926;

Her Cardboard Lover, by Wodehouse and Valerie Wyngate, New York, Empire Theatre, 21 March 1927;

Good Morning, Bill, London, Duke of York's Theatre, 28 November 1927;

A Damsel in Distress, by Wodehouse and Ian Hay, New York, New Theatre, 13 August 1928;

Baa, Baa, Black Sheep, by Wodehouse and Hay, New York, New Theatre, 22 April 1929;

Candlelight, adapted by Wodehouse from Siegfried Geyer, *Kleine Komödie,* New York, Empire Theatre, 30 September 1929;

Leave It to Psmith, by Wodehouse and Hay, London, Shaftesbury Theatre, 29 September 1930;

Who's Who, by Wodehouse and Guy Bolton, London, Duke of York's Theatre, 20 September 1934;

Anything Goes, by Wodehouse and Bolton, London, Palace Theatre, 14 June 1935;

The Inside Stand, London, Saville Theatre, 20 November 1935;

Don't Listen, Ladies, by Wodehouse and Bolton, New York, Booth Theatre, 28 December 1948.

SELECTED MOTION PICTURES: *Rosalie,* screenplay by Wodehouse, M-G-M, 1930;

Summer Lightning, screenplay by Wodehouse, British and Dominion Films, 1932;

A Damsel in Distress, screenplay by Wodehouse, Ernest Pagano, and S. K. Lauren, R-K-O, 1937.

OTHER: *A Century of Humour,* edited by Wodehouse (London: Hutchinson, 1934);

William Anthony Macguire, *The Three Musketeers: A Romantic Musical Play,* lyrics by Wodehouse and Clifford Grey (London & Sydney: Chappell, 1937; New York: Harms, 1937);

The Best of Modern Humor, edited by Wodehouse and Scott Meredith, with a general introduction by Wodehouse (New York: Metcalf, 1952);

The Week-End Book of Humor, edited by Wodehouse and Meredith, with a general introduction by Wodehouse (New York: Washburn, 1952).

P. G. Wodehouse is an anomaly in twentieth-century fiction. In an age of relentless artistic experimentation, he wrote fiction firmly rooted in the Edwardian world of his childhood. In an age of rapidly changing moral and sexual values, he created characters and situations remarkable for their purity and innocence. In an age whose mood was decidedly serious, he wrote fiction designed solely for amusement. And in an age of artistic angst and alienation, for nearly eighty years Wodehouse wrote novels and short stories that succeeded in pleasing his readers, his critics, and himself.

Pelham Greville Wodehouse was born on 15 October 1881, the third of four sons of Henry Ernest Wodehouse, a member of the British civil service in Hong Kong, and Eleanor Deane Wodehouse, the daughter of a minister, Rev. Deane of Bath. Sent back to England as early as 1884 with his older brothers, Philip and Armine, for schooling, Wodehouse began his education at Bath with a Miss Roper. In 1886 he began attending a dame school run by Flossie and Cissie Prince; there he wrote his first story, about a thrush, at age seven. He then attended Elizabeth College in Guernsey and Malvern House, a navy prepara-

tory school, in Kearnsey. Wodehouse's most important educational experience began on 2 May 1894, when at age twelve he first attended Dulwich College, where he stayed for six years. During his last year there Wodehouse received his first payment for writing "Some Aspects of Game Captaincy," an essay published in the *Public School Magazine.*

The enormous influence of Dulwich in Wodehouse's work has long been recognized. J. B. Priestley voiced the common sentiment that Wodehouse remained "a brilliant super-de-luxe schoolboy" throughout his life, a belief that explains the sexless young women, terrifying aunts, and eccentric aristocrats who fill his pages. It also explains his success, as Priestley added: "Most of us who enjoy him still have a schoolboy somewhere in us, and to reach that schoolboy (aged about fifteen or sixteen), to let himself enjoy himself, is a perfect escape from our adult problems and trials." That Wodehouse remained a schoolboy is absurd, but his work does reflect a schoolboy sensibility. Even Wodehouse recognized the important influence of Dulwich in his life: he wrote to his lifelong friend Charles Townend in 1945 that he had read a review of a book that he thought was "apparently the same old anti-public school stuff. I often wonder if you and I were unusually fortunate in our schooldays. To me the years between 1896 and 1900 seem like Heaven." In his fiction Dulwich becomes Valley Fields, a paradisaical location where the best characters are allowed to settle at the end.

Wodehouse's most important early work consisted, appropriately, of school stories. These stories are still admired in England, but to American readers the world of the English public school may seem even stranger than later worlds of Wodehouse's imagining. In these school stories, though, Wodehouse began to use materials from conventional novels for his own ends, spicing his stories with the literary allusions and quotations that became characteristic features of his later work. With the appearance of the character Psmith, based on Richard D'Oyly Carte, Wodehouse began to create his own new world. Psmith was introduced in "The Lamb" (1907) and appeared in *The Captain: A Magazine for Boys & "Old Boys"* and then in *Mike: A Public School Story* (1909). Psmith provides the first important instance of the typical Wodehouse incongruity, ultra-correct form applied to ultra-absurd content, and *Psmith in the City* (1910), based on Wodehouse's bank experience, connects the school stories with the later novels.

Wodehouse's experience as a bank clerk occurred because he could not proceed to Oxford — the usual path for a boy of his background and one

PSMITH SEIZED AND EMPTIED JELLICOE'S JUG OVER SPILLER

Illustration from Mike: A Public School Story *(courtesy of Special Collections, Thomas Cooper Library, University of South Carolina)*

pursued by his brother Armine – because his father's pension was paid in rupees, the value of which fell so precipitously at the time that, even had a scholarship been available, the family could not afford another son at the university. Wodehouse already knew he wanted to write and suggested that he become a freelance writer, but his father would not hear of such impracticality. So Wodehouse became a clerk at the London branch of the Hong Kong and Shanghai Bank, a training post for those later to be sent to the Far East. His time as a clerk proved to be not entirely unproductive: in the evenings he wrote, primarily sports-related articles for the *Public School Magazine,* and during his tenure at the bank he sold eighty stories and articles.

Wodehouse always recalled that his "total inability to grasp what was going on made me something of a legend" in the bank, and he soon undertook the more congenial profession of journalism. He was first a substitute writer for the "By the Way" column in *The Globe,* and in August 1903 he was employed full-time by the paper. Fascinated with boxers and wishing to meet James J. Corbett and other fighters, Woodhouse fulfilled a longtime

ambition by making a first trip to America, arriving in New York in 1904. After a short stay he returned to England as editor of the "By the Way" column, but his love for America, and for the possibilities he felt it promised writers, continued. He made many later trips to the United States, later writing that "Being there was like being in heaven without going to all the bother and expense of dying," and in a 7 November 1915 *New York Times* interview with Joyce Kilmer he predicted that the years following World War I would "afford a great opportunity for the new English humorist who works on the American plan."

Wodehouse eventually seized this opportunity and exploited it so well that years later in a review of *Young Men in Spats* (1936) Robert Strunsky remarked that Wodehouse was "the only Englishman who can make an American laugh at a joke about America." Strunsky reasoned that Wodehouse was perhaps capable of such humor because of "the amount of time he [has] spent here and the amount of money he has taken away," but he concluded that the real secret of Wodehouse's American popularity was that he "really likes Americans." One American whom Wodehouse particularly liked was Ethel Newton Rowley, a widow with one child named Leonora. Wodehouse had met Ethel on one of his many visits to America, and he married her on 30 September 1914.

Another great influence on Wodehouse's fiction was his theatrical writing, which began in 1904 when Owen Hall asked Wodehouse to compose a lyric for a song in the show *Sergeant Bruce.* Wodehouse responded with "Put Me In My Little Cell," sung by three crooks. In 1906 Sir Seymour Hicks hired Wodehouse as lyricist for his Aldwych Theatre shows, the first of which, *The Beauty of Bath,* marked also the first collaboration between Wodehouse and Jerome Kern. When Kern introduced Wodehouse to Guy Bolton in 1915, the three men shared ideas about a new kind of musical comedy and decided to join forces to create what became known as the Princess Theatre shows. Their musicals began with *Have a Heart* (January 1917), followed by *Oh, Boy!* (February 1917), *Leave It to Jane* (August 1917), and *Oh, Lady! Lady!* (February 1918).

The Kern-Bolton-Wodehouse team set new standards for musical comedy, and the *Oxford Companion to the American Theatre* states that Wodehouse "may well be considered the first truly great lyricist of the American musical stage, his easy colloquially flowing rhythm deftly intertwined with a sunny wit." The Princess Theatre shows, though highly successful and influential in their time, are now seldom-revived period pieces. Their real and lasting influence was on Wodehouse's fiction, which he now began to structure in the fashion of the musical comedy. According to David Jasen, Wodehouse himself "described his books as musical comedies without the music."

Throughout the 1920s Wodehouse's work as a journalist, lyricist, and fiction writer made him increasingly famous and wealthy, and his success inevitably attracted the attention of Hollywood, where Wodehouse first went in 1929. After being subjected to the typically shrewd business negotiations of Ethel Wodehouse, Samuel Goldwyn in 1930 offered Wodehouse $2,000 a week for six months, with a further six-month option. Wodehouse's contribution amounted to little more than adding a few lines to already-completed scripts, and this caused him to tell an interviewer for the *Los Angeles Times* (7 June 1931) that "They paid me $2000 a week – $104,000 – and I cannot see what they engaged me for. They were extremely nice to me, but I feel as if I cheated them."

Wodehouse's remarks caused a minor scandal and were said to have caused New York banks to examine studio expenditures more closely. That he actually influenced Hollywood finance seems doubtful, especially since three years after this interview, with the Depression continuing, he was asked to return to Hollywood. His final film project, *Damsel in Distress* (1937), was not a success, and in that year Wodehouse left Hollywood for good. Film scripts constitute the only type of writing Wodehouse attempted without success. The Hollywood experience did, however, give him abundant material for his fiction, notably in the stories about Jacob Z. Schnellenhamer, subliterate head of Perfecto-Zizzlebaum studios. This figure, whom "The Castaways" describes as "a stout man with a face rather like that of a vulture which has been doing itself too well on the corpses," bears a more than passing resemblance to Louis B. Mayer.

The Hollywood experience aside, the 1920s and 1930s were remarkably productive and successful years for Wodehouse. In addition to his work in the theater and in journalism, at this time he began to introduce characters and situations in stories that began to show Wodehouse's most characteristic devices: a mixture of strong, convoluted plots; comic timing; stereotypical characters; travesties of popular fiction (what Wodehouse called "bilge literature" and of which he was a voracious reader); and, above all, Wodehouse's own invented language. This last consists of odd personifications, a thorough confusion of vocabulary, an abundance of puns, and the wild similes and metaphors that transport both characters and readers far beyond the bounds of logical, or indeed sane, discourse. Wodehouse wrote several hundred short stories, most of which have astonishingly complex, farcical plots. Given the quantity and quality of such a fictional canon, a short survey can only enumerate the types of short stories Wodehouse wrote and attempt to give something of their flavor.

Stanley Featherstonehaugh Ukridge, the first of the comic heroes to populate Wodehouse's fictional world, appeared in the short stories collected in *Ukridge* (1924). With his yellow macintosh resembling "an animated blob of mustard," his glasses held together by ginger-beer wire, and his tendency to give a false name as "just an ordinary business precaution," Ukridge is the most amoral of Wodehouse's heroes. His amorality appears in continuing attempts to amass unearned wealth, as he is "profoundly stirred – as ever – by a tale of easy money." These schemes for easy money include "Ukridge's Dog College," devoted to training dogs (beginning with six Pekingese stolen from his aunt) to perform in music halls. "Ukridge's accident syndicate" seeks to swindle insurance companies by involving members of the syndicate in nonaccidental accidents. In "Ukridge Sees Her Through" the scheme involves selling to members of the Warner's Stores Social and Outing Club (a lower-class group) seven hundred tickets for the annual highbrow dance of the Pen and Ink Club (a group of pretentious writers), a scheme that considerably enlivens the club's dance; and in "Ukridge Rounds a Nasty Corner" Ukridge provides medicine to cure a supposedly sick parrot – which is actually suffering from a hangover induced by his having plied the bird with alcohol. Although Wodehouse always retained a partiality for Ukridge, the character was not so successful with readers, and Wodehouse wrote relatively few Ukridge stories after his first collection. Most of the other characters introduced in his fiction written between the wars, however, remained staples of Wodehouse's fiction.

Wodehouse's best work in the short story is in those family sagas narrated by Mr. Mulliner and the golf stories narrated by The Oldest Member, a sage who conjures up thoughts of Coleridge's Ancient Mariner in the minds of those usually unwilling audiences listening to him. In the Oldest Member's world, all persons and things are evaluated in terms of the golf course. He advises that "the only way . . . of really finding out a man's true character is to play golf with him," and he describes a pleasant morning as one on which "all nature shouted Fore!" and "the sun, peeping above the trees, looked like a giant golf-ball lofted by the mashie of some unseen god and about to drop dead by the pin of the eighteenth."

The essential pattern of these golf stories was set as early as Wodehouse's first such tale, "The Clicking of Cuthbert," in 1916. In this story Cuthbert Banks loves Adeline Smethurst, niece of Mrs. Willoughby Smetherst, president of the Wood Hills Literary and Debating Socicty. Wood Hills is divided into the warring camps of The Golfers and The Cultured, however, and Adeline is initially attracted to Raymond Parsloe Divine, a young novelist "more Russian than any other young English writer." The famous Russian novelist Vladimir Brusilloff, attending his eighty-second suburban literary party at Wood Hills, declares "No novelists anywhere any good except me" and showers contempt upon Devine, but when Brusilloff discovers that Cuthbert has played in the French Open, he calls Cuthbert a great man — and Adeline turns her favor upon the golfer. Devine leaves the neighborhood and begins writing scenarios for the Flicker Film Company; Cuthbert and Adeline marry, and Adeline becomes such an avid golfer that she wants to name their eldest son Abe Mitchell Ribbed-Face Mashie Banks.

The most notable of the later golf stories are those concerning Jane Packard, William Bates, and Rodney Spelvin ("Rodney Fails to Qualify," "Jane Gets Off the Fairway," "The Purification of Rodney Spelvin," and "Rodney Has a Relapse"). These stories trace the slow courtship of Jane and William, whose love rests securely on their mutual devotion to golf. Their romance is intermittently interrupted by Rodney Spelvin, a vers libre poet who appeals to Jane's romantic nature until Rodney, as a joke, makes his first drive on a golf course. He immediately becomes so addicted to the game that he gives up poetry to write lucrative mystery thrillers and marries William's sister Anastasia, who gives him golf lessons.

For sixty years Wodehouse continued writing variations on this plot of true love interrupted but saved by devotion to golf. Though these golf stories reflect Wodehouse's usual care and his great love for the game, there is an obvious sameness about them. This cannot be said of the Mr. Mulliner stories, for although they also follow certain patterns, the patterns admit a much greater variety of character, plot, and style.

Mr. Mulliner, who regales the habitués of the Angler's Rest Pub, is the perfect narrator for the de-

cidedly tall tales of the Mulliner saga, for like the proverbial fisherman, he is "traditionally careless of the truth." Mr. Mulliner seems to have as many nephews as Bertie Wooster has aunts; all of his relatives are paragons or prodigies of one kind or another, and they are used to parody the popular romance novels, "success" novels, and other fads and curiosities of the period. In "A Slice of Life" brother Wilfred Mulliner produces "Mulliner's Magic Marvels" cream potion. Nephew George Mulliner loves Angela Purdue, whose guardian, Sir Jasper ffinch-ffarrownere, wants her to marry his son, Percy, to keep money in the family. Wilfred, believing Angela's rejection letter to him has been forced, goes to Sir Jasper's home disguised as the valet, Straker. He finds that Angela is in hiding because Rover Gipsy Face-Cram has made her piebald, and he cures her with Snow of the Mountain lotion and wins Sir Jasper's good will with Mulliner's Reduc-O.

Typically, the perils of the melodramatic thriller — "Give me that key, you Fiend," and "Wilfred Mulliner, look upon your handiwork!" — are reduced by Wodehouse to problems that can be solved by love and ingenuity. Similarly, "Mulliner's Buck-U-Uppo," another of Wilfred's concoctions, comes to the aid of Augustine Mulliner, who loves Jane Brandon but fears her father, the Reverend Stanley Brandon. Angela sends Augustine some of Mulliner's Buck-U-Uppo, a tonic of "a slightly pungent flavor, rather like old boot-soles beaten up in sherry," and this so mightily emboldens Augustine that he performs such daring deeds as chasing away a dog who has treed a bishop and convincing the bishop's wife not to make her husband wear thick winter woolies on warm days. Augustine's heroism leads to his becoming the bishop's secretary and winning Jane. When his Uncle Wilfred sends Augustine a letter telling him not to use the potion, as it was meant for Indian elephants and not for humans, Augustine promptly orders three cases.

Perhaps the most typical and funny of these absurd love plots is found in "The Reverent Wooing of Archibald," concerning Archibald Mulliner's love for Aurelia Cammarleigh, whose aunt is devoted to proving that Sir Francis Bacon wrote Shakespeare's plays. Archibald's only real talent is his ability to imitate a hen laying an egg, but he tries to impress Aurelia and her aunt with his moral earnestness until he overhears Aurelia telling a friend that she would never marry anyone so stuffy and serious. Archibald then performs an overwhelming imitation of a hen laying an egg, admits to smoking and drinking, and wins Aurelia's love.

The Mulliner tales are clearly written to a formula, like all of Wodehouse's best short stories, but in these the formula permits a wide range of characters and situations. They show Wodehouse at the top of his form in inventing farcical plots and in using language, and his mastery of these fictional features is also apparent in two other Mulliner stories – "Unpleasantness at Bludleigh Court" and "Something Squishy." These are also of interest because they connect the Mulliner saga with Wodehouse's other fiction.

"Unpleasantness at Bludleigh Court" concerns, atypically, a Mulliner niece, Charlotte – a poet who loves Aubrey Trefusis, writer of *Pastels in Verse*. Aubrey's family cares only for hunting and shooting at Bludleigh Court, which, Aubrey insists, "exercises a spell" that arouses in anyone present a desire to kill things. An incredible parody of sentimental love talk between Aubrey and Charlotte ends when Aubrey suddenly starts beating at a rat with his parasol. Charlotte refuses to believe that this violence is a result of the spell, but her own poem, "Good Gnus," begins, "When cares attack and life seems black / How sweet it is to pot a yak," and is filled with hunting imagery highly unsuitable for the *Animal-Lovers Gazette,* where it is to appear. Since "all nature seemed to call to her to come out and kill things," Charlotte shoots Aubrey's Uncle Francis in the backside with an airgun while he is sunbathing, and since "the fascination of shooting as a sport depends almost wholly on whether you are at the right or wrong end of the gun," the colonel "with an agility which no gnu, unless in the very pink of condition, could have surpassed," escapes and hides behind the bishop of Stortford. The spell wears off, and Aubrey and Charlotte flee from Bludleigh Court – although Aubrey wistfully asks Charlotte about taking one more shot.

"Something Squishy" concerns the rivalry of Roland Attwater and Sir Claude Lynn for the hand of Roberta "Bobbie" Wickham, daughter of Mr. Mulliner's cousin. Roland's uncle wants him to marry Lucy, a quiet conventional girl. When an owner of a bird and snake shop in Seven Dials, a shopowner whose life Roland has once saved, sends him a snake, Bobbie – who "resembled a particularly good-looking schoolboy who had dressed up in his sister's clothes" – puts the snake in Sir Claude's bed. Roland sneaks into his room to retrieve it; Claude returns; Roland hides in a cupboard; the snake appears; and all is chaos. Bobbie Wickham refuses to marry Claude after seeing him in his mauve pajamas, and she is not interested in Roland, who runs away from her and is now ready for a quiet life with Lucy. These two stories, respectively, take us into Wodehouse's best-known fictional worlds – the world of Blanding Castle inhabited by Lord Emsworth and his family, and the world of the Drones Club and Mayfair inhabited by Bertie Wooster and Jeeves.

The Blandings Castle stories, like the novels, concern Lord Emsworth, an amiable and woolen-headed peer whose only desire is to be left alone to tend his prize sow, the Empress of Blandings, but whose home at Blandings Castle is constantly infested by his domineering sisters, his idiot son Freddie Threepwood, a steady succession of impostors visiting the castle under false pretenses, and especially by Rupert Baxter, a bespectacled young man whose efficiency drives Lord Emsworth to distraction. Of the relatively few Blandings short stories, "Lord Emsworth and the Girl Friend" is of interest because it comes as close to sentimentality as Wodehouse ever does. Two others are among the very best of Wodehouse's short stories. "The Crime Wave at Blandings" parodies the mystery thrillers Wodehouse loved in recounting how everyone from Lord Emsworth to Beach the butler ends up shooting Rupert Baxter with an air gun. In "Uncle Fred Flits By," Frederick Twistleton, Lord Ickenham – a friend of Lord Emsworth's brother Galahad – achieves his goal of "spreading sweetness and light" by entering a strange house to avoid a rain storm, pretending to be the owner, and so facilitating a marriage between two young people whose families oppose the match. Most of the Blandings stories, however, are not as successful as the Blandings novels, for the often incredibly intricate plot twists these tales depend on need more room for development than the short story provides, and even Wodehouse described the stories as "the short snorts between the solid orgies."

Despite the comfortably familiar humor of the Blandings stories and the variety and brilliance of the Mulliner saga, Wodehouse's best-known short stories remain those devoted to his best-known characters, Bertie Wooster and his gentleman's personal gentleman, Jeeves. Bertie, the quintessential silly young ass, would have a carefree life if he were not "impeded and generally snookered by about as scaly a collection of aunts as was ever assembled" – and if as a result of the machinations of these aunts he did not constantly find himself in situations from which Jeeves must rescue him. Indeed, with a change of proper name the title of the first Jeeves story, "Extricating Young Gussie," could describe all of the Jeeves tales, for in each of them Jeeves must extricate young Bertie from various absurd situations.

Low Wood, the Wodehouses' residence near Le Touquet, where they lived from 1935 until they were captured by the Germans in 1940

Jeeves must extricate Bertie and his fellow Drones Club members from the consequences of their usually ridiculous wagers – including those on which minister in a rural county will preach longest ("The Great Sermon Handicap") and on who will win the choirboys' Handicap Race ("The Purity of the Turf"). Jeeves generally must extricate Bertie from those unpleasant family situations "on the occasions when Aunt is calling to Aunt like mastodons bellowing across primeval swamps." Above all, Jeeves must rescue Bertie from a series of young women who are determined to marry and reform him – including such women as Florence Craye, "steeped to the gills in serious purpose"; Honoria Glossop, who is the daughter of the loony doctor Sir Roderick Glossop and "the sort of girl who reduces you to pulp with sixteen sets of tennis and a few rounds of golf and then comes down to dinner as fresh as a daisy expecting you to take an intelligent interest in Freud"; Madeline Bassett, an overly sentimental type given to such beliefs as that the stars are God's daisy chain; and Bobbie Wickham, the most dangerous because she is more interested in enlisting Bertie to help with her absurd schemes than in reforming him.

Jeeves can manage all the situations in which Bertie finds himself, because he acts on his beliefs that "employers are like horses. They require managing," and that "in an employer brains are not desirable." Jeeves thus finds Bertie the perfect employer, as "mentally he is negligible – quite negligible," though generous and good-hearted.

Wodehouse continued to write occasional short stories concerning all of his major characters, but after the war he concluded that the plots used in his short fiction could better serve as plots for his novels, and his production of short stories declined. Thus, his best and most productive time as a writer of short fiction falls during the period between the wars, at the end of which Wodehouse was honored by being made a doctor of letters by Oxford University in 1939.

Shortly after this honor came perhaps the only truly unpleasant time of Wodehouse's life. Wodehouse was unable to get out of Le Touquet, where he was living at the time that France fell to the Germans. On 21 July 1940 Germany decreed that all male aliens were to be interned, and Wodehouse was imprisoned in Tost, Upper Silesia. In June 1941 Wodehouse was to be released, because he was approaching the age at which all such internees were released, and CBS correspondent Harry Flannery arranged for Wodehouse to broadcast to America from a script written by Flannery.

The German Foreign Office then asked Wodehouse, using his own scripts, to make a series of broadcasts to America. Unfortunately Wodehouse agreed and broadcast a series of talks called "How to Be an Internee in Your Spare Time without Previous Experience." The talks treated his experiences in prison camp with Wodehouse's usual humor, and when read today seem harmless enough. But at the time the reaction of the British press and government approached hysteria. William Connor ("Cassandra" of the *Daily Mirror*) referred to Wodehouse as an "elderly playboy" and accused him of broadcasting Nazi propaganda, though Connor never mentioned what Wodehouse actually said in the broadcasts. Ironically, the U.S. War Department used recordings of the broadcasts as "models of anti-Nazi propaganda" in its intelligence school, but members of the British government were unforgiving. Their continued attacks on Wodehouse are described with bitter accuracy by Benny Green as "a conventional and indubitably English story of political chicanery and bureaucratic moral imbecility reacting to bumbling foolishness, of madness in triplicate conspiring with intellectual dishonesty to ruin a life."

After this bitter experience Wodehouse left England for New York in 1947. Malcolm Muggeridge described Wodehouse's reaction as that of "a man who has parted, in painful circumstances, from someone he loves and whom he both longs and dreads to see again." Wodehouse seldom spoke of the broadcasts later and at least publicly held no grudges. He became an American citizen in 1955 and never returned to England, although he frequently discussed doing so, especially when he was granted a knighthood on New Year's Day 1975. He remained on Long Island, New York, where he lived a happy life "Just writing one book after another." He was working on another novel, *Sunset at Blandings,* when he died on 14 February 1975.

Wodehouse did not receive much critical attention during his career, and he described himself as "a pretty insignificant sort of blister, not at all the type that leaves footprints on the sands of time," because "I go in for what is known in the trade as 'light writing' and those who do that — humorists they are some-

Wodehouse with his wife, Ethel, in Paris in 1945

times called — are looked down upon by the intelligentsia and sneered at." Other writers, however, to say nothing of millions of readers, have found in Wodehouse's world a wonderful escape from their own. Evelyn Waugh, in a broadcast of 15 July 1961 explained Wodehouse's continuing attraction:

For Mr. Wodehouse there has been no Fall of Man, no aboriginal calamity. His characters have never tasted the forbidden fruit. They are still in Eden. The Gardens of Blandings Castle are that original garden from which we are all exiled. The chef Anatole prepares the ambrosia for the immortals of high Olympus. Mr. Wodehouse's world can never stale. He will continue to release future generations from captivity that may be more irksome than our own. He has made a world for us to live in and delight in.

As early as 1935 Frank Swinnerton concluded, in a remark that is surely the best praise a humorist can receive, that Wodehouse was so popular because "in a period when laughter has been difficult, he has made men laugh without shame."

Bibliographies:

David A. Jasen, *A Bibliography and Reader's Guide to the First Editions of P. G. Wodehouse* (Hamden, Conn.: Archon, 1970);

Eileen McIlvaine, Louise S. Sherby, and James Heineman, *P. G. Wodehouse: A Comprehensive Bibliography and Checklist* (New York: Heineman, 1990).

Biographies:

David A. Jasen, *P. G. Wodehouse: A Portrait of a Master* (New York: Mason & Lipscomb, 1974; London: Garnstone, 1975);

Joseph Connolly, *P. G. Wodehouse: An Illustrated Biography with Complete Bibliography and Collector's Guide* (London: Orbis, 1979);

Benny Green, *P. G. Wodehouse: A Literary Biography* (London: Joseph, 1981);

Iain Sproat, *Wodehouse at War* (London: Milner, 1981);

Frances Donaldson, *P. G. Wodehouse: A Biography* (New York: Knopf, 1982);

Barry Phelps, *P. G. Wodehouse: Man and Myth* (London: Constable, 1992).

References:

Thelma Cazalet-Keir, ed., *Homage to P. G. Wodehouse* (London: Barrie & Jenkins, 1973);

Owen Dudley Edwards, *P. G. Wodehouse: A Critical and Historical Essay* (London: Brian & O'Keefe, 1977);

Thomas Edwards, "P. G. Wodehouse," *Raritan,* 7 (Winter 1988): 86–107;

Richard Harter Fogle, "Saki and Wodehouse," in *The English Short Story 1880–1945: A Critical History,* edited by Joseph M. Flora (Boston: Twayne, 1985), pp. 83–111;

R. B. D. French, *P. G. Wodehouse* (London: Oliver & Boyd, 1966; New York: Barnes & Noble, 1967);

Geoffrey Jaggard, *Blandings the Blest* (London: Macdonald, 1968);

Jaggard, *Wooster's World* (London: Macdonald, 1967);

Robert A. Hall, *The Comic Style of P. G. Wodehouse* (Hamden, Conn: Archon, 1974);

Richard Usborne, *Wodehouse at Work to the End* (London: Barrie & Jenkins, 1976);

Richard Voorhees, *P. G. Wodehouse* (New York: Twain, 1966);

Evelyn Waugh, "An Act of Homage and Reparation to P. G. Wodehouse," *Sunday Times Magazine,* 16 July 1961, pp. 21, 23;

Herbert Warren Wind, *The World of P. G. Wodehouse* (New York: Praeger, 1972; London: Hutchinson, 1981).

Virginia Woolf

(25 January 1882 – 28 March 1941)

Susan Dick
Queen's University

See also the Woolf entries in *DS 10: The Bloomsbury Group; DLB 36: British Novelists, 1890–1929: Modernists;* and *DLB 100: Modern British Essayists, Second Series.*

BOOKS: *The Voyage Out* (London: Duckworth, 1915; revised edition, New York: Doran, 1920; London: Duckworth, 1920);

The Mark on the Wall (Richmond, Surrey: Hogarth Press, 1917);

Kew Gardens (Richmond, Surrey: Hogarth Press, 1919);

Night and Day (London: Duckworth, 1919; New York: Doran, 1920);

Monday or Tuesday (Richmond, Surrey: Hogarth Press, 1921; New York: Harcourt, Brace, 1921);

Jacob's Room (Richmond, Surrey: Hogarth Press, 1922; New York: Harcourt, Brace, 1923);

Mr. Bennett and Mrs. Brown (London: Hogarth Press, 1924);

The Common Reader (London: Hogarth Press, 1925; New York: Harcourt, Brace, 1925);

Mrs. Dalloway (London: Hogarth Press, 1925; New York: Harcourt, Brace, 1925);

To the Lighthouse (London: Hogarth Press, 1927; New York: Harcourt, Brace, 1927);

Orlando: A Biography (New York: Crosby Gaige, 1928; London: Hogarth Press, 1928);

A Room of One's Own (New York: Fountain Press / London: Hogarth Press, 1929; New York: Harcourt, Brace, 1929);

Street Haunting (San Francisco: Westgate Press, 1930);

On Being Ill (London: Hogarth Press, 1930);

Beau Brummell (New York: Rimington & Hooper, 1930);

The Waves (London: Hogarth Press, 1931; New York: Harcourt, Brace, 1931);

A Letter to a Young Poet (London: Hogarth Press, 1932; Folcroft, Pa.: Folcroft, 1932);

Virginia Woolf in 1939 (photograph by Gisèle Freund)

The Common Reader: Second Series (London: Hogarth Press, 1932); republished as *The Second Common Reader* (New York: Harcourt, Brace, 1932);

Flush: A Biography (London: Hogarth Press, 1933; New York: Harcourt, Brace, 1933);

Walter Sickert: A Conversation (London: Hogarth Press, 1934);

The Roger Fry Memorial Exhibition: An Address (Letchsworth, Hertsford: Garden City Press, 1935);

The Years (London: Hogarth Press, 1937; New York: Harcourt, Brace, 1937);

Three Guineas (London: Hogarth Press, 1938; New York: Harcourt, Brace, 1938);

Reviewing (London: Hogarth Press, 1939; Folcroft, Pa.: Folcroft, 1969);

Roger Fry: A Biography (London: Hogarth Press, 1940; New York: Harcourt, Brace, 1940);

Between the Acts (London: Hogarth Press, 1941; New York: Harcourt, Brace, 1941);

The Death of the Moth and Other Essays (London: Hogarth Press, 1942; New York: Harcourt, Brace, 1942);

A Haunted House and Other Short Stories (London: Hogarth Press, 1944; New York: Harcourt, Brace, 1944);

The Moment and Other Essays (London: Hogarth Press, 1947; New York: Harcourt, Brace, 1948);

The Captain's Death Bed and Other Essays (New York: Harcourt, Brace, 1950; London: Hogarth Press, 1950);

A Writer's Diary: Being Extracts from the Diary of Virginia Woolf, edited by Leonard Woolf (London: Hogarth Press, 1953; New York: Harcourt, Brace, 1954);

Hours in a Library (New York: Harcourt, Brace, 1958);

Granite and Rainbow: Essays by Virginia Woolf (London: Hogarth Press, 1958; New York: Harcourt, Brace, 1958); republished as *Granite and Rainbow: Essays* (New York: Harcourt, Brace, 1975);

Contemporary Writers (London: Hogarth Press, 1965; New York: Harcourt, Brace & World, 1966);

Nurse Lugton's Golden Thimble (London: Hogarth Press, 1966);

Collected Essays, 4 volumes (London: Hogarth Press, 1966–1967; New York: Harcourt, Brace & World, 1967);

Stephen Versus Gladstone (Headington Quarry, 1967);

A Cockney's Farming Experiences, edited by Suzanne Henig (San Diego: San Diego State University Press, 1972);

Mrs. Dalloway's Party: A Short Story Sequence, edited by Stella McNichol (London: Hogarth Press, 1973; New York: Harcourt, Brace & World, 1975);

The London Scene: Five Essays (New York: Hallman, 1975);

The Waves: The Two Holograph Drafts, edited by John W. Graham (Toronto: University of Toronto Press, 1976);

Moments of Being: Unpublished Autobiographical Writings, edited by Jeanne Schulkind (Sussex: University Press, 1976; New York & London: Harcourt Brace Jovanovich, 1977; revised and enlarged edition, London: Hogarth Press, 1985);

Freshwater: A Comedy, edited by Lucio P. Ruotolo (New York & London: Harcourt Brace Jovanovich, 1976; London: Hogarth Press, 1976);

The Diary of Virginia Woolf, 5 volumes, edited by Anne Olivier Bell (London: Hogarth Press, 1977–1984; New York & London: Harcourt Brace Jovanovich, 1977–1984);

Books and Portraits, edited by Mary Lyon (London: Hogarth Press, 1977; New York & London: Harcourt Brace Jovanovich, 1978); republished as *Some Further Selections from the Literary and Biographical Writings of Virginia Woolf: Books and Portraits* (N.p.: Panther Books, 1979);

The Pargiters, edited by Mitchell A. Leaska (New York: New York Public Library, 1977; London: Hogarth Press, 1978);

Virginia Woolf's Reading Notebooks, edited by Brenda R. Silver (Princeton, N.J. & Guildford, Surrey: Princeton University Press, 1982);

Melymbrosia: An Early Version of The Voyage Out, edited by Louise A. DeSalvo (New York: New York Public Library, 1982);

To the Lighthouse: The Original Holograph Draft, edited by Susan Dick (Toronto: University of Toronto Press, 1982; London: Hogarth Press, 1982);

'Pointz Hall': The Earlier and Later Typescripts of 'Between the Acts,' edited by Leaska (New York: University Publications, 1983);

The Complete Shorter Fiction, edited by Dick (London: Hogarth Press, 1985; New York: Harcourt Brace Jovanovich, 1985; expanded and revised, London: Hogarth Press, 1989; New York: Harcourt Brace Jovanovich, 1989);

The Essays of Virginia Woolf, 4 volumes, edited by Andrew McNeillie (London: Hogarth Press, 1986–1993; San Diego: Harcourt Brace Jovanovich, 1986–1993);

A Passionate Apprentice: The Early Journals, 1897–1909, edited by Leaska (London: Hogarth Press, 1990; San Diego: Harcourt Brace Jovanovich, 1990);

Women & Fiction: The Manuscript Versions of 'A Room of One's Own,' edited by S. P. Rosenbaum (Oxford: Blackwell, 1992).

OTHER: Fyodor M. Dostoyevsky, *Stavrogin's Confession and the Plan of the Life of a Great Sinner,* translated by Woolf and S. S. Koteliansky (Richmond, Surrey: Hogarth Press, 1922); republished as *Stavrogin's Confession* (New York: Lear, 1947);

Paul Biryukov, *Tolstoi's Love Letters, with a Study on the Autobiographical Elements in Tolstoi's Work,* translated by Woolf and Koteliansky (Richmond, Surrey: Hogarth Press, 1923);

A. B. Goldenveizer, *Talks with Tolstoi,* translated by Woolf and Koteliansky (Richmond, Surrey: Hogarth Press, 1923);

Julia Margaret Cameron, *Victorian Photographs of Famous Men & Fair Women,* introductions by Woolf and Roger Fry (London: Hogarth Press, 1926; New York: Harcourt, Brace, 1927); expanded and revised edition, edited by Tristram Powell (London: Hogarth Press, 1973);

Laurence Sterne, *A Sentimental Journey through France and Italy,* introduction by Woolf (London: Humphrey Milford, 1928);

George Gissing, *Selections Autobiographical and Imaginative,* introduction by Woolf (London: Cape, 1929);

Vanessa Bell, *Recent Paintings by Vanessa Bell,* foreword by Woolf (London: London Artists' Association, 1930);

Co-operative Working Women, *Life as We Have Known It,* introductory letter by Woolf (London: Hogarth Press, 1931);

Bell, *Catalogue of Recent Paintings by Vanessa Bell,* foreword by Woolf (London: Reid & Lefevre, 1934).

Although Virginia Woolf published only eighteen works of short fiction, she was engaged in writing short stories, sketches, and even experimental prose poems throughout her writing career. Recent research has shown that the eighteen published pieces are but a fraction of the total number of stories and sketches Woolf wrote. *The Complete Shorter Fiction* (1985) contains forty-six complete works as well as a dozen incomplete ones by Woolf. These range from four stories written in 1906 (when Woolf, who was twenty-four years old and already an accomplished reviewer, turned her attention to the writing of fiction) to two sketches written early in 1941, only a few weeks before her death. Short-

Virginia and Leonard Woolf in 1914

fiction writing was always important to her, for her shorter works were often testing grounds for themes, characters, prose styles, and narrative techniques she developed at greater length in her novels.

Born in London, Virginia Woolf was the third child of Julia and Leslie Stephen. While her brothers, Thoby and Adrian, were sent to school, Virginia and her sister, Vanessa, were taught at home by their parents and by tutors. Theirs was a highly literary family. Sir Leslie Stephen, philosopher, critic, and editor of the *Dictionary of National Biography* (1882–1891), encouraged Virginia to read widely and freely in his extensive library. Julia Stephen wrote children's stories that Leslie Stephen sometimes illustrated, and from an early age Virginia Stephen also wrote stories and kept a journal.

Woolf's earliest extant stories, the four written in 1906, are apprentice pieces, literary exercises in the art of telling a story, which she appears to have made no attempt to publish. In them she experiments with various narrative voices and forms. The earliest story, untitled but now known as "Phyllis and Rosamond," is an account of two "daughters at home," familiar types at the turn of the century, the narrator tells us, whose story has seldom been told. This is the first of many works by Woolf that explores what one of the characters in her first novel, *The Voyage Out* (1915), calls "this curious silent unrepresented life" of women.

The narrator tells their story by first generalizing about the pattern of their day and then focusing on a few scenes: a luncheon given for a prospective suitor, a party they attend with their parents, and then another party that they attend alone in "distant and unfashionable" Bloomsbury. These social occasions anticipate the many luncheons, teas, dinners, and parties that occur in Woolf's later stories and novels. She recognized early in her career the great narrative potential afforded by the party. Her characters meet new people and new ideas at her parties, and often these encounters give rise to unexpected revelations.

In this story Phyllis and Rosamond glimpse at the final party a world totally unlike their own. The sisters' lives are shaped by the assumption that their future is marriage. The people they meet at the party live far freer lives, and marriage for them is possible but by no means inevitable. The sisters return home enlightened and saddened by their brief excursion into a more open way of life that will never be theirs.

In writing this story Woolf drew upon her own unhappy experiences during the period between the deaths of her mother in 1895 and of her father in 1904, when her half brother, George Duckworth, insisted that the reluctant Stephen sisters accompany him to evening parties in the drawing rooms of his fashionable friends. When Vanessa and Virginia Stephen moved to Bloomsbury soon after their father's death, they freed themselves from George's attentions and began to enjoy the freer life denied Phyllis and Rosamond.

The second early story, "The Mysterious Case of Miss V.," is a shorter, slighter piece in which Woolf explores another aspect of contemporary London life: the isolation and anonymity that threaten one who lives in a large city. The narrative voice Woolf uses in this story closely resembles that of her early essays and reviews, and she may have written this with plans to publish it. The Miss V. of the title is a woman whom the narrator does not actually know but has become accustomed to seeing at concerts and other functions. The impetus for the story is the narrator's realization that she has not seen Miss V. lately. One morning after awakening at dawn and calling out, "Mary V., Mary V.!!," the narrator feels compelled to go to Miss V.'s flat. There she discovers that Miss V. has died, perhaps

at the precise moment that the narrator awoke calling her name. This curious story looks forward to the mysterious pairings of characters that occur in some of Woolf's later works, as in the uncanny sympathy that links Clarissa Dalloway to Septimus Warren Smith in *Mrs. Dalloway* (1925).

Such sympathetic pairing also occurs in the most ambitious of Woolf's early stories, untitled but now known as "The Journal of Mistress Joan Martyn." Woolf wrote this in August 1906, while she and her sister, Vanessa, were staying at Blo' Norton Hall, the Elizabethan manor house in Norfolk that became the setting of the story. Woolf creates two distinctive voices in this work. The first is that of Rosamond Merridew, a medieval historian who relates in the opening pages how, having been offered several medieval records of the Martyn family to read, she chose the journal of Joan Martyn. The journal then begins. The contrast between the vigorous, self-assured voice of the middle-aged historian and the contemplative, poetic style of the young diarist is striking. Joan Martyn never comments on her reasons for keeping this journal, which covers a single year, nor does she contemplate its being read in the future. This absence of self-consciousness — so different from Rosamond Merridew's spirited defense of her methods — contributes to the vivid impression Woolf creates of the young fifteenth-century "daughter at home."

The fourth early story, "A Dialogue Upon Mount Pentelicus," contrasts sharply to the three previous ones, for it is set in Greece, not in England; its unnamed characters are all men, and its narrator, who could be male or female, is aloof from the scene rather than its sympathetic observer or a participant in it. Woolf apparently wrote this story soon after she had returned from visiting Greece in the autumn of 1906 with her sister, Vanessa, and brothers, Thoby and Adrian. The narrative turns on the moment when the sudden appearance of a monk from a nearby monastery interrupts six Englishmen who are descending Mount Pentelicus and discussing the glories of ancient Greece and the contrasting barbarism of Greece now. Although the monk's only contribution to the dialogue is the Greek equivalent of "good evening," his intense gaze makes the Englishmen feel that they are experiencing the spirit of ancient Greece not as history studied in their distant English university, but as a living presence. Their glib generalizations about the decay of modern Greece are silenced by the encounter. This is one of many dialogues in Woolf's writings in which what is said is overshadowed by something that is unsaid — something that resides, as she put it in her essay "On Not Knowing Greek" (1925), on "the far side of language."

Woolf had begun publishing essays and reviews in 1904, so when she wrote the last of the early short fictions, "Memoirs of a Novelist" (1909), she was an experienced reviewer. She draws upon that experience in this work, an amusing "review" of an imaginary biography by a Miss Linsett – who has written about her friend, Miss Willatt, an imaginary nineteenth-century novelist. Woolf clearly had fun writing "Memoirs of a Novelist," which she hoped would be the first in a series of fictional portraits she would write. The editor of *Cornhill Magazine,* to whom she submitted it, turned it down, however, and she seems to have written no others.

Miss Linsett failed as a biographer, Woolf 's reviewer argues, for lack of imagination. While claiming to have known her well, Miss Linsett was unable to discover the person whom the reviewer believes to have been the real Miss Willatt – the one who existed behind the facade of pious platitudes that abound in her works, popular romances with titles such as *Lindamara: A Fantasy.* Similarly, the reviewer argues, Miss Willatt failed to reflect in her writings the ordinary life around her, for she "thought it indecent to describe what she had seen." The reviewer's lively scorn of Miss Linsett's biography and Miss Willatt's romances reflects Woolf's own impatience with nineteenth-century literary conventions, both of style and subject matter, which threw up barriers between the writer (and thus the reader) and reality.

Woolf began her own efforts to dismantle those barriers in her first novel, *The Voyage Out,* which she wrote between 1907 and 1913. She appears to have written no short fiction other than "Memoirs of a Novelist" during this time. Her personal life was especially demanding during those years. In August 1912 she married Leonard Woolf, who had been at Cambridge with her brother Thoby and who had recently returned from a civil-service post in Ceylon. *The Voyage Out* was accepted for publication in the spring of 1913, but it was not published until two years later because of Virginia Woolf's mental illness. This began early in 1912, became acute in September 1913 (when she attempted suicide), and lasted into 1916. During her recuperation in 1916 she began her second novel, *Night and Day* (1919), and while she was writing it she also wrote the short work that initiated an extremely fruitful period of short-fiction writing for her. This was "The Mark on the Wall," which was published along with Leonard Woolf's "Three

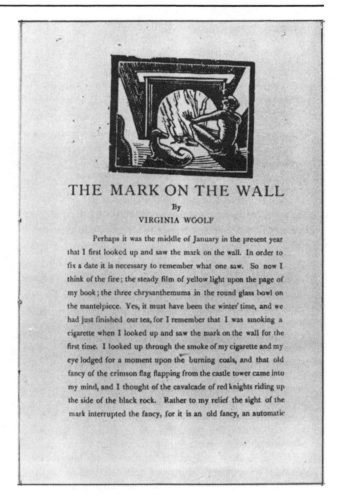

The first page of Virginia Woolf's contribution to Two Stories *(1917), the first book that the Woolfs published at their Hogarth Press*

Jews" in *Two Stories* (1917), the first publication of the Woolfs' fledgling Hogarth Press.

"The Mark on the Wall" is more a fictional reverie than a traditional short story with characters, incidents, and plot – a reverie that has affinities with the informal personal essays of Montaigne, Charles Lamb, Thomas De Quincey, and others. The entire piece re-creates the wide-ranging thoughts the narrator had one day while sitting in her chair by the fire and contemplating a mysterious mark on the wall. Although it begins in the past tense and is cast as a memory, most of "The Mark on the Wall" is narrated in the present tense, thus giving the impression that the reader is overhearing the narrator's thoughts as she thinks them, rather than as she remembers having thought them. Her periodic shifts of attention back to the vexatious mark and her languid refusal to get out of her chair and see what it is ground this "flight of the mind" (to use one of Woolf 's phrases) in a particular time and place and contribute to the playfulness in it. The reader senses the liberation Woolf told her friend Ethel Smyth that she had felt as she wrote this piece — "all in a flash," she recalled in a letter on 16 October 1930, "as if flying, after being kept stone breaking for months."

While visiting Perugia in 1908, Woolf had written a passage in her journal in which she had anticipated showing in her work "all the traces of the minds passage through the world; . . . the flight of the mind," but until she wrote "The Mark on the Wall" she had not found a way to do that. She may have been led toward her discovery of this new narrative method by the Russian writers she was reading and reviewing in the new translations by Constance Garnett that were then being published. In "More Dostoevsky," a 22 February 1917 *Times Literary Supplement* review of Fyodor Dostoyevsky's *The Eternal Husband and Other Stories,* Woolf marveled at the way Dostoyevsky presents the processes of thought. Her description of his method could characterize her own in "The Mark on the Wall." "Alone among writers Dostoevsky has the power of reconstructing those most swift and complicated states of mind," she wrote, the power

> of rethinking the whole train of thought in all its speed, now as it flashes into light, now as it lapses into darkness; for he is able to follow not only the vivid streak of achieved thought, but to suggest the dim and populous underworld of the mind's consciousness where desires and impulses are moving blindly beneath the sod. Just as we awaken ourselves from a trance of this kind by striking a chair or a table to assure ourselves of an external reality, so Dostoevsky suddenly makes us behold, for an instant, the face of his hero, or some object in the room.

Woolf felt that Dostoyevsky, like Anton Chekhov, whose "inconclusive" stories also deeply impressed her, looked at the soul. By contrast, the English novelists who were her immediate precursors, Woolf would repeatedly argue, preoccupied themselves with appearances.

Woolf wrote other experimental short fiction at this time — "The Evening Party," which is narrated mainly in dialogue; "Sympathy," in which the narrator reacts to the news of a friend's death; and "Cracked Fiddles," a series of prose poem sketches. But it was "The Mark on the Wall" that she published and later recognized as the first in a series of three works that formed a bridge leading from her largely conventional first two novels to her radically experimental third one, *Jacob's Room* (1922): ". . . conceive mark on the wall, K[ew]. G[ardens]. &

unwritten novel taking hands & dancing in unity," she wrote in her diary on 26 January 1920, the day she discovered "a new form for a new novel" would eventually become *Jacob's Room.*

"Kew Gardens," first published in 1919 by the Hogarth Press with woodcuts by Woolf's sister, the painter Vanessa Bell, was probably written in the summer of 1918, while Woolf was at work on *Night and Day.* In contrast to "The Mark on the Wall," which is shaped by the flight of the narrator's mind, "Kew Gardens" is a carefully patterned work narrated by an impersonal narrator who takes no part in the scenes described. The narrator's attention shifts from the intricate world of a flower bed, in which a snail is slowly progressing from one side to the other, to the thoughts and conversations of four couples as they pass by it.

This juxtaposing of scenes also juxtaposes ways of seeing. In the opening paragraph Woolf seems to be experimenting with what might be called pure description. The flowers are described as if they are being seen by someone who has never seen flowers before. The shapes and brilliant colors of the leaves and petals are presented with painterly care, and, as in a painting, they are unnamed. These are not roses or lilies or carnations but colored, living objects. Only the snail is identified.

The transition from the flower bed to the people in the garden is made by way of perception: as the breeze stirs the flowers, the color is "flashed . . . into the eyes of the men and women who walk in Kew Gardens in July." In describing what these people see and say, the narrator adopts their points of view and enters freely into their minds. Thus throughout the story Woolf juxtaposes the objective description of the flower bed, to which the narrator regularly returns, and brief scenes in which the characters see their own preoccupations reflected in the world around them. Such carefully patterned shifts of perspective, which occur throughout *Jacob's Room,* became a hallmark of Woolf's fiction.

The third work that Woolf wrote at this time and named in the 1920 diary entry quoted above, "An Unwritten Novel," was, she later recalled in her letter to Ethel Smyth, "the great discovery." It "showed me," she added, "how I could embody all my deposit of experience in a shape that fitted it." The "shape" closely resembles that of "The Mark on the Wall," for, like the earlier work, this one begins with the narrator perceiving something in front of her that initiates a richly imaginative train of thought. The impetus for the thoughts in this story, however, is another person, a woman sitting opposite the narrator during a train journey to East-

Frontispiece and title page for Kew Gardens, *experimental narratives by Woolf, illustrated with two woodcuts by her sister, Vanessa Bell*

bourne. The unwritten novel is the story the narrator tells herself as she imagines a life for her fellow passenger, whom she silently names "Minnie Marsh."

The situation is one Woolf would use again in a modified way in a later story, "The Shooting Party." It is also a central metaphor in "Character in Fiction" (1924), a talk she first gave in 1923 under the title "Mr. Bennett and Mrs. Brown" and then published as an essay in which she explored the major but changing role of character in fiction. "I believe that all novels begin with an old lady in the corner opposite," she stated. "I believe that all novels, that is to say, deal with character." The challenge that the writer faces, Woolf explained, is to find a way to portray character – character embodied in the essay in the figure of Mrs. Brown and in "An Unwritten Novel" in Minnie Marsh. Woolf argues in "Character in Fiction," as she had in her

earlier essay "Modern Novels" (1919), that the methods used by Edwardian novelists such as Arnold Bennett, John Galsworthy, and H. G. Wells tell much about the material world of their characters but little about what the Russian writers had succeeded so well in portraying, a character's soul. "An Unwritten Novel" brilliantly chronicles the challenges that Woolf felt her generation of writers faced as they attempted to find a fictional method that would enable them to write about this elusive subject.

Throughout the story the narrator struggles with the constraints of conventional realism. She assumes that these oblige her, for example, to clutter her story with the impedimenta of the middle-class world in which she has placed her heroine. It is "all a matter of crusts and cruets, frills and ferns," she says after toying with the notion of including a rhododendron in her scene – a flower that, she must admit, is unlikely to be found in Eastbourne in December. The narrator's struggle with the conventions of storytelling is a story in itself, and it develops in amusing counterpoint to the imagined life of "Minnie Marsh."

A story for Minnie does get told, and her elusive soul is celebrated by the narrator, who is undaunted at the end by the discovery that the unhappy life she has imagined in such detail probably bears no resemblance to her traveling companion's actual circumstances. The "mysterious figures" who walk away from the train – "Minnie Marsh" and her son – are representative of the subjects this novelist will continue to celebrate.

Woolf published "An Unwritten Novel" in the July 1920 *London Mercury* and then reprinted it, along with "The Mark on the Wall" and "Kew Gardens," in *Monday or Tuesday,* a collection of eight works of short fiction (illustrated with four woodcuts by Vanessa Bell) that the Hogarth Press published in 1921. This was the first full-length book that the Hogarth Press published, the only collection of short fiction that Woolf ever published, and the only one of her books never reprinted. Leonard Woolf included six of the works from it in *A Haunted House and Other Short Stories,* a collection of eighteen stories that he brought out in 1944, three years after his wife's death. He did not include "A Society" or "Blue & Green," for he assumed that Woolf had not wanted to reprint them. (Besides the other six stories from *Monday or Tuesday,* he included seven stories that had appeared in periodicals and five stories that had not been published before.)

With the exception of "A Society," the stories in *Monday or Tuesday* all reflect Woolf's desire to "invent a competely new form" in fiction, as she wrote to David Garnett on 26 July 1917. The opening story, "A Haunted House," is a lyrical evocation of the narrator's sense of the benign ghosts with whom she shares her house. "A Haunted House" is followed by "A Society," a long story written in a spirited, direct style that resembles that of *Night and Day.* The narrator, Cassandra, joins a group of her friends in a quest to discover to what extent men can attain the "objects of life," which the friends judge to be the production of "good people and good books." Men do not fare well in the story, especially when World War I, which is seen to be men's latest production, interrupts the society's researches. Their question, "Why do men go to war?," is left unanswered.

An overtly feminist work, "A Society" was a bold statement for a woman writer to make in 1921, as Woolf knew. In "The Mark on the Wall," which is placed last in *Monday or Tuesday,* the narrator imagines a world in which the "masculine point of view . . . will be laughed into the dustbin where the phantoms go, . . . leaving us all with an intoxicating sense of illegitimate freedom – if," she adds, "freedom exists." "A Society" presents some compelling reasons for desiring that overthrow.

"A Society" is followed by the one-page title story, "Monday or Tuesday." The phrase *Monday or Tuesday* suggested to Woolf the randomness of our impressions of an ordinary day. As the "myriad impressions" that the mind receives "shape themselves into the life of Monday or Tuesday," Woolf wrote in "Modern Fiction" (1925), "the accent falls differently from of old." "Monday or Tuesday," which along with "Blue & Green" has some affinities with the prose poem, illustrates one way that new accent may fall. In the opening paragraph the narrator's vision moves beyond the "lazy and indifferent" heron flying across the London skyline and adopts the Olympian perspective of the sky itself. This expansion of vision, which recalls the "flight of the mind" in "The Mark on the Wall," may be the impulse behind the desire for "truth" that is repeated in the following brief paragraphs. This desire draws the narrator toward abstraction and away from the immediate scene; that scene, like the mark on the wall and the figure of "Minnie Marsh," periodically reasserts its presence. Woolf's flights always return to solid ground.

"Monday or Tuesday" is followed by "An Unwritten Novel" and then by "The String Quartet," a story in which the narrator searches for ways to describe her impressions while attending a performance of a string quartet. Woolf's experiment with translating impressions of music into words recalls her friend E. M. Forster's description in *Howards End* (1910) of the visual images evoked in Helen Schlegel's mind by Beethoven's Fifth Symphony. T. S. Eliot told Woolf that he especially liked this story, and this may be because it also recalls how, in some of his early poems that the Hogarth Press had published, Eliot found in music analogies for subtle states of feeling.

The images awakened by music give way in the next piece, "Blue & Green," to images that particular colors may suggest. In her letter to Ethel Smyth, Woolf dismissed both "Monday or Tuesday" and this two-paragraph experiment in verbal painting as "mere tangles of words." While "Blue & Green" is certainly the most obscure piece in the collection, it does effectively set the scene for the story that follows it – "Kew Gardens," the penultimate story in *Monday or Tuesday.* In "Kew Gardens" the colors and shapes of the flowers form major elements in the story's overall design.

The failure of the reviewer for the *Times Literary Supplement* to see that in *Monday or Tuesday* Woolf was "after something interesting," as she noted in her diary on 8 April 1921, did not deter her. She continued writing *Jacob's Room,* a novel composed of many brief, often loosely related scenes. While revising her novel Woolf removed one chapter that she later published in *Atalanta's Garland* (1926) as a separate story called "A Woman's College from Outside." She wrote another highly experimental story called "In the Orchard" (*Criterion,* 1923), in which the same scene is described three times with slight but significant changes of emphasis. And in October 1922 she began to write her next novel. This would be composed, she first thought, of six or seven chapters that would be independent, yet also somehow related. She finished the first of these, the story "Mrs. Dalloway in Bond Street" (*The Dial,* 1923), and began the second, "The Prime Minister," but then abandoned her plan and wrote *Mrs. Dalloway,* which has no chapter divisions at all.

While writing "Mrs. Dalloway in Bond Street" Woolf discovered the narrative method she would use with such success in *Mrs. Dalloway, To the Lighthouse* (1927), and the short fiction closely related to these novels. The narrator moves with ease inside the characters' minds and narrates their thoughts, perceptions, and emotions as these occur. As Big Ben chimes eleven in the morning, Mrs. Dalloway leaves her house and walks to Bond Street , where she buys a pair of gloves. She thinks about the scene around her and about events in her past that the immediate scene brings to mind. These brief and unconnected memories give the reader glimpses of Mrs. Dalloway's past but tell no complete story. Writing in her diary on 15 October 1923, Woolf called this use of memory her "tunnelling process, by which," she observed, "I tell the past by instalments, as I have need of it." It had taken her a "year's groping," she noted, to discover it. One can see seeds of this method in some of Woolf's earlier short narratives, especially in "The Mark on the Wall" and "Kew Gardens."

Woolf wrote the first draft of her children's story, "Nurse Lugton's Curtain," while she was writing *Mrs. Dalloway,* and she may also have written her only other extant children's story, "The Widow and the Parrot: A True Story," during this period. ("Nurse Lugton's Curtain" is an early version of *Nurse Lugton's Golden Thimble* (1966), and it has been collected in its early version in *The Com-*

plete Shorter Fiction.) These lively tales not only exhibit Woolf's flair for fun and fantasy, but in their playful use of animals they also recall the children's stories that her mother had told.

As soon as she finished *Mrs. Dalloway,* Woolf returned to her earlier plan of writing a series of stories. She quickly wrote a group of eight, all of which are set at Mrs. Dalloway's party. These include "The New Dress," "Happiness," "Ancestors," "The Introduction," "Together and Apart," "The Man Who Loved His Kind," "A Simple Melody," and "A Summing Up." Woolf wrote in her diary on 27 April 1925 that she was interested in exploring various states of consciousness in these stories, for "my present reflection," she wrote, "is that people have any number of states of consciousness: & I should like to investigate the party consciousness, the frock consciousness &c." In each story she focuses on one or two characters at the party. Their private dramas are portrayed through a mixture of description, dialogue, and the narration of their thoughts. Each story relies less on action as a unifying device than "Mrs. Dalloway in Bond Street" had, and in each Woolf uses the functions of memory more extensively than she had in the earlier story. Woolf employs her "tunnelling process" to great effect in these brief stories, as the characters recall particular moments from the past that contribute to their present states of consciousness.

In "Together and Apart," for example, memories of Canterbury unite two middle-aged people who meet for the first time at Mrs. Dalloway's party. Casting about for something to say to the reputedly "falsely melancholy" writer Mr. Serle, Miss Anning recalls, "There was a Miss Serle who lived at Canterbury when I was a girl there." After Mr. Serle tells her that his ancestors came from that city, she asks, "Do you know Canterbury yourself?" Only the reader, who overhears Mr. Serle's thoughts, knows that "the best years of his life, all his memories, things he had never been able to tell anybody, but had tried to write – ah, had tried to write (and he sighed) all had centred in Canterbury: it made him laugh."

Miss Anning is equally guarded and does not at first want to tell Mr. Serle that the three months she spent in Canterbury as a child had been "amazing." Soon, however, she persuades herself to overcome her habitual reticence and tell him the truth: "I loved Canterbury," she says. Her unexpected admission creates one of the brief moments when the essential loneliness of the characters in these stories is overcome. "Their eyes met," the narrator says; "collided rather, for each felt that behind the eyes the secluded being, who sits in darkness while his shallow agile companion does all the tumbling and beckoning, and keeps the show going, suddenly stood erect; flung off his cloak; confronted the other. It was alarming; it was terrific." This confrontation is soon over and the characters are apart again, but its occurrence is significant, and probably memorable, for them both.

Woolf submitted only "The New Dress" for publication, and it appeared in the American periodical *Forum* in 1927. The editor of *Forum,* H. G. Leach, had apparently raised some objections to the story when Woolf had sent it to him in July 1925, so when in October of that year he asked her if she had any more stories, she replied, "The stories I have at present are much in the same style as The New Dress and are open to the same objections." She would not waste his time, she said, by submitting them. Although the rest of the stories would remain unpublished for many years, from Woolf's point of view they had served their main purpose. In a notebook in which she outlined this series of stories she observed that they might provide a corridor leading from *Mrs. Dalloway* to a new book. That book was *To the Lighthouse,* which she began to write in August 1925.

Between the time she finished *To the Lighthouse* in the autumn of 1926 and her death in March 1941, Woolf wrote at least seventeen stories and sketches. These can be divided into two groups: eight stories that Woolf wrote for publication and nine less polished sketches that she seems not to have considered publishing. She was by this time a widely read novelist and critic, and though she wrote less short fiction during these years than she had before, she continued to find it a challenging and useful vehicle for some of the many ideas that constantly came to her – ideas both for stories and for new ways to tell them.

Of the eight stories Woolf wrote for publication, only five were actually published. The first of these, "Moments of Being: 'Slater's Pins Have No Points'" was one of the "side stories" that were "sprouting in great variety," she noted in her diary on 5 September 1926, as she finished *To the Lighthouse.* Like many of the later stories, this one grew from her memory of a scene. She might now write a "book of characters," she noted in her diary, "the whole string being pulled out from some simple sentence, like Clara Pater's, 'Don't you find that Barker's pins have no points to them?'" Clara Pater had been Woolf's Greek tutor, and her simple observation must have been for Woolf a key to her character.

In this story Fanny Wilmot's music teacher, Julia Craye, comments on the bluntness of Slater's pins when a rose falls out of Fanny's dress. While Fanny searches for the fallen pin, she thinks about Miss Craye's observation and then proceeds to speculate about her teacher's life. The situation recalls that in "An Unwritten Novel," but in this story the two women are much more closely linked than in the earlier one. The story ends when Fanny, finding the pin, glances up to see a look of exquisite happiness on Julia Craye's face. Miss Craye's sudden kiss confirms Fanny's realization that her teacher is not the lonely woman Fanny had imagined her to be, but rather "steadily, blissfully, if only for a moment, a happy woman." What Fanny thinks of this brief embrace we are not told, though the plural in the story's title suggests that both women have had an intense and memorable experience, a "moment of being." Fanny pins the flower back on her dress, the narrator says, "with trembling fingers."

The editor of *Forum,* who published "Moments of Being: 'Slater's Pins Have No Points'" in January 1928 seems to have had some difficulty understanding this story, as he had "The New Dress." On 14 October 1927 Woolf wrote her friend Vita Sackville-West about having just received "Sixty pounds . . . from America for my little Sapphist story of which the Editor has not seen the point, though he's been looking for it in the Adirondacks."

The second of the published stories, "The Lady in the Looking-Glass: A Reflection" (first published in *Harper's Magazine* in December 1929), was written in the spring of 1929, when Woolf was preparing to begin the first draft of her most radically experimental novel, *The Waves* (1931). She wrote in her diary on 28 May 1929 that she felt "no great impulse" to begin her book. "Every morning I write a little sketch," she added, "to amuse myself." The earliest typescript draft of "The Lady in the Looking-Glass: A Reflection" is also dated 28 May 1929.

Like "Moments of Being: 'Slater's Pins Have No Points,' " "The Lady in the Looking-Glass: A Reflection" grows from Woolf's memory of a scene. After visiting her friend Ethel Sands, Woolf recalled how Ethel had looked at her letters but not opened them. "One might write a book of short significant separate scenes," she had written in her diary when the idea first came to her on 20 September 1927: "She did not open her letters." In this story, as in "An Unwritten Novel" and "Moments of Being: 'Slater's Pins Have No Points,' " one person tries to imagine a life story for another. The narrator, who is sitting alone in the drawing room of her friend Isabella Tyson, uses the knowledge she has about her friend, the objects in the room, and the scene outside that is reflected in the hallway looking glass to construct Tyson's story.

Woolf's fascination with this recurring plot reflects her sense of the essential unknowability of other people. We may feel compelled to tell ourselves stories about others, but only they know the true story about themselves. "The Lady in the Looking-Glass: A Reflection" ends as the narrator has a desolating vision of Tyson. Unlike Julia Craye, whom Fanny sees filled with happiness, the narrator sees Tyson as "perfectly empty. She had no thoughts. She had no friends. She cared for nobody. As for her letters, they were all bills. . . . [S]he did not even trouble to open them." Readers do not know whether this bleak reading of Tyson's character is true.

Woolf wrote at least two other sketches at this time but did not submit them for publication. "The Fascination of the Pool" (typescript dated 29 May 1929) is a meditation on the presence of the past. The narrator sits by the side of a pool and sees reflected in it scenes that took place beside the pool in previous centuries. In the third piece, "Three Pictures" (probably written in June 1929), the narrator describes three scenes – a sailor's jubilant homecoming, a loud and terrifying cry heard in the middle of the night, and then the same village with the sun shining on a graveyard where the gravedigger's family is picnicking on a newly dug grave. The grave is for the sailor, the narrator learns, who has died "of some foreign fever." In each of these three short works Woolf explores the ways our preconceptions shape, and are challenged by, the world we perceive. This is one of the aspects of human experience she explores far more fully in *The Waves*.

The stories Woolf wrote immediately after she completed *The Waves* reflect her growing interest in the potentialities of caricature. She had first recognized these when writing her fantasy/novel/biography *Orlando: A Biography* (1928), in which Orlando lives for several centuries, first as a man and then as a woman. This playful treatment of character was followed by her profound reconception of character in *The Waves*. Writing in her diary on 9 April 1930, as she was finishing the first draft of *The Waves,* Woolf observed, "What I now think (about the Waves) is that I can give in a very few strokes the essentials of a person's character. It should be done boldly, almost as caricature." The six speakers in *The Waves* (Woolf would not call them characters) have names and distinguishing characteristics and

are caricatures of familiar personality types, but they are also linked in ways that suggest they could all be aspects of a single person. Like Orlando but to a far greater extent, they are both fluid and fixed, multiple and one.

At the end of 1931 Woolf was still recovering from the strain of writing *The Waves*. On 29 December she wondered in her diary what she would write next. "Books come gently surging round me, like icebergs. I could write a book of caricatures. Christabel's story of the Hall Caines suggested a caricature of Country house life, with the red-brown pheasants." Woolf's manuscripts show that she wrote at this time drafts of three stories that were conceived as "Caricatures": "Scenes from the Life of a British Naval Officer," "The Duchess and the Jeweller," and "The Shooting Party," her caricature of country-house life. The latter two were among the stories that Woolf prepared for publication in the late 1930s.

The first of these tells no story but presents a succession of scenes in which a British naval officer, Captain Brace, performs his daily routine. The perspective is wholly external, making Captain Brace as "inscrutable" to the reader as he is to the narrator. Throughout the brief sketch Captain Brace's movements are described in terms that make him seem an extension of the instruments and machinery that surround him. Even his name contributes to this caricature of military life, all rules and regimentation.

"The Duchess and the Jeweller" (*Harper's Bazaar,* 1938) is the comic tale of a social-climbing jeweler, Oliver Bacon ("a giant hog in a pasture rich with truffles"), who must decide whether to pay £20,000 for pearls that are most certainly fake to the debt-ridden Duchess of Lambourne – "very large, very fat, tightly girt in pink taffeta, and past her prime." He has the money; she has the title, country house, and nubile daughters. In the end the Duchess gets her money, and he gets an invitation for the weekend. "Alone in the woods with Diana!" he thinks as he writes the check.

No summary can do justice to the comic vitality and subtle structure of the third caricature, "The Shooting Party" (*Harper's Bazaar,* 1938). The story of the elderly Rashleigh sisters and their brother the Squire is framed by the description of a woman who has boarded a train carrying a brace of pheasants. Although she is not directly associated with the Rashleigh family, several details in her description hint that she could be their housekeeper, Milly Masters. Indeed, like the narrator in "An Unwritten Novel" who begins to speculate about her fellow passenger, this story's speculating narrator suggests that this woman may be remembering the story that follows.

In the story Woolf presents scenes of the sisters sitting in their drawing room, talking cryptically of the past, and eating a meal of roast pheasant — while she interweaves these scenes with others of the Squire's shooting party as it moves toward the house. The layering of events as one scene is reflected in another, the dreamlike and comic mirroring of the sisters in the Squire's yellow-toothed dogs and in the dead and dying pheasants, and the frenetic collapse of the house around their heads in the end all contribute to the impression that this story is being told in the memory of the woman on the train.

Woolf's experimentation with caricature led her to write about a wider range of character types than had appeared in her fiction before. In another short sketch from this period she describes the activities of a tiresome but tireless do-gooder suitably named Miss Pryme, who lives in a village that closely resembles Rodmell, the Sussex village where the Woolfs had lived, when not in London, since 1919. But the most unusual short work of this period also has a most unusual title: "Ode Written Partly in Prose on Seeing the Name of Cutbush Above a Butcher's Shop in Pentonville." In one of the few poems Woolf ever wrote, she recounts the life story of the butcher John Cutbush, who has read Byron and dreamed of swimming the Hellesponte but who marries Louie the kitchenmaid and watches as she grows fat and his shop declines. "Ode" vividly evokes the atmosphere of life in this working-class section of north London, a world far removed from the one Woolf inhabited in Bloomsbury. Like the scenes depicting the servant Crosby in *The Years* (1937), which Woolf was working on when she wrote "Ode" in 1934, her sympathetic account of John Cutbush's life reflects the way her highly developed powers of observation supplemented her remarkable imagination.

"Ode" appears to be the only short fiction Woolf wrote during the long period from October 1932 to the end of 1936, during which she wrote *The Years*. Soon after its completion she and Vanessa Bell were discussing a collaborative work, tentatively called "Faces and Voices," for which Woolf wrote a series of brief portraits, but these were never published.

It was probably because of the popularity of *The Years*, which in June 1937 headed the *New York Herald Tribune* best-seller list for several weeks, that in 1937 Woolf was commissioned to write short stories for *Harper's Bazaar*. She revised "The Duchess

and the Jeweller" and "The Shooting Party" and wrote or revised a third story, "Lappin and Lapinova" (1939).

"Lappin and Lapinova" is the story of a marriage that works for a while and then goes wrong. The husband, Ernest Thorburn, is a familiar type in popular romances: handsome, wellborn, hardworking, and rather dull. Rosalind, his wife, is also a type: an imaginative woman stifled rather than nurtured by her marriage. Woolf is returning in this story to a theme she had explored in an early story called "Solid Objects" (*The Athenaeum,* 1920), that of the person whose imaginative life becomes a refuge from, and eventually threatens to usurp, everyday reality. In "Solid Objects" a young man named John becomes so obsessed with finding beautiful bits of stone, glass, and so on that he eventually abandons his career and his friends. In "Lappin and Lapinova" Rosalind invents a fantasy during her honeymoon in which she and her husband are rabbits. Ernest is King Lappin; Rosalind is Queen Lapinova. Ernest is amused by this game of "let's-pretend" for a while, as is the reader, and he goes along with it. But in time the couple grow apart, and Rosalind comes to rely more and more on the solace of her fantasy, which Ernest is no longer willing to share. One evening, in response to Rosalind's cry that she has lost Lapinova, Ernest coldly announces that Lapinova is dead: "'Caught in a trap,' he said, 'killed,' and sat down and read the newspaper. So that," the narrator concludes, "was the end of that marriage."

The playful quality in this story, like that in the lives of Rosalind and Ernest, is tempered by this stark ending. The death of Lapinova is not only the death of the marriage, but of the fantasy that has given Rosalind's life meaning. In being unable to establish a life independent of her husband, Rosalind resembles a character in another of Woolf's late stories, "The Legacy," which Woolf sent to *Harper's Bazaar* in October 1940 in response to their request for a story. Inexplicably, the magazine then rejected it.

Like many other late stories, this one grew out of an actual event. In May 1938 Woolf had visited Philip Morrell, whose wife, Lady Ottoline, had recently died. During the visit she had been shown Lady Ottoline's diaries. In "The Legacy," by reading his late wife's diaries, Gilbert Clandon slowly comes to learn the truth about her, after she has been recently hit and killed by a car. Both are familiar types. Gilbert Clandon is a self-centered, self-satisfied man, a successful politician who has assumed that his wife, Angela, has been content to bask in his reflected glow. Angela Clandon, however, had not been fulfilled in that role, and, as her diary reveals, she had eventually found in another man the companionship and love that her husband did not provide. The portrait of their marriage and of Angela's unhappiness is skillfully presented through the interplay of Gilbert's thoughts and the passages from Angela's diary that he reads. Through these passages the reader pieces together, as her husband does, the story of the events that have led up to Angela's death. By telling Angela's story in this indirect way, by giving her a voice only through her diary, Woolf emphasizes the prison that her life must have been.

A second story that Woolf submitted to *Harper's Bazaar* – this time in response to their request in October 1939 for a "dog story" – but which they did not publish (although they paid her £170 for it) is "Gipsy, the Mongrel." This is an episodic story, a "character study" of Tom and Lucy Bagot's dog Gipsy; it is unusual among Woolf's stories in being told mainly in dialogue. Although it is a dog story, it is also a story about friendship and the loss of friends. The Bagots tell how Gipsy came into their lives, recount her antics and their affection for her, and then describe how one snowy night she disappeared. "They had a sense of vast empty space round them," the narrator says after Tom tells of Gipsy's disappearance, "of friends vanishing for ever, summoned by some mysterious voice away into the snow."

The third late story that appears to have been prepared for publication but was apparently not submitted is "The Searchlight." Like "The Shooting Party," "The Searchlight" reflects Woolf's interest in ways that the "residue" of events, as she calls it in that story, is shaped by memory into vivid scenes. Further, like many of the other late stories, this one also grew from an anecdote. In his *Autobiography* (1885) senior civil servant Sir Henry Taylor recounts a boyhood memory of looking through his telescope at a neighboring farm and seeing the farmer's daughter rush into the arms of her brother, who was returning home after a long absence. This scene lodged in Woolf's memory too, for between 1929 and 1941 she wrote at least thirteen complete drafts of versions of "The Searchlight," all of which center on Henry Taylor's anecdote. It may also have been in her mind when she wrote "Three Pictures," as in the first picture the narrator watches a young sailor returning home to his wife and child.

In "The Searchlight" Woolf again uses a framing narrative. Mrs. Ivimey tells a group of friends a story that her great-grandfather had told her, a story of how as a young man he had seen through his telescope a young couple meet and kiss. Mrs. Ivimey re-creates with such energy the vivid scene and the excitement of the young man who threw down his telescope and ran through the fields to the young woman, that she seems to have been there herself. As in "The Shooting Party," the frame and the story merge at the end when Mrs. Ivimey almost acknowledges that she was the young girl in the story.

Woolf makes no reference in her diary or her letters to the last complete works of short fiction that she wrote, "The Symbol" and "The Watering Place." These were written approximately three weeks before she drowned herself on 28 March 1941. She had finished her novel *Between the Acts* (1941) at the end of February, and although she was feeling severely depressed, she was nevertheless considering what she might write next. That she should turn to short fiction at this time movingly illustrates the important role that it continued to play in her life.

These two short works also illustrate a recurring interplay in Woolf's fiction between what she sometimes called "fact" and "vision." "The Watering Place" is as firmly based on observation as "The Symbol" is on introspection. In "The Watering Place" the narrator describes a seaside town, then a local fish restaurant, and then, surprisingly, patrons in the ladies' lavatory of the restaurant. Woolf repeats here a conversation she overheard in the Sussex Grill in Brighton and recorded in her diary on 26 February 1941. The sketch ends with a haunting description of the town seen from the distance at night: "The town has sunk down into the water," she writes. "And the skeleton only is picked out in fairy lamps."

It is impossible not to see "The Symbol" as a projection of Woolf's own state of mind. A woman sits on a balcony in an Alpine village and writes a letter to her elder sister; she recounts scenes from the past and attempts to articulate her despondency in the present. The woman cannot find words to express what the mountain symbolizes or to say what she feels about the young mountain climbers whom she watches departing in the morning and then sees being brought home dead in the evening: "They died in an attempt to discover . . . , " she writes, but she cannot complete the sentence. Throughout the piece the unnamed woman's inability to tell her sister what she is feeling reflects the accuracy of the title Woolf originally gave it: "Inconclusions."

"Inconclusions" could also be the title of this survey of Woolf's short fiction, for there has not been room in it to address the question that the short fiction of many writers raises: what is the short story? Woolf had sought terms to replace *novel* to describe her long fictions, but she continued to call her short fictions *stories,* even though many of these works do not tell a story in any traditional way.

What links the forty-six complete works of short fiction by Virginia Woolf, besides their relative brevity, is the fact that in each of them Woolf draws upon the resources of the novel and the short story, as well as of poetry and drama, to explore in a fictional context aspects of human experience. And because Woolf was a writer who always sought new ways to tell stories, a writer whose insights into human experience were profound, her short fictions are remarkably varied. Anyone setting out to define the short story, to explore the range and the potentialities of the short-story form or to consider its use among the modernists, might well begin by contemplating the rich achievement of the short fiction of Virginia Woolf.

Letters:

The Flight of the Mind: The Letters of Virginia Woolf, Volume I: 1888–1912, edited by Nigel Nicolson and Joanne Trautmann (London: Hogarth Press, 1975); republished as *The Letters of Virginia Woolf, Volume I: 1888–1912* (New York & London: Harcourt Brace Jovanovich, 1975);

The Question of Things Happening: The Letters of Virginia Woolf, Volume II: 1912–1922, edited by Nicolson and Trautmann (London: Hogarth Press, 1976); republished as *The Letters of Virginia Woolf, Volume II: 1912–1922* (New York & London: Harcourt Brace Jovanovich, 1976);

A Change of Perspective: The Letters of Virginia Woolf, Volume III: 1923–1928, edited by Nicolson and Trautmann (London: Hogarth Press, 1978); republished as *The Letters of Virginia Woolf, Volume III: 1923–1928* (New York & London: Harcourt Brace Jovanovich, 1978);

A Reflection of the Other Person: The Letters of Virginia Woolf, Volume IV: 1929–1931, edited by Nicolson and Trautmann (London: Hogarth Press, 1978); republished as *The Letters of Virginia Woolf, Volume IV: 1929–1931* (New York & London: Harcourt Brace Jovanovich, 1979);

The Sickle Side of the Moon: The Letters of Virginia Woolf, Volume V: 1932–1935, edited by Nicolson and Trautmann (London: Hogarth Press, 1979); republished as *The Letters of Virginia Woolf, Volume V: 1932–1935* (New York: Harcourt Brace Jovanovich, 1979);

Leave the Letters Till We're Dead: The Letters of Virginia Woolf, Volume VI: 1936–1941, edited by Nicolson and Trautmann (London: Hogarth Press, 1980); republished as *The Letters of Virginia Woolf, Volume VI: 1936–1941* (New York: Harcourt Brace Jovanovich, 1980).

Bibliographies:

Robin Majumdar, *Virginia Woolf: An Annotated Bibliography of Criticism, 1915–1974* (New York: Garland, 1976);

B.J. Kirkpatrick, *A Bibliography of Virginia Woolf* (Oxford: Clarendon Press, 1980);

Thomas Jackson Rice, *Virginia Woolf: A Guide to Research* (New York: Garland, 1984).

Biographies:

Aileen Pippett, *The Moth and the Star: A Biography of Virginia Woolf* (New York: Viking, 1953);

Quentin Bell, *Virginia Woolf* (London: Hogarth Press, 1972);

George Spater and Ian Parsons, *A Marriage of True Minds: An Intimate Portrait of Leonard and Virginia Woolf* (London: Cape/Hogarth Press, 1977; New York: Harcourt Brace Jovanovich, 1977);

Lyndall Gordon, *Virginia Woolf: A Writer's Life* (Oxford: Oxford University Press, 1978);

Phyllis Rose, *A Woman of Letters: A Life of Virginia Woolf* (Oxford: Oxford University Press, 1984);

Louise DeSalvo, *Virginia Woolf: The Impact of Childhood Sexual Abuse on Her Life and Work* (Boston: Beacon, 1989);

Jane Dunn, *A Very Close Conspiracy: Vanessa Bell and Virginia Woolf* (London: Cape, 1990);

John Mepham, *Virginia Woolf: A Literary Life* (London: Macmillan, 1991).

References:

Dean R. Baldwin, *Virginia Woolf: A Study of the Short Fiction* (Boston: Twayne, 1989);

Patricia Clements and Isobel Grundy, eds., *Virginia Woolf: New Critical Essays* (London & Totowa, N.J.: Vision / Totowa, N.J.: Barnes & Noble, 1983);

Susan Dick, *Virginia Woolf* (London: Arnold, 1989);

Mark Hussey, ed., *Virginia Woolf and War: Fiction, Reality, and Myth* (Syracuse, N.Y.: Syracuse University Press, 1991);

Robin Majumdar and Allen McLaurin, eds., *Virginia Woolf: The Critical Heritage* (London & Boston: Routledge & Kegan Paul, 1975);

Jane Marcus, ed., *New Feminist Essays on Virginia Woolf* (Lincoln: University of Nebraska Press, 1981);

Marcus, ed., *Virginia Woolf: A Feminist Slant* (Lincoln: University of Nebraska Press, 1983);

Marcus, ed., *Virginia Woolf and Bloomsbury* (London: Macmillan, 1987);

Kathleen McCluskey, *Reverberations: Sound and Structure in the Novels of Virginia Woolf* (Ann Arbor: University of Michigan Press, 1986);

Harvena Richter, *Virginia Woolf: The Inward Voyage* (Princeton: Princeton University Press, 1970);

S. P. Rosenbaum, "The Philosophical Realism of Virginia Woolf," in his *English Literature and British Philosophy* (Chicago: University of Chicago Press, 1971), pp. 316–356;

Brenda R. Silver, *Virginia Woolf's Reading Notebooks* (Princeton: Princeton University Press, 1982);

Alex Zwerdling, *Virginia Woolf and the Real World* (Berkeley: University of California Press, 1986).

Papers:
The three major collections of Virginia Woolf's manuscripts and correspondence include the Henry W. and Albert A. Berg Collection of the New York Public Library; the Monks House Papers in the Manuscripts Section of the University of Sussex Library; and the Charleston Papers, King's College, Cambridge. The Berg Collection Woolf manuscripts and the Monks House Papers are available on microfilm. Smaller collections of Virginia Woolf papers are also found in the Leonard Woolf Papers, University of Sussex Library; the British Library Reference Division, Department of Manuscripts; the Frances Hooper Collection, Smith College Library Rare Book Room; the Lilly Library, Indiana University; the Harry Ransom Humanities Research Center, University of Texas at Austin; and the Beinecke Rare Book and Manuscript Collection, Yale University Library.

Checklist of Further Readings

Allen, Walter. *The Short Story in English.* Oxford: Clarendon Press, 1981; New York: Oxford University Press, 1981.

Bates, H. E. *The Modern Short Story: A Critical Survey.* London & New York: Nelson, 1941.

Bayley, John. *The Short Story: Henry James to Elizabeth Bowen.* New York: St. Martin's Press, 1988.

Beachcroft, T. O. *The Modest Art: A Survey of the Short Story in English.* London & New York: Oxford University Press, 1968.

Bergonzi, Bernard. *Reading the Thirties: Texts and Contexts.* Pittsburgh: University of Pittsburgh Press, 1978.

Burke, Daniel. *Beyond Interpretation: Studies in the Modern Short Story.* Troy, N.Y.: Whitson, 1991.

Canby, Henry S. *The Short Story in English.* New York: Holt, 1909.

Cunningham, Valentine. *British Writers of the Thirties.* Oxford & New York: Oxford University Press, 1988.

Evans, Benjamin Ifor. *English Literature between the Wars.* London: Methuen, 1948.

Flora, Joseph M., ed. *The English Short Story 1880–1945: A Critical History.* Boston: Twayne, 1985.

Fonlon, Bernard. "The Philosophy, the Science and the Art of the Short Story," *Abbia,* nos. 34–37 (June 1979): 427–438.

Fussell, Paul. *Abroad: British Literary Traveling between the Wars.* New York: Oxford University Press, 1980.

Fussell. *The Great War and Modern Memory.* Oxford: Oxford University Press, 1975.

Gindin, James M. *British Writers of the Thirties: The Dispiriting Decade.* New York: St. Martin's Press, 1993.

Grabo, Carl H. *The Art of the Short Story.* New York: Scribners, 1913.

Graves, Robert, and Alan Hodge. *The Long Weekend: A Social History of Great Britain, 1918–1939,* second edition. London: Faber & Faber, 1950.

Hanson, Clare. *Short Stories and Short Fictions, 1880–1980.* New York: St. Martin's Press, 1985.

Hynes, Samuel. *The Auden Generation: Literature and Politics in England in the 1930s.* London: Bodley Head, 1976; New York: Viking, 1977.

Kenner, Hugh. *A Colder Eye: The Modern Irish Writers.* New York: Knopf, 1983.

Kenner. *The Pound Era.* Berkeley: University of California Press, 1971.

Kenner. *A Sinking Island: The Modern English Writers.* London: Barrie & Jenkins, 1988.

Kilroy, James, ed. *The Irish Short Story: A Critical History*. Boston: Twayne, 1984.

Leavis, Q. D. *Fiction and the Reading Public*. London: Chatto & Windus, 1932.

Lohafer, Susan. *Coming to Terms with the Short Story*. Baton Rouge: Louisiana State University Press, 1983.

Magill, Frank N., ed. *Critical Survey of Short Fiction,* 2 volumes. Englewood Cliffs, N.J.: Salem Press, 1981. Revised edition, Pasadena, Calif.: Salem Press, 1993.

Martin, Peter. "The Short Story in England: 1930s Fiction Magazines," *Studies in Short Fiction,* 14 (Summer 1977): 233–240.

May, Charles E., ed. *Short Story Theories*. Athens: Ohio University Press, 1976.

McCave, Heather. *Women Writers of the Short Story*. Englewood Cliffs, N.J.: Prentice-Hall, 1980.

O'Connor, Frank. *The Lonely Voice*. Cleveland: World, 1963.

O'Faoláin, Seán. *The Short Story*. New York: Devin Adair, 1951.

Pain, Barry. *The Short Story*. New York: Doran, 1916.

Reid, Ian. *The Short Story*. London: Methuen, 1977.

Shaw, Valerie. *The Short Story: A Critical Introduction*. New York: Longmans, 1983.

Summers, Hollis, ed. *Discussions of the Short Story*. Boston: Heath, 1963.

Symons, Julian. *The Thirties: A Dream Revolved*. London: Cresset, 1960.

Thompson, Richard. *Everlasting Voice: Aspects of the Modern Irish Short Story*. Troy, N.Y.: Whitson, 1989.

Thurston, Jarvis, and others. *Short Fiction Criticism: A Checklist of Interpretation since 1925 of Stories and Novelettes (American, British, Continental) 1800–1958*. Denver: Swallow Press, 1960.

Walker, Warren S., comp. *Twentieth-Century Short Story Explication*. Hamden, Conn.: Shoe String Press, 1980.

Ward, A. C. *Aspects of the Modern Short Story: English and American*. London: University of London Press, 1924.

Contributors

Thomas J. Campbell ....Silver Spring, Maryland
Kevin J. H. Dettmar..Clemson University
Susan Dick..Queen's University
Paul A. Doyle............................Nassau Community College, State University of New York
Alexander M. Forbes ....University College of the Cariboo
James Ginden ....University of Michigan
John Harris ....University of Wales
George Johnson ....University College of the Cariboo
Shirley Laird..Tennessee Tech University
Lana Hartman Landon...Bethany College
Kathryn Ledbetter...Oklahoma Baptist University
Archie K. Loss ....Pennsylvania State University – The Behrend College
Joseph Lovering..Canisius College
Rachael Jane Lynch ....University of Connecticut at Waterbury
Mary S. Millar..Kingston, Ontario
Brian Murray ....Loyola College at Baltimore
Neil Nehring...University of Texas at Austin
John Orlet ....Kaskaskia College
Sally A. Paulsell ....IUPU-Columbus
John Rogers ....Vincennes University
Frank P. Riga ....Canisius College
Frank Edmund Smith ....William Rainey Harper College
Laurel Smith..Vincennes University
Michael Steinman....................Nassau Community College, State University of New York
Richard J. Thompson ....Canisius College
Jan Peter F. van Rosevelt...University of South Carolina
Carroll Viera ....Tennessee Tech University

Cumulative Index

Dictionary of Literary Biography, Volumes 1-162
Dictionary of Literary Biography Yearbook, 1980-1994
Dictionary of Literary Biography Documentary Series, Volumes 1-13

Cumulative Index

DLB before number: *Dictionary of Literary Biography,* Volumes 1-162
Y before number: *Dictionary of Literary Biography Yearbook,* 1980-1994
DS before number: *Dictionary of Literary Biography Documentary Series,* Volumes 1-13

B

C

G

N

O

Q

R

ISBN 0-8103-9357-3

90000

9 780810 393578

*For Marina, my companion on yet another crossing
of the Rubicon*

A
WARRIOR'S
LIFE

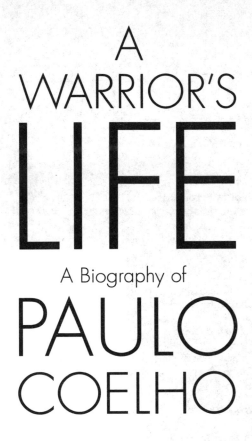

A WARRIOR'S LIFE

A Biography of

PAULO COELHO

Fernando Morais

HarperCollins*Publishers*

HarperCollins*Publishers*
77–85 Fulham Palace Road,
Hammersmith, London W6 8JB

www.harpercollins.co.uk

First published in Brazil by Editora Planeta Do Brasil Ltda. 2008
First published in the UK by HarperCollins*Publishers* 2009

10 9 8 7 6 5 4 3 2 1

www.fernandomorais.com.br/omago

A catalogue record of this book is
available from the British Library

HB ISBN 978-0-00-728138-1
PB ISBN 978-0-00-728140-4

Printed and bound in Great Britain by
Clays Ltd, St Ives plc

Mixed Sources
Product group from well-managed
forests and other controlled sources
www.fsc.org Cert no. SW-COC-1806
© 1996 Forest Stewardship Council
FSC

FSC is a non-profit international organisation established to promote the
responsible management of the world's forests. Products carrying the FSC
label are independently certified to assure consumers that they come
from forests that are managed to meet the social, economic and
ecological needs of present and future generations.

Find out more about HarperCollins and the environment at
www.harpercollins.co.uk/green

CONTENTS

When the world fails to end in the year 2000, perhaps what *will* end is this fascination with the work of Paulo Coelho.

Wilson Martins, literary critic, April 1998, O Globo

Brazil is Rui Barbosa, it's Euclides da Cunha, but it's also Paulo Coelho. I'm not a reader of his books, nor am I an admirer, but he has to be accepted as a fact of contemporary Brazilian life.

Martins again, July 2005, O Globo

CHAPTER 1

Paulo today: Budapest–Prague–Hamburg–Cairo

I T'S A DREARY, GREY EVENING in May 2005 as the enormous white Air France Airbus A600 touches down gently on the wet runway of Budapest's Ferihegy airport. It is the end of a two-hour flight from Lyons in the south of France. In the cabin, the stewardess informs the passengers that it's 6.00 p.m. in Hungary's capital city and that the local temperature is 8°C. Seated beside the window in the front row of business class, his seat belt still fastened, a man in a black T-shirt looks up and stares at some invisible point beyond the plastic wall in front of him. Unaware of the other passengers' curious looks, and keeping his eyes fixed on the same spot, he raises the forefinger and middle finger of his right hand as though in blessing and remains still for a moment.

After the plane stops, he gets up to take his bag from the overhead locker. He is dressed entirely in black – canvas boots, jeans and T-shirt. (Someone once remarked that, were it not for the wicked gleam in his eye, he could be mistaken for a priest.) A small detail on his woollen jacket, which is also black, tells the other passengers – at least those who are French – that their fellow traveller is no ordinary mortal, since on his lapel is a tiny gold pin embossed in red, a little larger than a computer chip, indicating to those around him that he is a Chevalier of the Legion of Honour. This is the most coveted of French decorations, created in

1802 by Napoleon Bonaparte and granted only at the personal wish of the President of the Republic. The award, which was given to the traveller at the behest of Jacques Chirac, is not, however, the only thing that marks him out. His thinning, close-cropped white hair ends in a tuft above the nape of his neck, a small white ponytail some 10 centimetres long. This is a *sikha*, the lock of hair worn by Brahmans, orthodox Hindus and Hare Krishna monks. His neat white moustache and goatee beard are the final touch on a lean, strong, tanned face. At 1.69 metres he's fairly short, but muscular and with not an ounce of fat on his body.

With his rucksack on his back and dying for a cigarette, he joins the queue of passengers in the airport corridor, with an unlit, Brazilian-made Galaxy Light between his lips. In his hand is a lighter ready to be flicked on as soon as it's allowed, which will not, it seems, be soon. Even for someone with no Hungarian, the meaning of the words '*Tilos adohanyzas*' is clear, since it appears on signs everywhere, alongside the image of a lighted cigarette with a red line running through it. Standing beside the baggage carousel, the man in black looks anxiously over at the glass wall separating international passengers from the main concourse. His black case with a white heart chalked on it is, in fact, small enough for him to have taken it on board as hand luggage, but its owner hates carrying anything.

After going through customs and passing beyond the glass wall, the man in black is visibly upset to find that his name does not appear on any of the boards held up by the drivers and tour reps waiting for passengers on his flight. Worse still, there are no photographers, reporters or television cameras waiting for him. There is no one. He walks out on to the pavement, looking around, and even before lifting the collar of his jacket against the cold wind sweeping across Budapest, he lights his cigarette and consumes almost half of it in one puff. The other Air France passengers go their separate ways in buses, taxis and private cars, leaving the pavement deserted. The man's disappointment gives way to anger. He lights another cigarette, makes an international call on his mobile phone and complains in Portuguese and in a slightly nasal voice: 'There's no one waiting for me in Budapest! Yes! That's what I said!' He repeats this, hammering each word into the head of the person at the other end:

'That's right – *there's no one waiting for me here in Budapest*. No one. I said *no one*!'

He rings off without saying goodbye, stubs out his cigarette and starts to smoke a third, pacing disconsolately up and down. Fifteen interminable minutes after disembarking he hears a familiar sound. He turns towards it, and his eyes light up. An enormous smile appears on his face. The reason for his joy is only a few metres away: a crowd of reporters, photographers, cameramen and paparazzi are running towards him calling his name, nearly all of them holding a microphone and a recorder. Behind them is a still larger group – his fans.

'Mister Cole-ro! Mister Paulo Cole-ro!'

This is how Hungarians pronounce the surname of the Brazilian author Paulo Coelho, the man in black who has just arrived in Budapest as guest of honour at the International Book Festival. The invitation was a Russian initiative, rather than a Brazilian one (Brazil doesn't even have a stand), Russia being the guest country at the 2005 festival. Coelho is the most widely read author in Russia, which, with 143 million inhabitants, is one of the most populous countries in the world. Along with the reporters come people bearing copies of his most recent success, *The Zahir*, all open at the title page, as they step over the tangle of cables on the ground and face the hostility of the journalists, simply to get his autograph. The flashbulbs and the bluish glow from the reflectors cast a strange light on the shaven head of the author, who looks as if he were on the strobe-lit dance floor of a 1970s disco. Despite the crowd and the discomfort, he wears a permanent, angelic smile and, even though he's drowning in a welter of questions in English, French and Hungarian, he appears to be savouring an incomparable pleasure: world fame. He is in his element. Mister Cole-ro with his sparkling eyes and the sincerest possible smile is once again Paulo Coelho, superstar and a member of the Brazilian Academy of Letters, whose books have been translated into 66 languages and dialects across 160 countries. He is a man accustomed to receiving a pop star's welcome from his readers. He tells the journalists that he has been to Hungary only once, more than twenty years before. 'I'm just afraid that fifteen years of capitalist tourism may have done Budapest more harm than the Russians did in half a century,' he says provocatively, referring to the period when the country was part of the former Soviet Union.

That same day, the author had another opportunity to savour public recognition. While waiting for the plane at Lyons airport he was approached by a fellow Brazilian, who told him that he had read and admired his work. On being called to take the bus to the plane, they walked together to the gate, but the other Brazilian, when asked to produce his boarding pass, couldn't find it. Anxious that the other passengers would grow impatient as the man searched clumsily through his things, the Air France employee moved him to one side, and the queue moved on.

Out of kindness, Paulo Coelho stood beside his fellow countryman, but was told: 'Really, you don't need to wait. I'll find it in a minute.'

All the other passengers were now seated in the bus, and the Air France employee was threatening to close the door. 'I'm sorry, but if you haven't got a boarding pass, you can't board the plane.'

The Brazilian began to see his holiday plans falling apart, but he wasn't going to give up that easily. 'But I know I've got it. Only a few minutes ago I showed it to the author Paulo Coelho, who was with me, because I wanted to know if we were going to be sitting next to each other.'

The Frenchman stared at him. 'Paulo Coelho? Do you mean that man is Paulo Coelho?' On being assured that this was so, he ran over to the bus, where the passengers were waiting for the problem to be resolved, and shouted, '*Monsieur Paulo Coelho!*' Once the author had stood up and confirmed that he had indeed seen his fellow Brazilian's boarding pass, the Frenchman, suddenly all politeness and cordiality, beckoned to the cause of the hold-up and allowed him to board the bus.

Night has fallen in Budapest when a tall, thin young man announces that there are to be no more photos or questions. To the protests of both journalists and fans, Paulo Coelho is now seated in the back of a Mercedes, its age and impressive size suggesting that it may once have carried Hungary's Communist leaders. Also in the car are the men who are to be his companions for the next three days: the driver and body-guard, Pal Szabados, a very tall young man with a crew cut; and Gergely

Huszti, who freed him from the reporters' clutches and who is to be his guide. Both men were appointed by the author's publisher in Hungary, Athenäum.

When the car sets off, and even before Gergely has introduced himself, Paulo asks for a moment's silence and, as he did in the plane, he gazes into the distance, raises his forefinger and middle finger, and for a few seconds prays. He performs this solitary ceremony at least three times a day – when he wakes, at six in the evening and at midnight – and repeats it in planes when taking off and landing and in cars when driving off, regardless of whether he is on a long-haul flight or a short trip in a cab.

On the way to the hotel, Gergely reads out the planned programme: a debate followed by a signing session at the book festival; a visit to the Budapest underground with the prefect, Gabor Demszky; five individual interviews for various television programmes and major publications; a press conference; a photo shoot with Miss Peru, one of his readers (who is in Hungary for the Miss Universe contest); two dinners; a show at an open-air disco …

Coelho interrupts Gergely in English. 'Stop there, please. You can cut out the visit to the underground, the show and Miss Peru. None of that was on the programme.'

The guide insists: 'I think we should at least keep the visit to the underground, as it's the third oldest in the world … And the prefect's wife is a fan of yours and has read all your books.'

'Forget it. I'll sign a book especially for her, but I'm not going to the underground.'

With the underground, the disco and Miss Peru scrapped, the author approves the schedule, showing no signs of fatigue in spite of the fact that he has had an exhausting week. With the launch of *The Zahir* he has given interviews to reporters from the Chilean newspaper *El Mercurio*, the French magazine *Paris Match*, the Dutch daily *De Telegraaf*, the magazine produced by Maison Cartier, the Polish newspaper *Fakt* and the Norwegian women's magazine *Kvinner og Klær*. At the request of a friend, an aide to the Saudi royal family, he also gave a long statement to Nigel Dudley and Sarah MacInnes from the magazine *Think*, a British business publication.

Half an hour after leaving the airport, the Mercedes stops in front of the Gellert, an imposing four-star establishment on the banks of the Danube, one of the oldest spa hotels in Central Europe. Before signing in, Paulo embraces a beautiful dark-haired woman who has just arrived from Barcelona and has been waiting for him in the hotel lobby. Holding her hand is a chubby, blue-eyed little boy. She is Mônica Antunes and the boy is her son. Although she acts as Paulo Coelho's literary agent, it would be a mistake to consider her, as people often do, as merely that, because it accounts for only a small part of the work she has been doing since the end of the 1980s.

Some people in the literary jet set say that behind her beautiful face, soft voice and shy smile lies a ferocious guard dog, for she is known and feared for the ruthlessness with which she treats anyone who threatens her author's interests. Many publishers refer to her – behind her back of course – as 'the witch of Barcelona', a reference to the city where she lives and from where she controls everything to do with the professional life of her one client. Mônica has become the link between the author and the publishing world. Anything and everything to do with his literary work has to pass through the modern, seventh-storey office that is home to Sant Jordi Asociados, named in Catalan after the patron saint of books, St George.

While her Peruvian nanny keeps an eye on her son in the hotel lobby, Mônica sits down with the author at a corner table and opens her brief-case, full of computer printouts produced by Sant Jordi. Today, it's all good news: in three weeks *The Zahir* has sold 106,000 copies in Hungary. In Italy, over the same period, the figure was 420,000. In the Italian best-seller lists the book has even overtaken the memoirs of the recently deceased John Paul II. The author, however, doesn't appear to be pleased.

'That's all very well, Mônica, but I want to know how *The Zahir* has done in comparison with the previous book in the same period.'

She produces another document. 'In the same period, *Eleven Minutes* sold 328,000 copies in Italy. So *The Zahir* is selling almost 30 per cent more. *Now* are you happy?'

'Yes, of course. And what about Germany?'

'There *The Zahir* is in second place on *Der Spiegel*'s best-seller list, after *The Da Vinci Code.*'

As well as Hungary, Italy and Germany, the author asks for information about sales in Russia and wants to know whether Arash Hejazi, his Iranian publisher, has resolved the problems of censorship, and what is happening regarding pirate copies being sold in Egypt. According to Mônica's figures, the author is beating his own records in every country where the book has come out. A week after its launch in France, *The Zahir* topped all lists, including the most prized, that of the weekly news magazine *L'Express*. In Russia, sales have passed the 530,000 mark, while in Portugal, they stand at 130,000 (whereas *Eleven Minutes* had sold only 80,000 copies six months after its launch). In Brazil, *The Zahir* has sold 160,000 copies in less than a month (60 per cent more than *Eleven Minutes* in the same period). And while Coelho is appearing in Hungary, 500,000 copies of the Spanish translation of *The Zahir* are being distributed throughout the southern states of America – to reach the Spanish-speaking communities there – and throughout eighteen Latin-American countries.

The only surprise is the last piece of news: the previous day, an armed gang stopped a lorry in a Buenos Aires suburb and stole the entire precious cargo – 2,000 copies of *The Zahir* that had just left the printer's and were on their way to bookshops in the city. Some days later, a literary critic in the *Diario de Navarra* in Spain suggested that the robbery had been a publicity stunt dreamed up by the author as a way of selling more copies.

All this stress and anxiety is repeated every two years, each time Paulo Coelho publishes a new book. On these occasions, he shows himself to be as insecure as a novice. This has always been the case. When he wrote his first book, *O Diário de um Mago* [*The Pilgrimage*], he shared the task of distributing publicity leaflets outside Rio's theatres and cinemas with his partner, the artist Christina Oiticica, and then went round the bookshops to find out how many copies they had sold. After twenty years, his methods and strategies may have changed, but he has not: wherever he is, be it in Tierra del Fuego or Greenland, in Alaska or Australia, he uses his mobile phone or his laptop to keep abreast of everything to do with publication, distribution, media attention and where his books are on the best-seller lists.

He has still not yet filled out the inevitable hotel form or gone up to his room, when Lea arrives. A pleasant woman in her fifties, married to the Swiss Minister of the Interior, she is a devoted reader of Coelho's books, having first met him at the World Economic Forum in Davos. When she learned that he was visiting Budapest, Lea took the train from Geneva, travelling over 4,000 kilometres through Switzerland, Austria and half of Hungary in order to spend a few hours in Budapest with her idol. It is almost eight o'clock when Coelho finally goes up to the suite reserved for him at the Gellert.

The room seems palatial in comparison with his modest luggage, the contents of which never vary: four black T-shirts, four pairs of coloured silk boxer shorts, five pairs of socks, a pair of black Levi's, a pair of denim Bermudas and a pack of Galaxy cigarettes (his stock of the latter is regularly topped up by his office in Rio or by kind visitors from Brazil). For formal occasions he adds to his luggage the coat he was wearing when he flew in from France, a shirt with a collar, a tie and his 'society shoes' – a pair of cowboy boots – again all in black.

Contrary to what one might think on first seeing him, his choice of colour has nothing to do with luck, mysticism or spirituality. As someone who often spends two-thirds of the year away from home, he has learned that black clothes are more resistant to the effects of hotel laundries, although on most occasions he washes his own socks, shirts and underpants. In one corner of his case is a small wash bag containing toothbrush and toothpaste, a razor, dental floss, eau de cologne, shaving foam and a tube of Psorex, a cream he uses for the psoriasis he sometimes gets between his fingers and on his elbows. In another corner, wrapped in socks and underpants, are a small image of Nhá Chica, a holy woman from Minas Gerais in Brazil, and a small bottle of holy water from Lourdes.

Half an hour later, he returns to the hotel lobby freshly shaved and smelling of lavender, and looking as refreshed as if he has just woken from a good night's sleep; his overcoat, slung over his shoulders, allows a glimpse of a small blue butterfly with open wings tattooed on his left forearm. His last engagement for the day is dinner at the home of an artist in the Buda hills above the city on the right bank of the Danube, with a wonderful view of the old capital, on which, this evening, a fine drizzle is falling.

In a candlelit room some fifty people are waiting for him, among them artists, writers and diplomats, mostly young people in their thirties. And, as usual, there are a lot of women. Everyone is sitting around on sofas or on the floor, talking or, rather, trying to talk above the noise of heavy rock blasting out from loudspeakers. A circle of people gathers round the author, who is talking non-stop. They soon become aware of two curious habits: every now and then, he makes a gesture with his right hand as if brushing away an invisible fly from in front of his eyes. Minutes later, he makes the same gesture, but this time the invisible fly appears to be buzzing next to his right ear. At dinner, he thanks everyone in fluent English for their kindness and goes on to praise Hungarian cooks, who can transform a modest beef stew into an unforgettable delicacy – goulash. At two in the morning, after coffee and a few rounds of Tokaji wine, everyone leaves.

At a quarter to ten the following morning, the first journalists invited to the press conference have already taken their places on the thirty upholstered chairs in the Hotel Gellert's small meeting room. Anyone arriving punctually at ten will have to stand. The person the reporters are interested in woke at 8.30. Had it not been raining he would have taken his usual hour-long morning walk. Since he dislikes room service ('Only sick people eat in their bedrooms'), he has breakfasted in the hotel's coffee bar, gone back to his room to take a shower, and is now reading newspapers and surfing the Internet. He usually reads a Rio newspaper and one from São Paulo, as well as the Paris edition of the *International Herald Tribune*. The remainder of his daily reading will arrive later in the form of cuttings and synopses focusing on the author and his books.

At exactly ten o'clock he enters the room, which is lit by reflectors and full of journalists, and sits down behind the small table provided, on which stand a bottle of mineral water, a glass, an ashtray and a vase of red roses. His guide, Gergely, takes the microphone, explains the reason for the author's visit to the country and announces the presence in the front row of his agent, Mônica Antunes. She stands shyly and acknowledges the applause.

Coelho speaks in English for forty minutes, which includes the time it takes for Gergely to translate each sentence into Hungarian. He recalls his visit to Budapest in 1982, and talks a little about his personal life and his career as a writer. He reveals, for example, that, following the success of *The Pilgrimage*, the number of pilgrims to Santiago de Compostela rose from 400 a year to 400 a day. In recognition of this, the Galician government has named one of the streets of Santiago 'Rua Paulo Coelho'. When the meeting is opened up for questions, it becomes clear that the journalists present are fans of his work. Some mention a particular book as 'my favourite'. The meeting passes without any indiscreet or hostile questions being asked; the friendly atmosphere is more like a gathering of the Budapest branch of his fan club. When Gergely brings the meeting to an end, the reporters reward the author with a round of applause. A small queue forms in front of the table and an improvised signing session exclusive to Hungarian journalists begins. Only then does it become apparent that nearly all of them have copies of his books in their bags.

The writer, who rarely lunches, has a quick snack in the hotel restaurant – toast with liver pâté, a glass of orange juice and an espresso. He makes use of a free half-hour before his next appointment to glance at the international news in *Le Monde* and *El País*. He's always interested in what's going on in the world and he's always well informed about any wars and crises that hit the headlines. It's quite usual to hear him speaking confidently (but without ever appearing to be dictatorial or superior) on matters as various as the growing crisis in Lebanon or the nationalization of oil and gas in Bolivia. He publicly defended the exchange of hostages held by Marxist guerrillas in Colombia for political prisoners being held by the Colombian government, and his protest letter in 2003 entitled 'Thank you, President Bush', in which he castigated the American leader for the imminent invasion of Iraq, was read by 400 million people and caused much debate.

Once he has read the newspapers, he gets back to work. Now it is time for Marsi Aniko, the presenter of RTL Club's *Fokusz2*, which regularly tops the Sunday evening ratings. The unusual thing about *Fokusz2* is that, at the end of each programme, the interviewee is given a Hungarian dish prepared by Marsi Aniko herself. In a small, improvised studio in the hotel, the face-to-face interview again holds no surprises, apart from the way she blushes when a cheerful Coelho decides to start talking about penetrative sex. At the end, he receives a kiss on each cheek, a tray of *almásrétes* – a traditional Hungarian tart filled with poppy petals that Aniko swears she has made with her own fair hand – and a bottle of Pálinka, a very strong local brandy. Within minutes, the set has been removed to make way for another jollier, more colourful one, for an interview with András Simon from Hungarian MTV. An hour later, once the recording is over, the journalist hands the author a stack of seven books to sign.

With a few minutes' break between each interview – time enough for the author to drink an espresso and smoke a cigarette – these interviews continue into the late afternoon. When the last reporter leaves the hotel, it is dark.

Coelho declares that he is not in the least tired. 'On the contrary. Talking about so many different things in such a short space of time only increases the adrenalin. I'm just getting warmed up ...'

Whether it is professionalism, vanity or some other source of energy, the fact is that the author, who is about to turn sixty, is on enviably good form. A shower and another espresso are all it takes for him to reappear at 8.30 in the hotel lobby, gleefully rubbing his hands. Mônica, Lea (who has managed to attach herself to the group), the silent bodyguard Szabados and Gergely are waiting for him. There is one more engagement before the end of the day: a dinner with writers, publishers and journalists at the home of Tamás Kolosi, who owns the publishing house Athenäum and is one of the people behind Coelho's visit to Hungary. When Gergely asks Coelho if he's tired after all the day's activities, the author roars with laughter.

'Certainly not! Today was just the aperitif. The real work begins tomorrow.'

After dinner with the publisher, Mônica uses the ten minutes in the car journey back to the hotel to tell him what she has organized with Gergely for the following day.

'The opening of the book festival is at two in the afternoon. You've got interviews at the hotel in the morning, so there'll be no time for lunch, but I've booked a restaurant on the way to the book festival so that we can grab a sandwich and some salad.'

Coelho's mind is elsewhere. 'I'm worried about the Israeli publisher. He doesn't like the title *The Zahir* and wants to change it. Call him tomorrow, will you, and tell him I won't allow it. Either he keeps the title or he doesn't get to publish the book. It was bad enough them changing the name of the shepherd Santiago in *The Pilgrimage* to Jakobi.'

He was equally stubborn before he became famous. Mônica recalls that the US publisher of *The Alchemist* wanted to re-name it *The Shepherd and His Dreams*, but the author refused to sanction the change.

Listening to her now, he says, smiling: 'I was a complete nobody and they were HarperCollins, but I stuck to my guns and said "No way," and they respected me for that.'

The following morning it is sunny enough to encourage the author to take his usual hour-long walk – this time along the banks of the Danube. Then after a shower, a quick glance at the Internet, breakfast and two interviews, he's ready for the second part of the day: the opening of the book festival. On the way there, they stop at the place reserved by Mônica, a snack bar, where all the other customers seem to have been driven away by the incredibly loud music coming from an ancient juke-box.

Coelho walks over, turns down the volume, puts 200 florins into the machine and selects a 1950s hit, 'Love Me Tender' by Elvis. He goes back to the table smiling as he imitates the rock star's melodious tones: '"Love me tender, love me true ..." I adore the Beatles, but this man is the greatest and will be around for ever ...'

Gergely wants to know why he's so happy, and Coelho flings wide his arms.

'Today is the feast of St George, the patron saint of books. Everything's going to be just fine!'

The International Book Festival in Budapest takes place every year at a convention centre located in a park – which, today, is still powdered with winter snow – and brings in hundreds of thousands of visitors.

Coelho is welcomed at a private entrance by three burly bodyguards and ushered into the VIP lounge. When he learns that there are almost five hundred people waiting at the publisher's stand to have their books signed, he says:

'We said that only 150 vouchers were to be handed out.'

The manager of the publishing house explains that they have no means of getting rid of the readers and fans. 'I'm sorry, but when the vouchers ran out, the other people in the queue simply refused to leave. There were even more people originally, but some of them have gone over to the auditorium where you're due to speak. The problem is that it only seats 350, and there are now 800 waiting to get in. We've had to erect screens outside for them.'

Mônica goes quietly out of the room to the Athenäum stand and returns five minutes later, shaking her head and looking worried. 'It's just not going to work. It's going to be bedlam.'

The security people say there's no danger, but suggest that Mônica's son and the nanny remain in the VIP lounge until the end of the programme.

Now, however, the news that the festival is crammed with fans and readers appears to have dispelled Coelho's initial feelings of irritation. He gets up smiling, claps his hands and makes a decision: 'So there are too many people? The more the merrier! Let's go and meet the readers. Just give me five minutes alone.'

He goes to the toilet as if for a pee, but once there he stands and stares into space, praying silently. Then he asks God to make sure that everything goes well during the day. 'Now it's up to You.'

God appears to have listened. Protected by the three bodyguards, and by Szabados, who has orders never to let him out of his sight, Paulo Coelho arrives in the Béla Bártok room lit by the lights of television crews and the flashlights of photographers. All the seats are taken and even the passageways, aisles and galleries are filled to capacity. The audience is equally divided between men and women, but most are young. He is escorted to the stage by the security guards and he acknowledges the applause, his hands pressed to his chest. The harsh lights and the crush of people mean that the heat is unbearable. The author speaks for half an hour in fluent French, talking about his life, his beliefs and the struggle to realize his dream to become a writer, all of which is then translated into Hungarian by a young woman. After this a small number of people are selected to ask questions, at the end of which the writer stands up to thank everyone for their welcome.

The audience don't want him to leave. Waving their books in the air, they yell: '*Ne! Ne! Ne!*'

In the midst of the uproar, the interpreter explains that '*ne*' means 'no' – those present do not want the author to leave without signing their books. The problem is that the security people are also saying '*ne*'. There are simply too many people. The cries of '*Ne! Ne!*' continue unabated. Coelho pretends not to have understood what the security people are saying, takes a pen out of his pocket and returns, smiling, to the microphone. 'If you can get yourselves in some kind of order, I'll try and sign a few.'

Dozens of people immediately start pushing forward, climbing on to the stage and surrounding the author. Fearing a stampede, the security guards decide to step in. They lift Coelho bodily off the floor and carry him through the curtains and from there to a secure room. He bursts out laughing.

'You could have left me there. I'm not frightened of my readers. What I fear is creating panic. In 1998, in Zagreb, a security man with a pistol at his waist tried to break up the queue and you can imagine how dangerous that was! My readers would never harm me.'

With two bodyguards in front of him and two behind, and under the curious gaze of onlookers, the author is accompanied down the corridors of the convention centre to the Athenäum stand, where copies of *The Zahir* await him. The queue of 500 people has become a crowd too large to organize. The 150 voucher holders wave their numbered cards in the air, surrounded by the majority, who have only copies of Paulo Coelho's books as their passport to an autograph. He is, however, used to such situations and immediately takes command. Speaking in French with an interpreter on hand, he raises his arms to address the multitude – and yes, this really is a multitude: 1,500? 2,000? It's impossible to know who is there to get his autograph or to get a glimpse of their idol and who has simply been attracted by the crowd. Finding it hard to be heard, he shouts: 'Thank you for coming. I know lots of you have been here since midday and I've asked the publisher to provide water for you all. We're going to have two queues, one for those who've got a voucher and the other for those who haven't. I'm going to try to deal with everyone. Thank you!'

Now comes the hard work. While waiters circulate with trays of cold mineral water, the author tries to create some order out of the chaos. He signs thirty books for those in the queue and then another thirty for those who have had to wait outside. Every fifty or sixty minutes he pauses briefly to go to the toilet or to a small area outside, the only place in the entire conference centre where he can smoke, and which he has named 'bad boy's corner'. On his third visit, he comes across a non-smoker, book in hand, waiting out of line for an autograph. He is Jacques Gil, a twenty-year-old Brazilian from Rio who has moved to Hungary to play for the oldest football club there, Újpest. Coelho quickly signs the book and takes four or five drags on his cigarette. He then hurries back to the stand, where the crowd is waiting patiently.

By the time the last of the fans reach the table, it is dark, and with the official programme at an end, it is time to relax. The original group – with the addition of half-a-dozen young men and women who refuse to leave – agree to meet after dinner in the hotel foyer for an evening's entertainment. At ten, everyone goes to a karaoke bar in Mammut, a popular shopping centre. The young Hungarians accompanying the author are disappointed when they learn that the sound system isn't working.

'That's too bad,' one complains to the manager. 'We managed to persuade Paulo Coelho to sing for us ...'

The mention of Coelho's name again opens doors, and the manager whispers something to a shaven-headed man, who immediately picks up a motorcycle helmet from the table and rushes off. The manager returns to the group, smiling. 'There's no way we're going to miss a performance by Paulo Coelho just because we've no karaoke equipment. My partner has gone to borrow some from another club. Please, take a seat.'

The motorcyclist takes so long to come back that the much-hoped-for performance becomes what musicians might call an 'impromptu' and a fairly modest one at that. Coelho sings Frank Sinatra's 'My Way' with

Andrew, a young American student on holiday in Hungary. He follows this up with a solo version of 'Love Me Tender', but declines to give an encore.

Everyone returns to the hotel at midnight, and the following morning, the members of the group go their separate ways. Mônica returns with her son and Juana to Barcelona, Lea goes back to Switzerland, and the author, after an hour's walk through the centre of Budapest, is once again sitting in the back of the Mercedes driven by Szabados. Next to him is a cardboard box full of his books. He opens one at the first page, signs it and hands it to Gergely, who is in the front seat. In the last two books, he writes a personal dedication to his driver and his guide. An hour later, he is sitting in business class in another Air France plane, this time bound for Paris, and again he is saying his silent prayer.

When the plane has taken off, a beautiful young black woman with her hair arranged in dozens of tiny plaits approaches him with a copy of *The Pilgrimage* in Portuguese. Her name is Patrícia and she is secretary to the famous Cape Verdean singer Cesária Évora. She asks him to sign the book. 'It's not for me, it's for Cesária, who's sitting back there. She's a big fan of yours, but she's really shy.'

Two hours later in Paris, at Charles de Gaulle airport, Coelho has yet another short but unexpected signing and photo session, when he's recognized by a group of Cape Verdean Rastafarians who are waiting for the singer. Their excitement attracts the attention of other people, who immediately recognize the author and ask to be allowed to take some photos as well. Although he's clearly tired, he cheerfully deals with all of them. At the exit, a chauffeur is waiting with a Mercedes provided by Coelho's French publisher. Although a suite costing 1,300 euros a day has been reserved for him at the Hotel Bristol, one of the most luxurious hotels in the French capital, he prefers to stay at his own place, a four-bedroom apartment in the smart 16th *arrondissement* with a wonderful view of the Seine. The problem is getting there. Today marks the anniversary of the massacre of the Armenians by the authorities of the Ottoman Empire, and a noisy demonstration is being held outside the Turkish Embassy, which is right near the apartment building. On the way, the Mercedes passes newspaper stands and kiosks displaying a full-page advertisement for *Feminina*, the weekly women's supplement with a circulation of 4 million, which is offering its readers an advance chapter from *The Zahir*. An enormous photo of the author fills the front page of the *Journal du Dimanche*, advertising an exclusive interview with him.

By dint of driving on the pavement and going the wrong way down one-way streets, Georges, the chauffeur, finally manages to park outside the apartment block. Despite having bought the place more than four years ago, Coelho is so unfamiliar with it that he still hasn't managed to learn the six-digit code needed to open the main door. Christina is upstairs waiting for him, but she has no mobile with her and, besides, he can't remember the phone number of the apartment. There are two alternatives: he can wait until a neighbour arrives or shout up to Christina for her to throw down the key. It's drizzling, and the wait is becoming uncomfortable. In a six-storey building with just one apartment per floor he might have to wait hours for a Good Samaritan to come in or out. The only thing to do is to shout and hope that Christina is awake.

He stands in the middle of the street and yells, 'Chris!'

No response. He tries again. 'Christina!'

He looks round, fearing that he might be recognized, and yells one more time, 'Chris-tiii-naaaaaa!'

Like a mother looking down at a naughty child, she appears, smiling, in jeans and woollen jumper, on the small balcony on the third floor and throws the bunch of keys to Coelho (who really does look tired now).

The couple spend only one night there. The following day they are both installed in suite 722 of the Hotel Bristol. The choice of hotel is deliberate: it is a temple to luxury in the Faubourg St Honoré and it is here that Coelho set parts of *The Zahir*, among the Louis XV sofas in the hotel lobby. In the book, the main character meets his wife, the journalist Esther, in the hotel café to drink a cup of hot chocolate decorated with a slice of crystallized orange. In recognition of this, the Bristol has decided to name the drink '*Le chocolat chaud de Paulo Coelho*' and the name is now written in gold letters on tiny bars of chocolate served to guests at 10 euros a go.

On this particular afternoon, the hotel has become a meeting place for journalists, celebrities and various foreign guests, all of whom have been invited to a dinner where Flammarion will announce the scoop of the year in the European publishing world: it has signed a contract to publish Paulo Coelho. Since 1994, the author has remained faithful to the small publisher Éditions Anne Carrière, which has achieved sales that have been the envy of even the most well-established publishing houses: in a little more than ten years it has sold 8 million copies of his books. After years of turning down ever-more enticing and hard-to-refuse offers, the author has decided to give way to what is reputed to be a 1.2 million-euro deposit in his bank account by Flammarion, although both parties refuse to confirm this sum.

Paulo and Christina appear in the hotel lobby. She is an attractive fifty-five-year-old, slightly shorter than Paulo, with whom she has been living since 1980. She is discreet and elegant, with fair skin, brown eyes and a delicate nose. On the inside of her left arm, she bears a tattoo of a small blue butterfly identical to Paulo's. Her glossy hair is cut just below her ears, and over her long black dress she's wearing a bright red shawl. But it is the two rings on her fingers ('blessed by a tribal leader', she explains) that attract most attention. They are a gift brought by Paulo from Kazakhstan. He, as ever, is dressed entirely in black – trousers, jacket, cowboy boots. The only slight change is that he is wearing a collar and tie.

The first friend to arrive is also a guest at the hotel and has come a long way. He is the Russian journalist Dmitry Voskoboynikov, a large, good-natured man who still bears the scars from the injuries he suffered during the 2004 tsunami in Indonesia, where he and his wife Evgenia were spending Christmas and New Year. A former London correspondent for TASS and the son of a member of the KGB, he is the owner of Interfax, a news agency with its headquarters in Moscow and which covers the world from Portugal to the farthest-flung regions of eastern Asia. The four sit round one of the small tables in the marble lobby and Evgenia, a magnificent blonde Kazak, gives the author a special present – a richly bound edition of *The Zahir* translated into her mother tongue. Four glasses of champagne appear on the table along with crystal bowls full of shelled pistachios. The subject changes immediately to gastronomy and Evgenia says that she has eaten a '*couscous à Paulo Coelho*' in Marrakesh, and Dmitry recalls dining in a Restaurant Paulo Coelho at Gstaad. The conversation is interrupted by the arrival of another well-known journalist, the Brazilian Caco Barcellos, the head of the European offices of Rede Globo de Televisão. He has arrived recently from their London office, having been sent to Paris solely to report on the Flammarion dinner. At seven in the evening, Georges arrives with the Mercedes to take Paulo and Christina to the ceremony. The choice of venue for this banquet for 250 guests leaves no doubt as to the importance of the evening: it is the restaurant Le Chalet des Îles, a mansion that Napoleon III ordered to be dismantled and brought over from Switzerland to be rebuilt, brick by brick, on one of the islands on the lake of the Bois de Boulogne as proof of his love for his wife, the Spanish Countess Eugenia de Montijo. The guests are checked by security guards on the boat that takes them across to the Île Supérieure. On disembarking, they are taken by receptionists to the main door, where the directors of Flammarion take turns greeting the new arrivals. Publishers, literary critics, artists, diplomats and well-known representatives of the arts in Europe are surrounded by paparazzi and teams from gossip magazines wanting photos and interviews. There are at least two ambassadors present, Sergio Amaral from Brazil and Kuansych Sultanov from Kazakhstan, where *The Zahir* is partly set. The only notable absentee is Frédéric Beigbeder, a former advertising executive, writer and provocative literary critic, who has worked as a publisher at Flammarion since 2003. Some years ago, when he was a critic for the controversial French weekly *Voici*, he wrote a very negative review of Paulo Coelho's *Manual of the Warrior of Light*. When everyone is seated, the author goes from table to table, greeting the other guests. Before the first course is served, there is a short speech from Frédéric Morel, managing director of Flammarion, who declares the new contract with Paulo Coelho to be a matter of pride for the publisher, which has launched so many great French writers. The author appears genuinely moved and gives a short address, thanking everyone for their good wishes and saying how pleased he is that so many people have come. After dessert, champagne toasts and dancing to a live band, the evening comes to an end. The following morning an hour-long flight takes the author and Christina to Pau in the south of France. There they take the car Coelho left in the car park some days earlier – a modest rented Renault Scénic identical to

Chris's. His obvious lack of interest in consumer goods, even a certain stinginess, means that although he's very rich, he didn't own his first luxury car until 2006, and even that was obtained without any money changing hands. The German car-makers Audi asked him to produce a short text – about two typed pages – to accompany their annual shareholders report. When asked how much he wanted for the work he joked: 'A car!' He wrote the article and sent it off by e-mail. A few days later, a truck from Germany delivered a brand-new, gleaming black Audi Avant. When he heard that the car cost 100,000 euros, a Brazilian journalist worked out that the author had earned 16 euros per character. 'Not bad,' Coelho remarked when he read this. 'Apparently Hemingway got paid 5 dollars a word.'

Half an hour after leaving Pau, Coelho and Christina are in Tarbes, a small, rather dismal town of 50,000 inhabitants on the edge of the French Basque country, a few kilometres from the Spanish border. Four kilometres out towards the south on a near-deserted road, they finally reach their house in Saint-Martin, a tiny community of 316 inhabitants and a few dozen houses set among wheatfields and pasturelands grazed by Holstein cows. The couple took the unusual decision to move here in 2001, when they made a pilgrimage to the sanctuary in Lourdes, 16 kilometres away. There wasn't a bed to be had in Lourdes, and they ended up staying in the Henri IV, a modest three-star hotel in Tarbes. It was the peacefulness of the region, its proximity to Lourdes and the incredible view of the Pyrenees that made them decide to settle there. While looking for a suitable house to buy and being in no hurry, Paulo and Christina spent almost two years in the only suite in the Henri IV, a rambling old house lacking any of the comforts they were accustomed to in large hotels. The absence of any luxury – which meant no Internet connection either – was more than made up for by the care lavished on them by the owner, Madame Geneviève Phalipou, and by her son, Serge, who, depending on the time of day, was manager, waiter or hotel porter. The so-called suite the couple occupied was, in fact, nothing more than a room with ensuite bath like all the others, plus a second room which served as a sitting room.

During their long stay in that small town, Coelho soon became a familiar figure. Since he has never employed secretaries or assistants, he was always the one who went to the post office, the chemist's or the butcher's, and shopped at the local supermarket, just like any other inhabitant. At first, he was regarded as a celebrity (particularly when foreign journalists started hanging around outside the Henri IV), but fame counts for little when one is standing in the queue at the baker's or barber's, and within a matter of months he had become a member of the Tarbes community. Even after he left the hotel and moved to his own house in Saint-Martin, the inhabitants of Tarbes continued to consider him one of their own – a compliment that Coelho is always eager to repay. He demonstrated his gratitude during an interview for *Tout le Monde en Parle*, a live programme on the French station France 2, whose presenter, Thierry Ardisson, is known for asking embarrassing questions. On this occasion, the singer Donovan and the designer Paco Rabanne were also on the programme.

Ardisson went straight to the point: 'Paulo Coelho, there's something I've been wanting to ask you for a long time. You're rich, world-famous, and yet you live in Tarbes! Isn't that rather stupid?'

The author refused to rise to the bait. He merely laughed and replied: 'Even the inhabitants were surprised, but it was love at first sight. Love is the only explanation.'

The presenter went on: 'Be serious now. What was the real reason you chose to live in Tarbes?'

'As I said, it was love.'

'I don't believe you. Admit it – you lost some bet and had to move to Tarbes.'

'No, I didn't!'

'Are they holding your wife hostage in order to force you to live there?'

'No, absolutely not!'

'But doesn't anyone who lives in Tarbes have to go to Laloubère or Ibos to do their shopping?'

'Yes, that's where I do all my shopping.'

'And does anyone there know you and know that you're Paulo Coelho?'

'Of course, everyone knows me.'

'Well, since you like it so much there, would you like to send a message to the inhabitant – sorry, the inhabitants – of Tarbes?'

'Absolutely. Tarbes people, I love you. Thank you for welcoming me as a son of your town.'

This was music to the ears of his new fellow citizens. A few days later, the newspaper *La Dépêche*, which covers the entire region of the Hautes-Pyrenées, praised Coelho's actions and stated: 'On Saturday night, Tarbes had its moment of national glory.'

Contrary to what one might read in the press, he doesn't live in a castle. The couple live in the old Moulin Jeanpoc, a disused mill that they have converted into a home. The living area is less than 300 square metres and is on two storeys. It's very comfortable but certainly not luxurious. On the ground floor are a sitting room with fireplace (beside which he has his work table), a small kitchen, a dining room and a toilet. While renovating the place the couple had an extension added, made entirely of strengthened glass, including the roof, where they can dine under the stars. They also converted an old barn into a comfortable studio, where Christina spends her days painting. On the first floor is the couple's bedroom, a guest room and another room, where Maria de Oliveira sleeps. She is the excellent cook whom Christina brought over from Brazil.

The most delightful part of the house, though, is not inside but outside, where there is a magnificent view of the Pyrenees. The view is even more beautiful between November and March, when the mountains are covered in snow. In order to enjoy this view, the author had to buy his neighbour's house and knock it down. He cannot remember exactly how much he paid for either his own house or the neighbour's, but agents in the area value the house alone, without the surrounding land, at about 900,000 euros. The author's property portfolio – which includes the house in Tarbes, the apartment in Paris and another in Copacabana – was substantially increased when His Highness Sheikh Mohammed bin Rashid Al Maktoum, Emir of Dubai and Prime Minister of the United Arab Emirates, gave him a fully furnished mansion worth US$4.5 million in one of the most exclusive condominiums in Dubai. The sheikh made similar gifts to the German racing driver Michael Schumacher, the English midfielder David Beckham and the Brazilian footballer Pelé.

Since they have no other help but Maria, not even a chauffeur, it is Coelho who is responsible for all the routine tasks: sawing wood for the fire, tending the roses, cutting the grass and sweeping up dead leaves. He is very organized and tries to keep some kind of discipline in the domestic timetable with a regime he laughingly calls 'monastic rules'. Apart from when he is involved in the launch of a new book or attending debates and talks around the world, his daily routine doesn't change much. Although he's no bohemian, he rarely goes to bed before midnight; he drinks wine in moderation and usually wakes in a good mood at about eight in the morning. He breakfasts on coffee, bread, butter and cheese, and, regardless of the weather, he goes out for an hour's walk every day, either in the wheat fields surrounding the house or, on a fine day, in the steep, stony hills near by, at the foot of the Pyrenees. Christina almost always goes with him on these walks, but if she's away or unwell, he goes alone. Any friends who stay at the house know that they will have to accompany their host – this is one of the monastic rules. One of his favourite walks takes him to the chapel of Notre Dame de Piétat in the *commune* of Barbazan-Debat, next to Saint-Martin and Tarbes. Here he kneels, makes the sign of the cross, says a brief prayer, puts a coin in the tin box and lights a candle in front of the small painted wooden image of the Virgin Mary holding the body of her dead son.

Back at the house, Coelho does some odd jobs in the garden, deadheads the plants and clears any weeds blocking the little stream that runs across the land. Only then does he go and take a shower and, afterwards, turn on his computer for the first time in the day. He reads online versions of at least two Brazilian newspapers and then takes a look at the electronic clippings agency that picks up on anything published about him and his books the previous day. Before pressing the enter key that will open up a site showing the best-seller lists, he places his outspread hands over the screen as though warming himself in front of a fire, closes his eyes and meditates for a moment, seeking, he says, to attract positive energy.

Today, he hits the key and smiles as the screen shows that, in the countries that matter most, he has only been beaten to number one in Germany and Brazil. In both these countries it is Dan Brown's *The Da Vinci Code* that heads the list. His e-mails also hold no great surprises. There are messages from no fewer than 111 countries, listed in alphabetical order from Andorra to Venezuela, passing through Burkina Faso, in Africa, to Niue off the coast of New Zealand and Tuvalu in Polynesia.

He says to Christina, who is sitting beside him: 'What do you make of that, Christina? When we got back from our walk it was 11.11 and the thermometer was showing 11°C. I've just opened my mailbox and there are messages from 111 countries. I wonder what that means.'

It's not uncommon to hear him say such things: while the majority of people would put something like that down to mere coincidence, Coelho sees such things as signs that require interpretation. Like the invisible fly he's always trying to drive away with his hand, his preoccupation with names, places, dates, colours, objects and numbers that might, in his view, cause problems, leads one to suspect that he suffers from a mild form of obsessive compulsive disorder. Coelho never mentions Paraguay or the ex-president Fernando Collor (or his Minister of Finance, Zélia Cardoso de Mello), and he only felt able to mention the name of Adalgisa Rios, one of his three long-term partners, after her death in June 2007. Indeed, if anyone says one of the forbidden names in his presence he immediately knocks three times on wood in order to drive away any negative energy. He crosses the road whenever he sees a pigeon feather on the pavement, and will never tread on one. In April 2007, in an eight-page article about him in *The New Yorker* magazine, he candidly confessed to the reporter Dana Goodyear that he refuses to dine at tables where thirteen people are seated. Christina not only understands this eccentric side of Coelho but shares his fears and interpretations and is often the one to warn him of potential risks when deciding whether or not to do something.

One afternoon a week is set aside for reading correspondence that arrives via ordinary mail. Once a week, he receives packages in the post from his Rio office and from Sant Jordi in Barcelona. These are stacked up on a table on the lawn and opened with a bone-handled penknife, and the letters arranged in piles according to size. From time to time, the silence is broken by a cow mooing or by the distant sound of a tractor. Any manuscripts or disks from aspiring authors go straight into the waste-paper bin, precisely as his various websites say will happen. At a time when letter bombs and envelopes containing poisonous substances have become lethal weapons, Coelho has begun to fear that some madman might decide to blow him up or contaminate him, but in fact he has never yet received any suspect package. However, because of his concern, he now meditates briefly over any parcels arriving from Rio or Barcelona, even when they're expected, in order to imbue them with positive vibes before they are opened. One cardboard package, the size of a shirt box, from his Rio office, contains replies to readers' letters that require his signature. The longer ones are printed on the official headed notepaper of the Brazilian Academy of Letters, of which Coelho has been a member since 2002. Shorter replies are written on postcards printed with his name. The session ends with the signing of 100 photos requested by readers, in which the author appears, as usual, in black trousers, shirt and jacket.

After a few telephone calls, he relaxes for an hour in an area in the garden (or in the woods around the house), where he practises kyudo, the Japanese martial art of archery, which requires both physical strength and mental discipline. Halfway through the afternoon, he sits down in front of his computer to write the short weekly column of 120 words that is published in thirty newspapers around the world, from Lebanon (*Al Bayan*) to South Africa (*Odyssey*), from Venezuela (*El Nacional*) to India (*The Asian Age*), and from Brazil (*O Globo*) to Poland (*Zwierciadlo*).

In other respects, the couple's day-to-day life differs little from that of the 300 other inhabitants of the village. They have a small circle of friends, none of whom are intellectuals or celebrities or likely to appear in the gossip columns. 'I can access 500 television channels,' Coelho declared years ago in an interview with the *New York Times*, 'but I live in a village where there's no baker.' There's no baker, no bar, no super-market and no petrol station. As is the case in the majority of France's 35,000 *communes*, there isn't a single commercial establishment in sleepy Saint-Martin. Tarbes is the nearest place for shops, as long as you get there before five in the afternoon, when the small town starts to shut down. Coelho's evening programme often consists of a visit to one of the three good restaurants there.

Eventually, it is time for Coelho to return to work. An e-mail from Sant Jordi contains a packed programme for the following three weeks which, if he agrees to it, will mean a round-the-world trip. On the programme are invitations to the launch of *The Zahir* in Argentina, Mexico, Colombia, Puerto Rico and Paris. He is also to receive the Goldene Feder prize in Hamburg, and there are signings as well in Egypt, Syria and Lebanon, plus a trip to Warsaw for the birthday of Jolanda, the wife of the President of Poland at the time, Aleksander Kwaśniewski. Then on to London to take part with Boris Becker, Cat Stevens and former secretary general of the UN Boutros Boutros-Ghali in a fund-raising dinner for the campaign against the use of land-mines. The following day he will return to France for dinner with Lily Marinho, widow of Roberto Marinho, the owner of Organizações Globo. Four days later, he is supposed to attend the launch of *The Zahir* in Japan and South Korea. On his return to Europe he will stop off in Astana, the capital of Kazakhstan, for the sixty-fifth birthday of the President, Nursultan Nazarhayev. The last engagement on the list cannot be missed: an invitation from Klaus Schwab, creator and president of the World Economic Forum held annually in Davos, for the author to speak at the opening of another of Schwab's enterprises, the Cultural Festival in Verbier, where young classical musicians from all over the world meet.

Coelho brushes away the invisible fly two or three times and mutters something along the lines of: 'No human being could possibly do all that.'

Christina hears the complaint and teases him gently: 'Look, you were the one who chose to be a Formula 1 champion, so get in your Ferrari and drive!'

The remark soothes him. He laughs and agrees that not only did he make that choice, but he fought his whole life to become what he is now, and so has no right to complain. 'But I still can't take on the whole programme. Some of the events are too close together and on three different continents!'

Usually, the stress of travel is caused not by the engagements themselves, but by the misery of modern air travel, especially since 9/11, when the consequent increase in vigilance and bureaucracy has created even longer delays for passengers. He faces the same queues, delays and over-bookings as his millions of readers, and one of the problems with the programme suggested by Sant Jordi is that it will have to be undertaken entirely on commercial flights. Coelho prints out the list and, pen in hand, starts by cutting out any engagements that entail intercontinental flights, which means putting off Latin America, Japan and South Korea, and the birthday party in Kazakhstan. Syria and Lebanon also go, but Egypt remains. Warsaw is replaced by Prague, where he wants to fulfil a promise made twenty years earlier. Finally, he decides that his first stop, in the Czech Republic, will be followed by Hamburg, where he will receive his prize and from where he will fly on to Cairo. However, the problem, once again, is flights. There are no connections that will allow him to stick to the timetables for Germany and Egypt. The Germans refuse to change the programme, which has already been printed and distributed, but they suggest an alternative: the private plane of Klaus Bauer, president of the media giant Bauer Verlagsgruppe, which sponsors the Goldene Feder prize, will take him and those in his party from Hamburg to Cairo as soon as the ceremony is over.

Hours later, when the programme has been agreed by all concerned, he telephones Mônica and jokes: 'Since we're going to Prague, what about putting on a "blitzkrieg" there?'

'Blitzkrieg' is the name Coelho gives to book signings that take place unannounced and with no previous publicity. He simply walks into a bookshop chosen at random, greets those present with 'Hi, I'm Paulo Coelho' and offers to sign copies of his books for anyone who wants him to. Some people say that these blitzkriegs are basically a form of exhibitionism, and that the author loves to put them on for the benefit of journalists. This certainly appeared to be the case when the reporter Dana Goodyear was travelling with him in Italy, where a blitzkrieg in Milan bore all the marks of having been deliberately staged for her benefit. In Prague, in fact, he is suggesting a middle way: to tell the publisher only the night before so that while there is no time for interviews, discussions or chat shows to be set up, there is time to make sure, at least, that there are enough books for everyone should the bookshop be crowded.

However, the objective of this trip to the Czech Republic has nothing to do with selling books. When he set out on the road back to Catholicism in 1982, after a period in which he had entirely rejected the faith and become involved in Satanic sects, Coelho was in Prague with Christina during a long hippie-style trip across Europe. They visited the church of

Our Lady Victorious in order to make a promise to the Infant Jesus of Prague. For some inexplicable reason, Brazilian Christians have always shown a particular devotion to this image of the child, which has been in Prague since the seventeenth century. The extent of this devotion can be judged by the enormous number of notices that have been published over the years in newspapers throughout Brazil, containing a simple sentence, followed by the initials of the individual: 'To the Infant Jesus of Prague, for the grace received. D.' Like millions of his compatriots, Coelho also came to make a request, and by no means a small one. He knelt at the small side altar where the image is displayed, said a prayer and murmured so quietly that even Christina, who was beside him, could not hear: 'I want to be a writer who is read and respected worldwide.'

He realized that this was quite a request, and that he would need to find a comparable gift to give in return. As he was praying, he noticed the moth-eaten clothes worn by the image, which were copies of the tunic and cloak made by Princess Policena Loblowitz in 1620 for the first known image of the Infant Jesus of Prague. Still in a whisper, he made a promise which, at the time, seemed somewhat grandiose: 'When I'm a well-known author, respected worldwide, I will return and bring with me a gold-embroidered cloak to cover your body.'

Three decades later the idea of the blitzkrieg is really an excuse to revisit Prague and repay the grace he has been granted. Made exactly to fit the image, which is about half a metre high, the red velvet cloak, embroidered with fine gold thread, is the result of weeks of work by Paula Oiticica, Christina's mother.

Packed in an acrylic box so that it can be transported safely, the gift creates a small incident at Charles de Gaulle airport, when the police demand that the package be passed through an X-ray machine in order to prove that it doesn't conceal drugs or explosives; unfortunately, it's too big for the machine. Coelho refuses to board without the cloak, while the police maintain that, if it can't be X-rayed, it can't travel. A superior officer notices the small crowd gathering, recognizes M. Coelho and resolves the deadlock: the cloak is taken on to the plane without being scanned.

When the couple arrive at the church in Prague, some two dozen faithful are there, all apparently foreigners. Since he speaks only Czech and

Italian, the Carmelite priest, Anastasio Roggero, appears not to understand quite who this person is and what he is doing in his church holding a red cloak. He listens to what Coelho is saying to him in English, smiles, thanks him and is preparing to stow the box away behind a cupboard in the sacristy when an old French woman recognizes the author.

In an inappropriately loud voice, she tells the members of her group: 'Look, it's the writer Paulo Coelho!'

All the tourist groups converge on him, clamouring for his autograph and to have their photo taken with him. Father Anastasio turns, looks again at the cloak he is holding and begins to realize his mistake. He apologizes to Coelho for not having recognized him or the significance of the gift the Infant Jesus has just received. He returns to the sacristy and comes back armed with a digital camera to take photos of the cloak, the tourists and, of course, himself with his famous visitor, whose work he claims to know well.

Once Coelho has settled his account with the Infant Child, the couple spend their free time revisiting the capital and seeing Leonardo Oiticica, Christina's brother, who is married to Tatiana, a diplomat at the Brazilian embassy in Prague. Two newspapers – *Pravó* and *Komsomólskaia* – have now publicized Paulo Coelho's presence in the city, and so the intended blitzkrieg cannot be a genuinely spontaneous event. By three in the afternoon, an hour before the agreed time, hundreds of people are lined up outside the Empik Megastore, the enormous modern bookshop chosen by Coelho's Czech publisher, Argo. He arrives at the agreed hour and finds things much as they were in Budapest. This time only 150 readers have managed to get vouchers, but hundreds of people are filling the aisles of the shop and spilling out into Wenceslas Square. They all want an autograph. The author does what he did in Hungary: he asks the bookshop to provide everyone with water, and divides the waiting crowd into those with vouchers and those without. At six in the evening, he looks at his watch and asks to be allowed a toilet break. Instead, he goes behind a screen only a few metres away in order to say his silent prayer. It's dark by the time he has signed the last book. He ends the evening enjoying Czech *nouvelle cuisine* in a smart restaurant in the old part of the city with a small group of friends.

The following day he is back in Paris for yet another signing, this time at the Fnac bookshop in the Place des Thermes. Although the shop is expecting only about a hundred people, the news has spread and about three hundred are packed into the small auditorium. Outside, people are trying to get to the display of CDs and DVDs, part of a small exhibition, not only of his books but also of his own literary, musical and cinemato-graphic favourites. Among the books are Albert Camus' *The Outsider*, Henry Miller's *Tropic of Cancer*, Jorge Luis Borges' *Fictions*, Jorge Amado's *Gabriela, Clove and Cinnamon* and the biography of the matador El Cordobés, *I'll Dress You in Mourning*, by Dominique Lapierre and Larry Collins. The films on display include *Blade Runner* (Ridley Scott), *Once Upon a Time in the West* (Sergio Leone), *2001: A Space Odyssey* (Stanley Kubrick), *Lawrence of Arabia* (David Lean) and *The Promise* (Anselmo Duarte), while the selection of CDs is even more eclectic: from The Beatles' *Abbey Road* to Beethoven's Ninth Symphony, from Pink Floyd's *Atom Heart Mother* to Chopin's First Piano Concerto. The French fans are as patient as the Hungarians and Czechs. After giving a half-hour talk and answering questions, the author signs books for all those present before leaving the shop.

In marked contrast to this relaxed atmosphere, the Goldene Feder award ceremony, the following day, is organized with almost military preci-sion. Hamburg has been in a permanent state of alert (and tension) since the discovery that the people behind the 9/11 attacks in the United States had been part of an Al Qaeda terrorist cell active there. Of the twenty men directly involved in the attack, nine lived in an apartment on the edge of the city, among them the leader of the group, the Egyptian Mohammed Atta. Judging by the number of private security guards present, the cere-mony is clearly considered a prime target. Bankers, industrialists, busi-nessmen, publishers and the famous have arrived from all corners of Europe to be here. In order to avoid any problems, the organizers of the event have allowed only five minutes for the press to photograph the guests and prize-winners (prizes are also being given to a scientist, a professor, a businesswoman and a priest). During the presentation cere-mony, the reporters, along with the security guards and chauffeurs, are relegated to a canteen where they can watch everything on TV monitors.

Five hours later, the writer and his rucksack are in the VIP lounge at Hamburg airport, ready to take a Falcon jet to Cairo. His arrival in Egypt coincides with a visit to Cairo by the First Lady of the United States, Laura Bush, which means that security measures are even tighter. Friends have expressed their concern for Coelho's safety, given the frequency with which tourists in Egypt have been the victims of terrorist attacks by radical Islamic groups. 'What if some group of religious fanatics kidnapped you and demanded the release of 100 political prisoners in exchange?' they ask. He, however, appears unconcerned. This is not only because he has previously consulted the oracles, but because he knows that during his visit he will be protected by Hebba Raouf Ezzar, the woman who invited him to speak at Cairo University. This forty-year-old Muslim mother of three, and visiting professor at Westminster University in London, is a charismatic political scientist who has overcome the prejudices of a society wedded to machismo and has become a major influence in the battle for human rights and the promotion of dialogue between Islam and other faiths. Being in Egypt at her invitation means being able to circulate freely – and safely – among a wide variety of political and religious groups.

There are other reasons, too, for Coelho to visit Egypt. The country is possibly the world champion when it comes to producing pirate editions of his books. Even though almost half the population is illiterate, it has been estimated that more than four hundred thousand illegal copies of his books – some 5 per cent of all pirate copies of his work worldwide – are available here. You can find Arabic translations of everything from *The Pilgrimage* to *The Zahir* in the windows of smart bookshops and on the pavements of Cairo, Alexandria and Luxor. And there are pirated editions for every pocket, from crude home-made versions to hardback editions printed on good-quality paper and produced by established publishers, some of them state-run. The author receives almost nothing in royalties from Egypt, but the real loser is the reader, who ends up buying copies either with chapters missing or in the wrong order, or that are translations intended for other Arab-speaking countries and not necessarily comprehensible to Egyptians. The pirate producers enjoy total immunity from prosecution; indeed, at the last International Book Fair in Cairo,

Paulo Coelho's works topped the best-seller lists, as if they had been produced by publishers complying with internationally agreed laws.

Keen to put a stop to the problem, Coelho lands in Cairo, accompanied by Mônica Antunes and Ana Zendrera, the proprietor of Sirpus in Spain, which specializes in Arabic publications destined for the Middle East and North Africa. Since May 2005, only two companies, All Prints in Lebanon and Sirpus, have been legally authorized to publish his books in Egypt.

At the airport, which is full of soldiers carrying sub-machine guns, the three are greeted by Hebba and her husband, the activist Ahmed Mohammed. He is dressed in Western clothes, but she is wearing a beige hijab. They all speak English, which is Egypt's second language. The small group goes straight to the Four Seasons Hotel, where a suite has been reserved for the author on the top floor with a view of Giza at the edge of the Sahara.

Hebba has drawn up a packed programme of events: interviews and TV appearances, visits to the famous (among them the Nobel Laureate Naguib Mahfouz, who is ninety and losing his sight, but determined to receive the author in his apartment for a cup of tea), a seminar at Cairo University and two talks, one at the Egyptian Association of Authors and the other at its rival, the Union of Egyptian Authors. At Paulo's request, Hebba has arranged a lunch in one of the dining rooms of the Four Seasons to which the principal publishers and booksellers in the country have been invited, along with representatives of the Ministry of Culture. It is here that the author is hoping to ram home his point about defending the rights of the author. He tells Hebba: 'You know perfectly well, Hebba, that when a warrior takes out his sword, he has to use it. He can't put it back in its sheath unbloodied.'

The following morning, the lobby of the Four Seasons Hotel is invaded by TV network people waiting for the interviews Mônica has organized. Cameras, tripods, reflectors, cables and batteries are stacked in corners and spread out on tables and sofas. Individual interviews are the privilege of the television reporters; newspaper and magazine journalists have to make do with a press conference. The only exception is *Al Ahram*, the main Egyptian newspaper – state-run as, it seems, most are –

which also has the privilege of being first in line. Once the interview is over, the reporter, Ali Sayed, opens his briefcase and asks the author to sign three books, *The Alchemist*, *Maktub* and *Eleven Minutes* – all of them pirate copies, bought in the street for US$7 each. In the early afternoon, the five go to a restaurant for a quick lunch washed down with Fanta, Coca-Cola, tea and mineral water. Although there is wine and beer available, the meal is going to be paid for by Ahmed, a Muslim, and good manners require that no alcohol be drunk.

Once the engagements with the press are over Coelho takes part in hurried debates at the two writers' associations. At both, the number of members of the public is two or three times greater than the venues' capacity and he attends kindly and good-naturedly to the inevitable requests for signings at the end. Before returning to the hotel, he is taken to Mohamed Heikal's apartment. Heikal is a veteran politician who started his career alongside President Nasser, who governed from 1954 to 1970, and he has so far managed to weather the political upheavals in Egypt. Surrounded by bodyguards, Heikal receives his visitor in a small apartment. The walls are covered in photos of him with great international leaders of the twentieth century, such as the Soviet leader Nikita Khrushchev, Chou En-Lai of China, Jawalarhal Nehru of India and Chancellor Willy Brandt, as well as Leonid Brezhnev and, of course, Nasser himself. Coelho's meeting with the Nobel Laureate Naguib Mahfouz is also subject to intense vigilance by security guards (years ago Mahfouz narrowly escaped death at his door when he was knifed in the neck by a Muslim fundamentalist who accused him of blaspheming against the Koran). The two speak rapidly in English, exchange signed copies of their books and that's it. With the day's agenda over, the evening is reserved for a boat trip on the Nile.

The following day the morning is free, allowing Coelho to wake later than usual, take his walk without hindrance and give some time to looking at news online. At one o'clock, he goes down to the hotel dining room for the lunch that he has suggested. In spite of the smiles and salaams during the presentations, it is clear that the idea is to set things to rights. Before the food is served and once all the guests are seated, one of the publishers stands up to greet the visitor and makes a point of stating that this is a meeting of friends.

'The author Coelho has proved his commitment to the Arab peoples not only in his work but in brave public statements such as in his letter "Thank you, President Bush", which clearly condemned the invasion of Iraq by the United States.'

Someone else speaks, and then it is Coelho's turn. Beside him at the table are three pirate copies of his books, deliberately placed there in order to provoke unease among the publishers – the elegant men in jackets and ties who are seated before him. He begins gently, recalling that some of his books have found inspiration in both Egyptian and Arabic culture. Then, face to face with the pirates themselves, he broaches the thorny topic of piracy, saying: 'Any author would, of course, love to see his books published in Egypt. My problem is precisely the opposite: I have too many publishers in Egypt.'

No one finds the joke funny, but he is unperturbed. He glances upwards, as if asking St George for the strength to defend his books, and then adopts a blunter approach.

He picks up a pirate copy of *The Alchemist* and waves it in the air. 'I am here as a guest of Dr Hebba, that is of the Egyptian people. But I have come here on my own account as well because I want to sort out, once and for all, the problem of the pirate copies of my books being published here.'

The guests shift uncomfortably in their seats. Some, embarrassed, are doodling on their napkins.

Coelho knows full well that some are important figures in the Ministry of Culture (which has shares in many of the publishing houses he is accusing of piracy) and he makes the most of this opportunity: 'The government neither punishes nor condemns piracy, but Egypt is a signatory to international treaties on royalties and must conform to them. I could get the best lawyer money can buy and win the case in international courts, but I'm not here merely to defend material values, I'm defending a principle. My readers here buy books at a cheap price and get cheap editions, and it's got to stop.'

Coelho's suggestion that they call an armistice doesn't seem to please anyone.

'I'm not interested in the past. Let's forget what's happened up to now. I'm not going to claim royalties on the 400,000 books published in a country where I've never even had a publisher. But from now on, any book of mine published in Egypt that is not produced by Sirpus or by All Prints will be considered illegal and therefore the subject of legal action.'

To prove that he's not bluffing, he announces that there will be a special blitzkrieg in the Dar El Shorouk bookshop, next to the hotel: he will sign the first book produced under the new regime (a pocket version of *The Alchemist* in Arabic with the Sirpus stamp on it) as well as copies of the English translation of *The Zahir*. This awkward meeting ends without applause and with the majority of those present looking stony-faced.

Everything seems to be going as he predicted. The signing is a success and he says to any journalist who hunts him out: 'I think the publishers have accepted my proposal. From now on, my Egyptian readers will read my books only in official translations published by Sirpus.' His confidence, however, will prove short-lived, because the only real change in the situation is that now the pirates have another competitor in the market – Sirpus.

The conference at Cairo University, the following day, the last engagement of his trip to Egypt, goes smoothly. The conference takes place in a 300-seat auditorium and there are exactly 300 people present. The majority are young women who, unlike Hebba, are wearing Western dress – tight jeans and tops revealing bare shoulders and midriffs. After his talk, idolatry gets the better of discipline, and they crowd around him, wanting him to sign copies of his books.

On the way back to the hotel, Hebba suggests doing something not on the schedule. Readers belonging to the Official Paulo Coelho Fan Club in Egypt who did not manage to get to any of his public appearances want to meet him at the end of the afternoon for a chat. Cheered by what he believes to have been the success of his lunch with the publishers, he agrees without asking for any further details. His response means that Hebba has to go off at once to mobilize the public. The place she has chosen is an improvised open-air auditorium under one of the bridges that cross the Nile. No one knows quite what methods she has used to gather so many people together, but there is general astonishment among the Brazilian contingent when they arrive and find a crowd of more than two thousand people. The venue appears to be a building that has been left half-finished with concrete slabs and bits of iron still visible. The place is packed, with people sitting in between the seats and in the side aisles. It seems quite incredible that so many could have been gathered together on a weekday without any prior announcement in the newspapers, on the radio or television. There are even people perched on the walls and in the trees surrounding the auditorium.

In the infernal heat, Hebba leads Coelho to a small dais in one corner of the area, where a coffee table and three armchairs await them. When he says his first words in English – 'Good afternoon, thank you all for being here' – a hush descends. He talks for half an hour about his life, his struggle to become a recognized author, his drug-taking, his involvement in witchcraft, the time he spent in mental institutions, about political repression and the critics, and how he finally rediscovered his faith and realized his dream. Everyone watches him entranced, as if they were in the presence not of the author of their favourite books but of someone who has lessons in life to teach them. Many are unable to hide their feelings and their eyes are filled with tears.

When he says his final 'Thank you' Coelho is crying too. The applause looks set to continue, and, making no attempt to conceal his tears now, Paulo thanks the audience again and again, folding his arms over his chest and bowing slightly. The people remain standing and applauding. A young girl in a dark hijab goes up on to the dais and presents him with a bouquet of roses. Although he is quite used to such situations, the author appears genuinely moved and is at a loss how to react. The audience is still applauding. He turns rapidly, slips behind the curtains for a moment, glances upwards, makes the sign of the cross and repeats for the umpteenth time a prayer of gratitude to St Joseph, the saint who, almost sixty years earlier, watched over his rebirth – because, but for a miracle, Paulo Coelho would have died at birth.

CHAPTER 2

Childhood

PAULO COELHO DE SOUZA was born on a rainy night on 24 August 1947, the feast of St Bartholomew, in the hospital of São José in Humaitá, a middle-class area of Rio de Janeiro. The doctors had foreseen that there might be problems with the birth, the first for twenty-three-year-old Lygia Araripe Coelho de Souza, married to a thirty-three-year-old engineer, Pedro Queima Coelho de Souza. The baby would be not only their first child but a first grandchild for the four grandparents and a first nephew for uncles and aunts on both sides. Initial examination had shown that the child had swallowed a fatal mixture of meconium – that is, his own faeces – and amniotic fluid. He was not moving in the womb and showed no inclination to be born, and finally had to be delivered by forceps. As he was pulled into the world, at exactly 12.05 a.m., the doctor must have heard a slight crack, like a pencil snapping. This was the baby's collarbone, which had failed to resist the pressure of the forceps. Since the baby, a boy, was dead, this was hardly a problem.

Lygia was a devout Catholic and, in a moment of despair, the first name that came to her lips was that of the patron saint of the maternity hospital: 'Please bring back my son! Save him, St Joseph! My baby's life is in your hands!'

The sobbing parents asked for someone to come and give the last rites to their dead child. Only a nun could be found, but just as she was about to administer the sacrament, there was a fainting mewing sound. The child was, in fact, alive, but in a deep coma. He had faced his first challenge and survived it.

He spent his first three days in an incubator. During those decisive seventy-two hours his father, Pedro, remained with him all the time. On the fourth day, when Paulo was taken out of the incubator, Pedro finally managed to get some sleep, and was replaced in his vigil by his mother-in-law Maria Elisa, or Lilisa as she was known. Six decades later, Paulo would state without hesitation that his earliest memory was of seeing a woman come into the room and knowing that she was his grandmother. In spite of weighing only 3.33 kilos at birth and measuring 49 centimetres, the child seemed healthy. According to Lygia's notes in her baby album, he had dark hair, brown eyes and fair skin, and looked like his father. He was named after an uncle who had died young from a heart attack.

Apart from a bout of whooping cough, Paulo had a normal, healthy childhood. At eight months, he said his first word, at ten months, his first teeth appeared and at eleven months, he began to walk without ever having crawled. According to Lygia, he was 'gentle, obedient, extremely lively and intelligent'. When he was two, his only sister, Sônia Maria, was born; he was always fond of her and, apparently, never jealous. At three, he learned to make the sign of the cross, a gesture that was later accompanied by requests to God for the good health of his parents, grandparents, cousins, uncles and aunts.

Until he was thirteen, he and his family lived on an eleven-house estate built by his father in Botafogo, a pleasant middle-class area of Rio. The best of the houses – the only one with a garden – was reserved for Pedro's in-laws, Lilisa and Tuca, who owned the land. Another of the houses, a modest, two-storey affair, was given to Pedro in payment for his work and the remaining nine were let, sold or occupied by relatives. The Coelhos were so concerned about security that, although the estate was protected by high gates, all the windows and doors in the house were kept shut. Paulo and the other children could play freely as long as they did so within the confines of the estate; although it was only a few blocks from Botafogo beach, they knew nothing of life beyond its walls. Friendship with children from 'outside' was unthinkable.

From a very young age, Paulo showed that he had an original way of thinking. When, at the age of three, Lygia caught him behaving badly, he said: 'Do you know why I'm being naughty today, Mama? It's because my guardian angel isn't working. He's been working very hard and his battery has run out.'

One of his greatest pleasures was helping his grandfather Tuca repair his enormous Packard car. His father felt that this was clear proof that his son would turn out to be an engineer like him. Pedro also had a car – a Vanguard – but it rarely left the garage. As far as Pedro Coelho was concerned, if the family could take the bus into the city, there was no reason to spend money on petrol.

One of Coelho's earliest memories is of his father's tight grip on domestic finances. Engineer Pedro Queima Coelho de Souza's dream was to build not just a modest house for his family, like those on the estate, but a really large house with drawing rooms, a conservatory, verandahs and several bathrooms. The first step towards building this cathedral was a present from his father-in-law, Tuca: a 400-square-metre plot in Rua Padre Leonel Franca in the smart district of Gávea. From then on all non-essential expenditure for the family was cut in favour of the house in Gávea. 'If we're going to build a house for everyone,' declared Dr Pedro, as he was known, 'then everyone is going to have to cut back on spending.' No new clothes, no birthday parties, no presents, no unnecessary trips in the car. 'At the time,' the author recalls, 'we had nothing, but we didn't lack for anything either.' Christmas was saved for the children by the German electric trains and French dolls that their maternal grandparents gave them.

The dream house in Gávea caused the family a further problem. Instead of placing his savings in a bank, Pedro preferred to invest them in building materials and, since he had no shed in which to store these treasures, he kept everything in the house until he had enough capital to begin the construction work. As a result, both Coelho and his sister recall spending their childhood among lavatory bowls, taps, bags of cement and tiles.

The cutbacks did not, however, impoverish Coelho's intellectual life. Although his father no longer bought any new records, he nevertheless listened to classical music every night. And anyone pressing his ear to the front door of No. 11 would have heard Bach and Tchaikovsky being played by Lygia on the piano that had been with her since before she was married. The house was also full of books, mainly collected by Lygia.

At the beginning of 1952, when he was four and a half, Coelho's parents enrolled him in kindergarten, where he spent two years. Then, in 1954, intending eventually to send their son to a Jesuit secondary school, St Ignatius College, he was moved to Our Lady Victorious School, which was seen as the best route to St Ignatius – the most traditional school of its kind in Rio, and one of the most respected educational establishments for boys in the city. St Ignatius was expensive, but it guaranteed the one thing that the Coelhos regarded as essential: strict discipline.

It was certainly true that, at least in Paulo's case, the *cordon sanitaire* placed around the estate to protect the children from the evil world outside had no effect. At five, he was already viewed by his adult neighbours as a bad influence on their children. As there were two other children on the estate called Paulo (his cousins, Paulo Arraes and Paulo Araripe), he was simply called 'Coelho'. To Lygia and Pedro's horror, suspicions that it was 'Coelho' who was responsible for many of the odd things that were happening in the small community began to be confirmed. First, there was the discovery of a small girl bound hand and foot to a tree so that she appeared to be hugging it and who was too afraid to tell on the culprit. Then came the information that, at dead of night, the boys were organizing chicken races, which ended with all the competitors, apart from the winner, having their necks wrung. One day, someone replaced the contents of all the cans of hair lacquer belonging to the young girls on the estate with water. It was one of the victims of this last jape – Cecília Arraes, an older cousin – who worked out who the culprit was. She found a satchel in one of the boys' hiding places containing papers that revealed the existence of a 'secret organization' complete with statutes, the names of the leaders and the minutes of meetings. This was the Arco Organization, its name being taken from the first two letters of the surnames of the chief perpetrators, Paulo Araripe and Paulo Coelho.

Cecília collared the future author and said: 'So what's this Arco business? What does the organization do? If you don't tell me, I'm going to your parents.'

He was terrified. 'It's a secret organization, so I'm forbidden to tell you anything.' When his cousin continued to threaten him, he said: 'No, really, I can't tell you. The only thing I can say is that Arco is an organization specializing in sabotage.' He went on to explain that both the water in the girls' hair lacquer and the girl being tied to the tree were punishments for their having crossed the chalk frontier scratched on the ground to mark the borders of Arco territory, beyond which lay an area 'forbidden to girls'.

When evidence of Paulo's involvement in the matter reached his parents, they were in no doubt that, when he was old enough, the boy should definitely be placed in the stern, wise hands of the Jesuits. While at Our Lady Victorious, he became accustomed to the regime that he would find at St Ignatius, for, unlike at other schools, the pupils had classes on Saturdays and were free on Wednesdays. This meant that Paulo only had Sunday to play with his friends on the estate. On Saturdays, when they were all off, he had to spend the day at school. On Wednesdays, when he was free but had no companions, he had no alternative but to stay at home reading and studying.

The children at Our Lady Victorious ranged in age from seven to eleven, and the school made a point of inculcating the pupils with a belief in the values of hard work and of respect for one's fellows. The children had to learn by heart the school rules, one of which was: 'It shows a lack of politeness, Christian charity and fellowship to wound less talented or less intelligent colleagues by words or laughter.' Coelho loathed all the subjects he was taught, without exception. The only reason he put up with the torment of spending his days bent over his books was that he had to get good marks in order to move up to the next year. In the first two years he spent at Our Lady Victorious, he managed to achieve well-above-average marks. However, from the third year on, things began to slip, as can be seen in a letter he sent to Pedro on Father's Day in 1956:

Papa,

I only got one in my maths test, so I'm going to have to study with you every night. My averages in the other subjects improved though. In religion I went from zero to six, in Portuguese from zero to six and a half, but in maths I went from four and a half to two and a half. My overall place in the class was still pretty bad, but I improved a bit, moving from twenty-fifth to sixteenth.

Love,

Paulo

Twenty-fifth was, in fact, bottom of the class, given that the classes at Our Lady Victorious had a maximum of twenty-five boys in them. However, the fact that he was bottom of the class didn't mean that the Coelhos were bringing up a fool. On the contrary. Their son may have hated studying, but he loved reading. He would read anything and every-thing, from fairy tales to Tarzan, and whatever his parents bought him or his friends lent him. Little by little, Coelho became the estate's resident storyteller. Years later, his aunt, Cecília Dantas Arraes, would recall the 'boy with skinny legs and baggy, wide-legged trousers': 'When he wasn't thinking up some mischief, he would be sitting on the pavement with his friends around him while he told stories.'

One night, he was with his parents and grandparents watching a quiz programme, *The Sky's the Limit*. A professor was answering questions about the Roman Empire and when the quiz master asked the professor who had succeeded Julius Caesar, Paulo jumped up and, to everyone's astonishment, said: 'Octavius Augustus', adding: 'I've always liked Octavius Augustus. He was the one August was named after, and that's the month I was born in.'

Knowing more than his friends was one way of compensating for his physical weakness. He was very thin, frail and short, and both on the estate and at school he was known as 'Pele' – 'skin' – a Rio term used at the time for boys who were always getting beaten up by their classmates. He may have been his peers' favourite victim, but he soon learned that knowing things no one else knew and reading stories none of his peers had read was one way of gaining their respect.

He realized that he would never come top in anything at school, but when he learned that there was to be a writing competition for all the boys in the third year, he decided to enter. The subject was 'The Father of Aviation', Alberto Santos Dumont. This is what Coelho wrote:

Once upon a time, there was a boy named Alberto Santos Dumont. Every day, early in the morning, Alberto would watch the birds flying and sometimes he would think: 'If eagles can fly, why can't I, after all, I'm more intelligent than the eagles.' Santos Dumont then decided to study hard, and his father and his mother, Francisca Dumont, sent him to an aeromodelling school.

Other people, such as Father Bartholomew and Augusto Severo, had tried to fly before. Augusto Severo flew in a balloon that he had built, but it fell to earth and he died. But Santos Dumont did not give up. He built a balloon that was a tube filled with gas and he flew, went round the Jefel [sic] Tower in Paris and landed in the same place he had taken off from.

Then he decided to invent an aeroplane that was heavier than air. Its shell was made of bamboo and silk. In 1906, in Champs de Bagatelle, he tried out the aeroplane. Lots of people laughed, convinced he would never fly. But Santos Dumont with his 14-bis travelled along for more than 220 metres and suddenly the wheels left the ground. When the crowd saw it there was a cry of 'Ah!' And that was it, aviation had been invented.

The best composition was to be chosen by a vote among the pupils. Paulo was so lacking in confidence that when it came to voting, he ended up choosing the work of another pupil. When the votes were counted, though, he was astonished to find that he was the winner. The pupil for whom he had voted came second, but was later disqualified when it was discovered that he had copied the text from a newspaper article.

However, Paulo's performance in the competition was not reflected in other subjects. When the time came for him to take the entrance exam for St Ignatius, the strict discipline and sacrifices imposed by the harsh regime at Our Lady Victorious proved useless and he failed. As punishment, in order to prepare for the retake, he was forced to stay in Rio having private lessons. This meant he had to forgo the annual family holiday in Araruama, where one of his uncles lived. To make sure that he had no spare time, his mother, who was also concerned by his lack of physical strength, decided that in the mornings he would attend PE classes at a holiday camp in Fortaleza de São João, an army unit in the peaceful, romantic area of Urca in the central region of Rio. Forced to do the two things he most hated – physical exercise in the morning and studying in the afternoon – Paulo felt as if he were spending two months in hell.

Every morning, Lygia took a bus with her son that went directly from Botafogo to Urca, where she handed him over to his tormentors. The climax of the nightmare was the dreaded jump into the river, which the boys – about fifty of them – were forced to do every day at the end of a seemingly endless session of bending, running and bar work. The boys, who were always accompanied by adult instructors, were placed in line and forced to jump from a bridge into the icy water of the river that cuts through the woods around the fortress. Even though he knew there was no chance of drowning or being hurt, the mere thought of doing this made Paulo panic. Initially, he was always last in line. His heart would pound, the palms of his hands would sweat and he felt like crying, calling for his mother, even peeing his pants: he would have done anything to avoid making that leap were it not for the fact that he was even more afraid of looking like a coward. Then he discovered the solution: 'If I was first in line, I would suffer for less time.' Problem solved. 'Not that I got over my fear of jumping,' he recalled years later, 'but the suffering ended and I learned my first lesson in life: if it's going to hurt, confront the problem straight away because at least then the pain will stop.'

These were, in fact, wasted days, in terms of both money and suffering, since he again failed the entrance exam. After spending the whole of 1958 preparing, however, he finally passed and did so with the excellent average mark of 8.3. High marks not only guaranteed admission to the school but also meant being given the title of 'Count'. If his performance improved still more he could become a 'Marquis' or even, as all parents dreamed of their children becoming, a 'Duke', a title reserved for those who ended the year with an average of 10 in all subjects.

But he never fulfilled his parents' dream. The entrance exam was the one moment of glory in his educational career. A graph based on his school reports for 1959 onwards shows a descending curve that would only end when he completed his science course in 1965 at one of the worst colleges in Rio de Janeiro. It was as though he were saying to his parents: 'Your dream of having a son at St Ignatius has come true, now leave me in peace.' As he himself remarked many years later, that mark of 8.3 was his final act in the world of the normal.

CHAPTER 3

Schooldays

IF THE DEVIL WAS HIDING in the hallowed walls of St Ignatius, paradise was 100 kilometres from Rio in Araruama, where Paulo Coelho usually spent the school holidays, almost always with his sister, Sônia Maria, who was two years younger. When family finances allowed, which was rare, they would go to Belém do Pará, where their paternal grandparents lived. Araruama, famous for its long beaches, was chosen by the Coelhos not for its natural beauty but because they had a guaranteed welcome at the home of Paulo's great-uncle, the eccentric José Braz Araripe. He had graduated in mechanical engineering and, in the 1920s, had been employed by the state-owned navigation company Lóide Brasileiro to run the ship repair yard owned by the company in the United States. With the help of another Brazilian engineer, Fernando Iehly de Lemos, Araripe spent all his free time in the Lóide laboratories working on the development of an invention that would change his life, as well as that of millions of consumers worldwide: the automatic gear box. Araripe based his invention on a prototype created in 1904 by the Sturtevant brothers in Boston, which was never taken up because it had only two speeds and would only work when the engine was on full power. It was not until 1932, after countless hours of tests, that Araripe's and Lemos's revolutionary invention was finally patented. That year, General Motors bought the rights from them for mass production, which began in 1938 when GM announced that the Oldsmobile had as an option the greatest thing since the invention of the automobile itself: the Hydra-Matic system, a luxury for which the consumer would pay an additional US$70, about a tenth of the total price of the car. Some say that the two Brazilians each pocketed a small fortune in cash at the time, and nothing else; others say that both opted to receive a percentage of each gearbox sold during their lifetime. Whatever the truth of the matter, from then on, money was never a problem for Araripe, or 'Uncle José', as he was known to his great-nephew and -niece.

With no worries about the future, Uncle José left Lóide and returned to Brazil. It might have been expected that he would live in Rio, close to his family; however, during his time in the United States, he had suffered a slight accident at work, which caused him to lose some movement in his left arm, and someone told him that the black sands of Araruama would be an infallible remedy. He moved there, bought a large piece of land on one of the main streets in the city, and built a six-bedroom house in which all the walls and furniture were retractable. At the command of their owner, walls, beds and tables would disappear, turning the residence into a large workshop where Uncle José worked and built his inventions.

In summer, walls and furniture would be restored in readiness to receive the children. One night a week during the holidays, the walls would disappear again in order to create an area for watching 35mm films on a professional film projector and the workshop would become a cinema. Some summers, Uncle José would have more than twenty guests, among them his great-nephews and -nieces, friends, and the few adults who had the impossible job of keeping an eye on the children. The children's parents were appalled by the man's unconventional behaviour, but the comfort he offered them outweighed their concerns. Anxious mothers whispered that, as well as being an atheist, José held closed sessions of pornographic films when there were only boys in the house – which was, indeed, true – and he took off his oil-stained dungarees (under which he never wore underpants) only on special occasions; but he was open and generous and shared the eccentricities of his house with his neighbours. When he learned that the television he had bought was the only one in town, he immediately turned the screen to face the street and thus improvised a small auditorium where, from seven to ten at night, everyone could enjoy the new phenomenon.

Michele Conte and Jorge Luiz Ramos, two of Coelho's friends in Araruama, recall that, every year, Coelho would arrive from Rio bearing some new 'toy'. Once, it was a Diana airgun with which he shot his first bird, a grassquit whose black wings he carefully plucked and stuck to a piece of paper with the date and a note of the bird's characteristics (a trophy that was to remain among his childhood mementoes in his house in Rio). The following year, he appeared with a diving mask and flippers, which prompted Uncle José to make him a submarine harpoon, its shafts propelled by a wire spring like a medieval man-of-war.

Like the other children, visitors and locals, Paulo woke every day when it was still dark. The town's residents recall a boy with skinny legs, knee-length socks and baggy shorts. The group would disappear off into the woods, explore the lakes, steal boats and go fishing, invade orchards or explore grottoes and caves. On returning home at the end of the day, they would hand over the spoils of their expedition – doves brought down with shot or fish spiked with Uncle José's harpoon – to Rosa, the cook, who would clean and prepare them for dinner. They would often return bruised or scratched or, as was the case once with Paulo, having been arrested by the forest rangers for hunting wild animals.

When Lygia arrived at the weekend to see her children, she would find herself in a party atmosphere. She would take up her guitar and spend the nights playing songs by Trini Lopez and by the rising star Roberto Carlos, accompanied by the children. The only thing Paulo did not enjoy was dancing. He found the parades in Rio fun, but hated dancing, and felt ridiculous when forced by his friends to jump around at Carnival dances in Araruama. To avoid humiliation, he would go straight to the toilets when he arrived at the club, hold his shirt under the tap and put it on again, soaking wet. If anyone invited him to dance he had his excuse ready: 'I've just been dancing. Look how sweaty I am. I'm going to take a break – I'll be back soon.'

Araruama was the place where he made various adolescent discoveries, like getting drunk for the first time. He and two friends went to one of the town's deserted beaches and swiftly downed two bottles of rum he had bought secretly in Rio and concealed among his clothes at the bottom of his suitcase. As a result, he fell asleep on the beach and woke with his body all swollen with sunburn. He was ill for several days. So bad was the hangover that, unlike most boys of his generation, he never became a serious drinker.

He also experienced his first kiss on one of these holidays. Although he liked to boast theatrically to his friends that destiny had reserved something rather different for his first kiss, namely a prostitute, that kiss in fact took place in the innocent atmosphere of Araruama and was shared with the eldest sister of his friend Michele, Élide – or Dedê – who was a little younger than he. It was in Araruama, too, that he experienced his first sexual impulses. When he discovered that his uncle had made the walls of the rooms of very light, thin wood so that they could easily be raised, Paulo managed secretly to bore a hole in one wall large enough for him to enjoy the solitary privilege, before falling asleep, of spying on his female cousins, who were sleeping naked in the next room. He was shocked to see that girls had curly hair covering their private parts. In his amazement, he grew breathless, his heart pounded and his legs shook, so much so that he feared that he might have an asthma attack and be caught in flagrante.

The respiratory problems he had suffered from since birth had developed, with puberty, into a debilitating asthma. The attacks, which were caused by a variety of things – changes in the weather, dust, mould, smoke – were unpredictable. They began with breathlessness, a cough and a whistling in his chest, and culminated in terrible feelings of asphyxia, when his lungs felt as if they were about to burst. He had to make sure that he always had his bag full of cough syrups, medication to dilate the bronchial tubes (usually in the form of cortisone tablets) and a 'puffer' to alleviate the symptoms.

Quite often his parents would take it in turns to sit by his bed at night in order to be there during an emergency and once, in despair, Lygia took him to a faith healer who had been recommended by friends. When they arrived at the consulting room, the man gazed fixedly into Paulo's eyes

and said just five words: 'I can see Dr Fritz.'* This was enough for Lygia
to take her son by the hand and leave, muttering: 'This is no place for a
Christian.' When the asthma manifested itself in Araruama, far from his
mother's care, the exchange of letters between Paulo and his mother
became more frequent and, at times, worrying: 'Could you come with
Aunt Elisa to look after me?' he asked, tearfully. Such requests would
provoke anxious telegrams from Lygia to the aunt who looked after the
children on holiday, one saying: 'I'm really worried about Paulo's asthma.
The doctor said he should be given one ampoule of Reductil for three
days and two Meticorten tablets a day. Let me know how things are.'

Although he said that he loved receiving letters, but hated writing
them, as soon as he could read and write, and when he was away from
home, Paulo would fill page after page, mostly addressed to his parents.
Their content reveals a mature, delicate child concerned with his reputation as a bad, ill-behaved student. His letters to Lygia were mawkish and
full of sentimentality, like this one, sent on Mother's Day 1957, when he
was nine:

> Dear Mama: No, no, we don't need May 8th to remember all the good
> things we've received from you. Your constant love and dedication,
> even though we're, very often, bad, disobedient children.
>
> [...] The truth is, it's your love that forgives us. That resilient love
> that never snaps like chewing gum. May God keep you, darling
> Mama, and forgive my errors because I'm still only small and I prom-
> ise to improve very very soon.
>
> Lots of love,
>
> Paulinho

The letters he sent to his father were more formal, even down to the
signature, and written in a rather complaining tone.

---

* Adolf Fritz, generally called Dr Fritz, was a hypothetical German surgeon whose
spirit was said to have been channelled by various psychic surgeons in Brazil,
starting with Zé Arigo in the 1950s and continuing up to the present. There is no
proof that he actually existed.

Papa,

Have you sent my leaflets to be printed? And how is the new house going? When are we going to move in?

I'm counting on your presence here the next time you come.

Love,

Paulo Coelho

As time went by, letter-writing became a regular thing for him. He would write to his parents, uncles and aunts, grandparents and friends. If he had no one to write to, he would simply jot down his ideas on small pieces of paper and then hide his scribbled thoughts in a secret place away from prying eyes. When he was about twelve he bought a pocket diary in which he began to make daily entries. He would always write in ink, in a slightly wobbly hand, but with few grammatical errors. He began by recording typical adolescent tasks – 'tidy my desk', 'Fred's birthday' and 'send a telegram to Grandpa Cazuza' – and gradually he also began to record things he had done, seen or merely thought. Sometimes these were short notes to himself, such as 'swap s. with Zeca', 'papa: equations' and 'do part E of the plan'. This was also the first time he sketched a self-portrait:

I was born on 24 August 1947 in the São José Hospital. I have lived on this estate since I was small. I have attended three schools and in all three I was regarded as a prince because of the way I dressed. I've always had good marks in all the schools I've been to.

I really like studying, but I also like playing. I've never been interested in opera or romantic music. I hate rock-and-roll, but I really like popular Brazilian music. I only like carnival when I'm taken to fancy-dress balls.

I really like adventures, but I'm scared of dangerous things [...] I've had several girlfriends already. I love sport. I want to be a chemist when I grow up because I like working with flasks and medicines. I love the cinema, fishing and making model aeroplanes.

I like reading comics and doing crosswords. I hate picnics and outings or anything that's boring.

This regular exercise of writing about himself or things that happened during the day attracted him so much that he began to record everything – either in a diary kept in a spiral notebook or by dictating into a cassette recorder and keeping the tapes. Later, with the arrival of computers he put together the entire set of records covering the four decades of confessions that he had accumulated up until then and stored them in a trunk, which he padlocked. In those 170 handwritten notebooks and 94 cassettes lay hidden the minutiae of his life and soul from 1959, when he was twelve years old, up to 1995, when he was forty-eight and began to write directly on to a computer. He was famous by then, and had stated in his will that immediately following his death, the trunk and its entire contents should be burned. However, for reasons that will be explained later, he changed his mind and allowed the writer of this biography free access to this material. Diaries are records produced almost simultaneously with the emotion or action described, and are often cathartic exercises for the person writing them. This is clear from Coelho's diaries, where he often speaks of the more perverse sides of his personality, often to the detriment of his more generous and sensitive side.

The diary gave the author the freedom to fantasize at will. Contrary to what he wrote in the self-portrait quoted above, Coelho rarely dressed smartly, he loathed studying just as he loathed sport and his love life was not always happy. According to his diary, his cousin Cecília, his neighbour Mónica, who lived on the estate, Dedê, with whom he shared his first kiss in Araruama, and Ana Maria, or Tatá, a pretty dark-haired girl with braces, were all girlfriends. Young love is often a troubling business, and the appearance of the last of these girls in his life was the subject of dramatically embroidered reports. 'For the first time, I cried because of a woman,' he wrote. At night, unable to sleep, he saw himself as a character in a tragedy: as he cycled past his lover's house, he was run over by a car and fell to the ground covered in blood. Somehow, Tatá was there at his side and knelt sobbing beside his body in time to hear him utter his last words: 'This is my blood. It was shed for you. Remember me ...'

Although the relationship was purely platonic, Tatá's parents took an immediate dislike to Coelho. Forbidden to continue her relationship with that 'strange boy', she nevertheless stood up to her family. She told Paulo that her mother had even hit her, but still she wouldn't give him up. However, when he was holidaying in Araruama, he received a two-line note from Chico, a friend who lived on the estate: 'Tatá has told me to tell you it's all over. She's in love with someone else.' It was as though the walls in Uncle José's house had fallen in on him. It wasn't just the loss of his girlfriend but the loss of face before his friends for having been so betrayed, cuckolded by a woman. He could take anything but that. He therefore invented an extraordinary story, which he described in a letter to his friend the following day. Chico was told to tell everyone that he had lied about his relationship with Tatá; he had never actually felt anything for her, but as a secret agent of the CIC – the Central Intelligence Center, a US spy agency – he had received instructions to draw up a dossier on her. This was the only reason he had got close to her. A week later, after receiving a second letter from Chico, he noted in his diary: 'He believed my story, but from now on, I have a whole string of lies to live up to. Appearances have been saved, but my heart is aching.'

Lygia and Pedro also had aching hearts, although not because of love. The first months their son had spent at St Ignatius had been disastrous. The days when he brought back his monthly grades were a nightmare. While his sister, Sônia Maria, was getting top marks at her school, Paulo's marks got steadily worse. With only rare exceptions – usually in unimportant subjects such as choral singing or craftwork – he hardly ever achieved the necessary average of 5 if he was to stay on at the school. It was only when he was forced to study for hours on end at home and given extra tuition in various subjects that he managed to complete the first year, but even then his average was only a poor 6.3. In the second year, things deteriorated still further. He continued to get high marks in choral singing, but couldn't achieve even the minimum average grade in the subjects that mattered – maths, Portuguese, history, geography, Latin and English. However, his parents were sure that the iron hand of the Jesuits would bring their essentially good-natured son back to the straight and narrow.

As time went by, he became more and more timid, retiring and insecure. He began to lose interest even in the favourite sport of his schoolmates, which was to stand at the gates of the Colégio Jacobina, where his sister was a pupil, to watch the girls coming out. This was a delight they would all remember for the rest of their lives, as the author and scriptwriter Ricardo Hofstetter, who was also a pupil at the Jesuit college, was to recall:

> It was pure magic to walk those two or three blocks to see them coming out. I still have the image in my mind: the girls' slim, exquisite legs, half on view, half hidden by their pleated skirts. They came out in groups, groups of legs and pleated skirts that the wind would make even more exciting. Anyone who experienced this knows that there was nothing more sublime in the world, although I never went out with a girl at the Jacobina.

Nor did Paulo, not at the Jacobina or anywhere else. Apart from innocent flirtations and notes exchanged with the girls on the estate or in Araruama, he reached young adulthood without ever having had a real girlfriend. When his friends got together to brag about their conquests – never anything more than holding hands or a quick kiss or a squeeze – he was the only one who had no adventure to talk of. Fate had not made him handsome. His head was too big for his skinny body and his shoulders narrow. He had fleshy lips, like his father's, and his nose, too, seemed over-large for the face of a boy of his age.

He became more solitary with each day that passed and buried himself in books – not those the Jesuits had them read at school, which he loathed, but adventure stories and novels. However, while he may have become a voracious reader, this still did not improve his performance at school. At the end of every year, in the public prize-giving ceremonies, he had become used to seeing his colleagues – some of whom went on to become leading figures in Brazilian public life – receiving diplomas and medals, while he was never once called to go up to the dais. He only narrowly avoided being kept down a year and thus forced to find another school, since at St Ignatius, staying down was synonymous with being thrown out.

While their son proved himself to be a resounding failure, his parents at least lived in hope that he would become a good Christian and, indeed, he appeared to be well on the way to this. While averse to study, he felt comfortable in the heavily religious atmosphere of the college. He would don his best clothes and happily attend the obligatory Sunday mass, which was celebrated entirely in Latin, and he became familiar with the mysterious rituals such as covering the images of the saints during Lent with purple cloths. Even the dark underground catacombs where the mortal remains of the Jesuits lay aroused his curiosity, although he never had the courage to visit them.

His parents' hopes were re-awakened during his fourth year, when he decided to go on a retreat held by the school. These retreats lasted three or four days, and took place during the week so that they would not seem like a holiday camp or mere recreation. They were always held at the Padre Anchieta Retreat House, or the Casa da Gávea, as it was known – a country house high up in the then remote district of São Conrado, 15 kilometres from the centre of Rio. Built in 1935 and surrounded by woods, it was a large three-storey building with thirty blue-framed windows in the front. These were the windows of the bedrooms where the guests stayed, each with a magnificent view of the deserted beach of São Conrado. The Jesuits never tired of repeating that the silence in the house was so complete that at any hour of the day or night and in any corner of the building you could hear the waves breaking on the beach below.

It was on a hot October morning in 1962 that Paulo left for his encounter with God. In a small suitcase packed by his mother, he took, as well as his clothes and personal belongings, his new, inseparable companions: a notebook and a fountain pen with which to make the notes that were more and more taking on the form of a diary. At eight in the morning, all the boys were standing in the college courtyard and as they waited for the bus to take them to the retreat house, Coelho was suddenly filled with courage. With two friends he went into the chapel in the dark, and walked round the altar and down the stairs towards the catacombs. Lit only by candles, the crypt, which was full of coffins, looked even gloomier. To his surprise, though, instead of being filled with terror, as he had always imagined he would be, he had an indescribable feeling of well-being. He seemed inspired to search for an explanation for his unexpected bravery. 'Perhaps I wasn't seeing death in all its terror,' he wrote in his notebook, 'but the eternal rest of those who had lived and suffered for Jesus.'

Half an hour later, they were all at the Casa da Gávea. During the days that followed, Paulo shared with another young boy a bare cubicle provided with two beds, a wardrobe, a table, two chairs and a little altar attached to the wall. In a corner was a china wash basin and above it a mirror. Once they had unpacked, both boys went down to the refectory, where they were given tea and biscuits. The spiritual guide for the group was Father João Batista Ruffier, who announced the rules of the retreat, the first of which would come into force in the next ten minutes: a vow of silence. From then on, until they left at the end of the retreat, no one was allowed to say a single word. Father Ruffier, who was a stickler for the rules, was about to give one of his famous sermons, one that would remain in the memory of generations of those who attended St Ignatius.

'You are here like machines going into the workshop for a service. You can expect to be taken apart piece by piece. Don't be afraid of the amount of dirt that will come out. The most important thing is that you put back each piece in its right place with total honesty.'

The sermon lasted almost an hour, but it was those opening words that went round and round in Paulo's head all afternoon, as he walked alone in the woods surrounding the house. That night he wrote in his diary, 'I have reviewed all my thoughts of the last few days and I'm ready to put things right.' He said a Hail Mary and an Our Father, and fell asleep.

Although Father Ruffier had made it clear what the retreat was for – 'Here you will drive away the temptations of life and consecrate yourselves to meditation and prayer' – not everyone was there for Christian reflection. Everyone knew that once dinner was over and after the final prayer of the day had been said, shadows would creep along the dark corridors of the house to meet secretly in small groups for whispered games of poker and pontoon. If one of the boys had managed to smuggle in a transistor radio – something that was expressly forbidden – someone would immediately suggest placing a bet on the races at the Jockey Club. From midnight to dawn the religious atmosphere was profaned by betting, smoking and even drinking contraband whisky concealed in shampoo bottles. Whenever a light in a cubicle warned of suspicious activities, one of the more attentive priests would immediately turn off the electricity. This, however, didn't always resolve the problem, since the heretical game would continue in the light from candles purloined from the chapel during the day.

On the second day, Paulo woke at five in the morning, his mind confused, although his spirits improved a little when he opened the bedroom window and saw the sun coming up over the sea. At six on the dot, still not having eaten, he met his colleagues in the chapel for the daily mass, prepared to put things right with God and do something he had been putting off for almost a year: taking communion. The problem was not communion itself but the horror of confession, with which all the boys were familiar. They would arrive at the confessional prepared to reveal only the most banal of sins, but they knew that, in the end, the priest would always ask the inevitable question: 'Have you sinned against chastity, my son?' Should the reply be in the affirmative, the questions that followed were more probing: 'Alone or with someone else?' If it was with someone else, the priest would continue, to the mortification of the more timid boys: 'With a person or an animal?' If the response was 'with a person', the sinner was not required to reveal the name of the partner, only the sex: 'With a boy or with a girl?'

Paulo found this an extremely difficult topic to deal with and he didn't understand how it could be a sin. He was so convinced that masturbation was not a shameful activity that he wrote in his notebook: 'No one on this earth can throw the first stone at me, because no one has avoided this temptation.' In spite of this, he had never had the courage to confess to a priest that he masturbated, and living in a permanent state of sin troubled him deeply. With his soul divided, he preferred merely to say the act of contrition and to receive communion without going to confession.

Following mass, Father Ruffier returned to the charge with a particularly harsh sermon. Before a terrified audience, he painted a terrifying picture of the place intended for all sinners: 'We are in hell! The fire is burning mercilessly! Here one sees only tears and hears only the grinding of teeth in mutual loathing. I come across a colleague and curse him for being the cause of my condemnation. And while we weep in pain and remorse, the Devil smiles a smile that makes our suffering still greater. But the worst punishment, the worst pain, the worst suffering is that we have no hope. We are here for ever.'

Paulo was in no doubt: Father Ruffier was talking about him. After twelve months without going to confession – so as not to have to touch on the taboo subject of masturbation – he realized that if he were to die suddenly, his final destiny would be hell. He imagined the Devil looking into his eyes and snickering sarcastically: 'My dear boy, your suffering hasn't even begun yet.' He felt helpless, powerless and confused. He had no one to turn to, but he knew that a Jesuit retreat was a place of certainties, not of doubts. Faced with a choice between suffering in the flames for all eternity as described by the priest and giving up his solitary pleasure, he chose faith. Deeply moved and kneeling alone on the stone floor of the mirador, he turned to God and made a solemn promise never to masturbate again.

His decision gave him courage and calmed him, but that feeling of calm was short-lived. The following day, the Devil counter-attacked with such force that he could not resist the temptation and, defeated, he masturbated. He left the bathroom as though his hands were covered in blood, knelt in front of the altar and implored: 'Lord! I want to change, but I can't stop myself! I've said endless acts of contrition, but I can't stop sinning. I sin in thought, word and deed. Give me strength! Please! Please! Please!' Full of despair, he only felt relief when, in a whispered conversation in the woods, he found that he had a companion in eternal suffering: a fellow pupil who had also been masturbating during the retreat.

Ashamed of his own weakness, Paulo was subjected to two more sermons from Father Ruffier, which seemed to have been chosen especially to instil fear into the minds of the boys. Once again, the priest deployed dramatic and terrifying images, this time to alert the boys to the perils of clinging on to material values. From the pulpit Father Ruffier gesticulated like an actor, shaking his short, muscular arms and saying: 'Truly, truly I say unto you, my children: the time will come when we shall all be laid low. Imagine yourselves dying. In the hospital room, your relatives white with fear. The bedside table is crammed with different medicines, all useless now. It is then that you see how powerless you are. You humbly recognize that you are powerless. What good will fame, money, cars, luxuries be at the fatal hour? What use are those things if your death lies in the hands of the Creator?' With his fists clenched, and as though possessed by divine fury, he declared vehemently: 'We must give up everything, my sons! We must give up everything!'

These words should not be confused with an exhortation to embrace socialism or anything of the sort. Not only were the sons of some of the wealthiest families in Rio de Janeiro in the congregation, but the college was politically conservative and was always showing films of executions by firing squads in Fidel Castro's Cuba in order to show the boys 'the bloodthirsty nature of communism'. And Father Ruffier himself was proud of the fact that he had had to leave Colombia in a hurry 'to flee communism' (he was referring to the popular uprising in Bogotá in 1948, known as the Bogotazo).

While the boys stared at each other in astonishment, the priest spoke again. The subject was, once again, hell. Just in case he had not made himself clear in the first part of his sermon, he once more described the eternal state of suffering to which sinners would be condemned: 'Hell is like the sea that is there before us. Imagine a swallow coming along every hundred years and taking a drop of water each time. That swallow is you and that is your penance. You will suffer for millions and millions of years, but one day the sea will be empty. And you will say: at last, it's over and I can rest in peace.' He paused, then concluded: 'But then the Creator will smile from the heights and will say: "That was just the beginning. Now you will see other seas and that is how it will be for all eternity. The swallow empties the sea and I fill it up again."'

Paulo spent the rest of the day with these words echoing in his head. He went into the woods that surrounded the retreat house and tried to distract himself with the beauty of the view, but Father Ruffier's words only resonated inside him more loudly. That night, he set down his thoughts before finally falling asleep, and the notes he made appear to demonstrate the efficacy of the spiritual retreat.

Here, I've completely forgotten the world. I've forgotten that I'm going to fail maths, I've forgotten that Botafogo is top of the league and I've forgotten that I'm going to spend next week on the island of Itaipu. But I feel that with every moment spent forgetting, I'm learning to understand the world better. I'm going back to a world that I didn't understand before and which I hated, but which the retreat has taught me to love and understand. I've learnt here to see the beauty that lies in a piece of grass and in a stone. In short, I've learnt how to live.

Most important was the fact that he returned home certain that he had acquired the virtue which – through all the highs and lows of his life – would prove to be the connecting thread: faith. Even his parents, who appeared to have lost all hope of getting him back on the straight and narrow, were thrilled with the new Paulo. 'We're very happy to see that you finally appear to have got back on the right track,' Lygia declared when he returned. Her son's conversion had been all that was missing to complete domestic bliss, for a few months earlier, the family had finally moved into the large pink house built by Pedro Coelho with his own hands.

In fact, the move to Gávea happened before the building was completed, which meant that they still had to live for some time among tins of paint, sinks and baths piled up in corners. However, the house astonished everyone, with its dining room, sitting room and drawing room, its ensuite bathrooms in every bedroom, its marble staircase and its verandah. There was also an inner courtyard so large that Paulo later thought of using it as a rehearsal space for his plays. The move was a shock to Paulo. Moving from the estate in Botafogo, where he was born and where he was the unchallenged leader, to Gávea, which, at the time, was a vast wasteland with few houses and buildings, was a painful business. The change of district did nothing to lessen his parents' earlier fears, or, rather, his father's, and, obsessively preoccupied with the harm that the 'outside world' might do to his son's character and education, Pedro thought it best to ban him from going out at night. Suddenly, Paulo no longer had any friends and his life was reduced to three activities: sleeping, going to classes at St Ignatius and reading at home.

Reading was nothing new. He had even managed to introduce a clause concerning books in the Arco statutes, stating that, 'besides other activities, every day must include some recreational reading'. He had begun reading the children's classics that Brazilian parents liked to give their children; then he moved on to Conan Doyle and had soon read all of Sherlock Holmes. When he was told to read the annotated edition of *The Slum* by Aluísio Azevedo at school, he began by ridiculing it: 'I'm not enjoying the book. I don't know why Aluísio Azevedo brings sex into it so much.' Some chapters later, however, he radically changed his mind and praised the work highly: 'At last I'm beginning to understand the book: life without ideals, full of betrayal and remorse. The lesson I took from it is that life is long and disappointing. *The Slum* is a sublime book. It makes us think of the sufferings of others.' What had initially been a scholastic exercise had become a pleasure. From then on, he wrote reviews of all the books he read. His reports might be short and sharp, such as 'weak plot' when writing about *Aimez-vous Brahms?* by Françoise Sagan, or, in the case of *Vuzz* by P.A. Hourey, endless paragraphs saying how magnificent it was.

He read anything and everything, from Michel Quoist's lyrical poems to Jean-Paul Sartre. He would read best-sellers by Leon Uris, Ellery Queen's detective stories and pseudo-scientific works such as *O Homem no Cosmos* by Helio Jaguaribe, which he classed in his notes as 'pure, poorly disguised red propaganda'. Such condensed reviews give the impression that he read with one eye on the aesthetic and the other on good behaviour. Remarks such as 'His poetry contains the more degrading and entirely unnecessary aspects of human morality' (on *Para Viver um Grande Amor* by Vinicius de Moraes) or 'Brazilians aren't yet ready for this kind of book' (referring to the play *Bonitinha, mas Ordinária* by Nelson Rodrigues) were frequent in his listings. He had even more to say on Nelson Rodrigues: 'It's said that he's a slave to the public, but I don't agree. He was born for this type of literature, and it's not the people who are making him write it.'

Politically his reactions were no less full of preconceptions. When he saw the film *Seara Vermelha*, which was based on the book of the same name by Jorge Amado, he regretted that it was a work that was 'clearly

communist in outlook, showing man's exploitation of man'. He was pleas-
antly surprised, however, when he read Amado's best-seller *Gabriela,
Clove and Cinnamon*; indeed, he was positively intoxicated: 'It's so natural ... There's not a trace of communism in its pages. I really liked it.' He
felt that Manuel Bandeira was the greatest Brazilian poet ('because he
leaves aside unhealthy aspects of life, and because of his simple, economical style'); he loathed João Cabral de Melo Neto ('I read some of his
verses and I shut the book immediately'); and he confessed that he didn't
understand Carlos Drummond de Andrade ('He has a confused, abstract
style, which makes it hard to interpret his poetry').

It was apparently at this time, when he was thirteen or fourteen, that
Paulo showed the first signs of an undying *idée fixe*, a real obsession that
he would never lose – to be a writer. Almost half a century later, as one
of the most widely read authors of all time, he wrote in *The Zahir*:

> I write because when I was an adolescent, I was useless at football, I
> didn't have a car or much of an allowance, and I was pretty much of
> a weed ... I didn't wear trendy clothes either. That's all the girls in
> my class were interested in, and so they just ignored me. At night,
> when my friends were out with their girlfriends, I spent my free time
> creating a world in which I could be happy: my companions were
> writers and their books.

In fact, he saw himself as a writer well before he said as much. Besides
being the winner of the writing competition at Our Lady Victorious, from
the time he could read he had become a full-time poet. He would write
short verses and poems for his parents, grandparents, friends, cousins,
girlfriends and even the saints revered by his family. Compositions such
as 'Our Lady, on this febrile adolescent night/I offer you my pure child-
hood/That the fire is now devouring/And transforming into smoke so
that it may rise up to you/And may the fire also free me from the past',
which was inspired by the Virgin Mary; or four-line verses written for his
parents: 'If the greatest good in the world/Is given to those who are
parents/Then it is also a certain truth/That it is they who suffer most.' If
there was no one to whom he could dedicate his verses, he would write

to himself: 'The past is over/And the future has not yet arrived/I wander through the impossible present/Full of love, ideals and unbelief/As if I were simply/Passing through life.'

When, at a later age, he grew to know more about books and libraries, he came across a quote attributed to Émile Zola, in which the author of *J'Accuse* said something along the lines of 'My poetic muse has turned out to be a very dull creature; from now on, I shall write prose'. Whether or not these words were true of Zola, Paulo believed that the words were written precisely for him. He wrote in his diary: 'Today I ended my poetic phase in order to devote myself solely to the theatre and the novel.' He made a bonfire in the garden of everything he had written up to then – vast quantities of poems, sonnets and verses.

Such a promise, if meant seriously, would have been a proof of great ingratitude to the art of verse, for it was a poem he wrote – 'Mulher de Treze Anos' ['Thirteen-year-old Woman'] – that rescued him from anonymity among the 1,200 students at St Ignatius. One of the Jesuit traditions was the Academy of Letters of St Ignatius (ALSI), which had been created in 1941 and was responsible for cultural development of the students. Great names in Brazilian culture attended the events held by the ALSI. At the age of fourteen, Paulo appeared for the first time in the pages of the magazine *Vitória Colegial*, the official publication of the ALSI, with a small text entitled 'Why I Like Books'. It was an unequivocal defence of writers, whom he portrayed dramatically as people who spent sleepless nights, 'without eating, exploited by publishers', only to die forgotten:

What does a book represent? A book represents an unequalled wealth of culture. It is the book that opens windows on to the world for us. Through a book we experience the great adventures of Don Quixote and Tarzan as though we ourselves were the characters; we laugh at the hilarious tales of Don Camilo, we suffer as the characters in other great works of world literature suffer. For this reason, I like to read books in my free time. Through books we prepare ourselves for the future. We learn, just by reading them, theories that meant sacrifice and even death for those who discovered them.

Every didactic book is a step in the direction of the country's glorious horizon. This is why I like books when I'm studying. But what did it take for that book to arrive in our hands? Great sacrifice on the part of the author, whole nights spent starving and forgotten, their room sometimes lit only by the spluttering flame of a candle. And then, exploited by their publishers, they died forgotten, unjustly forgotten. What willpower on the part of others was needed for them to achieve a little fame! This is why I like books.

Months later, the ALSI announced the date for entries for its traditional annual poetry prize. Paulo had just seen the Franco-Italian film *Two Women*, directed by Vittorio de Sica, and left the cinema inspired. Based on the novel *La Ciociara*, by Alberto Moravia, the film tells the story of Cesira (Sophia Loren) and her thirteen-year-old daughter Rosetta (Eleanora Brown), both of whom have been raped by Allied soldiers during the Second World War. Paulo based his poem 'Thirteen-year-old Woman' on the character of Rosetta, and it was that poem which he then entered for the competition.

The day the poems were to be judged was one of endless agony. Paulo could think of nothing else. That evening, before the meeting when the three prize-winners were to be announced, he overcame his shyness and asked a member of the jury, a Portuguese teacher, whom he had voted for. He blushed at the response: 'I voted for you, Átila and Chame.'

Twenty poems were selected for the final. Paulo knew at least one of the chosen poems, 'Introduce', by José Átila Ramos, which, in his opinion, was the favourite. If his friend won, that would be fine, and if he himself managed at least third place, that would be wonderful. At nine in the evening, the auditorium was full of nervous boys soliciting votes and calculating their chances of winning. There was total silence as the jury, comprising two teachers and a pupil, began to announce in ascending order the three winners. When he heard that in third place was 'Serpentina and Columbina' and in second 'Introduce', he felt sure he hadn't been placed at all. So he almost fell off his chair when it was announced: 'The winner, by unanimous vote, is the poem ... "Thirteen-year-old Woman", by Paulo Coelho de Souza!'

First place! He couldn't believe what he was hearing. Heart pounding and legs shaking, the slight young boy crossed the room and stepped up on to the stage to receive the certificate and the prize, a cheque for 1,000 cruzeiros – about US$47. Once the ceremony was over, he was one of the first to leave the college, desperate to go straight home and for once give his parents some good news. On the tram on the way back to Gávea, he began to choose his words and work out the best way to tell his father that he had discovered his one and only vocation – to be a writer.

He was therefore somewhat surprised on reaching the house to find his father standing outside on the pavement, angrily tapping his watch and saying: 'It's almost eleven o'clock and you know perfectly well that in this house the doors are closed at ten, no argument.'

This time, though, Paulo had up his sleeve a trump card that would surely move his father's cold heart. Smiling, he brandished the trophy he had just won – the cheque for 1,000 cruzeiros – and told his father everything: the prize, the unanimous vote, the dozens of contestants, the discovery of his vocation.

But even this failed to win over his grim father. Apparently ignoring everything his son had said, Pedro poured cold water on the boy's excitement, saying: 'I'd prefer it if you got good marks at school and didn't come home so late.'

The thought that at least his mother would be thrilled by his win was dispelled in an instant. When he saw her waiting at the front door, he told her, eyes shining, what he had just told his father. To her son's dismay, Lygia quietly gave him the same lecture: 'My boy, there's no point dreaming about becoming a writer. It's wonderful that you write all these things, but life is different. Just think: Brazil is a country of seventy million inhabitants, it has thousands of writers, but Jorge Amado is the only one who can making a living by writing. And there's only one Jorge Amado.'

Desperately unhappy, depressed and close to tears, Paulo did not get to sleep until dawn. He wrote just one line in his diary: 'Mama is stupid. Papa is a fool.' When he woke, he had no doubt that his family was determined to bury for ever what he dramatically called 'my only reason for living' – being a writer. For the first time, he seemed to recognize that he was prepared to pay dearly to realize his dream, even if this meant clashing with his parents. Lygia and Pedro Queima Coelho were not going to have long to wait.

CHAPTER 4

First play, first love

A T THE END OF 1962, at his father's insistence, Paulo was forced to
enrol in the science stream rather than the arts as he had hoped. His
scholastic performance in the fourth year had been disastrous, and he had
finished the year having to re-sit maths, the subject at which his father so
excelled. In the end, he passed with a 5 – not a decimal point more than
the mark required to move on to the next year and remain at St Ignatius.
In spite of this and Paulo's declared intention to study the arts, his parents
insisted that he study engineering and, following his appalling scholastic
performance, he was in no position to insist.

However, from his point of view, the practical Pedro Coelho had
reasons for hoping that his son might yet be saved and become an engineer.
These hopes lay not only in the interest Paulo had shown in his grandfather's success as a mechanic – professional and amateur. As a boy, Paulo
had frequently asked his parents to buy him copies of the magazine
Mecânica Popular, a publication dating from the 1950s that taught readers
how to do everything from fixing floor polishers to building boats and
houses. When he was ten or eleven he was so passionate about aeroplane
modelling that any father would have seen in this a promising future as an
aeronautical engineer. The difference was that, while lots of children play
with model aeroplanes, Paulo set up the Clube Sunday, of which he and his

cousin Fred, who lived in Belém, were sole members. Since a distance of 3,000 kilometres separated them and their aeroplanes, the club's activities ended up being a chronological list of the models each had acquired. At the end of each month, Paulo would record all this information in a notebook – the names and characteristics of the small planes they had acquired, the serial number, wing span, date and place of purchase, general construction expenses, the date, place and reason for the loss of the plane whenever this occurred. Not one of these pieces of information served any purpose, but 'It was best to keep things organized,' Paulo said. When the glider Chiquita smashed into a wall in Gávea, it was thought worthy of special mention: 'It only flew once, but since it was destroyed heroically, I award this plane the Combat Cross. Paulo Coelho de Souza, Director.'

This fascination for model aeroplanes rapidly disappeared, but it gave way to another mania, even more auspicious for anyone wanting his son to be an engineer: making rockets. For some months Paulo and Renato Dias, a classmate at St Ignatius, spent all their spare time on this new activity. No one can say how or when it began – not even Paulo can remember – but the two spent any free time during the week in the National Library reading books about such matters as 'explosive propulsion', 'solid fuels' and 'metallic combustibles'. On Sundays and holidays, the small square in front of the Coelho house became a launch pad. As was almost always the case with Paulo, everything had to be set down on paper first. In his usual meticulous way, he started a small notebook entitled 'Astronautics – Activities to be Completed by the Programme for the Construction of Space Rockets'. Timetables stated the time taken on research in books, the specifications of materials used in the construction and the type of fuel. On the day of the launch, he produced a typewritten document with blank spaces to be filled in by hand at the time of the test, noting date, place, time, temperature, humidity and visibility.

The rockets were made of aluminium tubing about 20 centimetres in length and weighing 200 grams and had wooden nose cones. They were propelled by a fuel the boys had concocted out of 'sugar, gunpowder, magnesium and nitric acid'. This concentrated mixture was placed in a container at the base of the rocket, and the explosive cocktail was detonated using a wick soaked in kerosene. The rockets were given illustrious names: Goddard I, II and III, and Von Braun I, II and III, in homage, respectively, to the American aeronautics pioneer Robert H. Goddard and the creator of the German flying bombs that devastated London during the Second World War, Wernher von Braun. However, although the rockets were intended to rise up to 17 metres, they never did. On launch days, Paulo would take over a part of the pavement outside their house 'for the public' and convert a hole that the telephone company had forgotten to close up into a trench where he and his friend could shelter. He then invited his father, the servants and passers-by to sign the flight reports as 'representatives of the government'. The rockets failed to live up to the preparations. Not one ever rose more than a few centimetres into the air and the majority exploded before they had even got off the ground. Paulo's astronautical phase disappeared as fast as it had arrived and in less than six months the space programme was abandoned before a seventh rocket could be constructed.

Apart from these fleeting fancies – stamp-collecting was another – Paulo continued to nurture his one constant dream – to become a writer. When he was sixteen, his father, in a conciliatory gesture, offered him a flight to Belém, which, to Paulo, was a paradise on a par with Araruama. Nevertheless, he turned it down, saying that he would rather have a typewriter. His father agreed and gave him a Smith Corona, which would stay with him until it was replaced, first, by an electric Olivetti and, then, decades later, by a laptop computer.

His total lack of interest in education meant that he was among the least successful students in his class in the first year of his science studies and at the end of the year he once again scraped through with a modest 5.2 average. His report arrived on Christmas Eve. Paulo never quite knew whether it was because of his dreadful marks or an argument over the length of his hair, but on Christmas Day 1963, when the first group of relatives was about to arrive for Christmas dinner, his mother told him bluntly: 'I've made an appointment for the 28th. I'm taking you to a nerve specialist.'

Terrified by what that might mean – what in God's name was a nerve specialist? – he locked himself in his room and scribbled a harsh, almost cruel account of his relationship with his family:

I'm going to see a nerve specialist. My hands have gone cold with fear. But the anxiety this has brought on has allowed me to examine my home and those in it more closely.

Mama doesn't punish me in order to teach me, but just to show how strong she is. She doesn't understand that I'm a nervous sort and that occasionally I get upset, and so she always punishes me for it. The things that are intended to be for my own good she always turns into a threat, a final warning, an example of my selfishness. She herself is deeply selfish. This year, she has never, or hardly ever, held my hand.

Papa is incredibly narrow-minded. He is really nothing more than the house financier. Like Mama, he never talks to me, because his mind is always on the house and his work. It's dreadful.

Sônia lacks character. She always does what Mama does. But she's not selfish or bad. The coldness I feel towards her is gradually disappearing.

Mama is a fool. Her main aim in life is to give me as many complexes as possible. She's a fool, a real fool. Papa's the same.

The diary also reveals that the fear induced by the proposed visit to the specialist was unjustified. A day after the appointment he simply mentions the visit along with other unimportant issues:

Yesterday I went to the psychiatrist. It was just to meet him. No important comment to make.

I went to see the play *Pobre Menina Rica*, by Carlos Lyra and Vinicius de Moraes and then I had a pizza.

I decided to put off my whole literary programme until 1965. I'm going to wait until I'm a bit more mature.

He managed to achieve the required grades to pass the year and, according to the rules of the house, he therefore had the right to a holiday, which, this time, was to be in Belém. His holidays with his paternal grandparents, Cencita and Cazuza, had one enormous advantage over those spent in Araruama. At a time when a letter could take weeks to arrive and a long-distance phone call sometimes took hours if not days to put through, the distance – more than 3,000 kilometres – between Rio and Belém meant that the young man was beyond the control of his parents or from any surprise visits. Adventures that were unthinkable in Rio were routine in Belém: drinking beer, playing snooker and sleeping out of doors with his three cousins, whose mother had died and who were being brought up by their grandparents. Such was the excitement and bustle of life there that within the first few days of his holiday, he had lost his penknife, his watch, his torch and the beloved Sheaffer fountain pen he had bought with his prize money. One habit remained: no matter what time he went to bed, he devoted the last thirty minutes before going to sleep to writing letters to his friends and reading the eclectic selection of books he had taken with him – books ranging from Erle Stanley Gardner's detective story *The Case of the Calendar Girl*, to the encyclical *Pacem in Terris*, published in March 1963 by Pope John XXIII ('Reading this book is increasing my understanding of society,' he wrote).

He filled his letters to friends with news of his adventures in Belém, but in his letters to his father there was only one subject: money.

> You've never put your money to such good use as when you paid for this trip for me. I've never had such fun. But if all the money you've spent on the trip is to produce real benefits, I need more cash. There's no point in you spending 140,000 on a trip if I'm not going to have fun. If you haven't got any spare money, then no problem. But it isn't right to spend all your money on the house while my short life passes me by.

Belém appears to have been a city destined to provoke strong feelings in him. Three years before, on another trip there, he had at last had the chance to clarify a question that was troubling him: how were babies made? Earlier, he had plucked up the courage to ask Rui, a slightly older friend, but the reply, which was disconcertingly stark, appalled him: 'Simple: the man puts his dick in the woman's hole and when he comes, he leaves a seed in her stomach. That seed grows and becomes a person.'

He didn't believe it. He couldn't imagine his father being capable of doing something so perverted with his mother. As this was not something that could be written about in a letter, he waited for the holidays in Belém so that he could find out from an appropriate person – his cousin, Fred, who as well as being older, was a member of the family, someone whose version he could trust. The first chance he had to speak to his cousin alone, he found a way of bringing the subject up and repeated the disgusting story his friend in Rio had told him. He almost had an asthma attack when he heard what Fred had to say: 'Your friend in Rio is right. That's how it is. The man enters the woman and deposits a drop of sperm in her vagina. That's how everyone is made.'

Paulo reacted angrily. 'You're only telling me that because you haven't got a mother and so you don't have a problem with it. Can you really imagine your father penetrating your mother, Fred? You're out of your mind!'

That loss of innocence was not the only shock Belém had in store for him. The city also brought him his first contact with death. Early on the evening of Carnival Saturday, when he arrived at his grandparents' house after a dance at the Clube Tuna Luso, he was concerned to hear one of his aunts asking someone, 'Does Paulo know?' His grandfather Cazuza had just died unexpectedly of a heart attack. Paulo was extremely upset and shocked by the news, but he felt very important when he learned that Lygia and Pedro – since they were unable to get there in time – had named him the family's representative at his grandfather's funeral. As usual, he preferred to keep his feelings to himself, in the notes he made before going to sleep:

Carnival Saturday, 8th February
This night won't turn into day for old Cazuza. I'm confused and over-whelmed by the tragedy. Yesterday, he was laughing out loud at jokes and today he's silent. His smile will never again spread happiness. His welcoming arms, his stories about how Rio used to be, his advice, his encouraging words – all over. There are samba groups and carnival floats going down the street, but it's all over.

That same night he wrote 'Memories', a poem in three long stanzas dedicated to his grandfather. The pain the adolescent spoke of in prose and verse appeared sincere, but it was interwoven with other feelings. The following day, with his grandfather's corpse still lying in the drawing room, Paulo caught himself sinning in thought against chastity several times, when he looked at the legs of his female cousins, who were there at the wake. On the Sunday evening, Cazuza's funeral took place – 'a very fine occasion', his grandson wrote in his diary – but on Shrove Tuesday, during the week of mourning, the cousins were already out having fun in the city's clubs.

That holiday in Belém was not only the last he would spend there: it also proved to be a watershed in his life. He knew he was going to have a very difficult year at school. He felt even more negative about his studies than he had in previous years; and it was clear that his days at St Ignatius were numbered and equally clear that this would have consequences at home. There were not only dark clouds hanging over his school life either. At the end of the month, the day before returning to Rio, he flipped back in his diary to the day when he had written of his grandfather's death and wrote in tiny but still legible writing: 'I've been thinking today and I've begun to see the terrible truth: I'm losing my faith.'

This was not a new feeling. He had experienced his first religious doubts – gnawing away at him implacably and silently – during the retreat at St Ignatius when, troubled by sexual desire and tortured by guilt, he had been gripped by panic at the thought of suffering for all eternity in the apocalyptic flames described by Father Ruffier. He had turned to his diary to talk to God in a defiant tone ill suited to a true Christian: 'It was You who created sin! It's Your fault for not making me strong enough to resist! The fact that I couldn't keep my word is Your fault!' The following morning, he read this blasphemy and felt afraid. In desperation, he took his fellow pupil Eduardo Jardim to a place where they would not be seen or heard and broke his vow of silence to open up his heart to him.

His choice of confidant was a deliberate one. He looked up to Jardim, who was intelligent, read a lot and was a good poet without being a show-off. A small group of boys from St Ignatius to which Paulo belonged would

meet in the garage at Jardim's house to discuss what each had been reading. But it was mostly the strength of Jardim's religious convictions that
made him not only a good example but also the perfect confidant for a
friend with a troubled soul. Paulo told him that everything had started with
one doubt: if God existed and if this God had created him in his own image
and likeness, then why did He delight in his suffering? As he asked these
questions Paulo had arrived at the really big one – the unconfessable
doubt: did God really exist? Fearing that others might hear him, Jardim
whispered, as though in the confessional, words that were like salt being
rubbed into his friend's wounds: 'When I was younger and was scared that
my faith in God would disappear, I did everything I could to keep it. I
prayed desperately, took cold baths in winter, but my faith was very slowly
disappearing, until, finally, it disappeared completely. My faith had gone.'

This meant that even Jardim had succumbed. The more Paulo tried
to drive away this thought, the less he was able to rid his mind of that
image of a small boy taking cold baths in the middle of winter just so that
God would not disappear – and God simply ignoring him. That day Paulo
Coelho hated God. And so that there would be no doubt regarding his
feelings he wrote: 'I know how dangerous it is to hate God.'

A perfectly banal incident when he was returning from the retreat had
soured his relations with God and His shepherds still more. On the way
from the retreat house to the school Paulo judged that the driver of the
bus was driving too fast and putting everyone's life at risk. What started
out merely as a concern became a horror movie: if the bus had an accident and he were to die, his soul would be burning in hell before midday.
That fear won out over any embarrassment.

He went to the front of the bus, where his spiritual guide was sitting,
and said: 'Father Ruffier, the driver is driving too fast. And I'm terrified of
dying.'

Furious, the priest snarled at the boy: 'You're terrified of dying and I'm
outraged that you're such a coward.'

As time passed, Paulo's doubts became certainties. He began to hate
the priests ('a band of retrogrades') and all the duties, whether religious
or scholastic, that they imposed on the boys. He felt the Jesuits had
deceived him. Seen from a distance, sermons he had once believed to

contain solid truths were now remembered as 'slowly administered doses of poison to make us hate living', as he wrote in his diary. And he deeply regretted ever having taken those empty words seriously. 'Idiot that I was, I even began to believe that life was worthless,' he wrote, 'and that with death always watching, I was obliged to go to confession on a regular basis so as to avoid going to hell.' After much torment and many sleepless nights, at almost seventeen years of age, Paulo knew that he no longer wanted to hear about church, sermons or sin. And he hadn't the slightest intention of becoming a good student during his second year on the science course. He was equally convinced that he would invest all his beliefs and energy in what he saw not as a vocation but as a profession – that of being a writer.

One term was more than enough for everyone to realize that the college had lost all meaning for him. 'I have gone from being a bad pupil to being a dreadful pupil.' His school report shows that this was no exaggeration. He was always near the bottom of the class, and he managed to do worse in each exam he sat. In the first monthly tests he got an average of just over 5, thanks to a highly suspect 9 in chemistry. In May, his average fell to 4.4, but alarm bells only started to ring in June, when his average fell to 3.7.

That month, Pedro and Lygia were called to a meeting at the school and asked to bring his report book. The news they received could not have been worse. A priest read out the fifth article of the school rules, which all parents had to sign when their son was admitted to the school and in which it was stated that those who did not achieve the minimum mark required would be expelled. If Paulo continued along the same path, he would undoubtedly fail and his subsequent expulsion from one of the most traditional schools in the country would thereafter blot his scholastic record. There was only one way to avoid expulsion and to save both student and parents from such ignominy. The priest suggested that they take the initiative and move their son at once to another school. He went on to say that St Ignatius had never done this before. This exception was being made in deference to the fact that the pupil in question was the grandson of one of the first pupils at the college, Arthur Araripe Júnior, 'Mestre Tuca', who had gone there in 1903.

Pedro and Lygia returned home, devastated. They knew that their son smoked in secret and had often smelled alcohol on his breath, and some relatives had complained that he was becoming a bad example for the other children. 'That boy's trouble,' his aunts would whisper, 'he's going to end up leading all his younger cousins astray.' What, up until then, had been termed Paulo's 'strange behaviour' was restricted to the family circle. However, if he were to leave St Ignatius, even without being expelled, this would bring shame upon his parents and reveal them as having failed to bring him up properly. And if, as his father was always saying, a son was a reflection of his family, then the Coelhos had more than enough reason to feel that their image had been tarnished. At a time when corporal punishment was commonplace among Brazilian parents, Pedro and Lygia had never lifted a hand against Paulo, but they were rigorous in the punishments they meted out. So when Pedro announced that he had enrolled Paulo at Andrews College, where he would continue in the science stream, he also told his son that any future holidays were cancelled and that his allowance was temporarily suspended – if he wanted money for cigarettes and beer he would have to work.

If this was meant as a form of punishment, then it backfired, because Paulo loved the change. Andrews was not only a lay college and infinitely more liberal than St Ignatius but co-educational, which added a delightful novelty to the school day: girls. Besides this, there were political discussions, film study groups and even an amateur drama group, which he joined before he even met any of his teachers. He had ventured into the world of the theatre a year earlier, when, during the long end-of-year holiday, he had locked himself in his room, determined to write a play. He would only come out for lunch and dinner, telling his parents that he was studying. After four days, he finished *The Ugly Boy*, which he pretentiously referred to as 'a *petit guignol* à la Aluísio Azevedo', a synopsis of which he recorded in his diary:

> In this play, I present the ugly person in society. It's the story of a
> young man rejected by society who ends up committing suicide. The
> scenes are played out by silhouettes, while four narrators describe
> the feelings and actions of the characters. During the interval

between the first and second acts, someone at the back of the stalls sings a really slow bossa nova [a style of Brazilian music that has its roots in samba and cool jazz] whose words relate to the first act. I think it will work really well. This year it's going to be put on at home in the conservatory.

Fortunately, his critical sense won out over his vanity, and a week later, he tore up this first incursion into play-writing and gave it a six-word epitaph: 'Rubbish. I'll write another one soon.' And it was as a playwright (as yet unpublished) that he approached the amateur theatre group at Andrews College, known as Taca.

As for schoolwork, teachers and exams, none of these seemed to concern him. On the rare occasions when these topics merited a mention in his diary, he would dismiss them with a short, usually negative sentence: 'I'm doing badly at school, I'm going to fail in geometry, physics and chemistry'; 'I can't even get myself to pick up my schoolbooks: anything serves as a distraction, however stupid'; 'Classes seem to get longer and longer'; 'I swear I don't know what's wrong with me, it's beyond description.' Admitting that he was doing badly at school was a way of hiding the truth: he was on the slippery slope.

Up until October, two months before the end of the year, all his marks in every subject had been below 5. His father thought that it was time to rein him in once and for all and carry out his earlier threat: his cousin, Hildebrando Góes Filho, found Paulo work in a dredging company that operated at the entrance to the port of Rio de Janeiro. The pay wasn't even enough to cover Paulo's travel and cigarettes. Every day after morning classes, he would rush home, have lunch and take a bus to Santo Cristo, an area by the docks. A tugboat would take him over to the dredger, where he would spend the rest of the day with a slate in his hand, making a cross each time the machine picked up the rubbish from the seabed and deposited it in a barge. It seemed to him utterly pointless and reminded him of the Greek myth of Sisyphus, who is forced to push a stone up to the top of a mountain only to have the stone roll back down to the bottom, so that he has to begin his task all over again. 'It's never-ending,' Paulo wrote in his diary. 'Just when I think it's finished, it starts again.'

The punishment had no positive result. He continued to do badly at school and when he knew he ran the risk of failing the whole year, he recorded the fact quite shamelessly: 'A friend has told me I'm going to be kept down in maths,' he wrote. 'And meanwhile the morning is so beautiful, so musical, that I'm even rather happy. Oh, God, what a life. What a life, what a life.' At the end of the year, his report confirmed the expected results: his final average of 4.2 meant that he had failed in every subject.

Paulo seemed to be growing ever more indifferent to the world in which he found himself. He accepted uncomplainingly the work on the dredger and didn't even care when all he received from his parents at Christmas was a penknife. The only thing that interested him was writing, whether in the form of novels, plays or poetry. He had recently returned to poetry and was writing furiously. After some thought, he had concluded that it was no disgrace to write verses if he was not yet ready to start writing his novel. 'I have so many things to write about! The problem is that I can't get started and I haven't got the patience to carry on with it,' he moaned, and went on: 'All the same, that is my chosen profession.'

As he settled into the house in Gávea, he discovered that there were others among the young who were interested in books and literature. Since there were fifteen boys and girls, they created a literary club, which they called Rota 15, the name Rota being derived from Rua Rodrigo Otávio, which crossed Rua Padre Leonel Franca, where Paulo's house was, and at the corner of which they would all meet. Paulo's poetic output was such that when Rota 15 decided to produce a mimeographed booklet of poetry he contributed an anthology of thirteen poems (among them the award-winning 'Thirteen-year-old Woman'), and he added at the end his biography: 'Paulo Coelho began his literary career in 1962, writing short articles, then moved on to poetry. He entered a poem in the Academia Literária Santo Inácio in 1963 and in the same year won the top prize.' Rota 15 collapsed amid scandal when Paulo accused the treasurer of stealing the petty cash in order to go and see the French singer Françoise Hardy in concert in Rio.

He already believed himself to be a poet of sufficient standing not to have to depend any more on insignificant little magazines produced locally or by small groups. With the self-confidence of an old hand he felt that the time had come for him to fly higher. His dream was to be praised for his work – a laudatory quote would work wonders – in the respected weekly literary column 'Escritores e Livros', produced by José Condé, from Pernambuco, in the newspaper *Correio da Manhã*. The waspish Condé, who was able to make or break reputations in one paragraph, was the joint author of *Os Sete Pecados Capitais* [*The Seven Cardinal Sins*], a collection published by Civilização Brasileira, the other authors being Guimarães Rosa, Otto Lara Resende, Carlos Heitor Cony and Lygia Fagundes Telles, among other equally important writers. Paulo admired Condé's dry style and hoped that the critic's sharp eye would perceive the talent hidden in his work.

He added new poems to the anthology published by Rota 15, typed it up and sent off the carefully bound volume to the editors of *Correio da Manhã*. The following Wednesday, when 'Escritores e Livros' appeared, he rushed to the newspaper stand, desperate to read Condé's opinion of his work. His surprise was such that he cut out the column and stuck it in his diary, writing above it: 'A week ago, I wrote to J. Condé sending him my poetry and asking for his opinion. This is what appeared in the news-paper today.' The reason for his fury was a ten-line postscript at the foot of the writer's column: 'To all young show-offs who are desperate to get themselves a name and publish books, it would be worthwhile recalling the example of Carlos Drummond de Andrade, who only published three volumes totalling 144 poems in 15 years ... And only the other day, a critic said that Ernest Hemingway rewrote that small masterpiece *The Old Man and the Sea* no fewer than twenty times.'

Paulo took this personally and felt crushed by such an aggressive response. While only a short while before he had been thanking God for the joy of having discovered his vocation, his self-confidence gave way to a sea of doubt. 'Maybe I'm not cut out to be a writer,' he wrote. But he soon recovered his self-belief. Like the friend who used to take cold baths in order not to lose faith in God, he had to fight to realize his dream. Condé had dealt him a blow, but he was not prepared to lie down. He spent the whole day thinking of nothing but that literary column. In order to take his mind off it he tried watching an episode of *Dr Kildare*, about a young doctor, played by Richard Chamberlain, working in a large hospital. He switched off before the end and wrote in his notebook: 'In today's episode of *Dr Kildare*, the director of the hospital says to the doctor: "I shouldn't have tried to change your life, Jim. We were all born with an ideal." I've applied these words to being a writer and have decided that's what I'll be.' Thrilled by his own determination, he wrote a parody of Kipling's 'If …':

> If you can ask your friends and enemies for a chance.
> If you can hear a 'no' and take it as a 'maybe'.
> If you can start from the bottom and yet still value the little that
>   you have.
> If you can improve yourself each moment and reach the heights
>   without succumbing to vanity.
> Then you'll be a writer.

Immersed in these lofty ideas, he viewed with horror the prospect of going back to Andrews College. Tormented by the mere thought of it, he dreamed up a plan which, if it succeeded, would free him from school for a good two years: to get a study grant and leave the country, as several of his schoolfriends had done. His parents found renewed hope when he applied to join the American Field Service, a cultural exchange programme that was much in vogue at the time. Judging by his marks, he wasn't entirely useless at English (a subject in which, by his standards, he always did fairly well), and that would certainly help in obtaining the grant. For two weeks, he dedicated his free time to getting together all the necessary documents: school certificates, passport-size photos, references. When the exams came around, the seven other applicants in his group for the one place were whittled down until there remained only Paulo and two others who were to take the decisive test – the interview in English with someone from the United States.

On the day, he was so nervous that as he sat down in front of the examiner – a girl his own age – he felt a jolt, as though he had been punched in the chest. He set aside his atheism and silently begged God to let this be a false alarm. It was not: he was having an asthma attack. A dry whistle rose from his lungs while, eyes bulging, he patted his pockets, searching for his inhaler. He tried to talk, but all that came out was a whisper. The American girl didn't know what to do. After a few minutes, the attack subsided. Pulling himself together, he managed to complete the interview, but he left with misgivings: 'I think that asthma attack has ruined my chances.' Indeed, a month before he would have been due to leave for the United States, a telegram arrived informing him that he had not been selected. Instead of feeling downhearted at this failure, Paulo attributed it not to his poor performance but to the fact that his mother had visited the States earlier. 'I think they'd prefer people whose relatives have never been to the United States,' he wrote, finishing with a statement worthy of the fox in the fable when faced with the bunch of grapes he cannot reach: 'They believe, at least this is how I interpret it, that I'm too much of an intellectual for America.'

It was at this time that a new, overwhelming passion entered his life: a flesh-and-blood passion with brown eyes and long legs and answering to the name of Márcia. At seventeen, Paulo was still skinny and rather short, even by Brazilian standards. He weighed 50 kilos, which was at least 10 kilos below the ideal for his height of 1.69 metres (he remains this height to this day). Added to this, he was not an attractive adolescent. 'I was ugly, skinny, lacking in charm and incapable of getting a girlfriend,' he has said in various interviews throughout his life. 'I had an inferiority complex about the way I looked.' While the majority of boys wore short-sleeved, close-fitting shirts, to show off their muscles, he would always wear a long-sleeved shirt that concealed his narrow shoulders and thin arms. A disproportionately wide leather belt held up his faded jeans which, as fashion decreed, were tight on the legs. He wore the same metal-framed spectacles with tinted lenses that, years later, would become the trademark of the Beatle John Lennon. His hair was almost shoulder-length, and he had started to cultivate a thin moustache and a tuft of hair under his lower lip.

Márcia was a year younger than Paulo and lived almost next door. She was also a pupil at Andrews College and a member of Rota 15. In spite of vigilance on the part of her parents and older brother, she was seen by her colleagues as a fun-loving girl and was, therefore, in great demand. With his self-confidence at rock bottom, Paulo didn't even notice her looking at him when he was arguing with the other 'intellectuals' in the group about films, books and plays. Although the majority of the group didn't even know the meaning of the word, they almost all felt that they were 'existentialists'. Paulo never wore smart clothes, he didn't have a car and he wasn't strong, but Márcia melted whenever she heard him talking about books or reciting famous poems. He, however, was oblivious to this until she took the initiative.

On New Year's Eve 1964, Paulo closed yet another notebook with the melancholy words: 'Today is the last day of 1964, a year that's coming to an end with a sob hidden in the dark night. A year crowned with bitterness.' And it was in this same downbeat mood that he met up with his friends two days later, on a Saturday, to go to the show *Opinião*, featuring the singer Nara Leão, at the Arena Theatre in Copacabana. The group took their seats and Márcia happened to sit next to him. When the lights dimmed and Nara began to sing, Márcia felt something brush her hand. She glanced sideways and saw Paulo's hand lying close to hers. She immediately entwined her fingers in his and squeezed lightly. He was so astonished that his first reaction was one of panic: what if he had an asthma attack right there? However, he calmed down. 'I was certain that God had guided Márcia's hand towards mine,' he recalled later. 'In that case, why would He give me an asthma attack?' So he began to breathe like any mortal and the two fell desperately in love.

When the show came to an end, Nara Leão gave several encores, but, still holding hands, the young couple took advantage of the dark, and escaped from the crowded theatre. They took off their shoes and walked barefoot, hand-in-hand, along Copacabana beach. Paulo put his arms around her and tried to kiss her, but Márcia pulled back gently, saying: 'I've never been kissed on the mouth before.'

He reacted like a veritable Don Juan: 'Don't worry. I've kissed lots of girls. You'll like it.'

In the suffocating heat and under the starry Rio night, the two liars shared a long kiss, which both would remember warmly more than forty years later. The year 1965 could not have got off to a more encouraging start.

Paulo's relationship with Márcia brought him a peace of mind he had never known before, not even during the best times in Araruama and

Belém. He wasn't even upset when he learned that he hadn't been placed in a poetry competition held by the Instituto Nacional do Mate. 'Who cares about prizes,' he wrote magnanimously, 'when they're loved by a woman like Márcia?' He now filled whole pages of his diary with drawings of hearts pierced by love's arrow and with their two names written on them.

This happiness was short-lived. Before the summer was over, Márcia's parents found out the name of her boyfriend, and they were adamant that he was not the one for her. And when she wanted to know the reason for this ban, her mother was disconcertingly frank: 'In the first place he's really ugly. I can't understand what a pretty girl like you could see in such an ugly, awkward boy. You're someone who likes parties, and he doesn't even know how to dance and would be embarrassed to ask a girl to dance. The only thing he's interested in is books. Added to that, he looks rather sickly ...'

Márcia retorted that he was perfectly healthy. He had asthma, like millions of others, but it could be cured and certainly wasn't a blot on his character. Her mother feared that he might have other, contagious illnesses: 'I've even been told that he's an existentialist and a communist. So we're not going to discuss it any further.'

For her daughter, the matter was far from being closed. She recounted the entire episode to her boyfriend and the two decided to deal with the situation as best they could. They began to meet secretly in the homes of mutual friends, but because there were very few safe places, their intimate moments together were exceedingly rare and usually occurred in a pedalo on Lake Rodrigo de Freitas. Not that they ever went beyond the preliminaries. Paulo pretended to be experienced, but in fact up until then he had had only one sexual relationship, some months earlier, when, taking advantage of his parents' absence, he had managed to convince Madalena, a pretty maid whom his mother had recently employed, to go up to his room with him. Although she was only eighteen, Madá – as she was known – was experienced enough for the boy to retain a happy memory of that first night.

When they learned that their daughter was still meeting 'that creature' behind their backs, Márcia's parents increased their vigilance and refused to allow her to speak to Paulo on the phone. However, it was soon discovered that they had each put an alarm clock under their pillow to wake them at four in the morning when, in the silence of the night, they could whisper words of love, their mouths pressed to the receiver. The punishment for this disobedience was still harsher: she was to remain in the house for a month. Márcia refused to give up. With the help of the maid she would send notes to her boyfriend in which she would say when he should go and stand beneath the window of her room, where she was shut away. One morning, she woke to find a declaration of love scrawled in the tarmac in enormous letters: 'M: I love you. P.'

Márcia's mother returned to the charge: Paulo wasn't right for her, it wouldn't work out, he had no future and no prospects. The girl responded, undaunted, that she would certainly not break up with her boyfriend. She planned to marry Paulo one day. On hearing this, one of her aunts suggested that a sickly boy like him might not have the physical strength to fulfil his conjugal obligations. 'You know what I'm talking about, don't you, my dear,' she went on. 'Marriage, sex, children ... Do you think that, weak as he is, he'll be able to lead a normal life?' Márcia appeared unconcerned by such threats. As soon as she had served her term of punishment, she went back to meeting Paulo. They had discovered an ideal spot: the church of Our Lady of the Conception, which was close to both their houses. They never sat next to each other, but one would sit in front of the other so that they wouldn't arouse suspicion, and there they would talk in whispers. Despite all their precautions, they were caught by Márcia's father, who dragged her home screaming and punished her by beating her with a belt.

She, however, seemed firmly determined to love, become engaged to and marry her Prince Charming. His parents weren't over-enthusiastic about their son's choice either. Since it was usual for his friends to hold small parties in their homes, Paulo managed to persuade his parents to allow him to hold one in theirs. It was a disaster. When they saw their son dancing cheek-to-cheek with his girlfriend, his father stood, arms crossed, beside them, staring angrily until Márcia, embarrassed, moved away and joined a group of girlfriends. And he did the same with Paulo's other guests. If he saw a boy and girl dancing too close or with the boy's hand below the girl's waist, he would stand right next to them until they 'showed some manners'. In addition, the master of the house had forbidden all alcohol, even an innocent beer.

This was the first and last party held in the Coelhos' large pink house. But nothing could shake Paulo's happiness. Márcia's birthday was approaching, and their love was not yet two months old, when her mother suggested they have a talk. Not being a believer in corporal punishment, she tried another tack: 'If you break up with him, you can go to the best boutique in Rio and buy all the clothes you want.' Her mother knew her daughter's weak spot: vanity. Márcia's initial reaction was that the suggestion was unacceptable – 'downright blackmail'. However, after some reflection, she decided that she had more than proved her love and that they both knew that they couldn't pursue their love against their parents' wishes. They were both under age and dependent – there was no future in it. If she had to give in, then at least it was at a good price. She accepted. When he read Márcia's letter telling him that their romance was over, Paulo burst into tears and wrote of his frustration: 'For someone like me, who dreamed of transforming Gávea into a Brazilian Verona, there could be no sadder end than being thrown over for a couple of dresses.'

Abandoned by his Great Love – as he described Márcia in his diary – he once again fell into depression. His parents were concerned about his state of mind and, taking pity on him, they decided to make an exception. Although holidays in Araruama had been forbidden because of his failure at Andrews College, he would be allowed to spend Carnival there with his cousins. Paulo arrived by bus on the Friday night and spent the weekend feeling miserable, not even wanting to go and see the girls at the dances in the city. On the following Monday evening, he accepted an invitation from three friends to have a beer in a bar near his Uncle José's house.

When the table was covered in beer mats, showing how many drinks had been consumed, one of the boys, Carlinhos, had an idea: 'My parents are away and the car is in the garage just waiting to be taken out. If any of you knows how to drive we can go for a spin round the town.'

Although he had never driven a car, Paulo announced: 'I can drive.'

They paid the bill, went to Carlinhos's house and took the car. While the four of them were driving up the main street, where there were crowds of people and carnival parades, there was a general power failure. Although it was pitch dark, Paulo drove on through the mêlée of pedestrians and carnival-goers. Suddenly he saw a group of revellers in carnival costumes making their way towards the car.

Not knowing how to react, he swerved and accelerated. Then one of his friends yelled: 'Watch out for the boy!'

It was too late. They all felt something hit the car's front bumper, but Paulo went on accelerating while his friends looked back, terrified, shouting: 'Put your foot down, Paulo! Put your foot down! Get out of here! You've killed the boy!'

CHAPTER 5

First encounter with Dr Benjamim

THE BOY WAS LUÍS CLÁUDIO, or Claudinho, the son of a tailor, Lauro Vieira de Azevedo. He was seven years old and lived in Rua Oscar Clark, near the house where Paulo was staying. The violence of the collision was such that the boy was thrown some distance, with his stomach ripped open and his intestines exposed. He was taken unconscious to the Casa de Caridade, the only hospital in Araruama, where it was found that the blow had ruptured his spleen. To control the haemorrhaging the doctor in A&E gave him a blood transfusion, but Claudinho experienced a sudden drop in blood pressure and nearly died.

After the collision, Paulo and his friends had not only failed to go to Claudinho's aid but also fled the scene of the accident. They took the car back to Carlinhos's house and, with the city still in darkness, went to the home of another of the boys who had been in the car, Maurício. On their way there, they realized that news of the accident was spreading. Terrified by rumours that the boy had died, they made a pact of silence: no one would ever utter a word about the incident. They all went their separate ways. In order not to arouse suspicion, when Paulo arrived at his uncle's home, he 'cynically' (his own word) acted as though nothing had happened. However, half an hour later came the moment of truth: Maurício and Aurélio, the fourth member of the group, had been named by a witness and arrested, and while in police custody they revealed the identity of the driver.

Paulo's uncle took him to a room and told him of the gravity of the situation: 'The boy's life is hanging by a thread. We must just hope that he survives, because if he dies, things will get very ugly for you. Your parents have been told everything and they're on their way from Rio to talk to the police and the magistrate. Meanwhile, you're not leaving the house. You're safe here.'

His uncle knew what the tailor was like and was concerned that he might do something crazy. His fears were confirmed that night. After visiting his dying son in hospital, Lauro appeared at the gates of the house where Paulo was hiding, along with two unpleasant-looking men. A revolver stuck in his belt, Lauro wagged a finger at José and said: 'Dr Araripe, we don't know yet whether Claudinho will live or die. As long as that's the case, your nephew is not to leave Araruama. And if my son dies, Paulo will die too, because I'll come here personally and kill him.'

Late that night, Lygia and Pedro arrived in Araruama and, even before going to see their son, they went to the magistrate's house, who told them that the 'perpetrator' could only leave the city with his permission. His parents' arrival did nothing to alleviate Paulo's despair and he spent a sleepless night. Lying in bed, he wrote in a tremulous hand:

> This is the longest day of my life. I feel terrible, not knowing how the child is. But the worst thing was when we arrived at Maurício's house, after the accident, and everyone was saying that the boy was dead. I wanted to run away, to disappear. I can't think of anything but you, Márcia. I'm going to be charged with driving without a licence. And if the child's condition worsens, I'll be tried and might be sent to prison.

This was hell on earth. On Shrove Tuesday news of the two incidents – the accident and the tailor's threat – had spread rapidly, drawing inquisitive crowds to Rua Oscar Clark, eager to witness the climax to the drama. Early on, Lygia and Pedro decided to visit Claudinho's parents to offer their apologies and to get news of the boy's condition, for Claudinho was still unconscious. Lygia put together a large basket of fruit for the boy's mother to take to him. As she and her husband were approaching the house, which was on the same side of the road as José's, Lauro ordered them to turn back, because he was not prepared to talk. He repeated his threat – 'Your son will only leave this town if my son survives' – and he said that Lygia could take the fruit back: 'No one here is dying of hunger. I don't want charity, I want my son back.'

Paulo left his room only to ask for news of the boy. He recorded each piece of information in his notebook:

> They went to the hospital this morning. The boy's temperature is going down, let's hope that his father withdraws his complaint to the police.
>
> [...] The whole town knows everything and I can't leave the house because they're out looking for me. I heard that yesterday, at the dance, there was a detective waiting for me at the door.
>
> [...] The boy's temperature has gone up again.
>
> [...] It looks as though I might be arrested at any moment, because someone told the police I'm over eighteen. Everything depends on the boy.

Claudinho's temperature rose and fell several times. He regained consciousness on the Wednesday morning, two days after the accident, but it wasn't until late that night that the agony ended, when the doctors reported that he was out of danger and would be discharged in a few days.

Early on the Thursday, Pedro Coelho took his son to make a statement to the magistrate, who had him sign an agreement to pay all the medical and hospital expenses. The boy survived and suffered no long-term consequences, apart from an enormous scar on his abdomen that would remain with him for life. Destiny, however, appears to have decided that his meeting with death was to be on Carnival Monday, for thirty-four years later, on 15 February 1999 – another Carnival Monday – Luís Cláudio, by this time a businessman, and married with two daughters, was dragged from his house in Araruama by two masked men with guns, who were apparently in the pay of a group of hijackers of transport lorries. He was viciously tortured, then tied up, soaked in petrol, set alight and burned to death.

Claudinho's survival in 1965 did nothing to improve Pedro Coelho's mood. When Paulo returned to Rio, he learned that, as a punishment for having caused the accident and for having lied, he would not be allowed out at night for a month. Added to this, his allowance, which he had regained after leaving his job on the dredger in December, was once again to be stopped until he had repaid his father the 100,000 cruzeiros (some US$1,750 in today's terms) for the hospital fees.

Two months after the beginning of term, the first report from Andrews College revived the hopes of the Coelho family: although he had done badly in some subjects, their son had received such good marks in Portuguese, philosophy and chemistry that his average had risen to 6.1, which may have been only so-so, but was certainly an improvement for someone who hadn't even been able to manage a 5. Everyone was hopeful: but in his second report, his average dropped to 4.6 and in the third he managed only 2.5. The days when the reports arrived became days of retribution for Paulo. Pedro Coelho would rant and rave, take away more of Paulo's privileges and threaten even worse punishments. Paulo, however, appeared indifferent to all of this. 'I'm fed up with school,' he would tell his friends. 'I'll leave as soon as I can.'

He channelled all the energy and enthusiasm he failed to put into his schoolwork into the idea of becoming a writer. Unwilling to accept the fact that he was not yet a famous author, and convinced of his own talent, he had decided that his problem could be summed up in four words: a lack of publicity. At the beginning of 1965, he would take long walks with his friend Eduardo Jardim along Copacabana beach, during which he would ponder what he called 'the problem of establishing myself as a recognized writer'.

His argument was a simple one: with the world becoming more and more materialistic (whether through communism or capitalism, it made no difference), the natural tendency was for the arts to disappear and, with them, literature. Only publicity could save them from a cultural Armageddon. His main preoccupation was with the written word, as he frequently explained to Jardim. Since it wasn't as widely disseminated as music, literature was failing to find fertile ground among the young. 'If someone doesn't enthuse this generation with a love of literature,' he would tell his friend, 'it won't be around much longer.' To conclude, he revealed the secret of success: 'That's why publicity is going to be the main element in my literary programme. And I'm going to control it. I'm going to use publicity to force the public to read and judge what I write. That way my books will sell more, but, more importantly, I'll arouse people's curiosity about my ideas and theories.' In spite of Jardim's look of astonishment when he heard this, Paulo continued with his plans for the final phase of his conquest of the reading public: 'Then, like Balzac, I shall write articles under a pseudonym both attacking and defending my work, but that's a different matter.'

Jardim did not appear to agree with anything he was hearing: 'You're thinking like a businessman, Paulo. Remember, publicity is an artificial thing that forces people to do what they don't want.'

Paulo was so convinced of the effectiveness of his ideas, though, that he had stuck to his desk at home a summary of the tasks he would have to carry out during that year in order to achieve fame:

Literary programme for the Year 1965
Buy all the Rio newspapers each day of the week.
Check the book reviews, who writes them and the names of the
    editors of the papers.
Send articles to the relevant people and a covering note to the
    editors. Telephone them, asking when the article will appear.
    Tell the editors what my ambitions are.
Find contacts for publication.
Repeat this process for magazines.
Find out whether anyone who has received my texts would like to
    receive them on a regular basis.
Repeat the same process with radio stations. Send my own
    proposal for a programme or send contributions to current
    programmes. Contact the relevant people by phone, asking
    when my contribution will be transmitted, if it is.

Find out the addresses of famous writers and write to them
sending my poetry and asking for their comments and for help
in placing them in the papers they write for. Write again if
there's no reply.

Go to all book signings, lectures, first nights of plays, and try to get
talking with the big names and get myself noticed.

Organize productions of plays I've written and invite people
belonging to the literary circle of the older generation, and get
their 'patronage'.

Try to get in touch with the new generation of writers, hold drinks
parties, go to places where they go. Continue with my internal
publicity campaign, keeping my colleagues informed of my
triumphs.

The plan seemed infallible, but the truth is that Paulo continued to be
humiliatingly, painfully unknown. He didn't manage to get anything
published; he didn't get to know any critics, journalists or anyone who
could open a door for him or reach out a hand to help him up the ladder
of success. To make matters worse, he continued to do badly in his studies and was clearly miserable at having to go to college every day – what
was the point when his marks went from bad to worse? He spent the days
in a state of abstraction, as if his mind were in another world.

It was during this state of lethargy that he got to know another boy
at school, Joel Macedo, who was studying classics. They were the same
age, but Joel was the opposite of Paulo: he was extrovert and politically
articulate, and one of the youngest members of the so-called 'Paissandu
generation' – film-lovers and intellectuals who would meet at the old-
fashioned Paissandu cinema in the Flamengo district. He was a cultural
activist, led the Taca drama group and was responsible for *Agora*, a small
newspaper published by the pupils of the college, whose editorial team he
invited Paulo to join. The newspaper was at loggerheads with the conservative directors of the college because it criticized the arrests and other
arbitrary measures taken by the military government.

A new world opened up to Paulo. Joining the Paissandu set meant
rubbing shoulders with Rio's intellectual elite and seeing close to the

leading lights of the left-wing opposition. The cinema and the two nearby bars – the Oklahoma and the Cinerama – attracted film directors, musicians, playwrights and influential journalists. The latest European films were shown at midnight sessions on a Friday, when the 700 available tickets sold out in minutes. Paulo wasn't much interested in political or social problems, but his deep existential anxieties fitted the profile of the typical denizen of Paissandu and he quickly made himself at home.

One day, he was forced to confess to Joel why he never went to the midnight film sessions, which were, after all, the most popular ones. 'Firstly because I'm not yet eighteen and the films shown there are usually banned for minors,' he explained, adding: 'And if I get home after eleven o'clock my father won't open the door to me.' Joel couldn't accept that someone of seventeen had a set time for getting home. 'The time has come for you to demand your freedom. The problem of your age is easy enough to solve: all you have to do is change your date of birth on your student card, as I did.' He also offered to solve the problem of the curfew: 'After the midnight sessions you can sleep in my parents' house in Ipanema.' From then on, with his card duly falsified and a guaranteed roof over his head, Paulo was free to enter the enchanted world of Jean-Luc Godard, Glauber Rocha, Michelangelo Antonioni, Ingmar Bergman and Roberto Rossellini.

However, one problem remained: tickets, beer, cigarettes and travel all cost money. Not a fortune, obviously, but with his allowance suspended he didn't have a penny to his name, nor any idea as to how to get some money. To his surprise, a partial solution came from his father. Pedro was a friend of Luís Eduardo Guimarães, the editor of the *Diário de Notícias*, which, at the time, was an influential newspaper in Rio. Guimarães was also the son-in-law of its owner, Ondina Dantas. Pedro fixed up a meeting between his son and the journalist, and a few days later Paulo began to work as a cub reporter. The work, alas, would be unpaid until he was given a proper contract. The problem of money remained, therefore, but there was one compensation: the job was a step towards liberating himself from parental control. He was almost never at home. He would go out in the morning to college, return home briefly for lunch, then spend the afternoon at the newspaper office and the evening at the Paissandu. He spent so many nights at Joel's parents' apartment that it became his second home.

As is the case with all publications, the least exciting tasks fell to the juniors, such as reporting on any potholes that were holding up the flow of traffic or any domestic arguments that ended up at the police station, or compiling lists of the dead in the public hospitals for the deaths section in the next day's edition. It was not unusual for the new boy to arrive at the office and be told by Silvio Ferraz, the chief reporter at the *Diário de Notícias*: 'Go and talk to shopkeepers to see whether business is suffering from the downturn.' He may have been earning nothing and dealing only with unimportant matters, but Paulo felt he was an intellectual, someone who wrote every day, no matter about what. There was also another great advantage. When his colleagues at college or someone from the Paissandu set asked what he was doing, he would say: 'I'm a journalist. I write for the *Diário de Notícias*.'

He was so busy with the newspaper, the cinema and amateur dramatics that he had less and less time left for Andrews College. His father was in despair when he discovered that, at the end of April, his son had an average of 2.5 (contributed to by a zero in Portuguese, English and chemistry), but Paulo seemed to be living in another world. He did exactly what he wanted to and came home at night when he wanted. If he found the door unlocked, he would go in. If his father had, as he usually did, carefully locked everything up at eleven, he would simply take the Leblon–Lapa bus and, minutes later, be sleeping in Joel's house. His parents didn't know what else they could do.

In May, a friend asked him for a favour: he wanted a job in the Crédito Real de Minas Gerais bank and needed two references. As this was the bank where Paulo's father had an account, perhaps he could be persuaded to write one of the necessary letters? Paulo promised to see to it, but when he brought up the subject with his father he received a blunt refusal: 'Absolutely not! Only you could possibly think that I would support your vagrant friends.'

Upset and too ashamed to tell his friend the truth, Paulo made a decision: he locked himself in his room and typed up a letter full of praise for the applicant, adding at the bottom 'Engenheiro Pedro Queima Coelho de Souza'. He signed it and put the letter in an envelope – problem solved. Everything went so well that the subject of the letter felt obliged to thank its writer for his kindness with a telephone call. Dr Pedro couldn't understand what the boy was talking about: 'Letter? What letter?' On hearing the words 'bank manager', he said: 'I wrote no letter! Bring that letter here. Bring it here immediately! This is Paulo's doing! Paulo must have forged my signature!' He rang off and rushed to the bank, looking for evidence of the crime – the letter, the proof that his son had become a forger, a fraudster. Paulo arrived home that evening, unaware of what had happened. He found his father in a fury, but that was nothing new. Before going to sleep, he wrote a short note in his diary: 'In a month and a half I've written nine articles for *Diário de Notícias*. I've got a trip to Furnas set up for 12th June, when I'm going to meet the most important people in the political world, such as the president, the most important governors and ministers of state.'

The following morning, he woke in a particularly good mood, since a rumour had been going round at the newspaper that he was going to be taken on officially, which would mean he would be a real journalist, with a press card and a guaranteed salary. When he went downstairs, he was surprised to find his parents already up and waiting for him. Pedro was beside himself with rage, but he said nothing.

It was Lygia who spoke: 'Paulo, we're worried about your asthma and so we've made an appointment with the doctor for a check-up. Eat your breakfast because we've got to leave soon.'

A few minutes later, his father took the Vanguard out of the garage – a rare occurrence – and the three drove along the coast road towards the city centre. Seated in the back, absorbed in thought, Paulo gazed out at the fog over the sea, which made Guanabara bay look simultaneously melancholy and poetic. When they were halfway along Botafogo beach the car took a left turn into Rua Marquês de Olinda, drove another three blocks and drew up alongside a wall more than 3 metres high. The three got out and went over to a wrought-iron gate. Paulo heard his father say something to the gatekeeper and, moments later, saw a nun arrive to take them to a consulting room. They were in the Casa de Saúde Dr Eiras, a large hospital occupying various buildings and large mansions in the woods at the bottom of a hill.

The nun went ahead, showing his parents the way, with Paulo behind, not understanding what was going on. The four of them took a lift to the ninth floor and, as they walked down a long corridor towards the consulting room, the nun opened a door and showed Pedro and Lygia a bedroom with two beds and a window with an iron grille. She smiled, saying: 'This is where the boy will sleep. As you can see, it's a nice bright, spacious room.'

Paulo couldn't understand what he was hearing and had no time to ask, since, by then, they were all in the doctor's consulting room. Seated behind a desk was the psychiatrist Dr Benjamim Gaspar Gomes, a fifty-two-year-old man, bald, with small eyes and a pleasant face.

Astonished, Paulo turned to his parents: 'If I've just come here for asthma tests, why have you booked a room for me?'

Pedro said nothing and Lygia gently tried to explain to her son that he was being admitted to an asylum. 'You're not going to school any more, and you're not going to sleep at home. You left St Ignatius so that you wouldn't be expelled and you've ended up failing at Andrews. On top of that you ran over the boy in Araruama ...'

Then his father spoke for the first time: 'This time, you've really overstepped the mark. Forging a signature, as you did mine, isn't just a prank – it's a crime.'

Things moved rapidly from then on. His mother said that she and his father had had a long talk with Dr Benjamim – a colleague of Pedro's and a person whom the family trusted implicitly – and that they were all agreed that he was too excitable and needed medication, so it would be a good idea for him to spend a few days in this 'rest home'. Before he could recover from the shock, his parents stood up, said goodbye and disappeared down the tiled corridor.

Suddenly he found himself alone, locked up in an asylum with his school file under his arm and a jacket over his shoulders, not knowing what to do. As though he thought it might still be possible to escape from this nightmare, he said to the doctor: 'You mean you're going to lock me up like a madman without examining me – no interview, nothing?'

Dr Benjamim smiled: 'You're not being admitted as a madman. This is a rest home. You're just going to take some medicine and rest. Besides, I don't need to interview you, I have all the information I need.'

No one with any common sense would think that the information given by Paulo's father could justify this treatment: his parents' complaints – that he was irritable, hostile, a bad student and 'even politically opposed to his father' – were not very different from the complaints that nine out of ten parents make about their adolescent children. His mother had more precise concerns and thought that her son 'had problems of a sexual nature'. The three reasons for this suspicion are surprising, coming as they do from an intelligent and sophisticated woman like Lygia: her son had no girlfriends, he had refused circumcision to correct an overtight foreskin – phimosis – and, finally, it seemed, lately, that his breasts were developing like those of a girl. There was, in fact, an explanation for all of these 'symptoms', including the change in his breasts, which was nothing more than the side effect of a growth hormone prescribed by a doctor to whom she herself had taken him.

The only problem of a psychiatric nature that might have concerned his parents was one of which they were in fact unaware. Some months earlier, during one of his many sleepless, anxiety-filled nights, he had decided to kill himself. He went into the kitchen and began to block all the air vents with sticky tape and dusters. However, when it came to turning on the gas inlet from the street to the oven, his courage failed him. He saw with sudden clarity that he didn't want to die: he only wanted his parents to notice his despair. He describes how, as he removed the last strip of tape from behind the door and started to go back to his room, he realized, terrified, that he had company: it was the Angel of Death. There was good reason for his panic, since he had read somewhere that, once summoned to Earth, the Angel never left empty-handed. He recorded the conclusion to this macabre encounter in his diary:

I could sense the smell of the Angel all around me, the Angel's breath, the Angel's desire to take someone away. I remained silent and silently asked what he wanted. He told me that he had been summoned and that he needed to take someone, to give an account of his work. Then I picked up a kitchen knife, jumped over the wall and landed in an empty plot of land where the people in the shanty towns kept their goats running free. I grabbed hold of one of them and slit its throat. The blood spurted up and went right over the wall, splattering the walls of my house. But the Angel left satisfied. From then on, I knew that I would never try to kill myself again.

Unless his parents had been so indiscreet as to read his diary – as he suspected some time later – the sacrifice of the goat, which at the time was attributed to some perverse evil-doer, could not have been one of their reasons for having him admitted to the asylum.

Still absorbing the shock of this new situation, Paulo was led to his room by a male nurse. As he leaned against the iron bars at the window, he was surprised by the beauty to be found in such a wretched place. From the ninth floor he had an unbroken view of the white sands of Botafogo beach, the Flamengo gardens and, in the background, the spectacular outline of Morro da Urca and Pão de Açucar. The bed beside his was empty, which meant that he would have to suffer his torment alone. In the afternoon, someone arrived from his house and handed over at the gate a suitcase with clothes, books and personal possessions. The day passed without incident.

Lying on his bed, Paulo thought of the options open to him: the first, of course, was to continue with his plan to be a writer. If this didn't work out, the best thing would be to go mad as a convenient means to an end. He would be supported by the state, he wouldn't have to work any more nor take on any responsibilities. This would mean spending a lot of time in psychiatric institutions, but, after a day wandering the corridors, he realized that the patients at the clinic didn't behave 'like the mad people you see in Hollywood films': 'Except for some pathological cases of a catatonic or schizophrenic nature, all the other patients are perfectly capable of talking about life and having their own ideas on the subject. Sometimes they have panic attacks, crises of depression or aggression, but they don't last for long.'

Paulo spent the following days trying to get to know the place to which he had been confined. Talking to the nurses and employees, he discovered that 800 mentally ill people were interned at the clinic, and divided up according to the degree of their insanity and social class. The floor he was on was for the so-called 'docile mad' and those referred by private doctors, while the remainder, the 'dangerously mad' and those dependent on public health services, were in another building. The former slept in rooms with a maximum of two beds and a private bathroom and during the day they could move freely around the entire floor. However, you could only take the lift, the doors of which were locked, when accompanied by a nurse and a guide nominated by a doctor. All the windows, balconies and verandahs were protected by iron grilles or walls made of decorative air bricks through which one could still see. Those being paid for by social services slept in dormitories of ten, twenty and even thirty beds, while those considered to be violent were kept in solitary confinement.

The Dr Eiras clinic was not only an asylum, as Paulo had originally thought, but a group of neurological, cardiological and detox clinics for alcoholics and drug addicts. Two of its directors, the doctors Abraão Ackerman and Paulo Niemeyer, were among the most respected neuro-surgeons in Brazil. While hundreds of workers dependent on social secu-rity lined up at their doors waiting for a consultation, famous people with health problems also went there. During his time in the clinic as a patient, Paulo received weekly visits from his mother. On one of these visits, Lygia arrived accompanied by Sônia Maria, who was fifteen at the time and had insisted on going to see her brother in hospital. She left in a state of shock. 'The atmosphere was horrendous, people talking to themselves in the corridors,' she was to recall angrily some years later. 'And lost in that hell was Paulo, a mere boy, someone who should never have been there.' She left determined to speak to her parents, to beg them to open their hearts and remove her brother from the asylum, but she lacked the courage to do so. If she was unable to argue in defence of her own rights, what could she do for him? Unlike Paulo, Sônia spent her life in submission to her parents – to such a point that, even when married and a mother, she would never smoke in front of her father and concealed from him the fact that she wore a bikini.

As for Paulo's suffering, this, according to Dr Benjamim, who visited him each morning, was not as bad as it might have been, thanks to 'a special way he had of getting himself out of difficult situations, even when he was protesting against being interned!' According to the psychiatrist, 'the fact that Paulo did not suffer more is because he had a way with words'. And it was thanks to that 'way with words' that he avoided being subjected to a brutal treatment frequently inflicted on the mentally ill at the clinic: electroshock treatment. Although he was well informed about mental illnesses and had translated books on psychiatry, Dr Benjamim was a staunch defender of electroconvulsive therapy, which had already been condemned in a large part of the world. 'In certain cases, such as incurable depression, there is no alternative,' he would say confidently. 'Any other therapy is a cheat, an illusion, a palliative and a dangerous procrastination.' However, while he was a patient, Paulo was subjected to such heavy doses of psychotropic substances that he would spend the whole day in a daze, slouching along the corridor in his slippers. Although he had never experimented with drugs, not even cannabis, he spent four weeks consuming packs and packs of medication that was supposedly detoxifying, but only left him more confused.

Since almost no one knew he was in the asylum, he had little news of his friends. One day, he had an unexpected visit from the friend who was indirectly responsible for his presence there by asking for a reference, and who left the clinic with a mad idea – never carried out: that of rallying the members of the defunct Rota 15 group to kidnap him. However, Paulo's tortured soul only found true peace when his latest love appeared: Renata Sochaczewski, a pretty girl whom he had met at an amateur theatrical group, who was to become a great actress under the name Renata Sorrah, and whom Paulo affectionately called 'Rennie' or 'Pato'. When she failed to get in to visit him, Renata would furtively send him little love notes. These contained such messages as 'Stand at the window because I'm waiting to wave goodbye to you', or 'Write a list of what you want and give it to me on Friday. Yesterday I phoned but they didn't tell you.'

When he was allowed out, four weeks after being admitted, Paulo was in a very fragile state, but he nevertheless tried to take a positive lesson from his journey into hell. It was only when he got home that he found the mental energy to make notes in his diary:

In the meantime, I've been in Casa de Saúde Dr Eiras, where I was admitted for being maladjusted. I spent twenty-eight days there, missed classes, lost my job and was released as if I had been cured, even though there was no reason for my ever having been admitted in the first place. My parents have really done it this time! They ruin my chances at the newspaper, ruin my academic year and spend loads of money only to find that there was nothing wrong with me. What I have to do now is start all over again, accepting what's happened as a joke and a well-intentioned mistake. (The worst of it is that the day I was admitted, I was going to be given a job on the permanent staff at the newspaper.)

All the same, it was OK. As a patient on my floor said, 'All experiences are good experiences, even the bad ones.' Yes, I've learned a lot. It gave me a chance to mature and gain in self-confidence, to make a more careful study of my friends and notice things I'd never really thought about before. Now I'm a man.

While Paulo may have left the clinic convinced that there was nothing wrong with him, this was not the opinion of the psychiatrist Dr Benjamim Gomes. The hospital file in the archives of the clinic held a dark prognosis that read more like a condemnation: 'A patient with schizoid tendencies, averse to social and loving contact. He prefers solitary activities. He is incapable of expressing his feelings or of experiencing pleasure.' Judging from this piece of paper, Paulo's suffering was only just beginning.

CHAPTER 6

Batatinha's début

T HE FEW FRIENDS WHO HAD WITNESSED Paulo's twenty-eight days of suffering in the clinic were surprised when he was let out. Although physically exhausted and looking more fragile, he made no attempt to hide the fact that he had been admitted to an asylum. On the contrary, when he reappeared in Rua Rodrigo Otávio, he boasted to a circle of friends that he had lived through an experience unknown to any of them: being treated as a madman. His descriptions of the people and events at the clinic, many of them invented, were so extraordinary that some of his friends even expressed envy at not having been in such an interesting place.

Lygia and Pedro were concerned about their son's behaviour. Fearing that his confinement might stigmatize him at school and at work, they treated the matter with total discretion. His father had decided to tell Andrews College and the *Diário de Notícias* that Paulo's absence was due to his having to go away unexpectedly. When they learned that their son was telling everyone the truth, Pedro warned him: 'Don't do that. If people get to know that you've had mental problems, you'll never be able to stand as a candidate for President of the Republic.'

Not having the least desire to be president of anything at all, Paulo appeared to have returned from the clinic with a renewed appetite for what he called 'the intellectual life'. Now he had a new place where he could hang out, besides the amateur theatre at the college and the Cine Paissandu. The director of the Serviço Nacional de Teatro (SNT), Bárbara Heliodora, had got permission from the government to transform the old headquarters of the Students' Union (which had been ransacked and burned by extreme right-wing groups on the day of the military coup) into the new National Drama Conservatory. Without restoring the building or painting over the marks left by the damage caused by the vandals, the Centro Popular de Cultura, as it had been known, was turned into the Teatro Palcão, a 150-seat theatre which, although it didn't enjoy the freedom it had previously enjoyed, would once again become a centre of cultural debate permanently filled by workshops, rehearsals and drama group productions. What would later become the Teatro Universitário Nacional (National University Theatre), an occasional drama group comprising only students, was also born there. Paulo's sole experience in this area was his play *The Ugly Boy*, which he had torn up soon after writing it, plus two or three other plays that had also gone no further than his own house. However, he was sure that he had some ability in the field and plunged into the newly formed Conservatory.

When he returned to the *Diário de Notícias*, it became clear to Paulo that his absence of almost a month had put paid to or at least delayed his chances of being taken on as a reporter, but he stayed on, unpaid and uncomplaining. Working in a place that allowed him to write every day, even if only on the trivial topics that usually fell to him, was a good thing. At the end of July 1965, he was sent off to report on the history of the Marian Congregation in Brazil. He was beginning to gain experience as a reporter and had no difficulty in carrying out the task; at the organization's headquarters, he interviewed members of the community, noted down numbers and wrote a short article describing the history of the Marians from the time they had arrived in Brazil with the first Portuguese Jesuit missionaries. The following morning on his way to school, he bought a copy of the *Diário de Notícias* at the newspaper stand and smiled proudly when he saw his article. The subeditors had made some small changes, but they were still essentially his words being read by thousands of readers at that very moment.

When he arrived at the newspaper office after lunch, he learned that his head was on the block. The Marians were furious about the article and had gone straight to the owner of the newspaper to complain. They accused him of having invented facts and attributing them to the organization's leaders. The cub reporter was indignant when he heard this, and although his colleagues told him to lie low until the whole thing had blown over, he decided that it would be best to clear up the matter straight away. He sat outside the owner's glass-walled office, the so-called 'fishbowl', and waited two hours for her to arrive.

On entering the fishbowl, he remained standing in front of her desk. 'Dona Ondina, I'm the person who wrote the article on the Marians and I've come to explain —'

She didn't even let him finish the sentence: 'You're sacked,' she said.

Surprised, he countered with: 'But Dona Ondina, I'm about to be taken on by the newspaper.'

Without even looking up, she said again: 'You're sacked. Please leave.'

Paulo left, regretting his naivety. If he had waited a few days, as he had been advised, she would probably have forgotten about the matter. Now there was no way of saving the situation. He returned home with his tail between his legs. Although shaken by the incident, his ability to fantasize seemed limitless. Recording in his diary his regret at having taken the initiative, he described his dismissal as if it were a case of political persecution:

> I could have done all kinds of things to avoid being fired! I could have given in and gone over to the right simply in order to keep my job on the newspaper. But no. I wanted to be a martyr, crucified for his ideas, and they put me on the cross before I could give any kind of message to humanity. I couldn't even say that I was innocent, that I was fighting for the good of all. But no! Die now, you filthy dog. I'm a worm. A C-O-W-A-R-D! I was sacked from the 'DN' for being a subversive. Now I've got nothing but night school and lots of time doing nothing.

The *Diário de Notícias* was not a right-wing newspaper; nor had he been dismissed for political reasons.

Paulo appeared prepared to take advantage of his time in the clinic. He had been labelled 'a madman', and he intended to enjoy the impunity that protects the mentally ill and do whatever he wanted. To hell with school and his parents: he wanted to follow his dream. In his own words, he had become a 'delinquent' who went around with gangs, but since he lacked the physical strength of other boys, he thought that he could become an 'intellectual delinquent' – someone who read things that none of his friends had read and knew things that no one else knew. He belonged to three different groups – Paissandu, the Conservatory and what remained of Rota 15 – but whenever there was any sign of violence, he felt ashamed that he didn't have the courage even to break up a fist-fight.

He knew, however, that displays of physical strength were not the way forward. Whereas before he had felt himself to be 'an existentialist on the road to communism', now he saw himself as 'a street communist'. He had read Henry Miller's famous trilogy *Sexus*, *Plexus* and *Nexus*, and glanced over the works of Marx and Engels, and he felt confident enough to talk on such topics as 'true socialism', 'the Cold War' and 'the exploitation of the worker'. In a text entitled 'Art in Brazil', he quotes Lenin as having spoken of the need to take two steps back when it was clear that this was the only way of taking one step forward. 'Art cannot flee from this premise. It must first adapt to man and then, having gained his confidence, respect and love, it can lead him along the road to reality.' His basis for taking a route he had earlier rejected was simple: 'I am an intellectual, and since all intellectuals are communists, I am a communist.' The mother of a girl he was friendly with accused him of 'putting ideas' in the heads of the poor people in the street. 'From Henry Miller to communism is only a step,' he wrote; 'therefore, I'm a communist.' What he would only confess to his diary was that he loathed Bergman and considered Godard 'a bore' and Antonioni 'annoying'. In fact what he really liked was to listen to The Beatles, but it wasn't quite right for a communist to say this in public.

As he had predicted, his studies were relegated firmly to the background. In August, fearing that he would fail the year, the school summoned Lygia and Pedro to deal with three issues: low grades, too many absences and 'the student's personal problems'. Since the start of classes after the July holidays he had not achieved marks above 2.5 in any subject and during that time he had not been to a single maths lesson, which explained why he had never got more than 3 in the subject since moving to the college. He would leave home every morning and go to school, but once there, involved as he was with the drama group, he would spend whole days without entering the classroom. The verdict presented to his parents was worrying: either their son paid more attention to his studies or he would be expelled. Although the college did not adopt the same strategy as that used at St Ignatius, the director of studies subtly suggested to his parents that 'to avoid the worst', it might be best to move him before the end of the year to a 'less demanding' educational establishment. Put bluntly: if they didn't want to have the shame of seeing their son fail again, the best thing would be to enrol him in a college where the pupil only had to pay his monthly fees promptly in order to guarantee success. Lygia and Pedro were indignant at this suggestion. Neither of them had lost hope of Paulo returning to the straight and narrow, and to accept such an idea meant a humiliating surrender. There was no way they would let him end up in a fifth-rate school.

Paulo, meanwhile, seemed to be living on another planet. His life within the world of theatre, which was a hotbed of opposition to the military regime, brought him close to young people who were becoming politically militant. Now all the films and plays he watched were political, and he had incorporated into his vocabulary left-wing slogans such as 'More bread, fewer guns' and 'United, the people will never be defeated'.

One night, when he went with a group of his friends to see *Liberdade, Liberdade* [*Freedom, Freedom*], which was being put on by Oduvaldo Viana Filho and Paulo Autran at the Teatro Opinião, the play was interrupted halfway through. A dishevelled young man got up on the stage and spoke out against the military dictatorship. He was Vladimir Palmeira, the student leader who went on to become a Member of Parliament and who was urging the audience to join yet another student march against the regime. On the few occasions when Paulo decided to take part in such marches, his real objective was to be seen by his father, whose office was in the centre of the city, where all the protest marches ended up. In fact, the world of politics that he was being drawn into had never much mattered to him. Apart from one or two notes, such as the results of the presidential elections in 1960 won by Jânio Quadros, his diary reflects his indifference to both politics and politicians. When the army had taken power in the April of the previous year, Paulo was speculating loftily in his diary on the existence of heaven and hell. Two weeks before the coup, when the whole country was in uproar, he filled several pages in his diary describing the misfortunes of a 'sixteen-year-old girl' he had met in the street: 'To think that this girl ran away from home and that in order to survive, she has been subjected to the most humiliating of things, although she has still managed to keep her virginity. But now she'll have to lose that just so she can eat.' And he ended: 'It's at times like this that I doubt the existence of God.'

However, that was the past. Now he felt himself to be a member of the resistance, although his criticisms of the dictatorship never went beyond the limits of his diary and even then were very timid. It was in his diary that he recorded his dissatisfaction with the existing situation, for example, in a satirical article entitled 'J'accuse', in which he placed The Beatles, Franco, Salazar and Lyndon B. Johnson on one side and on the other de Gaulle, Glauber Rocha and Luís Carlos Prestes:

I accuse the rich, who have bought the consciences of the politicians. I accuse the military, who use guns to control the feelings of the people. I accuse the Beatles, Carnival and football of diverting the minds of a generation that had enough blood to drown the tyrants. I accuse Franco and Salazar, who live by oppressing their compatri- ots. I accuse Lyndon Johnson, who oppresses countries too poor to resist the flow of dollars. I accuse Pope Paul VI, who has defiled the words of Christ.

But is there anything good in the world around me? Yes, it's not all disappointment. There's de Gaulle, who revived France and wants to spread freedom throughout the world. There's Yevtushenko, who raised his voice against a regime, knowing that he could be crushed without anyone knowing, but who saw that humanity was prepared to accept his thoughts, free as doves. There's Khrushchev, who

allowed the poet to express himself as he wished. There's Francisco
Julião and Miguel Arraes, two true leaders who knew how to fight to
the end. There's Ruy Guerra and Glauber Rocha, who brought to
popular art a message of revolt. There's Luís Carlos Prestes, who
sacrificed everything for an ideal. There's the life beating inside me
so that one day I can speak out too. There's the world in the hands of
the young. Perhaps, before it's too late, they will realize what this
means. And fight to the death.

The first job opportunity to arise, meanwhile, was light years away from
the battle against the military dictatorship and the exploitation of under-
developed countries by American imperialism. An actors' cooperative
called Grupo Destaque was rehearsing a dramatized version of the children's classic *Pinocchio*, which was to be performed at the end of 1965,
and the directors had a problem. The show required seven scene-changes,
and the directors were worried that each time the curtain fell, the audience, mostly children, would start wandering around the theatre and delay
the start of the next scene. The producer, the Frenchman Jean Arlin,
came up with a simple solution: they would get another actor to appear
on the stage during each interval and distract the children until the
curtain rose again. He recalled an ugly, awkward, but witty young man,
Paulo Coelho, who had been introduced to him by Joel Macedo. He would
be perfect for the role. This was hardly resistance theatre, and the role
didn't even have a script, which meant he would simply have to improvise,
and it was unlikely he would get paid very much. As a cooperative
venture, after each show, the takings would be shared out, most of them
going to pay first for the hire of the theatre, and then the technicians,
lighting assistants and scene-shifters. If anything was left over, then it
would be divided equally among the actors, each of whom would get only
enough to pay for a snack. All the same, Paulo accepted the invitation on
the spot.

During his first rehearsal, he chose to wear a ragged pair of dungarees
and an old hat and waited in the wings to make his entrance. The only
instruction he had received from the director, the Argentine Luís Maria
Olmedo, who was known as Cachorro, was to improvise. When the

curtain fell for the first scene-change, he went on stage, pulling funny faces, and said whatever came into his head: 'When Little Potato starts to grow, he spreads across the ground. When Little Mama falls to sleep she puts her hand upon her heart.'

From then on, to his friends in the theatre he was known as Batatinha, or Little Potato. Although he considered himself to be a useless actor, during the following weeks he worked so hard at his role that when *Pinocchio* was about to open, his appearances had become so much part of the show that his name appeared in the programme and on the posters. At each rehearsal, he elaborated a little more on his performance – although always sticking to the time allowed for the scene-change – inventing strange names, making faces, jumping around and shouting. Deep down, he thought the whole thing ridiculous, but if that was the door that would allow him to enter the world of the theatre, he would go through it. In Grupo Destaque he worked with professionals who made their living from the theatre. After the rehearsals, the cheerful, lively group would leave the Miguel Lemos theatre, walk along the beach to Rua Sá Ferreira, four blocks away, and make an obligatory stop at the Gôndola bar, where the actors, technicians and directors who packed the stages of Copacabana's twenty theatres would meet every night.

Paulo felt he was in heaven. He was eighteen now, which meant he could drink when he wanted, go to any film or play and stay out all night without having to answer to anyone. Except, of course, to his father, Pedro Coelho, who took a dim view of his son's burgeoning theatrical vocation. This was not only because he hardly ever went to school and was on the verge of being expelled again. For his parents, the world of the theatre was a 'den of homosexuals, communists, drug addicts and idlers' with whom they would prefer their son not to mix. At the end of December, though, they gave in and accepted his invitation to the preview of *Pinocchio*. After all, this was a children's classic, not the indecent, subversive theatre that was enjoying such success in the country.

Paulo had reserved seats for his parents, his sister and his grandparents and, to his surprise, they all turned up. On the first night, the cultural section of the *Jornal do Brasil* published an article and his name appeared in print for the first time. He was last on the list, but for someone who was just beginning it was the right place. He recorded the feeling of being on stage in a short but emotional note in his diary: 'Yesterday was my début. Excitement. Real excitement. It was just unbelievable when I found myself there in front of the audience, with the spotlights blinding me, and with me making the audience laugh. Sublime, truly sublime. It was my first performance this year.' The family's attendance at the first night did not mean an armistice, however. When they learned that Paulo had failed at Andrews, his parents forced him to attend group therapy three times a week, still convinced that he had mental problems.

Indifferent to the hostility on the domestic front, he was having a wonderful time. In a matter of weeks, he had practically created a new character in the play. When the curtain fell on one scene, he would sit on the edge of the stage, unwrap a delicious toffee or sweet and start to eat it.

The children would watch greedily and when he asked one of the children in the front row: 'Would you like one?' the whole audience would yell: 'I want one! I want one!'

To which he would reply heartlessly: 'Well, too bad. I'm not going to give you one!'

Batatinha would take another bite or lick and turn to the audience again: 'Would you like one?'

More shouting, and again he would refuse. This would be repeated until the curtain rose for the next act.

A month and a half after the first night, *Pinocchio* moved to the Teatro Carioca, which was on the ground floor of an apartment block in Flamengo, a few metres from the Paissandu cinema. One afternoon when he was rehearsing, Paulo noticed that a very beautiful girl with blue eyes and very long hair had sat down in one of the rear stalls seats and seemed to be watching him closely. It was Fabíola Fracarolli, who lived on the eighth floor of the building, had noticed the open door and, out of curiosity, gone in to take a look. The following day, Fabíola returned and, on the third day, Paulo decided to approach her. She was sixteen and she lived in a small rented apartment with her widowed mother, who was a dressmaker, and her maternal grandmother, a nutty old woman who sat all day clutching a bag full of old papers, which she said were 'her fortune'.

Up to the age of fifteen, Fabíola had been afflicted with an enormous, grotesque nose à la Cyrano de Bergerac. When she learned that the only boy she had managed to attract had been paid to take her out by her cousins, she didn't think twice. She climbed on to the window ledge and said to her mother: 'Either you pay for plastic surgery or I'll jump!' Weeks later, when she had recovered from the surgery, she was parading a neat, sculptured nose. It was this new Fabíola who fell madly in love with Paulo.

Things were going well for Paulo when it came to women. While continuing his relationship with Renata Sorrah, he had decided to forgive Márcia and take her back as a girlfriend. This didn't stop him beginning a steady relationship with Fabíola. Her mother seemed to take pity on the puny young man with breathing problems and welcomed him into the family. He would have lunch and dinner with them almost every day, which made his life as Batatinha all the more comfortable. As if such kindness were not enough, soon Fabíola's mother, Beth, moved her bed into her sick mother's bedroom, thus freeing up a small room, which Paulo began to use as a studio, office and meeting room. To make the place seem less domestic, he covered the walls, ceiling and even the floor with pages from newspapers. When Beth was not around, his workspace became the bedroom where Fabíola had her first sexual experience. However, Paulo still could not understand why such a beautiful girl like her would be attracted to the rather sickly person he thought himself to be.

Riddled with insecurity and driven by what was certainly a mad streak, he gave her an ultimatum: 'I can't believe that a woman as beautiful as you, with your charm, your beautiful clothes, can be in love with me. I need to know that you really love me.'

When Fabíola replied confidently 'I'll do whatever you want me to do', he said: 'If you really love me, let me stub this cigarette out on your thigh. And you're not to cry.'

The girl lifted the edge of her long Indian wrapover skirt, like someone waiting to have an injection. Then she smiled at him without saying a word. Paulo took a long drag on his cigarette and stubbed it out on her smooth, tanned leg. With her eyes closed, Fabíola heard the hiss and smelled the repellent stench of the hot ash burning her skin – she would bear the scar for the rest of her life – but she didn't utter a sound or shed a tear. Paulo said nothing, but thought: She really does love me.

Although he made constant declarations of love, his feelings for Fabíola were ambiguous. While, on the one hand, he was proud to be seen in the fashionable places of Rio hand-in-hand with such a beautiful girl, on the other, he was embarrassed by her silliness and her extraordinary ignorance about almost everything. Fabíola was what, in those days, was known as a *cocota* or bimbo. When she announced over a few beers that Mao Tse Tung was 'the French couturier who created the Mao suits', Paulo wished the ground would open up and swallow him. But it was such a comfortable relationship, which made no demands on him, and she was so pretty that it was worth putting up with her stupid remarks with good grace.

The day she was invited to his house, she was astonished. Judging by her boyfriend's ragged appearance and his lack of money (she often gave him some of her allowance so that he could buy cigarettes and take the bus), Fabíola had always imagined that he was poor and homeless. Imagine her surprise, then, when she was received by a butler wearing white gloves and a jacket with gold buttons. For a moment, she assumed Paulo must be the son of one of the employees, but no, he was the son of the master of the house – 'an enormous pink house with a grand piano and vast courtyard gardens', she said later, recalling that day. 'Just think – in the middle of the drawing room there was a staircase that was identical to the one in *Gone With the Wind* ...'

Although he was eighteen and enjoying relative independence, Paulo still sometimes behaved like a child. One night, he stayed late at Márcia's house, listening to recordings of poetry (her family had given in and decided to accept him), and on returning home, which was only a few metres away, he came across what he called 'a group of nasty-looking individuals'. In fact, they were simply some boys with whom he'd had words a few days earlier when he complained about the noise they were making playing football. However, when he saw them armed with sticks and bottles he was terrified, went back to Márcia's apartment and called home, waking his irascible father. Dramatic and theatrical as ever, he begged: 'Papa, come and collect me from Márcia's house. But come with a revolver because twelve criminals are threatening to kill me.' He would not leave until he looked out of the apartment window and saw his father in pyjamas, with a catapult in his hand, thus guaranteeing him a safe return home.

This paternal zeal did not mean that the situation at home had improved. Things were still as tense as ever, but his parents' control over his life had slackened. His performance during the second term at Andrews had been so dreadful that he wasn't actually allowed to take the end-of-year exams and was thrown out. The only solution was to take the route Pedro had sworn never to accept: to look for a college that was 'less demanding'. The choice was Guanabara, in Flamengo, where Paulo hoped to finish his schooling and then apply for a university course, although not in engineering, as his father so wanted. By opting to take the evening course at the college, he forced his parents to relax their vigilance on his timekeeping and give him a key to the house, but this freedom was won at a price: if he wanted independence and to choose a college for himself, to do drama and get home whenever he wanted, then he would have to find work. Pedro found his son a job where he could earn money selling advertising space in the programmes for the Jockey Club races, but after weeks and weeks of trying, the new entrant into the world of work hadn't managed to sell a single square centimetre of advertising space.

His lack of success did not dismay his father, who suggested another option, this time with Souza Alves Acessórios, a company specializing in the sale of industrial equipment. Although he hated doing anything he was forced to do, Paulo decided to agree for the sake of financial independence, because this was a job with a fixed salary and he wouldn't have to sell anything to anyone. On the first day, he turned up in a suit and tie with his unruly hair slicked down. He wanted to know where his desk would be and was surprised when the manager led him to an enormous shed, pointed to a broom and told him: 'You can start here. First you can sweep out this storeroom. When you've finished, let me know.'

Sweep out a storeroom? But he was an actor, a writer. Had his father fixed him up with a job as a cleaner? No, this must be some kind of joke, a prank they played on all the new employees on their first day at work. He decided to play the game, rolled up his sleeves and swept the floor until lunchtime, by which time his arms were beginning to ache. When the job was finished, he put on his jacket and, smiling, told his boss that he was ready. Without even looking at the new employee, the man handed him a sales slip and pointed to the door: 'Get twenty boxes of hydrometers from that room and take them to dispatch, on the ground floor, with this sales slip.'

This could only have been done deliberately to humiliate him: his father had found him work as a mere factory hand. Despondently, he did what he had been ordered to do and, after a few days, discovered that the routine was always the same: carrying boxes, packing water and electricity meters, sweeping the floor of the storeroom and the warehouse. Just as when he had worked on the dredger, he again felt like Sisyphus. As soon as he finished one thing, he was given something else to do. Weeks later, he wrote in his diary: 'This is like a slow suicide. I'm just not going to cope with waking up at six every morning, starting work at seven thirty to sweep the floor and cart stuff around all day without even stopping for lunch, and then having to go to rehearsals until midnight.'

He survived only a month and a half in the job and had no need to ask if he could leave. The manager decided to call Pedro and tell him that the boy was no good 'for this type of work'. When he left the building for the last time, Paulo had 30 cruzeiros in his pocket – the wages to which he was entitled. It was understandable that he couldn't do the work. Apart from performing in *Pinocchio*, which was on six days a week, he had begun rehearsing another children's play, *A Guerra dos Lanches* [*The War of the Snacks*], which was also directed by Luís Olmedo. 'I've got a role in this new play,' he wrote proudly, 'thanks to my spectacular performance as Batatinha in *Pinocchio*.' Now he was going to work as a real actor, sharing the stage with his friend Joel Macedo and a pretty brunette called Nancy, the sister of Roberto Mangabeira Unger, the perfect student who had come first in almost every subject at St Ignatius. After the tiring routine of rehearsals, the play had its first night in the middle of April 1966. Seeing how nervous Paulo was, Luís Olmedo kissed him on the forehead and said: 'You can do it, Batatinha!'

Paulo got off to a good start. Dressed as a cowboy, all he had to do was to step on to the stage to provoke roars of laughter from the audience, and so it continued. When the show ended, he was fêted as the best actor of the night. As the compliments came flooding in, Luís Olmedo hugged and kissed him (much to the embarrassment of Paulo's parents, who had attended the first night), saying: 'Batatinha, there are no words to describe your performance tonight. You were the hit of the evening, you had the audience eating out of your hand. It was wonderful.'

On the final night of *Pinocchio*, he repeated his success. Batatinha was the only actor – even though he wasn't really an actor – who merited an extra round of applause. If it weren't for the total absence of money, he would have been leading the kind of life he had always dreamed of. He had several girlfriends, he was reasonably successful as an actor, and he had also learned to play the classical guitar and now went everywhere with the instrument on his shoulder, just like his bossa nova idols. However, as had been happening for some time now, his waves of happiness were always cut short by bouts of deep depression. For example, this diary entry, written after reading a biography of Toulouse-Lautrec, dates from that apparently happy and exciting period of his life:

I've just this minute finished one of the most moving real-life stories I've ever read. It's the biography of a wealthy, talented artist, from an aristocratic family, who had achieved fame in his youth, but who, despite this, was the unhappiest man in the world, because his grotesque body and his incredible ugliness meant that he was never loved. He died of drink in the prime of life, his body worn down by his excesses. He was a man who, in the dark, noisy cafés of Montmartre, spent time with Van Gogh, Zola, Oscar Wilde, Degas, Debussy, and from the age of eighteen lived the kind of life all intellectuals aspire to. A man who never used his wealth and social position to humiliate others, but, on the other hand, his wealth and social position never brought a crumb of sincere love to a heart hungry for affection. In some ways, this man is very like me. Henri de Toulouse-Lautrec, whose life is brilliantly described by Pierre La Mure, in the 450 pages of *Moulin Rouge*. I'll never forget this book.

He continued reading a lot, but now, as well as making a note in his diary of each book he read, as he had always done, he would give each book a classification, like that given by professional critics. One star, bad; two, good; three, very good; four, brilliant. On one page in June, he wrote of his surprise at his own voracious literary appetite: 'I've beaten my record: I'm reading five books at the same time. This really can't go on.' And he wasn't reading lightweight stuff either. That day, he had on his bedside table *Crime and Punishment* by Dostoevsky; *Fear and Trembling* by Kierkegaard; *For People Under Pressure: A Medical Guide* by David Harold Fink; *Masterpieces of World Poetry*, edited by Sérgio Milliet; and *A Panorama of Brazilian Theatre* by Sábato Magaldi.

In that same month in 1966, Paulo finally got up the courage to show Jean Arlin the first play he had written as an adult: a three-act play, *Juventude sem Tempo* [*Timeless Youth*]. This was, in fact, a miscellany of poetry, speeches and texts by various authors: Bertolt Brecht, Carlos Lacerda, Morris West, Manuel Bandeira, Vinicius de Moraes, Carlos Drummond de Andrade, Jean-Paul Sartre and, of course, Paulo Coelho. Arlin found it interesting, fiddled with it here and there and decided to try it out. And there was more – since it was a simple play with hardly any scenery or props, he decided to put it on at the first Festival de Juventude, which was going to be held during the holidays in Teresópolis, 100 kilometres from Rio.

Since, besides being an author, he was also an actor, in the second week of July, Paulo went to Teresópolis with Grupo Destaque, against his parents' orders, naturally. He was excited by the festival and even entered a poem in the festival competition, which was to be judged by the poet Lêdo Ivo and the critic Walmir Ayala. The play was a disaster and the result of the poetry competition wouldn't be announced until a month later, but what mattered was that he'd had the courage to try.

The atmosphere at home hadn't changed at all. Besides continuing to nag him about getting home early – he rarely returned before one in the morning – his parents were now insisting that he have his hair cut, something he hadn't done for six months. When he arrived back late at night, he could rely on having to listen to a half-hour lecture before he could go to bed.

On one such night, Pedro was waiting for him at his bedroom door, looking very threatening: 'Once again you've overstepped the mark. As from tomorrow, we're going back to the old regime: the doors of this house will be locked at eleven at night; anyone left outside then can sleep in the street.'

Paulo spent the following day going from his 'studio' in Fabíola's home to rehearsals of *A Guerra dos Lanches*, for which the audiences were becoming smaller and smaller. In the evening, he went to the Paissandu to see Godard's latest film, *La Chinoise*; although he didn't much like the director, he was interested in attending the debate on the film that was to be held afterwards. There he met Renata and at the end of the evening the two went out to supper together. There was hardly anyone else in the restaurant when they finally asked for the bill and set off towards Leblon. Hand-in-hand, they walked almost 3 kilometres along the beach to Rua Rita Ludolf, where Renata lived. Exhausted, Paulo hoped desperately that a bus on the Lapa–Leblon route would come by, and it must have been almost four in the morning when he put his key in the front door, except that the key wouldn't go in. It was only then that he realized that his father must have had the lock changed.

At that hour in the morning, he couldn't possibly go to Joel's or Fabíola's. Furious, he grabbed a handful of stones and began to break all the glass in windows and doors at the front of the house. Woken by the noise, his parents at first decided to ignore him, but fearing that the neighbours would call the police, Pedro went downstairs and opened the door to his son. Making no secret of the fact that he had drunk too much, Paulo stalked across the glass-strewn drawing room and went upstairs without listening to a word his father was saying.

That night he went straight to sleep, but he had a dreadful nightmare. He dreamed that there was a doctor sitting on the edge of his bed taking his blood pressure and two male nurses standing at the door of the room holding a straitjacket. It was only then that he realized with horror that this was no dream. His father had called the emergency services of the mental asylum to admit him again. This time by force.

CHAPTER 7

Ballad of the Clinic Gaol

Wednesday, 20 July

08:00 I was woken up to have my blood pressure taken. Still groggy with sleep, I thought it was a dream, but gradually, the reality of the situation began to sink in. It was the end. They told me to get dressed quickly. Outside the house stood a car from the Emergency Psychiatric Service. I had never imagined how depressing it would be to get into such a car.

A few neighbours watched from a distance as the thin youth with long hair bowed his head to get into the car. Yes, bowed his head. He was defeated.

09:30 All the necessary bureaucratic documents have been filled out. And here I am again on the ninth floor. How fast things happened! Yesterday, I was happily walking with my girlfriend, a little worried, but certainly not expecting this. And here I am again. If I'd stayed out all night rather than gone home, I wouldn't have had that scene with my parents. I think of my girlfriend sometimes. I miss her.

Here everyone is sad. There are no smiles. Eyes stare into emptiness, seeking something, perhaps an encounter with the self. My room-mate is obsessed with death. To tease him, I play the Funeral

March on the guitar. It's good to have my guitar here. It brings a little joy into this atmosphere laden with sadness – the profound sadness of those who aspire to nothing in life and want nothing. The only thing that consoles me is that they still know how to sing.

15:00 I was talking to a young man who has been in here for two years now. I told him I couldn't bear it and wanted to get out. And he said in all sincerity: 'Why? It's great here. You don't have to worry about anything. Why struggle? Deep down, nobody cares about anything anyway.' I felt afraid, afraid that I might start thinking like him. I now feel real anguish, the anguish of not knowing when I will stop seeing the world through bars. It's indescribable. The anguish of the man sentenced to life imprisonment, knowing that one day he'll be given parole. But when will that day come? In a month? Three months? A year? Never?

17:00 Never?

19:20 I can't leave this floor, I can't phone anyone or write letters. A little while ago, I tried (in secret) to phone my girlfriend. She couldn't come to the phone, she was having supper. But what if she hadn't been having supper? What would I have said to her? Would I have complained about my lot, got angry? What would I have said? Who would I have been saying it to? Can I still speak?

I'm shocked at how calmly people accept being shut up in here. I'm afraid I might come to accept it too. If every man is an incendiary at 20 and a fireman at 40, then I reckon I must be 39 years and eleven months old. I'm on the brink of defeat. I felt this when my mother was here this afternoon. She looks down on me. This is only the first day, and yet I already feel half-beaten. But I must not let myself be beaten.

Thursday, 21 July
08:00 Yesterday they gave me a really powerful drug to make me sleep and I'm only just coming to. During the night, for no apparent reason, my room-mate woke me to ask if I was in favour of masturbation. I

said I was and turned over. I really don't understand why he would ask me that. Or perhaps I dreamed it, but it was certainly strange. Flávio, my room-mate, normally spends long periods in complete silence. When he does speak, he always asks the same question: How are things outside? He still wants to maintain contact with the outside world. Poor thing. He's proud of his bohemian lifestyle, but now he's in here and admits that he's ill.

I will never do that. I'm fine.

11:30 I've just realized that they've emptied my wallet. I can't buy anything. Rennie, my girlfriend, promised to visit me today. I know it's forbidden, but I need to talk to her. I spoke to her on the phone, but I kept the tone light, to disguise my depression.

The people here like to show me new things. I'm fond of them really. Roberto is always showing me things – a way of calculating someone's age, a voltmeter, etc. Flávio is obsessed with knowing important people. There are endless interesting cases here. One man is always sniffing his food, another doesn't eat anything for fear of getting fat, a third talks only about sex and sexual aberrations. My room-mate is lying down, staring into space, looking fed up. They're playing a love song on the radio. I wonder what he's thinking about. Is he desperately searching for himself or is he just drifting aimlessly, lost and defeated?

I talk to some of the other patients. Some have been here for three months, others nine; still others have been here for years. I won't be able to bear this.

'Now from the sixth hour there was darkness over all the land unto the ninth hour. And about the ninth hour Jesus cried with a loud voice, saying: My God, my God, why hast thou forsaken me?'

Music, the sun beyond the barred windows, dreams, all of this brings with it a terrible melancholy. I remember the theatre at Teresópolis, where we put on my play *Timeless Youth*. It flopped, but it was still a great experience. Those were happy days, when I was free to see the sun come up, go horseback riding, to kiss my girlfriend and to smile.

Not any more. Not any more. Sleep dulls the ability to reason, and I'll end up like everyone else in here.

14:10 I'm waiting for Rennie. My doctor came to my room to bring me an anthology of French poets. That's good, because I'm starting to learn French. He remarked on the fact that I seemed calm, that I appeared to be enjoying myself. And sometimes I do enjoy it here. It's a world apart, where one just eats and sleeps. That's all. But there always comes a moment when I remember the world outside and then I feel like leaving. Not so much now. I'm getting used to it. All I need is a typewriter.

I know that my girlfriend will come (or try to come) today. She must be curious to find out what's happening to me. She'll visit another two or three times and then she'll forget about me. *C'est la vie.* And I can do nothing about it. I'd like her to come every day to cheer me up as only she can, but that won't happen. I don't even know if they'll let her visit me today. Still, it's a pleasant prospect – the enjoyable suspense of waiting.

14:45 It's a quarter to three and she hasn't arrived. She won't come now. Or perhaps they wouldn't let her in.

Friday, 22 July
11.50 Rennie came yesterday. She brought me a load of photos of her in the States and promised to write a dedication on one of them for me. I like Rennie. I feel sad to think that I haven't treated her as well as I should. I was cold and distant. And she was so affectionate.

So far, the rest of my things from home haven't arrived. As soon as my typewriter gets here, I'm going to have to type out an essay on psychiatry that Dr Benjamim set me. I've finished the anthology of French poets he lent me. Now I'm going to read *The Leopard* by Lampedusa.

It's odd, I'm starting to get used to the idea of staying here.

12:00 I'm beginning to allow sleep to overwhelm me. A heavy, dream-less sleep, sleep-as-escape, the sleep that makes me forget that I'm here.

14:00 I've stopped reading *The Leopard*. It's one of the most boring books I've ever read. Monotonous, stupid and pointless. I abandoned it on page 122. It's a shame. I hate leaving anything half-finished, but I couldn't stand it. It makes me sleepy. And I must avoid sleep at all costs.

14:30 It's not good to leave something half-done.

14:45 Conversation with my room-mate:

'I don't want to live here, in Flamengo, in Copacabana, or in any of those places.'

'So where do you want to live, Flávio?'

'In the cemetery. Life has lost all meaning for me since Carnival in 1964.'

'Why?'

'The person I loved most in the world didn't want to go with me to the Carnival ball at the Teatro Municipal.'

'Oh, come on Flávio, don't be so silly. There are plenty more fish in the sea. [Pause.] Do you still love her?'

'Him. He was a boy. Now he's doing his entrance exams to study medicine and I'm stuck in here, waiting for death.'

'Don't talk nonsense, Flávio.'

'He phoned me yesterday. He's a bit effeminate. It would make me so happy if he came to see me. I attempted suicide because of him. I drank ether spray mixed with whisky on the night of the ball. I ended up in the Emergency Department. Now he's out there and I'm in here, waiting for death.'

He's a strange guy, Flávio. He seems totally schizoid, but some-times he talks perfectly normally, like now. I feel sad and powerless. He's made several suicide attempts in here. He's often spoken to me about the bohemian life he used to lead, and I've noticed a certain pride in his voice when he did so. I know from my own experience that all bohemians feel proud of being bohemian.

Flávio is crying.

15:00 The patients here can sometimes be very funny. Ápio, for example, who's fifty-six, told me yesterday that the Bolshevik Revolution was financed by the Americans. And there's a young man, the only other patient who's about the same age as me, who makes everybody laugh.

I can't write any more. Flávio is crying.

Saturday, 23 July

10:00 Last night, I managed to phone Rennie, who told me that she was still my girlfriend and still loved me very much. That made me so happy, and I probably said a load of silly things. I'm a sentimental fool. When I stopped talking, the telephonist butted in and I couldn't say anything else. Rennie's coming here on Monday. I hope I don't spend all the time complaining. It's awful, I feel inferior.

Luís said he'd come at midday.

Beside me is a boring guy called Marcos. He's been here since I got out, that's a year ago now. He keeps taking my radio so that he can listen to the football.

I diplomatically expelled him from my room.

20:30 It's half past eight at night, but it feels much later here. Luís came. He raised my spirits a little. I phoned Rennie and spouted more nonsense.

Sunday, 24 July

It's Sunday morning. I'm listening to the radio and I'm filled by a terrible sense of solitude, which is slowly killing me. It's Sunday morning, a sad, dull Sunday. I'm here behind bars, not talking to anyone, immersed in my solitude. I like that phrase: immersed in my solitude.

It's Sunday morning. No one is singing; the radio is playing a sad song about love and weeping. A day with few prospects.

Rennie is far away. My friends are far away. Probably sleeping off a night of partying and fun. I'm all alone here. The radio is playing an old-fashioned waltz. I think about my father. I feel sorry for him. It must be sad for someone to have a son like me.

On this Sunday morning, I feel my love for Rennie die a little. I'm sure her love for me must be dying too. My hands are empty, I have nothing to offer, nothing to give. I feel powerless and defence-less like a swallow without wings. I feel bad, wicked, alone. Alone in the world.

Everything here is at once monotonous and unpredictable. I cling fearfully to my photos of Rennie, my money and my cigarettes. They are the only things that can distract me a little.

Monday, 25 July

I long for you and the nearer the time gets to your visit, the more I long to see you. Yesterday, on the phone, you said that you were still my girlfriend, and I'm very glad to have a girlfriend. It makes me feel less alone in here, the world seems a nicer place, even from behind bars. And it will be even nicer when you arrive. And so this morning, I open myself entirely to you, my love, and give you my heart. I feel a bit sad because you're far away and can't be with me all the time, but I'm a man now and have to survive this ordeal alone.

It's funny, I feel possessive. Yesterday, I talked to Luís and Ricardo on the phone. They'll come and see me on Tuesday. I know it's an effort for them. Luís's father is in hospital and Ricardo has to study. But they'll come. And that makes me glad. I've learned that people can get happiness and joy out of the saddest things. I've learned that I'm not as alone as I thought. There are people who need me and care about me. I feel a bit nostalgic, but happy.

Tuesday, 26 July

Yesterday, I read the whole of *Our Man in Havana* by Graham Greene. I haven't yet had time (ha, ha, ha) to write anything about the book. But it distracted me. I enjoyed it.

Sunday, 31 July

13:00 At this hour on this day, in this hospital, I have just received the news that in the poetry competition run by the newspaper *Diário de Notícias*, I came ninth out of 2,500 entries in the general category and second in the honourable mention category. My poem will probably appear in the anthology they're going to publish.

I'm happy. I wish I was outside, telling everyone, talking to everyone. I am very, very happy.

Here, behind bars, I wonder if Tatá still remembers me, her first boyfriend. I don't know if she's grown a lot, if she's thin or fat, if she's an intellectual or a member of high society. She might have been crippled or lost her mother, she might have moved into a mansion. I haven't seen her for eight years, but I'd like to be with her today. I haven't heard from her once since then. The other day, I phoned and asked if she used to go out with a guy called Coelho. She just said 'Yes' and hung up.

Saturday, 6 August

Rennie, my love, I feel a terrible need to speak to you. Now that Dr Benjamim has threatened me with insulin and electroconvulsive therapy, now that I've been accused of being a drug addict, now that I feel like a cornered animal, utterly defenceless, I want so much to talk to you. If this was the moment when my personality was about to be completely transformed, if in a few moments' time the systematic destruction of my being was about to begin, I would want you by my side, Rennie.

We'd talk about the most ordinary things in the world. You'd leave smiling, hoping to see me again in a few days' time. You would know nothing and I would pretend that everything was fine. As we stood at the door to the lift, you'd see my eyes fill with foolish tears, and I'd say it was because our conversation had been so boring it had made me yawn. And downstairs, you'd look up and see my hand through the bars waving goodbye. Then I'd come up to my room and cry my heart out thinking about what was and what should have been and what can never be. Then the doctors would come in with the black bag, and the electric shocks would enter me and fill my whole body.

And in the solitude of the night, I would pick up a razor blade and look at your photo next to the bed, and the blood would flow; and I would say to you softly, as I looked at your smiling face: 'This is my blood.' And I would die without a smile on my face, without shedding a tear. I would simply die, leaving many things undone.

Sunday, 7 August

Conversation with Dr Benjamim:

'You've no self-respect. After your first admission, I thought you'd never be back, that you'd do all you could to become independent. But, no, here you are again. What did you achieve in that time? Nothing. What did you get from that trip to Teresópolis? What did you get out of it? Why are you incapable of achieving anything on your own?'

'No one can achieve anything on their own.'

'Maybe, but tell me, what did you gain by going to Teresópolis?'

'Experience.'

'You're the sort who'll spend the rest of his life experimenting.'

'Doctor, anything that is done with love is worthwhile. That's my philosophy: if we love what we do, that's enough to justify our actions.'

'If I went and fetched four schizophrenics from the fourth floor, I mean real schizoids, even they would come up with a better argument than that.'

'What did I say wrong?'

'What did you say wrong?! You spend your whole time creating an image of yourself, a false image, not even noticing that you're failing to make the most of what's inside you. You're a nothing.'

'I know. Anything I say is pure self-defence. In my own eyes, I'm worthless.'

'Then do something! But you can't. You're perfectly happy with the way things are. You've got used to the situation. Look, if things go on like this, I'm going to forget my responsibilities as a doctor and

call in a medical team to give you electroconvulsive therapy, insulin,
glucose, anything to make you forget and make you more biddable.
But I'm going to give you a bit more time. Come on, be a man. Pull
yourself together!'

Sunday, 14 August – Father's Day
Good morning, Dad. Today is your day.
For many years, this was the day you'd wake up with a smile on
    your face
and, still smiling, accept the present I brought to your room,
and, still smiling, kiss me on the forehead and bless me.
Good morning, Dad, today is your day,
and I can neither give you anything nor say anything
because your embittered heart is now deaf to words.
You're not the same man. Your heart is old,
your ears are stuffed with despair,
your heart aches. But you still know how to cry. And I think you're
    crying
the timid tears of a strict, despotic father:
you're weeping for me, because I'm here behind bars,
you're weeping because today is Father's Day and I'm far away,
filling your heart with bitterness and sadness.

Good morning, Dad. A beautiful sun is coming up,
today is a day of celebration and joy for many,
but you're sad. And I know that I am your sadness,
that somehow I became a heavy cross
for you to carry on your back, lacerating your skin,
wounding your heart.
At this very moment, my sister will be coming into your room
with a lovely present wrapped in crêpe paper,
and you'll smile, so as not to make her sad too. But inside you,
your heart is crying,
and I can say nothing except dark words of revolt,
and I can do nothing but increase your suffering,

and I can give you nothing but tears and the regret
that you brought me into the world.

Perhaps if I didn't exist, you'd be happy now,
perhaps you'd have the happiness of a man who only ever wanted
     one thing:
a quiet life,
and now, on Father's Day,
you receive the reward for your struggle, in the form of kisses,
trinkets bought with the small monthly allowance
that has remained untouched for weeks in a drawer
so that it could be transformed into a present,
which, however small, assumes vast proportions in the heart of
     every father.

Today is Father's Day. But my Dad had me admitted
to a hospital for the insane. I'm too far away
to embrace you; I'm far from the family,
far from everything, and I know that
when you see other fathers surrounded by their children,
showering them with affection, you'll feel a pang
in your poor embittered heart. But I'm in here
and haven't seen the sun for twenty days now,
and if I could give you something it would be the darkness
of someone who no longer aspires to anything or yearns for
     anything in life.
That's why I do nothing. That's why I can't even say:
'Good morning, dear father, may you be happy;
you were a man and one night you engendered me;
my mother gave birth to me in great pain,
but now I can give you a little of the treasure
placed in my heart
by your hard-working hands.'
I can't even say that. I have to stay very still
so as not to make you even sadder,

so that you don't know that I'm suffering, that I'm unhappy in here,
in the midst of this quietness, normally only to be found in heaven,
if, of course, heaven exists.
It must be sad to have a son like me, Dad.

Good morning, Dad. My hands are empty,
but I give you this rising sun, red and omnipotent,
to help you feel less sad and more content,
thinking that you're right and I'm happy.

Tuesday, 23 August

It's dawn, the eve of my birthday. I'd like to write a message full of optimism and understanding in this notebook: that's why I tore out the previous pages, so devoid of compassion and so sad. It's hard, especially for someone of my temperament, to withstand thirty-two days without going out into the courtyard and seeing the sun. It's really hard, believe me. But, deep down, I know I'm not the most unfortunate of men. I have youth flowing in my veins, and I can start all over again thousands of times.

It's the eve of my birthday. With these lines written at dawn, I would like to regain a little self-confidence.

'Look, Paulo, you can always do your university entrance exams next year: you've still got many years ahead of you. Make the most of these days to think a little and to write a lot. Rosetta, your type-writer, your loyal companion-at-arms, is with you, ready to serve you whenever you wish. Do you remember what Salinger wrote: "Store away your experiences. Perhaps, later, they'll be useful to someone else, just as the experiences of those who came before were useful to you." Think about that. Don't think of yourself as being alone. After all, to begin with, your friends were a great support. Being forgotten is a law of life. You'd probably forget about one of your friends if they left. Don't be angry with your friends because of that. They did what they could. They lost heart, as you would in their place.'

Thursday, 1 September

I've been here since July. Now I'm becoming more and more afraid. I'm to blame for everything. Yesterday, for example, I was the only one to agree to having an injection to help me sleep, and I was the only one to obey the nurse and lie down; the others, meanwhile, continued kicking up a ruckus. One of the nuns who help out here took a dislike to my girlfriend and so she's not allowed to visit me any more. They found out I was going to sell my shirts to the other patients and they wouldn't let me: I lost an opportunity to earn some money. But I managed to persuade my friends to bring me a gun, a Beretta. If I need to, I'll use it.

Interruption for a hair cut.

Right, my hair's all gone. Now I'm left with a baby face, feeling vulnerable and mad as hell. Now I feel what I feared I might feel: the desire to stay here. I don't want to leave now. I'm finished. I hadn't cut my hair since February, until the people in this hospital gave me an option: cut your hair or stay here for good. I preferred to cut my hair. But then came the feeling that I'd destroyed the last thing remaining to me. This page was going to be a kind of manifesto of rebellion. But now I've lost all will. I'm well and truly screwed. I'm finished. I won't rebel again. I'm almost resigned.

Here ends this ballad and here ends me.
With no messages to send, nothing, no desire to win,
a desire that had its guts ripped out by human hatred.
It was good to feel this. Total defeat.
Now let's start all over again.

CHAPTER 8

Shock treatment

ONE SUNDAY IN SEPTEMBER 1966, Paulo was wandering along the corridors of the clinic after lunch. He had just been re-reading 'The Ballad of the Clinic Gaol', which he had finished writing the day before, and he felt proud of the thirty-five typewritten pages that he had managed to produce in a month and a half at the mental asylum. In fact, it was not so very different from the work that had inspired him, Oscar Wilde's 'The Ballad of Reading Gaol', written in 1898, after his release from prison, where he had served two years for homosexual offences. Paulo's final sentence on the last page – 'Now let's start all over again' – might seem like mere empty words, a rather glib ending. Starting all over again meant only one thing: to get out of the hell that was the clinic as quickly as possible and restart his life. However, a terrifying idea was daily becoming more of a reality: if it was up to the doctors or his parents, he would continue to rot on the ninth floor for a long time.

Absorbed in these thoughts, he hardly noticed the two male nurses who came over to him and asked him to go with them to another part of the building. They led him to a cubicle with tiled floor and walls, where Dr Benjamim was waiting. In the centre of the room was a bed covered with a thick rubber sheet and, to one side, a small machine that looked like an ordinary electric transformer with wires and a handle, much like the equipment used clandestinely by the police to torture prisoners and extract confessions.

Paulo was terrified: 'Do you mean I'm going to have shock treatment?'

Kindly and smiling as ever, the psychiatrist tried to calm him: 'Don't worry, Paulo. It doesn't hurt at all. It's more upsetting seeing someone else being treated than receiving the treatment yourself. Really, it doesn't hurt at all.'

Lying on the bed, he watched a nurse putting a plastic tube in his mouth so that his tongue wouldn't roll back and choke him. The other nurse stood behind him and stuck an electrode that looked like a small cardiac defibrillator to each of his temples. While he stared up at the peeling paint on the ceiling, the machine was connected. A session of electroconvulsive therapy was about to begin. As the handle was turned, a curtain seemed to fall over his eyes. His vision was narrowing until it was fixed on one point; then everything went dark.

At each subsequent turn of the handle his body shook uncontrollably and saliva spurted from his mouth like white foam. Paulo never knew how long each session lasted – Minutes? An hour? A day? Nor did he feel any sickness afterwards. When he recovered consciousness he felt as though he were coming round after a general anaesthetic: his memory seemed to disappear and he would sometimes lie for hours on his bed, eyes open, before he could recognize and identify where he was and what he was doing there. Apart from the pillowcase and his pyjama collar, which were wet with dribble, there was no sign in the room of the brutality to which he had been subjected. The 'therapy' was powerful enough to destroy his neurones, but the doctor was right: it didn't hurt at all.

Electroconvulsive therapy was based on the idea that mental disturbance resulted from 'electrical disturbances in the brain'. After ten to twenty sessions of electric shocks applied every other day, the convulsions caused by the succession of electric charges would, it was believed, 'reorganize' the patient's brain, allowing him to return to normal. This treatment was seen as a great improvement on other treatments used at the time such as Metazol and insulin shock: it caused retrograde amnesia, blocking any memory of events immediately prior to the charges, including their application. The patient would therefore have no negative feelings towards the doctors or his own family.

After that first session, Paulo woke late in the afternoon with a sour taste in his mouth. During the torpor that dulled both mind and body after the treatment, he got up very slowly, as if he were an old man, and went over to the grille at the window. He saw that it was drizzling, but he still did not recognize his room, where he had been taken following the treatment. He tried to remember what lay beyond the door, but couldn't. When he went towards it, he realized that his legs were trembling and his body had been weakened by the shocks. With some difficulty, he managed to leave his room. There he saw an enormous, empty corridor and felt like walking a little through that cemetery of the living. The silence was such that he could hear the sound of his slippers dragging along the white, disinfected corridor. As he took his first steps, he had the clear impression that the walls were closing in around him as he walked, until he began to feel them pressing on his ribs. The walls were enclosing him so tightly that he could walk no further. Terrified, he tried to reason with himself: 'If I stay still, nothing will happen to me. But if I walk, I'll either destroy the walls or I'll be crushed.'

What should he do? Nothing. He stayed still, not moving a muscle. And he stayed there, for how long, he doesn't know, until a female nurse led him gently by the arm, back to his room, and helped him to lie down. When he woke, he saw someone standing beside him, someone who had apparently been talking to him while he slept. It was Luís Carlos, the patient from the room next door, a thin mulatto who was so ashamed of his stammer that he would pretend to be dumb when meeting strangers. Like everyone else there, he also swore that he wasn't mad. 'I'm here because I decided to retire,' he would whisper, as though revealing a state secret. 'I asked a doctor to register me as insane, and if I manage to stay here as a madman for two years, I'll be allowed to retire.'

Paulo could not stand hearing such stories. When his parents visited, he would kneel down, weep and beg them to take him away, but the answer was always the same: 'Wait a few more days. You're almost better. Dr Benjamim is going to let you out in a few days.'

His only contacts with the outside world were the ever-more infre-quent visits from the friends who managed to get through the security.

By taking advantage of the comings and goings at the gate, anyone with a little patience could get through, taking in whatever he or she wanted. So it was that Paulo managed to get a friend to smuggle in a loaded 7.65 automatic revolver, hidden in his underpants. However, once rumours began to spread among the other patients that Paulo was walking around armed, he quickly stuffed the Beretta into Renata's bag, and she left with the gun. She was his most frequent visitor. When she couldn't get through security, she would leave notes at the gate to be given to him.

> The fool in the lift knows me now and today he wouldn't let me come up. Tell the people there that you had a row with me, and maybe that band of tossers will stop messing you around.
>
> I feel miserable, not because you've made me miserable, but because I don't know what to do to help you.
>
> [...] The pistol is safe in my wardrobe. I didn't show it to anyone. Well, I did show it to António Cláudio, my brother. But he's great; he didn't even ask whose it was. But I told him.
>
> [...] I'll deliver this letter tomorrow. It's going to be a miserable day. One of those days that leave people hurting inside. Then I'm going to wait for fifteen minutes down below looking up at your window to see if you've received it. If you don't appear, it will be because they haven't given you the letter.
>
> [...] Batata, I'm so afraid that sometimes I want to go and talk to your mother or Dr Benjamim. But it wouldn't help. So if you can, see if you can sit it out. I mean it. I had a brilliant idea: when you get out, we'll take a cargo ship and go to Portugal and live in Oporto – good idea?
>
> [...] You know, I bought a pack of your favourite cigarettes because that way I'll have a little bit of the taste of you in my mouth.

On his birthday, it was Renata who turned up with a bundle of notes and letters she had collected from his friends with optimistic, cheerful messages, all of them hoping that Batatinha would soon return to the stage. Among this pile of letters full of kisses and promises to visit there was one message that particularly excited him. It was a three-line note from Jean Arlin: 'Batatinha my friend, our play *Timeless Youth* is having its first night on 12 September here in Rio. We're counting on the presence of the author.'

The idea of running away surfaced more strongly when Paulo realized that with his newly cropped hair he was unrecognizable, even to his roommate. He spent two days sitting on a chair in the corridor pretending to read a book but in fact watching out of the corner of his eye the movements of the lift – the only possible escape route, since the stairs were closed off with iron grilles. One thing was sure: the busiest time was Sunday, between midday and one in the afternoon, when the doctors, nurses and employees changed shift and mingled with the hundreds of visitors who were getting in and out of the packed lift.

In pyjamas and slippers the risk of being caught was enormous. But if he were dressed in 'outdoor clothes' and wearing shoes, it would be possible to merge unnoticed with the other people crowding together so that they wouldn't miss the lift; then he could leave the building complex. Concealed behind his open book, Paulo mentally rehearsed his escape route dozens, hundreds of times. He considered all the possible obstacles and unexpected incidents that might occur and concluded that the chances of escaping were fairly high. It would have to be soon, though, before everyone got used to his new appearance without his usual shoulder-length curly mane.

He spoke of his plan to only two people: Renata and Luís Carlos, his 'dumb' neighbour in the clinic. His girlfriend not only urged him on but contributed 30 cruzeiros – about US$495 today – from her savings in case he should have to bribe someone. Luís Carlos was so excited by the idea that he decided to go too, as he was fed up with being stuck in the clinic. Paulo asked whether this meant he was giving up his idea of using mental illness as a way of retiring, but his fellow inmate replied: 'Running away is part of the illness. Every mad person runs away at least once. I've run away before, and then I came back of my own accord.'

Finally the long-awaited day arrived: Sunday, 4 September 1966. Duly dressed in 'normal people's clothes', the two friends thought the lift ride down, stopping at every floor, would never end. They kept their heads lowered, fearing that a doctor or nurse they knew might get in at any moment. It was a relief when they reached the ground floor and went up to the gate, not so fast as to arouse suspicion, but not so slowly as to be easily identified. Everything went exactly to plan. Since there had been no need to bribe anyone, the money Renata had given Paulo was enough to keep them going for a few days.

Still with Luís Carlos, Paulo went to the bus station and bought two tickets to Mangaratiba, a small town on the coast, a little more than 100 kilometres south of Rio. The sun was starting to set when the two of them hired a boat to take them to an island half an hour from the mainland. The tiny island of Guaíba was a paradise as yet unspoiled by people. Heloísa Araripe, 'Aunt Helói', Paulo's mother's sister, had a house on Tapera beach, and it was only when he arrived there, still with the 'dumb' man in tow, that he felt himself safe from the wretched clinic, the doctors and nurses.

The place seemed ideal as a refuge, but hours after getting there, the two realized that they wouldn't be able to stay there for long, at least not the way things were. The house was rarely used by Aunt Helói, and had only a clay filter half full with water – and this of a highly suspicious green colour. The caretaker, a man from Cananéia who lived in a cabin a few metres from the house, showed no interest in sharing his dinner. They were by now extremely hungry, but the only relief for their rumbling stomachs was a banana tree. When they woke the following day, their arms and legs covered in mosquito bites, they had to go to the same banana tree for breakfast, lunch and, finally, dinner. On the second day, Luís Carlos suggested that they should try fishing, but this idea failed when they discovered that the stove in the house had no gas and that there was no cutlery, oil or salt in the kitchen – nothing. On the Tuesday, three days after their arrival, they spent hours in the depot waiting for the first boat to take them back to the mainland. When the bus from Mangaratiba left them at the bus station in Rio, Paulo told his fellow fugitive that he was going to spend a few days in hiding until he had decided what to do with his life. Luís Carlos had also concluded that their adventure was coming to an end and had decided to go back to the clinic.

The two said goodbye, roaring with laughter and promising that they would meet again some day. Paulo took a bus and knocked on the door of Joel Macedo's house, where he hoped to remain until he had worked out what to do next. His friend was delighted to receive him, but he was worried that his house might not be a good hiding-place, as Lygia and Pedro knew that Paulo used to sleep there when he stayed out late. If he were to leave Rio, the ideal hiding-place would be the house that Joel's father had just finished building in a condominium at Cabo Frio, a town 40 kilometres from Araruama. Before setting out, Joel asked Paulo to have a bath and change his clothes, as he didn't fancy travelling with a friend who hadn't washed or had clean clothes for four days. A few hours later, they set off in Joel's estate car, driven by Joel (after the trauma of the accident, Paulo hadn't even touched a steering wheel).

The friends spent the days drinking beer, walking along the beach and reading Joel's latest passion, the plays of Maxim Gorki and Nikolai Gogol. When the last of Renata's money had gone, Paulo thought it was time to return. It was a week since he had run away and he was tired of just wandering about with nowhere to go. He went to a telephone box and made a reverse-charge call home. On hearing his voice, his father didn't sound angry, but was genuinely concerned for his physical and mental state. When he learned that his son was in Cabo Frio, Pedro offered to come and fetch him in the car, but Paulo preferred to return with Joel.

Lygia and Pedro had spent a week searching desperately for their son in mortuaries and police stations, and this experience had changed them profoundly. They agreed that he should not return to the clinic and even said that they were interested in his work in the theatre; and they appeared to have permanently lifted the curfew of eleven o'clock at night. Paulo distrusted this offer. 'After a week of panic, with no news of me,' he was to say later, 'they would have accepted any conditions, and so I took advantage of that.' He grew his hair again, as well as a ridiculous beard, and no one told him off. In his very limited free time, he devoted himself to girls. Besides Renata and Fabíola (Márcia was not around much), he had also taken up with Genivalda, a rather plain, but very intelligent girl from the northeast of Brazil. Geni, as she preferred to be called, didn't dress well, she didn't live in a smart part of town and she didn't study at the Catholic university in Rio or at one of the smart colleges. However, she seemed to know everything and that ensured her a place in the Paissandu circle.

Paulo's growing success with women was due not – as with Fabíola – to any surgical intervention but to a change in fashion. The 'counterculture' revolution that was spreading across the world was transforming not only political patterns and behaviour but also people's idea of what was attractive. This meant that men who had always been considered ugly up until then, such as the rock star Frank Zappa or, in Brazil, the musician Caetano Veloso, had overnight become ideals of modern beauty. The new criterion for beauty demanded that the virile, healthy and carefully shaven man be replaced by the dishevelled, ill-dressed and physically frail variety.

As a beneficiary of this new trend, Paulo had only one problem: finding a place where he could make love. He was eager to make up for lost time, and as well as his long-standing girlfriends, there were various others whom he chanced to meet. At a time when motels did not exist and morality demanded a marriage certificate when registering in a hotel, there were few alternatives for the young who, like him, did not have a bachelor pad. Not that he could complain, though, since as well as the lenient attitude of Fabíola's mother and grandmother, who shut their eyes and ears to what was going on in the newspaper-plastered 'studio', he could count on the assistance of Uncle José, in Araruama, whose door was always open to whomever Paulo might bring back at the weekends or on holidays.

Even so, when he made an unexpected conquest, he always managed to find a solution to suit the situation. On one occasion, he spent hours indulging in amorous preliminaries with a young aspiring actress in a pedalo on Lake Rodrigo de Freitas. After visiting numerous dives and by then feeling pretty high – on alcohol, since neither took any drugs – Paulo and the girl ended up having sex in the apartment where she lived with a great-aunt. As it was a one-room apartment, they enjoyed themselves before the astonished eyes of the old woman, who was deaf, dumb and senile – an experience he was to repeat several times. On another occasion, he confessed to his diary that he had had sex in still more unusual circumstances:

> I invited Maria Lúcia for a walk on the beach with me; then we went to the cemetery to talk some more. That's why I'm writing today: so that, later, I'll remember that I had a lover for one day. A young girl

completely devoid of preconceptions, in favour of free love, a young girl who's a woman too. She said that she could tell from my physical type that I would be hot stuff in bed. And the two of us, with a few interruptions due to exhaustion or a burial taking place, made love the whole afternoon.

Weeks after he ran away from the clinic, however, the problem of having to find somewhere to make love was resolved. Thanks to the mediation of his maternal grandfather, Tuca, Paulo's parents gave him permission to try an experiment: living alone for a while. His new home was one offered by his grandfather: a small apartment that he owned in the Marquês de Herval building on Avenida Rio Branco, right in the commercial centre of Rio.

The apartment, which was a few blocks from the red light district, could not have been worse. During the day, the area was a noisy tumult of street vendors, traders, beggars and sellers of lottery tickets, with buses and cars travelling in every direction. From seven in the evening, there was a complete change of scene. As the brightness of day gave way to darkness, the day workers were replaced by prostitutes, layabouts, transvestites, pimps and drug traffickers. It was entirely unlike the world Paulo came from, but it didn't matter: it was his home, and he, and no one else, was in charge. As soon as he contacted his friends in the Grupo Destaque, Paulo learned that the promised production of *Timeless Youth* in Rio had been cancelled for lack of funds. Some of the group who had been in *Pinocchio* and *A Guerra dos Lanches* were now engaged on another venture, in which Paulo immediately became involved: a play for adults. For some weeks, under the auspices of the Teatro Universitário Nacional, the group had been rehearsing an adaptation of *Capitães da Areia* [*Captains of the Sands*], a novel written thirty years before by the Brazilian writer Jorge Amado. Blond, blue-eyed and tanned, the director and adapter, Francis Palmeira, looked more like one of the surfers who spent their time looking for waves in Arpoador; but, as a precocious fifteen-year-old, he had already had one play, *Ato Institucional*, banned by the censors. Jorge Amado was so thrilled to see this group of young people putting on drama by established writers that he not only authorized the adaptation but also wrote a foreword for the programme:

> I have entrusted the students with the adaptation of my novel *Capitães da Areia* and have done so confidently and gladly: students nowadays are in the vanguard of everything that is good in Brazil. They are the untiring fighters for democracy, for the rights of man, for progress, for the advance of the Brazilian people, against dictatorship and oppression. In the novel on which they have based their play, I also conveyed my faith in the Brazilian people and registered my protest against all forms of injustice and oppression. The first edition of *Capitães da Areia* was published a week before the proclamation of the 'Estado Novo', a cruel and ignorant dictatorship – which seized and banned the book. The novel was a weapon in the struggle. Today it has taken on a new dimension: the stage, which makes contact with the public all the more immediate. I can only wish the students of the Teatro Universitário Nacional the greatest success, certain that they are, once again, working for the good of democracy and of Brazil.

It was obvious that there would be problems. The first was with the Juizado de Menores (the Juvenile Court), which acted in the interests of minors and threatened to ban the rehearsals unless those under eighteen were able to show that they had permission from their parents. This meant all the young people in the group, starting with the show's director. Then, just a few days before the first night, the rehearsals were interrupted by the arrival of Edgar Façanha, Member of Parliament and the head of censorship in Rio, together with a member of the Serviço Nacional de Informações, or SNI, who wanted to see a certificate from the censor's office, without which the play could not be performed. When it became clear that no such certificate existed, during the ensuing argument the police arrested one of the actors, Fernando Resky, and left a warning that if they wanted to open on 15 October 1966, as planned, they should submit a copy of the script to the censor as soon as possible. Days later, the script was returned with certain words deleted – 'comrade', 'dialogue', 'revolution' and 'freedom' – and one entire sentence cut: 'All homes would be open to him, because revolution is a homeland and a family for all.' As they had already had such difficulty putting on the play, the group thought it best to accept the cuts without protest or appeal.

Although there were thirty actors in the play, Paulo had a reasonably prominent part. He was Almiro, the homosexual lover of Barandão, who dies of smallpox at the end of the play. Jorge Amado had promised to be at the preview, but as he was in Lisbon for the launch of his most recent novel, he asked no less a figure than 'Volta Seca', one of the street boys from Salvador who had been the inspiration for the main characters in the book, to represent him. The news in the Rio papers that *Capitães da Areia* had been censored proved a magnet to audiences. On the first night, all 400 seats in the Teatro Serrador in the centre of Rio were filled. Only two of the people Paulo had invited were missing: Renata and Dr Benjamim.

After his second period at the clinic, Paulo had formed a strange relationship with the psychiatrist. It wasn't just affection, despite all that Paulo had been through there: it was more that being close to the doctor and being able to talk to him about his doubts gave him a sense of security he hadn't felt before. At the time, such a relationship between doctor and patient was considered one of the side effects of retrograde amnesia. Many years later, however, Paulo himself diagnosed it as what came to be called Stockholm Syndrome, the sudden and inexplicable feelings of emotional dependence some hostages feel towards their hostage-takers. 'I established the same relationship of hostage and hostage-taker with Dr Benjamim,' he said in an interview. 'Even after leaving the clinic, during the great crises of my youth and problems with my love life, I would go and talk to him.'

Capitães da Areia ran for two months. Apart from that first night, it wasn't a wild success, but the takings were large enough to pay the expenses and there was even some money left over to be shared out among the actors and technicians. There was also praise from respected critics.

After the euphoria of the production, Paulo once again became depressed. He felt empty and lost, and frequently kicked to pieces anything that got in his way in his grandfather's apartment. Alone in that hostile, unfamiliar neighbourhood, with no one to turn to during his periods of melancholy and no one to share his rare moments of joy, he would often fall into despair. When these crises arose, he poured out his heart to his diary. Once, he sat up all night filling page after page with something he called 'Secrets of a Writer': 'Suddenly my life has changed. I've been left high and dry in the most depressing place in Brazil: the city, the commercial centre of Rio. At night, no one. During the day, thousands of distant people. And the loneliness is becoming such that I've begun to feel it's like something alive and real, which fills every corner and every street. I, Paulo Coelho, aged nineteen, am empty-handed.'

His proximity to the red light district meant that he became a regular client in the brothels that lined the streets from the bottom of the Lapa to Mangue. It didn't matter that these women weren't very elegant and bore no physical resemblance to the rich girls he fancied. He could talk about anything to a prostitute and realize all his secret fantasies without scandalizing anyone – even when these fantasies meant doing absolutely nothing, as he recorded in his diary:

Yesterday I went with the oldest woman in the area – and the oldest woman I've slept with in my whole life (I didn't screw her, I just paid to look). Her breasts looked like a sack with nothing in it and she stood there in front of me, naked, stroking her cunt with her hand. I watched her, unable to understand why she made me feel both pity and respect. She was pure, extremely kind and professional, but she was a really old woman, you can't imagine just how old. Perhaps seventy. She was French and had left a copy of *France Soir* lying on the floor. She treated me with such care. She works from six in the evening to eleven o'clock at night; then she catches a bus home and there she's a respectable old lady. No one says, Oh my God! I can't think of her naked because it makes me shudder and fills me with such a mixture of feelings. I'll never forget this old woman. Very strange.

While sometimes he would pay and not have sex, on other occasions he would have sex and pay nothing, or almost nothing ('Yesterday I was on inspired form and I managed to get a prostitute without paying anything – in the end she took a sweater that I'd pinched from a friend'). Then, for weeks on end, he devoted every page in his diary to his crazed love for a young prostitute. One day, the woman disappeared with another client, without telling him, and once again he went crazy. He may have been an adult, but only the innocence of a boy in matters of love could explain his jealousy at having been betrayed by a prostitute. 'I wanted to cry as I've never cried before, because my whole being resided in that woman,' he moaned. 'With her flesh I could keep loneliness at bay for a while.' On hearing that his loved one had returned and that she was revealing inti- mate facts about him to all and sundry, he wrote: 'I've heard that she's slandering me … I've realized that as far as she's concerned, I'm a nobody, a nothing. I'm going to give away the name of the woman to whom I gave everything that was pure in my putrefied being: Tereza Cristina de Melo.'

During the day, Paulo continued to live the life of his dreams: girl- friends, rehearsals, study groups, debates about cinema and existential- ism. Although he had hardly set foot in his new college, he had managed to move up a year, which allowed him to think of taking the entrance exam for a degree. On the few occasions when he appeared at the family home – usually in order to scrounge a meal or ask for money – he made up stories in order to shock his parents, saying that he had been in the most outlandish places in Rio. 'I read in the newspapers about the places frequented by free-living young people and lied, saying that I had been there, just to shock my father and mother.' Although he almost never played his guitar, he took it with him everywhere, 'just to impress the girls!'

When night fell, though, the bouts of melancholy and loneliness returned. There came a time when he could take them no more. For three months, night after night, he had done battle with a constant nightmare, and he felt he had to take a step back. He packed up all his belongings in a box and, sad and humiliated, he asked his parents to have him back in the house to which he had never imagined he would return.

CHAPTER 9

The great escape

THE EASE WITH WHICH HE MIXED with women of all classes, from prostitutes in Mangue to elegant young bimbos at the Paissandu, gave everyone the impression that Paulo had no doubts about his sexual proclivities. This, however, was merely an impression. His life in the world of the theatre, where homosexuality was practised freely, had aroused a doubt so secret that he didn't even reveal it to his diary: did he have 'sexual problems', as his mother had suspected when she had first had him admitted to the clinic? Or, in plain language, was he homosexual? Although he was almost twenty, this was still a dark, mysterious area for Paulo. Unlike most Brazilian boys of the time, he had had his first sexual encounter with a woman, the sexually precocious and experienced Madá, rather than with a male friend. He had never felt the desire to have physical relations with a man, and had never even fantasized about such an encounter. Several times, though, when he saw groups of homosexual friends talking during intervals in rehearsals, he tormented himself with troubling questions: 'What if they're right? What if their sexual choice is better than mine?'

Life had taught him that it was better to be the first to jump into the icy river than to suffer in line until it was his turn. Instead of continuing to torment himself with endless doubts, he knew that there was only one way to resolve the problem: try it out. When he read a text from Marx saying something like 'practice is the deciding factor', he interpreted it as a prompt to take action. One evening, when he was still living in his grand-father's apartment in the city centre, he summoned up his courage and went round various of the gay bars until, fortified by a few whiskies, he decided to take the plunge. He went up to a boy of his age, a professional, who was waiting for customers, and got straight to the point.

'Hi. How do you fancy going to bed with me?'

Paulo was ready for anything, but certainly not the reply he got: 'No. I don't want to.'

Paulo felt as surprised as if he had been punched. How come? He was going to pay, after all! The boy turned his back on him and left him standing, glass in hand. When he tried again in another nightclub and received a second 'No', he brought his brief homosexual experiment to an end. Weeks later, frantically engaged in work, he appeared to have forgot-ten the matter.

While the career of Paulo Coelho the writer continued to be an evident failure, the same could not be said about Coelho the playwright and producer. His first solo foray into the world of the arts, in children's theatre, was a production of a cinema classic, *The Wizard of Oz*. He not only adapted the script but also directed the play and cast himself as the Lion. Lacking funds for costly props and costumes, he simply painted whiskers on his face and stuck two cloth ears on his head; the tail was a rope sewn on to his trousers, the end of which he would twist round his forefinger during the show. Almost the only thing he took from the film was the song 'Somewhere Over the Rainbow'. The remainder of the score was composed by Antônio Carlos Dias, or Kakiko, a musician and actor with whom Paulo had shared a dressing room during the production of *Capitães da Areia*. To everyone's surprise, *The Wizard of Oz* took in enough to cover the costs of the production and the salaries of actors and tech-nicians *and* made a profit – money that Paulo squirreled away for their next production. Having his name appear on the entertainment pages of the newspapers was also something akin to success: on one day in 1967, his name appeared in three different places in the cultural sections of the Rio press. At the Teatro de Arena he was the author and director of *O*

Tesouro do Capitão Berengundo [*The Treasure of Captain Berengundo*]; at the Santa Terezinha his name was on the posters for an adaptation of his, *Aladdin and his Magic Lamp*; and at the Teatro Carioca he was appearing as an actor in Walmir Ayala's *A Onça de Asas* [*The Winged Jaguar*].

Children's plays brought in a little money, but it was only in adult theatre that he could achieve the fame and prestige he craved. The production of *Capitães da Areia* had made this clear. In March, he was asked to act in a big production of Brecht and Weil's *The Threepenny Opera*. The show had been a great success in São Paulo with a cast of famous actors, and the Rio cast did not lag far behind, and was also full of well-known stars. The play was to be the first production at the theatre in the Sala Cecília Meirelles. Paulo played a blind beggar, a role that needed little acting ability, but his name would be printed in the programme alongside all the big names.

After several weeks of rehearsal, they were ready for the first night. A few days before, the company was invited to give a live performance of the play in the studios of TV Rio, the most important of the city's television stations. When it was due to go out, someone realized that the actor Oswaldo Loureiro, who was to sing the theme song, was missing. Since Paulo was the only one of the group who knew the words of 'Mack the Knife' by heart, he received the most exposure on the programme. The reasonable success of the production established him further in his new profession.

He was back in his parents' house and the play was still showing when the Devil of homosexuality decided to tempt him again. This time the initiative was not his but that of an actor of about thirty who was also working on the play. In fact the two had only exchanged a few words and looks, but one night, after the show, the older man approached him.

He came straight to the point: 'Would you like to come back to my place and have sex?'

Nervous and rather taken aback, Paulo said the first thing that came into his head: 'Yes, I would.'

They spent the night together. Although much later, Paulo recalled feeling rather disgusted to find himself exchanging caresses with a man, he nevertheless had sex with him, penetrating and being penetrated.

Paulo returned home the following day even more confused than before. He had felt no pleasure and yet he still remained unsure as to whether or not he was homosexual. Some months later, he decided to try again and chose someone from among his stage friends. In the man's studio flat in Copacabana, he felt horribly embarrassed when his partner suggested they take a bath together. His feelings of unease continued throughout the night, and they only managed to have full sex when the sun was already coming up. Paulo Coelho was now convinced, once and for all, that he was not homosexual.

Despite his doubts about his sexuality, he continued to find success with women. He had left Márcia and finished his friendship with Renata, but he continued his relationship with Fabíola, who seemed to be growing more beautiful by the day. He had become a gifted bigamist, though, having fallen for Genivalda, from Sergipe, the ugly, brilliant Geni whose witty comments delighted the intelligentsia who hung out at the Paissandu. After besieging her unsuccessfully for weeks, he finally took her away for a weekend at Uncle José's house in Araruama. On their first night together, he was surprised to hear Geni, who seemed such a woman of the world, asking him in a whisper to be gentle because this was her first sexual experience. Since there was no suitable place for them to meet, the first months of their 'honeymoon' were awkward, but they were fruitful: at the beginning of June, Geni telephoned him to say that she was pregnant with his child. Paulo immediately decided that he wanted the child, but had no time to say so, as she immediately announced that she was going to have an abortion. He suggested a meeting so that they could talk, but Geni was determined: she had made her decision and, besides, she wanted to put an end to their relationship. She rang off and disappeared from his life as if she had never existed.

Paulo entered another downward spiral. Upset by the news of the pregnancy and Geni's sudden disappearance, he set about looking for her everywhere until he learned that she had returned to her hometown of Aracaju, where she was intending to have the abortion. Keen to dissuade her, but with no means of finding her when she was almost 2,000 kilometres away, he once again succumbed to fits of depression, interrupted by short periods of euphoria. Pages and pages of his diary, written during sleepless nights, reflect this:

> I breathe solitude, I wear solitude, I crap solitude. It's awful. I've never felt so alone. Not even during the long bitter days of my adolescence. Not that solitude is anything new. It's just that I'm getting tired of it. Soon I'll do something mad that will terrify the world.
>
> I want to write. But what for? Why? Alone, my brain fills with existential problems, and I can only make out one thing in all that noise and confusion: a desire to die.

This rather melodramatic vein also appears in his moments of happiness. He recorded these rare and short-lived moments of optimism with a total lack of modesty: 'My hour to give birth has arrived, as foreseen in a poem I wrote in the clinic. This morning I was born, along with the morning light. The time has come for me to show the world who I am.'

In 1967, the world still did not know who Paulo Coelho was; indeed, it ran the risk of losing him, judging by his frequent bouts of depression and the insistence with which he spoke of death and suicide. At the end of June, after enduring another sleepless night, he had a sudden attack of rage. He put his diary away in the drawer, locked his bedroom door and began to break everything. He started with his guitar, which he smashed over his desk with a crash that sounded like a bomb exploding. The neighbours, who at that time, around six in the morning, had not yet got up, were astonished to hear the racket coming from the Coelho household. He broke his portable red plastic tape recorder and his short-wave radio and anything else he came across.

There was nothing left to destroy, but his fury was not yet spent. He went over to his bookcase and set to work on the ten volumes of his Sherlock Holmes collection. He ripped them up one by one and then went to the shelf containing books by Brazilian authors and continued his destruction until the bedroom floor was covered in the tattered remains of books. He went into the small bathroom next door and, using the fingerboard of his guitar as a cudgel, smashed the mirror. When the noise stopped for a moment, he heard his father pounding on the door, demanding that he open up, but he would not stop. He ripped down and tore into tiny pieces the two texts he had stuck on his door – a prayer by St Francis of Assisi and the words of 'Barbara' by the French poet Jacques Prévert, and then he did the same thing with the posters decorating his room: Goya's *La Maja Desnuda*, Bosch's *Garden of Delights* and *The Crucifixion* by Rubens. Panting, he saw that only one thing had remained intact: the white armchair where, as he once wrote, he would sit and cry or look up at the starry sky. Having nothing he could use to smash it, he opened the window and hurled it out into the garden at the side of the house. It was only then, when there was nothing left standing or intact, that he decided to open the door. He hardly had time to notice that it was no longer his father who was knocking. Two male nurses held him down and one injected him with what seemed to be a powerful sedative.

When he opened his eyes, he recognized the peeling paint on the ceiling. He was back lying on a bed on the ninth floor of the clinic. The first precaution the nurses had taken as soon as he came round from sedation was to take him to the liftmen and tell them: 'This is the patient who ran away from here last year. Take a good look at his face and this time be more careful.'

Nothing in the clinic had changed since his previous stays there. Except for Flávio, who had tried to kill himself with whisky and ether spray, they were all there, including Luís Carlos, his companion in flight. The faces were the same as before, as was the suffering. On the first day, Paulo was submitted to a session of electroshock therapy so strong that when Fabíola came to visit him some hours later, he was still unconscious, drooling and with his face contorted by the violence of the electrical charges to his brain. In spite of the love and care shown him by his girlfriend – this time, Fabíola was the only person, apart from his parents, to visit him – he could not get the absent Geni and the baby out of his mind.

A week after being admitted to the clinic, during which time he was subjected to three electroshock sessions, Paulo was once again thinking of running away. And once again his chosen companion was Luís Carlos, who was unable to bear the routine of the hospital any longer. The opportunity arose on a day when a member of Dr Benjamim's team was checking his mouth and noticed that a wisdom tooth was coming through. He thought that he had found the cause of Paulo's problems: 'Now I know what's wrong. It's a tooth coming through and causing pressure in your head. That's what's making you agitated and causing your crises. I'm going to ask the dentist to take out the tooth and then you'll be all right.'

While they were looking for a nurse to take him to the dental clinic, he found Luís Carlos and told him: 'It's now or never! They're going to take me to the dentist and I'm going to try to escape. See if you can too. If all goes well, we'll meet in an hour at the café opposite the clinic.'

He walked down the paths separating the different clinic buildings, constantly watched by the male nurse, who, when they reached the door of the consulting room, looked at his watch and agreed with the dentist that since the extraction would take about half an hour, he would go to the toilet and then return straight away to take the patient back to the unit housing the mentally ill. However, the consultation lasted less than five minutes. After a quick examination, the dentist told him he could go: 'I don't know who invented such a stupid story! Since when has a wisdom tooth made anyone mad? You can sit outside and wait for the nurse to take you back to your floor.'

This was the moment. Paulo hurried along the corridors and, keeping his head down, crossed the woods on the edge of the complex and joined the crowd of visitors and doctors at the gate. Minutes later, he was free.

He ran to the café on the corner of Rua Assunção and Rua Marquês de Olinda and, to his surprise, saw Luís Carlos waiting for him with a glass of beer in his hand – it was all he could afford with the few coins he had in his pocket. They celebrated their success and decided to get out of the café before anyone on the ninth floor noticed they were missing and came looking for them (security seems to have been somewhat lax that day, since it was only two days later, on 9 July, that the doctors realized the two had disappeared). As they were leaving, Paulo managed to sell his wristwatch at the bar, although since there was no time for haggling, he received only 300 new cruzeiros (US$380), less than half its true value. The fugitives walked three blocks along Rua Marquês de Olinda, sat on the grass and spent hours in silence, enjoying the delicious pleasure of

Lygia Araripe Coelho de Souza holding her baby Paulo, Rio de Janeiro, 1947.

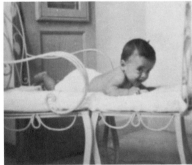

Paulo as a baby (*above*) and playing with his cousins (in sandals and shorts, *left*), Rio de Janeiro, 1950s.

Paulo, aged ten (second from left, first row), at Our Lady Victorious School, Rio de Janeiro, 1957.

Paulo, aged fifteen (fourth from left, second row from top), at St Ignatius College, a respected boys' school in Rio de Janeiro, in 1962.

Left The forged school document Paulo used to get into the left-leaning 'Paissandu set' in 1965. Adding two years to his age gained him admittance to this group of intellectual film-lovers.

Below Paulo used to classify and rank the books he read. In this list, Martin Luther King wins his highest rating.

50	Os direitos ao escuro	Solschenizin	ensaio - Censura	—
51	Um dia na vida de Ivan	''	romance	★★★
52	O Terceiro Homem	Cook ripe	espionagem	★
53	Explosão Biologica	Retray	ensaio	★★
54	Quatro Quartetos	T.S. Eliot	poesia	★★★★
55	A vida dos Beatles	Hunter Davies	biografia	★★
56	A nuvem negra	Fred Hoyle	Ficção Cientifica	★★★★
57	Amor 5 Dimensões	vários	''	★★
58	O Colosso de Marousi	Henry Miller	ensaio	★★★★
59	Anabel - Pintor	Anabel	teatro	★★★★
60	O Atentado - Kleitch	Jon Houst	documentário	★★★
61	Minha vida com Hané	Elsa Soares	biografia	★★★
62	Magia e Ciencia	Lourenço Braga	espiritismo	★★
63	O mundo de H. Miller	Vários autores	ensaios	—
64	O mundo do sexo	Henry Miller	biografia	★★★
65	Ritual de Umbanda	Benedito Ramos	ensaio	○
66	Submarino Amarelo	Nelson Motta (adap)	conto	○
67	Sexo em Clichy	Henry Miller	biografia	★★★★
68	Gritos Consciencia	M. Luther King	discurso	★★★★★
69	Ecce Homo	Nietzche	filosofia	★★
70	Livro das Profecias	Joaquim Monteiro	profecias	○
71	Nostradamus	M. da Cruz	''	○
72	Ate 1984 e depois	Sena-khan	''	★
73	Interpretação Apocalipse	Isaac Newton		★
74	Horoscopo Ashoscabalistico	Waldomiro Lorenz	Astrologia	
75	d'Astrologia	Varios autores	Astrologia	—

Left Fabíola Fracarolli in 1967, one of Paulo's many girlfriends during the late 1960s.

Right Paulo and Fabíola.

Paulo with fellow actors in an adaptation of Jorge Amado's *Capitães da Areia* at the Teatro Serrador in Rio de Janeiro, 1966.

Paulo (fifth from left, front row) with cast and crew on the opening night of *Capitães da Areia*.

Paulo as Captain Hook (far right) and the other actors in his production of *Peter Pan*, 1969. Fabíola, who subsidised the production, played Peter Pan and Paulo's friend Kakiko (centre, front row) wrote the score.

Kakiko, Paulo, Vera and Arnold (left to right) make their first stop in Registro on their ill-fated trip to Asunción, Paraguay, 1969.

Above Paulo during his trip across the United States, 1971.

Left Paulo during his 24-hour marijuana experiment at Kakiko's house in Friburgo, 1971.

Paulo and his girlfriend Gisa (also *right*).
Following the termination of her pregnancy,
she took an overdose of barbiturates and
nearly drowned.

Paulo used black magic techniques and rituals in the drama courses he ran
in 1973 at schools in Mato Grosso, Brazil.

Right Paulo breaks his hour-long pact with the Devil, 11 November 1971.

Far right Paulo's registration card as prisoner no. 13720. He and Gisa were imprisoned on account of the *Krig-Ha, Bandolo!* comic strip, 1974.

Right A leaflet advertising a presentation by the Crowleyites and the launch of Paulo's *Arquivos do Inferno*.

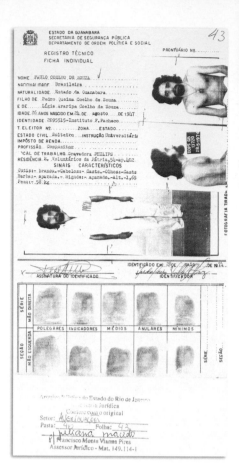

The psychedelic comic strip accompanying the *Krig-Ha, Bandolo!* LP, written by Paulo and Raul Seixas and illustrated by Gisa, that so intrigued the Brazilian police, 1974.

seeing the shimmering Urca beach with Sugar Loaf Mountain in the background. It was exactly the same view that they had from the windows of the asylum, only now there was no grille in front of them.

Paulo told Luís Carlos what he was planning: 'I'm going to the bus station to buy a ticket to Aracaju. I need to find a girlfriend of mine who is or was expecting my baby. If you want to come with me, the money from the watch is enough to pay for you, too.'

Luís Carlos was surprised at the thought of such a long journey, but having no better plan and having nowhere to go, he accepted the invitation. As the bus did not leave until eight the following morning, the pair spent the night on the benches at the bus station. The tickets had cost them 80 cruzeiros, leaving more than enough money to buy food on the long bus ride. Luís Carlos wanted to know how they were going to survive when they reached their destination, but Paulo reassured him, saying: 'There are people there who will take care of that.' After crossing the states of Rio de Janeiro, Minas Gerais and Bahia, with stops at fifteen towns along the way, two days later, on the morning of 9 July 1967, they arrived in Aracaju. It was only then that Luís Carlos learned that Paulo had no address, telephone number or any other way of finding his beloved Genivalda in a town of 170,000 inhabitants. His sole local reference was the name of Mário Jorge Vieira, a young poet and militant member of the banned Brazilian Communist Party (PCB).

Thanks to the lies he invented, a day later, Paulo and his friend, whom he introduced as 'my dumb secretary', were installed in journalist Marcos Mutti's comfortable home, and he appeared in the social columns of the local press, described either as 'university student and actor' or as 'young playwright from Rio'. These references were always accompanied by extravagant stories: 'Mingling with the artistic community of Aracaju is the theatre actor Paulo Coelho, who recently appeared in Rio in the play *Oedipus Rex* alongside Paulo Autran. It seems that Coelho has come to admire our green landscape and to plant new seeds in the region's almost non-existent theatrical history.'

After a week of searching, he lost all hope of finding Geni. He heard nothing of her until many years later, when he learned that she had indeed had an abortion and that, some time later, when still young, she had been run over and killed. Frustrated in the one objective that had taken him to Aracaju, he planned to return to Rio, but the hospitality he was receiving was such that he stayed on. Treated with the respect granted to a star, he gave a long interview to the *Gazeta de Sergipe*, in which he was presented to the newspaper's readers: 'A strange individual arrived here on the 9th. Long-haired, unshaven, thin, and rather odd-looking, but with lots of ideas in his head, lots of hope and an enormous desire to propagate art throughout Brazil. He is, in short, an artist. A young man of twenty who has left his home (he is the son of one of the best-known families in Rio de Janeiro) for the love of art. His is a mind turned towards Humanity.'

Feeling himself to be at a safe distance (or protected perhaps by the impunity granted to the mad, to children and to native Indians), Paulo suddenly grew courageous and made use of the piece in the newspaper in order, for the first time, to criticize the military dictatorship – or rather, even more dangerous, the then President of the Republic, Marshal Artur da Costa e Silva. 'I'm not going to keep quiet just because some superannuated marshal picks up a rifle and claims to be defending the morals and freedom of a people who don't even know what freedom is.' This was starting to look less like an interview and more like a manifesto, a call to arms. 'I haven't travelled thousands of kilometres to Aracaju in order to keep quiet. I won't lie to myself or to those around me.' The result of this vehemence was that he was offered a space in the newspaper to write a signed political article for the following Saturday's edition.

On the Friday, however, he discovered that there were two people in the city who were looking for 'the guy from Rio', wanting to kill him. He was convinced that these must be Geni's relatives, intent on defending their daughter's honour by spilling the blood of her abuser, and his courage disappeared in a flash. He decided to make a run for it and was just about to leave when Luís Carlos reminded him about the article he had promised for the newspaper. Paulo opened up the leather bag he was wearing slung over his shoulder and took out a cutting from a Rio newspaper he had picked up on a bench at the bus station in Vitória da Conquista, in Bahia, one of the fifteen stops on the way to Aracaju. He asked his hosts whether he could use their typewriter and copied, word for word, an article castigating the military dictatorship for having disenfranchised Brazilians. He kept the title and simply changed the author's name to his. Still with Luís Carlos, he spent the remainder of his money on two bus tickets to Salvador – the furthest his money would take him.

Years later, furious to learn that they had been duped and the article plagiarized, the people in Sergipe who had met Paulo at the time gave a rather different account of his sudden departure from Aracaju. 'He and his so-called dumb secretary didn't take a shower for two weeks and smoked cannabis all day,' recalls Ilma Fontes. 'That's why Paulo Coelho was thrown out of Marcos Mutti's house: for spending the day smoking cannabis in a strictly residential street.' Two weeks without washing was not perhaps anything new in his life, but smoking cannabis was certainly not one of Paulo's habits in July 1967.

When they got off the bus in the Salvador capital of Bahia without a penny in their pockets, the two men walked 10 kilometres to the Obras Sociais Irmã Dulce, a charitable institution known throughout Brazil. After joining a long line of beggars holding aluminium bowls for their daily soup ration, they went up to a small table, where the poor were received individually by the nun, to whom Paulo referred in his diary as 'Irma la Douce'. He explained to the sad-eyed little nun that he needed money to buy two bus tickets to Rio. The ragged appearance of these two mendicants spoke volumes, and so she asked no questions and wrote in tiny writing on a piece of paper bearing the name of the institution:

These young men are requesting free transport to Rio.
    Irmã Dulce – 21/7/67

All they needed to do was to exchange the slip of paper at the bus station for two tickets. In Bahia, any piece of paper signed by the nun had the value of a voucher for a plate of food, having a relative taken into hospital or, as in their case, a bus ticket.

Paulo spent the forty-hour journey from Salvador to Rio drawing up the synopsis of a book about their escape and their journey to the northeast of the country. No – not just one book: in keeping with his megalomaniac temperament, he planned to write no fewer than nine books, each with twelve chapters. By the end of the journey, he had filled fifteen pages of his diary with details of each volume and their chapter titles ('Preparing the Escape'; 'My Travelling Companions'; 'The General's Son'; 'My Long Hair and Other People's Short Ideas'; 'Pedro's Pistol, or When the Bahians Shit Themselves'; 'Sleeping in Kerosene Cans at 7° Centigrade' ...), but the project never got any further than that.

At the Rio bus station, he and Luís Carlos sadly parted company. Once again, Paulo was going home and the 'dumb' man was on his way back to the clinic, where he was to remain, playing the part of madman, for as long as it took to gain his dreamed-of pension.

Less than a year later, Paulo was plunged into misery and despair again, and he again smashed up his room. This time, when he opened his door, he found not the male nurses bearing syringes or straitjackets but a pleasant young doctor, who asked politely: 'May I come in?'

It was the psychiatrist Dr Antônio Ovídio Clement Fajardo, who often used to send patients for treatment at the Dr Eiras clinic. When Lygia and Pedro had heard the first sounds of things being broken in their son's room, they had called Dr Benjamim, but when he couldn't be found and since it was an urgent matter, they had contacted Dr Fajardo. When he spoke on the telephone to Pedro, the doctor had asked for basic information about Paulo.

'Is he armed?'

'No.'

'Is he an alcoholic?'

'No.'

'Is he a drug addict?'

'No.'

This made matters simpler.

Fajardo asked again: 'May I come in?'

Hearing this unusual question repeated, Paulo didn't know how to respond. 'Come in? But haven't you come to take me to the clinic?'

The doctor replied: 'Only if you want me to. But you haven't answered my question: may I come in?'

Seated on the bed, the doctor looked around the room, as though assessing the extent of the damage, and continued quite naturally: 'You've broken everything, haven't you? Excellent.'

Paulo couldn't understand what was going on. The doctor went on, explaining in professorial tones: 'What you've destroyed is your past. That's good. Now that it's no longer here, let's begin to think about the future, all right? My suggestion is that you start coming to see me twice a week so that we can talk about your future.'

Paulo was astonished. 'But doctor, I've just smashed up my room again. Aren't you going to send me to the clinic?'

The doctor replied dispassionately: 'Everyone has their mad side. I probably do, but you don't put people away just like that. You're not mentally ill.'

Only after this episode did peace return to the Coelho household. Much later, he wrote: 'I think my parents were convinced I was a hopeless case and preferred to keep an eye on me and to support me for the rest of my life. They knew I would get into "bad company" again, but it didn't enter their heads to have me re-admitted to the clinic.' The problem was that their son was not prepared to continue living under parental control. He was ready to accept anything but a return to his grandfather's depressing studio flat in the city centre. The short-term solution, which would last for a few months, came once again from his grandparents. Some years earlier, Tuca and Lilisa had moved into a house near by, which had over the garage a small apartment with a bedroom, bathroom and independent entrance. If Paulo wished – and if his father was in agreement – their grandson could move in there.

Their grandson wanted this so much that, before his father had time to say no, he had moved everything that remained from the wreck of his room into his new home – his bed, his desk, his few clothes and his typewriter, which he had carefully protected from his frenzy. He soon realized that the apartment was like a gateway to paradise: given his grandparents' extreme liberality, he could come and go as he pleased and, within the broad limits of decency, he could entertain whomever he wanted, day or night. His grandparents' tolerance was such that, years later, Paulo vaguely recalled that it was probably there that he tried cannabis for the first time.

With no control over their son and with his grandparents making no attempt to control his behaviour either, some months later, Paulo's father suggested he should move somewhere more comfortable. If interested, he could go back to living alone, not in Tuca's studio but in a comfortable apartment Pedro had been given in payment for a building he had constructed in Rua Raimundo Correa in Copacabana. Paulo was suspicious of this generosity, and discovered that the offer concealed another reason: his father wanted to get rid of a tenant who was frequently late in paying his rent. Since the law said that a contract could only be broken by the landlord if the dwelling was to be used by a close relative of the owner, this was the solution to two problems, both Paulo's and his father's. Like almost any offer coming from Pedro, it had its drawbacks: Paulo could use only one of the three bedrooms, since the other two were permanently locked and empty. Also, access was always to be by the door in the basement, since the main entrance was to be kept locked and the key to remain with his father. Paulo only had to go to a local second-hand shop to buy some lamps and a bookcase and the place was ready to live in.

Paulo retained happy memories of the days he spent in Rua Raimundo Correa. Other affairs with other girls began and ended, but Fabíola remained faithful to him. She swallowed her jealousy and, as she later recalled, put up with the 'Renatas, Genis and Márcias ... but in the difficult times, I was there for him, it was pure love – pure love.' Many years later, when he was famous, Paulo recalled that time with nostalgia: 'I experienced a period of enormous happiness, enjoying the freedom I needed in order, finally, to live the "artist's life". I stopped studying and devoted myself exclusively to the theatre and to going to bars frequented by intellectuals. For a whole year, I did exactly what I wanted. That was when Fabíola really came into my life.'

Now a full-time playwright – he had managed to complete his course at Guanabara, but had no plans as yet to take the university entrance exam – he turned the dining room of his new apartment into a workshop for scenery, costumes, compositions and rehearsals. He annoyed his neighbours by painting in Italian over the front door – which he never used – the words written above the gates of Dante's Inferno: '*Lasciate ogni speranza, voi che entrate*' ['Abandon hope all ye who enter here']. He translated plays, directed and worked as an actor. The more successful productions made up for the failures, and so he was able to live without depending exclusively on support from his parents. When he needed more funds, he tried to make money at poker and snooker tables and by betting on horses at the Jockey Club.

At the end of 1968, he resolved to try the only aspect of theatre he had not yet worked on: production. He adapted the classic *Peter Pan*, which he wanted to direct and in which he also wanted to perform, but he was shocked to find that his savings were not nearly enough to cover the production's costs. He was still pondering how to resolve the problem when Fabíola came to his apartment one night, opened her bag and took out bundles of notes in rubber bands – more than 5,000 cruzeiros (US$11,600), which she scattered over the bed, explaining: 'This is my present for your production of *Peter Pan*.'

Fabíola told him that as she was about to turn eighteen, she had decided to tell her mother, grandmother and all her other relatives and friends that instead of clothes and presents she would prefer money. She had contacted people everywhere – her mother's rich clients and godparents whom she hadn't seen for years – and here was the result: the bundles on the bed were not a fortune, but the money was more than enough to make putting on the play a viable proposition. Paulo was overwhelmed by the gift: 'One girlfriend swapped me for two dresses and now you've exchanged all the dresses and presents for me. Your action has entirely changed my view of women.'

Fabíola not only got the money for the production but also sold advertising space in the programme and came to an agreement with the restaurants around the Teatro Santa Terezinha in the Botanical Gardens: in exchange for their names being printed on any advertising material, they would allow the actors and technicians to have dinner for free. Paulo repaid all he owed her by inviting her to take the title role. He was to be Captain Hook. With a score by Kakiko, *Peter Pan* played to packed houses throughout its run, which meant that every cent invested was recovered. And contrary to the notion that says that public success means critical failure, the play went on to win a prize at the first Children's Theatre Festival in the state of Guanabara. Paulo's dream remained the same – to be a great writer – but meanwhile, he had no alternative but to live by the theatre. These cheering results made him decide to turn professional, and soon he was a proud member of the Brazilian Society of Theatre Writers (SBAT).

In 1969, he was invited to work as an actor in the play *Viúva porém Honesta* [*A Widow but Honest*], by Nelson Rodrigues. In a break in rehearsals, he was drinking a beer in the bar beside the Teatro Sérgio Porto when he noticed that he was being watched by an attractive blonde woman seated at the counter. He pretended to look away, but when he turned round again, there she was, with her eyes fixed on him and with a discreet smile on her lips. This flirtation cannot have lasted more than ten minutes, but she made such an impression on Paulo that he wrote in his diary: 'I can't say how it all started. She appeared suddenly. I went in and immediately felt her looking at me. Despite the crowd, I knew that she had her eyes fixed on me and I didn't have the courage to look straight back at her. I had never seen her before. But when I felt her gaze something happened. It was the beginning of a love story.'

The beautiful mysterious blonde was Vera Prnjatovic Richter, eleven years Paulo's senior, who at the time was trying to end her fifteen-year marriage to a rich industrialist. She was always well dressed, she had a car – which was still fairly rare among women at the time – and she lived in a huge apartment in one of the most expensive areas of Brazil, Avenida Delfim Moreira, in Leblon. From Paulo's point of view she had only one obvious defect – she was going out with the actor Paulo Elísio, a bearded Apollo known for his bad temper and for being a karate black belt. However, the feelings recorded in his diary were to prove stronger than any martial arts.

CHAPTER 10

Vera

B RAZIL BEGAN 1969 immersed in the most brutal dictatorship of its
entire history. On 13 December 1968, the President of the Republic,
Artur da Costa e Silva – the 'superannuated marshal' to whom Paulo had
referred in his interview – had passed Institutional Act number 5, the AI-
5, which put paid to the last remaining vestiges of freedom following the
military coup of 1964. Signed by the President and countersigned by all
his ministers, including the Minister of Health, Leonel Miranda, the owner
of the Dr Eiras clinic, the AI-5 suspended, among other things, the right
to *habeas corpus* and gave the government powers to censor the press,
the theatre and books, as well as closing down the National Congress.

It was not only Brazil that was about to erupt. In its sixth year of war
in Vietnam, where more than half a million soldiers had been sent, the
United States had elected the hawkish Richard Nixon as president. In
April 1968, the black civil rights leader Martin Luther King, Jr, had been
assassinated, and just over two months later it was the turn of Robert
Kennedy. One of the symbols of counterculture was the musical *Hair*, in
which, at one point, the actors appeared naked on stage. Also in May,
French students had occupied the Sorbonne and turned Paris into a
battlefield, forcing General Charles de Gaulle to hold talks with the French
military chiefs in Baden-Baden, Germany. This worldwide fever had

crossed the Iron Curtain and reached Czechoslovakia in the form of the Prague Spring, a liberalizing plan proposed by the Secretary General of the Czech Communist Party, Alexander Dubček, which was crushed in August by the tanks of the Warsaw Pact, the Soviet Union's military alliance with its political satellites.

In Brazil, opposition to the dictatorship was beginning to grow. Initially, this took the form of peaceful student marches, in which Paulo rarely participated and, when he did so, it was more for fun and for the adventure of 'confronting the police' than as an act of political commitment. The political temperature rose with a rash of strikes called by workers in São Paulo and Minas Gerais, and reached alarming levels when the military intelligence services detected a growth in the number of guerrilla groups, which the regime loosely termed 'terrorists'. By the end of the year, there were, in fact, at least four armed urban guerrilla organizations: the Vanguarda Armada Revolucionária (VAR-Palmares), Ação Libertadora Nacional (ALN), Vanguarda Popular Revolucionária (VPR) and the Comando de Libertação Nacional (Colina). The Brazilian Communist Party, which took its inspiration from the Chinese Communist Party, had sent its first militants to Xambioá, in the north of Goiás (now on the frontier with the state of Tocantins), to mount a rural guerrilla assault in the region of the Araguaia River, on the edge of the Amazon rainforest. The extreme left attacked banks and set off bombs in barracks, while the extreme right organized attacks on one of the most visible centres of opposition to the regime: the theatre. Theatres in São Paulo and Rio were attacked or destroyed and there were an increasing number of arrests at street demonstrations as well as arrests of prominent people such as the ex-governor of Guanabara and civil leader of the 1964 coup, Carlos Lacerda, the composers Caetano Veloso and Gilberto Gil, and the journalist Carlos Heitor Cony, whose article Paulo had plagiarized in Aracaju.

Although he boasted of being 'the communist in the group', and although he was a witness to the violence being perpetrated on his profession – he was, after all, a playwright now and a member of the theatre union – Paulo seemed quietly indifferent to the political storm ravaging Brazil. As with the military coup, the new law and its consequences didn't merit a mention in his diaries. The first words he wrote in 1969 are revealing as to the focus of his energies: 'It's New Year's Day. I spent the evening with adulterers, homosexuals, lesbians and cuckolds.'

In 1964, he could have attributed his lack of interest in politics to his youth, but now he was nearly twenty-two, the average age of most of those leading the political and cultural movements rocking the country. If any important change was occurring in his life, it was due not to the political maelstrom Brazil found itself in but to his new passion, Vera Richter.

Petite, blonde and elegant, she had been born in 1936 in Belgrade, the capital of the then kingdom of Yugoslavia (now the capital of Serbia), the daughter of a wealthy landowning family. Until the age of twenty, she had lived a normal upper-class life; then, when she was in her first year at the theatre studies department of the university, she began to sense political changes occurring across Central Europe. That, and the collectivization programme begun in Yugoslavia by Tito, seemed to indicate that it was time for the rich to leave the country.

Since they had friends living in Rio de Janeiro, the Prnjatovic family – widowed mother, elder sister and Vera – decided this was to be their destination. Her mother and sister went first, and it was only some months later, when they were settled in Copacabana, that they sent a ticket for Vera. Speaking only English and the Italianate dialect of the area in which she had lived, she felt uncomfortable in Brazil. She ended up agreeing to a marriage arranged by her family – to a Yugoslav millionaire twelve years her senior. She recalled years later that even those who didn't know her well noticed how incompatible the two were. Like most twenty-year-old girls, she liked dancing, sports and singing, whereas her husband was shy and quiet and, when he wasn't running his import/export business, loved reading and listening to classical music.

When her eyes met Paulo's that night in the theatre bar, Vera's marriage was merely a formality. She and her husband lived under the same roof, but were no longer a couple. She had been attracted to the Teatro Carioca by an announcement in the newspaper saying that a young director from Bahia, Álvaro Guimarães, was selecting students for a drama course. Almost four decades later, she recalls that her first impression of

Paulo was not exactly flattering. 'He looked like Professor Abronsius, the scientist with a big head in Roman Polanski's film *Dance of the Vampires* – an enormous head on a tiny body. Ugly, bony, big lips and protruding eyes, Paulo was no beauty.' But he had other charms: 'Paulo was a Don Quixote! He was crazy. Everything seemed easy for him, everything was simple. He lived in the clouds, he never touched the ground. But his one obsession was to be someone. He would do anything to be someone. That was Paulo.'

At the time of Vera's arrival on the scene, Paulo's relationship with Fabíola was doomed anyway, but it finally ended when she caught him with Vera. Fabíola suspected that Paulo was secretly meeting a young Dutch actress who had appeared during rehearsals and she decided to find out if her suspicions were true. One night, she sat on the doorstep of the apartment in Rua Raimundo Correa and did not move until late in the morning when he finally left with Vera. Deeply hurt, she ended the affair. Some months later, she scandalized Lygia and Pedro, to whom she had become quite close, by appearing nude on the cover of the satirical weekly *Pasquim*.

As Paulo was to recall some years later, it was the experienced Vera who really taught him how to make love, to speak a little English and to dress a little better. But she could not help him overcome the trauma of Araruama: he still shook at the mere thought of driving a car. Their convergence of tastes and interests extended to their professional lives, and Vera's money was the one thing that had been lacking in Paulo's attempts to become immersed in the theatre. He divided his time between his Copacabana apartment and Vera's luxurious apartment in Leblon, where he would sleep almost every night, and where he bashed away for weeks on end at his typewriter until he was able to announce proudly to his partner that he had completed his first play for adults, *O Apocalipse* [*The Apocalypse*]. The couple seemed made for each other. Vera not only understood the entire play (a feat achieved by very few) but liked it so much that she offered to put it on professionally, acting as its producer – the person investing the money – while Paulo would be the director.

Everything went so well that, at the end of April 1969, the critics and editors of the arts sections of newspapers received an invitation to the preview and a copy of the programme listing the cast, in which Vera had the star part. Paulo's friend Kakiko, who had recently qualified as an odontologist and divided his time between his dental practice and his music, was to write the score.

Along with their invitation and the programme, journalists and critics received a press release written in pretentious, obscure language but which gave some idea of what *The Apocalypse* would be about. 'The play is a snapshot of the present moment, of the crisis in human existence, which is losing all its individual characteristics in favour of a more convenient stereotype, since it dogmatizes thought,' the blurb began, and it continued in the same incomprehensible vein. It then promised a great revolution in modern drama: the total abolition of characters. The play began with scenes from a documentary on the Apollo 8 mission to the moon, after which the cast performed dance that was described as 'tribal with oriental influences'. Actors followed one another on to the stage, spouting excerpts from Aeschylus' *Prometheus Bound*, Shakespeare's *Julius Caesar* and the Gospels. At the end, before hurling provocative remarks at the audience, each actor acted himself, revealing traumatic events in his childhood.

The Apocalypse meant that Paulo would, for the first time, experience the thing that would persecute him for the rest of his life: negative criticism. On the days that followed the preview, the play was slated in every Rio newspaper. *The Apocalypse* was as big a disaster with the public as it was with the critics. It played for only a few weeks and left a large hole in the accounts of Paulo's first joint initiative with Vera – a hole that she quickly decided to fill.

The production coincided with an important change in their life as a couple. Vera's marriage had rapidly deteriorated, but since her husband continued to live in their shared apartment, she decided to put an end to that rather awkward situation and move with her lover to a place that had become a symbolic address in the counterculture movement in Rio at the end of the 1960s: Solar Santa Terezinha. Originally created as a night shelter for beggars, the Solar was a vast rectangular building with a central courtyard around which people had their bedrooms. It had the look of a large, decadent refuge, but it was considered 'hip' to live there.

In the majority of cases each tenant had to share a bathroom with half a dozen other residents, but Paulo and Vera occupied a suite – a room with bathroom – for which the monthly rent was about 200 cruzeiros (US$210).

At the end of July 1969, they decided to do something different. In the middle of August, the Brazilian football team was going to play Paraguay in Asunción in a World Cup qualifier, the finals of which were to be held in Mexico in 1970. Although he wasn't that interested in football, one Sunday, Paulo thrilled his foreign girlfriend by taking her to a match between Flamengo and Fluminense at the packed Maracanã stadium. Vera was mesmerized and began to take an interest in the sport, and it was she who suggested that they drive to Paraguay to watch the match. Paulo didn't even know that Brazil was going to play, but he loved the idea and started making plans.

He immediately discounted the idea of just the two of them driving the almost 2,000 kilometres to Asunción, a marathon journey on which Vera would be the only driver, since he had still not summoned up the courage to learn to drive. The solution was to call on two other friends for the adventure: the musician-dentist Kakiko and Arnold Bruver, Jr, a new friend from the theatre. They thought of Kakiko for another reason too: as well as being able to drive, he could guarantee hospitality for all in Asunción, in the home of a Paraguayan girlfriend of his father's. Bruver, like almost all those in Paulo's circle, was an unusual fellow. The son of a Latvian father and a Galician mother, he was thirty-three, a dancer, musician, actor and opera singer, and had been ejected from the navy, in which he had reached the rank of captain, for alleged subversion. It was only after accepting the invitation that Arnold revealed that he couldn't drive either. The next precaution was to ask Mestre Tuca, who had travelled with Lilisa by car to Foz do Iguaçu, on the frontier with Paraguay, to give them a route with suggestions of places to fill up the car with petrol, have meals and sleep.

On the cold, sunny morning of Thursday, 14 August, the four got into Vera's white Volkswagen. The journey passed without incident, with Vera and Kakiko taking turns at the wheel every 150 kilometres. It was evening when the car stopped at the door of the small hotel in Registro in the state of São Paulo. After twelve hours on the road they had covered 600 kilometres, about a third of the total distance. The locals eyed any strangers with understandable suspicion. Since the Department of Political and Social Order (the political police of the time, known as Dops) had disbanded the Student Union Congress some months earlier in Ibiúna, 100 kilometres from there, the small towns in the region were often visited by strangers and the locals had no way of telling if they were police or something else entirely. However, the four travellers were so tired that there was no time for their presence to arouse anyone's curiosity, for, on arriving, they went straight to bed.

On the Friday, they woke early, because the next stretch of the journey was the longest and they hoped to cover it in just a day. If all went well, by suppertime they would be in Cascavel, in the western region of Paraná, a 750-kilometre drive from there, and the last stop before reaching Asunción. But all did not go well: they were slowed down by the number of trucks on the road. The result was that, by ten o'clock that night, they were all starving and still had 200 kilometres to go.

It was at this point that Vera stopped the car in a lay-by and asked Kakiko to get out to see whether there was a problem with one of the tyres, because the car seemed to be skidding. As there was no sign of anything wrong, they decided that it must be the thick mist covering the area that was making the road slippery. Kakiko suggested that Vera should sit in the back and rest while he drove the rest of the way to Cascavel. After travelling for a further hour, he stopped at a petrol station to fill up. All their expenses were to be shared among the four, but when Vera looked for her purse, she realized that she had lost her bag with her money and all her documents, including her driving licence and car registration papers. She concluded that she must have dropped it when she had handed over the driving to Kakiko. They had no alternative but to go back to the place where they had stopped, 100 kilometres back, to try to find the bag. It took three hours to get there and back, without success. They looked everywhere, with the help of the car headlights, but there was no sign of the bag and no one in the local bars and petrol stations had seen it either. Convinced that this was a bad omen, a sign, Paulo suggested that they turn back, but the other three disagreed. They continued the journey and didn't reach Cascavel until early on the Saturday morning, by which time the car had a problem – the clutch wasn't working, and so it was impossible to carry on.

Because of the Brazil game, on the following day, almost everything in Cascavel was closed, including all the garages. They decided that they would continue on to Asunción by bus. They bought tickets to Foz do Iguaçu and, as Vera had no documents, they had to mingle with the crowds of tourists and supporters in order to cross the bridge separating Brazil from Paraguay. Once in Paraguay, they took another bus to the capital.

Immediately after settling into the home of Kakiko's father's girlfriend, they discovered that all tickets for the match had been sold, but they didn't mind. They spent the weekend visiting tribes of Guarani Indians on the outskirts of the city and taking tedious boat trips on the river Paraguay. On the Monday morning they began to think about getting the car repaired in Cascavel. With the disappearance of Vera's bag, they would have to take special care on the return journey: without the car documents they mustn't get caught breaking any laws and, without Vera's money, their expenses would have to be divided by three, which meant eating less and spending the night in cheaper places. They rejigged Tuca's route map and decided to go to Curitiba, where they would sleep and try to get a duplicate copy of the car documents and of Vera's driving licence.

At about ten at night – none of them remembers quite what time it was – hunger forced them to stop before reaching Curitiba. They parked the car by a steak house, just outside Ponta Grossa, having driven about 400 kilometres. To save money they used a ruse they had been practising since Vera had lost her bag: she and Paulo would sit alone at the table and ask for a meal for two. When the food arrived, Kakiko and Arnold would appear and share the meal with them.

Duly fed and watered, they were just about to resume their journey when a group of soldiers belonging to the Military Police entered the restaurant, armed with machine guns.

The man who appeared to be the head of the group went over to their table and asked: 'Is the white VW with Guanabara number plates parked outside yours?'

Kakiko, who was the only one officially allowed to drive, replied: 'Yes, it's ours.'

When the soldier asked to see the certificate of ownership, Kakiko explained in detail, watched by his terrified friends, how Vera had left her bag next to the car door and lost her purse and everything in it, and how the plan was to stay in Curitiba and see whether they could get a duplicate of the lost documents.

The man listened, incredulous, then said: 'You're going to have to explain all this to the police chief. Come with us.'

They were taken to a police station, where they spent the night in the freezing cold, sitting on a wooden bench until six in the morning, when the police chief arrived to give them the news himself: 'You are accused of terrorist activities and carrying out a bank raid. It's nothing to do with me now – it's up to the army.'

Although none of them had been taking much interest in the matter, the political situation had been getting worse in Brazil in the previous few months. Since the publication of the new law, AI-5, in December 1968, more than two hundred university professors and researchers had been compulsorily suspended, arrested or exiled. In the National Congress, 110 Members of Parliament and four senators had been stripped of their mandate and, elsewhere, about five hundred people had been removed from public office, either directly or indirectly accused of subversion. With the removal of three ministers from the Supreme Federal Tribunal, violence in the country had reached its height. In January, Captain Carlos Lamarca had deserted an army barracks in Quitaúna, a district of Osasco, taking with him a vehicle containing sixty-three automatic guns, three sub-machine guns and other munitions for the urban guerrilla movement. In São Paulo, the recently nominated governor Abreu Sodré had created Operação Bandeirantes (Oban), a unit that combined police and members of the armed forces, which was intended to crush any opposition. It immediately became a centre for the torture of enemies of the regime.

Two days before Paulo and his friends had been arrested, four guerrillas armed with machine guns – three men and a blonde woman – and driving a white Volkswagen with Guanabara number plates had attacked a bank and a supermarket in Jandaia do Sul, a town 100 kilometres north of Ponta Grossa. The police were now assuming that Paulo and his friends must be those people. Shivering with cold and fear, the four were taken in a prison van guarded by heavily armed soldiers to the headquarters of the 13th Battalion of the Armed Infantry (BIB), in the district of Uvaranas, on the other side of the city. Scruffy, dirty and cold, they climbed out of the van and found themselves in an enormous courtyard where hundreds of recruits were doing military exercises.

Half an hour after being placed in separate cells, made to undress and then dress again, interrogation began. The first to be called was Kakiko, who was taken to a cell furnished only with a table and two chairs, one of which was occupied by a tall, dark, well-built man in boots and combat gear with his name embroidered on his chest: 'Maj. Índio'. Major Índio ordered Kakiko to take a chair and then sat down in front of him. Then he spoke the words that Kakiko would remember for the rest of his life: 'So far no one has laid a finger on you, but pay very close attention to what I'm going to say. If you give just one bit of false information – just one – I'm going to stick these two fingers in your left eye, and rip out your eyeball and eat it. Your right eye will be preserved so that you can witness the scene. Understood?'

The first of the crimes of which Paulo and his friends were accused – an armed raid on a supermarket in Jandaia do Sul – had left no victims. But during the attempted raid on a bank in the same city, the guerrillas had shot the manager. The similarities between the four travellers and the guerrillas appeared to justify the suspicions of the military in Ponta Grossa. Although the raiders used nylon stockings to cover their faces, there was no doubt that they were three white men, one of them with long hair, like Paulo, and a blonde woman, like Vera, and that, like Paulo and his friends, they were driving a white Volkswagen with Guanabara number plates. Paulo's map also seemed to the authorities to be too careful and professional to have been produced by a grandfather eager to help his hippie grandson. Besides this, the chosen route could not have been more compromising: information from military intelligence had reported that the group led by Captain Carlos Lamarca might be preparing to establish a guerrilla nucleus in Vale do Ribeira – which was on the very route the friends had taken on their journey to Asunción. A dossier containing files on all four plus information on the car had been sent to the security agencies in Brasilia, Rio and São Paulo.

Besides their illegal arrest and the ever more terrifying threats, none of the four had as yet experienced physical violence. Major Índio had repeated his promise to eat one of their eyeballs to each of the others, insisting that this was not a mere empty threat: 'Up to now no one has laid a finger on you. We're giving you food and blankets on the assumption that you are innocent. But don't forget: if there's a word of a lie in your statements, I'll carry out my promise. I've done it before to other terrorists and I'll have no problems doing the same to you.'

The situation worsened on the Tuesday morning, when some of the supermarket employees were taken to the barracks to identify the suspects. With Paulo and Vera, the identification was made through a small opening in the cell doors, without their knowing that they were being observed. In the case of Arnold and Kakiko, the doors were simply opened, allowing the people – who were as terrified as the prisoners – a quick look inside. Although the assailants had had their faces covered when committing the crimes, and despite the very cursory identification procedure, in unlit cells, the witnesses were unanimous: those were the four who had committed the crime. The interrogations became more intense and more intimidating, and the same questions were repeated four, five, six, ten times. Vera and Arnold had to explain over and over to the succession of civil and military authorities who entered the cells to ask questions just what a Yugoslav woman and a naval officer suspended for subversion were doing in the area. Coelho cannot recall how often he had to answer the same questions: after such a long journey, how come they hadn't even bothered to see the match? How had Vera managed to cross the frontier with Paraguay in both directions without documents? Why did the map suggest so many alternative places to stay and fill up the car with petrol? Paulo commented to Arnold, in one of the rare moments they were alone in the same cell, that this was a Kafkaesque nightmare: even the presence of his nebulizer to relieve his asthma attacks had to be explained in detail several times.

The nightmare continued for five days. On the Saturday morning, armed soldiers entered the cells and gave orders for the prisoners to collect their things because they were being 'moved'. Squashed in the back of the same olive-green van, the four were sure that they were going to be executed. When the vehicle stopped minutes later, much to their surprise, they got out in front of a bungalow surrounded by a garden of carefully tended roses. At the top of the stairs, a smiling soldier with grey hair and a bouquet of flowers in his hands was waiting for them. This was Colonel Lobo Mazza, who explained to the dazed travellers that everything had been cleared up and that they were indeed innocent. The flowers, which the officer had picked himself, were given to Vera by way of an apology. The colonel explained the reasons for their imprisonment – the growth of the armed struggle, their similarity to the assailants in Jandaia do Sul, the drive through Vale do Ribeira – and he made a point of asking each whether they had suffered any physical violence. Seeing their dirty, ragged appearance, he suggested they use the bathroom in the house and then offered them canapés accompanied by some good Scotch whisky. So that they would have no problems getting back to Rio, they were given a safe-conduct pass signed by Colonel Mazza himself. The journey was over.

CHAPTER 11

The marijuana years

ONCE HE WAS BACK IN RIO, Paulo entered the 1970s propelled by a new fuel: cannabis. This would be followed by other drugs, but initially he only used cannabis. Once they had tried the drug together for the first time, he and Vera became regular consumers. Being new to the experience, they had little knowledge of its effects, and before starting to smoke they would lock away any knives and other sharp household objects in a drawer 'to prevent any accidents', as she said. They smoked every day and on any pretext: in the afternoon so that they could better enjoy the sunsets, at night to get over the fact that they felt as if they were sleeping on the runway of Santos Dumont airport, with the deafening noise of aeroplanes taking off and landing only a few metres away. And, if there was no other reason, they smoked to allay boredom. Paulo recalled later having spent days in a row under the effect of cannabis, without so much as half an hour's interval.

Completely free of parental control, he had become a true hippie: someone who not only dressed and behaved like a hippie but thought like one too. He had stopped being a communist – before he had ever become one – when he was lectured in public by a militant member of the Brazilian Communist Party for saying that he had really loved the film *Les Parapluies de Cherbourg* – a French musical starring Catherine Deneuve.

With the same ease with which he had crossed from the Christianity of the Jesuits to Marxism, he was now a devout follower of the hippie insurrection that was spreading throughout the world. 'This will be humanity's final revolution,' he wrote in his diary. 'Communism is over, a new brotherhood is born, mysticism is invading art, drugs are an essential food. When Christ consecrated the wine, he was consecrating drugs. Drugs are a wine of the most superior vintage.'

After spending a few months at the Solar Santa Terezinha, he and Vera rented, together with a friend, a two-bedroom apartment in Santa Teresa, a bohemian district at the top of a hill near the Lapa, in the centre of the city, which had a romantic little tramway running through it that clanked as it went up the hill. In between moves, they had to live for some weeks in the Leblon apartment, along with Vera's husband, who had not yet moved out.

Cannabis usually causes prolonged periods of lethargy and exhaustion in heavy users, but the drug seemed to have the opposite effect on Paulo. He became positively hyperactive and in the first months of 1970, he adapted for the stage and produced *The War of the Worlds* by H.G. Wells, took part in theatre workshops with the playwright Amir Haddad and entered both the Paraná Short Story Competition and the Esso Prize for Literature. He even found time to write three plays: *Os Caminhos do Misticismo* [*The Paths of Mysticism*], about Father Cícero Romão Batista, a miracle worker from the northeast of Brazil; *A Revolta da Chibata: História à Beira de um Caís* [*The Chibata Revolt: History on the Dockside*], about the sailors' revolt in Rio de Janeiro in 1910; and *Os Limites da Resistência* [*The Limits of Resistance*], which was a dramatized compilation of various texts. He sent the latter off to the National Book Institute, an organ of the federal government, but it failed to get beyond the first obstacle, the Reading Commission. His book fell into the hands of the critic and novelist Octavio de Faria who, while emphasizing its good points, sent the originals straight to the archives with the words:

> I won't deny that this strange book, *The Limits of Resistance*, left me completely perplexed. Even after reading it, I cannot decide which literary genre it belongs to. It claims to comprise 'Eleven Fundamental

Differences', bears an epigraph by Henry Miller, and sets out to 'explain' life. It contains digressions, surrealist constructions, descriptions of psychedelic experiences, and all kinds of games and jokes. It is a hotchpotch of 'fundamental differences', which, while undeniably well written and intelligent, does not seem to me the kind of book that fits our criteria. Whatever Sr. Paulo Coelho de Souza's literary future may be, it's the kind of work that 'avant-garde' publishers like, in the hope of stumbling across a 'genius', but not the publishers of the National Book Institute.

At least he had the consolation of being in good company. The same Reading Commission also rejected at least two books that would become classics of Brazilian literature: *Sargento Getúlio*, which was to launch the writer João Ubaldo Ribeiro in Brazil and the United States, and *Objeto Gritante*, by Clarice Lispector, which was later to be published as *Água Viva*.

As if some force were trying to deflect him from his *idée fixe* of becoming a writer, drama continued to offer Paulo more recognition than prose. Although he had high hopes for his play about Father Cícero, foreseeing a brilliant future for it, only *A Revolta da Chibata* went on to achieve any success. He entered it in the prestigious Concurso Teatro Opinião, more because he felt that he should than with any hope of winning. The prize offered was better than any amount of money: the winning play would be performed by the members of the Teatro Opinião, which was the most famous of the avant-garde theatre groups in Brazil. When Vera called to tell him that *A Revolta* had come second, Paulo reacted angrily: 'Second? Shit! I always come second.' First prize had gone to *Os Dentes do Tigre* [*Tiger's Teeth*] by Maria Helena Kühner, who was also starting out on her career.

However, if his objective was fame, he had nothing to complain about. Besides being quoted in all the newspapers and praised by such critics as João das Neves and José Arrabal, that despised second prize brought *A Revolta* a place in the Teatro Opinião's much-prized series of readings, which were open to the public and took place every week. Paulo may have been upset about not winning first prize, but he was very anxious during the days that preceded the reading. He could think of nothing else all week and was immensely proud when he watched the actress Maria Pompeu reading his play before a packed house.

Months later, his acquaintance with Teatro Opinião meant that he met – very briefly – one of the international giants of counterculture, the revolutionary American drama group the Living Theatre, which was touring Brazil at the time. When Paulo learned that he had managed to get tickets to see a production by the group, he was so excited that he felt 'quite intimidated, as though I had just taken a big decision'. Fearing that he might be asked to give his opinion on something during the interval or after the play, he read a little Nietzsche before going to the theatre 'so as to have something to say'. In the end, he and Vera were so affected by what they saw that they wangled an invitation to the house where the group – headed by Julian Beck and Judith Malina – were staying, and from there went on to visit the shanty town in Vidigal. Judging by the notes in his diary, however, the meeting did not go well: 'Close contact with the Living Theatre. We went to the house where Julian Beck and Judith Malina are staying and no one talked to us. A bitter feeling of humiliation. We went with them to the *favela*. It was the first time in my life that I'd been to a *favela*. It's a world apart.'

The following day, although they had had lunch with the group and been present at rehearsals, the Americans' attitude towards them remained unchanged. 'Julian Beck and Judith Malina continue to treat us with icy indifference,' he wrote. 'But I don't blame them. I know it must have been very difficult to get where they are.' The next Paulo heard of the group and its leaders was some months later, when he heard that they had been arrested in Ouro Preto, in Minas Gerais, accused of possession and use of cannabis. The couple had rented a large house in the city and turned it into a permanent drama workshop for actors from all over Brazil. A few weeks later, the police surrounded the house and arrested all eighteen members of the group and took them straight to the Dops prison in Belo Horizonte.

In spite of protests from the famous across the world – Jean-Paul Sartre, Michel Foucault, Pier Paolo Pasolini, Jean-Luc Godard and Umberto Eco among others – the military government kept the whole group in prison for sixty days, after which they expelled all the foreign members, accusing them of 'drug trafficking and subversion'.

As for Paulo, some months after he and Vera had first been introduced to cannabis, the artist Jorge Mourão gave them a tiny block the size of a packet of chewing gum that looked as though it were made of very dark, almost black, wax. It was hashish. Although it comes from the same plant as cannabis, hashish is stronger and was always a drug that was consumed more in Europe and North Africa than in South America, which meant that it was seen as a novelty among Brazilian users. Obsessive as ever about planning and organizing everything he did, Paulo decided to convert a mere 'puff' into a solemn scientific experiment. From the moment he inhaled the drug for the first time he began to record all his sensations on tape, keeping a note of the time as well. He typed up the final result and stuck it in his diary:

Brief notes on our Experiment with Hashish
To Edgar Allan Poe

We began to smoke in my bedroom at ten forty at night. Those present: myself, Vera and Mourão. The hashish is mixed with ordinary tobacco in a ratio of approximately one to seven and put into a special silver pipe. This pipe makes the smoke pass through iced water, which allows for perfect filtration. Three drags each are enough. Vera isn't going to take part in the experiment, as she's going to do the recording and take photos. Mourão, who's an old hand at drugs, will tell us what we must do.

3 minutes – A feeling of lightness and euphoria. Boundless happiness. Strong inner feelings of agitation. I walk backwards and forwards feeling totally drunk.

6 minutes – My eyelids are heavy. A feeling of dizziness and sleepiness. My head is starting to take on terrifying proportions, with images slightly distorted into a circular shape. At this phase of the experiment, certain mental blocks (of a moral order) surfaced in my mind. Note: the effects may have been affected by over-excitement.

10 minutes – An enormous desire to sleep. My nerves are completely relaxed and I lie down on the floor. I start to sweat, more

out of anxiety than heat. No initiative whatsoever: if the house caught fire, I'd rather die than get up from here.

20 minutes – I'm conscious, but have lost all sense of where sounds come from. It's a pleasant phase that leads to total lack of anxiety.

28 minutes – The sense of the relativity of time is really amazing. This must be how Einstein discovered it.

30 minutes – Suddenly, I lose consciousness entirely. I try to write, but I fail to realize that this is just an attempt, a test. I begin to dance, to dance like a madman; the music is coming from another planet and I exist in an unknown dimension.

33 minutes – Time is passing terribly slowly. I wouldn't have the courage to try LSD ...

45 minutes – The fear of flying out of the window is so great that I get off my bed and lie on the floor, at the back of the room, well away from the street outside. My body doesn't require comfort. I can stay lying on the floor without moving.

1 hour – I look at my watch, unable to understand why I'm trying to record everything. For me this is nothing more than an eternity from which I will never manage to escape.

1 hour 15 minutes – A sudden immense desire to come out of the trance. In the depths of winter, I'm suddenly filled by courage and I decide to take a cold bath. I don't feel the water on my body. I'm naked. But I can't come out of the trance. I'm terrified that I might stay like this for ever. Books I've read about schizophrenia start parading through the bathroom. I want to get out. I want to get out!

1 hour and a half – I'm rigid, lying down, sweating with fear.

2 hours – The passage from the trance to a normal state takes place imperceptibly. There's no feeling of sickness, sleepiness or tiredness, but an unusual hunger. I look for a restaurant on the corner. I move, I walk. One foot in front of the other.

Not satisfied with smoking hashish and recording its effects, Paulo was brave enough to try something which, in the days when he was under his father's authority, would have ended in a session of electroshock therapy in the asylum: he made a copy of these notes and his parents almost died of shock when he gave it to them to read. From his point of view, this was perhaps not simply an act of provocation towards Lygia and Pedro. Although he confessed to his diary that he had 'discovered another world' and that 'drugs are the best thing in the world', Paulo considered himself to be no ordinary cannabis user but, rather, 'an activist ideologue of the hippie movement' who never tired of repeating to his friends the same extravagant claim: 'Drugs are to me what the machine gun is to communists and guerrillas.' As well as cannabis and hashish, the couple had become frequent users of synthetic drugs. Since the time when he had first been admitted to the clinic, he had been prescribed regular doses of Valium. Unconcerned about the damage these drug cocktails might cause to their nervous systems, the lovers became enthusiastic users of Mandrix, Artane, Dexamil and Pervitin. Amphetamines were present in some of these drugs and acted on the central nervous system, increasing the heartbeat and raising blood pressure, producing a pleasant sensation of muscular relaxation, which was followed by feelings of euphoria that would last up to fourteen hours. When they became tired, they would take some kind of sleeping drug such as Mandrix, and crash out. Drugs used in the control of epileptic fits or the treatment of Parkinson's disease guaranteed neverending 'trips' that lasted days and nights without interruption.

One weekend at Kakiko's place in Friburgo, 100 kilometres from Rio, Paulo carried out an experiment to find out how long he could remain drugged without stopping even to sleep, and was overjoyed when he managed to complete more than twenty-four hours, not sleeping and completely 'out of it'. Only drugs seemed to have any importance on this dangerous path that he was following. 'Our meals have become somewhat subjective,' he wrote in his diary. 'We don't know when we last ate and anyway we don't seem to miss food at all.'

Just one thing seemed to be keeping him connected to the world of the normal, of those who did not take drugs: the stubborn desire to be a writer. He was determined to lock himself up in Uncle José's house in Araruama and just write. 'To write, to write a lot, to write everything' was his immediate plan. Vera agreed and urged him on, but she suggested that before he did this, they should relax and take a holiday. In April 1970, the couple decided to go to one of the Meccas of the hippie movement, Machu Picchu, the sacred city of the Incas in the Peruvian Andes, at an altitude of 2,400 metres. Still traumatized by his journey to Paraguay, Paulo feared that something evil would happen to him if he left Brazil. It was only after much careful planning that the couple finally departed. Inspired by the 1969 film *Easy Rider*, they had no clear destination or fixed date of return.

On 1 May they took a Lloyd Aéro Boliviano aeroplane to La Paz for a trip that involved many novelties, the first of which Paulo experienced as soon as he got out at El Alto airport, in the Bolivian capital: snow. He was so excited when he saw everything covered by such a pure white blanket that he could not resist throwing himself on the ground and eating the snow. It was the start of a month of absolute idleness. Vera spent the day in bed in the hotel, unable to cope with the rarefied air of La Paz at 4,000 metres. Paulo went out to get to know the city and, accustomed to the political apathy of a Brazil under a dictatorship, he was shocked to see workers' demonstrations on Labour Day. Four months later, Alfredo Ovando Candia, who had just named himself President of the Republic for the third time, was ousted.

Taking advantage of the low cost of living in Bolivia, they rented a car, stayed in good hotels and went to the best restaurants. Every other day, the elegant Vera made time to go to the hairdresser's, while Paulo climbed the steep hills of La Paz. It was there that they encountered a new type of drug, which was almost non-existent in Brazil: mescalito, also known as peyote, peyotl or mescal – a hallucinogenic tea distilled from cut, dried cactus. Amazed by the calmness and tranquillity induced by the drink, they wallowed in endless visual hallucinations and experienced intense moments of synaesthesia, a confusion of the senses that gives the user the sense of being able to smell a colour or hear a taste.

They spent five days in La Paz drinking the tea, visiting clubs to listen to local music and attending *diabladas*, places where plays in which the Inca equivalent of the Devil predominated. They then caught a train to Lake Titicaca, the highest navigable lake in the world, where they took a boat across and then the train to Cuzco and Machu Picchu, after which they went by plane to Lima.

In Lima, they rented a car and headed for Santiago de Chile, passing through Arequipa, Antofagasta and Arica. The plan was to spend more time on this stretch, but the hotels were so unprepossessing that they decided to carry on. Neither Paulo nor Vera enjoyed the Chilean capital – 'a city like any other', he wrote – but they did have the chance to see Costa-Gavras's film *Z*, which denounced the military dictatorship in Greece and was banned in Brazil. At the end of their three-week trip, still almost constantly under the influence of mescalito, they found themselves in Mendoza, in Argentina, on the way to Buenos Aires. Paulo was eaten up with jealousy when he saw the attractive Vera being followed by men, particularly when she began to speak in English, which he still could not understand that well. In La Paz it had been the sight of snow that had taken him by surprise; in Buenos Aires it was going on the metro for the first time. Accustomed to low prices in the other places they had visited, they decided to dine at the Michelangelo, a restaurant known as 'the cathedral of the tango', where they were lucky enough to hear a classic of the genre, the singer Roberto 'Polaco' Goyeneche. When they were handed a bill for $20 – the equivalent of about US$120 today – Paulo almost fell off his chair to discover that they were in one of the most expensive restaurants in the city.

Although his asthma had coped well with the Andean heights, in Buenos Aires, at sea level, it reappeared in force. With a temperature of 39°C and suffering from intense breathing difficulties, he had to remain in bed for three days and only began to recover in Montevideo, on 1 June, the day before they were to leave for Brazil. At his insistence, they would not be making the return journey on a Lloyd Aéro Boliviano flight. This change had nothing to do with superstition or with the fact that they would have to travel via La Paz. Paulo had seen the bronze statue of a civilian pilot at La Paz airport in homage 'to the heroic pilots of LAB who have died in action': 'I'd be mad to travel with a company that treats the pilots of crashed planes as heroes! What if our pilot has ambitions to become a statue?' In the end, they flew Air France to Rio de Janeiro, where they arrived on 3 June in time to watch the first round of the 1970 World Cup, when the Brazilian team beat Czechoslovakia 4–1.

The dream of becoming a writer would not go away. Paulo came nowhere in the short story competitions he entered. He wrote in his diary: 'It was with a broken heart that I heard the news ... that I had failed to win yet another literary competition. I didn't even get an honourable mention.' However, he did not allow himself to be crushed by these defeats and continued to note down possible subjects for future literary works, such as 'flying saucers', 'Jesus', 'the abominable snowman', 'spirits becoming embodied in corpses' and 'telepathy'. All the same, the prizes continued to elude him, as he recorded in his notes: 'Dear São José, my protector. You are witness to the fact that I've tried really hard this year. I've lost in every competition. Yesterday, when I heard I'd lost in the competition for children's plays, Vera said that when my luck finally does arrive, it will do so all in one go. Do you agree?'

On his twenty-third birthday, Vera gave him a sophisticated micro-scope and was pleased to see what a success it was: hours after opening the gift, Paulo was still hunched over it, carefully examining the glass plates and making notes. Curious to know what he was doing, she began to read what he was writing: 'It's twenty-three years today since I was born. I was already this thing that I can see under the microscope. Excited, moving in the direction of life, infinitesimally small but with all my hereditary characteristics in place. My two arms, my legs and my brain were already programmed. I would reproduce myself from that sperm cell, the cells would multiply. And here I am, aged twenty-three.' It was only then that she realized that Paulo had put his own semen under the microscope. The notes continue: 'There goes a possible engineer. Another one that ought to have become a doctor is dying. A scientist capable of saving the Earth has also died, and I'm impassively watching all this through my microscope. My own sperm are furiously flailing around, desperate to find an egg, desperate to perpetuate themselves.'

Vera was good company, but she could be tough too. When she real-ized that, if he had anything to do with it, Paulo would never achieve anything beyond the school diploma he had got at Guanabara, she almost forced him to prepare for his university entrance exams. Her vigilance produced surprising results. By the end of the year, he had managed to be accepted by no fewer than three faculties: law at Cândido Mendes, theatre direction at the Escola Nacional de Teatro and media studies at the Pontifícia Universidade Católica (PUC) in Rio.

This success, needless to say, could not be attributed entirely to Vera: it had as much to do with Paulo's literary appetite. Since he had begun making systematic notes of his reading four years earlier, he had read more than three hundred books, or seventy-five a year – a vast number when one realizes that most Brazilians read, on average, one book a year. He read a great deal and he read everything. From Cervantes to Kafka, from Jorge Amado to Scott Fitzgerald, from Aeschylus to Aldous Huxley. He read Soviet dissidents such as Alexander Solzhenitsyn and Brazilians who were on police files such as the humourist Stanislaw Ponte Preta. He would read, make a short commentary on each work and rate them accordingly. The highest accolade, four stars, was the privilege of only a few writers, such as Henry Miller, Borges and Hemingway. And he blithely awarded 'zero stars' to books as varied as Norman Mailer's *American Dream*, Régis Debray's *Revolution in Revolution* and two Brazilian classics, *Os Sertões* [*Rebellion in the Backlands*] by Euclides da Cunha and *História Econômica do Brasil* [*An Economic History of Brazil*] by Caio Prado, Jr.

In this mélange of subjects, periods and authors, there was one genre that appeared to arouse Paulo's interest more than others: books dealing with the occult, witchcraft and satanism. Ever since he had read a short book written by the Spanish sorcerer José Ramón Molinero, *The Secret Alchemy of Mankind*, he had devoured everything relating to the invisible world beyond the human senses. When he finished reading *The Dawn of Magic* by the Belgian Louis Pauwels and the French-Ukrainian Jacques Bergier, he began to feel he was a member of this new tribe. 'I'm a magician preparing for his dawn,' he wrote in his diary. At the end of 1970, he had collected fifty works on the subject. During this time he had read, commented on and given star ratings to all six of the Hermann Hesse books published in Brazil, as well as to Erich von Däniken's best-sellers *The Chariots of the Gods* and *Return to the Stars*, Goethe's *Faust*, to which he gave only three stars, and to absurd books such as *Black Magic and White Magic* by a certain V.S. Foldej, which didn't even merit a rating.

One of the most celebrated authors of this new wave was Carlos Castaneda. Not only did he write on the occult: his own story was shrouded in mystery. He was said to have been born in 1925 in Peru (or in 1935 in Brazil, according to other sources) and had graduated in anthropology at the University of California, in Los Angeles. When he was preparing his doctoral thesis he decided to write autobiographical accounts of his experiences in Mexico on the use of drugs such as peyote, mushrooms and stramonium (known as devil's weed) in native rituals. The worldwide success of Castaneda, who even featured on the cover of *Time* magazine, attracted hordes of hippies, in search of the new promised land, from the four corners of the earth to the Sonora desert on the border where California and Arizona meet Mexico, where the books were set.

For those who, like Paulo, did not believe in coincidences, the fact that it was at precisely this moment that his mother made him the gift of a trip to the United States seemed like a sign. His grandmother Lilisa was going to Washington to visit her daughter Lúcia, who was married to the diplomat Sérgio Weguelin, and he would go with her and, if he wanted, extend the trip and go travelling alone or with his cousin Serginho, who was a few years younger. Besides giving him the opportunity to get to know first-hand the area about which Castaneda had written, the trip was useful in another way. His relationship with Vera appeared to be coming to an end. 'Life with her is getting complicated,' he complained at the beginning of 1971 in his diary. 'We don't have sex any more, she's driving me mad, and I'm driving her mad. I don't love her any more. It's just habit.' Things had reached such a low ebb that the two had stopped living together. Vera had returned to her apartment in Leblon and he had moved from Santa Teresa back to his grandparents' house before moving to Copacabana. Besides this, he announced in his diary that he was 'half-married' to a new woman, the young actress Christina Scardini, whom he had met at drama school and with whom he swore he was passionately in love. This was a lie, but during the month and a half he was away in America, she was the recipient of no fewer than forty-four letters.

At the beginning of May, after a celebratory farewell dinner given by his parents, he took a Varig flight with his grandparents to New York, where they were to catch an internal flight to Washington. When they arrived at Kennedy airport, Paulo and his grandmother couldn't understand why Tuca was in such a hurry to get the eleven o'clock plane to

Washington, for which the check-in was just closing. Lilisa and her grand-son argued that there was no reason to rush, because if they missed that plane they could take the following flight, half an hour later. Out of breath from running, the three boarded the plane just as the doors were about to be closed. Tuca only calmed down once they were all sitting with their seatbelts buckled. That night, when they were watching the news at his uncle's house, Paulo realized that the hand of destiny had clearly been behind Tuca's insistence that they catch the 11.00 flight. The 11.30 flight, a twin-engined Convair belonging to Allegheny (later US Airways), had experienced mechanical problems and when the pilot tried to make an emergency landing near New Haven, 70 kilometres from New York, the plane had crashed, killing the crew and all thirty passen-gers on board.

While staying at his diplomat uncle's house in Bethesda, Maryland, half an hour from Washington, instead of writing a travel diary Paulo decided to use his copious correspondence with Christina to record his impressions. He seemed to be astounded by everything he saw. He could stand for ages, gazing at the automatic vending machines for stamps, newspapers and soft drinks, or spend hours on end in department stores without buying anything, amazed by the sheer variety of products. In his very first letter he regretted not having taken with him 'a sack of change' from Brazil, since he had discovered that all the machines accepted the Brazilian 20 centavo coin as if it were a 25 cent piece, even though it was worth only one fifth of the value. 'I'd have made great savings if I'd brought more coins,' he confessed, 'because it costs me 25 cents to buy a stamp for Brazil from the vending machines and to get in to see the blue movies they show in the porn shops here.'

Everything was new and everything excited him, from the supermar-ket shelves stacked with unnecessary items to the works of art at the National Gallery, where he wept as he actually touched with his own hands the canvas of *Death and the Miser* by Hieronymus Bosch. He knew perfectly well that touching a painting is a cardinal sin in any serious museum, but he placed his fingers not only on Bosch's 1485 work but on several other masterpieces too. He would stand in front of each work for some minutes, look around and, when he was certain he wasn't being watched by the security guards, commit the heresy of spreading all ten fingers out on the canvas. 'I touched a Van Gogh, a Gauguin, and a Degas, and I felt something growing in me, you know,' he told his girlfriend. 'I'm really growing here. I'm learning a lot.'

Nothing, however, seems to have struck him more, while in Washington, than the visits he made to the military museum and the FBI museum. The first, with its many exhibits relating to the participation of the United States in the two world wars, appeared to him to be a place 'where children are sent to learn to hate the enemies of the United States'. Not only children, to judge by his reaction. After visiting every bit of the museum and seeing planes, rockets and films about American military power, he left 'hating the Russians, wanting to kill, kill, kill, spitting hatred'. On his tour of the FBI museum, with a federal agent as his guide, he saw the Gangster Museum, with the original clothes and weapons used by famous gangsters, such as Dillinger, 'Baby Face', 'Machine Gun Kelly' and others, as well as the actual notes written by kidnapped hostages. In the corner of one room he was surprised to find a blinking light, under which was a plaque bearing the following words: 'Each time this light blinks, a type A crime (murder, kidnap or rape) is committed in the United States.' The problem was that the light blinked every three seconds. On the gun stand, the agent was proud of the fact that in the FBI, they shoot to kill. That night, on a card peppered with exclamation marks, he recorded his feelings:

> These guys don't miss! They shot with revolvers and machine-guns, and always at the target's head! They never missed! And there were children, my love, watching all this! There were whole school parties at the FBI gun stand to find out how they defend the country! ... The agent told me that to join the FBI you have to be taller than 1.80m, have a good aim and be prepared for them to examine the whole of your past life. Nothing else. There's no intelligence test, only a shooting test. I'm in the most advanced country in the world, in a country enjoying every comfort and the highest social perfection. So why do such things happen here?

Concerned with his public image, Paulo usually appended a footnote, asking Christina not to show the letters to anyone. 'They're very private and written with no thought for style,' he explained. 'You can say what I've written, but don't let anyone else read them.' At the end of a marathon week of visits, he bought a train ticket to New York, where he was going to decide on his next move. In a comfortable red-and-blue second-class carriage on an Amtrak train, minutes after leaving the American capital, he felt a shiver run through him when he realized the purpose of the concrete constructions beside the railway line: they were fall-out shelters built in case of nuclear war. These dark thoughts were interrupted by a tap on his shoulder when the train was about to make its first stop in Elizabeth, New Jersey.

It was the conductor, wearing a blue uniform and with a leather bag round his waist, who said to him: 'Morning, sir, may I see your ticket?'

Surprised, and not understanding what he meant, Paulo responded in Portuguese: '*Desculpe.*'

The man seemed to be in a hurry and in a bad mood: 'Don't you understand? I asked for your ticket! Without a ticket nobody travels on my train.'

It was only at this point that Paulo understood, with deep dismay, that all Vera's efforts to make him into a model English speaker had been in vain. Without her to turn to, he realized that it was one thing to read books in English, and even then with the help of his lover or of dictionaries. It was quite another to speak it and, most of all, to understand what people were saying in the language. The disappointing truth was that there he was alone in the United States and he couldn't say a single, solitary word in English.

CHAPTER 12

Discovering America

PAULO'S FIRST IMPRESSION OF NEW YORK could not have been worse. In marked contrast to the cleanliness and colour he was accustomed to seeing on cinema screens and in books, the city that opened up to him through the train windows as soon as he passed through the Brooklyn tunnel and entered Manhattan Island appeared to be infested with beggars and ugly, poorly dressed, threatening-looking people. But this sight did not dishearten him. He wanted to stay only a few days in the city and then set off to find the original objective of his journey: the Grand Canyon in Arizona and the magical deserts of Mexico. He had US$300 and wanted to spend two months 'wandering from one side of the United States to the other'. The first thing he should do was to stop travelling by train and switch to Greyhound buses. He remembered having seen these buses in films, an elegant greyhound painted on the side. A pass costing US$99 gave you the right to travel for forty-five days to anywhere on the Greyhound network, more than two thousand towns across the United States, Mexico and Canada. Since his plan was to spend two months travelling, this meant that, with the money that remained, he could only afford to stay in YMCA hostels, which charged 6 dollars a night, including breakfast and dinner.

Two days was enough for New York to dispel the disappointment he had felt on arrival. Firstly, because, although the YMCA rooms were small – half the size of his room at his grandmother's house – and they had no bathroom, television or air conditioning, they were single and very clean, with bed linen changed daily. The staff were polite and while the food was not exactly haute cuisine, it was well cooked and tasty. Were it not for the discomfort of having to share a bathroom with all the other guests on the corridor, Paulo could happily have stayed there longer. The continuing problem was the language. Every day, in the dining room, he would annoy everyone else in the hungry, impatient queue with his inability to communicate to the cook what it was he wanted to eat. It was a relief to learn that the delicious beans served at the YMCA were called 'poroto'. Since this was a word he had no difficulty in pronouncing, the problem was solved: he would eat nothing but 'poroto' until his English improved.

New York's tolerant, liberal atmosphere also helped to reconcile him to the city. Paulo discovered that sex, cannabis and hashish were all available in the streets, especially in the areas around Washington Square, where groups of hippies spent their days playing guitars and enjoying the first rays of spring sunshine. One night, he arrived at the hostel restaurant only five minutes before the doors were to be closed. Even though almost all the tables were empty, he picked up his tray and sat down opposite a slim girl of about twenty, wearing what seemed to be the official uniform of hippie women the world over – an ankle-length Indian dress in multicoloured cotton. A smile appeared on her freckled face and Paulo, sure that he had enough English to be polite, said: 'Excuse me?'

The girl didn't understand: 'What?'

Realizing that he was incapable of pronouncing even a banal 'excuse me', he relaxed and started to laugh at himself. Feeling more relaxed made communication easier, and, later that night, he and the girl, Janet, walked together through the city streets. However hard he tried to find out what it was she was studying, Paulo could not understand what the word 'belei' meant. Belei? But what did studying 'belei' mean? Janet drew back and jumped up, her arms wide, performed a pirouette, and then curtseyed deeply. So that was what it was! She was studying ballet!

At the end of the evening, on the way back to the hostel, where men and women slept on different floors, the young couple stopped on the steps of a building in Madison Square Garden to say goodbye. Between kisses and hugs, Janet slipped her hand below Paulo's waist, over his jeans, and then started back and said, almost spelling out the words so that he could understand: 'I've been with other boys before, but you … Wow! You're the first one I've known who's had a square one.' Laughing, he had to explain that no, he did not have a square dick. Rather than leaving his documents in the wardrobe in the YMCA, he had put all his money and his return ticket to Brazil in his passport and put the whole lot in a supposedly safe place – his underpants.

It was under the guidance of Janet, with whom he would often have sex in quiet corners of parks and gardens, that he came to know a new world: the New York of the 1970s. He joined demonstrations against the war in Vietnam, went to concerts of baroque music in Central Park and was thrilled to go down some steps and find Pennsylvania station magically lit up. 'It's bigger than Central station in Rio,' he wrote to his girlfriend, 'only it's constructed entirely underground.' He was excited when he went to Madison Square Garden, 'where three months ago Cassius Clay was beaten by Joe Frazier'. His passion for the boxer who would later take the name Muhammad Ali was such that he not only watched all his fights but also compared his tiny physical measurements with those of the American giant. Although he had no specific date to return home, time seemed too short to enjoy everything that New York had to offer a young man from a poor country under a military dictatorship.

When he could, he tried to record in his letters the excitement he was experiencing:

There are areas where everything – books, newspapers, posters – is written in Chinese, or Spanish or Italian. My hotel is full of men in turbans, Black Panther militants, Indians in long clothes, everything. Last night, when I left my room, I broke up a fight between two old guys of sixty! They were bashing the hell out of each other! I haven't even told you anything about Harlem yet, the black district, it's amazing, fantastic. What is NY? I think NY is the prostitutes walking the streets at midday in Central Park, it's the building where *Rosemary's Baby* was filmed, it's the place where *West Side Story* was filmed.

Before sealing the envelopes he would cover the margins of his letters with sentimental declarations of love ('adored, loved, wonderful woman', or 'I'll telephone you even if I've got to go without food for a day just to hear your voice for a minute') and a few lies, such as 'Don't worry, I won't cheat on you'.

At the end of a torrid, two-week affair with New York, Paulo realized that he was limited by two things: neither his hesitant English nor his savings would be enough for him to travel alone across the United States for two months. The question of money could be resolved with a clever piece of belt-tightening suggested by Janet: if he used his Greyhound ticket for night journeys lasting more than six hours, the bus would become his hotel bedroom. The language problem, though, seemed insoluble. His schoolboy vocabulary might be enough to cope with basic needs, such as sleeping and eating, but Paulo knew that the journey would lose its charm if he couldn't properly understand what other people were saying. Faced with a choice between returning to Brazil and asking for help, he opted for the latter: he made a reverse-charge call to his aunt's house in Washington and invited his cousin Sérgio, who spoke English fluently, to go with him. A few days later, the two young men, rucksacks on their backs and using the Greyhound buses as a hotel, headed off to Chicago, the first stop on the long haul to the Grand Canyon, in the heart of Arizona, more than 4,000 kilometres from Manhattan and so far away that the time there was two hours earlier than in New York.

The only records of this period are the letters he sent to Christina, and one notes the absence of any reference to his companion who was, after all, his saviour on the journey. This is not just a lapse, because, besides overlooking Sérgio's presence, Paulo told his girlfriend that he was travelling alone. 'Perhaps I'll leave my camera with Granny during the journey,' he wrote, 'because I'm alone and can't take photos of myself, and it's better to buy postcards than to waste film on landscapes.' He wanted to make this marathon trip sound like a bold adventure.

With no money to spare, he recorded all his expenses on a piece of paper with the amounts in dollars and Brazilian cruzeiros: a packet of cigarettes 60 cents, a hamburger 80 cents, a subway ticket 30 cents, a cinema ticket 2 dollars. Each time they missed the night Greyhound bus, his savings would shrink by 7 dollars, the price of a room in one of the more modest roadside hotels. New York, with its mixture of civilization and barbarism, had left him 'shaken up', and it was hard for him to adjust to the more rural states in the Midwest. 'After NYC I've got little to say,' he complained to Christina in a near unintelligible scrawl written as the bus was moving. 'I'm only writing because I'm really missing my woman.' The majority of the cities he visited merited only superficial mention in his correspondence. His impression of Chicago was that it was the 'coldest' city he had so far encountered. 'The people are absolutely neurotic, and totally and uncontrollably aggressive. It's a city where they take work very seriously.'

After spending five days on the road, Paulo's eyes lit up at the sight through the dusty bus window of a road sign saying 'Cheyenne – 100 miles'. In the state of Wyoming, on the border with Colorado, in the heart of the American West, this was a city he felt he had known since childhood. He had read so many books and magazines and seen so many westerns set in Cheyenne that he thought himself capable of reconstructing from memory the names of the streets, hotels and saloons where the cowboy and Indian adventures had taken place. His astonishment at seeing the road sign stemmed from the fact that he hadn't realized the city actually existed. In his mind, Cheyenne was a fantasy appropriated by the authors of books, films and cartoons in stories of the Wild West that he had read and seen during his childhood and adolescence.

He was disappointed to discover that while there were still cowboys in the city, in boots, stetsons and belts with bull's buckles, and revolvers in holsters, they now travelled in convertible Cadillacs. The only traces of the Cheyenne he had seen in John Ford's *Cheyenne Autumn* were the carriages used by the local Amish community, which forbids the use of such modern inventions as lifts, telephones and cars. But his greatest disappointment was when he discovered that Pioneer Street, the favourite place for cowboys to hold duels in the evening in the mythical Cheyenne, had been transformed into a busy four-lane highway lined with shops selling electronic gadgets.

The obvious route to the Grand Canyon was to travel some 1,000 kilo-metres southwest, then cross Colorado and part of New Mexico into Arizona. However, because they both wanted to go to Yellowstone Park and make the most of their Greyhound ticket, they travelled in the opposite direction, northwards. When they realized that the closest stopping-off place to the park was Idaho Falls, 300 kilometres from Yellowstone, Paulo decided to take two risks. First, he spent US$30 on hiring a car. Second, since he had not taken his driving test he lied to the car-hire firm and presented his membership card of the Actors' Union in Rio as a Brazilian driving licence.

Although he was aware that he risked being arrested if stopped by a traffic policeman, he drove for the whole day past the glaciers in the park and the geysers spewing out hot water and sulphur on to the snow, and saw bears and deer crossing the road. In the evening, they went to return the car and decided to catch a Greyhound bus where they could shelter from the cold. Although it was the middle of summer and the two had experienced temperatures of up to 38°C, two hours from the Canadian border, the cold was so unbearable that the heating in the car wasn't enough to keep them warm. As neither had suitable clothes for such low temperatures, when they arrived at the bus station in Boise, the capital of Idaho, they rushed to the Greyhound ticket office to ask what time the next night bus left. Going where? Anywhere that wasn't so cold. If the only destination with available seats at that time of night was San Francisco, then that was where they would go.

In the middle of the night, as the bus was crossing the Nevada desert, he wrote a letter to Christina boasting of how he had tricked the man at the car-hire firm with his false licence, but regretting the fact that the extra expense of hiring the car had 'messed up my budget'. He also said that he had discovered the reason for the strong smell of whisky pervading the Greyhound bus: 'Everyone here has a small bottle in his pocket. They drink a lot in the United States.' The letter is interrupted halfway through and starts again some hours later:

> I was going to go straight to San Francisco, but I discovered that
> gambling in Nevada is legal, so I spent the night here. I wanted to

play and see how other people play. I didn't make any friends at the casino; they were all too busy gambling. I ended up losing 5 dollars in a one-armed bandit – you know, those betting machines where you pull a handle. There was a cowboy sitting next to me wearing boots, hat and neckerchief, just like in the films. In fact the whole bus is full of cowboys. I'm in the Far West on the way to San Francisco, where I'm due to arrive at eleven at night. In seven hours' time, I'll have crossed the American continent, which not many other people have.

When they reached San Francisco, exhausted after travelling for twenty-two days, the cousins signed in at a YMCA hostel and spent the day sleeping, in an attempt to catch up on more than a hundred hours spent sitting in cramped buses.

The cradle of the hippie movement, San Francisco had as great an impact on Paulo as New York. 'This city is much freer than NYC. I went to a really smart cabaret and saw naked women making love with men on the stage in front of rich Americans with their wives,' he told her, excited but regretting the fact that he'd been unable to see more. 'I went in quickly and saw just a bit of the show, but as I didn't have enough money to buy a seat, I got thrown out.' He was astonished to see adolescents buying and consuming LSD pills quite openly; he bought some hashish in the hippie district, smoked it on the street and no one stopped him. He also took part in demonstrations against the war in Vietnam and saw a pacifist march by Buddhist monks being broken up by a gang of young blacks with truncheons. 'You breathe an air of complete madness in the streets of this city,' he said in a letter to Christina.

After five 'mind-blowing' days, the cousins caught another bus in the direction of the Grand Canyon. They got off halfway there, in Los Angeles, but as it was 4 July, Independence Day, the city was dead, and they stayed only a few hours. 'Nothing was open, and it was almost impossible to find somewhere to have a coffee,' he complained. 'The famous Hollywood Boulevard was a complete desert, with no one on the streets, but we did see how luxurious everything here is, even the most ordinary bar.' And since the cost of living in Los Angeles was incompatible with the backpackers' funds, they didn't stay the night. They took another bus and, twenty-four hours after leaving San Francisco, reached Flagstaff, the entrance to the Grand Canyon.

The extortionate prices of the hotels and restaurants were almost as impressive as the beauty of the canyon. Since there were no YMCA hostels in the area, they bought a nylon tent, which meant a 19-dollar hole in their tiny stash of savings, and spent the first night in a hippie camp, where at least free hashish was guaranteed. As soon as the sun began to rise, they took down their tent, filled their rucksacks with bottles of water and tinned food, and left on foot for the Grand Canyon. They walked all day beneath the blazing sun and when they decided to stop, exhausted and hungry, they discovered that they were at the widest point of the Canyon, which measures 20 kilometres from side to side. It is also the deepest; between them and the river was a drop of 1,800 metres. They pitched their tent, lit a small bonfire to heat up their tins of soup and fell asleep, exhausted, not waking until dawn the next day.

When Sérgio suggested they go down to the river, Paulo was terrified. As there was absolutely no one around, apart from them, and they were on a path little used by tourists, he was worried that should they get into difficulties, there would be no one to come to their aid. However, Sérgio was determined: if Paulo didn't want to, he would go alone. He put all his stuff in his rucksack and began the descent, oblivious to his cousin's protests: 'Serginho, the problem isn't going down, but coming back! It's going to get really hot and we've got to climb the equivalent of the stairs in a 500-storey building! In the blazing sun!'

Impervious, his cousin didn't even turn round. There was nothing for Paulo to do but pick up his rucksack and follow him down. The beauty of the area dispelled some of his fears. The Grand Canyon looked like a 450-kilometre gash in the desert of red sand, at the bottom of which was what appeared to be a tiny trickle of water. This was, in fact, the torrential Colorado River, which rises in the Rocky Mountains in the state of Colorado and flows more than 2,300 kilometres until it runs into the Sea of Cortez in Mexico, crossing six more American states (Arizona, California, Nevada, Utah, New Mexico and Wyoming). To be down there was indescribable.

After walking for some five hours, Paulo stopped and suggested to his cousin that they end their adventure there and begin the climb back up, saying: 'We didn't eat much last night, we haven't had a proper breakfast and up to now we haven't had any lunch. Take a look and see how far we've got to climb.'

His cousin remained determined. 'You can wait for me here, because I'm going down to the river bank.'

He continued walking. Paulo found some shade where he could sit, smoked a cigarette and enjoyed the splendour of the landscape as he sat in total silence. When he looked at his watch, he realized it was midday. He walked on a few metres, trying to see Sérgio, but there was no sign of him. Indeed, as far as the eye could see, there was no one, no tourist, no Indians, not a soul for kilometres and kilometres. He realized that if he were to go down a little further, he would come to a rocky ledge from where he would have a wider view of the area. However, even from there, he couldn't see his cousin. He began to shout out his name, waiting a few seconds after each shout, before shouting again. His voice echoed between the walls of red stone, but there was neither sign nor sound of his cousin. He was beginning to think that they had taken the wrong path. From fear to panic was but a step. Feeling entirely defenceless and alone, he became terrified. 'I'm going to die here,' he kept saying: 'I'm going to die. I can't take any more. I'm not going to get out of here. I'm going to die here, in this wonderful place.'

He was aware that, in midsummer, the temperatures around the Grand Canyon could be over 50°C. His water had run out and it was unlikely that there would be a tap in the middle of that desert. Added to which, he had no idea where he was, since there were so many intersecting paths. He started to shout for help, but no one appeared, and he heard nothing but the echo of his own voice. It was past four in the afternoon. Desperate to find his cousin, he began to run, stumbling, in the direction of the river, knowing that every step he took meant another he would have to climb up on his return.

The sun was burning his face when he finally reached a sign of civilization. Fixed to a rock was a metal plate with a red button and sign saying: 'If you are lost, press the red button and you will be rescued by helicopters or mules. You will be fined US$500.' He had only 80 dollars left and his cousin must have about the same in his pocket, but the discovery of the sign made him certain of two things: they were not the first to be so foolish as to take that route; and the risk of dying began to fade, even though it might mean a few days in jail until their parents could send the money for the fine. However, first of all, Paulo had to find Sérgio. He went another 200 metres further down, never taking his eyes off the red button, which was his one visible reference mark, and after a bend in the path, he came across a natural belvedere where there was a metal telescope with a coin slot. He inserted 25 cents, the lens opened and he began to scan the river banks, looking for his travel companion. There he was, in the shadow of a rock and apparently as exhausted as Paulo. He was sound asleep.

Rejecting the idea of summoning a helicopter, they climbed up to the top again, and it was midnight by the time they got there. They were exhausted, their skin was puffy with sunburn, but they were alive. After the long day, the idea of spending another night in the hippie camp was so appalling that Paulo made a suggestion: 'I think we deserve two things tonight: dinner in a restaurant and a night in a hotel.'

They found a comfortable, cheap motel, left their rucksacks in their room and went into the first restaurant they came to, where each ordered a T-bone steak so big it barely fitted on the plate. It cost 10 dollars – the amount they usually spent each day. They barely had the strength to pick up knife and fork. They were both starving, though, and ate as quickly as they could. Five minutes later, however, they were in the toilet, throwing up. They returned to the motel and collapsed on to their beds for the last night they would spend together on their journey: the following day Sérgio would be returning home to Washington and Paulo was to go on to Mexico.

The original reason he had accepted his mother's gift of a plane ticket had been that it would give him the chance to make a pilgrimage to the mysterious deserts that had inspired Carlos Castaneda, but he had been so thrilled by the novelty of the country as a whole that he had almost forgotten this. Now, with his entire body aching after his adventure in the Grand Canyon, and with money fast running out, he felt a great temptation to return to Brazil. His Greyhound pass was still valid for a few more days, though, and so he carried on as planned. Grown accustomed to the wealth of America, he was appalled by the poverty he found in Mexico, which was much like Brazil. He tried all the mushroom syrups and hallucinogenic cactus teas that he could, and then caught the bus back to New York, where he spent three more days, after which he flew home to Brazil.

CHAPTER 13

Gisa

A WEEK AFTER RETURNING TO BRAZIL, having recovered from his trip, Paulo had still not decided what to do with his life. One thing was certain: he was not going back to the law faculty, so he left the course in the middle of the academic year. He continued to attend classes in theatre direction at the Guanabara State Faculty of Philosophy – which would later become the University of Rio de Janeiro – and he did everything he could to get his articles published in Rio newspapers. He wrote an article about the liberal attitude towards drugs in the United States and sent it to the most popular humorous weekly of the period, *Pasquim*, which went on to become an influential opponent of the dictatorship. He promised St Joseph that he would light fifteen candles to him if the text was published and, every Wednesday, he was the first to arrive at the newspaper stand on the corner near his home. He would avidly leaf through the magazine only to return it to the pile, disheartened. It was not until three weeks later that he realized the article had been rejected. Although this rejection tormented him for days, it was not enough to put paid to his dream of becoming a writer. When he realized that *Pasquim*'s silence was a resounding 'No', he made a strange note in his diary: 'I've been thinking about the problem of fame and have concluded that my good fortune hasn't yet turned up. When it does, it's going to be quite something.'

The problem was that while he waited for it to turn up, he needed to earn a living. He still enjoyed working in the theatre, but the returns weren't usually enough even to cover the costs of putting on the production. This led him to accept an invitation to teach on a private course preparing students for the entrance exam for theatre courses given by the Federation of Isolated State Schools in the State of Guanabara. It wouldn't contribute anything to his future plans, but, on the other hand, it wouldn't take up much time and it guaranteed him a monthly salary of 1,600 cruzeiros, some US$350.

On 13 August 1971, a little more than a month after his return from the United States, Paulo received a phone call from Washington. His grandfather, Arthur Araripe or Tuca, had just died. He had suffered severe cranial trauma when he fell down the stairs at his daughter's house in Bethesda, where he was staying, and had died instantly. Appalled by the news, Paulo sat in silence for a few minutes, trying to collect his thoughts. One of the last images he had of Tuca, smiling and sporting a beret as they arrived at the airport in Washington, seemed so fresh that he could not accept that the old man had died. Paulo felt that if he went out on to the verandah he would find Tuca dozing there, mouth open, over a copy of the *Reader's Digest*. Or, as he loved to do, provoking his hippie grandson with his reactionary ideas, saying for instance that Pelé was 'an ignorant black man' and that Roberto Carlos was 'an hysterical screamer'. Then he would defend right-wing dictators, starting with Salazar in Portugal and Franco in Spain (on these occasions, Paulo's father would join in and insist that 'any idiot' could paint like Picasso or play the guitar like Jimi Hendrix). Instead of getting annoyed, Paulo would roar with laughter at his obstinate grandfather's over-the-top remarks, because, for all his conservatism, and perhaps because he himself had been a bit of a bohemian during his youth, he was the only member of the family who respected and understood the strange friends Paulo went around with. Having known him for so many years, and having built a closer relationship with him during the time he spent in his grandparents' small house, Paulo had come to consider Tuca to be almost a second father to him. A generous, tolerant father, the very opposite of his real father, the harsh and irascible Pedro. For these reasons, his grandfather's unexpected death was all the more painful, and the wound opened up by that loss would take time to heal.

Paulo continued to teach and to go to his theatre course, with which he was beginning to find fault. 'In the first year, the student learns to be a bit of a chiseller and to use personal charm to achieve whatever he or she wants,' he wrote in his diary. 'In the second year, the student loses any sense of organization he had before and in the third, he becomes a queer.' His proverbial paranoia reached unbearable levels when he learned that the detective Nelson Duarte, who was accused of belonging to the Death Squad, was going around the Escola Nacional de Teatro looking for 'cannabis users and communists'. On one such visit, the policeman was confronted by a brave woman, the teacher and speech and hearing therapist Glória Beutenmüller, who wagged her finger at him and said: 'My students can wear their hair as long as they like – and if you arrest one of them, they'll have to be dragged out of here.'

Protected by the secrecy of his diary, Paulo made a solitary protest against these arbitrary arrests:

> Nelson Duarte again issued a threat against students and teachers with long hair, and the school issued a decree, banning long hair. I didn't go to the class today because I haven't decided whether I'm going to cut mine or not. It's affected me deeply. Cutting my hair, not wearing necklaces, not dressing like a hippie ... It's unbelievable. With this diary I'm writing a real secret archive of my age. One day, I'll publish the whole thing. Or else I'll put it all in a radiation-proof box with a code that's easy to work out, so that one day someone will read what I've written. Thinking about it, I'm a bit worried about even keeping this notebook.

In fact, he had already made plenty of notes showing that he didn't share the ideas of many of his left-wing friends who opposed the dictatorship. His diary was peppered with statements such as: 'There's no point getting rid of this and replacing it with communism, which would just be the same shit' and 'Taking up arms never solved anything'. But the repression of any armed conflict was at its height and mere sympathizers as well as their friends were being rounded up. Censorship meant that the press could not publish anything about the government's use of violence against its opponents, but news of this nevertheless reached Paulo's ears, and the shadow cast by the security forces seemed to get closer by the day. One of his friends was imprisoned by the political police merely because he had renewed his passport in order to go to Chile during the period of Salvador Allende's rule. A year earlier, Paulo had learned that a former girlfriend of his, Nancy Unger, had been shot and apprehended in Copacabana while resisting arrest. He found out that Nancy, along with sixty-nine other political prisoners, had been exiled from Brazil, in exchange for the Swiss ambassador Enrico Giovanni Bucher, who had been kidnapped by command of the Popular Revolutionary Front. In the end, the repression became too much even for those who weren't part of the armed resistance. Persecuted by the censors, the composer Chico Buarque went into self-imposed exile in Italy. Gilberto Gil and Caetano Veloso moved to London after having their heads shaved in an army barracks in Rio. Gradually, Paulo was starting to hate the military, but nothing would make him overcome his fear and open his mouth, and say in public what he felt. Appalled that he could do nothing against a regime that was torturing and killing people, he fell into depression.

In September 1971, the army surrounded and killed Captain Carlos Lamarca in the interior of Bahia. When Paulo read excerpts from the dead guerrilla's diary that were published by the press, he wrote a long and bitter outburst that gives a faithful picture of his inner conflicts. Once again, he confessed that he avoided talking about the police in his diary for one reason only: fear. But how could he continue not protesting against what was going on around him? It was when he was alone, locked in his room that he gave expression to his pain:

> I'm living in a terrible climate, TERRIBLE! I can't take any more talk about imprisonment and torture. There is no freedom in Brazil. The area in which I work is subject to vile and stupid censorship.
>
> I read Lamarca's diary. I admired him only because he fought for his ideas, nothing more. Today, though, when I see the demeaning

comments in the press, I felt like shouting, like screaming. I was really angry. And I discovered in his diary a great love for someone, a poetic love that was full of life, and the newspaper called it 'the terrorist's dependence on his lover'. I discovered a man who was full of self-doubt and hyper-honest with himself, even though he fought for an idea that I consider wrong.

The government is torturing people and I'm frightened of torture, I'm frightened of pain. My heart is beating far too fast now, simply because these words could compromise me. But I have to write. The whole thing is fucked. Everyone I know has either been imprisoned or beaten up. And none of them had anything to do with anything.

I still think that one day they're going to knock on the door of this room and take this diary. But St Joseph will protect me. Now that I've written these lines, I know that I'm going to live in fear, but I couldn't continue to keep quiet, I needed to let it out. I'm going to type because it's faster. It needs to be fast. The sooner this notebook is out of my room the better. I'm really frightened of physical pain. I'm frightened of being arrested like I was before. And I don't want that to happen ever again: that's why I try not to think about politics at all. I wouldn't be able to resist. But I will resist. Up until now, 21st September 1971, I was scared. But today is an historic day – or perhaps just a few historic hours. I'm liberating myself from the prison that I built, thanks to all Their practices.

It was very difficult for me to write these words. I'm repeating this so that I won't ever delude myself when I re-read this diary in a safe place, thirty years from now, about the times I'm living through now. But now I've done it. The die is cast.

Sometimes he would spend all day locked in his room at the back of his grandmother's house, smoking cannabis and trying to make a start on that dreamed-of book, or at least a play, or an essay. He had notebooks full of ideas for books, plays and essays, but something was missing – inclination? inspiration? – and when evening came, he still hadn't written a line. Otherwise, he taught for three hours a day and then went to the university. He would go in, talk to various people and, when he got fed up with doing that, end up alone in a bar near by, drinking coffee, chain-smoking and filling pages of notebooks with ideas.

It was on one such evening that a girl appeared, wearing a miniskirt and high boots. She had very long thick dark hair. She sat down beside Paulo at the bar, ordered a coffee and struck up a conversation with him. She had just qualified as an architect and her name was Adalgisa Eliana Rios de Magalhães, or Gisa, from Alfenas in Minas Gerais; she was two years older than Paulo. She had left Minas for Rio in order to study at the Federal University and was now working for the Banco Nacional da Habitação, although what she liked best was drawing comic strips. She was as slender as a catwalk model, and had an unusual face in which her dark melancholy eyes contrasted with a sensual mouth. They talked for some time, exchanged telephone numbers and parted. Once again, Paulo dismissed any possibility of a relationship developing, writing: 'She's ugly and has no sex appeal.'

Unlike Paulo – and this was something he never knew – Gisa had been an active militant in opposition to the military regime. She had never taken part in armed action or anything that might involve risking her life – and this, in the jargon of repression, meant that she was a 'subversive', rather than a 'terrorist' – but following her first year in architecture, she had been a member of several clandestine left-wing cells that had infiltrated the student movement. It was through the students' union at the university that she joined the Brazilian Communist Party, or PCB, where she handed out pamphlets at student assemblies with copies of *Voz Operária* [*The Worker's Voice*]. She left the party and joined the Dissidência da Guanabara, which changed its name in 1969 to Movimento Revolucionário 8 de Outubro, or MR-8, and was one of the groups responsible for the kidnapping of the United States ambassador Charles Elbrick. Although she herself was never anything more than a low-ranking militant, Gisa was nevertheless an activist, and, when she met Paulo, she was having an affair with a young architect from Pernambuco, Marcos Paraguassu de Arruda Câmara. He was the son of Diógenes de Arruda Câmara, a member of the elite in the Partido Comunista do Brasil, who had been in prison in Rio since 1968, and was himself a militant.

In spite of Paulo's scornful remark after their first meeting, over the next few days, the two met up again every night in the small bar next to the theatre school. A week later, he walked her back to the apartment where she lived with her brother, José Reinaldo, at Flamengo beach. She invited him up, and they listened to music and smoked cannabis until late. When her brother arrived home at two in the morning, he found them lying naked on the sitting-room carpet. Less than a month later, Gisa broke up with Marcos Paraguassu: she and Paulo had decided to live together. Paulo moved in three weeks later, once she had managed to get rid of her brother, and immediately proposed that they get married in a month and a half, on Christmas Eve. Gisa accepted, despite feeling slightly uncomfortable about the speed with which he had moved into her home and his habit of walking around the apartment naked.

Hoping perhaps that marriage would help her son to settle down, Paulo's mother reacted as warmly as she had with his previous girl-friends. Then, on 22 November, three months after they had met, Paulo recorded in his diary: 'Gisa is pregnant. It looks as though we're going to have a son.' The fact that the baby would be a boy born under the sign of Leo appears to have made him still more excited at the thought of fatherhood. 'My powers will be re-born with this son,' he wrote delight-edly. 'In the next eight months I'll redouble my energy and climb higher and higher.'

The dream lasted less than a week. After his initial excitement, Paulo began to feel a sense of horror whenever he thought of it, which was all the time. When reality dawned, and he saw that it would be absolute madness to have a child when he had no permanent employment and no means of supporting a family, the first person to be told of his decision was not Gisa but his mother. To Paulo's surprise, Lygia turned out to be not quite the committed Catholic when he told her that he was going to suggest to his girlfriend that she have an abortion. She agreed that having the child was not a good idea. Gisa resisted at first, before agreeing that she, too, was convinced that it would be irresponsible to have the baby. With the help of friends they found a clinic that specialized in clandestine abortions – abortion being a crime – and arranged the operation for 9 December 1971.

Neither managed to sleep the night before. In the morning, they got up in silence, had a bath and went in search of a taxi. They arrived at the clinic at seven on the dot, the time of the appointment. It was a surprise for them both when they saw that there were about thirty women there, the majority very young, and many with their husbands or boyfriends – all looking miserable. On arrival, each woman gave her name to the nurse, left a small pile of notes on the table – cheques were not accepted – and waited to be called. Although there were plenty of chairs, the majority preferred to stand. Five minutes later, Gisa was taken by another nurse to a staircase going up to the second floor. She left with her head bowed, without saying goodbye. In a matter of minutes, all the women had been called, with only a few men remaining in the waiting room.

Paulo sat on one of the chairs, took a notebook out of his bag and began to write – in a very small hand so that his partners in misfortune would not be able to read what he was writing. Whether knowingly or not, each tried to conceal his concern with some gesture or other. Paulo was constantly blinking; the man on his right would empty half the tobacco from his cigarette into the ashtray before lighting up; another kept flipping through a magazine, meanwhile staring into space. Despite his tic, Paulo did not appear to be nervous. He was, it was true, feeling an unpleasant sense of physical smallness, as though he had suddenly become a shrunken dwarf. Background music was coming from two loud-speakers, and although no one was really listening to it, they all kept time by tapping their feet or rattling their key rings. As he watched these move-ments, Paulo noted in his diary: 'They are all trying to keep their bodies as busy as possible and in the most varied ways, because their subcon-scious is clearly telling them: "Don't think about what's going on in there".' They all kept looking at the clock, and each time footsteps were heard, heads would turn toward the staircase. Occasionally, one would complain about how slowly time seemed to be passing. A small group tried to put aside their thoughts by talking quietly about football. Paulo merely observed and wrote:

A young man next to me is complaining about the delay and says that he's going to be late collecting his car from the garage. But I know he's not really like that. He's not thinking about his car, but he wants me to believe that so that he can play the part of the strong man. I smile and gaze into his neurones: there's his wife with her legs open, the doctor is inserting forceps, cutting, scraping and filling everything up with cotton wool once it's over. He knows that I know, turns the other way and is still, without looking at anything, breathing only deeply enough to stay alive.

At 8.30 in the morning, half the women had left and there was no sign of Gisa. Paulo went to the bar around the corner, had a coffee, smoked a cigarette and went back to the waiting room and his notebook, impatient and concerned that perhaps things were not going well for his girlfriend. An hour later, there was still no news. At 9.30 he put his hand in his pocket, hurriedly took out his fountain pen and wrote: 'I felt that it was now. My son returned to the eternity he had never left.'

Suddenly, no one knew from where, or why, they heard a sound that no one had really expected to hear in such a place: a loud, healthy baby's cry, followed immediately by a shout of surprise from a young lad in the waiting room: 'It's alive!'

For a moment, the men appeared to have been freed from the pain, misery and fear that united them in that gloomy room and they broke into a wild, collective burst of laughter. Just as the laughter stopped, Paulo heard footsteps: it was Gisa, returning from the operation, almost three hours after their arrival. Paler than he had ever seen her and with dark rings around her eyes, she looked very groggy and was still suffering from the effects of the anaesthetic. In the taxi on the way home, Paulo asked the driver to go slowly, 'because my girlfriend has cut her foot and it's hurting a lot'.

Gisa slept the whole afternoon and when she woke she couldn't stop crying. Sobbing, she told him that just as she was about to be anaesthetized, she had wanted to run out: 'The doctor put a thin tube inside me and took out a baby that was going to be born perfect. But now our son is rotting somewhere, Paulo ...'

Neither could sleep. It was late at night when she went slowly over to the desk where he was sitting writing and said: 'I hate to ask you this, but I've got to change the dressing and I think I'll manage to do it alone. But if it's very painful, can you come into the bathroom with me to help?'

He smiled and replied with a supportive 'Of course', but once the bathroom door was shut, Paulo begged St Joseph a thousand times to save him from that unpleasant task. 'Forgive me my cowardice, St Joseph,' he murmured, looking up, 'but changing that dressing would be too much for me. Too much! Too much!' To his relief, minutes later, she released him from that obligation and lay down on the bed again. Since leaving the abortion clinic, Gisa had only stopped crying when she fell asleep.

On the Saturday, Paulo took advantage of the fact that she seemed a little better and went off to do his teaching. When he got back in the evening, he found her standing at the bus stop in front of their building. The two returned home and only after much questioning from him did she confess what she had been doing in the street: 'I left the house to die.'

Paulo's reaction was astonishing. He immediately said: 'I'm really sorry I interrupted such an important process. If you've decided to die, then go ahead and kill yourself.'

Her courage had failed her, though.

On the third night without sleep, Gisa only opened her mouth to cry, while he could not stop talking. He explained carefully that she had no way out: after being called to Earth, the Angel of Death would only go back if he could take a soul with him. He said that there was no point in turning back, because the Angel would follow her for ever, and even if she didn't want to die now, he could kill her later, for example by letting her be run over. He recalled how he had faced the Angel when he was an adolescent and had cut the throat of a goat so that he would not have to hand over his own life. The way out was to stand up to the Angel: 'You need to challenge him. Do what you decided to do: try to kill yourself but hope that you'll escape with your life.'

When Gisa closed her eyes, exhausted, he went back to his diary, where he pondered the mad course of action he was proposing to his girl-friend:

I know that Gisa isn't going to die, but she doesn't know it and she can't live with that doubt. We have to give a reply to the Angel in some way or other. Some days ago, a friend of ours, Lola, slashed her whole body with a razor blade, but she was saved at the last moment. Lots of people have been attempting suicide recently. But few succeeded and that's good, because they escaped with their lives and managed to kill the person inside them whom they didn't like.

This macabre theory was not just the fruit of Paulo's sick imagination but had been scientifically proven by a psychiatrist whom he frequently visited, and whom he identified in his diary merely as 'Dr Sombra', or 'Dr Shadow'. The theory was that one should reinforce the patient's traumas. The doctor had told him quite categorically that no one is cured by conventional methods: 'If you're lost and think that the world is much stronger than you are,' he would say to his patients, 'then all that's left for you is suicide.' According to Paulo, this was precisely where the brilliance of his thesis lay: 'The subject leaves the consulting room completely devastated. It's only then that he realizes that he has nothing more to lose and he begins to do things that he would never have had the courage to do in other circumstances. All in all, Dr Sombra's method is really the only thing in terms of the subconscious that I have any real confidence in. It's cure by despair.'

When they woke the following day – a brilliant, sunny summer Sunday – Paulo did not need to try to convince Gisa any further. He realized this when she put on a swimsuit, took a bottle of barbiturates from the bathroom cupboard – he thought it was Orap, or pimozide, which he had been taking since his first admission to the clinic – and emptied the contents into her mouth, swallowing it all down with a glass of water. They went out together into the street, she stumbling as she walked, and proceeded down to the beach. Paulo stayed on the pavement while Gisa waded into the water, where she began swimming out to sea. Although he knew that with that amount of medication in her she would never have the strength to swim back, he waited, watching until she was just a black dot among the glittering waves, a black dot that was moving farther and farther away. 'I was scared, I wanted to give in, to call her, to tell her not to do it,' he wrote later, 'but I knew that Gisa wasn't going to die.'

Two men doing yoga on the beach went up to him, concerned that the girl was nearly out of sight, and said: 'We should call the lifeguard. The water's very cold and if she gets cramp she'll never get back.'

Paulo calmed them with a smile and a lie: 'No need, she's a professional swimmer.'

Half an hour later, when a group of people had begun to collect on the pavement, foreseeing a tragedy, Gisa began to swim back. When she reached the beach, pale and ghostly looking, she threw up, which probably saved her life, because she vomited up all the tablets. The muscles in her face and arms were stiff from the cold water and from the overdose. Paulo held her as they went to the house and then wrote the results of that 'cure by despair' in his diary:

> I'm thinking: Who's the Angel going to content himself with this time, now that Gisa is in my arms? She cried and was very tired, and of course she did still have eight tablets inside her. We came home, and she fell asleep on the carpet, but woke up looking quite different, with a new light in her eyes. For a while, we didn't go out for fear of contagion. The suicide epidemic was spreading like anything.

If anyone had looked through his diaries during the months prior to Gisa's attempted suicide, they would not have been surprised by Paulo's bizarre behaviour. Since reading Molinero's book, *The Secret Alchemy of Mankind*, he had become deeply immersed in the occult and in witchcraft. It was no longer just a matter of consulting gypsies, witch doctors and tarot readers. At one point, he had concluded that 'The occult is my only hope, the only visible escape'. As if he had put aside his dream of becoming a writer, he now concentrated all his energies on trying to 'penetrate deep into Magic, the last recourse and last exit for my despair'. He avidly devoured everything relating to sorcerers, witches and occult powers. On the bookshelves in the apartment he shared with Gisa, works by Borges and Henry Miller had given way to things such as *The Lord of Prophecy*, *The Book of the Last Judgement*, *Levitation* and *The Secret Power of the Mind*.

He would frequently visit Ibiapas, 100 kilometres from Rio, where he would take purifying baths of black mud administered by a man known as 'Pajé Katunda'.

It was on one such trip that Paulo first attributed to himself the ability to interfere with the elements. 'I asked for a storm,' he wrote, 'and the most incredible storm immediately blew up.' However, his supernatural powers did not always work. 'I tried to make the wind blow, without success,' he wrote a little later, 'and I ended up going home frustrated.' Another trick that failed was his attempt to destroy something merely by the power of thought: 'Yesterday Gisa and I tried to break an ashtray by the power of thought, but it didn't work. And then, would you believe it, straight afterwards, while we were having lunch here, the maid came to say that she had broken the ashtray. It was bizarre.'

Sects had also become an obsession with Paulo. It might be Children of God or Hare Krishnas, followers of the Devil's Bible or even the faithful of the Church of Satan, whom he had met on his trip to the United States. All it took was a whiff of the supernatural – or of sulphur, depending on the case. Not to mention the myriad groups of worshippers of creatures from outer space or UFO freaks. He became so absorbed in the esoteric world that he eventually received an invitation to write in a publication devoted to the subject, the magazine *A Pomba*. Published by PosterGraph, a small publishing house dedicated to underground culture and printing political posters, this contained a miscellany of articles and interviews on subjects of interest to hippie groups: drugs, rock, hallucinations and paranormal experiences. Printed in black and white, every issue carried a photographic essay involving some naked woman or other, just like men's magazines, the difference being that the models for *A Pomba* appeared to be women recruited from among the employees in the building where the magazine was produced. Like dozens of other, similar publications, *A Pomba* had no influence, although it must have had a reasonable readership, since it managed to survive for seven months. For half the salary he received at the school, Paulo accepted the position of jack-of-all-trades on the magazine: he would choose the subjects, carry out the interviews, write articles. The visual aspect – design, illustrations and photographs – was Gisa's job. It appears to have been a good idea, because after only two issues under Paulo's editorship, the owner of PosterGraph, Eduardo Prado, agreed to his proposal to launch a second publication, entitled *2001*. With two publications to take care of, his salary doubled, and he had to give up teaching.

While he was doing research for an article on the Apocalypse, it was suggested to Paulo that he should go and see someone who called himself 'the heir of the Beast in Brazil', Marcelo Ramos Motta. He was surprised to find that the person he was to interview lived in a simple, austere apartment with good furniture and bookcases crammed with books. There was just one eccentric detail: all the books were covered with the same grey paper, without any indication as to the content apart from a small handwritten number at the foot of the spine. The other surprise was Motta's appearance. He wasn't wearing a black cloak and brandishing a trident, as Paulo had expected, but instead had on a smart navy-blue suit, white shirt, silk tie and black patent-leather shoes. He was sixteen years older than Paulo, tall and thin, with a thick black beard, and a very strange look in his eye. His voice sounded as if he were trying to imitate someone. He did not smile, but merely made a sign with his hand for the interviewer to sit down, and then sat down opposite him.

Paulo took his notepad out of his bag and, to break the ice, asked: 'Why are all the books covered in grey paper?'

The man did not appear in the mood for small talk and said: 'That's none of your business.'

Startled by his rudeness, Paulo began to laugh: 'I'm sorry, I didn't mean to offend you. I was just curious.'

Motta continued in the same vein: 'This is no matter for children.'

When the interview was over, Paulo wrote and published his article, but he couldn't stop thinking about that strange man and his library of books with blank spines. After several refusals, Motta agreed to meet him again and this time he opened the conversation by saying: 'I'm the world leader of a society called AA – Astrum Argentum.' He got to his feet, picked up a copy of The Beatles' record *Sgt. Pepper's Lonely Hearts Club Band* and pointed out one of the figures on the crowded collage on the cover. This was a bald, elderly man, the second along in the photo, next to an Indian guru: 'This man is called Aleister Crowley, and we are the proponents of his ideas in the world. Go and find out about him, and then we'll talk again.'

It was only after searching through libraries and second-hand book-shops that Paulo discovered that there were very few books available in Brazil about the old man on the cover of The Beatles' album, lost among the images of Mae West, Mahatma Gandhi, Hitler, Jesus Christ and Elvis Presley. While he was preparing to go back to speak to the mysterious Motta, he continued to produce the two magazines with Gisa. Since the budget was not enough to take on even one collaborator, he wrote almost everything. So that the readers would not realize what a tiny budget the magazines had to survive on, he used a variety of pseudonyms as well as his own name.

At the beginning of 1972, a stranger appeared in the office, which was a modest room on the tenth floor of a commercial building in the centre of Rio de Janeiro. He was wearing a shiny suit – one of those crease-resistant ones – and a thin tie, and carried an executive briefcase, and he announced that he wanted to talk to 'the writer Augusto Figueiredo'. At the time, Paulo did not connect the visitor with the person who had phoned him some days earlier, also asking for Augusto Figueiredo. It was enough to awaken his dormant paranoia. The man had the look of a policeman and must have come there after a tip-off, looking for drugs, perhaps. The problem was that Augusto Figueiredo did not exist; it was one of the names Paulo used to sign his articles.

Terrified, but trying to appear calm, he attempted to get rid of the visitor as quickly as possible, saying: 'Augusto isn't here. Do you want to leave a message?'

'No. I need to talk to him. Can I sit and wait for him?'

The man was definitely a policeman. He sat at a table, picked up an old copy of *A Pomba*, lit a cigarette and started to read, with the air of someone with all the time in the world. An hour later, he was still there. He had read every past copy of the magazine, but showed no sign of wanting to leave. Paulo recalled the lesson he had learned as a child, when jumping off the bridge into the river: the best way to curtail suffering was to face the problem head on. He decided to tell the truth – for he was absolutely certain this man was a policeman. First, though, he took the precaution of going through all the drawers in the office to make sure that there were no butts left over from cannabis joints.

He summoned up his courage and, blinking nervously, confessed that he had lied: 'You must forgive me, but there is no Augusto Figueiredo here. I'm the person who wrote the article, Paulo Coelho. What can I do for you?'

The visitor smiled broadly, held out his arms as if about to embrace him and said: 'Well, you're the person I want to talk to, man. How do you do? My name is Raul Seixas.'

CHAPTER 14

The Devil and Paulo

APART FROM THEIR INTEREST in flying saucers and having both been disastrous students during their adolescence, Raul Seixas and Paulo Coelho appeared to have little in common. Seixas was working as a music producer for a multinational recording company, CBS; his hair was always tidy and he was never seen without a jacket, tie and briefcase. He had never tried drugs, not even a drag on a cannabis joint. Coelho's hair, meanwhile, was long and unruly, and he wore hipsters, sandals, necklaces, and spectacles with octagonal purple lenses. He also spent much of his time under the influence of drugs. Seixas had a fixed address, and was a real family man, with a daughter, Simone, aged two, while Paulo lived in 'tribes' whose members came and went according to the seasons – in recent months his 'family' had been Gisa and Stella Paula, a pretty hippie from Ipanema who was as fascinated as he was by the occult and the beyond.

The differences between the two men were even more marked when it came to their cultural baggage. At twenty-five, Paulo had read and given stars to more than five hundred books, and he wrote articulately and fluently. As for Raul, despite having spent his childhood surrounded by his father's books – his father worked on the railways and was an occasional poet – he didn't seem particularly keen on reading. However, one date in their lives had different meanings but was equally important to each of them. On 28 June 1967, when Paulo was drugged and taken to the ninth floor of the Dr Eiras clinic for his third admission, Seixas was twenty-two and getting married to the American student Edith Wisner in Salvador, Bahia, where he was born. Both believed in astrology, and if they had studied their respective astrological charts they would have seen that the zodiac predicted one certain thing: the two were destined to make a lot of money, whatever they did.

When Raul Seixas entered his life, Paulo Coelho was immersed in the hermetic and dangerous universe of satanism. He had begun meeting Marcelo Ramos Motta more frequently and, after devouring weighty volumes on pentacles, mystical movements, magical systems and astrology, he could understand a little of the work of the bald man on The Beatles' LP cover. Born in Leamington Spa, England on 12 October 1875, Aleister Crowley was twenty-three when he reported that he had encountered in Cairo a being who transmitted to him the *Liber AL vel Legis* [*The Book of the Law*], which was his first and most important work on mysticism, the central sacred text of Thelema.

The Law of Thelema proclaimed the beginning of an era in which man would be free to realize all his desires. This was the objective contained in the epigraph 'Do what thou wilt shall be the whole of the Law', which was considered the basic rule of conduct by Crowley's followers. Among the instruments recommended to achieve this state were sexual freedom, the use of drugs and the rediscovery of oriental wisdom. In 1912, Crowley entered the sect known as Ordo Templi Orientis (OTO), a Masonic, mystical, magical type of organization of which he soon became the head and the principal theorist. He called himself 'the Beast', and built a temple in Cefalu, in Sicily, but was expelled from Italy by the Mussolini government in 1923, accused of promoting orgies. During the Second World War, Crowley was summoned by the writer Ian Fleming, creator of James Bond and an officer in British Naval Intelligence, to help the British consider how superstitions and mysticism among the Nazi leaders could be put to good use by the Allies. It was also Aleister Crowley who, through Fleming, suggested to Winston Churchill that he should use the V for Victory sign, which was, in fact, a sign of

Apophis-Typhon, a god of destruction capable of overwhelming the energies of the Nazi swastika.

Crowley's occult theories attracted various rock artists and groups
such as Black Sabbath, Iron Maiden and Ozzy Osbourne (who wrote the
classic 'Mr Crowley'). The famous Boleskine House, where Crowley lived
for several years, later became the property of Jimmy Page, the Led
Zeppelin guitarist. But the English Beast's ideas also inspired terrible
tragedies: in August 1969, his American disciple Charles Manson headed
the massacre of four people who were shot, stabbed and clubbed to death
in a mansion in Malibu. Among the victims was the actress Sharon Tate,
aged twenty-six, who was expecting a baby by her husband, the director
Roman Polanski.

Paulo appeared to be so influenced by these readings and supernatural practices that not even the atrocities committed by Manson brought
him back down to earth. The murderer of Sharon Tate was described as
'the most evil man on Earth' by the jury that condemned him to death,
although this sentence was subsequently commuted to life imprisonment.
When he read the news, Paulo wrote in his diary: 'The weapons of war
nowadays are the strangest you can find. Drugs, religion, fashion ... It's
something against which it's impossible to fight. When looked at like this,
Charles Manson is a crucified martyr.'

Until he met Paulo Coelho, Raul Seixas had never heard of Crowley
or of the nomenclature used by those people. He knew nothing about
Astrum Argentum, OTO or *Liber Oz*. He liked reading about flying
saucers, but the main object of his interest had always been music, and
more precisely rock and roll, a musical genre with which Paulo had only
a glancing relationship – he liked Elvis Presley, knew the most famous
groups and that was it. Seixas' passion for rock music had meant him
repeating his second year at São Bento College in Salvador three times,
and at eighteen he had had some success in performances in Bahia as
leader of the group Os Panteras – The Panthers. However, at the insistence of his future father-in-law, an American Protestant pastor, he abandoned his promising musical career and returned to his studies. He made
up for lost time with a revision course, and when he took his entrance
exams for the law faculty, he was among the top entrants. 'I just wanted

to prove to people, to my family, how easy it was to study and pass exams,' he said many years later, 'when for me it wasn't important in the least.' During the first months of his marriage, he supported the family by giving guitar and English lessons. Before he was even three months into his marriage, though, Seixas succumbed to temptation.

In October 1967, the singer Jerry Adriani went to Salvador after being hired for a show at the smart Bahian Tennis Club, where the muse of bossa nova, Nara Leão, was also performing, along with the comedian Chico Anysio. Adriani was, by then, regarded as a national star among the youth music movement, Jovem Guarda, but dismissed by more sophisticated audiences as tacky. On the day of the show, a tennis club employee told the singer that his performance had been cancelled: 'The group you've hired has got several black musicians in it, and no blacks are allowed in the club.'

Although the Afonso Arinos law had been in place since 1951, making racial discrimination a crime, 'Blacks didn't enter the Club even through the kitchen door', in the words of the song 'Tradição', by another famous Bahian, Gilberto Gil. This prejudice was even harsher here, since this was a club in Bahia, a state where more than 70 per cent of the population were black and of mixed race. Instead of calling the police, the show's impresario chose to hire another group. The first he could think of were the defunct Os Panteras, who in the past few months had changed their name to The Panthers. Seixas was thrilled at the idea of reviving the group and went off into the city to look for his old accompanists: the bassist Mariano Lanat, the guitarist Perinho Albuquerque and the drummer Antônio Carlos Castro, or Carleba – all of them white. The show was a great success, and Os Panteras left the stage to loud applause. At the end of the show, Nara Leão whispered in Jerry Adriani's ear: 'That group are really good. Why don't you ask them to play with you?'

When, that evening, he received an invitation from the singer for the group to go with him on a tour of the north and the northeast, due to start the following week, Seixas was thrilled. An invitation to tour with a nationally famous artist such as Jerry Adriani wasn't one that was likely to come around twice. However, he also knew that accepting the proposal would be the end of his marriage, and that was too high a cost.

He said he was sorry, but he had to refuse: 'It would be an honour to go on tour with you, but if I leave home now, my marriage will be finished.'

Jerry Adriani doubled the stakes: 'If that's the problem, then problem solved: your wife is invited too. Bring her with you.'

As well as giving the couple a rather amusing, unusual honeymoon, the tour was so successful that when it ended, Jerry Adriani convinced Raul and his musicians to move to Rio and turn professional, and at the beginning of 1968 they were all in Copacabana. This adventure did not end happily. Although they managed to record one LP of their own, in the years that followed, the only work that came their way was playing as a backing group to Adriani. There were times when Seixas had to ask his father for a loan to pay the rent on the house where he, Edith and the other members of the group were living. Going back to Bahia because they had run out of money was a very hard thing to do, particularly for Raul, the leader of the group, but there was no other solution. Much against his will, he started giving English lessons again and was beginning to think that his musical career was over when a proposal came from Evandro Ribeiro, the director of CBS, to return to work in Rio, not as a band leader but as a music producer. His name had been suggested to the management of the record company by Jerry Adriani, who was interested in getting his friend back on the Rio–São Paulo circuit, which was the centre of Brazilian music production. Wanting to get even with the city that had defeated him, Seixas did not think twice. He asked Edith to organize the move and, a few days later, he was working, in jacket and tie, in the polluted city centre of Rio, where the CBS offices were. Within a few months, he had become music producer to various well-known artists, starting with Adriani.

At the end of May 1972, Raul had walked the seven blocks between the CBS building and the offices of *A Pomba* not merely to praise the non-existent Augusto Figueiredo's writings on extraterrestrials. He had in his briefcase an article that he himself had written on flying saucers and wanted to know if *A Pomba* might be interested in publishing it. Paulo politely accepted it, said that he would indeed be happy to publish the article, and drew him out on the subject of UFOs and life on other planets. He had an ulterior motive for this. The mention of CBS had sparked a rather more materialistic interest: since Raul enjoyed the magazine and was an executive in a multinational, he might well be persuaded to place advertisements for CBS in *A Pomba*. The short meeting ended with Raul inviting Paulo to dinner at his house the following night, a Thursday. At the time, Coelho never took any decision without consulting his 'family', Gisa and their flatmate, Stella Paula. Even something as banal as whether or not to go to someone's house was subjected to a vote: 'We had a truly ideological discussion in that tiny hippie group to decide whether or not we should go and have a drink at Raul's house.'

Even though he realized that, apart from an interest in UFOs, the two appeared to have nothing in common, Paulo, with one eye on the possibility of getting some advertising revenue from CBS, decided to accept the invitation. Gisa went with him, while Stella Paula, who was outvoted, felt no obligation to go along as well. On that Thursday evening, on his way to supper, Paulo stopped at a record shop and bought an LP of Bach's Organ Preludes. The bus taking them from Flamengo to Jardim de Alah – a small, elegant district between Ipanema and Leblon, in the south of Rio, where Raul lived – was stopped at a police checkpoint. Since the crackdown by the dictatorship in December 1968, such checks had become part of life for Brazilians in the large cities. However, when Gisa saw the police get on the bus and start asking the passengers to show their papers, she felt it was a bad sign, a warning, and threatened to call off the meeting. Paulo, however, would not be moved, and at eight that evening, as agreed, they rang the bell of Raul's apartment.

The meeting lasted three hours. When he left, the obsessive Paulo stopped at the first bar they came to and scribbled on the cover of his Bach LP every detail of their visit to the man he still referred to as 'the guy'. Every blank space on the record cover was taken up with tiny, almost illegible writing:

> We were greeted by his wife, Edith, and a little girl who must have been three at most. It was all very respectable, very proper. They brought in little dishes with canapés … It's years since I've eaten in

someone's house where they had little dishes with canapés. Canapés, how ridiculous!

So then the guy comes in: 'Would you like a whisky?'

Well, of course we wanted a whisky! A rich man's drink. Dinner was hardly over and Gisa and I were desperate to leave.

Then Raul said: 'Oh, I wanted to play you some of my music.'

Oh, shit, we were going to have to listen to music as well. All I wanted was to get some advertising out of him. We went into the maid's room and he picked up his guitar and played some marvellous music. When he finished, the guy said to me: 'You wrote that stuff on flying saucers, didn't you? Well, I'm planning on going back to being a singer. Would you like to write some lyrics for me?'

I thought: Write lyrics? Me write lyrics for this guy who's never touched drugs in his life! Never put a joint in his mouth. Not even an ordinary cigarette. Anyway, we were just leaving and I hadn't yet mentioned the advertisement. I plucked up courage and asked: 'Since we're going to publish your article, do you think you could manage to get an advertisement for CBS in the magazine?'

Imagine my astonishment when he said that he had resigned from CBS that very day: 'I'm moving to Philips because I'm going to follow my dream. I wasn't born to be a manager, I want to be a singer.'

At that moment I understood: I'm the conventional one, this guy deserves the greatest respect. A guy who leaves a job that gives him everything, his daughter, his wife, his maid, his family, his canapés! I left feeling really impressed with the guy.

Gisa's premonitions were not entirely unfounded. She had mistaken the year, but not the date. While it marked Paulo's first step in the direction of one of his dreams – fame – 25 May was, by coincidence, going to be a crucial date, a watershed in his life: the day chosen by destiny, some years later, for his first appointment with the Devil, a ceremony he was preparing for when he met Raul Seixas. Under Marcelo Ramos Motta's guidance he felt he was a disciple of the Beast's battalions. He was determined to immerse himself in the malignant forces that had seduced Lennon and Charles Manson, and began the process by being accepted into the OTO as a 'probationer', the lowest rank in the sect's hierarchy. He was fortunate that his guide was not Motta but another militant in the organization, a graduate employee of Petrobras, Euclydes Lacerda de Almeida, whose magical name was Frater Zaratustra, or Frater Z, and who lived in Paraíba do Sul, 150 kilometres from Rio. 'I received a letter, rude as ever, from Marcelo,' Paulo wrote to Frater Z when he heard the news. 'I'm forbidden from contacting him except through you.' It was a relief to have a well-educated man like Euclydes as his instructor rather than the uncouth Marcelo Motta, who treated all his subordinates appallingly. Extracts from letters sent to militants of the OTO by Parzival XI (as Motta self-importantly called himself) show that Paulo was being quite restrained when describing the leader of the followers of the Devil as 'rude':

> I'd prefer you not to write to me any more. If you do, send a stamped, addressed envelope for the reply – or you won't get a reply.
>
> [...] Be aware of just where you are on the vertebrate scale, monkey!
>
> [...] If you're incapable of getting up on your own two legs and looking for the Way through your own efforts then stay on all fours and howl like the dog you are!
>
> [...] You're no more than a drop of shit on the end of the monkey's cock.
>
> [...] If suddenly your favourite son, or you, were to fall ill with a fatal disease that required an expensive operation and you could only use OTO money, then rather let your son die, or die yourself, than touch the money.
>
> [...] You haven't seen anything yet. Wait until your name is known as a member of the OTO. The Army's secret service, the CIA, Shin-Beth [Israeli military intelligence], the Russians, the Chinese and innumerable Roman priests disguised as members of the sect will try to get in contact with you.

On at least two occasions Paulo's name appears in correspondence from Parzival XI to Euclydes. In the first, one gets the impression that Paulo will be working on the publication by Editora Três, in São Paulo, of the book *The Equinox of the Gods*, by Crowley and translated into Portuguese by Motta: 'I got in touch with Editora Três through their representative in Rio, and we shall soon see whether or not they're going to publish *Equinox of the Gods*. Paulo Coelho is young, enthusiastic and imaginative, but it's too early for us to assume that they really will publish the book.' In the second, Euclydes is castigated for having told Paulo too much and too soon about Parzival XI's power: 'Paulo Coelho said that you told him I destroyed the Masons in Brazil. You talk too much. Even if it were true, Paulo Coelho doesn't have the magical maturity to understand how these things are done, which is why he's confused.'

At the time, Paulo had had his own experiences of being in contact with the Devil. Some months before getting to know Motta and the OTO, during one of his regular anxiety crises, he was full of complaints. The reasons were many, but behind them lay the usual fact: he was nearly twenty-five and still just a nobody, without the remotest chance of becoming a famous writer. The situation seemed hopeless and the pain this time was such that, instead of asking for help from the Virgin Mary or St Joseph as he usually did, he decided to make a pact with the Prince of Darkness. If the Devil gave him the power to realize all his dreams, Paulo would give him his soul in exchange. 'As an educated man who knows the philosophical principles that govern the world, humanity and the Cosmos,' Paulo wrote in his diary, 'I know perfectly well that the Devil does not signify Evil, but just one of the poles in the equilibrium of humanity.' Using a fountain pen with red ink ('the colour of this supernatural being'), he began to write out his pact in the form of a letter to the Devil. In the first line he made it clear that he was setting out the conditions and was not willing to deal with intermediaries:

> You have wanted this for a long time. I felt that You were beginning to close the circle around me and I know that You are stronger than I am. You are more interested in buying my soul than I am in selling it. Whatever the case, I need to have an idea of the price that You

are going to pay me. For this reason, from today, 11 November 1971, until 18 November, I'm going to do an experiment. I will speak directly to You, the King of the Other Pole.

In order to confirm this agreement he took a flower out of a vase and crushed it, at the same time proposing to Satan a kind of spectral test: 'I'm going to crush this flower and eat it. From now on, for the next seven days, I'm going to do everything I want and I'm going to get what I want, because You will be helping me. If I'm satisfied with the results, I will give You my soul. If a ritual is necessary, I take it upon myself to carry it out.'

As a proof of good faith, Paulo promised the Devil that, during this experimental period, he would reciprocate by not praying to or saying the names of those considered sacred by the Catholic Church. But he did make it clear that this was a test, not a lifelong contract. 'I retain the right to go back,' he went on, still in red, 'and I want to add that I'm only doing this because I find myself in such a state of complete despair.'

The agreement lasted less than an hour. He closed his notebook, and went out to have a cigarette and walk along the beach. When he returned home, he was deathly pale, terrified at the mad thing he had done. He opened his notebook again and wrote in capital letters that took up the whole page:

PACT CANCELLED
I OVERCAME TEMPTATION!

Paulo felt sure that he had tricked the Devil, but this ruse did not work for long. Although he and the Devil did not meet this time, he continued to invoke the spirit of evil in his articles for *A Pomba* and in a new enterprise in which he had become involved, the storyboards for comic strips. Beings from the Beyond created by him were brought to life in Gisa's drawings and began to illustrate the pages of the magazine. The positive reaction to the series *Os Vampiristas*, which told of the troubles and adventures of a small, peaceful solitary vampire, convinced Gisa to send her work to King Features, an American agency that distributed comic strips, but she received no reply. The couple did, though, manage to get some of their work into two of the main daily Rio newspapers, *O Jornal* and *Jornal do Brasil*, creating a special cartoon about the little vampire for the latter's children's supplement, which came out on Sundays. They also created a highly popular character, Curingão, whose image was used on lottery tickets. From time to time, one of their comic strips even appeared in *Pasquim*, the magazine favoured by the Rio intelligentsia.

A Pomba was managing to survive with almost no advertising revenue and even achieved sales of 20,000, a real achievement in the tiny counterculture market; however, by the middle of 1972, it was heavily in debt, and looked set to take *2001* down with it. When the publisher, Eduardo Prado, announced that he was thinking of closing both publications, Paulo and Gisa moved to the newspaper *Tribuna da Imprensa*, where they produced a whole page that was published on Saturdays and given the name of the magazine that had died after only two issues – *2001*.

This change of medium was another step towards their work emerging from the subworld of flying saucers, elves and sorcerers to reach a wider public. Although in comparison with the other Rio dailies, *Tribuna* didn't publish many copies, it had earned respect as a fighter. It had been founded in 1949 by the journalist Carlos Lacerda in order to combat the ideas, the supporters and the future government of President Getúlio Vargas (1951–4) and now, under the editorship of Hélio Fernandes, it was the favourite target for the military dictatorship's censors. The arrival of Paulo and Gisa in the old building on Rua do Lavradio, near Lapa, coincided with the most repressive period in the entire history of the dictatorship, and this was reflected in the daily life of the paper. For three years, the offices of *Tribuna* had been visited every night by army officers, who would read everything and then decide what could and could not be published. According to Hélio Fernandes, a fifth of their daily output was thrown in the rubbish bin by the censors. He himself was an example of what happened to those targeted by the regime's violence, for he had been arrested no fewer than twenty-seven times since 1964 and imprisoned twice. However, since the military were not too concerned about alchemy and the supernatural, the page produced by Paulo and Gisa remained untouched.

The visibility they achieved in the paper encouraged Paulo to go to the advertising department of Petrobras and show them a comic strip he and Gisa had created to be handed out at their petrol stations.

The man they met had approved the idea, but then Paulo, eager to make the project a success, said: 'Just so that there's no risk to Petrobras, we can work for free for the first month.'

The man turned round and said: 'For free? Sorry, but you're clearly a real amateur. Here no one does anything for free. Go and do a bit more work and try again when you're a professional.'

In August, while he was still smarting from this rejection, Paulo received an invitation to go with his mother and maternal grandmother, Lilisa, for a three-week trip to Europe. He was heavily into his journalistic work, and hesitated before agreeing, but then it wasn't every day that one was invited on a trip to Europe with all expenses paid. Added to this, he could leave several cartoons ready as well as the *Tribuna* page for Gisa to illustrate and design while he was away, since his mother's invitation did not include his girlfriend. During the twenty-one day trip, which started in Nice and ended in Paris, with stops in Rome, Milan, Amsterdam and London, Paulo visited museums, ruins and cathedrals. Apart from two or three occasions in Amsterdam, when he escaped his mother's vigilance in order to smoke a joint, the trip meant that he went almost a month without his daily intake of drugs.

Having been brought up by a methodical, obsessive mother, Paulo was furious with what he found when he arrived home. He wrote: 'The house is a complete tip, which really annoyed me. It hasn't even been swept. The electricity bill hasn't been paid, nor has the rent. The page for *Tribuna* hasn't been handed in, which is utterly irresponsible. I'm so upset by all this that I have nothing else to say.'

However, not everything was bad. While he was away, a tempting invitation had arrived in the post. Professor Glória Albues, who worked for the education department in Mato Grosso, had finally organized a project that the two had thought up when they had met up in Rio. The idea was that Paulo would spend three weeks every two months in three cities in Mato Grosso – Campo Grande, Três Lagoas (now in Mato Grosso do Sul, a state that did not exist at the time) and Cuiabá – teaching a course in

theatre and education for teachers and pupils in state schools. The salary
was tempting – 1,500 cruzeiros a month, which was double what he
earned on *A Pomba* and *2001*. There was another reason that led Paulo to
exchange the delights of Rio for the inhospitable lands of Mato Grosso.
When the idea for the course had first come up, he hadn't been involved
with the OTO, but now, eager to spread Crowley's ideas, the thought came
to him: Why not change the course into a black magic workshop?

CHAPTER 15

Paulo and Raul

EITHER ALONE OR WITH GISA, who was following him on his journey to satanism, Paulo began to try out some so-called magical exercises. One he frequently performed consisted in going to a park to pick a leaf of *Sansevieria trifasciata*, a plant with hard, pointed leaves, popularly known in English as mother-in-law's-tongue and in Brazil as St George's sword. Performed in public, this exercise was likely to expose the novice to a certain amount of ridicule, since it was then necessary to walk ten steps holding the plant as though it were a real sword, turn towards the setting sun and then bow to the four points of the compass, pointing the 'sword' at each and shouting at the top of one's voice: 'Strength lies in the West!' Each step to the left was accompanied by a roar, with eyes raised heavenwards: 'Knowledge lies in the South! Protection lies in the East! Victory lies in the North!'

He would then take the leaf home, where he would cut it into eleven pieces (eleven being the Thelemites' magic number) with a penknife or an ordinary knife that he had previously thrust into the ground, and then heated over a fire and washed in sea water. After this he would arrange the eleven pieces on the kitchen table to form the symbol of Mars – a circle topped by a small arrow, which also represents the male sex – while boiling up some water in a saucepan. He would then mix the pieces up with the torn petals of two yellow roses and add them to the boiling water. The entire ceremony had to be performed so that the thick, viscous liquid thus produced would be ready at precisely eleven at night, which, according to the *Liber Oz*, is the hour of the Sun. He would then add it to his bath water, in which he would immerse himself until midnight, the hour of Venus. After performing one such ceremony, Paulo dried himself and wrote in his diary, with the house in almost total darkness and his notebook lit just by a single candle:

> I realize that this ritual might appear naive. It lasted in total almost two hours. But all I can say is that for the greater part of the time I was in touch with a different dimension, where things are interconnected in the Laws (Second Causes). I can feel the mechanism, but I am not yet able to understand it. Nor can I rationalize the mechanism. I feel only that intuition works in close conjunction with rationalization and that these two spheres almost touch each other. Something leads me to believe that the Devil really does exist.

Another ceremony he frequently performed was the so-called 'Ritual of the Lesser Pentagram', which involved spreading out on the floor a white sheet on which one had to paint a green five-pointed star. The star was surrounded by a length of twine dipped in sulphur, with which Paulo would draw the symbol of Mars. He would turn off all the lights, and then hang a lamp from the ceiling, immediately above the centre of the pentagram, so that it created a column of light. With sword in hand and completely naked, he would turn to the south, step into the middle of the sheet and adopt the 'Dragon pose' – a yoga position in which the person crouches on the floor with one leg forward and the other back – and then jump up and down like a toad while repeating invocations to the Devil. On one of these occasions, the ceremony ended very strangely, as he recorded in his diary:

> After half an hour, my personal problems began seriously to interfere with my concentration, thus wasting a great deal of energy. I

changed from the Dragon pose to the Ibis pose, finally crouching in
the centre of the circle, shaking my body. This made me sexually
excited and I ended up masturbating, even though I was only thinking about the column of light over the circle. I ejaculated into the
column of light in several successive spasms. This brought me a feeling of total confirmation. Obviously I felt very guilty while I was
masturbating, but this soon passed, so profound was my state of
ecstasy.

It was during this time that Paulo was preparing for his first stay in Mato
Grosso. He left various texts and storyboards ready for *Tribuna* and the
other publications he was working for and typed out a programme for the
course. Anyone not in the know would have had difficulty identifying any
magical or satanic content. 'I used this trick on purpose, so that no one
would realize,' he confessed years later, 'because I knew it was an act of
supreme irresponsibility to use magical techniques and rituals in order to
give classes to teachers and adolescents … There I was performing black
magic: I was using them without their knowledge, innocently, for my own
magical experiments.' Before leaving, Paulo asked permission from Frater
Zaratustra to use Hermes Trismegistus' *Emerald Tablet* on the course. This
was a text containing such statements as: 'By this means wilt thou partake
of the honours of the whole world. And Darkness will fly from thee', and
'With this thou wilt be able to overcome all things and transmute all that
is fine and all that is coarse.'

Unaware that they were to be used as guinea pigs in the experiments
of a satanic sect, the people of Mato Grosso received him with open
arms. The local press heralded his arrival at each of the towns partici-
pating in the project with praise, hyperbole and even a pinch of fantasy.
After comparing him with Plínio Marcos and Nelson Rodrigues, two of the
greatest names in Brazilian drama, the Campo Grande *Diário da Serra*
congratulated the government for having invited Paulo to bring to Mato
Grosso a course 'that was crowned with success in Rio de Janeiro, Belém
do Pará and Brasília'. The treatment conferred on him by the *Jornal do
Povo*, in Três Lagoas, was even more lavish:

Now it's the turn of Três Lagoas. We have the opportunity to experience one of the great names in Brazilian theatre: Paulo Coelho. He
may not look it, but Paulo Coelho is a great man! The prototype of
concrete art, in which everything is strong, structured and growing ...
Such a figure could not help but be noticed, and that is what drives
him on and what makes of him a natural communicator. While not
wishing to exaggerate, we could compare him symbolically with
Christ, who also came to create.

He had not received such reverential attention since Aracaju, when he
had plagiarized an article by Carlos Heitor Cony. Cast in the role of full-
time missionary, Paulo took advantage of his few free hours to become
still more steeped in mysticism, and it didn't much matter to him how he
gained access to this mysterious world. In Três Lagoas, 'with the help of
a Tibetan who is there fulfilling a mission', he went to the headquarters
of the Brazilian Society of Eubiosis, a group that argued for living in
harmony with nature, and also the Masonic lodge of the Grand Order of
Brazil. When he learned that there was a village of acculturated Indians
on the edge of the city, he decided to visit them in order to find out about
native witchcraft. After his three weeks were up, he recorded the first
results of his time there:

At the beginning my work with the *Emerald Tablet* was a real disappointment. No one really understood how it worked (not even me,
despite all the workshops and improvisations I had done). All the
same the seed was sown in the minds of the students and some of
them really changed their way of thinking and began to think in
different ways. One female pupil went into a trance during a class.
The vast majority reacted negatively and the work only took on
some meaning on the last day of the classes when I managed one
way or another to break down their emotional barriers. Obviously,
I'm talking about a purely theatrical use of the *Tablet*. Perhaps if the
last day had been the first I could have done something interesting
with them.

Ah, before I forget: one day, I went for a walk in the city to collect some plants (I had just finished reading Paracelsus and was going to perform a ceremony) and I saw a cannabis plant growing outside a branch of the Bank of Brazil. Imagine that!

On his return to Rio, Paulo learned from a colleague at *Tribuna* that the editorial team at *O Globo* was looking for staff. The idea of writing for what claimed to be 'the greatest newspaper in the country' was very tempting, and he managed to arrange an interview with Iran Frejat, the much-feared editor. If he got a job there, he would have at his disposal a fantastic means of spreading the ideals of the OTO. Several times in his correspondence with Frater Zaratustra he had suggested allowing the weekly page in *Tribuna* to be used by the sect, but they had never asked him to do so. When he told Raul Seixas of his interest in a position at *O Globo*, his friend tried to dissuade him from the idea, again suggesting a musical partnership: 'Forget it. Don't go and work for some newspaper, let's write music. TV Globo are going to re-record *Beto Rockefeller* [an innovative and very successful soap opera that was shown on the now defunct TV Tupi from 1968 to 1969] and they've asked me to write the soundtrack. Why don't we do it together? I'll write the music and you can write the lyrics.'

While Paulo was still torn between the supernatural and the need to earn a living, Raul was building his career as a singer, devoting himself entirely to music. He had an LP on sale – *Sociedade da Grã Ordem Kavernista*, which was recorded almost secretly at CBS a few weeks before he resigned – and he was getting ready for the seventh International Song Festival being put on by Rede Globo. For Paulo, accepting a partnership would mean going back to poetry, which he had sworn never to do. For the moment at least the position at *O Globo* seemed more achievable and this was what he was going to try for.

He turned up at the appointed time for his interview with Frejat, introduced himself to the chief reporter, who appeared to be in a very bad mood, and sat down in a corner of the office waiting to be called. Before leaving home, he had put a book of poems by St John of the Cross in his bag to help take his mind off things while waiting. At two in the afternoon, an hour after he had arrived, Frejat had still not even so much as glanced at him, although he had walked past him several times, giving orders and handing out papers to various desks. Paulo stood up, got himself a coffee, lit a cigarette and sat down again. When the clock showed three he lost patience. He ripped the pages out of the book he was reading, tore them into tiny pieces, gathered them up and deposited them on Frejat's desk.

This unexpected gesture caught the journalist by surprise, and he burst out laughing and said: 'What's up, boy? Have you gone mad?'

Paulo said quietly, but forcefully: 'I've been waiting for two hours – didn't you notice? Are you behaving like this just because I want a job? That's so disrespectful!'

Frejat's response was a surprising one: 'Oh, I'm sorry. I didn't realize you were here for the job. Well, let's give you a test. If you pass it, the job's yours. You can start now. Go to the Santa Casa and count the dead.'

The dead? Yes, one of his daily tasks would be to go to the Santa Casa de Misericórdia and to two other large hospitals in Rio to get lists of the names of the dead, which would then appear on the newspaper's obituary pages the following day. In spite of his previous experience on *Diário de Notícias* and *Tribuna*, he was going to start at *O Globo* as a cub reporter. As a trainee, on the lowest rung of the ladder, he would work seven hours a day, with one day off a week, for a salary of 1,200 cruzeiros a month – some US$408. His first weeks at the paper were spent on 'reports on still lives', or 'coverage of a pacifist demonstration' as he called his daily visits to the city's mortuaries. The famous, such as politicians and artists, were the domain of the more experienced reporters, who would write obituaries or 'memorials'. When this macabre daily round finished early he would go to the red light district of Mangue to chat to the prostitutes.

Although he didn't have a formal contract, which was the case with the majority of cub reporters on most Brazilian newspapers (meaning that they had no form of social security), he could have his meals at *O Globo*'s very cheap canteen. For a mere 6 cruzeiros – US$1.75 – he could have lunch or dinner in the canteen, along with the owner of *O Globo*, Roberto Marinho. A few days after meeting Marinho in the canteen queue, Paulo learned from Frejat that 'Dr Roberto', as he was known, had issued an ultimatum: either Paulo cut his hair, which at the time was down to his shoulders, or he need not return to the office. Working on *O Globo* was more important than having long hair, and so he gave in to the demand without protest and trimmed his black mane.

Paulo was, in fact, used to report on two or three emergency situations, which meant that his superiors could see that this cub reporter with dark circles under his eyes knew how to write and had the confidence to carry out an interview. While he was never singled out to report on matters of major importance, he went out on to the streets every day with the other more experienced reporters, and, unlike some of them, he almost never returned empty-handed. What his superiors didn't know was that when he failed to find the interviewees he needed, he simply made them up. On one such occasion, he was told to file a report on people whose work centred on Carnival. He spent the day out in the streets, returned to the office and, in the early evening, handed to his editor, the experienced Henrique Caban, five pages of interviews with, among others, 'Joaquim de Souza, nightwatchman', 'Alice Pereira, waitress' and 'Adilson Lopes de Barros, bar owner'. The article ended with an 'analysis of the behaviour of the inhabitants of Rio during Carnival', a statement made by a 'psychologist' going by the highly suspicious name of 'Adolfo Rabbit'. That night Paulo noted at the top of his carbon copy of the article, which he had taken home, something that neither Caban nor anyone else would ever know: 'This material was COMPLETELY invented.'

While he may occasionally have resorted to such low stratagems, he was, in fact, doing well at the newspaper. Less than two months after starting work, he saw one of his interviews – a real one this time – with Luis Seixas, the president of the National Institute of Social Security (INPS), on the front page of the next day's edition of *O Globo*: 'Free medicine from the INPS'. Following this he was given the news that if he moved to being *pauteiro de madrugada* (sub-editor on the early-morning shift), he would receive a 50-per-cent salary increase. Most applicants for the position were put off by having to work every day from two until nine in the morning; however, for an insomniac like him, this was no problem.

The *pauteiro* began by reading all the competing newspapers, the first editions of which had been bought at the newspaper stands in the centre

of town, and comparing them with the early edition of *O Globo*, in order
to decide which items might be worth including in later editions of *O
Globo*. Once this was done, he would listen to the radio news to see what
were going to be the major news items of the day and then draw up
guidelines for the reporters when they arrived at nine o'clock as to what
they should investigate and whom they should interview. He also had to
decide which of the night's events, if any, merited the presence of a
reporter or photographer. At first, he longed for something important to
happen while he was working. 'One of these days, some really big news
story will break while I'm on duty, and I'll have to cover it,' he noted in his
diary. 'I'd prefer a different shift, but working this one isn't unpleasant, if
it weren't for that bastard Frejat, who keeps me hanging on here in the
morning.' During his six months in the post, only one thing required him
to mobilize reporters and photographers: the murder of the footballer
Almir Albuquerque, or 'Pernambuquinho', a forward in the Flamengo football team, who was shot by Portuguese tourists during a fight in the Rio
Jerez restaurant in the South Zone of the city. Mostly, though, the nights
passed without incident, which left time for him, as he sat alone in the
office, to fill pages of notes that he later stuck into his diary.

I don't think Frejat likes me. He told someone that I'm a 'pseudo-
intellectual'.

[…] As I said to Gisa, what I like about journalism is that no one
lasts long … Frejat's fall is long overdue and it's going to happen,
because the whole production team is pressing for it. There are no
nice people in journalism. Anyone nice is basically fucked.

[…] I read in the newspaper that someone knifed his wife to death
because she never did anything. I'm going to cut out the article and
leave it for Gisa to read. I hope she gets the message.

[…] Adalgisa went to Minas leaving the house a complete tip. She
didn't hand in our pages to *Tribuna*, she didn't pay the electricity bill
and she didn't even wash any clothes. These things make me so
angry. It seems that she hasn't got the slightest idea of what living
together means. Now I've got no cash to pay the electricity bill and
the house is going to be in darkness. When she spoke to me on the

phone she said that she's had too much work, but it's nothing to do with that. She's just completely irresponsible.

Before joining *O Globo* Paulo had agreed to lead the drama course in Mato Grosso, and at the end of 1972, after much insistence, he managed to get the newspaper to give him three weeks' unpaid leave. However, at the beginning of the following year the problem arose again. 'I'm going to have to choose between the course in Mato Grosso and the work here on the biggest newspaper in the country,' he wrote in his diary. 'Caban says I can't go, and if I have to give up one of them, I'm going to have to leave the paper.' Besides, Raul Seixas was continuing to pursue him with the idea of working together, and to show that his interest in having him as a lyricist was genuine, Seixas had done a very seductive thing: he let it be known that the song 'Caroço de Manga', which he had written for the theme music of the new version of *Beto Rockefeller*, was in fact by him and Paulo Coelho. Although it was not uncommon in the recording world for a composer to 'share authorship' of a composition with a friend, this also meant an equal division of any royalties. Raul Seixas was slowly beginning to win a place in his life. Paulo wrote:

> It's so peaceful working at night. I didn't take a bath today. I slept from nine in the morning until seven at night. I got up to find that Gisa hadn't done any work. We telephoned Raul telling him that we can't meet him today.
>
> [...] I'm tired. I spent all day typing and now I can't remember the music I promised Raul.
>
> [...] Raul is full of silly scruples about writing commercial music. He doesn't understand that the more you control the media, the more influence you have.

As he had foreseen, in April 1973, Paulo had to decide whether or not to continue at *O Globo*. As had become his normal practice whenever he had to make a decision, however unimportant, he left it to the I Ching or the Book of Changes, to choose. He was alone at home and, after a period of concentration, he threw the three coins of the Chinese oracle on the table and noted in his diary the hexagrams that were revealed. There was no doubt: the I Ching warned him against working on the newspaper and advised him that it would mean 'a slow and prolonged exercise leading to misfortune'. He needed nothing more. The following morning, his short-lived career on *O Globo* came to an end. The outcome had been good, even as regards his bank balance. The money he had earned by selling his and Gisa's cartoons, along with what he had been paid for the course at Mato Grosso, their page in *Tribuna* and his work at *O Globo*, not only covered his day-to-day expenses but meant that he, ever cautious, could start investing his modest savings in the stock market. 'I lost my money buying shares in the Bank of Brazil. I'm ruined ...' he recorded at one stage in his diary, only to cheer up a few days later. 'The shares in Petrobras that were only 25 when I bought them are at 300 today.'

Between the time when he resigned from *O Globo* and the start of his partnership with Raul Seixas, Paulo did a little of everything. Alongside the various other bits of work he had been doing, he did some teaching and some theatre directing, and worked as an actor in a soft-porn movie. No longer having to spend his nights working in the editorial office, which had meant he had to sleep during the day, he began to meet up with Raul either at his place or his own in order to begin their much-postponed part-nership. The thought of working together had another attraction for Paulo: if 'Caroço de Manga' was already generating substantial royalties, what would he earn if he were the lyricist on a hit song?

As someone who, in a very short space of time, had composed more than eighty songs recorded by various artistes – although he claimed not to like any of them – Raul had enough experience to be able to rid Paulo of any negative feelings he might still have about writing poetry. 'You don't have to say things in a complicated way when you want to speak seriously to people,' Raul would say during their many conversations. 'In fact, the simpler you are the more serious you can be.' 'Writing music is like writing a story in twenty lines that someone can listen to ten times without getting bored. If you can do that, you'll have made a huge leap: you'll have written a work of art everyone can understand.'

And so they began. As the months went by, the two became not just musical partners but great friends or, as they liked to tell journalists, 'close enemies'. They and their partners went out together and visited each other often. It did not take much for Raul and Edith to be seduced by the disturbing allure of drugs and black magic. At the time, in fact, drugs had taken second place in Paulo's life, such was his fascination for the mysteries revealed to him by Frater Zaratustra and the OTO. The much proclaimed 'close enmity' between Paulo and Raul wasn't just an empty expression, and appears to have arisen along with their friendship. While Raul had opened the doors of fame and fortune to his new friend, it was Paulo who knew how to reach the world of secret things, a universe to which ordinary mortals had no access. Raul held the route to fame, but it was Paulo who knew the way to the Devil.

The first fruits of their joint labours appeared in 1973 as an LP, *Krig-Ha, Bandolo!*, the title being taken from one of Tarzan's war cries. Of the five songs with lyrics by Paulo, only one, 'Al Capone', became a hit that people would hum in the street. *Krig-Ha* also revealed Raul Seixas to be an excellent lyricist in his own right. At least three of the songs he composed and wrote – 'Mosca na Sopa', 'Metamorfose Ambulante' and 'Ouro de Tolo' – continued to be played on the radio years after his death in 1989. The LP may not have been a blockbuster, but it meant that Paulo finally saw money pouring into his bank account. When he asked for his balance at his branch of the Banco do Brasil in Copacabana a few weeks after the launch of *Krig-Ha*, he couldn't believe it when he saw that the record company, Philips, had deposited no less than 240 million cruzeiros – about US$200,000 – which, to him, was a real fortune.

The success of the disc meant that Paulo and Gisa, Raul and Edith could really push the boat out. They flew to the United States and, after spending a childish week at Disney World in Florida, visited Memphis, the birthplace of Elvis Presley, and then spent a glorious, hectic month in New York. On one of their many outings in the Big Apple, the two couples knocked at the door of the Dakota building, the grey, neo-Gothic, somewhat sinister apartment block opposite Central Park where John Lennon lived and which had also provided the setting for that classic of satanism, *Rosemary's Baby*, directed by Roman Polanski. With typical Brazilian immodesty, Paulo and Raul seemed to assume that the success of *Krig-Ha* was recommendation enough for these two puny rockers to fraternize with the unassailable writer of 'Imagine'. On their return to Brazil, Paulo and Raul gave several interviews, some for international publications, in which they gave details of their conversation with Lennon, who despite a heavy cold had, according to them, received them with his wife, Yoko Ono, to chat, swap compositions and even consider the possibility of working together. A press release described their meeting:

> We only got to meet John Lennon the day before our return. We went there with a journalist from a Brazilian TV channel. As soon as we sat down, the journalist asked about his separation from Yoko. John immediately told the journalist to leave, saying that he wasn't going to waste his time on gossip. Because of this, the meeting began rather tensely, with John warning us that he would take a very dim view of any attempt on our part to capitalize on our meeting for the purposes of promoting ourselves in Brazil. After a few minutes, the tension lifted and we talked non-stop for half an hour about the present and the future. The results of this meeting will be revealed bit by bit as the situation develops.

It was a complete lie. As time went by the truth behind the story emerged. Paulo and Raul never visited John Lennon's apartment; nor were they received by Yoko Ono. The nearest they got to John Lennon was the porter at the Dakota building, who merely informed them over the intercom that 'Mr Lennon is not at home'. The same press release included another invention: that Lennon had been most impressed by the project Paulo and Raul were preparing to launch in Brazil, the Sociedade Alternativa, the Alternative Society.

The plan was to create a community based on an experiment developed by Aleister Crowley at the beginning of the twentieth century in Cefalu, in Sicily. The place chosen as the site of the 'City of the Stars', as Raul called it, was Paraíba do Sul, where Euclydes Lacerda, or Frater Zaratustra, lived. Raul had absorbed the world of drugs and magic so quickly that a year after his first meeting with Paulo, there was no sign of the smart businessman who had come to the office of *Pomba* to discuss flying saucers. He now sported a thick beard and a magnificent mane of black hair, and had started dressing extravagantly as well, favouring flares that were very tight in the leg and very wide at the bottom, and lamé jackets which he wore without a shirt underneath, thus revealing his pale, sunken, bony chest.

When they returned from their American trip, Raul and Paulo began to create what was to be by far their greatest success – the LP *Gita*. Of the eleven songs chosen for the disc, seven had lyrics by Paulo and of these at least three became the duo's theme tunes – 'Medo da Chuva', 'Gita' and 'Sociedade Alternativa'. 'Medo da Chuva' revealed the lyricist's somewhat unorthodox views on marriage ('It's a pity that you think I'm your slave/Saying that I'm your husband and I can't leave/Like the stones on the beach I stay at your side/Knowing nothing of the loves life brought me, but that I never knew ...'). The title song, 'Gita', was no more than a translation of the dialogue between Krishna and Arjuna found in *Bhagavad Gita*, the Hindu sacred text which they had just read. The most intriguing song on the album, though, was the sixth, 'Sociedade Alternativa' – or, rather, what was intriguing was what the words concealed. At first sight, the words appear to be an innocent surrealist game based on a single chorus, which is repeated throughout the song:

> If I want and you want
> To take a bath in a hat
> Or to wait for Father Christmas
> Or to talk about Carlos Gardel
> Then let's do it!

It was the refrain that opens and closes the piece that concealed the mystery.

> Do what you want is the whole of the law.
> Viva! Viva! Viva the Sociedade Alternativa!

As if wanting to leave no doubt as to their intentions, the authors transcribed word for word entire texts from the *Liber Oz*, finally showing their hand and making their allegiances crystal clear. While Raul sang the refrain, a backing track of his own voice sang:

> Number 666 is called Aleister Crowley!
> Viva! Viva!
> Viva the Sociedade Alternativa!
> The law of Thelema
> Viva! Viva!
> Viva the Sociedade Alternativa!
> The law of the strong
> That is our law and the joy of the world
> Viva! Viva!
> Viva the New Age!

Although only the few initiates to the world of Crowley would understand this, Paulo Coelho and Raul Seixas had decided to become the spokesmen of OTO and, therefore, of the Devil. For many of their audience this was a coded message written to confuse the censors and arguing for a new society as an alternative to the military dictatorship. This also seemed to be the government's view, because when 'Sociedade Alternativa' was released, the censors forbade Raul to sing it when he toured Brazil.

With or without censorship, the fact is that everything was going so well that Paulo concluded that his days of material and emotional penury were over. That evening, as he sometimes did, instead of writing, he recorded his diary on tape, talking as if he were on stage:

> On 15 April 1974, at the age of twenty-six, I, Paulo Coelho, finally finished paying for my crimes. Only at twenty-six did I become fully aware of this. Now give me my reward.
> I want what's due to me.
> And what's due to me will be whatever I want!
> And I want money!
> I want power!
> I want fame, immortality and love!

While he was waiting for his other wishes to come true, he enjoyed the money, fame and love that had already come his way. At the beginning of May, Raul invited him and Gisa to go to Brasília, where he was going to do three shows during the Festival of the Nations being held in the federal capital on 10, 11 and 12 May. At the same time, they were going to start promoting the LP *Gita*, which was to be launched a few weeks later. A slave to the I Ching, Paulo threw the three coins several times until it was confirmed that the trip would present no danger.

They were staying at the smart Hotel Nacional when, on the Friday afternoon, the day of the first show, the two were summoned by the Federal Police to be given the usual talk by the censors as to what could and could not be sung in public. The colonel and bureaucrat who received them explained that in their case the only banned song was 'Sociedade Alternativa'. The sports stadium where the show was to be held was packed, and the first two shows passed off without incident. On the Sunday, the night of the final show, Raul, after spending the afternoon and evening smoking cannabis, had what he called 'a turn'. He was unable to remember a single word of the songs on the programme. While the band kept the audience entertained, he squatted at the edge of the stage and whispered to his partner, who was sitting in the first row: 'Help me, will you? I'm in deep shit. Get up here and keep the public quiet for a while, while I go and splash my face with water.' With the microphone in his hand, Raul introduced Paulo to the crowd as 'my dear partner' and left him to deal with the problem. Since the audience were already clapping in time to the band, shouting out the banned refrain, Paulo simply did the same and began to sing along with them:

Viva! Viva! Viva the Sociedade Alternativa!
Viva! Viva! Viva the Sociedade Alternativa!

When he returned to Rio, he described the weekend in Brasília in just a few lines: 'It was a very quiet trip. On Friday we talked to the censor and a colonel from the Federal Police. On Sunday, I talked to the crowd for the first time, although I was completely unprepared. Any mention of the Alternative Society is restricted to interviews.'

During that week Paulo made an important decision: he formalized his acceptance into the OTO as a probationer or novice, when he swore 'eternal devotion to the Great Work'. From 19 May 'of the year 1974 of the Common Era' onwards, for followers of the Devil, Paulo Coelho de Souza's 'profane name' would disappear and be replaced by the 'magical name' that he himself had chosen: Eternal Light, or Staars, or, simply, 313. After sending his oath off in the post, he noted in his diary: 'Having been invoked so often, He must be breathing fire from his nostrils somewhere near by.' He was. On the morning of 25 May, six days after his entrance into the world of darkness, Paulo was finally to have his much-desired meeting with the Devil.

CHAPTER 16

A devil of a different sort

T HE LARGE AMOUNT OF MONEY that Philips had deposited in Paulo's bank account the previous year was just a hint of what was to come. Following the enormous success of *Krig-Ha, Bandolo!* the recording company launched a single featuring 'Gita' and 'Não Pare na Pista', the latter written on the Rio–Bahia highway when the two were returning from a few days' rest in Dias d'Ávila, in the interior of Bahia, where Raul's parents lived. The aim of the single was merely to give the public a taster of the LP that would be released in June, but in less than a month it had sold more than a hundred thousand copies, which won the creators an unexpectedly early Gold Disc, the first of six prizes that the two songs went on to win. Each time a radio station unwittingly made an invocation to the Devil as they played the refrain 'Viva! Viva a Sociedade Alternativa!' meant more money for Raul and Paulo. In April 1974, Paulo bought a large apartment in Rua Voluntários da Pátria, in Botafogo, a few blocks from the estate where he had been born and spent his childhood, and he moved in there with Gisa.

On Friday, 24 May, two weeks after their short stay in Brasília, Raul telephoned to say that he had been ordered to go to the political police – known as the Dops – on the following Monday in order to 'provide some information'. Being accustomed to frequent invitations to discuss which songs could appear in shows or on records, he didn't appear to be worried, but just in case, he asked his partner to go with him. As soon as he rang off, Paulo consulted the I Ching as to whether there was any risk in going to the Dops. Since the answer seemed to be 'No' – or at least so it seemed, for according to its followers, the interpretation of the oracle is not always very precise – he thought no more about the matter.

When he woke on the Saturday morning, Paulo found a note on the bedside table from Gisa, saying that she had gone out early and would be back soon. As he scanned the front page of the *Jornal do Brasil*, the date on the masthead caught his eye: it was exactly two years since he had met Raul, a meeting that had totally changed his life. He drank a cup of coffee, lit a cigarette, glanced through the window from where he could see the sun beating down on the pavement below and then went into his bedroom to put on some shorts before going for his usual hour-long walk. He could detect a slight smell of burning and checked the sockets and domestic appliances, but found nothing wrong. And yet the smell was getting stronger. No, it wasn't the smell of a fuse blowing, it was something else, something very familiar. He felt a chill in his stomach as his memory took him back to the place where he had smelled the same smell now filling the apartment: the morgue in the Santa Casa de Misericórdia that he had visited daily for some months when collecting data for the obituary page of *O Globo*. It was the macabre smell of the candles that appeared to be permanently burning in the hospital morgue. The difference was that the odour permeating everything around him now was so strong that it seemed to be coming from 100, even 1,000, candles all burning at the same time.

As he bent down to do up his trainers, he had the impression that the parquet floor was rising up and coming dangerously close to his face. In fact, his legs had unexpectedly given way beneath him, as if he were about to faint, throwing his chest forwards. He almost crashed to the ground. When the dizziness intensified, he tried to remember whether he had eaten anything strange, but no, it was nothing like that: he wasn't feeling nauseous, he was simply caught up in a kind of maelstrom that seemed to be affecting everything around him. As well as the attacks of giddiness, which came and went, he realized that the apartment was full of a dark mist, as though the sun had suddenly disappeared and the place was being invaded by grey clouds. For a moment, he prayed that he was merely experiencing the moment most feared by drug addicts – a bad trip, provoked by the use of LSD. This, however, was impossible. He hadn't taken LSD in ages, and he'd never heard of cannabis causing such hellish feelings.

He tried to open the door and go outside, but fear paralysed him. It might be worse outside than in. By now, along with the dizziness and the smoke, he could hear terrifying noises, as though someone or some being were breaking everything around him, and yet everything remained in its place. Terrified and lacking the strength to do anything, he felt his hopes revive when the telephone rang. He prayed to God to let it be Euclydes Lacerda – Frater Zaratustra – who could put an end to his suffering. He picked up the phone, but almost immediately put it down again when he realized that he was invoking God's name in order to speak to a disciple of the Devil. It was not Euclydes: the person calling was his friend Stella Paula, whom he had also recruited into the OTO. She was sobbing, as terrified as he was, and was calling to ask for help because her apartment was filled with black smoke, a strong smell of decomposition and other vile smells. Paulo broke down into uncontrollable sobs. He rang off and, remembering what he usually did when he'd had too much cannabis, he went to the refrigerator and drank several glasses of milk, one after the other, and then put his head under the cold-water tap in the bathroom. Nothing happened. The smell of the dead, the smoke and the dizziness continued, as did the noise of things breaking, which was so loud that he had to cover his ears with his hands to deaden it.

It was only then that he began to understand what was happening. Having broken all ties with Christianity, he had spent the last few years working with negative energies in search of something that not even Aleister Crowley had achieved: a meeting with the Devil. What was happening that Saturday morning was what Frater Zaratustra called a 'reflux of magical energies'. All his prayers had been answered. Paulo was face to face with the Devil. He felt like throwing himself out of the window, but jumping from the fourth floor might not necessarily kill him, and might do terrible damage and perhaps leave him crippled. Crying like an abandoned baby, his hands shielding his ears and his head buried between his knees, he recalled fragments of the threats that Father Ruffier had pronounced from the pulpit of the chapel at St Ignatius College.

> We are in hell! Here you can see only tears and hear only the grinding of teeth caused by the hatred of some against others.
> [...] While we cry in pain and remorse the Devil smiles a smile that makes us suffer still more. But the worst punishment, the worst pain, the worst suffering is that we have no hope. We are here for ever.
> [...] And the Devil will say: my dear, your suffering hasn't even begun!

That was it: he was in hell – a hell far worse than Father Ruffier had promised and which he seemed to be condemned to suffer alone. Yes, how long had this been going on – two hours? three? He had lost all notion of time, and there was still no sign of Gisa. Had something happened to her? In order to stop thinking, he began to count the books in the apartment, and then the records, the pictures, the knives, spoons, forks, plates, pairs of socks, underpants ... When he reached the end, he started again. He was standing bent over the kitchen sink with his hands full of cutlery when Gisa returned. She was as confused as he was, shivering with cold, and with her teeth chattering. She asked him what was happening, but Paulo didn't know. She became angry, saying: 'What do you mean, you don't know? You know everything!'

They clung to each other, knelt down on the kitchen floor and began to cry. When he heard himself confessing to Gisa that he was afraid to die, the ghosts of St Ignatius College again rose up before him. 'You're afraid of dying?' Father Ruffier had bawled at him once in front of his classmates. 'Well, I'm shamed by your cowardice.' Gisa found his cowardice equally shameful, especially in a man who, until recently, had been the great macho know-it-all, and who had encouraged her to become involved with the crazy warlocks of the OTO. However, in the midst of that mayhem, Paulo really didn't care what that priest or his girlfriend or his parents might think of him. The only thing he knew was that he didn't want to die, far less deliver his soul to the Devil.

He finally plucked up the courage to whisper in Gisa's ear: 'Let's go and find a church! Let's get out of here and go straight to a church!'

Gisa, the left-wing militant, couldn't believe her ears. 'A church? Why do you need a church, Paulo?'

He needed God. He wanted a church so that he could ask God to forgive him for having doubted His existence and to put an end to his suffering. He dragged Gisa into the bathroom, turned on the cold-water tap of the shower and crouched beneath it with her. The evil smell, the grey clouds and the noise continued. Paulo began to recite out loud every prayer he knew – Hail Mary, Our Father, Salve Regina, the Creed – and eventually she joined in. They couldn't remember how long they stayed there, but the tips of their fingers were blue and wrinkled by the time Paulo got up, ran into the sitting room and grabbed a copy of the Bible. Back in the shower, he opened it at random and came upon verse 24, chapter 9, of St Mark's gospel, which he and Gisa began to repeat, like a mantra, under the showerhead:

Lord, I believe! Help thou my unbelief …
Lord, I believe! Help thou my unbelief …
Lord, I believe! Help thou my unbelief …

They repeated these words out loud hundreds, possibly thousands of times. Paulo renounced and forswore, again out loud, any connection with OTO, with Crowley and with the demons who appeared to have been unleashed that Saturday. When peace returned, it was dark outside. Paulo felt physically and emotionally drained.

Terrified by what they had experienced, the couple did not dare to sleep in the apartment that night. The furniture, books and household objects were all in their usual places, as if that emotional earthquake had never taken place, but it seemed best not to take any chances and they went to spend the weekend with Lygia and Pedro in Gávea. Since she had been with Paulo, Gisa had become a regular visitor to the Coelho household and was always made welcome, particularly by Lygia. Gisa's one defect – in the eyes of Paulo's parents – was her political radicalism. During the long Sunday lunches in Gávea when Paulo's parents, aunts, uncles and grandparents would meet, Gisa would always defend her ideas, even though she knew she was among supporters of Salazar, Franco and the Brazilian military dictatorship. Although everything indicates that she had gradually distanced herself from the political militancy of her student days, her views had not changed. When the couple left on Monday morning, Lygia invited them to a small dinner she was going to hold that evening for her sister Heloísa, 'Aunt Helói'. The two took a taxi back to their apartment – for Paulo had still not learnt to drive. There were no smells, no mists, no shards of glass, nothing to indicate that two days earlier the place had been the scene of what both were sure had been a battle between Good and Evil. When he chose the clothes he was going to wear after his shower, Paulo decided that he would no longer be a slave to superstition. He took from his wardrobe a pale blue linen shirt with short sleeves and pockets trimmed with embroidery, which was a present his mother had given him three years earlier and which he had never worn. This was because the shirt had been bought on a trip his parents had made to Asunción, the capital of the neighbouring country whose name, since his imprisonment in Ponta Grossa, he had never again pronounced. In wearing that shirt from Paraguay he wanted, above all, to prove to himself that he was free of his esoteric tics. He had lunch with Gisa and, at two in the afternoon, went over to Raul's apartment to accompany him to the Dops.

It took more than half an hour to travel the traffic-ridden 15 kilometres that separated Jardim de Alah, where Raul lived, and the Dops building in the centre of the city, and the two men spent the time discussing plans for the launch of their LP *Gita*. A year earlier, when the *Krig-Ha, Bandolo!* album had been released, the two, at Paulo's suggestion, had led a 'musical march' through the streets of the commercial area in old Rio, and this had been a great success. This 'happening' had garnered them valuable minutes on the TV news as well as articles in newspapers and magazines. For *Gita* they wanted to do something even more extravagant.

Calmly going to an interview with the political police when Brazil still had a military dictatorship, without taking with them a lawyer or a representative of the recording company, was not an irresponsible act. Besides being reasonably well known – at least Raul was – neither had any skeletons in the cupboard. Despite Paulo's arrest in Ponta Grossa in 1969 and their skirmishes with the censors, they could not be accused of any act that might be deemed to show opposition to the dictatorship. Besides, the regime had eradicated all the armed combat groups operating in the country. Six months earlier, at the end of 1973, army troops had destroyed the last centres of guerrilla resistance in Araguaia in the south of Pará, leaving a total of sixty-nine dead. Having annihilated all armed opposition, the repressive machinery was slowly being wound down. The regime was still committing many crimes and atrocities – and would continue to do so – but on that May Monday morning in 1974, it would not have been considered utter madness to keep an appointment with the political police, especially since any allegations of torture and the killing of prisoners were mostly made against the intelligence agencies and other sectors of the army, navy and air force.

When the taxi left them at the door of the three-storey building in Rua da Relação, two blocks away from the Philips headquarters, it was three on the dot on 27 May. While Paulo sat on a bench, reading a newspaper, Raul showed the summons to the man at a window and then disappeared off down a corridor. Half an hour later, the musician returned. Instead of going over to Paulo, who was getting up ready to leave, he went over to a public telephone opposite, pretended to dial a number, and began to sing in English: 'My dear partner, the men want to talk to you, not to me ...'

When Paulo failed to understand that Raul was trying to alert him to the fact that he might be in danger, Raul continued tapping his fingers on the telephone and repeating, as though it were a refrain: 'They want to talk to you, not to me ... They want to talk to you, not to me ...'

Paulo still didn't understand. He stood up and asked, smiling: 'Stop messing around, Raul. What are you singing?'

When he made to leave, a policeman placed a hand on his shoulder and said: 'You're not going anywhere. You've got some explaining to do.'

Paulo only had time to murmur a rapid 'Tell my father' to Raul before being led away. He was taken through a labyrinth of poorly lit corridors and across a courtyard until they reached a corridor with cells on either side, most of which appeared to be empty and from which emanated a strong smell of urine combined with disinfectant. The man with him stopped in front of one of them, occupied by two young men, shoved him inside and then turned the key in the lock. Without saying a word to the others, Paulo sat down on the floor, lit a cigarette and, panic-stricken, tried to work out what could possibly lie behind this imprisonment.

He was still immersed in these thoughts when one of the men, who was younger than him, asked: 'Aren't you Paulo Coelho?'

Startled, he replied: 'Yes, I am. Why?'

'We're Children of God. I'm married to Talita. You met her in Amsterdam.'

This was true. He recalled that during his trip to Holland, a young Brazilian girl had come up to him on seeing the Brazilian flag sewn on to the shoulder of his denim jacket. Like Paulo, the two young men had no idea why they were there. The Children of God sect, which had been started in California some years earlier, had managed to attract hundreds of followers in Brazil and now faced serious allegations, among which was that they encouraged sex with children, even between parents and their own children. The presence of the three in the Dops cells was like a snapshot of the state of political repression in Brazil. The much-feared, violent machine created by the dictatorship to confront guerrillas was now concerned with hippies, cannabis users and followers of eccentric sects.

It wasn't until about six in the evening that a plainclothes policeman with a pistol in his belt and holding a cardboard folder in his hand opened the door of the cell and asked: 'Which one of you is Paulo Coelho de Souza?'

Paulo identified himself and was taken to a room on the second floor of the building, where there was only a table and two chairs.

The policeman sat on one of them and ordered Paulo to sit in the other. He took from the folder the four-page comic strip that accompanied *Krig-Ha, Bandolo!* and threw it down on the table. Then he began a surrealist dialogue with the prisoner.

'What kind of shit is this?'

'It's the insert that accompanies the album recorded by me and Raul Seixas.'

'What does *Krig-Ha, Bandolo!* mean?'

'It means "Watch out for the enemy!"'

'Enemy? What enemy? The government? What language is it written in?'

'No! No, it's not against the government. The enemy are African lions and it's written in the language spoken in the kingdom of Pal-U-Don.'

Convinced that this skinny, long-haired man was making a fool of him, the policeman looked as if he was about to turn nasty, thus obliging Paulo to explain carefully that it was all a work of fiction inspired by the places, people and language of the Tarzan cartoons which were set in an imaginary place in Africa called Pal-U-Don.

The man was still not satisfied. 'And who wrote this stuff?'

'I did, and my partner, who's an architect, illustrated it.'

'What's your partner's name? I want to interview her too. Where is she now?'

Paulo panicked at the thought of involving Gisa in this nightmare, but he knew that there was no point in lying; nor was there any reason to lie, since they were both innocent. He looked at his watch.

'Her name is Adalgisa Rios. We were invited to supper this evening at my parents' house. She should be there by now.'

The policeman gathered up the papers, cigarettes and lighter he had scattered on the table, got up and ordered the terrified prisoner to follow him, saying: 'Right, let's go. Let's go and find your old lady.'

As he was being bundled into a black-and-white van bearing the symbol of the Rio de Janeiro Security Police, Paulo felt momentary relief. This meant that he had been officially arrested and, in theory at least, was under state protection. Hell meant being picked up in unmarked cars with false number plates by plainclothes policemen, men with no orders and no official mandate, and who had been linked with many cases of torture and with the disappearance, so far, of 117 political prisoners.

His parents could hardly believe it when they saw their son get out of the car, surrounded by four armed men. They said that Gisa had not yet arrived and wanted to know what was going on. Paulo tried to calm them down, saying that it was just a minor problem with *Krig-Ha, Bandolo!* It would soon be resolved, and he and Gisa should even be back in time for dinner.

One of the policemen backed him up, assuring Lygia and Pedro: 'Yes, they'll be back before you know it.'

As on the outward journey, he sat in the back of the van with an armed policeman on either side and the other two in the front. Halfway there, Paulo asked if they could stop at a public telephone, saying that he needed to tell the recording company that there were some problems with the record. One of the policemen said 'No', but calmed him by saying that in a few hours he and Gisa would be free. His plan had not worked: in fact, Paulo had been hoping to call home to ask Gisa to get rid of a jar full of cannabis that was on the bookcase in the sitting room. He sat frozen and silent until they reached the door of the building where he lived. A policeman stayed with the van while the other three went upstairs with him, crowding into the small, slow lift which on that occasion seemed to take about an hour to arrive at the fourth floor. Inside, wearing an Indian sari, Gisa was just turning out the lights, ready to leave, when Paulo came in with the policemen.

'Sweetheart, these men are from the Dops and they need some information about the record I made with Raul and about the comic strip you and I did for Philips.'

Gisa was a bit frightened, but she seemed to take the matter calmly enough: 'Fine. Tell me what you want. What do you want to know?'

A policeman said that it didn't work that way: 'We can only take statements at the Dops headquarters, so we'll have to go back there.'

She didn't understand. 'Do you mean we're being arrested?'

The policeman answered politely: 'No. You're being detained so that you can provide us with some further information and then you'll be released. But before we leave, we'll just take a quick look around the apartment.'

Paulo's heart was beating so fast he thought he'd have a heart attack: they were sure to find the cannabis. Standing in the middle of the room with his arm around Gisa's shoulder, he followed the movements of the policemen with his eyes. One of them took a pile of about a hundred *Krig-Ha, Bandolo!* comic strips, while another rummaged through drawers and cupboards, and the third, who seemed to be the leader, scrutinized the books and records. When he saw a Chinese lacquered jar the size of a sweet tin, he picked it up, took off the lid and saw that it was full to the brim with cannabis. He sniffed the contents as though savouring a fine perfume, put the lid back on and restored it to its original place. It was only then that Paulo realized that the situation was infinitely worse than he had supposed: if the policeman was prepared to overlook a jar of cannabis, it was because he was suspected of far graver crimes. The Ponta Grossa incident came to mind: could it be that he was once again being confused with a terrorist or a bank robber?

It was only when they arrived at the Dops headquarters that he and Gisa realized that they would not be dining with his parents that evening. They were separated as soon as they arrived and ordered to exchange the clothes they were wearing for yellow overalls with the word 'PRIS-ONER' written in capital letters on the top pocket. During the night of the twenty-eighth they were both photographed and identified and finger-printed for the police files that had been created in their names; Paulo's number was 13720 and Gisa's 13721. They were then interrogated sepa-rately for several hours. Among the personal items confiscated along with their clothes were their watches, which meant that they lost all idea of time, particularly in the circumstances in which they found themselves – imprisoned in a place where there was no natural light.

The interrogation did not involve any physical torture and mainly had to do with the psychedelic comic strip that accompanied the *Krig-Ha, Bandolo!* LP and what exactly was meant by Sociedade Alternativa. This, of course, was after they had spent hours dictating to clerks what in the jargon of the Brazilian police is called the *capivara* – a careful, detailed history of a prisoner's activities up to that date. When Paulo said that he had been in Santiago in May 1970 with Vera Richter the police pressed him for information on Brazilians who lived there, but he had nothing to tell them, for the simple reason that he'd had no contact with any Brazilian exiled in Chile or anywhere else. Gisa, for her part, had a problem convincing her interrogators that the title of *Krig-Ha, Bandolo!* had come up during a brainstorming session at Philips when Paulo, standing on a table, had bellowed out Tarzan's war cry.

In Gávea, the Coelhos were frantic with worry. With the help of a friend, the secretary of the governor of what was then the state of

Guanabara, the journalist and businessman Antônio de Pádua Chagas Freitas, Lygia managed to find out, to everyone's relief, that her son had been arrested by the Dops and was being detained in their prison in Rua da Relação. This was some guarantee, however flimsy, that he would not join the list of the 'disappeared'. Since *habeas corpus* no longer existed, all they could do was to try to find people who might have some kind of link, either family or personal, with influential individuals in the security forces. Paulo's brother-in-law, Marcos, suggested seeking the help of a friend, Colonel Imbassahy, who had connections with the SNI (Brazil's National Intelligence Service), but Pedro decided to try legal routes first, however fragile these might be. It was Aunt Helói who suggested the name of the lawyer Antônio Cláudio Vieira, who had worked in the offices of 'Uncle Candinho', as the Coelho family called the ex-procurator general of the Republic, Cândido de Oliveira Neto, who had died a year earlier.

By five in the afternoon, they were all at the door of the prison. When he was told that only the lawyer, Vieira, could enter, Pedro mentioned that he knew one of the stars of the dictatorship. 'We're friends of Colonel Jarbas Passarinho.' He was speaking of the ex-governor of Pará, who had held ministerial positions in three military governments (he had been one of the signatories of the AI-5) and had been re-elected senator for Arena, a party that supported the regime. The policeman was unimpressed, saying that even someone in Jarbas's position had no influence in Dops.

While the lawyer was trying to get news about Paulo from the officer on duty, Pedro, Lygia, Sônia and her husband Marcos had to wait on the pavement in the drizzle.

After some minutes, Vieira came out with good news: 'Paulo is here and should be released today. The officer in charge is phoning his superior to see whether they will allow me to see him for a few minutes.'

The lawyer was summoned by the doorman and taken to a room where he would be allowed to speak to Paulo briefly. He was shocked by Paulo's appearance: while he hadn't been the victim of any physical violence, Paulo was very pale with dark rings under his eyes and had a strange zombie-like expression on his face. Vieira reassured him, saying he had been given a promise that he would be freed in the next few hours. And that was that. Lygia insisted that they remain on the pavement outside the Dops until her son was released, but the lawyer dissuaded her from this idea.

At about ten o'clock on the Tuesday night, one of the policemen, who had always seemed to Paulo to be the most sympathetic and least threatening, opened the cell door and gave him back the clothes and documents he'd had with him when he was arrested: he and Gisa were free to go. Paulo dressed quickly and met Gisa in the lobby, and the policeman accompanied the couple to the café next to the Dops, where they smoked a cigarette.

Anxious to get away from such a terrifying place, Paulo hailed a taxi and asked the driver to take them to his parents' house in Gávea. The driver set off; then, as the cab was travelling at speed past Hotel Glória, it was brought screeching to a halt by three or four civilian vehicles, among them two Chevrolet Veraneio estate cars, which at the time were the trademark vehicle used by the security police. Several men in plain clothes jumped out and opened the two rear doors of the taxi in which the couple were travelling and dragged Paulo and Gisa out by force. As Paulo was handcuffed and dragged along on his stomach across the grass, he caught sight of Gisa being thrown into an estate car, which drove off, tyres squealing. The last thing he saw before his head was covered in a black hood was the elegant white building of the Hotel Glória, lit up like fairyland.

Once in the back seat of the car, Paulo managed to murmur a question to one of the men with him: 'Are you going to kill me?'

The agent realized how terrified he was and said. 'Don't worry. No one's going to kill you. We're just going to interrogate you.'

His fear remained undiminished. His hands shaking, Paulo was able to overcome his fear and shame enough to ask his captor: 'Can I hold on to your leg?'

The man seemed to find this unusual request amusing. 'Of course you can. And don't worry, we're not going to kill you.'

CHAPTER 17

Paulo renounces the Devil

IT WAS NOT UNTIL THIRTY YEARS LATER, with the country's return to democracy, that Paulo learned he had been kidnapped by a commando group of the DOI-Codi (Department of Information Operations – Centre for Internal Defence Operations). Pedro Queima Coelho was concerned about the damage all this might inflict on his son's fragile emotional state and made a point of being at home so that he would be there to receive Paulo when he was freed. He spent a sleepless night beside a silent telephone and at eight in the morning took a taxi to the Dops. When he arrived, he was astonished to be told by the officer at the desk:

'Your son and his girlfriend were freed at ten o'clock last night.'

When Paulo's father stared at him in disbelief, the agent opened a file and showed him two stamped sheets of paper. 'This is the document for release and here are their signatures,' he said, trying to appear sympathetic. 'He was definitely released. If your son hasn't come home, it's probably because he's decided to go underground.'

The nightmare had begun. Paulo and Gisa had been added to the list of the regime's 'disappeared'. This meant that whatever might happen to them, it was no longer the responsibility of the state, since both had been released safe and sound after signing an official release document.

What happened after their kidnapping is still so swathed in mystery that in 2007, when he turned sixty, the author still had many unanswered questions. Records kept by the security police confirm that Raul was not detained and that on 27 May the Dops arrested the couple, having identified and questioned them during the night and throughout the day of the twenty-eighth. Documents from the army also show that following their kidnapping outside the Hotel Glória, Paulo and Gisa were taken separately to the 1st Battalion of the Military Police in Rua Barão de Mesquita, in the north of Rio, where the DOI-Codi had its offices, although there is no information about how long they were held at the barracks. Some family members state, albeit not with any certainty, that he could have spent 'up to ten days' in the DOI-Codi, but on Friday, 31 May, Paulo was in Gávea writing the first entry in his diary following his release: 'I'm staying at my parents' house. I'm even afraid of writing about what happened to me. It was one of the worst experiences of my life – imprisoned unjustly yet again. But my fears will be overcome by faith and my hatred will be conquered by love. From insecurity will come confidence in myself.'

However, among the documents taken from the archives of Abin, the Brazilian Intelligence Agency (the successor to the SNI, the National Intelligence Service), is a long interrogation with Paulo lasting from eleven o'clock on the night of 14 June until four in the morning of 15 June in the offices of the DOI-Codi. The mystery lies in the fact that he swears that he never returned to the DOI-Codi following his release. The lawyer Antônio Cláudio Vieira also states with equal certainty that he never accompanied him to Rua Barão de Mesquita; nor was he called a second time by the Coelho family to help their son. The same version is corroborated by Pedro, Paulo's sister Sônia Maria and her ex-husband, Marcos, who witnessed everything at close hand. Any suspicion that Paulo, in his terror, had betrayed his friends or put others in danger and now wanted to remove this stain from his record does not stand up to a reading of the seven pages typed on the headed notepaper of the then 1st Army. The first four pages are filled with a reiteration of the statement that Paulo had made in the Dops, a detailed history of his life up until then: schools, work in the theatre, trips within Brazil and abroad, prison in Paraná, *O Globo*, the course in Mato Grosso, *A Pomba*, his partnership with Raul …

The part referring to his and Raul's membership of the OTO is so incomprehensible that the clerk had to write '*sic*' several times, just to make it clear that this really was what the prisoner had said:

That in 1973 the deponent and Raul Seixas had concluded 'that the world is experiencing an intense period of tedium' [*sic*]; that on the other hand they realized that the career of a singer, when not accompanied by a strong movement, tends to end quickly. That the deponent and Raul Seixas then resolved 'to capitalize on the end of hippiedom and the sudden interest in magic around the world' [*sic*]; that the deponent began to study the books of an esoteric movement called 'OTO'. That the deponent and Raul Seixas then decided to found the 'Sociedade Alternativa', 'which was registered at the register office to avoid any false interpretations' [*sic*]; that the deponent and Raul Seixas were in Brasília and explained the precepts of the Sociedade Alternativa to the chiefs of the Federal Police and the Censors, stating 'that the intention was not to act against the government, but to interest youth in another form of activity' [*sic*].

When the police asked him to give the names of people he knew with left-wing tendencies, Paulo could recall only two: someone who used to go to the Paissandu, 'known by everyone as the Philosopher', and an ex-boyfriend of Gisa's in the student movement, whose name he also could not remember, but which he believed 'began with the letter H or A'. The certainty with which everyone states that he did not return to the DOI-Codi after being kidnapped is corroborated by his diary, in which there is absolutely no record of his making a further statement on the night of 14–15 June. The theory that the clerk had typed the wrong date doesn't hold up when one considers the fact that the statement is seven pages long, with the date – 14 June – typed on every page. The definitive proof that Paulo was indeed at the DOI-Codi on some date after 27 May, however, is to be found in one small detail: when he was photographed and identified in the Dops some hours after his arrest on 27 May, he had a moustache and goatee beard. On 14 June, he is described as having 'beard and moustache shaven off'.

As for Gisa, during the time in which she remained in the DOI-Codi she underwent two interrogations. The first started at eight on the morning of 29 May and only ended at four in the afternoon, and the second was held between eight and eleven on the morning of the following day, Thursday. On both occasions, she was treated as a militant member of the radical group Ação Popular (Popular Action) and of the Brazilian Communist Party, but, as in Paulo's case, she had little or nothing to tell them, apart from her work in the student movement when she was involved in several left-wing organizations.

During one of the nights when they were being held in the DOI, something happened that caused the final break between the two. With his head covered by a hood, Paulo was being taken to the toilet by a policeman when, as he walked past a cell, he heard someone sobbing and calling him: 'Paulo? Are you there? If it's you, talk to me!'

It was Gisa, probably also with a hood on her head: she had recognized his voice. Terrified at the thought that he might be placed naked in the 'refrigerator' – the closed cell where the temperature was kept deliberately low – he stayed silent.

His girlfriend begged for his help: 'Paulo, my love! Please, say yes. Just that, say that it's you!'

Nothing.

She went on: 'Please, Paulo, tell them I've got nothing to do with all this.'

In what he was to see as his greatest act of cowardice, he didn't even open his mouth.

One afternoon that week, probably Friday, 31 May, a guard appeared with his clothes, told him to get dressed and to cover his head with the hood. He was put on the rear seat of a car and, having been driven some way, thrown out in a small square in Tijuca, a middle-class district 10 kilometres from the barracks where he had been held.

The first days in his parents' house were terrifying. Every time someone knocked on the door, or the telephone rang, Paulo would lock himself in his room, afraid of being taken away again by the police, the military or whoever it was who had kidnapped him. In order to calm him a little, Pedro, touched by his son's paranoia, had to swear that he would not allow him to be imprisoned again, whatever the consequences. 'If anyone comes to take you without a legal summons,' he promised, 'he'll be greeted with a bullet.' Only after two weeks holed up in Gávea did Paulo have the courage to go out in the street again, and even then he chose a day when it would be easy to spot if someone was following him: Thursday, 13 June, when Brazil and Yugoslavia were playing the first match of the 1974 World Cup in Germany, and the whole country would be in front of the television supporting the national team. With Rio transformed into a ghost town he went by bus to Flamengo and then, after much hesitation, he plucked up the courage to go into the apartment where he and Gisa had lived until the Saturday on which they believed they had received a visit from the Devil. It was exactly as the police had left it on the Monday evening after searching it. Before the referee blew the final whistle of the match, Paulo was back in the shelter of his parents' home. One of the penances he imposed on himself, though, so that everything would return to normal as quickly as possible, was not to watch any of the World Cup matches.

The most difficult thing was finding Gisa. Since that dreadful encounter in the DOI-Codi prison he had had no more news of his girlfriend, but her voice crying 'Paulo! Talk to me, Paulo!' kept ringing in his head. When he eventually managed to call her old apartment, where she had gone back to live, it suddenly occurred to him that the phone might be tapped and so he didn't dare to ask whether she had been tortured or when she had been released. When he suggested a meeting in order to discuss their future, Gisa was adamant: 'I don't want to live with you again, I don't want you to say another word to me and I would prefer it if you never spoke my name again.'

Following this, Paulo fell into such a deep depression that his family again sought help from Dr Benjamim Gomes, the psychiatrist at the Dr Eiras clinic. Luckily for Paulo, this time the doctor decided to replace electric shocks with daily sessions of analysis, which, during the first weeks, were held at his home. Paulo's persecution mania had become so extreme that, on one outing, he became so frightened that he fainted in the street in front of a bookshop in Copacabana and was helped by passers-by. When Philips sent him the proofs for the record sleeve for *Gita*, which was about to be released, he couldn't believe his eyes: it was a photo of Raul with a Che Guevara beret bearing the red five-pointed star of the communists. Appalled, he immediately phoned Philips and demanded that they change the image; if they didn't, he would not allow any of his songs to appear on the record.

When they asked why, he replied so slowly that he seemed to be spelling out each word: 'Because I don't want to be arrested again and with that photo on the record sleeve, they'll arrest me again. Understood?'

After much discussion, he accepted that Raul could be shown wearing the Che beret, but he demanded a written statement from Philips stating that the choice was the entire responsibility of the company. In the end, a suggestion by a graphic artist won the day: the red star was simply removed from the photo, so that it looked as though the beret was merely an innocent beret with no sinister communist connotations.

Since Gisa refused to answer his calls, Paulo began to write her letters each day, asking forgiveness for what he had done in the prison and suggesting that they live together again. In one of these letters he wrote of his feelings of insecurity during the three years they had spent together:

> I didn't understand why, when you moved in with me, you brought just the bare minimum of clothes. I never understood why you insisted on continuing to pay the rent on the other empty apartment. I wanted to put pressure on you with money, saying I wouldn't pay any more, but you still kept on the other apartment. The fact that the other apartment existed made me really insecure. It meant that from one moment to the next you could escape my grasp and regain your freedom.

Gisa never replied, but he continued to write. One day, his father, clearly upset, took him to one side. 'Look, Gisa phoned me at the office,' he told him, his hand on his son's shoulder. 'She asked me to tell you not to write to her again.' Paulo ignored the request and went on writing: 'Today my father told me that you don't want to see me again. I also learned that you're working, which is good, and I felt both hurt and happy. I had just heard "Gita" on the radio. I was wondering whether you think of me when you hear that song. I think they were the most beautiful lyrics I've written so far. It contains all of me. Now I don't read, don't write and I've no friends.'

This was one of the symptoms of his paranoia, that all his friends had supposedly abandoned him for fear of being close to someone who had been seized and imprisoned by the security police. Whether this was real or imagined, what mattered was his belief that, apart from Raul, only two people held out a hand to him: the journalist Hildegard Angel and Roberto Menescal, one of the creators of the bossa nova and, at the time, a director of Polygram. Together with Phonogram, Polydor and Elenco, the company was one of the Brazilian arms of the Dutch multinational Philips, and one of its greatest rivals in Brazil was CBS, a subsidiary of the American company Columbia. Hilde, as she was and is known, continued to be a friend to Paulo even though she had painful reasons to avoid risking any more confrontations with the dictatorship: three years earlier, her youngest brother, Stuart Angel, who was a member of the guerrilla group MR-8, had been brutally asphyxiated at an air force barracks, with his mouth pressed to the exhaust pipe of a moving jeep. His wife, the economist Sônia Moraes Angel, a member of the ALN (National Liberationist Movement), had also died while being tortured by the DOI-Codi in São Paulo a few months earlier, at the end of 1973. As if these two tragedies were not enough for one family, Hilde and Stuart's mother, the designer Zuzu Angel, was to die two years later in a car accident that had all the hallmarks of an assassination attempt and became the subject of the film *Zuzu Angel*.

It was Hilde who, after much insistence, convinced Paulo to get back into circulation. She invited him to attend the debate 'Women and Communication' at which she was to participate with the feminist Rose Marie Muraro at the Museu Nacional de Belas-Artes. Paulo's justified paranoia would have reached unbearable levels had he known that among the audience was a spy, Deuteronômio Rocha dos Santos, who wrote a report on the meeting for the Section of Special Searches (part of the Dops) in which he said: 'among those present was the journalist and writer Paulo Coelho, a personal friend of Hildegard Angel'.

As soon as he felt strong enough to go around without fear of being kidnapped again, Paulo's first important step after what he referred to as the 'black week' was to search out the OTO. He had two reasons for going to see Frater Zaratustra: first, he wanted to understand what had happened in his apartment on that dreadful Saturday and, second, whatever the explanation, he was going to distance himself permanently from the sect. His fear of the Devil was such that he asked Euclydes-Zaratustra to meet him during the day at his parents' house, where he had gone back to live, and, for good measure, he invited Roberto Menescal to be there as a witness. This turned out to be a good idea: to his surprise, on the appointed day, who should appear at the house in Gávea but Parzival XI, the self-crowned world head of the sect – the sinister and uncouth Marcelo Ramos Motta. Paulo decided to come straight to the point. After summarizing what had happened at his home and in prison, he asked: 'I want to know what happened to me that Saturday and on the following days.'

Parzival XI eyed him scornfully. 'You always knew that with us what counts is the law of the strongest. I taught you that, remember? According to the law of the strongest, whoever holds out succeeds. Those who don't, fail. That's it. You were weak and failed.'

Menescal, who was listening to the conversation from a distance, threatened to attack the visitor – something that would have endangered the Coelhos' china and crystal, since Menescal practised aikido and the Crowleyite Ramos Motta was a black belt in ju-jitsu.

But Paulo restrained him and, for the first time, addressed the high priest by his real name: 'So is that what the OTO is, Marcelo? On Saturday, the Devil appears in my house, on Monday, I'm arrested and on Wednesday, I'm abducted? That's the OTO, is it? Well, in that case, my friend, I'm out of it.'

As soon as he found himself free from the sect, it was with great relief, as though he had sloughed off a great burden, that Paulo sat down at his typewriter and wrote an official document formalizing his rejection of the mysterious Ordo Templi Orientis. His brief and dramatic incursion into the kingdom of darkness had lasted less than two months:

Rio de Janeiro, 6 July 1974

I, Paulo Coelho de Souza, who signed my declaration as a Probationer in the year LXX, 19 May, with the sun in the sign of Taurus, 1974 e.v., ask and consider myself to be excluded from the Order because of my complete incompetence in realizing the tasks given me.

I declare that, in taking this decision, I am in a perfect state of physical and mental health.

93 93 / 93

As witness my hand,

Paulo Coelho

What Paulo believed to be a break with the Devil and his followers did not mean the end of his paranoia. In fact he felt safe only when at home with his parents and with the doors locked. It was during this period of despair that the idea of leaving Brazil for a while, at least until the fear subsided, first surfaced. With Gisa out of his life there was nothing to keep him in Brazil. The sales of *Gita* had outstripped even the most optimistic expectations and the money kept pouring into his bank account.

This coincided with another important moment in Paulo's progress: the launch of his first book. Although it was not the Great Work he dreamed of producing, it was nevertheless a book. It had been published at the end of 1973 by the highly regarded Editora Forense, which specialized in educational books, and was entitled *O Teatro na Educação* [*Theatre in Education*]. In it he explained the programme of courses he had given in state schools in Mato Grosso. Not even an admiring review by Gisa published on their weekly page in *Tribuna* had been able to get sales moving: a year after its launch, the book had sold only 500 copies out of an initial print run of 3,000. Although it was predictable that the work would pass almost unnoticed in the world of letters, this was still his first book and therefore deserved to be celebrated. When Gisa had arrived home on the day it came out, on the dining table stood two glasses and a miniature of Benedictine liqueur that Paulo had won at the age of fifteen and kept all that time, promising not to open it until he published his first book.

Not even this initial lack of success as an author or the wealth that came with fame, however, could shake the dream that he himself admitted had become an obsession: to be a writer known throughout the world. Even after he had become well known as a lyricist, that dream would return as strongly as ever when he was alone. A rapid flick through his diaries reveals, in sentences dotted here and there, that public recognition as a lyricist had not changed his plan one jot: he wanted to be not just another writer but 'world-famous'. He regretted that by the time they were his age, The Beatles 'had already conquered the world', but Paulo didn't lose hope that, one day, his dreams would be realized. 'I'm like a warrior waiting to make his entrance on the scene,' he wrote, 'and my destiny is success. My great talent is to fight for it.'

Raul had been very shaken by his friend's imprisonment, and Paulo had no difficulty in convincing him, too, to go abroad for a while. Less than ten days after their decision to leave Brazil, they were ready for departure. The fact that they had to go to the Dops to receive a visa to leave the country – a requirement imposed by the dictatorship on anyone wanting to travel abroad – so frightened Paulo that he had a serious asthma attack. But on 14 July 1974, a month and a half after his kidnapping, the two partners landed in New York with no fixed return date.

They each had on their arm a new girlfriend. Raul had separated from Edith, the mother of his daughter, Simone, and was living with another American, Gloria Vaquer, the sister of the drummer Jay Vaquer. Abandoned by Gisa, Paulo had started a relationship with the beautiful Maria do Rosário do Nascimento e Silva, a slim brunette of twenty-three. She was an actress, scriptwriter and film producer. She was also the daughter of a judge from Minas Gerais, Luiz Gonzaga do Nascimento e Silva, who, a week before the trip, had been named Minister for Social Services by General Ernesto Geisel, the President of the Republic. Despite her father's political activities, Rosário was a left-wing activist who hid those being persecuted by the regime and who had been arrested when filming statements by workers at the Central do Brasil railway station in Rio. When she met Paulo, through Hilde Angel, she was just emerging from a tempestuous three-year marriage to Walter Clark, the then director-general of the Globo television network.

The bank balance of any of those four travellers was more than enough for them to stay in comfort at the Hotel Plaza opposite Central Park or in the Algonquin, both natural staging posts for stars passing through New York. In the crazy 1970s, however, the in thing was to stay in 'exciting' places. So it was that Paulo, Rosário, Raul and Gloria knocked at the door of the Marlton Hotel, or, to be more precise, on the iron bars that protected the entrance of the hotel from the street gangs of Greenwich Village.

Built in 1900, the Marlton was famous for welcoming anyone, be they pimps, prostitutes, drug-dealers, film stars, jazz musicians or beatniks. Such people as the actors John Barrymore, Geraldine Page and Claire Bloom, the singers Harry Belafonte, Carmen McRae and Miriam Makeba and beat writer Jack Kerouac had stayed in some of its 114 rooms, most of which shared a bathroom on the landing. The fanatical feminist Valerie Solanas left one of those rooms in June 1968, armed with a revolver, to carry out an attack on the pop artist Andy Warhol that nearly killed him. Raul and Gloria's apartment, which had a sitting room, bedroom and bathroom, cost US$300 a month. Paulo and Rosário had only a bedroom and bathroom, which cost US$200, but there was no refrigerator, which meant they had to spend their days drinking warm Coke and neat whisky – this, of course, when they weren't smoking cannabis or sniffing cocaine, their main pastimes.

On 8 August 1974, the eyes of the whole world were turned on the United States. After two years and two months of involvement in the Watergate scandal, Richard Nixon's Republican government was suffering a very public death. The big decisions were taken in Washington, but the heart of America beat in New York. There seemed to be a more than usually electric atmosphere in the Big Apple. It was expected that at any moment either the President would be impeached or he would resign. After a night spent in a fashionable nightclub, Paulo and Rosário woke at three in the afternoon, went out for a big breakfast at Child, a rough bar a block away from the Marlton, and then returned to their room. They had a few lines of cocaine and when they came to, it was getting dark. On the radio on the bedside table, the reporter was announcing that in ten minutes there was to be a national radio and television transmission of an announcement by President Nixon.

Paulo jumped off the bed, saying: 'Come on, Maria! Let's go down and record the reactions of the people when he announces his resignation.' He put on a denim jacket but no shirt and his knee-high riding boots, grabbed his portable recorder – a heavy thing the size of a telephone directory – filled his pockets with cassette tapes and hung his cine camera round Rosário's neck, telling her to hurry: 'Come on, Maria! We can't miss this. It's going to be better than the final of the World Cup!'

He turned on the recorder when they got outside and began describing what he could see, as though making a live radio report:

> Paulo – Today is 8th August 1974. I am on 8th Street, heading for the Shakespeare restaurant. In five minutes' time the President of the United States is going to resign. Right, we've arrived. We're here in the Shakespeare, the TV is on but the broadcast hasn't started yet ... What did you say?
>
> Rosário – I said I still think the American people aren't cold at all. Quite the contrary!
>
> Paulo – It's like a football match. The TV's on here in the bar of the Shakespeare restaurant. The broadcast hasn't started yet but there are already loads of people out in the street.
>
> Rosário – Everyone's shouting, can you hear?
>
> Paulo – I can!

In the crowded restaurant, the two managed to find a place in front of the television that was suspended from the ceiling, its volume on maximum. Wearing a navy-blue suit and red tie, Nixon appeared on the screen, looking very sombre. A church-like silence fell in the bar as he began to read the speech in which he resigned from the most important position in the world. For almost fifteen minutes, the people standing around made not a sound as Nixon explained the reasons that had led him to this dramatic decision. His speech ended on a sad note: 'To have served in this office is to have felt a very personal sense of kinship with each and every American. In leaving it, I do so with this prayer: may God's grace be with you in all the days ahead.'

As soon as the speech had ended Paulo was out in the street, closely followed by Maria do Rosário, with the microphone to his mouth like a radio announcer.

Paulo – Christ! I was really moved, Rosário, I really was! If one day I have to resign, I hope it's like that … But look! Nixon has just resigned and there's some guy dancing on the corner.

Rosário – Dancing and playing the banjo. This country's full of madmen!

Paulo – My feelings, at this moment, are completely indescribable. We're walking along 8th Street.

Rosário – The people are really so happy. Oh, it's just too much!

Paulo – They really are! They're sort of half-surprised, Maria. Really! The television crews are interviewing people in the streets! This is an historic day!

Rosário – There's a woman crying, a girl crying. She's genuinely upset.

Paulo – It's a truly fantastic moment, isn't it? Really, really fantastic!

The two returned to the Marlton, feeling very excited. Rosário got out at the third floor, where their apartment was, and Paulo took the lift up to the seventh, because he wanted Raul to listen to the tapes recording the madness that had taken hold of New York that evening. When he opened the door, without knocking, as was their habit, he found his partner lying flat out on the sofa, sleeping with his mouth open. On the small table next to him was a line of cocaine ready to be sniffed, a half-drunk bottle of whisky and a pile of money amounting to about US$5,000 in one hundred dollar bills. For someone coming from a public celebration as Paulo had, after having been witness to a spontaneous street festival, the shock of seeing his friend lying there, completely out of it, a victim of drugs and alcohol, was a real wake-up call. He was sad not only to see a friend in that state – a friend whom he had introduced to the world of drugs – but also because he realized that cocaine was leading him down the same path. Paulo had never confessed this to anyone, not even to his diary, but he knew he was becoming drug-dependent. He returned to his room in a state of shock. He saw Rosário's slim body lying naked on the bed, lit only by the bluish light from the street.

He sat shamefaced beside his girlfriend and gently stroked her back as he announced in a whisper: 'Today is an historic day for me too. On 8 August 1974, I stopped sniffing cocaine.'

CHAPTER 18

Cissa

THEIR PLAN TO REMAIN IN NEW YORK for a few months was cut short by an unforeseen incident. One evening, Paulo was trying out an electric can-opener and accidently let the sharp blade slip, catching his right hand. Rosário tried to staunch the flow of blood with a bath towel, and it immediately became a ball of blood. He was taken by ambulance to a first-aid station in Greenwich Village, where he learned that the gadget had sliced the tendon in the third finger of his right hand. He had emergency surgery and ended up with nine stitches in his finger and had to wear a metal splint for several weeks, which immobilized his hand. A few days later, he and Rosário left for Brazil, while Raul and Gloria travelled on to Memphis.

On his return to Rio, Paulo found that he was strong enough to confront his ghosts and decided to live alone in the apartment where he had lived with Gisa. However, his courage was short-lived. On 10 September, after two weeks, he was once again berthed in the secure port of his parents' house in Gávea. Anxious to free himself of everything that might remind him of demons, prisons and abductions, before moving to their house, he sold all his books, records and pictures. When he saw his bare apartment, with nothing on the walls or shelves, he wrote in his diary: 'I have just freed myself from the past.' But it wasn't going to be that easy. His paranoia, fears and complexes continued to trouble him. He frequently confessed that he continued to feel guilty even about things that had happened during his childhood, such as having 'placed my hand on a girl's private parts', or even 'dreaming of doing sinful things with Mama'. But at least at home it was unlikely that anyone could simply abduct him, with no questions asked.

At a time when sexual promiscuity appeared to carry few risks, he recorded in his diary the women who came and went in his life without saying anything much about them, apart from some statement as to how well this woman or that had performed in bed. Sometimes he set up meetings with ex-girlfriends, but the truth is that he had still not got over the end of his affair with Gisa, to whom he continued to write and from whom he never received a reply. When he learned that Vera Richter was back with her ex-husband he noted: 'Today I went into town to resolve my psychological problem with a few shares in the Bank of Brazil. I was thinking of selling them and giving the money to Mário in exchange for having possessed Vera for more than a year. In fact it was Vera who possessed me, but in my muddled head I always thought it was the other way round.'

His partnership with Raul continued to produce impressive results, but the ship of the Sociedade Alternativa was beginning to let in water. Even before the 'dark night' and Paulo's imprisonment, disagreements between them and Philips as to the meaning of the Sociedade Alternativa had begun to arise. Everything indicates that Raul had been serious about creating a new community – a sect, religion or movement – that would practise and spread the commandments of Aleister Crowley, Parzival XI and Frater Zaratustra. For the executives of the recording company, however, the Sociedade Alternativa was nothing more than a brand name they could use to boost the sales of records. The president of Philips in Brazil, André Midani, a Syrian who had become a Brazilian national, had created an informal working group to help the company market its artists better. This dream team, which was coordinated by Midani and the composer Roberto Menescal, consisted of the market researcher Homero Icaza Sánchez, the writer Rubem Fonseca and the journalists Artur da Távola, Dorrit Harazim, Nelson Motta, Luis Carlos Maciel, João Luís de Albuquerque and Zuenir Ventura. The group would meet once a week in a suite in some luxury hotel in Rio and spend a whole day there discussing the profile and work of a particular Philips artist. At the first meeting, they would simply talk among themselves, and then the following week, they would repeat the exercise with the artist present. Those taking part were paid well – Zuenir Ventura describes how for each meeting he would receive 'four thousand or four million, I can't remember which, but I know that it was the equivalent of my monthly salary as a director of the Rio branch of the magazine *Visão*'.

When it was time for Paulo and Raul to face the group, it was Raul who was in the grip of paranoia. He was sure he was being followed by plainclothes policemen and had taken on a bodyguard, the investigator Millen Yunes, from the Leblon police department, who, in his spare time, was to accompany the musician wherever he went. When Paulo told him that Menescal had invited them to be questioned by the select group of intellectuals, Raul declared: 'It's a trick on the part of the police! I bet you the police have infiltrated the group in order to record what we say. Tell Menescal we're not going.'

Paulo assured his partner that there was no danger, that he knew most of the participants and that some were even people who were opposed to the dictatorship; finally he promised that neither Midani nor Menescal would play such a trick. Since Raul refused to budge, Paulo went alone to the meeting, but because of Raul's concerns, he placed a tape recorder on the table so that he could give the tapes to his partner afterwards. Before the discussion began, someone asked Paulo to explain, in his own words, what exactly the Sociedade Alternativa was. From what he can remember more than three decades later, he hadn't taken any drugs or been smoking cannabis; however, to judge by what he said, which was all captured on tape, you would think he must have taken something:

The Sociedade Alternativa reaches the political level, the social level, the social stratum of a people, you see? Shit, it also reaches the intellectuals in a country whose people are coming down from a trip, who are being more demanding ... So much so that there was a discussion in São Paulo about the magazine *Planeta*. I reckon *Planeta* is going to go bust in a year from now because everyone who reads *Planeta* is bound to think that *Planeta* is a stupid magazine, well, it failed in France, and so they invented *Le Nouveau Planète*, then *Le Nouveau Nouveau Planète*, do you see what I mean? They ended up closing down the magazine. That's what's going to happen with all these people who are into macumba. No, no, no! I don't mean the proletariat, but what people call the middle classes. The bourgeoisie who suddenly decided to take an interest, you know. Intellectually, like. Obviously there's another aspect to the question which is the aspect of faith, of you going there and making a promise, and getting some advantage, you know, things like that. Right, but in cultural terms there's going to be a change, right? And the change is going to come from abroad, just like it always does, do you see what I'm saying? And it's never going to be filtered through a Brazilian product called spiritualism. That's on the spiritual level, of course, because I think on the political level I've been clear enough.

Clarity was obviously not his strong point, but the working group seemed to be used to people like him. Paulo paused a second for breath, and then went on:

So ... there's going to be this filtering. In my opinion, it's not filtering, but no one's ever going to stop getting a buzz out of Satan, because it's a really fascinating subject. It's a taboo like ... like virginity, do you understand? So, when everyone starts talking about Satan, even if you're afraid of the Devil and hate him, you really want to get into it, do you understand? Because it's aggression, State agression turned against itself, the aggression of repression, right? A series of things turn up inside this scheme and you start to get into it ... It's not a trip that's going to last very long, it hasn't even happened yet, the Satan trip. But it's a phenomenon. It's the result of aggression, of the same thing as free love, of the sexual taboo that the hippies opened up.

[...] I haven't given, like, an overview of the Sociedade Alternativa. I've just noted a few things, but I wanted to give an overview of everything that we created, a general vision of the thing, right? Anyway, where does Raul Seixas fit in with all this? The

Sociedade Alternativa serves Raul Seixas and he's not going to change his mind because we've spent two days talking about the Sociedade Alternativa and nothing but, right? The Sociedade Alternativa serves Raul Seixas in the sense that Raul Seixas is a catalyst for this type of movement, all right? It's been judged to be a myth. No one can explain what the Sociedade Alternativa is.

Do you see what I mean?

'More or less,' the journalist Artur da Távola replied. Since most of those present had understood none of this nonsense, the problem the group put to Paulo was a simple one: if this was the explanation he and Raul were going to give to the press, then they should prepare themselves to see the idea made mincemeat of by the media. Dorrit Harazim, who, at the time, was editor of the international section of the magazine *Veja*, thought that if they wanted to convince the public that the Sociedade Alternativa was not merely a marketing strategy but some kind of mystical or political movement, then they would need far more objective arguments: 'First of all, you need to decide whether the Sociedade Alternativa is political or metaphysical. With the arguments you put to us, it will be very hard for you to explain to anyone what the Sociedade Alternativa actually is.'

This was the first time the working group had reached a unanimous decision about anything, and it fell to Artur da Távola to remind them that they risked losing a gold mine: 'We need to be very careful because we're pointing out defects in a duo who sell hundreds of thousands of records. We mustn't forget that Raul and Paulo are already a runaway success.'

However, there was another matter bothering the group: Raul and Paulo's insistence on telling the press that they had seen flying saucers. They all believed that this was something that could affect the commercial standing of the duo, and they suggested that Paulo tell Raul to stop it. They had good reason to be concerned. Some months earlier, Raul had given a long interview to *Pasquim* and, inevitably, he was pressed by the journalists to explain the Sociedade Alternativa and his sightings of flying saucers, giving him the chance to ramble on at will. He explained that it was a society that wasn't governed by any truth or any leader, but had arisen 'like a realization of a new tactic, of a new method'. As his reply was somewhat unclear, he made another attempt to explain what he meant: 'The Sociedade Alternativa is the fruit of the actual mechanism of the thing,' he went on, adding that it had already crossed frontiers. 'We're in constant correspondence with John Lennon and Yoko Ono, who are also part of the Society.' With no one there to keep a check on him, Raul even made up facts about things that were public knowledge, such as his first meeting with Paulo. 'I met Paulo in Barra da Tijuca,' he told *Pasquim*. 'At five in the afternoon, I was there meditating and he was too, but I didn't know him then – it was then that we saw the flying saucer.' One of the interviewers asked whether he could describe the supposed UFO and he said: 'It was sort of ... silver, but with an orange aura round it. It just stood there, enormous it was. Paulo came running over to me, I didn't know him, but he said, "Can you see what I see?" We just sat there and the saucer zigzagged off and vanished.' It was statements like these that made the Philips work group fear that the duo risked exposing themselves to public ridicule.

When the session ended, Paulo took the recorded tapes to his partner. Since the working group's comments had not been exactly flattering, instead of telling Raul to his face what had happened, Paulo preferred to record another tape on arriving home, in which he gave Raul his version of the meeting:

The working group's great fear is that the Sociedade Alternativa might work out and that you, Raul – listening to this tape – won't be up to the challenge. They're afraid that the Sociedade Alternativa will grow and that when you go to give an interview on what the Sociedade Alternativa is ... as Artur da Távola said, you'll talk a lot but won't explain things. And the press will fall about laughing, will say it's a farce and your career will go up in smoke. What I mean is, Philips' main concern is that you're not up to it. The meeting was extremely tense. There's one point I really feel they won't budge on: your inability, Raul, to hold out. You'll hear that on the tape and I'm talking about it now because that's the impression I got.

Another thing that came up was the problem of the flying saucer, with everyone saying that it's stupid. They said, for example, that every time you repeat the story about the flying saucer, the press will just laugh at you. I decided to stay quiet and not say whether it was true or false. But the working group reckon that the flying saucer story should gradually be abandoned. I didn't say as much, but I left it open at least to the working group that we might deny the story about the flying saucer.

Although the idea of the Sociedade Alternativa proved alluring enough to attract hundreds of thousands of record buyers and an unknown number of Devil-worshippers from all over Brazil, time would prove the working group right. As time went on, the expression 'Sociedade Alternativa' would be remembered only as the chorus of a song from the 1970s.

Now, not long after his return from New York with his hand strapped up, and at the height of the success of *Gita* (which had been released in their absence), Paulo was invited by Menescal to join the working group as a consultant, with the same pay as the other members, which meant an additional US$11,600 per month. Money was flooding in from all sides. When he received the first set of accounts from the recording company for initial sales of *Gita*, he wondered whether to invest the money in shares or to buy a summer house in Araruama, but finally decided upon an apartment in the busy Rua Barata Ribeiro, in Copacabana. At this time, Paulo also wrote three sets of lyrics – 'Cartão Postal', 'Esse Tal de Roque Enrow' and 'O Toque' – for the LP *Fruto Proibido*, that the singer Rita Lee released at the beginning of 1975, and he also produced film scripts for Maria do Rosário. In between, he acted in the porn movie *Tangarela, a Tanga de Cristal*. In December 1974, the recording company abandoned the working group, but then, at Menescal's suggestion, André Midani contracted Paulo Coelho to work as a company executive, managing the creative department.

His new financial and professional security did not, however, have the effect of comforting his tortured soul. Until May 1974, he had just about managed to live with his feelings of persecution and rejection, but following his imprisonment, these appeared to reach an unbearable level. Of the 600 pages of his diary written during the twelve months following his release, more than 400 deal with the fears resulting from that black week. In one notebook of 60 pages chosen at random, the word 'fear' is repeated 142 times, 'problem' 118 times, and there are dozens of instances of words such as 'solitude', 'despair', 'paranoia' and 'alienation'. He wrote at the bottom of one page, quoting Guimarães Rosa: 'It is not fear, no. It's just that I've lost the will to have courage.' In May 1975, on the first anniversary of his release from the DOI-Codi, he paid for a mass of thanksgiving to be celebrated at the church of St Joseph, his protector.

Since leaving prison, the person who gave him the greatest sense of security – more even than Dr Benjamim and even perhaps his father – was the lawyer Antônio Cláudio Vieira, whom Paulo considered responsible for his release. As soon as he returned from the United States, he asked his father to make an appointment for him to thank Vieira for his help. When he arrived at the lawyer's luxurious apartment with its spectacular view of Flamengo, Paulo was completely bowled over by the lawyer's dark, pretty daughter, Eneida, who was a lawyer like her father and worked in his office. During that first meeting, the two merely flirted, but exactly forty-seven days later, Paulo proposed to Eneida, and she immediately accepted. According to the social values of the time, not only was he in a position to marry, but he was also a good prospect – someone with enough money to maintain a wife and children. The new album he had made with Raul, *Novo Aeon*, had been released at the end of 1975. The two had written four of the thirteen tracks ('Rock do Diabo', 'Caminhos I', 'Tú És o MDC da Minha Vida' and 'A Verdade sobre a Nostalgia'). The record also revealed Raul's continued involvement with the satanists of the OTO: the ill-mannered Marcelo Motta had written the lyrics of no fewer than five of the tracks ('Tente Outra Vez', 'A Maçã', 'Eu Sou Egoísta', 'Peixuxa – O Amiguinho dos Peixes' and 'Novo Aeon'). Although Raul and his followers considered the record a masterpiece, *Novo Aeon* was not a patch on the previous albums, and sold only a little over forty thousand copies.

Paulo clearly had enough money to start a family, but asking for the girl's hand so quickly could only be explained by a burning passion, which, however, was not the case. As far as Paulo was concerned, he had not only found a woman he could finally marry and 'settle down' with – as he had been promising himself he would do since leaving prison – but he would also have the guarantor of his emotional security, Antônio Cláudio Vieira, as his father-in-law. On the evening of 16 June 1975, after smoking a joint, Paulo decided that it was time to resolve the matter. He called Eneida, asking her to tell her parents that he was going to formalize his offer of marriage: 'I just need time to go home and pick up my parents. Then we'll come straight over.'

His parents were fast asleep, but were hauled out of their beds by their crazy son who had suddenly decided to become engaged. Whether it was the effects of the cannabis, or whether it was because he had never before played such a role, the fact is that when it came to speaking to his future father-in-law, Paulo's mouth went dry, and he choked and stammered and was unable to say a single word.

Vieira saved the situation by saying: 'We all know what you want to say. You're asking for Eneida's hand in marriage, aren't you? If so, the answer is "Yes".'

As they all toasted the engagement with champagne, Paulo produced a beautiful diamond ring that he had bought for his future wife. The following day, Eneida reciprocated Paulo's present by sending to his house an Olivetti electric typewriter, which the author continued to use until 1992, when he changed to working on a computer.

Not even three weeks had passed before his diary began to reveal that the engagement had perhaps been over-hasty: 'I have serious problems with my relationship with Eneida. I chose her for the security and emotional stability that she would give me. I chose her because I was looking for a counter-balance to my naturally unbalanced temperament. Now I understand the price I have to pay for this: castration. Castration in my behaviour, castration in my conversation, castration in my madness. I can't take it.'

To go back on his word and break off the engagement did not even enter his head, because it would mean not only losing the lawyer but gaining an enemy – the mere thought of which made his blood run cold. But Paulo realized that Eneida was also getting fed up with his strange habits.

She didn't mind if he continued to smoke cannabis, but she didn't want to use it herself, and Paulo was constantly on at her to do just that. As for his 'sexual propositions', she made it quite clear: he could forget any ideas of having a *ménage à trois*. Eneida was not prepared to allow his girlfriends to share their bed. A split was, therefore, inevitable. When the engagement was only forty days old Paulo recorded in his diary that it had all come to an end:

> Eneida simply left me. It's been very difficult, really very difficult. I chose her as a wife and companion, but she couldn't hack it and suddenly disappeared from my life. I've tried desperately to get in touch with her mother, but both her parents have disappeared as well. I'm afraid that she has told her parents about my Castaneda-like ideas and my sexual propositions. I know that she told them about those. The break-up was really hard for me, much harder than I had imagined. My mother and father are going to be very shocked when they hear. And it's going to be difficult for them to accept another woman in the way they accepted my ex-fiancée. I know that, but what can I do? Go off again and immediately start looking for another companion.

The companion on whom he had his eye was a trainee, Cecília Mac Dowell, who was working on the press team at Philips. But before declaring himself to Cissa, as she was known, Paulo had a lightning romance with Elisabeth Romero, who was also a journalist and had interviewed him for a music magazine. They started going out together, and the affair took off. Beth rode a large Kawasaki 900 motorbike, and Paulo took to riding pillion. Although the affair was short-lived, it allowed Beth to witness an episode which Paulo was to describe dozens, if not hundreds of times in interviews published in the international press: the meeting he never had with his idol Jorge Luis Borges.

With the Christmas holidays approaching, Paulo invited Beth to go with him to Buenos Aires, where he intended to visit the great Argentinean writer. He had been putting off the trip for some time, reluctant to go to the police in order to ask for an exit visa to travel to the neighbouring country, fearing that he might be arrested again. They made no attempt to get in touch with Borges beforehand or to obtain some kind of letter of introduction, but the couple were nevertheless prepared to put up with the forty-eight-hour bus journey between Rio and Buenos Aires, armed only with Borges's address: Calle Maipu 900. As soon as they arrived, Paulo went straight there. The porter of the apartment block, in the centre of the city, told him that Don Jorge Luis was on the other side of the road having a coffee in the bar of an old hotel. Paulo crossed the road, went into the lobby and saw through the window the unmistakable silhouette of the great author of *El Aleph*, then seventy-six years old, seated alone at a table, drinking an espresso. Such was his excitement that Paulo didn't have the courage to go up to him. Creeping out as silently as he had entered, he left without saying a word to Borges – something he would always regret.

At the age of twenty-eight, he was to spend his first Christmas away from his family. On the path to Christian reconversion, on 24 December he invited Beth to go with him to midnight mass. Surprised by her refusal – she preferred to spend the night walking through the streets of Buenos Aires – he simply ended the relationship. He telephoned Cissa in Rio on the pretext of wishing her a happy Christmas and declared: 'I'm in love with you and I'll be home in three days' time. If you promise to meet me at the airport, I'll take a plane so we can be together as soon as possible.'

Small, like him, with brown eyes and a slightly aquiline nose, Cecília Mac Dowell was nineteen and doing media studies at university in Rio de Janeiro when she met Paulo. She was the daughter of Patricia Fait, an American, and the wealthy and respected TB specialist Afonso Emílio de la Rocque Mac Dowell, the owner of a large clinic in Jacarepaguá. She had been educated at the traditional Colégio Brasileiro de Almeida in Copacabana, which had been set up and run by Nilza Jobim, the mother of the composer Tom Jobim. Although she came from a conservative background – her father came from the northeast and her mother had received a strict Protestant education – the Mac Dowells welcomed with open arms the hippie who had fallen in love with their youngest child. As the months went by, Patricia and Afonso Emílio shut their eyes to the fact that Cissa spent every weekend with her boyfriend (who had rented out his apartment in Voluntários da Pâtria and moved to the two-roomed apartment in noisy Barata Ribeiro). Thirty years later, Cissa would look back and see some ulterior motives behind her parents' broadmindedness: 'I think that because my two older sisters hadn't married, my parents lowered their expectations regarding future sons-in-law. They thought it best not to frighten off any potential candidates.'

Whatever her parents' reasoning, the fact is that at the end of the week, when the Mac Dowells went to their country house in Petrópolis, Cissa would put a few clothes and possessions into a cloth bag and set off to the apartment in Barata Ribeiro. The memory of his disastrous engagement to Eneida, however, continued to trouble Paulo whenever such a situation threatened to reappear: He wrote in his diary: 'This evening, we're having supper at Cissa's house and I hate that because it looks like we're engaged, and the last thing I want at the moment is to be someone's fiancé.' During one of his sessions with the psychiatrist, which he continued to attend frequently, Dr Benjamim Gomes suggested that his nervous tension arose from his problems with sexual relationships: 'He said that my lack of interest in sex is causing the tension I'm experiencing. In fact, Cissa is a bit like me: she doesn't insist that much on having sex. This suited me fine because I wasn't under any obligation, but now I'm going to use sex as a therapy to relieve tension. Dr Benjamim told me that the curve on the graph produced by electroshock treatment is the same as for an orgasm or for an epileptic fit. That's how I discovered sex as therapy.'

Although he still avoided any mention of an engagement, in March 1976, when his girlfriend returned from a three-week trip to Europe, Paulo proposed marriage. Cissa accepted with genuine happiness, but she laid down certain conditions: she wanted a real marriage, both in a register office and in church, with a priest, and with the bride in white and the groom in jacket and tie. He burst out laughing, telling her that he would accept all her demands in the name of love; 'besides I really needed to do something conventional and there was nothing better than marriage for that'.

Before the ceremony Paulo consulted the I Ching several times to discover whether he was doing the right thing, and he recorded in his diary his feelings of insecurity: 'Yesterday I was filled with a real dread of marriage and I was terrified. I reacted violently. We were both feeling a bit suspicious of each other and things turned ugly.' Two days later, his state of mind was quite different: 'I've been sleeping away from the apartment because I'm suffering from paranoia. I'm desperate for Cissa to come and live with me now. We really do love each other and understand each other and she's a very easy person to be with. But before she can do that, we have to go through the farce of the wedding.'

On 2 July, however, Paulo was even more dressed up than his fiancée had demanded. Punctually, at seven in the evening, as Chopin's Nocturne No. 2 was playing, he took his place to the right of the priest in St Joseph's Church. Compared with the Paulo Coelho who had allowed himself to be photographed drunk and dishevelled in New York two years earlier, the man at the altar looked like a prince. With short hair, and his moustache and goatee neatly trimmed, he was wearing a modern morning suit, with a double-breasted jacket, striped trousers, black shoes, a white shirt with cufflinks and a silver tie – identical clothes to those worn by his father and father-in-law, although not by his two best men, Roberto Menescal and Raul Seixas.

To the sound of Elgar's 'Pomp and Circumstance', five bridesmaids led the way for the bride, who arrived on her father's arm and wearing a long white dress. Among the dozens of guests filling the church, Raul Seixas was a most striking figure, in dark glasses, red bowtie and a jacket with matching red stitching. At the blessing of the rings, music filled the nave and the ceremony ended to the chords of Albinoni's Adagio. Afterwards, everyone went back to the bride's parents' apartment, where the civil ceremony was performed, followed by a magnificent dinner.

The honeymoon was nothing special. Since both had to get back to work, they spent a week in a summer house that belonged to Paulo's parents on the island of Jaguanum, off the Rio de Janeiro coast. Neither has particularly fond memories of that time. There is no reference to the trip in Paulo's diaries, and Cissa commented: 'Paulo wasn't very happy. I don't think he wanted all that formality … He agreed to it, but only, I think, because I insisted. But it wasn't the sort of honeymoon, where you'd say, oh, it was marvellous, we were so in love. No. No, I don't recall that. I know we spent a few days there, I can't say how many, and then went back to our little life in Rio.'

Their 'little life' was to start with a slight disagreement between husband and wife. Paulo insisted on living in his two-room apartment in Barata Ribeiro, not because it was cheap, but because it was near his parents, who had sold their house in Gávea and moved to a new apartment in Rua Raimundo Correia, in Copacabana, just a block away. The memories Cissa has of the first months of her marriage are not very encouraging:

> Living there was dreadful. The only bedroom looked directly out on to Rua Barata Ribeiro, which was incredibly noisy. But he was in his maternal phase and wanted it so that he could be close to his mother, who lived in the same district. Our apartment would hardly have fitted into a decent-sized living room. He had another apartment, but wanted to stay close to his mother. I had been brought up to be a good Protestant, and so I did everything I could for the sake of the marriage and learned to fall asleep to the noise from the street. We got married in July, and I think we stayed there for about six months.

This may not have been one of the most promising starts to a marriage, but the marriage survived. Sometimes, however, their fights were very noisy, as in the early hours of 24 August, Paulo's twenty-ninth birthday. Cissa was woken at two in the morning by a loud bang, as if a bomb had gone off in the building. She got up, terrified, and found her husband in the sitting room with a burnt-out firework in his hand. With the inevitable spliff in the other hand, he had decided to let off some rockets, to the despair of the neighbours. Everything was, of course, recorded on tape:

> Paulo – It's 1:59 on 24th August 1976. I'm twenty-nine. I'm going to let off a rocket commemorating who I am and I'm going to record the noise [sound of the rocket exploding]. Great! Everyone is coming to their windows.
>
>   Cecília – Paulo!!
>
>   Paulo – What? Everyone's awake, the dogs are barking ...

Cecília – This is absurd!

Paulo – What?

Cecília – Are you mad?

Paulo – It made a fantastic noise! It echoed all over the city! I'm the champion! [laughing a lot]. It's great that I bought these rockets the other day! It's great! God, it was fun! [laughing a lot]. Fantastic! I think that I've really freed myself of a lot of things letting off that rocket!

Cecília – Come and sit here with me for a while. I'm frightened.

Paulo – Why are you frightened? Have you had a premonition or something?

Cecília – No Paulo, it's because I've had a difficult day.

Paulo – Ah, thank God for that! Jesus, this has been a real liberation, Cecília. Go on, you let off a rocket and you'll feel calm too, straight away. Stand here at the window and let off a rocket.

Cecília – No! Anyone hearing the noise will know where it came from. Forget about the rockets. Stay a bit with me, will you?

Paulo – [laughing a lot] Oh, this is so cool! Two o'clock in the morning, a rocket celebrating my birthday, the stars filling the sky. Oh, thank you, God! I'm going to let off my fireworks across the city! [sound of rockets exploding]

Cecília – Paulo! The porters in all the other buildings will see it's coming from here.

Cissa was in fact an easy person to live with, but she had a strong character and wouldn't be forced to do anything against her will. She accepted her husband's 'Castaneda-inspired ideas', as Eneida had, and would sometimes even join him in smoking a cannabis joint, but she wouldn't hear of any marital extravagances, which he called 'sexual propositions'. One day, Paulo woke late in the morning when, as usual, Cissa was at work. She had left a piece of paper on the bedside table with a handwritten note that seemed to burn his fingers as he read it. It said that if her husband had decided to 'settle down', then this certainly hadn't happened at home.

To whom it may concern:

I am quite relaxed about the 500 women Paulo has had in the past because none of them is a threat. But today I felt really worried about my marriage. When Paulo joked with a secretary that he was going to grab her arse, I thought that was really low-class, but it was much worse when I heard him suggest paying 'some guys' in Cinelândia to join in our sexual relationship. I knew he had done this before, but I never thought he would suggest something so disgusting to me, knowing me as Paulo knows me, and knowing what I think about it. So this morning I feel more alone than ever because I know I can't talk about it to anyone. The only thing I can see, and what I actually want at this moment, is to separate from Paulo as soon as possible, as soon as this stupid society allows it, but I know that it's going to be a real trauma for me and for my family.

They hadn't even been married for a year and already the marriage was floundering.

CHAPTER 19

London

H IS MARRIAGE MIGHT BE FALLING APART, but the same could not be said of Paulo's professional life. In December 1976, Philips released the fifth LP produced by Paulo and Raul, *Há Dez Mil Anos Atrás*, on which ten of the eleven tracks had lyrics written by him. It immediately became a phenomenal success. The album took its title from 'I Was Born Ten Thousand Years Ago', a traditional American song of which there were several versions, the most famous of which had been recorded by Elvis Presley four years earlier. It was also only the second time that Paulo had dedicated a song to anyone; in this case, the dedication was to his father, Pedro Queima Coelho. It was an unusual way of paying him homage, since the lyrics speak of the differences between himself and his father and are slightly condescending. Although he only admitted it years later, anyone who knew a little about his family history would realize that the 'Pedro' of 'Meu Amigo Pedro' ['My Friend Pedro'] was his father:

> Every time that I touch paradise
> Or else burn in hell,
> I think of you, my poor friend,
> Who always wears the same suit.

Pedro, I remember the old days
When we two used to think about the world.
Today, I call you square, Pedro
And you call me a bum.

Pedro, where you go I go too,
But everything ends where it started

And I've got nothing to say to you,
But don't criticize me for being the way I am,
Each one of us is a universe, Pedro,
Where you go I go too.

Success was synonymous with money and, as far as Paulo was concerned, money had to be transformed into bricks and mortar. By the end of 1976, he was the owner of a third property, a two-bedroom apartment in Rua Paulino Fernandes, in Flamengo, a few steps from the estate where he had been born and brought up. Despite the pleasure he took in being a property owner, there was a problem in being rich: the possible envy of other people, particularly communists. In this aspect, Paulo had become very conventional indeed. The long-haired hippie who, only a short time before, had challenged the consumer society and written ironical songs about materialism was now terrified of losing the money he had so eagerly accumulated. 'Today at the cinema I was gripped by this terrible fear of communism coming and taking away all my apartments,' Paulo confessed to his diary and added bluntly, 'I would never fight for the people. These words may come back to haunt me, but I would never do that. I fight for free thought and perhaps for an elite of privileged people who choose a society apart.'

The material stability that the world of music gave him, however, never seems to have diverted him from his old dream of becoming a great writer. In anxious moments he got to the point of feeling 'almost certain' that he would not achieve this. He was appalled each time he thought how close his thirtieth birthday was, the deadline he had given himself, and beyond which, he believed, he wouldn't have the slightest chance of being a literary success. But all it took to restore his enthusiasm was to read that Agatha Christie had accumulated a fortune of US$18 million simply from her book sales. On these occasions Paulo would plunge back into his daydreams: 'There's no way I want to publish my novels in Brazil. There's no market for them here. In Brazil, a book that sells 3,000 copies is deemed a success, while in the United States that would be considered a complete flop. There's no future here. If I want to be a writer I'm going to have to get out of here.'

Meanwhile, Paulo was obliged to submit to the routine of meetings and trips to São Paulo demanded by his position as a Philips executive. The company had decided to concentrate all its departments in one office, in the then remote Barra da Tijuca, a modern district that was just beginning to develop in Rio. He was against the move, not just because his work would then be 40 kilometres from his home – which meant he had to get over the trauma of that accident in Araruama, buy a car and take his driving test – but also because he was given a really tiny office. He complained to no one except his diary: 'I'm sitting in my new office, if that's what you can call the place I'm in now. Me and my team, comprising two secretaries, an assistant and an office boy, occupy an area of 30 square metres, i.e. 5 metres per person. This would be bad enough if it weren't for the fact that we also have to take into consideration the pile of obsolete furniture that has also been crammed into this small space.'

As well as the distance and discomfort, he realized that his job was all to do with vanity, prestige and squabbles over space in the media. This world of embattled egos and back-stabbings was hardly the ideal place for someone so tormented by fear and paranoia. If some big shot was less than effusive when he met him in the lift, Paulo would immediately see in this a threat to his job. Not being invited to a show or to some major launch in the music world was a guarantee of sleepless nights and page after despairing page in his diary. Being excluded from a company meeting could trigger an asthma attack. His insecurity reached extreme levels. A music producer who ignored him could provoke an internal crisis that almost prevented him from working. When a number of these symptoms coincided, Paulo would lose direction entirely.

I'm in a really bad way today, completely in the grip of paranoia. I think no one likes me, that they're going to play some dirty trick on me at any moment and that they don't pay me as much attention as they used to.

It all started when I was practically thrown out of a meeting this morning. It left me with a runny nose. Maybe the colds I get are psychosomatic. André Midani, the president of the company, came into the room and didn't even speak to me; my partner was in a foul mood, and I'm sure he's plotting against me. My name isn't mentioned in a newspaper column, when it should be.

To add to my persecution mania, I wasn't even invited to the launch of Nelson Motta's book. He's pretty much avoided me, and I've never been able to conceal my dislike of him.

I think people only tolerate me because I'm a friend of Menescal's. It really winds me up.

His dual role – as lyricist and Philips executive – also became a source of irrepressible fears. Paulo often had to produce lengthy reports for the Philips board containing critical appraisals of the most important artists contracted to the company, namely, his colleagues. Although only Midani, Menescal, Armando Pittigliani and one or two other directors read this information, it made him go cold just to think of that material falling into the hands or reaching the ears of the artists he had assessed. His fear was justifiable, as he was usually niggardly in his praise and harsh in his criticism. Paulo was nevertheless a more than dedicated worker whose enthusiasm for what he was doing often meant working late into the night. His work with Philips was one of the supports on which his fragile emotional stability was balanced. The second was his somewhat shaky marriage and the third, a new interest into which he threw himself body and soul, yoga. As well as this, and when things got too much, he asked for help from Dr Benjamim Gomes, who would get him back on track with an assortment of antidepressants.

In January 1977, Paulo had been convinced that Cissa was different from his previous partners. 'She is what she is, she's unlikely to change,' he wrote. 'I've stopped trying to change her because I can see how useless that is.' Gradually, however, he managed to interest his wife in at least one facet of his world – drugs. Cissa would never become a regular consumer, but it was because of him that she smoked cannabis for the first time and then experimented with LSD. Following a ritual similar to that adopted by Vera Richter when she smoked hashish for the first time, they had their first experiment with LSD on 19 March, St Joseph's feast day, after first kissing the saint's image. They turned on a tape recorder when Cissa placed the small tablet on her tongue and from then on she described her initial feelings of insecurity, how she felt, at first, sleepy and then experienced itching all over her body, finally reaching a state of ecstasy. At that moment, she began to hear 'indescribable' sounds. Sobbing, she tried unsuccessfully to describe what she felt: 'No one can stop what's going in my ears. I'll never forget what I'm hearing now. I need to try and describe it … I know that you heard what I heard. I was looking at the ceiling of our little home. I don't know … I think it's impossible to describe it, but I must … Paulo, it's such an amazing thing.' Her husband monitored this 'research' and also provided the sound track. The opening was a headline from *Jornal Nacional*, on TV Globo, announcing high numbers of traffic accidents in Rio. Then came Bach's Toccata and Fugue, and Wagner's Wedding March. To calm his guinea pig he promised that should she have a bad trip, a simple glass of freshly squeezed orange juice would quickly reverse the effects of the lysergic acid.

While drugs may have masked his anxieties, they were not enough to drive them away. It was during one of his deep depressions that a super-hero appeared to him in his room, on a mission to save him. This was the heavyweight Rocky Balboa, the character played by Sylvester Stallone in the film *Rocky*. In the early hours, in March 1977, as he and Cissa sat in bed watching the Oscar awards on TV, Paulo was moved to see *Rocky* win no fewer than three statuettes, for best film, best director and best editing. Like Balboa, who had come back from nothing to become a champion, he, too, wanted to be a winner and was determined to win his prize. And still the only thing he was interested in becoming was a writer with a worldwide readership. It was already clear in his mind that the first step on the long road to literary glory was to leave Brazil and write his books abroad. The following day he went to Menescal and told him he was leaving. If it had been up to Paulo, the couple's destination would have been Madrid, but Cissa's preference won the day and in early May 1977, the two disembarked at Heathrow airport in London, the city chosen as the birthplace of his first book.

A few days later, they were settled in a studio flat in 7 Palace Street, halfway between Victoria station and Buckingham Palace, for which they paid £186 a month. It was a tiny apartment, but it was in a good location and there was a further attraction: a bath. When they arrived in London, they opened an account at the Bank of Brazil with US$5,000. Money was not exactly a problem for Paulo, but as well as being known for his parsimony, he had a legal problem, which was the limit of US$300 a month that could be transferred to Brazilians living abroad. In order to get round this, at the end of each month Paulo and Cissa mobilized grandparents, uncles, aunts and cousins to each send US$300 to Brazilian friends who were resident in London and they would then deposit the money in the couple's account in the Bank of Brazil. Thus they received about US$1,500 a month without paying any tax.

Paulo's incomings included payment for a music column he wrote in the weekly magazine *Amiga*. Cissa did some journalistic work for the Brazilian section of the BBC and published the occasional short, signed article in the *Jornal do Brasil*, as well, of course, as doing all housework, since her husband's contribution in this area was nil. Worse, he refused to allow any frozen food in the house and politely asked his wife to buy a cookery book. The problem was translating the recipes. The two spent hours trying to understand a recipe so that she could transform it into a meal. A weekly menu listing each day's meals was solemnly posted in a prominent place on one of the walls of the apartment. From these menus it can be seen that they only allowed themselves meat once a week, although they made up for this with frequent visits to Indian and Thai restaurants.

They never lacked for money and what they received was enough to cover their expenses, including the classes in yoga, photography and vampirism that Paulo attended, as well as outings, short trips and taking in London's many cultural highlights. Paulo and Cissa were always first in the queue when something was shown that would have been banned by the censors in Brazil, such as the film *State of Siege*, directed by Costa-Gavras, which was a denunciation of the dictatorship in Uruguay. Three months went by without any real work being done. Paulo wrote: 'I have worked a maximum two days a week. That means that, on average, in these three months in Europe I've worked less than a month. For someone who wanted to conquer the world, for someone who arrived full of dreams and desires, two days' work a week is very little.'

As there seemed no way to write the wretched, longed-for book, Paulo tried to fill his time with productive activity. The classes in vampirism inspired him to write a film script, *The Vampire of London*. He sent it by post to well-known producers, all of whom replied politely, making it clear that, as far as they were concerned, vampires did not make good box office. One of them very kindly offered 'to look at the film when it's finished and give you my opinion as to whether or not we are prepared to distribute it'.

By July, Paulo and Cissa realized that it would not be easy to find friends in London. To compensate for this lack in their lives they had a short visit from his parents. The exchange of correspondence with Brazil was growing, in the form of letters or, as Paulo preferred, tapes, whenever there was someone who could take them back to Brazil. Piles and piles of cassette tapes collected in the houses of his parents and friends, particularly in that of his dearest friend, Roberto Menescal, from whom he learned that Rita Lee had found a new writing partner – which, added to the rejections from producers and publishers, led to pages of lamentation:

> My partner has found another writing partner. I've been forgotten far more quickly than I imagined: in just three months. In just three months I've lost any importance I had to cultural life over there. No one's written to me for several days.
>
> What's been going on? What lies behind the mysteries that led me here? The dream I've dreamed all my life? Right now I'm close to realizing that dream and yet I feel as though I'm not ready for it.

At the end of 1977, when it was time to renew the six-month contract with their landlord, the couple decided to leave the apartment in Palace

Street for a cheaper one. They put a five-line advertisement in the classified column of a London newspaper saying: 'Young professional couple need flat from November 15th, London area with telephone.' Days later, they had settled in Bassett Road, in Notting Hill, near Portobello, where Paulo would later set his novel *The Witch of Portobello*. It was not such a smart address as Palace Street, but they were now living in a far larger apartment that was also better and cheaper than the other one.

While the course in vampirism didn't help Paulo become a screenplay writer, it nevertheless left a mark on his life. There he met and fell in love with a charming twenty-four-year-old Japanese masseuse, Keiko Saito, who was as interested as he was in that lugubrious subject. As well as being his colleague on the course, Keiko became his companion in handing out pamphlets in the street, one day protesting against the mass killings perpetrated by 'Marshal' Pol Pot in Cambodia, and another collecting signatures in favour of the legalization of cannabis in Great Britain. Paulo broached the subject with Cissa: 'I'm in love with Keiko and I want to know how you feel about me inviting her to come and live with us.' On the only occasion when he spoke publicly about this episode – an interview in 1992 with the journalist W.F. Padovani, who was working for *Playboy* at the time – Paulo revealed that his wife happily accepted his proposal:

> *Playboy* – And what about your marriage to Cecília Mac Dowell?
> Paulo – It took place in church.
> *Playboy* – With the full regalia?
> Paulo – Yes, and Raul Seixas was my best man. Cecília and I then
>   went to live in London, where we enjoyed a *ménage à trois*.
> *Playboy* – How did that happen?
> Paulo – I did a course on vampires and fell in love with one of the
>   students, a Japanese girl called Keiko. Since I loved Cecília too,
>   I decided to live with them both.
> *Playboy* – Did they meet?
> Paulo – Oh, yes, we lived together for a year.
> *Playboy* – And how was it in bed?

Paulo – I had sex with them both at the same time, but they didn't
    have sex with each other.

Playboy – Wasn't one jealous of the other?

Paulo – No, never.

Playboy – Wasn't there a time when you felt you wanted to make
    love just to one of them alone?

Paulo – As far as I can remember, no. It was a very intense love
    affair *à trois*.

Playboy – Cecília and Keiko didn't have sex, but what exactly did
    they feel for each other?

Paulo – They were very fond of each other. They knew how much I
    loved them and I knew how much they loved me.

Just as the Chinese and Soviet communist leaders used to do with political dissenters in official photos, Paulo airbrushed from the scene
described in *Playboy* an important character in this story, a young, long-
haired Brazilian music producer known as Peninha, who was also living
in London at the time. Paulo had always believed that Cissa was an easy
person to live with, but after living with her for a year he had learned that
he had married a woman who would not put up with any excesses. When
she realized that he was suggesting living with two women, like an
Arabian sheikh, in an apartment that had just one room and one bed, he
was astonished at her reaction:

'Keiko can come and live here, as long as you agree that Peninha can
move in too, because I'm in love with him as well.'

Paulo had no alternative but to agree to the involvement of this fourth
member of what he came to call 'the extended family', or the 'UN General
Assembly'. Whenever a relative of Cissa's or Paulo's arrived, Keiko and
Peninha had to vanish, as, for example, when Gail, Cissa's elder sister,
spent a week at the apartment.

To celebrate the New Year – the first and only one they spent in
England – the Coelhos travelled by train with the 'extended family' to
spend a few days in Edinburgh. The end of the year was always a time
for Paulo to weigh up triumphs and failures. He clearly wasn't going to
lay his hands on the imaginary Oscar that had been one of his reasons

for leaving Brazil in March. Months and months had passed without his producing a single line of the much dreamed-of book. Defeat followed defeat, as he confessed to his diary:

> It's been a time of rejections. Everything I've submitted to the various competitions I was eligible to enter has been rejected. The last remaining results arrived today. All the women I've wanted to go out with have rejected me. This isn't just my imagination. When I say 'all' I mean that there is not one exception.
>
> [...] Ever since I was a child I've dreamed of being a writer, of going abroad to write and becoming world-famous. Obviously London was the step I dreamed of taking when I was a child. The fact is that the results haven't been what I was hoping for. My first and greatest disappointment has been with myself. I've had six months here to feel inspired and I haven't had enough discipline to write a single line.

The image Paulo gave to other people was of a successful lyricist whose hobby was writing about London for Brazilian magazines. His old friend Menescal, however, with whom he corresponded frequently, began to suspect that his protégé was not very happy and thought that it was time for him to end his stay in London. Paulo agreed to return to Brazil, but he didn't want to return with his tail between his legs, as though defeated. If Philips invited him to go back to work there, he would return to Rio de Janeiro the next day. Menescal not only flew to London to make the offer but took with him Heleno Oliveira, a top executive of the multinational company. The job would not begin until March 1978, but it was the invitation Paulo needed, not the job. The day before leaving, he collected together the few pieces of writing he had managed to produce during those sterile months in London and put them in an envelope on which, after sealing it, he wrote his own name and address. Then, as he was drinking a whisky with Menescal in a modest pub in the Portobello Road, he 'accidentally' left the envelope on the bar. On his last night in the city, he explained to his diary the reason for this act: 'I've left everything I've written this year in that bar. It's the last chance for someone to discover me and say: this guy's brilliant. So there's my name and address. If they want to, they can find me.'

Either the package was lost or whoever found it did not consider its contents particularly brilliant. The couple returned to Brazil in February 1978. During the flight, Cissa broke down in tears and Paulo summarized the situation thus: 'In London all my hopes of becoming a world-famous writer were dashed.'

As various of the characters he created later on would say: this was just another defeat, not a failure. He and Cissa returned to the apartment in Rua Barata Ribeiro, which had seemed unsuitable even before their trip to England. As soon as they were back, Paulo began to predict dark times for his marriage, if the 'emotional flexibility' that had prevailed in London did not extend to Brazil:

> My relationship with Cissa could prove lasting if she showed the same emotional flexibility that existed in London. We have already advanced far enough for a small step back to be acceptable. On the other hand, there will be no opportunities. It is just going to be a question of time. Let's hope that everything turns out all right. Although I think that our return to Brazil means that we're more likely to split up than to stay together, because here we're less forgiving of each other's weaknesses.

Some months later, they moved to the fourth property that Paulo had added to his small urban portfolio. Bought with the royalties that had accumulated during his absence, this was a comfortable three-bedroom apartment in Rua Senador Eusébio in Flamengo, two blocks from the Paissandu cinema, three from the home of his ex-fiancée Eneida and a few metres from where Raul Seixas lived. They decorated half the sitting-room wall with photos and souvenirs of their trip to London, which began to take on another meaning: while on the one hand, they reminded the couple of the happy times they had spent there, on the other, they were, for Paulo, a permanent reminder that he had not succeeded in writing 'the book'.

In March he took up his job as artistic producer with Philips and during the months that followed, he resumed his routine as executive at a recording company. Since he disliked getting up early, he was frequently woken at ten in the morning with a telephone call from his secretary, telling him that someone had been asking for him. He would drive from home to Barra da Tijuca in his own car and spend the rest of the day in endless meetings, many out of the office, with artists, directors of the company and journalists from the music world. In his office he ended up dealing with everything. In between fielding numerous telephone calls, he would sort out administrative matters, approve record sleeves and write letters to fans on behalf of famous artists.

The fact that Raul Seixas was near by didn't mean that the partners became close again. Indeed, at the end of the year, the two 'close enemies' were invited by WEA, Raul's new recording company, to try to recreate the partnership that had taken Brazil by storm, but the attempt failed. The LP *Mata Virgem*, for which Paulo wrote five lyrics ('Judas', 'As Profecias', 'Tá na Hora', 'Conserve seu Medo' and 'Magia de Amor'), was released at the beginning of 1979, but did not achieve even a tenth of the sales of such albums as *Gita* and *Há Dez Mil Anos Atrás*.

The fame that the two had experienced between 1973 and 1975 became a thing of the past, but Paulo had absorbed the lesson that Raul had taught him – 'Writing music is like writing a story in twenty lines that someone can listen to ten times without getting bored' – and was no longer dependent on his partner. Besides the five songs he wrote for *Mata Virgem*, in 1978 he wrote almost twenty songs in partnership with all the performers who were making a mark on the popular Brazilian music of the time. He had become a sort of jack-of-all-trades in show business, writing songs, directing and scripting shows, and when Pedro Rovai, a director of porn films, decided to make *Amante Latino*, he invited Paulo to write the script for that.

As was usually the case with his fragile emotional state, when his work was going well, his emotional life wasn't – and vice versa. This time was no different. The clear skies he was enjoying professionally clouded over when he returned home. The bitterness between him and Cissa gave way to ever more frequent arguments, and then came the endless silences that could last for days. In February 1979, he decided to go alone on a boat trip to Patagonia. When the liner anchored in Buenos Aires on the way back to Brazil, he phoned Cissa and suggested that they separate. Given how concerned he was with signs, it's surprising that he failed to realize that, three years earlier, he had proposed marriage to her by telephone and from Buenos Aires.

The separation took place on 24 March 1979, when Cissa left the apartment in Rua Senador Eusébio, and it was legally ratified on 11 June in a family court 50 metres from St Joseph's Church, where they had married. The hearing nearly didn't take place. Firstly, because Cissa had to go out at the last minute to buy a skirt, because the judge would not allow jeans in the court. Then, the lawyer had forgotten a document, which meant that they had to bribe an employee in the register office in order to get their certificate of legal separation.

Setting aside their disagreements, the two went out afterwards to have a civilized lunch in a restaurant. They each had a very different memory of the end of their marriage. Paulo wrote: 'I don't know how unhappy she is, but she certainly cried a lot. I didn't find the procedure in the least traumatic. I left and went back to work in other offices, other rooms, other worlds. I had a good dinner and enjoyed it more than I have for a long time, but that had nothing to do with the separation. It was all down to the cook, who made a really delicious meal.' Cissa, on the other hand, set down her feelings in a brief note written in English, which she posted to him. She found fault with him in the one area where he considered himself to be good – in bed: 'One of our main problems, in my view, was sex. I never understood why you didn't think about me in bed. I could have been much better if I had felt that you were thinking about my pleasure in bed. But you didn't. You never thought about it. So I began not to think about your pleasure either.'

For someone whose emotional stability was so dependent on a stable relationship with a woman who would help him through his psychological storms, the end of the marriage was sure to presage more depression and more melancholy. Not that he lacked for women – on the contrary. The problem now was that Paulo had got it into his head that they were sucking out the energy that he should be putting into his career as a writer. 'I've gone out a lot, had sex a lot, but with female vampires,' he wrote, 'and I don't want that any more.'

The person who appears to have been most seriously shaken by the separation was his mother. During Easter she wrote a long letter to her son, typewritten in single spacing. It does not appear to have been written by 'a fool', as Paulo called his mother more than once. The document reveals someone who had a knowledge of psychoanalytical jargon, which was unusual in a non-professional. She also insisted that it was he who was responsible for the separation, with his insecurities and his inability to recognize what he had lost:

My dearest son,

We have much in common, including the ease with which we express ourselves in letters. That's why, on this Easter Sunday, I'm sending you these lines in the hope that they will be of some help to you or at least let you know how much I love you, which is why I suffer when you suffer and am happy when you're happy.

As you can well imagine, you and Cissa are much on my mind. There's no need to tell me again that it's your problem and that I should simply keep out of it. That's why I don't really know whether I'll actually send you this letter.

When I say that I know you well I'm basing this simply on my mother's intuition, because much of you, unfortunately, was created far from us, and so there are lots of things I don't know. You were repressed during childhood and then suffocated by your own problems and ended up having to break off close relationships, break with convention and start from scratch. And although you were anxious, fearful, insecure, you succeeded. And how! But you also let go of a very repressed side to you, something you didn't know how to live with.

I only know Cecília a little, but she seems to me a practical woman. Strong. Fearless. Intuitive. Uncomplicated. It must have been a real shock to you when she paid you back in kind ... with her dependency, her hang-ups, her needs. She refused to carry your burden any more and that's what tipped the balance in your relationship. I don't know how it all ended, but you took it as a rejection, as lack of love, and couldn't accept it. There is only one way of resolving the problem: recognizing it. Identifying it. You told me that you don't know how to lose. We can only live life fully if we accept winning and we accept losing.

Lygia

Note: As you can see, I'm still a dreadful typist. But I've decided to beard the lion in his den, and I'm sending the letter.

My dear son: I prayed a lot for you today in my way. I prayed that God would encourage in you the certainty that it's in your hands to build your life, and that your life will always be the same as it has been up to now: full of conscious and honest decisions and full of moments of happiness and joy.

Much love,

L.

As he himself often wrote in his diary, there is nothing new under the sun. And as had been the case so often before in his life, the only way of compensating for an emotional defeat was to find new victories at work. So it seemed like a gift from God when he received an invitation in April 1979 – not even a month after his separation – to swap his job at Philips for that of product manager with their largest competitor, CBS. Included in the proposal was the prospect of prompt promotion to the post of artistic director. Following a succession of amorous and professional failures – the poor performance of the *Mata Virgem* album, the short-lived engagement to Eneida, the literary sterility in London, the end of his marriage – the invitation was a great relief, in large part because it would put him back in the media world of Rio and São Paulo, a world he hadn't frequented for some time. But it also awoke an unfamiliar and unpleasant side to his character: arrogance. Since one of his duties was to reorganize the artistic department, he started by rocking the boat. 'It's true, I did behave very arrogantly when I started work there,' he was to recall years later. 'I went round giving orders and giving the yes-men a really hard time; pure authoritarianism!' He suspected that money was being channelled out of the company and began to refuse to sign notes and invoices about which there might be any doubt.

Unaware that he was digging his own grave, he hired and fired, cut costs and closed departments, adding fuel to what was already a bonfire of egos and vanities. Meanwhile, those who had suffered most in his clean-up operation were plotting against him. One Monday, 13 August 1979, after two months and ten days in the job, he arrived at the company late in the morning and, having sent yet more heads rolling, was summoned to the office of Juan Truden, the president of CBS in Brazil. He was standing waiting for Paulo, smiling, his hand outstretched and with these words on his lips: 'My friend, you're fired.' Nothing more. No 'Good afternoon', no 'Hope it goes well'.

The impact was enormous, not simply because of the coldness of the dismissal but because he knew that this meant the end of his career as a recording executive. 'I was dismissed from the highest post, from the highest position in the profession, and I couldn't go back, I couldn't go back to being what I was at the beginning,' Paulo recalled years later in a statement at the Museum of Image and Sound in Rio de Janeiro. 'There were only six recording companies in Brazil and all the six positions I might really want were occupied.' Before packing his bags, he wrote a long, angry letter to Truden in which he said that, in view of the lack of structure in the company, 'CBS artists at the moment enjoy the dubious pleasure of being the most poorly served in the Brazilian market.' He finished dramatically, using an expression that had remained in the popular imagination since it had been used by the ex-president Jânio Quadros in his letter of resignation: 'And the same hidden forces that are responsible for my dismissal will one day have to face the truth. For you cannot hide the sun with a sieve, Sr Juan Truden.'

His dismissal ('for incompetence', as he learned later) was celebrated by the group of disaffected individuals he had created as manager, and would cause him still more humiliation. Some days later, at a social function, Paulo met Antônio Coelho Ribeiro, who had just been made president of Philips, the company Coelho had left in order to try his luck with CBS. When he saw him, Ribeiro said, in front of everyone: 'You always were a bluffer.'

Ten months later, Antônio Ribeiro, too, got the sack. When he heard the news, Paulo took from a drawer a present he had bought shortly after Ribeiro had publicly insulted him. He went to the Ribeiros' apartment and, when Ribeiro opened the door, Paulo hurriedly explained the reason for his presence there: 'Do you remember what you said to me when I was sacked? Right, now you can repeat those words every day as you look into your own eyes.' He unwrapped the object and handed it to Ribeiro. It was a wall mirror on which he had had the wretched words painted in capitals: 'YOU ALWAYS WERE A BLUFFER.' Once he had returned the insult, he turned, took the lift and left.

It was time for Paulo to heal his wounds. Now that he had been ejected from the world of show business, his name did not appear again in the press until the end of the year, when the magazine *Fatos&Fotos* published an article entitled 'Vampirology: a Science that Now Has its Own Brazilian Master'. He was the master, presenting himself as a specialist in the subject, and he announced that he was writing the script for a feature film on vampires, which was, in fact, never made. His unexpected dismissal from CBS had caught him unawares, and with the scars from the recent breakdown of his marriage still open he was unable to bear the setback alone. In his solitude, his mind oscillated between delusions of grandeur and feelings of persecution, which, at times, he managed to bring together in his diary in one sentence: 'Every day it seems harder to achieve my great ideal: to be famous and respected, to be the man who wrote the Book of the Century, the Thought of the Millennium, the History of Humanity.'

This seemed to be simply a repeat of what various doctors had diagnosed as paranoid schizophrenia or manic depression. The problem was that it was nearly time for his traditional end-of-year taking stock and, at thirty-two, he had still not succeeded in realizing his dream. There were moments when he seemed to accept being a writer like any other. 'Sometimes I think about writing an erotic story, and I know it would get published,' he noted in his diary. 'Besides which, I could devote myself to that one genre, which is gaining ground here now that pornographic magazines are being published again. I could think up some really good pseudonym.' These plans were followed by questions he could not answer. Why write erotic books? To earn money? He was already earning money and he still wasn't happy. In order not to have to accept that his problems were caused by no one but himself, he returned to the old story: he hadn't written before because he was married and Cissa didn't help. Now it was because he was alone and loneliness was preventing him from writing.

> I carry on with the same plans, which haven't yet died in me. I can resuscitate them whenever I want to; all I have to do is find the woman of my life. And I really do want to find her soon …
>
> […] I've been very, very lonely. I can't be happy without a woman at my side.
>
> […] I'm tired of searching. I need someone. If I had a woman I could love, I'd be all right.

In his misery Paulo seemed to be confirming the popular belief that there's none so blind as those who will not see, because 'the woman of his life' had been right there before him for more than ten years without ever receiving from him a smile or even a handshake. It's surprising that such a pretty girl – petite, with dark hair, gentle eyes and porcelain skin – had gone unnoticed for such a long time by Paulo, the confirmed womanizer.

Paulo had met Christina Oiticica in 1968, when her uncle, Marcos, asked Sônia, Paulo's sister, to marry him. At Lygia's insistence, all the women invited to the formal engagement dinner were to wear long dresses. For the men, including Paulo, who was sporting a great dark mane of hair at the time and appeared to be completely out of it on drugs during the supper, she demanded dark suits. Christina and Paulo met several times in the years that followed at family gatherings and dinners without either really noticing the other. Naturally, one of these celebrations was for the marriage of Cissa and Paulo. When Paulo's sister took him to Christmas lunch in 1979 at Christina's parents' house, she was going out with Vicente, a young millionaire whose inheritance included, among other luxuries, a vast yacht. Destiny, however, had decided that she was to be the woman Paulo had so longed for. A week later, just as in a fairy tale, the two were together for ever.

CHAPTER 20

Christina

AFTER HER PRIMARY EDUCATION, Christina had been to Bennett College, a traditional Protestant establishment, where the Bible stories told during the Religious Knowledge lessons were the only thing that awoke in her a flicker of interest. She consistently failed in all other subjects, which meant that she had to leave the college and go from school to school until, like Paulo, she gave up completely. When she was seventeen, however, she was able to take a different educational route that would allow her to complete her secondary school studies in less than a year. It was only then that she returned to Bennett College, which had become a college of higher education, where she studied art and architecture. And at the end of 1979, when Paulo arrived at her parents' house for Christmas dinner, she was working as an architect.

Although they were practising Christians, Christina's parents were exceptionally liberal. If she wanted to go to lessons, she went. If she preferred to go to the cinema, no problem. And as soon as she was old enough, she was allowed to have her boyfriends sleep over at her parents' house without any objections on their part. Not, however, that she had that many boyfriends. Although she was very pretty, Chris was no flirt. She was a thoughtful girl, who enjoyed reading and, although she was not particularly religious, joined a choir at one of the Protestant churches.

On the other hand, she also went to see films at the Paissandu, bought clothes at Bibba, the fashion boutique in Ipanema, and consumed large quantities of whisky at Lama's. She went out every night and would often not get home until dawn, her legs unsteady. 'My drug was alcohol,' she confessed years later. 'I simply loved alcohol.'

It was growing dark by the time coffee was being served at the end of Christmas lunch in the Oiticica household. Paulo had had his eye on Chris since he arrived and, even though she was going out with someone else, he decided to use his cousin Sérgio Weguelin, who was also present, to find out whether or not she was doing anything that evening. When it was time to leave, he asked his cousin to invite her to go with them to see Woody Allen's latest hit, *Manhattan*. She was taken by surprise and didn't know what to say. The next thing she knew, she was alone in the cinema with Paulo, not watching *Manhattan*, which was sold out, but a re-run of *Airport*, which had been released almost ten years earlier.

Paulo behaved like a true gentleman throughout the film, and didn't even try to hold Chris's hand. When they left, they found the square outside the cinema full of jugglers, fortune-tellers, tarot readers, chiromancers, fire-eaters and, of course, several religious choirs each singing a different hymn. They walked along until they came to a fake Indian sitting in front of a wicker basket in which was coiled a terrifying reptile 6 metres in length. It was an enormous anaconda, a non-poisonous snake that was, however, capable of asphyxiating an ox or a human, swallowing it whole and spending weeks digesting the remains of its prey.

With a mixture of fear and disgust for the creature the couple went up to the Indian. As naturally as if he were merely asking the time, Paulo said to Chris: 'If I kiss the snake on the mouth will you kiss me on the mouth?'

She couldn't believe what she was hearing. 'Kiss that monster? Are you mad?'

When she realized that he was serious, she accepted the dare. 'Fine: if you kiss the snake, I'll kiss you on the mouth.'

To her astonishment and to that of the Indian and all the bystanders, Paulo stepped forward, grabbed the head of the snake in both hands and kissed it. Then, in front of dozens of wide-eyed spectators, he turned, took Chris in his arms and gave her a long, movie-style kiss on the lips, a kiss that was greeted with a round of applause by those present. Paulo got more than a kiss. A few hours later, the two were sleeping together in his apartment.

On the last day of the year – having first consulted the I Ching – he invited her to spend New Year with him in the sixth of the properties he owned, a small, pleasant summer house he had just bought in the seaside resort of Cabo Frio. The little white chalet, with red windows and a thatched roof, was exactly the same as the other seventy-four in a condominium called Cabana Clube designed by Renato Menescal, the architect brother of Paulo's friend Roberto. On their way there, Paulo told Christina that the previous night he had dreamed of a voice that kept saying over and over: 'Don't spend New Year's Eve in the cemetery.' Since neither could work out what this meant, and since they had no plans to see in the New Year in a cemetery, the matter was forgotten.

Immediately after they arrived in Cabo Frio, they both sensed a strange atmosphere in the house, although they were unable to pinpoint what it was. It wasn't something they could smell or see; it was what Paulo would call negative energy. As night fell, they began to hear noises, but couldn't work out where they were coming from – it sounded as though some creature, human or animal, was dragging itself through the rooms, but apart from the two of them there was no one else there. Feeling both intrigued and frightened, they went out for dinner.

In the restaurant, they told the waiter about these strange occurrences and were given an explanation that made their hair stand on end: 'Are you staying at the Cabana Clube? There used to be an Indian cemetery there. When they were building the foundations, they found the bones of hundreds of Indians, but built the houses on top of them anyway. Everyone in Cabo Frio knows that it's haunted.'

So that was what the warning in Paulo's dream had meant. Paulo and Chris stayed in a hotel that night and didn't go back to the house until the next morning, and even then, they only went to collect their clothes. A few weeks later, the chalet was sold for the same US$4,000 it had cost a few months earlier.

No ghosts darkened their relationship, however. After breaking up with her boyfriend during the first days of the New Year, Chris moved

into Paulo's apartment, with all her clothes, furniture and personal possessions, including the easel she needed for her work as an architect. There
then began a partnership which, though it has never been formalized, has
remained solid ever since.

The start of their life together was not easy, though. As preoccupied
as Paulo was with interpreting signs, Chris was most upset to find in the
apartment a biography of Count Dracula open on a Bible lectern. It was
not that she had anything against vampires or vampirologists – she even
liked films on the subject – but she was appalled that a sacred object
should be used as a joke, something which she believed would attract
negative energies into the house. She was so shocked that she went out
into the street and from the first available public telephone called the
Baptist pastor who used to counsel her and told him what she had seen.
They prayed together over the phone and, before returning to the apartment, Chris thought it prudent to go into a church. She only calmed down
when Paulo explained that his interest in vampirology had absolutely
nothing to do with satanism, OTO or Aleister Crowley, saying: 'The myth
of the vampire existed a hundred years before Christ. I haven't had any
contact with anyone involved in the dark arts for years.'

In fact, he hadn't had anything to do with Marcelo Motta's satanists
since 1974, but he continued to appear publicly here and there as a
specialist on the work of Aleister Crowley. Indeed, some months later he
wrote a long article on the English occultist in *Planeta*, which was illustrated with drawings by Chris. Their relationship went through further
rocky times before it finally settled down. Paulo was still racked with
doubt: was Chris really the 'marvellous companion' he had been waiting
for? He feared that deep down the two were only together for the same,
unspoken reason, what he called 'the paranoiac desire to escape solitude'.
However, even while he was saying that he was afraid of falling in love
with her, he broke out in a cold sweat at the thought of losing her. 'We had
our first serious argument a few days ago, when she refused to go to
Araruama with me. Suddenly I was terrified to think how easily I could
lose Chris. I did everything to get her and have her close. I like her, she
brings me peace, calm, and I feel that we can try and build something
together.'

These ups and downs at the start of their life together did not stop them celebrating their partnership unofficially. On 22 June 1980, a dreary Sunday, they blessed their union with a lunch for their parents, relatives and a few friends in the apartment where they were living. Christina took charge of the hippie-style decorations and on each invitation she wrote a psalm or proverb illustrated with a drawing. Chris's eclectic interest in religion seems to have helped the couple's relationship. When they met, she was already a specialist in tarot, on which she had read numerous books, and, even though she didn't consult the I Ching as often as Paulo, she knew how to interpret its predictions. When Paulo read *The Book of Mediums* by Allan Kardec, the couple decided to see if they could be mediums. Just as Cissa had been a guinea pig in the experiment with LSD, now Paulo was trying to get Chris to write down messages from the Beyond. He wrote: 'I have performed a few experiments. We began last week, when I bought the book. Chris has acted as a medium, and we have achieved some elementary communications. I've found this all very troubling. My concept of things has changed radically since I arrived scientifically at the conclusion that spirits do exist. They exist and are all around us.' Much later, Chris confirmed that the experiment had worked. 'I'm sure that a table really did move,' she recalls, 'and I also wrote down some texts that were dictated to me.'

The suspicion that she might have powers as a medium continued to grow from the moment when she was gripped by strange, inexplicable feelings of dread whenever she went into the bathroom of their apartment. They were odd sensations which she herself had difficulty understanding and of which she never spoke to anyone. More than once it entered her mind to turn on the gas for the shower, seal up the exits and kill herself. On the afternoon of Monday, 13 October, she left her easel and went into the bathroom. This time the desire to kill herself seemed uncontrollable, but fearing that death by asphyxiation might be very slow and painful she decided to turn to medication. She calmly took a taxi to her parents' house in Jardim Botânico, where she knew she would find the tranquillizers that her mother took regularly – Somalium, she recalls, or Valium in Paulo's version of events. Whatever the name of the medication, the fact is that she emptied a whole pack into her mouth, wrote a short note to Paulo and collapsed on the bed.

When he arrived home and Chris wasn't there, Paulo went to her parents' apartment, where they both often used to have dinner, and found Chris unconscious on the bed and, beside her, as well as the note, an empty pack of Valium. With the help of Chris's mother, who had just arrived, he managed to get her to the lift, having first made Chris put her finger down her throat and vomit up what she could. Outside, they stopped the first taxi that passed and went to the St Bernard clinic in Gávea, where the doctors pumped out her stomach. Once recovered, hours later, she was well enough to go home.

While she was sleeping and having spoken to her about what happened, Paulo kept asking himself where those strange emanations in the bathroom came from. With the question still going round and round in his head, he went downstairs to talk to the porter, tell him what had happened to Chris and see if he had an answer to the mystery. The man said: 'The last person who lived in that apartment, before you, was an airline captain who gassed himself in the bathroom.' When he went back upstairs and told Chris the story, she didn't think twice: despite having been in hospital only a few hours earlier, she got up, collected together a change of clothes for them both, as well as other personal items, threw everything into a suitcase and announced: 'We're going to my mother's house. I never want to set foot in this apartment again.'

Neither of them did, not even to move house. They spent a little more than a month with Chris's parents, long enough for work on the seventh property Paulo had bought to be completed so that they could move in there. This was a ground-floor apartment with a lovely garden and one particularly priceless feature: it was in the same building as Lygia and Pedro's apartment. He could only have felt more emotionally secure if he were actually living with his parents.

Chris's rules regarding Paulo's sexual excesses always prevailed, but they were still far from being an average couple. One day, for example, Paulo suggested that they should both try an experiment that had its origins in the Middle Ages, and to which he gave the grand name of 'a reciprocal test of resistance to pain'. Chris agreed, although she knew what was involved: stark naked, they began to whip each other with a thin bamboo cane. They took it in turns to beat the other on the back, the blows growing harder and harder, until they reached the limit of physical endurance. This occurred only when they were both bleeding from their wounds.

Their relationship gradually began to settle down. The first two years passed without anything untoward disrupting their life together. Encouraged by her partner, Chris began to paint again, something she had given up four years earlier, while Paulo began to direct so-called TV 'specials'. Not that they needed money to live on. Besides the forty-one songs he had written with Raul Seixas, in the past few years, Paulo had written more than a hundred lyrics – originals or versions of foreign hits – for dozens of different artists. This meant that the royalties continued to flow into his bank account. He tried to keep busy, however, fearing that idleness would lead him into depression again. Besides the TV specials, he gave talks and took part in round-table discussions on music and, occasionally, on vampirism. But the cure only worked for a while, because even when he was fully occupied, he would still suffer occasional anxiety attacks.

When this occurred, as it did at the end of 1981, he continued to give vent to his feelings in his diary:

These last two days, I missed two appointments, on the pretext that I was having a tooth extracted. I'm completely confused as to what to do. I can't even be bothered to write a short press release that would bring in a tiny amount of money. The situation inside me is this. I can't even write these pages and this year, which I was hoping would be better than last, has turned out precisely as I described above. Oh, yes: I haven't had a bath for the last few days.

The crisis appears to have hit him so badly that he even changed his behaviour regarding something that had always been very dear to him – money: 'I haven't paid attention to anything, including one of the things that I really like: money. Just imagine, I don't know how much is in my bank account, something I've always known down to the minutest detail.

I've lost interest in sex, in writing, in going to the cinema, in reading, even in the plants I've been tending so lovingly for so long and that are now dying because I only water them sporadically.'

If he had lost interest in both money and sex, things were very bad indeed, and so he did what he always did in such situations – he went back to Dr Benjamim, visiting him once a week. Whenever he felt like this, he would always ask Chris the same question: 'Am I on the right path?' And so, at the end of 1981, she made a suggestion that struck a chord in his nomadic soul: why not just leave everything and go off travelling with no fixed destination and no date set for their return? Her instincts told her that this was the right path. Years later, Chris would recall: 'Something was telling me that it would work. Paulo trusted my instinct and decided to drop everything.' Determined to 'search for the meaning of life', wherever it might be, he asked permission to leave his unpaid post with TV Globo, bought two air tickets to Madrid – the cheapest he could find – and promised that he and Chris would return to Brazil only when the last cent of the US$17,000 he took with him had run out.

Unlike all Paulo's other trips, this one, which was to last eight months, was made without any forward planning. Although he took more than enough for a comfortable trip, with no need to cut corners, he was never one to squander money. He chose Iberia, the airline that not only offered the cheapest flights but added in a free night in a hotel in Madrid. From Spain he and Chris went on to London at the beginning of December 1981, where they rented the cheapest car available, a tiny Citroën 2CV. In London, they also established the first rule of the trip: neither should carry more than 6 kilos of luggage. This meant sacrificing the heavy Olivetti typewriter that Paulo had taken with him; this was shipped back to Brazil.

While pondering what direction to take, Paulo and Chris remained in London until the middle of January 1982, when they took to the road, determined to visit two places: Prague, where he wanted to make a promise to the Infant Jesus, and Bucharest, the capital of Romania and birthplace, 550 years earlier, of the nobleman Vlad Tepeş, who was the inspiration behind Bram Stoker's creation: the most famous of all the vampires, Count Dracula. On the afternoon of Tuesday, 19 January, they arrived in Vienna frozen to the bone, after almost a day travelling the 1,200 or so kilometres separating London from the capital of Austria. Their modest 2CV had no heater, which meant that they had to travel wrapped in woollen blankets in order to withstand the low winter temperatures. The stop in Vienna was so that they could obtain visas for Hungary, which they would have to cross in order to reach Romania.

Once this was done, they went to the Brazilian embassy, where Chris needed to sort out a small bureaucratic matter. Paulo waited for her out in the street, smoking and walking up and down. Suddenly, with a sound like a bomb, a vast sheet of ice several metres long slid off the roof of the building five storeys above and crashed on to the street, ripping open the bodywork of a car that was parked only a few centimetres from where Paulo was standing. He had been that close to death.

After spending the night in Budapest, they left for the capital of Yugoslavia, where they decided to stay for three days. Not that Belgrade held any special attraction, but they couldn't face getting back into the freezing Citroën. The car had become such a problem that they decided to hand it back to the rental company. With the help of the hotel manager they found a real bargain: the Indian embassy was selling a light-blue Mercedes – nine years old, but in good condition – for a mere US$1,000. Although well used, it had a 110-horse-power engine and was equipped with an efficient heating system. This would be the only large expense of the trip. For advice on hotels, restaurants and places to visit, they relied on *Europe on 20 Dollars a Day*.

Now that they had a proper car, the 500 kilometres between Belgrade and Bucharest, the couple's next destination, could be done in one day. However, precisely because they now had a fast, comfortable car, they chose to take a more roundabout route. Having crossed Hungary and part of Austria, driving a little more than 1,000 kilometres, they arrived in Prague, where Paulo was to make the promise to the Infant Jesus that he would honour almost twenty-five years later. It was only then that they turned towards Romania, which meant another 1,500 kilometres. For anyone not in a hurry or concerned about money, this was wonderful.

During this criss-cross journey across Central Europe, chance placed another destination in their path. It was not until a few weeks after buying the Mercedes that Paulo discovered that the car had originally come from the old Federal Republic of Germany (or West Germany) and that the change of ownership had to be registered at the licensing authority in Bonn, the then capital of West Germany. Travelling from Bucharest to Bonn meant a journey of almost 2,000 kilometres, a distance that now held no worries for them. Two days after leaving the capital of Romania, the blue Mercedes was crossing the frontier into West Germany. From Bucharest to Munich, the first German city they went through, the odometer showed that they had driven 1,193 kilometres. Munich was completely covered in snow, it was almost midday and since neither of the travellers was hungry, instead of lunching there, they decided to stop in Stuttgart, about 200 kilometres further on. Minutes after passing through Munich, the capital of Bavaria, Paulo turned the car off the road into an avenue of bare trees with a sign written in German: 'Dachau Konzentrationslager'. It had long been in his mind to visit the sadly famous Nazi concentration camp in Dachau – since he was a boy he had been a passionate reader of books and stories about the Second World War – but little did he imagine that this visit, which lasted only a few hours, would radically change his life.

CHAPTER 21

First meeting with Jean

ALTHOUGH HE WOULD NOT PUBLISH his first real book until 1987, Paulo Coelho the author was born on 23 February 1982 at the age of thirty-five in Dachau concentration camp in Germany. Five days earlier, he had had a strange experience in Prague. Immediately after making his promise to the Infant Jesus of Prague, he had gone out with Chris for a walk round the city which, like almost all of Central Europe, was covered in snow and with below-zero temperatures. They crossed the river Vltava by the imposing Charles Bridge. One end of the bridge is in the Old City; the other comes out into the Street of Alchemists where, according to legend, lies the entrance to hell through which, naturally, Paulo was determined to go. The object of his interest was a medieval dungeon, which had been opened to the public some years before. In order to get in, he and Chris had to wait until the place had emptied of an enormous group of Soviet recruits – who appeared to be there as tourists.

Minutes after going through the doors of the dark dungeon and entering the cells, Paulo felt as though the ghosts from which he had believed himself to be free were reviving – the electroshock therapy, his supposed meeting with the Devil, his imprisonment by the Dops, his abduction, his cowardly betrayal of Gisa. From one moment to the next, all those events seemed to rise up, as though they had only just happened. He began to sob convulsively and Chris led him away. The gloomy surroundings had reawakened memories that threatened to propel him into a fit of deep depression, and he was thousands of kilometres from the security provided by his parents, Dr Benjamim's consulting rooms or Roberto Menescal.

This time, the origins of his torment were not metaphysical but all too real and visible on the pages of the newspapers and on the TV news: dictatorships, the state oppression of people, wars, abductions and clandestine imprisonments, which appeared to be sweeping the planet. Civil war was to claim almost 80,000 lives in the tiny state of El Salvador. In Chile, the savage dictatorship of General Pinochet was about to celebrate ten years of its existence and appeared to be as firmly entrenched as ever. In Brazil, the military dictatorship seemed exhausted, but there was still no guarantee that democracy was within reach. This was the worst possible state of mind in which to visit the site of a Nazi concentration camp, but this was precisely how Paulo was feeling when he parked the Mercedes in the visitors' car park in Dachau.

Dachau was the first camp built by the Third Reich and was the model for the remaining fifty-six scattered across ten European countries. It operated from 1933 until April 1945, when its gates were opened by the Allied troops. Although it was planned to house 6,000 prisoners, on the day of its liberation there were more than 30,000. During that tragic period, about 200,000 people of sixteen nationalities were taken there. Although the majority were Jews, there were also communists, socialists and others opposed to Nazism, as well as Gypsies and Jehovah's Witnesses. For reasons as yet unknown, the gas chamber in Dachau was never put to use, which meant that any prisoners who were condemned to death had to be taken by bus to Hartheim Castle, halfway between the camp and Linz, in Austria, which had been transformed into a centre of mass execution. The first surprise for Paulo and Chris as they went through the entrance gates of Dachau was that there was absolutely no one there. It was understandable that the freezing wind might have kept away the tourists, but they didn't see any porters, guards or officials who could give them any information. They were – or they appeared to be – alone in that enormous 180,000-square-metre rectangle surrounded on all sides by walls and empty watch towers. Paulo had not yet got over the dark thoughts that had assailed him in Prague some days before, but he didn't want to miss the opportunity of visiting one of the largest Nazi concentration camps. They followed the arrows and took the suggested route for visitors – the same as that taken by the prisoners. They went into the reception area, where the newly arrived prisoners would receive their uniforms, have their heads shaved and be 'disinfected' in a collective bath of insecticide. Then they walked down the corridors lined by cells, in which they saw the hooks attached to the ceiling beams from which the prisoners were hung by their arms during torture sessions; then they went into the sheds where, until the end of the war, bunk beds were stacked three or four high and where the prisoners slept like animals, packed into wooden cages. In total silence, their horror only grew with each new revelation.

Although Paulo was clearly upset, he saw the concentration camps as a tragedy of the past, part of the Nazism that was defeated in a war that had ended even before he was born. However, in the room set aside for the relatives of the dead to pay their respects, he felt that the emotions aroused in Prague were returning. The cards pinned on bunches of fresh flowers that had been put there only a few days earlier were living proof that Dachau was still an open wound. The 30,000 dead were not meaningless names taken from books, but human beings whose cruel deaths were recent enough still to awaken the grief of widows, children, brothers and sisters.

Paulo and Chris returned to the open area of the camp feeling overwhelmed. They walked along an avenue of bare trees whose branches looked like bony claws reaching for the sky. In the north part of the camp there were three small religious buildings – Catholic, Protestant and Jewish – beside which a fourth – Russian Orthodox – was to be built in the 1990s. The couple walked straight past these buildings, following a sign indicating the most chilling place in Dachau: the crematorium. At that point, they noticed a radical change in the landscape. Unlike the barren camp itself, which is a lunar landscape of grey stones with not a hint of greenery, the path leading to the crematorium passes through a small wood. Even in the hardest of winters this is covered by vegetation of tropical exuberance, with gardens, flowers and pathways between rows of shrubs. Planted in a clearing in the middle of the wood is a modest, rustic, red-brick building, which can only be distinguished from a traditional family house by the chimney, which seems disproportionately large. This was the crematorium oven, where the bodies of more than thirty thousand prisoners would have been burnt after their execution or death from starvation, suicide or illness, such as the typhoid epidemic that devastated the camp a few months before its liberation.

His experience in the medieval prison in Prague was still very clear in Paulo's mind. He saw all eight red-brick ovens and the metal stretchers on which the bodies would have been piled for incineration, and he stopped in front of a peeling door on which one word was written: 'Badzimmer'. This was not an old bathroom, as the name indicated, but the Dachau gas chamber. Although it was never used, Paulo wanted to feel for himself the terror experienced by millions in the Nazi extermination camps. He left Chris alone for a moment, went into the chamber and shut the door. Leaning against the wall, he looked up and saw, hanging from the ceiling, the fake showerheads from which the gas would be released. His blood froze and he left that place with the stench of death in his nose.

When he stepped out of the crematorium he heard the small bell of the Catholic chapel chiming midday. He went towards that sound and as he re-entered the harsh grey of the camp, he saw an enormous modern sculpture, which recalled Picasso's *Guernica*. On it was written in several languages 'Never again!' As he read the two words on entering the small church, a moment of peace came to him, as he was to remember many years later: 'I'm entering the church, my eye alights on that "Never Again!" and I say: Thank God for that! Never again! Never again is that going to happen! How good! Never again! Never again will there be that knock on the door at midnight, never again will people just disappear. What joy! Never again will the world experience that!'

He went into the chapel feeling full of hope and yet in the short space of time between lighting a candle and saying a quick prayer, he suddenly felt overwhelmed again by his old ghosts. In a moment, he went from faith to despair. As he crossed the frozen camp, a short way behind Chris, he realized that the 'Never again!' he had just read was nothing more than a joke in several languages:

> I said to myself: what do they mean 'Never again!'? 'Never again', my eye! What happened in Dachau is still happening in the world, on my continent, in my country. In Brazil, opponents of the regime were thrown from helicopters into the sea. I myself, on an infinitely smaller scale, lived for several years in a state of paranoia after being the victim of that same violence! I suddenly remembered the cover of *Time* with the killings in El Salvador, the dirty war waged by the Argentine dictatorship against the opposition. At that moment, I lost all hope in the human race. I felt that I had reached rock bottom. I decided that the world is shit, life is shit, and I'm nothing but shit for having done nothing about it.

While he was thinking these contradictory thoughts, a sentence began going round and round in his head: 'No man is an island.' Where had he read that? Slowly, he managed to rebuild and recite to himself almost the entire passage: 'No man is an island entire of itself; every man is a piece of the continent, a part of the main; if a clod be washed away by the sea, Europe is the less, as well as if a promontory were, as well as if a manor of thy friends or of thine own were; any man's death diminishes me, because I am involved in mankind ...' For a moment he could not remember the rest, but when he did, it seemed to have opened all the doors of his memory: 'and therefore never send to know for whom the bell tolls; it tolls for thee'. It was from one of John Donne's *Meditations*, from which Ernest Hemingway took the title for his novel. What happened in the following minutes is something that will remain for ever cloaked in mystery; indeed Paulo himself, on one of the few occasions when he has been urged to describe what occurred, became so emotional that he wept copiously: 'We were in the middle of a concentration camp, Chris and I, alone, absolutely alone, without another living soul around! At that moment I heard the sign: I felt that the bells of the chapel were ringing for me. That's when I had my epiphany.'

According to him, the revelation in Dachau took the form of a beam of light, under which a being of human appearance apparently told him something about possibly meeting again in two months' time. This message was given not in a human voice but, as Paulo himself put it, 'in a communication of souls'. Even the most sceptical would perhaps agree that something took place in Dachau, so radical was the change in Paulo's life from that day on. When he reached the car park, he wept as he told Chris what he had just experienced, and the first, horrifying suspicion fell on the OTO. What if what he had seen minutes earlier were the reincarnation of the Beast? Had the ghosts of Crowley and Marcelo Motta returned to frighten him eight years on? When they reached Bonn, six hours later, Paulo settled on the most rational explanation: he would consider the vision as a delirium, a brief hallucination provoked by the fear and tension he was feeling.

The couple planned to stay in Bonn just long enough to sort out the paperwork for the car and to meet Paula, a niece who had been born a few months earlier. Since they were staying at the home of Chris's sister, Tânia, and so were free of hotel expenses, they decided to extend their stay to a week. In early March, the couple set off once again, this time to cover the 250 kilometres between them and the liberal city of Amsterdam, which had so enchanted Paulo ten years earlier.

They stayed in the Hotel Brouwer, on the edge of the Singel Canal, where they paid US$17 a day for bed and breakfast. In a letter to his parents Paulo talked of the pot shops, 'cafés where you can freely buy and smoke drugs that are considered soft, like hashish and cannabis, although cocaine, heroin, opium and amphetamines, including LSD, are prohibited', and he took the opportunity to add a subtle apology for the liberalization of the drugs: 'This doesn't mean that the Dutch youth are drugged all the time. On the contrary, government statistics show that there are far fewer drug addicts here, proportionally speaking, than in the USA, Germany, England and France. Holland has the lowest rate of unemployment in the whole of Western Europe, and Amsterdam is the fourth largest commercial centre of the world.'

It was in this liberal atmosphere, where the two smoked cannabis until they got tired of it, that Chris tried LSD for the first and only time. Paulo was so shocked by the devastating effects of heroin on its users – zombies of various nationalities wandered the streets of the city – that he wrote two articles for the Brazilian magazine *Fatos&Fotos* entitled 'Heroin, the Road of No Return' and 'Amsterdam, the Kiss of the Needle'. His relationship with this underworld, however, was strictly professional, that of an investigative reporter. Judging by the letters he sent to his father, their European tour was a hippie journey in appearance only: 'We haven't deprived ourselves of anything, lunching and dining every day. And although we have a very thirsty child to support (the 110-horse-power Mercedes), we go to cinemas, saunas, barbers, nightclubs and even casinos.'

There seemed to be no end to the good life. After several weeks in the city, Paulo became bored by so much cannabis. He had tried varieties from places as far away as the Yemen and Bolivia. He had smoked blends of every strength and experimented with plants that had won prizes in the Cannabis Cup, the marijuana world cup which was held once a year in Amsterdam. He had even tried a new product called skunk – cannabis grown in a hot house and fed with fertilizers and proteins. And it was there, in that hippie paradise, that Paulo discovered that the plant had nothing more to offer him. He was, he said, 'fed up' with its repetitious effects. He repeated the oath he had made eight years earlier in New York regarding cocaine: he would never again smoke cannabis.

He was explaining all this to Chris in the hotel café when he felt a cold shiver run through him, just as he had in Dachau. He glanced to one side and saw that the shape he had seen in the concentration camp had taken physical form and was there having tea at a table nearby. His first feeling was one of terror. He had heard of societies which, in order to preserve their secrets, would pursue and even kill those who had left. Was he being followed by people belonging to a satanist group from the other side of the world? He suddenly remembered the lesson he had learned during those PE classes in Fortaleza de São João: to avoid unnecessary pain, confront the fear straight away.

He looked at the stranger – a man in his forties of European appearance, in jacket and tie – and summoned up his courage to address him in English in a deliberately hostile way: 'I saw you two months ago in

Dachau and I'm going to make one thing clear: I have not, nor do I wish to have, anything to do with occultism, sects or orders. If that's why you're here, then you've had a wasted journey.'

The man looked up and reacted quite calmly and, to Paulo's surprise, he replied in fluent Portuguese, albeit with a strong accent: 'Don't worry. Come and join me so that we can talk.'

'May I bring my partner?'

'No, I want to talk to you alone.'

Paulo made a sign to Chris to reassure her that everything was all right. Then he went and sat at the other man's table and asked: 'Talk about what?'

'What's all this about a concentration camp?'

'I thought I saw you there two months ago.'

The man said that there must be some confusion. Paulo insisted: 'I'm sorry, but I think that we met in February in the concentration camp at Dachau. You don't remember?'

The man then admitted that Paulo might have seen him, but that it could also have been a phenomenon known as 'astral projection', something Paulo knew about and to which he had referred many times in his diary. The man said: 'I wasn't at the concentration camp, but I understand what you're saying. Let me look at the palm of your hand.' Paulo cannot remember whether he showed him his left or his right hand, but the mysterious man studied it hard and then began to speak very slowly. He did not seem to be reading the lines on his hand; it was more as if he were seeing a vision: 'There is some unfinished business here. Something fell apart around 1974 or 1975. In magical terms, you grew up in the Tradition of the Serpent, and you may not even know what the Tradition of the Dove is.'

As a voracious reader of everything to do with magic, Paulo knew that these traditions were two different routes leading to the same place: magical knowledge, understood as the ability to use gifts that not all humans succeed in developing. The Tradition of the Dove (also known as the Tradition of the Sun) is a system of gradual, continuous learning, during which any disciple or novice will always depend on a Master, with a capital 'M'. On the other hand, the Tradition of the Serpent (or Tradition of the Moon) is usually chosen by intuitive individuals and, according to its initiates, by those who, in a previous existence, had some connection with or commitment to magic. The two routes are not mutually exclusive, and candidates to the so-called 'magical education' are recommended to follow the Tradition of the Dove once they have followed that of the Serpent.

Paulo began to relax when the man finally introduced himself. He was French, of Jewish origin, worked in Paris as an executive for the Dutch multinational Philips and was an active member of an old, mysterious Catholic religious order called RAM which stood for Regnus Agnus Mundi – Lamb of the Kingdom of the World – or 'Rigour, Adoration and Mercy'. He had gained his knowledge of Portuguese from long periods spent in Brazil and Portugal working for Philips. His real name – which could be 'Chaim', 'Jayme' or 'Jacques' – has never been revealed by Paulo, who began to refer to him publicly as 'the Master', 'Jean' or simply 'J'.

In measured tones, Jean said that he knew Paulo had started out along the road towards black magic, but had interrupted that journey. He said: 'If you want to take up the road to magic again and if you would like to do so within our order, then I can guide you. But, once you have made the decision, you will have to do whatever I tell you without argument.'

Astonished by what he was hearing, Paulo asked for time to reflect. Jean was uncompromising: 'You have a day to make your decision. I shall wait for you here tomorrow at the same time.'

Paulo could think of nothing else. While he had felt great relief at leaving the OTO and rejecting the ideas of Crowley, the world of magic, as opposed to black magic, continued to hold an enormous fascination for him. He recalled later: 'Emotionally I was still connected to it. It's like falling in love with a woman, and sending her away because she really doesn't fit in with your life. But you go on loving her. One day she turns up in a bar, as J did, and you say: "Please, go away. I don't want to see you again, I don't want to suffer again."'

Unable to sleep, he spent all night talking to Chris, and it was dawn when he finally made up his mind. Something was telling him that this was an important moment and he decided to accept the challenge, for good or ill. Some hours later, he met for the second (or was it the third?)

time the mysterious man who from that moment was to be his Master –
always with a capital M. Jean explained to Paulo what the first steps
towards his initiation would be: on the Tuesday of the following week he
was to go to the Vikingskipshuset, the Viking Ship Museum in Oslo.

'Go to the room where you will find three ships called the *Gokstad*,
Oseberg and *Borre* on display. There someone will hand you something.'

Not quite understanding what he was being asked to do, Paulo
wanted to know more. 'But what time should I be at the museum? How
will I recognize the person? Is it a man or a woman? What will they give
me?'

As Jean stood up, leaving a few coins on the table in payment for the
cup of tea he had drunk, he satisfied only a part of Paulo's curiosity: 'Be
in the room when the museum opens its doors. The other questions need
no answer. You will be told when we are to see each other again.' And
then he vanished, as if he had never existed – if indeed he ever did exist.
Whether real or supernatural, one thing was certain: he had left his new
disciple a task that would begin with a journey of almost 1,000 kilometres
to the capital of Norway, a city Paulo had never been to before. They
drove there through the snow via Holland, Germany and Denmark. On
the appointed day, Paulo woke early, worried that he might arrive late and
fearing that any queues and groups of tourists at the museum might delay
him. The publicity leaflet from the museum, which he had picked up in the
lobby of the hotel, informed him that the doors opened at nine in the
morning, but he set off a whole hour earlier. Situated on the Bygdøy
Peninsula, ten minutes' drive from the centre of the city, the
Vikingskipshuset is a large yellow building in the shape of a cross, with no
windows and a pointed roof. It was only when he arrived that Paulo realized he had misunderstood the opening hours. The museum was open
from nine in the morning until six in the evening during the high season,
but from October to April, the doors only opened at eleven. He spent the
time reflecting on the decision he had just taken. 'I had tried everything
in order to realize my dream to be a writer, but I was still a nobody,' Paulo
was to recall later. 'I had abandoned black magic and the occult sciences
when I discovered that they were of no help to me at all, so why not try
the route Jean was suggesting?'

At eleven on the dot, he joined the half-dozen Japanese tourists who were also waiting and followed the arrows to the room with high, curved walls like a church nave, where the *Gokstad*, *Oseberg* and *Borre* were displayed. There was only one other person there – a pretty blonde woman of about forty, who seemed to be absorbed in reading a plaque on one of the walls. When she heard his footsteps, she turned, revealing that she was holding something long, like a walking stick or a sword. She said nothing, but walked towards him, took a silver ring bearing the image of an ouroboros – the snake that devours its own tail – from the ring finger of her left hand and placed it on the middle finger of his left hand. She then traced an imaginary circle on the floor with the stick or sword, indicating that Paulo should stand inside it. Then, she made a gesture as if pouring the contents of a cup into the circle. She moved her right hand across Paulo's face without touching it, indicating that he should shut his eyes. 'At that moment I felt that someone had liberated stagnant energies,' he said years later, 'as though the spiritual floodgate of a lake had been opened, allowing fresh water to enter.' When he opened his eyes again, the only sign left by the mysterious woman was the strange ring, which he would wear for the rest of his life.

Paulo would only be in contact with Jean again much later, when he returned to Brazil. At the end of April 1982, he was supposed to return to his job with TV Globo, but after discussing it at length with Chris, he decided not to return to work but to remain in Europe. They had more than enough money to allow them to stay for another three months in Amsterdam.

And so it wasn't until the middle of July that they drove the 1,900 kilometres from Amsterdam to Lisbon – a journey of three days – from where they would take a plane to Brazil. However, the first visible change in Paulo Coelho's behaviour following his meeting with his Master took place on European soil. Only some supernatural force could have persuaded someone as careful with money as he was to donate the Mercedes to a charitable institution, the Sisterhood of the Infant Jesus for the Blind, rather than selling it and pocketing the thousand dollars.

CHAPTER 22

Paulo and Christina – publishers

WHEN THEY ARRIVED IN RIO, reinvigorated by their eight long months in Europe, Paulo and Chris settled back into the ground-floor apartment in Rua Raimundo Correia, in which her parents had been living since their departure. He began his initiation tasks. These so-called 'ordeals', which would lead to his being admitted to RAM, would arrive in either a letter or a phone call from Jean. The first of these, 'the ritual of the glass', involved a short ceremony that he was to perform alone each day for six months, always at the same hour. He had to fill a glass that had never been used with water, and place it on the table. He then had to open the New Testament at any page, read out loud a paragraph at random and drink the water. The passage he had read was to be marked with the date of the reading. If, on the following days, he alighted on the same text, then he should read the following paragraph. If he had read that one too, then he was to find another that had not been previously read. Paulo chose the early morning as the best time to perform this penance, so that it would not clash with anything else. And since no specific instruction had been given as to the size or shape of the glass, he bought a small shot glass, which could, if necessary, be discreetly carried around with a copy of the New Testament.

Fortunately, none of the trials demanded by Jean prevented him from leading a normal life. Money continued to be no problem, but his partnership with Raul had clearly fallen out of fashion. Their records continued to sell, but royalties from the recording company were not pouring in as they had before. Although a regular income from the five apartments he rented out guaranteed a comfortable lifestyle, his lack of activity was likely to propel him once more into depression. Therefore the best thing to do would be to find some more work as soon as possible.

A year before his trip to Europe, Paulo had persuaded Chris that she should start a company, Shogun Editora e Arte Ltda, which was primarily created for tax purposes to cover the architectural work she was doing, but which also meant that they both had business cards, letterheads and envelopes stating that they were a legal entity. In addition, as he said, when the time came for him to write his books, why not publish them himself? On returning to Brazil, he decided to put this idea into action and rented two rooms in a building on Rua Cinco de Julho in Copacabana, two blocks from the apartment where they lived. Although it managed to grow and even to bring in some income, Shogun was never more than a small family firm whose day-to-day business was handled by its two owners, with the accounts done by Paulo's father, who had just retired. They had only one paid employee – an office boy.

Less than three months after their return to Brazil, in October 1982, the publishing house launched its first book: *Arquivos do Inferno* [*Archives of Hell*], a collection of sixteen texts written by the proprietor, Paulo Coelho. On the cover was a picture of the author sitting cross-legged in front of a typewriter, holding a cigarette and apparently deep in thought, while, beside him, are two young women with bare breasts: one was Chris, and the other was Stella Paula, his old colleague from his Crowley witchcraft days. In the photo she had such long hair that it not only covered most of her breasts but fell below her waist. Although it was little more than a booklet (it was only 106 pages long), *Arquivos do Inferno* was certainly a record-breaker in terms of prefaces, forewords and notes on the inside flaps. The preface, entitled 'Preface to the Dutch Edition', was signed by the pop genius Andy Warhol (who, as Paulo confessed years later, never read the book):

I met Paulo Coelho at an exhibition of mine in London, and discovered in him the kind of forward-looking nature one finds in very few people. Rather than being a literary man in search of clever ideas, he coolly and accurately touches on the concerns and preoccupations of the present time. Dear Paulo, you asked for a preface to your book. I would say that your book is a preface to the new era that is just beginning, before the old one has even ended. Anyone who, like you, strides forward, never runs the risk of falling into a hole, because the angels will spread their cloaks out on the ground to catch you.

The second was written by Jimmy Brouwer, the owner of the hotel where the couple had stayed in Amsterdam; the third by the journalist Artur da Távola, Paulo's colleague at Philips; the fourth by the psychiatrist Eduardo Mascarenhas, who at the time was the presenter of a television programme and a Member of Parliament; and the fifth by Roberto Menescal, who was one of the book's two dedicatees, the other being Chris. Nothing about the book quite fits. According to the cover, it was supposedly a co-edition by Shogun with a Dutch publisher, the Brouwer Free Press, a firm that apparently never existed. A press release distributed by Shogun confused things still more by stating that the book had been published abroad, which was not true: 'After its successful launch in Holland, where it was acclaimed by critics and public alike after only two months in the shops, *Arquivos do Inferno*, by Paulo Coelho, will be in all the bookshops in Brazil this month.' The information given about the author's previous works muddied the waters still further, including as it did something entitled *Lon: Diário de um Mago*, which had apparently been published by Shogun in 1979, even though the firm did not exist at that time and *Diário de um Mago* (translated as *The Pilgrimage* in English) wasn't published until 1987. On one of the few occasions, years later, when he spoke about the matter, Paulo gave a strange explanation: 'It can only have been a prophecy.' On the imprint page, in tiny print, is another peculiarity: '300 copies of the first editions in Portuguese and Dutch will be numbered and signed by the author and sold at US$350 each, the money to be donated to the Order of the Golden Star.'

Paulo and Cissa leave the altar of
St Joseph's Church, Rio de Janeiro,
as man and wife, 2 July 1976.

Right Paulo on his visit to
London in 1976.

Left Paulo and Christina in
January 1980.

Paulo and Christina bought this Mercedes-Benz from the Indian embassy in Budapest for their European trip in 1982 after having struggled in their previous car, a Citröen 2CV.

Left Paulo's visit to Dachau concentration camp in 1982 saw his birth as an author.

Below Nandor Glid's bronze memorial at the camp.

Left The cover of *Arquivos do Inferno* featured Paulo with Christina and his old Crowleyite colleague Stella, 1982. The preface was by 'Andy Wharol', who never read the book.

Left Béla Lugosi on the cover of *Manual Prático do Vampirismo*, 1985. Though credited as the main author, Paulo didn't write a single word and persuaded a friend to produce his chapters.

Left Paulo asked the I Ching in 1988 how to ensure 100,000 sales of *The Alchemist*. The oracle replied, 'The great man brings good luck.'

Below Paulo in Egypt in 1987. The trip would provide inspiration for *The Alchemist*.

Paulo and Christina in the Mojave desert in 1988, where they practised the spiritual exercises of St Ignatius Loyola.

Paulo cemented an image of Our Lady of Aparecida in a grotto in Glorieta Canyon, New Mexico, writing a message in the wet mortar beneath it. The image was subsequently stolen.

The cartoon that appeared in *Jornal do Brasil*, 1993. According to the accompanying article, putting books by Paulo on the school curriculum would make students more stupid.

Jacques Chirac congratulates Paulo at the Paris Expo convention centre in 1998, after he had been ignored by the official Brazilian delegation. Brazilian First Lady Ruth Cardoso looks on.

Paulo takes a photo of himself in the hotel bathroom, wearing the Légion d'Honneur with which he has just been decorated by the French president in 1999.

Below Paulo is received by Pope John Paul II in the Vatican, 1998.

Left Mônica Antunes, Paulo's literary agent, with Paulo and friends in Dubai.

Right Paulo and Christina in Prague in 2005 with their gift to the Infant Jesus of a gold-embroidered cloak, fulfilling a promise Paulo made three decades earlier.

Left Paulo signing books in Cairo, 2005. Egypt is the world's leading producer of pirate editions of his books.

In 2002 Paulo was chosen as one of the forty lifetime members of the Brazilian Academy of Letters. He is pictured here with four of his fellow 'immortals'.

Paulo, Marisa Letícia (First Lady of Brazil), Christina and President Lula (left to right) at a state banquet in the president's honour at Buckingham Palace, 2006.

Right Paulo meeting
Vladimir Putin.

Left Fulfilling an old dream: Paulo
pauses during his journey on the
Trans-Siberian Railway, 2007.

Above The *Sunday
Times* journalist
Christina Lamb, the
inspiration for the
character of Esther
in *The Zahir*.

Below The pamphlet
commemorating 100
million books sold.

PAULO COELHO
100,000,000 COPIES

The book did not contain a single chapter or essay that dealt with the theme mentioned in the title – hell. The sixteen texts are a jumble of subjects arranged in no particular order, covering such disparate matters as the proverbs of the English poet William Blake, the rudiments of homoeopathy and astrology, and passages from manuscripts by a certain Pero Vaz and from Paulo's own works, such as 'The Pieces':

> It is very important to know that I have scattered parts of my body across the world. I cut my nails in Rome, my hair in Holland and Germany. I saw my blood moisten the asphalt of New York and often my sperm fell on French soil in a field of vines near Tours. I have expelled my faeces into rivers on three continents, watered some trees in Spain with my urine and spat in the English Channel and a fjord in Oslo. Once I grazed my face and left some cells attached to a fence in Budapest. These small things – created by me and which I shall never see again – give me a pleasant feeling of omnipresence. I am a small part of the places I have visited, of the landscapes I have seen and that moved me. Besides this, my scattered parts have a practical use: in my next incarnation I am not going to feel alone or unprotected because something familiar – a hair, a piece of nail, some old, dried spit – will always be close by. I have sown my seed in several places on this earth because I don't know where I will one day be reborn.

The most striking feature of the book is the second chapter, entitled 'The Truth about the Inquisition'. Paulo makes it clear that this was not written by him, but was dictated by the spirit of Torquemada, the Dominican friar who was in charge of the trials held by the Holy Office in Spain at the end of the fifteenth century. As though wanting to clear himself of any responsibility for its content, the author explains that not only the spelling and the underlinings but also 'some syntactical errors' were retained exactly as dictated by the spirit of the Grand Inquisitor. The eight pages of the chapter are filled with celebrations of torture and martyrdom as instruments in the defence of the faith:

It is therefore most just that the death penalty be applied to those who obstinately propagate heresy and so ensure that the most precious gift of man, Faith, is lost for ever!

[...] Anyone who has the right to command also has the right to punish! And the authority that has the power to make laws also has the power to ensure that those laws are obeyed!

[...] Spiritual punishment is not always enough. The majority of people are incapable of understanding it. The Church should, as I did, have the right to apply physical punishment!

Apparently wanting to attribute a scientific character to this psychic writing, Paulo ends the text with a curious parenthetical observation: '[After these words, no other communication was made by what called itself the "spirit of Torquemada". As it is always important to note the conditions in which a transmission was made – with a view to future scientific investigations – I recorded the ambient temperature (29°C), the atmospheric pressure (760 mmHg), weather conditions (cloudy) and the time the message was received (21h15m to 22h07m)].'

This was not the first occasion on which Paulo had shown an interest in the Holy Office of the Inquisition. In September 1971, he had thought of writing a play on the subject and during his research he came across a book by Henrique Hello, published by Editora Vozes in 1936 and reprinted in 1951, the title of which was *The Truth about the Inquisition*. The ninety-page text is a long peroration in defence of the objectives and methods used by the Inquisition. Part had been quoted in the preface to *O Santo Inquérito* [*The Holy Inquisition*], written in 1966 by the playwright Dias Gomes. When he finished reading it, Paulo had concluded ironically: 'I set to work on the play about the Inquisition. It's an easy play. It simply plagiarizes what someone called Henrique Hello said about it. No, it doesn't plagiarize, it criticizes. The guy wrote a book called *The Truth about the Inquisition* in favour of the Inquisition!'

Probably because of his imprisonment and abduction in 1974, Paulo held back from criticizing the author and simply transcribed his words. A comparison between the content of *Arquivos do Inferno* and the 1936 publication shows that if it was in fact an example of psychic writing, the spirit that dictated 'The Truth about the Inquisition' was that of Henrique Hello and not Torquemada, since 95 per cent of the text is simply copied from Hello's work.

None of this, however, surpasses the extraordinary piece of information the author gives at the beginning of 'The Truth about the Inquisition'. He states there that the automatic writing had occurred 'on the night of 28 May 1974'. The fact is that, between 21.15 and 22.07 on the night of 28 May 1974, Paulo was lying handcuffed on the floor of a car with his head covered by a hood and was being driven to the buildings of the DOI-Codi. It is hard to believe that the prison guards of one of the most violent prisons of the Brazilian dictatorship would have allowed a prisoner to write such an essay, even though it was a treatise in praise of torture. The author seems to have realized that *Arquivos do Inferno* would not stand up to scrutiny, and once the first, modest print run had sold out, he did not publish it again. When he had become an international name, the work was mentioned discreetly on his website: 'In 1982 he published his first book, *Arquivos do Inferno*, which made no impact whatsoever.'

A quarter of a century after this major failure, *Arquivos* became a rarity sought by collectors in auctions on the Internet with starting prices of about US$220, as though Paulo's initial fantasy were finally coming to fruition.

The lack of success of Shogun's debut book acted as an important lesson, since it made it clear that this was an undertaking requiring a professional approach. Determined to do things properly, Paulo took over the management of the business, and his first step was to take a seven-week correspondence course on financial planning. The course seems to have borne fruit, since in 1984, two years after it was set up, Shogun was ranked thirty-fourth among Brazilian publishers listed in the specialist magazine *Leia Livros*, rivalling traditional publishing houses such as Civilização Brasileira and Agir, and even Rocco (which some years later would become Paulo's publisher in Brazil). Shogun rented stands at book fairs and biennials and had a backlist of more than seventy titles.

Among the authors published, besides the proprietors themselves, there were only two well-known names, neither of whom was exactly a writer: the rock singer Neusinha Brizola, the daughter of the then-governor of Rio, Leonel Brizola (*O Livro Negro de Neusinha Brizola* [*The Black Book of Neusinha Brizola*]), and the ever-present 'close enemy', Raul Seixas (*As Aventuras de Raul Seixas na Cidade de Thor* [*Raul Seixas' Adventures in the City of Thor*]). Shogun's success was, in fact, due to hundreds and thousands of anonymous poets from all over Brazil who, like the owner of Shogun, had dreamed for years of one day having a book of their poetry published. In a country where hundreds of young authors were desperate to publish, Shogun came up with the perfect solution: the 'Raimundo Correia Poetry Competition'.

Paulo placed small advertisements in newspapers and left flyers at the doors of theatres and cinemas, inviting unpublished poets from across Brazil to take part in the competition, which had been named after the street in which Paulo and Chris lived, in turn named after an influential Brazilian poet who had died in 1911. The rules were simple. The competition was open to poems written in Portuguese by 'authors, whether amateur or professional, published or not, and of any age'. Each person could submit up to three poems of a maximum length of two pages double-spaced, and a 'committee of critics and experts of high standing' (whose names were never revealed) would select those to be included in an anthology to be published by Shogun. Those selected would receive a contract under which they committed themselves to paying US$175, for which they would receive ten copies. To the couple's surprise, one of the competitions received no fewer than 1,150 poems, of which 116 were selected for a book entitled *Poetas Brasileiros*. The publishers ran no financial risk at all, because the work was published only after the authors had paid up. Each contributor would receive, along with the books, a certificate produced by Shogun and signed by Chris, and a handwritten note from Paulo:

Dear So and So,

I have received and read your poems. Without going into the merits of the material – which, as you yourself know, is of the highest quality – I should like to compliment you on not having let your poems stay in a drawer. In today's world, and during this particularly exceptional period of History, it is necessary to have the courage to make one's thoughts public.

Once again my congratulations,

Paulo Coelho

What at first sight had appeared to be an amateur enterprise turned out to be very good business indeed. When the couple sent off the last package of books in the post, Shogun had earned the equivalent of US$187,000. The success of an apparently simple idea encouraged Paulo and Chris to repeat the project on a larger scale. A few weeks later, Shogun announced competitions to select poems to be published in four new anthologies, entitled *Poetas Brasileiros de Hoje, A Nova Poesia Brasileira, A Nova Literatura Brasileira* and *Antologia Poética de Cidades Brasileiras*. In order to motivate those who had been rejected in the first anthology, Chris sent each of them an encouraging letter in which she explained that the number of poems to be awarded the prize of publication was to rise from 116 to 250:

Rio de Janeiro, 29 August 1982

Dear Poet,

A large number of the works that failed to be placed in the Raimundo Correia Poetry Competition were of very high quality. Therefore, although we are forced to restrict the number of winning poems to 250, we have decided to find a solution for those poems which, either because they did not comply with the rules or because they were not selected by the Committee of Judges, were not included in the Anthology.

The book *Poetas Brasileiros de Hoje* – another Shogun publication – is to be published this year. We would love one of your poems to be included in this anthology. Each of the authors will pay the amount stated in the attached agreement and, in exchange, will receive ten copies of the first edition. This means that, for each copy, you will be paying only a little more than you would pay for a weekly news magazine, and you will be investing in yourself, increasing the sphere of influence of your work and, eventually, opening doors to a fascinating career.

As stated in the attached agreement, Shogun will send copies of *Poetas Brasileiros de Hoje* to the best-known literary critics in the country, and publicity material will be sent to more than two hundred important newspapers and magazines. Copies of the first edition will also be donated to state and municipal libraries, thus ensuring that thousands of readers will, over the years, have access to your poetry.

Lord Byron, Lima Barreto, Edgar Allan Poe and other great names in Literature had to finance the publication of their own books. Now, with this system of sharing the costs, it is possible to produce the book quite cheaply and for it to be read and commented upon throughout the country. In order to take part in *Poetas Brasileiros de Hoje*, all you have to do is fill in the attached agreement, sign it and send it with the stated amount to Shogun.

If you have any questions, please write to us.

Christina Oiticica

The Shogun anthologies grew in popularity, and poets of every sort sprang up in every corner of the country. On the evenings when the diplomas and other awards were handed out, there were so many present that the publisher was forced to hire the Circo Voador in Lapa, one of the newest venues in Rio, to accommodate the winning bards and their guests. Chris also organized public events, usually held in busy places, where the authors would recite their prize-winning poetry to passers-by, who would stop, genuinely interested, to listen to the poetry. There was, of course, always some problem, such as those who took a long time to pay or the poet who wrote a letter of protest to the *Jornal do Brasil*:

> I took part in the Fifth Raimundo Correia Poetry Competition and was awarded a prize for my poem 'Ser humano'. In order for my poem to be published, I had to pay a fee of Cr$380,000 in four instalments, for which I would receive ten copies of the book. When I paid the final instalment, I received the books. When I saw them and opened them, I was so disappointed that I didn't even want to read them. I realized, then, that I had fallen for a confidence trick.

The book uses very old-fashioned typography, and the design itself is one of the worst I've ever seen, muddled and ugly. It is Shogun's philosophy that he who does not pay is not published. I know of several people who were excluded because they couldn't pay all the instalments. 116 poets were published. By my calculations, Shogun have made a total of Cr$44 million, and have the right to use our money as they wish from the very first instalment.

Considering the amount we paid, we deserved something better. I work in the field of graphic design myself, and so feel able to make these criticisms. I wouldn't give the book away as a present or even sell it to my worst enemy.

Rui Dias de Carvalho – Rio de Janeiro

A week later, the *Jornal do Brasil* published Shogun's reply in which the director Christina Oiticica stated that the printers who produced their books were the same as those who worked for such publishing giants as Record and Nova Fronteira. As for making money from the anthology, she responded by saying that this was used to finance projects that would never interest large publishers, such as *Poesia na Prisão* (a competition held among prisoners within the Rio de Janeiro prison system), without depending upon public funds: 'We do not beg for support from the state for our cultural activities. We are independent and proud of the fact, because all of us – publishers and poets – are proving that it is possible for new artists to get their work published.'

The complaints did not seem to be shared by other authors published by Shogun. Many years later, the poet Marcelino Rodriguez recalled proudly in his Internet blog seeing his 'Soneto Eterno' included in the publisher's anthology: 'My first literary venture was produced by Shogun, owned by Paulo Coelho (who is now our most important writer, although many "academics" do not recognize his worth, perhaps because they do not understand the content of his work) and Christina Oiticica, who is a highly talented artist (I still haven't forgotten the smile she gave me when I visited the office once).'

The fact is that, as well as encouraging young authors, the project proved to be a successful business enterprise. By organizing four anthologies a year, Shogun could earn some 160 million cruzeiros a year. Between 1983 and 1986, there was a boom in anthologies and poetry competitions, and so these sums may have been even greater, particularly when Shogun doubled the number of prize-winners. At the age of nearly forty, Paulo's life finally seemed to be working out. Chris was proving to be a wonderful partner – their relationship grew more solid by the day – and business was flourishing. All that was needed to complete his happiness was to realize his old dream of becoming a world-famous writer. He continued to receive spiritual guidance from Jean, but this did not prevent him from reading about and entering into public debates on esoteric subjects and indulging his old curiosity for vampirism. It was as a vampirologist that, in 1985, he accepted an invitation to give a talk in the largest conference centre in the city, Riocentro, which was holding the first Brazilian Esoteric Fair, an initiative by the guru Kaanda Ananda, the owner of a shop selling esoterica in the Tijuca district in Rio, who had invited Paulo to open the meeting with a talk on vampirism.

When he arrived on the afternoon of Saturday, 19 October, Paulo was greeted by the reporter Nelson Liano, Jr, who had been selected by the Sunday magazine of the *Jornal do Brasil* to interview him. Although he was only twenty-four, Liano had worked on the main Rio publications and, like Paulo, had experimented with every type of drug. If there is such a thing as love at first sight between esoterics, this is what happened between Paulo and Liano. Such was their reciprocal delight in each other's company that their conversation only ended when Kaanda Ananda told them for the third time that the auditorium was full and that an impatient public was waiting for Paulo. The two exchanged phone numbers and took their leave of each other with a warm embrace. While Paulo went into the auditorium, Liano headed off to have a coffee with his friend Ernesto Emanuelle Mandarino, the owner of the publishing house Editora Eco.

Eco was a small publishing house founded in the 1960s. Although it was unknown in intellectual circles, during its twenty years in existence, it had become a reference point for anyone interested in umbanda and candomblé (the Brazilian forms of voodoo), magic, etc. Over coffee with Mandarino, Liano told him that he had just interviewed a vampirologist.

'The guy's called Paulo Coelho and he trained in vampirism in England. He's talking at the moment to a packed auditorium of people on the subject. Don't you think it might make a book?'

Mandarino opened his eyes wide: 'Vampirism? It sounds like something out of the movies. Would a book like that sell? When he finishes his talk bring him over here to the stand for a coffee.'

Minutes after being introduced to Paulo, Mandarino told him point-blank: 'If you write a book on vampirism, Eco will publish it.'

Paulo replied: 'I'll do it, if Nelson Liano will write it with me.'

Mandarino was astonished: 'But Nelson told me that you had only just met!'

Paulo chuckled: 'That's true, but we're already life-long friends.'

The deal was done. The two left, having agreed to write a book entitled *Manual Prático do Vampirismo* [*Practical Manual on Vampirism*]. The work was to be arranged in five parts, the first and fifth to be written by Paulo, the second and fourth by Liano and the third divided between the two. Paulo and Chris wondered afterwards whether it wouldn't be better if Shogun published the book, but they were dissuaded from this idea by Liano, who felt that only a publisher of Eco's standing would be able to market such a book, whereas Shogun's speciality was poetry anthologies. On the assumption that it would be a best-seller, Paulo demanded changes to Eco's standard contract. Concerned about inflation, he asked to receive monthly rather than quarterly accounts. Even though Liano was going to write half the book and edit the final text, Paulo asked Mandarino's secretary to add this clause at the bottom of the contract: 'Only the name Paulo Coelho will appear on the cover, with the words "Edited by Nelson Liano, Jr." on the title page under the title.'

In effect, Liano was going to write half the book and edit the whole thing, but was to appear only as its coordinator (and this only on the inside pages). And, following a final addendum suggested by Paulo, he was to receive only 5 per cent of the royalties (0.5 per cent of the cover price of the book), the remaining 95 per cent going to Paulo. As though anticipating that this was going to be the goose that laid the golden egg, Mandarino patiently accepted his new author's demands and since Liano also made no objections, they signed the contract a week after their first meeting.

However, only Liano handed in his chapters on the agreed date. Saying that he had too much work at Shogun, Paulo had not written a single word of his part. Time went on, and still the text did not appear. It was only after much pressure and when he realized that all deadlines had passed that Paulo finally handed his text to Eco. At the last minute, perhaps feeling that he had been unfair to his partner, he allowed the inclusion of Liano's name on the cover, but in small print, as though he were not the co-author but only an assistant.

The launch of the *Manual*, with waiters serving white wine and canapés, was held in the elegant Hotel Glória, in front of which, eleven years earlier, Paulo had been seized by the DOI-Codi. The cover, designed by Chris, bore the title in gothic characters over a well-known photograph of the Hungarian-American actor Béla Lugosi who, in 1931, had become world-famous when he played Count Dracula in the Tod Browning film. The texts covered subjects ranging from the origins of vampirism to the great 'dynasties' of human bloodsuckers, which were divided into the Romanian, British, German, French and Spanish branches. One chapter explained how to recognize a vampire. At social gatherings this could be done by observing certain habits or gestures. For example, if you come across a person with a particular liking for raw or undercooked meat, who is also studious and rather verbose, you should be on your guard: he could be a true descendant of the Romanian Vlad Tepeș. It would be even easier, the *Manual* explained, to know whether or not you were sleeping with a dangerous bloodsucker because vampires don't move their pelvis during the sexual act and the temperature of their penis is many degrees below that of ordinary mortals.

The *Manual* concealed some even greater mysteries. None of the guests in the lobby of the Hotel Glória could know that, although his name appeared in larger print than Liano's on the cover, Paulo had not written a single word, a single syllable, of the 144 pages of the *Manual*. The author never revealed that, under pressure of the deadline and disinclined to keep his part of the agreement, he had secretly taken on someone else to write his parts of the book.

His choice fell on a strange man from Minas Gerais, Antônio Walter Sena Júnior, who was known in the esoteric world as 'Toninho Buda' or

'Tony Buddha', a somewhat inappropriate name for a very skinny man who never weighed more than 55 kilos. He had graduated in engineering at the Universidade Federal in Juiz de Fora, where he still lived, and had met Paulo in 1981 during a debate on vampirism at the Colégio Bennett in Rio. He had studied subjects such as magic and the occult, had closely followed the career of Paulo and Raul Seixas, and dreamed of resurrecting the old Sociedade Alternativa. He felt greatly honoured at the thought of seeing his name alongside that of Paulo Coelho in a book and he accepted the task in exchange, as he said later, 'for the price of lunch in a cheap restaurant in Copacabana'. He wrote all the chapters that Paulo was supposed to write.

On 25 April 1986, Toninho Buda was recovering after being run over some weeks earlier. He was shocked to read in a column in the *Jornal do Brasil* that Paulo Coelho would be signing his new book, *Manual Prático do Vampirismo*, that evening in the Hotel Glória. He thought it rude that he hadn't been invited to the launch, but preferred to believe that the invitation had not arrived on time. Still walking with the aid of a stick, he decided to go to the launch of a book that was, after all, also his. He went to the bus station, took the bus and, after two hours on the road, arrived in Rio de Janeiro as night was falling. He crossed the city by taxi and hobbled up the four white marble steps at the main entrance of the Hotel Glória. It was only then that he realized that he was the first to arrive: apart from the employees of the publishing house, who were stacking books on a stand, there was no one else there, not even the author.

He decided to buy a copy – as well as receiving no invitation he hadn't even been sent a complimentary copy – and sat in an armchair at one end of the room to enjoy his creation in peace. He admired the cover, ran his eyes over the first pages, the frontispiece, the two flaps, but his name did not appear anywhere in the book, of which half had been entirely written by him. He was about to take a taxi back to the bus station when he saw Paulo enter, smiling, with Chris, Liano and Mandarino.

At that moment, he decided that he wasn't going to waste the journey and so he gave vent to his feelings: 'Dammit, Paulo! You didn't even put my name on the book, man, and that was the only thing I asked for! The only thing I asked for, man!'

Paulo pretended not to understand, asked to see a copy of the *Manual*, flipped quickly through it and said regretfully: 'It's true, Toninho. They didn't add your name. But I promise you: I'll ask for a special stamp to be made and we'll stamp the whole of the first edition. I'll correct it in the next edition, but with this one, we'll stamp every book. Forgive me.'

Although deeply upset, Toninho Buda didn't want to ruin Paulo's evening and felt it best to end the conversation there: 'Paulo, I'm not an idiot. Don't talk to me about a stamp, man. Go off to your launch, where there are loads of people wanting your autograph. Go on and I'll just leave.'

Toninho swallowed the insult in the name of a higher ambition: to get Paulo interested in reinstituting the Sociedade Alternativa. His strategy was a simple one: to use public debates and popular demonstrations to gain the attention of the media and public opinion. Some months earlier, he had written a long letter to Paulo from Juiz de Fora suggesting 'public actions' by the group, among which he suggested rushing on to the stage of the first international rock concert in Rio on the night when stars such as Whitesnake, Ozzy Osbourne, the Scorpions and AC/DC were perform-ing. Toninho's plan was to seize the microphone and start talking about the Sociedade Alternativa: 'This will depend almost entirely on you and your contacts in Rio. I'm prepared to go there myself. If you agree, you can start to work on things, but please don't forget to keep me informed as to how it's going.'

In January 1986, some months after the book signing, the threesome had taken part in an event in Rio. They decided to use a protest by inhab-itants of the South Zone against the decision of the Prefecture to close a public park in order to announce the launch of a newspaper, *Sociedade Alternativa*, the first draft of which had been designed entirely by Toninho. It was he who enrolled with the organizers of the demonstration in order to get his message heard. As soon as his name was called, he went up to the improvised rostrum in suit and tie and in front of the television cameras began to read what he had entitled 'Manifesto Number 11'. It was an entire page of statements such as 'Free space, everyone should occupy their space'; 'Time is free, everyone has to live in their time'; and 'The artistic class no longer exists: we are all writers, housewives, bosses and employees, radicals and conservatives, wise and mad'. It wasn't the content that mattered though, but the manner of his performance. As Toninho Buda read out each sentence, paragraph or thought, Chris carefully and silently cut off a piece of his clothing: first his tie, then a sleeve of his suit, then a leg of his trousers, then another sleeve, a collar, another sleeve ... When he pronounced the final sentence (something like 'The great miracle will no longer be being able to walk on water, but being able to walk on the earth') he was completely naked, without a square centimetre of cloth on his body.

That night, when they were all celebrating the repercussions of their 'public action' in the park, Paulo was still muttering about the need to do something even more scandalous, with greater impact. However, Chris and Paulo were flabbergasted when Toninho told them that what he hoped to do would, in his words, 'leave the Sociedade Alternativa engraved for ever in the memory of millions of Brazilians': neither more nor less than blowing the head off the statue of Christ the Redeemer. He explained the plan to explode the monument's 3.75-metre-high, 30-ton head, a monument which, in 2007, would be named one of the seven new wonders of the modern world. Any normal person would have thrown such a madman out of the house, but Paulo didn't do that. On the contrary, he simply said: 'Go ahead.'

This was what Toninho wanted to hear. 'Just imagine the population of Rio de Janeiro waking up one morning and seeing Christ there, without his head and with that great mound of twisted iron struts sticking out of his neck towards the indigo sky! Think of the Pope's edict for making amends, the crowds climbing up Corcovado looking for pieces to keep as a relic. Imagine that! The Church collecting tithes for the miracle of its reconstruction! That's when we would go in singing "Viva, Viva, Viva a Sociedade Alternativa!" and distributing the first edition of our newspaper with the hot news on the dreadful episode ...'

This was a heresy too far, particularly for someone who was in the process of reconciliation with the Church, and Paulo preferred to bring the conversation to a close and never return to the subject. As Toninho would only find out months later, Paulo was very close to being admitted as a Master of RAM, the religious order to which Jean had introduced him. His first failed attempt to acquire this rank in the secret organization had occurred in January that year. Taking advantage of a business trip to Brazil, Jean had appointed 2 January 1986 as the date for a secret ceremony during which Paulo would receive a sword, the symbol of his ordination as a Master. The site for this was to be the summit of one of the mountains in Mantiqueira, on the frontier between Minas Gerais and Rio de Janeiro, next to one of the highest points in Brazil, the peak of Agulhas Negras. As well as Jean and Paulo, Chris, a hired guide and another man who was to be initiated into the order were also to be there. The sole instruction Paulo had received was to take with him the old sword that he had been using for years in his esoteric exercises.

As Paulo himself describes in the prologue to *The Pilgrimage*, they all met around a bonfire and the ceremony began when Jean pointed a brand-new sword, which he had not yet removed from its sheath, towards the sky, saying: 'And now before the sacred countenance of RAM, you must touch with your hands the Word of Life and acquire such power as you need to become witness to that Word throughout the world!' After digging a long, shallow hole with his bare hands, Paulo received from Chris his old sword, which was to be buried there, and in a tremulous voice, he pronounced the words of the ritual. As he finished, he saw that Jean was placing the new sword on top of the hole.

He then goes on to say that they were all standing with their arms outstretched when something happened. 'The Master, invoking his power, created a strange light that surrounded us; it didn't illuminate, but it was clearly visible, and it caused the figures of those who were there to take on a colour that was different from the yellowish tinge cast by the fire.' The high point, not just of the ceremony but of the whole long day, was approaching. Still not believing what he was experiencing, he heard the words Jean was saying while he made a slight cut on his forehead with the point of the blade of the new sword: 'By the power and the love of RAM, I anoint you Master and Knight of the Order, now and for all the days of your life. R for Rigour, A for Adoration, and M for Mercy; R for *regnum*, A for *agnus*, and M for *mundi*. Let not your sword remain long in its scabbard, lest it rust. And when you draw your sword, it must never be replaced without having performed an act of goodness, opened a path or tasted the blood of an enemy.' Paulo was not shaking quite so much and, for the first time since he had arrived, he felt relief. When his hand touched the sword that Jean had laid down on the ground, he would finally be a magus.

At that moment, someone stepped roughly on the fingers of his right hand, which he had just reached out to touch the sword. He looked up and saw that the foot that had almost maimed him was Jean's. Furious, the Frenchman snatched up the sword, replaced it in its scabbard and gave it to Chris. Paulo realized then that the strange light had disappeared and that Jean was looking at him coldly, saying: 'You should have refused the sword. If you had done so, it would have been given to you, because you would have shown that your heart was pure. But just as I feared, at the supreme moment, you stumbled and fell. Because of your avidity you will now have to seek again for your sword. And because of your pride you will have to seek it among simple people. Because of your fascination with miracles, you will have to struggle to recapture what was about to be given to you so generously.'

The ceremony ended miserably. Alone in the car on the return to Rio de Janeiro, Paulo and Chris remained silent for a long time, until Paulo was unable to restrain his curiosity and asked her what the Master had said to her. Chris tried to reassure him, saying that she was sure he would get the sword back. She had received precise instructions from Jean as to where she was to hide the sword so that Paulo could try to regain it.

Still more troubled, he wanted to know what place had been chosen as the hiding place, but she was unable to reply precisely: 'He didn't explain very well. He just said that you should look on the map of Spain for a medieval route known as the Road to Santiago.'

CHAPTER 23

The road to Santiago

WHEN HE ENQUIRED AT TRAVEL AGENCIES, Paulo discovered that in 1986, there was hardly any interest in the so-called Road to Santiago. Each year, fewer than 400 pilgrims ventured along the 700 inhospitable kilometres of the mystical route between St-Jean-Pied-de-Port, in the south of France, and the cathedral in Santiago de Compostela, the capital of Galicia, in the northwest of Spain. From the first millennium of Christianity onwards, this road had been taken by pilgrims seeking the supposed tomb of the Apostle James. All Paulo needed to do was to pluck up the courage and leave. Instead, he handed over the day-to-day management of Shogun to Chris, while he spent his days at home filling pages and pages of diaries with a constant lament: 'I haven't felt this angry for a long time. I'm not angry at Jesus, but at myself for not having sufficient willpower to realize my dreams.'

He felt that he lacked the strength he needed and frequently said that he felt like becoming an atheist. However, he never lost sight of the commitment he had made to Jean. Since, though, he seemed determined to put off the trip for ever, it fell to Chris to take the initiative. Without telling him, at the end of July she went to a travel agency, bought two tickets and came home to announce: 'We're going to Madrid.'

He tried to put off their departure yet again, saying that the publishing house couldn't function on its own and that the business about him finding the sword, which Chris was to hide somewhere on a 700-kilometre-long road, seemed utter madness: 'Has my Master set me an impossible task, do you think?'

Chris, however, was determined: 'You've done nothing for the last seven months. It's time to fulfil your commitment.'

So at the beginning of August 1986, they landed in Barajas international airport in Madrid, where skinny Antônio Walter Sena Júnior, the same Toninho Buda who had dreamed of blowing off the head of Christ the Redeemer, was waiting for them.

Once Paulo had made the decision to follow the Road to Santiago, he had taken on Toninho as his assistant and, since then, had started to refer to him as 'slave'. Toninho had barely recovered from his frustration over the *Manual Prático do Vampirismo* and was setting up a macrobiotic restaurant in Juiz de Fora when he received Paulo's proposal, in which Paulo made it clear that this wasn't an invitation to travel together but an employment contract.

When he learned the details of the proposal over the telephone, Toninho had a surreal conversation with his friend – surreal because this was to be paid slavery.

'But what you're suggesting is slavery!'

'Exactly. I want to know if you'll agree to be my slave for the two months I'll be in Spain.'

'But what am I going to do there? I haven't got a penny to my name, I've never been outside Brazil, I've never been on a plane.'

'Don't worry about money. I'll pay your fare and give you a monthly salary of 27,000 pesetas.'

'How much is that in dollars?'

'It must be about US$200, which is a fortune if you take into account that Spain is the cheapest country in Europe. Do you accept?'

Aged thirty-six, single and with no responsibilities, Toninho saw no reason to refuse: after all, it wasn't every day that someone invited him to go to Europe, regardless of what he would have to do when he got there. And if things didn't work out, all he had to do was take the plane back. But it was only when he arrived in Rio, with his bags packed, and read the contract drawn up by Paulo that he discovered that things were not quite like that. In the first place, while Paulo and Chris were taking an Iberia flight that included a free night in a hotel, Paulo had bought him a much cheaper flight on the ill-fated Linhas Aéreas Paraguaias. Apart from the risks involved in flying with a company that was hardly a world champion in safety, he had to go to Asunción, in Paraguay, in order to get the plane to Madrid. In addition, the ticket could not be exchanged and could only be used on the specified dates, which meant that, whatever happened, he could not return to Brazil until the beginning of October, two months later. The contract, grown yellow over time and lost at the bottom of a trunk in Rio de Janeiro, shows how draconian were the conditions Paulo imposed on his slave, who is referred to here as 'Tony':

Agreements

1 If Tony sleeps in my room, he will only do so when it is time to sleep, since I will be working there day and night.

2 Tony will receive an allowance of US$200 a month which will be reimbursed to him when he returns to Rio, but this is not obligatory.

3 Should my room or apartment be occupied by someone else, Tony will sleep elsewhere at his own expense.

4 Any visits I want to make and for which I require Tony's company will be at my expense.

5 Tony will not make the journey with me and Chris. He will wait for us in Madrid.

6 Tony has been advised of the following items:

6.1 That the air ticket does not allow him to change the date of his return;

6.2 That it is illegal for him to work in Spain;

6.3 That, apart from his monthly allowance of US$200, he will have to find money himself;

6.4 That if he changes his return date he will have to pay the equivalent of a normal fare (US$2080) to be discounted from the US dollars already paid for the non-refundable ticket.

1 August 1986
Antônio Walter Sena Júnior
Paulo Coelho

On reading these monstrous requirements, Toninho Buda considered returning to Minas Gerais, but the desire to know Europe won out and so he had no alternative but to sign the agreement. Since their respective flight times did not coincide, he took a flight the day before Paulo and Chris on a journey that started badly. On arriving in Madrid, without knowing a word of Spanish, he spent three hours trying to explain to the authorities how he was planning to stay sixty days in Spain with the four 10-dollar notes in his wallet. He found himself in the humiliating position of being undressed and interrogated before, finally, being allowed to go. On the following day, Tuesday, 5 August, he was once again at Barajas airport, awaiting the arrival of his boss. Toninho had found somewhere to stay with an old blind woman who hated Brazil (a 'country full of shame-less hussies', she would mutter) and who would lock the front door at eleven at night, after which whoever was still out in the street slept in the street. The only advantage of Doña Cristina Belerano's boarding house was the price – a paltry 600 pesetas (US$7 in today's terms) a day, which included a modest breakfast. Chris and Paulo spent only the first night together in Madrid: the following day Chris rented a car and went off to hide Paulo's sword in the place indicated by Jean.

It was suffocatingly hot in the Spanish capital on 7 August 1986, when Paulo left the city in a hired car. He drove about 450 kilometres north, crossed the frontier with France and left the car at a branch of the hire firm in Pau, where he spent two nights. On the Sunday morning, 10 August, he took a train to the Pyrenees and there wrote what was to be the final note in his diary before returning from his pilgrimage:

11h57 – S.-Jean-Pied-de-Port
A fiesta in town. Basque music in the distance.

Immediately below, on the same page, was a stamp on which one can read an inscription in Latin – 'St. Joannes Pedis Portus' – beside which there is a handwritten note in French signed by someone called 'J.', whose surname looks something like 'Relul' or 'Ellul':

Saint-Jean-Pied-de-Port
Basse-Navarre
Le 10 Août 1986
J.........

Could this initial J be for Jean? As is usually the case whenever someone tries to cross the frontier of his mystical world by asking too many questions, Paulo Coelho neither confirms nor denies this. Everything indicates that Jean was the person in St-Jean-Pied-de-Port (presumably, as the official representative of the religious order RAM) to ensure that his disciple really was beginning the ordeal imposed on him.

Paulo's pilgrimage would end in the Spanish city of Cebrero, where he found the sword and broke off his journey. An episode in which a taxi driver claimed that Paulo had in fact made the journey in the back of his comfortable, air-conditioned Citroën, and was proved by a Japanese television company to have been lying, led Paulo to include in the preface to the subsequent editions of *The Pilgrimage* a short piece in which he invites the reader to believe whichever version he prefers, thus only increasing the mystery surrounding the journey:

I've listened to all kinds of theories about my pilgrimage, from me doing it entirely by taxi (imagine the cost!) to my having secret help from certain initiating societies (imagine the confusion!).

My readers don't need to be sure whether or not I made the pilgrimage: that way they will seek a personal experience and not the one I experienced (or didn't).

I made the pilgrimage just once – and even then I didn't do the whole thing. I finished in Cebrero and took a bus to Santiago de Compostela. I often think of the irony: the best-known text on the Road at the end of this millennium was written by someone who didn't follow it right to the end.

The most important and mysterious moment of the whole journey, which is not revealed until the end of the book, occurred when Paulo was nearing Cebrero, some 150 kilometres from Santiago. At the side of the road, he came across a solitary lamb, still unsteady on its feet. He began to follow the animal, which plunged off into the undergrowth until it reached a little old church built beside a small cemetery at the entrance to the town, as he describes in the book:

> The chapel was completely lit when I came to its door. [...] The lamb slipped into one of the pews, and I looked to the front of the chapel. Standing before the altar, smiling – and perhaps a bit relieved – was the Master: with my sword in his hand.
>
> I stopped, and he came toward me, passing me by and going outside. I followed him. In front of the chapel, looking up at the dark sky, he unsheathed my sword and told me to grasp its hilt with him. He pointed the blade upward and said the sacred Psalm of those who travel far to achieve victory:
>
> 'A thousand fall at your side and ten thousand to your right, but you will not be touched. No evil will befall you, no curse will fall upon your tent; your angels will be given orders regarding you, to protect you along your every way.'
>
> I knelt, and as he touched the blade to my shoulders, he said:
>
> 'Trample the lion and the serpent. The lion cub and the dragon will make shoes for your feet.'

Paulo tells how at the exact moment when Jean finished speaking, a heavy summer shower began to fall. 'I looked about for the lamb, but he had disappeared,' he wrote, 'but that did not matter: the Water of Life fell from the sky and caused the blade of my sword to glisten.' Like a child celebrating some form of rebirth, Paulo returned to Madrid, moved into a pleasant furnished flat in the elegant Alonso Martínez district, and gave himself over body and soul to the city's vibrant lifestyle. Until October, he could count on the assistance of Toninho Buda – whom he referred to in his diary as 'the slave', or simply 'the sl.' – but he soon realized that he had chosen the wrong man to be his servant. While Paulo had become a sybarite eager to drain Madrid's night-life to the last drop, Toninho turned out to be a radical vegetarian who would eat only minute portions of macrobiotic food and drink no alcohol. Nor could he spend his evenings with his boss, since he had to be back at Doña Cristina's boarding house by eleven, when the night in Madrid had barely begun. He also complained with increasing frequency that his salary was not enough to live on. On one such occasion, they had a bitter argument.

'Paulo, the money isn't enough even for me to buy food.'

'I think you'd better read our contract again. It's says there that if the pay isn't enough, then you have to earn some extra money yourself.'

'But Paulo, the contract also says that it's forbidden for foreigners to work here in Spain!'

'Don't be so stupid, slave. Other people manage to get by. It's not as if you were crippled or anything, so do something!'

Toninho had no option. When he was down to his last penny, he took his guitar, which he had brought with him from Brazil, chose a busy underground station, sat on the floor and began to sing Brazilian songs. Beside him was a cap waiting for the coins and, more rarely, notes thrown in by passers-by. He could never stay long in the same place before being moved on, but an hour's singing would usually bring in 800–1,000 pesetas (US$9–11), which was enough to buy a plate of food and pay for his board and lodging. Another way of earning money was by using his rudimentary knowledge of Asian massage, in particular shiatsu, which wouldn't require him to speak Spanish or any other language. The cost of putting an advertisement in one of the Madrid newspapers was prohibitive, but with the help of a friend, he managed to find a kind soul willing to print a number of cards on which he offered to perform therapeutic massage for 'back, muscular pain, insomnia, tiredness, stress, etc'. On the day when the cards were ready, he stuck a copy in his diary and wrote above it:

Thursday, 25 Sep 86

I woke late, but went for a run in the Retiro Park. I had diarrhoea when I got back and felt very weak. Paulo phoned me, and I told him that it was going to take a miracle for them to keep me here ... I had the business card made to hand it out in strategic places in Madrid, but I'm the one who needs a massage! I need to get stronger. The tension is killing me.

Given Paulo's indifference to the sufferings of his 'slave', Toninho returned to Brazil at the beginning of October without saying goodbye.

All Paulo wanted to do was enjoy himself. He would lunch and dine in good restaurants, he would go to cinemas and museums, and he found himself giving way to two new passions: bullfights and pinball machines. With the latter, he would usually only stop playing once he had broken the record set by the previous player. He gradually became such an aficionado of bullfights that he would travel for hours by train to see a particular fighter in action. If there were no bullfights, he would spend his afternoons standing in bars full of adolescents, eyes glued to the illuminated screen of the pinball machine. He even joined a course to learn how to play the castanets.

It did not take long, though, for him to fall once more into depression. He had US$300,000 in the bank and five apartments bringing in a regular income, he was in a stable relationship and he had just received the sword of a Master or Magus, but he was still unhappy. In spite of the busy life he was leading, he found time to fill more than five hundred pages of his diary between September and January, when he was due to return to Brazil. Most of these pages repeated for the umpteenth time the monotonous complaint he had been making for the last twenty years, which had now become a tearful mantra: 'I'm still not an established writer.'

At the end of October, Chris came to Madrid for a few weeks and rubbed more salt into his wounds. One day, when Paulo was saying how prolific Picasso was, she said: 'Look, Paulo, you have as much talent as he has, but since we got together six years ago, you haven't produced anything. I've given and I'll continue to give you all the support you need. But you have to have a concrete objective and pursue it tenaciously. That's the only way you'll get where you want to be.'

When Chris returned to Brazil at the beginning of December, Paulo was in an even worse mental state than before. He was lamenting the fact that he had lost the ability to tell 'even stories about myself or my life'. He found his diary 'boring, mediocre and empty', but eventually recognized that, if he did, this was his own fault: 'I haven't even written here about the Road to Santiago. Sometimes I think about killing myself because I'm so terrified of things, but I have faith in God that I shall never do that. It would be exchanging one fear for a greater fear. I've got to get away from the idea that writing a book would be an important thing to do in Madrid. Perhaps I could dictate a book to someone.'

In the middle of December, Chris phoned to say that she could no longer stand working with Pedro: 'Paulo, your father is being very difficult. I need you to come back here straight away.'

Pedro Queima Coelho did not agree with the expenses that the publishing house incurred in advertising, and this created permanent friction between him and Chris. The phone call was an ultimatum for Paulo to start the countdown and think about returning, with or without his book. He handed over this final responsibility to God, begging in his diary for the Creator to give him a sign when the time came to start writing.

Some days later, one icy Tuesday morning, he left early to go for a walk in the Retiro Park. When he returned home, he went straight to his diary and wrote: 'I had hardly gone any distance when I saw the particular sign I had asked God for: a pigeon feather. The time has come for me to give myself entirely to that book.'

In biographies and on official websites, *The Pilgrimage* is described as having been written in Rio during the Carnival of 1987, but there are clear indications in the author's diary that he began to write the first lines of the book when he was still in Spain. A day after receiving what he believes to have been a sign from heaven he wrote:

15/12 – I can't write this book as though it were just any book. I can't write this book just to pass the time, or to justify my life and/or my idleness. I have to write this book as though it were the most important thing in my life. Because this book is the beginning of something very important. It's the beginning of my work of indoctrination in RAM and that is what I must devote myself to from now on.

18/12 – I wrote for an hour and a half. The text came easily, but there are lots of things missing. It seemed very implausible, very

Castaneda. Using the first person worries me. Another alternative would be an actual diary. Perhaps I'll try that tomorrow. I think the first scene is good, so I can make variations on that theme until I find the right approach.

The miracle was apparently taking place.

CHAPTER 24

The Alchemist

PAULO'S FIRST MOVE when he returned to Brazil was to persuade his father to leave Shogun so that Chris could work in peace, which he managed to do without causing any resentment. During his absence, she had dealt very competently with the firm's business, and knowing that Chris was looking after the firm as well as or even better than he could was a further inducement for Paulo to dedicate himself entirely to the book. He was still full of doubts, though. Was he really just writing a book about his pilgrimage? Weren't there enough books on that topic? Why not abandon the idea and try writing something else, such as a *Manual of Practical Magic*? And whatever the subject, should the book be published by Shogun or given to Eco, as had been the case with *Manual Pratico do Vampirismo*?

These uncertainties lasted until 3 March 1987, a Tuesday during Carnival. That day Paulo sat down in front of his typewriter, determined to leave the apartment only when he had put the final full stop on the last page of *The Pilgrimage*. He worked frenetically for twenty-one days, during which time he did not set foot outside the house, getting up from his chair only to eat, sleep and go to the toilet. When Chris arrived home on the twenty-fourth, Paulo had a package in front of him containing 200 pages ready to be sent to the printer. The decision to have Shogun publish it was growing in his mind and he even put some small classified ads in the Saturday edition of *Jornal do Brasil*, announcing: 'It's on its way! *The Pilgrimage* – Editora Shogun.'

The person who once again dissuaded him from the idea of being at once author and publisher was the journalist Nelson Liano, Jr., who advised him to knock on Ernest Mandarino's door. Paulo thought about it for a few days, and it wasn't until mid-April that he signed the contract for the first edition of *O Diário de um Mago*, or *The Pilgrimage*, standing at the counter of a small bar next to the publisher's office in Rua Marquês de Pombal.

The contract contains some odd things. First, Paulo demanded that, instead of the usual five- or seven-year contract, he should have a contract that would be renewed with every edition (the first had a print run of 3,000 copies). He did not, as he had with *Manual Prático do Vampirismo*, ask for monthly rather than quarterly accounts, but accepted what he was offered, even though inflation in Brazil had reached almost 1 per cent a day. The other strange thing is that at the foot of the contract the author put in an apparently meaningless addendum – which would, however, prove to be prophetic: 'Once the book has sold 1,000 (one thousand) copies, the publisher will be responsible for the costs of producing the book in Spanish and English.' If, among his gifts, Paulo had had the ability to predict the future, he could have taken the opportunity to make it Mandarino's responsibility to produce versions not only in English and Spanish but also in the other forty-four languages into which *The Pilgrimage* would subsequently be translated, among them Albanian, Estonian, Farsi, Hebrew, Hindi, Malay and Marathi.

Although sales got off to a very slow start, they soon overtook all of Eco's other titles. Years later, when he was retired and living in Petrópolis, 70 kilometres from Rio de Janeiro, Ernesto Mandarino was to recall how much of this success was due to a virtue that few authors possess – a desire to publicize the book: 'Authors would leave the finished manuscript with the publisher and do nothing to publicize their work. Paulo not only appeared in all the media, newspapers, radio and television, but gave talks on the book wherever he was asked.'

On the advice of his friend the journalist Joaquim Ferreira dos Santos, Paulo took an initiative rare even among established authors: at his own expense he employed the twenty-year-old journalist Andréa Cals to work exclusively on publicizing the book in the media. The salary was modest – 8,000 cruzados a month, the equivalent in 1987 of about US$400 – but he offered a tempting bonus. Should the book sell 20,000 copies by the end of 1987, Andréa would get a return flight from Rio to Miami. The contract also included the publicity for an exhibition of art by Chris entitled 'Tarô', and if all twenty-two works on show were sold before the exhibition closed, Andréa would earn a further 5,000 cruzados. Meanwhile, Paulo and Chris printed flyers about *The Pilgrimage*, which they themselves handed out nightly in cinema, theatre and stadium queues.

All this was an attempt to make up for the resistance of large media companies to give space to something as specific as *The Pilgrimage* – which seemed to be of interest only to the shrinking underground press. Andréa recalls trying in vain to get a copy of *The Pilgrimage* included in *Mandala*, a TV soap being shown by Globo and whose theme was in some ways similar to that of the book, but it was down to her hard work that the book got its first mention in one of the major newspapers. Beside the very brief mention in the *Jornal do Brasil* was a photo of the author who, at Joaquim's suggestion, was wearing a black cape and holding a sword. The picture caught the attention of the producers of *Sem Censura*, a chat show that went out every afternoon on the national television network Educativa, to which Paulo was invited.

In response to a question from the presenter, Lúcia Leme, and in front of millions of television viewers, Paulo revealed for the first time in public the secret that had been known only to a few friends and his diary: yes, he was a magus and among his many powers was that of making it rain. The strategy worked. The reporter Regina Guerra, from the newspaper *O Globo*, saw the programme and suggested to her boss an interview with this new individual on the Rio cultural scene: the writer who could make it rain. Her boss thought it all complete nonsense, but when his young reporter persisted, he gave in. The result was that, on 3 August, the cultural section of the newspaper devoted its entire front page to Paulo Coelho, who was given the title of 'the Castaneda of Copacabana'. In a sequence of photos, he appears among the leaves of his garden wearing the same black cloak and dark glasses and holding a sword. The text preceding the interview seems made to order for someone claiming to have supernatural powers:

> The thick walls of the old building mean that the apartment is very quiet, in spite of the fact that it's in one of the noisiest parts of the city – Copacabana, Posto Quatro. One of the bedrooms acts as a study and opens on to a miniature forest, a tangle of bushes, climbing shrubs and ferns. To the question – 'Are you a magus?' Paulo Coelho, who has just launched *The Pilgrimage*, his fifth book, replies with another: 'Is it windy outside?'
>
> A glance at the dense leaves is enough to make one shake one's head and murmur a casual 'No', implying that it really doesn't matter if there's a breeze outside or not: 'Right, take a look' – he remains as he was, seated on a cushion and leaning against another, doing nothing.
>
> First, the tip of the highest leaf of a palm tree starts to sway gently. In the next instant, the whole plant moves, as does all the vegetation around. The bamboo curtain in the corridor sways and clicks, the reporter's notes fly off her clipboard. After one or two minutes, the wind stops as suddenly as it began. There are a few leaves on the carpet and a question: was it coincidence or is he really a magus who knows how to summon up the wind? Read on and find out more.

Apart from *O Globo*, the only other coverage the rain-making author received was in *Pasquim* and the magazine *Manchete*. He was always friendly and receptive towards journalists, posing in a yoga position and allowing himself to be photographed behind smoking test tubes and putting on or removing his cloak and sword according to the demands of his clients. The barriers began to fall. His telephone number was soon in the diaries of social columnists, among them his friend Hildegard Angel, and he was often reported as having been seen dining in such-and-such a restaurant or leaving such-and-such a theatre. For the first time Paulo could feel the wind of fame in his face – something he had never experienced even at the height of his musical success, since, at the time, the star of the partnership was Raul Seixas. This media exposure did increase the sales of the book, but *The Pilgrimage* still seemed far from becoming a best-seller.

In order to try and capitalize on his new-found 'almost-fame', as he himself called it, Paulo and the astrologer Cláudia Castelo Branco, who had written the preface to *The Pilgrimage*, joined forces with the specialist travel firm Itatiaia Turismo to organize a spiritual package holiday named 'The Three Sacred Roads', which were to be Christianity, Judaism and Islam. Those interested would be guided by Paulo and Cláudia on a journey that would start in Madrid and end in Santiago de Compostela, via a zigzag route through Egypt (Cairo and Luxor), Israel (Jerusalem and Tel Aviv), France (Lourdes) and then back to Spain (Pamplona, Logroño, Burgos, León, Ponferrada and Lugo). Whether it was the fault of the dreadful advertisement published in the newspapers (which did not even say how long the excursion would last) or the high price of the package (US$2,800), they received not a single enquiry. However, although it produced no results, the project had cost them both time and money, and in order to pay them for their work, the agency gave them a half-price trip to the Middle East, one of the places suggested for the failed magical mystery tour.

Paulo and Cláudia set off on 26 September with Paula, Chris's mother, but as soon as they arrived in Cairo, he decided to continue alone with Paula. On their second day in the Egyptian capital, he hired a guide named Hassan and asked him to take them to the Moqattam district, in the southwest of the city, so that he could visit the Coptic monastery of St Simon the Shoemaker. From there they crossed the city by taxi, and night was falling when, after driving through an enormous slum, they reached the sandy fringe of the largest desert on the planet, the Sahara, a few hundred metres from the Sphinx and the famous pyramids of Cheops, Chephren and Mykerinos. They left the taxi and continued their journey to the pyramids on horseback (Paulo was frightened of falling off a camel, the only other available means of transport from there on). When they drew near, Paulo decided to proceed on foot, while Hassan looked

after the horses and read the Koran. Paulo says that, near one of the illuminated monuments, he saw a woman in the middle of the desert wearing a chador and carrying a clay pot on her shoulder. This, according to
him, was very different from what had occurred in Dachau. 'A vision is
something that you see and an apparition is something almost physical,'
he explained later. 'What happened in Cairo was an apparition.' Although
used to such phenomena, he found what he had seen strange. He looked
at the endless stretch of sand surrounding him on that moonlit night and
saw no one else apart from Hassan, who was still reciting sacred verses.
As the shape approached Paulo, it disappeared as mysteriously as it had
appeared. However, it left such a strong impression that, months later, he
could reconstruct the apparition in detail when describing it in his second
book.

When he flew back to Brazil some weeks later, he received the first
major news regarding his career while still on the plane. The stewardess
handed him a copy of *O Globo* from the Saturday before, and he placed
the folded newspaper on his lap, closed his eyes, meditated for a moment
and only then opened the paper at the arts section – and there was *The
Pilgrimage* on that week's best-sellers' list. Before the end of the year, he
would sign contracts for five new editions of the book, the sales of which
went on to exceed 12,000 copies. This success encouraged him to enter
The Pilgrimage for the Prêmio Instituto Nacional do Livro, an award
supported by the Ministry of Education for published novels. The jury
that year was to meet in Vitória, the capital of Espírito Santo, and its
members were the poet Ivan Junqueira, the writer Roberto Almada and
the journalist Carlos Herculano Lopes. *The Pilgrimage* didn't even appear
on the list of finalists and only got Junqueira's vote. 'The book was
unusual for us, because it mixed reality with fantasy,' the poet recalled
later. 'For me personally it was interesting in that I like travel literature
very much and also this kind of half-ghost-story.'

Immediately after the results were announced, Paulo suffered yet
another disappointment. The magazine *Veja* had published a long report
on the boom in esoteric books in Brazil and made no mention of *The
Pilgrimage*. This was such a hard blow that Paulo once again thought of
giving up his career as a writer. 'Today I seriously thought of abandoning

everything and retiring,' he wrote in his diary. Weeks later, however, he seemed to have recovered from those two setbacks and returned to the I Ching, already with an idea for a new book. He wrote a question in his diary: 'What should I do to make my next book sell 100,000 copies?' He threw the three coins on the table and stared in delight at the result. Usually vague and metaphorical in its responses, the Chinese oracle was, according to Paulo, astonishingly clear: 'The great man brings good luck.'

That piece of good luck – the new book – was already in his head. The next work by Paulo Coelho was to be based on a Persian fable that had also inspired the Borges story 'Tale of the Two Dreamers', published in 1935 in *A Universal History of Infamy*. It is the tale of Santiago, a shepherd who, after dreaming repeatedly of a treasure hidden near the Egyptian pyramids, resolves to leave the village where he was born in search of what the author calls a 'personal legend'. On the journey to Egypt Santiago meets various characters, among them an alchemist, and at each meeting he learns a new lesson. At the end of his pilgrimage he discovers that the object of his search was in the very village he had left. Paulo had also chosen the title: *O Alquimista*, or *The Alchemist*. It's odd to think that a book that would become one of the greatest best-sellers of all time – at the beginning of 2000 it had sold more than 35 million copies – started out as a play that would combine Shakespeare and the Brazilian humourist Chico Anysio, as the author recorded in his diary in January 1987:

Menescal and [the actor] Perry [Salles] called me asking me to write a play for one actor alone on the stage. By coincidence, I was watching *Duel* on video, which is a film about a man alone.

I had an idea: a large laboratory in which an old man, an alchemist, is searching for the philosopher's stone, for wisdom. He wants to discover what man can achieve through inspiration. The alchemist (perhaps that would be a good title) recites texts by Shakespeare and by Chico Anysio. He will perform songs and hold dialogues with himself, playing more than one character. He could be an alchemist or a vampire. I know through personal experience that vampires really excite the human imagination, and it's some time since I've seen anything that combines horror and humour on the stage.

But, like Faust, the alchemist realizes that knowledge lies not in books but in people – and the people are in the audience. In order to get them in the mood, he gets them to chant or sing something all together. Perry would be the alchemist, in the role of the discoverer. Again, I stress that this must all be done with great good humour.

This sketch never became a play, but went on to become a novel. Paulo knew the story so intimately that when it came to writing the book, it took him only two weeks to produce 200 pages. At the beginning was a dedication to Jean, to whom Paulo gave the privilege of being the first to read the original manuscript:

For J.,
An alchemist who knows and uses the secrets of the Great Work.

When *The Alchemist* was ready for publication in June 1988, sales of *The Pilgrimage* had exceeded 40,000 copies and it had spent nineteen uninterrupted weeks in the main best-seller lists of the Brazilian press. The sublime indifference with which the media had treated it gave a special savour to Paulo's success, a success that was entirely down to the book itself and to the guerrilla warfare that Paulo, Chris and Andréa Cals had engaged in to publicize it. The I Ching, as interpreted by Paulo, recommended that he renew his contract with Andréa, but since she had taken on other work and he required her to devote herself entirely to him, her responsibilities were transferred to Chris.

She and Paulo adopted the same tactics for *The Alchemist* as had been used for the first book: the couple once again distributed flyers at the doors of theatres, bars and cinemas, visited bookshops and presented booksellers with signed copies. With his experience of the record industry, Paulo brought to the literary world a somewhat reprehensible practice – the *jabaculê*, a payment made to radio stations to encourage them to make favourable comments about a record, or in this case, a book.

Evidence of this can be found in spreadsheets – *certificados de irradiação* – sent to him by O Povo AM-FM, the most popular radio station in Fortaleza, Ceará. These show that during the entire second half of July, *The Alchemist* was mentioned three times a day in programmes presented by Carlos Augusto, Renan França and Ronaldo César, who were, at the time, the station's most popular presenters.

Paulo and Chris knew that they were in a world where anything goes – from sending signed copies to the grandees of the Brazilian media to becoming a full-time speaker, albeit unpaid. He had eight themes for organizers of talks to choose from: 'The Sacred Paths of Antiquity'; 'The Dawn of Magic'; 'The Practices of RAM'; 'The Philosophy and Practice of the Occult Tradition'; 'The Esoteric Tradition and the Practices of RAM'; 'The Growth of the Esoteric'; 'Magic and Power'; and 'Ways of Teaching and Learning'. At the end of each session, the audience could buy signed copies of *The Pilgrimage* and *The Alchemist*, and it was, apparently, very easy to get people to come and listen to him. Paulo's diary at the time shows that he spoke frequently at theatres and universities, as well as in country hotels and even people's homes.

However, this campaign produced slow results and the effects on sales of *The Alchemist* took time to appear. Six weeks after its launch, a few thousand copies had been sold – a vast number in a country like Brazil, it's true, but nothing when compared with the success of *The Pilgrimage* and far fewer than he had planned: 'Up to now,' he wrote, 'the book hasn't reached 10 per cent of the goal I set myself. I think what this book needs is a miracle. I spend all day by the telephone, which refuses to ring. Why the hell doesn't some journalist call me saying that he liked my book? My work is greater than my obsessions, my words, my feelings. For its sake I humiliate myself, I sin, I hope, I despair.'

With *The Pilgrimage* still high in the best-seller lists and *The Alchemist* heading in the same direction, it had become impossible to ignore the author. A great silence had greeted the publication of the first book, but the launch of *The Alchemist* was preceded by full-page articles in all the main Brazilian newspapers. And because most of the press had totally ignored *The Pilgrimage* on its publication, they felt obliged to rediscover it following the success of *The Alchemist*. However, most restricted themselves to printing an article on the author and a summary of the story. The journalist and critic Antônio Gonçalves Filho, in *Folha de São Paulo*, was the first to publish a proper review. He commented only that *The Alchemist* was not as seductive a narrative as *The Pilgrimage* and that the story adopted by the author had already been the subject of a considerable number of books, plays, films and operas, something that Paulo himself had commented on in his preface to the book.

'This is why *The Alchemist*, too, is a symbolic text. In the course of the book I pass on everything I have learned. I've also tried to pay homage to great authors who managed to achieve a Universal Language: Hemingway, Blake, Borges (who also used the Persian story for one of his tales) and Malba Tahan, among others.'

In the second half of 1988, Paulo was just wondering whether to move to a larger, more professional publisher than Eco, when he was set yet another trial by Jean. He and Chris were to spend forty days in the Mojave Desert in southern California. A few days before they were due to leave, he had an unsettling phone conversation with Mandarino, the owner of Eco, who, although he was still enthusiastic about *The Pilgrimage*, did not believe that *The Alchemist* would enjoy the same success. The best thing to do would be to postpone the trip and try to resolve the problem immediately, but Master J would not be moved. And so in the middle of September, Paulo and Chris found themselves practising the spiritual exercises of St Ignatius Loyola in the extreme heat of the Mojave Desert, which could reach 50°C. Four years later, he wrote *As Valkirias* [*The Valkyries*], which was based on this experience.

At the end of October, they returned to Rio. Paulo wanted to resolve his difficulties with Eco immediately, but leaving the small publishing house without having anywhere else to go was not a good idea. One night, wanting to forget these problems for a while, he went with a friend to a poetry recital that was being held in a small fashionable bar. During the entire evening, he had the strange feeling that someone in the audience behind him was staring at him. It was only when the evening came to an end and the lights went up that he turned and caught the fixed gaze of a pretty dark-haired young girl in her early twenties. There was no apparent reason for anyone to look at him like that. At forty-one, Paulo's close-cropped hair was almost entirely white, as were his moustache and goatee. The girl was too pretty for him not to approach her.

He went up to her and asked straight out: 'Were you by any chance looking at me during the reading?'

The girl smiled and said: 'Yes, I was.'

'I'm Paulo Coelho.'

'I know. Look what I've got here in my bag.'

She took out a battered copy of *The Pilgrimage*.

Paulo was about to sign it, but when he heard that it belonged to a friend of hers, he gave it back, saying: 'Buy your own copy and I'll sign it.'

They agreed to meet two days later in the elegant old Confeitaria Colombo, in the centre of the city, so that he could sign her book. Although his choice of such a romantic venue might seem to indicate that he had other intentions, this was not the case. He arrived more than half an hour late, saying that he couldn't stay long because he had a meeting with his publisher, who had just confirmed that he was not interested in continuing to publish *The Alchemist*. So that they could talk a little more, Paulo and the girl walked together to the publisher's office, which was ten blocks from the Colombo.

Her name was Mônica Rezende Antunes, and she was the twenty-year-old only daughter of liberal parents whose sole demand had been that she take a course in classical ballet, which she abandoned almost at once. When she met Paulo, she was studying chemical engineering at the Universidade Estadual do Rio de Janeiro. What Mônica remembers most vividly about that meeting was that she was 'dressed ridiculously': 'Imagine going to discuss contracts with your publisher in the company of a girl in tiny shorts, a flowery blouse and hair like a nymphet!'

Mônica ended up being a witness to the moment when Mandarino at Eco decided not to continue to publish *The Alchemist*. He didn't believe that a work of fiction such as this could have the same degree of success as a personal narrative like *The Pilgrimage*. Although she had only read *The Pilgrimage*, Mônica couldn't understand how anyone could reject a book by an author who had made such an impact on her. Perhaps in an attempt to console himself, Paulo gave her a not very convincing explanation for what might be Ernesto Mandarino's real reason: with annual inflation in the country running at 1,200 per cent it was more profitable to put his money in financial deals than to publish books that ran the risk of not selling. The two of them walked on together a little further, exchanged telephone numbers and went their different ways.

A few days later, before Paulo had decided what to do with the rights to *The Alchemist*, he read in a newspaper column that Lya Luft would be signing her book of poetry, *O Lado Fatal* [*The Fatal Side*], at a cocktail party given by her publisher, Paulo Roberto Rocco. Paulo had been keeping an eye on Editora Rocco for some time. It had only been in existence for just over ten years, but its catalogue already included heavyweights like Gore Vidal, Tom Wolfe and Stephen Hawking. When Paulo arrived, the bookshop was crammed with people. Squeezing his way past waiters and guests, he went up to Rocco, whom he knew only from photographs in newspapers, and said:

'Good evening, my name's Paulo Coelho, we don't know each other but …'

'I already know you by name.'

'I wanted to talk to you about my books. I've a friend, Bona, who lives in the same building as you and had thought of asking her to give a dinner so she could introduce us.'

'You don't need to ask anything of anyone. Come to my office and we'll have a coffee and talk about your books.'

Rocco arranged the meeting for two days later. Before making a decision, though, Paulo turned to the I Ching to find out whether or not he should hand *The Alchemist* to a new publisher, since Rocco had clearly shown an interest. From what he could understand from the oracle's response, it seemed that the book should be given to the new publisher only if he agreed to have it in the bookshops before Christmas. This was a highly convenient interpretation since, as any author knows, Christmas is the best time of the year for selling books. As he was about to leave to meet Rocco, the phone rang. It was Mônica, whom he invited to go along with him.

After a brief, friendly conversation with Rocco, Paulo left copies of *The Pilgrimage* and *The Alchemist* with him. The publisher thought it somewhat strange that Paulo should want him to publish the book so quickly, but Paulo explained that all he had to do was buy the camera-ready copy from Eco, change the name of the publisher and put the book on the market. Rocco said that he would think about it and would reply that week. In fact, two days later, he called to say that the new contract was ready for signature. Rocco was going to publish *The Alchemist*.

CHAPTER 25

The critics' response

R EJECTED BY MANDARINO, *The Alchemist* became one of the most popular gifts not only that Christmas but on many other Christmases, New Years, Easters, Carnivals, Lents and birthdays in Brazil and in more than a hundred other countries. The first edition to be launched by his new publisher sold out within a few days, creating a most unusual situation: an author with two books in the best-seller lists, one, *The Alchemist*, fiction and the other, *The Pilgrimage*, non-fiction. *The Alchemist* never stopped selling.

The phenomenon that the book became in the hands of Rocco encouraged Paulo to take *The Pilgrimage* from Eco as well and give it to his new publisher. Needing a pretext for such a change, he began to make demands on his old publisher. The first of these was an attempt to protect his royalties from the erosion caused by an astonishing 1,350 per cent annual rate of inflation: instead of quarterly payments (a privilege accorded to very few authors), he wanted Mandarino to make them weekly, which he agreed to do even though it was against market practice. Taking advantage of Mandarino's infinite patience (and his clear interest in retaining the book), Paulo then added two clauses hitherto unknown in Brazilian publishing contracts: daily monetary correction, linked to one of the mechanisms that existed at the time, and the use of a percentage of gross sales for marketing the book. These tactics seemed to be of particular interest to Mônica Antunes, who now went everywhere with Paulo. At the beginning of 1989, she told him over dinner in a pizzeria in Leblon that she was thinking of giving up her degree course at the university (she had just finished her second year in chemical engineering) and moving abroad with her boyfriend, Eduardo. The author's eyes lit up, as if he had just seen a new door opening, and he said: 'Great idea! Why don't you go to Spain? I've got various friends there who can help you. You could try to sell my books. If you succeed, you'll get the 15 per cent commission every literary agent earns.'

When she told her boyfriend about this, he discovered that the company for which he was working had a factory in Barcelona and it appeared, at first glance, that it would be fairly easy to get a transfer there, or at least a paid placement for a few months. Mônica, meanwhile, had learned that some of the most important Spanish publishers had their headquarters in Barcelona.

In the last week of May 1989, Mônica and Eduardo arrived in Madrid, where they stayed for three weeks before going on to Barcelona. During their first year in Spain, Mônica and Eduardo lived in an apartment in Rubí, just outside Barcelona. At book fairs they would go to all the stands collecting publishers' catalogues and would then spend the following days sending each a small press release offering the Spanish language rights to *The Alchemist* and other foreign language rights to publishers in other countries for *The Pilgrimage,* which had been taken on and translated by the Bolivian agency H. Katia Schumer and published in Spanish by Martínez Roca.

Meanwhile, in Brazil *The Pilgrimage* and *The Alchemist* remained at the top of the best-seller lists. Although Mandarino had accepted all the author's demands, at the end of 1989, he received a visit from Paulo Rocco, who brought bad news. For an advance of US$60,000, his company had acquired the publication rights to *The Pilgrimage.* Nearly two decades later, Ernesto Mandarino still cannot hide the hurt caused by the author on whom he had gambled when he was still a nobody: 'New editions were continuing to come out – to the envy of other publishers. When he visited me, Rocco said that he was offering Paulo Coelho an advance of US$60,000. I said that if that was what he wanted, there was nothing I could do, as the contracts were renewable after each edition. After twenty-eight editions of *The Pilgrimage* he left us. That really hurt. Almost as hurtful was the fact that, in interviews and articles, he never mentioned that he began with us.'

Bad feelings apart, Mandarino recognizes the importance of the author not only in the publishing world in Brazil but also in Brazilian literature: 'Paulo Coelho made books into a popular consumer product. He revolutionized the publishing market in Brazil, which used to limit itself to ludicrously small runs of 3,000 copies. With him the market grew. Paulo Coelho brought respect for books in Brazil and for our literature in the world.'

In a very small publishing market such as that in Brazil, it was only natural that large publishers should feel interested in an author who, with only two titles to his name, had sold more than five hundred thousand copies. Despite the Olympian indifference of the media, his books vanished from the bookshop shelves and thousands crowded into auditoriums across the country, though not to listen to the usual promotional rubbish. Readers seemed to want to share with the author the spiritual experiences he wrote of in his works. Paulo's talks were incredibly popular, and scenes such as that in the Martins Pena auditorium in Brasília – when it was necessary to put up loudspeakers outside the 2,000-seater auditorium for those arriving late – were not uncommon. One interview which he gave to the journalist Mara Regea, of Rádio Nacional de Brasília, had to be repeated three times at the request of listeners wanting to hear him talk for an hour and a half on alchemy and mysticism. Such enthusiasm was repeated across the country. In Belo Horizonte, the 350-seat Banco do Desenvolvimento de Minas Gerais auditorium wasn't large enough for the almost one thousand people who turned up to hear him, forcing the young Afonso Borges, the organizer of the event, to place televisions in various parts of the building so that no one would miss the author's words.

When the press woke up to this phenomenon, it seemed confused and at a loss to explain his overwhelming success. Reluctant to judge the literary content of the books, the newspapers preferred to regard them as yet another passing marketing phenomenon. In the opinion of a large number of journalists, the author Paulo Coelho was nothing more than a fad, like the hula hoop, the twist and even the lyricist Paulo Coelho and his Sociedade Alternativa. Since *O Globo* had called him 'the Castaneda of Copacabana' on the front page of its arts section two years earlier, the media had practically forgotten him. It was only when his books reached the top of the best-seller lists and the newspaper *O Estado de São Paulo* learned that *The Pilgrimage* and *The Alchemist* had sold more than half a million copies that the critics took note of the fact that two years was a long time for something that was merely a fad. The man with the prematurely white hair who talked about dreams, angels and love seemed to be here to stay, but it took a while for the press to understand this.

He did not appear prominently in the newspapers again until October 1989, in a full-page feature in the arts supplement of *O Estado de São Paulo*, which was divided into two parts. The first was a profile written by Thereza Jorge on the author's career in rock music. At the end, she stated unequivocally: 'But it is in literature that Coelho has clearly found his place.' However, proof that opinions on his work were divided appeared on that same page, in the form of a twenty-line item signed by Hamilton dos Santos. He summarized Paulo's work as 'a cloying synthesis of teachings drawn from everything from Christianity to Buddhism'. As the author himself confessed, this was 'the first real blow' that he had received from a critic: 'I just froze when I read it. Absolutely froze. It was as though the person who wrote it was warning me about the price of fame.'

Even the monthly literary tabloid *Leia Livros*, a cult publication edited by Caio Graco Prado, found itself bowing to the sheer force of numbers. On the cover of the December 1989 edition, Paulo appeared with sword in hand, hair bristling and gazing Zen-like into infinity. The treatment meted out to him by *Leia Livros*, however, was no different from the approach normally adopted by other members of the press. Of the twelve pages of the article, eleven were taken up with a detailed profile of the author, with no evaluation of his work. The actual review, signed by Professor Teixeira Coelho of the University of São Paulo, occupied only half a page. The average Brazilian – as one presumes most readers of *The Pilgrimage* and *The Alchemist* were – might have had difficulty in understanding whether Paulo was being praised or insulted, so convoluted was the reviewer's language:

> The time when vision, imagination, the non-rational (albeit with its own rationality) were considered an integral part of the real and came 'from above'; it was just a mental habit. This norm defined a cultural paradigm, a way of thinking and knowing about the world. This paradigm was replaced by the new rationalist paradigm of the eighteenth century. Today, it is this paradigm that appears to be (temporarily) exhausted. The Paulo Coelho phenomenon is a symbol of the decadence of this paradigm and implies a distrust of rationalism as we have known it over the last two centuries.
>
> [...] I prefer to see in the sales success of Paulo Coelho's works the primacy of the imagination, which continues to exert its power in different forms (religions, 'magic', 'alternative' medicine and sex, the poetic road to knowledge), forms that old-fashioned emblematic Cartesian thinking would designate as 'irrational'.
>
> [...] Within the Paulo Coelho genre, Lawrence Durrell with his 'Avignon Quintet' is a better writer, and Colin Wilson more intellectual. However, such judgements are superfluous.

While the press was racking its brains as to how to understand the phenomenon, it continued to grow. In a rare unguarded moment – especially when it came to money – Paulo revealed to the *Jornal da Tarde* that the two books had so far earned him US$250,000. It may well have been more. Assuming that the amounts he and Rocco disclosed were true, the 500,000 copies sold up until then would have brought him at least $350,000 in royalties.

With two best-sellers, a new publisher, hundreds of thousands of dollars or more invested in property and his international career showing signs of taking off, Paulo was summoned by Jean to fulfil another of the four sacred paths that initiates to RAM must follow. After the Road to Santiago, he had performed a further penance (the trip to the Mojave Desert), but there was still the third and penultimate stage, the Road to Rome. The fourth would be the road towards death. The so-called Road to Rome was merely a metaphor, since it could be followed anywhere in the world, with the added advantage that it could be undertaken by car. He chose Languedoc, on the edge of the Pyrenees in southwestern France, where a Christian religious sect, Catharism or Albigensianism, had flourished in the twelfth and thirteenth centuries, only to be stamped out by the Inquisition. Another peculiarity of the Road to Rome was that the pilgrim must always follow his dreams. Paulo thought this too abstract and asked for more information, but the reply was less than illuminating: 'If you dream of a bus stop during the night, the following morning go to the nearest bus stop. If you dream of a bridge, your next stop should be a bridge.'

For a little more than two months he wandered through the valleys and across the mountains and rivers of what is one of the most beautiful regions of Europe. On 15 August he left the Hotel d'Anvers in Lourdes, where he had been staying, and continued on towards Foix, Roquefixade, Montségur, Peyrepertuse, Bugarach and dozens of other tiny villages which were, in the majority of cases, no more than a handful of houses. Since Jean had made no restrictions on the matter, Paulo travelled part of the route in the company of Mônica, who skipped work in Barcelona for a week in order to go with him.

On the evening of 21 August 1989, when they reached Perpignan, he used a public phone to call Chris in Brazil, because he was missing her. Chris told him that his ex-partner Raul Seixas had died in São Paulo from pancreatitis, brought on by alcoholism.

This was an enormous loss for Paulo. After not seeing one another for several years, he and Raul had met up again four months earlier in Rio de Janeiro during a show Raul was giving in Canecão, which would prove to be one of his last. It was not a reconciliation, since they had never quarrelled, but it was an attempt on the part of Raul's new musical partner, the young rock star Marcelo Nova, to bring them back together again. During the show, Paulo was called up on to the stage to sing the chorus 'Viva! Viva! Viva a Sociedade Alternativa!' with the band. According to his ex-slave Toninho Buda, the author sang with his hands in his pockets, 'because he was being forced to sing Crowley's mantra in public and had to keep his fingers crossed'. Parts of the show were filmed by an amateur fan and put on the Internet years later. They show a shaky Raul Seixas, his face puffy and with all the appearance of someone ruined by drink.

The last work the two had done together was the LP *Mata Virgem*, which had been recorded long ago, in 1978. In 1982 the Eldorado label, based in São Paulo, tried to revive the duo with a new album, but as a Rio journalist put it, they both seemed to be 'inflicted by acute primadonnaitis': Paulo lived in Rio and Raul in São Paulo, and both refused to travel to where the other was in order to start work. Solomon-like, Roberto Menescal suggested a solution. He had been invited to produce the record and suggested meeting exactly halfway between the two cities in the Itatiaia national park. They arrived at the Hotel Simon on a Sunday, and when Paulo woke early on the Monday, before even having a coffee, he left a note under the door of Raul's room: 'I'm ready to start work.' Raul didn't even show his face. The same thing happened again on Tuesday. On the Wednesday, the owner went to Paulo, concerned that Raul had been shut up in his room for three days, drinking and not even touching the sandwiches he had ordered by phone. Any hope of reuniting the duo who had revolutionized Brazilian rock music died there and then.

Six days after the news of the death of his 'close enemy', still shaken and still on the Road to Rome, Paulo had what he describes as another extrasensory experience. He was heading for one of the small towns in the region where he was to take part in the so-called 'ritual of fire', during which invocations are made in the light of a bonfire. On the way, he says, he felt the presence beside him of no less a person – or thing – than his guardian angel. It wasn't a tangible or audible being, nor even an ectoplasm, but a being whose presence he could clearly feel and with whom he could only communicate mentally. According to his recollection, it was the being that took the initiative, and a non-verbal dialogue took place.

'What do you want?'

Paulo kept his eyes on the road and said: 'I want my books to be read.'

'But in order for that to happen you're going to have to take a lot of flack.'

'But why? Just because I want my books to be read?'

'Your books will bring you fame, and then you're really going to get it in the neck. You've got to decide whether that really is what you want.'

Before disappearing into the atmosphere, the being said to him: 'I'm giving you a day to think about it. Tonight you will dream of a particular place. That's where we shall meet at the same time tomorrow.'

In the hotel where he was staying in Pau, he dreamed of a small 'tram' taking passengers to the top of a very high mountain. When he woke the following morning, he learned at reception that one of the city's attractions was precisely that: a cable car, the Funiculaire de Pau, which set off only a few metres from the hotel, next to the railway station. The hill where the dark-green cable car let off its thirty or so passengers every ten minutes was not as high as the one in his dream, but there was no doubt that he was on the right route. When it was getting dark, more or less twenty-four hours after the apparition of the previous day, Paulo joined a short queue and minutes later, reached a terrace surrounded by fountains – the Fontaine de Vigny, where he had an amazing view of the lights in the city coming on. The writer recalls clearly not only the date – 'It was 27 September 1989, the feast-day of Cosmos and Damian' – but also what he said to the apparition: 'I want my books to be read. But I want to be able to renew my wish in three years' time. Give me three years and I'll come back here on 27 September 1992 and tell you whether I'm man enough to continue or not.'

The seemingly interminable seventy days of the pilgrimage were drawing to a close, when one night, following the 'ritual of fire', a fair-skinned, fair-haired young woman went up to him and began a conversation. Her name was Brida O'Fern, and she was a thirty-year-old Irish woman who had reached the rank of Master in RAM and, like him, was following the Road to Rome. Brida's company proved to be not only a pleasant gift that would alleviate his weariness as he completed the pilgrimage, for Paulo was so delighted by the stories she told him that he decided to base his third book on her, which, like her, would be called *Brida*. Writing about the Road to Rome could come later.

Once he had completed the trial set by Jean, he set about writing *Brida*, using a method he would continue to use from then on: he would ponder the subject for some time and then, when the story was ready, write the book in two weeks. The novel tells the story and adventures of the young Brida O'Fern, who, at twenty-one, decides to enter the world of magic. Her discoveries start when she meets a wizard in a forest 150 kilometres from Dublin. Guided by the witch Wicca, she starts her journey and, after completing all the rituals, finally becomes a Master in RAM. In the very first pages the author warns his readers:

> In my book *The Diary of a Magus*, I replaced two of the practices of RAM with exercises in perception learned in the days when I worked in drama. Although the results were, strictly speaking, the same, I received a severe reprimand from my Teacher. 'There may well be quicker or easier methods, that doesn't matter; what matters is that the Tradition remains unchanged,' he said. For this reason, the few rituals described in *Brida* are the same as those practised over the centuries by the Tradition of the Moon – a specific tradition, which requires experience and practice. Practising such rituals without guidance is dangerous, inadvisable, unnecessary and can greatly hinder the Spiritual Search.

Encouraged by the success of *The Pilgrimage* and *The Alchemist*, Rocco, when he learned that Paulo had a new book on the boil, took the initiative and offered him US$60,000 for *Brida*. Although the amount offered was high by Brazilian standards, it certainly didn't break any records (a few months earlier Rocco had paid US$180,000 for the right to publish Tom Wolfe's novel *The Bonfire of the Vanities*). What was so different was the way in which Paulo proposed that the money should be divided up, a method he would continue to use in almost all negotiations over his future publications in Brazil: US$20,000 would be spent by the publisher on promotion and advertising; a further US$20,000 would be used to cover the journeys he would have to make within Brazil to promote the book; and only US$20,000 would go to him as an advance against royalties. The biggest surprise, which was kept secret by the publisher until a few days before its launch during the first week of August 1990, was that the first edition of *Brida* would have a print run of 100,000 copies – a run surpassed among Brazilian authors only by Jorge Amado, whose novel

Tieta do Agreste [translated as *Tieta, the Goat Girl*] was launched in 1977 with an initial print run of 120,000 copies.

The angel Paulo met near Pau was absolutely right when he predicted that the author would be massacred by the critics. *The Pilgrimage* and *The Alchemist* had been treated fairly gently by the press, but when *Brida* was launched, the critics appeared to want blood. Merciless and on many occasions almost rude, the main newspapers in Rio and São Paulo seemed determined to demolish him:

> The author writes very badly. He doesn't know how to use contractions, his use of pronouns is poor, he chooses prepositions at random, and doesn't know even simple things, like the difference between the verbs 'to speak' and 'to say'.
>
> (Luiz Garcia, *O Globo*)

> In aesthetic terms, *Brida* is a failure. It is an imitation of Richard Bach's tedious model seasoned with a little Carlos Castaneda. Paulo Coelho's book is full of stereotypes.
>
> (Juremir Machado da Silva, *O Estado de São Paulo*)

> What he should perhaps announce more boldly is that he can make it rain. For that is precisely what Paulo Coelho does – on his own garden.
>
> (Eugênio Bucci, *Folha de São Paulo*)

> … one of those books which, once you've put it down, you can't pick up again.
>
> (Raul Giudicelli, *Jornal do Commercio*)

The insults came from all sides, not only from newspapers and magazines. A few days after the launch of *Brida*, the author was interviewed on a popular Brazilian television chat show, *Jô Soares Onze e Meia*, which was broadcast nationally by SBT. Although they were friends and had worked together on the soft-porn movie *Tangarela, a Tanga de Cristal*, the presenter joined the attack on Paulo Coelho and opened the programme with a list of dozens of errors he had discovered in *The Alchemist*. The interview provoked a parallel squabble. Two days later, the Rio newspaper *O Dia* carried a note in the column written by Artur da Távola, Paulo's ex-colleague in the working group at Philips and someone who had contributed a preface to *Arquivos do Inferno*, entitled 'Credit where credit's due, Jô':

> Although we weren't given due credit – he did, after all, go into the studio with a fax of the article published in this paper listing the eighty-six [grammatical] mistakes found in *The Alchemist*, requested from us by the producers of their programme on SBT – Jô Soares interviewed the writer Paulo Coelho the day before yesterday going on about the errors overlooked by Editora Rocco.
>
> The magus justified the publisher's editorial laxity by stating that all the errors had been made on purpose. 'They're codes,' said Paulo Coelho. 'If they weren't, they would have been corrected in later editions.'

There remained, however, a faint hope that someone in the media might read his books with the same unprejudiced eyes as the thousands of people who were flocking to bookshops across the country looking for one of his three books. Perhaps it would be Brazil's most widely read and influential weekly, *Veja*, which had decided to put him on its next cover? After giving a long interview and posing for photographs, the writer waited anxiously for Sunday morning, when the magazine would arrive on the news-stands in Rio. The first surprise was seeing the cover, where, instead of his photo, he found the image of a crystal ball under the title 'The Tide of Mysticism'. He quickly leafed through the magazine until he came to the article, entitled 'The All-High Wizard' and illustrated with a photograph of him in a black cloak and trainers and holding a crook in his hand. He began to skim-read, but needed to go no further than the tenth line to realize that the journalist (the article was unsigned) was using heavy artillery fire: *Brida*, *The Pilgrimage* and *The Alchemist* were all classed as 'books with badly told metaphysical stories steeped in a vague air of mysticism'. In the following six pages, the bombardment continued with the same intensity, and hardly a paragraph went by that did not contain some criticism, gibe or ironic remark: 'crazy superstitions'; 'it's impossible to know where genuine belief ends and farce begins'; 'yet another surfer on the lucrative wave of mysticism'; 'he pocketed US$20,000 as an advance for perpetrating *Brida* and is already thinking of charging for his talks'; 'surely the worst of his books'; 'pedestrian fiction'. Not even his faith was spared. Referring to the religious order to which he belonged, *Veja* stated that Regnum Agnus Mundi was nothing more than 'an assemblage of Latin words that could be translated approximately as Kingdom of the Lamb of the World'. Despite the hours of interviewing time he had given them, only one sentence was used in its entirety. When he was asked what was the reason for his success, he had replied: 'It's a divine gift.'

The author reacted by writing a short letter to *Veja*, saying: 'I should like to make just one correction to the article "The All-High Wizard". I do not intend to charge for my talks to the public. The remainder came as no surprise: we are all idiots and you are very intelligent.' He sent a long article to the journalist Luiz Garcia of *O Globo*, which was published under the headline 'I am the Flying Saucer of Literature', and in which for the first time Paulo complained about the treatment he had received from the media:

> At the moment I am the flying saucer of literature – regardless of whether or not you like its shape, its colours and its crew. So I can understand the astonishment, but why the aggression? For three years the public has been buying my books in ever greater numbers and I really don't think I could fool so many people in so many age groups and from all social classes at the same time. All I've done is try to show my truth and the things in which I sincerely believe – although the critics haven't even spared my beliefs.

The author of the review replied on the same page, at the end of which he adopted as abrasive a tone as he had before: 'Resigned to the fact that he will continue, as he says in his all too mistakable style, to "fight the good fight", I would simply advise him not to persist with his thesis that writing simply and writing badly are the same thing. It does him no favours.'

Fortunately for Paulo, the bacteria of the critics' remarks did not infect sales. While the journalists, magnifying glass in hand, searched for misused verbs, doubtful agreements and misplaced commas, the readers kept buying the book. A week after it went on the market, *Brida* topped the best-seller lists throughout the country, bringing the author a new record, that of having three books simultaneously in the national best-seller lists. The popular phenomenon that Paulo Coelho had become meant that public figures, intellectuals and artists had to have an opinion about him. Curiously enough, to judge by the statements in various newspapers and magazines of the time, while the critics may have been unanimous, the world of celebrities seemed divided:

He's a genius. He teaches that enlightenment doesn't lie in complicated things.

(Regina Casé, actress)

Who? Paulo Coelho? No, I've never read anything by him. But it's not because I'm not interested. It's just that I'm completely out of touch.

(Olgária Matos, philosopher and professor
at the University of São Paulo)

The Alchemist is the story of each of us as individuals. I found the book very illuminating, in fact I recommended it to my family.

(Eduardo Suplicy, economist and politician)

I read and there was light. The narrative explores intuition and flows as naturally as a river.

(Nelson Motta, composer)

I found both books very enlightening. I understood things in them that are very hard to explain.

(Técio Lins e Silva, lawyer and politician)

I've read *The Pilgrimage*, but I prefer the lyrics he wrote in partnership with Raul Seixas.

(Cacá Rosset, theatre director)

It's all extraordinarily enlightening. He converses with the mystery.

(Cacá Diegues, film director)

In spite of the critics' bile, a year after its launch, *Brida* had been through fifty-eight editions and continued to top all the best-seller lists with sales which, combined with those of the previous books, were edging towards the one million mark, something very few Brazilian authors had achieved up to then. Encouraged by his success, Paulo was preparing to write a non-fiction book, a real bombshell that he intended to be in the shops in 1991. It was an autobiographical book that would describe his adventures with Raul Seixas in the world of black magic and satanism – including, of course, the 'black night', when he believed that he had come face to face with the Devil. He usually only gave Chris the text to read when he had finished the book, but this time he handed it to her a chapter at a time. While Paulo spent his days bent over his computer, she was electrified by what she was reading. When he was already on page 600, though, she gave him a piece of harsh advice.

'Paulo, stop writing that book.'

'What!'

'I love the book. The problem is that it's all about Evil. I know Evil is fascinating, but you can't go on writing it.'

He tried to talk her out of this crazy idea 'first, with arguments and then by kicking anything that happened to be near': 'You're mad, Chris! You might have told me that on page 10, not page 600!'

'OK, I'll tell you the reason for my concerns: I looked at Our Lady of Aparecida, and she said that you can't write this book.' (She was referring to the black patron saint of Brazil.)

After much discussion, Chris's point of view won the day, as usually happened. When he decided that the wretched work would die, unpublished, Paulo printed out one version of the book and then deleted all traces of it from his computer.

He arranged to have lunch with his publisher, Paulo Rocco, in the elegant Portuguese restaurant Antiquarius, in Leblon, and put the great thick tome on the table, saying: 'Here's the new book. Open it at any page.'

Rocco, out of superstition, normally never read any of Paulo's original texts before sending them off to the printer; this time, though, he thought that he should do as the author suggested. He opened the typescript at random and read the page, and when he finished, Paulo said: 'Besides myself and Christina, you will have been the only person to read any part of this book, because I'm going to destroy it. The only reason I'm not asking the waiter to flambé it right here and now is because I don't want the negative energy to turn to fire. I've already deleted it from my computer.'

After lunch, Paulo went alone to Leblon beach, looking for somewhere to bury the book for good. When he saw a rubbish truck chewing up the contents of the litter bins outside the buildings along the seafront, he went up to it, threw the package containing the original into the rotating drum and, in a matter of seconds, the book that would never be read had been utterly destroyed.

CHAPTER 26

Success abroad

DESTROYING A BOOK laden with so much negative energy may have saved Paulo from future metaphysical problems, but it presented him and his publisher with a new problem: what to launch in 1991 in order to capitalize on the phenomenal success of the three previous best-sellers. Paulo suggested to Rocco that he adapt and translate into Portuguese a small book, little more than a pamphlet, containing a sermon given in England in 1890 by the young Protestant missionary Henry Drummond: *The Greatest Thing in the World*, based on St Paul's letter to the Corinthians in which the author talks of the virtues of patience, goodness, humility, generosity, kindness, surrender, tolerance, innocence and sincerity as manifestations 'of the supreme gift given to Humanity: love'. It was given the new title of *The Supreme Gift* [*O Dom Supremo*] and despite being published with little fuss and almost entirely ignored by the media, in a matter of weeks, *The Supreme Gift* had entered the best-seller lists, where his other three books, *The Pilgrimage*, *The Alchemist* and *Brida*, had become permanent fixtures.

Its success did not, however, appear to satisfy the author. In the long run, this was not a work of his own but a translation produced in order to fill a gap. Paulo decided on a story that had been in his mind since 1988: his adventure with Chris in the Mojave Desert. The task that had been entrusted to him by Jean, Paulo says, was precise: he and Chris were to spend forty days in the Mojave Desert, one of the largest of the American national parks. The desert is known for its hostile climate and its unique geological formations, notably the Valley of Death; it is a place where the rivers and lakes disappear for half the year, leaving behind only dried-up beds. In order to fulfil the trial set by the Master – to find his guardian angel – the writer would have to employ a guide in the immense desert that stretches across California, Nevada, Utah and Arizona. The person chosen by Jean was Took.

On 5 September 1988, the couple landed at Los Angeles airport, where they hired a car and drove south towards the Salton Sea, a saltwater lake 50 kilometres long and 20 wide. After hours of driving, they reached one of those half-abandoned gas stations that are so common in films about the American West. 'Is it far to the desert?' Paulo asked the girl who was working the pump. She said no, they were about 30 kilometres from the small town of Borrego Springs, on the edge of the desert, and gave them some important advice: not to turn on the air-conditioning when the car was stationary, to avoid overheating the engine; to put four gallons of water in the boot; and not to leave the vehicle should anything unforeseen happen. Paulo was astounded to learn that the desert was so close: 'The climate there was comfortable and the vegetation was a luxuriant green. I found it hard to believe that a fifteen-minute drive away everything would change so radically, but that is precisely what happened: as soon as we crossed a chain of mountains the road began to descend and there in front of us lay the silence and the immensity of the Mojave.'

During the forty days they spent camping or, when they could, staying in hotels, Paulo and Chris lived with the historical remnants that form part of the legend of the desert: abandoned gold mines, the dusty carcases of pioneers' wagons, ghost towns, hermits, communities of hippies who spent the day in silent meditation. Besides these, the only living beings they came across were the so-called 'Mojave locals': rattle snakes, hares and coyotes – animals that come out only at night in order to avoid the heat.

The first two weeks of the forty days were to be spent in total silence, with the couple not being allowed to exchange so much as a 'good morning'. This period was to be entirely devoted to the spiritual exercises of St Ignatius Loyola. These exercises, which were approved by the Vatican in 1548, are the fruit of the personal experience of the founder of the Society of Jesus. It is a spirituality that is not to be preached about or intellectualized but experienced. 'It is through experience that the mystery of God will be revealed to each person, in a singular, individual form,' the manuals produced by the Jesuits explain, 'and it is this revelation that will transform your life.' St Ignatius' aim was that each individual practising these exercises should become a contemplative during this time, 'which means seeing in each and every thing the figure of God, the presence of the Holy Trinity constructing and reconstructing the world'. And that was what Paulo and Chris did during the first two weeks, offering up prayers and reflections in their search for God.

One night, a week after their arrival, they were sitting immersed in this atmosphere of spirituality, beneath a sky filled with millions of stars, when a great crash shattered the peace and silence, immediately followed by a second, and then another and another. The deafening noise was coming from the sky and was caused by gigantic balls of fire exploding and breaking up into thousands of coloured fragments, briefly illuminating the entire desert. It took a few seconds for them to be convinced that this was not Armageddon: 'Startled, we saw brilliant lights falling slowly from the sky, lighting up the desert as if it were day. Suddenly, we began to hear crashes around us: it was the sound of military planes breaking the sound barrier. Illuminated by that phantasmagorical light, they were dropping incendiary bombs somewhere on the horizon. It was only the next day that we learned that the desert is used for military exercises. It was terrifying.'

At the end of those first two weeks of spiritual practices, and still following the instructions given by Jean, they finally reached Took's old trailer, permanently parked near Borrego Springs. Both Paulo and Chris were surprised to see that the powerful paranormal to whom Jean had referred was a young man of twenty. Guided by the young magus, Paulo was to travel through dozens of small towns on the frontier between the United States and Mexico until he met a group known in the region as the 'Valkyries'. These were eight very attractive women who wandered through the towns of the Mojave dressed in black leather and driving powerful motorbikes. They were led by the eldest of the eight, Valhalla, a former executive of Chase Manhattan Bank, who, like Paulo and Took, was also an initiate in RAM. It was through contact with her that, on the thirty-eighth day of their journey, Paulo – without Chris this time – came across a blue butterfly and a voice which, he says, spoke to him. After this, the author states, he saw his angel – or at least the materialization of part of his angel: an arm that shone in the sunlight and dictated biblical words which he wrote down, shaking and terrified, on a piece of paper. Trembling with emotion, he could not wait to tell Chris what he had experienced and to explain that 'seeing the angel was even easier than talking to it'. 'All you had to do was to believe in angels, to need angels, and there they were, shining in the morning light.'

To celebrate the event, Paulo drove into the desert with Chris and Took to a village known as Glorieta Canyon. After walking across an area of barren, stony ground, the author stopped in front of a small grotto. Then he took bags of cement and sand and a flagon of water from the boot of the car and began to prepare some mortar. When it was the right consistency, he covered the floor of the grotto with the cement and, before the mixture began to harden, he affixed a small image of Our Lady of Aparecida, which he had brought with him. At the foot of the image he wrote in the still-wet cement the following words in English: 'THIS IS THE VIRGIN OF APARECIDA FROM BRAZIL. ASK FOR A MIRACLE AND RETURN HERE.' He lit a candle, said a quick prayer and left.

On his return to Brazil, Paulo was to spend three more years pondering those events in the Mojave Desert. It was only at the end of 1991, when he felt that the typescript he had destroyed required a replacement, that he decided to write *The Valkyries*. According to the records of his computer's word-processing program, he typed the first words of the book at 23.30 on 6 January 1992. After seventeen uninterrupted days of work, as had become his custom, he typed the final sentence of the 239th and final page of the work: 'And only then will we be able to understand stars, angels and miracles.'

On 21 April, when the book had gone through all the editorial processes and was ready to be printed, Paulo sent a fax from his apartment in Rio to Editora Rocco saying that Jean was not suggesting but 'ordering' and 'demanding' changes to the text:

> Dear Rocco:
>
> Half an hour ago, I received a phone call from J. (the Master), ordering me to delete (or change) two pages in the book. These pages are in the middle of the book and refer to a scene called 'The ritual that demolishes rituals'. He says that in the scene I must not describe things exactly as they happened, that I should use allegorical language or break off the narrative of the ritual before I reach the forbidden part.
>
> I have decided to opt for the second alternative, but this is going to mean me doing some rewriting. I will make these changes over the holiday, but I was anxious to let you know this. You can send someone to collect the following on Thursday:
>
> – the changes demanded by my Master;
>
> – the new 'Author's Note'
>
> If I can't manage this, I'll send you another fax, but my Master said that I was to contact the publisher immediately and that's precisely what I'm doing (even though I know that today is a holiday).
>
> Paulo Coelho

Besides Jean, the author and Paulo Rocco, no one would ever know what the censored passages contained. The removal of those passages doesn't in any way appear to have compromised the success of *The Valkyries*. Less than twenty-four hours after the book's launch in August 1992, 60,000 copies of the initial 120,000 print run had vanished from the bookshop shelves. A fortnight later, *The Alchemist* lost its number one spot in the best-seller lists, where it had remained for 159 consecutive weeks, to give way to *The Valkyries*. The author was breaking one record after another. With *The Valkyries*, he became the first Brazilian to have no fewer than five books in the best-seller lists. Besides the new launch, there were *The Alchemist* (159 weeks), *Brida* (106 weeks), *The Pilgrimage* (68 weeks) and *The Supreme Gift* (19 weeks) – something which had only been bettered at the time by Sidney Sheldon. What most caught the attention of the press, apart from the astonishing sales figures, were the details of the author's contract with Rocco. One newspaper stated that Paulo was to receive 15 per cent of the cover price of the book (as opposed to the usual 10 per cent), while another revealed that he would have a bonus of US$400,000 when sales passed the 600,000 mark. A third speculated about the money spent by the publisher on publicity and said that, in order to protect himself against inflation, the author had demanded payments every fortnight. The *Jornal do Brasil* stated that in the wake of the success of *The Valkyries* the market would be 'inundated with plastic knickknacks with the inscription "I believe in angels", posters announcing that "the angels are among us" and china replicas of the author, complete with goatee, as well as 600 shirts with a company logo and the Archangel Michael'. One Rio columnist said that the author had supposedly turned down a payment of US$45,000 to appear in an advertisement for an insurance company in which he would say: 'I believe in life after death, but, just in case, get some insurance.' A further novelty was that, from then on, Paulo was also able to influence the cover price of the book – an area in which, generally speaking, authors do not become involved. Concerned to keep his work accessible to those with less buying power, he went on to set a ceiling price for his books which, in the case of *The Valkyries*, was US$11.

Once the initial interest in numbers, records and figures had passed, the criticisms started to pile in, couched in much the same terms as the reviews of his earlier books:

> The literary mediocrity of *The Valkyries* does at least have one positive effect. It could have been thrilling, but is, in fact, dull, and is, therefore, easier to read.
>
> (*Folha de São Paulo*)

> In terms of literature, if one understands by that the art of writing, *The Valkyries* is generously endowed with the same qualities as Coelho's previous books, namely, none at all.
>
> (*Veja*)

Paulo Coelho's books, and *The Valkyries* is no exception, do not stand out for their stylistic excellence. Plot-line apart, the books consist of crudely constructed sentences that appear to have been taken from a school composition.

(*O Estado de São Paulo*)

In the midst of this bombardment, however, the newspapers had quietly let it be known that the Ministry of Education in Rio wanted to use Paulo Coelho's works as a means of getting students to read. The two reactions to the idea, both published in the *Jornal do Brasil*, were even harsher than the words of the critics. In the first of these, entitled 'Stupidities', the journalist Roberto Marinho de Azevedo said that he was astounded and accused the ministry of 'feeding these innocents with eighth-hand mysticism written in sloppy Portuguese'. Even worse was the illustration accompanying the article, a caricature of a student with the ears of a donkey holding a copy of *The Pilgrimage*. Having published four books and become one of the greatest literary successes of all time in Brazil, Paulo could count on the fingers of one hand the positive reviews he had received. Unable to offer readers an explanation as to why an author whom they considered mediocre was so successful, the media flailed around for answers. Some preferred to put it all down to publicity, but this left one question unanswered: if it was so simple, why didn't other authors and publishers adopt the same formula? When she was travelling in Brazil before the launch of *The Valkyries*, Mônica Antunes was sought out by the *Jornal do Brasil* and asked the same old question: to what do you attribute Paulo Coelho's success? She replied with the prophetic words: 'What we are witnessing is only the start of a fever.'

Another argument used to explain his success – the low cultural level of Brazilians, who are little used to reading – was soon to be demolished by the arrival of Paulo's books in the two most important publishing markets, America and France. This began in the United States at the end of 1990. Paulo was staying in Campinas, 100 kilometres from São Paulo, preparing for a debate on his book *Brida* with students at the Universidade Estadual de Campinas (Unicamp), when the telephone rang. On the other end of the line was Alan Clarke, a man in his fifties, owner of the Gentleman's Farmer, a five-room bed-and-breakfast hotel in the small town of West Barnstable, in Massachusetts. Speaking fluent Portuguese, Clarke explained that during his free time, he worked as a certified translator and had worked for some years in Brazil as an executive with ITT, which dominated the telecommunications industry in a large part of the world until the end of the 1980s. He had read and enjoyed *The Pilgrimage* and was offering to translate it into English.

Paulo knew that the American market could be a springboard to the rest of the world, but he was not excited by the idea and said: 'Thank you for your interest, but what I need is a publisher in the United States, not a translator.'

Clarke was not put off: 'All right, then, can I try and find a publisher for the book?'

Sure that the conversation would lead nowhere, Paulo agreed. Never having worked before on a literary project, Alan Clarke translated the 240 pages of *The Pilgrimage* and set off with his English translation under his arm. After hearing the word 'No' twenty-two times, he came across someone who was interested. All his efforts had been worth it, because the publisher was none other than HarperCollins, at the time the largest in the United States. It was not until 1992, when Paulo was launching *The Valkyries* in Brazil, that *The Pilgrimage*, under the title *The Diary of a Magician*, was published (the title was changed much later). Days and weeks went by and it immediately became clear that the book was never going to be a blockbuster. 'The book simply didn't happen,' the author recalls. 'It got no media coverage and was practically ignored by the critics.'

However, this lack of success did not dishearten his agent-cum-translator. Some months after its launch, Clarke took his translation of *The Alchemist* to HarperCollins, and the book won the hearts of all the professional readers invited to give their opinion as to whether or not to launch it on the American market. HarperCollins' enthusiasm for the book can be judged by the size of the initial print run: 50,000 hardback copies. HarperCollins' instincts were shown to be right: in a few weeks, the book was in the best-seller lists of important newspapers such as the *Los*

Angeles Times, the *San Francisco Chronicle* and the *Chicago Tribune*. The hardback version was so successful that the publisher didn't put the paperback version on the market until two years later.

The explosion of *The Alchemist* opened doors to markets of which the author had never even dreamed. Published in Australia immediately after its publication in the United States, *The Alchemist* was acclaimed by the *Sydney Morning Herald* as 'the book of the year'. The newspaper stated that it was 'an enchanting work of infinite philosophical beauty'. Australian readers seemed to agree, since weeks after arriving in the bookshops it was number one on the *Herald*'s own best-seller list. However, Paulo was dreaming of greater things. He knew that recognition as an author would come not from New York or Sydney but from the other side of the Atlantic. His dream was to be published, and above all read, in France, the land of Victor Hugo, Flaubert and Balzac.

At the beginning of 1993, during a short trip to Spain, Paulo was asked by the agent Carmen Balcells if she could represent him. The owner of the most respected literary agency in Europe, Balcells counted among her authors Mario Vargas Llosa and Gabriel García Márquez. Her request was a huge temptation, especially since, unlike most literary agents, among them Mônica Antunes, who received 15 per cent, the agency took only 10 per cent of its authors' royalties.

Paulo had been concerned for some time about his and Mônica's complete lack of experience in the foreign publishing world. Neither of them had the necessary contacts. He was worried that Mônica would waste her youth on trying to sell his work abroad, a venture that had so far lasted four years and brought no real results. 'It was my duty to tell her that she could never make a living working solely as my international agent,' the author recalled some time later. 'For her to be able to live well I would have to sell millions of books abroad, and that wasn't happening.' They needed to have a talk. After giving the matter serious thought, he invited her for a coffee in a small bar in Barcelona and came straight to the point. More than a dialogue, their conversation was a kind of tense verbal arm-wrestle.

'You know who Carmen Balcells is, don't you?'

'Yes.'

'Well, she sent me this letter proposing that her agency represent me. You're investing in someone you believe in, but let's be realistic: we're not getting anywhere. This business needs experience; it's a serious gamble.'

Mônica did not appear to understand what she was hearing, but Paulo went on: 'Let's accept that our work hasn't, as we hoped, borne fruit. There's nothing wrong with that. It's my life that's at stake, but I don't want you also to sacrifice yours in search of a dream that seems impossible.'

She could hardly believe what she was hearing.

'So, realistically speaking, what do you think about us terminating our professional relationship? If I want to go to Carmen Balcells now, I will. I'll pay you for all the years of work you've put in and I'll get on with my life. But the final decision is up to you. You've invested four years of your life in me, and I'm not going to be the one who gets rid of you. It's just that you have to understand that it would be best for both of us to call a halt. Do you agree?'

'No.'

'What do you mean "No"? I'm going to pay you for the time you've given me, for all your efforts. It's not as if I had a contract with you, Mônica.'

'No way. If you want to get rid of me, you can, but I'm not going to ask to leave.'

'You know who Carmen Balcells is, don't you? You're asking me to say "No" to her? She's going to announce that she is taking me on by filling the Frankfurt Book Fair with posters of my books, and you want me to say "No"?'

'No. I'm saying that you can sack me, if you want. You're free to do as you wish. After all, you made a separate deal with Alan Clarke in the States, didn't you? I think that I could do much better than him.'

Her utter conviction meant that Paulo could go no further. In a second, his dream of posters in Frankfurt and being in the same catalogue as García Márquez and Vargas Llosa had evaporated. He had swapped the elegant offices in central Barcelona occupied by Carmen Balcells and her dozens of employees for Sant Jordi Asociados, which was nothing more than a bookshelf with some cardboard files in the small apartment where Mônica lived.

In September, she plucked up her courage and prepared to face her first big challenge: to try to sell Paulo Coelho at the most important annual meeting of publishers and literary agents, the Frankfurt Book Fair.

At twenty-five, with no experience in the field and afraid of facing this challenge alone, she decided she needed the company of a friend, her namesake Mônica Moreira. The first surprise when she arrived in Frankfurt was the discovery that there wasn't a single hotel room to be found in the city. It hadn't occurred to them to make reservations in advance and so they ended up having to sleep in a youth hostel in a neighbouring town. For the four days that the fair lasted, Mônica worked like a Trojan. Unlike the posters and banners used by Balcells, her only weapon was a modest publicity kit – a brief biography and a summary of the success Paulo's books had enjoyed in Brazil and in other countries. She visited the stands of publishers from all over the world one by one, arranging as many meetings as possible. Her efforts were royally rewarded: by the end of the year, Mônica had sold the rights of Paulo Coelho's books in no fewer than sixteen languages.

The first contract she negotiated in Frankfurt, with the Norwegian publisher ExLibris, also had the virtue of changing her personal life: four years later, in 1997, the owner of ExLibris, Øyvind Hagen, and Mônica decided to marry. In a matter of months, she drew up contracts for the publication of *The Pilgrimage*, *The Alchemist*, or both, not only in Norway but also in Australia, Japan, Portugal, Mexico, Romania, Argentina, South Korea and Holland.

In the same year, 1993, Paulo entered the Brazilian version of *The Guinness Book of Records* after *The Alchemist* had been in *Veja*'s best-seller list for an impressive 208 consecutive weeks. However, there was still no sign from France. Mônica had sent the American version of *The Alchemist* to several French publishers, but none showed any interest in this unknown Brazilian. One of those who turned down Paulo Coelho's books was Robert Laffont, the owner of a traditional, reputable publishing house founded during the Second World War. The indifference with which *The Alchemist* was received was such that a reader's report – so important in deciding the fate of a book – was delegated to the only person in the company who spoke Portuguese, an administrative secretary, who was responsible for the book's rejection.

Destiny, however, seems to have decided that the literary future of Paulo Coelho in France would lie with the Laffont family anyway. At the beginning of 1993, Robert's daughter Anne had left her position as adviser in her father's company to set up her own publishing house, the tiny Éditions Anne Carrière. This was not a hobby to fill her time but a business in which she and her husband, Alain, had invested all their money and for which they still had to beg loans from banks, friends and relatives. The company was not yet three months old when Brigitte Gregony, Anne's cousin and best friend (and one of the investors who had put money into the new publishing house), telephoned from Barcelona, where she was on holiday, to say that she had read the Spanish translation 'of a fascinating book called *El Alquimista*, written by an unknown Brazilian'. Unable to read a word of Spanish or Portuguese, Anne simply relied upon her cousin's opinion (and a quick reading by her son, Stephen, who knew a little Spanish), and asked her to find out whether the publishing rights were held by anyone in France. When she found Mônica, Brigitte learned that *The Alchemist* was coming out in the United States in May and that the agent would send her a copy as soon as it was published.

Anne appeared prepared to put all her energies into the project. Although she offered a mere US$5,000 advance on royalties, to compensate she called upon a top translator, Jean Orecchioni, who had translated the entire works of Jorge Amado into French. Brigitte, who had been the fairy godmother of the publication, did not live long enough to see the success of *The Alchemist* in France: in July, before the book was ready, she died of a brain tumour. Many years later, Anne Carrière dedicated her memoirs to her, *Une chance infinie: l'histoire d'une amitié* (Éditions la Table Ronde), in which she talks about her relationship with Paulo Coelho and reveals the behind-the-scenes story of how he came to be the most successful Latin-American writer in France.

The wheels of the publishing business grind exceeding slow all over the world, and the launch of the book was pushed forward to March 1994, when Paulo was about to publish his fifth title in Brazil, *Na Margem do Rio*

Piedra eu Sentei e Chorei, or *By the River Piedra I Sat Down and Wept*. Anne was faced by a double problem: how to launch the book of an unknown author published by an equally unknown publishing house? How to make booksellers stop to look at one book among thousands? She decided to produce a special, numbered edition of *The Alchemist*, which would be sent to 500 French booksellers a month before its launch. On the fourth page of the book was a short statement written by her: 'Paulo Coelho is a Brazilian author famous throughout Latin America. *The Alchemist* tells the story of a young shepherd who leaves his homeland to follow a dream: the search for a treasure hidden at the foot of the pyramids. In the desert he will come to understand the language of signs and the meaning of life and, most important of all, he will learn to let his heart speak. He will fulfil his destiny.' On the book's spine was a sentence used by HarperCollins for the launch in the United States: '*The Alchemist* is a magical book. Reading this book is like getting up at dawn and seeing the sun rise while the rest of the world is still sleeping.'

While half the road to success was guaranteed by the booksellers' favourable reception, the other half would be determined by the critics, whose reaction could not have been better. The most important of the French newspapers and magazines, among them *Le Nouvel Observateur* (which, years later, became a harsh critic of the author), carried highly favourable reviews, as Anne Carrière describes in her memoirs:

> With what appears to be a simple tale, Paulo Coelho soothes the hearts of men and makes them reflect upon the world around them. A fascinating book that sows the seeds of good sense in the mind and opens up the heart.
>
> (Annette Colin Simard, *Le Journal du Dimanche*)

> Paulo Coelho is a testament to the virtue of clarity, which makes his writing like a cool stream flowing beneath cool trees, a path of energy along which he leads the reader, all unwitting, towards himself and his mysterious, distant soul.
>
> (Christian Charrière, *L'Express*)

It is a rare book, like an unexpected treasure that one should savour and share.

(Sylvie Genevoix, *L'Express*)

It is a book that does one good.

(Danièle Mazingarbe, *Madame Figaro*)

Written in a simple, very pure language, this story of a journey of initiation across the desert – where, at every step, one sign leads to another, where all the mysteries of the world meet in an emerald, where one finds 'the soul of the world', where there is a dialogue with the wind and the sun – literally envelops one.

(Annie Copperman, *Les Échos*)

The joy of his narrative overcomes our preconceptions. It is very rare, very precious, in the torrid, asphyxiating present day to breathe a little fresh air.

(*Le Nouvel Observateur*)

Now all that was needed was to wait and reap the harvest, and that was not long in coming. The cautious initial print run of 4,000 copies ran out in the bookshops in a matter of days and at the end of April, when 18,000 copies had been sold, *The Alchemist* appeared for the first time on a best-seller list in the weekly *Livres Hebdo*. Intended for the publishing world, this was not a publication for the public at large and the book was only given twentieth place, but, as Mônica had predicted, this was just the start. In May, *The Alchemist* was in ninth place in the most important best-seller list, that of the weekly magazine *L'Express*, where it remained for an incredible 300 consecutive weeks. The book was a success in several countries besides Brazil, but its acclaim in the United States and France would mean that the author would no longer be considered merely a Latin-American eccentricity and would become a worldwide phenomenon.

CHAPTER 27

World fame

WHILE THE WORLD WAS BOWING THE KNEE to Paulo Coelho, the Brazilian critics remained faithful to the maxim coined by the composer Tom Jobim, according to which 'in Brazil someone else's success is felt as a personal affront, a slap in the face', and they continued to belittle his books. The massive success of *The Alchemist* in France seems to have encouraged him to confront his critics. 'Before, my detractors could conclude, wrongly, that Brazilians were fools because they read me,' he declared to the journalist Napoleão Sabóia of *O Estado de* São *Paulo*. 'Now that my books are selling so well abroad, it's hard to universalize that accusation of stupidity.' Not so. For the critic Silviano Santiago, who had a PhD in literature from the Sorbonne, being a best-seller even in a country like France meant absolutely nothing. 'It's important to demystify his success in France,' he told *Veja*. 'The French public is as mediocre and as lacking in sophistication as the general public anywhere.' Some did not even go to the trouble of opening Paulo's books in order to condemn them. 'I've not read them and I don't like them,' was the judgement given by Davi Arrigucci, Jr, another respected critic and professor of literature at the University of São Paulo. However, none of this seemed to matter to Paulo's Brazilian readers, still less his foreign ones. On the contrary. Judging by the numbers, his army of readers and admirers

seemed to be growing in the same proportion as the virulence of his critics. The situation was to be repeated in 1994 when, as well as *By the River
Piedra I Sat Down and Wept*, he launched a 190-page book, *Maktub* – a
collection of the mini-chronicles, fables and reflections he had been
publishing in the *Folha de São Paulo* since 1993.

Just as *The Valkyries* had been inspired by the penance Paulo and
Chris had undertaken in 1988 in the Mojave Desert, in *By the River Piedra
I Sat Down and Wept* Paulo shares with his readers yet another spiritual
experience, the Road to Rome, which he undertook in the south of
France, partly in the company of Mônica Antunes. In the 236 pages of the
book he describes seven days in the life of Pilar, a twenty-nine-year-old
student who is struggling to complete her studies in Zaragoza in Spain
and who meets up again with a colleague with whom she'd had an adolescent affair. The meeting takes place after a conference organized by the
young man – who remains nameless in the book, as do all the other characters apart from the protagonist. Now a seminarian and a devotee of the
Immaculate Conception, he confesses his love for Pilar during a trip from
Madrid to Lourdes. The book, according to Paulo, is about the fear of
loving and of total surrender that pursues humanity as though it were a
form of original sin. On the way back to Zaragoza, Pilar sits down on the
bank of the river Piedra, a small river 100 kilometres south of the city, and
there she sheds her tears so that they may join other rivers and flow on
out into the ocean.

Centred more upon the rituals and symbols of Catholicism than on
the magical themes of his previous books, *By the River Piedra I Sat Down
and Wept* received unexpected praise from the clergy, such as the
Cardinal-Archbishop of São Paulo, Dom Paulo Evaristo Arns, but there
were no such surprises from the critics. As had been the case with all five
of his previous books, both *By the River Piedra* and *Maktub* were torn apart
by the Brazilian media. The critic Geraldo Galvão Ferraz, of the São Paulo
Jornal da Tarde, branded *By the River Piedra I Sat Down and Wept* as 'a
poorly mixed cocktail of mediocre mysticism, religion and fiction, full of
clichés and stereotypical characters who spend the greater part of their
time giving solemn speeches'. The author's approach to what he calls 'the
feminine side of God' was ridiculed by another journalist as 'a Paulo

Coelho for girls'. The magazine *Veja* handed the review of *Maktub* to Diogo Mainardi, who derided certain passages, comparing *Maktub* to a pair of dirty socks that he had left in his car:

> In truth all this nonsense would mean nothing if Paulo Coelho were merely a charlatan who earns a little money from other people's stupidity. I would never waste my time reviewing a mediocre author if he simply produced the occasional manual of esoteric clichés. However, things aren't quite like that. At the last Frankfurt Book Fair, the theme of which was Brazil, Paulo Coelho was marketed as a real writer, as a legitimate representative of Brazilian literature. That really is too much. However bad our writers might be, they're still better than Paulo Coelho. He can do what he likes, but he shouldn't present himself as a writer. When all's said and done, there's about as much literature in Paulo Coelho as there is in my dirty socks.

As on previous occasions, such reviews had no effect whatsoever on sales. While derided in the pages of newspapers and magazines, *By the River Piedra I Sat Down and Wept* sold 70,000 copies on the first day, more than *The Valkyries*. Some weeks after its launch, *Maktub* also appeared in the best-seller lists. The only difference was that this time, the victim of the attacks was thousands of kilometres from Rio, travelling through France with Anne Carrière in response to dozens of invitations for talks and debates with his growing number of French readers.

Despite the enormous success achieved by the author, Paulo's presence at the Frankfurt Book Fair in 1994, the first in which he had taken part, had made it clear that preconceptions about his work were not just the privilege of Brazilian critics but also of his fellow writers. Although the position of Minister of Culture was, at the time, held by an old friend of the author's, the diplomat Luiz Roberto do Nascimento e Silva, the brother of his ex-girlfriend Maria do Rosário, when it came to organizing a party of eighteen writers to represent Brazilian literature – Brazil was the guest of honour – Paulo was not included. According to Nascimento e Silva, writers were chosen who were popular with or familiar to German readers. Paulo's trip, therefore, was paid by Editora Rocco. In order to celebrate the contracts being signed around the world, his German publisher at the time, Peter Erd, owner of the publishing house of the same name, gave a cocktail party to which he invited all of Paulo's publishers present at the book fair and, naturally enough, all the members of the Brazilian delegation. The party was well attended, but not entirely a success because only two other Brazilian writers were present, and of the other delegation members, only Chico Buarque was polite enough to phone to give his excuses, since he would be giving a talk at the same time. A lone voice, that of Jorge Amado, who was not part of the delegation, spoke out loudly in Paulo's defence: 'The only thing that makes Brazilian intellectuals attack Paulo Coelho is his success.' In spite of this, in 1995, the fever that the British magazine *Publishing News* called 'Coelhomania' and the French media '*Coelhisme*' reached pandemic proportions. Sought out by the French director Claude Lelouch and then by the American Quentin Tarantino, both of whom were interested in adapting *The Alchemist* for the cinema, Paulo replied that the giant American Warner Brothers had got there first and bought the rights for US$300,000. Roman Polanski had told journalists that he hoped to be able to film *The Valkyries*. In May, when Anne Carrière was preparing for the launch of an edition of *The Alchemist* to be illustrated by Moebius, HQ, owners of Hachette and *Elle*, announced that the Elle Grand Prix for Literature that year had been awarded to Paulo Coelho. This caused such a stir that he earned the privilege of being featured in the 'Portrait' section of the magazine *Lire*, the bible of the French literary world.

But the crowning glory came in October. After thirty-seven weeks in second place, *The Alchemist* dethroned *Le Premier Homme*, an unfinished novel by Albert Camus, and went on to head the best-seller list in *L'Express*. Two famous critics compared *The Alchemist* to another national glory, *Le Petit Prince* by Antoine de Saint-Exupéry. 'I had the same feeling when I read both books,' wrote Frédéric Vitoux in his column in the magazine *Le Nouvel Observateur*. 'I was enchanted by the sensibility and the freshness, the innocence of soul.' His colleague Eric Deschot, of the weekly *Actuel*, shared his opinion: 'It is not a sacrilegious comparison, since the simplicity, transparency and purity of this fable remind me of the mystery of Saint-Exupéry's story.'

Paulo received news that he had leapt into first place in *L'Express* while he was in the Far East, where he had gone with Chris to take part in a series of launches and debates with readers. One afternoon, as the *shinkansen*, the Japanese bullet train taking them from Nagoia to Tokyo, was speeding past the snow-covered Mount Fuji, the writer made a decision: when he returned to Brazil, he would change publishers. The decision was not the result of some sign that only he had noticed: it came after a long period of reflection on his relationship with Rocco. Among other disagreements, Paulo was demanding a distribution system that would open up sales outlets other than bookshops, such as newspaper stands and supermarkets, so that his books could reach readers on lower incomes. Rocco had asked for a study by Fernando Chinaglia, an experienced newspaper and magazine distributor, but the plan went no further. On 15 February 1995, the columnist Zózimo Barroso do Amaral published a note in *O Globo* informing his readers that 'one of the most envied marriages in the literary world' was coming to an end.

The other newspapers picked up the scoop and some days later, the entire country knew that, for US$1 million, Paulo Coelho was moving from Rocco to Editora Objetiva, who would publish his next book, *O Monte Cinco*, or *The Fifth Mountain*. This vast sum – more than had ever been paid to any other Brazilian author – would not all go into his pocket, but would be divided up more or less as it had been with Rocco: 55 per cent as an advance on royalties and the remaining 45 per cent to be invested in publicity. This was a big gamble for Roberto Feith, a journalist, economist and ex-international correspondent with the television network Globo, who had taken control of Objetiva five years earlier. The US$550,000 advance represented 15 per cent of the publisher's entire turnover, which came mostly from sales of its three 'big names', Stephen King, Harold Bloom and Daniel Goleman. The experts brought in by the firm were unanimous in stating that if *The Fifth Mountain* were to repeat the success of *By the River Piedra I Sat Down and Wept*, Objetiva would get the US$1 million investment back within a matter of months. Apparently the change caused no resentment on the part of his ex-publisher, for although Paulo had moved to Objetiva, he left with Rocco his entire backlist, the profitable collection of seven books published there since 1989.

In fact, a month after announcing the move, Paulo Rocco was among the author's guests at Paulo's traditional celebration of St Joseph's feast day on 19 March.

Inspired by a passage from the Bible (1 Kings 18: 8–24), *The Fifth Mountain* tells of the suffering, doubts and spiritual discoveries of the prophet Elijah during his exile in Sarepta in Phoenicia, present-day Lebanon. The city, whose residents were well educated and famous for their commercial acumen, had not known war for 300 years, but it was about to be invaded by the Assyrians. The prophet encounters religious conflicts, and is forced to face the anger both of men and of God. In the prologue, Paulo once again reveals how he interweaves his personal experiences with the themes of his books. When he states that, with *The Fifth Mountain*, he had perhaps learned to understand and live with the inevitable, he recalls his dismissal from CBS seventeen years earlier, which had brought to an end a promising career as an executive in the recording industry:

> When I finished writing *The Fifth Mountain*, I recalled that episode – and other manifestations of the unavoidable in my life. Whenever I thought myself the absolute master of a situation, something would happen to cast me down. I asked myself: why? Can it be that I'm condemned to always come close but never to reach the finishing line? Can God be so cruel that He would let me see the palm trees on the horizon only to have me die of thirst in the desert? It took a long time to understand that it wasn't quite like that. There are things that are brought into our lives to lead us back to the true path of our Personal Legend. Other things arise so we can apply all that we have learned. And, finally, some things come along to *teach* us.

The book was ready to be delivered to Editora Objetiva when Paulo unearthed information on periods in Elijah's life that had not been dealt with in the Scriptures, or, more precisely, about the time he had spent in Phoenicia. This exciting discovery meant that he had to rewrite almost the entire book, which was finally published in August 1996 during the fourteenth São Paulo Book Biennial. The launch was preceded by a huge publicity campaign run by the São Paulo agency Salles/DMB&B, whose owner, the advertising executive Mauro Salles, was an old friend and informal guru on marketing matters, and the book's dedicatee. The campaign included full-page advertisements in the four principal national newspapers (*Jornal do Brasil, Folha de São Paulo, O Estado de São Paulo* and *O Globo*) and in the magazines *Veja-Rio, Veja-SP, Caras, Claudia* and *Contigo*, 350 posters on Rio and São Paulo buses, eighty hoardings in Rio, and displays, sales points and plastic banners in bookshops. Inspired by Anne Carrière's idea, which had worked so well in the French launch of *The Alchemist*, Paulo suggested and Feith ordered a special edition of numbered, autographed copies of *The Fifth Mountain* to be distributed to 400 bookshops across Brazil a week before the ordinary edition reached the public. In order to prevent any disclosure to the press, every recipient had to sign a confidentiality agreement.

The result was proportionate to the effort invested. The books were distributed on 8 August and in less than twenty-four hours 80,000 of the 100,000 copies of the first edition had been sold. Another 11,000 were sold in the week of the Book Biennial, where seemingly endless queues of readers awaited Paulo and where he signed copies for ten hours non-stop. *The Fifth Mountain* had barely been out for two months when sales rose to 120,000 copies, meaning that the publisher had already recouped the US$550,000 advance paid to the author. The remaining US$450,000 that had been spent would be recouped during the following months.

In the case of *The Fifth Mountain*, the critics appeared to be showing signs of softening. 'Let's leave it to the magi to judge whether Coelho is a sorcerer or a charlatan, that's not what matters,' wrote the *Folha de São Paulo*. 'The fact is that he can tell stories that are easily digested, with no literary athletics, and that delight readers in dozens of languages.' In its main competitor, *O Estado de São Paulo*, the critic and writer José Castello did not hold back either. 'The neat, concise style of *The Fifth Mountain* proves that his pen has grown sharper and more precise,' he said in his review in the cultural supplement. 'Whether or not you like his books, Paulo Coelho is still the victim of terrible prejudices – the same [...] which, if you transfer them to the religious field, have drowned the planet in blood.' A week before the launch, even the irascible *Veja* seemed to have bowed to the evidence and devoted a long and sympathetic article to him, entitled 'The Smile of the Magus', at the end of which it published an exclusive excerpt from *The Fifth Mountain*. However, in the middle of this torrent of praise, the magazine summarized the content of Coelho's work as 'ingenuous stories whose "message" usually has all the philosophical depth of a Karate Kid film'.

At the following launch, however, when *Manual do Guerreiro da Luz*, or *Manual of the Warrior of Light*, came out, the critics returned with renewed appetite. This was the first of Paulo's books to be published abroad before coming out in Brazil, and was the result of a suggestion from Elisabetta Sgarbi, of the Italian publisher Bompiani. Encouraged by the success of the author's books in Italy, she went to Mônica to see whether he might have any unpublished work for the *Assagi* collection, which Bompiani had just created. Coelho had for some time been thinking of collecting together various notes and reflections recorded over the years into one book, and this was perhaps the right moment. Some of these had already been published in the *Folha de São Paulo*, and this led him to stick to the same eleven-line limit imposed by the newspaper. Using metaphors, symbolism and religious and medieval references, Paulo reveals to readers his experiences during what he calls 'my process of spiritual growth'. In his view, the *Manual* was such a fusion between author and work that it became the 'key book' to understanding his universe. 'Not so much the world of magic, but above all the ideological world,' he says. '*Manual of the Warrior of Light* has the same importance for me as the *Red Book* had for Mao or the *Green Book* for Gaddafi.' The term 'Warrior of Light' – someone who is always actively trying to realize his dream, regardless of what obstacles are placed in his way – can be found in several of his books, including *The Alchemist*, *The Valkyries* and *By the River Piedra I Sat Down and Wept*. And should there remain any doubts as to its meaning, the home page of the author's then recently created website took on the task of responding to those doubts: 'This book brings together a series of texts written to remind us that in every one of us there is a Warrior of Light. Someone capable of listening to the silence of his heart, of accepting defeats without allowing himself to be weakened by them and of nourishing hope in the midst of dejection and fatigue.'

When it was launched in Brazil, the *Manual* was preceded by the success of the book in Italy, but this did not seem to impress the Brazilian critics – not even the *Folha de São Paulo*, which had originally published several of the mini-articles reproduced in the book. In a short, two-column review, the young journalist Fernando Barros e Silva, one of the newspaper's editors, referred to the launch as 'the most recent mystical spasm from our greatest publishing phenomenon' and dismissed the author in the first lines of his article:

> Paulo Coelho is not a writer, not even a lousy writer. There's no point in calling what he does 'subliterature'. That would be praise indeed. His model is more Edir Macedo [the 'bishop' of the Universal Church of the Kingdom of God] than Sidney Sheldon. [...] Having said that, let us turn to the book itself. There is nothing new. The secret, as ever, lies in lining up platitudes so that the reader can read what best suits him. As with the I Ching, this is about 'illuminating' routes, 'suggesting' truths by using vague metaphors, sentences that are so cloudy and surrounded by metaphysical smoke that they are capable of saying everything precisely because they say absolutely nothing. [...] Every cliché fits into this successful formula: an ecological and idyllic description of nature, allusions to interminable conflicts between good and evil, touches of Christian guilt and redemption – all stitched together in a flat, unpolished language that seems to be the work of an eight-year-old child and is aimed at people of the same mental age. Each time you read Paulo Coelho, even with care and attention, you become more stupid and worse than you were before.

Such reviews only proved to the author the tiresome and repetitive abyss that separated the views of the critics from the behaviour of his readers. As had been the case since his very first book – and as would be the case with the rest – despite being ridiculed in newspapers such as the *Folha de São Paulo*, the *Manual* appeared a few days later in all the best-seller lists. Paulo went on to achieve something that probably no other author ever had: being number one in best-seller lists of both non-fiction (in this case in *O Globo*) and fiction (in the *Jornal do Brasil*). Things were no different in the rest of the world: the *Manual* was translated into twenty-nine languages, and in Italy it sold more than a million copies, becoming, after *The Alchemist* and *Eleven Minutes*, the most successful of the author's books there – and a decade after its launch by Bompiani it still had an average sale of 100,000 copies a year. Its popularity in Italy became such that at the end of 1997, the designer Donatella Versace announced that her collection for 1998 had taken its inspiration from Coelho's book. In France, *The Alchemist* had sold two million copies and *By the River Piedra I Sat Down and Wept* 240,000, which led Anne Carrière to buy the publishing rights to *The Fifth Mountain* for US$150,000. Some months before, the author had been overwhelmed to receive from the French government the title of Chevalier de l'Ordre des Arts et des Lettres. 'You are an alchemist for millions of readers who say that you write books that do good,' the French Minister of Culture, Philippe Douste-Blazy, said as he presented him with the medal. 'Your books do good because they stimulate our power to dream, our desire to seek and to believe in that search.'

Some Brazilians, however, continued to turn their noses up at their compatriot, for whom the red carpet was rolled out wherever he walked. This attitude was made even more explicit at the beginning of 1998, when it was announced that Brazil was to be guest of honour at the 18th Salon du Livre de Paris to be held between 19 and 25 March that year. The Brazilian Minister of Culture, Francisco Weffort, had given the president of the National Library, the academic Eduardo Portela, the task of organizing the group of writers who would take part in the event as guests of the Brazilian government. Following several weeks of discussion, only ten days before the event the press received the list of the fifty authors who were to spend a week in Paris. Exactly as had happened four years earlier in Frankfurt, Paulo Coelho's name was not among those invited. It was a pointless insult by a government that the author had supported. Invited, instead, by his publisher, he spent the afternoon of the opening day signing copies of the French translation of *The Fifth Mountain*, which had an initial run of 250,000 copies (hardly too many for someone who had already sold five million books in France).

In fact, the author had arrived in Paris a week before the Brazilian delegation and been faced with a plethora of interviews with newspapers, magazines and no fewer than six different French television programmes. Finally, on 19 March, to the sound of a noisy Brazilian percussion group, President Jacques Chirac and the Brazilian First Lady, who was representing her husband, President Fernando Henrique Cardoso, officially declared the salon open and, surrounded by a crowd of journalists and security guards, walked along some of the aisles down the centre of the Paris Expo convention centre where the event was being held. At one point, to the dismay of the Brazilian contingent, President Chirac made a point of going over to the Éditions Anne Carrière stand, shook hands with the publisher and, with an enormous smile on his face, warmly embraced Paulo Coelho. He heaped praise on, as it was later discovered, the only Brazilian author he had read and on whom, two years later, he would bestow the Légion d'Honneur – an honour previously given to such international celebrities as Winston Churchill, Dwight D. Eisenhower and even some famous Brazilians, such as Santos Dumont, Pelé and Oscar Niemeyer. Before moving on, Chirac then turned to Anne Carrière, saying: 'You must have made a lot of money with Monsieur Coelho's books. Congratulations!'

The following day, the Salon du Livre de Paris opened to the public and was witness to another world record: an author signing autographs for seven hours non-stop apart from short trips to the toilet or to smoke a cigarette. However, the best was yet to come for Anne Carrière. Some days before the close of the event, she took over the Carrousel du Louvre, an elegant, exclusive gallery beneath the famous Paris museum where shows were held by the famous European fashion houses. There Paulo hosted a banquet to which he invited booksellers, publishers, journalists and famous intellectuals. Throwing down the gauntlet to those who had snubbed him, the host made sure that every member of the Brazilian delegation received a personal invitation to the dinner. One of these was the journalist and writer Zuenir Ventura, who had just published a book entitled, appropriately enough, *Inveja* [*Envy*]. He recalled Paulo's concern that the Brazilians were being well looked after: 'He didn't eat, he went round to every table. Although at the time, he had everyone who mattered in the literary world at his feet, Paulo was exactly the same person as ever. When he came to my table, instead of talking about himself, he

wanted to know how my book *Inveja* was going, whether I had any translation offers, whether he could help ...'

When it came to the time for toasts, the author asked the band to stop
playing for a while so that he could speak. Visibly moved and speaking in
good French, he thanked everyone for being there, heaped praise on his
Brazilian colleagues and dedicated the evening to one absentee: 'I should
like this night of celebration to be a homage from all of us to the greatest and best of all Brazilian writers, my dear friend Jorge Amado, to whom
I ask you all to raise your glasses.'

Then, to the sound of Brazilian music, the 600 guests turned the
hallowed marble rooms of the Carrousel into a dance floor and danced
the samba into the early hours. On their return to the hotel, Paulo had yet
another surprise: a special edition of *The Fifth Mountain*, produced for the
occasion. Each book in its own velvet case contained the same sentence,
written in French and signed by the author: 'Perseverance and spontaneity are the paradoxical conditions of the personal legend.' When Paulo
boarded the plane back to Brazil, three weeks after landing in Paris,
200,000 copies of *The Fifth Mountain* had been bought by the French
public.

Now firmly and comfortably established as one of the most widely
sold authors in the world, Paulo Coelho became an object of interest in
the academic world. One of the first essayists to turn his attention to his
work was Professor Mario Maestri of the University of Passo Fundo, in
Rio Grande do Sul, the author of a study in 1993 in which he had recognized that Coelho's books 'belong by right to the national literary-fictional
corpus'. Six years later, however, when he published his book *Why Paulo
Coelho is Successful*, Maestri seems to have been infected by the ill will of
literary critics:

Replete with proverbs, aphorisms and simplistic stories, full of
commonplaces and clichés, Paulo Coelho's early fiction nevertheless
has an important role in self-help. It allows readers demoralized by a
wretched day-to-day existence to dream of achieving happiness
swiftly and as if by magic. The worn-out modern esoteric suggests to
his readers easy ways – within the reach of all – of taking positive

action in their own lives and in the world, usually in order to gain material and personal advantage. It is essentially a magical route to the virtual universe of a consumer society.

The many MA and PhD theses being written throughout the country confirmed that, apart from a few exceptions, Brazilian universities were as hostile towards the writer as the Brazilian media. This feeling became public in a report published in the *Jornal do Brasil* in 1998, in which the newspaper described the experience of Otacília Rodrigues de Freitas, literature professor at the University of São Paulo, who had faced fierce criticism when she defended a doctoral thesis entitled 'A best-seller from the reader's point of view: *The Alchemist* by Paulo Coelho' – a thesis considered by her colleagues to be sympathetic towards the author. The professor told the *Jornal do Brasil* indignantly: 'They said that Paulo Coelho had paid me to write the thesis, that I was his mistress.'

Indifferent to what academics might think of his work, Paulo was preparing once again to face the whirlwind of activity that now accompanied the launch of each new book. Set in Slovenia, the story of *Veronika Decide Morrer*, or *Veronika Decides to Die*, has as its backdrop the romance between Eduard, the son of a diplomat, and the eponymous heroine who, after attempting suicide, is placed in a mental asylum by her parents and subjected to brutal electroshock treatment. The explosive nature of the book lay in Paulo's revelation that he had been admitted to the Dr Eiras clinic in Rio during the 1960s on three separate occasions, something he had never spoken about in public before. By doing so, he was breaking an oath he had made that he would deal with the subject in public only after the death of his parents. His mother had died five years earlier, in 1993, of complications arising from Alzheimer's disease, and he had been unable to be at her funeral because he received the news while he was in Canada, working on the launch of *The Alchemist*, and was unable to get back to Brazil in time. Although his energetic father, Pedro, was not only alive but, as he appears in the book, 'in full enjoyment of his mental faculties and his health', *Veronika Decides to Die* exposes in no uncertain terms the violence to which the author was subjected by his father and his late mother. 'Veronika is Paulo Coelho', the author declared to whoever wanted to listen.

Concerned as always that his books should reach poorer readers, this time he decided to change his launch tactics. He told Objetiva to cut by half the US$450,000 spent on advertising *The Fifth Mountain*, thus allowing a reduction of almost 25 per cent on the cover price. Another move intended to make his work more accessible was a contract with the supermarket chain Carrefour, which included *Veronika* in its promotional package of presents for Father's Day. The book's publication coincided with an intense debate in Brazil about the treatment of people being held in public and private mental asylums. The Senate was discussing a bill drawn up to bring about the gradual eradication of institutions where patients with mental problems were held as virtual prisoners, and during that debate, passages of *Veronika* were read out. On the day on which the vote was to be held and the law ratified, Senator Eduardo Suplicy quoted from a letter he had received from Paulo Coelho in praise of the bill: 'Having been a victim in the past of the violence of these baseless admissions to mental hospitals – I was committed to the Casa de Saúde Dr Eiras in 1965, '66 and '67 – I see this new law not only as opportune, but as absolutely necessary.' Together with the letter the author sent a copy of the records of his admissions to the clinic. Two years later, Paulo was invited to join the team of the International Russell Tribunal on Psychiatry, an institution created by the European Parliament, and in 2003, he was one of the speakers at a seminar on the Protection and Promotion of the Rights of Persons with Mental Health Problems organized by the European Committee on Human Rights.

Veronika broke all Paulo's previous records. What was new was the respectful treatment accorded to the book by the media. Perhaps moved by the shocking revelations contained in the book, the newspapers and magazines devoted pages and pages to accounts of the horror of his three internments.

One of the few dissenting voices was that of a friend of his, the writer and journalist Marcelo Rubem Paiva. Asked by the *Folha de São Paulo* to review *Veronika*, he did so tongue in cheek and even suggested stylistic changes to the text, only to pull himself up short: 'What am I saying? Here I am giving tips to a writer who has sold millions and won commendations and prizes abroad!'

Exactly. To judge by all those sales, prizes and commendations, it would seem that his readers preferred his texts as they were. Immediately following the publication of *Veronika* in Brazil, the journalist and professor Denis de Moraes published an essay entitled *The Big Four*. These were Stephen King, Michael Crichton, John Grisham and Tom Clancy. Moraes used a list of Paulo's achievements and engagements in 1998 to show that the Brazilian already had a foot in that select group of world best-sellers:

He spoke about spirituality at the Economic Forum in Davos, in Switzerland.

He was granted an audience at the Vatican and blessed by Pope John Paul II.

He beat the world record for a book signing at the eighteenth Salon du Livre de Paris with *The Fifth Mountain*, which has sold almost 300,000 copies in France.

He recorded a statement for the documentary *The Phenomenon*, based on his life, for a Canadian/French/American co-production.

His book *Manual of the Warrior of Light* inspired the 1998/1999 Versace collection.

He spent a week in Britain publicizing *The Fifth Mountain*.

On his return to Rio de Janeiro in May, he gave interviews to the Canadian TV5 and to the English newspapers the *Sunday Times* and the *Guardian*.

Between August and October, he undertook engagements in New Zealand, Australia, Japan, Israel and Yugoslavia.

He returned to Rio for interviews with French and German television, before setting off for a series of launches in Eastern Europe (Poland, the Czech Republic, Slovakia, Slovenia and Bulgaria).

Before returning to Brazil for the end-of-year festivities he went to Finland and Russia.

Hollywood wants to adapt four of his books for the cinema.

The French actress Isabelle Adjani is fighting Julia Roberts for the film rights to *By the River Piedra I Sat Down and Wept*.

The Arenas Group, with links to Sony Entertainment, wants to bring

The Valkyries to the screen, while Virgin is interested in *The Pilgrimage*.

Awarded the Ordem do Rio Branco by President Fernando Henrique Cardoso.

Named special UN envoy for the Spiritual Convergence and Intercultural Dialogue programme.

All this feverish travelling was only interrupted in 2000, when he finished his new book, *O Demónio e a Srta. Prym*, or *The Devil and Miss Prym*. The launch this time was rather different. Firstly, the author decided to stay at home (the book was launched simultaneously in Brazil and other countries), preferring to receive foreign journalists in his new apartment in Copacabana. This was an apartment occupying an entire floor, which he had transformed into a vast bedroom-cum-sitting room, for which he had paid about US$350,000 and from where he enjoyed a wonderful view of Brazil's most famous beach. The idea of asking journalists to come to him had arisen some weeks earlier, when the North American television network CNN International recorded a long interview with him that was shown in 230 countries.

During the weeks that followed, at the invitation of his agent, teams from all the major newspapers and television stations began to arrive in Rio from Germany, Argentina, Bolivia, Chile, Colombia, Ecuador, Spain, France, Greece, England, Italy, Mexico, Portugal and the Czech Republic. Many used the trip to Brazil to file reports on Rio de Janeiro as well, and Mônica commented: 'That amount of publicity would have cost the Prefecture of Rio a fortune.' The other unusual thing about the launch in Brazil was the choice of venue. Coelho preferred to hold it in the Brazilian Academy of Letters. You didn't have to be very sharp to guess what this choice meant: Paulo Coelho, who had been so mistreated by Brazilian critics, clearly had his eye on a seat in the Olympus of Brazilian literature.

CHAPTER 28

Becoming an 'immortal'

THE DEVIL AND MISS PRYM was not the book Coelho had wanted to publish at the turn of the millennium. He had written a novel about sex, which had been carefully checked by Mônica and a friend of the author, the theologian and ex-impresario Chico Castro Silva, but it did not survive Chris's reading of it, and, as with his book on satanism, she refused to give it her approval.

This was not the first time he had been down this route. At the end of the 1980s, a little after publishing *The Alchemist* in Brazil, he had tried to write a book in which he treated sex with a starkness rarely found in literature. Between January and March 1989, he produced a 100-page novel telling the story of a man who is identified simply as 'D.', with the book being given the provisional title *A Magia do Sexo, A Glória de Deus* [*The Magic of Sex, The Glory of God*] or, simply, *Conversas com D.* [*Conversations with D.*].

Tormented by doubts about his sexuality, the main character is only able to find sexual satisfaction with his wife, but has terrible dreams in which he sees his mother naked and being abused by several men who, having raped her, urinate over her. What troubles the forty-year-old D. is not just the nightmare in itself but also the fact that witnessing this violence gives him pleasure. Lost in the midst of these terrible fantasies,

D. starts to tell his problems to a friend, who becomes the narrator of the plot. The two meet every evening for a beer. As he describes his innermost secrets and insecurities, D. ends up confessing that, although he is not homosexual, he experiences enormous pleasure when dreaming that he is being raped by men ('I like the humiliation of being on all fours, submissive, giving pleasure to the other man'). Coelho never finished *Conversas com D.*, and it ends without one knowing what fate the author will choose for the central character – whose story bears a certain resemblance to his own. The book ended up in the trunk full of diaries that Coelho had said should be burned after his death.

The Devil and Miss Prym arose from a visit Coelho made to the French town of Viscos, on the Spanish frontier. In the main square, he saw a strange sculpture in which the water flowed out of a sun and into the mouth of a toad, and, however much he quizzed the inhabitants, no one could explain to him the significance of this odd creation. The image remained in his head for months, until he decided to use it as a representation of Good and Evil. With *The Devil and Miss Prym*, Coelho was completing a trilogy that he called 'And on the Seventh Day', which began with *By the River Piedra I Sat Down and Wept* (1994) and was followed by *Veronika* (1998). According to him, 'they are three books that describe a week in the life of normal people who suddenly find themselves confronted by love, death and power'.

The story takes place in a small imaginary village of 281 inhabitants, all of whom are believed to be extremely honest. The village routine is interrupted by the arrival of Carlos, a foreigner who is at once identified by the widow Berta, the eldest of the inhabitants, as someone bringing evil to their peaceful town, i.e. the Devil. The stranger stays in a hotel where the only single woman in town, Chantal Prym, works in the snack bar. Miss Prym is an orphan and rather frowned on by the other inhabitants, and she is chosen by the visitor as an instrument to test their honesty. Presenting himself as a businessman who has lost his wife and two daughters to a dreadful crime, the mysterious Carlos offers the young woman the chance to become rich and leave the tedious life of the town. In exchange, she must help him to convince the local inhabitants to take part in a macabre competition: if, within a week, someone can commit the motiveless murder of at least one local inhabitant, the town will receive ten bars of gold which he has hidden in a secret place. The book deals with the conflicts generated by this extraordinary offer and concludes by identifying the possible simultaneous existence within every human soul of a personal angel and a personal devil.

In March 2000, after delivering *The Devil and Miss Prym* to Editora Objetiva, Paulo took a plane to Paris in time to see the start of the huge publicity campaign organized by Anne Carrière for the launch of *Veronika Decides to Die*. On a cold, grey Monday morning, along with the millions of Parisians and tourists who daily cross the city, he was shown a number 87 bus bearing a gigantic close-up of his face printed against a blue back-drop, announcing that *Veronika* was in all the bookshops. The number 87 buses departed from Porte de Reuilly, to the east of the capital, and trav-elled some 30 kilometres through the streets until reaching their final stop in Champs de Mars, having passed through some of the busiest areas of Paris, such as Gare de Lyon, the Bastille and St Germain-des-Près. The same scene was being repeated in fourteen other French cities. This time, however, the publicity campaign did not produce the hoped-for results. The reaction of French readers was lukewarm, perhaps because they found it odd to see a book being advertised like soap or toothpaste. Although it sold more than the previous books, the sales of *Veronika* in France were below expectations. Even so, the book was warmly received by the French press, including *L'Express* and the serious and conservative *Figaro*, one of the most influential newspapers in the country. At the same time, although without the same fanfare, *Veronika* was beginning to arrive in bookshops in Taiwan, Japan, China, Indonesia, Thailand and the United States.

The globalization of his literary success was finally introducing the author to another circle – the international jet set. As he had been doing since 1998, Coelho had taken part in the World Economic Forum some weeks earlier. The forum is an organization created in 1971 by the profes-sor and economist Klaus Schwab and every year it brings together in Davos the elite of world politics and economics (at Schwab's invitation, the author has been a member of the Schwab Foundation since 2000). The most important guest at the 2000 meeting, the American President

Bill Clinton, had been photographed some months earlier clutching a copy of *The Alchemist* as he stepped out of a helicopter in the gardens of the White House. On hearing that Paulo was in Davos as well, Clinton took the opportunity to meet him. 'It was my daughter Chelsea who gave me the book – in fact she ordered me to read it,' the President joked. 'I liked it so much that I gave it to Hillary to read as well,' he went on, ending the meeting with an invitation that would not in fact be followed up: 'Let me know if you're visiting the United States. If I'm home, my family and I would love to have you over for dinner.' Seven years later, in 2007, at the request of Hillary Clinton's team, Paulo produced a text in support of her candidature for nomination for the presidency of the United States.

The meeting in Davos in 2000 and in subsequent years meant that he could personally meet some of his most famous readers – such as the former Israeli prime minister and winner of the Nobel Peace Prize, Shimon Peres, the American actress Sharon Stone and the Italian author Umberto Eco – and could mingle with such world-famous names as Bill Gates and political leaders such as the Palestinian Yasser Arafat and the German Gerhard Schroeder. Interviewed during one of the 'literary teas' held during the forum, Umberto Eco revealed that he had read Paulo's works, saying: 'My favourite book by Paulo Coelho is *Veronika*. It touched me deeply. I confess that I don't like *The Alchemist* very much, because we have different philosophical points of view. Paulo writes for believers, I write for those who don't believe.'

In the second half of 2000, the 'fever' predicted by Mônica Antunes ten years earlier had spread through all the social, economic and cultural classes regardless of race, sex or age, far less ideology. Some months before, the author had been appalled to read in the English newspaper the *Guardian* that *The Alchemist* and *The Fifth Mountain* were the favourite bedside reading of the Chilean ex-dictator Augusto Pinochet, who was at the time being held in England at the request of the Spanish courts, accused of 'torture, terrorism and genocide'. He declared to the press: 'I wonder if General Pinochet would continue to read my books if he knew that their author was imprisoned three times during the Brazilian military regime and had many friends who were detained in or expelled from Chile during the Chilean military regime.' Some time later, when interviewed by the Caracas newspaper *El Universal*, the Venezuelan Miguel Sanabria, the ideological leader of an organization that supported President Hugo Chávez, revealed the bibliography used in his political degree course: Karl Marx, Simón Bolivar, José Carlos Mariátegui and Paulo Coelho. Books by Coelho appeared in the strangest hands and on the oddest bookshelves, such as those of the Tajik ex-major Victor Bout, who was captured at the beginning of 2008 in Thailand by American agents. In a rare interview, the retired KGB official, who was considered the biggest arms dealer in the world (and who inspired the film *Lord of War*, starring Nicolas Cage), candidly stated to *New York Times* reporter Peter Landesman that, when not selling anti-aircraft missiles, he would relax by reading Paulo Coelho. In the war launched by the United States against the Al Qaeda network, Coelho's books were read on both sides. According to the British *Sunday Times*, *The Alchemist* was the most borrowed book in the barracks library of the American soldiers of the 10th Mountain Division, who were hunting for Osama Bin Laden in the Afghan caves. And on visiting Number 4 concentration camp in Guantanamo Bay, where those suspected of having links with Bin Laden were imprisoned, the reporter Patrícia Campos Mello, of *O Estado de São Paulo*, discovered versions in Farsi of *The Pilgrimage* among the books offered to the prisoners by their American gaolers.

Coelho himself was surprised when he saw the film *Guantanamera*, directed by the Cuban Tomás Gutiérrez Alea, to see that, on the protagonist's long trip across the island in order to bury a relative, he was carrying a copy of *The Alchemist*. Since his books are not published in Cuba, he did some research and discovered that it was a Spanish copy, sold on the black market for an incredible US$40. 'I had no qualms about contacting the Cubans and giving up my rights as author, without getting a cent,' he later told newspapers, 'just so that the books could be published there at lower prices and more people could have access to them.' In an incident that shows that rudeness has no ideological colour, in 2007, Paulo was the victim of a gratuitous insult from the Cuban Minister of Culture, Abel Prieto, who was responsible for the organization of the Havana Book Fair. 'We have a problem with Paulo Coelho,' Prieto declared to a group of foreign journalists. 'Although he is a friend of Cuba and speaks out against the blockade, I could not invite him because that would lower the tone of the fair.' Not a man to take insults lying down, the author paid him back on his Internet blog with a six-paragraph article that was immediately reproduced in the daily *El Nuevo Herald*, the most important Spanish-language newspaper published in Miami, the heart of anti-Castroism. 'I am not at all surprised by this statement,' he wrote. 'Once bitten by the bug of power, those who have fought for liberty and justice become oppressors.'

His international prominence did not distance him from his country of origin. The choice of the Brazilian Academy of Letters for the launch of *The Devil and Miss Prym* in October 2000 was seen as a step towards his entry into the Brazilian Academy. This was not the first such step. When Anne Carrière had organized that dinner at the Carrousel du Louvre in 1998, all the members of the Brazilian delegation in Paris had been invited, but only three writers received personal telephone calls from Paulo reiterating the invitation – Nélida Piñon, Eduardo Portela and the senator and ex-president of the Republic José Sarney. Needless to say, all three were members of the Academy.

For the launch of *The Devil and Miss Prym* 4,000 invitations were sent out. The size of the crowd meant that the organizers of the event had to increase the security and support services. At the insistence of the author, one thousand plastic glasses of iced mineral water were distributed among those present, and he regretted that he could not do as he had in France, and serve French champagne.

To everyone's surprise, the Brazilian critics reacted well to *The Devil and Miss Prym*. 'At the age of fifty-three, Paulo Coelho has produced his most accomplished work yet, with a story that arouses the reader's curiosity and creates genuine tension,' wrote the reviewer in the magazine *Época*. One of the exceptions was the astrologist Bia Abramo, in the *Folha de São Paulo*, who was asked by the newspaper to write a review. 'Like his other books, *The Devil and Miss Prym* seems to be a well-worn parable,' she wrote, 'that could have been told in three paragraphs, like the various little anecdotes that tend to fill his narratives.'

Any careful observer of the author at this time would have realized that his energies were focused not on the critics but on being given a chair in the Brazilian Academy. Paulo had no illusions and he knew, from someone else who had been rejected as a candidate, that 'it's easier to be elected as a state governor than to enter the Academy'. It was well known that some of the thirty-nine academicians despised him and his work. 'I tried to read one of his books and couldn't get beyond page eight,' the author Rachel de Queiroz, a distant cousin, told newspapers, to which the author replied that none of his books even started on page eight. The respected Christian thinker Cândido Mendes, rector and owner of the Universidade Cândido Mendes (where Paulo had almost obtained a degree in law), gave an even harsher evaluation:

> I have read all his books from cover to cover, from back to front, which comes to the same thing. Paulo Coelho has already had more glory heaped on him in France than Santos Dumont. But he's not really from here: he's from the global world of facile thinking and of ignorance transformed into a kind of sub-magic. Our very pleasant little sorcerer serves this domesticated, toothless imagination. This subculture disguised as wealth has found its perfect author. It isn't a text but a product from a convenience store.

Convinced that these views were not shared by the majority of the other thirty-seven electors in the Academy, Paulo did not respond to these provocative comments and went ahead with his plan. He courted the leaders of the several groups and subgroups into which the house was divided, lunched and dined with academics, and never missed the launch of a book by one of the 'immortals', as the members of the Academy are known. At the launch of his novel *Saraminda*, José Sarney, who was also a favourite target of the critics, posed smiling for the photographers as he signed Paulo's copy, Paulo being the most sought-after by the hundreds of readers queuing to receive a dedication. The fact is that his objective had soon become an open secret. At the end of the year, the celebrated novelist Carlos Heitor Cony, who held seat 3 at the Academy, wrote in the *Folha do Sul*:

I wrote an article about the contempt with which the critics treat the singer Roberto Carlos and the writer Paulo Coelho. I think it's a miracle that the two have survived, because if they had been dependent on the media, they would be living under a bridge, begging and cursing the world. That isn't quite how it is. Each one has a faithful public, they take no notice of the critics, they simply get on with life, they don't retaliate and, when they can, they help others. I am a personal friend of Paulo Coelho, and he knows he can count on my vote at the Academy. I admire his character, his nobility in not attacking anyone and in making the most of the success he has achieved with dignity.

From the moment the idea of competing for a chair at the Academy entered his head, Coelho had nurtured a secret dream: to occupy chair number 23, whose first occupant had been Machado de Assis, the greatest of all Brazilian writers and founder of the Academy. The problem was that the occupant of this chair was the academic whom Paulo most loved, admired and praised, Jorge Amado. This meant that every time the matter came up he had to be careful what he said: 'Since the chair I want belongs to Jorge, I only hope to put myself forward when I am really old,' he would say, 'because I want him to live for many many more years.'

Already eighty-eight, Jorge Amado had suffered a heart attack in 1993 and, in the years that followed, he was admitted to hospital several times. In June 2001, he was taken into a hospital in Salvador with infections in the kidneys and right lung, but recovered sufficiently to be able to celebrate at home with his family the fortieth anniversary of his election to the Academy. However, only three weeks later, on the afternoon of 6 August, the family let it be known that Jorge Amado had just died. Chair number 23 was vacant. The news reached Coelho that night via a short phone call from the journalist and academic Murilo Melo Filho: 'Jorge Amado has died. Your time has come.'

Paulo was filled by strange and contradictory feelings: as well as feeling excited at the thought of standing as a candidate for the Academy, he was genuinely saddened by the death of someone who had been not only one of his idols but also both a friend and faithful ally. However, this was no time for sentimentality. Paulo realized that the race for a chair in the

Academy began even before the lilies had withered on the coffin of the deceased incumbent. His first campaign phone call met with disappointment, though. When he called the professor and journalist Arnaldo Niskier, who occupied chair number 18 and was one of the first to have learned, months earlier, of Paulo's intentions, Niskier poured cold water on the idea. 'I don't think it's the right moment,' Niskier told him. 'It looks as if Zélia is going to put herself forward, and if that happens the Academy is sure to vote in her favour.' Zélia was the writer Zélia Gattai, Jorge Amado's widow, who had decided to compete for her late husband's chair.

Alongside the many obituaries, the following morning, the newspapers announced the names of no fewer than five candidates: Zélia, Paulo, the astronomer Ronaldo Rogério de Freitas Mourão, the humourist Jô Soares and the journalist Joel Silveira. When taking his daily walk along the promenade above Copacabana beach, Coelho heard one of the few voices capable of convincing him to do – or not do – something: that of Chris. With her customary gentleness, she said that she had a bad feeling about the competition: 'Paulo, I don't think you're going to win.'

This was enough for him to give up the idea. His candidature, which had not even been formally registered, had lasted less than twelve hours. Paulo sent a fax to Zélia expressing his sorrow at her husband's death, packed his bags and left with Chris for the south of France. The couple were going to fulfil their old dream of spending part of the year in Europe, and the place they had chosen was a region near Lourdes. One of the reasons for the trip was to look for a house to buy. While they were still hunting, their address in France was the modest but welcoming Henri IV hotel in the small city of Tarbes.

On Tuesday, 9 October, the two were in Odos, a small village 5 kilometres from Saint-Martin, where some months later they would choose to settle. As though tempted by the Devil whom he had long ago driven away, Coelho had decided to add to his property portfolio something more suited to a rock star than to a man of almost monastic habits (a millionaire monk, that is): a castle. The castle the couple had their eye on was Château d'Odos, where Marguerite de Valois, or Margot, the wife of Henri IV, had lived and died. However, the whole affair came to nothing – 'If I bought a castle,' he said to a journalist, 'I wouldn't possess it, it would possess me.' That afternoon, he left Chris in the hotel in Tarbes and took a train to Pau, where he boarded a flight to Monte Carlo, where he was to be a member of the film festival jury. In the evening, he was having a coffee with the director Sydney Pollack, when his mobile rang.

On the other end he heard the voice of Arnaldo Niskier: 'Roberto Campos has just died. May I give the secretary of the Academy the signed letter you left with me putting your name forward for the first position available?'

'If you think it's the right time, yes.'

On his return to France a few days later, he stopped off at the chapel of Notre Dame de Piétat, in the small town of Barbazan-Débat, and made a silent prayer: 'Help me get into the Brazilian Academy of Letters.'

A few hours later, in his hotel room in Tarbes, he gave a long interview over the telephone to the reporter Marcelo Camacho, of the *Jornal do Brasil*, an interview that began with the obvious question: 'Is it true that you're a candidate for the Brazilian Academy of Letters?'

He replied without hesitation: 'Absolutely.'

And the next day's *Jornal do Brasil* devoted the front page of its arts section to the scoop. In the interview, Coelho explained the reasons for his candidature ('a desire to be a colleague of such special people'); dismissed his critics ('if what I wrote wasn't any good my readers would have abandoned me a long time ago, all over the world'); and vehemently condemned George W. Bush's foreign policy ('What the United States is doing in Afghanistan is an act of terror, that's the only word for it, an act of terror'). The campaign for the vacant chair was official, but Coelho told the journalist that, because of a very full international programme, he would not be back in Brazil for another two months, in December, when he would carry out the ritual of visits to each of the thirty-nine electors. This delay was irrelevant, because the election had been set for March 2002, following the Academy's end-of-year recess.

In the weeks that followed, two other candidates appeared: the political scientist Hélio Jaguaribe and the ex-diplomat Mário Gibson Barbosa. Both were octogenarians and each had his strong and weak points. The presence in the competition of one of the most widely read authors in the world attracted the kind of interest that the Academy rarely aroused. The foreign media mobilized their correspondents in Brazil to cover the contest. In a long, sardonic article published by the *New York Times*, the correspondent Larry Rother attributed to the Academy the power to 'transform obscure and aged essayists, poets and philosophers into celebrities who are almost as revered as soccer players, actors or pop stars'. Rother included statements from supporters of Coelho such as Arnaldo Niskier ('he is the Pelé of Brazilian literature'), and added:

> Mr Coelho's public image is not that of a staid academic who enjoys the pomp of the Thursday afternoon teas for which the Academy is famous. He began his career as a rock 'n' roll songwriter, has admitted that he was heavily into drugs at that time, spent brief periods in a mental institution as an adolescent and, perhaps worst of all, refuses to apologize for his overwhelming commercial success. Brazilian society 'demands excellence in this house', the novelist Nélida Piñon, a former president of the Academy, said in the newspaper *O Globo* in what was interpreted as a slap at Mr Coelho's popularity. 'We can't let the market dictate aesthetics.'

Ignoring all the intrigues, Paulo did what he had to do. He wrote letters, visited all the academicians (with the exception of Padre Fernando Ávila, who told him curtly that this would not be necessary) and received much spontaneous support, such as that of Carlos Heitor Cony and ex-president Sarney. On the day of the election, involving four successive ballots, none of the three candidates obtained the minimum nineteen votes required under the rules. As tradition directed, the president burned the votes in a bronze urn, announced that chair number 21 was still unoccupied and called for further elections to be held on 25 July.

That evening, some hours after the announcement of the result of the first round, a group of 'immortals' appeared at Paulo's house to offer the customary condolences. One of them – Coelho cannot remember precisely who – said:

It was very good of you to put yourself forward as a candidate, and
our short time together has been most enjoyable. Perhaps on another
occasion you could try again.

Since he had received a modest ten votes as opposed to the sixteen given
to Jaguaribe, the group was somewhat taken aback by their host's immediate reaction: 'I'm not going to wait for another opportunity. I'm going to
register my candidature tomorrow. I'm going to stand again.'

It's likely that the date of the new election was of no significance to
the majority of the academicians, but Coelho saw in it an unmistakable
sign that he should put himself forward as a candidate: 25 July is the feast
day of St James of Compostela, the patron saint of the pilgrimage that
had changed his life. Nevertheless there was no harm in asking for confirmation from the old and, in his opinion, infallible I Ching. He threw the
three coins of the oracle several times, but they always gave the same
result: the hexagram of the cauldron, synonymous with certain victory.
The I Ching had also made a strange recommendation: 'Go travelling and
don't come back for a while.' He did as he was told.

Paulo flew to France, installed himself in the hotel in Tarbes and for
the following three months conducted his campaign with mobile phone
and notebook in hand. When he arrived, he saw on the Internet that he
was only going to have one opponent in the contest: Hélio Jaguaribe.
Christina recalls being surprised by Paulo's self-confidence: 'I discovered
that Paulo had negotiating skills about which I knew nothing. His
sangfroid in taking decisions and talking to people was a side of him I
didn't know.'

Although many of Paulo's supporters thought it risky to run his
campaign from a distance, the I Ching insisted: 'Do not return.' The pressure to return to Brazil grew stronger, but he remained immovable. 'My
sixth sense was telling me not to go back,' the writer recalls, 'and faced
by a choice between my sixth sense and the academicians, I chose the
former.' But the campaign began to get serious when one of his supporters started canvassing votes during the Thursday afternoon teas using a
seductive argument: 'I'm going to vote for Paulo Coelho because the corn
is good.' In the jargon of the Academy, 'good corn' was a metaphor used

to refer to candidates who, once elected, could bring both prestige and material benefits to the institution. From that point of view, the 'immortal' argued, the author of *The Alchemist* was very good corn indeed. There was not only his indisputable international fame, evidenced by the extraordinary interest in the election shown by the foreign media: what softened even the most hardened of hearts was the fact that the millionaire Paulo Coelho had no children, something which fuelled the hope that, on his death, he might choose the Academy as one of his heirs – as other childless academicians had in the past.

Unaware that there were people with an eye on the wealth it had cost him such effort and energy to accumulate, three weeks before the election, Coelho returned to Rio de Janeiro. There, contrary to what the oracles had been telling him, he was not greeted with good news. His opponent's campaign had gained ground during his absence and even some voters whom he had considered to be 'his' were threatening to change sides.

On the evening of 25 July 2002, the photographers, reporters and cameramen crowding round the door of the building in Avenida Atlântica in Copacabana were invited up to the ninth floor to drink a glass of French champagne with the owners of the apartment: Paulo had just been elected by twenty-two votes to fifteen. Jaguaribe appeared not to have taken in his defeat, and was not exactly magnanimous when expressing his dismay at the result. 'With the election of Paulo Coelho, the Academy is celebrating the success of marketing,' he moaned. 'His sole merit lies in his ability to sell books.' To one journalist who wanted to know whether he would be putting his name forward again, Jaguaribe was adamant: 'The Academy holds no interest for me any more.' Three years later, though, once he had got over the shock, he returned and was elected to the chair left vacant by the economist Celso Furtado. A year after that, it was the turn of Celso Lafer, the foreign minister, who took the chair left vacant by Miguel Reale.

If, in fact, any of the 'immortals' really had voted for Paulo Coelho in the hope that 'the corn' would be good, they would have been bitterly disappointed. In the first place, the international spotlight that followed him around never once lit up the Academy, for the simple reason that he has attended only six of the more than two hundred sessions held in the Academy since his election, which makes him the number one absentee. Those who dreamed that a percentage of his royalties would flow into the Academy's coffers were also in for a disappointment. In his will, which Paulo has amended three times since his election, there is no reference to the Academy.

Enjoying a honeymoon period following his victory, and being hailed by an article in the weekly American *Newsweek* as 'the first pop artist of Brazilian literature to enter the Academy, the house which, for the past 105 years, has been the bastion of the Portuguese language and a fortress of refined taste and intellectual hauteur', Coelho began to write his speech and prepare for his investiture, which was set for 28 October. He decided to go to Brasília in person to give President Fernando Henrique his invitation to his inauguration. He was cordially received at Planalto Palace, and was told that the President had appointments in his diary for that day, but would send a representative. While waiting for his plane at Brasília airport, he visited the bookshop there and saw several of his books on display – all of them produced by Editora Rocco and not one by Objetiva. At that moment, he began to consider leaving Objetiva and going back to his previous publisher.

At the inaugural ceremony, the guests wore black tie while the academicians wore the uniform of the house, an olive-green gold-embroidered cashmere jacket. To complete the outfit, the 'immortals' also wore a velvet hat adorned with white feathers and, at their waist, a golden sword. Valued at US$26,250, the uniform used by Paulo had been paid for, as tradition decreed, by the Prefecture of Rio, the city where he was born. Among the hundreds of guests invited to celebrate the new 'immortal' were Paulo's Brazilian publishers, Roberto Feith and Paulo Rocco. The polite remarks they exchanged gave no hint of the conflict to come.

The episode in the bookshop at Brasília airport had brought to the surface concerns that had, in fact, been growing for a while. Something similar had occurred some months earlier, when Paulo's agent Mônica, on holiday with her husband Øyvind in Brazil, decided to extend their trip to Natal, in Rio Grande do Norte. Mônica discovered that there were no books by Coelho on sale anywhere in the capital of Rio Grande (which at the time had more than six hundred thousand inhabitants), not even in the bookshop in the city's international airport.

However, the author had far more substantial reasons to be concerned. According to his calculations, during the period between 1996 and 2000 (when Objetiva launched *The Fifth Mountain, Veronika* and *The Devil and Miss Prym*), he had lost no fewer than 100,000 readers. The book whose sales he used as a reference point for this conclusion was not his blockbuster *The Alchemist* but *By the River Piedra I Sat Down and Wept*, which was the last book published by Rocco before his move to Objetiva. What he really wanted to do was to leave Objetiva immediately and go back to Rocco; there was, however, a problem: the typescript of his next novel, *Eleven Minutes*, was already in the hands of Objetiva and Roberto Feith had already suggested small changes to which the author had agreed.

As so often before, though, Paulo let the I Ching have the last word. Four days after taking his place in the Academy, he posed two questions: 'What would happen if I published my next book, *Eleven Minutes*, with Editora Objetiva?' and 'What would happen if I published my next book and my entire backlist with Rocco?' When the three coins had been thrown, the answer didn't appear to be as precise as the questions: 'Preponderance of the small. Perseverance furthers. Small things may be done; great things should not be done. The flying bird brings the message: It is not well to strive upward, it is well to remain below. Great good fortune.' On reading this response, most people would probably have been as confused as ever, but for Paulo Coelho the oracle was as clear as day: after seven years and four books, the time had come to leave Objetiva and return to Rocco.

Annoyed by the news of the change, and particularly by the author's decision to take with him a book that was ready for printing, Roberto Feith decided that he would only release the typescript of *Eleven Minutes* if Objetiva were reimbursed for the production costs. Paulo saw this as a threat and unsheathed his sword: he took on a large law firm in Rio and prepared for a long and painful legal battle. He announced that he was going back to Rocco – the publisher who, he stated, would launch *Eleven*

Minutes during the first few months of 2003 – and left for Tarbes with Chris, leaving the Brazilian publishing market seething with rumours. Some said that he had left Objetiva out of pique, because Luís Fernando Veríssimo was now their main author. Others said that Rocco had offered him US$350,000 to return.

Things only began to calm down when Chris, on her daily walk with Paulo, advised him to bring an end to the conflict with Feith. 'It looks as though you want a fight more than he does! What for? Why?' she asked. 'Do what you can to see that it ends amicably.' After some resistance, Paulo finally gave in. He stopped in front of a crucifix and asked God to remove the hatred from his heart.

A few weeks later, after some discussion between representatives of the two parties, Feith not only released *Eleven Minutes* but also returned to Paulo the four titles in his backlist that Paulo wanted to go to Rocco. There was just one point on which the owner of Objetiva dug in his heels: he refused to allow the insertion of his suggestions in the Rocco edition and in any foreign versions. This obliged Mônica to take back the copies of the text that had already been sent to translators in several countries. The problem had been resolved, but Coelho and Feith haven't spoken to each other since.

The book that had caused the uproar had its origins some years earlier, in 1997, in Mantua, in the north of Italy, where Coelho had given a lecture. When he arrived at his hotel, he found an envelope that had been left by a Brazilian named Sônia, a reader and fan who had emigrated to Europe in order to work as a prostitute. The packet contained the type-script of a book in which she told her story. Although he normally never read such typescripts, Coelho read it, liked it and suggested it to Objectiva for publication. The publisher, however, wasn't interested.

When Sônia met him again three years later in Zurich, where she was living at the time, she organized a book signing such as probably no other writer has ever experienced: she took him to Langstrasse, a street where, after ten at night, the pavement teems with prostitutes from all parts of the world. Told of Coelho's presence in the area, dozens of them appeared bearing dog-eared copies of his books in different languages, the majority of which, the author noted, came from countries that had been part of the former Soviet Union. Since she also worked in Geneva, Sônia suggested a repetition of this extraordinary event in the red light district there. That was where he met a Brazilian prostitute whom he called Maria and whose life story was to provide the narrative for *Eleven Minutes*: the story of a young girl from northeastern Brazil who is brought to Europe in order, she thinks, to be a nightclub dancer, but who, on arriving, discovers that she is to be a prostitute. For the author, this was 'not a book about prostitution or about the misfortunes of a prostitute, but about a person in search of her sexual identity. It is about the complicated relationship between feelings and physical pleasure.'

The title he chose for the 255-page book is a paraphrase of *Seven Minutes*, the 1969 best-seller in which Irving Wallace describes a court case involving an attempt to ban a novel about sex. Seven minutes, according to Wallace, was the average time taken to perform a sexual act. When *Eleven Minutes* was published in the United States, a reporter on *USA Today* asked Paulo why he had added four minutes. With a chuckle, he replied that the American's estimate reflected an Anglo-Saxon point of view and was therefore 'too conservative by Latin standards'.

Eleven Minutes was launched in Brazil during the first quarter of 2003 and was received by the media with their customary irony – so much so that a month before its launch the author predicted the critics' reaction in an interview given to *IstoÉ*: 'How do I know that the critics aren't going to like it? It's simple. You can't loathe an author for ten of his books and love him for the eleventh.'

As well as not liking *Eleven Minutes*, many journalists predicted that it would be the author's first big flop. According to several critics, the risqué theme of the book, which talks of oral sex, clitoral and vaginal orgasms, and sadomasochistic practices, was too explosive a mixture for what they imagined to be Paulo Coelho's average reader. Exactly the opposite happened. Before the initial print run of 200,000 copies had even arrived in Brazilian bookshops in April 2003, Sant Jordi had sold the book to more than twenty foreign publishers after negotiations that earned the author US$6 million. Three weeks after its launch, *Eleven Minutes* was top of the best-seller lists in Brazil, Italy and Germany. The launch of the English edition attracted 2,000 people to Borders bookshop in London. As had been the case with the ten previous books, his readers in Brazil and the rest of the world gave unequivocal proof that they loved his eleventh book as well. *Eleven Minutes* went on to become Paulo Coelho's second most-read book, with 10 million copies sold, losing out only to the unassailable *Alchemist*.

CHAPTER 29

The Zahir

PAULO AND CHRIS spent the first few months of 2004 working on making the old mill they had bought in Saint-Martin habitable. The plan to spend four months there, four in Brazil and four travelling had been scuppered by the suggested programme Mônica had sent at the beginning of the year. Sant Jordi had been overwhelmed by no fewer than 187 invitations for Paulo to present prizes and participate in events, signings, conferences and launches all over the world. If he were to agree to even half of those requests there would be no time for anything else – not even his next book, which was just beginning to preoccupy him.

He had been working on the story in his head during the second half of the year, at the end of which time just two weeks were enough for him to set down on paper the 318 pages of *O Zahir*, or *The Zahir*, the title of which had been inspired by a story by Jorge Luís Borges about something which, once touched or seen, would never be forgotten. The nameless main character, who is easily recognizable, is an ex-rock star turned world-famous writer, loathed by the critics and adored by his readers. He lives in Paris with a war correspondent, Esther. The narrative begins with the character's horror when he finds out that she has left him. Written at the end of 2004, in March of the following year, the book was ready to be launched in Brazil and several other countries.

However, before it was discovered by readers around the world, Brazilians included, *The Zahir* was to be the subject of a somewhat surprising operation: it was to be published first in, of all places, Tehran, capital of Iran, where Coelho was the most widely read foreign author. This was a tactic by the young publisher Arash Hejazi to defeat local piracy which, while not on the same alarming scale as in Egypt, was carried out with such impunity that twenty-seven different editions of *The Alchemist* alone had been identified, all of them pirate copies as far as the author was concerned, but none of them illegal, because Iran is not a signatory to the international agreements on the protection of authors' rights. The total absence of any legislation to suppress the clandestine book industry was due to a peculiarity in the law, which only protects works whose first edition is printed, published and launched in the country. In order to guarantee his publishing house, Caravan, the right to be the sole publisher of *The Zahir* in the country, Hejazi suggested that Mônica change the programme of international launches so that the first edition could appear in bookshops in Iran.

Some days after the book was published, it faced problems from the government. The bad news was conveyed in a telephone call from Hejazi to the author, who was with Mônica in the Hotel Gellert in Budapest. Speaking from a public call box in order to foil the censors who might be bugging his phone, the terrified thirty-five-year-old publisher told Coelho that the Caravan stand at the International Book Fair in Iran had just been invaded by a group from the Basejih, the regime's 'morality police'. The officers had confiscated 1,000 copies of *The Zahir*, announced that the book was banned and ordered him to appear two days later at the censor's office.

Both publisher and author were in agreement as to how best to confront such violence and ensure Hejazi's physical safety: they should tell the international public. Coelho made calls to two or three journalist friends, the first he could get hold of, and the BBC in London and France Presse immediately broadcast the news, which then travelled around the world. This reaction appears to have frightened off the authorities, because, a few days later, the books were returned without any explanation and the ban lifted. It was understandable that a repressive and moralistic state such as Iran should have a problem with a book that deals with

adulterous relationships. What was surprising was that the hand of repression should touch someone as popular in the country as Paulo Coelho,
who was publicly hailed as 'the first non-Muslim writer to visit Iran since
the ayatollahs came to power' – that is, since 1979.

In fact, Coelho had visited the country in May 2000 as the guest of
President Mohamed Khatami, who was masterminding a very tentative
process of political liberalization. When they landed in Tehran, and even
though it was three in the morning, Paulo and Chris (who was wearing a
wedding ring on her left hand and had been duly informed of the stric-
tures imposed on women in Islamic countries) were greeted by a crowd
of more than a thousand readers who had learned of the arrival of the
author of *The Alchemist* from the newspapers. It was just before the new
government was about to take office and the political situation was tense.
The streets of the capital were filled every day with student demonstrations in support of Khatami's reforms, which were facing strong opposition from the conservative clerics who hold the real power in the country.
Although accompanied everywhere by a dozen or so Brazilian and foreign
journalists, Coelho was never far from the watchful eyes of the six security guards armed with machine guns who had been assigned to him.
After giving five lectures and various book signings for *Brida*, with an audience of never fewer than a thousand, he was honoured by the Minister of
Culture, Ataolah Mohajerani, with a gala dinner where the place of
honour was occupied by no less a person than President Khatami. When
the seventy-year-old Iranian novelist Mahmoud Dolatabadi turned down
an invitation to be present at the banquet given in honour of his Brazilian
colleague, of whom he was a self-confessed admirer, he referred to the
limitations and the fragility of Khatami's liberalization process. Hounded
by the government, he refused to fraternize with its censors. 'I cannot be
interrogated in the morning,' he told the reporters, 'and in the evening
have coffee with the president.'

Some weeks after *The Zahir*'s publication in Iran, 8 million copies of
the book, translated into forty-two languages, arrived in bookshops in
eighty-three countries. When it was launched in Europe, the novel came
to the attention of the newspapers – not in the political pages, as had
been the case with the Iranian censorship, but in the gossip columns. In

the spring of 2005, a question had been going round the press offices of the European media: who was the inspiration behind the book's main female character, Esther? The first suspect, put forward by the Moscow tabloid *Komsomólskaia Pravda*, was the beautiful Russian designer Anna Rossa, who was reported to have had a brief affair with the author. When he read the news, which was reproduced on an Italian literary website, Coelho was quick to send the newspaper a letter, which his friend the journalist Dmitry Voskoboynikov translated:

> Dear readers of *Komsomólskaia Pravda*
>
> I was most intrigued to learn from your newspaper that I had an affair with the designer Anna Rossa three years ago and that this woman is supposedly the main character in my new book, *The Zahir*. Happily or unhappily, we shall never know which, the information is simply not true.
>
> When I was shown a photo of this young woman at my side, I remembered her at once. In fact, we were introduced at a reception at the Brazilian embassy. Now I am no saint, but there was not and probably never will be anything between the two of us.
>
> *The Zahir* is perhaps one of my deepest books, and I have dedicated it to my partner Christina Oiticica, with whom I have lived for twenty-five years. I wish you and Anna Rossa love and success.
>
> Yours
>
> Paulo Coelho

In the face of this quick denial, the journalists' eyes turned to another beautiful woman, the Chilean Cecília Bolocco, Miss Universe 1987, who, at the time, was presenting *La Noche de Cecília*, a highly successful chat show in Chile. On her way to Madrid, where she was recording interviews for her programme, she burst out laughing when she learned that she was being named as the inspiration for Esther in *The Zahir*: 'Don't say that! Carlito gets very jealous ...' The jealous 'Carlito' was the former Argentine president, Carlos Menem, whom she had married in May 2000, when he was seventy and she was thirty-five. Cecília's reaction was understandable. Some years earlier, the press had informed readers that she had had an affair with Coelho between the beginning of 1999 and October 2000, when she was married to Menem. Both had vehemently denied the allegations. Suspicions also fell on the Italian actress Valeria Golino.

However, on 17 April 2005, a Sunday, the Portuguese newspaper *Correio da Manhã* announced on its front page that the woman on whom Paulo had based the character was the English journalist Christina Lamb, war correspondent for the *Sunday Times*. When she was phoned up in Harare, where she was doing an interview, she couldn't believe that the secret had been made public. She was the 'real-life Esther', the newspaper confirmed. 'All last week I fielded phone calls from newspapers in Spain, Portugal, Brazil, South Africa, even Britain, asking how I felt being "Paulo Coelho's muse",' she said in a full-page article in the *Sunday Times Review*, entitled 'He stole my soul' and with a curious subtitle: 'Christina Lamb has covered many foreign wars for the *Sunday Times*, but she had no defences when one of the world's bestselling novelists decided to hijack her life.'

In the article, the journalist says that she met Coelho two years earlier when she was chosen to interview him about the success of *Eleven Minutes*. At the time, the writer was still living in the Henri IV hotel. This was their only meeting. During the following months, they exchanged e-mails, he in the south of France and she in Kandahar and Kabul, in Afghanistan. Coelho so enjoyed Christina's *The Sewing Circles of Herat* that he included it in his 'Top Ten Reads' on the Barnes & Noble website. When she checked her e-mails in June 2004 she found, 'among the usual monotonous updates from the coalition forces in Kabul and junk offering penis enlargement', a message from Coelho with a huge attachment. It was the Portuguese typescript of his just completed book *The Zahir*, with a message saying: 'The female character was inspired by you.' He then explained that he had thought of trying to meet, but she was always away, so he had used her book and Internet research to create the character. In the article published in the *Sunday Times*, she describes what she felt as she read the e-mail:

I was part astonished, part flattered, part alarmed. He didn't know me. How could he have based a character on me? I felt almost naked. Like most people, I guess, there were things in my life I would not wish to see in print. […]

So with some trepidation I downloaded the 304-page file and opened it. As I read the manuscript I recognized things I had told him in Tarbes, insights into my private world, as well as concerns I had discussed in my book.

The first paragraph began: 'Her name is Esther, she is a war correspondent who has just returned from Iraq because of the imminent invasion of that country; she is thirty years old, married, without children.'

At least he had made me younger.

What had at first seemed amusing ('I was starting to enjoy the idea that the heroine was based on me, and now here she was disappearing on page one,' Christina wrote) was becoming uncomfortable as she read on:

I was slightly concerned about his description of how Esther and her husband had met. 'One day, a journalist comes to interview me. She wants to know what it's like to have my work known all over the country but to be entirely unknown myself … She's pretty, intelligent, quiet. We meet again at a party, where there's no pressure of work, and I manage to get her into bed that same night.'

Astonished by what she had read, Christina told her mother and her husband – a Portuguese lawyer named Paulo:

Far from sharing my feeling of flattery, he was highly suspicious about why another man should be writing a book on his wife. I told a few friends and they looked at me as though I was mad. I decided it was better not to mention it to anyone else.'

If the *Correio da Manhã* had not revealed the secret, the matter would have ended there. The revelation would not, after all, have caused any further discomfort for the journalist, as she herself confessed in her article:

> Once I got used to it, I decided I quite liked being a muse. But I was not quite sure what muses do. [...] I asked Coelho how a muse should behave. 'Muses must be treated like fairies,' he replied, adding that he had never had a muse before. I thought being a muse probably involved lying on a couch with a large box of fancy chocolates, looking pensive. [...] But being a muse is not easy if you work full time and have a five-year-old. [...] In the meantime, I have learnt that going to interview celebrity authors can be more hazardous than covering wars. They might not shoot you but they can steal your soul.

The book seemed destined to cause controversy. Accustomed to the media's hostility towards Coelho's previous books, Brazilian readers had a surprise during the final week of March 2005. On all the news-stands in the country three of the four major weekly magazines had photos of Coelho on the cover and inside each were eight pages about the author and his life. This unusual situation led the journalist Marcelo Beraba, the ombudsman of the *Folha de São Paulo*, to dedicate the whole of his Sunday column to the subject.

The 'case of the three covers', as it became known, was only deemed important because it revealed a radical change in behaviour in a media which, with a few rare exceptions, had treated the author very badly. It was as though Brazil had just discovered a phenomenon that so many countries had been celebrating since the worldwide success of *The Alchemist*.

Whatever the critics might say, what distinguished Paulo from other best-sellers, such as John Grisham and Dan Brown, was the content of his books. Some of those authors might even sell more books, but they don't fill auditoriums around the world, as Paulo does. The impact his work has on his readers can be measured by the hundreds of e-mails that he receives daily from all corners of the earth, many of them from people telling him how reading his books has changed their lives. Ordinary letters posted from the most remote places, sometimes simply addressed to 'Paulo Coelho – Brazil', arrive by the sackload.

In February 2006 – as if in acknowledgement of his popularity – Coelho received an invitation from Buckingham Palace – from Sir James Hamilton, Duke of Abercorn and Lord Steward of the Household. This was for a state banquet to be given some weeks later for the President of Brazil, Luiz Inácio Lula da Silva, by Queen Elizabeth II and Prince Philip during the President's official visit to Britain. The invitation made clear that the occasion called for 'white tie with decorations'. As the date of the banquet approached, however, newspapers reported that, at the request of the Brazilian government, both President Lula and his seventy-strong delegation had been relieved of the obligation to wear tails. When he read this, Coelho (who had dusted off his tails, waistcoat and white tie) was confused as to what to do. Concerned that he might make a blunder, he decided to send a short e-mail to the Royal Household asking for instructions: 'I just read that President Lula vetoed the white tie for the Brazilian Delegation. Please let me know how to proceed – I don't want to be the only one with a white tie.'

The reply, signed by a member of the Royal Household, arrived two days later, also by e-mail:

Mr Coelho:

Her Majesty The Queen Elizabeth II has agreed that President Lula and members of his official suite need not wear white tie to the State Banquet. However, that will be just a small number of people (less than 20). The remainder of the 170 guests will be in white tie, so I can reassure you that you will not be the only person wearing white tie. The Queen does expect her guests to wear white tie and you are officially a guest of Her Majesty The Queen, not President Lula.

CHAPTER 30

One hundred million copies sold

SOME WEEKS AFTER HANDING HIS PUBLISHERS the typescript of *The Witch of Portobello*, which he had finished a week prior to the banquet at Buckingham Palace, Coelho was preparing for a new test. Two decades had passed since 1986, when he had followed the Road to Santiago, the first and most important of the penances imposed by Jean. In the years that followed, the mysterious Master had, in agreement with Coelho, regularly ordered further trials. At least one of these the author has confessed to having fulfilled purely out of respect for the duty to find disciples to whom he should transmit the knowledge he had received from Jean and show them the route to spiritual enlightenment. 'I have disciples because I am obliged to, but I don't enjoy it,' he told journalists. 'I'm very lazy and have little patience.' In spite of this resistance, he has acted as guide to four new initiates as demanded by RAM.

Besides following the Routes, the name given by members of the order to the different pilgrimages, he was ordered by Jean to submit to various tests. Some of these did not require much will power or physical strength, such as praying at least once a day with his hands held beneath a jet of flowing water, which could be from a tap or a stream. Coelho does, however, admit to having been given tasks that were not at all easy to perform, such as submitting to a vow of chastity for six months, during which time even masturbation was forbidden. In spite of this deprivation, he speaks with good humour about the experience, which happened in the late 1980s. 'I discovered that sexual abstinence is accompanied by a great deal of temptation,' he recalls. 'The penitent has the impression that every woman desires him, or, rather, that only the really pretty ones do.' Some of these tests were akin to rituals of self-flagellation. For three months, for example, he was obliged to walk for an hour a day, barefoot and without a shirt, through brushwood in thick scrubland until his chest and arms were scratched by thorns and the soles of his feet lacerated by stones. Compared with that, tasks such as fasting for three days or having to look at a tree for five minutes every day for months on end were as nothing.

The task Jean set his disciple in April 2006 may seem to a layman totally nonsensical. The time had come for him to take the External Road to Jerusalem, which meant spending four months (or, as the initiates prefer to say, 'three months plus one') wandering about the world, wherever he chose, without setting foot in either of his two homes – the house in France and his apartment in Rio de Janeiro. For him this meant spending all that time in hotels. Did this mean that only those with enough money to pay for such an extravagance could join the order? Coelho had been troubled by this very question twenty years earlier, just before setting off along the Road to Santiago, and he recalls Jean's encouraging reply: 'Travelling isn't always a question of money, but of courage. You spent a large part of your life travelling the world as a hippie. What money did you have then? None. Hardly enough to pay for your fare, and yet those were, I believe, some of the best years of your life – eating badly, sleeping in railway stations, unable to communicate because of the language, being forced to depend on others even for finding somewhere to spend the night.'

If the new Road to Jerusalem was unavoidable, the solution was to relax and put the time to good use. He devoted the first few weeks to carrying out a small number of the engagements that had accumulated in Sant Jordi's diary, among which was the London Book Fair. While there, he chanced to meet Yuri Smirnoff, the owner of Sophia, his publisher in Russia. Coelho told him that he was in the middle of a strange pilgrimage and that this might be the perfect opportunity to realize an old dream: to take the legendary Trans-Siberian Railway which crosses 9,289 kilometres and traverses 75 per cent of Russia, from Moscow to Vladivostok. Some weeks later, he received a phone call while he was touring in Catalonia, in northern Spain. It was Smirnoff calling to say that he had decided to make Coelho's dream come true and was offering him a fortnight on one of the longest railway journeys in the world.

Coelho assumed that the gift would be a compartment on the train. Much to his surprise, when he arrived in Moscow on 15 May, the agreed date for his departure, he discovered that Smirnoff had decided to turn the trip into a luxurious 'happening'. He had hired two entire coaches. Paulo would travel in a suite in the first, and the other two compartments would be occupied by Smirnoff, his wife and Eva, an admirer of Coelho's work, who would act as his interpreter during the two-week journey. He was also provided with a chef, two cooks and a waiter, as well as two bodyguards from the Russian government to ensure their guest's safety. The second coach was to be given over to thirty journalists from Russia and other European countries, who had been invited to accompany the author. Altogether, this kind gesture cost Smirnoff about US$200,000, and it proved to be a very poor investment indeed: some months later Coelho left Sophia for another publisher, Astrel.

It turned out to be an exhausting fortnight, not just because of the distance covered, but because he was constantly besieged by his readers. At every stop, the platforms were filled by hundreds and hundreds of readers wanting an autograph, a handshake, or even just a word. After crossing the provinces in the far east of Russia and skirting the frontiers of Mongolia and China, on a journey that crossed eight time zones, the group finally arrived in Vladivostok on the edge of the Sea of Japan on 30 May.

During the interviews he gave while on his Trans-Siberian journey Coelho made it clear that, in spite of the comfort in which he was travelling, it was not a tourist trip. 'This is not just a train journey,' he insisted several times, 'but a spiritual journey through space and time in order to complete a pilgrimage ordered by my Master.' Despite all these years of being a constant presence in newspapers and magazines across the world,

no journalist has ever been able to discover the true identity of the mysterious character to whom Paulo owes so much. Some months after the end
of the World Cup in 2006, someone calling himself simply a 'reader of
Paulo Coelho' sent a photo to the website set up for collecting information
for this book. It showed Coelho wearing a Brazilian flag draped over his
shoulders, Christina and a third person walking down a street. The third
person was a thin man, with grey hair, wearing faded jeans, a Brazilian
football shirt and a mobile phone hanging around his neck. It was hard to
identify him because he was wearing a cap and sunglasses and his right
hand was partly covering his face. The photograph bore a short caption
written by the anonymous contributor: 'This photo was taken by me in
Berlin during the 2006 World Cup. The man in the cap is Jean, Paulo
Coelho's Master in RAM.' When he saw the photo, the author was deliberately vague: 'What can I say?' he said. 'If it isn't him, it's very like him.'

Two months after the end of the World Cup, Brazilian bookshops
were receiving the first 100,000 copies of *The Witch of Portobello*. It was
a book full of new ideas. The first of these, to be found right at the beginning, is the method used by the author to relate the travails of Athena, the
book's protagonist. The story of the young Gypsy girl born in
Transylvania, in Romania, and abandoned by her biological mother is
narrated by fifteen different characters. This device brought eloquent
praise for his work in the *Folha de São Paulo*. 'One cannot deny that, in
literary terms, this is one of Paulo Coelho's most ambitious novels,' wrote
Marcelo Pen. The book is the story of Athena's life. Adopted by a
Lebanese couple and taken to Beirut, from where the family is driven out
by the civil war that raged in Lebanon from 1975 until 1990, she then
settles in London. She grows up in Britain, where she is educated, marries
and has a son. She works for a bank before leaving her husband and going
to Romania in order to find her biological mother. She then moves to the
Persian Gulf, where she becomes a successful estate agent in Dubai. On
her return to London, she develops and seeks to deepen her spirituality,
becoming, in the end, a priestess, who attracts hundreds of followers. As
a result of this, however, she becomes a victim of religious intolerance.

The second innovation was technological. The book appeared on the
author's website before the printed version reached the Brazilian and

Portuguese bookshops, and in just two days his web page received 29,000 hits, which took everyone, including the author, by surprise. 'It was just amazing, but it proved that the Internet has become an obligatory space for a writer to share his work with the readers,' he told newspapers. To those who feared that the initiative might rob bookshops of readers, he replied: 'In 1999, I discovered that the edition of *The Alchemist* published in Russia was available on the Internet. Then I decided to confront piracy on its own ground and I started putting my books on the web first. Instead of falling, sales in bookshops increased.'

As though wanting to reaffirm that these were not empty words, the site where he began to make his books available (www.piratecoelho.word-press.com) has a photo of the author with a bandana on his head and a black eye patch, as though he were a real pirate. Convinced that someone only reads books on-screen if he has no other option, and that printing them out at home would cost more than buying them in the bookshops, Coelho began to make all his books available online. 'It has been proved that if people read the first chapters on the Internet and like it,' he states, 'they will go out and buy the book.'

Since the middle of 2006, he and Mônica and Chris, as well as some of his publishers, had been hoping that the number of books sold would pass the 100-million mark around the feast day of St Joseph, 19 March, the following year, when he had decided he would celebrate his sixtieth birthday. As it turned out, the 100-millionth book was not sold until five months later, in August, which was his real birthday. Although he had told the newspapers that being sixty was no more important than being thirty-five or forty-seven, in February, he decided that he would celebrate St Joseph's day in the Hotel El Peregrino, in Puente la Reina, a small Spanish town 20 kilometres from Pamplona, halfway along the Road to Santiago. That day he announced on his blog that he would be glad to welcome the first ten readers to reply in Puente la Reina. When the messages began to arrive – coming from places as far away as Brazil, Japan, England, Venezuela and Qatar – Paulo feared that those who replied might think that the invitation included air trips and accommodation, and hastened to clarify the situation. To his surprise, they had all understood what he meant and were prepared to bear the cost. On the actual day, there were five Spaniards (Luís Miguel, Clara, Rosa, Loli and Ramón), a Greek (Chrissa), an Englishman (Alex), a Venezuelan (Marian), a Japanese (Heiko) and an American who lived in northern Iraq (Nika), as well as the ex-football star Raí and Paulo's old friends, among them Nelson Liano, Jr, his partner on the *Manual do Vampirismo*, and Dana Goodyear, the American journalist. In his blog, Liano summed up the atmosphere at El Peregrino:

> It was a celebration in honour of St Joseph in four languages. Paulo adopted the feast day of the patron saint of workers to celebrate his birthday, following an old Spanish Christian tradition. While the party was going on, a snowfall left the Road to Santiago completely white. Salsa, French regional music, the bolero, tango, samba and the unforgettable hits that Paulo had written with Raul Seixas gave a pan-musical note to the party, accompanied by the very best Rioja wine.

Five months later, as his real birthday was approaching, the team led by Mônica at Sant Jordi was working flat out on the preparation of a smart forty-page folder in English, the cover of which bore a photo of a beaming Paulo Coelho and the words 'PAULO COELHO – 100,000,000 COPIES'. The urgency was due to the fact that the folder had to be ready by the first week of October, for the Frankfurt Book Fair.

While the people at Sant Jordi were engaged on this, on 24 August, the man himself was, as usual, devoting himself to more spiritual matters. Anyone strolling along the narrow, sunny little streets in Barbazan-Debat, 10 kilometres from Saint-Martin, at three o'clock that afternoon, might not even have noticed the presence of the man with close-cropped white hair, wearing trainers, T-shirt and bermudas. Coelho had just come out of the small chapel of Notre Dame de Piétat and sat down on a wooden bench, where he placed a notebook on his lap and began to write. The few tourists who drove past would have found it hard to associate that slight, rather monk-like figure with the author courted by kings, emirs and Hollywood stars and acclaimed by readers all over the world. Christina, who was watching from a distance, went over to him and asked what he was writing.

'A letter,' he replied, without looking up.

'Who to?' she went on.

'To the author of my biography.'

Posted some hours later at Saint-Martin post office, the letter is reproduced in its entirety below.

Barbazan-Debat, 24 August 2007

Dear Fernando

I'm sitting here outside this small chapel and have just repeated
the usual ritual: lighting three candles to Notre Dame de Piétat. The
first asking for her protection, the second for my readers and the third
asking that my work should continue undiminished and with dignity.
It's sunny, but it's not an unbearably hot summer. There is no one in
sight, except for Chris, who is looking at the mountains, the trees and
the roses that the monks planted, while she waits for me to finish this
letter.

We came on foot – 10 kilometres in two hours, which is reasonable. We shall have to go back on foot, and I've just realized that I
didn't bring enough water. It doesn't matter; sometimes life gives you
no choice, and I can't stay sitting here for ever. My dreams are waiting for me, and dreams mean work, and I need to get back home,
even though I'm thirsty.

I turn sixty today. My plan was to do what I always do, and that's
how it's been. Yesterday at 23.15 I went to Lourdes so that I would be
there at 00.05 on the 24th, the moment when I was born, before the
grotto of Our Lady, thank her for my life so far and ask for her protection for the future. It was a very moving moment, but while I was
driving back to Saint-Martin, I felt terribly alone. I commented on
this to Chris, who said: 'But you were the one who chose to spend the
day like this!' Yes, I chose it, but I began to feel uncomfortable. There
we were, the two of us alone on this immense planet.

I turned on my mobile. At the same moment, it rang – it was
Mônica, my agent and friend. I got home and there were other
messages waiting for me. I went to sleep happy, and in the morning
I realized that there was no reason for last night's gloom. Flowers and

presents, etc. began to arrive. People in Internet communities had created extraordinary things using my images and texts. Everything had been organized, for the most part, by people I had never seen in my life – with the exception of Márcia Nascimento, who created something really magical that made me glad to say 'I'm a writer who has a fan club (of which she is the world president)!'

Why am I writing to you? Because today, unlike other days, I have an immense desire to go back to the past, using not my own eyes, but those of someone who has had access to my diaries, my friends, my enemies, to everyone who has been a part of my life. I should like very much to be reading my biography right now, but it looks like I'm going to have to wait.

I don't know what my reaction will be when I read what you've written, but in the chapel, it says: 'You will know the truth, and the truth will set you free.' Truth is a complicated word – after all, many religious crimes have been committed in its name, many wars have been declared, many people have been banished by those who believed themselves to be just. But one thing is certain: when the truth is a liberating truth, there is nothing to fear. And that was basically why I agreed to a biography: so that I can discover another side to myself. And that will make me feel freer.

A plane's flying by overhead, the new Airbus 380, which has not yet been put into service and is being tested near here. I look at it and think: How long will it take for this new marvel of technology to become obsolete? Of course, my next thought is: How long before my books are forgotten? Best not to think about it. I didn't write them with one eye on eternity. I wrote them to discover what, given your training as a journalist and given your Marxist convictions, will not be in your book: my secret corners, sometimes dark and sometimes light, which I only began to be aware of when I set them down on paper.

Like any writer, I always flirted with the idea of an autobiography, but it's impossible to write about yourself without ending up justifying your mistakes and magnifying your successes – it's human nature. So that's why I accepted the idea of your book so readily, even though

I know I run the risk of having things revealed that I don't think need to be revealed. Because, if they're a part of my life, they need to see the light of day. That's why I decided – a decision I've often regretted over the past three years – to give you access to the diaries that I've been writing since I was an adolescent.

Even if I don't recognize myself in your book, I know that there will be a part of me there. While you were interviewing me and I was forced to look again at certain periods of my life, I kept thinking: What would have become of me if I hadn't experienced those things?

It's not worth going into that now: Chris says we should go back home, we have another two hours to walk, the sun's getting stronger and the ground is dry. I have asked her for another five minutes to finish this. Who shall I be in your biography? Although I haven't read it, I know the reply: I shall be the characters who crossed my path. I shall be the person who held out his hand, trusting that there would be another hand waiting to support me in difficult times.

I exist because I have friends. I have survived because they were there on my path. They taught me to give the best of myself, even when, at some stages in my life, I was not a good pupil. But I think that I have learned something about generosity.

Chris says that my five minutes are up, but I've asked for a little more time so that I can write here, in this letter, the words that Khalil Gibran wrote more than a hundred years ago. They're probably not in the right order, because I learned them by heart on a distant, sad and gloomy night when I was listening to Simon & Garfunkel on that machine we used to call a 'gramophone', which has now been superseded (just as, one day, the Airbus 380 will and, eventually, my books). They are words that speak about the importance of giving:

'It is only when you give of yourself that you truly give. Therefore give now, that the season of giving may be yours and not your inheritors.

'People often say: "I would give, but only to the deserving." The trees in your orchard say not so. They give that they may live, for to withhold is to perish.

'Therefore, when you share something out, do not think of your-selves as generous people. The truth is, it is life that divides things up and shares them out, and we human beings are mere witnesses to our own existence.'

I'm going to get up now and go home. A witness to my own exis-tence, that is what I have been every day of the sixty years I am cele-brating today.

May Our Lady of Piétat bless you.

Paulo

When this biography was completed, in February 2008, the A380 was in commercial operation. Given how fast new technology becomes obso-lete, it is highly likely that manufacture of the A380 will have ceased long before the hundreds of millions of copies of Paulo Coelho's books disap-pear and, with them – despite what the literary critics may think – the profound effect they have had on readers in even the most far-flung corners of the planet.

FACTS ABOUT PAULO COELHO

BOOKS PUBLISHED

	English title
Teatro na Educação (1973)	
Arquivos do Inferno (1982)	
Manual Prático do Vampirismo (1985)	
O Diário de um Mago (1987)	*The Pilgrimage*
O Alquimista (1988)	*The Alchemist*
Brida (1990)	*Brida*
O Dom Supremo (1991)	
As Valkírias (1992)	*The Valkyries*
Na Margem do Rio Piedra eu Sentei e Chorei (1994)	*By the River Piedra I Sat Down and Wept*
Maktub (1994)	
O Monte Cinco (1996)	*The Fifth Mountain*
Manual do Guerreiro da Luz (1997)	*Manual of the Warrior of Light*
Cartas de Amor do Profeta (1997)	
Veronika Decide Morrer (1998)	*Veronika Decides to Die*
Palavras Essenciais (1999)	
O Demônio e a Srta. Prym (2000)	*The Devil and Miss Prym*
Histórias para Pais, Filhos e Netos (2001)	
Onze Minutos (2003)	*Eleven Minutes*
O Gênio e as Rosas (2004)	
O Zahir (2005)	*The Zahir*

Ser como o Rio que Flui (2006)   *Like the Flowing River*
A Bruxa de Portobello (2006)   *The Witch of Portobello*
O Vencedor está só (2008)   *The Winner Stands Alone*

Excluding pirate editions, his books have sold over 100 million copies in 455 translations, published in 66 languages and 160 countries.

MAIN PRIZES AND DECORATIONS

Golden Book – Yugoslavia, 1995, 1996, 1997, 1998, 1999, 2000 and 2004
Grand Prix Littéraire Elle – France, 1995
Guinness Book of Records – Brazil, 1995/1996
Chevalier des Arts et des Lettres – France, 1996
Livre d'Or – France, 1996
ABERT Prize, Formador de Opinião – Brazil, 1996
Premio Internazionale Flaiano – Italy, 1996
Super Grinzane Cavour Literary Prize – Italy, 1996
Finalist in the International IMPAC Literary Award – Eire, 1997 and
    2000
Protector de Honor – Spain, 1997
Comendador da Ordem do Rio Branco – Brazil, 1998
Diploma da Ordem Fraternal do Cruzeiro do Sul – Brazil, 1998
Fiera Del Libro per i Ragazzi – Italy, 1998
Flutuat Nec Mergitur – France, 1998
Libro de Oro for *La Quinta Montaña* – Argentina, 1998
Medaille de la Ville de Paris – France, 1998
Senaki Museum – Greece, 1998
Sara Kubitschek Prize – Brazil, 1998
Top Performance Nacional – Argentina, 1998
Chevalier de l'Ordre National de la Légion d'Honneur – France, 1999
Huésped Distinguido de la Ciudad de Nuestra Señora de la Paz –
    Bolívia, 1999
Książka Zagraniczna – Poland, 1999
Libro de Oro for *Guerrero de la Luz* – Argentina, 1999

Libro de Oro for *Veronika Decide Morir* – Argentina, 1999
Libro de Platina for *El Alquimista* – Argentina, 1999
Medalla de Oro de Galicia – Spain, 1999
Crystal Prize of the World Economic Forum – Switzerland, 1999
Crystal Mirror Prize – Poland, 2000
Member of the Pen Club Brazil – Brazil, 2001
Bambi Prize for Cultural Personality of the Year – Germany, 2001
Ville de Tarbes – France, 2001
XXIII Premio Internazionale Fregene – Italy, 2001
Diploma of the Academia Brasileira de Letras – Brazil, 2002
Miembro de Honor – Bolivia, 2002
Club of Budapest Planetary Arts Award in recognition of his literary
    work – Germany, 2002
International Corine prize for the best work of fiction for *The Alchemist*
    – Germany, 2002
Prix de la Littérature Consciente de la Planète – France, 2002
Ville d'Orthez – France, 2002
Médaille des Officiers des Arts et des Lettres – France, 2003
Medal from the Lviv Book Fair – Ukraine, 2004
Nielsen Gold Book Award for *The Alchemist* – United Kingdom, 2004
Order of Honour of Ukraine – Ukraine, 2004
Order of Saint Sophia for contribution to knowledge and culture –
    Ukraine, 2004
Premio Giovanni Verga – Italy, 2004
Golden Book award from the newspaper *Vecernje Novosti* – Serbia, 2004
Budapest Award – Hungary, 2005
Ex Libris award for *Eleven Minutes* – Serbia, 2005
Goldene Feder Award – Germany, 2005
International Author's Award from DirectGroup Bertelsmann –
    Germany, 2005
8th Annual International Latino Book Award for *The Zahir* – United
    States, 2006
I Premio Álava en el Corazón – Spain, 2006
Kiklop Award for *The Zahir* in the Best-Seller of the Year Category –
    Croatia, 2006

ARTICLES

Weekly articles written by Paulo Coelho are published in 109 publications in 60 countries: Albania, Argentina, Armenia, Austria, Bolivia, Bosnia and Herzegovina, Brazil, Bulgaria, Canada, Chile, China, Colombia, Costa Rica, Croatia, Czech Republic, Dominican Republic, Ecuador, Egypt, Eire, El Salvador, Estonia, Finland, France, Georgia, Germany, Greece, Guatemala, Honduras, Hungary, India, Indonesia, Iceland, Italy, Japan, Lithuania, Mexico, Netherlands, Nicaragua, Norway, Oman, Panama, Peru, Poland, Portugal, Puerto Rico, Romania, Russia, Serbia, Slovakia, Slovenia, South Africa, South Korea, Spain, Sweden, Switzerland, Taiwan, Ukraine, United Arab Emirates, United Kingdom and Venezuela.

CINEMA

The film rights for four of his books have been negotiated with the following American studios:

The Alchemist (Warner Brothers)
The Fifth Mountain (Capistrano Productions)
Eleven Minutes (Hollywood Gang Productions)
Veronika Decides to Die (Muse Productions)

INTERNET

Apart from his website, www.paulocoelho.com, which is available in sixteen languages, the author has a blog, www.paulocoelhoblog.com, and a Myspace page, www.myspace.com/paulocoelho.

PAULO COELHO INSTITUTE

The Paulo Coelho Institute is a non-profit-making organization financed entirely from the writer's royalties and managed by Belina Antunes, the mother of his agent, Mônica. From time to time, Paulo makes large contributions from his other activities. The Institute's main aim is to give opportunities to underprivileged and excluded members of Brazilian society, particularly children and the elderly. The Solar Meninos da Luz, founded in 1996, is co-sponsored by the Paulo Coelho Institute, which makes an annual contribution of US$400,000. The school offers entirely free education to 430 needy children in the Pavão-Pavãozinho e Cantagalo *favela* in Rio de Janeiro.

ACKNOWLEDGEMENTS

AUTHOR'S NOTE

This book started life at the beginning of 2005 at Saint-Exupéry airport, in Lyons, in the south of France, when I met Paulo Coelho for the first time. As a journalist, I was used to accompanying international names and stars and imagined I would find him surrounded by bodyguards, secretaries and assistants. To my surprise, the man with whom I would spend much of the following three years turned up alone, with a rucksack on his back and dragging a small suitcase on wheels. It was there that the excavation began that would reveal one of the most extraordinary individuals I have ever worked with.

After six weeks at his side, I returned to Brazil. Since the entire course of his life has revolved around Rio, I moved there and spent eight months following the trails left by the writer. I looked for Paulo Coelho everywhere and probed behind the events that had left so many scars. I searched for him in the dark alleys of the roughest areas of Copocabana, among the records of the insane and the ruins of what had once been Dr Eiras's clinic, in the dangerous world of drugs, in files dating from the years of political repression in Brazil, in satanism, in mysterious secret societies, in his partnership with Raul Seixas, in his family and his genealogy. I talked to friends and those who had fallen out with him, interviewed many of his ex-lovers and spent some time with his present – and, he vows, his last – partner, the artist Christina Oiticica. I rummaged through his life, dug deep into his private affairs, read his will, studied his medications, read his bank statements, felt in his pockets and searched for the children I imagined must have resulted from his various relationships and love affairs.

I won a bet with him that gave me access to a treasure that he had decided was to be burnt after his death: a trunk that held forty years of diaries, many of them recorded on cassette tapes. I spent weeks closeted in the Paulo Coelho Institute scanning documents, photos, old diaries and letters both received and sent. Once my time in Rio was over, I again accompanied him on trips to various corners of the earth with a recorder slung over my shoulder, listening to his nasal voice and to his comments, and watching that strange tic he has of flicking away non-existent flies from his eyes. I went with him on the road to Santiago de Compostela, I saw how moved he was on meeting a group of ordinary readers in Oñati, in the Spanish Basque country and in Cairo, and I watched him being acclaimed by men in black ties and women in long dresses at banquets held in his honour in Paris and Hamburg.

I put together the pieces left behind by Paulo Coelho throughout his sixty years, and the result is this book. Although the responsibility for everything written here is mine alone, I must acknowledge the help of the dozens of people who helped me along the way. Firstly, my old friend Wagner Homem. I asked him to apply his expertise to organizing the vast quantity of data, interviews and documents that I accumulated during three years of research. He ended up moving into my house, where for ten uninterrupted months he worked on that, as well as reading and re-reading the final text and making valuable suggestions for improving it. My gratitude must also go to two brothers: one putative, Ricardo Setti, who has long been in charge of quality control with regard to my books and whose talent has saved me at the most difficult moments, and one real, Reinaldo Morais, who moved heaven and earth to make sure that the book reached its final destination safely.

I must also thank all those who generously collaborated on this book, the many people I interviewed and the researchers, journalists, trainees and stringers who found and interviewed the individuals who have given life, colour and human warmth to this story. These are: Adriana Negreiros, Afonso Borges, Aldo Bocchini Neto, Alfonso Molinero, Ana Carolina da

Motta, Ana Paula Granello, Antônio Carlos Monteiro de Castro, Armando Antenore, Armando Perigo, The Association of Old Boys of the St Ignatius College, Áurea Soares de Oliveira, Áureo Sato, Beatriz de Medeiros de Souza, Belina Antunes, Carina Gomes, Carlos Augusto Setti, Carlos Heitor Cony, Carlos Lima, Célia Valente, Cláudio Humberto Rosa e Silva, César Polcino Milies, Dasha Balashova, Denis Kuck, Devanir Barbosa Paes, Diego de Souza Martins, Eliane Lobato, Eric Nepomuceno, Evanise dos Santos, Fernando Eichenberg, Firmeza Ribeiro dos Santos, Francisco Cordeiro, Frédéric Bonomelli, Gemma Capdevila, Herve Louit, Hugo Carlo Batista Ramos, Ibarê Dantas, Inês Garçoni, Instituto Paulo Coelho and Sant Jordi Associados, Ivan Luiz de Oliveira, Ivone Kassu, Joaquim Ferreira dos Santos, Joca do Som, José Antonio Martinuzzo, Juliana Perigo, Klecius Henrique, Leonardo Oiticica, Lourival Sant'Anna, Lúcia Haddad, Luciana Amorim, Luciana Franzolin, Luiz Cordeiro Mergulhão, Lyra Netto, Marcio José Domingues Pacheco, Marcio Valente, Marilia Cajaíba, Mário Magalhães, Mário Prata, Marisilda Valente, Mariza Romero, Marizilda de Castro Figueiredo, Pascoal Soto, Raphael Cardoso, Ricardo Hofstetter, Ricardo Schwab, Roberto Viana, Rodrigo Pereira Freire, Samantha Quadrat, Silvia Ebens, Silvio Essinger, Sylvio Passos, Talles Rodrigues Alves, Tatiana Marinho, Tatiane Rangel, Véronique Surrel, Vicente Paim and Wilson Moherdaui.

Finally, I would like to thank the hundreds of people from more than thirty countries who sent data, documents and photos to the website http://www.cpc.com.br/paulocoelho/, which was created in order to receive such contributions, some of whom supplied important information that I have used in this book.

Fernando Morais
Ilhabela, March 2008

THOSE INTERVIEWED FOR THIS BOOK

Acácio Paz
Afonso Galvão
Alan Clarke
Amapola Rios
André Midani
Andréa Cals
Antonio Carlos Austregésilo de
   Athayde
Antonio Carlos 'Kakiko' Dias
Antonio Cláudio de Lima Vieira
Antônio Ovídio Clement Fajardo
Antônio Walter Sena, Jr. ('Toninho
   Buda')
Arash Hejazi
Ariovaldo Bonas
Arnaldo Niskier
Arnold Bruver, Jr.
Artur da Távola
Basia Stepien
Beatriz Vallandro
Cecilia Bolocco
Cecília Mac Dowell
Chico Castro Silva
Christina Oiticica
Cristina Lacerda
Darc Costa
Dedê Conte
Eduardo Jardim de Moraes
Élide 'Dedê' Conte
Ernesto Emanuelle Mandarino
Eugênio Mohallen
Fabíola Fracarolli

Fernando Bicudo
Frédéric Beigbeder
Frédéric Morel
Geneviève Phalipou
Gilles Haeri
Glória Albues
Guy Jorge Ruffier
Hélio Campos Mello
Henrique Caban
Hildegard Angel
Hildebrando Goes Filho
Ilma Fontes
Índio do Brasil Lemes
Isabela Maltarolli
Ivan Junqueira
Jerry Adriani
José Antonio Mendonça Neto
Joel Macedo
Jorge Luiz Costa Ramos
Jorge Mourão
José Antonio 'Pepe' Domínguez
José Mário Pereira
José Reinaldo Rios de Magalhães
José Wilker
Julles Haeri
Kika Seixas
Leda Vieira de Azevedo
Lizia Azevedo
Marcelo Nova
Márcia Faria Lima
Márcia Nascimento
Marcos Medeiros Bastos

Marcos Mutti

Marcos Paraguassu Arruda
 Câmara

Maria Cecília Duarte Arraes de
 Alencar

Maria Eugênia Stein

Marie Christine Espagnac

Marilu Carvalho

Mário Sabino

Maristela Bairros

Maurício Mandarino

Michele Conte

Milton Temer

Mônica Antunes

Nelly Canellas Branco

Nelson Liano, Jr.

Nelson Motta

Orietta Paz

Patrice Hoffman

Patricia Martín

Paula Braconnot

Paulo Roberto Rocco

Pedro Queima Coelho de Souza

Regina Bilac Pinto

Renato Menescal

Renato Pacca

Ricardo Sabanes

Rita Lee

Roberto Menescal

Rodrigo Meinberg

Rosana Fiengo

Serge Phalipou

Sidney Magal

Silvio Ferraz

Soizik Molkhou

Sônia Maria Coelho de Souza

Stella Paula Costa

Vera Prnjatovic Richter

Zé Rodrix

Zeca Araújo

Zuenir Ventura

PHOTOGRAPHIC ACKNOWLEDGEMENTS

All plate images provided courtesy of Instituto Paulo Coelho with the exception of the following images:

page 1 (bottom left): personal collection of Maria Cecilia Duarte de
 Arraes Alencar
page 4 (top left): personal collection of Fabíola Fracarolli
page 5 (bottom right), page 6 (top and bottom left): personal collection
 of Antonio Carlos Dias ('Kakiko')
page 7 (top and middle): personal collection of Amapola Rios
page 8 (top right): Public Archive of the State of Rio de Janeiro

page 10 (bottom left and right): Dachau Concentration Camp Memorial
    Site: www.kz-gedenkstaette-dachau.de
page 13 (top): Gerard Fouet/Associated Press
page 13 (middle): Paulo Coelho
page 14 (middle): Fernando Morais
page 15 (bottom): Ricard Stuckert Filho
page 16 (bottom left): Sant Jordi Asociados
page 16 (middle left): Yuri Zolotarrev/Getty Images

While every effort has been made to trace the owners of copyright
material reproduced herein and secure permissions, the publishers would
like to apologise for any omissions and will be pleased to incorporate
missing acknowledgements in any future editions of this book.

INDEX

Life is a
journey

Make sure you don't miss a thing.
Live it with Paulo Coelho.

What are you searching for?

A transforming journey on the pilgrims' road to Santiago – and the first of Paulo's extraordinary books.

The Pilgrimage

Do you believe in yourself?

A modern-day adventure in the searing heat of the Mojave desert and an exploration of fear and self-doubt.

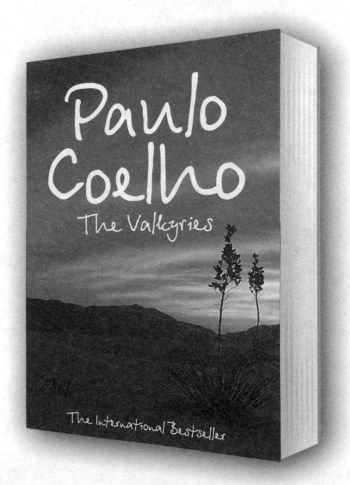

The Valkyries

How can you find your heart's desire?

A world-wide phenomenon; an inspiration
for anyone seeking their path in life.

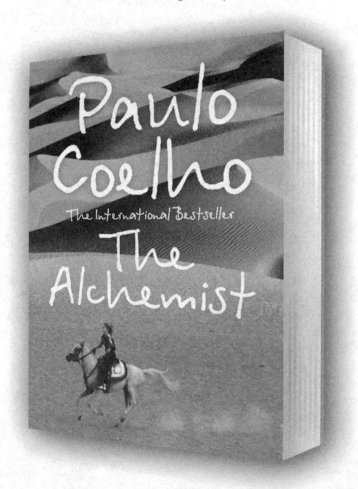

The Alchemist

How do we see the amazing in every day?

When two young lovers are reunited, they discover
anew the truth of what lies in their hearts.

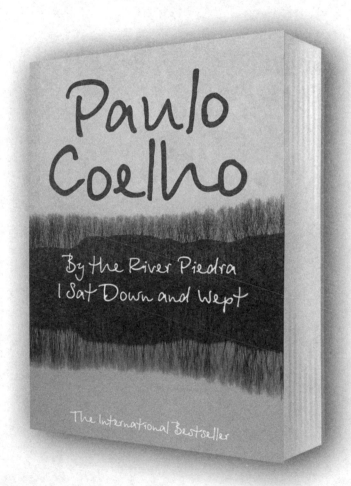

By the River Piedra I Sat Down and Wept

Is life always worth living?

A fundamental moral question explored as only
Paulo Coelho can.

Veronika Decides to Die

How far would you go for your obsession?

A sweeping story of love, loss and longing that spans the world.

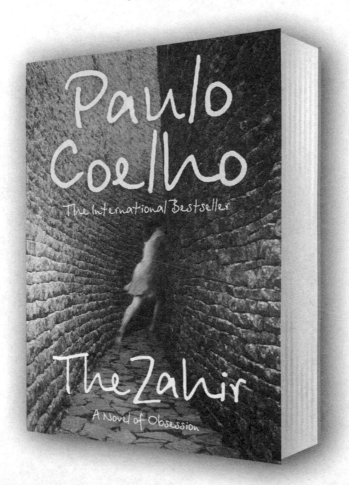

The Zahir

Could you be tempted into evil?

The inhabitants of a small town are challenged by a mysterious stranger to choose between good and evil.

The Devil and Miss Prym

Can faith triumph over suffering?

Paulo Coelho's brilliant telling of the story of Elijah, who was forced to choose between love and duty.

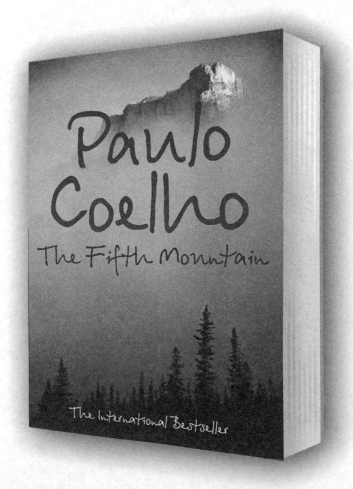

The Fifth Mountain

Can sex be sacred?

An unflinching exploration of the lengths we go to in our search for love, sex and spirituality.

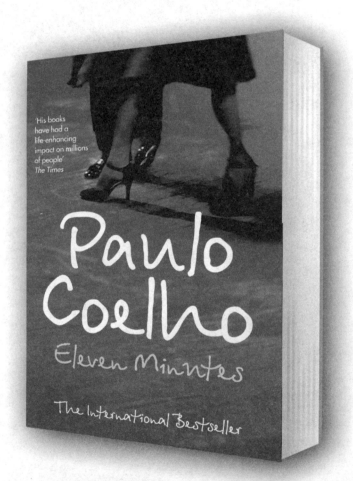

'His books have had a life-enhancing impact on millions of people'
The Times

Paulo Coelho

Eleven Minutes

The International Bestseller

Eleven Minutes

Are you brave enough to follow your dream?

Strategies and inspiration to help you
follow your own path in a troubled world.

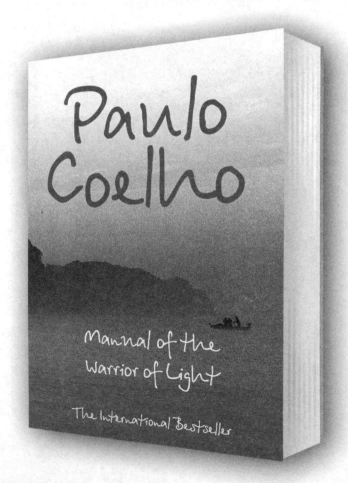

Manual of the Warrior of Light

What does it mean to be truly alive?

Powerful tales of living and dying,
destiny and choice and love lost and found.

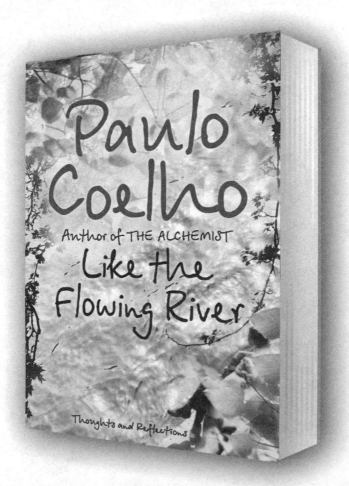

Like the Flowing River

Can we dare to be true to ourselves?

A story that will transform the way we
think about love, passion, joy and sacrifice.

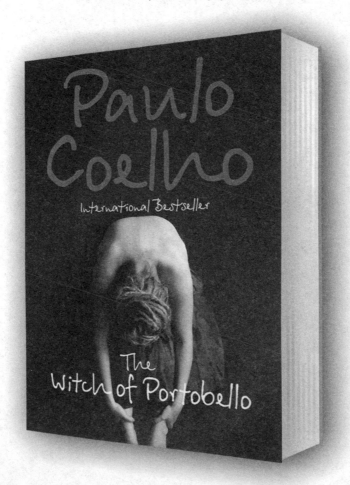

How will you know who your soulmate is?

A moving tale of passion,
mystery and spirituality.

Feeling
inspired?

Discover more about the
world of Paulo Coelho.

What happens when obsession turns to murder?

An enthralling story of jealousy, death and suspense.

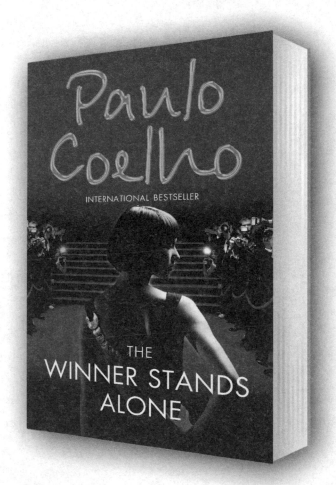

The Winner Stands Alone

Feeling
inspired?

Discover more about the
world of Paulo Coelho.

Visit his official international website
www.paulocoelho.com